THE OXFOR

VICTORIAN
POETRY

'I am inclined to think that we want new forms . . . as well as thoughts', confessed Elizabeth Barrett to Robert Browning in 1845. *The Oxford Handbook of Victorian Poetry* provides a closely-read appreciation of the vibrancy and variety of Victorian poetic forms, and attends to poems as both shaped and shaping forces. The volume is divided into four main sections. The first section on 'Form' looks at a few central innovations and engagements—'Rhythm', 'Beat', 'Address', 'Rhyme', 'Diction', 'Syntax', and 'Story'. The second section, 'Literary Landscapes', examines the traditions and writers (from classical times to the present day) that influence and take their bearings from Victorian poets. The third section provides 'Readings' of twenty-three poets by concentrating on particular poems or collections of poems, offering focused, nuanced engagements with the pleasures and challenges offered by particular styles of thinking and writing. The final section, 'The Place of Poetry', conceives and explores 'place' in a range of ways in order to situate Victorian poetry within broader contexts and discussions: the places in which poems were encountered; the poetic representation and embodiment of various sites and spaces; the location of the 'Victorian' alongside other territories and nationalities; and debates about the place—and displacement—of poetry in Victorian society. This Handbook is designed to be not only an essential resource for those interested in Victorian poetry and poetics, but also a landmark publication—a provocative, seminal volume that will offer a lasting contribution to future studies in the area.

Matthew Bevis is University Lecturer and Fellow in English at Keble College, Oxford. He is the author of *The Art of Eloquence: Byron, Dickens, Tennyson, Joyce* (OUP, 2007) and *Comedy: A Very Short Introduction* (OUP, 2012). He is the editor of *Some Versions of Empson* (OUP, 2007).

THE OXFORD HANDBOOK OF

VICTORIAN POETRY

Edited by

MATTHEW BEVIS

OXFORD

UNIVERSITY PRESS

Great Clarendon Street, Oxford, OX2 6DP,
United Kingdom

Oxford University Press is a department of the University of Oxford.
It furthers the University's objective of excellence in research, scholarship,
and education by publishing worldwide. Oxford is a registered trade mark of
Oxford University Press in the UK and in certain other countries

Published in the United States of America by Oxford University Press
198 Madison Avenue, New York, NY 10016, United States of America

British Library Cataloguing in Publication Data
Data available

Library of Congress Cataloging in Publication Data
Data available

ISBN 978-0-19-957646-3 (Hbk.)
ISBN 978-0-19-871371-5 (Pbk.)

Acknowledgements

I am very grateful to the Leverhulme Trust for awarding me a Philip Leverhulme Prize from 2008 to 2010; work on this volume began during that time. I would also like to thank Keble College, Oxford, for a research grant that provided me with editorial assistance. I am indebted to Robert Stagg and Kathryn Bevis for reading everything with such careful eyes and ears, and to the anonymous readers at the Press for their responses to the initial proposal. Finally, I am especially grateful to Jacqueline Baker for suggesting the idea in the first place and for supporting the book along the way.

MB

2013

CONTENTS

PART III   READINGS

PART IV   THE PLACE OF POETRY

Illustrations

Notes on Contributors

Isobel Armstrong is a Fellow of the British Academy and Emeritus Professor of English (Geoffrey Tillotson Chair) at Birkbeck, University of London. She has published widely on nineteenth-century literature and culture and feminist thought. Among her works is a critical history of Victorian Poetry (1993), currently being revised for a new edition. Her most recent book, *Victorian Glassworlds: Glass Culture and the Imagination 1830–1880*, won the Modern Language Association's James Russell Lowell Prize for the best book of 2008.

Derek Attridge is the author of several studies of poetry, including *The Rhythms of English Poetry* (1982), *Poetic Rhythm: An Introduction* (1995), and *Moving Words: The Forms of English Poetry* (2013). He has published a number of other books on literary theory, James Joyce, and South African literature. He is Professor of English at the University of York and a Fellow of the British Academy.

Matthew Bevis is a University Lecturer and Fellow in English at Keble College, Oxford. His publications include *Tennyson: Lives of Victorian Literary Figures* (2003), *The Art of Eloquence: Byron, Dickens, Tennyson, Joyce* (2007), *Some Versions of Empson*, ed. (2007), *Comedy: A Very Short Introduction* (2012), and *Lessons in Byron* (2013). He is currently co-editing a collection of essays on *Edward Lear and The Play of Poetry* and writing a book entitled *Wordsworth's Laughter*.

Kirstie Blair is a Professor in English Literature at the University of Stirling. She has published widely on Victorian literature, including two monographs on Victorian poetry: *Form and Faith in Victorian Poetry and Religion* (2012) and *Victorian Poetry and the Culture of the Heart* (2006). Recent publications on Victorian literature and religion include essays on Tennyson for *The Blackwell Companion to Literature and the Bible*, on Keble and *The Christian Year* for the *Oxford Handbook of Literature and Theology*, and on 'Poet Preachers' for the *Oxford Handbook of the British Sermon*.

J. B. Bullen has held two chairs in English Literature, one at the University of Reading, the other at Royal Holloway, University of London. The main focus of his work has been on word and image, and some of his papers have been collected in *Continental Crosscurrents: British Criticism and European Art 1810–1910* (2005). He is also the author of *The Pre-Raphaelite Body: Fear and Desire in Painting, Poetry, and Criticism* (1998) and *Rossetti: Painter and Poet* (2011). He has written the entry for Rossetti in the new *DNB*. His book *Thomas Hardy: the World of his Novels* appears with Frances Lincoln in 2013, and he is the editor of Walter Pater's *Renaissance* for the forthcoming ten-volume Oxford edition of *The Collected Works of Walter Pater*.

Matthew Campbell teaches modern literature at the University of York. He has published on Romantic, Victorian, and contemporary poetry from Britain as well as Ireland, and is the editor of *The Cambridge Companion to Contemporary Irish Poetry* (2003) and *The Voice of the People: Writing the European Folk Revival, 1761–1914* (2012). His most recent book is *Irish Poetry Under the Union, 1801-1924* (2013).

Robert Douglas-Fairhurst is Fellow and Tutor in English at Magdalen College, Oxford. He is the author of *Becoming Dickens: The Invention of a Novelist* (2011) and *Victorian Afterlives: The Shaping of Influence in Nineteenth-Century Literature* (2002), and has also edited Dickens's '*A Christmas Carol*' and Other Christmas Books, Henry Mayhew's *London Labour and the London Poor*, and Charles Kingsley's *The Water-Babies* for Oxford World's Classics.

Martin Dubois is a Lecturer in Victorian Literature at Newcastle University. He has published articles on a range of Victorian poets, including Hopkins and William Barnes, and is currently completing a monograph on Hopkins and religious poetry.

Andrew Elfenbein is Professor of English at the University of Minnesota, Twin Cities. He has written *Byron and the Victorians*, *Romantic Genius: The Prehistory of a Homosexual Role*, and *Romanticism and the Rise of English*. He has also edited Oscar Wilde's *The Picture of Dorian Gray* and Bram Stoker's *Dracula* for Longman Cultural Editions.

Mark Ford is a Professor in the English Department at University College London. Recent publications include a volume of poetry, *Six Children* (2011), a collection of essays on British and American poets, *Mr and Mrs Stevens and Other Essays* (2011), a translation of Raymond Roussel's *Nouvelles Impressions d'Afrique* (*New Impressions of Africa* (2011)), and an anthology of the poetry of London from the fourteenth century to the present day, *London: A History in Verse* (2012).

Janet Gezari is the Lucretia L. Allyn Professor of Literatures in English at Connecticut College. She is the editor of the Penguin *Emily Jane Brontë: The Complete Poems* and the author of *Last Things: Emily Brontë's Poems*. She is currently working on an annotated edition of *Wuthering Heights* and writing a book on late style in the work of four contemporary artists.

Erik Gray is Associate Professor of English and Comparative Literature at Columbia University. He is the author of *The Poetry of Indifference* (2005) and *Milton and the Victorians* (2009), and he has edited Tennyson's *In Memoriam* and co-edited Spenser's *The Faerie Queene*. His current work focuses on love poetry.

Emily Harrington is Assistant Professor of English at Penn State University where she teaches courses on Victorian literature and culture, poetry, and women's writing. She has published essays in *Victorian Studies*, *Victorian Poetry*, *Nineteenth-Century Literature* and *Literature Compass*. She is currently finishing a book project on fin-de-siècle women poets entitled *Second Person Singular: The Bonds of Verse*.

Constance W. Hassett is Professor of English at Fordham University. She is the author of *Christina Rossetti: The Patience of Style* (2005) and *The Elusive Self in the Poetry of Robert Browning* (1982).

Hugh Haughton was born in Cork and is Professor in the Department of English and Related Literatures, York. He is the author of *The Poetry of Derek Mahon* (2007) and co-editor (with Valerie Eliot) of the first two volumes of *The Letters of T. S. Eliot* (2009).

Anna Henchman joined Boston University's English Department in 2008, after three years as a Junior Fellow at Harvard's Society of Fellows. She recently completed a book manuscript entitled *The Starry Sky Within: Astronomy and the Reach of the Mind in Victorian Literature*, parts of which have been published in *Victorian Poetry* and *Victorian Studies*. Other articles have appeared in *English Language Notes* and *Victorian Review*. She is writing a new book on the inner lives of tiny creatures as they were imagined by Victorian literary and scientific writers.

Peter Howarth is Senior Lecturer in English at Queen Mary, University of London and a National Teaching Fellow. His most recent book is *The Cambridge Introduction to Modernist Poetry* (2011). He is currently working on the rise of performance aesthetics in modern poetry.

Linda K. Hughes is Addie Levy Professor of Literature at Texas Christian University in Fort Worth, Texas. She writes about gender and publishing history across literary genres and media. Recent titles include *Graham R.: Rosamund Marriott Watson, Woman of Letters* (2005) and *The Cambridge Introduction to Victorian Poetry* (2010). Her current project examines Victorian women writers and Germany in the context of female cosmopolitanism, study abroad, and a transnational women's literary tradition.

Michael D. Hurley is a Lecturer in English at the University of Cambridge, and Fellow of St Catharine's College. He is the author of *G. K. Chesterton* (2012), co-author, with Michael O'Neill, of *Poetic Form: an Introduction* (2012) and editor of the new Penguin Classics edition of *The Complete Father Brown Stories* (2012). *A History of Poetics: from Classical Antiquity to the Present* is forthcoming with Cambridge University Press.

Isobel Hurst is Lecturer in the Department of English and Comparative Literature at Goldsmiths, University of London. She is the author of *Victorian Women Writers and the Classics: The Feminine of Homer* (Oxford University Press, 2006), and of chapters on Elizabeth Barrett Browning and Arthur Hugh Clough for volume 4 of the *Oxford History of Classical Reception in English Literature*.

Simon Jarvis is the Gorley Putt Professor of Poetry and Poetics in the Faculty of English at the University of Cambridge. He is the author of *Wordsworth's Philosophic Song* (2007) and of many essays on the poetics of verse.

Daniel Karlin is the Winterstoke Professor of English Literature at the University of Bristol. He taught previously at University College London, Boston University, and the University of Sheffield. He has published numerous books and articles on Victorian poetry, especially Robert Browning, whose poetry he has edited in the Longman Annotated English poets series. He has also edited the *Penguin Book of Victorian Verse* (1997) and Edward FitzGerald's *Rubáiyát of Omar Khayyám* (2009). His most recent book is *The Figure of the Singer* (2013).

Tim Kendall is Professor of English Literature at the University of Exeter. He has published a book of poems, *Strange Land*, and full-length studies of Muldoon and Plath. From 1994 until 2003 he edited the international poetry magazine *Thumbscrew*. Recent publications include *Modern English War Poetry* (2006), *The Art of Robert Frost* (2012), and *Poetry of the First World War* (2013).

Rolf P[eter] Lessenich is Professor Emeritus of English Literature in the Department of English, American, and Celtic Studies of Bonn University, Germany. He is the author of *Elements of Pulpit Oratory in Eighteenth-Century England 1660–1800* (1972), *Lord Byron and the Nature of Man* (1978), *Aspects of English Preromanticism* (1989), and *Neoclassical Satire and the Romantic School 1780–1830* (2012). In preparation is a work on 'Romantic Disillusionism'. He is the author of about sixty periodical and festschrift essays, contributions to books, and dictionary articles on English and comparative literature from Shakespeare to Modernism as well as on the Classical Tradition.

Caroline Levine is Professor of English at the University of Wisconsin-Madison and author of two books, *The Serious Pleasures of Suspense: Victorian Realism and Narrative Doubt* (2003) and *Provoking Democracy: Why We Need the Arts* (2007). She is the nineteenth-century editor of the *Norton Anthology of World Literature* and is currently finishing a book on form, called *Strategic Formalism: Shape, Rhythm, Hierarchy, Network*.

Meredith Martin is an Associate Professor in the English Department at Princeton University. She works in historical poetics and prosody, poetry in English from 1830 to 1930, and the literature of war. Her book, *The Rise and Fall of Meter: Poetry and English National Culture, 1860–1930*, was published by Princeton University Press in 2012.

Samantha Matthews is a Senior Lecturer at the University of Bristol. She is the author of *Poetical Remains: Poets' Graves, Bodies, and Books in the Nineteenth Century* (2004). Her current work is on album poetry and the relations between manuscript and print in nineteenth-century culture.

Catherine Maxwell is Professor of Victorian Literature at Queen Mary, University of London, and author of *The Female Sublime from Milton to Swinburne: Bearing Blindness, Swinburne,* and *Second Sight: The Visionary Imagination in Late Victorian Literature.* She has edited Swinburne's poetry for Everyman's Poetry Library, and co-edited with Patricia Pulham, Vernon Lee's *Hauntings and Other Fantastic Tales*, and the collection, *Vernon Lee: Decadence, Ethics, Aesthetics.* She is guest-editor of 'Victorian Literature and Classical Myth', *Victorian Review* 34 (2008), and guest-editor with Stefano Evangelista of *The Yearbook of English Studies—The Arts in Victorian Literature* (2010). *Algernon Charles Swinburne: Unofficial Laureate*, a collection co-edited with Stefano Evangelista, is forthcoming from Manchester University Press in 2013.

Peter McDonald is Christopher Tower Student and Tutor in Poetry in the English Language at Christ Church, Oxford. His books include *Mistaken Identities: Poetry and Northern Ireland* (1997), *Serious Poetry: Form and Authority from Yeats to Hill* (2002), *The Collected Poems of Louis MacNeice* (2007), and *Sound Intentions: The Workings of Rhyme in Nineteenth-Century Poetry* (2012). He has published five volumes of poetry, as well as his *Collected Poems* (2012). He is currently editing a three-volume edition of *The Complete Poems of W. B. Yeats* for the Longman Annotated Poets series.

Elisa New is the Powell M. Cabot Professor of American Literature at the University of Harvard. Her books include *The Regenerate Lyric: Theology and Innovation in American Poetry* (1993) and *The Line's Eye: Poetic Experience, American Sight* (1999).

Francis O'Gorman was C. S. Deneke Organ Scholar of Lady Margaret Hall, Oxford, and has written widely on classical music. He is Professor of Victorian Literature at the University of Leeds and recent publications include essays on the poetry of Coleridge, Tennyson, Larkin, James Joyce, Gerard Manley Hopkins, and T. S. Eliot, and an edition of John Ruskin's *Praeterita*.

Michael O'Neill is Professor of English at Durham University. He is the author (with Michael D. Hurley) of *The Cambridge Introduction to Poetic Form* (2012), the co-editor (with Mark Sandy and Sarah Wootton) of *Venice and the Cultural Imagination* (2012), the co-editor (with Anthony Howe and with the assistance of Madeleine Callaghan) of *The Oxford Handbook of Percy Bysshe Shelley* (2012), and an associate editor of volume III of The *Complete Poetry of Percy Bysshe Shelley* (2012).

Ruth Padel is a Fellow of the Royal Society of Literature, has published eight poetry collections, most recently *The Mara Crossing*, poems and prose on migration in the medieval form of the *prosimetrum*. She was born in London and started out as a classical scholar. Her awards include First Prize in the National Poetry Competition; her critical books include two on Greek tragedy and three on reading contemporary poetry: *52 Ways of Looking at a Poem*, *The Poem and the Journey*, and *Silent Letters of the Alphabet*. See <www.ruthpadel.com>.

Seamus Perry is a Fellow of Balliol College. He is the author of *Coleridge and the Uses of Division* (1999) and *Alfred Tennyson* (2005), and the editor, with Christopher Ricks, of the Oxford journal *Essays in Criticism*.

Joseph Phelan is Professor of Nineteenth-Century Literature at De Montfort University, Leicester. He is the editor of *Clough: Selected Poems* (1995), and the author of *The Nineteenth-Century Sonnet* (2005) and *The Music of Verse: Metrical Experiment in Nineteenth-Century Poetry* (2012). He is also, along with John Woolford and Daniel Karlin, an editor of the Longman Annotated English Poets edition of *The Poems of Robert Browning*, volume 4 of which appeared in 2012.

Adam Phillips is an author, a psychoanalyst in private practice in London, and an Honorary Visiting Professor at the Department of English and Related Literature at the University of York. He is the author of several books, including *On Kissing, Tickling, and Being Bored* (1994), *The Beast in the Nursery* (1998), *On Balance* (2011), and *Missing Out: In Praise of the Unlived Life* (2012).

Adam Piette is a Professor of Modern Literature at the University of Sheffield. He is the author of *Remembering and the Sound of Words: Mallarmé, Proust, Joyce, Beckett* (Oxford University Press, 1996), *Imagination at War: British Fiction and Poetry, 1939–1945* (Macmillan, 1995), and *The Literary Cold War, 1945 to Vietnam* (Edinburgh University Press, 2009). He co-edited *The Edinburgh Companion to Twentieth-Century British and American War Literature* (Edinburgh University Press, 2012) and is co-editor of the poetry journal *Blackbox Manifold*.

Justin Quinn is Associate Professor at the University of West Bohemia and the Charles University, Prague. He has published two studies of twentieth-century American poetry and most recently *The Cambridge Introduction to Modern Irish Poetry, 1800–2000* (2008). The author of five poetry collections, he also translates poetry from Czech and Irish.

Peter Robinson is Professor of English and American Literature at the University of Reading, an award-winning poet, translator from the Italian, and poetry editor for Two Rivers Press. His recent publications include *Poetry & Translation: The Art of the Impossible* (2010), *Poems by Antonia Pozzi* (2011), and *The Returning Sky* (2012), a Poetry Book Society Recommendation. He has also edited *An Unofficial Roy Fisher* (2010), Bernard Spencer's *Complete Poetry, Translations & Selected Prose* (2011), and the anthologies *Reading Poetry* (2011) and *A Mutual Friend: Poems for Charles Dickens* (2012). His poetry is the subject of *The Salt Companion to Peter Robinson* edited by Adam Piette and Katy Price (2007).

Garrett Stewart is James O. Freedman Professor of Letters at the University of Iowa. He has written several books on nineteenth-century literature, including most recently *Novel Violence: A Narratography of Victorian Fiction*, and winner of the 2011 Perkins Prize from the International Society for the Study of Narrative. He is a member of the American Academy of Arts and Sciences.

Bharat Tandon lectures at the University of East Anglia on literature from 1700 to the present day. He is the author of *Jane Austen and the Morality of Conversation* (Anthem Press, 2003), editor of an annotated edition of Jane Austen's *Emma* (Harvard University Press, 2012), and is currently completing a book on echoing and haunting in Victorian literature.

Matthew Townend is Reader in the Department of English and Related Literature, and the Centre for Medieval Studies, at the University of York. His research interests include language and literature in Viking Age England, Old Norse poetry, and nineteenth- and twentieth-century medievalism. His books include *Language and History in Viking Age*

England (2002) and *The Vikings and Victorian Lakeland: The Norse medievalism of W. G. Collingwood and his contemporaries* (2009).

Herbert F. Tucker holds the John C. Coleman Chair in English at the University of Virginia, where he is also an associate editor for *New Literary History* and an editor for the series, Victorian Literature and Culture, for the University Press. *Epic: Britain's Heroic Muse 1790–1910* is his most recent (2008) of several books on nineteenth-century poetry. He revisits Victorian verse and prose narrative in a chapter on 'Epic' in *The Cambridge History of Victorian Literature*, edited by Kate Flint (2012). His current project is to study the language of charm.

Marcus Waithe is a Fellow in English and University Lecturer at Magdalene College, Cambridge. He is the author of *William Morris's Utopia of Strangers: Victorian Medievalism and the Ideal of Hospitality* (2006). Recent work includes essays on John Ruskin, Thomas Carlyle, William Empson, and Geoffrey Hill. In 2010 he launched a web-based 'reconstruction' of Ruskin's St George's Museum (<www.ruskinatwalkley.org>).

Stephanie Kuduk Weiner teaches nineteenth-century British literature at Wesleyan University. The author of *Republican Politics and English Poetry, 1789–1874* (Palgrave, 2005), she is currently at work on a book entitled *Clare's Lyric: Mimetic Fidelity in Clare, Symons, Blunden, and Ashbery.*

David Wheatley is a Senior Lecturer at the University of Aberdeen. He is the author of four collections of poetry with Gallery Press: *Thirst* (1997), *Misery Hill* (2000), *Mocker* (2006), and *A Nest on the Waves* (2010), and has edited the work of James Clarence Mangan for Gallery Press and Samuel Beckett's *Selected Poems 1930–1989* for Faber and Faber. His work features in *The Penguin Book of Irish Poetry.*

James Williams is Lecturer in English at the University of York. He is the author of articles on Lewis Carroll, Alfred Tennyson, and Samuel Beckett, and is currently preparing a monograph study of Edward Lear. In 2012–13, he was Eleanor M. Garvey Visiting Fellow in Printing and Graphic Arts at the Houghton Library, Harvard University.

Clive Wilmer is an Emeritus Fellow of Sidney Sussex College, Cambridge, and the Master of John Ruskin's Guild of St George. He edited William Morris's *News from Nowhere and Other Writings* for Penguin Classics, and has written many articles on Ruskin, William Morris, and Victorian poets. His *New and Collected Poems* was published by Carcanet in 2012.

Ross Wilson is Lecturer in Criticism at the Faculty of English, University of Cambridge. His work focuses on poetry from 1750 to 1900 and on the history, theory, and practice of literary criticism. He is the author of *Subjective Universality in Kant's Aesthetics* (2007), *Theodor Adorno* (2007), *Shelley and the Apprehension of Life* (2013), and editor of *The Meaning of 'Life' in Romantic Poetry and Poetics* (2009). He has also published essays on Coleridge, Shelley, Clare, and Adorno.

Michael Wood is the Charles Barnwell Straut Professor of English and Comparative Literature at the University of Princeton. He has written books on Vladimir Nabokov, Luis Buñuel, Franz Kafka, and Gabriel García Márquez, as well as *The Road to Delphi, a study of the ancient and continuing allure of oracles*. His recent books include *Literature and the Taste of Knowledge* (2005), *Yeats and Violence* (2010), and *Film: A Very Short Introduction* (2012).

Jane Wright is a Lecturer in English Literature at the University of Bristol. She has published essays on Coleridge, Browning, Carlyle, and Tennyson. She has recently completed a book on Sincerity and Victorian Poetry, and begun a new one on Poetry and Honey.

CHAPTER 1

INTRODUCTION: AT WORK WITH VICTORIAN POETRY

MATTHEW BEVIS

pkkkffffffffrrrffff-fff! pkkkffffffffrrrffff-fff!
pkkkffffffffrrrffff-fff! pkkkffffffffrrrffff-fff!
Hobble leg, hobble leg,
hobble leg owhmmm!
Into the bottle of fluff, rubbed the stuff under!
pkkkffffffffrrrffff-fff! pkkkffffffffrrrffff-fff!
  pkkkffffffffrrrffff-fff! pkkkffffffffrrrffff-fff![1]

'THIS is what Tennyson sounds like,' claims Paul Chowder, the narrator of Nicholson
Baker's novel, *The Anthologist*. Or rather, this is what the static on Edison's recording
makes him sound like. As the momentum of 'Half a league onward' is revised into 'hobble leg owhmmm', and as 'the valley of Death' is shrunk to 'the bottle of fluff', Tennyson's
act of ennobling is met by a belittling echo. This transcription of the Laureate reading
'The Charge of The Light Brigade' could be taken as a wry commentary on the transmission and reception of Victorian poetry, for Paul is not the first anthologist to sense that
there might be a problem with how Victorian poets have come to be heard. In his preface
to the first *Oxford Book of Victorian Verse*, Arthur Quiller-Couch admitted that to refer to
the verse as 'Victorian' was not likely to endear it to the reading public, before adding that
'the present misprision' of the past era would 'surely go its way as a flippancy of fashion'.[2]
The fashion proved enduring, as many subsequent anthologists have pointed out: 'even
now', Christopher Ricks wrote in 1987, 'to travesty or to calumniate the Victorians is still
such a cheap holiday'.[3] Daniel Karlin later referred to 'the imputation...which still clings
to their collective achievement'.[4] Valentine Cunningham has claimed that 'Victorian
poetry is well recognised to have, taken as a whole, a difficulty over the words. Its diction
can so often be slack, so breezily casual and cliché-ed, seemingly so uncared-for'.[5]

The poetic output of any age, 'taken as a whole', could test a reader's good will (that's
one reason to be grateful to anthologists); besides, Cunningham's 'seemingly' hedges its
bets and may imply that lack of care lies with readers rather than writers. Many Victorian

poems ask their audiences to think about clichés, not simply to accept them. Recalling that most Victorian of occasions—the Queen's Jubilee in 1887—A. E. Housman turned his attentions to a people's wish to sing 'God save the Queen':

> From Clee to heaven the beacon burns,
>   The shires have seen it plain,
> From north and south the sign returns
>   And beacons burn again.
>
> Look left, look right, the hills are bright,
>   The dales are light between,
> Because 'tis fifty years to-night
>   That God has saved the Queen.
>
> Now, when the flame they watch not towers
>   About the soil they trod,
> Lads, we'll remember friends of ours
>   Who shared the work with God.[6]

That God has saved the Queen for this long, and that he has required assistance, prompts the raising of an eyebrow as well as a smile. 'From Clee to heaven' does not quite set about building Jerusalem in England's green and pleasant land: the phrasing perhaps elevates the Shropshire village a little, but it also brings heaven down to earth. Contractions are ceremonious (''tis', not 'it's fifty years', has the quality of a toast) yet also off-duty ('we'll'); the formal is heard alongside the conversational. Both registers jostle for priority in 'Now', which could stress commemorative decorum ('here and now, on this most special of occasions…'), or something more colloquial and urgent ('Now lads, listen up…'). In this poem—and in many Victorian poems—words seem to have more than one kind of reader or listener in mind. Patriotic souls, those who admire how a single beacon is really a sign for many, may or may not be wholly in tune with that other, possibly more disgruntled group, the speaker and the lads who remember 'friends of ours'. If the poem sympathizes with the wish to shelter under the unity provided by anthems for queen and country, it also makes space for a different kind of feeling, one that Richard Howard found good words for when he imagined another of the Queen's poets saying: 'I will not / be Victorian in their way'.[7]

Housman's '1887' became the introductory poem to *A Shropshire Lad,* and its attempt to read and to address the signs of the times is a good place to begin an introduction to a new set of essays on Victorian poetry—not least because the poem weighs up the dangers as well as the values of the homogenizing impulse. In 'Victorian Poetry: An Overview' in *The Cambridge History of English Poetry,* Richard Cronin begins by reminding us that 'there is no style that Victorian poets share'.[8] Many of them, though, do share a discernible set of preoccupations about style—and about how style should be put to work. One of the ways in which Housman's poem inhabits as well as enquires into its own Victorianness is through its cognizance of labour: remembering the friends who 'shared the work with God' invites consideration of how far the poet's work could be said to share in their aspirations and actions. Housman was not renowned for his patience with those who wanted to take things easy: 'How the world is managed, and why it was created, I cannot tell; but it is no feather-bed for the repose of sluggards'.[9]

If the poet wasn't to be a sluggard, what was he to be? This was the period, Philip Davis claims, in which 'poetry first began to lose its nerve and its place': 'Swamped by the thought of its questionable relevance within a new mass industrial and democratic society, poetry became self-consciously peripheral'.[10] Austin Dobson's 'On the Hurry of this Time' would seem to support this diagnosis:

> With slower pen men used to write,
> Of old, when 'letters' were 'polite':
>   In ANNA'S, or in GEORGE's days,
>   They could afford to turn a phrase,
> Or trim a straggling theme aright.
>
> They knew not steam; electric light
> Not yet had dazed their calmer sight;—
>   They meted out both blame and praise
>   With slower pen.
>
> Too swiftly now the Hours take flight!
> What's read at morn is dead at night:
>   Scant space have we for Art's delays,
>   Whose breathless thought so briefly stays,
> We may not work—ah! would we might!—
>   With slower pen.[11]

The longing for the good old days is gently teased (just how 'polite' were they back then? And is today's electric light really *that* bad?). Still, the poem's smile is a nervous one, and the idea that 'Art' might itself aspire to be a form of 'work' if it were accorded more time and space is not laughed off.

The 'we' to whom Dobson appealed was at once growing and shrinking. More poems were being written and published than ever before (Tennyson grumbled about being sent 'such shoals of poems . . . the two hundred million poets of Great Britain deluge me daily'),[12] but those producing and consuming prose were swimming in a much bigger sea. Although the *OED* records new words springing up in the period that could signal poetry's growth in stature ('poeticalness', 'poethood'), other Victorian coinages are less flattering ('poetast', 'poetastic', 'poetastical', 'poeticule', 'poeticism', 'poetism'). If poeticalness was becoming an increasingly defined category, then it was also an increasingly marginal or distant or debatable one—as though people harboured suspicions that the real article (Poetry with a capital P) was disappearing from view or being dispersed into a competing set of definitions and questionable voices (who, after all, wants to be a poetast or to write a poeticule?). Matthew Arnold came up with a word not cited in the *OED* in order to express his frustration at a distinctly 'modern situation' of 'unpoetrylessness'.[13]

For Arnold, the unpoetrylessness of the age was summed up in its attachment to work (he himself was brought up on the precept, '"*Work*". Not, work at this or that—but,

Work').[14] As the Victorians kept reminding themselves, to grow up was to get working; the full title of the Great Exhibition was 'Great Exhibition of the Works of Industry in All Nations', and its accompanying motto was 'The workers, of all types, stand forth as the really great men'. *All* types? Henry Mayhew's novel, entitled *1851*, sees the exhibition as the first national event to mark 'the dignity and artistic quality of labour',[15] but it is not clear whether the poets are being invited to join the party. Despite this—or because of it—Victorian disquisitions on poetry are often haunted by work, and by the need to clarify how the work of the imagination might best be valued and measured in relation to the demands of the age. Take Carlyle and Pater, commentators from opposing ends of the period and figures who, for many, represent opposing ends of the spectrum (the Argufier versus the Aesthete). Carlyle is credited by the *OED* for bringing the word 'worksome' into the language in the year of Victoria's accession to the throne, but while he is sometimes a defender of poetry as a form of labour, he is wary of certain appeals to aims and outcomes. In 'The Hero as Poet' he asks: 'The uses of this Dante? We will not say much about his "uses." A human soul who has once got into that primal element of *Song*, and sung forth fitly somewhat therefrom, has worked in the *depths* of our existence . . . in a way that "utilities" will not succeed well in calculating!'[16] Pater's refined sensitivity to stylistic polish, meanwhile, does not preclude an awareness of the toil that goes into style—nor of the variety of things that issue from it: 'all the excellences of literary form', he writes in *Appreciations*, 'are reducible to various kinds of painstaking; this good quality being involved in all "skilled work" whatever, in the drafting of an act of parliament, as in sewing'.[17]

This feeling for words at work—and for words *as* work—is mindful of the many ways in which literary form can be seen as both a shaped and shaping force. 'I am inclined to think that we want new *forms* . . . as well as thoughts',[18] confessed Elizabeth Barrett to Robert Browning in 1845, and a central aim of this *Handbook* is to provide a closely read appreciation of the vibrancy and variety of Victorian poetic forms. Those forms, however, do not get worked on in a vacuum; like her author, Aurora Leigh is adamant that 'the world of books is still the world', later adding that 'When God helps all the workers for his world, / The singers shall have help of Him, not last'.[19] If poetry had become—in Davis's words—'self-consciously peripheral', this self-consciousness also helped to recalibrate relations between work and song: from Thomas Hood's 'The Song of The Shirt', where 'A Woman sat, in unwomanly rags, / Plying her needle and thread—/ . . . Work! work! work!',[20] to John Davidson's 'Thirty Bob a Week', where 'the difficultest job a man can do, / Is to come it brave and meek with thirty bob a week',[21] some of the most arresting poems of the age find words for those *on* the periphery and explore what kinship the poet might establish with them. For Davidson, Hood's poem was 'the most important English poem of the nineteenth century': 'The poet is on the street, the hospital. He intends the world to know that it is out of joint. He will not let it alone . . . And it will be sung in all keys and voices. Poetry has other functions, other aims; but this also has become its province'.[22]

New maps were being drawn up, new territory staked out, and some essays in this volume explore these developments. Davidson's comments emphasize a growing sense of division and debate about what poetry should be doing with its time—'other functions, other aims' are acknowledged without being formulated—but another purpose of this volume is to examine how different voices colluded as well as clashed. Davidson pointed out that 'the newspaper is one of the most potent factors in moulding the character of contemporary poetry', and Hood's poem certainly advertised itself as an address to the moment (it drew on a report in *The London Times* about a woman named Biddell, and first appeared in the 1843 Christmas number of *Punch*). But 'The Song of The Shirt' is responding to the sound of early Tennyson too, just as Tennyson was himself an admirer and imitator of Hood's gruesomely punning energy.[23] Hood's seamstress is 'weary and worn' ('worn' doubling up to turn the exhausted labourer into a product much like the one she makes). She is a relative of the 'aweary' Mariana who is stuck gazing upon her 'weeded and worn' surroundings (this in turn glances forward to *In Memoriam*: 'In words, like weeds, I'll wrap me o'er / Like coarsest clothes against the cold').[24] The seamstress hears the 'the cock crowing aloof', recalling Mariana listening to 'The cock' who 'sang out an hour ere light'; she notices that 'underneath the eaves / The brooding swallows cling', just as Mariana heard 'the sparrow's chirrup on the roof'; she laments 'a wall so blank, my shadow I thank / For sometimes falling there!', echoing Mariana's torment at how 'the shadow of the poplar fell'. And perhaps the Lady of Shalott is also a brooding presence behind Hood's poem, for she is another woman whose stitching is felt to be a predicament (significantly, the only people to see or hear the Lady are the workers, 'reapers, reaping early... by the moon the reaper weary').[25]

Looking back to Wordsworth's encounter with the solitary reaper, J. H. Prynne has noted that 'the poet can only feel alien to the reality of this work; but to feel and bear the reality for him of its alien distance is part of his own work also'.[26] This dual sense of alienation and engagement is passed down to Victorian poets, and Tennyson's poems provide some of the age's most oblique yet enduring surrogates for the figure of the modern poet-worker, a figure who somehow does and doesn't work. John Millais's version of Mariana captures this duality by giving her a job to do (see figure 1.1). In his painting, she is engaged in the act of sewing. Or: she *was* engaged. Millais depicts her taking a break from her task—stretching her back, perhaps looking for a distraction from the work that was meant to be distracting her from her suffering.

The period's mixed feelings about aesthetic spaces can be heard in Ruskin's response to this figure: 'The picture has always been a precious memory to me, but if the painter had painted Mariana at work in an unmoated grange instead of idle in a moated one it had been more to the purpose—whether of art or life'.[27] The sage sounds confident here about what *the* purpose is, and about art's duty to present a certain kind of life, but many Victorian poets were in dialogue with the age—and with themselves—about what sort of work poetry should be committed to. Tennyson's Ulysses may intone 'How dull it is to pause, to make an end, / To rust unburnished, not to shine in use!', but when he praises the 'labour' of Telemachus he himself sounds laboured because he offers his compliments whilst looking for a way of justifying his own need to get away from 'the sphere / Of common duties': 'He works his work, I mine'.[28] Elsewhere in Tennyson, eloquent voices draw attention to the victims and the costs of the gospel of work: 'All things have rest: why should we toil alone, / We only toil', sing the lotus-eaters.[29] If one strand of

FIGURE 1.1 'Mariana, 1851' by Sir John Everett Millais. © Tate, London 2013

Victorianism reified work as a release from melancholy or as a therapy for despair (a guarantor of personal as well as of economic progress), other commentators were less cheery. When, in his *Principles of Political Economy,* John Stuart Mill noted that 'the majority of Englishmen and Americans have no life but in their work; that alone stands between them and ennui,'[30] he was reading work as a kind of repression, not as a form of salvation. 'There is always the danger that people who work hard become blinded by work itself and, by a paradox, lazy-minded,'[31] V. S. Pritchett later remarked. The poets frequently considered what this diligent docility was running from or trying to hide, and how it might be resisted through the play of poetic form, a play which need not be conceived as the opposite of work, but as an enquiry into the usefulness of any schematic division of labour between work and play. To recall Davis again: if poetry is indeed 'swamped by the thought of its questionable relevance within a new mass industrial and democratic society', it is also shaping questions about how relevance is to be defined and decided. The essays in this volume often pay close attention to how poets' formal daring seeks to engage with society by refusing to play by society's rules.

Notwithstanding its hostility to certain strands of Victorian poetics, the modernist critique included an appreciation of this daring. T. S. Eliot observed that 'the surface of Tennyson stirred about with his time; and he had nothing to which to hold fast except his unique and unerring feeling for the sounds of words'; the poet was, Eliot ventured, 'the most instinctive rebel against the society in which he was the most perfect conform-ist'.[32] So the sounds themselves could be heard as rebellious and conformist, as Mallarmé intimated when paying tribute to the poet in 1892: 'This chaste arrangement of sylla-bles, *Tennyson,* now said solemnly like this: *Lord Tennyson*...full of determination, but above all reticent...ingenuous and taciturn'.[33] The final syllable of the name here (heard in French as *son,* 'sound') is a reminder that one syllable can say two things at once, and it's Mallarmé's way of implying that what the Tennysonian had already come to stand for (the lordly, the chaste, the solemn, the Victorian) was not the whole story. There is cer-tainly a side of the poet that feels the need to be determined; in *In Memoriam,* for exam-ple, when the speaker tells readers 'That nothing walks with aimless feet'. But another side of Tennyson is drawn to set poetic feet moving in less straightforward ways. Elsewhere in *In Memoriam,* these lines about the earth contain a perplexed admiration as well as an anxious concern, and part of their power comes from the poet's conjurings with 'work':

> This round of green, this orb of flame,
>   Fantastic beauty; such as lurks
>   In some wild Poet, when he works
> Without a conscience or an aim.[34]

Shaped round the line-end, 'works' is both determined and reticent. For a brief moment, the verb sounds intransitive; for the Poet to work is for him 'to act in the desired way, do what is required; to be practicable or effectual, to succeed' (*OED*). But the journey into the next line brings a small shock and a new apprehension of what success might mean. The enjambed lines seem to vouch for the uncertainty they embody, and in this respect they have much in common with Tennyson's attitude to the fantastical, beguil-ing beauty of sound—something he is willing to trust to on occasion without knowing exactly where it will lead him. To rhyme 'works' with 'lurks' is to imagine poetic form as a darkly ludic kind of labour. This wild work is not necessarily without its uses: it just doesn't presuppose the result of its activities in advance.

Formal questions are, then, at the heart of this volume, but discussion about the for-mal takes in matters of social decorum as well as the finer points of literary style. Indeed, the Victorians could be said to be the inventors of good form: '*good (*or *bad) form*: said of behaviour, manners, etc. which satisfy (or offend) the current ideals of "Society"; (good or bad) manners. *colloq.* [first recorded usage 1868]' (*OED*). Given their circum-stances, the poets had all the more reason to wonder whether Society (or the appari-tion of it signalled by the *OED*'s scare-quotes) should be dictating terms. When Aurora Leigh asks 'What form is best for poems?' (Book V, l. 223), she is also asking what duties poems have to themselves as well as to those who would have poems be on their best behaviour. Poets could do some of their most assiduous work 'without a conscience' by asking what conscientiousness was acting as a cover-story for. Samuel Smiles insisted that 'Honourable industry travels the same road with duty...The gods, says the poet, have placed labour and toil on the way leading to the Elysian fields'.[35] 'The poet' here is meant to be a spokesman for Poetry itself, but the best poets travelled less straightfor-ward roads. Arthur Hugh Clough probed 'the pure nonentity of duty...With the form conforming duly, / Senseless what it meaneth truly,[36] and his willingness to play devil-ish havoc with what the *OED* politely terms 'current ideals' was in part shaped by his relationship with Arnold, who confessed in private to his friend that he was unlike those 'who set to work at their duty self-denial &c like furies in the dark'. Arnold wanted 'a distinct seeing of my way as far as my own nature is concerned', not a dutiful craving for 'profound thoughts, mighty spiritual workings &c. &c.'[37] 'Work', 'workings', &c, &c: for many Victorian poets, 'work' and its cognates are envisaged as traps—or as words that need to be rescued or redefined—because the terms have been cheapened by commen-tators who use them too narrowly and too easily.

When defending his *Poems and Ballads* against the reviewers in 1866, Swinburne wrote:

> The question at issue is wider than any between a single writer and his critics, or it might well be allowed to drop. It is this: whether or not the first and last requisite of art is to give no offence; whether or not all that cannot be lisped in the nursery or fingered in the schoolroom is therefore to be cast out of the library; whether or not the domestic circle is to be for all men and writers the outer limit and extreme horizon of their world of work?[38]

Not just 'work' or 'world', but 'world of work': the phrasing highlights both the exter-nal reach and the internal force of what might now be referred to as the 'artwork' (the word is another Victorian coinage). For Swinburne, the extreme horizon is—as one of Browning's speakers has it—'on the dangerous edge of things', dealing with 'The honest thief, the tender murderer, / The superstitious atheist'.[39] The poet again has recourse to work in 'The Leper' as the scribe-speaker tells how he did a good work by taking in an outcast gentlewoman. Yet he may have done other things too ('Falling on her, such joy I had / To do the service God forbids'):

> It may be all my love went wrong—
>   A scribe's work writ awry and blurred,
> Scrawled after the blind evensong—
>   Spoilt music with no perfect word.[40]

Poems like this, where feeling turns textual and where the textual becomes tricky to decipher, go beyond the merely shocking in their resistance to what Swinburne saw as the critics' stipulation that 'the first and last requisite of art is to give no offence'. They aim to make readers hesitant about deciding what, precisely, the offence might be—and about their ability to clarify where the offence begins and ends.

Not being too sure of themselves is something that many Victorian poets work at. The growing uncertainty about poetry's form and function becomes a resource as well as a predicament as writers stage the uncertainty in and around the poems themselves:

> Well. Now it's anything but clear,
> What is the tone that's taken here;
> What is your logic? What's your theology?
> Is it or is it not neology?[41]

The spirit's questions in Clough's *Dipsychus and The Spirit* spill beyond the poem's bounds into its prose epilogue, where the poet's listener gets the chance to respond: "'I don't very well understand what it's all about,' said my uncle.'[42] His perplexity foreshadows Alice's when she hears the poem about the Jabberwocky a few years later: 'It seems very pretty…but it's rather hard to understand…Somehow it seems to fill my head with ideas—only I don't exactly know what they are!'[43] These small dramas of perception and reception are representative not just of demands that poems be explicable, knowable, subject to para-phrase (with form as a mere container of content); they are also a way of saying that the work of poetry should remain incomplete. In Victorian poems, the sense of an ending is frequently resisted or twisted as inherited expectations and ways of reading are confronted by new forms of experimental energy. This energy can be felt acutely in the poets' rhyming, in their very need to stick with rhyme whilst they take other kinds of risk—as though the ordered nature of rhyme was itself a way of luring readers into a false sense of security. Take this sampling of final lines from a range of genres and modes, all rhyming on the same vowel-sound to different effect. From Browning's dramatic monologues and dramatic lyrics, where the lyric 'I' and its addressee are re-cast as a troubling, serio-comic double-act:

> Notice Neptune, tho',
> Taming a sea-horse, thought a rarity,
> Which Claus of Innsbruck cast in bronze for me.[44]

> 'No, the book
> Which noticed how the wall-growths wave' said she
> 'Was not by Ruskin.'
> I said 'Vernon Lee?'[45]

From Dante Gabriel Rossetti's strangely blocked elegies, where readers can no longer be sure that the work of mourning has been completed:

> From perfect grief there need not be
> Wisdom or even memory:
> One thing then learnt remains to me,—
> The woodspurge has a cup of three.[46]

From Thomas Hardy's war poetry, where epic motifs—the honouring, burial, and stellification of the dead—are shaped into traumatic forms of damage and displacement:

> Yet portion of that unknown plain
>   Will Hodge for ever be;
> His homely Northern breast and brain
>   Grow to some Southern tree,
> And strange-eyed constellations reign
>   His stars eternally.[47]

From Robert Louis Stevenson's children's verse, where sing-song is ghosted by solitariness, as though the Ancient Mariner had stumbled into the nursery:

> We sailed along for days and days,
> And had the very best of plays;
> But Tom fell out and hurt his knee,
> So there was no one left but me.[48]

From Swinburne's contribution to the development of Victorian parody, where aspirations towards grand designs in poetry are heard as nonsensical:

> God, whom we see not, is: and God, who is not, we see:
> Fiddle, we know, is diddle: and diddle, we take it, is dee.[49]

And from Lewis Carroll's nonsense verse itself, where quest narratives are re-imagined as wild goose chases:

> In the midst of the word he was trying to say,
>   In the midst of his laughter and glee,
> He had softly and suddenly vanished away—
>   For the Snark *was* a Boojum, you see.[50]

We do see, but we also wonder whether we see aright—and whether we might have missed something.

'What is the tone that's taken here?' is a question that could be asked of many Victorian poems, and the difficulty of providing an answer is part of the poetry's strength. Writing in another context about the sound of nineteenth-century writing, Stanley Cavell has observed: 'A natural effect of reading such writing is to be unsure whether the writer is perfectly serious. I dare say that the writer may himself or herself be unsure, and that this may be a good sign that the writing is doing its work, taking its course'.[51] This is a conception of work that Victorian poets often entertain and encourage. When, in Christina Rossetti's 'Winter: My Secret', the speaker says 'Or, after all, perhaps there's none: / Suppose there is no secret after all, / But only just my fun',[52] it might be inferred that she has seen through the importance of being earnest. But it could also be a mistake to assume that the speaker herself knows the answer. The writing may be taking its own course, may be on its way to revealing a secret the speaker didn't know she had, asking readers for assistance as well as asking them to think about what it is they want from poems like this one. The poem closes with another 'or': one day, 'Perhaps my secret I may say, / Or you may guess'. It is as though the lessons of the Victorian dramatic monologue have been taken to heart and applied to the figure of the poet herself; the ending provides a space for the self to be occluded, invented, or revised, not merely discovered, and imagines the reader-auditor as a vital part of a continuing process.

Rossetti's final appeal to 'you'—at once conversable and cagey—is heard across Victorian poetry in varying keys, and it speaks of the poets' need to see themselves as situated within a wider community, even as they acknowledge the difficulty of how they find themselves placed. 'You cannot see in the world the work of the Poet's pen: / Yet the Poet is master of words, and words are masters of men', writes William Allingham.[53] The couplet echoes the rousing final paragraph of Shelley's defence, in which poetry allows

us 'to work a beneficial change in opinion or institution' and poets are 'the unacknowledged legislators of the world'.[54] But Allingham's lines also sound frustrated (it's not clear
that the 'You' is necessarily going to see things differently now that the poem has set
him straight). In his 'Prelude' to *Departmental Ditties and Other Verses*, Rudyard Kipling
underlines the awkwardness of the modern poet's task: he needs somehow to find a way
to make poetry speak to more than one kind of reader at once:

> I have written the tale of our life
>   For a sheltered people's mirth,
> In jesting guise—but ye are wise,
>   And ye know what the jest is worth.[55]

David Bromwich suggests that the jest here is another name for truth, and adds that
'one might say more conditionally that jest is truth, accommodated to an audience with
whom the poet's relation is tactical, but ready for another audience with whom his relation may be moral'.[56] This blending of tactical accommodation and implicit provoca-
tion is felt throughout the period, although other poets ready themselves for their ideal
readers by providing less shelter from the outset. Ruskin voiced his exasperation at
Browning's poetry in workaday terms: 'Being hard worked at present, & not being able
to give the cream of the day to poetry', he found that the poems in *Men and Women*
asked too much of him.[57] This might imply that reading poetry should be understood
simply as time-off from hard work. Browning took issue in his reply: 'We don't read
poetry the same way, by the same law; it is too clear. I cannot begin writing poetry till my
imaginary reader has conceded licences to me which you demur at altogether'.[58] He is
not just saying that he wants to be left alone to write what he wants, but that his utterance
takes shape only *after* a reader has been imagined for it, a reader who is in search of a
poem that will disorient him. The work of the poet here foreshadows that of Browning's
Euripides in *Aristophanes' Apology*:

>   he worked:
> And, as he worked, he wanted not, be sure,
> Triumph his whole life through, submitting work
> To work's right judges, never to the wrong—[59]

Just as for Kipling, the 'right judges' are those who are able to include themselves in
the judgement—readers like George Eliot, who in her review of Browning's *Men and
Women* acknowledged that 'in his best poems he makes us feel that what we took for
obscurity in him was superficiality in ourselves'.[60] The imaginary readers of such poems
are in their turn required to take liberties as well as to concede licences; in his response
to *The Ring and The Book*, Henry James said of Browning that 'he takes his wilful way
with me, but I make it my own': 'To glance at these things...is fairly to be tangled, and at
once, in the author's complexity of suggestion, to which our own thick-coming fancies
respond in no less a measure...From the moment I am taking liberties I suffer *no* awkwardness...Browning works the whole thing over—the whole thing as originally given
him—and we work *him*; helpfully, artfully, boldly, which is our whole blest basis'.[61]

This collection of essays tries to continue the artful work. The volume is divided into four sections. The first on 'Form' focuses on the complexity of suggestion generated by style (chapters explore 'Rhythm', 'Beat', 'Address', 'Rhyme', 'Diction', 'Syntax', and 'Story'). The second section, 'Literary Landscapes', examines traditions and writers that have influenced and taken their bearings from Victorian poets. It attends to some of the age's most pressing debates—about the uses of the past, the value of tradition, the varied meanings of 'progress', the condition of belatedness—by focusing on how writers shaped their work in relation to other poets, before moving on to a consideration of the afterlives of Victorian poetry in Modernist writing and beyond. The third section offers 'Readings' of twenty-three poets by concentrating on particular poems or collections of poems. These essays are not pitched as overviews or as introductions, but as focused, nuanced engagements with the pleasures and challenges offered by particular styles of thinking and writing. The final section, 'The Place of Poetry', explores place in a range of ways in order to situate Victorian poetry within broader discussions: the places in which poems were encountered; the poetic representation and embodiment of various sites and spaces; the location of the Victorian alongside other territories and nationalities; and discussions about the place—and displacement—of poetry in Victorian society.

In 1918 Ezra Pound pronounced: 'For most of us, the odour of defunct Victoriana is so unpleasant…that we are content to leave the past where we find it'. Nearly one hundred years later, this *Handbook* considers the many ways in which the past refuses to be left, and how it continues to find us. Pound's stridency was also a form of defensiveness: he—and the majority for whom he claimed to speak—were still too close to their predecessors, and sometimes too quick to turn the varied inflections of the Victorian into 'Victoriana' (the *OED* credits Pound with the first recorded usage of the word), or into 'Victorianism' (*OED*; first usage 1905). This volume includes many different types of approach and outlook, providing an opportunity to listen again to Victorian poetry from a wide range of positions. Throughout the volume, though, contributors study the poets as *writers*. Essays frequently come back to questions of form foregrounded in the opening section—not in order to retreat from other kinds of question (be they philosophical, scientific, cultural, or socio-political), but rather to concentrate and to complicate them, or to find new ways of asking them. So whilst the volume builds on recent theoretical, cultural, and historical scholarship, it remains committed to a sustained focus on the craft of poems themselves.

Essays in appreciation often benefit from attempts to discriminate between what does and what doesn't work, and this volume takes Pound's comments on board without taking them on trust. It opens, for example, with a couple of essays on the range of Victorian metrical experiment and achievement, and ends with a study of 'Bad Verse'. The volume, then, is not exactly intended as a celebration of Victorian poetry (although there *is* much to celebrate), but as a revaluation of it—a revaluation which envisages poetic craft as a kind of act. In his discussion of the relations between art and society in the nineteenth century, Geoffrey Hill considers two poems by Gerard Manley Hopkins:

> In 'Harry Ploughman' the man is in stride, his craft requires it; and the poem itself, in
> its rhythm and 'burden lines', is the model of a work song. In the companion-piece,

'Tom's Garland', the dispossessed are thrown out of work and out of stride and the piece is, both discursively and rhythmically, perhaps the harshest, the most crabbed, of all Hopkins's poems. It is as though the poet is implying that, because the men cannot work, therefore the poem itself cannot.[62]

This reads the work of rhythm as a form of witness and of conscience—work that sounds out the age by understanding its own sounds as taking shape within and against it. Indeed, when, in 'Harry Ploughman', Hopkins watches how 'one crew, fall to; / Stand at stress', or when in 'Tom's Garland' he zeroes in on the 'mighty foot',[63] the terms are meant to be understood as at once metrical and physical, with the life of the verse seeking to embody and respond to the lives of those outside it. Hopkins conceded to R. W. Dixon that 'Tom's Garland' and 'Harry Ploughman' were 'works of infinite, of over great contrivance, I am afraid, to the annulling in the end of the right effect',[64] yet the contrivance that led to weakness of the former is not entirely to be dissociated from the achievement of the latter. As Hill goes on to add: '"Tom's Garland" is a failure, but it fails to some purpose; it is a test to breaking point of the sustaining power of language'.[65] Such testing failures do not merely miss out on rightness. They help to create an appetite for new apprehensions of what poetry might be and do—and they prompt consideration of whether writers and readers should always be sure of what 'the right effect' actually is. In Hopkins's last poem, 'To R. B.', he dreams of an artistry that could come to fruition, 'with aim / Now known and hand at work now never wrong'.[66] To be 'at work', though, is to be not quite there yet, as the poem recognizes. Victorian poems are often hoping to arrive at a replenished sense of the known, and are often aware of the pressing need for an aim. But they respond to other, less predictable needs too—not the least of which is the wish to give themselves and their readers something to work with.

NOTES

1. Nicolson Baker, *The Anthologist* (London: Simon and Shuster, 2009), 151–2.
2. Arthur Quiller-Couch, ed., *The Oxford Book of Victorian Verse* (Oxford: Clarendon Press, 1912), ix.
3. Christopher Ricks, ed., *The Oxford Book of Victorian Verse* (Oxford: Oxford University Press, 1987), xxv.
4. Daniel Karlin, ed., *The Penguin Book of Victorian Verse* (London: Penguin, 1997), xxxiii-iv.
5. Valentine Cunningham, ed., *The Victorians: An Anthology of Poetry and Poetics* (Oxford: Blackwell, 2000), xlii.
6. A. E. Housman, '1887', *The Poems of A. E. Housman*, ed. Archie Burnett (Oxford: Clarendon Press, 1997), 3.
7. Richard Howard, 'November, 1889', in *Selected Poems*, ed. Hugh Haughton and Adam Phillips (London: Penguin, 1991), 67.
8. Richard Cronin, 'Victorian poetry: An Overview', in *The Cambridge History of English Poetry*, ed. Michael O'Neill (Cambridge: Cambridge University Press, 2010), 576.
9. A. E. Housman, 'Preface to Manilius', in *A. E. Housman: Collected Poems and Selected Prose*, ed. Christopher Ricks (London: Penguin, 1988), 378.

10. Philip Davis, *The Victorians* (Oxford: Oxford University Press, 2004), 457.

11. Austin Dobson, 'On the Hurry of This Time', in *Decadent Verse: An Anthology of Late Victorian Poetry, 1872–1900*, ed. Caroline Blyth (London: Anthem, 2011), 455.

12. Alfred Tennyson, quoted in Hallam Tennyson, ed., *Tennyson and His Friends* (London: Macmillan, 1911), 357.

13. Matthew Arnold, quoted in Ian Hamilton, *A Gift Imprisoned: The Poetic Life of Matthew Arnold* (London: Bloomsbury, 1999), 156.

14. Thomas Arnold, *Passages in a Wandering Life* (London: Edward Arnold, 1900), 243.

15. Henry Mayhew, *1851: or, The Adventures of Mr and Mrs Sandyboys and Family* (London: Bogue, 1851), 129.

16. Thomas Carlyle, 'The Hero as Poet', in *On Heroes, Hero-Worship, & The Heroic in History* (London: James Fraser, 1841), 161. On Carlyle's complex engagements with the idea of poetry as a form of work, see Marcus Waithe, 'The Pen and the Hammer: Thomas Carlyle, Ebenezer Elliott, and the "Active Poet"', in *Class and the Canon: Constructing Labouring-Class Poetry and Poetic 1780–1900* (Basingstoke: Palgrave Macmillan, 2012), 116–135.

17. Walter Pater, in *Selected Writings of Walter Pater*, ed. Harold Bloom (New York: American Library, 1974), 105.

18. Elizabeth Barrett, letter to Robert Browning (20 March 1845), in *The Brownings' Correspondence*, ed. P. Kelley and S. Lewis (Winfield: Kansas: Wedgestone Press, 1992), x. 103.

19. Elizabeth Barrett Browning, *Aurora Leigh*, ed. Margaret Reynolds (New York: Norton, 1996), 27, 72 (Book I, lines 747–8, & Book II, lines 1233–4).

20. Thomas Hood, 'The Song of the Shirt', in *Selected Poems of Hood, Praed and Beddoes*, ed. Susan Wolfson and Peter J. Manning (London: Penguin, 2000), 141.

21. John Davidson, 'Thirty Bob a Week', in *The Poems of John Davidson*, ed. Andrew Turnbull, 2 vols (Edinburgh: Scottish Academic Press, 1973), i. 65.

22. John Davidson, 'Pre-Shakespearianism', *Speaker*, XIX (28 January 1899), 258–9.

23. See Matthew Bevis, 'Tennyson's Humour', in *Tennyson Among the Poets: Bicentenary Essays*, ed. Seamus Perry and Robert Douglas-Fairhurst (Oxford: Oxford University Press, 2009), 240, 253.

24. Alfred Tennyson, 'Mariana' and *In Memoriam* (section V), in *Tennyson: A Selected Edition*, ed. Christopher Ricks, rev. edn. (Harlow: Pearson Longman, 2007), 4, 349.

25. Alfred Tennyson, 'The Lady of Shalott', *Tennyson: A Selected Edition*, 21.

26. J. H. Prynne, *Field Notes: The Solitary Reaper and Others* (Cambridge: Barque Press, 2007), 89.

27. John Ruskin, 'Notes on Millais', in *The Library Edition of the Works of John Ruskin*, ed. E. T. Cook and Alexander Wedderburn, 39 vols. (London: George Allen, 1903–12), xiv. 496.

28. Alfred Tennyson, 'Ulysses', in *Tennyson: A Selected Edition*, 142–4.

29. Alfred Tennyson, 'The Lotos-Eaters', in *Tennyson: A Selected Edition*, 74.

30. John Stuart Mill, *Principles of Political Economy*, ed. Stephen Nathanson (Indianapolis, IN: Hackett, 2004), 39.

31. V. S. Pritchett, quoted in Stefan Collini, *Common Reading: Critics, Historians, Publics* (Oxford: Oxford University Press, 2009), 21.

32. T. S. Eliot, '*In Memoriam*', in *Selected Essays* (London: Faber and Faber, 1951), 337.

33. Stéphane Mallarmé, 'Tennyson, Seen From Here', in *Mallarmé in Prose*, ed. Mary Ann Caws (New York: New Directions, 2001), 72.

34. Alfred Tennyson, *In Memoriam* (section XXXIV), in *Tennyson: A Selected Edition*, 377.

35. Samuel Smiles, *Self-Help*, ed. Peter W. Sinnema (Oxford: Oxford World's Classics, 2002), 37.

36. Arthur Hugh Clough, 'Duty,—that's to say complying', in *Clough: Selected Poems*, ed. J. P. Phelan (London: Longman, 1995), 42.

37. Matthew Arnold, quoted in Hamilton, *A Gift Imprisoned*, 118.

38. Algernon Charles Swinburne, 'A Rejoiner', in *An Anthology of Pre-Raphaelite Writing*, ed. Carolyn Hares-Stryker (Sheffield: Sheffield Academic Press, 1997), 171.

39. Robert Browning, 'Bishop Blougram's Apology', in *Robert Browning: Selected Poems*, ed. John Woolford, Daniel Karlin, and Joseph Phelan (Harlow: Pearson Longman, 2010), 306.

40. Algernon Charles Swinburne, 'The Leper', in *Major Poems and Selected Prose*, ed. Jerome McGann (New Haven: Yale University Press, 2004), 115–6.

41. Arthur Hugh Clough, *Dipsychus and The Spirit*, in *Clough: Selected Poems*, 200.

42. Arthur Hugh Clough, *Dipsychus and The Spirit*, in *Clough: Selected Poems*, 231.

43. Lewis Carroll, *Alice's Adventures in Wonderland and Through the Looking-Glass*, ed. Hugh Haughton (London: Penguin, 1998), 134.

44. Robert Browning, 'My Last Duchess' in *Robert Browning: Selected Poems*, 200.

45. Robert Browning, 'Inapprehensiveness', in Ricks, ed., *Victorian Verse*, 162.

46. Dante Gabriel Rossetti, 'The Woodspurge', in *Dante Gabriel Rossetti: Collected Poetry and Prose*, ed. Jerome McGann (New Haven: Yale University Press, 2003), 177.

47. Thomas Hardy, 'Drummer Hodge', in *Thomas Hardy: The Complete Poems*, ed. James Gibson (Basingstoke: Palgrave Macmillan, 2001), 91.

48. Robert Louis Stevenson, 'A Good Play', in *A Child's Garden of Verses* (Ware: Wordsworth Classics, 1993), 32.

49. Algernon Charles Swinburne, 'The Higher Pantheism in a Nutshell', in *Major Poems and Selected Prose*, 204.

50. Lewis Carroll, *The Hunting of The Snark*, ed. Martin Gardner (London: Penguin, 1995), 96.

51. Stanley Cavell, *In Quest of The Ordinary: Lines of Skepticism and Romanticism* (Chicago: University of Chicago Press, 1994), 121.

52. Christina Rossetti, 'Winter: My Secret', in *Christina Rossetti: The Complete Poems*, ed. R. W. Crump and Betty S. Flowers (London: Penguin, 2001), 41.

53. William Allingham, 'You cannot see in the world the work of the Poet's pen', in *Blackberries* (London: Longman, 1893), n. p.

54. Percy Shelley, 'A Defence of Poetry', in *Percy Bysshe Shelley: The Major Works*, ed. Zachary Leader and Michael O'Neill (Oxford: Oxford University Press, 2003), 700–1.

55. Rudyard Kipling, 'Prelude', in *The Complete Verse* (London: Kyle Cathie, 1990), 1.

56. David Bromwich, 'Kipling's Jest', in *A Choice of Inheritance: Self and Community from Edmund Burke to Robert Frost* (Cambridge, MA: Harvard University Press, 1989), 188.

57. John Ruskin, letter to Browning (2 December 1855), in *Robert Browning: Selected Poems*, 878.

58. Robert Browning, letter to Ruskin (10 December 1855), in *Robert Browning: Selected Poems*, 881.

59. Robert Browning, *Aristophanes' Apology*, in *The Poems: Volume Two*, ed. John Pettigrew and Thomas J. Collins (London: Penguin, 1981), lines 255–8.

60. George Eliot, unsigned review of *Men and Women*, in *The Westminster Review*, 65 (January 1856), 291.

61. Henry James, *Notes on Novelists, with some other Notes* (New York: Scribner's, 1914), 402, 404–5, 406.

62. Geoffrey Hill, 'Redeeming the Time', in *Collected Critical Writings*, ed. Kenneth Haynes (Oxford: Oxford University Press, 2008), 102.

63. Gerard Manley Hopkins, 'Harry Ploughman' and 'Tom's Garland: upon the Unemployed', in *Gerard Manley Hopkins: A Critical Edition of The Major Works,* ed. Catherine Phillips (Oxford: Oxford University Press, 1986), 177–8.

64. Gerard Manley Hopkins, *The Correspondence of Gerard Manley Hopkins and Richard Watson Dixon,* ed. C. C. Abbott (Oxford: Oxford University Press, 1955), 153.

65. Hill, 'Redeeming the Time', in *Collected Critical Writings,* 102.

66. Gerard Manley Hopkins, 'To R. B.', in *Gerard Manley Hopkins: A Critical Edition of The Major Works,* 184.

PART I

FORM

CHAPTER 2

···

RHYTHM

···

MICHAEL D. HURLEY

HOPKINS thought Swinburne had 'no real understanding of rhythm',[1] which seems arch coming from an unpublished part-timer whose own efforts in 'sprung rhythm' raised eyebrows—of both incomprehension and disapproval—even among his friends. But since the posthumous rise in Hopkins's reputation, initially as a poet (following Bridges's 1918 edition of his poems), and more recently as 'a literary theorist of first importance',[2] we may be inclined to take his aspersion seriously. And if we cannot summarily dismiss his contention as cloth-eared ignorance, the question sharpens: how *could* he have doubted the artisanal aptitude of the man George Saintsbury would in his eight-century conspectus crown England's 'prosodist magician'?[3] For all their obvious differences in world view, in terms of rhythmical practice, there are peculiar affinities between these diminutive red-headed Balliol men who were both steeped in the Classics and yet also seemingly proto-modern, some even say postmodern, in their poetics. Here are two representative samples of their verse styles, from Hopkins and Swinburne respectively:

> Is out with it! Oh,
> We lash with the best or worst
> Word last! How a lush-kept plush-capped sloe
> Will, mouthed to flesh-burst,
> Gush!—flush the man, the being with it, sour or sweet,
> Brim, in a flash, full!

> And as the august great blossom of the dawn
> Burst, and the full sun scarce from sea withdrawn
> Seemed on the fiery water a flower afloat,
> So as a fire the mighty morning smote
> Throughout her, and incensed with the influent hour
> Her whole soul's one great mystical red flower
> Burst, and the bud of her sweet spirit broke
> Rose-fashion, and the strong spring at a stroke

> Thrilled, and was cloven, and from the full sheath came
> The whole rose of the woman red as flame:
> And all her Mayday blood as from a swoon
> Flushed, and May rose up in her and was June.[4]

While these excerpts diverge thematically, poetically—and more specifically, prosodically—they seem rather to converge. The outcome is a curious one. Dramatized through their patterns of sound moving in time, what distinctions exist between the semantic material of these passages becomes blurred. Under the pressure of his prosody, Hopkins's account of a metaphysical experience simultaneously reads as a thoroughly physical event, and Swinburne's evocation of orgasm, as something gesturing beyond itself. Divine and sexual communions take on provokingly similar identities: bursting-gushing-flushing through alliteration, consonance, and vowel chiming set in expressive strain across line-endings, the reader encounters something that is at once sheerly felt but at the same time insistently transitive, teleological, seeking transcendence. 'Fleshly' was the pejorative term associated with Swinburne during his lifetime, but that seems at least as apt a description for Hopkins's synaesthetic—touching, tasting—richness here. And a parallel observation may be made about Swinburne, who describes one 'thrilled' beyond mere fleshliness. John Buchanan derided Swinburne's 'sensualism' for exciting the 'inference that the body is greater than the soul';[5] but it is truer to say that the way his 'great mystical' imagery folds into the 'whole soul' here excites self-witnessing spiritual implications *through* sensualism.

Part of what makes these poets an illuminating pairing is that they suggest the diversity but also the common perspectives of that vast and heterogeneous literary-historical category called 'Victorian Poetry'. Setting the chaste religious orthodox beside the sado-sexual atheist iconoclast indicates both the range of different and occasionally hostile interests of the period's verse, as it also suggests how certain apparently incompatible thematic preoccupations may connect in unexpected ways, through rhythm. To continue only the theme of Swinburne's coital climaxing as it imbricates with Hopkins's religious rapture, it is intriguing to compare the lush afterglow of conjugal pleasure in Dante Gabriel Rossetti's 'Nuptial Sleep' ('yet still their mouths, burnt red'),[6] with the greedy corporeality of another celebrated Christian poet of the period, that of his sister, Christina. Her best-known poem, *Goblin Market*, obviously revels in the transgressive temptations of forbidden fruit as experienced by 'Laura', who 'sucked and sucked and sucked the more', who 'sucked until her lips were sore'. But less obviously too, her later devotional poetry expresses a 'yearning' for spiritual satisfactions (notably, in 'Like as the hart desireth the water brooks'), satisfactions that are figured in vividly voluptuous terms: 'I thirst for Thee, full fount and flood; / My heart calls thine, as deep to deep' ('I Know You Not').[7]

Recent studies on Victorian prosody have shown how thoroughly the identity and function of rhythm was, for both poets and their readers, implicated in wider cultural and political contexts.[8] Other scholars have emphasized the importance of interpreting those same rhythms as a physical experience, one that was understood as part of

Victorian scientific discourse on rhythm in general and on its specific analogical and actual relation to the body's fixed-but-variable patterns of breath, gait, speech, heartbeat, and entire physiological being.[9] Much of the most trenchant work in historical recovery has demonstrated the commerce between these perspectives: how the poetics of physicality comes to be associated with the rhythms of cosmic processes (what Tennyson called 'the deep pulsations of the world'),[10] and how the tendency to understand verse rhythms as responding to and affecting the bodies of poets and readers 'must be read within a larger political framework for nineteenth-century poetry and poetic theory'.[11] Whatever ideology might be inscribed in this or that prosodic choice is enmeshed also in a powerful and pervasive belief in rhythm's somatically affective power.

While poetry's sensate richness is therefore in an obvious sense determined semantically ('the mind often governs the ear', as Dr Johnson reminds us),[12] in preparing the ground to discuss questions of rhythm it is well to make clear from the outset how far a poem's subject is also governed by its presentation. To speak of rhythm as an isolated category abstracted from words (their lexical meanings and sound textures) would be artificial. For it is only by, with, and through its rhythms that a poem's subject is shaped and animated. In the examples considered above, it is the sound patterning that makes the fleshy diction *fleshly*. Such is the vogue for experimentation and revival in the period that there is very much more to 'Victorian rhythm' than could be satisfied by generalization. The most striking quality of the period's verse forms is indeed its multiformity. It is, however, precisely because of this formal variety that generalizing about a poetics of fleshliness may prove useful as a way into a subject that is otherwise (to adapt Henry James's verdict on the nineteenth-century novel) a forbiddingly large, loose, baggy monster. For even where the period's poems are not about flesh as such—and, naturally, very many of them are not—there is often nonetheless something fleshly about them.

Without wishing to collapse all distinctions between poems, poets, and the movements with which they were associated, it might be said, then, that Victorian verse is conspicuously ambitious to rouse the quiddity of physical experience—experience not merely read about but read aloud, even chanted or declaimed—and felt in the act of reading. Seen in this way, it is possible to trace a network of allegiances across seven decades of otherwise divergent poetic practices: from what Arthur Hallam, with Tennyson in mind, recommends in 1831 as a 'poetry of sensation',[13] to those mid-century 'Spasmodics', to Hopkins's wish to instantiate a Scotian *haecceitas* (or 'thisness'), to the Pre-Raphaelite concern with evoking sensual particulars as a way of expressing feelings that eluded straightforward description, to Robert Browning's fractured, consonant-clustering dissonance, to Swinburne's Decadent hurrah for the saturate senses.

Importantly, such fleshly poetics may be observed criss-crossing between these poets, movements, and decades, rather than as a chronological progression culminating in *fin de siècle* excess. When Swinburne's 'Anactoria' raised alarm among those 'moral milkmen' for its lusty description of Sappho's desire for her female lover, Alfred Austin was right to point out that 'Mr Tennyson, of whose extreme moral propriety some people have made such an absurd parade, has written something very similar, to the full as impassioned'.[14] 'Fatima'—which was indeed published some thirty-four years before 'Anactoria'—likewise invokes Sappho (in its epigraph) and thrives on the diction of erotic tussle and release: 'Sudderest', 'strain', 'Throbbing', 'thirsted', 'tender', 'crushed', 'breast', 'mouth', 'burning', 'swoon', 'Faints', 'desire', 'fierce', 'delight', 'naked', 'possess', 'clasped', and, inevitably, 'Bursts'.[15] What makes Tennyson's poem 'to the full as impassioned', though, is not to be found so much in the poem's words as in how they are propelled. Words establish the narrative, but the *drama* of that narrative does not inhere in discrete lexical units: it is realized in the play between them. Priming and recalling each other between and across lines and stanzas, these words appeal in a way that is cumulative, arising from their interplay; and there is a sense in which the speaker's desired climax, which is the climax of the poem, is also realized through word-play, in the conventional *petit mort* pun. But another kind of word-play is more thoroughly at work here, one that is neither lexical nor grammatical, though it informs both the way we read words' meanings and construe their relations: a play of words through rhythm. Here are the last two of six stanzas:

> The wind sounds like a silver wire,
> And from beyond the noon a fire
> Is poured upon the hills, and nigher
> The skies stoop down in their desire;
>   And, isled in sudden seas of light,
>   My heart, pierced through with fierce delight,
>   Bursts into blossom in his sight.
>
> My whole soul waiting silently,
> All naked in a sultry sky,
> Droops blinded with his shining eye:
> I *will* possess him or will die.
>   I will grow round him in his place,
>   Grow, live, die looking on his face,
>   Die, dying clasped in his embrace.[16]

Lingering on those first four loamish dipthongs ('wire', 'fire', 'nigher', 'desire'), and then snapping shut the tighter chimes that follow, these end-rhymes ask to be noticed, and they collaborate also with intra-lineal alliteration and assonance to thicken the overall sonic texture. But against this luxuriating sound runs a rhythm that is impatient and builds to a pitch. The contrasting effect creates great pressure, caught most fully in the syntactically halted step of the last couple of lines that paraphrase the speaker's condition—'Grow, live, die'—which last condition, carrying the orgasm pun, then doubly redounds across the final line ('Die, dying'). It is a bravura bit of writing; not his most subtle or lastingly satisfying, but a fair example of how even the institutionally respectable Lawn Tennyson could wield prosody 'to the full as impassioned' as his peers.

'Fleshly' is one word for it; though perhaps, from the point of view of the reader rather than the poem itself, it might be more helpful to talk in terms of the lines' 'mouthability'. That coinage comes from Christopher Ricks, and he is thinking about how it was the

urge to roll poetry around in his mouth that first excited Tennyson's poetic imagination. Ricks goes on to concede in a parenthetical aside, 'His detractors might say that
he never progressed much beyond a childish delight in such poetic sound.'[17] But it is
not only his detractors who might say this: his would-be champions may wish to say
the same, by substituting 'childish' for 'childlike', and insisting that prosody is powerful
precisely because it is primal. 'Now the fatal mistake about poetry, and more than half of
the fatal mistake about humanity', suggests G. K. Chesterton, 'consists in forgetting that
we should have the first kind of [simple] pleasure as well as the second', 'sophisticated
pleasure': 'It might be said that we should have the first pleasure as the basis of the second; or yet more truly, the first pleasure inside the second'.[18] The imaginative hold that a
nursery rhyme may possess is in this sense a species of religious ritual. Hegel's description of music's 'elemental might' registers not only the sense in which music is elemental and mighty, but also that it is mighty because it is elemental.[19] Not sound as such,
sounding: or, as E. S. Dallas nicely imagines it in *Poetics: An Essay on Poetry* (1852), 'time
heard'.[20] Tennyson's own account of 'the force of melody in poetry' weighs 'the sound
of words', but ranks 'the beauty of rhythm most important';[21] as indeed other poets and
verse theorists of the period also aver (following Kant's insight that poetic affect is an
expression of the subjective perception of time processes).[22] For all the praise lavished
on Tennyson's 'ear'—T. S. Eliot calls it 'the finest…since Milton', W. H. Auden thinks
it 'the finest, perhaps, of any English poet'[23]—his verse is more satisfyingly tasted than
heard. We hear his verse best not as sound abstracted from words, and still, but as performing our mouths; and through our mouths, our whole bodies.

Nietzsche is struck by the modern misreading that relegates rhythm to a merely
structural or ornamental function, when, in the origin of poetry, there was thought
to be nothing more 'useful'. It can give 'thoughts a new colour', making them 'darker,
stranger, more distant': 'rhythm is a compulsion; it engenders an unconquerable desire
to yield, to join in; not only the stride of the feet but also the soul itself gives in to the
beat—probably also, one inferred, the souls of the gods!' Nietzsche is here talking about
the origin of poetry, but his interest in 'the presumption that rhythmic quality exercises
a magical force', that 'incantation and conjuration seem to be the primordial form of
poetry', is not merely historical: 'still today,' he claims (he is writing in 1882), 'after millennia of work at fighting such superstition, even the wisest of us occasionally becomes
a fool for rhythm, if only insofar as he *feels* a thought to be *truer* when it has metric form
and presents itself with a divine hop, skip, and jump'.[24] It is hard to disagree. Yet, the
very suggestion that rhythm exposes an atavistic foolishness might itself be interpreted
as an ancient bit of superstition. Treating rhythmic power as merely meretricious, as
something that can 'fool' us into mistaking lies for truth, rather than being something
that articulates its own truth, rests on a doubly dubious Platonic distinction: between
form and content, and between thinking and feeling.[25]

Insofar as late nineteenth-century poetics was abuzz with debates about rhythm as
a force able to engage our physical being, it is unsurprising that readers—'still today'—
should worry over prosodically winning lines distracting from the semantics of the
poem, and so perverting right judgement. Being fraught between admiration and

anxiety, this lingering suspicion over rhythm's sirenic potency expresses itself with special urgency when imputed to those most celebrated for their compositional prowess. 'Fascinated as everybody must be by the music of his verse,' writes John Morley of Swinburne, 'it is doubtful whether part of the effect may not be traced to something like a trick of words and letters'.[26] 'Nay, he will write you a poem with nothing in it except music,' worries R. H. Horne, this time about Tennyson.[27] Such comments presume that the 'music' of verse is self-evidently, constitutively, meaningless. Seamus Perry does brilliant work in charting the ways in which, actually, 'music and meaning are always crossing paths' in Tennyson's poetry; and Jerome McGann has offered similar advocacy for Swinburne.[28] But Simon Jarvis perhaps takes us further than either of these single-author studies in advancing the general proposition that 'music and meaning' may not after all be two separate and stable categories: that there may be such a thing called 'musical thinking', 'which is not thinking about music, or thinking which accompanies music, but a thinking which takes place in music; a thinking which is made up of music itself'.[29]

If Morley and Horne betray a Victorian suspicion about the value or possibility of such 'musical thinking', that suspicion only hardened into overt scepticism in the early twentieth century. And so fell the reputation of the Victorian poets. Their rhythmic facility that could not be denied was said to have been won at the expense of verbal precision. 'Reading the poets of the nineteenth century,' writes Auden, 'I am continually struck by the contrast between the extraordinarily high standard of their prosodic skill and the frequent clumsiness and inadequacy of their diction'. '[B]oth the virtue and the defect', he goes on to observe, may be explained by the fact that 'for most of them, their first experience of writing verse was in a language syntactically and rhythmically very different from their own', and this encouraged a 'habit of approximation', an 'undue tolerance' for 'the first word he could think of that fitted the metre or supplied a needed rhyme'.[30]

An early and intimate acquaintance with Latin and Greek verse would surely have encouraged a unique *habitus* of hearing. But it is less clear that this uniqueness need declare itself in the Victorians being straightforwardly sloppier in their phrasing. James I. Wimsatt makes an alternative suggestion: because studying Classical verse traditionally begins with a study of its form (by analysis of feet and line units), it 'implicitly predicates that rhythmic pattern rather than Aristotelian mimesis represents the beginning of poetic life.' Far from encouraging complacency towards the meaning of words, such an education promotes the possibility that the sounds of words and their rhythmic arrangement carry 'a prior and positive value'.[31] From this perspective, words are not debased in their meanings but re-estimated; they are valued not so much for how well they imitate but for what they constitute; not for the realities they reflect but for those they might inspire. In short, Victorian rhythms make energetic impressions that are both linguistic—in that, as Coventry Patmore suggests, 'every variation [of stress or tone] involves a variation of meaning'[32]—but also non-discursive, something Patmore well expresses too, in his description of 'the song that is the thing it says'.[33] Bound up in this notion of poetry saying what it is and being what it says is the recognition that verse 'must have a body',[34] and that by extension its appeal is physical as well as purely intellectual.

Challenging what kinds of thought—specifically, what kinds of *thinking*—rhythms might enable in verse—and more specifically still, in *Victorian* verse—makes it possible to return with fresh purpose to the protagonists of this essay's story, viewed as opposing but complementary emblems of an embodied poetics. As a way back into Hopkins's arresting belief that Swinburne 'had no real understanding of rhythm', it is helpful to begin by setting his remark beside Coleridge's similarly surprising claim that Tennyson wrote 'without very well understanding what metre is'.[35] Poets have always doubted each other's verse craft, here and there, from time to time, but something different, something unprecedented, takes hold in the nineteenth century, something that reaches histrionic heights towards its close. In this sense, Hopkins's carping is not noteworthy because it is exceptional but because it is exemplary. Everyone is at it, and Swinburne himself more than most: from his comments on Robert Browning's 'moans of tormented metre', to Arnold's 'ugly bastards of verse', to Clough's 'studies in graduated prose'.[36]

Within Victorian verse theory, confusion and conflict turn most persistently on the respective identities and functions of rhythm and metre, and especially on the relation between the two. Whether to scan by feet or according to musical notation; whether scansion should measure syllabic stress, or duration, or both; and the extent to which scansion is a description rather than a prescription for an actual or imagined or idealized rhythmical performance. These are only some of the hard-nut conundrums that trouble Victorian accounts of rhythm, and each refracts a number of competing cultural concerns, about everything from philology to the politics of empire. Confessed privately in journals, diaries, and letters, or cast publicly in books, essays and verse parodies, like never before in English literary history—far exceeding even those Renaissance debates on the relation of Classical quantities to English stress metres—Victorian poets, readers, and critics come to re-assess and re-imagine the absolute fundamentals of prosodic theory and practice; and they often strenuously disagree. Screeds are devoted to arguing over what might be called technicalities of verse craft (the number of treatises on prosody doubled in the 1860s, and had doubled again by the 1880s),[37] but there are deeper disagreements motivating these arguments, disagreements that are, at their deepest, essentially epistemological. Sidney Lanier was rehearsing a platitude among prosodists when he opened *The Science of English Verse* (1880) by observing that 'it still cannot be said that we possess a theory, or even a working-hypothesis, of the technic of English verse'.[38] But Lanier's ambition to explain prosody in scientific terms already rests on a disputed metaphysics (Hegel being the most influential disputant for Victorian verse theorists) as to whether rhythm can ever be theorized in the absence of a theory about subjectivity.[39]

Questions over 'technic' are, then, so thoroughly embroiled in other questions that even disputes seemingly framed in technical terms frequently devolve onto disagreements that are less clearly formulated. So it is that, although both Hopkins's and Coleridge's complaints are forcibly expressed, both are also, on inspection, enigmatically elusive. What Jesuitical subtlety lies buried in that cavilling distinction between understanding and *really* understanding poetic rhythm, and what Idealist insight, between knowing and *very well* knowing what metre is? Biographers and critics miss the more illuminating inference in speculating as to what cocktail of ignorance and envy—what ungenerous defensiveness—might excite such unspecific libels. Taking these remarks in earnest and on their own oblique terms reveals something more far reaching than prosodical pettifogging or ad hominem grudges. It is indeed the argument of this article that Hopkins's comment is poised, instructively, on the threshold of a poetic principle that simultaneously defines and divides the entire field of Victorian verse theory.

Bridges described the late nineteenth century as being in a 'stage of artistic exhaustion of form'.[40] The way poets of the period reacted to this perceived stylistic staleness incites tensions that are at once ideological and also keenly literary. Two modes of writing in particular are to be found jostling in Victorian poetics: the Anglo-Saxon and alliterative verse revival of (what Conybeare called) the 'good barbarians',[41] and the urbane sophistications of Classical verse. Put in this way, it might look like a choice between 'native' versus 'foreign', and something of those nationalistic (and attendant religious) politics do play. But as may be seen in the contrasting preferences of Hopkins and Swinburne, these debates have significant implications for the way verse may express itself *as* verse.

Insofar as Hopkins impressed an early twentieth-century readership specifically for how distinctively *un*-Victorian his style seemed to be—unpublished and unpublishable in his lifetime—he has been misrepresented as 'an eccentric...who worked in isolation'.[42] His letters and journals suggest how much he was influenced by the recommendations of contemporary philologists and verse theorists such as George Marsh, who identified the vigorous rhythms of the stress-timed Anglo-Saxon example as a way to 'infuse fresh life and spirit into movements of the muses which perpetual repetition has made wearisome'.[43] And while he would offer post hoc rationalizations for his prosody according to Classical principles (invoking the 'logaoedic' licence, and scanning by feet), his verse practice confirms this sympathy for the oral, strong-stress tradition. Sprung rhythm's prosodic intricacies are to some extent peculiar to him, of course, but insofar as stress is, as he says, the 'life' of it, that it is 'a matter of accent only', defined as 'an easily felt principle of equal strengths',[44] his innovative style finds common cause with a significant cohort of Victorian versifying. That includes not only poets such as William Morris who explicitly sought to revive an alliterative mode of stress timing, but also those who looked to ballads, songs, and broadsides in fashioning the 'dolnik' measures explored by Derek Attridge in 'Beat'.

In contrast, Swinburne's lush trill emulates the august example of Virgil and Sappho; and in this, for all his singularity of style, he too connects with a vast community of writers: from those like Longfellow, Clough, and Arnold who sought to compose in Classical metres adapted into English, to those such as William Whewell and John Stuart Blackie at the fore of translating Classical verse itself. This connection to other writers might indeed be said to extend beyond those who took their cue from Greek and Latin models to the so-called 'English Parnassians' who sought a kindred counter-cultural refinement in recherché medieval French rhythms. 'In all this battle for form and for pure literature', wrote Edmund Gosse to Swinburne (on sending him his essay promoting 'the six most important of the poetic creations of old France'), 'we fight as a mere handful against a whole army of Philistia.'[45]

It follows from the contrasting rhythmic traditions in which Hopkins and Swinburne participate that, even though their verses are both—as they liked to call it—'passionate',[46] that passion is expressed contrastingly too. Put simply: Hopkins is pugnacious and concentrated in his patterning ('the word Sprung which I use for this rhythm means something like *abrupt*', he explains, 'and applies by rights only where one stress follows another running, without syllable between'[47]), where Swinburne is euphonious, dilatant, and modal. What emerges from these divergent rhythmical textures is a divergent way of livening their poems' words. '[A]bove all remember what applies to all my verse,' implores Hopkins, 'that its performance is . . . with long rests, long dwells.'[48] Swinburne's verse refuses to let the mind rest and dwell. The subjects of his sentences are always chasing their verbs and objects that seem forever out of sight, relentlessly deferred by subordinate clauses. And chase is the right word, because the reader's attempt to catch the semantic sense is hurried, if not harried, by the urgent undertow of his alliterating anapaests. The defining importance of his triple rhythms here may be taken from the fact that Hopkins also alliterates heavily and also favours such suspensions, but without generating anything like the same scudding effect. Even where his 'lettering' is most marked, and his syntax suspended most spectacularly—such as in the first sentence of 'The Golden Echo and the Leaden Echo' (about which poem he said, 'I never did anything more musical'[49])—the reader is still required by sprung rhythm's abruptness to check and ponder. How different that is to the reading experience which awaits us in the first sentence of, say, *Tristram of Lyonesse*, in which some forty-two rampantly lilting lines separate the subject from its predicate.[50]

Because Hopkins is led by the stress of his rhetoric—which is why he typically spoke about rhythm rather than metre, and the whole strain of the stanza rather than the line unit—his scansion is 'imitative'.[51] Swinburne, working by an accentual-syllabic system, privileges instead the metrical set, and so the pattern of ictus which designates the position in the line where the stress is to be *expected*, demoting and promoting medial stresses accordingly to fulfil that expectation strongly established through triple rhythm. The significance of this difference cannot be explained in purely rhythmical terms, because verse rhythms acquire their identity not only in relation to the reading subject who experiences it, but also to the lexical medium through which it is realized. Even if there may be such a thing as 'musical thinking' that eschews referential explicitness, the life of rhythm is breathed through *words*, words that are, apart from anything else, conventions of referring. Writing on *Milton's Prosody* in 1889, Bridges presses this case:

> The relation of the form of the verse to the sense is not to be taken exactly; it is a matter of feeling between the two, and is misrepresented by any definition. Poetry would be absurd in which there was perpetual verbal mimicry of the sense; but that is not to deny that matter and form should be in live harmonious relation.[52]

That Hopkins might admire Swinburne's rhythms while regretting their relation to his poems' 'matter' offers an attractively neat resolution to the teaser heading this essay; but thus simply stated, it risks a double irony. For a start, the idea of harmonious relation—and indeed the very word 'harmony' itself—plays a central part in Swinburne's poetics. Prosodic competence is, he thinks, a necessary but not a sufficient condition for poetry. There must be also a 'harmony' between that 'outer music' and an elusive kind of 'inner music', which is spiritual and emotional in its origin and import. Critics have often mis-represented Swinburne in this respect by quoting out of context his commitment to 'revere form or harmony as the high one law of all art'.[53] Thomas E. Connolly rightly observes about this passage that the conjunction 'or' indicates that 'form' is not here being opposed to 'content' or 'matter', it is being used as a synonym for 'harmony'. And indeed Swinburne elsewhere makes explicit that he allowed this special use of the word 'form', not 'in the abstract and absolute sense' of outer music, but in the ways he con-sistently used the word 'harmony'.[54] To some extent his poetic theory remains unclear on quite what harmony is or how it might be achieved. The fact that he makes a dis-tinction between inner and outer music and insists on their appropriate relation should nonetheless give us pause before finding his poems lacking in precisely these terms, as if he were neither aware of, nor cared about, such a relation. To take only one example: it would surely have provoked some reflection in A. E. Housman if he had known, before contrasting Milton with Swinburne as poets of inner versus outer music, that Swinburne had himself characterized Milton exactly antithetically, as a paradigmatic poet of merely outer music.[55]

The second potential irony attends the fact that Hopkins himself has been read by many critics, including his admirers, as inverting (those less admiring say sub-verting) the right relationship between form and matter, such that, 'like the non-sense poet, he begins with the sounds of the words and lets the sense come tumbling after'.[56] Choice moments in his letters and journals appear to support this view; for instance:

> Poetry is speech framed for contemplation of the mind by the way of hearing or speech framed to be heard for its own sake and interest even over and above its interest in meaning. Some matter and meaning is essential to it but only as an element necessary to support and employ the shape which is contemplated for its own sake.[57]

Hopkins uses 'matter and meaning' here to refer to semantics. In the broader terms of his writings, however, the 'shape which is contemplated for its own sake' may be said to have 'meaning' too. That is not to suggest it may have meaning solely in terms of its 'shape'. Some 'matter and meaning' is 'essential' to support this 'shape'; but the 'matter and meaning' can no more exist without 'shape' than the 'shape' without 'matter and meaning'. Almost as often as the last passage is quoted, his significant qualifier is omit-ted: that verse 'might be composed without meaning (as nonsense verse and choruses—'Hey nonny nonny' or 'Willie wau wau wau' etc.) and then alone it would not be poetry'. For Hopkins, then, form and matter are mutually informing: 'It is plain that metre, rhythm, rhyme, and all the structure which is called verse both necessitate and engender a difference in diction and thought'.[58] It follows from this that he does not 'fail' to be limpid, because limpidity is not his priority. He derides Wordsworth's 'Parnassian' lucidity, and tries to avoid 'obscurity' only 'in so far as is consistent with excellences higher than clearness at first reading':

> Plainly if it is possible to express a subtle and recondite thought on a subtle and recondite subject in a subtle and recondite way and with great felicity and perfection in the end, something must be sacrificed, with so trying a task, in the process, and this may be the thing at once, nay perhaps even the being without explanation at all, intelligible.[59]

'Excellences higher than clearness at first reading' are, it seems, the subtle and recondite expression of subtle and recondite thoughts, for which clarity may be 'sacrificed'. Except that the figure of immolation distracts from the notion that temporary obscurity is, in a specific sense, purposeful. His verse is inspired by the insight that 'an effect is nothing but the way in which the mind ties together, not the sequences, but all the condition it sees ... a condition of a thing considered as contrasted with the whole thing, an effect a whole as contrasted with its conditions, elements, or parts'.[60] This insight is achieved through an aesthetics of delay whereby, because 'dark at first reading, when once made out', the poem's higher excellences, its collective parts taken as the whole, may 'explode'.[61]

It is at this fringe and limit where the prosodies of our protagonists are ultimately irreconcilable, such that Hopkins cannot believe Swinburne *really* understands rhythm at all. For if Hopkins's poems express themselves through abruptness and explosion, Swinburne's rhythms collude with alliteration and syntax in winging the reader along. This is not merely a matter of his anapaests speeding things up. As Veronica Forrest-Thomson well observes, in shifting between monosyllabic and polysyllabic words, he uses his anapaests for slowness as well as speed, for weight as well as lightness; and speed does not necessarily equate with lightness, nor slowness with weight. His anapaests are nonetheless crucial in defining the character of his verse, including, most of all, what his detractors have found to be 'diffuse'. For as Forrest-Thomson also notices, Swinburne's anapaests are 'most usually obtained by using many adverbial and adjectival phrases',[62] and it is the conspicuous preponderance of adjectives, prepositions, and adverbs that distracts the referential 'meaning' by perpetual qualification. Here is the last of ten stanzas from 'A Forsaken Garden':

> Till the slow sea rise and the sheer cliff crumble,
>   Till terrace and meadow the deep gulfs drink,
> Till the strength of the waves of the high tides humble
>   The fields that lessen, the rocks that shrink,
> Here now in his triumph where all things falter,
>   Stretched out on the spoils that his own hand spread,
> As a god self-slain on his own strange altar,
>   Death lies dead.[63]

Each of the nine previous stanzas is likewise self-contained (although the narrative progresses from one to the next, there is no grammatical run-on). But whereas the previous stanzas all break into two or more sentences, this final stanza runs and runs, switching breathlessly—the reader is given no time to catch breath—from its opening anaphoric 'Till', which three times marks out its prepositional postponement, to the resolving impulse, 'Here now'. As the mounting expectation finally realizes its paradoxical climax ('Death lies dead'), the words are charged not so much by stresses drawing out individual words as by the increscent rhythmical drama: what Empson called a poem's 'atmosphere', which 'it is very necessary for the critic to remember', but which requires the critic to 'concentrate on the whole…rather than on the particular things he can find to say'.[64] If Hopkins's poems repay the closest scrutiny of individual, etymologically and phonosymbolically loaded words enriched by their prosody, Swinburne must be read for the compound momentum with which his words are cast that accommodates how and what these words 'mean'. The way Swinburne's rhythms work with his diction is not a fixed relation; he sometimes manages to be every bit as diffuse even without anapaests. It is indeed his untypically anapaest-light verse drama *Locrine* that rouses Hopkins to complain that 'words only are only words' where there is 'a perpetual functioning of genius without truth, feeling, or an adequate matter to be at function on'.[65] But the general point holds: whereas Hopkins's words impend great and specific import as stress fetches out significances (as on, say, 'Buckle!' in 'The Windhover',[66] or on his many portmanteau coinages), Swinburne's rhythms encourage a cantering and constellated reading that disburses words' meanings into aggregating motifs (his handling of 'Love' and 'Fate' in *Tristram of Lyonesse* being only the most obvious example). Put another way: Swinburne's words are forever flinging onwards and (adverbially-adjectivally) outwards, centrifugally, as against Hopkins's centripetal densities.

Although the differences between their verse styles are, then, real and significant, on balance, Hopkins's plaint is not quite so stark as it first appears. He does after all grant that there is some 'matter' in Swinburne's verse. He regrets only that, to his mind, it is not 'adequate' to his rhythms; and if he thinks at times 'he misses badly', he also concedes that 'he sometimes hits brilliantly'.[67] Such conciliations may seem nugatory. But when compared with the dominant poetic practice of the next generation of poets, what rhythmic purpose unites Hopkins and Swinburne—their passionately embodied poetics—is greater than what divides them. What divides them might indeed be said to be what defines them as most characteristically Victorian. For what is at odds in their rhythms arises from a mutual commitment to verse music. Both use their prosodies to transform what and how their poems 'mean'; the only difference is in method, and in degree. However it is inflected, that faith in verse music's transformative—because performative—possibilities is what unites both men with Tennyson too, who in his verse drew on both strong stress and Classical measures; as it is what locates them more broadly still in their literary-historical moment of poetry's mouthability.

The danger of overstating the similarity between coeval verse styles is less pressing here than that of exaggerating dissimilarities. Late nineteenth-century disputes over poetry and poetics are, as noted, many, varied, and vigorous, but their number, range, and tenor is to some extent a false index. Contemporary testimonies, especially by the poets themselves, typically urge oppositions swollen with the caricature of contradistinction. The result can be to occlude affinities more fundamental than the contrasts being adduced. That is what has been argued for Hopkins on Swinburne, but this essay might, with the same thesis in view, have been framed in terms of other leading poets too; most obviously, by pairing Tennyson with Robert Browning. The former's claim that 'it doesn't matter so much in poetry written for the intellect—as much of Browning's is, perhaps; but in mine it's necessary to know how to sound it properly',[68] looks at first blush to abet the tendency to regard their verses as 'opposites in all respects, and perhaps specially in prosody'.[69] This tendency is as pervasive now as it appeared to Saintsbury a century ago, but more careful consideration of Tennyson's phrasing reveals that he stops short of such a polarized view; and inspecting his provisionality—'so much', 'as much', 'perhaps'—offers a way back into parsing Browning's poetry as one that, differently rather than not at all, makes its appeal to the 'intellect' *through* its prosody. Given that the signal formal innovation of Victorian verse was in developing a genre through which speakers unwittingly betray themselves in the very act of utterance, and that Browning was the pre-eminent practitioner of that genre (the dramatic monologue), he may indeed be viewed at the frontier of a literary culture whose aesthetic burden is of knowing 'how to sound it properly': rendering the full expressive pressures of verse rhythm with an ardent, incarnated voice.

Reading the shared, contemporary rhythmic cause behind the discord between Hopkins and Swinburne may, finally, be clarified by ending this essay as this essay began: in puzzling at Hopkins's dissatisfaction with one of his celebrated peers; this time, Walt Whitman. While some embraced him, and others, such as Gosse, believed he heralded a cultural apocalypse ('before the English poets take' him for their 'model in style…I hope I may be dead'[70]), Swinburne changed his mind from first admiring to decrying. Hopkins was more tempered and consistent in judging that Whitman wrote 'rhythmic prose and that only'.[71] Bridges and other readers since have wondered whether Hopkins was protesting too much here, whether he was disparaging Whitman out of a reflexive urge to safeguard his own originality or deviance—because he knew at some level that he was really only writing a kind of rhythmic prose himself. But to conflate their rhythmic practice in this way misses a more salient distinction between them. Without needing to accept Hopkins's claim that sprung rhythm is indeed 'stricter, not looser than the common rhythm',[72] it is clear he heightens his rhythms as a means to expression in a way Whitman avowedly does not. More specifically, Hopkins defined his verse as 'oral, made away from paper', such that he 'put it down with repugnance',[73] whereas Whitman's proto-free verse pays explicit homage to its printedness. Acknowledging, and without regretting, that 'the poetic work of literature is more than nineteen-twentieths of it by print', he privileges 'the content not the music of words'. 'Perhaps the music happens', he allows, in which case 'it does no harm'.[74] Resigned to an accidental feature of expression, Whitman's rhythms assume a status apart from that spurred by the Victorian heterogeneous collective, for whom verse mouths an embodied music which confounds the prior category of 'content' with its song.

NOTES

1. Gerard Manley Hopkins, *The Letters of Gerard Manley Hopkins to Robert Bridges*, ed. Claude Colleer Abbott, 2nd imp.rev. (London: Oxford University Press, 1955), 304.

2. James I. Wimsatt, *Hopkins's Poetics of Speech Sound: Sprung Rhythm, Lettering, Inscape* (Toronto: University of Toronto Press, 2006), 150.

3. George Saintsbury, *A History of English Prosody, from the Twelfth Century to the Present Day*, 3 vols. (London: Macmillan, 1906–10), iii. 335.

4. Hopkins, 'The Wreck of the Deutschland', in *Gerard Manley Hopkins: The Poetical Works of Gerard Manley Hopkins*, ed. N. H. MacKenzie (Oxford: Oxford University Press, 1990), 121; *Tristram of Lyonesse*, I.461–72 in *Algernon Charles Swinburne: Major Poems and Prose*, ed. Jerome McGann and Charles L. Sligh (New Haven & London: Yale University Press, 2004), 223.

5. John Buchanan (published under the pseudonym Thomas Maitland), 'The Fleshly School of Poetry', *The Contemporary Review*, October 1871.

6. Dante Gabriel Rossetti, 'Nuptial Sleep', in *Dante Gabriel Rossetti, Collected Poetry and Prose*, ed. Jerome McGann (New Haven: Yale University Press, 2003), 130.

7. Christina Rossetti, 'I Know You Not', in *The Complete Poems of Christina Rossetti*, ed. R. W. Crump (London: Penguin, 2001), 8; 416–7; 563–4.

8. See works by Armstrong, Prins, Reynolds, Hall (ed.), Martin, and the special issue of *Victorian Poetry* on Prosody, given in the bibliography.

9. See works by Blair, Campbell, Griffiths, and Rudy, given in the bibliography.

10. *In Memoriam*, XCV. 40. *The Poems of Tennyson*, ed. Christopher Ricks, 2nd edn., 3 vols. (London: Longman, 1987), iii. 413. See Blair's contextualization of this quotation: *Culture of the Heart*, ch. 2.

11. Rudy, *Electric Meters*, 5.

12. Samuel Johnson, 'Essay on Pope', in *The Lives of the Poets*, ed. John H. Middendorf, 3 vols. (New Haven & London: Yale University Press, 2010), iii. 1225.

13. 'On Some of the Characteristics of Modern Poetry, and on the Lyrical Poems of Alfred Tennyson' appeared unsigned in *Englishman's Magazine* (August 1831), 616–628.

14. Alfred Austin, 'The Poetry of the Period. Mr Swinburne', *Temple Bar*, 26 (July 1869), 462. These poems and Austin's quotation are discussed by Linda K. Hughes in her essay '"Frater, Ave"? Tennyson and Swinburne', in *Tennyson Among the Poets*, eds. Seamus Perry and Robert Douglas-Fairhurst (Oxford: Oxford University Press, 2009), 296–314 (306–7).

15. Alfred Tennyson, 'Fatima', in *The Poems of Tennyson*, 417–9.

16. Alfred Tennyson, 'Fatima', 417–9.

17. Christopher Ricks, *Tennyson* (London: Macmillan, 1972), 13.

18. G. K. Chesterton, 'The Romance of Rhyme', in *Fancies Versus Fads* (London: Methuen & Co., 1923), 2.

19. G. W. F. Hegel, *Hegel's Aesthetics*, trans. T. M. Knox, 2 vols. (Oxford: Clarendon Press, 1975), ii. 908.

20. E. S. Dallas, *Poetics: An Essay on Poetry* (London: Smith, Elder, and Co., 1852); repr. in William E. Fredeman, Ira Bruce Nadel, John F. Stansy, eds., *The Victorian Muse: Selected Criticism and Parody of the Period* (New York: Garland, 1986), 164.

21. Reported from a conversation of 1885; quoted in *Tennyson Among the Poets*, ii.

22. See Blair, *Culture of the Heart*, 85, who notices the direct influence of Kant's account of rhythm on E. S. Dallas's 1852 *Poetics: An Essay on Poetry*, and that influence may be more generally felt in verse theory of the period even where Kant is never cited as such.

23. See Angela Leighton's 'Tennyson, by Ear' (*Tennyson Among the Poets*, 337), which weighs both these quotes from Eliot and Auden. On the dubious praise for Tennyson's 'ear', see also Seamus Perry's *Alfred Tennyson* (Tavistock: Northcote House, 2005).

24. Friedrich Nietzsche, 'On the Origin of Poetry', in *The Gay Science*, trans. Josefine Nauckhoff, ed. Bernard Williams (Cambridge: Cambridge University Press, 2001), 83–6.

25. See Michael Hurley, 'How Philosophers Trivialize Art: *Bleak House, Oedipus Rex*, "Leda and the Swan"', *Philosophy and Literature* 33 (2009), 107–125.

26. *Swinburne: The Critical Heritage*, ed. Clyde K. Hyder (London: Routledge & Kegan Paul, 1970), 26.

27. *Tennyson: The Critical Heritage*, ed. John D. Jump (London: Routledge & Kegan Paul, 1967), 155.

28. Seamus Perry, *Alfred Tennyson*, 19; Jerome McGann, *Swinburne: An Experiment in Criticism* (Chicago: University of Chicago Press, 1972).

29. Simon Jarvis, 'Musical Thinking: Hegel and the Phenomenology of Prosody', *Paragraph* 28 (2005), 57.

30. *Nineteenth-Century Minor Poets*, ed. with intro. by W. H. Auden (London: Faber & Faber, 1967), 22.

31. Wimsatt, *Hopkins's Poetics of Speech Sound*, 12.

32. Coventry Patmore, *Coventry Patmore's 'Essay on English Metrical Law': A Critical Edition with a Commentary*, ed. Mary Augustine Roth (Washington, DC: Catholic University Press of America, 1961), 13.

33. Quoted in J. C. Reid, *The Mind and Art of Coventry Patmore* (London: Routledge & Paul, 1957), 31.

34. Patmore, *English Metrical Law*, 7.

35. *Tennyson: The Critical Heritage*, 418.

36. *Browning: The Critical Heritage*, ed. Boyd Litzinger and Donald Smalley (London: Routledge & Kegan Paul, 1970), 214; Algernon Charles Swinburne, *Poems & Ballads and Atalanta in Calydon*, ed. Kenneth Haynes (Harmondsworth: Penguin, 2000), 357.

37. Dennis Taylor, *Hardy's Metres and Victorian Prosody* (Oxford: Clarendon, 1988), 20.

38. Sidney Lanier, *The Science of English Verse* (New York: Charles Scribner's Sons, 1893), vi.

39. See Simon Jarvis's exploration, via Hegel, of Henri Meschonnic's insight that 'There can be no theory of rhythm without a theory of the subject, and no theory of the subject without a theory of rhythm', in 'Musical Thinking', 57. See also Armstrong's 'four epistemologies of meter' as conceived in Victorian poetics, in *Meter Matters*, 26–52.

40. Robert Bridges, 'Wordsworth and Kipling' (1912), in *Collected Essays, Papers, &c.*, 30 vols., ed. Mary Monica Bridges (London: Oxford University Press, 1933), viii. 31.

41. Quoted in Joseph Phelan, *The Music of Verse: Metrical Experiment in Nineteenth-Century Poetry* (Basingstoke: Palgrave Macmillan, 2011), 95. See ch. 3 on the 'native' claim of Anglo Saxon and alliterative verse in the nineteenth century.

42. Yvor Winters, *The Function of Criticism* (London: Routledge and Kegan Paul, 1967), 86.

43. George Marsh, *Lectures on the English Language*, 4th edn. (London: Sampson Low, Son and Co., 1863), 570.

44. Hopkins, *The Correspondence of Gerard Manley Hopkins and Richard Watson Dixon*, ed. Claude Colleer Abbott (London: Oxford University Press, 1955), 39, 22.

45. *The Life and Letters of Sir Edmund Gosse*, ed. Evan Charteris (London: W. Heinemann Ltd, 1931), 99–100.

46. The very purpose of sprung rhythm's 'abruptness' is that it may be employed to 'good effect' in 'passionate passages' (*Hopkins to Bridges*, 203); Swinburne distinguishes between a lower

form of 'passion', as equated with suffering and pathos, and a higher 'moral passion'. See Thomas E. Connolly, *Swinburne's Theory of Poetry* (Syracuse: State University of New York, 1964), 56–8; and also Antony H. Harrison, 'Swinburne's Losses: The Poetics of Passion', *ELH* 49 (1982), 689–706.

47. Hopkins, *Hopkins to Bridges*, 23.
48. Hopkins, *Hopkins to Bridges* 246.
49. Hopkins, *Hopkins to Dixon*, 149.
50. See McGann, *An Experiment in Criticism*, 149–50.
51. 'I forgot to answer about my metres', he writes on a postcard of 9 June 1878, before offering the telling parenthetical qualification: '(rhythms rather, I suppose)'; 'I don't see the difficulty...Is it in the scanning? Which is imitative as usual.' Hopkins, *Hopkins to Bridges*, 55; 50.
52. Bridges, *Milton's Prosody* (Oxford: Oxford University Press, 1921), 63.
53. Swinburne, *The Complete Works of Algernon Charles Swinburne*, ed. Edmund Gosse and Thomas James Wise (New York, Russell & Russell, 1968), 115.
54. See Connolly, *Swinburne's Theory of Poetry*, ch. 4.
55. A. E. Housman, 'Swinburne', *Collected Poems and Selected Prose*, ed. Christopher Ricks (Harmondsworth: Penguin, 1988), 282.
56. David Sonstroem, 'Making Earnest of Game: G. M. Hopkins and Nonsense Poetry', *Modern Language Quarterly*, 28 (1967), 192–206 (200).
57. Hopkins, *The Journals and Papers of Gerard Manley Hopkins*, ed. Humphry House and Graham Storey (London: Oxford University Press, 1959), 289.
58. Hopkins, *Journals and Papers of Hopkins*, 84.
59. Hopkins, *Hopkins to Bridges*, 54, 265–6.
60. Oxford, Campion Hall, MS. D.vi.2. Quoted and discussed in Tom Zaniello, *Hopkins in the Age of Darwin* (Iowa City: University of Iowa Press, 1988), 33–34.
61. Hopkins criticizes one of Bridges's poems for failing to 'explode' in this way: Hopkins, *Hopkins to Bridges,* 90.
62. Veronica Forrest-Thomson, 'Swinburne as Poet: A Reconsideration', *Journal of Pre-Raphaelite Studies* 15 (2006), 51–71.
63. Swinburne, 'A Forsaken Garden', in *Major Poems and Prose*, 160.
64. William Empson, *Seven Types of Ambiguity*, 3rd edn. (London: Penguin, 1995), 36–7.
65. Hopkins, *Hopkins to Bridges,* 304. He elsewhere complains to Bridges that verse of 'the Swinburnian kind...expresses passion but not feeling' (79). Of Canon Dixon's 'Mano', he similarly objects that 'it either has not or else I have hitherto missed finding a leading thought to thread the beauties on' (189); and of Richard Crawley's 'Venus and Psyche', that 'it is not serious', that 'the story [is] treated as a theme for trying style on' (225).
66. Hopkins, 'The Windhover', in *The Poetical Works*, 144.
67. Hopkins, *Hopkins to Bridges*, 304.
68. Tennyson, *The Letters of Alfred Lord Tennyson*, 3 vols, ed. Cecil Y. Lang and Edgar F. Shannon (Oxford: Clarendon Press, 1990), iii. 328.
69. Saintsbury, *History of English Prosody*, iii. 183.
70. Edmund Gosse, 'A Plea for Certain Exotic Forms of Verse', *Cornhill Magazine* (July 1877). For fuller discussion, see Michael Hurley, 'On or about July 1877', in Bianca Tredennick, ed., *Victorian Transformations: Genre, Nationalism, and Desire in Nineteenth-Century Literature*, (Farnham Ashgate, 2011), 61–78.
71. Hopkins, *Hopkins to Bridges*, 156.

72. Hopkins, *Further Letters of Gerard Manley Hopkins including his Correspondence with Coventry Patmore*, ed. Claude Colleer Abbott, 2nd edn. (London: Oxford University Press, 1956), 335. He goes further: that with all his 'licences, or rather laws', he is stricter than Bridges or than 'anybody' he knows; *Hopkins to Bridges*, 44.
73. Hopkins, *Further Letters*, 379.
74. Horace Traubel, *With Walt Whitman in Camden* (London: Gay and Bird, 1906), I.163 (16 May 1888). Phelan discusses this passage from Whitman in *The Music of Verse*, 171.

SELECT BIBLIOGRAPHY

Armstrong, Isobel, *Victorian Poetry: Poetry, Poetics, and Politics* (London and New York: Routledge, 1993).
Blair, Kirstie, *Victorian Poetry and the Culture of the Heart* (Oxford: Clarendon Press, 2006).
Campbell, Matthew, *Rhythm and Will in Victorian Poetry* (Cambridge: Cambridge University Press, 1999).
Griffiths, Eric, *The Printed Voice of Victorian Poetry* (Oxford: Oxford University Press, 1988).
Hall, Jason David ed., *Meter Matters: Verse Cultures of the Long Nineteenth Century* (Athens: Ohio University Press, 2011).
Martin, Meredith, *The Rise and Fall of Meter: Poetry and English National Culture, 1860–1930* (Princeton: Princeton University Press, 2012).
Phelan, Joseph, *The Music of Verse: Metrical Experiment in Nineteenth-Century Poetry* (Basingstoke: Palgrave Macmillan, 2011).
Prins, Yopie, 'Victorian Meters', in Joseph Bristow, ed., *The Cambridge Companion to Victorian Poetry* (Cambridge: Cambridge University Press, 2000), 110–111.
Reynolds, Matthew, *The Realms of Verse 1830–1870: English Poetry in a Time of Nation-Building* (Oxford: Oxford University Press, 2001).
Rudy, Jason, *Electric Meters: Victorian Physiological Poetics* (Athens: Ohio University Press, 2009).
Taylor, Dennis, 'Introduction' to *Hardy's Metres and Victorian Prosody* (Oxford: Clarendon, 1988).
Victorian Poetry, Special issue on Prosody, 49 (2011).
Wimsatt, James I., *Hopkins's Poetics of Speech Sound: Sprung Rhythm, Lettering, Inscape* (Toronto: University of Toronto Press, 2006).

CHAPTER 3

....

BEAT

....

DEREK ATTRIDGE

ONE of the best known lines in Victorian poetry has only three words—or, rather, only one word occurring three times: 'Break, break, break'. Given to a reader who doesn't know the poem (not an easy task among poetry-lovers), it presents a metrical puzzle. Is it perhaps the beginning of an iambic pentameter modelled on Milton's 'Rocks, Caves, Lakes, Fens, Bogs, Dens, and shades of death', in which case the first and third occurrences of 'break' are, nominally at least, in weaker positions than the second? Alternatively, has Tennyson ventured into free verse ahead of his time? But given with the rest of the stanza to a reader who is a native speaker of English, it poses no problems:

> Break, break, break,
>   On thy cold gray stones, O Sea!
> And I would that my tongue could utter
>   The thoughts that arise in me.[1]

The rhythm emerges easily when the lines are read aloud, any uncertainty about the opening line being quickly resolved when the others are read. And it is the immediacy and strength of that rhythm, and in particular its manifestation in the opening three words, that has played a major part—perhaps *the* major part—in making the poem so well-known and well-loved. Yet this poem has provoked at least as much debate about its metrical form as any from the Victorian period. Yopie Prins notes that in 1892 the interest of its rhythms for composers was made manifest by its being singled out in a *Musical Times* article on settings of Tennyson's poems, and that at a 2008 conference on metre in Victorian poetry at Exeter University it was nominated as the 'adopted conference poem'.[2] Prosodists who favoured musical scansion repeatedly returned to the poem, as Prins shows, though with different suggestions as to how its rhythm might be represented by musical notes. Dana Gioia states the metrical conundrum clearly:

> What is the metre of Tennyson's poem? A traditionalist might label it anapaestic, but that scansion does not adequately account for the opening line, which can only

be explained as stress metre. The lines range from three to nine syllables in length, and, if one divides them into accentual-syllabic feet, one discovers as many iambs as anapaests (not to mention the recurring monosyllabic feet). To label this poem iambic or anapaestic, therefore, is misleading since almost every line would then, to some degree, be irregular. Yet the poem is tangibly metrical—one hears a steady beat common to both the three syllable and nine syllable line.[3]

The poem's most significant forebear was a poem at least partly completed by 1798 and first published in 1816, with a preface explaining its unusual metre: Coleridge's 'Christabel'. 'The metre of Christabel,' Coleridge famously wrote, 'is not, properly speaking, irregular, though it may seem so from its being founded on a new principle: namely, that of counting in each line the accents, not the syllables. Though the latter may vary from seven to twelve, yet in each line the accents will be found to be only four.' Coleridge's counting is mistaken: in fact, the lower limit on the number of syllables per line is well below seven. The opening five lines, for example, have syllable-counts of eleven, eleven, four, and six:

> 'Tis the middle of night by the castle clock,
> And the owls have awakened the crowing cock;
> Tu—whit!——Tu—whoo!
> And hark, again! the crowing cock,
> How drowsily it crew.[4]

Not only does the syllable-count contradict Coleridge's prefatory statement, but his comment on the number of accents seems wrong: even if we read the third line with four strong stresses, as the long dashes imply, a normal reading of the fifth line would unquestionably give it three accented syllables. Nevertheless, the general observation that the lines vary greatly in numbers of syllables but observe near consistency in the number of accents—the most frequent variation being an occasional line with two accents—and that the metre is not 'irregular' in that it produces a strong and regular rhythm holds true of the poem as a whole. Gioia's observation about 'Break, break, break' is equally true of 'Christabel': to label it with the traditional names of metrical feet would mislead, yet it is 'tangibly metrical'.

Why did Coleridge choose to introduce his new metre with lines of four accents, and not, for instance, five, which would have associated it with the noble tradition of the iambic pentameter? Whatever model he was consciously following, his ear would have told him that the 'new principle' would only work if based on groups of four accents or, to use a more precise term (since 'accent' may be used of linguistic stress-patterns irrespective of their role in the metre), and one very familiar to Victorian poets and prosodists, *beats*.[5] Four-beat lines had for centuries been the staple of popular verse and song, including ballads, hymns and nursery rhymes, and the last category in particular had shown that certain variations in numbers of syllables can actually strengthen the regularity of the rhythm rather than diminishing it. Examples in which the number of beats per line remains four but the number of syllables varies extensively come to mind very easily (an upper-case, bold **B** under the relevant syllable marks the beat; the intervening figures show the number of syllables between the beats)[6]:

```
Tom, Tom, the piper's son
B   0 B    1 B 1       B

Stole a pig and away did run.
B   1 B     2 B   1 B

Star light, star bright,
B 0 B   0   B 0 B

The first star I see tonight.
1 B   0 B 1 B   1 B
```

Here, the absence of unstressed syllables between many of the beats encourages the emergence of a strong, regular rhythm, propelling the reader away from the modulations of the spoken language and towards something more like a chant. The double off-beat in the second line ('and a-') slips easily into the governing movement. It is worth noting, too, that rhyme plays an important structural role.

Historically, these popular forms are all associated with song, and it may well be that the tendency to vary unstressed syllables with some freedom while observing the count of the stresses was encouraged by the musical rhythm, which took care of any potential irregularities or ambiguities; nevertheless, it is clear that verse of this type doesn't need a musical setting in order to be perceived as having a salient and consistent rhythm. It is equally clear that it doesn't lend itself to prosodic analysis in terms of traditional (which is to say Greek and Latin) 'feet.' An analogous form is a staple in Russian verse, where it is called *dol'nik*, and the Anglicized version, 'dolnik,' is often used of the English metre.[7]

What Coleridge had intuited is an important fact about spoken English: there is a tendency for stressed syllables to occur at equal temporal intervals. This 'stress-timing' or 'isochrony' is only a tendency, and can be as much a matter of perception as of any objectively measurable duration, but it is a crucial factor in English metre—it is the reason, for instance, why purely syllabic verse in English is not rhythmically regular. What Coleridge may also have intuited, as is suggested by 'Christabel''s fifth line, is a fact about the insistent rhythms established by groups of four beats:[8] beats can continue to be felt even when they are not realized in vocal utterance. Nursery rhymes again provide vivid examples (the felt but not spoken beat is indicated here by an unbolded B).

```
Pease pudding hot,
B   0 B 1   B   0 B

Pease pudding cold,
B   0 B 1   B   0 B
```

```
Pease pudding in the pot,
B    0 B  1    B    1  B

Nine days old.
B    0 B   0B   0 B
```

The standard ballad stanza relies on this rhythmic fact, the second and fourth lines containing only three realized beats and an additional unrealized or 'virtual' beat; common measure in hymnody follows the same pattern, while short measure has four realized beats only in the third line (as is also the case in 'Pease pudding hot'). The virtual beat is made particularly evident in musical settings, in which the accompaniment continues while the voice remains silent (or a line-final syllable is extended over two beats). The dolnik form, of which 'Christabel' is a variant, has a long history in literary as well as popular verse, although poets in the seventeenth and eighteenth centuries showed a strong preference for regular accentual-syllabic verse. If we go back to medieval lyrics, to Skelton, or to Shakespeare's songs, however, we find many examples. (Some would trace the form back to the four-stress mode of Anglo-Saxon verse, though the two forms are rhythmically distinct, in spite of the centrality of the four-beat group to both. The form known as 'accentual' or 'strong-stress' or 'stress' metre—such as Gioia attributes to the first line of Tennyson's poem—is a modern imitation of such verse, and doesn't induce the regular rhythm of the dolnik.) A poet who began to explore the potential of dolnik verse well before Coleridge wrote 'Christabel' was Blake, though his example counted for little in the nineteenth century. In popular verse, however, the dolnik remained a staple, and in the nineteenth century numerous examples are to be found, for instance, among collections of ballads and of Chartist verse.

Literary verse in the Victorian period, in contrast to the dominance of the five-beat line—and in particular the iambic pentameter—in the previous century, saw a flowering of both shorter and longer lines, most of them based on the four-beat rhythm. The taste for such poetry from earlier periods was enshrined in Palgrave's *Golden Treasury*, first published in 1861; Palgrave explains in his Preface that 'blank verse and the ten-syllable couplet[...] have been rejected as alien from what is commonly understood by Song, and rarely conforming to Lyrical conditions in treatment'.[9] A later anthology that included a significant quantity of Victorian poetry in these song-like forms, the immensely popular 1900 *Oxford Book of English Verse* edited by Sir Arthur Quiller-Couch ('Q'), is testimony to this preference, and served to project it well into the twentieth century.[10](It is no accident that all the seven 'well-known and representative' nineteenth-century poems named—and disparaged—by F. R. Leavis in the 1932 study that reshaped the poetic canon for a generation, *New Bearings in English Poetry*, are in four-beat forms).[11]

When used in conjunction with end-stopping and rhyme, the four-beat metrical norm produces a verbal movement that evokes the regularity of song rather than the variety of speech; and the occurrence of virtual beats in the appropriate places enhances that rhythmic foregrounding. By the same token, judicious enjambment and avoidance of virtual beats can temper the song-like movement with something closer to speaking qualities; the pre-eminent nineteenth-century example of such poetry is Tennyson's *In Memoriam*. Triple rhythms, on the other hand, usually serve to increase rhythmic insistence, as does the introduction of a dipodic quality to duple rhythm—that is, a tendency for beats to alternate in strength. Browning's 'How They Brought the Good News from Ghent to Aix'—'I sprang to the stirrup, and Joris, and he'—is a good example of the former, while 'A Toccata of Galuppi's'—'Oh Galuppi, Baldassaro, this is very sad to find'—illustrates well his handling of the latter. These strongly rhythmic forms are close to the dolnik (which often has an underlying triple swing, and sometimes evinces a dipodic alternation),[12] though each has its own distinctive character.

Let us return now to Tennyson and 'Break, break, break.' Here are the first and last stanzas, with the beats, actual and virtual, and numbers of intervening syllables marked:

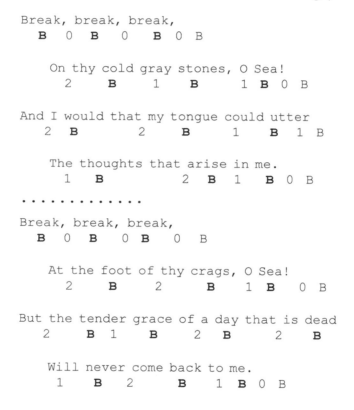

```
Break, break, break,
  B   0  B   0   B  0  B

    On thy cold gray stones, O Sea!
       2   B    1   B      1 B  0  B

And I would that my tongue could utter
  2  B           2   B     1   B  1  B

    The thoughts that arise in me.
       1   B          2  B  1  B  0  B

. . . . . . . . . . . .

Break, break, break,
  B   0  B   0  B  0   B

    At the foot of thy crags, O Sea!
       2    B     2    B    1  B   0  B

But the tender grace of a day that is dead
  2   B  1   B     2   B       2     B

    Will never come back to me.
       1   B   2    B    1  B  0  B
```

In reading the poem aloud it is possible to ignore the virtual beats at the end of most lines, but the result is unpleasantly hurried; whereas a pause allows the implicit sadness in the contemplation of the scene to emerge more fully. The various attempts at musical scansion of the poem clearly show rests in these positions (see Prins, 'Break, Break, Break into Song'). The penultimate line is one of only two in the poem in which the final beat is sounded, making the stanza a version of short measure, with lines of 3, 3, 4, and 3 realized beats.

Much has been written about the mimetic appropriateness of these rhythms to the unstoppable crashing of the waves and the plangent tones of the speaker's grief,[13] but less about the simplicity of the metrical scheme underlying the apparent complexity of the lines, which vary in length from three to eleven syllables (not nine, as Gioia claims). The memorability of the poem is largely due to this simple, strong rhythm, heightened by the striking first line, with its syntactically and metrically induced pauses making up for the lack of unstressed syllables.[14] It thus provides a clear template for the rest of the poem, in which—apart from the repeat of the first line—the beats are separated by one or two syllables. It is an unambiguous example of dolnik verse's characteristic four-beat line (usually, as in this poem, in groups of four lines), varied offbeats, and strong, easily grasped rhythm. Although most Victorian poets and prosodists still thought in terms of classical feet, the age was one in which the dolnik—for which classical prosody is inappropriate—was widely and inventively used. One way of putting this is that, among the richly various explorations of verse form that characterize the age, Victorian poets fully exploited the power of the rhythmic beat.

There is, of course, no sharp division between dolnik verse on one hand and accentual-syllabic verse with occasional variations in syllable-count on the other, although it has been shown that English poetry tends to gravitate either towards the more syllabically regular forms or towards the full-blown dolnik.[15] There is also a gradation between unmistakable dolnik verse with its four-beat foundation and verse in which the number of beats varies freely from line to line, disrupting the swing of the rhythm, a freedom which reached an extreme in the so-called 'Spasmodic' poets of the mid nineteenth century. From the start of his career as a poet Tennyson enjoyed varying both the numbers of beats in the line and the number of syllables between the beats; the 1830 and 1832 volumes of his verse contain many such examples. The following lines from 'Ode to Memory,' for example, begin with what could be the opening of a dolnik stanza but then move into a freer rhythmic mode:

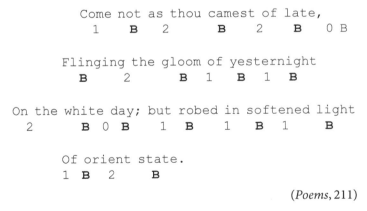

```
            Come not as thou camest of late,
              1   B   2       B   2   B   0 B


        Flinging the gloom of yesternight
          B      2        B  1  B  1  B


    On the white day; but robed in softened light
      2       B  0 B    1  B   1   B   1      B


        Of orient state.
          1 B   2      B
```

(*Poems*, 211)

The potential dolnik rhythm produced by the variation between single and double offbeats and the different line-openings is dissipated by a number of features: the move from three to four realized beats (instead of four to three); the run-on after two lines, which in the dolnik is the major internal break; and the lines of five and two beats. It remains the case, however, that classical prosody cannot account for Tennyson's practice here, and merely imposes divisions on what is a freely varying rhythm.[16]

Tennyson was writing dolnik verse from an early age, however. If we go back to the 1827 *Poems by Two Brothers*, containing poems written by Alfred as a teenager together with poems by his brothers Charles and Frederick, we find imitations of traditional ballads in dolnik rhythms, including a poem that identifies clearly one of Tennyson's major sources for this metrical style. 'The Old Chieftain' has as epigraph the opening line of the third canto of Sir Walter Scott's *Lay of the Last Minstrel* (1805), one of Scott's many four-beat poems with the distinctive dolnik character. Here is the opening of the first canto:

> The feast was over in Branksome tower,
> And the Ladye had gone to her secret bower;
> Her bower that was guarded by word and by spell,
> Deadly to hear, and deadly to tell—
> Jesu Maria, shield us well!
> No living wight, save the Ladye alone,
> Had dared to cross the threshold stone.[17]

Although Scott doesn't group his lines into quatrains here (something he does in many places in the poem), the characteristic dolnik lilt is produced by the salient four stresses in each line, standing out from the varied interval between them. The varied line-openings are typical of the dolnik: whether the line starts with one unstressed syllable (lines 1, 3, 6, and 7) or two unstressed syllables (line 2), or lacks an upbeat altogether (lines 4 and 5), it is the initial stress that sets the insistent rhythm of the line going.

Tennyson's poem is in four-line stanzas rhyming *a b a b*, though they vary between stanzas with the usual ballad form of 4, 3, 4, and 3 realized beats, and stanzas with four realized beats in every line. Here is the third stanza:

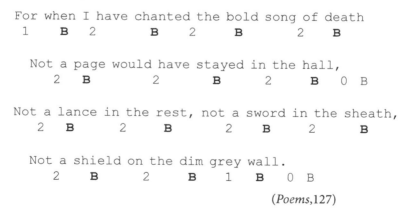

(*Poems*, 127)

We may note the phrase 'dim grey wall,' echoed by Tennyson many years later in 'cold gray stones': the strong rhythm of the dolnik allows a stressed syllable to appear in the position of the offbeat, and in so doing create a distinctive movement in which all three syllables are stressed, but the outer two attract the beat. This rhythmic figure became a distinctive feature of much later dolnik verse, a notable example being the poetry of Swinburne. We may also note that the words 'song of' constitute an offbeat, where the stressed word 'song' has to lose some of its normal emphasis to sustain the momentum of the line. (Among the other well-known forebears of this metre are Charles Wolfe's one remembered poem, the 1816 'Burial of Sir John Moore after Corunna'—'Not a drum was heard, not a funeral note, /As his corse to the rampart we hurried'—and Shelley's 1820 poem 'The Cloud'). The link back to 'Christabel' is evident in Scott's line 'Jesu Maria, shield her well,' which comes straight from Coleridge's poem.[18] It's not fanciful, therefore, to regard 'Break, break, break' as a direct descendant of Coleridge's path-breaking metrical experiment.[19]

Tennyson continued to explore the possibilities of the dolnik, along with many other verse forms. The memorability of its rhythm contributed to the success of some of his most popular lyrics, including the haunting 'Poet's Song', 'Sweet and low' from *The Princess* (*Poems* 772), and 'Come into the garden, Maud' from *Maud* (*Poems* 1075–8). 'Sweet and low' begins with a superb manipulation of the dolnik's possibilities of rhythmic strength and variation:

```
Sweet and low, sweet and low,
 B   1   B  0 B   1    B

Wind of the western sea
 B    2   B 1   B 0 B
```

Many of the songs in Tennyson's plays, as one might expect given the Shakespearean model, use dolnik verse. In his later life he developed a fondness for a six-beat dolnik, a form that breaks naturally in mid-line as well as at the end, though the reader can choose how much weight, if any, to give the mid-line break. Here is the opening of the final stanza of 'Rizpah', showing the possible virtual beat at the halfway mark:

```
Madam, I beg your pardon! I think that you mean to be
 B    2  B    1  B 1 B1  B       2      B    2
    kind,
    B   0 B
But I cannot hear what you say for my Willy's voice
  2  B  1   B       2     B0B 2   B  1    B
    in the wind—
    2    B    0 B
The snow and the sky so bright—he used but to call
  1 B     2    B   1  B  0B1 B      2     B
    in the dark,
    2    B   0 B
And he calls to me now from the church and not from the
  2  B    2   B      2      B  0B1   B      2
    gibbet—for hark!
    B    2   B 0 B
```

(*Poems*, 1249)

Much dolnik verse, like this example, has a predominantly triple rhythm, intermittently varied by the use of single-syllable offbeats ('**beg** your **pard**-,' '**can**not **hear**,' '**Willy's voice**') and different line openings ('**Mad**am,' 'But I **can**not,' 'The **snow**'). On the other hand, Tennyson's eight-beat lines, such as 'Locksley Hall,' use regular accentual-syllabic verse, beginning and ending on the beat.

Another poet who knew well how to exploit the robust rhythms of the dolnik was Robert Browning. The first set of poems in his first volume of short poems, the 1842 collection *Dramatic Lyrics*, is entitled 'Cavalier Tunes'; the initial poem, 'Marching Along', begins:

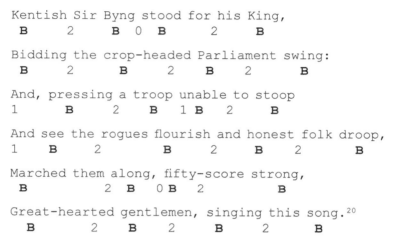

```
Kentish Sir Byng stood for his King,
B    2    B  0 B     2     B

Bidding the crop-headed Parliament swing:
B    2    B    2    B    2      B

And, pressing a troop unable to stoop
1     B    2    B  1 B  2     B

And see the rogues flourish and honest folk droop,
1  B   2      B     2    B    2      B

Marched them along, fifty-score strong,
B       2  B   0 B  2        B

Great-hearted gentlemen, singing this song.²⁰
B        2    B    2    B    2    B
```

The first line—unsurprisingly, one of Browning's most catchy openings—announces its rhythmic lineage immediately: the predominantly duple rhythm is enhanced, not weakened, by the missing syllables at the midway point of the line, an effect repeated in line 5, where the anticipated four-line group is extended by a further two lines in marching mode. The placing of this implied offbeat is crucial: the rhythm would have been entirely different had it occurred elsewhere in the line ('Kentish Sir Philemon played King,' for example, has none of the rhythmic immediacy of the original). The other two poems in this group are also examples of dolnik verse, the third with an opening line that serves as a refrain and demands an early virtual beat if the rhetorical emphasis on the first word, and the rhythm of four realized beats, is to be preserved:

```
Boot, saddle, to horse, and away!
B    0 B    2    B      2 B
```

Omitting the offbeat in this position doesn't produce the memorable rocking rhythm of 'Kentish Sir Byng', though the imagined musical setting—these are 'tunes,' after all—would ensure the appropriate emphases.²¹

Many of Browning's most famous poems draw on dolnik rhythms, including 'Meeting at Night' and 'Parting at Morning', 'Evelyn Hope', 'Up at a Villa—Down at the City', 'The Patriot', and 'Prospice'. The first stanza of 'Home—Thoughts from Abroad' is in dolnik verse, and 'The Pied Piper of Hamelin' utilizes the dolnik's hyper-rhythmicality in many places. 'AbtVogler' is in the same six-beat dolnik that Tennyson used for poems such as 'Rizpah'. Like Tennyson, Browning was an extraordinarily versatile handler of metre; he pushed the regularities of five-beat accentual-syllabic verse to the limit in represent-ing emotional speech at the same time as he capitalized on the song-like properties of the dolnik and other four-beat forms. And like Tennyson, though less frequently, he wrote poems with varying line-lengths and offbeats that don't settle into an insistent rhythm and are correspondingly less likely to imprint themselves on the memory ('In a Gondola', 'The Flight of the Duchess').

Although Elizabeth Barrett Browning didn't favour dolnik for the most part, she used it for one of her most anthologized poems, 'A Musical Instrument', in which we hear the characteristic lilt right from the start, produced by the shift from double offbeats with two unstressed syllables to a single offbeat with a stressed syllable, and clinched by the familiar pattern of four realized beats followed by three:

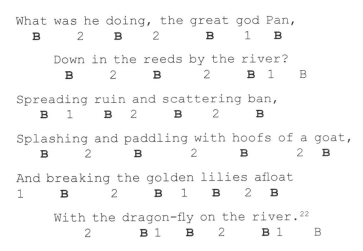

Part of the effectiveness of Barrett Browning's use of the stanza here lies in the thwart-ing of the reader's expectation of a shorter fourth line, as in the ballad stanza: instead, we get two additional lines with four realized beats until reaching the concluding short line—two lines in which evidence of Pan's destructive violence continues to accumulate. She also used a variant of the dolnik for a long, and not at all light-hearted, poem: 'The Runaway Slave at Pilgrim's Point'.

'A Musical Instrument' was included by Q in his *Oxford Book of English Verse*, as were dolnik poems by James Clarence Mangan ('The Nameless One'), William Allingham ('The Fairies'), George Meredith ('Love in the Valley'), Wilfred Scawen Blunt ('The Desolate City'), and Robert Louis Stevenson ('Requiem'). As the titles of these poems alone reveal, the dolnik was used for a large variety of themes, with no sense that it was only suited to light verse. (It did, however, have a strong presence in comic verse, to which we shall turn later.) Also in Q's anthology were dolnik poems by poets seldom heard of today, such as John Todhunter ('Maureen'), William Watson ('Ode in May'), and Henry Charles Beeching ('Going Down Hill on a Bicycle'). James Thomson's 'Gifts' and 'The Vine' and John Davidson's 'Song' may be included in the list of dolnik verse by somewhat better known poets.

To Q's own selection of dolnik poems by lesser-known Victorian authors many more could be added: Sir Alfred Lyall, Alfred Austin, Sir Henry Newbolt, Arthur Munby, and Lord Alfred Douglas.[23] Charles Kingsley used the dolnik rhythm in several poems, often reminiscent of Tennyson, as in the opening lines of 'Alton Locke's Song'—'Weep, weep, weep and weep'[24]—and 'The Tide River'—'Clear and cool, clear and cool.'[25] William Morris's 'Judgement of God' starts as dolnik, but run-on lines soon disrupt the swing of the rhythm. Another longer work that bears signs of the dolnik tradition is Matthew Arnold's 'Tristram and Iseult'. Many genuine ballads that have made it into anthologies of Victorian verse, as well as many literary ballads, use dolnik rhythms; among the latter are Barrett Browning's 'Lord Walter's Wife', Christina Rossetti's 'Noble Sister', and Newbolt's 'Gillespie'. The short lines of Rossetti's 'Goblin Market' fall at times into a dolnik rhythm, but the frequent variations in line-length and rhyme-pattern prevent it from sustaining that rhythm over any extended span.

This is an appropriate place to mention Gerard Manley Hopkins, whose 'sprung rhythm' illustrates the fact that the dolnik rhythm is not entirely free in its disposition of stresses and intervening syllables. Hopkins goes beyond the limited variation and preferred patterns of dolnik verse to create a rhythmic style marked by torsion and overspill, requiring the reader to wrestle the language into the mould of the metre—a very different experience from the easy alternations of the dolnik. A version of dolnik rhythm contributes to the effectiveness of what is perhaps Hopkins's first wholly successful poem, 'Heaven-Haven', and two of his most quoted poems, 'Spring and Fall' and 'Inversnaid' draw on dolnik rhythms (though Hopkins referred to the former as being in sprung rhythm). The latter is a particularly brilliant deployment of the dolnik lilt:

```
This darksome burn, horseback brown,
  1   B   1    B   0  B   1      B

His rollrock highroad roaring down,
  1   B   1    B   1   B   1    B

In coop and in comb the fleece of his foam
  1  B     2   B     1 B     2      B

Flutes and low to the lake falls home.26
   B   1   B   2    B    1    B
```

Where 'Spring and Fall' moves only between single and implied offbeats, 'Inversnaid' also introduces double offbeats that quicken and lighten the rhythm.

Although serious verse that uses a dolnik rhythm with a strong triple base is now hard to appreciate, its success as a medium for comic poetry remains undimmed. Edward Lear is the master, using dolnik variations to heighten rhythmicality in most of his classic poems, including 'The Jumblies', 'The Dong with a Luminous Nose', and 'The Pobble Who Has no Nose'.[27] 'The Jumblies', for example, exploits the dolnik's variations between

single and double offbeat to heighten rhythmicality, and inserts an additional four-beat
line into the 4.3.4.3 stanza:

```
They went to sea in a Sieve, they did,
 1   B   1  B    2  B         1   B

In a Sieve they went to sea:
 2   B       1  B   1  B  0 B

In spite of all their friends could say,
 1   B   1  B    1    B       1    B

On a winter's morn, on a stormy day,
 2   B  1    B        2    B 1 B

In a Sieve they went to sea!28
 2   B       1   B    1  B  0 B
```

We could also include much of W. S. Gilbert's comic verse, written to be set by Arthur
Sullivan, which often utilizes triple or dipodic rhythms, with metrical rests in places
where the music can sustain the momentum.

Another domain of Victorian verse which saw the dolnik flourish, in an odd
coming-together of the learned and the popular, was the enterprise of imitating classical Greek metres. The dactylic hexameter, when translated into an English accentual
hexameter, happens to produce a swinging dolnik rhythm (which has very little to do
with the rhythm of the quantitative Greek original), thanks to its basically triple metre
with allowable shifts into duple everywhere except before the last beat, and the tendency
of the six-beat line to fall into two three-beat groups. The pre-eminent English poet in
this mode is Arthur Hugh Clough. Here is the opening of part VII of *Amours de Voyage*
(I haven't marked the potential silent beats after every three realised beats, as Clough's
verse rattles along without much in the way of pauses, so that virtual beats are registered
only very faintly as articulations of the rhythm into lines and half-lines):

```
So, I have seen a man killed! An experience that, among others!
 B   2    B   2   B    2        B  2     B    2  B  1

Yes, I suppose I have; although I can hardly be certain,
 B   2    B  1 B  1  B      2    B   2  B  1

And in a court of justice could never declare I had seen it.29
 B    2   B  1 B    2      B  2   B   2    B  1
```

This metre is not very far removed from the six-beat dolnik used by Tennyson in
'Rizpah', a few lines of which I quoted earlier, or the many Victorian poems in a similar
metre, though one important difference is that Clough, following classical precedent,
doesn't use regular rhyme.

Another classical metrical form, carried, like the dactylic hexameter, from Ancient
Greek into Latin, was the Sapphic; and here it was not the replacement of the Latin

quantitative ictus by a stressed syllable but the original accentual pattern of the Latin that, fortuitously, produce a version of the dolnik rhythm, with three four-beat lines and a two-beat coda. The following is a characteristic stanza in Sapphic metre by Horace (*Odes* 1.38), showing the beats that emerge in a reading attentive to Latin stressing:

```
        Persicos odi, puer, apparatus,
        B    2  B    B     3   B 1

        desplicent nexae philyra coronae,
        B    2     B 1   B    3    B 1

        mitte sectari, rosa quo locorum
        B    2     B 1   B    3   B 1

            sera moretur³⁰
            B   2   B 1
```

Henry Dearmer's translation of a hymn attributed to Gregory the Great, included in the former's *English Hymnal* of 1906, will give us an example of the English Sapphic:³¹

```
        Father, we praise thee, now the night is over;
        B    2   B       1   B      3      B 1

        Active and watchful, stand we all before thee;
        B    2   B    1      B     3     B    1

        Singing, we offer prayer and meditation;
        B    2   B 1  B     prayer   3  B 1

        Thus we adore thee.³²
        B   2  B    1
```

The eleven-syllable lines have four main beats, and the first and second offbeats are, respectively, double and single (and the final five-syllable line follows the pattern of the openings of the earlier lines). It is between the third and fourth beats that the distinctive rhythm of the accentual Sapphic is created: three unstressed syllables, with the suggestion of a weaker beat on the middle one. Outside of the context of music, in fact, the longer lines come very close to iambic pentameter with an initial inversion, and a single line of this type would not be out of place in pentameter verse. The consistent opening, so typical of the stronger dolnik rhythm, however, encourages a four-beat reading, and hence a speeding up of the second part of the line to accommodate it. A slow chant of these lines will reveal that a dipodic rhythm underlies them:

```
        Fa-ther, we praise thee, now the night is o-ver
        B   b     B    b   B       b      B b
```

Emily Brontë's 'Remembrance' is probably most often read now as in somewhat free iambic pentameters, but if we hear it with a Victorian ear its rhythmic allegiance to the English Sapphic is clear, giving it a plangent musicality (I quote a stanza where this allegiance is especially clear):

```
Sweet Love of youth, forgive, if I forget thee,
   B       2   B     1 B         3     B     1

While the world's tide is bearing me along;
   B       2         B   1 B         3   B

Other desires and other hopes beset me,
  B    2   B    1   B       3      B    1

Hopes which obscure, but cannot do thee wrong!³³
   B          2    B      1    B    3        B
```

Brontë removes the final unstressed syllable of the second line, and repeats this metre in place of the short final line; but the distinctive Sapphic form of the dolnik four-line stanza is still evident.³⁴

Since the practice of many Victorian poets indicates an acute awareness of the poetic potential of dolnik verse and its characteristic beat prosody, and since, presumably, their readers were able to appreciate their exploitation of that potential, we might expect that prosodic theory of the period would provide us with a clear account of its workings. Unfortunately, however, theorizations of the mechanics of versification in Western poetry have, from the beginnings, been dogged by the difficulties of representing, either in linguistic or in graphic form, the experiences of the ear and body in respond-ing to rhythmic arrangements in sound. Although the ear finds dolnik verse the easiest metrical form to grasp, the prosodist working with the traditional tools finds it highly problematic. Nevertheless, there are some signs that the features of spoken English capi-talized on by dolnik verse, and more generally by four-beat forms, were brought into consciousness more fully during Victoria's reign than in previous eras. Joshua Steele, in his *Essay towards Establishing the Melody and Measure of Speech* (1775)—later entitled *Prosodia Rationalis*—had led the way in using musical notation to represent the tempo-ral relations of English speech, including pauses or silences. Edwin Guest's monumental *History of English Rhythms*, first published in 1838 and issued in a posthumous second edition in 1882, while approaching English metre as a matter of accent rather than time, registered in a few places the existence of dolnik verse and its dependence on temporal relations. Beats and offbeats felt by the reader but not manifested in the voice are termed 'sectional pauses', and Guest gives several examples, including the opening of Puck's song in *A Midsummer Night's Dream*:³⁵

```
On the ground
B   1   B

Sleep sound
 B   0   B
```

The dolnik's variation between single and double offbeats he discusses under the head-ing of 'tumbling-metre'; among his examples are the February eclogue in Spenser's *Shepheardes Calender* (535), which begins:

```
        There grew an aged Tree on the greene
        1     B 1  B 1   B    2        B
```

The most important contribution to the Victorian understanding of the song-rhythms of the dolnik and other four-beat forms was made by Coventry Patmore, in a study that first appeared in 1857, and was subsequently revised for further publication in editions of Patmore's poetical works, finally appearing as 'Essay on English Metrical Law' at the end of the second volume of his *Poems* (1886).[36] Patmore's basic premise is that 'metre, in the primary degree of a series of isochronous intervals, marked by accents, is as natural to spoken language as an even pace is natural to walking' (224). On this basis, he is able to give Guest's 'sectional pauses' a fundamental role in metre, appreciating that the temporal movement set up by a regular alternating rhythm makes it possible for beats to be experienced even when they have no material embodiment. He is thus able to say that 'there are two indispensable conditions of metre,' first, that the vocal utterance represented by the written line of verse is divided into 'equal or proportionate spaces,' and second, '*that the fact of that division shall be made manifest* by an "ictus" or "beat," actual or mental' (230). (Patmore's use in 1857 of the term 'beat' to refer to verse rhythm is considerably earlier than the *OED*'s first citation – a notebook entry by Hopkins made in 1873 or 1874.) These 'mental' beats, which I have been calling virtual beats, are a product of the isochronous tendency of the spoken language that Patmore has already emphasized; they exist, it is important to note, not in some abstract realm of mathematical relations but as realities in the mind as perceiver of rhythm.[37] When he goes on to say that this 'time-beater' has, 'for the most part, [. . .] *no material and external existence at all*,' but is a result of the mind's delight in marking measure 'with an imaginary "beat"' (231), he is not arguing for a mechanical grid against which the realities of vocal rhythm are played, but for the immediacy in the reader's experience of rhythmic pulses, continuing beyond the sounding of the voice. It is ironic that a prosodist who understood the significance of felt temporality in the mind's experience of regular verse should sometimes be hailed as the forefather of the prosodic theory of New Criticism, for which metre was exactly that abstract, mechanical grid. So taken was Patmore by this insight into the experiential reality of beats that he over-generalized it, and claimed to find 'catalexis'—missing syllables 'substituted by an equivalent pause'—in a wide variety of verse. This argument was linked to a view that English verse is fundamentally dipodic, so that any uneven number of beats in a line will always imply one more unsounded beat. Although, as we have seen, many Victorian poets found in dipodic verse a satisfying form, there are too many counter-examples (including most five-beat verse) to allow Patmore's argument to stand.[38]

We may end by turning briefly to three poets towards the end of the Victorian period who exploited the potential of the dolnik to the full, though in very different ways: Algernon Charles Swinburne, Rudyard Kipling, and Thomas Hardy. Swinburne's most characteristic poems employ a variant of the dolnik that he developed early in his career and continued to exploit until its end. It is used in 'The Triumph of Time', 'Hymn to Proserpine', 'The Garden of Proserpine', 'A Forsaken Garden', and the famous choruses from 'Atalanta in Calydon'. Here is the opening of 'The Garden of Proserpine':

```
Here, where the world is quiet;
  B         2     B   1  B 1   B

    Here, where all trouble seems
    B         2     B   1 B    OB

Dead winds' and spent waves' riot
 1   B    1    B     1     B 1  B

    In doubtful dreams of dreams;
    1   B    1    B    1    B    OB

I watch the green field growing³⁹
1  B     1   B    1     B 1    B
```

As usual with verse that is consistently in lines of three beats, the fourth, virtual beat is only a slight presence, and Swinburne's enjambments contribute to its containment. One feature of his dolnik verse is the use of demotion in single offbeats, that is, the use of a stressed syllable between two other stressed syllables that take beats (recall Tennyson's 'dim grey wall' and 'cold gray stones'). (This is a variation that may owe something to the classical example of the allowable substitution of a spondee for a dactyl in the dactylic hexameter). Demotion doesn't require a forced pronunciation, as the persistence of the four-beat rhythm in the mind—as Patmore understood—allows the alternation to be felt even if it is not objectively present. So 'waves' and 'field' in the lines above take their natural stress, but aren't experienced as beats. Initial stressed syllables—such as 'Dead'—can also be demoted in this way.

Where Swinburne cultivated a suave, melodic rhythm (further discussed by Michael Hurley in this volume), Kipling explored the dolnik, and other four-beat metrical forms, to achieve a jauntiness that contributed to his enormous popularity as a poet. Along with extensive use of dipodic and triple verse we find poems such as 'The Ballad of East and West', written in the seven-beat line realization of the 4.3.4.3. ballad stanza:

```
Oh, East is East, and West is West, and never the twain shall
1   B   1  B    1   B    1  B    1   B   2    B       1

    meet,
    B   0  B

Till Earth and Sky stand presently at God's great Judgment
 1   B    1    B   1     B 1   B 1  B      1   B 1

    Seat;
    B   0  B

But there is neither East nor West, Border, nor Breed, nor
 1   B    1  B    1  B     1   B  0 B    2      B    0

    Birth,
    B   0  B
```

```
When two strong men stand face to face, though they come from
    1   B   1   B   1   B   1 B         2      B        2

    the ends of the earth!40
        B    2 B       0  B
```

Whatever we may think of the sentiments expressed, there can be no doubt that this is a highly skilful deployment of dolnik verse, from the strong opening alternation of beats and single offbeats, through the suggestion of syncopation when the offbeat is skipped between 'West' and 'Border', to the run of five stressed monosyllables in the first part of the fourth line, followed by the rapid sequence of beats and double offbeats that finish the stanza. Among the other well-known poems of Kipling in dolnik metres are 'The 'eathen', 'The Light that Failed', 'When Earth's Last Picture is Painted', and several of the poems in *The Jungle Book* and *Just So Stories*. A dipodic poem that relies on the possibility of implied offbeats for its distinctive march rhythm is 'Boots' ('We're foot - slog - slog - slog - sloggin' over Africa').

Hardy, by contrast with Kipling, was able to encompass a much wider range of rhythmic styles, and found a way of eliciting from the dolnik emotional resonances of great depth and subtlety. His first collection, *Wessex Poems and Other Verses* (1898), contains several dolnik poems, including 'Postponement' (light verse dating from 1866), 'Neutral Tones' (contrastingly dark, from 1869), 'San Sebastian' (a plaintive spoken narrative), and 'Her Death and After' (a longer narrative poem, full of emotion). Examples of dolnik verse in *Poems of the Past and the Present* (1901) include the potent meditation on insect life, 'An August Midnight', the fourteeners of 'In Tenebris II', and the unmistakably Hardeian lament at the irreversibility of time, 'On the Departure Platform'. The last stanza of 'Neutral Tones' will have to suffice as an example of Hardy's metrical brilliance:

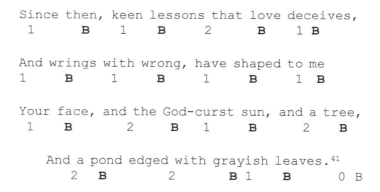

```
    Since then, keen lessons that love deceives,
      1     B    1   B    2     B    1 B

    And wrings with wrong, have shaped to me
    1    B    1    B     1    B     1 B

    Your face, and the God-curst sun, and a tree,
      1  B      2   B   1     B     2     B

    And a pond edged with grayish leaves.41
        2  B       2       B 1   B      0 B
```

The first two lines move steadily forward, all but one of the offbeats being single, and the only moment of heightening is on 'keen,' requiring stress but serving as an offbeat. Then the run-on after 'shaped to me' pushes against the four-beat expectation of a pause, while the following line piles on the elements in the scene with two double offbeats and a strong emphasis on the powerful word 'curst' (in the second line of the poem the sun was merely 'chidden' by God). Finally, the three-beat closing line42 tenses the rhythm by including the strongly-stressed word 'edged' as part of a double offbeat—there is a temptation to give it a beat, allowing a pause after 'pond' to take a beat, and it is largely the clearly three-beat lines of the three previous stanzas that determine the rhythm here.

Victorian verse in metrical forms that rely on the popular rhythms of ballad, song, and nursery rhyme has been consistently underestimated since the poetic revaluation effected by Pound, Eliot, Leavis, and others in the first third of the twentieth century. A full appreciation of its achievements requires that we learn to appreciate once more the potential of a poetic form that, instead of tempering rhythm in the interests of dramatic speech, heightens its regular beating to create movements of language that are vivid, memorable, and often deeply affecting.

Notes

1. Tennyson, *Poems*, ed. Christopher Ricks (London: Longmans, 1969), 602.
2. "'Break, break, break' into Song", in *Meter Matters: Verse Cultures of the Long Nineteenth Century*, ed. Jason David Hall (Athens, OH: Ohio University Press, 2011), 105–34; references on 107 and 109.
3. Dana Gioia, 'Meter-Making Arguments', in *Meter in English: A Critical Engagement*, ed. David Baker (Fayetteville: University of Arkansas, 1986), 75–96; reference on p. 93. J. F. A. Pyre, in *The Formation of Tennyson's Style* (New York: Phaeton, 1968), is equally bemused: 'Scarcely two verses have precisely the same movement. In the 16 lines there are twelve different combinations of iambs and anapaests' (107).
4. Coleridge, *Poetical Works*, ed. Hartley Coleridge (London: Oxford University Press, 1969), 215.
5. Another term with roughly the same meaning that appears in Victorian prosodic discussion is *ictus*; its use is complicated by its Latin inheritance, however.
6. A zero indicates an implied or unrealized offbeat, felt as a moment of relaxation between successive beats. A fuller scansion would also show the implied offbeats felt between the end of one line and the next, since the four-line, four-beat group functions as a single rhythmic whole; this would, however, complicate the visual representation even further.
7. See, for example, Marina Tarlinskaja, *Strict Stress-Meter in English Poetry Compared with German and Russian* (Calgary: University of Calgary Press, 1993); Martin Duffell, *A New History of English Metre* (London: MHRA and Maney, 2008); and Derek Attridge, 'The Case for the English Dolnik, or, How Not to Introduce Prosody', *Poetics Today* 33.1 (2012): 1–26. There is some inconsistency in the employment of the term; I use it for verse that has a strong four-beat rhythm and does not fall into the regular syllabic patterns scannable in terms of repeated feet.
8. Strictly speaking, the group of four is one level in a hierarchy that moves from single beats to pairs to fours, eights, and sixteens; it is, however, the level on which the verse line is usually based.
9. *The Golden Treasury of the Best Songs and Lyrical Poems in the English Language*, selected and arranged with notes by F.T. Palgrave (London: Macmillan, 1861 Preface), n.p.
10. Sir Arthur Quiller-Couch, *The Oxford Book of English Verse 1250–1900* (Oxford: Oxford University Press, 1900).
11. F. R. Leavis, *New Bearings in English Poetry* (1932) (Harmondsworth: Pelican, 1972), 14.

12. Four-beat forms involving virtual beats imply a dipodic rhythm, since the stronger beats are all realized while some of the weaker beats are omitted.

13. For a recent example, see Jason Rudy, *Electric Meters: Victorian Physiological Poetics* (Athens, GA: Ohio University Press, 2009), 71–2. Rudy interestingly relates Tennyson's poem to Thomas Hood's popular parody, 'The Song of the Shirt.'

14. The role of these pauses can be judged by comparing this opening to 'Star bright star light,' where the reciter has to use a somewhat artificial pronunciation in order to stress the words equally and allow the four beats to emerge.

15. See Tarlinskaja, *Strict Stress-Meter*, 35–41.

16. Ricks, surprisingly, states the that the poem is in iambics (Tennyson, *Poems*, 211).

17. Sir Walter Scott, *Selections from the Poems*, ed. Alexander Hamilton Thompson (Cambridge: Cambridge University Press, 1922), 6.

18. Although 'Christabel' was published after Scott's work, it was recited to Scott by John Stoddart in 1802, when the former was working on the *Lay*. Scott eventually acknowledged the indebtedness of his poem to Coleridge's. See Margaret Russett, *Fictions and Fakes: Forging Romantic Authenticity, 1760–1845* (Cambridge: Cambridge University Press, 2006), 82–90.

19. The importance to the young Tennyson of Scott's four-beat verse comes across in a notebook comment quoted by Hallam Tennyson in his memoir of his father: 'At about twelve and onward I wrote an epic of six thousand lines *à la* Walter Scott. . .with Scott's regularity of octo-syllables and his occasional varieties. Though the performance was very likely worth nothing I never felt myself more truly inspired. I wrote as much as seventy lines at one time, and used to go shouting them about the fields in the dark' (Hallam Tennyson, *Alfred, Lord Tennyson: A Memoir* (London: Macmillan, 1897), 12).

20. Robert Browning, *The Poems*, ed. John Pettigrew, vol. 1, 347.

21. Browning, too, may have been influenced by Scott, since these 'Cavalier Tunes' appear to contain echoes of the latter's *Woodstock; or the Cavalier*: see R. L. Lowe, 'Scott, Browning, and Kipling,' *Notes and Queries* 197.5 (1952): 103–4.

22. Elizabeth Barrett Browning, *Selected Poems*, ed. Marjorie Stone and Beverly Taylor (Peterborough, Ontario: Broadview, 2009), 298.

23. It is unfortunate that for the twentieth century the steady beating of the dolnik was often associated with militarism; see, for example, Meredith Martin's discussion of Newbolt (*The Rise and Fall of Meter: Poetry and English National Culture, 1860–1930* [Princeton: Princeton University Press, 2012], 122–30. His most famous poem, 'Drake's Drum,' successfully combines dipodic dolnik verse with strongly rhythmic five-beat lines.

24. Charles Kingsley, *Andromeda and Other Poems* (London: John W. Parker and Son, 1858), 129.

25. Charles Kingsley, *The Water-Babies* (Boston: Burnham, 1864), 42.

26. Gerard Manley Hopkins, *The Major Works*, ed. Catherine Phillips (Oxford: Oxford University Press, 2002), 153.

27. Lewis Carroll, by contrast, prefers to observe the regularity of accentual-syllabic verse—as does Lear in his limericks.

28. Lewis Carroll and Edward Lear, *Utter Nonsense: Selected Poems* (n.p.: Lonely Scribe, 2004), 21.

29. Arthur Hugh Clough, *Poems* (London: Macmillan, 1862), 181.

30. John Conington's Victorian translation reads: 'No Persian cumber, boy, for me; / I hate your garlands linden-plaited; / Leave winter's rose where on the tree / It hangs belated' (*The Odes and Carmen Saeculare of Horace* (London: George Bell and Sons, 1882)).

31. I am terming it the 'English Sapphic' rather than the 'accentual Sapphic,' which, on the model of the accentual hexameter, replaces the quantitative scheme with an accentual one without producing a dolnik rhythm.

32. Henry Dearmer et al., eds., *The English Hymnal* (London: Oxford University Press, 1906), 238.

33. Emily Brontë, *Poems*, ed. Barbara Lloyd Evans (London: Batsford, 1992), 130.

34. For a fuller discussion of the Horation Sapphic and English imitations, see Derek Attridge, *Well-weighed Syllables: Elizabethan Verse in Classical Metres* (Cambridge: Cambridge University Press, 1974), 211–16.

35. Edwin Guest, *A History of English Rhythms*, second edition, ed. W. W. Skeat (London: George Bell and Sons), 1882, p. 281.

36. Coventry Patmore, *Poems: Second Collective Edition*, 2 vols. (London: George Bell and Son), 1886.

37. Rudy reveals clearly the problems that beset the prosodist who puts abstract metrical grids before the experience of the ear: he chides Patmore for placing 'a great deal of trust in the reader, who must intuit (physically? intellectually?) the poem's metrical structure' and asks, a propos of isochrony, 'what sort of regulation might come from a poem that most readers cannot scan?' (*Electric Meters*, 122). The regular beats of strongly isochronic English verse are felt by both the mind and the body, and scanning difficulties are the product not of a complex metre but of inappropriate tools.

38. In his own poetry, Patmore—though he made extensive use of four-beat verse, for instance in the lengthy *Angel in the House*—did not favour dolnik verse.

39. Algernon Charles Swinburne, *Selected Poems*, ed. L. M. Findlay (Manchester: Carcanet, 1982), 75.

40. Rudyard Kipling, *The Complete Verse* (London: Kyle Cathie, 1996), 190.

41. Thomas Hardy, *The Complete Poems*, ed. James Gibson (London: Macmillan, 1976), 12.

42. All the dolnik verse in *Wessex Poems* involves a shorter last line or pair of lines, and it may well be, as Dennis Taylor has argued, that Hardy's fascination with the Sapphic and its mixture of dactyls and trochees is evident in these poems; see *Hardy's Metres and Victorian Prosody* (Oxford: Clarendon Press, 1988), 258–62. Although Matthew Campbell, in *Rhythm and Will in Victorian Poetry* (Cambridge: Cambridge University Press, 1999), analyzes the poem in terms of classical feet, he notes of one of these shorter lines that 'it creates the very effect that Coleridge had envisaged in *Christabel*' (59).

CHAPTER 4

....

ADDRESS

....

ROBERT DOUGLAS-FAIRHURST

SOME of Tennyson's earliest surviving lines were written in his schoolboy copy of Virgil:

1. A. Tennyson
2. Somersby
3. in Lincolnshire
4. in England
5. in Europe
6. in the world
7. in the air
8. in space[1]

A similar mixture of specificity and vagueness characterizes many of the locations imagined in his early poems: 'a golden clime' ('The Poet'), 'holy ground' ('The Poet's Mind'), 'a lonely place' ('The Poet's Song'), a garden that is 'Not wholly in the busy world, nor quite / Beyond it' ('The Gardener's Daughter').[2] These are not the sort of descriptions that might help anyone locate Tennyson's settings on a map, because their primary function is topological rather than topographical: they are imaginative spaces in which he can work out his place in poetic tradition, and the broader place of poetry in nineteenth-century culture. Similar questions lie at the heart of many Victorian poems. Is the poet a central or a marginal figure in society? Should a poem be a public platform, with its lines working like bridges to link poet and reader together, or a private retreat, in which the same lines work more like barriers to keep them apart?

At first sight, Tennyson's response to such questions might seem fairly straightforward. Educated at Cambridge University, where the presence of the Apostles and the Union debating society promoted the development of an influential 'oratorical environment', many of his contributions to *Poems by Two Brothers* (1827), his first published volume, begin by appealing to a known individual ('thou' or 'ye') or to some matter of shared concern ('we' or 'our').[3] Yet even in these early poems, abstract models of poetic address can be heard snagging on the local details of his writing. For example, when Tennyson refers to 'our fancy' in 'Midnight' ('Imperfect, half-seen objects meet the sight, / The other half our fancy must portray'), he could be describing the workings of his own imagination, or asking his readers to collaborate in the construction of this shadowy world: 'our' stretches and shrinks to accommodate different interpretations.[4] The referent of 'To—', published three years later, is equally opaque. Opening with an address to a 'Clear-headed friend', the decision to make its subject anonymous is at once a specific act of friendship (Tennyson's shyness made him wary of revealing too much about those who were close to him as well as about himself) and an overture to a more general audience. 'The first lines were addressed to [J. W.] Blakesley', Tennyson explained, 'but the poem wandered off to describe an imaginary man'.[5] However, even if Tennyson conjured up this 'imaginary man' as his ideal reader, always attractively clear-headed and friendly, his title cannot quite extinguish the fear that '—' might equally reflect the absence of any reader at all, as if his poem was a fragmentary SOS message sent out into the world without any certainty that it would be intercepted.

By the time Tennyson published 'To—' in *Poems, Chiefly Lyrical* (1830), these anxieties had established themselves as one of the period's imaginative home-keys. Although Wordsworth had argued that the poet should 'address himself' to his audience as 'a man speaking to men',[6] and followed his own advice (expanding the gender of 'men' to include women) by writing many poems with titles such as 'Address to my Infant Dora' or 'To Joanna',[7] in addition to *The Prelude*—described on the title page of an 1805 manuscript as a 'Poem / Title not yet fixed upon / by / William Wordsworth / Addressed to / S. T. Coleridge'—many of his contemporaries were not convinced.[8] Byron's *Childe Harold's Pilgrimage* uses the word 'address' just once, and even then it is put into a compromising position: 'It came to pass, that when he did address / Himself to quit' (II, 613–14). As Matthew Bevis points out, the line-ending 'translates public invocation into private communing',[9] as if the speaker suddenly lost his nerve when confronted with the space his voice must cross. However, like many literary jokes, Byron's syntactic recoil also reflects a genuine fear about his own poem and the fate of poetry more generally. A literary address might be followed by the silence of incomprehension or indifference, but the gap between poet and audience might equally have become too large for anyone to traverse, no matter how powerful the speaker's voice or how sharp their listener's ears.

John Martin's painting 'The Bard' (*c.*1817) had earlier translated the dilemma into spatial terms. Based on Thomas Gray's 'The Bard' (1757), an ode 'founded on a Tradition current in Wales, that Edward the First, when he compleated the conquest of his country, ordered all the Bards, that fell into his hands, to be put to death',[10] it depicts a poet standing on a crag, clutching his lyre and gesticulating angrily, while a waterfall crashes and the wind makes his cloak billow out like a pair of wings. He is a magnificent figure, who dwarfs the puny soldiers below him, yet there is no indication that they are remotely bothered by his lofty rhetoric. Having a calling does not necessarily mean that anyone is listening. In fact, if this painting depicts the poet's escape from his pursuers, all the indications from later in the century were that he had succeeded only too well.

'Reflect...how deeply *unpoetical* the age and all one's surroundings are,' Matthew Arnold observed in an 1849 letter to A. H. Clough. 'Not unprofound, not ungrand, not unmoving—but *unpoetical*'.[11] That self-consciously archaic word 'unpoetical' carried Arnold's fear that poetry was the relic of a bygone age, and he was not alone in expressing it. In Dickens's novels, similarly, the characters who appeal to poetry tend to be either ancient or fraudulent or both, like the simpering crone Mrs Skewton in *Dombey and Son*, who reveals her true colours when she cries out 'If they would only leave us a little more of the poetry of existence in these terrible days!'[12] Elsewhere, poets were still occasionally defended in traditional terms as leaders or prophets: Carlyle published an essay on 'The Hero as Poet', while Elizabeth Barrett Browning celebrated poets as 'the only truth-tellers now left to God'.[13] Their contemporaries were not always so sure, either of themselves or their writing. Wordsworth's famous question 'Whither is fled the visionary gleam? / Where is it now, the glory and the dream?' continued to reverberate across the century, and Victorian poets were especially nervous about how to respond.[14] What did it mean to be a post-Romantic poet? Was Victorian poetry a natural extension of earlier writing or an unnecessary supplement? When Arnold wrote about 'Wandering between two worlds, one dead, / The other powerless to be born' ('Stanzas from the Grande Chartreuse'),[15] he was mostly thinking about how to confront the decline of religious faith, but he was also reflecting on his own situation as a poet. Victorian poetry was equally caught between two worlds, keen to find a voice suitable for modern life, but worried that it could offer only a thin parody of what had come before. It produces a painful ambiguity in another line of Arnold's poem, 'the best are silent now', which could mean that the real poets are now all dead, or that only the worst kind of writer would consider breaking into song in such a self-consciously 'unpoetical' age.

Of the many reasons for Victorian poetry's self-doubts, several were generated specifically by the problem of literary address. The development of a large reading public—frequently characterized as indiscriminate and unknowable—threatened to remove the last vestiges of personal contact between poets and their audience.[16] Similarly, it was argued, old-fashioned ideas about poems as unique works of art were being lost in the din of an age of mechanical reproduction, as steam-powered presses threatened to flatten out the distinct contours of each poet's voice; when one of Tennyson's reviewers complained that his poems were 'curious mental manufactures which should rather come under the head of mechanism than anything else', he was using the language of the factory to suggest that even writers with a recognizable style had started to turn out poems like wallpaper patterns or mass-produced toys.[17] Most significant of all, the rise of the novel meant that poetry was being supplanted by a form that deliberately appealed to the crowd. In the case of a novelist like Dickens, starting with the preface he added to the second series of *Sketches by Boz* (1836), this was not always easy to distinguish from a sales pitch:

> *Publisher* (to author)—You knock.
> *Author* (to publisher)—No—you. [Here the publisher seizes the knocker, and gives a loud rap at the door.]
> *Public* (suspiciously, and with the door a-jar)—Well; what do *you* want?[18]

Dickens's answer to this question was clear: he wanted to establish himself in the hearts and homes of his public; to encourage them to make the real world a better match for the virtual world of fiction; to make them realize that what *they* wanted was a lack only he could supply. Occasionally Dickens's ambition bubbles to the surface of his writing, as when he ends *Hard Times* with a direct appeal: 'Dear reader! It rests with you and me, whether, in our two fields of action, similar things shall be or not. Let them be!'[19] For all its local ambiguities ('rests' sits oddly with 'action', just as 'Let them be!' seems unsure whether it is a call to action or an acceptance of the status quo), this was simply another manifestation of Dickens's longstanding dream of being able '*to write a book in company* instead of in my own solitary room'.[20] Like his speeches and public readings, his chosen method of serial publication—which each month produced letters from readers expressing their views on what had appeared so far—allowed him to remain audibly in contact with his audience. Calling upon his readers to right social wrongs was simply an explicit version of the contract he had established with them over the years.

Compared to this sort of easy familiarity, even the chattiest of Victorian poets were in danger of sounding strained or stilted when addressing their readers, their subjects, or even themselves. Their responses varied widely. In the case of Walt Whitman, it was to create a voice that sought out readers with urgent intimacy. A poem like 'To You' borrows the form of a classical inscription ('Stay, traveller'), and conjures up its future audience through rhythmical incantation:

> Stranger! if you, passing, meet me, and desire to speak to me, why
> > should you not speak to me?
> And why should I not speak to you?[21]

Such questions are not without their own form of knowing comedy, as Whitman's repetition of 'speak to me' hints at the pub bore button-holing a reluctant listener. They also contain the seeds of their own answers. It is by responding to Whitman's call that he can speak to us: a form of reciprocal activity that encourages a meeting of minds liberated from the vagaries of historical circumstance. To pick up Whitman's poem and read it with the same care that went into its composition is to grasp a hand being held out to us across the years.

Such examples suggest that when J. S. Mill sought to define poetry, he was too quick to make clear distinctions between public and private forms of speech: 'Poetry and eloquence are both alike the expression or uttering forth of feeling. But if we may be excused the seeming affectation of the antithesis, we should say that eloquence is *heard*, poetry is *over*heard. Eloquence supposes an audience; the peculiarity of poetry appears to us to lie in the poet's utter unconsciousness of a listener'.[22] This is both grandly sweeping and nervously concessive, and Mill was right to be wary of the opposition he was attempting to establish. As the period developed, although a handful of poems detached themselves from an imaginary reader, withdrawing into private grumbling and brooding, far more situated themselves on the fault-line between Mill's categories. The development of the dramatic monologue, in particular, created a form that could capture the stutterings and thwartings of ordinary speech, and at the same time absorb them into an argument directed towards an imagined interlocutor; it offered the sound of someone thinking as well as a set of finished thoughts. Some monologues complicated this picture still further, by deliberately confusing whether the speaker was addressing a listener directly or merely thinking aloud in their presence. When Tennyson's speaker addresses God in 'St Simeon Stylites', for example, the fact that he receives no reply could be because his listener is non-existent, or blankly indifferent, or choked with compassion, a doctrinal argument in which, as the poem's other invisible power, Tennyson himself gleefully refuses to take sides. Similarly, when Dante Gabriel Rossetti addresses a prostitute in 'Jenny', it only takes a few lines for the reader to realize that her 'head upon my knee to-night / Rests' not because she is being lovingly submissive, but because she is asleep, thereby turning the whole poem into a sophisticated thought bubble—one that encourages intimate revelations because the listener is unconscious, not because the speaker is unconscious of her.[23]

Even where Victorian poets engaged in more traditional forms of verse, they recognized that knowing how to address an audience could be as complex on paper as it was in real life. Readers could be invoked confidently or more tentatively; poets could seek a response or merely an appreciative silence; they could approach their task with an original turn of phrase or in a voice muffled by convention. Translation and parody allowed them to project a voice that both was and was not their own; alternatively, they could avoid the question of their readership altogether, by replacing human addressees with more compliant alternatives: 'Sonnet: To Tartar, a Terrier Beauty'; 'To a Snow-Flake'.[24] Occasionally these poems draw attention to the fact that they have taken old-fashioned forms of invocation and turned them in a new direction, as when Joanna Baillie composes an 'Address to a Steamvessel' in couplets that try to steer a course between tradition and modernity:

> Thou holdst thy course in independent pride;
> No leave ask'st thou of either wind or tide.
> To whate'er point the breeze inconstant veer,
> Still doth thy careless helmsman onward steer...[25]

Baillie's verse echoes the mechanical straightforwardness of its subject. Only the third line exhibits any irregularity, but this airy reference to 'the breeze' (and by extension, according to a standard Romantic analogy, the natural inspiration of the writer) is quickly pulled back into the underlying pattern of the verse, just as the steamer chugs through obstacles to produce a neatly measured wake. Yet although such lines deliberately over-pitch their rhetoric, hinting at how much has changed since earlier poets addressed the elements or the gods (the final phrase is a playful echo of Milton's sonnet about submitting to God's will: 'I...still bear up and steer / Right onward'),[26] they can also be read as a dawning realization that perhaps the conventions of direct address in poetry (*apostrophe*) no longer fitted the modern world.

In an influential discussion of apostrophe, Jonathan Culler has argued that it always risks sounding embarrassingly insincere. When Shelley cries out 'O wild West Wind', he is seeking to establish his identity as a visionary with access to nature's hidden secrets: far from being a lone voice, he is 'the embodiment of poetic tradition and of the spirit of poesy'. And because such claims are always likely to be frustrated, according to Culler, apostrophic poems tend to 'display in various ways awareness of the difficulties of what they purport to seek'. Even the most canonical Romantic poems, such as Keats's 'Ode to a Nightingale', collapse in queries and self-qualifications: 'Was it a vision, or a waking dream?...Do I wake or sleep?'[27] The question is one that Victorian poetry repeatedly confronts in its own workings. In addressing subjects such as political reform, love, and death, the period's poets also find themselves addressing their own capacity to deal adequately with such questions. In seeking to project a personal voice, the Victorian poet is often obliged to incorporate a sceptical counter-voice, and the result is what Matthew Arnold memorably described as 'the dialogue of the mind with itself',[28] as lines of verse simultaneously address the world beyond the page and turn back to reflect upon their own cultural predicament.

Confronted by such large questions, Victorian poetry gravitates towards some of the smallest words in the language: pronouns. 'Me', 'you', 'we', 'they', and so on, can carry a heavy weight of implication, not just by gesturing towards arguments they do not state explicitly, but also by obliging poets to consider the extent of their personal involvement in a particular subject. Consider Keats's lyric 'This Living Hand':

> This living hand, now warm and capable
> Of earnest grasping, would, if it were cold
> And in the icy silence of the tomb,
> So haunt thy days and chill thy dreaming nights
> That thou wouldst wish thine own heart dry of blood
> So in my veins red life might stream again,
> And thou be conscience-calmed. See here it is—
> I hold it towards you.[29]

Much critical attention has been devoted to these puzzling lines. They have been read variously as an appeal by the dying Keats to his fiancée Fanny Brawne, or as a passage intended for a play; their tone has been heard as sincere or playfully gothic. What is usually less remarked upon is the speaker's grammatical shift from 'thou' to 'you'. This enacts in miniature a much larger change in the grammar of poetic address, which can conveniently be dated to the period between the composition of 'This Living Hand' in c.1819 and its first publication in 1898.[30] By the start of the nineteenth century, 'thou' had attracted a certain tonal ambiguity, equally capable of suggesting a form of intimacy or a lofty rhetorical detachment, but a speaker's attitude towards 'you' was even less clear. In particular, the relatively narrow choice of pronouns in English, unlike those available in some other languages, meant that 'you' did not discriminate between an individual and a group. For Keats to claim that he is extending his hand 'towards you', whether directly or at one remove through his writing, therefore allows him to sustain the illusion that he is addressing each reader individually and as a collective whole. The final pronoun is at once personal and impersonal, tactfully discriminating and tactically indiscriminate.

The rise of 'you' as the default form of second-person pronoun over the course of the nineteenth century did not occur without resistance. 'While *you* was undoubtedly the standard form', Lynda Mugglestone observes, '*thou* and *thee* (as well as *ye/you* distinctions) remained a composite feature of many regional grammars', and writers such as Thomas Hardy and William Barnes 'had evident facility in pronominal systems of both kinds.'[31] Theory and practice were no less at odds in the work of writers who adopted a formal 'you' for published work, while retaining a more intimate 'thee' or 'ye' in private letters. Some went further still, by attempting to retain traditional distinctions between public and private forms of address even after their removal from everyday use. As late as 1898, Alice Meynell complained that the 'modern monotony of "you"' revealed the 'slovenliness of our civilisation' in linguistic matters, and proposed that 'thee' should be preserved for poetic and religious experience: 'our unique plot of disregarded language that the traffic of the world passes by.'[32] However, the idea that poetry might cut itself off from everyday speech was precisely what earlier nineteenth-century poets had most feared, and Meynell's ambition to turn all poems into opportunities for silent meditation was unlikely to have won acceptance from any poet who sought an audience wider than the space between their own ears.

An alternative was offered by E. S. Dallas in Book 3 of his *Poetics* (1852). According to Dallas, the main orientation of modern poetry was towards the reader, and this made 'you' its essential form of address. Moreover, he argued, because of the quirk of grammar that allows 'you' to refer to any number of people, it precludes thinking about the second person as a 'unity' or a 'totality', and instead encourages us to think about him or her as a 'plurality.'[33] Dallas's argument is perhaps of greater philosophical than critical interest, but it does suggest how the ambiguity of 'you' could be exploited in Victorian poetry as an imaginative resource. It provided a convenient piece of literary shorthand for poets wishing to explore some of the forces that brought people together or forced them apart.

Political poetry was especially attracted to the ambiguous potential of 'you', and its attention was sharpened by the recognition that poetry's traditional consumers did not necessarily want to read about messy social problems: addressing an issue did not necessarily mean addressing a public. Poems written in support of the Chartist movement often exploit this uncertainty, by explicitly addressing one readership (their antagonists) while implicitly addressing another (their supporters):

> Go! treasure well your miser's store
> With crown, and cross, and sabre!
> Despite you all—we'll break your thrall,
> And have our land and labour.
> You forge no more—you fold no more
> Your cankering chains about us;
> We heed you not—we need you not
> But you can't do without us.

This rousing call to action, Ernest Jones's 'A Chartist Chorus', was originally published in the radical periodical *The Northern Star* (6 June 1846), and was probably intended to be 'sung aloud during demonstrations or meetings to deepen solidarity'.[34] This solidarity is established by a simple opposition of 'you' and 'us', but the poem's attack on the 'cotton lords and corn lords' is more subtle than crude hectoring or preaching to the converted. Until the final 'you' is reached, not one of the stanza's pronouns occupies a metrically stressed position. This allows for an accusatory tone to swell towards 'But *you* can't *do* with*out* us', at once pointing the finger at a common enemy and singling out each of its members, but it also quietly suggests that nobody fits comfortably into traditional patterns any more. The jarring counterpoint of syntax and form works something like a metrical heckle: it hints at the need to address society's underlying structures if neither owners nor workers are to feel at odds with their time.

The tonal blankness of 'you', which can be used in a way that is either involved or detached, affectionate or chilly, means that such repetitions carry particular force in poems which concern themselves with how far human compassion can stretch. An example is Gerard Manley Hopkins's 'The Wreck of the Deutschland':

> Ah, touched in your bower of bone,
> Are you! turned for an exquisite smart,
> Have you! make words break from me here all alone,
> Do you!—mother of being in me, heart.[35]

Not until the final line do we realize that the speaker has been addressing himself: a piece of introspection that turns the repetitions of 'you' into a syntactic heartbeat, a way for him periodically to check his sympathies, rather as he might take his own pulse. The same tonal blankness can also register the struggle to retrieve personal affection from an indifferent or actively hostile world. Sometimes this is a matter of prudence or flirtatiousness rather than explicit argument. A good deal of poetry produced by gay writers, for example, employs the pronoun 'you' as a way of tackling questions of sexual identity that could not yet be discussed more openly. When we read of 'We Two' in George Cecil Ives's *Eros's Throne* (1890), who is the 'We' he sighs over? For readers outside his immediate homosocial circle it is hard to tell: as Valentine Cunningham has pointed out, the threat of legal sanctions meant that 'Although he was a public crusader for the legalizing of homosexuality, he was not going to let on by indulging in genderizing pronouns'.[36] Swinburne is equally careful in his deployment of 'you': 'Should love disown or disesteem you / For loving one man more or less?'[37] Is this 'you' a man or a woman? An individual or a social group? And by implication, who is the 'I' that speaks? Does this address constitute a sympathetic act of solidarity, or is it a tacit claim to being part of the group to which this ambiguous 'you' belongs?

More mainstream verse was often equally careful in its use of pronouns. The textual evolution of Matthew Arnold's 'To Marguerite—Continued' between 1852 and 1869 shows him experimenting with titles that ranged from the highly personal ('To Marguerite, in Returning a Volume of the Letters of Ortis') to the highly impersonal ('Isolation'), before referring back to the title of an earlier poem that was at once generic and intimate: 'Isolation. To Marguerite'.[38] The ambiguity of this earlier poem is developed in the grammar of 'To Marguerite—Continued':

> Yes! in the sea of life enisled,
> With echoing straits between us thrown,
> Dotting the shoreless watery wild,
> We mortal millions live *alone*.[39]

Beginning with an emphatic 'Yes!', Arnold's opening stanza gives every indication of being a direct address to Marguerite. Not until the reference to 'We mortal millions' is it clear that 'us' could refer equally to one couple or the whole human race: a grammatical ambiguity that neatly encapsulates the paradox that many of our most personal feelings, such as isolation, are those we share with other people. Not until the penultimate stanza does the speaker succeed in finding a personal significance within this common predicament, as he produces the poem's second exclamation mark, and recovers the intimate tone of his opening: 'Now round us spreads the watery plain—/ Oh might our marges meet again!' It is the poem's first use of 'our', and because it occupies an unstressed position in the line, it shows the speaker suddenly narrowing the focus of his interest. It is the sound of someone suddenly realizing that even if he and Marguerite are physically separated, they can be reunited by a voice that asserts itself against shared rhetorical patterns.

Arnold demonstrates a similarly sharp ear for creative uses of grammar in 'Dover Beach', and here again it is the ambiguity of 'you' that carries his main line of thought:

> The sea is calm tonight.
> The tide is full, the moon lies fair
> Upon the straits; on the French coast the light
> Gleams and is gone; the cliffs of England stand,
> Glimmering and vast, out in the tranquil bay.
> Come to the window, sweet is the night-air![40]

The speaker's invitation confirms the intimate tone of his opening, although the same lines retain a capacity for sounding far less involved. The thudding repetition of 'the' ('The sea', 'The tide', 'the moon', and so on), in particular, risks turning them into a geography lesson, merely listing facts rather than reflecting a shared set of experiences. This ambiguity is developed in the poem's personal pronouns. 'Listen! you hear the grating roar' could intend anything from 'my dear' to 'one' by its use of 'you'; not until the final stanza is this uncertainty resolved, with a clearly personal style of address ('Ah, love, let us be true / To one another') that echoes in the poem's closing lines:

> And we are here as on a darkling plain
> Swept with confused alarms of struggle and flight,
> Where ignorant armies clash by night.

Once again a speaker asserts a personal bond against the indifferent forces that threaten to swamp it. Once again this bond is concentrated into a pronoun that transforms a mode of address into a way of contemplating the speaker's place in the world.

A further feature that Arnold shares with the period's gay poets, beyond the uncertain reach of his pronouns, is his development of the Romantic conversation poem.[41] In poems such as Coleridge's 'Frost at Midnight' or 'This Lime-Tree Bower My Prison', as in the eighteenth-century literary epistle the conversation poem had adopted, the speaker addresses a specific interlocutor, but with the expectation that his words will be eavesdropped upon by a much larger set of readers. Such poems provide another point of overlap between poems that are 'heard' and those that are 'overheard', because although they assume a model of conversation between friends, they also implicitly invite the general reader to join their circle. The conversation poem promotes a model of friendship in which the line between insiders and outsiders is generously smudged.

This too is a common pattern in Victorian poetry, where old forms and conventions are repeatedly tested to see if they are still capable of adding extra volume or direction to a speaker's voice. The results are mixed. While a poem like Tennyson's 'To E. FitzGerald' (1885) can happily draw out a single sentence for fifty-six lines, affirming the constancy of their friendship in the reliable meetings of its rhymes, A. H. Clough's earlier *Amours de Voyage* (1849) offers a far more uncertain relationship between form and content. Purportedly a set of letters sent by a group of modern tourists in Italy, their often superficial thoughts are at once underpinned and undermined by Clough's hexameters, a form traditionally used to carry the action of classical epic. Both poems adopt the conventions of the literary epistle and turn them enquiringly in new directions: Tennyson, by using them to register the endurance of a friendship through time's vicissitudes, and Clough, by using them to suggest the growing gap between heroic action in the past and anxious reflection in the present.

Elsewhere, the conventions of poetic address were capable of being twisted into a kind of literary in-joke. A poem like Robert Browning's 'Any Wife to Any Husband' (1855) works in the same way as a modern greetings card. It is a type of speech that can be converted into a loving utterance only through performance: addressing the poem's opening words, 'My love', to a named individual has the same effect as placing a shop-bought Valentine's card in their hands. Such conventions could also be applied less optimistically. George Meredith's sonnet sequence *Modern Love* (1862) not only describes the breakdown of a marriage, but allows readers to hear it happening, as the couple's relationship repeatedly fractures against the romantic ideals traditionally carried by the sonnet form. When the speaker addresses his wife with 'O bitter, barren woman! what's the name? / The name, the name, the new name thou hast won?',[42] the answer (presumably 'adulteress' or 'harlot') is unspoken, but it unavoidably works itself into his way of asking the question, as the traditional rhythms of a sonnet are disrupted by his introduction of 'the new name', and the repetitions that usually feature as the backbone of such poems are twisted into a snarling parody of erotic obsession.

Conventions of address were no less significant for non-literary speakers in the period. From the 1840s onwards, working alongside an increased interest in matters of elocution and social etiquette, hundreds of books were published on the techniques of polite conversation, giving advice on everything from tone of voice to how to approach potentially tricky topics such as politics.[43] Central to these books was the importance of knowing how to facilitate conversational exchange, thereby preventing a friendly social encounter from turning into a monologue or a harangue. Theory and practice were sometimes comically at odds. Acquaintances of Robert Browning, in particular, recalled his habit of 'monopolizing' conversation, employing an eloquence that was sometimes hard to distinguish from bullying; 'Those whom he was expecting will never forget his welcome', Edmund Gosse recalled, '—the loud trumpet-note from the other end of the passage, the talk already in full flood at a distance of twenty feet.'[44] However, like many writers, Browning was adept at turning his personal weaknesses into literary strengths: poems such as 'My Last Duchess' use the conventions of the dramatic monologue, in which only one side of a verbal exchange is printed, to show how readily conversation could be used as a weapon to dominate and control. Some of the period's other dramatic monologues were more open than this—their ellipses and line-endings leave spaces for the reader to imagine interruptions from the poem's interlocutor—but even their speakers sometimes worry that they are talking to nobody but themselves. For although the development of the dramatic monologue provided one answer to anxieties about literary reception, by absorbing a listener into the poem and making their responses a crucial part of its workings, it also compounded these anxieties. No matter how much a Victorian poem might look and sound like a dramatic monologue, at its heart there was always the fear that words sent out in search of a listener might end up boomeranging back on the speaker.

The period's finest failed dramatic monologue is Tennyson's *Maud* (1855). The poem's original subtitle was 'Or The Madness', but in 1875 Tennyson altered it to 'A Monodrama', probably in response to R. J. Mann's critical study *Maud Vindicated* (1856), which had used the term 'monodrama' as part of its analysis. The truth lies somewhere between these alternatives, because as the poem develops it quickly becomes clear that one mark of the speaker's madness is that he is not aware of being in a poem where events are seen only from his own distorted perspective. His muddle is revealed in the way he wields 'you'—longingly, despairingly, sometimes accusingly—because often it is not certain when he is talking *to* Maud (whether or not she is aware of his presence) and when he is merely talking *about* her. Lines such as 'you wrong your beauty, believe it, in being so proud',[45] or 'Ah Maud, you milkwhite faun, you are all unmeet for a wife' (I.iv.10), at first sound like straightforward private reflections. However, as they accumulate, and as the speaker becomes more frenzied and fanciful, they start to sound suspiciously like rehearsals for the moment when he will confront her directly. The key scene occurs when he urges her to 'Come into the garden, Maud', and the poem swells into an invocation, as if the speaker finally had enough confidence to employ the language of Romantic apostrophe:

> The slender acacia would not shake
>   One long milk-bloom on the tree;
> The white lake-blossom fell into the lake,
>   As the pimpernel dozed on the lea;
> But the rose was awake all night for your sake,
>   Knowing your promise to me.

(I.xxii.8)

What happens next is unclear, but it seems likely that Maud comes into the garden accompanied by her protective older brother, which leads to a confrontation and eventually her death. The words 'you' and 'your' are never used again in the poem. Instead they are replaced by the far less personal 'one', which starts by drawing attention to the speaker's isolation ('Before I am quite sure / That there is one to love me', I.xi.2), and as he goes off to fight in the Crimea ambitiously ends by trying to reconcile him to the whole of humanity: 'I have felt with my native land, I am one with my kind, / I embrace the purpose of God, and the doom assign'd' (III.vi.5). Yet even this resonant public statement cannot altogether drown out some private murmurs of doubt. The rhyme of 'kind' and 'assign'd' may sound perfect, dramatizing the idea of a fated coming together, but to the eye it is slightly skewed. Even in claiming solidarity with his kind—falling into line as a soldier, and eventually joining the democratic ranks of the dead—*Maud's* speaker retains an awkward trace of separateness.

One way in which Tennyson's speaker does match his contemporaries is in his attempts to lasso Maud, himself, and even the dead, with the same indiscriminate 'O': 'O child', 'O clamorous heart', 'O father!' (I.iv.3, I.xvi.3, I.i.2). Victorian poets display particular sensitivity to the apostrophic 'O'.[46] In traditional verse this 'O' summons the poet's subject into being, and is invoked with all the confidence of an expert marksman aiming at a target. Much Victorian verse, by contrast, answered Spenser's question, 'O pierlesse Poesye, where is then thy place?' by deploying an 'O' that turned inward rather than outward; it suggested private murmuring rather than public declamation.[47] A poem like Tennyson's 'Break, break, break', written as an early response to Arthur Hallam's death, works in a similar way to the abba stanza of *In Memoriam*. Although it starts by appealing to something outside the poem, it quickly rounds on itself:

> Break, break, break,
>   On thy cold gray stones, O Sea!
> And I would that my tongue could utter
>   The thoughts that arise in me.
>
> O well for the fisherman's boy,
>   That he shouts for his sister at play!
> O well for the sailor lad,
>   That he sings in his boat on the bay!
>
> And the stately ships go on
>   To their haven under the hill;
> But O for the touch of a vanished hand,
>   And the sound of a voice that is still![48]

From an apostrophic 'O Sea', to an ambiguous 'O well for the sailor lad' that could be either a smattering of public applause or a private nod of approval, to the sigh 'O for the touch of a vanished hand', these 'O's are spaces in which Spenser's question resonates with particular force. Edward FitzGerald remembered Tennyson 'mouthing out his hollow oes and aes' as he read aloud,[49] but what a phrase like 'O for the touch of a vanished hand' cannot do is tell us how this 'O' should be expressed. It catches the moment between a voice emerging into articulate speech and that same voice disintegrating into empty cries and whispers. It could be hollow because the world now seems empty of meaning, or in the way that the mouthpiece of a megaphone is hollow, as Tennyson's speaker uses it to rail against the indifference of a natural world in which life goes on without the unique life that once gave it meaning.

Where Victorian elegy successfully bridged the gap between private and public speech, often it was by encouraging grief-stricken readers to adopt the poet's lyrical 'I' as their own. A poem like *In Memoriam* could articulate their own situation, finding words for what eluded their own powers of expression—as when the recently bereaved Queen Victoria, who confessed to her diary that 'only those who have suffered as I do, can understand these beautiful poems', annotated her copy with personal reflections that included changing 'widower' in section XIII ('Tears of the widower, where he sees / A late-lost form that sleep reveals') to 'widow'.[50] Tennyson was sympathetic to such impulses, telling James Knowles that *In Memoriam* was 'a very impersonal poem as well as personal', and the 'I' who speaks was 'rather the cry of the whole human race than mine'.[51] However, one anxiety that the poem cannot quite shake out of its voice is that if 'the whole human race' is a category that extends in time as well as space, its appeal to future readers might be limited by factors beyond its control. Traditionally, poets address themselves to posterity either in the hope that posthumous success will redeem their neglect while alive, or with the expectation that their words will live for ever. Yet starting with its title page, which brings together a dead language ('In Memoriam AHH') and a set of figures that resist being spoken aloud ('Obit MDCCCXXXIII'), Tennyson's poem acknowledges that languages, like people, can decay, die, or change out of all recognition. When Hopkins's father read *In Memoriam*, he was more exercised by the loving tone of the speaker—a 'strange manner of address' for one man to use towards another, he concluded nervously.[52] In one sense he was correct: Tennyson's poem is much concerned with how we should address each other, especially when the changes wrought by death mean that it is no longer clear to whom we are speaking. However, by far the most anxious version of this question is the one that *In Memoriam* turns on itself:

> What hope is here for modern rhyme
>   To him, who turns a musing eye
>   On songs, and deeds, and lives, that lie
> Foreshorten'd in the tract of time?
>
> These mortal lullabies of pain
>   May bind a book, may line a box,
>   May serve to curl a maiden's locks;
> Or when a thousand moons shall wane
>
> A man upon a stall may find,
>   And, passing, turn the page that tells
>   A grief, then changed to something else,
> Sung by a long-forgotten mind.

(LXXVII, ll. 1–12)

Once Tennyson has been forgotten, and literature has moved on, the title of his elegy might turn out to be prophetic as well as merely commemorative: it might anticipate its own demise. One of *In Memoriam*'s key rhymes is 'strange' and 'change', a little verbal tic that allows Tennyson's speaker to steady himself in the face of the unknown, but here even that stamp of certainty has been removed. Instead, the off-rhyme of 'turn the page that tells' and 'changed to something else' offers a glimpse of the past and the future no longer being on speaking terms. In many ways it is the nightmarish culmination of Victorian anxieties surrounding poetic address: the fear that no matter how eloquently a poet attempted to speak to the public, over time his or her voice would inevitably wither and fade.

Such anxieties animated Tennyson's poetry from early in his career. 'The Lady of Shalott' (1832) has often been interpreted as a poem that reflects nervously on the act of writing, but it can equally be interpreted as a fable about reading. The lady's barge is named 'The Lady of Shalott', like the poem, and once it reaches Lancelot he begins by 'muse[ing]' on what he sees, like a reader sympathetic to the pains of literary inspiration, but quickly confirms his own priorities by contemplating the Lady's 'lovely face'.[53] It is like a mocking echo of Tennyson's own critical reception, as he sent his poems out into the world in search of a sympathetic hearing, only for them to reach critics who preferred to dwell on their most superficial features. Not until 'Crossing the Bar' (1889) did he arrive at a more optimistic alternative:

> For though from out our bourne of Time and Place
> The flood may bear me far,
> I hope to see my Pilot face to face
> When I have crost the bar.[54]

Primarily this is a poem that anticipates death: the 'Pilot' is God, and the sandbar is a metaphor for what separates the river of life from the 'boundless deep' of eternity. However, it would not be altogether fanciful to view it also as Tennyson's final allegory of reading, concerned with how far his voice would stretch (there is just a quiver of doubt in 'The flood *may* bear me far'), and what later readers would make of him once he had passed beyond his final line. If Tennyson is like a ship heading out to sea, his poem is more like a message in a bottle—a form of writing that is free to drift across the years until intercepted by a reader. And if that reader happens to be me, Osip Mandelstam memorably observes, then it becomes a message that was written for me: 'The message in the bottle was addressed to its finder. I found it. That means, I have become its secret addressee.'[55]

Such questions were not limited to Victorian poetry. Indeed, their twentieth-century successors were, if anything, even more nervous about where the craft of poetry was heading. By the time T. S. Eliot published 'The Love Song of J. Alfred Prufrock' (1917), the intimacy of poet and reader that Whitman had attempted to bring into being was being eroded still further. 'Let us go then, you and I',[56] the opening line of a poem in which 'you' is never identified, is only a faded echo of the way Whitman ended his 'Inscription' to the fourth edition of *Leaves of Grass* (1867):

> (O friend, whoe'er you are, at last arriving hither to com-
>   mence, I feel through every leaf the pressure of your
>   hand, which I return.
> And thus upon our journey...link'd together let us go.)[57]

If Eliot's 'Let us go' was a wary reply to Whitman's 'let us go', allusion being one way in which he could take the earlier poet's hand in his own, it was also a natural climax to the anxieties surrounding poetic address that had been explored during the previous century. While some Victorian poets directed their words towards a reader with a degree of scepticism, and others were more trusting, the best calibrated the strength of their anxieties against their chosen form. 'This is my letter to the World / That never wrote to me', explains Emily Dickinson in one poem, where the deictic 'This' brings together the handwritten letter in which she composed the poem in *c*.1862 and the printed text in which we now read it. The conclusion goes further still, as she writes that her 'Message is committed / To Hands I cannot see—'.[58] If the line-break between 'committed' and 'To Hands' delicately intimates the gaps of space and time across which she must throw her voice, that final dash comes as close as any other feature in Victorian poetry to capturing the period's ambivalent attitudes towards literary address. For although it breaks her voice off, it also draws it out, pushing into the future like an arrow.

NOTES

1. Christopher Ricks, *Tennyson*, 2nd edn. (Berkeley and Los Angeles: University of California Press, 1989), 11.
2. Alfred Tennyson, various poems (see main text), in *The Poems of Tennyson*, ed. Christopher Ricks, 3 vols. (Harlow: Longman, 1987), i. 243, i. 246, ii. 178, i. 556.
3. See Matthew Bevis, *The Art of Eloquence: Byron, Dickens, Tennyson, Joyce* (Oxford: Oxford University Press, 2007), 149; Bevis notes that between them such forms of address account for two-thirds of the opening lines in Tennyson's contributions to the volume.
4. Tennyson, 'Midnight', in *The Poems of Tennyson*, i. 123.
5. *The Poems of Tennyson*, i. 209–10.
6. William Wordsworth, 'Preface to *Lyrical Ballads*' (1802), repr. in *William Wordsworth: The Major Works*, ed. Stephen Gill (Oxford: Oxford University Press, 2000), 603.
7. See J. Douglas Kneale, 'Romantic Aversions: Apostrophe Reconsidered', *ELH* 58 (1991), 141–165.
8. Wordsworth, *The Prelude*, ed. Stephen Gill (Cambridge: Cambridge University Press, 1991), 15.
9. Bevis, *The Art of Eloquence*, 41.
10. Thomas Gray, 'Advertisement' (1757), cited in *The Poems of Gray, Collins and Goldsmith*, ed. Roger Lonsdale (London: Longman, 1969), 180.
11. Matthew Arnold, *The Letters of Matthew Arnold*, 6 vols., ed. Cecil Y. Lang (Charlottesville; London: University Press of Virginia, 1996–2001), i. 131.
12. Charles Dickens, *Dombey and Son*, ed. Dennis Walder (Oxford: Oxford University Press, 2001), 407.

13. Thomas Carlyle, *On Heroes, Hero-Worship, and the Heroic in History* (London: Chapman and Hall, 1840), 93–136; Elizabeth Barrett Browning, *Aurora Leigh*, ed. Margaret Reynolds (Athens: Ohio University Press, 1992), 197.

14. Wordsworth, 'Ode: Intimations of Immortality from Recollections of Early Childhood', in *William Wordsworth: The Major Works*, 301.

15. Arnold, 'Stanzas from the Grande Chartreuse', in *The Poems of Matthew Arnold*, ed. Kenneth Allott (London: Longmans, Green & Co., 1965), 288.

16. Raymond Williams, *Culture and Society: 1780–1950*, 2nd edn. (New York: Columbia University Press, 1983), 33–4, discusses the period's distinction between 'the people' and 'the public.'

17. Fanny Kemble Butler, 'Tennyson's Poems', *United States Magazine and Democratic Review* 14 (January 1844), 64.

18. Dickens, *Sketches by Boz: Second Series* (London: John Macrone, 1836), ii.

19. Dickens, *Hard Times*, ed. Paul Schlicke (Oxford: Oxford University Press, 1989), 274.

20. Dickens, *The Letters of Charles Dickens*, 12 vols., ed. Madeline House, Graham Storey *et al.* (Oxford: Clarendon Press, 1965–2002), viii. 367.

21. Walt Whitman, 'To You', in *Leaves of Grass*, ed. Harold W. Blodget and Sculley Bradley (New York: New York University Press, 1865), 14. The example is discussed in William Waters, *Poetry's Touch: On Lyric Address* (Ithaca and London: Cornell University Press, 2003), 121–22. On Whitman's addresses to a future reader, see also Helen Vendler, *Invisible Listeners: Lyric Intimacy in Herbert, Whitman, and Ashbery* (Princeton: Princeton University Press, 2005).

22. John Stuart Mill, 'What is Poetry?' (1833), repr. in *Collected Writings of John Stuart Mill*, 33 vols., ed. J. M. Robson *et al* (1963–9, repr. London: Routledge & Kegan Paul, 1996), i. 348.

23. Dante Gabriel Rossetti, 'Jenny', in *The Poems of Dante Gabriel Rossetti*, ed. W. M. Rossetti (London: Ellis & Elvey, 1904), 53.

24. Thomas Lovell Beddoes, 'Sonnet: To Tartar, a Terrier Beauty', in *The Poems, Posthumous and Collected of Thomas Lovell Beddoes*, 2 vols. (London: William Pickering, 1851), i. 164; Francis Thompson, 'To a Snow-Flake', in *Selected Poems of Francis Thompson*, 3rd edn. (London: Methuen, 1909), 85.

25. Joanna Baillie, 'Address to a Steamvessel', in *The Dramatic and Poetical Works of Joanna Baillie* (London: Longman, Brown, Green, and Longmans, 1851), 816.

26. John Milton, 'To Mr Cyriack Skinner Upon his Blindness', in *The Poems of John Milton*, ed. John Carey and Alastair Fowler (London: Longmans, 1968), 414.

27. Jonathan Culler, 'Apostrophe', repr. in *The Pursuit of Signs: Semiotics, Literature, Deconstruction* (Ithaca, N.Y.: Cornell University Press, 1981), 143.

28. Arnold, 'Preface to the First Edition of *Poems* (1853)', repr. in *The Poems of Matthew Arnold*, 591.

29. John Keats, 'This Living Hand', in *Keats: The Complete Poems*, ed. Miriam Allott (London and New York: Longman, 1970), 701.

30. The fragment was written on a sheet of paper containing stanza 51 of Keats's comic poem *The Cap and the Bells*, and was first published in the 6th edition of H. Buxton Forman's *The Poetical Works and Other Writings of John Keats* (1898).

31. Lynda Mugglestone, *The Oxford History of English* (Oxford: Oxford University Press, 2006), 285.

32. Alice Meynell, 'The Second Person Singular' (1898), repr. in *The Second Person Singular and Other Essays* (London: Oxford University Press, 1922), 133–38. Meynell's essay is

discussed by Adela Pinch, *Thinking About Other People in Nineteenth-Century British Writing* (Cambridge: Cambridge University Press, 2010), 83–4.

33. E. S. Dallas, *Poetics: An Essay on Poetry* (London: Smith, Elder & Co., 1852), 99–101.

34. See Linda K. Hughes, *The Cambridge Introduction to Victorian Poetry* (Cambridge: Cambridge University Press, 2010), 72, where this stanza is quoted.

35. Gerard Manley Hopkins, 'The Wreck of the Deutschland', in *The Oxford Authors: Gerard Manley Hopkins*, ed. Catherine Phillips (Oxford: Oxford University Press, 1986), 114.

36. Valentine Cunningham, *Victorian Poetry Now: Poets, Poems, Poetics* (Chichester: John Wiley, 2011), 255–8.

37. Charles Algernon Swinburne, 'The End of a Month', cited ibid. 255.

38. See the headnotes to both poems in *The Poems of Matthew Arnold*, 121–3. Arnold's revisions are discussed by Anne Ferry, *The Title to the Poem* (Stanford: Stanford University Press, 1996), 124–5.

39. Arnold, 'To Marguerite—Continued', in *The Poems of Matthew Arnold*, 124.

40. Arnold, 'Dover Beach', in *The Poems of Matthew Arnold*, 240.

41. Nils Clausson has argued convincingly that Coleridge's 'The Eolian Harp' is an important source for 'Dover Beach': see 'Arnold's Coleridgean Conversation Poem: "Dover Beach" and "The Eolian Harp"', *Papers on Language and Literature* 44 (2008), 276–304. On the relationship between Romantic conversation poems and the Victorian dramatic monologue, see W. David Shaw, *Origins of the Monologue: The Hidden God* (London: University of Toronto Press, 1999).

42. George Meredith, *Modern Love* VI, in *Selected Poems of George Meredith*, ed. Graham Hough (London: Oxford University Press, 1962), 24.

43. See E. A. W. St George, *Browning and Conversation* (Basingstoke: Macmillan, 1993).

44. E. A. W. St George, *Browning and Conversation*, 45.

45. Tennyson, *Maud* I.iv.3, in *The Poems of Tennyson*, ii. 529.

46. On 'O' (and 'oh') as both 'locked in the interiority of the uttering subject' and a 'form of appeal or invocation', see J. H. Prynne, 'English Poetry and Emphatical Language', *Proceedings of the British Academy* 84 (1988), 135–69.

47. Edmund Spenser, 'October', from *The Shepheardes Calender* in *The Poetical Works of Edmund Spenser*, 3 vols., ed. Ernest de Sélincourt (Oxford: Clarendon Press, 1910), i. 99.

48. Tennyson, 'Break, break, break', in *The Poems of Tennyson*, ii. 24.

49. Hallam Tennyson, *Alfred Lord Tennyson: A Memoir*, 2 vols. (London: Macmillan & Co, 1897), i. 162.

50. *Dear and Honoured Lady: The Correspondence Between Queen Victoria and Alfred Tennyson*, ed. Hope Dyson and Charles Tennyson (London: Macmillan, 1969), 67.

51. Tennyson, *The Poems of Tennyson*, ii. 312.

52. Anonymous review, *The Times*, 28 November 1851.

53. Tennyson, 'The Lady of Shalott', in *The Poems of Tennyson*, i. 395.

54. Tennyson, 'Crossing the Bar', in *The Poems of Tennyson*, iii. 254.

55. Osip Mandelstam, 'On the Addressee', in *The Collected Critical Prose and Letters*, ed. Jane Gary Harris (London: Collins Harvill, 1991), 68.

56. T. S. Eliot, 'The Love Song of J. Alfred Prufrock', in *The Complete Poems and Plays of T. S. Eliot* (London: Faber and Faber, 1969), 13.

57. Whitman, 'Inscription', in *Walt Whitman: Complete Poetry and Selected Prose & Letters*, ed. Emory Holloway (London: Nonesuch Press, 1938), 469.

58. See Waters, *Poetry's Touch*, 162–3.

SELECT BIBLIOGRAPHY

Anderman, Gunilla, 'Untranslatability: The Case of Pronouns of Address in Literature', *Perspectives: Studies in Translatology*, 1 (1993), 57–67.

Burr, Zofia, *Of Women, Poetry, and Power: Strategies of Address in Dickinson, Miles, Brooks, Lorde, and Angelou* (Urbana, Illinois: University of Illinois Press, 2002).

Chandler, David, 'Coleridge's "Address to a Young Jack-Ass": A Note on the Poetic and Political Context', *Notes and Queries* 42 (1995), 179–80.

Craft, Christopher, '"Descend, and Touch, and Enter": Tennyson's Strange Manner of Address', in Herbert Tucker, ed., *Critical Essays on Alfred Lord Tennyson* (New York: G. K. Hall, 1993), 153–73.

Edwards, Jessie, 'The Mode of Address in Victorian Fiction: Dickens, Wilde, and Stevenson', *Ball State University Forum* 19 (1978), 35–40.

Kennedy, William, '"Voice" and "Address" in Literary Theory', *Oral Tradition*, 2 (1987), 214–230 [electronic publication].

Waters, William, *Poetry's Touch: On Lyric Address* (Ithaca, NY: Cornell University Press, 2003).

CHAPTER 5

··

RHYME

··

MATTHEW CAMPBELL

AMONG the treasures of the poet's library held in the Tennyson Research Centre in Lincoln is an undated copy—possibly the 1819 edition—of John Walker's *A Rhyming Dictionary*.[1] It seems an odd possession for a writer who was so certain of the accuracy of his ear: 'My father confessed', Hallam Tennyson said, 'that he believed he knew the quantity of every English word, except perhaps "scissors"'. In Tennyson's time controversy simmered over that word 'quantity', and it would be odd when used by such a musically sophisticated poet, for whom quantitative verse in English was only an experiment. Perhaps Hallam misheard, and his father said he knew a *rhyme* for every English word except 'scissors'. Hallam tells us that Robert Browning boasted to Tennyson and his son that 'he could make a rhyme for every word in the English language,'[2] but there is no rhyme for scissors in Walker's *Rhyming Dictionary*.[3]

At the end of his copy of Walker, Tennyson had sketched in a draft of 'The Skipping Rope', a poem Tennyson's editor Christopher Ricks dates to 1836, and which, while published in 1842, was omitted by Tennyson from collected editions after 1850. The lyric replicates a number of Walker's instances of rhymes for the ending, '-ope':

> Sure never yet was Antelope
>   Could skip so lightly by,
> Stand off, or else my skipping-rope
>   Will hit you in the eye.
> How lightly whirls the skipping-rope!
>   How fairy-like you fly!
> Go, get you gone, you muse and mope—
>   I hate that silly sigh,
> Nay, dearest, teach me how to hope,
>   Or tell me how to die.
> There, take it, take my skipping-rope,
>   And hang yourself thereby.[4]

Such fun is actually not so rare in Tennyson, and it is a shame that he allowed this poem to slip from his published work during his lifetime. With its exotic creature (Antelope) and its excursion into the darker areas of the nursery (the skipping-rope becomes a noose), the poem might have been happier in the hands of Tennyson's friend Edward Lear. The propulsions of sense into the necessities of rhyme produce effects which court 'nonsense', of which this little lyric appears to offer an understanding. Ricks quotes Hallam Tennyson on his father's dissatisfaction with rhyming dictionaries: 'There was no natural congruity between the rhymes thus alphabetically grouped together'.[5] The restrictions of rhyming possibility set by the rhyming task here lead to the natural incongruities of the joke, and a comic verse with which Tennyson often played but was never entirely comfortable.

Given that, like Lear's limericks, say, the rhyme words establish drastically diminished semantic options for the poet and the characters in his poem, the child-speaker of the lyric very quickly exits the poem as the rhyming game runs out. Alternating with rope/rope/mope/hope and rope yet again, the rhymes for 'by' head inexorably through 'eye' and 'sigh' to 'die', after which '-by' effects a very slight resurrection in its repeat at the end: 'hang yourself thereby'. The poem ends like the enclosed thing which is the limerick, seemingly without issue beyond its own fun, but nevertheless somehow unsettled both by word and rhyme games, and by comic incongruity. To take just one of any possible number of examples from Lear,

> There was an Old Person of Burton,
> Whose answers were rather uncertain;
> When they said, 'How d'ye do?' he replied, 'Who are you?'
> That distressing Old Person of Burton.[6]

A compassionate comedy of nonsense and misunderstanding allows 'distressing' to modulate the inevitable repeat of the first line, creating a little sympathetic forum in which age and forgetting can comport with the memory game of rhyme. In 'The Skipping Rope', Tennyson's eventual double repeats of 'rope' and 'by' end the fun, as his speaker stomps off, not playing any more.

To say that the Victorian period was the last age to allow its poetry to be determined by the search for rhyme would be unfair both to the persistence of rhyme in the work of their successors and to the great nineteenth-century exponents of blank verse, Tennyson and Browning among them. But as the examples above show, issues of naturalness of speech and comic incongruity which lie behind many considerations of rhyme were pressing for the sense of craft practised by the Victorian poets, readers of rhyming dictionaries or not. Rhyme is the most obviously 'unnatural' thing about verse, one difference between poetry and prose or between stanza and speech. There are many ways in which verse might rhyme: pararhyme, off rhyme, median rhyme, cross-rhyme, slant-rhyme, internal rhyme, even sight rhyme. But to start with terminal rhyme, after six to ten syllables or so of any given line of poetry, the reader hears a word which announces the end of the line to the ear. The sound of that word will either have been an echo of, or will echo on through, a different word or words at a similar position at the end of one or more of the preceding or following lines. We mostly notice rhyme at the end of the line and, despite various claims to the contrary over the centuries and up to the present day, we have yet to come to the end of the line for rhyme in English. If for the enthusiastic adopter of blank verse, John Milton, it was an 'invention of a barbarous age',[7] he never quite civilized it out of the English language, even from his own poetry. In these poems by Tennyson and Lear, terminal, or end, rhyme is a memory game, played by the young and the infirm. Yet a desire for naturalness still governs a Victorian poetry alert to the competing aesthetic risks of congruousness and incongruity, formally alert to the unsettling or unnerving of content by the multiplications of sense in the sonic relations of rhyme.

One answer to attempts to purge English poetry of the barbarities of rhyme was given in Alexander Pope's emphasis on congruity in matters of prosody. 'The sound must seem an echo to the sense', he said, but that aphorism exists as a rhyming completion of the insufficiency expressed in the line with which it forms a couplet: "Tis not enough no harshness make offense.'[8] Consonance of rhyme is not enough in itself, rhyme must reason, mere taste must give way to sense. Eric Griffiths has suggested that poetry in the nineteenth century went some way to the edge of breaking up these double acts of rhyme and reason. For Griffiths, the 'double nature' of poetry as print and voice—or to use a phrase from Browning's *The Ring and the Book*, the 'printed voice'—was first suggested by William Wordsworth in 1801. Wordsworth emphasizes that metre need not be mimetic of feeling: 'metre cannot but have great efficacy in tempering and restraining the passion by an intertexture of ordinary feeling, and of feeling not strictly and necessarily connected with the passion'. Like the regularities of metre, the returns of rhyme also enable the reader to endure the suffering enacted in the sense of the poem. The 'old ballads', Wordsworth tells us, enact this incongruity between narratives of suffering and the pleasures of repetition and return in rhyme and refrain.[9]

So in one possible construction, nineteenth-century rhyme plays between the matter of aesthetic decorum (congruity and incongruity) and that of authenticity (naturalness of speech or the real language of men). Thus in Samuel Taylor Coleridge's 'Rime of the Ancient Mariner', one of the poems to which Wordsworth's thoughts on verse and endurance acted as preface, poetry is compulsion and repetition, the need to speak and the reiteration of the now-renovated barbarities of the 'common measure' of the old ballads:

> 'Forthwith this frame of mine was wrench'd
> With a woeful agony,
> Which forced me to begin my tale;
> And then it left me free.

> 'Since then, at an uncertain hour,
> That agony returns;
> And till my ghastly tale is told,
> This heart within me burns.

> 'I pass, like night, from land to land;
> I have strange power of speech;
> That moment that his face I see,
> I know the man that must hear me;
> To him my tale I teach.'

The alternate rhyming of the measure of the ballad verse is both replicated and adapted in Coleridge's loosened modern version, where in the stretched five-line stanza above, 'speech' and 'teach' are brought together in delayed full rhyme as the mariner concludes his account of his predicament. Exactly what the hapless wedding guest who has been listening to this 'strange power of speech' has been taught is moot. He has both endured the rime and been stupefied:

> He went, like one that hath been stunned,
> And is of sense forlorn:
> A sadder and a wiser man
> He rose the morrow morn.[10]

In the 'Rime of the Ancient Mariner', rhyme is not the natural partner of reason. The rhymes of 'Sense forlorn / morrow morn' and the half-rhyming or even internal rhyming consonance of 'one…stunned', 'forlorn', 'man', 'morrow morn' give a version of rhyme as both a repetition of the mystery and a moving on.

The Victorian poets learned much from such compulsion to perform rhyme as both the necessity and contingency of verse. It is at one and the same time an oppressive determination of sense and the self-conscious indeterminacy of mere sound. It is the marker of a form seeking liberation from formality while doomed to find its endings in the recurrence of like sounds. Rhyming is one of the liberal arts, but it can have the rigidity of a discipline. In a bravura account of Victorian poetry which places rhyme and repetition at its centre, Valentine Cunningham says that rhyme is repetition: 'poetic words are *bound* words—words tied together, held together by the repetition of verbal components. By repetition, that is, by rhyme.'[11] In refrain, limerick, nursery, and nonsense verse, the repeated word is used as a temporal marker, either of return or closure or both. It also binds the writer. The return of the word 'rope' in Tennyson's poem ends the rhyming game since the rhymes appear to have run out of the sense needed to hold them together. But rhyme per se is not only repetition. Repetition can close off alternatives, bind itself up in tautology. The dangers of incongruity when putting unlike meanings beside each other while seeking for likeness of sound need not make way for the congruousness of monotony. Victorian poetry did play with such effects, from the refrain of Tennyson's 1830 'Mariana' (the rhyme sounds 'dreary' / 'aweary' are repeated eighteen times in the poem) to W. B. Yeats's 1899 'He Wishes for the Cloths of Heaven', which prostrates itself before the loved one at its line-endings in full repetition with minimal modulation ('cloths' / 'light' / 'cloths' / 'half-light' / 'feet' / 'dreams' / 'feet' / 'dreams': just to list the words at the end of the lines invites symbolist immersion).[12] In such poems of psychic and amorous self-absorption, repetition does more than play with the sound of words, as in nonsense or comic verse. For Tennyson and later Yeats, the writers' deployment of it prolongs stilled time into stasis.

Writing in 1900, Yeats said that the purpose of rhythm in verse is to 'prolong the moment of contemplation', and that it encourages 'that state of perhaps real trance, in which the mind liberated from the pressure of the will is unfolded in symbols'.[13] Yeats's trance is that of a symbolist latecomer to Victorian prosody, expressing a desire to quieten the English line. Poetic rhythm performs the time, the duration, of the poem, as both tempo and beat. Given a poem as a score to read from and a voice to perform it, the reader can describe the probable metre of any given poem as founded on a comparison or sample of lines sounded and perceived forwards and backwards through the poem. I say 'probable' because in any given line, the actual perceived rhythm may not accord with that metre, and it is always caught in a singular forward movement, spatially and temporally completing itself only on reaching the end of the line. When hearing rhythm we have to hear the next stress in order to hear how and where it takes us, and if it takes us to terminal rhyme then it can avoid stasis or abjection by tugging two ways. In verse with terminal rhyme endings, the movement of the line is carried both forwards in anticipation from the sound at a line-ending and backwards in recollection from the recurrence of words which sound similar but are not the same.

A rhyme or a refrain is burdened with the problem of making sense, and a 'burden' is the repetitive play of refrain and chorus, the echoing backwards and forwards movement of like sounds and unlike sense through the performance of verse. The echoes of first rhyme and recurring rhyme linger in the ear as mnemonic and chronicle of duration, burrowing in on the Victorian preoccupation with memory, mind, and meaning, or even the meaning of mind and memory. According to Gillian Beer, one chronicler of the Victorian struggle with the materialist challenges of the new sciences of mind and of the recently revealed long geological and astronomical time of the universe,

> Rhyme drags words back from the abyss of obliteration, to put it at its most animistic. Rhyme plays in with auditory memory, whose absolute span is under four seconds (so I am informed), a duration of memory which is repeated and prolonged each time the chime occurs. So words loop across from line to line, making skeins of meaning not wholly under the control of the poem in consciousness. In long narrative poems, particularly, rhyme often tells another story, moving askance the surface plot. Rhyme keeps connections floating. Sometime it describes boundaries, knits up connectives. But always it includes the likelihood of further rhyme words. For that reason rhyme can sometimes in the nineteenth century represent the new vision of the cosmos without close, ever extending as waves pulse through the universe, transformed as heat, as light, as sound.[14]

To go from 'under four seconds' to 'the cosmos without close' is quite a leap for the auditory memory of rhyme to negotiate, but it is a moving forward always, and then a correspondent tug back into memory. It is 'not wholly under the control of the poem in consciousness', but it can by turns be either floating or knitting. Rhyme is both a boundary and something 'moving askance the surface plot', like Wordsworth's 'not strictly and necessarily connected with the passion'.

Beer's endlessly looping rhyme is maybe more Dantean than Tennysonian, the ever-forward moving of end rhyme into eternity of the terza rima, and not the struggle with long time and the finality of death which is conveyed in *In Memoriam* and its *abba* stanza. It will take the careful reader more than four seconds to read between the rhyme sounds at the end of the first and fourth lines of one stanza of *In Memoriam*, so it may be that Beer's four seconds might be adjusted to four lines. What Henry James had to say about the ending of Tennyson's blank verse monologue 'Tithonus' can equally be applied to the rhyme scheme of the *In Memoriam* stanza and its writer's habitual way of thinking, his deeply sonic temperament: 'when [Tennyson] wishes to represent movement, the phrase always seems to me to pause and slowly pivot upon itself, or at most to move backward'.[15] At the beginning of the twentieth century, in the great unsystematic act of opinionated retrospect which is his *History of English Prosody*, George Saintsbury also invokes a psychology of rhyme when echoing James's great insight about Tennyson's thinking as a sort of rhyme. This is Saintsbury in 1910, on *In Memoriam*, psychology, and rhyme:

> ...it is a text from which to prove the folly, not merely of those who pooh-pooh prosody in general, but of those who belittle rhyme. This is the day of (among other things) a special form of 'removing our ignorance further back' by stating things in terms of what is called psychology. And psychology may, if it will, give its own statement (calling it an explanation) of the curious fact that if you take four sounds corresponding in pairs, arrange them with trains of other sounds behind them, and then change the tip-arrangement from *abab* to *abba*, the *total* effect will be quite different. The fact is the fact. The alternate-rhymed quatrain gives, with no unpleasant touch, the effect of something like a ratchet-bar motion, with checks. The included rhyme gives that of a sweep, in which the variation of rhyme in the first pair is obliterated or compensated by the reverse of this same variation in the second pair, and seems to constitute an unbroken circle. In other words, the *In Memoriam* quatrain is much more continuous, and has a more bird-like motion, than the ordinary 'long measure', of which it is a displacement; and yet, like the Spenserian itself, it invites to continuation, though its own internal movement is so perfect.[16]

'The fact is the fact', Saintsbury says, as if 'psychology' so invoked were a wholly empirical science. What he uses psychology to describe is not fact but effect—in fact, '*total* effect' (his emphasis). If the common measure or alternate rhyming quatrain proceeds mechanically, the *In Memoriam* stanza appears to the listener to lose the ratchets and checks of one type of rhyming in order to replace them with a perfect sweep. It is like 'an unbroken circle', and as such both self-contained and ongoing.

This is not necessarily the rhyme of eternity—the perfection of the stanza can close itself off in its swinging backwards to the past rather than the future. To that extent, it can also be like the dead thing for which it was constructed as memorial, a sort of recycling of the remains of memory, of remains in memory. Saintsbury's example of the 'unbroken circle' is the second section of the poem, which is a graveyard lyric.

II

Old Yew, which graspest at the stones
 That name the under-lying dead,
 Thy fibres net the dreamless head,
Thy roots are wrapt about the bones.

The seasons bring the flower again,
 And bring the firstling to the flock;
 And in the dusk of thee, the clock
Beats out the little lives of men.

O not for thee the glow, the bloom,
 Who changest not in any gale,
 Nor branding summer suns avail
To touch thy thousand years of gloom:

And gazing on thee, sullen tree,
 Sick for thy stubborn hardihood,
 I seem to fail from out my blood
And grow incorporate into thee.[17]

The stanzas are all either end-stopped at the enclosing terminal rhymes or checked by strong punctuation: the penultimate stanza ends with a colon, betraying the distended sonnet-shape which lies behind many of the sixteen-line sections of *In Memoriam*. It is as if the poem were about to shift from its quatrains into a sonnet-sestet and to prove something: the poet seems to grow bodily ('in-corporate') into the tree which has lived for a thousand years in this place of the human dead. Elegiac poet and the thousand years of gloom of the tree become as one, performing the same function of memorial and unseeing stupefaction. Time is a heedless, punishing determinant ('The clock / Beats out the little lives of men'), and rhythm and rhyme conspire to enclose human poem and human remains.

But of course this is placed at the very verge of the human, and in such an interchange of grim suffering the poet tempts the pathetic fallacy of complete absorption in the object of contemplation, seeking the heedless knowledge of near-eternity by gazing on the ancient tree. Reading for sound and thus seeming not to read for the near unbearable desire for oblivion in the poem, Saintsbury finds this to be its aesthetic consolation:

> …though each verse is sufficiently self-contained when looked at *in* itself, there is intimate connection between them. And when the thing ends you feel that the end is an organic completion, not a mere cutting short because enough seems to have been given, a mere absence from adding another course because the bricks are used up.[18]

If 'The Skipping Rope' (a poem written in the period in which Tennyson was still composing the *In Memoriam* sections) gives the impression of having run out of the bricks of rhyme, this poem seeks rhyme as completion, both perfect ending and the thought of death. Tennyson said of the last two stanzas: 'Yet it is better to bear the wild misery of extreme grief than that Time should obliterate the sense of loss and deaden the power of love.'[19] This is not quite a bearing up, but it is the kind of thing that rhymed verse alone can bear, carrying thought and suffering in a medium that tends towards the strong endings of terminal rhyme, yet must hold out against termination. In these stanzas, rhyme is sound and sense working in divergent ways, yet touching one another, both as Saintsbury describes ('the end is an organic completion'), and in the yew's eerie embrace of the corpse, grasping the gravestones, netting the head, wrapping the bones.

Organic form in this instance goes in divergent ways, primarily between life and death (the seemingly deathless tree and human remains), but also between the temptations to closure of terminal rhyme and the need to bear the misery. Obliteration of loss can also be obliteration of meaning, where sound and sense come too close together, but the rhymed words of this Victorian poetic language must be wary of knitting them too closely. If Tennyson's language seems so aware of the dangers of the obliteration and deadening of this language, Robert Browning's verse can appear not so much to be bearing up as letting go. For a poet like Browning, one solution to this problem is to write a poetry that is in the best sense a 'liberal art': in 'Two in the Campagna', a poem about equality and liberty in love, one poet-speaker tells the loved one that after 'I touched a thought', his tantalizing attempts to pin it down were simply, 'for rhymes / To catch at and let go'.[20] To let the caught thing go is primarily to release it, but letting go is also a surrender to the spontaneous, the unforeseen, and the ungraspable. If this makes Browning a 'difficult' poet, then so be it, since rhyme can seem to be the only binding on a famously contorted syntax. But the bindings of grammar and the bindings of rhyme can work creatively in divergent ways that need not necessarily seek to state that 'the end is an organic completion' and the corresponding temptations of the terminal. Browning's rhymes are often tightly bound together (in couplets or elaborate stanzaic structures) but they never quite suggest completion of the thought—as if thinking could be completed.[21]

To take a troubled poet, this time a character who has been compelled to work through sound and sense, 'to try the stuff / That held the imaged thing...his Language', this is Browning's 1840 recreation of the medieval Italian troubadour poet Sordello da Goito and

> How he sought
> The cause, conceived a cure, and slow re-wrought
> That Language,—welding words into the crude
> Mass from the new speech around him, till a rude
> Armour was hammered out,...
>
>   (ii, 573–577)[22]

The difficulty is that if language clothes experience like a suit of armour, this armour does not fit:

> Piece after piece that armour broke away,
> Because perceptions whole, like that he sought
> To clothe, reject so pure a work of thought
> As language: thought may take perception's place
> But hardly co-exist in any case,
> Being its mere presentiment—of the whole
> By parts, the simultaneous and the sole
> By the successive and the many. Lacks
> The crowd perception? Painfully it tacks
> Thought to thought, which Sordello, needing such,
> Has rent perception into; it's to clutch
> And reconstruct—his office to diffuse,
> Destroy; as hard then to obtain a Muse
> As to become Apollo.

(ii. 588–601)

Most readers find *Sordello* as 'hard' to read as its hero did with writing his songs, and this can at first sight certainly seem to be a re-wrought, diffused, even destroyed poetic language. A paraphrase might help slightly. If language is the medium of the poet-artist, and as such is the clothing of perception, then Sordello's poetic language is like a suit of armour. His task is to weld poetry from the 'new speech' of the people around him. The problem is, the quality of the poet's perceptions is such that they break out of the suit of armour fashioned for him by language, and language is the 'work of thought' and not perception. The resulting mis-fit of thought in language (a 'mere presentiment') and 'perceptions whole' (unified in mind and body, actual lived and living experience) creates a challenge for the two main participants in art. These are on the one hand the 'crowd', or audience, which 'lacks' the original perception but painfully 'tacks' together the thoughts presented in language; and the poet, who has forced his perception into the ill-fitting suit of poetry. The result is a violence of misrepresentation and misunderstanding, neither party wholly satisfied with a system of figuration which reveals itself by metonymy ('the whole / By parts') or in anachronism and incongruity ('the simultaneous and the sole / By the successive and the many'). As if to demonstrate this, the passage mixes metaphors and registers, where 'welding words' continues into 'armour' but then returns us from the blacksmith's forge to the tailor's workshop. The tailor-poet 'tacks / Thought to thought', in a preliminary assembly of the suit, but this has been made up from the torn cloth which Sordello has 'rent perception into', where 'rent' means both tearing the cloth and giving a rendition of the song.

What has this got to do with rhyme? As in the breakthrough into monologue of Browning's much-admired 'My Last Duchess' (1842), which it predates by a matter of a year or two, *Sordello* is written wholly in pentameter rhyming couplets, the 'heroic' couplets of Dryden or Pope. Unlike 'My Last Duchess' and perhaps more in common with Dryden and Pope, we are rarely fooled into privileging speech over verse or thinking that it doesn't rhyme. One material making the suit of armour is rhyme, and a rhyme carrying on a commentary, as it were, on the contorted and contorting aesthetic and grammatical problems of art, perception, representation, and communication Sordello has set himself. The rhymes are sometimes subtle, subliminally linked with the sense of other words around them. For instance, in the first passage above, getting from 'crude' to its rhyme 'rude', the passage passes over an assonantal, or vowel rhyme, in the word 'new', which is the challenge of innovation and experiment that writing in the 'new speech' of the people sets this poet. Again, the sound-string from 'Such', 'clutch', and then into the delayed assonantal 'reconstruct' which follows the clutching, seeks to put things together again. Otherwise, rhyme is more obtrusive: 'Sought' and 'thought' (will and intellect) find congruities of opposition with each other, as do 'whole' and 'sole'. But 'Lacks' (something missing) and 'tacks' (putting something together again), along with 'diffuse' (scatter) and 'Muse' (a creative power which should assist the re-unifying of poetry) push the rhymes into semantic opposition, courting an ambivalence of meaning which approaches paradox.

    A few lines later, Sordello finds himself in a pickle with all this, subject to adulation by his audience, yet almost entirely misunderstood:

> He found that, every time
> He gained applause by any ballad-rhyme,
> His auditory recognised no jot
> As he intended, and mistaking not
> Him for his meanest hero, ne'er was dunce
> Sufficient to believe him—all at once.
> His will ... conceive it caring for his will!

(ii. 621–627)

The rhymes are forced, and jar: 'jot' / 'not', 'dunce' / 'once'. But Browning has constructed a verse in which an artist's agony of representation and effect is played out with increasing semantic and syntactical exasperation, while the rhyming form of the couplets plays in a complementary swivel between acts of mimesis and incongruity. The verse form is enacted in a rhythm of will, welding and hammering and destroying just as it lacks what it tacks. 'His will ... conceive it [the audience] caring for his will!' Artistic control is flexed everywhere in the daring of the rhyme, while the subject-matter, poetic language itself, seems to be the cause of anguished disorder and near-defeat. In both *In Memoriam* and *Sordello*, rhyme moves thus between freedom and control, in which freedom of thought pays the price of anguish of communication at the very verge of the communicable. It is on the one hand, as Beer says, 'not wholly under the control of the poem in consciousness'. On the other, it is desirous of organic completion and thus an ending. In both poems the rhymes strive to sound an unbound consciousness, not carried in the sense at all, but sounding something beyond themselves as harmony or discord, consonance or overtone, something caught at but then let go.

    If Browning breaks through this dilemma, grasping and liberating all at once, then rhyme affords the poet's material various freedoms just as it seems to be wrapping them up at the end of the line. The 'Prologue' to Browning's 1876 *Pacchiarotto* collection starts as a little parable poem about the unknowability of other lives behind the walls which separate us. It ends, though, as a dedication of a poetry which can communicate freedoms of soul and thought, given that they are freedoms perhaps only realized in immortality:

> Wall upon wall are between us; life
>   And song should away from heart to heart
> I—prison-bird, with a ruddy strife
>   At breast, and a lip whence storm-notes start—
>
> Hold on, hope hard in the subtle thing
>   That's spirit; though cloistered fast, soar free;
> Account as wood, brick, stone, this ring
>   Of the rueful neighbours, and—forth to thee!

What follows in the volume is no 'subtle thing', rather it is the extravagantly rich sonic performance in 'Of Pacchiarotto and How he Worked in Distemper', a poem of immense 'spirit' about criticism and freedom of thought carried in 581 double-and triple-syllable-rhymed couplet and triple-rhyming lines. In a way it is also a poem about rhyme itself, a good-humoured defence of the poet against his critics, even if now and then invoking the rather less good-humoured vehemence of a Victorian Pope writing his own *Dunciad*.

A paraphrase of 'Of Pachiarotto' separate from its sonic form is nearly impossible—which is not to say that sound and sense are exactly comfortable with each other in the poem. Remove the rhymes and we have something which is part parable and part broadside. Its story is ostensibly that of the fifteenth-century Sienese artist who dared to dabble in active politics and had to hide in a grave from his persecutors when he said just too much. The lesson is not so much of the poet as a Shelleyan 'unacknowledged legislator', as what happens when Sordello's anguish about his failure to communicate with the crowd is exchanged for a Hyde-Park-Corner harangue. Thoroughly repentant of his intemperance of speech and emerging traumatized from the sepulchre in which he has been hiding for two days, Pachiarotto relates to a priest his hallucination of what the corpse in the crypt has told him of the vanity of the didactic artist and the limits of art in this mortal world:

> '*Things rarely go smooth at Rehearsal.*
> *Wait patient the change universal,*
> *And act, and let act, in existence!*
> *For, as thou art clapped hence or hissed hence,*
> *Thou hast thy promotion or otherwise.*
>   . . .
> *So, back nor disturb play's production*
> *By giving thy brother instruction*
> *To throw up his fool's-part allotted!*
> *Lest haply thyself prove besotted*
> *When stript, for thy pains, of that costume*
> *Of sage, which has bred the imposthume*
> *I prick to relieve thee of,—Vanity!*'

(xxii)

That word 'Vanity' then rhymes across the stanza break with 'So, Father, behold me in sanity!' The artist has learnt his lesson: 'I'm back to the palette and mahlstick' (xxiii).

So much for the story of Pachiarotto the painter; what of his Victorian author? The story is followed up with an extraordinary digression or coda:

> Nay, here shall my whistling and singing
> Set all his street's echoes a-ringing
> Long after the last of your number
> Has ceased my front-court to encumber
> While, treading down rose and ranunculus,
> You *Tommy-make-room-for-your-Uncle* us!
> Troop, all of you—man or homunculus,
> Quick march! for Xanthippe, my housemaid,
> If once on your pates she a souse made
> With what, pan or pot, bowl or *skoramis*
> First comes to her hand—things were more amiss!
> I would not for worlds be your place in—
> Recipient of slops from the basin!
> You, Jack-in-the-Green, leaf-and-twiggishness
> Won't save a dry thread on your priggishness!
> While as for Quilp-Hop-o'-my-thumb there,
> Banjo-Byron that twangs the strum-strum there—
> He'll think, as the pickle he curses,
> I've discharged on his pate his own verses!
> "Dwarfs are saucy," says Dickens: so, sauced in
> Your own sauce, . . .

> (xxvii)

Few authors can resist the urge to exercise the right to reply to criticism, but a basic tenet is not to repeat the solecisms of which your critics have complained.[23] This passage seems to take great relish in stacking up more rhyme crimes, and various critics, including Sainstbury, have adverted since to this very passage: '*Uncle*-us / ranunculus / homunculus. . .*skoramis* / more amiss. . .thumb there / strum-strum there'.

In his highly readable 1903 biography of Browning, perhaps more enamoured of the man than the poet, G. K. Chesterton said of the passage, 'It ends up with a voluble and largely unmeaning malediction upon the poet's critics, a malediction so outrageously good-humoured that it does not take the trouble even to make itself clear to the objects of its wrath.'[24] But Chesterton either gave up figuring out the object of ridicule or tactfully held back. A footnote for the unfinished rhyme above is signed by 'Printer's Devil' and goes, 'No, please! For "Who would be satirical / On a thing so very small?"' The unprinted words 'Alfred Austin' would fill out the missing rhyme. Austin had attacked Browning in 1870, but he was Poet Laureate in the time of Chesterton (from 1895 to 1913), and Browning's biographer may not have wanted to repeat the libel that the printer's devil footnote actually exacerbates: whether homunculus or dwarf or 'a thing so very small', we are left in no doubt of Austin's shortness of physical and intellectual stature. A 'skoramis' is a chamber pot (or, in Edward Berdoe's the *Browning Cyclopedia*, 'a vessel of dishonour'),[25] and in the scatology of *The Dunciad* that the poem adopts here, Browning's housemaid throws its contents over the hapless Austin, by turns 'Quilp Hop-o'-my thumb' (the dwarf villain in Dickens's *Old Curiosity Shop*) or 'Banjo-Byron'.

The Victorian banjo which 'twangs' here was a popular music-hall joke instrument, which by the end of the century could be found doing military service for Kipling as 'the war-drum of the White Man around the world!'[26] In Browning, the banjo does suggest that something else is going on with the twang and dissonances or overtones of sound and sense in the passage and the poem as a whole. Like most modern versions of the instrument it was sounded off a drum head and played with a distinctive droning spare or fifth string. The word 'banjo' first appears in an English poem in the Literature Online database in 1876 in this poem, and seems to have been imported from American popular and minstrel song by Browning.[27] Attached to a description of Austin as 'Banjo-Byron', it is certainly no compliment, but in the environs of a poem by a poet who is answering criticism of his own lack of musicality, the banjo's distinctive percussive and supposedly droning unmusicality is doing other work where rhyme is the drone, the discordant accompaniment to the satire. That satire can thus seem unintelligible, so distracting is the strum or twang or dissonant rhyme. Chesterton describes 'Of Pacchiarotto' thus: 'galloping energy, an energy that has nothing intellectual or even intelligible about it, a purely animal energy of words...the brute force of language'.[28] That is either to misread a poem so *bound*, as Cunningham might say, in its rhyming as sense-less, or at best to read it positively as a freeing experience of body. Contemporary theorists of the sound of poetry emphasize it as somatic rather than phenomenological, as an experience *of* body or mind rather than an object *in* ear or mind. For Derek Attridge, rhythm 'is the apprehension of a series of events as a regular repeated pulse of energy, and experience which has a muscular as well as a mental dimension'. For Simon Jarvis, 'It would be possible to begin thinking about the birth of prosody only upon condition that we stopped thinking of the bodily, and of the musical, as the non-cognitive vessels for a cognitive content.'[29] As I am suggesting here, Browning's version of this is a late answer to Sordello's angst at the division of perception (or experience) and thought (or language), where he and his readers might reconcile themselves to that division. 'Of Pacchiarotto' both reconciles necessary divisions of sound and sense and perpetuates those divisions, while sounding something else entirely in overtone and wilful dissonance.

This is the state of mind of the writer thinking about his poetry's supposed lack of musicality, the oft-repeated canard about Browning having 'no ear':

> And, what with your rattling and tinkling,
> Who knows but you give me an inkling
> How music sounds, thanks to the jangle
> Of regular drum and triangle?
> Whereby, tap-tap, chink-chink, 'tis proven
> I break rule as bad as Beethoven.

'That chord now—a groan or a grunt is't?
Schumann's self was no worse contrapuntist.
No ear! or if ear, so tough-gristled—
He thought that he sung while he whistled!

(xxvi)

Ashby Crowder tells us that Browning 'whistles while he works',[30] and the image, or sound-image, of Browning and Schumann whistling while singing[31] is picked up again and carried on throughout the rest of the poem.

Hopkins said that Browning made his characters talk 'with the air and spirit of a man bouncing up from the table with his mouth full of bread and cheese and saying that he meant to stand no blasted nonsense',[32] and here the rhymes are wilfully munching their way through clarity and elegant articulation. In this passage, the musicians and the poet are resolutely doing more than one thing at once, whistling while at work on their various compositions, musical and poetical. Are the tunes they whistle the same as those they are writing? Is the beat of Browning's whistled tune the same as his poem? Are the 'drum and triangle' timing the beat and rhymes of the poem or something else entirely? The 'tap-tap, chink-chink' is the deaf Beethoven playing around with sounds he cannot hear, the chords sounding in the music of his later years providing the harmonies of 'a groan or a grunt'. 'Grunt is't' sounds an outrageous rhyme against 'contrapuntist', but this is more than a counterpoint of rhythm and metre. It is of the writing and reading mind sustaining a number of activities, apprehensions, perceptions, and pleasures all at once, where the rhyme marks the time while the words just keep on letting go.

The not-quite rhyme of 'jangle' / 'triangle' is the rhyme of a sort of multi-tasking poetry, keeping to one time while the thinking is happily distracted, 'away' somewhere else. That word 'away' features three times in odd grammatical positions in the 'Prologue' to the Pachiarotto volume, and finally as quoted above, 'life / And song should away from heart to heart'. This transfer from 'prison-bird' to uncloistered 'spirit' from behind the wall is such an important movement in Browning's belief in things which will not be constrained, not even by death. In the words of 'Two in the Campagna', it must be let go, to be itself. Such are the constraints of the rhymes in 'Of Pachiarotto' that Browning sets the poem free from them just as they hammer things down against the double-rhyming jangle of that triangle. 'Of Pachiarotto' happily sounds the overtones around and beyond pitch of the sibilant whistle or the twang and drone of the banjo. The poem's penultimate stanza ends with geese: 'You'd know as you hissed, spat and sputtered, / Clear cackle is easily uttered!'

Such moments of liberation, of the artist and of the art itself, are typical of Browning. Somehow that sheer 'galloping energy', or the 'brute force of words' that Chesterton noticed with disparagement also means that Browning gets away with it. He resists doggerel while writing at that edge as well, and if not all of his critics have been indulgent, certain excuses have been made: Saintsbury can forgive Browning rhyming 'Manchester' and 'haunches stir',[33] but not Elizabeth Barrett Browning, for whom solecisms of rhyme when set against her otherwise impeccable rhythm, make reading her 'something like eating with a raging tooth—a process of alternate expectation and agony'. But this is again a doubling, in which the physicality of the reading experience carries pleasure and pain through rhyme. About Christina Rossetti's extraordinary experiment with mono-rhymed stanzas, 'The Poor Ghost' of 1866, Sainstbury said, 'The fact is that the poetess has chosen a kind of "croon-patter" or musical doggerel, relying mainly on monorhymes and a central pause.'[34] Those paradoxes, 'musical doggerel', or 'croon-patter' (where to croon is to sing softly but to patter is to speak rapidly), suggest that Victorian poetry's first readers heard in rhyme something which would be not be bound, either to sense or to concord.

It can, however, suggest that there is a certain inevitability of result. Two of the Tennyson and the Browning poems discussed above, by turns elegiac and satiric, had taken a turn in the grave, and in the dialogue of 'The Poor Ghost' (1863–66), the poet's conversation with a dead loved one returned from that place suggests to her only that she join him. The poem is haunted by its terminal monorhymes, which suggest finality, as the ghost is given the last word:

> 'Indeed I loved you, my chosen friend,
> I loved you for life, but life has an end;
> Thro' sickness I was ready to tend:
> But death mars all, which we cannot mend.
>
> Indeed I loved you; I love you yet
> If you will stay where your bed is set,
> Where I have planted a violet
> Which the wind waves, which the dew makes wet.'
>
> 'Life is gone, then love too is gone,
> It was a reed that I leant upon:
> Never doubt I will leave you alone
> And not wake you rattling bone with bone.
>
> I go home alone to my bed,
> Dug deep at the foot and deep at the head,
> Roofed in with a load of lead,
> Warm enough for the forgotten dead.
>
> But why did your tears soak thro' the clay,
> And why did your sobs wake me where I lay?
> I was away, far enough away:
> Let me sleep now till the Judgment Day.'[35]

The croon-patter or musical doggerel is in those rhymes which are only going one way as they repeat in monosyllables admitting only minimal variation: 'friend', 'end', 'tend', 'Death mars all, which we cannot end'; or 'bed', head', 'a load of lead / Warm enough for the forgotten dead'; or eventually 'away', as in Robert Browning, or as pre-prepared answer to Gillian Beer's 'cosmos without close': 'I was away, far enough away / Let me sleep now till the Judgement Day.'

For Valentine Cunningham, 'When a rhyme returns…with a difference, the action is sometimes known as *incremental repetition*. But whatever the nature of the repeat, of the return, it is all—to keep insisting—rhyme. Tagging of like unto like. The tag-wrestling match of the poetic.'[36] Rossetti's rhymes tag like unto like so much that the living and the dead submerge into one another in the coffin, roofed in and unable to escape the cloistered prison which is one graveyard determination of sense by sound. Terminal rhyme is only reinforced by the act of changing one letter in the shutting out of the crypt under 'a load of lead'. Victorian rhyme moves between these possibilities, as it also moved between mortality and that shaken sense that the end of the mortal was simply a provisional state, in the words of Pachiarotto's speaking corpse, a '*Rehearsal. / Wait patient the change universal, / And act, and let act, in existence!*' In one way, rhyme is a constraint, but if we must 'act', we must also 'let act', both limiting and allowing freedoms. The account of rhyme I have been giving here is involved in this question of freedom and its limits, and the freedoms of the artist can be terrifying when trying to write a 'free verse'. If Cunningham sees rhyme as a form of tag-wrestling match, the American poet and critic James Longenbach takes issue with one defender of the sense of form that rhyme gives to poetry thus: 'Robert Frost once said rather impishly that writing free verse is like playing tennis with the net down; in fact writing any kind of poem is more like playing tennis on a court in which the net is in motion at the same time that the ball is in motion.'[37] This is not just about rhyme, the freedoms of poetry for the Victorians were the freedoms of just such a difficult game, in which the rules seem to recalibrate at every point of contact with sense, resisting the urge to end it.

In *In Memoriam* LXXVII, Tennyson wondered whether rhyme would have a future in the modern world:

> What hope is here for modern rhyme
> To him, who turns a musing eye
> On songs, and deeds, and lives, that lie
> Foreshorten'd in the tract of time?

The 'tract of time' is both the theological controversy of the Victorian English church ('tracts for the times') and the wasted place where controversy is forgotten by history long after the heat has gone out of ideological difference. The forgetting happens in the foreshortening of the poetic line and of 'modern rhyme' itself, where the four lines between 'rhyme' and one of its longer-standing wrestling partners in the English language, 'time', are both a time-lapse and the provider of perspective. Tennyson wonders for two stanzas what might happen if someone were to read his poems in a future when he had been forgotten by history, but then rejects the irrelevance of the thought:

> But what of that? My darkened ways
> Shall ring with music all the same;
> To breathe my loss is more than fame,
> To utter love more sweet than praise.

From 'tract of time' to 'darkened ways', the poem 'Shall ring with music all the same'. The repetitions of rhyme are in a way 'music all the same', but this sameness follows a change, and this poetry faces its future as a place of sound, rhymes without reason, breath, or utterance, but nevertheless to be heard.

NOTES

1. Nancy Campbell, ed., *Tennyson in Lincoln: A Catalogue of the Holdings in the Research Centre*, 2 vols. (Tennyson Society: Lincoln, 1971–73), I, 104.
2. Hallam Tennyson, *Tennyson: A Memoir, By His Son*, 2 vols. (London: Macmillan, 1897), ii. 230–231.
3. See John Walker, *A Rhyming Dictionary*, 2 vols., 3rd edn. (London: Cadell and Davies et al, 1819). On either side of 'scissors', Walker lists the words 'posteriors' and 'champertors' (which means, 'Those who move suits for sinister views').
4. Alfred Tennyson, 'The Skipping Rope', in *The Poems of Tennyson*, ed. Christopher Ricks, 3 vols. (London: Longmans, 1987), ii. 85.
5. H. Tennyson, *Memoir*, ii. 496.
6. Edward Lear, 'There was an Old Person of Burton', in *The Complete Nonsense and Other Verse*, ed. Vivien Noakes (London: Penguin, 2001), 78.
7. John Milton, 'The Verse', headnote to *Paradise Lost in Poetical Works*, ed. Douglas Bush (Oxford: Oxford University Press, 1966), 211.
8. Alexander Pope, *Essay in Criticism*, 366–7, in *Poetical Works* ed. Herbert Davis (Oxford: Oxford University Press, 1966), p.74.
9. 'Preface' (1801–2) to William Wordsworth and Samuel Taylor Coleridge, *Lyrical Ballads*, ed. Michael Mason (London: Longmans, 1992), 81; Eric Griffiths, *The Printed Voice of Victorian Poetry* (Oxford: Oxford University Press, 1989), 75.
10. Coleridge, *The Rime of the Ancient Mariner*, in *Lyrical Ballads*, 203–204.
11. Valentine Cunningham, *Victorian Poetry Now* (Oxford: Blackwell, 2011), 56.
12. Tennyson, 'Mariana' in *Poems*, i. 205–209; W. B. Yeats, 'He Wishes for the Cloths of Heaven', in *The Poems*, ed. Daniel Albright (London: Dent, 1990), 90.
13. Yeats, 'The Symbolism of Poetry', in *Essays and Introductions* (London: Macmillan, 1961), 159.
14. Gillian Beer, 'Rhyme as Resurrection', in *Memory and Memorials, 1789–1814*, eds. Matthew Campbell, Jacqueline Labbe and Sally Shuttleworth (London: Routledge, 2000), 196–197.
15. Henry James, 'Tennyson's Drama', in *Views and Reviews*, ed. Le Roy Phillips (Boston: Bail, 1908).
16. George Saintsbury, *A History of English Prosody from the Twelfth Century until the Present Day*, 3 vols. (Macmillan: London, 1906–10), iii. 204–5.
17. Tennyson, *In Memoriam A.H.H*, in *Poems*, II, 315–459.
18. George Saintsbury, *A History of English Prosody from the Twelfth Century until the Present Day*, iii., 205–206.
19. Tennyson quoted in *Poems* ii, 320n.
20. Robert Browning, 'Two in the Campagna', 9–10, in *The Poetical Works of Robert Browning*, 15 vols., ed. Ian Jack et al. (Oxford: Oxford University Press, 1988–), v, 450–3.
21. See the final stanza of 'By the Fireside', which simply resolves that 'the whole is well worth thinking o'er /...which I mean to do / One day, as I said before'.

22. Browning, *Sordello, Poems* II, 195–498.
23. Cunningham, *Victorian Poetry Now*, 99–105, presents an entertaining digest of the most telling criticisms.
24. G. K. Chesterton, *Robert Browning* (London: Macmillan, 1903), 125.
25. Edward Berdoe, *The Browning Cyclopedia*, 3rd edn. (London: Swann Sonnenschein, 1897), 307.
26. Rudyard Kipling, 'The Song of the Banjo' (1894), in *A Choice of Kipling's Verse*, ed. T. S. Eliot (London: Faber, 1941).
27. The word is used throughout Stephen Foster's work, based as it was on minstrel songs. *Literature Online* records that the word appears as early as 1856 in Walt Whitman's *Leaves of Grass*, with thirteen entries across various editions.
28. Chesterton, *Browning*, 125.
29. Derek Attridge, *The Rhythms of English Poetry* (London: Longmans, 1982), 77; and Simon Jarvis, 'Poety as Cognition', *Critical Quarterly*, 40 (1998), 11.
30. Ashby Bland Crowder, 'Browning and How He Worked in Good Temper: A Study of the Revisions of "Pacchiarotto"', *Browning Institute Studies*, 17 (1989), 94.
31. Robert Schumann is supposed to have whistled the melodies of the tunes he composed, although this may have been as a consequence of his appearance: most portraits show him with pursed lips, as if he were whistling.
32. Gerard Manley Hopkins, *The Correspondence of Gerard Manley Hopkins and Richard Watson Dixon*, ed. C. C. Abbott (London: Oxford University Press, 1935), 74–75.
33. See Browning, 'Christmas Eve and Easter Day' in *Poetical Works*, iv. 251 and 254.
34. Saintsbury, *A History of English Prosody*, iii. 244, 357.
35. Christina Rossetti, 'The Poor Ghost', in *Christina Rossetti: The Complete Poems of Christina Rossetti*, ed. R. W. Crump (London: Penguin, 2001), 114.
36. Cunningham, *Victorian Poetry Now*, 66.
37. James Longenbach, *The Art of the Poetic Line* (Graywolf: Minneapolis, 2008), 39.

SELECT BIBLIOGRAPHY

Attridge, Derek, *The Rhythms of English Poetry* (London: Longmans, 1982).
Campbell, Matthew, Labbe, Jacqueline, and Shuttleworth, Sally, *Memory and Memorials, 1789–1814* (London: Routledge, 2000).
Berdoe, Edward, *The Browning Cyclopedia*, 3rd edn. (London: Swann Sonnenschein, 1897).
Chesterton, G. K., *Robert Browning* (London: Macmillan, 1903).
Crowder, Ashby Bland, 'Browning and How He Worked in Good Temper: A Study of the Revisions of "Pacchiarotto"', *Browning Institute Studies*, 17 (1989), 93–113.
Cunningham, Valentine, *Victorian Poetry Now* (Oxford: Blackwell, 2011).
Griffiths, Eric, *The Printed Voice of Victorian Poetry* (Oxford: Oxford University Press, 1989).
Hopkins, Gerard Manley, *The Correspondence of Gerard Manley Hopkins and Richard Watson Dixon*, ed. C. C. Abbott (London: Oxford University Press, 1935).
James, Henry, 'Tennyson's Drama', in *Views and Reviews*, ed. Le Roy Phillips (Boston: Bail, 1908).
Jarvis, Simon, 'Poetry as Cognition', *Critical Quarterly*, 40 (1998), 3–15.
Kipling, Rudyard, *A Choice of Kipling's Verse*, ed. T. S. Eliot (London: Faber, 1941).
Longenbach, James, *The Art of the Poetic Line* (Minneapolis: Graywolf, 2008).

Saintsbury, George, *A History of English Prosody from the Twelfth Century until the Present Day*, 3 vols. (London: Macmillan, 1906–10).

Tennyson, Hallam, *Tennyson: A Memoir, By His Son*, 2 vols. (London: Macmillan, 1897).

Walker, John, *A Rhyming Dictionary*, 2 vols., 3rd edn. (London: Cadell and Davies et al, 1819).

Yeats, W. B., *The Poems*, ed. Daniel Albright (London: Dent, 1990).

—— *Essays and Introductions* (London: Macmillan, 1961).

CHAPTER 6

···

DICTION

···

GARRETT STEWART

THREE exhibits, by no means chosen as extreme examples, can ferry us—in initial overview—across a meandering century and more of word use from Romantic to modernist. Of the river-borne boat as vehicle of the poetic spirit in Shelley's *Alastor* (1816), symbolic through and through, we hear (and are hailed to hear by typical Romantic apostrophe): 'Beneath a woven grove it sails, and, hark! / The ghastly torrent mingles its far roar'.[1] The encroaching sublime, implicitly woven in the (text)ture of the poet's words to begin with, takes the assonance of 'woven grove' and transmutes its long-vowelled diction through the melodramatic 'ghastly torrent' toward the lexical mingling of that double-*r*'ed and farther-off 'far roar' to which the reader is enjoined to listen by direct address ('hark!')—as if to a phonic drama of the verse itself. This is Exhibit A.

Exhibit B offers a diction somewhat more relaxed and less closely 'woven', but still flagging its own phonetics. As prelude to a lovelorn suicide in Dante Gabriel Rossetti's 'Down Stream' (1871), we hear at first, in an easy paratactic flow of syntax—and via the typically hyphenated and alliterating Victorian diction of a coined substantive—how 'Between Holmscote and Hurstcote / The river-reaches wind'.[2] It is as if, for a split second, before the actual verb falls into place, we are hearing how the river 'reaches' between two villages. Instead, in grammar's own further extension, it is the 'reaches' that are said in themselves to 'wind', but with the next clause washing over this one so quickly that the verb seems swept forward as well, in the unsounded but still fluttering form of the short-*i* substantive 'wind', across the run-on into 'The whispering trees accept the breeze, / The ripple's cool and kind'. We then hear further, with the verbal rather than nominal diction hyphenated this time, how the setting is completed by either— we're not sure yet (since it isn't narratively focalized)—a personified pathetic fallacy or, more likely, an actual lovers' tryst: 'With love low-whispered 'twixt the shores, / With rippling laughters gay'. That the love could be a yearning 'twixt' the banks, rather than a human desire professed somewhere afloat between them, is an ambiguous and vestigially Romantic possibility enhanced, not just by the archaism 'twixt', but even more by the repetition of 'ripple' as part of that chiastic (quintessentially Victorian) flange of adjectives on either side of the unusual plural (the insistently mutual) 'laughters'. As the plot unfolds, the scene is quickly disclosed as an erotic meeting ironically harmonized with nature—and soon to turn tragic, its rhetorical symmetry itself a part of this narrative poem's dramatic irony, abetted from the outset by the very cast of its diction.

Exhibit C could, even at a glance, be neither Romantic nor Victorian. Shelley's 'woven grove' of diction, of interleaved phonemes, as well as described arching vegetation, has, in T. S. Eliot's *The Waste Land* (1922), become the wasted, frayed tent of modernist emotional dilapidation: 'The river's tent is broken: the last fingers of leaf'—the least Romantic of alliterative personifications here, almost ghoulish—'Clutch and sink into the wet bank'.[3] The reader's need to adjust the expected parallel predicate from the single transitive verb 'clutch' to the arythmic verb phrase 'sink into', with its own metrical slump, mucks up the flat-toned verse as much as it does the forlorn image. Under the force of diction's excluded euphony, a more echoic and Tennysonian 'tent is rent' has been so thoroughly avoided that 'broken' can seem thrust into prominence almost to personify the autumn tree's unsaid *limbs* in the injury of their dismembered (defoliated) extremities.

Given evolving protocols of word use in verse, it isn't easy to dip your pen in the same river twice. Nonetheless, certain familiar, as well as unique, effects of poetry in the Victorian age offer an ongoing laboratory for the nineteenth-century question of diction in its relation to the phrasing of verse thought, more flaunted at times than in the period's Romantic forebears. Then, too, the term 'diction' locates, not just a stylistic topic, but a recurrent problem in the assessment of Victorian writing, one best faced head-on before setting the bad press aside to concentrate on certain masterstrokes of poetic phrase. Among the rumours and truisms about Victorian poetry, diction is a recurrent flashpoint, or lightning rod, both of critical detraction and of textual innovation alike. Such poetry is certainly never as cosy, even in its filigree, as cliché chooses to remember. Yet even what is new and strange in Victorian verse can be skewed and strained, even recondite, without being genuinely surprising. The premium on rhyme may at times take the edge off oddness by making it not only melodic but routinized, however ingenious. Rhyming diction (with its constraints on the 'naturally right' word) widens the gap between verse and the ever-more popular novel, a genre that absorbs more porously all the new diction of the epoch, technological, geopolitical, and otherwise, without turning it decorative or precious under the needs of metrical compression. Let alone cacophonous. Like Victorian furnishing, though, Victorian poetry is often mistakenly remembered as being quaint even in its excess, either lush, gushing, or both, overstuffed in its conceits as well as overstressed in its chiming.

Another cliché, the hackneyed charge of prudery or sentimentality, may be simple to dismiss in a given case, as with the necrophile masochism of Swinburne. So, too, even the expectations of frill and trill may be easy to dissipate with counter-examples. But the institutionalized and carefully maintained distance between poetry and prose, even as novelists of the age were increasingly waxing extensively metaphoric and even intermittently iambic (Dickens especially), is advertised everywhere by diction in Victorian poetry, often in service to the prevalent habits of rhyme. This is the dominant tendency despite cases where the diction is so far from 'high' that it finds no precedent in any landmark articulations from Milton to Keats. But even the gnarled Victorian vernacular, as in Browning or Hopkins or Hardy, can feel unventilated by the familiar, wrung to rare purpose, specialized in its own right, thickly oblique and clotted. And especially earlier in the period, the rhythmic prefixes and hyphenates, the displaced grammatical usages, the chiastically arrayed adjectival diction—all this can easily become the stuff of facile travesty, as when (in one of my own) a concoction like this to describe poetry's 'wave-deep pace sail-spread and mist-encurtained' (the adjectival compounds pitched by turns port and starboard) might find only a truncated near rhyme (to prolong this mock citation) in '. . . athirst with a searcher's burden / Compassed nearward and far in the grand uncertain.' Turning adjectives, or verbs, to nouns (or vice versa) may work to 'orb' (an actual Tennysonian instance) the verse with the aura of exotic vision.[4] But in this and similar casts of phrase, even when locally effective, the habits are indeed all too easy to parody. Harder to see is the accomplishment that, at their best, they leverage. And the literary historical energies such diction channels and transmits.

Checklists of 'Victorianisms' have been thoroughly tabulated by Bernard Groom and Bernard Richards, but the immediate phrasal context often lends more force to the effect, as we are to see, than would appear from mere taxonomy. Beyond Victorian poetry's fondness for archaism as well as contemporaneous eclecticism in the lexical register, there are circumlocutions so extreme that they actually redefine the object they circle. In the realm of adjectival or adverbial modification, hyphenated epithets may also throw new weight on a latent sense of the descriptor, including those torqued into unlicensed uses of comparative and superlative degrees ('richlier', 'completest'). And along with exotic affixes of all sorts, especially prefixes, such as 'a-seethe' or 'en-haloed', which can seem by turns stagey or spontaneous, there are bundled negatives that highlight the contours of a described scene or feeling precisely by its cancellation, as in Arnold's 'unallied unopening earth' in 'Empedocles on Etna'.[5] And if meaning is not defined by contrast in this way, it may be transferred by more direct association from one part of speech to another. Three lines apart in Tennyson's 'The Princess', for instance, the faintly oxymoronic 'twilight dawned' is matched by its looming again in 'twilight gloomed'.[6] In one of the epoch's leading Romantic inheritances, description is thus dynamized as narrative by the working (over) of diction.

'POETIC DICTION' VS POETICS OF DICTION

Diction. The very word needs some historicizing, even as an interest in its literary manifestations has yielded centre-stage lately to many other levels of literary attention, historicist included. The term also benefits from some quick dictionary work, before any given 'piece of diction' claims the spotlight. For the Victorian Browning, diction was the watchword of poetic appreciation. For the moderns, it is, in a more specific sense, what Browning helped rescue poetry from. That's where definition comes in. As if it were an instance of the multivalence it often triggers in poetry, diction means two different things in regard to poetic writing, as it does (differently) in the larger field of discourse. For poetry, on the one hand, the term identifies either the words of the poem, any poem, lexicon to its syntax, or the specific fund or subset of words deemed appropriate for verse expression in a given literary-historical period or genre, a matter of general stylistic decorum or even a mandated 'poeticism' from an established reservoir of available phrasing. In general usage, on the other hand, diction refers either to the choice of words or to the spoken articulation of them, 'phrasing' or 'enunciation', so that, in a further splitting of designation, even the former term can mean the latter in the performance of a musical lyric.

In poetic writing, by contrast, aesthetic force comes when verse on the page, seemingly restricted to distinctions between the first two senses of the lexical register apart from oral delivery—its aptness to meaning in general or more narrowly (and datedly) to generic occasion—turns out to involve an almost palpable (if not actually audible) sense of enunciation as well. This is an enunciation evoked, if not strictly vocalized, by the silent echoes and collisions of word sounds in sequence. Even when not orally delivered, poetry can deliver the forms of orality. This is what the modernist standard-bearer Eliot means when he speaks of Tennyson as having the 'finest ear of any English poet'[7]—even when the Victorian poet himself knew he was always wrestling with the inert graphic stuff of scripted diction in 'matter-moulded forms of speech'.[8] Perfect pitch must be translated into something even the reader's silent reading can, let's say, 'audialize'. But in poetry, diction is always 'sounded' in another sense too: its composite depth of association plumbed, its echoes charted.

Yet 'poetic diction' so-called is, as suggested, what the Victorians had to get over rather than put across—with the flexed vernacular of Browning's monologues leading the charge. The project was begun with early Romanticism, of course, Wordsworth warning his readers that there will be 'little of what is usually called poetic diction' in his *Lyrical Ballads*, their phrasing closer than usual in verse to 'the language of men'[9]—less artifice, more of the natural, both in focus and formulation: a more democratic power of address as well as topic. The second generation of Romantics was not so strict with itself, especially Keats and Shelley, but the strongest Victorian poetry for the most part continued to take few prisoners in the forced march against diction's formulaic 'figures of speech' (in the terms of Wordsworth's dismissal), often by transcribing instead the imagined vocal spontaneity of speaking figures in dramatic monologues—and elsewhere by opening poetry's ears to the new discourses of biological and physical science, economy, psychology, and social relations in the period, to arcane vocabularies and ad hoc collocations, including the increased prominence (when less vaporous than in my opening parody) of those hyphenated compounds meant to wed impressions under metrical stress in new and peculiar forms of the traditional epithet. A prototypical incursion of specialized vocabularies into verse occurs when Arthur Hugh Clough isolates two contemporary physiological conditions together in the same line, the second rare and five-syllabled term having only come into English usage in the late 1820s. The line in fact offers a double synonym for the self-rephrasing of the poem's own title, 'Duty—that's to say complying', with Clough's satire of a central Victorian virtue as in fact 'Atrophy, exi-nanition!'[10] On offer there is a poetics of diction in the key of irony.

Choice Words vs Word Choice

When Walter Pater, noticing the vocabulary absorbed earlier in the century from picto-rial art, German metaphysics, and mysticism, suggests that English 'phraseology' may be occupied for years to come in 'the naturalisation of the vocabulary of science', he has the work of Tennyson in mind as an exemplary site for a resourceful and 'eclectic' assim-ilation: 'How illustrative of monosyllabic effect, of sonorous Latin, of the phraseology of science, of metaphysic[s], of colloquialism even, are the writings of Tennyson'.[11] Freeing poetry from the shackles of poeticized diction—as a euphonious nexus of received asso-ciation and its phrasing—is one main historical agenda, then, and trajectory, inherited by the Victorians and pressed further, in its turn, by modernist experiment. No longer in the next century, for instance, will the chiastic modification of noun bolstered by epi-thets on each flank—as in Coventry Patmore's vestigial delectation of 'love's abysmal ether rare' (so rare indeed that it half names and then swallows up ordinary 'air')—be the showy mark of verse distinction, especially under a title like 'The Poet's Humility'.[12]

Moreover, on the analytic front, 'choice of words' is a notion that, quite apart from the formulaic mould of a pre-designated Verse Thesaurus and its companion volumes in grammatical etiquette, also calls to attention the ongoing residue of indecisiveness and variability even in an elected phrasing. If the relation of modifier to substantive, verb to its adverb, is coined through fresh feats of diction, rather than taken as overdraft from a depleted phrase bank, the shock of this newly forged relation must be measured against the earned pressure of its occasion. No longer of prime concern is the on/off toggle of 'poetic' versus 'un(poetic)'. Of keener interest is the sensed tension generated by possibilities still latent and available, sifted through already by scripted phrase, yet still adrift in and between words as self-generated undertones. This developed tolerance for the flux of utterance rather than its crystalline fixity helps explain the premium on grit rather than gemology in the later Victorian strain of diction, as capped by Hardy's eccentric phrasing: a taste for surprise over polish, for the forcefully rough rather than burnished contours of expression. Edginess of this sort cuts to the jugular of another cliché. One hears, by mostly false rumour, about 'Victorian certainties' in the ethos and poetic themes of the era. Pinpointed by diction, but only in its multifaceted state of play, the precision of Victorian poetry is often, instead, that of enacted relativity rather than installed absolutes, a language less complacent than exactingly wary and pertinently ambivalent.

This is partly to say that the truly vivid word choice in Victorian poetry, enhancing its own residual vitality, may keep the matter of choice uppermost in view, or at least in mind's ear. This is a facet of its Romantic heritage. Frequently enough, near alterna-tives are not quite evicted from the line, laying claim to squatter's rights until decidedly ousted or forgotten in the turn-over of sense. The gifted choice doesn't wrap things up too neatly: it is instead the proverbial gift that keeps on giving. Not just predictably seductive in their music, words appeal *to each other* across a line, a rhyme, a stanza—and sometimes call each other out as well, like a duel for priority in reception. Frequently it's an intertextual allusion that inflects the choice of diction, throws down a gauntlet to the given, impinges with its own alternative. Or sometimes a pun bursts open a word from within. In other cases the calling-out results instead from a proximate and encroaching word in the actual diction of the written line itself, asserting the unsaid in collision with its inscribed predecessor, skirting the written word or hemming it in, nibbling at its syllabic heels or sweeping it forward into echoic ligatures and accumulations undue, undulant, undoing. The force of a given choice of diction is, therefore, not just what the dictionary says it is, says the word means, but what the contextual setting shadows it with—or what the contingencies of enunciation insinuate.

LEXICAL ENGINEERING

On the matter of such diction, we have on the books the homage of one Victorian master to his great Romantic predecessor, however different their lexical habits—the Romantic forebear all sonority and heady metaphysics, the Victorian testimonial from an exaggerated naturalist of the vernacular. This is the exemplary case of Browning celebrating Shelley for the ringing clarity of his word choice: an uncanny match of language to its subject in both description and figuration. It is a match that Browning also strives for, of course, not in bardic visions of the Shelleyan sort, but in the rougher grain of secular dailiness in the character-drenched idiolects of his dramatic monologues. Without mentioning his own debt or aspiration in this regard, Browning's encomium singles out Shelley for a 'diction' (his specific and signal triumph) more reliable, more pliable, and more original than in any poet before him, as if, almost inevitably, to suggest that such a legacy is the most challenging and fruitful one to build on for a poet of the new era. Shelley's diction is 'more adequate to the task' than 'can be attributed to any other writer whose record is among us'.[13] This is all part of the spiritualized mechanics, as it were, of Shelley's craft, and it is apparent, according to Browning's retrospect, from the first stirrings of his Romantic genius, where already the 'complete enginery' of a poet was to be seen and of course heard. For sound is part of the effect, as well as harmony its metaphor. Shelley's diction has a 'natural and acquired richness'—its phrases, in other words, both effortlessly found and lavishly fashioned by turns. His is a wording whose 'material colour and spiritual transparency', or say whose lucid hues, are, in the synesthetic turn of Browning's own testament (from optical to vocal tonality) 'moved by and suffused with a music at once of the soul and the sense'.[14] The lesson to be learned is, we may note, not just attested but already in practice. For by the harmonics of Browning's own eulogistic diction in glorifying Shelleyan vocabulary, the chord-changes of syllabic action suggest the cumulative force, subtending any obvious alliteration, by which 'm*o*ved' + 'm*u*sic' = the volatile phonemic redistribution of '*suffused*,' a word, like 'inter-fused', dear to Wordsworth as well as Shelley. Such effects are for Browning almost a mode of analysis by allusion. In Shelley, on Browning's account, intuitive energy is at one with the intricacies of rhythmic calculation, so that sponsoring impulse and its prosodic pulse are wholly synchronized and ultimately transparent to each other. The result is 'expressive', therefore, 'both of an external might of sincere passion and an internal fitness and consonancy'.[15] That last, almost redundant and certainly formal, term—in its technical understanding rather than just as a metaphor for correlation—can be taken to set off, as complement to alliteration, those internal echoes that are indeed a hallmark of Browning's diction and its own chiming consonantal patterns (as of Shelley's before him).

Con/son/an/cy. So it is that the consonant-heavy term associated with the phonetic amalgam of certain (con-sounded) syllables and words becomes a metaphor for the very relation among them in the extended iteration of sonorous interplay. Laudation is both metapoetic and self-referential in this case, with Browning in a sense, to paraphrase a Wordsworthian dictum, creating the taste by which Shelley should be judged as well as enjoyed. We're not just expected to know what he means, but actually to feel it by present exemplum in the strenuous lilt of appreciation (the quatra syllabic play of sound). A further piece of diction can be taken to clinch this performative witness. Into the most ornate syntax of the essay, Browning drops a rare and striking term coined during Shelley's own lifetime (*c.*1800), a noun form for that nexus of pertinence and flexibility in verse engineering that, according to Browning's mandarin parallelism, is 'as signal in the excellence of its several *adaptitudes* as transcendent in the combination of effects'.[16] Adaptability in invention, one is reminded by these conflated substantives, is the truest aptitude of poetic diction. In this one word's exemplary reaching for ingenuity and exactitude alike, celebratory diction enacts its own panegyric within a delimited and unmistakable field of effect, abetting in the process the reflexive aura of Browning's dedication to his own inherited (if also redirected) craft, whose 'enginery' has an internal momentum beyond the mere girded structures of 'engineering': pistons as much as pylons, say, in the drive of meaning.

It was the Victorian Lewis Carroll who coined the term *portmanteau* for such a tight-folded packing—as in one lexical suitcase—of two different words.[17] The principle applies even to conflated forms that have their own accepted meaning apart from poetic coinage. Adaptation plus aptitude = adaptitude. Again, then, a choice of words is made to overlap in the dovetailed succession of wording, and this even within a single lexical unit of prose. Word choice, which in normal practice is thought to precede sentence construction, can sometimes see its principle—the selection among synonyms, the opting for one equivalent over another—returned instead into the ordering of a grammatical span rather than just the ordering *up* of a single word. In any case, it's no accident that Carroll seems to have lent subsequent generations a dead metaphor for the analysis of literary writing when we set about 'unpacking' the meaning of a word or phrase. And long since Carroll wrote, a modern linguist has given us one definitive model for the procedure of literary packing, and sometimes nesting, in the first place.

Roman Jakobson's influential definition of 'the poetic function' (as it 'projects the principle of equivalence from the axis of selection into the axis of combination') amounts to saying that the choice, for instance, of a name from the paradigm of proper nouns, on the basis of functional equivalence in a given grammar of identification or description, would, if operating poetically, induce in the combinatory axis of syntax a surplus or echo of that name pulsing across the line.[18] In the spirit of Browning's admiration, think Shelley: 'I weep for Adonais—he is dead!', where the drowned 'Adonais' is already recalled in this opening line by paradoxical predication in the 'he *is*' of non-being.[19] In Jakobson's model, choosing *among* equivalents is transferred into a repetition *across* their dispersal as sequence.

SYLLABIC DISTRIBUTION

Browning, we may say, selects for repetition in a way that can make his diction seem, not just seamless, but self-embedded, as in 'Paracelsus' with the prefix-cued phrasing (chosen over *en*) of '*Ingulfed in icy night*' that sinks further into itself around the subsequent *i-n-i* chiasm.[20] Or there is the even more complex phonic braid of Charlotte Brontë's 'hour of sorrow sore'.[21] In Browning's 'Pippa Passes', echoic pressure springs from diction an etymological stem that throws the morphemic glow of a (past-tense) pun over its own chromatic ambience, so that 'the whole sun*rise*, not to be suppressed, / *Rose*, reddened' along the vocalic groove of *su/ri/su/res/ros/red*.[22] Elsewhere, Elizabeth Barrett Browning is at her most Keatsian in the onomatopoetic murmur and regrouping of sounds that make for a kind of anagrammatic roll of the lexical dice: 'With a murmurous stir uncertain, in the air the purple curtain / Swelleth in and swelleth out'.[23] The systole and diastole of repetition in the second line only intensifies the off-echo in the first, its *ur/ur/ir/er/air/ur/ur*—where the long *a* in 'air' is diffused as cause across the bifold ripple in this curtain, this undulating waterfall, of sound. Diction, again, is a choice from a paradigm slotted into overt recurrence where there could have been more predictable distinctions. In this mode, there is also Robert Browning's virtually self-referential phonetic attentiveness in the savagely ironic 'all th*is* exqu*is*ite sol*i*ci*tu*de' from *The Ring and the Book* (XI, 1806), spat out by the doomed murderer Guido about those waiting for his execution.[24] And at the melancholic and depleted end of the lexical spectrum, in Thomas Hardy's 'Afterwards' the tailing-off of recurrence is arranged to align with the flagged powers of the attentive subject who, awash in evocative sound, 'hears it not now, but used to notice such things', where '-s it not' is the felt phonetic decline—a kind of slack anagrammatic denigration—of 'notice'.[25]

For a less concentrated but more encompassing dose of such bonded diction, take one of the most famous works by the laureate Tennyson, 'The Lady of Shalott', and its initial play with the paradigm of proper names. On a river running down to 'Camelot' is an island thus, by echo's dictate, named 'Shalott', whose embowered damsel—in purely erotic distress—has her mirrored bower invaded finally (after eight paired rhymes of

'Camelot' with 'Shalott' over as many stanzas) by the flashing image of 'bold Sir Lancelot' (as if impending in the rhyme scheme as an erotic inevitability). What results is a threatened collapse of the distance between sequestered isle and teeming world that springs an extra off-rhyme in recoil; rather than the echoing keynote 'the Lady of Shalott', we find instead the repeated phrasing (with its vowelled downbeat from long to short *o*) 'beside rem*o*te Shal*o*tt' at the end of two subsequent stanzas—marking with its stiffer iambic beat a starker cordoning-off of her sphere.

The tacitly 'piercing' ('Lance-') vision of the knight's glamorous form is captured by indirection through a mere metaphor (and hyphenated coinage) for the distance of his remove, the whole scene complicated in its portrayed disorientation by a phonetic instability in the diction itself. This happens just as the apparition of 'Lancelot' has broken with the phonetic pattern of lexical echo to this point, so that the bracketing sound frame of 'Shalott' suddenly, in the first line of the ensuing stanza, contracts to 'sh--ot'. In the sense of 'a stone's-throw', we read of his passing no more than 'A bow-shot from her bower-eaves'. The phonic projection that has precipitated the initial alphabetic doubling (out of 'Shalott') is matched there by a subvocal 'correction' in the sudden need, not just to distinguish across the parallel hyphenations the actual diction from the haze of false etymology (in the 'bough' that contributes to each), but also to distinguish the alternative pronunciation of 'bow' (long *o*) from the first syllable of 'bow(er)'. The minor cognitive dissonance induced by diction in that adverbial phrase—wholly avoidable in prose, fully exploitable in poetry—has timed its abrupt shift of vocal gear to exactly this moment of imploded distance between embowered privacy and the unsaid sting of cupid's arrow.

DOUBLE(D) DICTION

With the Lady instantaneously smitten and entranced, moving finally to evacuate altogether the distance between her enclave and the knight's gleaming world of desire by embarking on the river of no return, the verse already predicts the foreclosure of this effort in the overt repetition of 'singing her last song'—where, in the manifest parsing of its effect, the chosen word (rather than 'chanting', say) is 'selected' twice over in the run of syntactic combination, once as predicate, once in the accusative case. This is what grammar calls the cognate object, what Jakobson might call projection degree zero, and what Victorian poets find frequent use for. In the Lady of Shalott's dying music, what is carried on the air is the syllabic reverb of 'carol' (rather than song, hymn, ditty, or dirge)— with the *ol* generating a phonetic matrix for the coming chiastic turn of 'm*o*urnf*ul*, h*o*ly, / Chanted l*o*w*ly*, chanted l*o*w*ly*' and ending with a look 'frozen sl*o*w*ly*' matched to a pair of eyes 'darkened wh*o*lly'. The full arc of the death scene is rounded by these sound patterns of diction, coming down in the end to 'Singing in her song she died', at which point the locative preposition seems striving somehow to delimit the 'in' of subjective extinction. In the midst of her singing she died, having given it her last breath? Into her song she died? If the latter, as it partly must be, here is a projection of equivalence, a blatant repetition, whose thematic work is so little redundant that it suggests the subsumption of agent into act—a proto-modernist anticipation of the later aesthetic difficulty, in Yeats, of telling 'the dancer from the dance'.[26]

Verb/object correlations of this Tennysonian sort in the interplay of diction have a prolific and varied career in Victorian poetry, both as emblems of balanced symmetry (in ready metrical implementation) and for more dramatic effects. And satiric ones too, as when Christina Rossetti's 'In an Artist's Studio' mocks the claustrophobia of a portrait painter's erotic *idée fixe*; despite the momentary open-ended promise of enjambment, 'every canvass means / The same one meaning'.[27] In any study of poetic word choice, cognate objects (even strained ones like this) invite notice as one of the purest and most unmistakable forms of diction's poetic functioning, a veritable conjugation and declension at once (paradigmatic processes par excellence) catching each other up in the syntagmatic axis. Tennyson's spiritual commitment in the elegiac regimen of *In Memoriam*, his vow to 'dream my dream, and hold it true' (CXXIII.10)—the dream in part of his dead friend's resurrection: truly hold on to it, hold to its faith as true—is an example tacitly pitched between faith and doubt. It is a dream of religious providence spelled out later, with less agnostic hedging, in 'I dream a dream of good, / And mingle all the world with thee' (CXXIX.11–12).

One appeal of cognate diction, in compressed forms like this, has certainly to do with the way it dictates, or at least facilitates, its own iambic beat, as when Elizabeth Barrett Browning's heroine, Aurora Leigh, mentions that, untutored and uncensored, she has, across a yet more emphatic enjambment, 'lived my life, and thought my thoughts, and prayed / My prayers without the vicar', where the arriving prepositional phrase may well seem to negate theological guidance in all three facets of consciousness at once.[28] Only later does this symmetry between action and its 'object' (in the everyday as well as grammatical sense) get inflected with an adjective that intensifies it, raising the chosen diction to a power of itself in 'Whoever lives true life will love true love' (I.1067). Here the shifting logic of the cognate relation is redoubled by the bracketing syllabic echo *l-ve* for both pairs of predicates and substantives.

Being one of the most common and least discussed functions of iteration-with-a-difference in Victorian poetic arrangements, such bracketing is a recursive framework—as in the emergence of sh-ot from Sh-al-ott in Tennyson—that operates over and above, or more to the point in and among, the more obvious doublings (often monosyllabic) of the cognate object. In his early poem 'Neutral Tones', Thomas Hardy's 'wrings with wrong' is a particularly concerted instance of a bracketing span more often embedded within lexical borders than framing whole parallel words. This more typical case, though subject to its own anomalies, can be seen in Hardy's 'Snow in the Suburbs', where the phrase 'overturns him' is found rhyming, in paraphrase of the normatively adverbial 'nearly buries him', with the more obscure and echoic '*near inurns him*'.[29] All such examples remind us that 'word choice' may, strictly speaking, hold little of interest until adjacent choices, interdetermined, are pertinently yoked.

SPLIT DICTION

Facing his own death rather than a figurative burial, the murderous Guido in *The Ring and the Book* boasts of hellfire purging him to his essence, his body shedding its 'accretions' and reduced to 'some *nucleus* that's myself' (XI.2397). Yet the accreting vowels, long and short, of that very boast topple over two lines later, as if via a hardening pre-diction itself, into 'You *soon* shall see the *use* of fire.' The transformative act of reading, rather than the words written, suggests that the only nucleus catalyzed is, just before death, the 'ire' and bile that is distilled on the brink of the guillotine from the junctural combustion 'of f/ire'. As if, in his festering rage, he is becoming a scapegoat to the genre of the dramatic monologue as a whole, we see Guido offering himself up there, unwittingly and despite his supposedly constelled ego, to the dispersed subjectivity of language in action, a subjectivity as unfixed as the syllables of self-aggrandizement he spews.

Guido is a monologist lost to the slippery inscriptions of his own self-indictment. And his medium is that of a diction denucleated in its own right. The only use ire has in this poem, all but posthumously revealed, is to be, like fire, self-consuming. Incapable of penitence or reform, the homicidal self-witness approaches the gallows locked into his own malice across a cognate object operating for once in the negative rather than the positive degree in a one-of-a-kind innovation of the lexicon: 'Nor is it in me to *unhate my hates*' (XI.2400). As it happens, in Browning's beloved Shelley the cognate grammatical pattern appears in its more familiar form in 'A Hate-Song', where the angry man 'sang a song which was more of a screech', thus wedging open a distinction between lyric and other tonalities of expression.[30] Browning drags this into a new kind of psychological morass, where Guido is so caught up in rancour that grammar's logic (after the mordant idiomatic turn on his not having it 'in me' to remake his inner life) is further warped by precisely the blocked option it rejects. To unhate one's hatreds is as impossible as it sounds.

Where Browning's diction lends an ear to Shelley in the 'enginery' and 'adaptitude' of its recurrence, Tennyson pays equal heed, and tribute, to the earlier laureate, Wordsworth—and not least in passages where sonic anomaly or dissonance (if nothing as extreme as 'hate-song') is the topic. As Sir Belvedere in 'Morte d'Arthur' trudges forward, he is paced by a mounting and spreading alliteration (b/b; cl/cl) in 'bare black cliffs clang'd round him', the verb itself offering an echo from his footfalls 'on juts of slippery crag that rang / Sharp-smitten with the dint of armed heels'.[31] Word choice is dramatically overdetermined here, both from within and from beyond the text. So that to hear, as it were, the din intrinsic to dint is an effect only enhanced by the further echo of Wordsworth's famous skating episode in *The Prelude*, where inverted grammar doesn't just note but virtually conveys, in the build-up to epiphany, how 'with the din / Smitten, the precipices rang aloud' (I.439–40).[32] In Tennyson's replay, noun, participle, and verb (*din/smitten/rang*) are all deployed from the borrowed trove of word choice and brandished together as soft-pedalled onomatopoeia.

And while 'song' or 'din' as topic (a question of music or ambient noise) may help elicit complex sonorities of phrasal selection and combination, other thematic energies bundle and bunch a poet's chosen words, stringing if not ringing them out along a looped rather than straightforward line. These effects may have nothing whatever to do with things harmonious. The actual murder by Guido of his wife in Browning's *Ring* is clocked to the beat of its grotesque efficiency: 'A moment of disquiet, working eyes, / Protruding tongue, a long sigh, then no more' (XI.1362–3). The guttural sounds work in oblique performance of a last gasp more evocative in Guido's own enunciation than in the euphemistic noun 'sigh' by which he coolly names it, where the finally silenced *g* of the death rattle seems placed to relieve that four-word sequence from 'dis*quiet*' through 'working *eyes*' and from 't*ong*ue' to 'l*ong*' that tracks her panicked 'eyes' to the brutal neutrality—and chiastic reversal—of the single-syllable 'sigh'. After which 'no more'—of struggle and of her alike.

And if such stressed recurrence joins with the overt forms of the cognate object in the imposition of pattern across the sequence of Victorian diction, there are more canonical rhetorical tropes of word order on hand for the same purpose, including related devices of under- rather than over- variation. These include either the forked diction of syllepsis (sometimes identified as zeugma) or the splayed and overlapped logic of hendiadys, each recruiting two nouns (usually as paired objects or paired subjects respectively) where one would do—and thus putting the separated units of diction into dubious relation with each other. The reason to stress the frequency, and interaction, of such devices in Victorian verse cadence is to note the inextricable relation of any instanced diction to the incremental grammatical sequence it inaugurates, sustains, or completes. Barrett Browning finds in metered deployment of a divided (rather than just redoubled and cognate) verbal object an equivalent of the former satiric effect of syllepsis from the Augustan poets down through Jane Austen. When Aurora Leigh 'Gave ear to her vicar, tea to her visitors' (a version of Pope's 'sometimes counsel take, and sometimes *tea*'),[33] it is a phrasing in which the choice of a split predicate skews an idiom like 'lend an ear' into a syncopated alliteration across the bracketing syllabification from 've-ear to 'vi-ar' as well as spreading out to the expanded 'vi-or' of 'visitors' (I.493). Syllepsis appears in its more idiomatic form in this same poem with the monosyllabic simplicity of Aurora's remark to Romney: 'You have read / My soul, if not my book' (II.245–6). This double-taxing of the single-word predicate takes, in context, a more emotionally vexed form in Romney's own commitment to 'vow away my years, my means, my aims' (II.320) in ministering to the needy—where a pledge to do something gives way to the negative or sacrificial word-choice of 'vow' when completed by its immediate phonetic uptake in the open-vowelled 'away'. The surrender of years, financial means, and other purposes each to the same cause but in different senses of the verb is all meant to be fused in the supposed vector of dedication *toward*. Diction all by itself marks, in short, the strain of this holier-than-thou commitment.

A tension in the phrasal verbs of metered speech between dictional composition and syntactic slant finds a more serene example at the start of Matthew Arnold's 'Dover Beach' where, against the dimming lights of the French Coast (as backdrop and foil

both), 'the cliffs of England *stand*, / Glimmering and vast, *out* in the tranquil bay'[34]—
both stationed there and emphatic, as if in a muted version of an over-yoked compound
like 'standing firm and out', to say nothing of that oscillating glimmer in the oxymoronic
oddity of 'out in'. That aside, such a cloven verb phrase as 'stand...out' recalls, in a drastically different mood, an unusual forked moment (syllepsis again) as Browning's Guido
nears the guillotine (as if it were his name's phonetic destiny). In his own so-called
'trope' of a battle to the death, Guido imagines—and with a self-inflicted pummelling
of monosyllabic diction at that—'The last bad blow that strikes fire in at eye/And on to
brain, and so out, life and all' (XI.2312–3). The unmarked diction of *in*, *at*, and *on* operates first as an aggressive burst of prepositions, whereas a phrasal verb kicks in retroac-
tively when 'strike out' must be reconfigured as an idiom for 'expunge'. All this blast and
ricochet of diction as if at one 'blow'. And if the panicking approach of death contorts his
language in this fashion, in a more sardonic vein the officiating Pope, anticipating the
execution, turns the notion of just deserts to a cross-lexical, rather than phrasal, word-
play. He does this by speaking of the beheading—to be staged between the hangings of
Guido's two accomplices—as designed (in avoidance of the more normal 'reward') to
'Carry the criminal to his crime'*s award*' (I.1326), a mock-euphemistic diction clouded
with the cross-word overlay (and enunciated overtone) of 'sword'-play and its associated descending blade.

SPLICED DICTION

Even setting pun aside (one word for two), brevity may be the soul of one kind of wit, but
redundancy (two for one) is the musculature of another. Poetic wit, its give and scintil-
lation both, often consists, as we've seen, in the looser economy of surprise recursions.
The charge of 'wordiness' in the student margin—like the question 'diction?'—can be
an apt reprimand. But wordiness, or make that wordness—with its much of a much-
ness—is at the core of Victorian poetry. And this is never clearer than when alternatives that should have been decided *between* are instead arrayed as poles of a new kind
of electrical charge that sparks an unsaid combination of the two. Or three. In his early
'Pauline', Browning's diction, across a run of subterranean phonetic recursion, is slotted
into hendiadys—the Shakespearean (noun) and (noun) of (noun) format—in 'The fever
and the stir of after years'.[35] The phrasing is deployed to characterize (and, in its distraction, to exemplify) something logically closer to the epithetical 'feverish stir', an update
of Keats's quasi-anagrammatic 'fever and fret' from the 'Ode to a Nightingale'; instead,
the prolongation in Browning leaves the verbal noun '*stir*' more obviously half-stirring
still in the downbeat of 'after'.
　　The most gripping poetic cases of such spliced diction are, however, more indisputably redundant and overlappingly emphatic. Barrett Browning's use of this two-for-one
formula (the etymology of 'hendiadys')—with attributes conjoined rather than subordinated one to the other—is most prominent in the dramatic interchanges of *Aurora Leigh*,

with their air at times of a headlong thinking-out-loud, and especially when hinged about the delayed footfall of enjambment. There is, for instance, the redundant—or perhaps half spiritual, half social—boon of being 'baptized into the grace / And privilege of seeing' (I.577–8), leading in turn to 'a noble trust / And use of your own instinct' (I.805–6; for 'trusting use') and on in certain vents of energy to the 'delight / And triumph of the poet' (I.901–2), rather than the limply celebratory 'delightful triumph' or 'triumphant delight'. The diction of synonym and functional equivalence is thus recombined in this case, instead, into an iterative and ultimately cumulative impact, even perhaps causal, almost as if the triumph begins in the passion of 'delight' per se, as elsewhere in the tacit causal logic (detonation plus overflow) of 'shock / And surge of natural feeling' (II.1127–8). But the poetically captured force of an enjambing shock can be negative as well in its overplayed distinctions, as in 'the wrong / and shock'—for shocking wrong or wrongful shock—'he gave my life' (II.531–2) or, again at the blunt fulcrum of enjambment, 'the social spasm / And crisis of the ages' (II.273–4). Elsewhere in *Aurora Leigh*, a less abrupt run-on enacts the wish-fulfilment of damage control in an extended metaphor drawn from the new geology and aimed at a dream meant to 'fill up, bridge at least / To smoother issues some abysmal cracks' in our social planet, at which point the object of the verb is doubled from literal to metaphoric usage at the line's turn: 'cracks / And feuds of earth, intestine heats have made / To keep men separate' (II.1220–3). After such separation, such line-broken fissures, hendiadys is the figure that pairs and repairs at once, banding together things discrete into continuous rhythms of thought.

SLIPPED DICTION

Two distinct words kept separate where a single modified one would do: such, in hendiadys, is a gesture that seems in part to release poetry from the constraints elsewhere of rhyme, where the paradigm of word choice is deliberately curtailed. But rhyme itself can split more differences than at first appears, spreading backward into the chain of syntax for the odd surprise. Given the notorious paucity of rhyme words in English, the ingenuity of a poet's diction is often tested and strained in end-slots whose bounds it strains to overstep. In Browning's 'A Grammarian's Funeral', the wry potential of such far-fetched rhymes accrues, in fact, to a self-referential parable of poetic construction. The design of the whole anticipates its implementation; the '*fabric*' of any structure determines how to '*dab brick*'—so that, like rhyme itself, schemata must precede execution in the mortar of monosyllabic compounding.[36] This ability to pipe out of hiding just the right word is instanced by such hard-won rhymes in 'The Pied Piper of Hamelin' as *ermine/determine/vermin*, or the momentary crossword puzzlers of '*robe ease*' chimed with 'obese' (the latter word about as far from neoclassical 'poetic diction' as one can get), or the even more baroque examples of 'Doom's tone' played off against 'tomb-stone' and the downright madcap howler of 'Vin-De *Grave, Hock*' slotted against, not just the lone rhyme-word 'havoc', but the whole intralexical run of '*rare havoc*'. Building on the

Romantic tradition of cross-lexical comic rhymes in Byron and Thomas Hood, random comedy is subsumed nonetheless to dramatic irony in this folkloric reworking of the Pied Piper tale. For these incidental lexical transgressions cannot dissipate the central force of a thematic matrix—and phonetic capper—that pitches forward the phrasing 'free from rats or from mice', with its emphatic junctural decoupling of '*from*' from '*mice*', so as to find the juncture slurred again by syllabic off-rhyme with 'promise'. In naming there a bond fatally broken in the plot of the cheated Piper, it is as if a plague of its own has been released from the word itself.

In departing like this from the high road of Victorian sonority, the low road of comic diction also intersects at times with the well-travelled bypass of dialect poetry, whose popularity in the period is often forgotten. At the opposite end of the spectrum from Latinate abstraction, and as mastered by Tennyson himself in little-known counterpoint to his laureate tonalities, the specialized diction of dialect poetry can well entail the schemata of the 'poetic function' wrung from the sequence of a quite aberrant phonetics of diction. An idea like 'So I turned and thought of those good old times that were gone' gains its own added sense of loss—not just of distance but of performed withdrawal— from its manifestation in Tennyson's dialect lines from 'Owd Roä': 'Saw I turn'd in ageän, an' I thowt o' the good owd times 'at was goan'.[37] Operating there is the retreating echo of '(s)aw' in 'ow(t)' and of 'owt' in 'owd', the dysllabic match up of 'ageän' and 'goan', and then its further rhyme with a phrasal verb from the dialect, 'coomin' on' rather than just coming—as if arriving from the future, as onset, rather than just as prospect, and thus answering phonetically to all that had *gone on* (gone by and past) in 'go-an'. Tennyson's ventriloquized diction is managed, that is, not just by an avocational linguist's but by a canonized poet's ear.

With poetic decorum breached in a different way, though sometimes evoking the cadence of dialect as well, the often bizarre torsion of language in Hopkins and Hardy rounds out the experiments of the century, exploiting a vein of wording already worked, though not fully mined. As a transitional poet at the launch of Victorian prosody, Letitia Landon has the unmated Sappho speaking of a poetic song in which 'each wild / High thought I nourished raised a pyre / For love to light'.[38] The line that begins in enjambment with the assonant shove of 'High' ends momentarily on the ear, before being grammatically rerouted, with 'up higher' as well as 'a pyre'. In this way can words renegotiate—and hence reinvest—their own gaps as a new dialectical twist of diction, with the collision of two terms detonating (by invisibly denotating) a third. This function of converted absence, or say 'pregnant silence', standing in contrast to the overt repletions of syllepsis or hendiadys, is also related to the ellipsis which metre sometimes compels: related and in fact conjoined in certain cases, where an elided term wedges open a space marked out as if for the diction of the unwritten. This is one of the ways rhythm is famously 'sprung' in Hopkins, part of his proto-modernist refusal of the smooth—and hence an apt place, in its vertiginous complexity, to conclude this sampler of an era's work of words.

After all our examples of doubled diction, then, a case—by subtraction—of less is more. And this from a poet who has elsewhere, in 'Morning, Midday, and Evening Sacrifice', taken the splayed substantives of hendiadys to a new pitch of multiplicity in

'The vault and scope and schooling / And mastery in the mind'[39] of life's encompassed mental reach. In contrast, Bernard Richards singles out an extreme elliptical hurdle from Hopkins's 'My own heart let me more have pity on' which laments 'I cast for comfort I can no more get'—as if it might mean an end-stopped 'no longer find'—until the belated analogic 'than' sets in by enjambment: 'By groping round my comfortless, than blind / Eyes in their dark can day...'[40] This would make more immediate sense if it read 'groping round me comfortless'. In the manuscript, as noted by Hopkins's 1918 editor Robert Bridges, 'comfortless' is placed, instead, to anticipate 'dark' as modifier of the postponed substantive 'world'.[41] But with that belated noun excised, the latter adjective seems instead nominalized and the former suspended in a suitably aimless blur—achieving grammatical satisfaction only if retrofitted (a point not entertained by either Bridges or Richards) in sprung rhythm with 'dark' as its adjectival substantive: 'my comfortless dark [analogous to]... *their* different one'.

The only *present* (rather than edited-out) alternative would be for 'comfortless' to take as antecedent the word 'mind', released by tripled overkill in the preceding two lines, lines whose ameliorative plea, obsessively phrased, is to 'not live this tormented mind / With this tormented mind tormenting yet'. We encounter there in that impacted mindfull-ness—beyond cognate patterns, and in keeping with a diction oscillating beyond any one determinate grammar—an iteration so invariant that it begins to forge a false etymological bond between the participial diction of *tor/mented* and ment/ality itself. And then, too, beyond the elisions and subdivisions of diction's metered sequence in the subsequent perplexing density, there is again the bridged interstice between word choices. By way of slipped diction and across what phonology terms the 'dental' ambiguity of a cross-lexical bond (the same *d* or *t/d* ligatures, for instance, of my last four subheadings above), the ellipsis—on one hearing of the analogic clause—makes a sudden continuous sense. It does so when the wording is downshifted phonetically from clause (no more can find day than I can) to phrase (than in the blindness of their day) across a double and dovetailing liaison, with comfort no more to be had by the speaker than by 'blind eyes in their dar*kened day*' (an aural melding or seaming of the monosyllabic triad 'dar*k can d*ay').

As the gap of ellipsis is thus sutured over by phonemic cross stitch, the oddness is both normalized and redistributed in the continuous groping of diction for its impossible therapeutic fitness. In the process, certain choices lie open—and closed again—in the waver and wager of reading. Hopkins offers in this regard a radical epitome of the period's rhetorical mood, committed to seeking out the 'inscape' and 'instress' of the single word (his famously elusive phrases for poetic in-formation), even before scanning the wider landscape of its assigned linkages. By exploiting this tendency even in moderated form, the Victorians continued, after Wordsworth's salient initiative, a nineteenth-century 'modern' assault on the frozen rather than pointedly chosen forms of verse expression. Though with a sometimes flagging vigilance, or even an only intermittent commitment, theirs was nonetheless, all told, an ongoing revolution against the bastion of poetic diction and its prescripts—in allegiance instead to a more exploratory poetics of the word, which is only to say a continuing romance with its invitations.

NOTES

1. Percy Bysshe Shelley, *Alastor in Shelley's Poetry and Prose*, eds. Donald H. Reiman and Neil Fraistat (London: Norton, 2002), 83.

2. Dante Gabriel Rossetti, 'Down Stream', in *The Collected Works of Dante Gabriel Rossetti*, ed. William Rossetti (London: Ellis and Elvey, 1897), 319.

3. T. S. Eliot, *The Annotated Waste Land with Eliot's Contemporary Prose*, ed. Laurence Rainey (New Haven: Yale University Press, 2005), 62.

4. See Bernard Richards, *English Poetry of the Victorian Period, 1830–1890* (London: Longman, 1988), 26–62. Richards mentions this verbalized coinage among others, along with unfamiliar compound epithets and prefixes and suffixes far from the beaten path of standard English, as hallmarks in the period's verse, along with other kinds of 'poeticism' on the one hand, colloquialism on the other, with a section as well on dialectic poetry—while alert throughout, in the higher rhetorical tradition, to the Victorian tendency towards wordings 'doctored by periphrasis'.

5. Matthew Arnold, 'Empedocles on Etna', in *Mathew Arnold: The Complete Poems*, ed. Kenneth Allott, 2nd edn. (London: Longman, 1979), 201. See Groom, Bernard, *The Diction of Poetry from Spenser to Bridges* (Toronto: University of Toronto Press, 1955) especially chapters on 'Tennyson, Browning, and Arnold' and 'Rossetti, Morris, and Swinburne'.

6. Alfred Tennyson, 'The Princess', in *The Poems of Tennyson*, 3 vols, ed. Christopher Ricks, 2nd edn. (London: Longman, 1987), ii. 280.

7. T. S. Eliot, *Essays Ancient & Modern* (New York: Haskell, 1974), 175.

8. Tennyson, *In Memoriam* (XCV.46), in *The Poems of Tennyson*, ii. 413.

9. William Wordsworth, 'Preface to the *Lyrical Ballads*', in *The Poetical Works of William Wordsworth*, ed. Ernest de Sélincourt, 2nd edn. (Oxford: Oxford University Press, 1952), 390.

10. Arthur Hugh Clough, 'Duty—that's to say complying', in *The Poems of Arthur Hugh Clough*, ed. F. L. Mulhauser, 2nd edn. (Oxford: Oxford University Press, 1974), 28.

11. Walter Pater, *Appreciations, with an Essay on Style* (London: Macmillan, 1924), 12–13.

12. Coventry Patmore, 'The Poet's Humility', in *'The Angel in the House' together with 'The Victories of Love'* (London: Routledge, 1905), 32.

13. Robert Browning, 'Introductory Essay', in *Letters of Percy Bysshe Shelley, With an Introduction by Robert Browning* (London: Edward Moxon, 1999; first pub. 1852), 20–1.

14. Robert Browning, 'Introductory Essay', in *Letters of Percy Bysshe Shelley*, 20.

15. Robert Browning, 'Introductory Essay', in *Letters of Percy Bysshe Shelley*, 21.

16. Robert Browning, 'Introductory Essay', in *Letters of Percy Bysshe Shelley*, 18–19.

17. Lewis Carroll, *Through the Looking-Glass* (New York: St. Martin's Press, 1977), 133.

18. Roman Jakobson, 'Linguistics and Poetics', in Seymour Chatman and Samuel R. Levin, eds., *Essays on the Language of Literature* (Boston: Houghton Mifflin, 1967), 302–3.

19. Shelley, *Adonais in Shelley's Poetry and Prose*, 411.

20. Ian Jack et al., ed., *The Poetical Works of Robert Browning* (Oxford: Clarendon Press, 1983—), iii. 22.

21. Charlotte Brontë, *The Professor*, ed. Margaret Smith and Herbert Rosengarten (Oxford: Oxford, University Press, 1987), 221.

22. Browning, 'Pippa Passes', in *The Poetical Works of Browning*, 44.

23. Elizabeth Barrett Browning, 'Lady Geraldine's Courtship', *The Works of Elizabeth Barrett Browning*, 5 vols, ed. Sandra Donaldson (London: Pickering & Chatto, 2010), i. 403.

24. Jack et al, ed., *The Poetical Works of Robert Browning*.

25. Thomas Hardy, 'Afterwards', in *The Complete Poetical Works of Thomas Hardy*, 5 vols., ed. Samuel Hynes (Oxford: Oxford University Press, 1984), ii. 309.

26. W. B. Yeats, 'Among School Children', in *The Collected Works of W.B. Yeats: The Poems*, ed. Richard J. Finneran, 2nd edn. (New York: Scribner, 1997), 221.

27. Christina Rossetti, 'In an Artist's Studio', in *The Complete Poems of Christina Rossetti*, ed. R. W. Crump (London: Penguin, 2001), 796.

28. Browning (E. B.), *The Works of Elizabeth Barrett Browning*, iii., 19 (I.699–700).

29. Hardy, *The Complete Poetical Works of Thomas Hardy*, iii. 13, iii. 43.

30. Shelley, 'A Hate-Song', in *The Complete Poetical Works of Percy Bysshe Shelley*, 2 vols., ed. Neville Rogers (Oxford: Oxford University Press, 1975), ii. 319.

31. Tennyson, 'Morte d'Arthur' in *The Poems of Tennyson*, ii. 15.

32. Wordsworth, *The Poetical Works of William Wordsworth*, ed. Thomas Hutchinson (Oxford: Oxford University Press, 1933), 638.

33. Alexander Pope, *The Rape of the Lock* in *Poems of Alexander Pope*, ed. John Butt (New Haven: Yale University Press, 1963), 227.

34. Allott, ed., *Matthew Arnold: the Complete Poems*, 254.

35. Browning, 'Pauline', in Ian Jack et al, eds., *The Poetical Works of Robert Browning*, i.

36. Browning, 'A Grammarian's Funeral' in Ian Jack et al., eds., *The Poetical Works of Robert Browning*, v. 459.

37. Tennyson, 'Owd Roä', in *The Poems of Tennyson* (London: Longman, 1987), iii. 171.

38. Letitia Landon, 'Sappho's Song', in *Poetical Works of Letitia Elizabeth Landon 'L.E.L.'*, ed. F. J. Sypher (Delmar, New York: Scholars' Facsimiles & Reprints, 1990), 5.

39. Gerard Manley Hopkins, 'Morning, Midday, and Evening Sacrifice', in *The Poetical Works of Gerard Manley Hopkins*, ed. N. H. MacKenzie (Oxford: Oxford University Press, 1990), 163.

40. Richards, *English Poetry of the Victorian Period, 1830–1890*, 50.

41. *Poems of Gerard Manley Hopkins*, ed. Robert Bridges (London: Humphrey Milford, 1918), 119.

SELECT BIBLIOGRAPHY

Armstrong, Isobel, *Language as Living Form in Victorian Poetry* (Brighton: Harvester, 1982).

Attridge, Derek, *Peculiar Language: Literature as Difference from the Renaissance to James Joyce* (London: Methuen, 1988).

Barfield, Owen, *Poetic Diction: A Study in Meaning*, 3rd edn. (Middletown, CT: Wesleyan University Press, 1973).

Browning, Robert, 'Introductory Essay', in *Letters of Percy Bysshe Shelley, with an Introduction by Robert Browning* (London: Edward Moxon, 1999; 1st pub. 1852).

Davie, Donald, *Purity of Diction in English Verse* (London: Routledge, 1967).

Dowling, Linda, *Language and Decadence in the Victorian Fin de Siècle* (Princeton, NJ: Princeton University Press, 1986).

Groom, Bernard, *The Diction of Poetry from Spenser to Bridges* (Toronto: University of Toronto Press, 1955).

Harrison, Anthony H., *Victorian Poets and the Romantic Poem: Intertextuality and Ideology* (Charlottesville: University of Virginia Press, 1990).

Jakobson, Roman, 'Linguistics and Poetics', in Seymour Chatman and Samuel R. Levin, eds., *Essays on the Language of Literature* (Boston: Houghton Mifflin, 1967).

Leighton, Angela, *On Form: Poetry, Aestheticism, and the Legacy of a Word* (New York: Oxford University Press, 2007).

Pater, Walter, *Appreciations, with an Essay on Style* (London: Macmillan, 1924; 1st pub. 1889).

Richards, Bernard, *English Poetry of the Victorian Period, 1830–1890* (London: Longman, 1988).

Ricks, Christopher, *The Force of Poetry* (Oxford: Oxford University Press, 1984).

Stewart, Garrett, *Reading Voices: Literature and the Phonotext* (California: University of California Press, 1990).

Tucker, Herbert F., *Tennyson and the Doom of Romanticism* (Cambridge, Mass: Harvard University Press, 1988).

Wolfson, Susan J., *Formal Charges: The Shaping of Poetry in British Romanticism* (Stanford, CA: Stanford University Press, 1997).

CHAPTER 7

···

SYNTAX

···

ISOBEL ARMSTRONG

In 1955 the poet, Donald Davie, wrote a book on syntax in English poetry, one of the rare studies of this theme, and called it *Articulate Energy*.[1] He was more interested in eighteenth-century poetry and its power in comparison with what he thought of as the syntaxless poetry of modernism than in Victorian poetry. Indeed, he skips over the corpus of Victorian poetry as if it never existed. Nevertheless, the title of his book is important for all poetry. He thought of syntax as 'articulate energy', though he never explained the subtle pun in his definition, which plays on two meanings of syntax. It is (first) a mode of making energy apparent as the words, sound, and sense that are its expression come into being, are at once made articulate and themselves *articulate* energy. It is (second) a mode of jointing together or articulating segments of language in such a way as to generate energy through the connections established. It is the function of joints to bring movement into play—the energy would not be there without them. Energy is both articulated and articulates. This way of reading syntax, as the life that creates the interlacings of words, makes it the source of communicative vitality in sentences. Its embodied connections are what makes possible other structural patterns, in poetry in particular, such as rhythm and rhyme, and brings them into being so that we can experience them in real time. Syntax brings form into being. It hosts meaningful sound.

By contrast, definitions of syntax by professional grammarians and specialists in linguistics look unexciting. In his authoritative *Cambridge Encyclopaedia of the English Language*, David Crystal defines syntax in two ways: '*syntax* 1 The study of word combinations; cf. morphology. 2 The study of sentence structure (including word structure)'. If we pass on to *morphology*, that is designated as 'The study of word structure, especially in terms of morphemes'. And if we pass on to the *morpheme*, that is designated as 'The smallest contrastive unit of grammar (*man, de-, -tion, -s*, etc)'.[2] In other words, 'syntax' is understood as a hierarchy of connective structures in descending order from the sentence, to the word, and to the smallest particle. An account of syntax in Victorian poetry necessarily works with both definitions of articulation, that of the poet and of linguistics. Nevertheless, it is hard to see how one can evolve an account of syntax that comprehends, for instance, the languages of Tennyson and Christina Rossetti, Swinburne, and Elizabeth Barrett Browning, Hopkins, and Amy Levy. 'The strongest slang of all is the slang of poets', Fred Vincy asserts in *Middlemarch*.[3] Since each poet builds an idiolect out of his or her own 'slang', any generalization about poetic language will miss the point. It may well be the case that poets shared in the historical changes that were occurring in English in the nineteenth century: to name some of the most prominent shifts in syntax, for instance, the increasingly free use of prepositions, the shift from non-count nouns to count nouns, the tendency to create noun strings, the gradual loss of importance of the subjunctive, the loss of the verb 'to be' in favour of 'have' as an auxiliary, the fluid use of progressive participle forms ending in -ing, and the tendency to omit relative pronouns.[4] But to document such usages—or their exceptions—across a large spectrum of poetry would provide a codification of textual practice without describing the specific 'slang' of individual poets. Therefore the strategy of this essay has been to consider a single poem by four poets across the long nineteenth century: Tennyson's 'Tears, Idle Tears' (included in *The Princess* but probably a poem of the 1830s), Browning's 'Two in the Campagna' (1855), Christina Rossetti's 'Winter Rain' (1862), and Michael Field's 'Ebbtide at Sundown' (1908). [5] Most people would accept, I think, that each poem is more or less typical of the poet's idiom—though this has to be an educated guess.

'Tears, idle tears, I know not what they mean' (Tennyson); 'I wonder do you feel to-day' (Browning); 'Every valley drinks' (Rossetti); 'How larger is remembrance than desire!' (Field). Two statements, a question, an exclamation, open these poems. Yet they all begin in the present tense, a tense that might be thought of as the ontological present tense for the nineteenth century, because it states what *is*. It makes the poem happen in real time. It is a tense about *being* here and now. A rapid census suggests that this is the preferred tense for many poets. 'I stand on the mark beside the shore' (Elizabeth Barrett Browning); [6] 'The sea is calm tonight.' (Matthew Arnold); [7] 'White rose in red rose-garden / Is not so white' (Swinburne); [8] 'Thou mastering me / God' (Hopkins); [9] 'Now the earth in fields and hills / Stirs with the pulses of spring' (Mathilde Blind).[10] The present tense brings into being the dramatic immediacy of an affective condition—it signals that its mode is what J. L. Austin called a 'perlocutionary' speech act, the language that moves, that deliberately makes an appeal to the other's emotion. But beyond this the present tense proposes that its essence is to be in act, *in* the moment of being, taken up by it. 'Each thing, as far as it can by its own power, strives to persevere in its being...*Striving* is nothing but the actual essence of the thing', Spinoza wrote.[11] The Victorian present tense attempts to live out the essence of striving as process. In the present tense every moment is a now, keeps us *in* the experience. Know, wonder, feel, remembrance, desire, these are all terms that denote what consciousness does and *is*. We do not strive *for* but strive *to be*. Even Rossetti's 'Every valley drinks', since it is the essence of the valley to persevere in its being by actively taking in moisture 'by its own power', has an affinity with these terms denoting mental acts. The present tense creates the syntax of striving.

Bound up with the key words of consciousness—knowing, wondering, feeling, remembering, desiring—is a sense of something inaccessible or lost. These words all have their correlative negations, the not known, the not understood, the forgotten, the lost object of desire. Tennyson's inexplicable tears, Browning's inaccessible thoughts, Rossetti's invisible water source, Field's 'vanishing' sun and seascape: there is a caesura in the 'nows' of the present tense that confronts the poet with a break. Breaks, syntactic, metrical, and conceptual (the latter often in the form of the non sequitur), characterize these poems. During this period we encounter many prefigurations of the unconscious, as Sally Shuttleworth and Jenny Bourne Taylor have demonstrated in their collection of documents of psychology of the nineteenth century. To quote from two discussions: 'How can we know that [i.e. the unconscious] to exist which lies beyond the one condition of all knowledge,—consciousness?' Things 'manifest their existence indirectly though the medium of their effects' (William Hamilton). 'Between the outer and the inner ring, between our unconscious and our conscious existence, there is a free and constant but unobserved traffic for ever carried on' (E. S. Dallas).[12]

How can this break between conscious and unconscious be articulated? How can the not known, the not understood, the invisible, the 'vanished' be made available in the material of words? One of the questions latent in these poems is: how can the horizontal, linear nature of syntax be used to articulate the vertical presence of unknown depths in the psyche or in the phenomenal world? How can linear syntax convey the 'depth' of despair (Tennyson), or that which is 'deeper' than longing (Field)? Finding a syntax for the unconscious meant using the possibilities of the caesura in conjunction with the open, fluid grammar inherited from the Romantics by the Victorians. The caesura brings the break into being performatively. A gap opens in syntax, disclosing an abyss or rift that becomes constitutive, disclosing a moment of non-connection. Opening up more than one meaning in the same words, a double or ambiguous syntax can explore contradictions and complexities as words and sentences become palimpsests, mapping a double possibility.

TENNYSON'S TINTERN ABBEY

> Tears, idle tears, I know not what they mean,
> Tears from the depth of some divine despair
> Rise in the heart, and gather to the eyes,
> In looking on the happy Autumn-fields,
> And thinking of the days that are no more.
>
> Fresh as the first beam glittering on a sail,
> That brings our friends up from the underworld,
> Sad as the last which reddens over one
> That sinks with all we love below the verge;
> So sad, so fresh, the days that are no more.
>
> Ah, sad and strange as in dark summer dawns
> The earliest pipe of half-awakened birds

To dying ears, when unto dying eyes
The casement slowly grows a glimmering square;
So sad, so strange, the days that are no more.

Dear as remembered kisses after death,
And sweet as those by hopeless fancy feigned
On lips that are for others; deep as love,
Deep as first love, and wild with all regret;
O Death in Life, the days that are no more. [13]

Christopher Ricks notes that 'Tears, idle tears', a lyric inset into *The Princess*, arose from Tennyson's visit to Tintern Abbey. 'This song came to me on the yellowing autumn-tide at Tintern Abbey, full for me of its bygone memories.'[14] Arthur Hallam was buried near Tintern, but one of these bygone memories must have been of Wordsworth's poem in *Lyrical Ballads* (1798), 'Lines written a few miles above Tintern Abbey'. Tennyson's compact, four-stanza poem, with its repeated refrain, 'the days that are no more', might seem and is alien to the flow of Wordsworth's blank verse paragraphs, but it recapitulates Wordsworth's unrhymed blank verse and almost insolently repeats the syntax of a key line while refiguring its prepositions—and propositions. Tears, Tennyson writes, 'Rise in the heart, and gather to the eyes'. 'Sensations sweet', Wordsworth wrote, are 'Felt in the blood, and felt along the heart'.[15] Tennyson's rearrangement enunciates the rearrangement of major components of Wordsworth's ideas through a highly elaborate and disjunctive revisionary syntax. Wordsworth's syntax is sufficiently stunning: we would expect the prepositions 'in' and 'along' to be reversed—'in' the heart, 'along' the blood, would have been the conventional use of these prepositions. But for him, 'sensations sweet', physical sense data from the outer world, and simultaneously a reflexive awareness of this (as registered by the past tense of 'felt' and the adjective 'sweet'), actually have their habitat 'in' the bodily blood, which is literally the conduit of organic life. Oxygen and nutrients originated 'in' the blood from external sources and the sense data that belong to organic life flow together interdependently. These are 'felt along the heart', not 'in' it, because they are in movement, the heart being the agent of circulation. Physiological and mental life are in joyous organic movement together and in interchange with the external world.

Tennyson rearranges the prepositions in a superficially more conventional way. Tears are generated internally. They are part of a closed circuit within the self and they are of the material body. Tears rise 'in' the heart, and gather 'to' the eyes. The prepositions replace Wordsworth's circulatory flow with a hydraulic flow, from depth upward. The heart is not the source of these tears but the medium by which they 'rise' 'from', the syntax insists, a further and yet deeper internal source, the antecedent, indeterminate 'depth' of 'some divine despair' in a sentence that is placed antecedently to make the point. Grief, emotion, exerts cardiac pressure. Is this despair sacred? Is it ecstatic and Dionysian? 'Some', that throwaway adjective with its indefinite generalizing force, refuses to make 'divine' more than speculative. 'Some', an indicator of quantity when used with count nouns ('some eggs'), deliberately repudiates the quantifying function in favour of indicating a wholly non-specific entity, despair. (In the background, there is the semantic hint of the way one can 'divine' water, the despair that detects the lachrymist's underground tears.) *Its* (despair's) source is indeterminate too. Wordsworth's 'sensations sweet' can pass into his 'purer mind', can become an aspect of pure thought. In another context, he can thus experience 'Thoughts that do often lie too deep for tears'. Tennyson's poem on the contrary, resolutely affirms that tears lie too deep for thought.

Mysterious secretions of the human body, tears are 'idle' and cannot 'mean' because they do no cathartic work of mourning and have neither exchange value nor use value. Nevertheless, the syntax allows them to be both subject and object and to take over the remaining stanzas that attempt to interpret them through loss, death, and Eros, so that the poem is suffused in tears, *lacrimae rerum*. Tears have a strange syntactic status in the first stanza. The articulations of the syntax put them in different places, making ambiguous connections and disconnections. Almost addressed as the detached subject of an apostrophe in the discrete first line—'Tears, idle tears, I know not what they mean'— the 'idle' tears addressed seem to be outside the speech act on first reading, particularly as the heavy ictus on 'Tears' isolates the word metrically. ('Tears' can almost pun on another form of tear, as they are torn apart from the rest of the sentence by the blow of the ictus.) The separate entity of the line at first makes these tears the object of 'I know not': I know not what they, tears, idle tears, mean. But in the second line they take over as subject, reinforced now as a thrice-reiterated noun. 'Tears, idle tears, . . . Tears. . . rise. . .' The 'I' of the first line gets lost. Taking advantage of those agent-free present participles that were increasingly part of linguistic practice in this period, the two lines 'In looking on the happy autumn-fields / And thinking of the days. . .' open three possibilities for the agent that have to be sought way back in the stanza—the tears themselves, the eyes to which they gather, and the 'I' of the first line. The tears intervene in the looking and thinking, the 'I' and the 'eyes', almost as an obstruction.

Compare the ambiguous syntax of 'Tintern Abbey': 'and connect / The landscape with the quiet of the sky' (7–8). Here it is unclear whether the 'I', the first person singular, or the cliffs, 'connect' landscape and sky. But these rival articulations, a structural pun on connection itself, extraordinary as they are, do not demand the same leaps across clauses and phrases as the dislocated connections of Tennyson's first stanza, where grammatical concord is not easily established. As if the first stanza were not complex enough, 'Tears' intervenes in the final three stanzas as a phantasmal subject: [Tears] 'Fresh as the first beam'; [Tears] 'Ah, sad and strange'; [Tears] 'Dear as remembered kisses'. The reason for this is that the refrain delays the real subject—'the days that are no more'—until the end of each stanza. The mind searches for an antecedent subject, and 'tears' is attracted to this slot by virtue of its reiteration. The upshot of this is that there are lost connections between tears and their meaning, even though tears pervade the poem.

The refrain in this and the three other stanzas of the poem attempts to establish what tears 'mean' by finding a correlative in 'the days that are no more'. That use of the primal verb 'to be' draws these days into the present—they *are* no more—by making the 'no moreness' of the days a lived experience in the present. It is this 'no moreness' rather than the days that is important syntactically. Ricks quotes Frederick

Locker-Lampson saying 'it was not a real woe, as some people might suppose; "it was rather the yearning that young people occasionally experience for that which seems to have passed away from them forever"'.[16] Since this not 'real' loss about loss has an elusive content, each of the three last stanzas of the poem attempts to elucidate this buried content by making as if to produce a simile for it. The result is an almost simile, a kind of near miss, generated by the carefully patterned anaphoric adverb 'as'—'Fresh as', 'Sad as', 'Ah, sad and strange as', 'Dear as', 'Sweet as', 'Deep as'. Alike in sound but different in function, these 'as' structures attempt to demonstrate what 'no moreness' is like. The second stanza, 'Fresh as the first beam glittering on a sail…Sad as the last', comes nearest to a simile. Invoking the 'as' as an adverb of comparative equality, it mimics without quite achieving the 'just as' of classical simile. It is the same with the substance of the description itself. There is no classical myth that quite matches this cyclical rising and sinking of a ship crewed with comrades from the 'underworld'. But what it does is to bring the inaccessible underworld briefly into cognizance along with its inevitable sinking. The sinking sun and the sinking ship fused syntactically, seem to sink forever, to drown as the poet drowns in tears. The 'as' structures in stanzas three and four are different. In stanza three 'as' is an adverb of time and place, designating 'when/while', 'at the point when'. It pulls the experience of death right into the present, divesting it of any metaphoric protection, as the ubiquitous -ing formation—'dying eyes', 'dying ears', 'glimmering square'—insists on the acute perception of the last moments of the sensoria. Death here is posited as pure sensation without the residue of thought.

The syntax ensures that these last moments are a series of 'nows'. Finally, death and Eros come together in ecstatic memory. 'Dear as remembered kisses after death'. We are back with the adverb of comparative equality, and as with the third stanza there is no metaphoric exchange value in this experience. A disturbing syntactic ellipsis suggests that past kisses are remembered after the death of a loved one, or that the kisses are remembered from the necrophilic act of kissing the dead, or that the dead themselves remember kisses. As the conjunction 'And' suggests, memory and desire are closely allied. 'And sweet as those [kisses] by hopeless fancy feigned / On lips that are for others'. Not *were*, but, as Jonathan Dollimore has brilliantly suggested, 'are'.[17] Transgressive desire belongs to the present, not the past. It goes on existing in the present of the poem. The chasm of a caesura follows this admission. The break is constitutive, performing that leap across the gap of the past as the weeper comes into possession of some measure for indeterminate depths—'deep as love, / Deep as first love…' Not deep as past love but deep as first love, as if that love begins all over again with recollection. The caesura marks a leap into the infinity of the present tense, when memory becomes a consummation and not a storehouse for the past. Unlike Wordsworth, whose memories form a store available to 'future life', Tennyson's poem is taken up with the rapture of the now and the pure expenditure of feeling. This is how the depths become accessible. This is how the text perseveres in its being.

Bataille's *The Tears of Eros* is a latter-day reading of those 'idle' tears secreted in the ecstasy of love and death.[18] The dissolution of tears for him becomes a marker of the continuum between life and death and the necessary pain caught up in the rapture of that transitional moment. Tennyson, of course, has been associated with rapture by Cornelia Pearsall, but I think her reading, like mine, comes short of this post-modern interpretation.[19] The intensity of the 'now', the poem's clinging to the present tense, places it just this side of life rather than death.

ROSSETTI: NON-TELEOLOGICAL SYNTAX

Every valley drinks,
  Every dell and hollow:
Where the kind rain sinks and sinks,
  Green of Spring will follow.

Yet a lapse of weeks
  Buds will burst their edges,
Strip their wool-coats, glue-coats, streaks,
  In the woods and hedges;

Weave a bower of love
  For birds to meet each other,
Weave a canopy above
  Nest and egg and mother.

But for fattening rain
  We should have no flowers,
Never a bud or leaf again
  But for soaking showers;

Never a mated bird
  In the rocking tree-tops,
Never indeed a flock or herd
  To graze upon the lea-crops.

Lambs so woolly white,
  Sheep the sun-bright leas on,
They could have no grass to bite
  But for rain in season.

We should find no moss
  In the shadiest places,
Find no waving meadow-grass
  Pied with broad-eyed daisies:

But miles of barren sand,
  With never a son or daughter,
Not a lily on the land,
  Or lily on the water. [20]

My discussion follows out of historical sequence with the ecological thirst of Christina Rossetti's 'Winter Rain' (1862) because the poem's fascination with aqueous flow and hydraulic movement, with depths, and the syntactic modes it finds for exploring these elements, belongs to the same concept-world of Tennyson, however different the lyric poem.

The caesura of this poem is not the metrical break that 'Tears, Idle Tears' exploits. It is rather a conceptual break between sentences and stanzas, often created by the meticulous punctuation of colon and semi-colon that accentuates the gaps between stanzas. The formal breaks raise the philosophical question of the non sequitur. These question formally what we take for granted in the physical world, repetition and connection—here the recurrence of irrigating rain and the continuance of biological plenitude. The poem uses repetition against itself. Its repeated pattern of rhyme and rhythm continues, but what its careful anaphora do is to break the connection between surface and depth, cause and effect. 'Every... Every... But for...But for... Never... Never...'. The first stanza, despite its gentle maternal imaging of the female containers of dell and hollow, establishes a voracious thirst through repetition. '*Every* valley drinks, / *Every* dell and hollow' [drinks]. The economic syntax of zeugma supplies the missing repetition of 'drinks' in the second line, lending a parallelism to 'sinks and sinks' in the third. Rossetti, mistress of the feints of syntax, sets up a conventional reading and denies it. The unwary reader tends to read the second and third lines of the first stanza in continuity: every dell and hollow drinks where the kind rain sinks and sinks. But the colon after 'hollow' disallows this reading and breaks the relative clause and the connection between the intake of water and the rainfall. Effectively a new sentence begins with the third line, only asserting that the green of spring follows from the downfall of rain. But a massive ecological non sequitur might be in waiting: perhaps there will not be rain and perhaps there will be no green to 'follow'—which stands for a translation of the grammatical 'sequitur'. It is a Humean point, that the repetition of the constant conjunction of rainfall and green surface is just that. Where we see cause and effect we actually only see repetition, misreading effect as cause and assuming a teleological necessity where none is guaranteed. There is an irony in the constantly doubled labials—valley, dell, hollow, *will*, that act out the morphology of repetition, concluding with the false certainty of 'will', with its mixed function of present tense affirmative and future tense. This disconnection is made more sinister by the repetition of 'sinks and sinks', which suggests an endless penetration of depths as the present tense goes on for ever, with the implication that the water sinks *away*. So we have a universe of successively smaller concavities in the landscape thirstily drinking and drinking, and water sinking and sinking in parallel. Like Tennyson's divine despair, these porous depths are endless, and the secret working of irrigation is an unknown and undiscoverable, the theological mystery of fertilization and germination. We only know it from the appearance of the surface. But the recurrence of 'rain' and 'green' is not inevitable, as the almost rhyme hints.

It is the surface that preoccupies the rest of the poem, the world above ground. This is all we can see, as the poem's prepositions indicate—in, above, on. The strange grammatical solecism in stanza six—'Sheep the sun-bright leas on'—corroborates this insistence on the surface. The poem celebrates that surface at first with a teleological affirmation and confidence.

Buds *will* burst, and, leaping across the chasm of the second to the third stanza, the grammar asserts that they *will* 'weave' a bower of love, *will* weave a canopy above the procreative trio of nest and egg and mother. Yet, despite its seeming equanimity, the syntax is as elliptical, disjunctive, and strange as anything in Tennyson's poem. There are gaps here, like the temporal gap in 'the lapse of weeks', so that it is possible to read 'Weave a bower of love' as an imperative. It is humans who are enjoined to weave a bower of love through the culture of 'woods and hedges', making possible the 'canopy' that ensures procreation: 'Nest and egg and mother'.

But behind human labour and nature as human artefact is 'fattening rain', an epithet that builds an atavistic solidity and bulk miraculously from the flow of water. Yet the last five stanzas, seeming always to aspire to reductive trimeters, proceed inexorably to dearth. We cannot presuppose the teleological necessity of rain 'in season', cause and effect. Its presence is a mystery. The verbs turn subjunctive, conditional, and as their repeated negations drain the world of water so there is an intransigent draining of affect, as if the loss of fertility dries up feeling. Interestingly, Rossetti uses the subjunctive insistently here, which, we are told, was gradually losing its importance in this period, as if to remind the reader of its necessity. If we isolate the overdetermined conditional structures of these stanzas and their negations—'But for...we should have no...Never...Never...Never...They could have no...But for...We should find no...Find no...But...never...Not'—we find that every visible living thing described, whether bird, animal, or vegetation, is in fact *invisible*, conjured through conditional negations, a figment of grammar. Rossetti's skill with verbal sleights is nowhere more powerful than in these feigned presences, phantoms of plenitude withdrawn. The final stanza modulates the 'But for' sequence and pares it to 'But': there are no exceptions, no 'But fors' now, simply the stark sense of 'only', 'alone'. Without rain there is only the depopulated 'miles of barren sand'. Not only the closest of procreative issue disappears, sons and daughters, but gender distinction itself. Only grammar conjures, in the final two lines, what is not and cannot exist – except in language: 'Not a lily on the land / Or lily on the water'. The steady annihilation of distinction proceeds to make another distinction disappear, that between land and water itself, and with it the 'flowers' of stanza four. These lilies are not just any flowers: they have been aesthetic objects and symbols for historic cultures and civilizations. With dearth, language, symbol-making, and belief systems die. This poem uses syntax to create—nothing. Perhaps its consolation is that syntax, articulation, is still possible.

BROWNING: ORGANIC SYNTAX

1

I wonder do you feel to-day
    As I have felt since, hand in hand,
We sat down on the grass, to stray
    In spirit better through the land,
This morn of Rome and May?

2

For me, I touched a thought, I know,
    Has tantalised me many times,
(Like turns of thread the spiders throw
    Mocking across our path) for rhymes
To catch at and let go.

3

Help me to hold it: first it left
    The yellowing fennel, run to seed
There, branching from the brickwork's cleft,
    Some old tomb's ruin: yonder weed
Took up the floating weft. . .

10

No. I yearn upward—touch you close,
    Then stand away. I kiss your cheek,
Catch your soul's warmth,—I pluck the rose
    And love it more than tongue can speak—
Then the good minute goes.

11

Already how am I so far
    Out of that minute? Must I go
Still like the thistle-ball, no bar,
    Onward, whenever light winds blow,
Fixed by no friendly star?

12

Just when I seemed about to learn!
    Where is the thread now? Off again!
The old trick! Only I discern—
    Infinite passion and the pain
Of finite hearts that yearn.[21]

Browning's great lyric is too lengthy to be discussed in its entirety: I will examine what links it with Rossetti's and Tennyson's texts: the not known, the invisible, the vanished, the elusive. The elliptical syntax of 'Two in the Campagna' is riven with breaks and disconnections. It is almost about the caesura, the gap between language and world, thought and experience, the gap between two people (despite being 'hand in hand'). The syntax is continually, to use the terms of stanza eleven, 'So far / Out of that minute', dislocating temporality and the self. The break of the caesura becomes a wound, as in stanza 8 ('What the core / O' the wound, since wound must be?'). The embedded clauses of stanza one, with their uncertain agreement and ambiguous temporal sequence suggest that experience has already vanished before it can be lived. 'I wonder, do you feel to-day / As I have felt since…' We are never given a content for what 'I have felt' may be, even though the poet assumes that the lover might share in it—'do you feel…as I have felt?' 'I wonder', with its homonymic similarity to 'wander', anticipating and catching up with

the later words ('to stray in spirit'), establishes a double concern with restless speculation and with open-ended exploration which is always losing its way. There is a rift after
'since': 'do you feel to-day / As I have felt since,...'. The suspended predicate, 'We sat
down on the grass', makes it possible for 'since' to register a time almost contemporary
with the act of sitting down on the grass in the immediacy of 'This morn of Rome and
May', or a time way before this event took place, a long time since 'This morn of Rome
and May'. To whom does the 'since' belong? 'Do *you* feel...since'? '*I* have felt since'? '*This*
morn of Rome and May' is a different 'this' according as it relates to speaker or lover.
That final line of the stanza hangs indeterminately. 'This', so deictic and specific is at the
same time highly generalized. The urgency of 'Do you feel to-day / As I have felt...' is
caught up in a tangle of tenses. The syntactic disjunctions and ambiguities go far beyond
the fluid amorphousness of Romantic syntax.

The stanza virtuosically captures the way that in thought process consciousness compresses, elides, jumps, in a forever unfinished process, fighting the disjunctions of its
own solipsism, seeking to find out what it feels in the act of feeling itself. The poem is
about and is the act of seeking, losing, and seeking again a train of thought. It is a psychological poem, attempting to mime out the association of ideas, the threads of connection that enable thought to be articulated, alluding to a theory of mind that was, despite
Coleridge's deconstruction of it, still highly important to Victorian thinkers. Indeed, it is
an effort to find the syntax of thinking, the syntax of the association of ideas. Just as 'This
time of Rome and May' floats unattached at the end of stanza one, so the poet speaks of
'the floating weft' in stanza three and the lost thread—'Where is the thread now?'—in
the final stanza. A weft is the weaver's thread that is woven into a supporting warp of
threads, but here the weft floats loose without anchor. Browning plays on this and the
meaning of thread as a 'clue', that which leads one to a terminal point of understanding.
A clue leads one back, a weft leads one forward, and it is this strange two-way aspect of
connection that gives the poem its ungrounded movement. The 'turns of thread' first
appears in stanza two, as the poet compares the tangled act of thinking to the multiple crossings of spiders' webs encountered as fragile barriers to movement. 'Turns' is an
apposite pun, for one of the meanings of 'turn' is the single line of a poem, as if the poet is
baffled and obstructed by his own lines.

'I would I could adopt your will, / See with your eyes...your part, my part / In life,
for good or ill'. In stanza nine, in one of the many echoes of Shelley's *Epipsychidion*, in
which the poet seeks absolute union with the beloved, the ontological or metaphysical
problem of thinking becomes urgent, going beyond the psychologism of the early part
of the poem. Is it possible to think the same thoughts, be one with the mind of the other,
and reciprocally, is it possible for the loved one to identify absolutely with the lover's
thoughts? If thinking is inaccessible to the self, how much more is the lover's thought
closed off from the beloved. The answer finally is the 'wound' (stanza eight) of separation, the caesura of division. Yet before this, Browning tries to see how a joint creation
of thought might be possible. The ever-moving thread of thought is potentially captured
by lover and beloved together: 'Help me to hold it!' (stanza three): 'Hold it fast!' (stanza
four). 'For me, I touched a thought, I know, / Has tantalized me many times', the poet

states, in stanza two. To 'touch' a thought is to be in material, physical relation with the phenomenology of thinking. To 'touch' a thought may simply mean that the poet has made contact with the impalpable abstraction of thinking. On the other hand it may be that he has 'touched' a thought as a concrete, sensory experience, an experience that can be shared because it is concrete. Thought is inherently mobile. Rhymes 'To catch at and let go' (stanza two) have to be created and given up in order for more rhymes to displace the earlier pairings. With extraordinary inventiveness—I know of no other poem of this kind—Browning and his speaker trace the 'weft' of thought by associating it with the sensory, visual detail thought attaches itself to in the external world, so that the material world becomes a kind of mnemonic or substitute for ideas, an interpreter of thought process which itself becomes organic, a biological process. Things 'manifest their existence indirectly through the medium of their effects', we have seen William Hamilton say. Here consciousness can grasp (literally 'hold') the effects of thought but not its hidden essence. That process itself is represented through an ambiguous syntax, for the connections being traced are volatile and unstable:

> First it left
> The yellowing fennel, run to seed
> There, branching from the brickwork's cleft,
> Some old tomb's ruin, yonder weed
> Took up the floating weft,
>
> Where . . .

So quick and mobile is the associative process that the fennel to which an idea attaches, 'run to seed / There . . .' may be 'branching', like the filaments of thought, from the brickwork's cleft, or it may be already superseded by 'yonder weed' which has 'gone to seed'. The 'brickwork's cleft' palimpsestically overrides 'Some old tomb's ruin' of which it may be part, but over which it takes precedence, placing the tomb as a parenthesis as it hurries on to 'one small orange cup' in the next stanza (stanza four). The tomb, belonging to ancient history, but possibly alluding to the tomb of Shelley's doomed love, is incorporated and abandoned in a rapid associative tally that can only make retrospective sense of the fragments it lives by.

As the poet's thought is lost, absorbed in the champaign's 'endless fleece', which suddenly presents a multiplicity of potential threads (a fleece, of course, is spun into thread), and the joint creation of mental life comes to an end, the poet turns from involuntary thought to the involuntary life of the natural organic world. I leave this part of the poem to return to the final stanzas that conclude with the inevitability of separation. Co-creation is impossible: the speaker will 'touch' the lover close, as he touched a thought, and as thoughts touch one another, 'catch' the soul's warmth, as he caught at rhymes, but relinquishes the impossible identity he yearned for. The other cannot be known. The poem ends with the poet caught in the paradox of forward-moving thought and retrospective understanding which forever displaces the self. 'Must I go . . . Onward?' 'Just when I seemed about to learn! / Where is the thread now? Off again!' In a final stanza riven with fragmenting caesura there is a pyrrhic recognition. The mind is not condemned to random thought, arbitrarily moved as the thistle ball by the wind. 'Only I discern': I alone now discern, I can only discern. The double syntax endows a poignancy to this reflexive perception, while the epistemological verb 'discern', rhyming so brilliantly with the failed cognition of 'learn', sets up the possibility not only of recognizing, but of at least distinguishing, separating out, and thus understanding what is seen. The solitary insight recognizes that it is possible to understand the logic but not the content of desire—'Infinite passion, and the pain / Of finite hearts that yearn'.

Michael Field: Idealist Syntax

> How larger is remembrance than desire!
> How deeper than all longing is regret!
> The tide is gone, the sands are rippled yet;
> The sun is gone; the hills are lifted higher,
> Crested with rose. Ah, why should we require
> Sight of the sea, the sun? The sands are wet,
> And in their glassy flaws huge record set
> Of the ebbed stream, the little ball of fire.
> Gone, they are gone! But oh, so freshly gone,
> So rich in vanishing we ask not where—
> So close upon us is the bliss that shone,
> And, oh, so thickly it impregns the air!
> Closer in beating heart we could not be
> To the sunk sun, the far, surrendered sea.[22]

Michael Field finds a syntax to discern the not seen, the invisible, just as Browning finds one to define the not known. Their sonnet, 'Ebbtide at Sundown', explores an extraordinary proposition, that what has vanished, the very process of disappearing—'So rich in vanishing'—is more potent, more perceptually intense, than its full presence could ever be. Indeed, perhaps full presence can only be known by its disappearance. Finding a syntax for transition is the task of the poem. In Virginia Woolf's *To The Lighthouse*, as Mrs Ramsay steps over a threshold the narrator comments that the moment had become 'already the past'.[23] It is this becoming past that the sonnet is about. Thus the poem lives in a present tense that has to do the duty of remaining with the immediate moment of perception and recording that the past *is*, simultaneously. Field uses the primal verb 'to be' with the past participle to insist on the immediacy of the past. 'The tide *is* gone, the sands *are* rippled yet; / The sun *is* gone; the hills *are* lifted higher...the sands *are* wet' [my italics]. The five times repeated verb, the gonglike 'gone', the verb that hinges the sestet to the octet, functions in that ninth hinging line—'Gone, they are gone! But, oh, so freshly gone...'—to express the tension between the past as a conclusive event and the past as a continuing experience, as trace. 'Gone' with an auxiliary verb—'they *are* gone!'—is enfolded between two appearances of the true past tense at either end of the line. Interestingly, Field prefers to use the almost archaic '*is* gone' and '*are* gone', using the verb 'to be' as auxiliary instead of the increasingly common and idiomatic 'have' to denote the actuality of the past. So the past *is*, just as much as the present.

We have to read 'So close upon us *is* [my italics] the bliss that shone' not as a discrete account of the bliss that is now past but as an unexpressed compound suggesting a trace—'bliss-that-shone'. For the sestet establishes that the immediacy of the '*is* gone' past has now moved into another phase of pastness. The sun, the sea, *and* the 'record' of sunset on the wet sand have now disappeared. The poem sets up gradations of pastness but still refuses to concede its finality. The sestet resorts to oxymoron—'so freshly gone'—and to the curious seemingly neologized present-tense verb, 'impregns'. This word, seemingly, is a contraction of 'impregnates', and it has the eccentricity of Christina Rossetti's 'leas on', though it is actually a dictionary word. To impregnate in its weakest sense is to diffuse, permeate, or saturate, but in its strongest sense, it is to fertilize, to make pregnant. The bliss of sensory memory, in a gendered image, fertilizes the air, makes it capable of reproduction, of generating further memories. The breaks and pauses so dominant in the octet are fewer in the sestet as if to confirm the continuities of the experience, but a warning caesura recurs when the last line returns to the double action of sunset and ebbtide in the empirical world with which the poem begins: 'Closer in beating heart we could not be / To the sunk sun, the far surrendered sea'.

The sea has given up its tidal flow, but it has also been 'surrendered' to perception and lives only in consciousness. The 'sunk sun', with its cacophonous assonance, really has finally 'sunk' rather than setting. The sonnet ends with the ambiguous syntax that is so characteristic of the Victorian poem and makes two irreconcilable claims. We could not be closer, in the bodily, cardiac intensity of memory, to the lost sun and the ebbed sea. On the other hand, we could *not* be closer empirically to all that has disappeared in the phenomenal world, the sun and the sea. Hence the regret of the final line, living proof of the first statement—'How deeper than all longing is regret!'

The force of Field's sonnet lies in its use of the comparative adjective, 'larger', 'deeper', 'closer', supported with the adverbs 'how' and 'so'. The anaphora that begin the poem— 'How larger is remembrance than desire! / How deeper than all longing is regret!'—take advantage of the fact that the comparative is always an indeterminate coordinate. The comparative marks an endless largeness, depth, and closeness unless or until it is closed down by its superlative. Thus remembrance and regret expand to infinity, while desire and longing, not actually semantically that distinct, recede. Memory and regret suffer because we cannot place them on a scale of difference, but the effect of these first two lines is to emancipate the passions of memory, regret, desire, and longing from the empirical world, unmeasurable where it is measurable. For them Michael Field chooses a regular *measure*, the iambic line, in contrast with the jolting caesura later in the octet, as if to suggest the continuity of the emotions, the discontinuity of the physical world.

To adapt Hamilton, the empirical world of sun and sea in the octet is already only apparent by its effects—the rippled sand that is the negative space of the waves, the glow of light cresting the hills. The glassy 'flaws' of sand, fragments of beach but also flawed by their very physicality, 'huge record set' of the ebbtide and the setting sun by reflecting them, just as the mind will reflect the physical scene through sense data and ultimately through memory. As in Browning, the model of mind is the surface that will accept associative patterns. But Michael Field explores the ultimate in idealist experience: that an idea of the world might displace its physical reality instead of being a supplement to it. Indeed, experience may be made up of time and memory, loss. 'Ah, why should we require / Sight of the sea, the sun?' Nevertheless there is as much desire and longing in the poem as regret and remembrance. The antitheses set up between desire and memory, longing and regret, then turn out to be questionable. Michael Field do not push syntax quite as far as Browning, who attempted to make it perform simultaneous rather than sequential acts of mind. But they are as much concerned with being 'out' of 'that minute' as he is.

Conclusion: Double Syntax, the Caesura: Voids and Interstices

Poetry enlarges the circumference of the imagination by replenishing it with thoughts of ever new delight, which have the power of attracting and assimilating to their own nature all other thoughts, and which form new intervals and interstices whose void forever craves fresh food.[24]

Shelley, 'A Defence of Poetry'

None of these four poems is a religious poem. Yet they exist in an era that was gradually losing a culturally shared language for the ineffable of teleological religious experience—literally a grammar of assent—and seeking another that would search into other forms of the ineffable. In the four poems under discussion these other, secular and sceptical forms of the ineffable are the unconscious, the sources of emotion, the pairing of Eros and death, the mystery of cause and effect in the created world, the phenomenology of thought processes, its connection with the unconscious and the association of ideas, the temporality of perception, the nature of desire and memory, longing, and regret. Since these are all poems that question the possibility of retrieving this experience they all turn reflexively on the nature of language, the morphology of the ineffable. Given that these poems are reaching for a new kind of metaphysics and psychology, I might have been writing about the syntax of idealist poetry that is present in all the texts here, and not just Michael Field. Certainly a double syntax that constantly proposes more than one possibility, and a use of the caesura that creates gaps and wounds which found the poems on breaks and disconnection, open up a form of secular ineffability at the same time as reaching to bring what cannot be defined within the sphere of the expressible and the circumscription of language. We can only call this an idealist syntax, however, if we accept that it also includes and registers the concrete immediacy of perceptual experience, which continues with an acute physiological intensity felt in the body. Whether it is the casement's 'glimmering square', the buds' 'glue-coats, streaks', beetles 'blind and green', or the wet sand's 'glassy flaws', language is alert to the sensoria and a Victorian descriptive detail that depends constantly on the physiological adjective of sight, sound, touch and colour.

This physiological intensity differentiates these poems from those of their forebears. Romantic poets like to find ways of describing the way energy comes up from the depths. A chasm in the mist, the wild sound of waters that culminate Wordsworth's *Prelude*, caverns measureless to man and the panting fountain of Coleridge's 'Kubla Khan', Shelley's thoughts which create 'new intervals and interstices' for more thought to arise—all are clear antecedents of these Victorian poems, and yet all lack that atavistic particularity that we associate with Victorian epistemological lyrics. I think Shelley's thinking provides the closest model for these poems and their syntax. He understood the constitutive nature of the void in thought. When thought as it were, reaches its negative space, that moment of negation is the moment when emptiness creates desire, when there is space to generate new thought. And this is no abstract process, as his bodily language of primal hunger and desire suggests: the void for ever craves fresh food. The void is greedy for Shelley. Syntactically this void is the break, the caesura. These are the interstices and disjunctions that ex nihilo create the possibility of the speculative double grammar that is a mode of exploration in these poems. If these poems open up the depths of a secular ineffable as a result, this is experienced through the craving body as much as through longing, desire, remembrance, and regret.

NOTES

1. Donald Davie, *Articulate Energy. An Inquiry into the Syntax of English Poetry* (London: Faber and Faber, 1955).
2. David Crystal, *Cambridge Encyclopaedia of the English Language*, 2nd edn. (Cambridge: Cambridge University Press, 2008), 469, 465.
3. George Eliot, *Middlemarch: A Study of Provincial Life*, ed. Felicia Bonaparte and David Carroll (Oxford: Oxford University Press, 2008), 92.
4. These changes are discussed in detail in *The Cambridge History of the English Language*, 5 vols., ed. Suzanne Romaine (Cambridge: Cambridge University Press, 1992–2001), iv. 96–274. See also Richard W. Bailey, *Nineteenth-Century English* (Ann Arbor: The University of Michigan Press, 1996).
5. Poems are from the following editions: Alfred Tennyson, *The Poems of Tennyson*, ed. Christopher Ricks (Harlow: Longman, 1969); Robert Browning, *The Poems of Browning: 1846–1861*, ed. Daniel Karlin, Joseph Phelan, John Woolford (London: Longman, 2007); Christina Rossetti, *Complete Poems*, ed. Betty Flower (London: Penguin, 2001); Michael Field, *Victorian Women Poets: An Anthology*, ed. Angela Leighton and Margaret Reynolds (Oxford: Blackwell, 1995).
6. Elizabeth Barrett Browning, 'The Runaway Slave at Pilgrim's Point', in *Victorian Women Poets*, 80.
7. Matthew Arnold, 'Dover Beach', in *The Complete Poems*, ed. Kenneth Allott, 2nd edn. (London: Longman, 1979), 239.

8. Algernon Charles Swinburne, 'Before the Mirror', in *Poems and Ballads* (London: Chatto and Windus, 1893), 146.
9. Gerard Manley Hopkins, 'The Wreck of the Deutchsland', in *The Poetical Works of Gerard Manley Hopkins*, ed. N. H. Mackenzie (Oxford: Oxford University Press, 1990), 51.
10. Mathilde Blind, 'The Street-Children's Dance', in *Nineteenth-Century Women Poets*, ed. Isobel Armstrong and Joseph Bristow, with Cath Sharrock (Oxford: Clarendon Press, 1996), 653.
11. *A Spinoza Reader. The Ethics and Other Works*, ed. E. M. Curley (Princeton: Princeton University Press, 1994), 159.
12. William Hamilton and E. S. Dallas, *An Anthology of Psychological Texts 1830–1890*, ed. Jenny Bourne Taylor and Sally Shuttleworth (Oxford: Clarendon Press, 1998), 82, 93.
13. Alfred Tennyson, 'Tears, Idle Tears', in *Poems of Tennyson*, 784.
14. Tennyson, 'Tears, Idle Tears'.
15. William Wordsworth, 'Tintern Abbey', in *Lyrical Ballads*, ed. Michael Gamer and Dahlia Porter (Claremont: Broadview, 2008), 283.
16. Quoted in Ricks, *Poems of Tennyson*, 785.
17. Jonathan Dollimore, *Death, Desire and Loss in Western Culture* (London: Routledge, 2001).
18. Georges Bataille, *The Tears of Eros*, trans. Peter Connor (London: City Lights Books, 1989).
19. Cornelia Pearsall, *Tennyson's Rapture: Transformation in the Victorian Dramatic Monologue* (Oxford: Oxford University Press, 2008), 51–120.
20. Christina Rossetti, 'Winter Rain', in *The Complete Poems of Christina Rossetti*, ed. Betty Flower, 23.
21. Robert Browning, 'Two in the Campagna', in *The Poems of Robert Browning*, ed. John Woolford, Daniel Karlin, Joseph Phelan, iii. 601.
22. Michael Field, 'Ebbtide at Sundown', in *Victorian Women Poets*, 501.
23. Virginia Woolf, *To The Lighthouse*, ed. Hermione Lee (London: Penguin, 2011), 121.
24. Percy Bysshe Shelley, 'A Defence of Poetry', in *Shelley's Poetry and Prose*, ed. Donald H. Reiman and Sharon B. Powers (New York, London: W. W. Norton and Company, 1977), 488.

SELECT BIBLIOGRAPHY

Agamben, Giorgio, *Language and Death: The Place of Negativity*, trans. Karen Pinkus (Minneapolis: University of Minnesota Press, 2006).
Bailey, Richard W., *Nineteenth-Century English* (Ann Arbor: The University of Michigan Press, 1996).
Barthes, Roland, 'From Work to Text', in Stephen Heath, ed., *Image Music Text* (London: Fontana Press, 1993), 155–164.
Crystal, David, *Cambridge Encyclopaedia of the English Language*, 2nd edn. (Cambridge: Cambridge University Press, 2008).
Davie, Donald, *Articulate Energy. An Inquiry into the Syntax of English Poetry* (London: Faber and Faber, 1955).
Empson, William, *Seven Types of Ambiguity* (1930), 2nd edn (London: Chatto and Windus, 1947).
——*The Structure of Complex Words*, 3rd edn (London: Chatto and Windus, 1951).
Pearsall, Cornelia, *Tennyson's Rapture: Transformation in the Victorian Dramatic Monologue* (Oxford: Oxford University Press, 2008).

Ricks, Christopher, 'Wordsworth: 'A Pure Organic Pleasure from the Lines', *Essays in Criticism*, 21 (1971), 1–32.

Romaine, Suzanne, ed., *The Cambridge History of the English Language*, 5 vols. (Cambridge: Cambridge University Press, 1992–2001).

Shuttleworth, Sally, and Bourne Taylor, Jenny, *An Anthology of Psychological Texts 1830–1890* (Oxford: Clarendon Press, 1998).

Prins, Yopie, *Victorian Sappho* (Princeton: Princeton University Press, 1999).

CHAPTER 8

....

STORY

....

HERBERT F. TUCKER

TRADITIONAL GROUNDS

....

THESE days everybody knows a couple of verse narratives, maybe by heart; but such acquaintance has little effect on our default assumption, inherited as we shall see from the last Victorians, that real storytelling gets done in prose while real poetry does something else. And yet once upon a time—indeed, for nearly the entire cultural history we have means of reconstructing—narrative and poetry were made for each other. Within the oral culture of archaic society, verse served both as a preservative technology and as an ornament dignifying those records whose importance justified elaborate safe-keeping. Equipped to survive the memory of a single individual or generation by especially marked verbal practices (a prosody), such records moreover tended to assume a narrative form. Elder societies tallied the knowledge they prized by telling it over; to account for a momentous phenomenon in natural or tribal history was to recount it in the designedly memorable, stepwise shape of myth, ritual, recipe. Thus in primary epics, whether orally or scribally recorded, a practical knowledge-how (to slay, to plant, to worship) consorts with a commemorative knowledge-that (Odysseus prevailed, Prometheus transgressed, Moses persisted), the ensemble being delivered in a narrative package distinctively clothed in measured language.

By the time of classical Rome and Alexandria, literacy had taught sophisticated poets to regard continuous major narrative as not an obligation but an option; and the same went for the stories they opted to retail. Nevertheless, the story poems Virgil and Ovid wrote formed a binding tradition within the scribal culture of medieval Latinity. In emergent vernaculars too the predominant poetic kinds remained firmly narrative— ballad, lay, romance—and the crowning genius of Dante and Chaucer was devoted to making narrative new. It was at the waning of the Middle Ages that major narrative began its epochal secession from verse into prose, a medium that asserted new bragging rights as the Renaissance ripened across Boccaccio and Rabelais towards Cervantes. The brisk arrival of the new fictional prose on one hand sent poets elsewhere, notably to cultivate subjectivities of unprecedented complexity in lyric forms like the sonnet. On the other hand, prose's new inroads on the realms of fiction let poets from Ariosto to Spenser lay afresh the classical poets' millennial wager on artfully learned verse as the vehicle of choice for a plot keyed to a *translatio imperii* that was now coursing west by north-west.

It was poems, not novels, that played for these high cultural stakes: novels had in hand the different game of subverting generic decorum, breaking the rules of genre in the name of a lower but truer mimesis of the world and the human condition than the venerable rules permitted. Arguably one such rule was the monopoly on epistemological authority that narrative had traditionally enjoyed. In lieu of that ancient accountancy, prose fiction with its burly inventories and farcical overturnings breathed a curiosity about the things of this life, and an accompanying empiricist scepticism as to ideas about things, that in alliance with science's new inductive method bid fair to sweep the seventeenth century before it.

In the face of these winds of change, Milton's breathtaking reclamation of poetry for the universal human story was the daring last stand of a forfeit dispensation. Within a couple of generations Dryden and Pope, although they cherished that dispensation dearly, were devoting their talents to verse polemics and essays: satiric and didactic modes of dazzling brilliance, which sharpened story to a burin's point for the scoring of a caricature or illustration of an aphorism. The best eighteenth-century verse being dedicated to Augustan controversy or Sensibility discursiveness, properly narrative energy flowed through prose channels into fiction and historiography. The cultural place once enjoyed by *Paradise Lost* was occupied a century later by the magisterial prose of Gibbon's *Decline and Fall*, with its sardonic supersession of all Milton had stood for: Christ's religion as the culture-summing expression of human potential, and verse's grandeur as the right medium in which to sing so lofty a theme.

ROMANTIC RECUPERATION

With the Romantic poets it was another story, a story to which Victorian verse narrative forms a long and eventful sequel. We should remember that 'Romanticism' denotes, as an -ism, not just a revival of 'romance' (extended narrative) but a revival undertaken with conscious deliberation. For the revival of romance took place on what Schiller hailed as *sentimental* rather than *naïve* terms. Romantic poetry was more often than not narrative, and on the whole it was consistent with a largely shared cultural theory. This theory revalourized narrative as a privileged category of knowledge. At the turn of the nineteenth century the thing that most urgently needed knowing was not a thing at all but a process, not a noun but a verb: not a fixed order, nor even a series of changes; but the law of change itself. In valourizing time over space, this theory broke decisively with eighteenth-century assumptions, by taking up the Enlightenment key of sceptical inquiry and using it to unlock the Enlightenment postulate of unconditioned, invariant rationality. The rock of vantage to which Descartes and Locke had pointed, and on which Pope and Gibbon had based their panoramic certitudes, was in Romantic hindsight a philosopher's mirage flitting across the slope of an active volcano.

Two powerfully efficient causes sustained this Romantic critique of Enlightenment in ways that, having affected primarily intellectuals during the Romantic era, soon spread their influence to touch every Victorian common reader: the spectacular failure of the French Revolution and the irresistible advance of the Industrial one. The former revolution showed that the price paid for repressing history, as Parisian ideologues had lately done on the best Enlightenment principles, was having to repeat it traumatically once the historically repressed came back. The latter revolution transvalued time itself, which emerged in the nineteenth century as the dimension along which to gauge the vast interlocking changes in production and consumption, transportation and residence, labour and leisure, that were refiguring human relations across the board. The political and economic consequences of these twinned developments gave denizens of the nineteenth century every reason to reckon on change as the paradoxically salient constant within modern experience; and their calculus for coping with change took preponderantly the shape of story. So influential was the new *modus vivendi* that it surged into the intellectual currents from which educated Victorians took their bearings. Ascendant disciplines near the turn of the century included chemistry and geology, philology and the analytic editing of classic and scriptural texts: each in its way was a science of change that characteristically asked, not what and why, but whence and whither; and its findings were in effect narratives. Once understanding a thing became coterminous with knowing how it had come to pass, the epochal appearance of a book called *The Origin of Species* was just a matter of time, and the difference between Darwin's dynamical plots and Newton's mechanical equations discloses what amounts to a tale of two cultures.

In the discipline of literature, accordingly, narrative swiftly recouped the ground it had recently lost to the discursive space of reason, whose synoptic array now looked quaint beside story's limber mutabilities; and it was in the medium of verse that Romantic sophistication about narrative was most clearly pronounced. True, Austen and Scott wove in supple prose their studies of a maturing protagonist's psychological development into the fabric of a society that was itself in throes of change; but by their time the commodity form of the novel was enforcing consistencies of marketplace presentation from which avant-garde poetry could depart more freely. The best poets' enthusiastic resumption of narrative's age-old duties was tempered by a more exigently critical spirit than had motivated even those elders like Ovid and Spenser who were most inspired by visions of change and becoming. Inquisitors of change, the Romantics broke story open in order to show how it worked, at once exalting and exposing the technique of narrative as just that—a human and instrumental creation, answerable to the devising imagination whose revolutionary interventions, for good and ill, were the most conspicuous phenomena of the new century.

Thus the prosodic reinforcement and tale-binding structure that in past centuries had conservatively stabilized cultural heirlooms were turned under Romanticism into diagnostic expedients. *Lyrical Ballads* revolutionized the folk poetry that antiquarian scholarship had recently revived by (the title says it) customizing the ballad form through systematic interruption. 'Simon Lee' sabotages its ostensible storytelling, challenging the reader to 'make a tale' of what's left; 'The Rime of the Ancient Mariner' fouls a putatively redemptive storyline with uncanny incongruities, then wraps the result in faux-scholarly apparatus that leaves readers wondering just what company they are keeping. 'La Belle Dame Sans Merci' follows ballad-mutant suit by puncturing the tale of Keats's knight-at-arms (a memoir tendered, like the Mariner's, by way of *explanation*) with a cautionary dream that is then punctured in its turn, and to no better issue than a cold hillside. For each of these poems the way to understanding lies through story, as it ever did of old. But now nothing stands in greater need of wary analysis than story as such: its givenness, its conventional and ideological presuppositions. The unfinished form of 'Christabel', mounted for good measure on a versification spectacularly experimental, solicits awareness of how narrative expectation gets aroused and frustrated. There—as in the sorely scrambled Bard's Song that Blake ladles into *Milton*, and Byron's self-perforating raconteurship in *Don Juan*—the truly engrossing story is that of the telling itself, a meta-fiction whereby the poet labours to promote into critical awareness the conscripted readerly involvement that he simultaneously elicits. This Romantic vanguard heralded what we find in Victorian poetry: a narrative regime that took the force of early-century experimentalism, even as without remission it listened, and danced, to the tempo of modern living.

Story Naïvetized: Epicry, Balladry, Nursery, Mockery

That the nineteenth-century poetic approach to narrative was self-consciously *sentimental* does not mean there wasn't plenty of residual *naïveté* to go around. In decade after decade, poet after poet produced straight-up narratives of epic scope and ambition, typically sporting the look, the tone, and the generic accessories that had been installed into the British tradition via Milton from Virgil and Homer. About stolid verse narratives of this kind—the pious sort exemplified by Jean Ingelow's *A Story of Doom* (1867), based on the biblical patriarchs; the chauvinistic sort whose Victorian flood tide, after much Romantic-era inundation, was John Fitchett's 1841 *King Arthur*, waterlogged in at some 130,000 lines—this essay will have nothing more to say, because the subject is one the present author has treated at length elsewhere. These white mastodons deserve a decent pen within the literary-historical menagerie, if only to countervail triumphalist accounts of the rise of the novel; but they stood so stubbornly apart from the defining energies of their time that literary history can do little more than gesture at them.

It's also the case that, in pure mint condition, the mastodon epic was almost as rare as were the handful of brilliantly successful adaptations of the genre that the most innovative Victorian poets produced: Barrett Browning's *Aurora Leigh* (1857), Browning's *The Ring and the Book* (1868–9), Morris's *Sigurd* (1876), Swinburne's *Tristram* (1882), Hardy's *Dynasts* (1903–10). More commonly met than either kind of epic outlier is a hybrid creature that superficially resembles epic but makes a point of winking or shrugging off its generic ambition; and the way such a work apologizes for its modern irrelevance could not be more modern. Southey pioneered such arts of generic disownment early in the century by the condescending prose in which he annotated his own deadpan epic verses; Scott did him one better when he built the disclaimer right into the poetry, by means of proem, epilogue, or more pervasively still the odd nudge confiding to readers that they were at an entertainment and not a sermon—a device Byron exploited to the hilt by inverting its proportions of earnest and game. It was Scott's lightly worn dubiety about heroic narrative that made verse romances on the model of *Marmion* the most imitated of nineteenth-century modes. The forgiving adaptability of the form made it the *sentimental* choice par excellence among narrative poets wishing to appear, however late in the day, in *naïf*'s clothing.

So did the nineteenth-century identification of Scott with history. For heroism was a quality that by modern lights belonged to the past, which remained an inexhaustible resource for the poet who sought to indulge heroic imaginings at safe distance, in that mix of admiration with patronage which typifies our first order of verse narrative. Victorian minds believed in the rising curve of progress—or believed they should so believe, which is what ideology means in practice—and therefore to look back on a prior stage of development, whether social or personal, was inevitably to look down on it too. Much of the appeal of early times was that they were simpler: primal in one aspect (innocent, authentic), primitive in another (barbarous, backward). Such was the ambivalence that drew narrative poets, not only to historical themes, but to settings remote in place: rural outlands within a national purview, colonial and imperial outposts within a global one. Such geographic dislocation made it possible to restage, in the historical present but a far-flung place, the same essential contrast that was afforded by the epic of distant retrospect. Neither William Allingham's *Laurence Bloomfield in Ireland* (1864) nor Alfred Domett's New Zealand epic *Ranolf and Amohia* (1872) was as hamfistedly jingoistic as other titles that will go unmentioned here, yet they all held a share in the metanarrative that melded progressivist modernity with the diffusion of civilization. In the associated campaign for minds and hearts, the heart went out to beautiful aboriginal losers, but that cordial impulse was trumped every time, as in Scott's poems and novels it had been, by the intellect's recognition that modernity depended on the cutting of just such losses. Being of two minds about simplicity was a part of outgrowing it, a rite of modern passage in which poetic narratives like these afforded practice.

Modernity's self-representation as cultural maturity fed directly into stories in verse for children, a subset of straight-ahead narrative in which the Victorian period excelled. Here childhood innocence served much the same function as did archaic or outlandish simplicity in the epics just considered, within a calculus that suited juvenile literature ideally for consumption by adults as well. As if to acknowledge this split audience, poets seized on plots involving a threshold experience, often set within something like a colonial contact zone, that brought the child protagonist up towards adulthood, and inducted the implied child reader likewise by proxy. Christina Rossetti's 'Goblin Market' (1862) is the locus classicus for this narrative dynamic, where through respectively transgressive and recuperative ordeals the two sisters have their fruit and eat it too; the dynamic may be even more drastically present in Browning's 'The Pied Piper of Hamelin' (1842), where the swindled Piper's seduction of an entire generation becomes narratable at all only by a crippled boy whom sole survivorship may now have lamed imaginatively into the bargain. A test case for this subgenre greets us in Macaulay's best-seller of 1842, *Lays of Ancient Rome*: a three-layered confection of tales in verse that are ostensibly englished from a classical Latin feint at celebrating Rome's Latian antecedents. Macaulay probably wrote them with grown-up readers in mind, but they were recruited into the juvenile section for the rest of the century, as if to prove how versatile the patronizing stance of Victorian condescension into indulged byways of make-believe could be.

Further along the continuum from brazen to pinchbeck narrative lie varieties of comic verse that retail some funny thing that happened on the way somewhere. 'Funny' can of course mean 'humorous' or 'bizarre', and it is remarkable how the funny stories Victorian poets found to tell are clustered near the bizarre end of the spectrum: take, for instance (please), Thomas Hood's 'Miss Kilmansegg and Her Precious Leg' (1840). The donnée of a golden limb tilts this kind of production so heavily in the direction of broad humour that subtlety of wit must assert its comic rights elsewhere—and precisely this is what the choice of a verse medium let Hood and others do, at the level of formal execution. Thus while Browning's 'Sibrandus Schafnaburgensis' (1845) tells a cute story about lobbing a boring tome into a hollow stump, this would be merely the 'garden fancy' he calls it were it not for a robust dividend of vigorously clever rhyming. The best known of Victorian comic rhymesters is W. S. Gilbert, and the principle of incongruity that comic rhyming localizes is writ large in the attitude his *Bab Ballads* (1868) take towards the ballad tradition his title alludes to. Of mock-epic on the Augustan scale, which had flared up again in Regency polemics and rocketed to greatness in Byron's last phase, the Victorian period produced nothing to speak of. But tongue-in-cheek balladry did much to supply the deficit, and it did so by contriving disparities between form and content that bear comparison with what lay at stake in mock-epic: namely, modern civilization and its discontents.

Even the strictly sober ballads that Elizabeth Barrett among other poetesses contributed to early Victorian gift-books were stiffened with gender resentments that now seem halfway down the road to the incisive ironies of *Aurora Leigh*. Their suppressed energies caught the ear of the young Tennyson, whose 'Ballad of Oriana' and ballad-based 'Mariana' (both 1830) stoked passion by inhibiting action, within poetic forms that ought to have made narrative progress but didn't; this is famously the case with 'The Lady of Shalott' (1832), whose balladic elaboration of confining rhymes underscores the protagonist's meagre budget of options for living out a love story that has been blighted in advance by a curse. The nightmarish quest of Browning's 'Childe Roland' (1855) takes him at last to a place where something at last might happen, but nothing, in the poem, actually does. The endurance of forbidden or balked desire forms as well the unprogressive plot typical of Pre-Raphaelite balladry. The terms 'refrain' and 'burden' seem cruel puns descriptive of a frustration that turns Dante Gabriel Rossetti's 'Sister Helen' (1854) back on itself in verbal as well as narrative terms; an opening like 'The blessed damozel leaned out / From the gold bar of Heaven' forecasts a story but proves, in Rossetti's dislocated portrayal, to be mere description of an inalterable state.[1] In 'The Ballad of Reading Gaol' (1898) Wilde tenders no grimmer irony than his choice of a genre that underscores its rendition of a dreary inferno without forward motion, life without parole.

By generic affiliation these ballads formed part of the era's ambivalent medievalism, which in turn participated in that Victorian historicism which on all sides bespoke the wholesale nineteenth-century revival of narrative itself. Where the Augustans had set classical epic grandeur in inconclusive stand-off against the tawdry triviality of contemporary life, for the Victorians it was balladry's medieval provenance and folk affinity that implied an ideal contrast to bourgeois manners, which triumphant capitalism was industriously spooling off into the separate spheres of the commercial and the domestic, the banal and the genteel. Gilbert's ballads, like the *Ingoldsby Legends* (1840) of R. H. Barham and the *Bon Gaultier Ballads* (1845) of W. E. Aytoun and Theodore Martin, played each side of this contest off the other. Incident parodied form in ways that were impossible to miss, and that were highlighted yet further by the habitual infusion of grotesquerie. All the while, however, the durable if tattered ballad forms spoke for a cultural heritage, conducted in accordance with rhythms and values contrary to those of industrial life, that the poets would not willingly let die. The result was not great poetry, but it made for good comedy, and like all good comedy it sprang more or less gaily painted from pervasive sources of malaise.

STORY EXPLODED: NONSENSE

Before Edward Lear taught it to the world, the limerick form had been around for a couple of decades, but it was *A Book of Nonsense* (1846) that put it on everybody's mind and earns it a place in this essay. For in Lear's hands the limerick is a relentlessly narrative device, albeit a perversely unproductive one. The standard 'There was a…' introduction could not look more like the opening of a story. But then the stories Lear starts go nowhere:

> There was an old man who screamed out
> Whenever they knocked him about;
> So they took off his boots, And fed him with fruits,
> And continued to knock him about.[2]

The sterile recycled rhyme of 'about' with itself enacts this limerick's failure to progress, in spite of the pains so consequentially taken ('So…And') with the old man's boots and fruits. Here is a kind of comic story—better take it that way, from the author of *Laughable Lyrics* (1877), than take the bait and chase after the red herring of sadistic violence, which also goes nowhere—but then what kind of comic story? A Bergsonian foregrounding of machinery over life, structure over sense, one that takes up the tendency that was already evident in mock-balladry from the 1840s and runs with it, around form's charmed circle, right back to where it started, in both the *a-a-b(-b)-a* rhyme and loose anapaestic 3-3-2(-2)-3 metre. It's not just that the story a limerick tells is trifling, but that Lear's entire practice is to trifle with story as such—and to trifle, thereby, with his century's deep investment in narrative understanding. The limerick is narrative, all right, but at the same time so ostentatiously nonprogressive that it has its laugh, lastly, at the expense of progressivism itself.

Poetry like this crosses a line that separates its game plan from the directness with which even Gilbert played at narrative. At bottom, the reader of a *Bon Gaultier* or *Bab* or even *Barrack-Room* ballad (Kipling, 1892) is enjoined to believe in the story it tells; there is a twinkle in the narrator's eye, but the eye stays on the ball. The show must go on, and the plot must fulfil itself conventionally in order for the parodic contrast to take effect. Not so Lear, whose purpose is to bankrupt the narrative system, and to show that in the end it is only form that abides. His great counterpart in the high arts of Victorian nonsense had a similarly subversive point to make:

> 'Twas brillig, and the slithy toves
>   Did gyre and gimble in the wabe:
> All mimsy were the borogoves,
>   And the mome raths outgrabe.[3]

Lewis Carroll's strategic objective in 'Jabberwocky' (1855) is one with Lear's: to expose the sense-making mechanism of narrative as the apparatus it is. The difference between Carroll's poetical ''Twas…' and Lear's flatfooted 'There was a…' corresponds, however, to a difference in tactics. In diction and syntax the limerick is by design plain, nay prosaic, so as to throw the burden of proof onto the abstract narrative formula of expectation and (non)fulfilment that bears the throwaway words along. Carroll too will end where he began: the quatrain quoted here is both the poem's first stanza and its last, so that the completion of the young swordsman's Jabberwock quest seems to have made no more difference than the old man's bootless diet of fruit in Lear. But to this Lear-like subversion of narrative's progressive destination Carroll adds subversion of the linguistic vehicle that gets narrative to its no place special. The arch locutions 'Did gyre' and 'All mimsy were…' express texturally a loftiness of aim that the rhetorically stilted lexicon of the poem as a whole sustains, and that it is Carroll's purpose to send up as all attitude, no substance.

Knock-down proof in support of Carroll's charge against narrative's vacant posturing lies in the semantic emptiness of the main words in his trademark stanza. After the initial postulate of ''Twas', the only words a candid reader of the lines can so much as recognize are connective prepositions, articles, conjunctions, plus that resonant adverbial intensifier of zero, 'All'. The verbs, nouns, and adjectives have nothing to tell except that those are the parts of speech they are. That a reader untutored by Humpty Dumpty may know this much with assurance from the syntax alone—may know even that 'outgrabe' is a strong past-tense form, probably of the inferred nonsense verb 'to outgribe'—is the focal point of Carroll's experiment. 'Jabberwocky' is an exposé, an investigative report on how, and how far, the vehicle of narrative can run on auto-pilot without real-world fuel. The execution of the Jabberwock illustrates the execution of a sheer programme, a story pattern that, because it is about next to nothing, might as well be about almost anything. What the framing stanza exposes about the mechanics of language, the whole poem exposes about the mechanics of narrative.

This is the job Lear does, just a little less deftly, in his verses about the Jumblies and the Dong with a luminous nose, whose tales we follow in spite of gross semantic roadblocks, and follow not only in the plot but in the plot's associated affects. Narratives groom the expectation they fulfil, a principle we may find obliquely acknowledged in a notorious choral syllepsis from 'The Hunting of the Snark': 'They pursued it with forks and hope'.[4] Carroll's demented pursuivants have both the right gear and the right stuff; for the attitudinal orientation that is reinforced by habituation to story-types is itself mightily formative, and adhesive, equipment for living. This is why stories should be both told and interrogated, and why for the latter service in Victorian times it was radical questioners of the status quo who volunteered most often. Witness the widely attested obscurity of Browning's *Sordello* (1840) or Morris's 'The Tune of Seven Towers' (1858): each is manifestly a narrative, both have long baffled readers, yet neither is classed—why not?—with nonsense verse.

Story Perspectivized: Monologue

Carroll's stunning coup against conventionality—his exposure of the robotic circuitry, and mindless stamina, of the unexamined mythic archetypes that underlie common sense—could not, by its nature, be repeated very often. Once you've got the point, a refresher course may be advisable now and then, but that is available through a fresh reading of 'Jabberwocky'. Full-monty exposure to yet another gutted plot peppered with yet another budget of nonsensical words seems beside the point: the 'Snark' and the 'Dong' soon take us to the limit of the rightly rare and wonderful sort of poem they are. And a dozen limericks go a long way. Much richer terrain for the poetic proving of narrative lay open to poets who cultivated different elements of the storyteller's art, such as narratorial perspective. Here was available a spectrum of possibilities as various as human psychology, and it was compounded, during a century that established the modern social sciences, by the myriad fractions of economic, political, ethnic, and credal difference whose impingement on character ordinary Victorians stood ready to concede in their own lives and to recognize in each other's. This dangerous edge of impingement was the breeding ground for that signal poetic innovation the dramatic monologue, as we now call it, though the poets did not; and indeed for our purposes we may as well put the term to one side and think of their great verse impersonations, for a change, as constituting a subset of narrative.

For the monologue emerges in hindsight as Victorian Britain's answer to the concurrent development of the short story in America and on the Continent. In each genre, as more broadly in the novel, the variable balance between character and conditioning is where the action is. The plot ordinarily consists of the mutual determination of subjective selves and objective circumstances (including other selves). Where a first-person standpoint is used, and in monologues by definition it always is, an additional wrinkle enters the picture with the soupçon, if not the wild-eyed reality, of narratorial unreliability. The device of the unreliable narrator is one that nineteenth-century verse monologues did much to establish. In the genre's more sophisticated instances the device remains legible as an artefact or deposit created within the psyche as a result, yet again, of specifically imagined outward conditions against which the narrator's symptomatic distortions attempt a defence. The heavy narratorial foregrounding that obscured *Sordello* and Tennyson's experiment in introversion 'The Lover's Tale' (1832?) suggests that narrative unreliability was the problem for which both poets went on to write monologues as the solution.

Admittedly, verse monologues do sometimes traffic in plot mysteries, and mystifications, of a more elementary kind; and these can upstage narratorial matters. It takes quite a while, when meeting Browning's 'The Bishop Orders His Tomb' (1845), to sort out even the big simple questions—who is speaking to whom, where, and when—before proceeding to the hermeneutic challenges of why. It was to obviate such trouble that Tennyson furnished introductory framing narratives in the third person for his early impersonations 'The Hesperides' (1830), 'Oenone', and 'The Lotos-Eaters' (both 1832); as late as 'Lucretius' (1868) he invoked it again lest the mental instability of his monologist induce too great a disorientation. Stories of social protest like Hood's 'Song of the Shirt' (1843) and Elizabeth Barrett Browning's 'Cry of the Children' (1844) likewise gave voice to the voiceless by ushering monologue in under the opening stanzas' chaperonage. Robert Browning preferred implication to explication in this as in all matters, gambling on the reader's capacity to infer the elements of story from the horse's mouth, the first-person discourse of the speaker. The insatiable curiosity felt by readers of 'My Last Duchess', or 'Count Gismond' (both 1842), as to what the Duke ultimately did to his late wife, or who had access when to the Countess's bed, demonstrates that these are not the best questions to ask about those poems. Yet pressing hard for an answer to these questions can be a way of posing better ones that lead closer to the perspectival nerve of the monologue genre. Why do the Duke and the Countess see themselves, and their world, as they do? What does a woman like Augusta Webster's 'Circe', or 'The Castaway', or 'The Happiest Girl in the World' (all 1870) want, and what has led her to frame her desire that way?

Considering Victorian monologues as narrative rather than dramatic texts should prompt us to answer questions like these in terms of the personal stories, and behind them the collective histories, that the texts imply. Suffice it here to note how a discrepancy opens between the story a speaker thinks s/he's in, and the story in which what the speaker discloses along the way, while telling that story, shows us s/he is more deeply entangled. With 'Circe', as with Webster's model Tennyson's 'Ulysses' (1842), the fuller story is intertextual: see the *Odyssey* and *Inferno* if you want to know what's really in the works. With the Italian Duke and the English Happiest Girl we encounter a more intricately elegant inside story. Each speaker is in possession of a cogent narrative dictating the place of man, woman, and desire within the institution of marriage—narratives distinct not just from each other, and from a reader's today probably, but also from what the poet shows each speaker dimly suspecting may be a truer narrative, one that arises from the unarticulated experience of the heart. Neither Browning's monologist nor Webster's can steer clear around the ideological story that is composed by the defining cultural and historical moment; but their intuition of an emergent alternative story, just beyond their capacity to think it in words, is both their most humanizing feature and their poems' most modernizing contribution to an understanding of history that is rooted, with the best nineteenth-century understandings, in processual change.

Not all strong Victorian monologues work this kind of interior narrative overlap. Amy Levy's 'Xantippe' (1881) stalks the masculine chauvinism of the Victorian academy so hard, under cover of the all-male monolithic Platonic academy it swore by, that there is nothing for us to know about her speaker's bitter intellectual frustration that straitened Xantippe doesn't know all too well already. History offers the cornered pagan speaker of Swinburne's 'Hymn to Proserpine' (1866) an exit from its oppressions, when on the occasion of Christianity's ascendancy in Rome he predicts its eventual doom by the same supersessive law that has swept it into power; but here as in 'Xantippe' the speaker's knowledge coincides with the reader's. These monologues and others imagined in a like rhetorical vein exemplify essentially testimonial narrative: etched in the spirit, and the service, of contemporary controversy, their portraiture is rather propagandistic than heuristic.

At the opposite extreme lies a species of monologue so deeply invested in the violation of norms as to be, like much in the study of abnormal psychology, actually norm-enforcing. Browning's homicidal narrator in 'Porphyria's Lover' (1836) is roughly reliable as to the circumstances of his tale—the whole poem evaporates on any other supposition—and yet the sympathetic reliance his opening lines have elicited blows up in our face the moment he improvises the sex-crime strangulation that his poem is really all about. The abhorrent recoil that Browning contrived with this strictly narrative prototype monologue detonates as sensationally as a bomb, but the chasm that thereafter sunders reader from speaker yawns too wide to permit the squirm or wiggle room on which the genre's more impressive narrative effects depend. The grim assessment of Romantic desire that Browning may have had in mind with this poem seems more successfully pursued through the unhurried gradualism of a diseased necrophiliac's self-accounting in 'The Leper' (1866) by Swinburne. Still, this story, like Browning's, resembles as much as anything a confession taken down in police custody, an effect that discourages the deputized reader from pursuing the study of perversion very far into the sponsoring medieval culture by which Swinburne's incident is framed. And yet, when police custody again provides the venue for Elizabeth Barrett Browning's infanticidal culprit in 'The Runaway Slave at Pilgrim's Point' (1848) and also for her husband's womanizing monk 'Fra Lippo Lippi' (1855), the opportunity for an enlarged and liberal understanding proves in each case ample. This is due, in the latter poem, to the way police arrest becomes a figure for less palpable mind-forged entrapments, all of which Lippo feels, but only some of which he can grasp. In the former, it is due to the very extremity of the speaker's literal enslavement within bonds of race and gender. This condition the speaker, for once in the history of the monologue genre, understands better than the reader, who is left with the stunned posse to ponder whether 'curse-free', at the bottom line, possesses greater moral shock-value as a malediction climactically hurled or as one mercifully withheld.

STORY SERIALIZED: SEQUENCE

Victorian poets, to resume our argument, kept time with a turbulent century by putting poetry and story back in each other's keeping. They deployed the consciousness-raising resources of verse as means of evaluating the pervasive cultural power that was wielded by narrative as a cognitive instrument. Unreconstructed epoists simply exploited that power (or died trying); so did parodists and writers for children, even though in doing so they also belittled and to that extent disowned it. This serious play reached an extreme when nonsense verse stripped plot down to the bare bones, showed it could live on nothing, and proposed that nothing might be all it was good for anyhow. With impersonative monologues, poets shifted attention from the narrative to the narratorial, there to patrol the thronged crossroads where the self met history. This was a junction ideologically fraught, since liberal individualism and transpersonal progressivism were as likely to thwart as abet one another; and Victorians' diligence to keep the traffic smoothly flowing emerges in the pains they took over yet another of story's primary dimensions: narrative continuity. One striking result was the sheer fluency of the poetic monologue, especially within the blank-verse format that, in Browning's hands, ballooned out into hundreds and even thousands of lines at a narrative stretch: 'Mr. Sludge' (1864) and the Balaustion poems (1871, 1875) are such prodigies of unstinting articulation that we marvel to think what phobic compulsion must be driving them on.

The cardinal manifestation, however, of the nineteenth century's anxiety over continuity was its proliferation of serial forms. Seriality is everywhere in Victorian literature, from the phenomenal explosion of the periodical press, through the part-issue of novels subdivided into time-released instalments, down to the period's fondness for stanza-staggered verse. It is among the poets that this proclivity for the express segmentation of narrative intake appears with utmost sharpness. Not only do the number-ticketed quanta comprised by *In Memoriam* (1850) and *The House of Life* (1870) regularly obtrude on a reader's notice, but they serve to focus the distinctive sort of plottedness to which an ordinal poetic sequence lays claim. Lyrically atomized in themselves, the constituent portions engross attention within an interlude which the work's larger design treats as momentary, and from whose tranceful suspense the narrative thrust of the sequence must be again and again reactivated. This iterated pattern of interruption and resumption, which is integral to the design of these and many other instances of serial narrative poetry, in effect trained readers to collaborate in the production of continuity: a survival skill seemingly indispensable to nineteenth-century bourgeois sanity. The cultural importance of this practice explains why, although Victorian poets did not invent the idea of stringing lyrics along a narrative thread, they seized on Renaissance sequence poetry so eagerly as a model and permuted it so inventively.

Sonnet sequences were the most patent of such derivatives. Elizabeth Barrett Browning's *Sonnets from the Portuguese* (1850) pioneered a Victorian mode with its slow but sure plot of erotic acceptance and spiritual uplift. Two decades later love's Victorian climax was regained, then excruciatingly relinquished, by Dante Gabriel Rossetti in *The House of Life*; and from this devastation his sister Christina went on, with the desperate serenity of 'Monna Innominata' (1881), to mount an a priori argument for love's human unsustainability. All three sequences are cardiogram printouts of the heart's events, which George Eliot's sonnets in 'Brother and Sister' (1874), and Webster's in 'Mother and Daughter' (1895), show beating for Victorians as poignantly with familial as with sexual affection. That George Meredith expanded the tale-bearing platform for *Modern Love* (1862) from fourteen lines to a quatrain-accommodating sixteen has kept no one from regarding that poem of marital disaster as a sonnet sequence squarely true to type.

But that type is only the most conspicuous within a category of serialized lyrics much larger than can be enumerated here. Tennyson's *In Memoriam* and *Maud* (1855) occupy a class by themselves for sheer visibility, and also perhaps for the subtlety with which they worry the question of their own continuity. But their congeners are legion, among them Arnold's 'Switzerland' (1852), Clough's *Amours de Voyage* (1858), Patmore's *The Angel in the House* (1862), and Browning's 'James Lee's Wife' (1864). All these works use forms other than the sonnet; nearly all incorporate a variety of metrical and stanzaic modes; and every one of them, like every sonnet sequence just mentioned, directly concerns the making and breaking of contact between lovers. This remarkable consistency of topic tempts one to claim that the Victorian lyric sequence embraced interpersonal connectedness as its theme because structural connectedness was its prescribed principle; and, in addition, that the structural challenge was the more exigent of the two. Lovers might win or lose, and more often than not they lost. Yet even where a tale came to catastrophic grief, it paid a formal bonus: the question of continuity that impended over Victorian life was favourably resolved by a tale's being brought to term, despite the gaps and obstacles that serial form placed in the way.

Discontinuity overcome: such was the watchword of sequential verse narrative, and it obtained all the way from the sonneteer's scanty plot of love into the higher order of magnitude where Victorians designed new prototypes of the epic. Tennyson starts *The Princess* (1847), as Browning does *The Ring and the Book*, by discussing explicitly what sort of continuity the poem aspires to and how the author has compassed it. *The Earthly*

Paradise (1868–70), for all its casual languor of presentation, stakes Morris's bet that an artful arrangement of many tales by many tellers will give structural support to a togetherness radically broader than Chaucer's had been, embracing now all Europe and not just England. Where Morris's epic and Browning's both appeared serially over months, *Idylls of the King* was published in instalments over as many years: the gradual emergence of Tennyson's epic across half a century (1833–1885 from first manuscript to twelfth idyll) gives unbeatable evidence of the era's patient craving for the fruits of slow-ripening time.

In this magnum opus, as in shorter poetic sequences, theme followed format. The rise and decline of Camelot hangs, like the poem's gestation over decades, on the question of unity: in epic statecraft as in sonnet courtship, getting it all together is a value that outlives the dashing of King Arthur's dreams as man of state and married man alike. The sovereign's task and the laureate's ultimately addressed the same Victorian problematic, which was how to rescue order from change under the sign of progressive continuity. The governing melancholy shared by poet and hero is symptomatic of the same ambivalence we have seen quickening the best narrative verse of the century. It was only poetic mediocrities, at the end of the day, who could endure to surf progressivism's rising tide without a grimace. One such was Tennyson's friend F. T. Palgrave, whose anthology *The Golden Treasury* (1861) had so effectually boosted the English lyrical tradition, and who went on to publish in *The Visions of England* (1881) a lyrical sequence of his own composition whose unifying through-line inhered in the foregone conclusion of his nation's ascent to world dominion. The complacency of Palgrave's facile chauvinist exercise shows how effortlessly full-blown imperial progressivism lent itself to a kind of ideological automatic writing, a slumbrous crooning at the narrative switch of cultural power.

Story Imploded: Lyric

A longer account of how the field of poetry lay open at the fin de siècle to Palgrave's brand of lyric sequencing would lead back to the dissociation of poetry from narrative with which this essay began. Victorian serial poetry had harboured from the first a possibility that its thread of continuity might be slit, its constituents spilled from the envelope of major narrative into the free-floating suggestiveness of vignette. Verse anecdotes about what just happened to happen had been attracting Victorian poets at least since Tennyson wrote 'Sir Lancelot and Queen Guinevere' (1842) and 'The Eagle' (1851). Each was subtitled 'A Fragment', and their intensity of appeal arises, as in Browning's zestful 1845 'Meeting at Night' and 'How They Brought the Good News', from their comparative narrative disconnection, their status as episodes unbeholden to epic. Abandoned or absorbed into the moment, these vagrant lyrics, like their obsessed speakers, deem the world well lost for that moment's passionate sake. Where the poems just mentioned were truants from their authors' still traditionally narrative regime, in the next generation Victorian poetry crested a lyric watershed when Morris filled his remarkable debut volume *The Defence of Guenevere* (1858) with poems typically taken not *from* history but clean *out of* it: incidents rough at the edges, which bristle with verisimilitude yet are extravagantly unrelated to each other or to any master narrative.

'The Haystack in the Floods' and 'Concerning Geffray Teste Noire' look from a distance like an epyllion and a ballad, respectively. But the closer we get, the less either poem has to do with narration as usual: the former's splendid tactical violence stands out the more shockingly for its disconnection from strategic motives and results; the latter's free-association transitivity throws into stronger relief an old man's memories that emerge the more vividly for their being inconsequential. These poems draw on none of the generalizing power that made of William Barnes' 'The Turnstile' (also 1858) a lucid, archetypal parable of familial grief at a child's death; nor are they didactic fables, of a kind whose potential for sophistication would appear in Barrett Browning's 'A Musical Instrument' (1862) and Meredith's 'Lucifer in Starlight' (1883), each of which carves from a classic narrative a modern parable of creative anomie. What Morris was up to is more nearly matched, indeed all but explicated, in Dante Gabriel Rossetti's 'The Woodspurge' (1870), which wears the shape of narrative but tells the story of, precisely, meaning's failure to emerge from events:

> From perfect grief there need not be
> Wisdom or even memory:
> One thing then learnt remains to me,—
> The woodspurge has a cup of three.[5]

Declining his own flirtatious gambit with the Trinitarian symbolism of 'three cups in one', Rossetti's speaker declines not only narrative's offer of meaning but even memory's offer of continuity. Here is neither antecedence nor succession, beyond the graven print of unaccommodated fact on life's tabula rasa. Narrative stringency on this Pre-Raphaelite order meets its apotheosis, if not its redemption, in Gerard Manley Hopkins, whose sonnets remain fiercely unsequenced and who aspired to convert chance happening to radiant epiphany. *The Wreck of the Deutschland* (1876) and flight of 'The Windhover' (1877) were narratable events; but all the effort of this poet's inspired reportage was to make events declare themselves not historically but sacramentally: to redeem the very significations Morris and Rossetti regarded as lost, yet still like them to situate phenomena in an order of meaning perpendicular to that of secular continuity.

An understated example drawn from a poet less dazzling than Hopkins will suggest, in closing, how the new ascendancy of lyrical anecdote slackened the sinews of nineteenth-century narrative in verse:

> The lake lay blue below the hill.
>   O'er it, as I looked, there flew
> Across the waters, cold and still,
>   A bird whose wings were palest blue.
>
> The sky above was blue at last,
>   The sky beneath me blue in blue.
> A moment, ere the bird had passed,
>   It caught his image as he flew.[6]

In 'L'Oiseau Bleu' (publ. 1908), nineties poet Mary E. Coleridge was practising the minimalist narrative of imagism avant la lettre, bending story back on itself in anticipation of the modernist spatial form towards which her painterly French title gestures. There's a plot here, just enough to let the poem glance before and after its one agent's one act. The cool wisp of a narratorial 'I' seems superfluous until we notice that the situation s/he occupies—the potentially limiting vantage that might define a persona, and so introduce some High Victorian irony—is as free and airy as the bird's, with blue sky not only above but beneath. The sky's reflection in the lake water, mimed aurally by the echoic 'blue in blue', feels foretold from the outset by the inlaid repetition of sounds, 'lake' clipping 'lay' and 'blue below' in line 1, the two word pairs converging in line 2 on the key word 'looked' and emerging again with a difference in 'flew'. Redundancy is in the air, the speaker's place doubling the bird's, the 'image' the bird makes in the lake tallying with the one left in the poem.

As the last line hovers between snapshot and filmclip, between the bird 'caught' in a phrase and the bird let fly in a passage, we confront poetry that has ingested its ostensibly narrative occasion. 'L'Oiseau Bleu' no longer tells a story, because it has become one. An act discovered in the world is embedded within the story of its discovery, what Wallace Stevens would call half a century later 'The poem of the mind in the act of finding / What will suffice'.[7] That 'act of finding' is already for Coleridge a nineteenth-century deed sufficient unto itself; its narrative *heuristic* is rooted etymologically, with *history* and thus with this essay's category of *story*, in the Greek verb *heuriskein* ('to find'). The past tense of that verb—*eureka*—epitomizes the story of modern poetry to which Victorian story-poems belong.

NOTES

1. Dante Gabriel Rossetti, 'The Blessed Damozel', in *The New Oxford Book of Victorian Verse*, ed. Christopher Ricks (Oxford and New York: Oxford University Press, 1987), 269.
2. Edward Lear, *Victorian Verse*, 217.
3. Lewis Carroll, 'Jabberwocky', in *Victorian Verse*, 190.
4. Carroll, 'The Hunting of the Snark', in *Victorian Verse*, 204.
5. Rossetti, 'The Woodspurge', in *Victorian Verse*, 275.
6. Mary E. Coleridge, 'L'Oiseau Bleu', in *The Penguin Book of Victorian Verse*, ed. Daniel Karlin (Harmondsworth: Penguin, 1997), 731.
7. Wallace Stevens, 'Of Modern Poetry', in *Collected Poems* (New York: Knopf, 1954), 239.

SELECT BIBLIOGRAPHY

Brooks, Peter, *Reading for the Plot: Design and Intention in Narrative* (Oxford: Clarendon Press, 1984).
Curran, Stuart, *Poetic Form and British Romanticism* (New York: Oxford University Press, 1986).
Dentith, Simon, *Epic and Empire in Nineteenth-Century Britain* (Cambridge: Cambridge University Press, 2006).

Edmond, Rod, *Affairs of the Hearth: Victorian Poetry and Domestic Narrative* (London and New York: Routledge, 1988).

Hughes, Linda K., and Michael Lund, *The Victorian Serial* (Charlottesville and London: University of Virginia Press, 1991).

Kroeber, Karl, *Romantic Narrative Art* (Madison: University of Wisconsin Press, 1960).

Markovits, Stefanie, *The Crisis of Action in Nineteenth-Century English Literature* (Columbus: Ohio State University Press, 2006).

Morgan, Monique R., *Narrative Means, Lyric Ends: Temporality in the Nineteenth-Century British Long Poem* (Columbus: Ohio State University Press, 2009).

PART II

LITERARY LANDSCAPES

CHAPTER 9

....

VICTORIAN POETRY AND THE CLASSICS

....

ISOBEL HURST

IN 'Development' (1889), Robert Browning traces an evolving engagement with Homer from childhood games based on stories of the Trojan war to the discovery of the Greek text. As in Keats's sonnet 'On First Looking into Chapman's Homer' (1816), discovering the Homeric poems is a joyful experience. The enjoyment of classical learning that this poem displays contrasts with the dull routines of formal education: repetitive study of a few key texts, endless grammatical and syntactic analysis, and prose and verse composition in Latin and Greek.[1] Browning learns through play to understand 'who was who and what was what', a method justified by his enduring pleasure in the poem:

> So far I rightly understood the case
> At five years old: a huge delight it proved
> And still proves—thanks to that instructor sage
> My Father, who knew better than turn straight
> Learning's full flare on weak-eyed ignorance.[2]

As he learns and relearns Homer, he explores new aspects of narrative, language, history and critical reception. The poem might be taken to exemplify different stages of the Victorian reception of Homer outside schools and universities. The increasing availability of translations encouraged the dissemination of classical epic and tragedy in literary and popular culture in a variety of forms, including theatrical burlesques, cartoons, and children's books, as well as more serious poems, paintings, and dramatic performances. For Browning's generation, reading Pope's translation of Homer was an enthralling experience: enthusiastic responses to this text by Tennyson, Ruskin, John Stuart Mill, and Elizabeth Barrett Browning contrast with Romantic poets' distaste for Pope (with the notable exception of Byron). Some youthful poets were inspired to emulate the stately heroic couplets: Tennyson, at 10 or 11, wrote 'hundreds and hundreds of lines in the regular Popeian metre', even claiming that he could, like an epic bard, 'improvise them'.[3] Barrett Browning later described her short epic, *The Battle of Marathon* (written when she was 14) as 'Pope's Homer done over again... or rather *undone*'.[4] Going on to read Homer in Greek was an experience mainly restricted to a privileged class of gentlemen and a few exceptional women, but it was one to which aspiring poets considered it worthwhile to devote 'year after year of studious life'.[5]

Having read the Greek text, Browning assumes that 'nothing more remains to know', a certainty that is undercut by the foreshadowing of his encounter with F. A. Wolf's *Prolegomena ad Homerum* (1795). This work is popularly identified as the source of the controversial 'Homeric Question': were the *Iliad* and *Odyssey* composed by a single poet, or were they compilations that evolved through generations of bards who recited and reshaped traditional narratives? Given the status of the Homeric poems as secular scriptures, the challenge to the authorship of the poems was not just an academic controversy. In *Aurora Leigh* (1857), Elizabeth Barrett Browning calls Wolf an 'atheist' and finds the idea that the *Iliad* is merely a 'fortuitous concourse of old songs' as unsettling as the notion that 'the universe' could have been created by chance (V. 1254–7).[6] 'Development' similarly invokes a faith that outweighs the mere 'knowledge' that there is no evidence of Homer's existence, 'no authentic text', but only a 'fiction'. Attempts to prove the historicity of the epics by means of archaeological and philological research proved disappointing for readers whose emotional attachment to the Homeric poems had developed early and persisted through numerous rereadings.[7] At the end of the poem, Browning questions whether his belief in the historical reality of the Homeric world was necessary for his development. He wonders whether he could have absorbed ethical lessons from a poem he had always known to be a fiction:

> My aim should be to loathe, like Peleus' son,
> A lie as Hell's Gate, love my wedded wife,
> Like Hector, and so on with all the rest.
> Could not I have excogitated this
> Without believing such men really were?

The idea that readers ought to model themselves on the heroes of ancient epic was not an eccentric digression from conventional thinking, although the trite messages that this immature reader derives from the text may suggest some scepticism about the use of classical literature and history for didactic purposes in the Victorian period.

Matthew Arnold spoke in his inaugural lecture as Professor of Poetry at Oxford (later published as 'On the Modern Element in Literature') of the literature of ancient Greece as 'a mighty agent of intellectual deliverance', offering solutions to the problems of contemporary life.[8] Outsiders were not convinced of the value of such cultural models: in Elizabeth Gaskell's *North and South* (1855), the industrialist Thornton is unimpressed by the argument that the 'heroic simplicity of the Homeric life' might be inspirational for a struggling worker, arguing that he has only returned to reading Homer in a time of prosperity because it is a luxury he can afford.[9] The future Prime Minister, Gladstone, attempted to apply principles from Homer to the problems of his own age. His three-volume *Studies in Homer and the Homeric Age* (1858) pointed out what he considered to be the absence of prostitution, homosexuality, and divorce in the Homeric poems. As Frank M. Turner observes, this is a 'domesticated Hellenism...unwilling to confront the full moral implications of Homer's epics'.[10] The Greek qualities Arnold wanted Victorian poets to emulate are 'the calm, the cheerfulness, the disinterested objectivity' he associates with the *Iliad* and Athenian tragedy.[11] In order to support his idea of a calm, serene, balanced culture, Arnold's readings of Greek literature are selective. In 'To A Friend' (1848), his mental props in a time of crisis include Homer and the 'even-balanced' Sophocles who 'saw life steadily and saw it whole / The mellow glory of the Attic stage'.[12] The equanimity he attributes to Sophocles here is not the most obvious characteristic of dramas such as *Antigone* and *Oedipus the King*: when Sophocles reappears in 'Dover Beach' (1867) he is more convincing as a tragedian sensitive to 'the turbid ebb and flow / Of human misery'.[13]

The exemplary Homer praised by Gladstone and Arnold is undermined by poems such as Tennyson's 'Ulysses' and 'The Lotos-Eaters', in which melancholy and pathos erode the manly virtues that Homer was supposed to be teaching. This is partly a question of the choice of source text: the tragic resonances, grand style, and noble qualities of the *Iliad* attracted readers like Arnold, whose contentious lectures 'On Translating Homer' demonstrate the importance of shaping readers' ideas about 'the most important poetical monument existing'.[14] The *Iliad* was not simply a source of models of manly virtue: there was some scope for pathos and reflections on the cost of war, as translations of passages such as Hector's farewell to Andromache (by Arnold and Barrett Browning, among others) suggest. The *Odyssey* had a complex structure, powerful and intelligent female characters such as Penelope and Circe, and details of hospitality and domestic life, as well as more fantastic elements such as adventure, magic, and monsters, which rendered the poem attractive to novel readers. Anthony Trollope suggested that both poems were ideal for newcomers to the classical tradition, 'very pleasant reading;—as good as a novel we might say...were it not that they are very much better than most novels'.[15]

Epic, the genre described by Herbert F. Tucker as 'the last rite of passage to full poetic majority, the summative test of art', continued to occupy the thoughts of ambitious and educated Victorian poets.[16] The most memorable responses to the epic tradition often represent an oblique approach to the genre, a recognition that it was hard to conceive of a traditional epic in the nineteenth century. Even Tennyson's Arthurian *Idylls of the King*, as Norman Vance observes, form 'a series of pictures rather than a full-scale epic, almost as if the steady heroism and sustained purpose of epic narrative were no longer possible in troubled and fragmented times'.[17] Byron's infusion of energy into the epic tradition by means of the generic hybridity of Romantic poetry inspired Barrett Browning's *Aurora Leigh* and Clough's *The Bothie of Toper-na-Fuosich: A Long Vacation Pastoral* (1848), which combine elements of epic form with contemporary settings and novelistic preoccupations. William Morris's epic experiments reflect a Pre-Raphaelite fascination with the past: he juxtaposes Greek myth, mediaevalism and the poetry of Chaucer, and Old Norse sagas in *The Earthly Paradise* (1868–70), a poem that was very popular at the time of its publication. Like Ovid's *Metamorphoses*, *The Earthly Paradise* could be said to be an epic made up of mythological episodes, but Morris's poem is extraordinarily long even for an epic—at over forty thousand lines, longer than the *Iliad*, the *Odyssey*, and the *Metamorphoses* put together. It would have been even more unwieldy had Morris not taken out and published separately his seventeen-book poem *The Life and Death of Jason* (1867). Morris follows Jason's adventures as told in an influential post-Homeric epic, the four-book *Argonautica* by Apollonius of Rhodes, in which the hero's journey is complicated with digressions and romantic distractions. He also translated *The Aeneids of Virgil* (1875) and *The Odyssey of Homer* (1887), making his contribution to the late-Victorian reception of ancient epic a substantial one.

Tennyson recognized early in his career that the way for a poet to make his mark might be 'by shortness, for the men before me had been so diffuse, and most of the big things…had been done'.[18] Features such as epic formulae or extended similes could be adapted for use in 'episodes' such as Matthew Arnold's 'Sohrab and Rustum' and 'Balder Dead': Herbert F. Tucker describes these poems as belonging to a 'classic-torso subgenre' that allows the poet to place an epic idea before the public, and to demonstrate the viability of the epic manner.[19] The episode, a self-contained poem that could be an extract from a work of epic length, resembles the Romantic fragment, which Anne Janowitz has described as 'a *partial whole*—either a remnant of something once complete…or the beginning of something that remains unaccomplished'.[20] The dramatic monologue enabled Tennyson to select an unexpected point of entry to a well-known story, just as epic poets like Homer did, and to explore the psychology of an individual character in a way that Homeric epic does not attempt. Less than seventy lines long, Tennyson's 'Ulysses' (1842) is considerably shorter than even a single book of the *Iliad* or *Odyssey*, but its aged and discontented hero is a significant presence in the history of Homeric receptions. Tennyson does not represent any of Ulysses' heroic exploits but shows him, after the return to Ithaca, frustrated and longing to set out on a new voyage. Ulysses retains his gift for persuasive oratory and vivid storytelling. The terms in which he urges his men to return for one last adventure are all the more stirring for their acknowledgment of the passage of time:

> We are not now that strength which in old days
> Moved earth and heaven; that which we are, we are;
> One equal temper of heroic hearts,
> Made weak by time and fate, but strong in will
> To strive, to seek, to find, and not to yield.[21]

To begin an epic was to embark on a great voyage, a metaphor Tennyson would have found in another familiar classical text. In *Odes* 1.3, Horace's prayer to the ship for Virgil's safe passage to the Homeric territory of Greece develops into a warning to the poet who is contemplating the creation of his *Aeneid*.[22] Horace stresses the audacity of those who travel by sea, comparing them with such renowned overreachers as Prometheus, Daedalus, and Hercules. By taking on the character of an epic hero, however briefly, Tennyson was declaring himself a major poet. His ambitious reworkings of classical materials, A. A. Markley suggests, 'contributed to a lifelong project of attempting to provide modern Britain with a new achievement in literature—a literature comparable to the great works of antiquity'.[23] 'Ulysses' renders the speaker's epic aspirations questionable: his heroic craving for adventure, exploration, and camaraderie is undercut by his appearance as a lonely, static figure whose projected voyage may never come to pass. Despite his rhetorical skill, there is, as Christopher Ricks suggests, a 'dragging sense of inertia, of *ennui*, played against the vocabulary of adventure and enterprise'.[24] The poem's jaded speaker ominously resembles Dante's Ulisse in his contempt for his home and his restless desire to sail beyond the limits of the world (a boundary-crossing ambition that precipitates him straight into Dante's hell):

> 'Tis not too late to seek a newer world.
> Push off, and sitting well in order smite
> The sounding furrows; for my purpose holds
> To sail beyond the sunset, and the baths
> Of all the western stars, until I die.

Ulysses addresses his fellow mariners, yet in the *Odyssey* his companions are all lost and Odysseus is the only one to reach Ithaca. He speaks of finding Achilles, who is already in the underworld and rethinking the heroic ideology that led him to prefer a glorious death in battle to a long and peaceful existence at home.

Far from the time and place by which he chooses to define his life, the battle on 'the ringing plains of windy Troy' in which the Greeks were victorious, Ulysses himself has finally reached home. His disparaging adjectives—'still', 'barren', 'savage'—reveal how little his power over the remote island and its people can satisfy him. Ithaca turns out to be just another digression, one of the series of islands on which Odysseus is forced to delay—and this time his companion is not the beguiling Calypso or Circe but the 'agèd' Penelope. There is a melancholy awareness that death is not far off. Despite the poem's emphasis on 'civic lessons' from a hero fascinated by 'men / And manners, climates, councils, governments', Ulysses wants to withdraw from his responsibilities: he is eager to hand over his authority to a dutiful son he seems to consider rather dull.[25] Tennyson's statement that 'Ulysses' gave his feeling about 'the need for going forward, and braving the struggle of life' suggests a kind of didacticism that the hero's melancholy self-indulgence questions and complicates.[26]

'Ulysses' was written in response to the death of Tennyson's friend Arthur Hallam (as were the first versions of its pendant monologues 'Tithonus' and 'Tiresias'). If 'Ulysses' represents 'the need for going forward, and braving the struggle of life', 'Tithonus' portrays an intense longing for death. The goddess of the Dawn, Eos (or Aurora) asks Zeus to grant her lover Tithonus eternal life, but does not think to ask for eternal youth. His life with the goddess is glorious until he grows old, when his weakness and dependence increases, while she remains the same. To be different from ordinary men, to 'pass beyond the goal', is characteristic of heroes like Ulysses, but Tithonus laments that he ever tried to evade the condition of mortality that connects man with nature:

> The woods decay, the woods decay and fall,
> The vapours weep their burthen to the ground,
> Man comes and tills the field and lies beneath,
> And after many a summer dies the swan.
> Me only cruel immortality
> Consumes; I wither slowly in thine arms,
> Here at the quiet limit of the world…
>   Let me go: take back thy gift:
> Why should a man desire in any way
> To vary from the kindly race of men,
> Or pass beyond the goal of ordinance
> Where all should pause, as is most meet for all?[27]

The immortality that Tithonus once craved and now sees as a burden may be a reflection on the desire for fame that lasts longer than a single lifespan. For the epic hero, this fame (*kleos*) is won by heroic deeds and is perpetuated in the songs of bards, but for warriors like Achilles it comes at the cost of a shortened life. For the poet, lasting fame confirms that he is set apart, more than an ordinary human but not quite divine. In *Odes* 3.1, Horace writes that the poet, the priest of the Muses, hates and keeps his distance from the uninitiated crowd. In Matthew Arnold's 'The Strayed Reveller' (1849), the 'wise bards' see all that the gods do, but also suffer acutely because they share the experiences they observe:

> They see the Centaurs
> On Pelion; then they feel,
> They too, the maddening wine
> Swell their large veins to bursting; in wild pain
> They feel the biting spears
> Of the grim Lapithae, and Theseus, drive,
> Drive crashing through their bones;
>   …such a price
> The Gods exact for song:
> To become what we sing.[28]

The Youth who speaks these words is himself a poet, but one who does not suffer for his art. He is like the lotos-eaters: he describes to Ulysses the contrast between the 'labour' of the subjective poet and his own intoxicated and painless visions. The bards are more like the 'true' poets described by Arthur Hallam, 'whose senses told them a richer and ampler tale than most men could understand, and who constantly expressed, because they constantly felt, sentiments of exquisite pleasure and pain, which most men were not permitted to experience'.[29]

As a poet and the beloved friend of a poet, Hallam was a fitting subject for the tradition of pastoral elegies such as the 'Lament for Bion' traditionally attributed to Moschus (influenced by Bion's 'Lament for Adonis', which Elizabeth Barrett Browning translated) and Milton's 'Lycidas'. The most recent of these elegies was Shelley's 'Adonais: An Elegy on the Death of John Keats, Author of *Endymion, Hyperion* etc.' (1821). Hallam had obtained a copy of 'Adonais' while travelling in Italy and arranged for its publication in England only a few years before his own death. Tennyson gradually constructed and revised the long sequence of elegies that make up *In Memoriam* (1850) over a period of 17 years, creating a poem that explores a longer mourning period (3 years) than earlier examples of the genre. Peter M. Sacks suggests that *In Memoriam* and 'Thyrsis', Matthew Arnold's elegy for Clough, differ from previous pastoral elegies because of their 'highly personalized sense of identity' and 'the Victorian elegist's almost novelistic fidelity to the empirical details of his own experience'.[30] Both Arnold and Tennyson draw attention to the incongruity of Arcadian or Sicilian pastoral conventions against an English background. *In Memoriam* also draws on another elegiac tradition, that of love poems by Latin authors such as Catullus, Propertius, Tibullus, and Ovid.[31] Elegists frequently complain about a distant and sometimes cruel mistress, and use forms such as the *paraclausithyron*, the poem addressed to the closed door of the beloved's house by the poet who languishes outside. Tennyson alludes to this lyric subgenre in poem 7 of *In Memoriam* (and again in poem 119):

> Dark house, by which I once more stand
>> Here in the long unlovely street,
>> Doors, where my heart was used to beat
> So quickly, waiting for a hand,
>
> A hand that can be clasp'd no more [32]

Poems 9–17 are a series of lyrics that echo the conventions of the *propemptikon*, an address to someone who is setting out on a voyage, or to the ship that carries him. The poem in which Horace entreats Virgil's ship to bring him back safely (*Odes* 1.3) is a notable example. Tennyson urges the 'Fair ship' that is carrying Hallam's body home for burial to take care of 'thy dark freight, a vanished life'. Men who had studied the classics at school and university, like Tennyson and Hallam, would easily recall lines from Horace's *Odes*, an apt source for poetry about masculine friendship and conviviality. Tennyson's 'To the Rev. F. D. Maurice', an invitation poem, is a light-hearted example of Horatian allusion, a poem that can accommodate private and public concerns in a genre that lies between the private, dissident world of elegy and the public world of epic.[33] The question of whether it is permissible to withdraw from the world into a solitary contemplation of beauty (or pain), or whether the poet has a duty to participate in society, is one that Horace shares with his Victorian interpreters.

In 'The Lotos-Eaters', another of Tennyson's Homeric poems, which appeared in revised form in 1842 after its initial publication in 1832, Ulysses' selfish reservations about life on Ithaca are anticipated by his companions on the return from Troy. Odysseus exhorts his men onward only in the first two lines of the poem, after which he is silenced by the overwhelmingly lethargic atmosphere of the island of the lotos-eaters; the lack of a closing narrative frame leaves it uncertain whether he will be able to drag the mariners back to his ship, as he does in the *Odyssey*.[34] The 'mild-eyed melancholy

Lotos-eaters' offer the mariners the narcotic fruit that distorts their senses and makes the external world seem far away. They exist in a waking dream and are too exhausted by the prospect of action to set sail again for Ithaca:

> Most weary seemed the sea, weary the oar,
> Weary the wandering fields of barren foam.
> Then some one said, 'We will return no more;'
> And all at once they sang, 'Our island home
> Is far beyond the wave; we will no longer roam.'[35]

As John Wilson Croker comments in his review of *Poems* (1832), they remain absorbed in indolent and solipsistic pleasures: 'Tennyson—himself, we presume, a dreamy lotos-eater, a delicious lotos-eater—leaves them in full song.'[36] Here poetry is connected with escapism, with a retreat from the world into an aesthetically and sensually pleasing environment depicted with a luxuriance reminiscent of the poetry of Keats. This is an appealing but morally questionable direction for a Victorian poet: Isobel Armstrong describes 'The Lotos-Eaters' as 'at once the culminating expression of the poetry of sensation and its greatest critique'.[37]

The description of the island with a languid climate of permanent afternoon focuses on a waterfall, a 'slender stream' that recalls one of the aesthetic prescriptions of the Hellenistic poet Callimachus. Acknowledging the pre-eminence of Homer to such an extent that he counselled future poets to create new forms rather than writing pseudo-Homeric epics, Callimachus writes in the prologue to the epyllion *Aetia* that Apollo told him to fatten up his flocks but keep his muse slender. This maxim is translated into Latin in Virgil's sixth Eclogue (a poem that Tennyson highlights in 'To Virgil'), and invoked by Ovid in the opening of his *Metamorphoses* in his claim that the poem will be an elegantly slender thread drawn out to epic length. The Callimachean epyllion (a fragment of epic narrative with an old story told in a new setting), and pastoral forms such as the Virgilian eclogue and the Theocritean idyll are sophisticated and learned shorter forms of poetry that Tennyson adopts as models for his reworkings of classical material. They are associated with love rather than war, with leisure rather than labour, with digressions rather than strictly linear narratives, and with metaliterary reflections on the art of poetry. These qualities suggest a greater affinity with the *Odyssey*, the Homeric precursor of the romance, than with the *Iliad*.

The choric song marks Tennyson's departure from the immediate Homeric source, but is in keeping with the *Odyssey*'s fascination with the power of song, such as the dangerously seductive music of the Sirens.[38] Despite the lotos-eating mariners' refusal to leave their tranquil retreat, their excuses for inaction reveal that some of their concerns about the Odyssean mission of *nostos* (the return home) are valid. Although they pay tribute to the remembered joys of married life, the singers anticipate the difficulties of returning to Ithaca: their sons are ready to inherit their estates and long-absent fathers would 'come like ghosts to trouble joy'. This is a recurring theme in the *Odyssey*: there are frequent reminders that Agamemnon returned home and was killed by his wife's lover, and that his son Orestes inherited only an obligation to avenge his father. The fear that 'the island princes over-bold' are consuming Ithaca's wealth is one that the *Odyssey* shows to be realistic, as is the idea that the 'great deeds' of the Trojan war have already been rehearsed in song by the court bards. However, the mariners' suspicion that they are already 'half-forgotten' is either excessively pessimistic or merely a convenient excuse.

The final section of the 1842 poem emphasizes the selfishness of the mariners. Their emotional detachment, achieved by lotos-eating, enables them to behave like the gods who, remote from humanity, amuse themselves by singing 'a lamentation and an ancient tale of wrong' while 'an ill-used race of men' suffers in war and labours in times of peace to produce the offerings that the gods expect to receive. The lotos-eaters' image of carefree, callous deities resembles the 'happy' gods in Matthew Arnold's 'The Strayed Reveller', who see everything but do not feel pain. Powerful but not necessarily benevolent, the Olympian gods could be criticized in a way that enabled poets to attack Christianity.[39] In Swinburne's *Atalanta in Calydon* (1865), the chorus sings about the gods' lack of care for humans and wishes that they could be forced to feel mortal pain and grief. Hostility towards the gods is then narrowed to focus on one powerful deity (referred to as 'God' not 'Zeus') and describes him with distinctly Old Testament language:

> The lord of love and loathing and of strife
>   Who gives a star and takes a sun away . . .
> Who makes desire, and slays desire with shame;
>   Who shakes the heaven as ashes in his hand
> Who, seeing the light and shadow for the same,
>   Bids day waste night as fire devours a brand,
> Smites without sword, and scourges without rod;
>   The supreme evil, God.[40]

In a world where religion could not offer consolation, melancholy might intensify into suicidal despair, as it does in Arnold's *Empedocles on Etna* (1852). A philosopher who is alienated from society and cannot be comforted by religion or the beauty of nature, Empedocles ends by throwing himself into a volcano. His despairing speeches are intermittently interrupted by Callicles, the harp player who represents Arnold's idealized Hellenism but whose art cannot save Empedocles. Arnold had originally intended to write a tragedy about the Roman poet Lucretius, seen as a modern type of melancholy by Tennyson, Hardy, Eliot, and Barrett Browning, but after the publication of Tennyson's dramatic monologue 'Lucretius' he chose to write about Empedocles instead.[41] In the 1853 Preface, he explained that he decided not to reprint *Empedocles* because the poem's representation of the 'modern' feeling of living in a period of transition was not uplifting, the 'dialogue of the mind with itself' too subjective, and the focus on a state of unrelieved suffering 'morbid'. Arnold also identifies Lucretius with 'modern *feeling*', depression and *ennui* resulting from the 'predominance of thought, of reflection'.[42] Lucretius's Epicurean materialist philosophy and religious scepticism made the *De Rerum Natura* an important reference point for poets who wanted to explore the unsettling effects of living in an era when scientific theories challenged traditional religion.[43] Lucretius castigates religion as useless superstition, a malignant force: his gods do not control the operations of natural law and are indifferent to mortals.

The crisis of faith in the Victorian period prompted some poets to look back to the time when Christianity began to take the place of ancient religions. Elizabeth Barrett Browning's 'The Death of Pan' (1844) shows the deserted shrines of the Olympian gods and the silencing of their oracles at the moment of Christ's crucifixion and Pan's simultaneous death. The pantheon of Greek gods is replaced by God and the resurrected Christ, the true subject of poetry and 'the best poet'.[44] In Swinburne's 'Hymn to Proserpine' (1866), however, the passing of the old religion and the proclamation of Christianity in Rome is regretted by the pagan speaker, who prefers the 'cruel' and 'lovely' deities to the 'young compassionate Gods'.[45] He counsels Proserpine to rest and await the return of the old faith after people tire of the 'bitter' and 'barren' religion of the 'pale Galilean' and recall the sensuous delights of paganism. Through this Roman speaker, Swinburne can articulate the provocative argument that Christianity will become obsolete in its turn:[46] 'O ghastly glories of saints, dead limbs of gibbeted Gods! / Though all men abase them before you in spirit, and all knees bend, / I kneel not neither adore you, but standing, look to the end'. Proserpine will return because she is not (unlike the Olympians) remote from darker human experiences of death and pain. Late-Victorian interest in Greek mystery religions, in particular the cults of the chthonic deities Persephone and Dionysus (Proserpina and Bacchus) enabled what Margot K. Louis describes as 'the repudiation of the transcendent, the perception of sex and violence as central to the development of religion'.[47] For Aesthetic writers, the irrational and destructive energies associated with chthonic divinities contributed to radical, counter-cultural versions of Hellenism that contradicted the sanitized images projected in Matthew Arnold's critical prose (already undermined by a more Dionysiac strain in poems such as 'The Strayed Reveller').[48]

The compelling self-justification of murderers and madmen in Browning's dramatic monologues offered a precedent for interpretations of transgressive characters such as Medea, a mother who kills her children. Froma Zeitlin remarks that women in Greek tragedy function as 'catalysts, agents, instruments, blockers, spoilers, destroyers, and sometimes helpers or saviours for the male characters'.[49] The limits to their agency resonated with Victorian women writers. Augusta Webster wrote her dramatic monologue 'Medea in Athens' (1870) after publishing an acclaimed translation of Euripides' *Medea* in 1868. Her rendering of the speech in which Medea pleads with the women of Corinth for sympathy and appeals to their common experience makes clear the relevance of Medea's speech to contemporary debates on marriage and divorce:

> Aye, of all living and of reasoning things
> Are women the most miserable race:
> Who first needs buy a husband at great price,
> To take him then for owner of our lives:
> For this ill is more keen than common ills.
> And of essays most perilous is this,
> Whether one good or evil do we take.[50]

'Medea in Athens' shows her after the death of her children, stranded in the stultifying boredom of her second marriage and shocked by the news of Jason's death. She looks back at the events of Euripides' drama, arguing that her sons were her only weapon against Jason (already established in Victorian literature as selfish and ruthless, a symbol of patriarchal injustice). She fantasizes that Jason came to regret his decision to abandon Medea and enter into a more politically advantageous alliance, and to recognize that she could have furthered his ambitions. Any sorcery she may practise lies in her nursing skills, and the exaggeration of feminine qualities to appeal to Jason. She represents herself as an innocent who was seduced and corrupted by Jason, a 'smooth adder / Who with fanged kisses changedst my natural blood / To venom in me'.[51] She claims that Jason compelled her 'treacherous flight' from her father's kingdom, the killing of her brother, and even the murder of their sons, claiming sympathy for herself as a bereaved mother. While her rhetorical skill cannot convince the reader to accept all of Medea's accusations against Jason, she does suggest that women's powerlessness in a patriarchal society creates victims whose vengeance is extreme and horrifying precisely because they feel they have nothing to lose.

Amy Levy's 'Medea (A Fragment in Drama Form, After Euripides)' (1891) similarly highlights the unexploited abilities of women in a misogynistic society. Medea is represented as a woman whose love is thwarted by her husband's indifference, and who is tormented by her desperate need for love. She experiences Jason's desertion as a liberation from the 'chains' of passion:

> Strong, stronger than the blast of wintry storms;
> And lifted up into an awful realm
> Where is nor love, nor pity, nor remorse,
> Nor dread, but only purpose.[52]

Levy's Medea, like Webster's, is isolated: there is no chorus of women to hear and perhaps sympathize with her condemnation of marriage as slavery. In foregrounding the heroine's loneliness among 'marble-cold' Greek citizens for whom a barbarian woman is doubly alien, and her incomprehension of the 'language of their souls', Levy recalls the anti-semitism she herself encountered. While neither Webster nor Levy attempts to make Medea an entirely sympathetic character, their versions of Medea express justified rage at Jason. By contrast, in *The Life and Death of Jason*, William Morris idealizes Jason's romantic idylls with Medea, and later Glauce, and pays relatively little attention to Jason's cruelty and Medea's violent revenge (based on Euripides). His Medea is, as Douglas Bush notes, 'more pathetic and wistful than tragic and vindictive'.[53] When she poisons the garment that she plans to send to Glauce, Morris emphasizes the careful craftsmanship that produced the 'fine web' rather than the heroine's rage and sense of betrayal.

Like Webster and Levy, Emily Pfeiffer uses Greek heroines in 'Studies from the Antique' (1879), a pair of double sonnets about Greek tragic heroines, 'Kassandra' and 'Klytemnestra'. These are not dramatic monologues but observations about the characters. In the *Iliad*, Cassandra appears only as the most beautiful of the Trojan princesses: her story develops further in tragedy, particularly in the *Agamemnon* of Aeschylus. Pursued by the god Apollo, Cassandra asks him for the power of prophecy and then rejects him once she has the gift, so Apollo adds the condition that her prophecies will never be believed. She foretells the fall of Troy and the disastrous homecoming of Agamemnon. Pfeiffer's openly sensual Kassandra, caressed by 'golden' and 'bold' rays, does not resist the sun god's seductive power: 'But best that day when, steeped in noontide dreams, / The young Apollo wrapped thee in his beams, / And quenched his love in thine as in a sea!'[54] After the idyllic scenes of the first sonnet, the second shows Kassandra's 'sun-stricken' life as Agamemnon's concubine: 'slave's employ / Had from thy trembling lip effaced quite / The kisses of the god, and heaven's light / Now shone upon thee only to destroy'. Kassandra's death is represented here as a release in response to her frantic prayers to Apollo. Klytemnestra is a much fiercer character, who seethes with rage at the limited sphere to which gods and men confine women until she is wounded by a greater wrong, the sacrifice of Iphigenia to secure the Greeks' safe passage to Troy.

Figures such as Medea could highlight the suffering of intelligent and resourceful women whose wasted energies might turn to destruction. Shanyn Fiske describes Augusta Webster and other poets as 'recuperating Greek women's voices to express the frustrations and desires for which Victorian women had yet to conceive a language'.[55] In Amy Levy's 'Xantippe' (1881), the speaker (Socrates' wife) is forced to give up her intellectual ambitions while the foreign courtesan, Aspasia, is permitted to engage in philosophical discourse with Socrates and Plato. She finds that the husband in whom she had hoped to find a mentor 'Deigned not to stoop to touch so slight a thing / As the fine fabric of a woman's brain—/ So subtle as a passionate woman's soul'.[56] Her frustration flames into 'a merciful fury', a rage in which she throws down a full wineskin that stains her white gown red and transforms her briefly into a kind of maenad. The empowerment she experiences is short-lived, and she withdraws into the life of an exemplary housewife amongst her maids. Limited to domestic tasks such as spinning and weaving, Xantippe takes a perverse pleasure in forcing other women to emulate her sacrifice.

Augusta Webster describes Medea's magic powers in terms of revealing truths about men and women: in 'Circe' (1870), the goddess argues that her 'cup of Truth' shows how easily the dividing line between man and animal is crossed.[57] In the *Odyssey* Circe transforms Odysseus' companions into pigs after they have feasted and drunk greedily at her palace (Odysseus is protected by an antidote bestowed on him by the messenger-god Hermes). Truth and falsehood are constantly open to question in the *Odyssey*, so the ability to show things as they are is a proof of Circe's power. Webster emphasizes the idea that the transformation only makes men manifest their true characters: they become 'yapping wolves / And pitiless stealthy wild-cats, curs and apes / And gorging swine and slinking venomous snakes' because self-indulgence wakens 'the beast in them':

> Change? there was no change;
> Only disguise gone from them unawares:
> And had there been one right true man of them
> He would have drunk the draught as I had drunk,
> And stood unchanged, and looked me in the eyes,
> Abashing me before him.

The man who will one day stand there unchanged is Odysseus, whose arrival she has long anticipated. Circe waits, looks out at the sea and hopes for a 'storm at last, storm, glorious storm' to interrupt the 'sickly sweet monotony' of her days. Her unchanging surroundings are reminiscent of the lotos-eaters' island, but there is no calming drug for Circe, who craves emotional stimulus: 'subtle joy / Of anguish and of hopes, of change and growth.' Her monologue returns obsessively to the projected arrival of her unknown lover, 'him whom fate will send / One day to be my master utterly'. This poem can be interpreted as a critique of romantic fantasy, of the idea that her life will be transformed by the arrival of a man.[58] Circe is confident in her power over men: in place of the morbid refrain of Tennyson's Mariana, 'He cometh not', Circe asserts 'Nay but he *will* come'. The reader of the *Odyssey* knows that Circe's desires will be both fulfilled and thwarted: the coming storm will bring Odysseus, he will linger for over a year and have to be reminded by one of his men to continue his journey home, but in time he will leave and Circe will be alone again. Living far from the turmoil of the world, 'like a lonely god, in a charmed isle', suits her no better than it does Tennyson's Ulysses: she is 'weary of this long bright calm; / Always the same blue sky, always the sea / The same blue perfect likeness of the sky'.

Earlier poets had accepted the Ovidian story of the Greek poet Sappho's passion for Phaon and her suicide when he rejected her. Late-Victorian writers, as Yopie Prins has demonstrated, began to exploit the association of Hellenism with a 'discourse of homosexual desire' to reimagine Sappho in a context of lesbian eroticism.[59] Katharine Bradley and Edith Cooper—who described themselves as '*closer married*' than the Brownings because of their poetic collaboration as 'Michael Field'—imaginatively restore Sappho's lost lyrics in the volume *Long Ago* (1889). The preface describes the poems as a response to Wharton's 1885 edition of the Sapphic fragments, an 'audacious' form of 'worship' that 'involves the blissful apprehension of the ideal': Sappho is the 'one woman who has dared to speak unfalteringly of the fearful mastery of love'.[60] The Sapphic text that acts as epigraph to poem XXXIII is equivalent to the first line of the first stanza:

> Maids, not to you my mind doth change;
> Men I defy, allure, estrange,
> Prostrate, make bond or free:
> Soft as the stream beneath the plane
> To you I sing my love's refrain;
> Between us is no thought of pain,
>   Peril, satiety.[61]

Despite the differences between Homer's epic and Sappho's lyric as poetic models, the speaker's approach to men—'defy, allure, estrange'—is not far from that of the Circean *femme fatale*. The 'pain' and 'peril' she and her maids avoid are dangers that the lotos-eaters also escape, and the 'soft' 'stream' evokes the 'slender stream' of the waterfall on their luxurious island. There is a shared sense that love and poetry involve a withdrawal from the world into a private paradise.

Poets who experimented with translating or adapting classical texts risked producing works that nineteenth-century readers would not be able to read: Matthew Arnold's *Merope* (1858), for example, is an academic exercise that the author acknowledged would not 'move deeply the present race of humans'.[62] Yet despite Arnold's censure of the melancholy *Empedocles*, Victorian poets produce compelling versions of classical figures when they imbue them with 'modern feeling'. In Robert Browning's *Balaustion's Adventure; Including a Transcript from Euripides*, Balaustion remarks that Euripides' play is only one way of treating the story of Alcestis, that Sophocles will create a new play with different characters, and that Balaustion herself, or anyone else, can also 'mould a new / Admetos, new Alkestis' (2145–6).[63] Greek and Roman literature flourished by producing competing reworkings of familiar myths and texts. Any story worth telling is also worth retelling, Balaustion suggests: it is open to any reader to 'share the poets' privilege, / Bring forth new good, new beauty, from the old' (2424–5).

Notes

1. See Christopher Stray, *Classics Transformed: Schools, Universities, and Society in England, 1830–1960* (Oxford: Clarendon Press, 1998).
2. Robert Browning, 'Development', in *The Poetical Works of Robert Browning*, 15 vols., ed. Ian Jack et al. (Oxford: Oxford University Press, 1988–) xv. 458.
3. Quoted in Hallam Tennyson, *Alfred, Lord Tennyson: A Memoir*, 2 vols (London: Macmillan, 1897), i. 11.
4. *The Brownings' Correspondence*, ed. Ronald Hudson, Philip Kelley, Scott Lewis and Edward Hagan, 18 vols. (Winfield: Wedgestone, 1984 –), vii. 353–4.
5. *The Brownings' Correspondence*, x. 222.
6. Elizabeth Barrett Browning, *Aurora Leigh*, ed. Margaret Reynolds (New York: W. W. Norton, 1996), 180.
7. Meilee Bridges, 'The Eros of Homeros: The Pleasures of Greek Epic in Victorian Literature and Archaeology', *Victorian Review* 34 (2008), 165–83.
8. Matthew Arnold, *On the Classical Tradition*, ed. R. H. Super (Ann Arbor: University of Michigan Press, 1960), 20.
9. Elizabeth Gaskell, *North and South*, ed. Angus Easson (Oxford: Oxford University Press, 2008), 85.
10. Frank M. Turner, *The Greek Heritage in Victorian Britain* (London: Yale University Press, 1981), 175–6.
11. Arnold, *On the Classical Tradition*, 1.
12. Arnold, 'To a Friend' in *The Complete Poems*, ed. Kenneth Allott, 2nd edn. (London: Longman, 1979), 110–1.
13. Arnold, 'Dover Beach', in *Poems*, 255.
14. Arnold, *On the Classical Tradition*, 97. See also David Ricks, 'Homer', in Peter France and Kenneth Haynes, eds., *The Oxford History of Literary Translation in English*, vol. 4: *1790–1900* (Oxford: Oxford University Press, 2006), 173–7.
15. Anthony Trollope, 'Ancient Classics for English Readers', *Saint Pauls*, 5 (1870), 667.

16. Herbert F. Tucker, *Epic: Britain's Heroic Muse, 1790–1910* (Oxford: Oxford University Press, 2008), 2.

17. Norman Vance, *The Victorians and Ancient Rome* (Oxford: Blackwell, 1997), 150.

18. Tennyson (H.), *Alfred, Lord Tennyson*, i. 166.

19. Tucker, *Epic*, 367.

20. Anne Janowitz, 'The Romantic Fragment', in Duncan Wu, ed., *A Companion to Romanticism* (Oxford: Blackwell, 1999), 442.

21. Alfred Tennyson, 'Ulysses', in *Poems of Tennyson*, 3 vols., ed. Christopher Ricks, 2nd edn. (London: Longman, 1987), i. 620.

22. See Richard F. Thomas, *Virgil and the Augustan Reception* (Cambridge: Cambridge University Press, 1988), 63–5.

23. A. A. Markley, *Stateliest Measures: Tennyson and the Literature of Greece and Rome* (Toronto: University of Toronto Press, 2004), 4.

24. Christopher Ricks, *Tennyson*, 2nd edn. (Basingstoke: Macmillan, 1996), 115.

25. Cornelia D. J. Pearsall, *Tennyson's Rapture: Transformation in the Victorian Dramatic Monologue* (Oxford: Oxford University Press, 2008), 185.

26. Tennyson (H.), *Alfred, Lord Tennyson*, i. 196.

27. Tennyson, 'Tithonus', in *Poems*, ii. 607–9.

28. Arnold, 'The Strayed Reveller', in *Poems*, 77.

29. A. H. Hallam, review of *Poems, Chiefly Lyrical* (1830), repr. in *Tennyson: The Critical Heritage*, ed. John D. Jump (London: Routledge, 1967), 38.

30. Peter M. Sacks, *The English Elegy: Studies in the Genre from Spenser to Yeats* (London: Johns Hopkins University Press, 1985), 167, 202.

31. See Markley, *Stateliest Measures*, 70–86.

32. Tennyson, *In Memoriam* in *Poems*, ii. 325–6.

33. See Niall Rudd, 'Two Invitations: Tennyson *To the Rev. F.D. Maurice* and Horace *to Maecenas (Odes* 3.29)', *Hermathena* 150 (1991), 5–19, repr. in *The Common Spring: Papers on Latin and English Poetry* (Bristol: Bristol Classical Press, 2005), 177–90.

34. Tennyson's source is *Odyssey* 9. 82–104: Homer, *The Odyssey: Books 1–12*, trans. A. T. Murray, revised by George E. Dimock (Cambridge, MA: Harvard University Press, 1995), 278–9. On their return from Troy, Odysseus and his men have been behaving like traditional warriors wherever they land, killing the men they find there and sharing out the women and valuables. After a storm at sea they reach the land of the lotos-eaters: here there is no fighting, but those of the men who eat the honey-sweet lotos lose all memory of home, and all desire to return there. Sleep or unconsciousness is always dangerous in the *Odyssey*: it is when Odysseus is asleep that the ship is most likely to be driven off course. Homer's Odysseus forces the weeping men back to the ship and they sail off to an even more perilous destination, the island of the Cyclops.

35. Tennyson, 'The Lotos-Eaters', in *Poems*, i. 470.

36. Quoted in David Riede, *Allegories of One's Own Mind: Melancholy in Victorian Poetry* (Columbus: Ohio State University Press, 2005), 57.

37. Isobel Armstrong, *Victorian Poetry: Poetry, Poetics and Politics* (London: Routledge, 1993), 87. See also 87–94 for a reading of the poem as a repudiation of the alienating conditions of 'mechanised labour and exploitation'.

38. See Lillian Eileen Doherty, *Siren Songs: Gender, Audiences, and Narrators in the* Odyssey (Ann Arbor: University of Michigan Press, 1996).

39. See Margot K. Louis, *Persephone Rises, 1860–1927: Mythography, Gender, and the Creation of a New Spirituality* (Aldershot: Ashgate, 2009), 14–17.

40. Algernon Charles Swinburne, *Atalanta in Calydon in Poems and Ballads & Atalanta in Calydon*, ed. Kenneth Haynes (Harmondsworth: Penguin, 2000), 283.

41. Donald Mackenzie, 'Two Versions of Lucretius: Arnold and Housman', *Translation and Literature* 16 (2007), 160–77. See also Markley, *Stateliest Measures*, 140–8; Vance, *Victorians and Ancient Rome*, 83–111.

42. Arnold, *On the Classical Tradition*, 1–3, 32.

43. See John Holmes, 'Lucretius at the Fin De Siècle: Science, Religion and Poetry', *English Literature in Transition, 1880–1920* 51 (2008), 266–80.

44. Elizabeth Barrett Browning, 'The Death of Pan', in *The Works of Elizabeth Barrett Browning*, 5 vols., ed. Sandra Donaldson (London: Pickering & Chatto, 2010), ii. 383.

45. Swinburne, 'Hymn to Proserpine', in *Poems*, 56.

46. See Thaïs E. Morgan, 'Swinburne's Dramatic Monologues: Sex and Ideology', *Victorian Poetry* 22 (1984), 192–3.

47. Louis, *Persephone Rises*, 17.

48. See Stefano Evangelista, *British Aestheticism and Ancient Greece: Hellenism, Reception, Gods in Exile* (Basingstoke: Palgrave Macmillan, 2009).

49. Froma Zeitlin, *Playing the Other: Gender and Society in Classical Greek Literature*, 2nd edn. (University of Chicago Press, 1996), 347.

50. Augusta Webster, *The Medea of Euripides, Literally Translated into English Verse* (London: Macmillan, 1868), 19.

51. Augusta Webster, 'Medea in Athens', in *Portraits and Other Poems*, ed. Christine Sutphin (Peterborough, ON: Broadview, 2000), 175.

52. Amy Levy, 'Medea (A Fragment in Drama Form, After Euripides)', in *A Minor Poet and Other Verse* (London: T. Fisher Unwin, 1884), 57.

53. Douglas Bush, *Mythology and the Romantic Tradition in English Poetry* (Cambridge, Mass: Harvard University Press, 1937), 309.

54. Emily Pfeiffer, 'Studies from the Antique in *Victorian Women Poets: A New Annotated Anthology*, ed. Virginia Blain (London: Longman, 2001), 96.

55. Shanyn Fiske, 'Augusta Webster and The Social History of Myth', *Women's Studies* 40 (2011), 478.

56. Amy Levy, 'Xantippe', in *The Complete Novels and Selected Writings of Amy Levy 1861–1889*, ed. Melvyn New (Gainesville: University Press of Florida, 1993), 360.

57. Webster, 'Circe', in *Portraits*, 183.

58. Christine Sutphin, 'The Representation of Women's Heterosexual Desire in Augusta Webster's 'Circe' and 'Medea in Athens'', *Women's Writing*, 5 (1998), 373–92.

59. Yopie Prins, *Victorian Sappho* (Princeton: Princeton University Press, 1999), 77.

60. 'Michael Field' (Katharine Bradley and Edith Cooper), *Michael Field, the Poet: Published and Unpublished Materials*, ed. Marion Thain and Ana Parejo Vadillo (Peterborough, ON: Broadview, 2009), 57.

61. 'Michael Field', *Michael Field, the Poet*, 68–9.

62. Arnold, *Merope in Poems*, 432.

63. Browning, *Balaustion's Adventure; Including a Transcript from Euripides in The Poems, Volume I*, ed. John Pettigrew and Thomas J. Collins (Harmondsworth: Penguin, 1981), 934.

SELECT BIBLIOGRAPHY

Bush, Douglas, *Mythology and the Romantic Tradition in English Poetry* (Cambridge, Mass: Harvard University Press, 1937).

Jenkyns, Richard, *The Victorians and Ancient Greece* (Oxford: Blackwell, 1980).

Louis, Margot K., *Persephone Rises, 1860–1927: Mythography, Gender, and the Creation of a New Spirituality* (Aldershot: Ashgate, 2009).

Markley, A. A., *Stateliest Measures: Tennyson and the Literature of Greece and Rome* (Toronto: University of Toronto Press, 2004).

Pearsall, Cornelia D. J., *Tennyson's Rapture: Transformation in the Victorian Dramatic Monologue* (Oxford: Oxford University Press, 2008).

Prins, Yopie, *Victorian Sappho* (Princeton: Princeton University Press, 1999).

Sacks, Peter, *The English Elegy: Studies in the Genre from Spenser to Yeats* (London: Johns Hopkins University Press, 1985).

The Oxford History of Literary Translation in English, Vol. 4: *1790–1900* ed. Peter France and Kenneth Haynes (Oxford: Oxford University Press, 2005).

Tucker, Herbert, *Epic: Britain's Heroic Muse, 1790–1910* (Oxford: Oxford University Press, 2008).

Turner, Frank, *The Greek Heritage in Victorian Britain* (London: Yale University Press, 1981).

Vance, Norman, *The Victorians and Ancient Rome* (Oxford: Blackwell, 1997).

CHAPTER 10

....

VICTORIAN MEDIEVALISMS

....

MATTHEW TOWNEND

ON 21 September 1898 a tall, decorated cross was unveiled in the churchyard of St Mary's Church, Whitby, just a few yards from the bench where, in a novel published only the previous year, the ill-fated Lucy Westenra had been assailed by Count Dracula. The inscription at its foot declares that the monument was erected 'To the glory of God and in memory of Cædmon, the father of English sacred song, fell asleep hard by, 680'. The narrower sides of the cross are adorned with Anglo-Saxon vine-scroll and foliage ornament, while its two main faces boast a number of human figures, four of them with large captions ('Christus', 'David', 'Hild', 'Cædmon'). The margins of the two narrower sides are also inscribed with the text of the short Old English poem known as *Caedmon's Hymn,* once in Anglo-Saxon minuscule and once in Northumbrian runes. A translation is provided at the back for those lacking fluency in such scripts.

Whitby's 'Caedmon Cross' is an extraordinary piece of Anglo-Saxonist sculpture.[1] Its prime mover was Canon Hardwicke Drummond Rawnsley (1851–1920), Vicar of Crosthwaite near Keswick and a man of manifold enthusiasms and stupendous energy. He is best remembered today as one of the founders of the National Trust, but his many other interests included literary history and *in situ* commemorations (not just memorial crosses, but also bonfires and jubilee beacons, with which he was greatly occupied in 1897). He also wrote scores of books and literally thousands of sonnets, and his father had been the clergyman who married Alfred Tennyson and Emily Selwood. And it was Tennyson's successor as Poet Laureate, Alfred Austin, who unveiled the Caedmon Cross in 1898. Just two years previously, Austin had declared himself an enthusiast for matters Anglo-Saxon through the publication of his verse-drama about King Alfred the Great, *England's Darling*—not, it has to be said, the most distinguished work to be discussed in this chapter, and a text with a number of comic or anachronistic moments: Alfred gives away the famous Alfred Jewel as a present, makes model ships in his study, and lets the cakes burn because he is too busy writing the Anglo-Saxon Chronicle.[2] But there are also echoes of Anglo-Saxon texts to be caught, from Alfred's Preface to *Pastoral Care* to

The Battle of Maldon, and these indicate something of the primary reading that the Poet Laureate had been doing.

Whitby's Caedmon Cross—altogether a more impressive production than *England's Darling*—forms an ideal opening vista for this chapter as, like Austin's play, it exemplifies many of the key features of nineteenth-century medievalism: a combination of scholarship and creativity, inspiration and elaboration; a preoccupation not just with England's medieval past, but with the literary products of that past; an assumption of continuity between medieval past and Victorian present; and a conviction that the medieval, or medievalist, had a public role to play in contemporary culture. The origins and genesis of the Victorian period's multifarious and imaginative engagement with the Middle Ages have been well established. Eighteenth- and early nineteenth-century foundations in literature included the antiquarian and editorial initiatives of Thomas Percy and his contemporaries, the rise of Gothic as a mode and idea, and the cultivation of romance as a poetic form by Coleridge and Scott.[3] Wider and deeper movements were also at work, of course, most importantly the increasingly historicist approach to both human culture and the physical world. As a result, the Middle Ages, and medieval literature, were able to be viewed as many things in the nineteenth century, and deployed to many ends, from the pious to the primitive, the patriotic to the proto-socialist. Victorian medievalism, in its countless forms, was not gently wistful or politically inert, and it was as often an expression of criticism as of complacency. The medieval period stretched from approximately 400 to 1500: how could more than a millennium of history and literature not exert a profound influence on the poetry of an historicist age?

Nationalism, Regionalism, Race

Perhaps the most frequent paradigm by which Victorian medievalism is construed in modern scholarship, or the lens through which it is viewed, is that of nationalism or national history.[4] The so-called romantic nationalism that re-shaped Europe in the nineteenth century typically looked back to a people's earliest history, or its earliest texts, to find a foundation for current community and identity.[5] According to such an interpretation, diagnostic projects of medievalism, within Britain at least, would include the choice of Gothic as the architectural style for the new Houses of Parliament, the vernacularist labours of the Early English Text Society, and, in poetry, precisely such works as *England's Darling*—and, perhaps, Tennyson's *Idylls of the King.* Inga Bryden, for example, states firmly that 'one form which nationalism took in a rapidly industrializing Victorian Britain was medievalism' (not 'one form which medievalism took…was nationalism').[6]

Clearly there is some truth in this position, but it is not the whole truth, and various qualifications must be made. As a way in, let us return to the example of the Caedmon Cross. This can, if one wishes, easily be viewed within a nationalist perspective. First, it celebrates the supposed founder of 'English sacred song', and thus it foregrounds vernacularity and continuity, as well as the role of Christianity as a unifying force for the English people. Second, the sole medieval source for the story of Caedmon, Bede's *Ecclesiastical History of the English People* (*Historia Ecclesiastica Gentis Anglorum*), is a text with the palpable ideological purpose of demonstrating the unity of the *gens Anglorum*.[7] Third, the full weight of English university scholarship stood behind the erection of the Cross, with a number of eminent philologists or archaeologists being involved (including G.F. Browne, Israel Gollancz, and W.W. Skeat). And fourth, the Cross was unveiled by the Poet Laureate, and masterminded by a public figure (Rawnsley) who had been busy the previous year with the celebration of Victoria's Diamond Jubilee.

But this nationalist interpretation can just as easily be queried or qualified. Bede's early eighth-century *History* locates the unity of the people in religious (or specifically, ecclesiastical) structures, not political ones: the idea of 'Englishness' existed in Bede's time, but the entity of 'England' did not, and the *gens Anglorum* lived in several regional kingdoms, not one nation-state—even though those separate kingdoms all recognized the primacy of one Archbishop, at Canterbury. Moreover, although he has a 'national' perspective, Bede is a Northumbrian writer, and on the whole he narrates Northumbrian history and celebrates Northumbrian saints; and so one could read the late nineteenth-century celebration of Caedmon as part of a broader Northumbrian interest in the region's Anglo-Saxon heritage: other examples would include the prominence given to Northumbrian saints in stained glass in the north of England, and the scenes from Northumbrian history painted by William Bell Scott at Wallington in Northumberland.[8] Indeed, one could narrow the focus even more, and read the Caedmon Cross in terms of local or civic significance, in the articulation and consolidation of Whitby's urban identity.

Other comparable cases, able to be construed either in terms of nationalism or regionalism/localism, or in terms of a creative tension between the two, can easily be found. One of the grandest of Anglo-Saxonist commemorations was the 'Alfred Millenary', celebrated in Winchester in 1901. (Most nineteenth-century scholars believed that King Alfred the Great died in 901; 899 is now the agreed date.) The unveiling of a colossal statue of Alfred by Hamo Thornycroft (Siegfried Sassoon's uncle) formed the centrepiece for the Millenary, and was complemented by processions, publications, and assorted public festivities.[9] Literary figures who were involved in some way included Thomas Hardy and (again) Alfred Austin, and H. D. Rawnsley had a finger in this commemorative pie as well, sending a rose-bowl to the City of Winchester on behalf of his Ruskinian 'Keswick School of Industrial Arts'. Planning for the Millenary was marked by a tug-of-war over tone and emphasis between, as it were, the 'national' camp and the 'Winchester' camp, and Winchester's (and, by extension, Hampshire's) claims as Alfred's supposed capital were disputed by other locations within the bounds of his old kingdom of Wessex—such as Athelney in Somerset, where he famously hid in the marshes, and Wantage in Berkshire (Hardy's 'Alfredston'), where he was born and where another, smaller statue of Alfred had already been erected, in 1877. Civic pride, county pride, regional pride, and national pride were all in evidence, and in competition, in the late nineteenth-century cult of King Alfred.

The point, then, is that in Victorian England what has been termed 'romantic region-alism' may have played just as great a role as romantic nationalism, or perhaps an even greater one; the medievalism of nineteenth-century England was not the same as that of Germany, or Finland, or Iceland, and nationalism does not supply some sort of 'key to all medievalisms'. The medievalist enthusiasms of many Victorians, both learned and popular, were directed at least as much to local or regional ends as to national or nation-alistic ones.[10] This should be no surprise: the surge of regional self-awareness in the sec-ond half of the nineteenth century is well known, and is amply attested in fiction from this period, while the proliferation of local antiquarian societies tells a similar story.[11] Moreover, certain brands of Victorian medievalism were by definition *not* national-ist or statist, and were committed instead to such devolved or decentralized political organisms as folk-moots, craft-guilds, and village communities. The figure of William Morris should by himself cause us to doubt the view that Victorian medievalism is best explained in terms of nationalism: the preoccupations of Victorian England's most prominent medievalist can hardly be construed in such terms.[12]

But Morris did sometimes talk about 'race', and this charged word also requires some attention in this context. Most famously, Morris and EiríkurMagnússon end the preface to their 1870 translation of the Old Norse *Völsunga Saga* as follows:

> In conclusion, we must again say how strange it seems to us, that this Volsung Tale, which is in fact an unversified poem, should never before have been translated into English. For this is the Great Story of the North, which should be to all our race what the Tale of Troy was to the Greeks—to all our race first, and afterwards, when the change of the world has made our race nothing more than a name of what has been—a story too—then should it be to those that come after us no less than the Tale of Troy has been to us.[13]

This peroration strikes two of the characteristic notes of what Andrew Wawn has termed Old Northernism, as it declares the availability of a northern, Germanic alter-native to a southern, Mediterranean culture, and a medieval alternative to a classical one.[14] But what does Morris mean by 'race' here? We should beware of back-projecting a twenty-first-century biological meaning onto all Victorian occurrences of the word. As the entry in the first edition of the *Oxford English Dictionary* makes clear (in a fascicule published in 1903 under the editorship of W.A. Craigie), when nineteenth-century writ-ers used the word 'race' it did not consistently bear a narrowly biological sense, though of course the word in some way assumed common origins or identity; in Victorian usage 'race' often stands for (what we would now call) 'people' or 'nation', or even sometimes 'speech community'.[15] When Morris writes 'race' in this preface, he is almost certainly thinking in terms of language and culture, not biology, and in terms of a language and culture that transcend national boundaries, to be shared among the Germanic-speaking peoples of northern Europe: his appeal is to a communal story-world that should be more widely appreciated.

Moreover, by the time of Morris' *Völsunga Saga* translation, the prevailing assump-tion was that the race or people would be mixed or hybrid, of varied origins. Robert

Young has argued that an important shift in thinking can be observed in the middle of the nineteenth century, with a pivot in perhaps the 1860s. Prior to this time, a common claim was for the single origins of peoples. For the English, as Young has shown, this can be seen in early Victorian emphases on the pure Saxon or German origins of the people, and of course such a position had a counterpart in thought about the English language. But after the mid-century there rapidly arose a new conviction, that the English were an irremediably mixed people, and arguably the better for it.[16] Ironically, one of the causes of this change was the researches of scientists, or pseudo-scientists, who were engaged in such practices as cranium measuring and facial taxonomy, and who realized that their findings, or pseudo-findings, were incompatible with an idea of single-origin purity ('in terms of modern preconceptions', Young writes, 'the paradox was that in the case of English ethnicity, far from proposing a new racialized identity for the English as constituting a pure race, it was racial science that was used to disprove the racial exclusivism of Saxonism').[17]

Young traces the mid-century shift especially in terms of England's political relations with its Celtic neighbours, and analyses Matthew Arnold's *On the Study of Celtic Literature* (1867) as a seminal text. But his argument can also be supported from non-Celtic perspectives, for example with the change in understanding effected by J. J. A. Worsaae's *An Account of the Danes and Norwegians in England, Scotland, and Ireland* (1852). In the first half of the nineteenth century, Britain's Viking past, and the consequences of Scandinavian settlement in the ninth and tenth centuries, had largely been neglected or disparaged. But Worsaae's book soon encouraged a more receptive view of this cultural inheritance:

> Foreigners, and particularly the German historians, usually assert, for instance, that the Danish and Norwegian Vikings brought nothing but misfortune upon the British Isles; whilst, on the contrary, everything great and good in England is mainly attributable to the Saxons, or Germans . . . What if we found that, by means of monuments, the popular character, public institutions, and other traits, a constant and beneficial influence could be traced from the expeditions of the Vikings or Northmen, so that the natives of the lands which they subdued accounted it an honour to descend from the bold natives of the North?[18]

As in political and ethnological thought, so also in literary criticism (and, we shall see, in language study). W. P. Ker's *Epic and Romance* (1896) has strong claims to be the most enduring critical work on medieval literature produced in Victorian Britain. Ker's book not only anatomizes Old English and Old Norse poetry and prose with magisterial insight, but it is also cosmopolitan and Europeanist in its perspectives: with a multilingual comparativism, Ker is as much at home among Greek or Latin as he is among Germanic languages, and the last quarter of his book is on the subject of French *chansons de geste*.[19] One implication of Ker's work is precisely that English readers should not be bound by narrow notions of nationalism, but rather should be interested in stories told in other languages or set in other countries—as, it was assumed, the Anglo-Saxons themselves were.

Although this discussion of nationalism, regionalism, and race has taken us away from concrete poetic examples, it has put us in a position to appreciate the heterogeneity of Victorian medievalism in the second half of the nineteenth century. The search for single-origin purity was, on the whole, outmoded; a nationalizing story was likely to be complemented, or undercut, by a local or regional one; and interests and sympathies among the peoples of Europe might be recognized as extending beyond modern national boundaries or political fault-lines.

METHODS AND MODES

Victorian medievalisms were founded upon medieval textual sources. Of course, not all writers and artists engaged directly with those primary sources, and one might offer a rough division into three categories: those who read the primary sources for themselves, in the original language(s); those who read the sources in translation; and those who worked at second- or third-hand, more from generalized (and often stereotyped) ideas about 'the medieval' than from specific medieval sources. Moreover, those medieval sources were composed in a variety of languages—Old English, Middle English, Old Norse, French, Italian, and of course Latin—and assumed a variety of literary forms—epic, elegy, ballad, panegyric, saga, chronicle, charter, homily. Thus the composition of medievalist literature in the nineteenth century, and especially of medievalist poetry, almost invariably raised questions of linguistic and generic translation. How should the source material be approached and re-imagined? How closely or obliquely should a medievalist work stand in relation to its medieval sources? What were some of the challenges of form and style? Medievalist poets found themselves in dialogue, not just with an historical period, but with particular literary forms from the past, often no longer current.

King Arthur posed particular problems, or opportunities. Whatever he was, Arthur was not English—or he could only be made so through creative manoeuvring. And the main medieval sources about Arthur were not exclusively English either, or written in the English language. Textually, nineteenth-century Arthurianism was built on texts written in Welsh (*The Mabinogion*), Latin (Geoffrey of Monmouth's *History of the Kings of Britain*), and French (Chrétien de Troyes' romances), as well of course as on Malory's *Morte Darthur*, written in fifteenth-century English prose.[20] This diversity of sources means that, if *Idylls of the King* is to be read as a nationalist text, then its nationalism is likely to be of the hybrid, post-1850 kind. But an appreciation of Tennyson's use of his medieval sources points up the difficulties of reading *Idylls* as straightforwardly celebratory in its nationalism, in spite of its book-ending poems to Albert and Victoria. Tennyson's main source was of course Malory, whose work he owned or consulted in various editions.[21] But Malory's fifteenth-century treatment of the Arthurian story is far more celebratory, and more explicitly nationalistic, than Tennyson's. Malory equates Arthur's Camelot with Winchester; Tennyson does not (at least explicitly), and he co-ordinates his Arthurian geography more with that of Wales than England (not least in the prominence he accords to Caerleon). Nor does Tennyson, unlike Malory, ever equate Arthur's realm with England or the English (there is nothing in Tennyson to compare with Malory's famous lament, 'Lo ye all Englysshemen, se ye nat what a myschyff here was?'), and for Tennyson, as for most nationalistic readings of the Arthurian legend, the Anglo-Saxons remain problematic, as we shall see.[22] Furthermore, Malory only brings Lancelot and Guinevere's relationship to the fore in the final part of his work; Tennyson, at least in his final ordering, accentuates it all the way through his *Idylls*, repeatedly signalling to the reader that a corrosive affair lies at the heart of Arthur's fragile polity.[23] Above all, Tennyson omits all mention of the overseas conquests which are so important in Malory (as also in Geoffrey of Monmouth and other medieval Arthurian texts).

For most of his later *Idylls,* as is well known, Tennyson's working method was to produce a prose summary or digest from his primary sources (reading the non-English texts in translation), and then, in a second step, to compose his verse from these prose synopses.[24] For a closer engagement with non-English medieval sources, by one with the linguistic skills to read the original language, we need to turn again to William Morris, and to his two long poems based on Old Norse literature, 'The Lovers of Gudrun' (originally published in 1870 as part of his *Earthly Paradise*) and *The Story of Sigurd the Volsung and the Fall of the Niblungs* (published in 1876).

Narrative was one of Morris' enduring loves. As his long time collaborator recalled, Morris responded to the sagas of medieval Iceland with an intense appetite for their narratives:

> His first taste of Icelandic literature was the story of 'Gunnlaug the Snaketongue'. I suggested we had better start with some grammar. 'No, I can't be bothered with grammar; have no time for it. You be my grammar as we translate. I want the literature, I must have the story. I mean to amuse myself'.[25]

Morris and Magnússon's first published translations were *Grettis Saga* (1869) and *Völsunga Saga* (1870), but there were several other sagas that they read in their early years together that did not result in published translations. The most important of these was *Laxdæla saga*, the central part of which tells of the tragic love-triangle of Guðrún, Kjartan, and Bolli (Kjartan and Bolli are best friends; Kjartan and Guðrún love each other, but Guðrún ends up marrying Bolli instead; eventually Guðrún forces Bolli to kill Kjartan). 'The Lovers of Gudrun', the poem that resulted from Morris' reading of *Laxdæla saga*, became for Victorian readers the most widely read work of Old Northernism: no translation of the saga was published in English until 1899, yet as a result of Morris' poem many Victorians felt that they knew the saga, and the arc of its central story.

Much of the time Morris follows the plot of *Laxdæla saga* quite closely, but 'Gudrun' is not a verse translation, and there are many omissions, simplifications, and embellishments.[26] *Laxdæla saga* supplied the story and the setting, but not much of the tone and mood, and still less the narrative technique. Old Norse saga style is famously 'impersonal': vocabulary is restricted; the narrator is highly reticent in terms of commentary or foreknowledge; and there is little access to characters' interiority, so that readers are forced to intuit feelings and motivations from how characters speak and act.[27] So, one of the most famous scenes in *Laxdœla saga* is that in which Guðrún learns of Kjartan's death:

> After Kjartan's body was taken to the farm at Tunga, Bolli rode back to Laugar. Gudrun went out to meet him, and asked how late in the day it was.
>
>   Bolli replied that it was almost mid-afternoon, and Gudrun said, 'A poor match they make, our morning's work—I have spun twelve ells of yarn while you have slain Kjartan.'[28]

How are we to construe Guðrún's emotions and conduct at this highly dramatic moment? What is she thinking? What is she feeling? The saga-author gives us no guidance, and we have to read behind her casual-seeming one-liner.

This is how Icelandic sagas habitually work, but it is not how Morris' poem works. This scene is in fact omitted from 'The Lovers of Gudrun'—perhaps it was too oblique, too under-stated, for the purposes and mood of Morris' poem. Instead, a series of passionate scenes are substituted, in which Guðrún comes face-to-face with Kjartan's corpse (something that does not happen in the saga—his body is taken away for burial without first making a halt at Guðrún's home):

> She raised her head, and clenched her hands, but nought
> Of sound from out her parched lips was there brought,
> Till at her breast she clutched, and rent adown
> With trembling hands the bosom of her gown,
> And cried out, panting as for lack of air:
>
>> "Alas, what do ye? have ye come to bear
>> My love a second time from me, O men?
>> Do ye not know he is come back again
>> After a long time? Ah, but evil heart
>> Must be in you such love as ours to part!"
>
>> Then, crying out, upon the corpse she fell,
>> And men's hearts failed them for pure ruth, and well
>> They deemed it, might she never rise again;
>> But strong are many hearts to bear all pain
>> And live, and hers was even such an one.
>> Softly they bore her back amidst her swoon.[29]

Morris targets emotional intensity, not through the saga's techniques of enigma and unspokenness, but through a range of colourful, un-saga-like strokes: a verb-based lexis of animation and suffering ('clenched', 'parched', 'clutched', 'trembling', 'panting', and so on); dramatic or even melodramatic gestures ('she ... rent adown ... the bosom of her gown'; 'upon the corpse she fell'; 'amidst her swoon'); full access to characters' interiority (the speech beginning, 'Alas what do ye?'); and a ready willingness on the part of the narrator to generalize ('strong are many hearts to bear such pain / And live'). There is also a strong element of the sensational or macabre here, as the deranged heroine pleads not to be separated from the dead body of her former lover.

Such changes in technique and emphasis, we can confidently say in Morris' case, are not the result of ignorance, or a failure to appreciate the manners and mode of the medieval original, but rather spring from a desire to marry a medieval plot with some contemporary techniques and sensibilities. Nonetheless, it is striking that *Sigurd the Volsung*, the long poem which Morris composed after his two visits to Iceland in 1871 and 1873, puts much less distance between itself and its sources in terms of mood and approach. In *Sigurd* Morris is much less analytic of motives, meanings, and emotions than he is in 'Gudrun'; instead, like the original prose of *Völsunga Saga* and the original poems of the Poetic Edda (both of which he had translated), Morris' poem presents to the reader its powerful sequence of stories—tender and violent, suggestive and inscrutable—with minimal guidance from an intervening narrator.[30]

Sigurd the Volsung is not composed in alliterative metre, as the poems of the Edda were, though Morris does reach for ornamental or emphatic alliteration with a frequency that gestures unmistakably towards the metre of his sources; the revival of formal alliterative metre, in original compositions rather than translations (from Old Norse and Old English), is mostly a twentieth-century story rather than a nineteenth-century one.[31] One eye-catching feature of Morris' style in *Sigurd the Volsung* is, however, his prominent use of kennings. A staple of so-called skaldic poetry in Old Norse, though also found in some Eddic verse (and, to a lesser degree, in Old English), kennings are compressed circumlocutions, often of a metaphorical type.[32] Most of the kennings in *Sigurd* are Morris' own inventions, but they are for precisely those categories for which kennings are most common in Old Norse, such as gold, the sea, and swords: consider, for example, 'the sea-flood's fire', 'the Candle of the Deep', and 'Fafnir's Bed'; 'the field of the fishes', 'the bath of the swan', and 'Ægir's acre'; and 'the serpent of death', 'the Flame of Strife', and 'the brand of Odin'. In its nuanced attention to the matter and mode of its textual sources, *Sigurd the Volsung* is one of the poetic high-points of Victorian medievalism.

PHILOLOGY AND POETRY

Arguably, the forms and functions of Victorian medievalism discussed so far are all over-shadowed in importance by the last area to be considered—namely philology. This new, nineteenth-century discipline revolutionized contemporary attitudes to language, so that the relations between different languages were fundamentally re-assessed, and the histories of individual languages—and of individual words—were able to be revealed and contemplated. In short, philology made people think about language historically, in an evolutionary manner.

The progress of the new 'science of language'—with its rise in the first half of the nineteenth century, and its acceptance and dissemination in the second half—has been well established.[33] In nineteenth-century Britain at least, 'philology' primarily meant Germanic philology, rather than comparative Indo-European philology on the grand scale. Germanic philologists spent their time doing two things above all, thoroughly inter-related: explicating older, especially medieval, states of the language (frequently by reference to contemporary spoken dialects), and producing editions of older, especially medieval, texts. Germanic philology was thus the linguistic wing of Victorian medievalism, and an essay on the medievalism of Victorian poetry must certainly take account of the several ways in which the new philological learning impacted on poets, and on poetic practice.

The greatest monument to Victorian philology (as also, therefore, to Victorian medievalism) is of course the *Oxford English Dictionary*—or, to give it the title by which the Victorians themselves first knew it, *A New English Dictionary on Historical Principles, Founded Mainly on the Materials Collected by the Philological Society*. Conceived in 1857, re-commenced in earnest in 1879 (with the appointment of James Murray as editor), and at long last concluded in 1928, the *Oxford English Dictionary* represents one of the heroic achievements of Victorian letters.[34] If the *Oxford English Dictionary* is to be read as a nationalist enterprise as well as a scholarly one, then we should again note the nature of its nationalism. In a manner consonant with Robert Young's mid-century shift, the *Oxford English Dictionary* can be read as a gigantic demonstration of the fundamentally mixed nature of the English language: it is a testament to Victorian perceptions of the receptivity of the English language, in terms of its promiscuous incorporation of elements from many other languages, and it thus stands in opposition to earlier desires for Saxon purity.

Philology brought awareness of older words and older states of the language, of older meanings and older methods of word-formation; above all, it brought a consciousness of the historical depth both of individual words and of the vocabulary as a whole—a sort of lexical-semantic equivalent of the dizzying sense of time expressed for geology most famously in *In Memoriam*. The two major poets who responded most fully and creatively to the opportunities presented by this aspect of philology were Hopkins and Hardy. Interestingly, neither can be regarded as 'medievalist' poets according to the more usual criterion of subject matter. Gerard Manley Hopkins might conceivably be included in the medievalist ranks on the basis of his Marian devotion and interest in Christian thinkers such as Duns Scotus, but it would surely be a misapprehension to regard Catholic piety as fundamentally 'medieval'. Moreover, the extent and importance of Hopkins' reading in Old and Middle English poetry may well have been exaggerated.[35] But there is abundant evidence from his journals and letters for Hopkins' commitment to philology in terms of etymology and dialectology (Joseph Wright's *English Dialect Dictionary* (1898–1905), to which Hopkins contributed material, is an important counterpart to the *Oxford English Dictionary*).[36] As James Milroy has written, '[it is not] correct to say that it was Hopkins who breathed life into philology; on the contrary, it was philology that helped to breathe life into Hopkins's poetry'.[37] The distinctive features of Hopkins' philologically-derived diction are of course very well known: an alertness to word roots and their phonaesthetic effects and associations; a very high frequency of innovative compounds, often arising through the creative redeployment of bound morphemes; and a preference for expressive dialect terms (which have often been misconstrued as archaisms).

Hardy's lack of medievalist subjects is more surprising, as his world-view was in many ways thoroughly historicist, and he was much moved by cross-temporal collisions between the ancient and the contemporary (see for example *A Pair of Blue Eyes* (1873), Chapter 22 (man meets trilobite), or *A Laodicean* (1881), Chapter 2 (telegraph-wire meets castle)). But Hardy showed little interest in the Middle Ages as a subject for his own writing, being more inspired by the Roman and prehistoric past.[38] A few poems on medieval subjects can be pointed to, such as 'The Lost Pyx' (in *Poems of the Past and the Present* (1901)) and 'The Abbey Mason' (in *Satires of Circumstance* (1914)), but Hardy's fullest medievalist enterprise, in terms of subject matter, did not appear until 1923: *The Famous Tragedy of the Queen of Cornwall,* in which the Arthurian love affair of Tristram and Iseult (which had previously attracted Arnold and Swinburne, among others) provides substance for a modern mumming-play.

But as has been well studied, Hardy's poetic language, like Hopkins', is profoundly indebted to the historicism of philology, and to his reading in the discipline.[39] In 1898 Hardy responded with some interest to a reviewer who described him, in his poems, as 'seeing all the words in the dictionary on one plane, so to speak, and regarding them all as equally available and appropriate for any and every literary purpose'.[40] Let us take, as an example, the short poem 'A Spot' (from *Poems of the Past and the Present*):

> In years defaced and lost,
> Two sat here, transport-tossed,
> Lit by a living love
> The wilted world knew nothing of:
>> Scared momently
>> By gaingivings,
>> Then hoping things
>> That could not be.
>
> Of love and us no trace
> Abides upon the place;
> The sun and shadows wheel,
> Season and season sereward steal;
>> Foul days and fair
>> Here, too, prevail,
>> And gust and gale
>> As everywhere.
>
> But lonely shepherd souls
> Who bask amid these knolls
> May catch a faery sound
> On sleepy noontides from the ground:
>> 'O not again
>> Till Earth outwears
>> Shall love like theirs
>> Suffuse this glen!'[41]

Hardy draws his lexis here from a characteristically wide catchment-area, and imparts boldness through collocation, compounding, and word-formation—though that boldness, for the most part, chooses perfectly common elements to work with. The first edition of the *Oxford English Dictionary* labels 'faery' as '*arch.*' and 'gaingiving' (in the sense 'misgiving') as '*Obs. exc. arch.*'. 'Wilted' is of course usually applied to vegetation, while 'transport' (in the sense of 'the state of being 'carried out of oneself'') is rarely found in compounds. The second element of 'sereward' is, in current language, no longer a productive suffix, while the first element is labelled 'now *poet.* or *rhetorical*' by the *Oxford English Dictionary*. The compound 'outwears' is less frequent than its phrasal alternative, 'wears out', and is very rarely recorded as an intransitive verb. 'Bask' is a loanword from Old Norse, and sits here alongside a number of Latinate words (such as 'transport', 'prevail', 'suffused', and others); 'glen' is of course a topographical term drawn from Scots. Furthermore, Hardy's revisions to his earlier version of this poem nearly all tend towards the philological enrichment of his diction (for example, 'trouble-tossed' > 'transport-tossed', and 'onward' > 'sereward'). Hardy's diversity of vocabulary, and his cross-period, cross-register approach to word-choice and word-formation, are the products of an immersion in Victorian language study; and we should also observe his feeling for two-stress alliterative phrases—the basic unit of the Old English half-line.

William Morris provides a different sort of case, as in his work we find an attempt to correlate medieval subject matter with an appropriate historical lexis, philologically informed. Morris was a fluent reader of Old Norse, had read widely in Middle English, and was evidently capable enough in Old English. His much-maligned archaism of style is not bogus: his archaisms and oddities of expression nearly always turn out to be historically correct or philologically justified, though one curiosity of his career as a writer is that the language of his poetry tends to be less distanced from contemporary usage than that of his medievalist prose. 'The Lovers of Gudrun' is far less remarkable in its diction than the saga translations that Morris was publishing around the same time, though a small number of loan-translations from Old Norse do appear, such as 'Hill of Laws' (<*lögberg*) and 'home-men' (<*heimamenn*, 'servants'), in addition to the many place-names which Morris anglicizes on an element-by-element basis ('Burgfirth' <*Borgarfjörður*, 'White-river' <*Hvítá*, and so on).

The modest nature of this undertaking is stepped up somewhat in *Sigurd the Volsung* ('mirk-wood' <*myrkviðr*, 'the Helm of Aweing' <*œgishjálmr*), but the full effect of Morris' philological approach only appears in his poetry (as opposed to his prose) with his translation of *Beowulf,* produced in 1895 in collaboration with the Anglo-Saxon scholar A. J. Wyatt:

> What! we of the Spear-Danes of yore days, so was it
> That we learn'd of the fair fame of kings of the folks
> And the Athelings a-faring in framing of valour.
> Oft then Scyld the Sheaf-son from the hosts of the scathers,
> From kindreds a many the mead-settles tore.[42]

It is important to understand what Morris is and is not doing in his *Beowulf* translation. He is not like some historical novelist who has plundered glossaries for a little bit of period detail to sprinkle over the surface of his or her language. Rather, his desire is to 'penetrat[e] into the thought of the old language', and so, through attention to cognates, older meanings, and supposed modern reflexes, to carry over qualities from the source text.[43] We can see this by comparing the original of the passage above:

> Hwæt! Wē Gār-Dena in gēar-dagum
> þēod-cyninga þrym gefrūnon,
> hū ðā æðelingas ellen fremedon.
> Oft Scyld Scēfing sceaþena þrēatum,
> Monegum mǣgþum, meodo-setla oftēah.[44]

All the compounds in the original have been rendered as compounds or two-element phrases by Morris: 'Spear-Danes' (*Gār-Dena*), 'yore days' (*gēar-dagum*), 'kings of the folks' (*þēod-cyninga*), and 'mead-settles' (*meodo-setla*). A number of simplexes have simply been transposed into Modern English: 'What!' (*Hwæt!*), 'Athelings' (*æðelingas*), and 'scathers' (*sceaþena*), the last a typically bold—or optimistic—attempt. Morris was no Germanic absolutist, though, and he is happy to select 'valour' for *ellen*. He is also alert to the syntax of the original, replicating the postponement of the main verb to the second line ('learn'd' / *gefrūnon*) and so reproducing the uncertainty of sense that the audience experiences in the first line (though he re-iterates the pronoun 'we', rather than endorsing the lengthy separation between subject and verb). This is, in short, a translation that is thoroughly aligned with the grain of its original, and fully confident in its linguistic strategies. As with Hardy, we should also note the prominent alliteration: for his period, Morris' is a distinguished performance in attempting the four-stress alliterative line. In every way, Morris' translation, or re-working, is one that would have been unimaginable before the rise of philology.

Finally, what about Tennyson in this context? In his young adulthood Tennyson was acquainted with the pioneering John Mitchell Kemble; he read widely in mid-century philology and subscribed to the Early English Text Society; and in 1880 he published a translation of the Old English *Battle of Brunanburh* that was significant in its attention to both diction and metre.[45] Matthew Reynolds has argued that in *Idylls of the King*, especially the later ones, Tennyson displays a strong preference for 'northern' (Anglo-Saxon) vocabulary, over 'southern' (Latinate, Romance).[46] It is certainly true that the *Idylls* do not consistently show the type of aureate diction evidenced in some of Tennyson's early poetry, but the claim can be overstated, and it is not difficult to find Latinate diction in almost every verse paragraph of the *Idylls*, and in some passages in almost every line.[47] What is more, almost all the terms of rank and status in Tennyson's Arthurian world are, of course, Romance-derived: *baron, liege-lord, seneschal, vassal, villain,* and so on, alongside important cultural terms such as *chivalry, courtesy,* and *gentleness* (all these from 'Gareth and Lynette'). One might argue that this is inevitable: the ahistoricism of Arthurian legend posed problems for poets who wished to achieve a consonance between history and language, and in its cultural trappings the Arthurian world was imagined in terms of period detail drawn from the high and late Middle Ages (1100–1500). Indeed, Anglo-Saxon vocabulary is from one point of view the least appropriate lexis with which to narrate Arthurian story. From Geoffrey of Monmouth onwards (and, if Arthur ever had an historical existence, in history too), it was the Anglo-Saxons—heathen, Germanic-speaking—who brought an end to the Table Round (as Tennyson usually calls it, demonstrating a French-derived syntax with a post-positioned adjective). Tennyson never uses the word '(Anglo-)Saxon' in his *Idylls,* evidently conscious of the problematic nature of Arthur's tale for English national history, but his heathen hordes are plainly to be identified as Anglo-Saxons, as indicated by the detail that the White Horse is their emblem (as, later, in an important work of Edwardian medievalism, G. K. Chesterton's *Ballad of the White Horse* (1911)).[48] Another way of explaining Tennyson's fondness for Anglo-Saxon words in his *Idylls*—and, indeed, other features of his style and tone—is to see them as arising from his admiration for, and indebtedness to, Malory (and occasional strings of Anglo-Saxon monosyllables are taken over verbatim from this source).[49] Malory's prose style has been well characterized as chronicle-like, showing a preference for paratactic syntax and a deliberately restricted vocabulary, and thus (as a consequence) yielding few clues as to motivation and causality.[50] Reynolds' observation that 'the *Idylls* make no attempt to ingratiate themselves with their readers...Rather, they are just there' would serve equally well as a characterization of Malory's stories, and this may suggest that certain Malory-like effects are what Tennyson was attempting to achieve.[51] Medieval sources, as argued above, often supplied nineteenth-century poets not only with their subject-matter, but also with their narrative mode and (as here) their lexical preferences.

Alfred Austin, the laureate unveiler of Whitby's Caedmon Cross, wrote:

> The English language, as it now exists, is indebted for its volume and variety to many tributaries; and we owe it to our mother-tongue not to allow it to be impoverished by gratuitous prejudice against any one of its sources. The attempt to exalt the Saxon over the Latin elements of our language can never be more than an exhibition of philological pedantry.[52]

He went on, however, referring to himself impersonally: 'But one perforce felt that, in portraying a period anterior to the days when the Latin and Romance literatures gradually enriched the vocabulary of Beowulf, one was bound to eschew, as far as might be, glaring anachronisms of speech'.[53] It cannot be claimed that the language of *England's Darling* resoundingly substantiates this claim, though there is a smattering of interesting compounds (such as 'gafolwood', 'time-token', and 'foam-fenced'). But in spite of these few features Austin's verse can hardly fail to appear anodyne when set next to the (philologically speaking) much denser and richer diction of Hopkins, Hardy, and Morris. Moreover, it is thought-provoking that all three of these exerted an important influence on the course of twentieth-century poetry (Morris, the least obvious example, was a significant figure for the young Ezra Pound), and that the first two largely escaped the reaction against 'Victorianism'. There is perhaps a story to be told here about the unexpected triumph of at least one form of Victorian medievalism.

NOTES

1. See 'The Caedmon Memorial at Whitby', *The Times*, 22 Sept. 1898; Canon [H.D.] Rawnsley, 'The Story of the Cædmon Cross', *The Sunday Magazine*, Oct. 1898, 691–96, and E. F. Rawnsley, *Canon Rawnsley: An Account of his Life* (Glasgow: Maclehose, 1923), 117–120.
2. Alfred Austin, *England's Darling* (London: Macmillan, 1896).
3. See for example Alice Chandler, *A Dream of Order: The Medieval Ideal in Nineteenth-Century Literature* (London: Routledge and Kegan Paul, 1971) and Michael Alexander, *Medievalism: The Middle Ages in Modern England* (New Haven: Yale University Press, 2007).
4. See, for example, Clare A. Simmons, *Reversing the Conquest: History and Myth in Nineteenth-Century British Literature* (New Brunswick: Rutgers University Press, 1990) and Stephanie L. Barczewski, *Myth and National Identity in Nineteenth-Century Britain: The Legends of King Arthur and Robin Hood* (Oxford: Oxford University Press, 2000).
5. See, for example, Joep Leerssen, *National Thought in Europe: A Cultural History* (Amsterdam: Amsterdam University Press, 2006) and Andrew Wawn, with Graham Johnson and John Walker, eds., *Constructing Nations, Reconstructing Myth: Essays in Honour of T. A. Shippey* (Turnhout: Brepols, 2007).
6. Inga Bryden, *Reinventing King Arthur: The Arthurian Legends in Victorian Culture* (Aldershot: Ashgate, 2005), 33.
7. See, for example, Patrick Wormald, 'The Venerable Bede and the 'Church of the English'', in Geoffrey Rowell, ed., *The English Religious Tradition and the Genius of Anglicanism* (Wantage: Ikon, 1992), 13–32.
8. See John Batchelor, *Lady Trevelyan and the Pre-Raphaelite Brotherhood* (London: Chatto and Windus, 2006), 125–144.
9. See Barbara Yorke, *The King Alfred Millenary in Winchester, 1901*, Hampshire Papers 17 (Winchester: Hampshire County Council, 1999) and Joanne Parker, *'England's Darling': The Victorian Cult of Alfred the Great* (Manchester: Manchester University Press, 2007), 1–32.
10. For an extended case study see Matthew Townend, *The Vikings and Victorian Lakeland: The Norse Medievalism of W. G. Collingwood and his Contemporaries* (Kendal: Cumberland and Westmorland Antiquarian and Archaeological Society, 2009).
11. See Philippa Levine, *The Amateur and the Professional: Antiquarians, Historians and Archaeologists in Victorian England, 1838–1886* (Cambridge: Cambridge University Press, 1986) and K.D. M. Snell, ed., *The Regional Novel in Britain and Ireland, 1800–1990* (Cambridge: Cambridge University Press, 1998).
12. See Marcus Waithe, *William Morris's Utopia of Strangers: Victorian Medievalism and the Ideal of Hospitality* (Cambridge: Brewer, 2006).
13. William Morris, 'Preface' to *Völsunga Saga*, in *The Collected Works of William Morris*, 24 vols., ed. May Morris (London: Longmans, Green, 1910–15), vii. 286.
14. Andrew Wawn, *The Vikings and the Victorians: Inventing the Old North in Nineteenth-Century Britain* (Cambridge: Brewer, 2000). See also David Ashurst, 'William Morris and the Volsungs', in David Clark and Carl Phelpstead, eds., *Old Norse Made New: Essays on the Post-Medieval Reception of Old Norse Literature and Culture* (London: Viking Society for Northern Research, 2007), 50.

15. See also Matthew Reynolds, *The Realms of Verse: English Poetry in a Time of Nation-Building* (Oxford: Oxford University Press, 2001), 212–215.

16. Robert J. C. Young, *The Idea of English Ethnicity* (Oxford: Blackwell, 2008). See also, from a different angle, T. A. Shippey, 'The Undeveloped Image: Anglo-Saxon in Popular Consciousness from Turner to Tolkien', in Donald Scragg and Carole Weinberg, eds., *Literary Appropriations of the Anglo-Saxons from the Thirteenth to the Twentieth Century* (Cambridge: Cambridge University Press, 2000), 215–236.

17. Young, *The Idea of English Ethnicity*, 125.

18. J. J. A. Worsaae, *An Account of the Danes and Norwegians in England, Scotland, and Ireland* (London: Murray, 1852), xxi–xxii. See also Joanne Parker, 'The Dragon and the Raven: Saxons, Danes and the problem of defining national character in Victorian England', *European Journal of English Studies*, **13** (2009), 257–273.

19. W. P. Ker, *Epic and Romance: Essays on Medieval Literature* (London: Macmillan, 1896). See Michael Lapidge, 'The Comparative Approach', in Katherine O'Brien O'Keeffe, ed., *Reading Old English Texts* (Cambridge: Cambridge University Press, 1997), 20–38.

20. On nineteenth-century Arthurianism, see for example Roger Simpson, *Camelot Regained: The Arthurian Revival and Tennyson 1800–1849* (Cambridge: Brewer, 1990) and Bryden, *Reinventing King Arthur*.

21. See Yuri Fuwa, 'Malory's Morte Darthur in Tennyson's Library', *Studies in Medievalism*, 4 (1992), 161–169.

22. Thomas Malory, *Works*, ed. Eugène Vinaver, 2nd edn. (Oxford: Oxford University Press, 1971), 708.

23. See Christopher Ricks, *Tennyson*, 2nd edn. (Basingstoke: Macmillan, 1989), 252–253.

24. Printed in David Staines, *Tennyson's Camelot: The Idylls of the King and its Medieval Sources* (Waterloo: Wilfrid Laurier University Press, 1982), 179–202.

25. Eiríkur Magnússon, 'Preface' to *The Stories of the Kings of Norway (Heimskringla)*, trans. William Morris and Eiríkur Magnússon, vol. 4 (London: Quaritch, 1905), xiii. On Morris and the sagas see further J. N. Swannell, *William Morris and Old Norse Literature* (London: William Morris Society, 1961) and Wawn, *The Vikings and the Victorians*, 245–79.

26. See Linda Julian, '"Laxdaela Saga" and "The Lovers of Gudrun": Morris' Poetic Vision', *Victorian Poetry*, 34 (1996), 355–371.

27. See Vésteinn Ólason, *Dialogues with the Viking Age: Narration and Representation in the Sagas of Icelanders*, trans. Andrew Wawn (Reykjavík: Mál og Menning, 1998).

28. *The Saga of the People of Laxardal and Bolli Bollason's Tale*, trans. Keneva Kunz (London: Penguin, 2008), 116. For the first, Victorian translation (with a variant reading), see *Laxdæla Saga*, trans. Muriel A. C. Press (London: Dent, 1899), 178.

29. Morris, 'The Lovers of Gudrun', in *Collected Works*, v. 389–90.

30. See further, Herbert F. Tucker, *Epic: Britain's Heroic Muse 1790–1910* (Oxford: Oxford University Press, 2008), 515–522.

31. See Chris Jones, *Strange Likeness: The Use of Old English in Twentieth-Century Poetry* (Oxford: Oxford University Press, 2006) and 'Anglo-Saxonism in Nineteenth-Century Poetry', *Literature Compass*, 7 (2010), 358–369.

32. See Margaret Clunies Ross, *A History of Old Norse Poetry and Poetics* (Cambridge: Brewer, 2005).

33. See Hans Aarsleff, *The Study of Language in England, 1780–1860*, 2nd edn. (Minneapolis: University of Minnesota Press, 1983), Anna Morpurgo Davies, *History of*

Linguistics: Volume IV Nineteenth-Century Linguistics (London: Longman, 1998), and Haruko Momma, *From Philology to English Studies: Language and Culture in the Nineteenth Century* (Cambridge: Cambridge University Press, 2013).

34. See K. M. Elisabeth Murray, *Caught in the Web of Words: James A. H. Murray and the Oxford English Dictionary* (Oxford: Oxford University Press, 1977) and Lynda Mugglestone, ed., *Lexicography and the OED: Pioneers in the Untrodden Forest* (Oxford: Oxford University Press, 2000).

35. See Alexander, *Medievalism*, 180–192.

36. See Manfred Markus, Clive Upton, and Reinhard Heuberger, eds., *Joseph Wright's English Dialect Dictionary and Beyond: Studies in Late Modern English Dialectology* (Frankfurt am Main: Lang, 2010).

37. James Milroy, *The Language of Gerard Manley Hopkins* (London: Deutsch, 1977), 39. See also Cary H. Plotkin, *The Tenth Muse: Victorian Philology and the Genesis of the Poetic Language of Gerard Manley Hopkins* (Carbondale: Southern Illinois University Press, 1989).

38. See Martin J. P. Davies, *A Distant Prospect of Wessex: Archaeology and the Past in the Life and Works of Thomas Hardy* (Oxford: Archaeopress, 2011).

39. See Ralph W. V. Elliott, *Thomas Hardy's English* (Oxford: Blackwell, 1984) and Dennis Taylor, *Hardy's Literary Language and Victorian Philology* (Oxford: Clarendon Press, 1993).

40. Thomas Hardy, *The Collected Letters of Thomas Hardy: Volume Two 1893–1901*, ed. Richard Little Purdy and Michael Millgate (Oxford: Clarendon Press, 1980), 207.

41. Hardy, 'A Spot', in *The Complete Poetical Works of Thomas Hardy: Volume One*, ed. Samuel Hynes (Oxford: Clarendon Press, 1982), 175–176.

42. *Beowulf*, trans. Morris, *Collected Works*, x. 179.

43. Magnússon, 'Preface', xiv. See further, P. M. Tilling, 'William Morris's Translation of *Beowulf*: Studies in his vocabulary', in P. M. Tilling, ed., *Studies in English Language and Early Literature in Honour of Paul Christophersen* (Coleraine: The New University of Ulster, 1981), 163–175, Waithe, *William Morris's Utopia of Strangers*, 90–106, and Chris Jones, 'The Reception of William Morris's *Beowulf*', in David Latham, ed., *Writing on the Image: Reading William Morris* (Toronto: University of Toronto Press, 2007), 197–208.

44. *Beowulf*, ed. A. J. Wyatt, 2nd edn. (Cambridge: Cambridge University Press, 1898), 1.

45. See Patrick Greig Scott, '"Flowering in a Lonely Word": Tennyson and the Victorian Study of Language', *Victorian Poetry*, 18 (1980), 371–381, and Edward B. Irving, Jr, 'The charge of the Saxon Brigade: Tennyson's *Battle of Brunanburh*', in Donald Scragg and Carole Weinberg, eds., *Literary Appropriations of the Anglo-Saxons from the Thirteenth to the Twentieth Century* (Cambridge: Cambridge University Press, 2000), 174–193.

46. Reynolds, *The Realms of Verse*, 238–43, 267–70.

47. See for example, simply as a selection, Tennyson, *Idylls of the King* in *Tennyson: A Selected Edition*, ed. Christopher Ricks (Harlow: Pearson Longman, 2007), 785 ('Geraint and Enid', lines 887–918), 915 ('Pelleas and Ettarre', lines 419–26), and 923–24 ('The Last Tournament' lines 89-107).

48. Tennyson, *Idylls of the King*, 843 ('Lancelot and Elaine', line 297), 885 ('The Holy Grail', line 312), and 942 and 956 ('Guinevere', lines 15 and 571); see also 786 ('Geraint and Enid', lines 934–36).

49. Tennyson, *Idylls of the King* 861 ('my good days are done': 'Lancelot and Elaine', line 942).

50. See P. J. C. Field, *Romance and Chronicle: A Study of Malory's Prose Style* (London: Barrie and Jenkins, 1971) and Jeremy Smith, 'Language and Style in Malory' in Elizabeth Archibald and A. S. G. Edwards, eds., *A Companion to Malory* (Cambridge: Brewer, 1996), 97–113.

51. Reynolds, *The Realms of Verse*, 271.

52. Austin, *England's Darling*, xvi.

53. Austin, *England's Darling*, xvi–xvii.

SELECT BIBLIOGRAPHY

Aarsleff, Hans, *The Study of Language in England, 1780–1860*, 2nd edn. (Minneapolis: University of Minnesota Press, 1983).

Alexander, Michael, *Medievalism: The Middle Ages in Modern England* (New Haven: Yale University Press, 2007).

Barczewski, Stephanie L., *Myth and National Identity in Nineteenth-Century Britain: The Legends of King Arthur and Robin Hood* (Oxford: Oxford University Press, 2000).

Bryden, Inga, *Reinventing King Arthur: The Arthurian Legends in Victorian Culture* (Aldershot: Ashgate, 2005).

Chandler, Alice, *A Dream of Order: The Medieval Ideal in Nineteenth-Century Literature* (London: Routledge and Kegan Paul, 1971).

Matthews, David, *The Making of Middle English, 1765–1910* (Minneapolis: University of Minnesota Press, 1999).

Momma, Haruko, *From Philology to English Studies: Language and Culture in the Nineteenth Century* (Cambridge: Cambridge University Press, 2013).

Milroy, James, *The Language of Gerard Manley Hopkins* (London: Deutsch, 1977).

Parker, Joanne, *'England's Darling': The Victorian Cult of Alfred the Great* (Manchester: Manchester University Press, 2007).

Scragg, Donald, and Weinberg, Carole, eds., *Literary Appropriations of the Anglo-Saxons from the Thirteenth to the Twentieth Century* (Cambridge: Cambridge University Press, 2000).

Simmons, Clare A., *Reversing the Conquest: History and Myth in Nineteenth-Century British Literature* (New Brunswick: Rutgers University Press, 1990).

Taylor, Dennis, *Hardy's Literary Language and Victorian Philology* (Oxford: Clarendon Press, 1993).

Waithe, Marcus, *William Morris's Utopia of Strangers: Victorian Medievalism and the Ideal of Hospitality* (Cambridge: Brewer, 2006).

Wawn, Andrew, *The Vikings and the Victorians: Inventing the Old North in Nineteenth-Century Britain* (Cambridge: Brewer, 2000).

CHAPTER 11

....

VICTORIAN MILTONS

....

ERIK GRAY

To understand the relation of Milton to Victorian poetry, it may be helpful to begin with a Victorian novel. In Elizabeth Gaskell's industrial novel *North and South* (1855), Milton is both nowhere and everywhere. The poet is never quoted or referred to over the course of the book. Yet the word 'Milton' appears on nearly every page, since that is the name Gaskell gives to her fictional version of Manchester, where the story is set. This may seem an insignificant coincidence: the primary reason for the choice of name is that Milton is, indeed, a mill town, and tensions between mill-owners and their labourers form a major focus of the narrative. But once the reader becomes conscious of the presence of 'Milton', it becomes clear that the name is no coincidence. *North and South* begins with the exile of Mr. Hale and his daughter Margaret from their Edenic home in the New Forest to a fallen world of labour and sickness.[1] Such a story is biblical, of course, not specifically Miltonic, but it is given a Miltonic twist by the figure of Mr. Hale. Like Milton himself, Hale is compelled by his own conscience to leave the Established Church and to make a living instead by offering instruction in Latin and Greek. Such parallels continue to multiply as the novel progresses, and cumulatively they serve an important function: the constant presence of Milton, the great poet of the Civil War, hovering over the text reminds the reader of the deep divisions that threaten Victorian England—a civil turmoil all the more ominous for remaining largely invisible.

In the works of the major Victorian poets, Milton is similarly both nowhere and everywhere to be seen. There has long existed a critical consensus that although Milton exerted an enormous, at times overwhelming influence on poets of the Romantic period, his direct influence on English poetry all but disappeared after the deaths of Byron, Percy Shelley, and John Keats in the mid-1820s. This notion is visible already in R. D. Havens' *The Influence of Milton on English Poetry* (1922), which ends with Keats; it is made explicit by Joseph Wittreich, who writes in *The Romantics on Milton* (1970) that the Victorians, in contrast to their predecessors, were 'repelled' by Milton; and it is everywhere implicit in the writings of Harold Bloom. Bloom's early, seminal works on literary influence all display the same pattern: they show Romantic poets struggling with the mighty presence of Milton, while Victorian poets confront the precedent of Romanticism; but Bloom almost never gives an instance of a Victorian poet engaging directly with Milton.[2] The same view continues into the twenty-first century: both *A Companion to Milton* (2001) and *The Oxford Handbook of Milton* (2009) devote whole sections to Milton's reception and influence; but their accounts end with the Romantics.[3]

There is a sense in which this viewpoint is clearly misleading. Milton, far from being absent, is detectable throughout Victorian poetry: the Victorians continued to read and admire Milton, and their poems are filled with allusions to his life and work. From the work of Alfred Tennyson alone (to look no further) one could compile a whole anthology of Miltonic echoes and borrowings—an influence Tennyson freely acknowledged, both in recorded conversations and in his poem 'Milton' (1864). And yet the common critical perception of Milton's disappearance remains oddly true. Although Milton certainly continues to exert an influence on Victorian poetry, he ceases to stand out from all other precursors as he had earlier in the century. A list of major Romantic poems—*The Prelude, Prometheus Unbound, Hyperion*—immediately, insistently calls to mind a Miltonic precedent, as a similar list of Victorian long poems—*Aurora Leigh, Empedocles on Etna, The Ring and the Book*—does not. Even the example of Tennyson is equivocal since, as I outline below, Milton's influence on Tennyson is much more oblique than might at first appear. In Tennyson, as in Victorian poetry more generally, Milton appears in much the same way he does in *North and South*: constantly present, yet strangely diffuse.

How should we understand this phenomenon? The explanation seems to be, not that Milton's influence declined, but the opposite: he did not disappear from the Victorian poetic consciousness, but pervaded it. Such a development not only follows logically from the Romantic precedent—the very fact that Romantic poets had so frequently and self-consciously invoked Milton rendered it unnecessary for Victorian poets to do the same—but is also consistent with the more general reception of Milton in this period. The Victorian era was steeped in Milton. Victorian editions of Milton's poetry, particularly those by Thomas Keightley (1859) and David Masson (1874), far outstripped anything produced in the previous generation. The canon of his poetry, meanwhile, was expanding, as readers and critics increasingly looked beyond his major works. ('[T]o appraise Milton', A. C. Swinburne reminded the reading public, 'is not merely "to appraise *Paradise Lost*".')[4] At the same time, following the publication of Milton's newly rediscovered treatise on *Christian Doctrine* in 1825, interest in Milton's polemical writings soared, and his prose began to be widely available for the first time.[5] Above all, the period was marked by an increased attention to Milton's life, as revealed both by Masson's monumental six-volume *Life of John Milton* (1859–80), which unlike earlier biographies placed Milton firmly in historical and literary context, and at a more popular level by Anne Manning's best-selling novel *The Maiden and Married Life of Mary Powell* (1849), which recounts Milton's life from the point of view of his first wife.

In short, if Milton seems less insistently present to the Victorian than to the Romantic imagination, it is not because he was unfamiliar to the Victorians, but overfamiliar. This familiarity was itself a commonplace: 'Of John Milton, what can be now said which may not be familiarly known by all who possess even a superficial acquaintance with the litera-ture of their country?' asked the *New Monthly Magazine* in 1834. George Gilfillan, writing a decade later, agrees: 'What more can be said or sung? Is it not impossible to add to … our sense of his greatness?'[6] Yet that greatness is not diminished, but strengthened, by the sense of familiarity. James White, in an essay comparing Milton to the early medieval poet St Avitus, quotes them side by side: 'Hear the saint', he writes before quoting Avitus, and then, before quoting *Paradise Lost*, 'Listen to John.'[7] To call Milton 'John' is an act both of cheeky familiarity and of literal canonization; White is treating Milton either as a very close friend or as a saint. This is the characteristic duality of the Victorian Milton: he is at once common and exalted. If Victorian poems seem to engage with Milton less energeti-cally than do their Romantic predecessors, that is because he seems not so much the giver of poetic tradition as the given—so obvious as to go without saying. Yet such familiarity represents no breach but an expansion of Milton's influence.

There is no room in the current chapter to explore this dynamic in every major Victorian poet. Instead in what follows I present three models: the Singular Milton (inherited from the Romantics), the Diffuse Milton, and the Invisible Milton. For each model of influence I offer illustrations from the works of Tennyson and Elizabeth Barrett Browning, perhaps the two Victorian poets who engage most consistently with Milton over the course of their careers, together with readings of other relevant poets and poems. Although it is impossible even to begin to discuss every notable instance of Milton's influence on Victorian poetry, I hope that these models will provide a helpful starting-point for further analyses.

THE SINGULAR MILTON

It is important to recognize that the forms of direct, conscious engagement with Milton's precedent that characterize Romantic poetry, and that have been the subject of so much critical debate, do continue into the Victorian period.[8] The continuities are most palpable in Victorian sonnets, which, as James Nelson observes in his illu-minating monograph *The Sublime Puritan: Milton and the Victorians*, offer the clear-est example of 'Milton's direct influence' on Victorian poetry.[9] In singling out Milton as their prime model, Victorian sonneteers resemble William Wordsworth, whose major period of sonnet writing was inspired, according to his own account, by a rereading of Milton's sonnets. Wordsworth acknowledged his debt in his sonnet 'London, 1802' ('Milton! thou shouldst be living at this hour'), and many Victorian poets followed his example. Henry Ellison (1811–90), for instance, a particularly prolific sonneteer, com-posed no fewer than seven sonnets entitled 'To Milton', all of them hewing very close to Wordsworth's example.

Yet it is not only minor Victorian poets (nor only sonneteers) who carry on the Romantic practice of singling out Milton, both explicitly and implicitly, as the precur-sor to whom their poetry responds. The longest and most ambitious piece in Elizabeth

Barrett Browning's 1844 collection, for example, is *A Drama of Exile*, a closet drama that picks up the story of Adam and Eve precisely where Milton left off at the end of *Paradise Lost*. Browning is acutely conscious of treading on Milton's territory, as she makes clear in her preface:

> My subject was the new and strange experience of the fallen humanity, as it went forth from Paradise into the wilderness; with a peculiar reference to Eve's allotted grief, which . . . appeared to me imperfectly apprehended hitherto, and more expressible by a woman than a man. . . . But when all was done, I felt afraid, as I said before, of my position. I had promised my own prudence to shut close the gates of Eden between Milton and myself, so that none might say I dared to walk in his footsteps. . . . It would not do. The subject, and his glory covering it, swept through the gates, and I stood full in it, against my will, and contrary to my vow,—till I shrank back fearing, almost desponding; hesitating to venture even a passing association with our great poet before the face of the public.[10]

This is a richly suggestive passage. Browning's protestations of humility at the end are complicated by her defiant claim at the beginning that, as a woman, she is more capable than Milton was of representing Eve. In the poem itself Browning continually challenges Milton, while also recognizing that such a challenge to authority is itself Miltonic; in this her work resembles Byron's closet dramas, especially *Cain*. But whether it continues *Paradise Lost* or contests it, either way *A Drama of Exile*, like *Cain* (and unlike *North and South*), clearly points to Milton as its primary literary model.

The same is true of many Tennyson poems, especially the early ones: his juvenile poem 'Armageddon' (*c*.1827), for instance, in which the speaker is visited by an angel and experiences sublime visions from a mountain top, clearly invites comparison with similar moments in both *Paradise Lost* and *Paradise Regained*. The debt is equally clearly signalled in such mature poems as 'Ulysses' (1842)—the one Victorian poem that Bloom marks out as deriving directly from Milton ('[Ulysses'] truest and largest ancestor is Milton's Satan in Book II of *Paradise Lost*').[11] Steven Dillon concurs with Bloom, noting that the final line of 'Ulysses'—'To strive, to seek, to find, and not to yield'—echoes Satan's 'courage never to submit or yield' (*PL* i. 108).[12] Similar moments, both in the work of Tennyson and in other poets, are easily found; this form of direct engagement with Milton's major works continues throughout the nineteenth century. But the peculiarly Victorian poetic response to Milton is even more widespread, and more unusual.

THE DIFFUSE MILTON

Browning's *Aurora Leigh* (1856) mentions dozens of poets by name. The eponymous narrator is a voracious reader as well as a poet, and she happily acknowledges her chief sources of inspiration. Milton, however, goes unmentioned, and this seems only appropriate, since *Aurora Leigh* does not appear particularly Miltonic. Although it is a long poem in blank verse, and the most ambitious of all Browning's works, the poem presents itself as a verse novel, discouraging any easy association with epic precedent. The absence of a clear Miltonic subtext comes out all the more strongly when *Aurora Leigh* is compared to Wordsworth's *The Prelude*, published just a few years earlier in 1850. Both poems offer autobiographical narratives describing, in Wordsworth's phrase, the 'growth of a poet's mind'.[13] Wordsworth, however, is conscious of Milton's precedent at every step. He famously echoes one of the last lines of *Paradise Lost* ('The World was all before them' [xii. 646]) at the opening of his own poem: 'The earth is all before me' (i. 14). And he self-consciously seeks out, as a subject for his epic endeavours, a 'tale by Milton left unsung' (i. 169). *The Prelude*, in other words, resembles *A Drama of Exile*—it explicitly picks up where Milton left off. *Aurora Leigh*, by contrast, makes no such gesture.

Yet this does not mean that Milton had no influence on *Aurora Leigh*, only that the influence takes a different form. Echoes and allusions to Milton appear scattered throughout the poem; Sarah Annes Brown, for instance, has noted a number of suggestive verbal and thematic parallels with *Paradise Lost*.[14] What distinguishes these connections is that, though numerous, they remain understated. When Aurora, 'creeping' around in a garret full of old books, first discovers poetry, she writes that 'my soul, / At poetry's divine first finger-touch, / Let go conventions and sprang up surprised' (i. 850–52). Her phrasing recalls the moment when Satan, prying about Eden in the shape of a toad, is discovered by an angel: 'Him thus intent *Ithuriel* with his Spear / Touch'd lightly;...up he starts / Discover'd and surpris'd' (*PL* iv. 810–14). Aurora does not specify which 'divine' poet sparks her transformation; but perhaps she does not need to.

The point is not that allusions to Milton are more subtle in *Aurora Leigh* than in *The Prelude*, but that Milton's influence is qualitatively different. Milton does not stand out in *Aurora Leigh* as the chief precedent for either Browning's or Aurora's poetic ambitions. Rather, he hovers constantly in the background, providing a model for every part of Aurora's career, minor as well as major—as, for example, when Aurora describes how she is reluctantly obliged to try her hand at writing prose.

> [B]eing but poor, I was constrained, for life,
> To work with one hand for the booksellers
> While working with the other for myself
> And art...
>
> I resolved by prose
> To make a space to sphere my living verse.
> I wrote for cyclopædias, magazines,
> And weekly papers...
>
> I wrote tales beside,
> Carved many an article on cherry-stones
> To suit light readers,—something in the lines
> Revealing, it was said, the mallet-hand.
>
> (iii. 302–20)

There are several allusions to Milton in this passage. The opening recalls his description, in *The Reason of Church Government* (1642), of his being compelled to write, however ham-handedly, in prose: 'I should not choose this manner of writing, wherein knowing myself inferior to myself...I have the use, as I may account it, but of my left hand.'[15] The end of the passage alludes to Samuel Johnson's comment, recorded by Boswell, explaining what he perceived as Milton's failure as a sonnet writer: 'Milton...was a genius that could cut a Colossus from a rock, but could not carve heads upon cherry-stones.'[16] These allusions are typically Victorian, first in being particularly light-handed: so familiar is Milton that Aurora (and Browning) can trust her audience to appreciate the most glancing allusions to his prose works or to his eighteenth-century reception. But even more importantly, Aurora is invoking Milton here as a precedent for her perceived *failures*. This is a frequent Victorian trope: Milton is remembered not only as a divinely inspired bard but, more familiarly, as a man who faces all the troubles and distractions of living in the world. Whereas Wordsworth's struggles and missteps at the beginning of *The Prelude* are implicitly set in contrast to a grand Miltonic precedent, here Aurora draws comfort from the example of a very different, more mundane Milton.

This tendency to invoke the unsublime or unremarkable Milton characterizes Victorian poetry as a whole. Tennyson, for instance, voices an explicit preference for Milton's earth over his heaven or hell. He begins his poem 'Milton' by enumerating the sublime aspects of *Paradise Lost*, but turns his attention halfway through to the 'charms' of the beautiful instead:

> Me rather all that bowery loneliness,
> The brooks of Eden mazily murmuring,
> And bloom profuse and cedar arches
> Charm...

This is Tennyson's practice throughout his career: he alludes frequently to Milton, but usually to the more inconspicuous or unexpected parts of Milton's work. *In Memoriam*, for instance, is shot through with Miltonic echoes, but they are rarely the ones we would expect. From the time of its publication in 1850, Tennyson's elegy drew comparisons with Milton's 'Lycidas'; but Henry Van Dyke, author of one of the earliest critical books about Tennyson's poetry (1889), grew frustrated at the analogy:

> The comparison of *In Memoriam* with *Lycidas* would certainly appear...easy and obvious; so obvious, indeed, that it has been made a thousand times, and is fluently repeated by every critic who has had occasion to speak of English elegies. But this is just one of those cases in which an external similarity conceals a fundamental unlikeness.[17]

Van Dyke's point, however, is not that Milton is irrelevant to *In Memoriam* but the contrary. Critics have focused so exclusively on the Milton they expect to find—the elegiac Milton of 'Lycidas'—that they have not remarked on Tennyson's more diffuse but profound engagement with *Paradise Lost*, which shares so many of the chief concerns of *In Memoriam*: the relation of spirit to body, for example, or the relevance of cosmological knowledge to daily existence.

Even when *In Memoriam* does specifically recall 'Lycidas', Tennyson continues to draw unexpected inspiration from *Paradise Lost*. A series of lyrics early in *In Memoriam* (sections 9–18) concerns the return of Hallam's body, by ship, from abroad—clearly recalling the shipwreck at the heart of 'Lycidas'.[18] But as he waits for the ship, the speaker twice remarks on the 'deep peace' that surrounds him: 'Calm and deep peace on this high wold'; 'Calm and deep peace in this wide air' (xi. 5, 13). The phrase derives from Book 7 of *Paradise Lost*, where God causes the created world to emerge out of the 'immeasurable Abyss / Outrageous as a Sea', commanding, 'Silence, ye troubl'd waves, and thou Deep, peace' (vii. 211–16). Tennyson called this 'a magnificent line': 'How much finer than "and billows, peace," the proper scansion, this break is, and the alliteration how subtle, "and thou dee*p, peace*"!'[19] The allusion is not only apt, since Milton is describing the emergence of a solid body out of 'a Sea' (which is what the speaker of *In Memoriam* awaits), but also representative. Tennyson's allusions to Milton more often than not focus on moments of concretion, on the material rather than the spiritual. Even in 'Armageddon', when the speaker 'seem[s] to stand / Upon the outward verge and bound alone / Of God's omniscience', he remains conscious of mundane details: 'the hum of men / …And notes of busy Life in distant worlds' (ii. 25–38). Yet this physical detail is just as Miltonic as the cosmic vision, since it derives from 'L'Allegro': 'Tow'red Cities please us then, / And the busy hum of men'. Like *Aurora Leigh*, Tennyson does not cherry-pick only the sublime or ethereal moments from Milton's life and writings, but imitates even the most humdrum.

Tennyson's imitations of Milton are rendered inconspicuous, not only because they tend to draw upon the less prominent or expected parts of Milton's work, but because they often appear buried amid echoes of other poets. This is the case, for instance, with 'Ulysses': although the character of the speaker is certainly indebted to Milton's Satan, the poem diverts attention away from the Miltonic precedent by drawing even more directly upon the figure of Ulysses in Dante's *Inferno*. This practice is common in Victorian poetry, nowhere more so than in the work of Matthew Arnold, who consistently places Milton amid a chorus of other voices. One of Arnold's early poems, for example, clearly recalls Milton's sonnet to Cyriack Skinner: Milton tells his addressee to pay no attention to 'what the *Swede* intend, and what the French'; Arnold similarly declares 'If France and we are really friends, / And what the Russian Czar intends, / Is no concern of ours'.[20] Yet the title of Arnold's piece, 'Horatian Echo', obscures the debt by acknowledging only another, classical source of inspiration. Similarly, critics have noted the highly Miltonic language at the end of 'Dover Beach':

> the world, which seems
> To lie before us like a land of dreams,
> So various, so beautiful, so new,
> Hath really neither joy, nor love, nor light,
> Nor certitude, nor peace, nor help for pain;
> And we are here as on a darkling plain
> Swept with confused alarms of struggle and flight,
> Where ignorant armies clash by night.

The 'world which [lies] before us' echoes the same line from *Paradise Lost* ('The World was all before them') Wordsworth had so prominently invoked at the opening of *The Prelude*, while 'neither joy, nor love' are Satan's words upon looking at lost paradise (*PL* iv. 509).[21] But it is easy to overlook these echoes, since the passage concludes with the more famous and more direct allusion to Thucydides' description of the battle of Epipolae. And the poem as a whole, like 'Horatian Echo', is more eager to draw attention to its classical sources: the only writer actually named in this densely allusive poem is Sophocles.

Yet the influence of Milton could be said to be all the greater for being hidden away. Arnold's poems tend to centre on figures who hide or retreat from the world rather than confront it directly: the strayed reveller; the poet of 'Resignation'; even the warriors Sohrab and Rustum, both of whom do their best to avoid their fatal duel. Arnold's heroes thus resemble Milton's, who similarly avoid direct confrontation. The Lady in *Comus*, for instance, overcomes the enchanter by refusing to argue with him, and the Son in *Paradise Regained* defeats Satan in much the same way. It is only fitting, then, that 'The Scholar-Gipsy', Arnold's archetypal poem of retreat, should allude to Milton repeatedly, but glancingly. The second line of 'The Scholar-Gipsy'—'Go, shepherd, and untie the wattled cotes'—derives its archaic diction directly from *Comus* ('might we but hear / The folded flocks penn'd in their wattled cotes'). Yet the echo is occluded by Arnold's explicitly attributing the poem's inspiration to another seventeenth-century source, Joseph Glanvill's *The Vanity of Dogmatizing*, from which he gives a long extract in a note. Similarly, the poem ends with another reminiscence of Milton: 'There, where down cloudy cliffs, through sheets of foam, / Shy traffickers, the dark Iberians come' recalls *Paradise Regained* and the 'cliffs / Of *Caucasus*, and dark *Iberian* dales' (iii. 317–18). But again, the allusion is embedded within a longer one: the whole of the final two stanzas of 'The Scholar-Gipsy' are derived from a passage in Herodotus. Milton, like the scholar-gipsy, haunts Arnold's imagination, but like the scholar-gipsy is only ever seen fleetingly.

Two final examples of Milton's peculiarly diffuse influence on Victorian poetry can be found in the work of Christina Rossetti (particularly *Goblin Market*) and Gerard Manley Hopkins. In both cases critics have often assumed that the later poets were responding directly to, or even 'rewriting', Milton's work; in both cases this seems highly unlikely. Yet Milton did exert a powerful shaping influence on the verse of Rossetti and Hopkins. That influence, however, is once again both more pervasive and more inconspicuous than a direct poetic response would suggest.

Although *Goblin Market* is probably the Victorian poem that has been most extensively discussed in relation to Milton, that discussion is still relatively recent. Critics have long recognized the biblical foundations of Rossetti's poem, which begins with a woman eating fruit and falling from innocence, and ends with a self-sacrificial act of redemption. But it was only after Sandra M. Gilbert and Susan Gubar classed Rossetti, together with other Victorian women writers, as a 'daughter of Milton' in their influential book *The Madwoman in the Attic* (1979) that critics began regularly to discuss Rossetti's poem as responding primarily to a Miltonic rather than a biblical precedent.[22] *Goblin Market* is now frequently read as perpetuating 'the Romantic penchant for rewriting Milton'.[23] Yet as Kathleen Vejvoda points out, this is a problematic assumption, since all evidence suggests that Rossetti's direct knowledge of Milton's epic, unlike her knowledge of the Bible, was limited. There is no reason to think that she devoted much time to reading *Paradise Lost*. To the contrary, she tended to avoid Milton's works on account of religious objections ('Anglo-Catholics were predisposed to despise Milton; and Rossetti was one of the most famous Anglo-Catholics'),[24] and she seems to have found him rebarbative for other reasons as well: as she wrote in a letter, 'Milton I cannot warm towards, even let alone all theological questions'.[25] Her brother William Michael Rossetti confirms that Milton did not form part of her regular reading: a 'great thing which she disliked was Milton's *Paradise Lost*: the only poems of his which she seems to me to have seriously loved were the sonnets'.[26]

On the other hand, not only was Rossetti sufficiently familiar with *Paradise Lost* to dislike it, but she was from a young age surrounded by Milton, even more than most Victorians. As Vejvoda notes, Rossetti's grandfather, to whom she was very much attached, translated Milton into Italian.[27] Rossetti was also intimately acquainted with the two leading Victorian editors of Milton: Thomas Keightley was a close friend of her family, and David Masson was also a friend, as well as being her editor at *Macmillan's Magazine*. Even Rossetti's recorded distaste for Milton suggests a high degree of familiarity. 'Milton I cannot warm towards': the comment implies that Milton, though constantly unappealing, is constantly present, like a disagreeable lodger. In short, Gilbert and Gubar and other critics are surely right in considering Rossetti a daughter of Milton; but it is important to distinguish the form the filiation takes. Poets like Wordsworth and Barrett Browning, who devotedly read and reread *Paradise Lost*, were so steeped in Milton that they felt obliged to respond directly to his example when they approached his poetic domain. The same cannot be said of Rossetti. Yet even if *Goblin Market* is not a response primarily to the version of the fall presented in *Paradise Lost*, it still shows evidence of Milton's pervasive influence.

Vejvoda, for instance, argues persuasively that Rossetti's poem draws to a remarkable extent upon Milton's *Comus*. The parallel is most notable in the scene of female solidarity at the end of *Goblin Market*: like Sabrina in Milton's masque, who releases the Lady from the trance brought on by her encounter with Comus and his crew, Lizzie heals Laura through her redemptive touch. But the similarities run throughout, both at the level of imagery (animal-headed tempters, descriptions of nature's lush variety) and of form (the abundant trochaic rhythms and rhymes). These parallels, Vejvoda suggests, draw attention to Milton's more general influence, notably on Rossetti's notion of chastity as a form of self-love or self-sufficiency.

Milton's influence can likewise be seen in the most distinctive rhetorical feature of *Goblin Market*, its lists of similes.[28] Throughout the poem Rossetti regularly rattles off rapid-fire strings of comparisons ('Laura stretched her gleaming neck / Like a rush-imbedded swan, / Like a lily from a beck, / Like a moonlit poplar branch, / Like a vessel at the launch').[29] There are several precedents for this device, the most obvious being the lists of similes in the Song of Songs, which are then imitated in the blazons of Petrarchan sonneteers. But although these may have been the models of which Rossetti was conscious—the Song of Songs is the book of the Bible she quotes most frequently, and she was a dedicated reader of Petrarch's poetry—they do not in fact provide the closest analogues for the device. Both in the Song and in the traditional Petrarchan blazon, every comparison applies to something different; each new vehicle, in other words, has a different tenor (thy lips are like scarlet threads, thy teeth like ewes, etc.). But Rossetti, far more unusually, piles all her comparisons onto a single object, thus producing a radically different effect. The images are all superimposed and so interfere with each other, or else displace each other, as if in a stutter of self-correction:

> Her locks streamed like the torch
> Borne by a racer at full speed,
> Or like the mane of horses in their flight,
> Or like an eagle when she stems the light
> Straight toward the sun,
> Or like a caged thing freed,
> Or like a flying flag when armies run.
>
> (500–506)

The *locus classicus* for this type of list is neither the Bible nor Petrarch but Milton. In both *Paradise Lost* and *Paradise Regained* Milton frequently piles similes upon his characters in this manner; the first epic simile in *Paradise Lost*, for instance, compares Satan to creatures '*Titanian*, or *Earth-born*...*Briareos* or *Typhon*...or that Sea-beast / *Leviathan*' (i. 198–201). Similarly, just before the Fall, Eve is said to be

> like a Wood-Nymph light,
> *Oread* or *Dryad*, or of *Delia's* train...
> To *Pales* or *Pomona* thus adorn'd,
> Likest she seem'd, *Pomona* when she fled
> *Vertumnus,* or to *Ceres* in her prime.
>
> (ix. 386–95)

Rossetti's practice shows that, to the extent that she was conscious of a precedent for this device, her model was biblical.[30] But it is a sign of Milton's influence that even a poet who sought specifically to adopt a biblical idiom could find herself echoing a Miltonic one instead.

Gerard Manley Hopkins presents a case similar to Rossetti's, but more extreme. If Milton was someone Rossetti '[could] not warm towards', Hopkins had a rather more decided opinion. 'I think he was a very bad man,' he writes to Robert Bridges in 1877. Not only Milton's puritanism but his stance on divorce, in Hopkins's view, literally damns him and classes him with other reprobates, and Hopkins upbraids Bridges for voicing any admiration of such a figure:

Those who contrary to our Lord's command...break the sacred bond of marriage, like Luther and Milton, fall with eyes open into the terrible judgment of God. Crying up great names, as for instance the reviews do now Swinburne and Hugo, those plagues of mankind, is often wicked and in general is a great vanity and full of impious brag and a blackguard and unspiritual mind.[31]

Accordingly there is very little visible influence of Milton on the phrasing or content of Hopkins's poems (in contrast, for instance, to the many echoes of Shakespeare). Even when he was writing on similar themes, Hopkins seems to have felt no need to respond to Milton, any more than he would respond to Luther, or Swinburne.[32]

At the same time, however, Milton exerts an enormous influence on the *form* of Hopkins's poetry, notably its metre. Unlike Rossetti, Hopkins read Milton's poems obsessively, and his imitation of their formal features was perfectly conscious. In the same letter in which he condemns Milton to hell, Hopkins writes, 'I have paid much attention to Milton's rhythm.... His achievements are quite beyond any other English poet's.' 'In fact', he later tells Bridges, 'all English verse, except Milton's, almost, offends me as "licentious".' Throughout his writings Hopkins consistently acknowledges that his characteristic use of 'counterpoint' and 'sprung' rhythms derives directly from Milton, since 'Milton is the great standard in the use of counterpoint'; he likewise notes that Milton's 'On the New Forcers of Conscience' provides the 'example' for his own caudated sonnets, 'Tom's Garland' and 'That Nature is a Heraclitean Fire'.[33] For all his divergences from the mainstream of Victorian poetry, Hopkins thus nevertheless participates in the typically Victorian relation to Milton. By consciously divorcing sound from sense, he allows Milton to be both everywhere and nowhere an influence on his poetry.

THE INVISIBLE MILTON

The unusual relation of Milton to Victorian poetry reveals a great deal about both, notably their shared interest in forms of influence that are the more powerful for being indirect or inconspicuous. Although we tend to think of Milton, as did the Romantics, in terms of his sublime displays of poetic power, Milton frequently makes use of understatement and of narratives in which power is latent or withheld, and these are the aspects of Milton's work to which Victorian poets characteristically turn. The effect is perhaps clearest in the poetry of Arnold, who can be detected quietly invoking Milton whenever he celebrates a stance of wise passiveness or tactical retreat. But similar uses of Milton are found throughout Victorian poetry. Hopkins, for instance, writes frequently about how God's power so pervades nature as to go unnoticed, perceived only at unexpected moments ('God's Grandeur', 'Hurrahing in Harvest'). It is appropriate that Hopkins expresses this latent power through the use of rhythms that he derived from Milton.

At times, therefore, the Victorian Milton seems not merely diffuse but entirely invisible; yet his importance is paradoxically made clearer by his apparent absence. In her 1842 essay 'The Book of the Poets', for example, Elizabeth Barrett Browning offers a summary of British poetry from Chaucer to Wordsworth, dividing her account into different eras. She concludes the 'third era' with Abraham Cowley, then follows with this:

> And then came 'glorious John', with the whole fourth era in his arms;—and eloquent above the sons of men, to talk down, thunder down poetry as if it were an exhalation. Do we speak as if he were not a poet? nay, but we speak of the character of his

influences! nay, but he was a poet—an excellent poet—in marble! and Phidias, with the sculptbut the sculpturesque ideal separated from his working tool, might have carved him. He was a poet without passion, just as Cowley was—but, then, Cowley lived by fancy, and that would have been poor living for John Dryden.[34]

Any reader familiar with the history of English poetry would expect this paragraph to name not Dryden but Milton, who should come next chronologically (he follows Cowley, for instance, in Samuel Johnson's *Lives of the Poets*), and who has not yet been discussed in the essay. Browning seems actively to court this confusion, by referring to Dryden as 'John', and by describing his poetry in particularly Miltonic language.[35] For at least a sentence or two, therefore, she appears to be disparaging Milton, or at least damning him with faint praise; but the result, when the reader realizes that she is not referring to Milton at all, is an exaltation greater than could have been achieved by outright panegyric. Milton is apparently so integral to the history of English poetry that one can with confidence overleap him in this way: he simply goes without saying. In the following paragraph Browning does 'return upon her steps for a breathing moment, and pause before MILTON', but her explicit appreciation has the feel of being almost superfluous. Milton's true greatness is made evident by his not initially being named—a type of 'omission that can be construed as itself a more complex form of deference'.[36]

A final example is furnished by Tennyson's *Idylls of the King* (1859–85), which illustrates all three Victorian responses to Milton. In the first place it contains numerous direct echoes and imitations of *Paradise Lost*—as might be expected of a twelve-book English epic about a lost golden age. These echoes are found throughout the work, most conspicuously in 'Merlin and Vivien': as several critics have noted, Vivien combines features of Milton's Eve and Milton's Satan as she tempts Merlin to his downfall.[37] Yet the greater Miltonic influence on 'Merlin and Vivien' is of a different, more diffuse kind, and is fully revealed only at the end of the idyll. Merlin, having resisted all Vivien's attempts to learn his secret, suddenly, inexplicably confesses it during a passing storm:

> Till now the storm, its burst of passion spent,
> Moaning and calling out of other lands,
> Had left the ravaged woodland yet once more
> To peace; and what should not have been had been,
> For Merlin, overtalked and overworn,
> Had yielded, told her all the charm, and slept.

(959–64)

The phrase 'passion spent' reveals the Miltonic inspiration for this scene, since these are the closing words of *Samson Agonistes* ('And calm of mind, all passion spent'). The whole passage in fact closely resembles Samson's description of his capitulation to Dalila:

> She surceas'd not day nor night
> To storm me over-watch't, and wearied out.
> At times when men seek most repose and rest,
> I yielded, and unlock'd her all my heart.

(404–7)

These verbal echoes reflect the more general influence of Milton's tragedy on Tennyson's idyll. Like Samson, who yields despite 'perceiving / How openly, and with what impudence / She purpos'd to betray me' (397–99), Merlin too brings on his own overthrow in perfect consciousness of what he is doing. In depicting Merlin's fall, which preludes the more general ruin of Camelot, Tennyson thus draws not only on Milton's Adam and Eve but more broadly, and more unexpectedly, on his Samson and Dalila.

In *Samson Agonistes*, a crucial event, Samson's decision to reveal his secret to Dalila, is given just a few lines of barely sufficient explanation. In 'Merlin and Vivien' the parallel decision is not described at all: having followed every moment of the two characters' interaction throughout the idyll, we are denied direct access to the climactic event and are only told in retrospect that 'what should not have been had been'. Herein lies Tennyson's greatest debt to Milton, not only in 'Merlin and Vivien' but in *Idylls of the King* as a whole. Many of Milton's most powerful effects derive from what he leaves unseen and unspoken, and Tennyson successfully imitates Milton's tactic of skilful omission. In this light it seems significant that when Tennyson's contemporaries noted the Miltonic nature of the *Idylls*, they singled out as its chief source neither *Paradise Lost* nor *Samson Agonistes* but a poem that Milton never wrote. In two of his early Latin compositions, Milton declared his intention to compose an epic about King Arthur; he never followed through on his plan, but Victorian critics saw Tennyson as the inheritor of Milton's unfulfilled aspiration. Van Dyke, for instance, rejoiced that Milton's project fell 'at last into the hands of the one man, since Milton died, who was able to carry it to completion'; E. C. Stedman claimed that in *Idylls of the King*, 'Milton's dream inconsonant with his own time and higher aspirations, has, at last, its due fulfilment.'[38] To both critics it seems clear that even an absence—an unwritten poem—can constitute a powerful influence.

The perception is apt, since both Milton's epic and Tennyson's centre on an absence, a critical failure that is never shown. In *Paradise Lost* Milton signally neglects to narrate Satan's first turn to evil—the decisive event that gives rise to all that follows. The moment is described allegorically in Book 2, when Sin recounts her own birth, but critics have notoriously struggled to reconcile the scene she describes with the rest of the poem's narrative.[39] The earliest narrated event in *Paradise Lost* comes in Book 5, when the angels assemble to celebrate the exaltation of the Son of God; after their celebration, when the others have retired to sleep, we are shown Satan, 'Deep malice thence conceiving and disdain', already plotting rebellion (v. 666). Either his fall occurred, unannounced, before the poem's narrative begins, or else it occurs here, in a single dependent phrase; either way, the crucial event is all but passed over.

The same is true of *Idylls of the King*. The downfall of Camelot comes about through the adultery of Lancelot and Guinevere. Yet their affair is not only never directly described, but never pinpointed: it is impossible to say when in the course of the twelve books the sin occurs that sets all the rest in motion. The nearest representation comes in 'Pelleas and Ettarre' when Pelleas catches sight, not of Lancelot and the queen, but of their debased doubles, Gawain and Ettarre:

> Then was he ware of three pavilions reared
> Above the bushes, gilden-peakt: in one,
> Red after revel, [slept] her lurdane knights...
> And in the third, the circlet of the jousts
> Bound on her brow, were Gawain and Ettarre.
> Back, as a hand that pushes through the leaf
> To find a nest and feels a snake, he drew:
> Back, as a coward slinks from what he fears.
>
> (419–29)

This passage contains two important echoes of *Paradise Lost*. The end clearly recalls the moment of Eve's fall, when 'Back to the Thicket slunk / The guilty Serpent' (ix. 784–85). But the opening lines more inconspicuously recall the 'Pavilions numberless, and sudden rear'd,/Celestial Tabernacles, where [the angels] slept' (v. 653–54)—the very scene in which we learn that Satan, like Pelleas unnoticed by all those sleeping around him, has already introduced sin into the world.

Idylls of the King can be considered Tennyson's most Miltonic work. The influence is largely oblique: Tennyson apparently draws inspiration from a poem Milton never composed, and his chief point of imitation is an omission. Yet this peculiar form of influence is characteristic of the Victorian Milton. Victorian poets did of course continue to engage directly and explicitly with the most salient aspects of Milton's poetry, as their predecessors had. But they also found in Milton an unfamiliar figure, one particularly appealing to their own times: a poet of understatement, who exerts his influence subtly, inconspicuously, but powerfully from the background.

Notes

1. There are originally three characters who are 'exiled' to Milton, since Mrs. Hale accompanies her husband and daughter. But Mrs. Hale soon dies, and Margaret, like Eve, more and more fills the role both of dutiful daughter and of partner or joint labourer with her father.

2. See Raymond Havens, *The Influence of Milton on English Poetry* (Cambridge: Harvard University Press, 1922); Joseph Wittreich, ed., *The Romantics on Milton* (Cleveland: Case Western Reserve University Press, 1970), 9; and Harold Bloom, in such works as *The Ringers in the Tower* (1971), *The Anxiety of Influence* (1973), *A Map of Misreading* (1975), *Poetry and Repression* (1976). For a fuller discussion of this debate, as well as of many of the issues and readings discussed in this chapter, see Erik Gray, *Milton and the Victorians* (Ithaca: Cornell University Press, 2009).

3. Thomas N. Corns, ed., *A Companion to Milton* (Oxford: Blackwell, 2001); Nicholas McDowell and Nigel Smith, eds., *The Oxford Handbook of Milton* (Oxford: Oxford University Press, 2009). Despite its title, the essay in the former volume called 'Milton: The Romantics and After' is devoted almost entirely to the Romantics.

4. Algernon Charles Swinburne, 'Short Notes on English Poets', *Fortnightly Review*, 34 (1880), 717.

5. A new edition of the prose works, edited by J. A. St. John (London, 1848), was welcomed by a reviewer as having made 'this part of our hereditary wealth [accessible] to the great mass of the people': see *British Quarterly Review*, 10 (1849), 224.

6. See 'The Prose Works of Milton', *New Monthly Magazine*, 40 (1834), 39; George Gilfillan, 'The Genius of John Milton', *Tait's Edinburgh Magazine*, 19 (1848), 511.

7. James White, 'Guizot and Milton', *Blackwood's Magazine*, 43 (1838), 311.

8. The literature on Milton and Romantic poetry is extremely extensive, but in addition to the works mentioned above, see especially Lucy Newlyn, *Paradise Lost and the Romantic Reader* (Oxford: Clarendon Press, 1993).

9. James G. Nelson, *The Sublime Puritan: Milton and the Victorians* (Madison: University of Wisconsin Press, 1963), 39.

10. Elizabeth Barrett Browning, 'Preface' to *A Drama of Exile* in *The Works of Elizabeth Barrett Browning*, 5 vols., ed. Sandra Donaldson et al. (London: Pickering and Chatto, 2010), ii. 567–68.

11. Bloom, *A Map of Misreading* (New York: Oxford University Press, 1975), 157.

12. Steven C. Dillon, 'Milton and Tennyson's "Guinevere"', *ELH*, 54 (1987), 133; Alfred Tennyson, 'Ulysses', in *The Poems of Tennyson*, 3 vols., ed. Christopher Ricks, 2nd edn. (London: Longman, 1987), i. 620; John Milton, *Paradise Lost* in *Complete Poems and Major Prose*, ed. Merritt Y. Hughes (Indianapolis: Hackett, 2003), 214.

13. The phrase is Wordsworth's subtitle; see Wordsworth, *The Prelude* (London: Moxon, 1850).

14. Sarah Annes Brown, '*Paradise Lost* and *Aurora Leigh*', *Studies in English Literature 1500–1900*, 37 (1997), 723–40.

15. Milton, *The Reason of Church Government* in *Complete Poems and Major Prose*, 667.

16. James Boswell, *Life of Johnson*, ed. R. W. Chapman (Oxford: Oxford University Press, 1980), 1301.

17. Henry Van Dyke, *The Poetry of Tennyson* (New York: Scribner's, 1889), 102.

18. See Joseph Sendry, '*In Memoriam* and *Lycidas*', *PMLA*, 82 (1967), 437–43, and Buck McMullen and James R. Kincaid, 'Tennyson, Hallam's Corpse, Milton's Murder, and Poetic Exhibitionism', *Nineteenth-Century Literature*, 45 (1990), 176–205.

19. Hallam Tennyson, *Alfred Lord Tennyson: A Memoir*, 2 vols. (London: Macmillan, 1897), ii. 522.

20. Matthew Arnold, 'Horatian Echo', in *The Complete Poems*, ed. Kenneth Allott, 2nd edition ed. Miriam Allott (London: Longman, 1979), 59.

21. See Martin Bidney, 'Of the Devil's Party: Undetected Words of Milton's Satan in Arnold's "Dover Beach"', *Victorian Poetry*, 20 (1982), 85–89; Maurice J. O'Sullivan, Jr., 'Matthew Arnold: *Un Milton jeune et voyageant*', *Milton Quarterly*, 7 (1974), 82–84; Ronald A. Sharp, 'A Note on Allusion in "Dover Beach"', *English Language Notes*, 21 (1983), 52–55.

22. See Sandra Gilbert and Susan M. Gubar, *The Madwoman in the Attic: The Woman Writer and the Nineteenth-Century Literary Imagination* (New Haven: Yale University Press, 1979), 564–75.

23. D. M. R. Bentley, 'The Meretricious and the Meritorious in Goblin Market: A Conjecture and an Analysis', in David A. Kent, ed., *The Achievement of Christina Rossetti* (Ithaca: Cornell University Press, 1987), 73; note that this claim is not central to Bentley's argument but is merely mentioned as a possibility. On Rossetti and Milton, see also Sylvia Bailey Shurbutt, 'Revisionist Mythmaking in Christina Rossetti's "Goblin Market": Eve's Apple and Other Questions Revised and Reconsidered', *Victorian Newsletter*, 82 (1992), 40–44, and Sarah

Fiona Winters, 'Questioning Milton, Questioning God: Christina Rossetti's Challenge to Authority in "Goblin Market" and "The Prince's Progress"', *Journal of Pre-Raphaelite Studies*, 10 (2001), 14–26.

24. Kathleen Vejvoda, 'The Fruit of Charity: Comus and Christina Rossetti's *Goblin Market*', *Victorian Poetry*, 38 (2000), 557.

25. Quoted in Nelson, *The Sublime Puritan*, 34.

26. Christina Rossetti, *Poetical Works*, ed. William Michael Rossetti (London: Macmillan, 1904), lxx.

27. Vejvoda, 'The Fruit of Charity', 558.

28. For more on this subject, see Erik Gray, 'Faithful Likenesses: Lists of Similes in Milton, Shelley, and Rossetti', *Texas Studies in Literature and Language*, 48 (2006), 291–311.

29. Christina Rossetti, *Goblin Market* ll. 81–5, in *The Complete Poems*, ed. R. W. Crump and Betty S. Flowers (London: Penguin, 2001), 7.

30. Rossetti's 'A Birthday', which closely follows 'Goblin Market' in the 1862 volume and which shares the same rhetorical device, explicitly recalls the Song of Songs; compare 'My heart is like an apple tree / Whose boughs are bent with thickset fruit' to 'As the apple tree among the trees of the wood, so is my beloved ... and his fruit was sweet to my taste' (Song 2:3).

31. Gerard Manley Hopkins, *Selected Letters*, ed. Catherine Phillips (Oxford: Clarendon Press, 1990), 88.

32. Among critics who argue otherwise, see John J. Glavin, '"The Wreck of the Deutschland" and "Lycidas": ubique naufragium est', *Texas Studies in Literature and Language*, 22 (1980), 522–46, and Dennis Sobolev, 'Contra Milton', *English Studies*, 84 (2003), 530–44.

33. Hopkins, *Selected Letters*, 87, 90, 108, 264.

34. Barrett Browning, 'The Book of the Poets', in *Works of Elizabeth Barrett Browning*, iv. 469.

35. The epithet 'Glorious John' was introduced earlier in the century by Walter Scott to describe Dryden, but was not applied only to him: James White, for instance, calls Milton 'Glorious John' in 1838 (White, 'Guizot and Milton', 303). The words 'thunder' and 'exhalation' in this passage both figure prominently in Book 1 of *Paradise Lost*; see especially i. 93, 701.

36. John Guillory, *Poetic Authority: Spenser, Milton, and Literary History* (New York: Columbia University Press, 1983), 94 (referring to Milton's not naming Spenser). Similarly, N. K. Sugimura writes that 'Tennyson's silence on certain subjects—such as Milton—are as significant as ... the pronouncements he chose to make'; see 'Epic Sensibilities: "Old Man" Milton and the Making of Tennyson's *Idylls of the King*' in Robert Douglas-Fairhurst and Seamus Perry, eds., *Tennyson Among the Poets* (Oxford: Oxford University Press, 2009), 160.

37. See Thomas P. Adler, 'The Uses of Knowledge in Tennyson's *Merlin and Vivien*', *Texas Studies in Literature and Language*, 11 (1970), 1397–1403; John D. Rosenberg, *The Fall of Camelot: A Study of Tennyson's 'Idylls of the King'* (Cambridge: Harvard University Press, 1973), 111–15; William W. Bonney, 'Torpor and Tropology in Tennyson's "Merlin and Vivien"', *Victorian Poetry*, 23 (1985), 351–67.

38. Van Dyke, *Tennyson*, 94; Edmund Clarence Stedman, *Victorian Poets* (Boston: James R. Osgood, 1876), 179–80.

39. See William Empson, *Milton's God* (London: Chatto and Windus, 1961), 57–59.

Select Bibliography

Bloom, Harold, *A Map of Misreading* (New York: Oxford University Press, 1975).

Brown, Sarah Annes, '*Paradise Lost* and *Aurora Leigh*', *Studies in English Literature 1500–1900*, 37 (1997), 723–40.

Dillon, Steven, 'Milton and Tennyson's "Guinevere"', *ELH*, 54 (1987), 129–55.

Gilbert, Sandra M., and Gubar, Susan, *The Madwoman in the Attic: The Woman Writer and the Nineteenth-Century Literary Imagination* (New Haven: Yale University Press, 1979).

Gray, Erik, *Milton and the Victorians* (Ithaca: Cornell University Press, 2009).

Maxwell, Catherine, *The Female Sublime from Milton to Swinburne: Bearing Blindness* (Manchester: Manchester University Press, 2001).

Nardo, Anna K., *George Eliot's Dialogue with John Milton* (Columbia: University of Missouri Press, 2003).

Nelson, James, *The Sublime Puritan: Milton and the Victorians* (Madison: University of Wisconsin Press, 1963).

Newlyn, Lucy, *Paradise Lost and the Romantic Reader* (Oxford: Clarendon Press, 1993).

Vejvoda, Kathleen, 'The Fruit of Charity: Comus and Christina Rossetti's Goblin Market', *Victorian Poetry*, 38 (2000), 555–578.

CHAPTER 12

....

VICTORIAN SHAKESPEARES

....

BHARAT TANDON

In his *Memoir* of his father, Hallam Tennyson (after the manner of many Victorian literary biographers) offers excerpts of the poet's opinions on various writers, most prominently Shakespeare. '*Hamlet*', Tennyson is reported as declaring, 'is the greatest creation in literature that I know of: though there may be elsewhere finer scenes and passages of poetry. Ugolino and Paolo and Francesca in Dante equal anything anywhere. It is said that Shakespeare was such a poor actor that he never got beyond the ghost in this play, but then the ghost is the most real ghost that ever was'.[1] On one level, Tennyson's praise shares its pitch and vocabulary with so many other Shakespearean encomia in the nineteenth century—witness Coleridge's vision of 'a nature humanized, a genial understanding directing self-consciously a power and an implicit wisdom deeper even than our consciousness',[2] or Keats's note to *Troilus and Cressida* in his copy of the Folio, remarking that Shakespeare 'could easily do Man's utmost'[3]—all unwitting contributions to that larger commodification of Shakespeare as heritage brand which eventually led Samuel Beckett to recoil in disgust on a visit to Stratford-upon-Avon ('unspeakable, everything His Nibs up to the vespasienne universelle').[4] However, the nature and context of Tennyson's praise deserve closer attention, as they tell other and deeper truths about Shakespeare's presences in Victorian poetic imaginations. First of all, Tennyson is drawn, not to the play's protagonist himself, a figure to whom earlier writers such as Schlegel and Coleridge had paid so much attention, but to the ghost of Old Hamlet, that spectral presence from the past who inspires his son with both obligation and resentment at once. In addition, this account itself is framed within a son's account of his own father (*Alfred Lord Tennyson/A Memoir/By His Son*), which adds another layer of resonance. For Victorian poets more generally, Shakespeare could often figure, like Old Hamlet, as an ancestor both disquietingly absent and vitally present, often at the same time—and as such, the constellation of the 'Shakespearean', from the smallest phrases and words to the grand connotations of the canonized national genius, offered not only an allusive resource, but a means of thinking about themselves and others. By thinking through Shakespeare, poetry could sound out the contours of its own voices, whilst remaining alert to those moments when those voices are inhabited by the elsewhere and elsewhen: 'but then the ghost is the most real ghost that ever was'.

One reason why Shakespeare offered himself as such a creative measure for poetic voices by the middle of the nineteenth century derives from a variety of opinions and arguments that had been abroad earlier in the century—arguments that frequently hinged on how and where his words were to be voiced, if indeed they were to be voiced at all. Jonathan Bate provides an excellent summary of the connections between 'Bardolatry' and poetic theories of imagination in the Romantic period. 'If we had to pick out a single premise at the core of English Romanticism', he observes, 'it would probably be the ascription of a central place to the power of the creative imagination, a belief that imagination, genius, and poetry are closely associated with each other... Those critics and aestheticians of the second half of the eighteenth century who laid the ground-work for the Romantics by exploring the creative power of imagination turned again and again to Shakespeare for examples of that power. The rise of Romanticism and the growth of Shakespeare idolatry are parallel phenomena'.[5] Indeed, it is hard to read the major works of Romantic-period Shakespeare criticism without being struck by the intensity with which the poet's own creative and sympathetic capacities are summoned up and analyzed. Take, for example, one of the most celebrated European readings of Shakespeare's imaginative characterization, that of August Wilhelm von Schlegel:

> If the delineation of all his characters, separately considered, is inimitably bold and correct, he surpasses even himself in so combining and contrasting them, that they serve to bring out each other's peculiarities. This is the very perfection of dramatic characterization: for we can never estimate a man's true worth if we consider him altogether abstractedly by himself; we must see him in his relations with others, and it is here that most dramatic poets are deficient. Shakespeare makes each of his principal characters the glass in which the others are reflected, and by like means enables us to discover what could not be immediately revealed to us.[6]

Schlegel's analysis is a fine example of the best early nineteenth-century Shakespeare criticism in its meticulous attention to the means by which dramatic poetry can be inward with the subtlest textures of psychology in action. That said, its very emphasis on different kinds of inwardness also marks it out as being of its time, and hints at some of the problems subsequent poets may have had with adapting Shakespeare to their own ends. '[W]e must see him'; 'the glass in which the others are reflected'; 'revealed to us': the insistent recourse to visual metaphors in Schlegel's description tells its own story about his priorities and emphases, and has the effect of making 'dramatic characterization' sound like an oddly static process, since in all this glittering exchange of reflections, it sounds as if the light is doing most of the moving. The tendency of Schlegel's view certainly does not sit entirely comfortably with the bluntly profound distinction that Ezra Pound drew in 1934: 'whereas the medium of poetry is WORDS, the medium of drama is people moving about on a stage and using words. That is, the words are only part of the medium and the gaps between them, or deficiencies in their meaning, can be made up by "action"'.[7] What one encounters all too often in Romantic poetic drama, whether Keats and Brown's *Otho the Great* (1819), or Byron's *Marino Faliero, Doge of Venice* (1821), are brilliant, mutually reflective imaginations of character, such as those Schlegel ascribes to Shakespeare, but ones where the impulse towards delicate psychological inwardness becomes such a priority that the more robust modes of 'people moving about on a stage and using words' can get lost. By the time the likes of Tennyson and Browning began their poetic careers, then, one strand of Romantic bardolatry had put such stress on imaginative delineations of character that there was a risk that Shakespeare might be 'Shakespeareanized' to death—but they may not have gone on to write as they did had things been otherwise.

Looking at Browning's earliest verse-dramas, it is easy to trace his inheritances from Romantic Shakespeare's championing of psychological interiority. That famous line from the published preface to *Strafford* (first performed in 1837 at the commission of the great actor-impresario W. C. Macready), sets out the play's priorities even more clearly than Schlegel's vision of Shakespeare ('Action in Character rather than Character in Action'[8])—all of which may work magnificently in the moment of reading, but may not carry quite the same charge when reluctantly presented on stage. As a result, reactions such as W. B. Scott's were understandable: 'From the first scene it became plain that applause was not the order. The speakers had every one of them orations to deliver, and no action of any kind to perform. The scene changed, another door opened, and another half-dozen gentlemen entered as long-winded as the last'.[9] For sure, *Strafford* has much in it that might prompt such reactions; this drama of loyalties during the English Civil War is willing to give its ideas full rein in the characters' minds and mouths, as witnessed by Strafford's remonstrance to the king in Act 2, Scene ii:

> *Strafford.* I! I! that was never spoken with
> Till it was entered on! That loathe the war!
> That say it is the maddest, wickedest...
> Do you know, sir, I think within my heart,
> That you would say I did advise the war;
> And if, through your own weakness, or what's worse,
> These Scots, with God to help them, drive me back,
> You will not step between the raging People
> And me, to say...
>   I knew it! from the first
> I knew it! Never was so cold a heart!
> Remember that I said it—that I never
> Believed you for a moment!
>   —And, you loved me?

Strafford's angry exclamation is shadowed—as much in manner as in diction—by Shakespearean predecessors such as Othello ('O monstrous! monstrous!');[10] however, Browning allows his characters to have their say, largely untrammelled by the possibilities of interruption that can make Shakespearean soliloquy so thrillingly fraught. *Strafford* may be, as many of its contemporary viewers and readers found, a work compromised by a certain kind of 'Shakespearean' orotundity, but its failures nevertheless point to Browning's desire to push the forms he inherited from Romantic drama in new directions. As it turned out, Browning, like so many of the best Victorian poets, was to become most truly Shakespearean once he learned to let go of Shakespeare's founding possession, the stage itself.

The first half of the 1840s saw the end of Browning's professional association with the theatre—and, not coincidentally, the development of his greatest achievements in dramatic verse, verse in which stage gives way to page. *A Blot in the 'Scutcheon* (1843) follows *Strafford* in adapting its formal inheritances from Shakespeare to more recent historical situations (in this case, eighteenth-century English dynastic feuds), although the latter play also makes an ironic virtue of the particular Shakespearean sources that it plunders. For instance, by making his central plot a patent transplantation of *Romeo and Juliet*, Browning can make some covert and overt suggestions about the futile and destructive nature of aristocratic feuds:

> Dear and ancient trees
> My fathers planted, and I loved so well!
> What have I done that, like some fabled crime
> Of yore, lets loose a Fury leading thus
> Her miserable dance amidst you all?[11]

However, in going so far as to provide a parallel balcony scene between the secret lovers Mildred and Mertoun, he succeeds only in showing up how the original has the better of the comparison:

> But soft, what light through yonder window breaks?
> It is the East, and *Iuliet* is the Sunne.
> Arise fair Sun and kill the enuious Moone,
> Who is already sicke and pale with griefe,
> That thou her Maid art far more faire then she:
>
> (Shakespeare)[12]
>
> Does a new life, like a young sunrise, break
> On the strange unrest of our night, confused
> With rain and stormy flaw—and will you see
> No dripping blossoms, no fire-tinted drops
> On each live spray, no vapour steaming up,
> And no expressless glory in the East?
>
> (Browning)

Simply in terms of commercial history, the poor time that *A Blot in the 'Scutcheon* had at Macready's hands was the beginning of the end of Browning as a stage-dramatist. It was his misfortune to be formally out of tune with many of the expectations which audiences were bringing to Shakespeare by the 1840s (and continued to hold until the early twentieth century), expectations finely enumerated by Adrian Poole: 'Audiences marvelled at the visual splendour of Macready's *Tempest* and *As You Like It*, at the gorgeous pageantry of the Keans' *King John* or the masque in *King Henry VIII*, at the luminous street and canal in their *Merchant of Venice*, at the extraordinary church in Irving's *Much Ado* and the unearthly landscape of his *Macbeth*, at the fantastic landscapes of Beerbohm Tree's *Twelfth Night* and *A Midsummer Night's Dream*.[13] This was not a stage environment naturally conducive to the more static oratory of *Strafford* or *A Blot in the 'Scutcheon*; thankfully, by the time of his estrangement from Macready, Browning's own writing had begun to create its own private Shakespearean space.

'Thus Conscience does make Cowards of vs all',[14] remarks Hamlet. Be that as it may, it seems that the depiction of conscience in action (more than 'Action in Character') is what drives Browning's Shakespearean imagination into new forms in the 1840s. *Pippa Passes* (1841) and *Dramatic Lyrics* (1842) apprehend 'conscience' in its fullest senses: not only '[t]he internal acknowledgement or recognition of the moral quality of one's motives and actions', but also '[i]nward knowledge and consciousness of something within or relating to oneself', and even at times 'knowledge or consciousness *of* something external to oneself, esp. God'.[15] In so doing they both draw on a central quality of Shakespearean verse and abstract it into new forms. As Romantic critics often noted, Shakespearean soliloquy is often turned inwards as well as outwards, 'speaking out' also serving as a way to listen to oneself (not for nothing were so many early nineteenth-century readers in thrall to *Hamlet*); Browning's poetic redirections of drama away from the stage uncover fresh resources in the interplays between eloquence, self-communion, and blank silence. In *Pippa Passes*, the shifts between the internal and external senses of 'conscience' are frequently enacted at the level of echo and re-sounding, with Pippa's songs sparking off unpredictable moral and acoustic associations in their auditors, as when the murderer Sebald and his lover Ottima are inhabited by the resonances of Pippa's famous '*God's in his heaven—/ All's right with the world!*'[16] First Sebald repeats the phrase, tellingly unable to locate their source ('God's in his heaven! Do you hear that! Who spoke?'), then works it into the curse his awakened conscience pronounces on Ottima ('I hate, hate—curse you! God's in his heaven!'), whose own final words in the scene are themselves distantly haunted by it, as well as Luke 18:13 ('Not me—to him, O God, be merciful!'). Measuring words and feelings from outside against those from the inside, *Pippa Passes'* shifts between speaking, hearing, and overhearing create sometimes startling contour-maps of selfhood, but these effects depend upon the drama's being a closet piece, a text for the page rather than the stage: a fact emphasized by its being one of those rare works of literature to get its title from a stage-direction (Philip Roth's *Exit Ghost* comes to mind, but not many more). And if *Pippa Passes* achieves its distinctive effects by employing the textual space of the page as its dramatic medium, Browning's first fully achieved dramatic monologues in *Dramatic Lyrics* explore the possibilities of channelling drama into the act of reader response itself, discovering in the process a fresh setting for that play of selfhood and otherness so central to his inheritance from Romantic Shakespeare.

'My voice', as Steven Connor has described it, 'comes from me first of all in a bodily sense. It is produced by means of my vocal apparatus—breath, larynx, teeth, tongue, palate, and lips. It is the voice I hear resonating in my head, amplified and modified by the bones of my skull, at the same time as I see and hear its effects upon the world'.[17]

The phenomenological double-movement that Connor traces so well here is particularly appropriate to the encounters that Browning's dramatic monologues stage between readers and the voices that the poems invite them to conjure up in the act of reading. To put it simply, if the act of enunciating also engages internal resonances in the body, if eloquence is, by necessity, shadowed by some form of inward colloquy, then a reader might not feel entirely at ease when temporarily lending his or her voice (and, by association, body) to the inhabitants of the two 'Madhouse Cells' in the original *Dramatic Lyrics*, Porphyria's Lover and Johannes Agricola:

> I have God's warrant, could I blend
>   All hideous sins, as in a cup,
>   To drink the mingled venoms up,
> Secure my nature will convert
> The draught to blossoming gladness fast:[18]

As these lines (with their glances to Lady Macbeth) show, 'Johannes Agricola in Meditation', first published in 1836, makes an unsettling creative virtue of its engagement with a reader's voice, since one of the questions that tends on any imaginative voicing of them is that of how literally Agricola, the Antinomian 'justified sinner', might mean them. Hence one of the disturbing aesthetic and ethical pleasures of dramatic monologue: the sudden emergence, from amid the supposed intimacies of voicing, of possible voices and values that can seem pathologically distant from a reader's own, or at least ones that a reader would *like* to think of as pathologically distant.

Given this formal quality of dramatic monologue, it is not surprising that it should lend itself so well to that Browning poem which is in most direct and searching dialogue with Shakespeare—the poet to whom Browning, like his Romantic predecessors, turned as a way of thinking about selfhood and otherness. 'Caliban Upon Setebos; or, Natural Theology on the Island', published in *Dramatis Personae* (1864) sets anxieties of literary influence alongside much larger questions about immanent design or its absence in the world, and manages to make them part of the same agonized disquisition. In this strangest and most painful of dramatic monologues (in which the abject Caliban can barely dare to speak of himself in the first person), Shakespeare is not so much an allusive reference point for Browning but a climate of thought, one part of what Sophie Ratcliffe has described as his 'heroic struggle with epistemological uncertainty—his sceptical attempt to make one realize that one is unable to be certain about what someone else is experiencing'.[19] One of the features of Romantic Bardolatry that Victorian poets inherited was a tendency to fall back on modes of allusive button-touching, to bolster the modern text with overt or subliminal Shakespearean 'soundbites' (even such works as George Eliot's *The Spanish Gypsy* (1868) and Oscar Wilde's *The Duchess of Padua* (1883) are not innocent in this regard). However, the Shakespearean echoes in Browning's poem work to more searching ends. When Caliban unconsciously echoes Hamlet ('But wherefore rough, why cold and ill at ease? / Aha, that is a question!'[20]), or Lear ('Sees, himself, / Yonder two flies, with purple films and pink, / Bask on the pompion-bell above: kills both'), the effect isn't just that of a Bardolatrous parading of Shakespeare's greatest hits.

On one level, this is because the uncanny, unconscious echoing of words from elsewhere is itself a Shakespearean technique—perhaps most famously in Macbeth's unwitting reworking of the Weird Sisters' 'faire is foule, and foule is faire'[21] in his very first line in the play ('So foule and faire a day I haue not seene').[22] Beyond this, though, the fact that Caliban appears to be unconscious of these echoes whilst at some level fearing his own condition of unoriginality (as witnessed by the sham version of his own life that he stages with captive animals and birds) puts an added pressure on any reading. A reader is tasked to consider whether the possible presence of a Shakespearean echo has any larger significance whatsoever (as happens later, for instance, in Beckett's *Endgame*); and if one can't be sure what a character means by an allusive line, or whether the character is even 'meaning' anything by the allusion at all, then how can one be sure where one stands in relation to them? '[S]o He', runs Caliban's refrain throughout the poem, as he attempts, like an exponent of Deistic 'natural theology', to pin the world he perceives analogically back to the unknowable works of Setebos. Yet the poem as a whole unpicks the possibility of there being any stable exchange-rate of comparison on which one could base a 'So'. If Pope could turn the relative scales of importance along the Great Chain of Being into refined humour

> Superior beings, when of late they saw
> A mortal Man unfold all Nature's law,
> Admired such wisdom in an earthly shape,
> And shew'd a NEWTON as we shew an Ape. [23]

Browning's poem brings that joke to book, opening up a frightening prospect of potentially infinite scales of being: Caliban's world, Setebos, the conjectural superior power known only as 'the Quiet', and so on, ad infinitum. In this extraordinary poem, Caliban squares up and bows down to Setebos, just as Browning does to Shakespeare;, but a reader has no objective measure that would enable him or her precisely to map one on to the other: thus, 'so He' is the last thing that a reader could say with any confidence. If Romantic aesthetics could stress the interplay of the internal and external in Shakespeare, Browning here folds that interplay out into a Möbius strip where inside and outside are indistinguishable. The epigraph to the poem, taken from Psalms 50:21, runs: 'Thou thoughtest that I was altogether such a one as thyself.' It might apply to Caliban and Setebos; it might apply to Browning and Shakespeare; and it certainly presses upon a reader, since if there is one thing that 'Caliban Upon Setebos'—Browning's most perversely Shakespearean and Shakespeareanly perverse poem—demonstrates, it is that human likeness can never be, or can never be known to be, 'altogether'. 1864, the year in which *Dramatis Personae* appeared, was also the tercentenary of Shakespeare's birth, and Browning was prompted to speak on the subject at a grand literary *soirée* held at Francis Palgrave's house in February of that year. Thomas Richmond, chaplain of St Thomas's Hospital, recalled Browning's public thoughts: '"Here we are called upon to acknowledge Shakespeare, we who have him in our very bones and blood, our very selves."'[24] The irony is that in this same year, Shakespeare gave Browning a means of unpicking much of what 'our very selves' signified.

Dramatic monologue afforded an especially stylized means by which Shakespeare might inform Victorian poetry's explorations of selfhood and estrangement. But even in ostensibly less experimental forms, Shakespeare—as both poetic precedent and canonical, cultural touchstone—often looms large. While Matthew Arnold's sonnet 'Shakespeare' may have come, with the benefit of hindsight, to crystallize the image of a conveniently inscrutable national treasure transcending history and politics, the poem also hints at subtler affinities:

> Others abide our question. Thou art free.
> We ask and ask—Thou smilest and art still,
> Out-topping knowledge. For the loftiest hill,
> Who to the stars uncrowns his majesty,
> Planting his steadfast footsteps in the sea,
> Making the heaven of heavens his dwelling-place,
> Spares but the cloudy border of his base
> To the foiled searching of mortality;
>
> And thou, who didst the stars and sunbeams know,
> Self-schooled, self-scanned, self-honoured, self-secure,
> Didst tread on earth unguessed at.—Better so!
>
> All pains the immortal spirit must endure,
> All weakness which impairs, all griefs which bow,
> Find their sole speech in that victorious brow.[25]

'Planting his steadfast footsteps in the sea': Arnold's apotheosis of Shakespeare's genius, out of Psalm 29 ('The LORD sitteth vpon the flood') by way of William Cowper's *Olney Hymns* ('He plants his footsteps in the Sea, / And rides upon the Storm'),[26] typifies a certain way of figuring Shakespeare that goes hand in hand with his more secular establishment as an icon of 'heritage' culture ('that victorious brow'). So, for example, Shakespeare features as part of the mythological pantheon of Englishness in W. C. Bennett's 'Our Glory Roll' ('Thy Shakespeare, greatest gift that God has given his Earth to own'),[27] and even the young Elizabeth Barrett was not immune to such gushing tributes:

> Beloved Shakespeare! England's dearest fame!
> Dead is the breast that swells not at thy name!
> Whether thine Ariel skim the seas along,
> Floating on wings etherial as his song—
> Lear rave amid the tempest—or Macbeth
> Question the hags of hell on midnight heath—
> Immortal Shakespeare! still, thy lips impart
> The noblest comment on the human heart.[28]

It would be difficult to deny a lineage stretching from this kind of nineteenth-century hyperbole to the overbearing presence of 'His Nibs' that so appalled Beckett in Stratford in 1935, and beyond that, to the biscuit tins and tea-towels of the modern Shakespeare industry. That said, Arnold's image of a Shakespeare who 'smilest and art still' and '[d]idst tread on earth unguessed at' suggests other possibilities. The stress that Arnold places on Shakespeare's refusal to fold under his readers' interrogations allows him to become a public possession while maintaining a Sphinx-like inscrutability, and it may even be that the latter condition *causes* the former. At once canonical and mysterious, then, Shakespeare may tower over his readers like Arnold's 'loftiest hill', but such a presence could be seen as a spur to exploration rather than a curb upon it, especially as mountains represented, by Arnold's time, a new frontier of discovery.[29] After all, as witnessed by what Shakespeare himself did to his sources, to become part of the literary folklore is to invite reworkings from the readers whose cultural possession one has become, and the sharpest Victorian poems can contest the 'authority' of Shakespeare, even in the act of venerating and continuing it.

One marker of the status that Shakespeare had gained by the middle of the century was that 'Shakespearean' and its cognates often served as the terms of choice for praising authors, regardless of how much or little their work resembled Shakespeare's. Jane Austen is a notable example: for Archbishop Whately, she had 'a regard to character hardly exceeded even by Shakespeare himself'; G. H. Lewes described her as a 'prose Shakespeare';[30] even Tennyson argued that the 'realism and life-likeness of Miss Austen's Dramatis Personæ come nearest to those of Shakespeare'.[31] Similarly, Elizabeth Barrett Browning's death in 1861 was mourned in comparable terms: she was variously 'the Shakespeare among her sex', and worthy of a place in the pantheon with 'Homer, Dante, Shakespeare, Milton, Goethe, and Shelley'.[32] If such terms may chime unfortunately with the register of 'Beloved Shakespeare! England's dearest fame!' in her juvenilia, her mature poetry—in particular, *Sonnets from the Portuguese* (written in 1845–46 and published in 1850)—marks a far subtler and more challenging engagement with Shakespeare as the voice of poetic and cultural authority, as Angela Leighton has detailed. 'To write a sonnet sequence', she argues, 'is of course to trespass on a male domain. Dante, Petrarch, Sidney and Shakespeare are the eminent "grandfathers" of this predominantly male line, and Barrett Browning is one of the first granddaughters. She thus enters into a tradition in which the roles are sexually delineated: there is the man who speaks, and there is the woman who is admired, described, cajoled and pleaded with from a distance…Barrett Browning must not only reverse the roles, but she must also be sensitive to the fact that Robert was a lover and a poet in his own right, and disinclined to be cast in the role of the superior muse'.[33] The pertinence of this analysis emerges when one considers what the *Sonnets from the Portuguese* so often do with modes and conventions of address, especially in their opening invocations (and exhortations): Sonnet III opens with 'Unlike are we, unlike, O princely Heart! / Unlike our uses and our destinies'; Sonnet VI starts with the imperative 'Go from me. Yet I feel that I shall stand / Henceforward in thy shadow'; whereas the voice in Sonnet XXXIII recasts the imperative mood into flirtatiousness ('Yes, call me by my pet-name! let me hear / The name I used to run at, when a child').[34] In each of these sonnets, Barrett Browning subtly changes the dynamics of the romantic and sexual power-relationships between the speaker and her addressee, refusing to be pinned down to any one fixed template, with the result that the sequence as a whole works less as a prolonged act of self-abnegation than as a multi-faceted medi-tation on how and when one might, rightly and willingly, offer oneself in love. Of course, Leighton is right to see this as a critical argument with the diffuse cultural associations that Shakespeare had gathered by the nineteenth century, and particularly with the gender-politics of authorship, and of desire itself. However, *Sonnets from the Portuguese* may be an argument with Shakespeare that also moves in the spirit of Shakespeare, since the Bard's original Sonnets shift their imagined grounds so lithely that many Victorians were tempted to read them as cryptograms—as witnessed in the multiple fakeries of Wilde's 'The Portrait of Mr W. H.' (1889). Barrett Browning's method of enlisting and engaging with Shakespeare may have been vastly different from that of her husband, but in their anxieties of influence and dramas of gratitude, they both attest to that distinc-tive presence that, as I have been tracing, Shakespeare had in Victorian poetry—as both a major part of a poetic inheritance and an enabling means by which individual writers might articulate their relations to it.

I mentioned above how another way in which poets might respond to Shakespeare's establishment as part of English cultural folklore was in recasting and reworking their great source; and I shall close this essay by looking closely at how Tennyson's Shakespearean reworkings help to find his—and others'—voices. Arthur Hallam remarked of *Poems, Chiefly Lyrical* (1830): 'The features of original genius are clearly and strongly marked. The author imitates no one; we recognize the spirit of his age, but not the individual form of this or that writer. His thoughts bear no more resem-blance to Byron or Scott, Shelley or Coleridge, than to Homer or Calderon, Firdusi or Calidas'.[35] It is noticeable that one poet missing from Hallam's list is Shakespeare, which is, on the surface, all the more surprising, considering that the volume con-tains 'Mariana', one of Tennyson's most direct improvisatory glosses in the margins of the plays. The poem takes its cue from the Duke's description of Mariana's aban-donment by Angelo in *Measure for Measure*, III, i.: 'I will presently to S. *Lukes*, there at the moated-Grange recides this deiected *Mariana*'. Yet from the beginning, the fit between the Shakepearean source-text and the new poem is neither a complete nor a comfortable one: first off, Tennyson's epigraph ('*Mariana in the moated grange*') is not an actual line from *Measure for Measure*, while his choice of '*in*' rather than '*at*' places Mariana in a different prepositional relationship to her circumstances. The predominant atmosphere of the poem is one of stagnation, both in terms of the grange's physical setting, and the seeming inescapability of the protagonist's plight:

> With blackest moss the flower-pots
> Were thickly crusted, one and all:
> The rusted nails fell from the knots
> That held the pear to the gable-wall[36]

In this context, '*in*' confines Mariana that much more than '*at*', since to be 'at the moated-Grange' implies a temporary stay, whereas '*in the moated grange*' (without even a full-stop to hint visually at a possible end to her suffering) leaves Mariana ringed about by the moat, worn down into part of her decayed surroundings, anticipating Dickens's Miss Havisham and the wraith-like survivors of Beckett's dramas. Indeed, as Christopher Ricks has famously contended, Tennyson's version, given where it ends, may not even have the same *dénouement* as Shakespeare's: 'a reader must inevitably make some decision about the known outcome in Shakespeare, and an open reader will bear in mind that "Mariana" is only one of innumerable poems by Tennyson in which the final ending is shrouded but magnetic'.[37] Nor is it only in its possible narrative direction that 'Mariana' departs from the source that simultaneously sustains it: form itself in this poem becomes a way of hearing the contours of a character. In each stanza of 'Mariana', the last four lines, rhyming *efef*, constitute her despairing refrain, which echoes, with small but important variations, throughout the poem: from

> She only said, 'My life is dreary,
>   He cometh not,' she said;
> She said, 'I am aweary, aweary,
>   I would that I were dead!'

through to

> Then, said she, 'I am very dreary,
>   He will not come,' she said;
> She wept, 'I am aweary, aweary,
>   Oh God, that I were dead!'

Yet it only exists as this kind of refrain in the form in which the poem has cast it, since the rhyme's continuation depends upon the narrator's interpolations of 'she said; / She said' or 'she said / She wept'; take them away and Mariana would sound very different. So, as with Browning's Caliban more than thirty years later, a reader can perceive at once a character written into being by Shakespearean precedent, and the contingent, asymmetric contours of a voice that isn't wholly determined by its intertextual DNA. The very title of Tennyson's volume offers an insight into his priorities: not only does *Poems, Chiefly Lyrical* denote broadly the division of different genres of verse within the book, but it also hints at a quality of his verse that was to become ever more prominent as his career went on. For Tennyson, even a poem that is 'chiefly lyrical' is potentially partly *dramatic* as well; and it is apt that his lifelong habit of employing the lyrical and the dramatic to interrogate each other should reach a particular peak in 1855, in a poem so haunted by 'the most real ghost that ever was': *Maud*.

'The presence of Hamlet in Romantic discourse', Jonathan Bate suggests, 'usually indicates that the artist is examining his own self...The self was a central problem for the Romantics; Shakespeare was thus brought to the centre of their thinking'.[38] While the presence of *Hamlet* in Victorian poetry is not so consistently a sign of autobiographical self-scrutiny, it continues to serve as a dramatic structure and shorthand for psychological, and frequently pathological introspection, or for an inability to negotiate adequately between thought and deed. Browning's Bishop Blougram can joke about Gigadibs' debts to Romantic criticism and psychology:

> You, Gigadibs, who, thirty years of age,
> Write statedly for Blackwood's Magazine,
> Believe you see two points in Hamlet's soul
> Unseized by the Germans yet—which view you'll print—[39]

Lord Howe, though, in Elizabeth Barrett Browning's verse-novel *Aurora Leigh*, uses Hamlet as an unflattering point of comparison for Aurora's cousin Romney:

> There's one thing true on earth,
> That's love! he takes it up, and dresses it,
> And acts a play with it, as Hamlet did,
> To show what cruel uncles we have been . . .[40]

So it is in this context that we need to read Hallam Tennyson's report of what his father thought *Maud* represented: 'As he said himself, "This poem is a little *Hamlet*", the history of a morbid poetic soul, under the blighting influence of a recklessly speculative age'.[41] It may only be a 'little' *Hamlet*—indeed, one in which most of the parts are played by one actor, and which is finally 'staged' in a reader's audio-visual imagination—yet *Maud* re-imagines in a contemporary setting much of what is central to the play, whilst remembering what it can never hope to reproduce. One of *Hamlet*'s most searching explorations involves the ways which characters listen to, or simply hear, themselves and others: there are dramas of mishearing (Hamlet's deliberate playing to Polonius's incomprehension of his 'Anticke disposition'),[42] overhearing (Polonius's fatal hiding behind the arras), and, perhaps saddest of all, those moments where Hamlet most wants to unburden himself, only to find that he is still his only true hearer ('I shall winne at the ods; thou would'st not thinke how ill all's heere about my hart, but it is no matter').[43] *Maud*, which Tennyson appropriately subtitled 'A Monodrama' from 1875 onwards, stages in the silent act of reading some of Victorian poetry's most startling sequences of speaking-out, speaking-in, and being spoken through, as the poem sets different modes of inheritance against each other. *Hamlet* lends itself to poets because it is not just a Shakespearean inheritance, but one of the plays that deals most directly with the matter of unwanted inheritance ('Oh cursed spight, / That euer I was borne to set it right'),[44] and both those aspects press on Tennyson here. At one level, the anxiety about parental inheritance is translated into the fear of hereditary madness, the madness which, along with the cut-throat world of speculation, did for his father:

> What! am I raging alone as my father raged in his mood?
> Must *I* too creep down to the hollow and dash myself down and die
> Rather than hold by the law that I made, nevermore to brood
> On a horror of shattered limbs and a wretched swindler's lie? [45]

But the speaker's fear runs farther than matters of psychopathology: when he asks 'am I raging alone as my father raged in his mood?', it is also a worry about unoriginality, about whether he is condemned to trot out the same worn old lines (and a reader in 1855 might well have felt the additional pressure of Poe's 'nevermore' from just a decade before). This feeds into the more diffuse 'replays' that *Maud* as a whole performs, in which the speaker is by turns the misanthropic Hamlet ('Why do they prate of the blessings of Peace? we have made them a curse, / Pickpockets, each hand lusting for all that is not its own'), the mad Ophelia ('See what a lovely shell, / Small and pure as a pearl, / Lying close to my foot, / Frail, but a work divine'), and, eventually, an awkward surrogate for Fortinbras ('And hail once more to the banner of battle unrolled!'). But if these roles don't quite fit, that is as it should be; for the speaker of *Maud* is, like Eliot's Prufrock, 'not Prince Hamlet, nor was meant to be'.[46] Then again, *Maud* repeatedly picks away at any secure position from which a reader might make such a claim, and, as I have been detailing elsewhere, Shakespeare is the channel along which familiarity is measured against estrangement.

I mentioned earlier how part of the challenge in reading dramatic monologues by Browning such as 'Johannes Agricola in Meditation' and 'Porphyria's Lover' lies in having to calculate, with no objective measure on which to rely, exactly how sincerely or literally the speakers might mean their words. This quandary is the basic condition of reading *Maud*, since a reader needs to bring his or her sense of literary, formal, and Shakespearean precedent to bear on the poem, even as the poem shows up that apparatus as possibly insufficient. Established poetic forms carry their own different baggages of 'poetic licence': for example, love-lyrics might be allowed a certain licence in talking up the beloved, as well as a certain figurative latitude. But, when encountering sequences such as I, xviii ('Has our whole earth gone nearer to the glow / Of your soft splendours that you look so bright? / *I* have climbed nearer out of lonely Hell'), or I, xxii, a reader might be on less certain ground:

> But the rose was awake all night for your sake,
>   Knowing your promise to me;
> The lilies and roses were all awake,
>   They sighed for the dawn and thee.

Of course, *we* know that lyric poetry permits such figurative excesses as the earth's becoming a satellite of Maud, or the anthropomorphic flowers' keeping the watches of the night along with the speaker; but can we ever be wholly sure that the speaker has the same sense of what's safely metaphorical? Likewise, the last two lines of the poem, which caused so much argument amongst its contemporary readers, retain a certain distance, an impunity: 'I have felt with my native land, I am one with my kind, / I embrace the purpose of God, and the doom assigned'. Writing in 1859, Gladstone found the suggestion of the Crimean War as a way out of individual madness irksome ('out of such fervid partial representations nearly all grave human error springs...we do not recollect that 1855 was a season of serious danger from a mania for peace and its pursuits').[47] But to object simply on these grounds would be to miss the care with which Tennyson arranges the end of *Maud* so as to make the speaker's precise justification a deliberate matter of mystery. The couplet offers some kind of summary, but it's hard to say exactly what it does summarize, and much of this comes down to the chime between 'I am one with my kind' and 'the doom assigned'. One feels that the speaker's reasons for choosing 'the doom assigned' might come into focus, if only it were possible fully to understand what it meant to be 'one with my kind'; then again, the genius of *Maud* is that by the time a reader comes to these lines, he or she will have been through a long, performative demonstration of the difficulty, if not the impossibility, of being absolutely 'one with my kind'. Instead, after the fashion of Shakespeare's Horatio, forever on the outside of Hamlet's self-expressions, he or she may recognize Victorian poetry's most Shakespearean inheritance and legacy—a meticulous inwardness that is nevertheless always incomplete, and which can only be won through the difficult affinities that are the least, and the most, that art can decently offer.

'All our past acclaims our future: Shakespeare's voice and Nelson's hand, / Milton's faith and Wordsworth's trust in this our chosen and chainless land / Bear us witness'.[48] Algernon Charles Swinburne's lines epitomize one Victorian Shakespeare, participant in a poetical, national, and ideological continuum; yet these other Victorian Shakespeares, as I have been exploring, are no less Victorian, and no less Shakespearean, for finding different ways of navigating an air so full of resonant noises, and finding in Shakespeare not just the comforts of togetherness but the cold shocks of the particular. Or as Browning's Strafford declares from the Tower of London: 'I want, just now, / To hear the sound of my own tongue. This place / Is full of ghosts'.

Notes

1. Hallam Tennyson, *Alfred Lord Tennyson, A Memoir by His Son*, 2 vols (London: Macmillan and Co., 1897), ii. 291.
2. Samuel Taylor Coleridge, lecture note of 1812–13, in Jonathan Bate, ed., *The Romantics on Shakespeare* (London: Penguin, 1992), 129.
3. John Keats, marginalia to the Folio, in Elizabeth Cook, ed., *The Oxford Authors: John Keats* (Oxford: Oxford University Press, 1990), 334.
4. Letter to Thomas McGreevy, 25 July 1935, quoted in James Knowlson, *Damned to Fame: The Life of Samuel Beckett* (London: Bloomsbury, 1996), 203.
5. Jonathan Bate, *Shakespeare and the English Romantic Imagination* (Oxford: Clarendon Press, 1986), 6.
6. A. W. von Schlegel, from *Lectures on Dramatic Art and Literature* [1808–11], in *The Romantics on Shakespeare*, 101.
7. Ezra Pound, *ABC of Reading* (New York: New Directions, 1960; 1st pub. 1934), 46.
8. Robert Browning, *Strafford* in *The Poetical Works of Robert Browning*, 10 vols, ed. Ian Jack et al. (Oxford: Clarendon Press, 1983–), ii. 500.
9. Quoted in Clyde de L. Ryals, *Becoming Browning: The Poems and Plays of Robert Browning, 1833–1846* (Columbus: Ohio State University Press, 1983), 53.
10. *Othello*, III. iii, Folio text.
11. Browning, *A Blot in the 'Scutcheon*, in *The Poetical Works of Robert Browning*, iii. 420.
12. *Romeo and Juliet*, II, i, Folio text.
13. Adrian Poole, *Shakespeare and the Victorians* (London: Arden Shakespeare/Thomson Learning, 2004), 23.
14. *Hamlet*, III. i, Folio text.
15. Senses I.1.a., II.7.a., and II.7.b. from the *OED*.
16. Browning, *Pippa Passes*, in *The Poetical Works of Robert Browning*, iii. 40.
17. Steven Connor, *Dumbstruck: A Cultural History of Ventriloquism* (New York: Oxford University Press, 2000), 3.

18. Browning, 'Johannes Agricola in Meditation', in *The Poetical Works of Robert Browning*, iii. 247.

19. Sophie Ratcliffe, *On Sympathy* (Oxford: Clarendon Press, 2008), 120.

20. Browning, 'Caliban Upon Setebos' (1864), in *Poetical Works, 1833–1864*, ed. Ian Jack (Oxford: Oxford University Press, 1970), 839.

21. *Macbeth*, I. i, Folio text.

22. *Macbeth*, I. iii, Folio text.

23. Alexander Pope, 'An Essay on Man' (1733–4), in *The Poems*, ed. John Butt (London: Methuen, 1963), 517.

24. Alexandra Leighton (Mrs Sutherland Orr), *Life and Letters of Robert Browning*, 2nd edn. (London: Smith, Elder & Co. 1908), 258.

25. Matthew Arnold, 'Shakespeare', in *The Poems of Matthew Arnold*, ed. Kenneth Allott (London: Longman, 1965; 2nd edn., ed. Miriam Allott, 1979), 39–40.

26. William Cowper, *Olney Hymns*, in *The Poems of William Cowper*, 3 vols, ed. John D. Baird and Charles Ryskamp (Oxford: Clarendon Press, 1980–95), i. 174.

27. William Cox Bennett, *Proposals for and Contributions to a Ballad History of England* (London: Hamilton, Adams, 1868), 127.

28. Elizabeth Barrett Browning, 'An Essay on Mind' (1826), in *The Works of Elizabeth Barrett Browning*, 5 vols, ed. Sandra Donaldson et al. (London: Pickering and Chatto, 2010), iv. 106.

29. See Robert Macfarlane, *Mountains of the Mind: The History of a Fascination* (London: Granta, 2003).

30. Quoted in B. C. Southam, ed., *Jane Austen: The Critical Heritage*, 2 vols. (London: Routledge & Kegan Paul, 1968-87), i. 98, 125.

31. Hallam Tennyson, *Memoir*, ii. 372.

32. Quoted in Gardner B. Taplin, *The Life of Elizabeth Barrett Browning* (London: John Murray, 1957), 407.

33. Angela Leighton, *Elizabeth Barrett Browning* (Brighton: Harvester, 1986), 98–99.

34. *The Works of Elizabeth Barrett Browning*, ii. 444, 447, 470.

35. Quoted in John D. Jump, ed., *Tennyson: The Critical Heritage* (London: Routledge and Kegan Paul, 1967), 42.

36. Alfred Tennyson, 'Marianna', in *The Poems of Tennyson*, 3 vols, ed. Christopher Ricks (London: Longman, 1969; 2nd edn., 1987), i. 206.

37. Christopher Ricks, *Tennyson* (London and Basingstoke: Macmillan, 1972), 50.

38. Bate, *Romantics*, 19.

39. Browning, 'Bishop Blougram's Apology', in *The Poetical Works of Robert Browning*, v. 252.

40. Elizabeth Barrett Browning, *Aurora Leigh* (1856), ed. Kerry McSweeney (Oxford and New York: Oxford University Press, 1993), 132–133.

41. Hallam Tennyson, *Memoir*, i. 396.

42. *Hamlet*, I.v., Folio text.

43. *Hamlet*, V.ii., Second Quarto text.

44. *Hamlet*, I. v., Folio text.

45. Tennyson, *Maud*, in *The Poems of Tennyson*, ii. 523.

46. T. S. Eliot, 'The Love Song of J. Alfred Prufrock', in *The Complete Poems and Plays* (London: Faber and Faber, 1969), 16.

47. *Tennyson: The Critical Heritage*, 248.

48. Algernon Charles Swinburne, 'England: An Ode' (1894), in *Swinburne's Collected Poetical Works*, 2 vols (London: Heinemann, 1924), ii. 1026.

SELECT BIBLIOGRAPHY

Armstrong, Isobel, *Victorian Poetry: Poetry, Poetics, Politics* (New York and London: Routledge, 1993).

Bate, Jonathan, *Shakespeare and the English Romantic Imagination* (Oxford: Clarendon Press, 1986).

Bloom, Harold, *The Anxiety of Influence* (New York and Oxford: Oxford University Press, 1973; 2nd edn., 1997).

Douglas-Fairhurst, Robert, *Victorian Afterlives: The Shaping of Influence in Nineteenth-Century Literature* (Oxford: Oxford University Press, 2012).

Marshall, Gail, ed., *Shakespeare in the Nineteenth Century* (Cambridge: Cambridge University Press, 2012).

Poole, Adrian, *Shakespeare and the Victorians* (London: Arden Shakespeare/Thomson Learning, 2004).

Ratcliffe, Sophie, *On Sympathy* (Oxford: Clarendon Press, 2008).

Ricks, Christopher, *Allusion to the Poets* (Oxford: Oxford University Press, 2002).

CHAPTER 13

....

THE ROMANTIC BEQUEST:
ARNOLD AND OTHERS

....

MICHAEL O'NEILL

CONNECTIONS

....

THE Victorians can sound peremptory in their rejection of their predecessors. In 'The Function of Criticism at the Present Time', Matthew Arnold laments that 'the poetry of the first quarter of this century, with plenty of energy, plenty of creative force, did not know enough. This makes Byron so empty of matter, Shelley so incoherent, Wordsworth even, profound as he is, yet so wanting in completeness and variety'.[1] Tennyson finds Shelley 'often too much in the clouds for me'.[2] Browning undergoes a severe disillusion with the same poet, only able to 'avoid despising' himself for his earlier 'fancy' of the Romantic poet by 'remembering that I judged in pure ignorance and according to the testimony of untruthful friends'.[3] Hopkins regrets in Keats the presence of 'an unmanly and enervating luxury'.[4]

Yet the story of Victorian poetry's relationship with Romantic poetry is full of criss-crossing strains. Arnold, the central figure in this essay because of his pervasive attention to questions of cultural bequest, also speaks in the same essay of '*our* Byron' and '*our* Wordsworth' (emphases added), affirming kinship.[5] Tennyson's ear resonates with echoes of Romantic poetry; even the 'bourne of Time and Place' in his late 'Crossing the Bar' engages intertextually with Shelley and Keats, to the poem's benefit. It wards off anything too homiletic through its glancing reference to the close of *Prometheus Unbound*, Act 3, Scene 3, when the Earth speaks of those who bear the 'torch of hope' (171): 'As thou hast borne it most triumphantly / To this far goal of time' (173–4).[6] Shelley's verb turns into Tennyson's noun by way of a recollection of Keats's 'bourn' at the close of 'To Autumn', both works, in turn, hailing back to Shakespeare's *Hamlet*.[7] Browning's own playful, riddlingly elusive voice is in evidence in 'Memorabilia' where his speaker marvels at someone who once saw 'Shelley plain', a seeing that the poem suggests is impossible, switching into a restless, elliptical anecdote in which 'I crossed a moor, with a name of its own'.[8] One might allegorize this 'moor' as a terrain composed of past and present cultures; 'a hand's-breadth of it shines alone', writes Browning alluding obliquely to Shelley, the 'eagle-feather' picked up.[9] 'Well, I forget the rest', the poem finishes, a gesture at once colloquial and brusque, suggesting, too, the significance of a single memory, but affecting a brisk rejection of the past. The idiom itself marks a point of difference between Victorian and Romantic poets, Browning reshaping the conversational manner which is among Romanticism's bequests into something curter, crisper, more rough-hewn, yet tightly rhymed.

Hopkins, for his part, never loses an affinity with the Keats who was a potent influence on early works such as 'A Vision of the Mermaids'. The poet who cries, 'I am gall, I am heartburn' in one of his late sonnets ('I wake and feel the fell of dark, not day'), understands the anguish of selfhood with a gustatory disrelish that recalls Hyperion's experience of lost authority when 'his ample palate took / Savour of poisonous brass and metal sick' (I. 187–8).[10] Hopkins agreed with Arnold in finding in Keats the stirrings of 'an interest in higher things and of powerful and active thought'.[11] He recognizes the ways in which Keats's writing evinces existential courage, a tragic zest, an awareness of the need to re-think poetry's role in a world subject to universal and time-specific ravages, in which 'old age shall this generation waste', as 'Ode on a Grecian Urn' has it, and 'all is seared with trade; bleared, smeared with toil', as Hopkins puts it in his ecologically saddened sonnet 'God's Grandeur'.[12]

Seamus Heaney, a later heir of both poets, illuminates the relationship between them, contrasting Keats's 'Close bosom-friend of the maturing sun' from 'To Autumn' with Hopkins's 'Warm-laid grave of a womb-life grey' from 'The Wreck of the Deutschland'.[13] Both poets pack experience into condensed phrases, and both reflect on processes of generation. But, for Heaney, 'Hopkins's consonants alliterate to maintain a design whereas Keats's release a flow.... Keats woos us to receive, Hopkins alerts us to perceive.'[14] This is helpful, and reminds us that Hopkins devotes his sensuousness to a re-imagining of Christ's incarnation, Keats to a more earth-bound evocation of seasonal 'fulfilment'. Yet Keats's poem prompts us both to 'receive' and 'perceive', to supply our understanding of what is entailed by his presentation of autumn, from which allegorizing or comment is excluded. Hopkins's imagery carries its burden of theological implication as though always straining against the sensory evocation to which it is drawn. One way of reading Hopkins's poetic theodicy is to see it as testing Keatsian concentration on the evidence of the senses to the limit, or to the point at which 'the heart, being hard at bay, // Is out with it!' Fascinatingly, it is at this point, at which the beleaguered 'heart' grasps the meaning of 'The dense and the driven Passion', that Hopkins produces the most Keatsian passage in the poem, as he compares the flooding in of realization with a 'lush-kept plush-capped sloe' that has been 'mouthed to flesh-burst'. Hopkins emerges as a tragic Catholic poet through strenuous engagement with his proto-humanist Romantic predecessor.

The gulf between the Romantic and Victorian periods turns out to be somewhat factitious in certain cases. Felicia Hemans and Letitia Landon appear in anthologies of Romantic and Victorian poetry, caught in the limbo between Shelley's and Byron's deaths, and the accession of Queen Victoria, but helping to shape what Susan Brown calls the 'Sapphic moment' which became 'a prime vehicle for poetic utterance' in the work of many Victorian women poets.[15] John Clare writes some of his greatest 'Romantic' poetry years after the death of Byron in 1824. In fact, a poem such as 'An Invite to Eternity' (published in 1848) shows Clare as the heir of Romantic quest and, in his wryly baffled yet lyrical evocation of a 'sad non-identity', the contemporary of the Tennyson for whom negation, too, is a way forward and a mode of circling back in 'Tears, Idle Tears'.[16] Both poems illustrate the applicability to Victorian poetry of Heidegger's remark that 'What is presumed to be eternal merely conceals a suspended transiency, suspended in the void of a durationless now'.[17] Poetry, for the Victorians, serves often as a liminal space, an interim, a temporal 'void' that creates a 'durationless now' that fends off endings. Romantic quest turns into Victorian gazing, in Tennyson's 'Ulysses', towards 'an arch wherethrough/Gleams that untravelled world, whose margin fades/For ever and for ever when I move'.[18] Movement here is the same as lack of motion; an interminable disappearance of closure is the reward for a yearning that has only itself as its goal.

The same dynamic, taken to an astonishing extreme, occurs in Swinburne's poems, which, among other things, serve as revisionary meditations on the Romantic legacy, their patternings of echo and reverberation indebted to poems by Shelley, their elegiac restlessness a tacit rebuke to modes of Wordsworthian reconciliation with temporality.[19] The poems swing, with metrical virtuosity, between the poles of origin and conclusion, life and death, until the poetry 'turns all sequential processes of beginnings, middles, and ends into self-contained circles'.[20] Emotions magnificently cancel one another out in this art of cycles and contraries wheeling over and upon one another, as at the end of 'Hymn to Proserpine'. Here the speaker turns his back on religion and, implicitly, notions of progress, in a decadent version of Greek acceptance of necessity: he will 'laugh not again, neither weep. / For there is no God found stronger than death; and death is a sleep'.[21] Swinburne said that the poem voiced 'the deathsong of spiritual decadence', but it is a 'deathsong' full of a courageous refusal to settle for solutions that would tame complexities too quickly.[22] In 'Anactoria', influenced by Shelley's practice in *Epipsychidion*, he finds a voice for his own longing to fuse eros and artifice in the persona of Sappho.[23] Here Sappho's measured, intense celebration of her supreme skills as a poet has the effect of a Wagnerian aria, a last will and testament with an endlessly dying fall. The end when reached seems to bear witness to poetry's role as a self-sustaining medium through which consciousness achieves a precarious if hypnotic heightening of self-awareness, a state in which nothing can 'Assuage me nor allay me nor appease'.[24] Romantic striving has turned into a clear-sighted sense that poetry's supreme gift to its reader is the occupation of a seemingly 'durationless now'.

CONFLICTS

It is salutary to recall that the Romantics presented to the Victorians a different profile and image than they do in the twenty-first century. Indeed, the very word 'Romantic' takes a long while to assume its epoch-defining nature. The growth of the reputations of the major Romantics went at irregular rates. Despite initial scepticism, Arthur Hallam became a 'furious Shelleyist' by the time he was elected to the Cambridge Apostles.[25] Keats figures largely in Tennyson's early work, contributing to its quality of sensuous finesse; in 1832 Mariana in the South 'From her warm brow and bosom down / Through rosy taper fingers drew / Her streaming curls of deepest brown'.[26] The 'warm' 'bosom' seems indirectly to allude to Madeline in 'The Eve of St. Agnes', though Keats displaces bosomy warmth onto the 'warmed jewels' next to Madeline's skin; 'taper fingers' reclaims for the human a phrase used by Keats in 'I stood tip-toe upon a little hill' for what in a cancelled draft he calls 'the tendrils of sweetpeas'.[27] Tennyson is responding, at such moments, to Romantic innovation; Keats and Shelley may not, by 1832, be quite the latest thing, but they affect Tennyson and others with the shock of the new.

Wordsworth, the author of *The Prelude*, was effectively unknown. Arnold, who 'dirged W.W. *in the grand style*', did so in the same year as the older poet's Romantic epic of subjectivity was first published.[28] His take on Wordsworth was not that of later critics such as A. C. Bradley who drew attention to the visionary strangeness central to the poetry. But this is not surprising, given the work available to him and the terms of Wordsworth's reception. In 'Memorial Verses', Arnold offers a magisterial survey of Romantic poetry. His feeling-laden octosyllabic couplets offer distilled critical views and demonstrate a poet's search to grasp the current state of the poetic art: a state that is at once predicament and opportunity. Arnold offers brief sketches of Byron and Goethe, before turning to Wordsworth. He praises Byron for exemplifying near-heroic struggle: 'He taught us little; but our soul / Had *felt* him like the thunder's roll. / With shivering heart the strife we saw / Of passion with eternal law'.[29] The initial dismissal is Goethean: 'The moment he reflects, he is a child'.[30]

But the following lines respond with 'reverential awe', pointed up by a triplet rhyme, to the 'strife' embodied in Byron's work. Arnold, too, plays out the strife 'Of passion with eternal law' in his poetry, even as he implies a critique of what he finds in Byron: 'the fount of fiery life / Which served for that Titanic strife'. In *On the Study of Celtic Literature* Arnold refers to 'the Titanism of the Celt, his passionate, turbulent, indomitable reaction against the despotism of fact', asking, 'of whom does it remind us so much as of Byron?'[31] As rebel against 'the despotism of fact', Byron is fighting a losing battle, which Arnold admires. As the stager of 'strife', he is both actor and creator, which Arnold also admires. Byron is the dying gladiator and also the poet who contrived the tragic pathos of the stanzas commemorating him.

Before considering Wordsworth, Arnold turns to Goethe, presented here as the analyst of cultural illness, presumably Romanticism (as in his assertion to Eckermann, 'I call the classic *healthy*, the romantic *sickly*'), 'happy' if

> to know
> Causes of things, and far below
> His feet to see the lurid flow
> Of terror, and insane distress,
> And headlong fate, be happiness.

The syntax serves to attach a lengthening and sardonic chain of qualifications to Goethe's 'happiness'. There may be a Virgilian allusion, but Virgil's happy man in *Georgics* who is able 'to know the causes of things' has the power to 'cast beneath his feet all fear and unyielding Fate, and the howls of hungry Acheron'.[32] Arnold's Goethe can merely 'see' 'far below / His feet', a way of putting it that suggests there may be relatively little difference between the engulfed participant (Byron) and the omniscient but ineffectual looker-on (Goethe).

Something in Arnold, then, cannot wholly acquiesce in Carlyle's advice in *Sartor Resartus*: 'Close thy *Byron*; open thy *Goethe*'.[33] The major turn in the poem involves a tribute to Wordsworth, and involves an explicit sense of parallels: the 'too' in 'He too upon a wintry time / Had fallen' links Wordsworth not only to Byron and Goethe but also to Arnold and his contemporaries. Wordsworth's special gift to later poets is, for Arnold, a capacity for feeling and responsiveness to nature. The poem speaks of the way in which Arnold feels addressed by Wordsworth, a finding that implies an earlier stage of loss:

> He found us when the age had bound
> Our souls in its benumbing round;
> He spoke, and loosed our heart in tears.
> He laid us as we lay at birth
> On the cool flowery lap of earth.

The first line's internal rhyme suggests that Wordworth's finding fights against the age's binding, while the repetition in 'He laid us as we lay' implies an emotional re-birthing. A guardedness accompanies the encomium: there is a hint of infantilizing, and the therapeutic effect is placed decisively in the past: 'Smiles broke from us and we had ease'. Arnold concludes by suggesting that Wordsworth's uniqueness lies less in his stoicism or courage than in his ability to offer 'healing power': 'The cloud of mortal destiny, / Others will front it fearlessly—/ But who, like him, will put it by?'. A line from Wordsworth's 'Ode: Intimations of Immortality' replays itself in those last words. Wordsworth speaks of the child's 'Immortality' as 'A Presence which is not to be put by'.[34] Arnold redirects the line: his Wordsworth does allow us to 'put...by' 'The cloud of mortal destiny'.

This putting-by has a slightly facile sound, and in his 'Stanzas in Memory of the Author of "Obermann"', Arnold asserts that 'Wordsworth's eyes avert their ken / From half of human fate'.[35] The judgement is unfair in its suggestion that Wordsworth did not attend to suffering or was not concerned with the darker side of 'human fate', but it allows Arnold to characterize a later generation as beset in ways unknown to Wordsworth. Ironically he depicts this condition in a revision of a Wordsworthian image. Wordsworth speaks in the Immortality Ode of moments when we 'see the Children sport upon the shore, / And hear the mighty waters rolling evermore'. Arnold uses the same image, but for an opposing end:

> Like children bathing on the shore,
> Buried a wave beneath,
> The second wave succeeds, before
> We have had time to breathe.[36]

Arnold's contemporaries, on this revisiting of Wordsworth, are not in touch with the 'mighty waters' of immortality; rather, they are the near-victims of forces which overwhelm them wave after wave. If anything, their mental states resemble the wave-besieged consciousness of Rousseau in Shelley's *The Triumph of Life*, 'Buried' by the first wave, not having time enough 'to breathe' before 'The second wave succeeds'. That Arnold wins vigour out of flagging energies, new life out of entombment, shows in the handling of the verse, with its expressive stress-shift in the second line and a syntax that conveys a breathless gulp as 'The second wave' assumes the subject-position that belongs by grammatical rights to 'We'.

Much of Arnold's poetry draws eloquence out of his sense of being the restless, self-divided inheritor of Romanticism. 'A Summer Night' is among those poems by him that combine technical skill and expressiveness with a lyrical but animated melancholy. Arnold defines his position with intelligence and flair, projecting onto the 'calm moonlight' a self-diagnosis that has a generation-defining authority:

> *Hast thou then still the old unquiet breast,*
> *Which neither deadens into rest,*
> *Nor ever feels the fiery glow*
> *That whirls the spirit from itself away,*
> *But fluctuates to and fro,*
> *Never by passion quite possessed*
> *And never quite benumbed by the world's sway?*[37]

The rhyming has eloquence (that on 'breast' continues through the paragraph), suggesting that the speaker undersells himself as a mere fluctuator; it is less that he is flogging a dead horse of lost inspiration than that he is deriving fresh resource from a poetry that invests definition with mood. The passage teems with Romantic tropes that identify Arnold's belated and distracted status. Men are either slaves or Romantic madmen, the madmen's representative sounding distinctly Shelleyan, as, tempest-driven, he is imagined as 'Still bent to make some port he knows not where, / Still standing for some false, impossible shore', his posture doomed (the rhyme of 'false, impossible shore' with 'comes no more' drives home the point). Yet the last stanza of *Adonais* on which Arnold calls is only too aware of the dangers as well as heroism of Romantic quest, and, as often in Arnold's poetic relationship with his predecessors, a gap narrows just as the poetry seems intent on exposing its width.[38] So, for his trope of 'most men' as slaves, living 'in a brazen prison', Arnold again turns to Wordsworth's Immortality Ode, and its description of how 'Shades of the prison-house begin to close / Upon the growing Boy'.

REVISIONARY VISIONS

Much Victorian poetry tackles the question of how to deal with Romantic poetry's sometimes productive divisions. In *Empedocles on Etna*, Arnold reorchestrates Romantic motifs as he sets, in Frank Kermode's words, 'Empedocles...the Romantic poet who knows enough' against 'Callicles the Romantic poet who does not know enough'.[39] The result is a dialectical poem which may have earned its creator's rejection for not allowing suffering to find vent in action, but which deserves our critical admiration. In 'The Darkling Thrush' Thomas Hardy evokes the apparent antithesis of Keats's nightingale or Shelley's skylark. Instead of 'full-throated ease' or 'profuse strains of unpremeditated art' that resonate with hints of transcendence, Hardy's bird appears amidst a landscape depicted in a near-parody of Romantic projection of feeling as a corpse in its grave.[40] The poem seems to punish the Romantic for not knowing enough, for not guessing at the 'fervourless' state of a culture shorn of idealistic aspirations.

Yet the poem does not merely debunk the finest hopes of Romanticism, even as the Romantics are themselves alert to the dangers that beset such hopes. In 'Ode to a Nightingale' Keats at once confers on the bird an emblematic status, as the representative of song's immortality, and backs away from any uncomplicated exaltation of art. Song's immortality belongs to 'fairy lands forlorn', though it can console, find 'a path / Through the sad heart of Ruth', and the poem ends with a seesawing question ('Do I wake or sleep?'), establishing equilibrium of sorts only through its capacity to depict vacillation and indeterminacy.[41] Shelley's 'To a Skylark' recognizes the gulf between the human condition and the rapturous vision suggested by the skylark's song, conceding that 'Our sweetest songs are those that tell of saddest thought'.[42] Hardy's end-of-century poem seems intent on depicting a 'growing gloom', yet it also recovers some of the Romantics' yearning in its description of the bird's decision to 'fling his soul / Upon the growing gloom'. The idea, implicit in the poem's self-conscious imagery, that pathetic fallacies can be avoided turns out to be wrong: interpretation, involving what in 'Mont Blanc' Shelley calls the 'human mind's imaginings', is always at work.[43] With syntactical tact and subtlety in deployment of the phrase 'could think', Hardy suggests that the very absence of any cause for celebration means that the speaker

> could think there trembled through
> His happy good-night air
> Some blessed Hope, whereof he knew
> And I was unaware.

In the last line, the 'I' is both put in its place and given due prominence (taking a strong iambic stress), as, like Coleridge's Mariner, Hardy alights on the virtues of being 'unaware'.[44] He alights, too, on the word's precariousness as the basis for trust in 'Some blessed Hope'.

Hardy's 'moments of vision', to borrow the title of his 1916 volume, differ from Shelley's in that they frequently arise from a source beyond the poet's conscious agency, as though some hidden hand rubbed away mist from a window, letting through an unexpected light. Yet to say, as Tim Armstrong does in suggestive annotation of '"For Life I Had Never Cared Greatly"', that in it 'Hardy's revelation is passive, in contrast to the self-born energies of the Romantics' downplays the fact that the later poet shapes the way in which his own expectations are overthrown.[45] If ever 'Life' 'uncloaked a star' to Hardy, it did so to a poet receptive to Romantic epiphanies, in however dimmed a form. Even when the 'sick leaves reel down in throngs' in 'During Wind and Rain', they do so with a conscious sense that they pitilessly reprise the death of the leaves in the first section of Shelley's 'Ode to the West Wind'.[46] And while Hardy's poem does not imagine the leaves' resurrection, as Shelley does when he commands the wind to 'Drive my dead thoughts over the universe / Like withered leaves to quicken a new birth', the poem cunningly sets the annihilation figured in each stanza's final lines against the cameos of lasting value sketched in each stanza's opening.[47] Memory fights against the threat of oblivion, indeed links hands with it, as is brought out in the rhyme connecting the first and last lines of each stanza. Romantic poetry is an impossible heaven towards which Hardy's poetry sometimes lifts its troubled eyes or on which it turns its obstinate shoulders. But it is also, as he intimates in his all-guns-blazing 'Apology' to *Late Lyrics and Earlier* (1922), the source of his poetry's '"questionings" in the exploration of reality', questionings that allude to Wordsworth's in his 'Ode: Intimations of Immortality' and take 'the first step towards the soul's betterment'.[48]

Recent criticism has sought, often helpfully, to point up differences as well as connections between Romantic and Victorian poetry. And yet critical constructions can simplify. E. Warwick Slinn distinguishes between 'the essentialist assumptions of organic poetics' at work in Romantic poetry and the Victorian emphasis upon 'the inseparability of material reality from the sentient subject's experience'.[49] The distinction holds only to the degree that the Romantics do embody such 'essentialist assumptions'. Much work has sought to demonstrate that the Romantics not so much embody as offer critiques of the coherent self or of the poem whose form aspires to the condition of a natural thing. True, 'Kubla Khan', for example, incorporates a notion of harmoniously reconciled opposites in the image of the 'miracle of rare device, / A sunny pleasure-dome with caves of ice!'[50] Yet it presents itself as a 'fragment' of more interest as 'a psychological curiosity', than on the ground of any supposed *poetic* merits', and it refuses to leave us with any straightforwardly achieved 'miracle'.[51] The close is the climax of an imperilled quest after inspiration, launched by a conditional sentence beginning 'Could I revive within me'.

No Victorian poet ever quite rivals the conclusion's suggestion of bardic triumph, even if it is one that draws a circle of 'holy dread' round the awe-inducing poet. But the relationship between Romantic and Victorian poetry is, here as elsewhere, often finer than that of contrast. J. C. Trench may seem to be criticizing an aestheticist super-dome towards which roads run from Xanadu when he told Tennyson that 'we cannot live in Art'.[52] Tennyson's resulting poem *The Palace of Art*, however, is as much riposte to, as affirmation of, Trench's sturdy truism. 'I built my soul a lordly pleasure-house' alludes to Coleridge's 'pleasure-dome' in the spirit of one following in Romantic footsteps too naively; but the horror, beauty and fascination of living in art work themselves out in a poem that cannot wholly bear to destroy art's blissful, claustrophobic edifice.[53] The poem concludes with the poet's soul wishing to leave behind the solipsism and sin of artistic gratification, and concerned that no one should 'pull . . . down my palace towers, that are / So lightly, beautifully built'. Tennyson cannot live in art or without it, and in so doing makes explicit an ambivalence that is also at work, if less propositionally, in Coleridge's poem.

Victorian poets may take as their default position the failure of vision which is among Romantic poetry's severest forms of anguish.[54] Yet at the moment when Victorian poets assert their difference from Romantic stances, they can also seem to be teasing out implications and sub-texts in their predecessors' work. Francis O'Gorman observes perceptively that 'Emily Brontë's poetry is in persistent negotiation with its Romantic inheritance'.[55] An example is 'To Imagination', where Brontë explains, almost brutally yet with empathy, the psychological drives at work behind the Romantics' trust in imagination. 'So hopeless is the world without; / The world within I doubly prize', her speaker says (and the poem has a dramatizing feel), glorying in the retreat to inwardness which is stigmatized by Jerome McGann as constituting the 'Romantic Ideology'.[56] Brontë's speaker is guarded, too, however, using vigilantly measured iambic tetrameters and a compactly rhymed stanzaic form as though to analyze as well as evoke a visionary voice at odds with 'Nature's sad reality'. Her final stanza conveys wariness about, and the lure of, the Romantic imagination. 'I trust not to thy phantom bliss', it begins, before 'Yet' sends the stanza in a different direction as the speaker welcomes the imagination as a 'Sure solacer of human cares, / And sweeter hope, when hope despairs'.

The Romantics prize imagination as a 'shaping spirit', as Coleridge has it in 'Dejection: An Ode'; Brontë as a 'solacer', a source of 'hope when hope despairs', at once, and subtly, a diminished and an acuter version of Shelley's imperative 'to hope, till Hope creates / From its own wreck the thing it contemplates' (*Prometheus Unbound*, 4. 573–4).[57] Shelley's lines are also a reply to despair, but they affirm a robust confidence. Brontë, here and in other poems, implies an intimate bond between a condition close to despair and the emergence of transcendent vision when, as she puts it in 'The Prisoner', 'the Unseen its truth reveals', even if that assertion is the prelude to an affectingly rendered account of vision's vanishing when normal sensory service is resumed, and 'the pulse begins to throb, the brain to think again'.[58] If, as O'Gorman notes, 'The poem is distinctive in presenting a female mystical experience', it also dramatizes the descent from mystical heights with a poignancy that is typical of Brontë and characteristic of a Victorian concern with affective authenticity.[59]

Brontë's poem differs from Romantic poetry through its greater explicitness ('the Unseen' is a phrase that suggests a codification of Romantic poetry's natural supernaturalism) and its more hard-pressed individuality.[60] The scenario of defiance amidst imprisonment may recall Romantic libertarianism, but the poem declines the prophetic or the hortatory. Continuity and discontinuity wear different expressions in different poems. When Slinn writes that in 'The Scholar-Gipsy' Arnold seeks 'aesthetic wholeness and transcendent truth but also wishes to incorporate the conflicting conditions of mid-nineteenth-century values' he may be right.[61] Yet his statement applies (if one substitutes 'early' for 'mid') to Romantic poems such as Keats's *Hyperion* or Shelley's *Adonais*. Keats and Shelley use the genre of epic and elegy to include their best hopes and worst fears; Arnold produces something closer to a combination of Keatsian ode and post-Wordsworthian meditation.

Inconveniently for one taxonomic criterion, the idea that the turn made in Victorian poetry is from 'Romantic, predominantly self-expressive poetry to a new, less personal poetry', Arnold is, arguably, as subjective in his poem as Shelley and Keats are in theirs.[62] It is true that Keats's struggle with the inherited idiom of Miltonic epic leads him to recast his poem in the openly subjective form of *The Fall of Hyperion*, with its foregrounded concern 'Whether the dream now purposed to rehearse' (I. 16) will turn out to be a true poem.[63] Arnold speaks for a culture as well as himself, when he leaves behind imaginings of the scholar-gipsy, emblem of freedom from 'the sick fatigue, the languid doubt, / Which much to have tried, in much been baffled, brings', to considering 'this strange disease of modern life'.[64] In constructing a poem whose structure and conduct enact 'divided aims', Arnold engages in complicated ways with Romantic practice. The scholar-gipsy who is praised for leaving 'the world, with powers / Fresh, undiverted to the world without' is kin to Shelley's Keats, raised in *Adonais* beyond 'the contagion of the world's slow stain'.[65]

But Arnold's Victorian originality is many-angled, and shows here in his engagement with Keatsian pastoral. He is lured by, yet holds back from, techniques used by Keats and Shelley to overcome temporality. Keats arrests natural process through descriptions that sensuously inhabit the apprehension of such process as though it were eternal. One side of his dialectically shaped poetry makes it seem 'rich to die' ('Ode to a Nightingale'), and invites us to linger over the false surmise that 'warm days will never cease' ('To Autumn'). Arnold does more than pay homage to Keats when he refers to 'the live murmur of a summer's day': he draws the phrase up into his critique of the 'Keatsian' by making the line, in the context of the poem as a whole, inevitably whisper of winter's approach, of a time when he will see his haunting alter-ego, the scholar-gipsy, 'Wrapped in thy cloak and battling with the snow'. And yet if this is critique, it also recognizes and brings to the fore tragic aspects of his predecessor's vision. Keats himself, Arnold half-suggests, never succumbs to the drug of escapism by which he is drawn.[66] Or, to put it differently, the scholar-gipsy is a Shelleyan quester who does not succumb to an Arnoldian version of Keatsian plenitude: Arnold produces tense-defying and Keats-saturated descriptions of 'Dark bluebells drenched with dews of summer eves' and 'wide fields of breezy grass / Where black-winged swallows haunt the glittering Thames', only to assert the scholar-gipsy's absence from the natural scene: 'But none hath words she can report of thee'; 'But, when they came from bathing, thou wast gone!'. Shelley's Poet in *Alastor* comes to mind, the 'fleeting visitant' who induces 'wondering awe'.[67] Shelley, indeed, comes to Arnold's aid with angelical effectualness in the poem. In *Adonais*, his assertion that the apparently expired Keats 'hath awakened from the dream of life' rejects through an act of rhetorical will the fact of mortality. It anticipates and underpins the strange switch made by Arnold from accepting that time cannot be overcome (the scholar-gipsy is laid to rest 'in some quiet churchyard') to conferring upon him 'an immortal lot, / And we imagine thee exempt from age'.

Arnold again spells out what in Shelley is implicit: that the need to imagine Keats as being 'exempt from age' is all that underpins claims for his immortality. But he is revising rather than rejecting his Romantic forebears, nowhere more so than at his poem's close. Where he differs from Shelley is that, having adumbrated a problem, he does not propose a solution; instead, he pours linguistic energy into exploring the idea of flight, rather than seeking to 'make war', as Peter Sacks puts it in describing the last movement of Shelley's elegy, 'on poetic language as an interpositional texture'.[68] By contrast, the concluding movement thrives on such 'texture' as it compares the scholar-gipsy to 'some grave Tyrian trader' and those whom he encounters, or might encounter, to a 'merry Grecian coaster' containing 'The young light-hearted masters of the wave'. The effect is suddenly to write the speaker's disconsolate self out of, yet also transform him within, his poem. The taxingly difficult extended simile shifts the poem away from lament into something more vigorous. As the 'Tyrian trader' spurns the Greek 'intruders on his ancient home', he 'day and night held on indignantly ... To where the Atlantic raves / Outside the western straits'. He leaves behind his home and searches for new spaces. The writing suggests a possibility of objective reconstruction that tilts the poem away from brooding over 'the infection of our mental strife', and hints at a mode of writing freed from introspection's sorrows and the eventual effect of ennui. That this hinting at impersonality tells us about the pressure of feeling from which escape is sought should not lead us to devalue it as a way of fruitfully reconceiving a post-Romantic dilemma: it is, for one thing, finding a new mode of representing the 'I' who has earlier ventriloquized the feelings of 'we' who 'wish the long unhappy dream would end'.

Glimpses of such a reconstruction of the self through what, in *A Defence of Poetry*, Shelley calls 'a going out' from it are staged in Romantic poetry, notably in the attempted objectivity of *Hyperion*.[69] The first book of Keats's poem closes with an account of Hyperion looking at the stars, an account that, in its concern with endurance and patience, anticipates thematic aspects of Victorian poetry: 'and still he kept them wide' (352), writes Keats of Hyperion's 'curved lids' (351), 'And still they were the same bright, patient stars' (353). Those 'bright, patient stars' serve, briefly and unforgettably, as an image of a mental stance proposed by Oceanus: 'to bear all naked truths, / And to envisage circumstance, all calm, / That is the top of sovereignty' (2. 203–5). Arnold's extended simile, for its part, takes the poem into new places: it suggests that flight can never be merely escapist, but must involve redefinition since there is no place available to the poet apart from the material world. The Tyrian trader belongs to a culture in which commerce and materialism are central, even if the 'Shy traffickers' with whom he finally does business are 'the honourable of the earth' (Isaiah 23. 8).[70] There is no refuge, the simile implies, from participation in the real: only the hope of eschewing its more corrupting aspects.

DIALOGIC MONOLOGUE AND MONODRAMA

In its revision of Romantic transcendentalism, the poem may repackage the 'corded bales' which compose the Romantic legacy. In a related manner, Martens suggests, in post-Bloomian style, that 'Browning offers creative misreading of Romantic poets which reduce the complexity of these predecessors'.[71] Summing up his sense of how he had been affected by Shelleyan subjectivity, Browning writes in his essay on the poet (1852) of the way in which his Romantic precursor sustains a

> simultaneous perception of Power and Love in the absolute, and of Beauty and Good in the concrete, while he throws, from his poet's station between both, swifter, subtler, and more numerous films for the connexion of each with each than have been thrown by any modern artificer of whom I have knowledge.[72]

Browning's mature response to this incarnation of 'subjective' artifice is to assume a mode of writing that is 'objective', a mode throwing 'swifter, subtler, and more numerous films' between the poetic self and his subject than can be decoded by any biographical or psychoanalytic critic. And yet the move is towards a framed subjectivity, one in which the self is paramount, even if studiedly not the poet's. *Pauline* shows Browning in the first flush of Shelley worship, dedicating himself to his predecessor's idealism and erotic quest: 'Sun-treader, I believe in God and truth / And love'.[73] By the time Browning revisits themes associated with Shelleyan erotic quest in dramatic lyrics, such as 'Two in the Campagna', he develops a mode that allows him to use the word 'I', yet to escape any assumption of subjective confessionalism.

That said, Browning's mode in his dramatic monologues owes much to Wordsworth's practice in his *Lyrical Ballads*: Wordsworth's speakers are often not identifiable with Wordsworth; the same is true of Blake's in his *Songs*, while Shelley's poetry shows a development towards work in which self-portraiture grows dramatic, as in his *Julian and Maddalo*. That poem's Preface half-mocks the 'I' with whom the poem seems to sympathize. The poem itself contains hints of criticism (Julian's 'dreams of baseless good' flutter like disconsolate fantasies), yet it passes the burden and privilege of interpretation to the reader in a way that anticipates Browning's practice in poems such as 'Andrea del Sarto'.[74] The work is among Browning's most satisfying monologues, because it allows its speaker a self-awareness that spoils the reader's pleasure in playing the role of superior therapist. Andrea may blame his wife for his relative failures, but he concedes that the failures arise from his choices: 'So—still they overcome / Because there's still Lucrezia,—as I choose'.[75] Those last three words complicate the view of Andrea that sees him as 'searching for excuses', as O'Gorman pithily has it.[76] Certainly he seeks to lay flattering unctions to his soul; the earlier idea that 'we are in God's hand', for example, insinuates an extenuating excuse. Yet 'So free we seem, so fettered fast we are' is a line characteristic of Browning's crossply poetics; it challenges our convictions even as we question its authenticity.

The degree of simplification involved in viewing the Romantic mode as 'predominantly self-expressive' is considerable (it ignores, for instance, the fact that the Romantic
self is often performed as much as expressed). But it comes close to explaining the
pressure to find objective modes of presentation in Victorian poetry, one that results
in fertile forms of experimentation. There is an explicitness in the Victorian attempt
to objectify (through monologues, dramatic lyrics, and monodramas) that wishes to
exorcize a troubling Romantic concern with the self. At the same time, what is expelled
returns with all the energy of the repressed. Tennyson may adopt a persona in *Maud*,
yet that persona is given over entirely to 'self-expression' in a venture in which the poet's
metrical skill is vibrantly and thrillingly complicit. The poem, a 'Monodrama' draws on
the practice of the so-called 'Spasmodics' in its commitment to the uninhibited expression of feeling.[77] It is as though the mask of monodrama permits an emotional licence
denied to the lyric 'I', of, say, Wordsworth's 'She dwelt among th'untrodden ways'. That
poem concludes, 'But she is in her Grave, and Oh! / The difference to me', exploiting
the power present in understatement.[78] The hero of *Maud*, after the heroine's death, is
equally affecting; but what one finds here is something close to metrically irresistible,
cunningly wrought overstatement; monodrama, monomania, and monorhyme combine to devastating effect in the long passage concluding,

> Always I long to creep
> Into some still cavern deep,
> There to weep, and weep, and weep
> My whole soul out to thee. (2. 235–8)[79]

'I' and 'thee' reach across an unspannable gulf throughout the poem, and one is enclosed
inside the speaker's projections throughout; if solipsism shadows affirmation of
self-presence in Romantic poetry, it takes centre-stage in *Maud*.

Tennyson anticipates modernist notions of an objective correlative in a poem such as
'Mariana' where the poet finds a way of exploring a lyric scenario in which suffering finds
no vent in action. The poet's 'I' is absent from the poem, and yet his presence is implicit in
that absence. Mariana undergoes a post-Romantic experience of sense-confusion in the
final stanza, an heir of the Rousseau dazzled by the shifting contradictions of the 'shape
all light' in Shelley's *The Triumph of Life*. The 'sparrow's chirrup on the roof, / The slow
clock ticking, and the sound / Which to the wooing wind aloof / The poplar made, did
all confound / Her sense' are lines which domesticate and humanize the shape all light's
potentially sinister sense-confusion.[80] Rousseau's experience is terrifying yet culturally revealing; Mariana's is one that allows the poet to practise a virtuosic narrowing of
Romantic scope. For Arthur Hallam, Tennyson's early poetry was marked by its 'vivid,
picturesque delineation of objects, and the peculiar skill with which he holds them all
fused ... in a medium of strong emotion'.[81] This recalls Coleridge on the imagination, yet
the 'strong emotion' which Tennyson excels at depicting takes Wordsworthian obsession
(itself bordering on compulsive rituals of repetition) into new pathologies of isolation
and erotic frustration: Martha Ray fixated on the spot where she has probably buried her

infant turns into Mariana who 'seem'd to walk forlorn', without hope even that the Keatsian adjective will recall her to her 'sole self' and a different mode of vision. Tennyson's presence in the poem is immensely restrained. Narrative comment is kept to a minimum, heard only as an implicit confession in the refrain that the poem's art stylizes suffering.

Comparable recognitions and techniques inform 'The Lady of Shalott'. In this poem, Shelley's aloof Witch of Atlas turns into an artist surrogate burdened by her separation from reality. Shelley's buoyant, graceful ottava rima gives way to a ballad-like stanza full of repeated phrases and triple rhymes, and often using tripping trochaic rhythms. Shelley's Witch disdains capture by a utilitarian readership desiring, like Mary Shelley, more 'HUMAN INTEREST'; the Lady of Shalott seeks release from her web-weaving and mirrored shelter on seeing Sir Lancelot, only to pursue a self-chosen death.[82] Shelley stages the fate of the imagination with inventive panache and evident self-involvement; Tennyson broaches the question of whether the artist can ever escape the mirror-world of representation with cautious indirection.[83]

'Their Age, Not Charlemagne's'

Over and over, then, one is aware of the Romantics as 'that which [the Victorian poets] know', in T. S. Eliot's phrase, or to give his account of tradition a Bloomian twist, that which they are compelled, as they seek to carve out their own creative space, to 'mis-know'.[84] Victorian poets are conscious of their times in ways that bear the impress of Romanticism's own historicism. Their stance can smack of despairing belatedness, as when Arnold sees himself as 'Wandering between two worlds, one dead, / The other powerless to be born' in 'Stanzas from the Grande Chartreuse'. Even here, Arnold's trope of being 'between two worlds' is post-Byronic ('Between two worlds life hovers like a star'), and derives creative excitement out of its post-Romantic 'wandering'.[85] Arnold looks before and after, though his sense of what is 'to be born' lacks the Utopian hope of Shelley's 'yet to be' (*Prometheus Unbound*, 3. 3. 56).

Elsewhere, Victorian poets suggest both a timeliness and an awareness of elsewhere through their developed historical consciousness. Browning locates contemporary concerns about the poet's role in a long, tangled, suggestive poem, *Sordello*, set in the time of medieval troubadours. Elizabeth Barrett Browning argues, conversely, in *Aurora Leigh*, that the poet's 'sole work is to represent the age, / Their age, not Charlemagne's'.[86] Arthur Hugh Clough's Claude, self-deprecating, snobbish successor to the suffering pilgrim of *Childe Harold's Pilgrimage* and the wry narrator of *Don Juan*, finds the *mot juste* for Rome to be 'Rubbishy', in part because of the Eternal City's evidence of 'All the incongruous things of past incompatible ages' (*Amours de Voyage*, I. i. 20, 22).[87] Such alertness to the self's fragmented positioning within history and the self's limits looks ahead to modernism.[88] Yet it also accompanies and prompts a pervasive sense of being, to borrow (and gloss) Arnold's phrasing from 'Stanzas in the Grande Chartreuse', the 'inheritors' of Romantic restlessness and its poem-inspiring 'distress'.

NOTES

1. Quoted from *Matthew Arnold: The Major Authors*, ed. Miriam Allott and Robet H. Super (Oxford: Oxford University Press, 1986), 320. This article sustains and broadens arguments broached in my essay, '"The Burden of Ourselves": Arnold as a Post-Romantic Poet', *The Yearbook of English Studies* 36 (2006), 109–124.

2. Alfred Tennyson quoted in Hallam Tennyson, *Alfred, Lord Tennyson: A Memoir by his Son*, 2 vols. (London: Macmillan, 1897), ii, 285.

3. Robert Browning, letter of 19 Jan., 1870, quoted from *Robert Browning: The Oxford Authors*, ed. Adam Roberts (Oxford: Oxford University Press, 1997), 726.

4. Gerard Manley Hopkins, *Selected Prose*, ed. Gerald Roberts (Oxford: Oxford University Press, 1980), 158.

5. *Matthew Arnold*, 321.

6. Alfred Tennyson, 'Crossing the Bar', in *The Poems of Tennyson*, ed. Christopher Ricks (London: Longmans, 1969), 1459. Percy Bysshe Shelley, *Prometheus Unbound*, in *Percy Bysshe Shelley: The Major Works*, ed. Zachary Leader and Michael O'Neill (2003; Oxford: Oxford University Press, 2009), 288.

7. John Keats, 'To Autumn', in *The Poems of John Keats*, ed. Miriam Allott (London: Longman, 1970), 654. For Tennyson's allusion to *Hamlet*, see *The Poems of Tennyson* 1459n.

8. Robert Browning, 'Memorabilia', in *Robert Browning*, 238.

9. See Herbert F. Tucker, Jr., 'Memorabilia: Mnemonic Imagination in Shelley and Browning', *Studies in Romanticism* 19 (1980), 295–325, for good discussion of the poem's 'process of belated but restorative representation' (325).

10. Hopkins, 'I wake and feel the fell of dark, not day', in *The Poems of Gerard Manley Hopkins*, 4th edn., ed. W. H. Gardener and N. H. MacKenzie (London: Oxford University Press, 1970), 101.

11. Hopkins, *Selected Prose*, 159.

12. Keats, 'Ode on a Grecian Urn', in *The Poems of John Keats*, 537; Hopkins, 'God's Grandeur', in *The Poems of Gerard Manley Hopkins*, 66.

13. Keats, 'To Autumn', in *The Poems of John Keats*, 651 (where 'bosom friend' is not hyphenated as it is in Heaney's essay); Hopkins, 'The Wreck of the Deutschland', in *The Poems of Gerard Manley Hopkins*, 53.

14. Seamus Heaney, 'The Fire i' The Flint: Reflections on the Poetry of Gerard Manley Hopkins', in *Preoccupations: Selected Prose 1968-1978* (London: Faber and Faber, 1980), 84, 85.

15. Susan Brown, 'The Victorian Poetess', in Joseph Bristow, ed., *The Cambridge Companion to Victorian Poetry* (Cambridge: Cambridge University Press, 2000), 183.

16. John Clare, 'An Invite to Eternity', in *John Clare: The Oxford Authors*, ed. Eric Robinson and David Powell (Oxford: Oxford University Press, 1984), 351.

17. Martin Heidegger, *Poetry, Language, Thought*, trans. Albert Hofstadter (New York: Harper, 1971), 142.

18. Tennyson, 'Ulysses', in *The Poems of Tennyson*, 563.

19. See Jerome McGann, *Swinburne: An Experiment in Criticism* (Chicago: University of Chicago Press, 1972), 73–78, 117–123, 175–176.

20. McGann, *Swinburne: An Experiment in Criticism*, 141.

21. Algernon Charles Swinburne, 'Hymn to Proserpine', in *Major Poems and Selected Prose*, ed. Jerome McGann and Charles L. Sligh (New Haven: Yale University Press, 2004), 104.

22. Swinburne, *Major Poems and Selected Prose*, 478.

23. For Shelley's influence, see *The Pre-Raphaelites and Their Circle*, ed. Cecil B. Lang, 2nd edn. (Chicago: University of Chicago Press, 1975), 523.

24. Swinburne, 'Anactoria' in *Major Poems and Selected Prose*, 100.

25. See Peter Allen, *The Cambridge Apostles: The Early Years* (Cambridge: Cambridge University Press, 2010), 45.

26. Tennyson, 'Mariana in the South', in *The Poems of Tennyson*, 363.

27. Keats, 'The Eve of St Agnes', in *The Poems of John Keats*, 468, 88n.

28. Matthew Arnold, quoted in *The Complete Poems*, ed. Kenneth Allott, 2nd edn. (London: Longman, 1979), 239.

29. Arnold, 'Memorial Verses', in *The Complete Poems*, 239–40.

30. Arnold, 'Memorial Verses', 239n.

31. Arnold, *On the Study of Celtic Literature*, quoted in *The Complete Poems* 240n.

32. Virgil quoted in Arnold, *The Complete Poems*, 241n.

33. Carlyle, quoted in Arnold, *The Complete Poems*, 239n.

34. William Wordsworth, 'Ode: Intimations of Immortality', in *21st-Century Oxford Authors: William Wordsworth*, ed. Stephen Gill (Oxford: Oxford University Press, 2010), 284.

35. Arnold, 'Stanzas in Memory of the Author of "Obermann"', in *The Complete Poems*, 138.

36. Arnold, 'Stanzas in Memory of the Author of "Obermann"', 139n.

37. Arnold, 'A Summer Night', in *The Complete Poems*, 283.

38. Arnold, *The Complete Poems*, 284n.

39. Frank Kermode, *Romantic Image* (London: Fontana, 1971; 1st pub. 1957), 25–26.

40. Thomas Hardy, 'The Darkling Thrush', in *Thomas Hardy: Selected Poems*, ed. Tim Armstrong (London: Longman, 1993), 89–91.

41. Keats, 'Ode to a Nightingale', in *The Poems of John Keats*, 530.

42. Shelley, 'To a Skylark', in *Percy Bysshe Shelley: The Major Works*, 466.

43. Shelley, 'Mont Blanc', in *Percy Bysshe Shelley: The Major Works*, 124.

44. Samuel Taylor Coleridge, 'The Rime of the Ancient Mariner', in *Coleridge's Poetry and Prose*, ed. Nicholas Halmi, Paul Magnuson, and Raimonda Modiano (New York: Norton, 2004), 77.

45. Hardy, '"For Life I Had Never Cared Greatly"', in *Thomas Hardy: Selected Poems*, 235n.

46. Hardy, 'During Wind and Rain', in *Thomas Hardy: Selected Poems*, 229.

47. Shelley, 'Ode to the West Wind', in *Percy Bysshe Shelley: The Major Works* 414.

48. Hardy, 'Apology', in *Thomas Hardy: Selected Poems*, 246.

49. E. Warwick Slinn, 'Experimental Form in Victorian Poetry', in Joseph Bristow, ed., *The Cambridge Companion to Victorian Poetry*, 522.

50. Coleridge, 'Kubla Khan', in *Coleridge's Poetry and Prose*, 182–183.

51. Coleridge, 'Kubla Khan', 180.

52. Quoted in *The Poems of Tennyson* 400.

53. Tennyson, *The Palace of Art*, in *The Poems of Tennyson*, 401.

54. See Richard Cronin's comment that 'Victorian poets assume a condition that their Romantic predecessors associated with dejection or with a state of imaginative loss', 'Victorian Poetry: An Overview', in Michael O'Neill, ed., *The Cambridge History of English Poetry* (Cambridge: Cambridge University Press, 2010), 588.

55. *Victorian Poetry: An Annotated Anthology* ed. Francis O'Gorman (Malden, Mass: Blackwell, 2004), 220.

56. Emily Brontë, 'To Imagination', in *The Complete Poems*, ed. Janet Gezari (London: Penguin, 2002), 19–20.

57. Coleridge, 'Dejection: An Ode', in *Coleridge's Poetry and Prose*, 157.

58. Emily Brontë, 'The Prisoner', in *The Complete Poems*, 15.

59. *Victorian Poetry: An Annotated Anthology*, 223.

60. The *OED* (1a) gives the following example from Thomas Carlyle (in 1829): 'The veil and mysterious Garment of the Unseen'.

61. *The Cambridge Companion to Victorian Poetry*, 53.

62. Britta Martens, *Browning, Victorian Poetics and the Romantic Legacy: Challenging the Personal Voice* (Farnham: Ashgate, 2011), 3.

63. Keats, *The Fall of Hyperion*, in *The Poems of John Keats*, 658.

64. Arnold, 'The Scholar-Gipsy', in *The Complete Poems*, 364.

65. Shelley, *Adonais*, in *Percy Bysshe Shelley: The Major Works*, 541.

66. See William A. Ulmer, 'The Human Seasons: Arnold, Keats, and "The Scholar-Gipsy"', in *Victorian Poetry* 22 (1984), 247–261. Ulmer argues that Arnold moves from critique of Keats to recognizing his 'worth' (259).

67. Shelley, *Alastor*, in *Percy Bysshe Shelley: The Major Works*, 99.

68. Peter Sacks, 'Last Clouds: A Reading of *Adonais*', in *Shelley*, ed. Michael O'Neill (London: Longman, 1993), 194.

69. Shelley, *A Defence of Poetry*, in *Percy Bysshe Shelley: The Major Works*, 682.

70. Arnold, 'The Scholar-Gipsy', in *The Complete Poems*, 369n.

71. Quoted in Arnold, *The Complete Poems* 42.

72. Browning, *Robert Browning: The Oxford Authors*, 589.

73. Browning, *Pauline*, in *Robert Browning: The Oxford Authors*, 28.

74. Shelley, *Julian and Maddalo*, in *Percy Bysshe Shelley: The Major Works*, 227.

75. Browning, 'Andrea del Sarto', in *Robert Browning: The Oxford Authors*, 246.

76. *The Cambridge Companion to Victorian Poetry*, 189.

77. J. H. Buckley in *The Victorian Temper* (1952), quoted in *The Poems of Tennyson*, 1038.

78. Wordsworth, 'She dwelt among th'untrodden ways', in *21st-Century Oxford Authors: William Wordsworth*, 103.

79. Tennyson, *Maud*, in *The Poems of Tennyson*, 1086.

80. Tennyson, 'Mariana', in *The Poems of Tennyson*, 190. Harold Bloom notes and brilliantly glosses the Shelleyan echo in Harold Bloom, *Poetry and Repression: Revisionism from Blake to Stevens* (New Haven: Yale University Press, 1976), 152.

81. Hallam, quoted in *Victorian Poetry: An Annotated Anthology*, ed. F. O'Gorman, 64.

82. *Percy Bysshe Shelley: The Major Works*, 486.

83. For further discussion, see Michael O'Neill, 'The Wheels of Being: Tennyson and Shelley', in Robert Douglas-Fairhurst and Seamus Perry, eds., *Tennyson among the Poets: Bicentenary Essays* (Oxford: Oxford University Press, 2009), 186–188.

84. See 'Tradition and the Individual Talent', in Frank Kermode, ed., *Selected Prose of T. S. Eliot*, (London: Faber and Faber, 1975), 40.

85. Arnold, 'Stanzas from the Grande Chartreuse', in *The Complete Poems*, 305.

86. Elizabeth Barrett Browning, *Aurora Leigh*, v. 202–3, ed. Margaret Reynolds (New York: Norton, 1996), 149.

87. Arthur Hugh Clough, *Amours de Voyage*, quoted in *The Cambridge Companion to Victorian Poetry*, 230.

88. For discussion of 'Victorian Modernismus', see Valentine Cunningham, *Victorian Poetry Now: Poets, Poems, Poetics* (Malden, Mass: Wiley-Blackwell, 2011), ch. 10.

SELECT BIBLIOGRAPHY

Bloom, Harold, *Poetry and Repression: Revisionism from Blake to Stevens* (New Haven: Yale University Press, 1976).

Bristow, Joseph, ed., *The Cambridge Companion to Victorian Poetry* (Cambridge: Cambridge University Press, 2000).

Cronin, Richard, 'Byron, Clough, and the Grounding of Victorian Poetry', *Romanticism* 14 (2008), 13–24.

—— Chapman, Alison, and Harrison, Anthony H., eds., *A Companion to Victorian Poetry* (Malden, MA: Blackwell, 2002).

Cunningham, Valentine, *Victorian Poetry Now: Poets, Poems, Poetics* (Malden, MA: Wiley-Blackwell, 2011).

Douglas-Fairhurst, Robert, *Victorian Afterlives: The Shaping of Influence in Nineteenth-Century Literature* (Oxford: Oxford University Press, 2002).

Harrison, Antony, H., *Victorian Poets and Romantic Poems: Intertextuality and Ideology* (Charlottesville: University Press of Virginia, 1990).

Kermode, Frank, *Romantic Image* (London: Fontana, 1971; 1st pub. 1957).

Lang, Cecil B., ed., *The Pre-Raphaelites and Their Circle*, 2nd edn. (Chicago: University of Chicago Press, 1975).

Martens, Britta, *Browning, Victorian Poetics and the Romantic Legacy: Challenging the Personal Voice* (Farnham: Ashgate, 2011).

McGann, Jerome, *Swinburne: An Experiment in Criticism* (Chicago: University of Chicago Press, 1972).

O'Gorman, Francis, ed., *Victorian Poetry: An Annotated Anthology* (Malden, MA: Blackwell, 2004).

O'Neill, Michael, '"The Burden of Ourselves": Arnold as a Post-Romantic Poet', *The Yearbook of English Studies* 36 (2006), 109–124.

—— ed., *The Cambridge History of English Poetry* (Cambridge: Cambridge University Press, 2010), esp. chs. 29–38.

Radford, Andrew and Sandy, Mark, eds., *Romantic Echoes in the Victorian Era* (Aldershot: Ashgate, 2008).

Ulmer, William A., 'The Human Seasons: Arnold, Keats, and "The Scholar-Gipsy"', *Victorian Poetry* 22 (1984), 247–261

Wootton, Sarah, *Consuming Keats: Nineteenth-Century Representations in Art and Literature* (Basingstoke: Palgrave Macmillan, 2006).

CHAPTER 14

....

AMERICAN INTERSECTIONS: POETRY IN THE UNITED STATES 1837–1901

....

ELISA NEW

MARK Twain's oft-quoted observation that the sixty odd years of Victoria's rule produced greater change than the prior two thousand cannot apply to the United States, which, sixty years prior to Victoria's ascent to the throne, had not yet been declared an independent nation. Transatlantic print networks exposed Americans to many of the same intellectual disruptions to traditional thought their English counterparts absorbed (Darwin, Lyell, Marx and the positivist turn; steam, railways, the grisly spectacle of modern war; the rise of science and the social sciences, imperial expansion, urban misery; the cry for female emancipation; new ideas of mind, brain, sex, and psyche; new doubts about old vices and virtues) and, of course, the physical pace of change on the North American continent was far more accelerated than in Britain.

But in the United States, the mere two-hundred years of cultural presence before 1837 had to do the cultural work of two thousand. America only had the sketchiest literary background to boast of in 1837 (as English visitors loved to point out), and it also had far less in the way of storied history to build a literature upon. The bannered medievalism so enriching, for instance, to English Victorian poetry had as its closest American analogue the hardly chivalric epoch of the French and Indian wars, scarcely eighty years back. America's Victorian era was, like England's, preceded by Romanticism (a Romanticism schooled especially in Wordsworth, whose example permitted American acolytes to boast their more immediate access to inspiriting Nature), but this Romanticism, and the neo-Classicism that preceded it, was coincident with, and complicated by, the exigencies of establishing a national literary tradition. It is as if Pope and Wordsworth had, in addition to being themselves, also to be Chaucer and Milton—when they were, in fact, only Dwight and Bryant.

If a past worthy of a literate and virtuous people had to be found, this was in spite of the fact that the past had scant prestige. America epitomized the evanescence Marx meant when he wrote 'all that is solid melts into air'.[1] Nineteenth-century American poetry of the Victorian period proves the point, for its history is one of major achievements processed by—and through—a culture of extreme disposability. All three of America's great poets of this period—Dickinson, Whitman, and Melville—had, by the 1890s, died undiscovered, sidelined, or fully forgotten, the latter two not only deprived of the laureateships enjoyed by their British peers, but living in modest (Camden, New Jersey, supported by contributions) or pathetic (Lower New York, depressed and anonymous) circumstances. The period of Victoria's reign saw the birth, maturity, and demise of American poetic culture. Inside of a generation, the rural ingenuousness and popular optimism of the start-up period (1820s–1850s) had already found its downward slope, a premature *fin de siècle* (precipitated by the Civil War) arriving as early as the late 1860s and persisting until the 1890s, when beneath the fraying formalities of postbellum verse one could suddenly see the lineaments of a precocious, but genuine, modernism.

All the more to be marked, then, that in 1837, a mere seventy years previously, American poetry was not really yet off the ground. It was in its infancy, the phenomenon of American literary production—a novelty, a patriotic necessity, and a cottage industry. It may be hard to imagine a time when the production and circulation of poetry in bulk was deemed so important that editors of periodicals would pay a flattering pittance to more or less anyone willing to produce some. But this was the case in mid-century, early Victorian America, where cultural pressures to create a genuine and distinctively American literature, *and* a literature earning European respect, *and* a literature meeting the needs and democratic aspirations of its highly diverse populace raised the value of poetic production and rewarded those who generated it in bulk.

In this culture, where ministers and housewives, collegians and teenagers, writers of dirges and writers of doggerel were all pressed into the manufacture of poetry, those with a longer view worried that *the* Poet, 'the sayer, the namer' who 'represents beauty', as Emerson called him, had not yet emerged.[2] How could he? 'The poets of aristocratic ages', as Tocqueville wrote, 'created admirable works by taking as their subject certain incidents in the life of a people or a man, but none of them ever dared to embrace the destinies of all mankind, whereas poets who write in democratic ages may undertake to do just this'.[3] His word 'undertake' captures the difficulty, for how could one be a poet of the present, of the moment, and also a poet for all time? As it happened, there was such a poet coming, one who spent the 1840s incubating the genuinely contemporary *and* genuinely cosmic poetics Emerson would pronounce 'a remarkable mixture of the Bhagvat Gita and the *New York Herald*'.[4] As this poet burnished what Emerson called his 'sunbeam'—developing his talent in upper Hudson schoolhouses and grimy Broadway taprooms, assembling the jottings he'd eventually print and then hawking himself in Brooklyn phrenology parlours as *Leaves of Grass*—the offices of American poetry were opened by others.

By mid-century a fully accredited culture of letters was up and running in Cambridge, Massachusetts. There, the New England stalwarts, James Russell Lowell, Oliver Wendell

Holmes, and Henry Wadsworth Longfellow, along with Emerson, manned an American outpost of mainstream Victorian culture: English poetry's satellite campus at Harvard. They published poems in every issue of the *North American Review* and then, beginning in 1857, in the *Atlantic Monthly*, in whose pages they established and cultivated transatlantic fraternity, welcoming Tennyson, Arnold, Hallam, Hardy, and Browning to these pages, and enjoying the reciprocations of their courtesies. By the 1880s, appreciative readers of Charles Gibbon's popular *Casquet of Literature, A Selection in Poetry and Prose from the Works of the Most Admired Authors* would find generous selections from the work of Lowell, Holmes, Emerson, and Longfellow (along with Lydia Maria Child, Nathaniel Hawthorne, and Harriet Beecher Stowe) in every one of the *Casquet*'s six volumes. Such contributors from New England's capitol of culture demonstrated American sophistication, alacrity, mastery, and scope. They demonstrated that fealty to the value of earnest writing so prized by their English contemporaries: faith in the vocation of letters as a moral enterprise.

Arnoldian would be one way of calling this capacity, except that, of the three, only Longfellow plumbed the deeper registers of Victorian faith. Only he admitted into his verse the doubt that distinguishes faith from mere confidence. Lowell and Holmes may be said to have run poetry as a public utility: they made sure the franchise was professionally run. But Longfellow really was a poet, his career an increasingly moving demonstration of two principles shared by all Victorians: the principle of service raised to Kantian ideal, and, that of forbearance before difficulty, tolerance before uncertainty, played for high, sometimes even Kierkegaardian, stakes.

The commitment to service is easiest to see, for it is writ all over Longfellow's style—a style which combines assured regularity and musicality with delicate, often surprising, local effects. What Tillotson once wrote of Tennyson is fairly said of Longfellow: his metres, though carefully considered and very consistently wrought, seem nevertheless 'as easily accomplished as a tree accomplishes leaves'.[5] Tightly woven patterns of diction, firm authority of voice, clearly imputed audience, and impeccable metrical regularity all work together to provide a comfort zone, a well-made domain in which feelings expand as they must, while the poet's voice guarantees understanding and reciprocity. Add to this Longfellow's visual sense, his gift for swift-moving narrative, his infectious curiosity, his learnedness without pedantry, his candour without crudity, and one sees why his poems were put, not only into circulation, but into practical use across the full range of human purposes—pedagogical, recreational, romantic, therapeutic, and national.

For all his remarkable cultural relevancy, Longfellow was not parochial. The cantering tetrameter of 'Listen my children and you shall hear / Of the midnight ride of Paul Revere'[6] does, of course, guide the American pursuit of independence toward a foregone conclusion, but Longfellow's definition of the 'American' is more nuanced, far less triumphalist, than most. Longfellow's American is the child of roundabout migrations, of fortuitous accidents, and of braided currents of cultural diffusion from elsewhere. Whether in such poems as 'Evangeline' of 1847 (an epic of the Acadian journey from the Canadian 'forest primeval' to French Louisiana, which Longfellow sets in dactylic, distinctly Homeric-sounding, verse), or 'The Song of Hiawatha' of 1855 (a Native

American epic set to the rhythms of the Finnish Kalevala), or even in the most 'native' of his American origin stories, 'The Courtship of Miles Standish' (which introduces Standish as a buccaneer—veteran of engagements in Damascus and Flanders—and a scholar of Hebrew and Latin, his statecraft learned from classical epics), Longfellow lets imaginative poetic syntheses represent cultural syncretisms: he offers the 'responsible poetic voice', in George Monteiro's phrase, as statecraft's firm and serviceable staff.[7] As if nationhood and *poesis* shared burdens of citizenship, Longfellow models a progress disciplined by earnest craft.

Human service is, then, a sort of categorical imperative in Longfellow's work. So much more interesting is the way Longfellow, like his most intrepid English cousins, braves categorical conundra, leading those steeled for rigour towards what Philip Davis calls, simply 'the hard thing'.[8] For even as the nation coheres, as fellowship endures, and as song firms the social covenant, Longfellow acknowledges an essential spottiness of the self and psyche, his verse exposing the reader to the chasms, breaks, and incommensurables any mature person eventually faces. Anxiety abounds in Longfellow's verse. Alert to the ways purposefulness breeds tension, to the ways ambition can feel, in the moment, exactly like dread, and to how fear can quicken the nerves like desire, Longfellow tests his fluency against the real vicissitudes of human psychology.

A poem like the 'The Bridge' of 1845, for example, puts Longfellow very much among British peers. It is a poem in which a yearning for consolation and resolution, and the discipline applied to achieve these, cannot produce the unity desired: the 'bridge'. In 'The Bridge', rather, a simple walk over a local river bisects discontinuous and irreconcilable ranges of experience. The golden light of the moon first glimpsed 'Behind the dark church-tower' sinks 'like a golden goblet' and also blends, and contends, with the 'redder' gleam of an industrial furnace.[9] Temporal registers are layered on one another as the speaker paces a scene that is provincially (New Englandly) civic, poetically (symbolically) archaic, and infernally (industrially) contemporary. The contest of registers in one medium, on one consciousness, produces, not synthesis, but its reverse: a heart 'hot and restless', 'burdened', 'care-encumbered'. A mind assimilating so much is burdened by, rather than embosomed, within its own interiority. Interference and disturbance are its native element, and, as Philip Davis puts it, the 'chronology of its feelings' is 'not in step with their importance'.[10] In Longfellow's already modern world, bridges are too trafficked and they open chasms as well.

Or consider 'The Fire of Driftwood' of 1850 which reunites some long-separated friends gathered in a 'farm-house old'. The poem seems to promise a sort of *nostos*, the redemptive classic return, with all the satisfactions of closure such a return might provide. But the house in which the friends meet is in a seaport town whose best days are past. There is a dismantled fort, one whose timbers fuel the fire of driftwood, and so much else that might be solid proves porous and brittle. Iambic tetrameter stanzas batten down the verse, but they, like the wooden windows, leak, giving 'to the sea breeze damp and cold / An easy entrance, night and day'.[11] And as with the fire of driftwood, which immolates the security of an old town (the familiar place where old friends huddle), so friendship and human rituals of sharing also seem to consume themselves. The pressure to find community quickens anxieties. Social occasion fuels misgivings genuinely existential. Loneliness takes its place in the intimate circle:

> The first slight swerving of the heart
>   That words are powerless to express
> And leave it still unsaid in part
>   Or say it in too great excess

Language, this poem discovers, may only draw us into a deeper sort of alienation:

> The very tones in which we spake
>   Had something strange, I could but mark;
> The leaves of memory seemed to make
>   A mournful rustling in the dark.
>
> Oft died the words upon our lips,
>   As suddenly, from out the fire
> Built of the wreck of stranded ships,
>   The flames would leap and then expire

Not that this poem, for all its sadness, or indeed any of Longfellow's poems, gives way to despair. This is saying quite a lot, since Longfellow himself endured and carried his whole life memory of the most horrifically sentimental tragedy ever to befall any Victorian poet—the evening in 1861 when his beloved wife, Fanny, engaged in preserving locks of her children's hair in sealing wax, accidentally set her voluminous skirts on fire and died a few days later. The speaker of Longfellow's greatest sonnet, 'The Cross of Snow' of 1876, is a prowling somnambulist whose grief drives him beyond his culture's succours to a place of deeper, more ravaged knowledge:

> In the long, sleepless watches of the night,
> A gentle face—the face of one long dead—
> Looks at me from the wall, where round its head
> The night-lamp casts a halo of pale light.
> Here in this room she died, and soul more white
> Never through martyrdom of fire was led
> To its repose; nor can in books be read
> The legend of a life more benedight.[12]

Winding through the octet, the speaker pauses at all the stops, at all the memorial or consolatory stations his culture has devised. Through the shrine-like rooms, the rituals, vigils, and formalized temporal intervals, past the icons and images and exercises of reflection that would give closure, and even peace, to the mourner, he passes. But closure eludes, and the mourning spaces crowd the speaker, who remains without solace. Sorrow, it turns out, is wilder, more remote and intransigent than our cultural machinations. And so the poet 'lights out', as Twain would later say, for the territories:

> There is a mountain in the distant West
> That, sun-defying, in its deep ravines
> Displays a cross of snow upon its side.
> Such is the cross I wear upon my breast
> These eighteen years, through all the changing scenes
> And seasons, changeless since the day she died.

Grief bounds beyond the forms devised to quell it. It finds a place where the heart can lie on the cold ground. The sensibility here is what I called, earlier, Kierkegaardian—its leap is out of the world of consolation and into a world harder, truer, than we understand. If there is something large and unmistakably American in the way this most refined of poets turns west, to the Rockies, one knows Longfellow's West as recognizably Victorian territory. Nations may rise in triumph, setting towns and building structures along alien coast, but mature persons know there are ranges of experience insusceptible to our buildings. There, ignorant armies clash by night, or, as in Longfellow's 'The Fire of Driftwood': 'Ships dismasted . . . / . . . sent no answer back again'.

Kierkegaardian is a good word, too, for the work of the mature Dickinson who, by the 1860s, was laying claim to, and venturing to the very edge of what she liked to call 'circumference', a poetic zone of spiritual and affective exposure she contrasted with 'Center'. As Dickinson explained in a letter to Thomas Wentworth Higginson, 'My business is circumference'.[13] In her most radical work of the 1860s Dickinson makes the Kiekegaardian leap, the leap into faith via doubt, one of her usual motions: 'A Doubt if it be Us / Assists the staggering Mind' she writes, 'In an extremer Anguish / Until it footing find'.[14] Caustic, she casts off the norms of stable Romantic selfhood, the security of security: 'On a Columnar Self / How ample to rely / In Tumult or Extremity / How good the Certainty' in pursuit of her own hard thing.[15] It is, as in Longfellow's case, a game played for truth, for the highest stakes.

But if the differences between scripture and poetry, orthodoxy and imagination, were what interested Dickinson at her period of most ferocious productivity, such interests were hardly the usual thing for a poetess of her day on either side of the ocean, within a culture of letters that, while encouraging rather than discouraging publication for women, drastically circumscribed poetic possibilities. The American woman poet had a job to do, and it was to represent the diminutive, the humble, and the unworldly. Situating childishness right next to godliness, she was meant to renounce all interest in the world beyond her proper sphere—that domestic realm of house, crib, and garden, that realm where protectiveness for the small and fragile growing thing (flower, child, season) equated with virtue. The genre is well represented by this selection from the most prolific, and popular, Mrs. Lydia Sigourney:

> A butterfly basked on a baby's grave
> Where a lily had chance to grow;
> Why art thou here with thy gaudy dye
> When she of the blue and sparkling eye
> Must sleep in the churchyard low?[16]

Especially in early verse, Dickinson voiced the same enthusiasm her contemporaries did for the charm of little things, for the most female of females, the diminutive female; for the most flowery of flowers, the diminutive flower; and for the most diminutive of diminutives, the juvenile, as childishness is the small things' authenticating stamp. For instance, Dickinson's poem #167: 'I'm the little "Heart's Ease"! / I don't care for pouting skies! / If the Butterfly delay / Can I, therefore, stay away?' turns a flower, via tone, into a girl-child, as if drawing a ruffled edge around them.[17] Tonally, these lines are atrophied in the singsong of immature valentine, and the vision they offer is a plea for arrested development as strength: 'Heaven does not change her blue. / Nor will I, the little Heart's Ease- / Ever be induced to do!'

Like the 'frog in its bog' of the lisping 'I'm Nobody / Who Are You?', here chiming and rhyming of identities between the human and the natural is overdone. Dickinson is indulging a stylization of innocence almost camp in its exaggeration, an explosion of conventions from within. Thus, her exploration of conventional cultural equivalencies between heaven and Heaven. In 'I'll tell you how the Sun rose- / A Ribbon at a time-', the poet uses lateral stripes, discrete and ribbon-like bands of colour, as an image for immature perceptions without temporal depth or dimensional integration.[18] Counting them off in an engaging recitation, her lines and rhymes mime the bands of sun, rising like harbingers of divine benevolence: the drenched layerings of the morning are reduced to a fixed set, the breadth and depth of the atmosphere to a sequence of stripes. Sequence literally shepherds, and then corrals, the splendours of the sky within the banded palette of conventional pastoral. Sunrise becomes a reproduction in half tones, tinted faintly by religious sentiment:

> There seemed a purple stile
> That little Yellow boys and girls
> Were climbing all the while-
> Till when they reached the other side-
> A Dominie in Gray-
> Put gently up the evening Bars-
> And led the flock away-

How very low this sky is! How very 'here', with the 'there' of heaven brought so close. Scarcely higher than a girl's hatband, no more various than her little paintbox, the sunrise we 'tell' from earth is a tot's rendering of a sun stuck in a corner.

From very early in her career, then, Dickinson's *oeuvre* shows her mastering, and then transcending, her culture's love of littleness. By the 1860s, she is moving steadily outside its precincts, yet still, one wants to note, working with a set of approved cultural topoi. The deservedly famous pair of poems beginning 'Safe in their Alabaster Chambers' illustrates this. Both versions of this poem return to the same scene Mrs. Sigourney frequents, the cemetery where the 'meek members of the Resurrection' lie 'Untouched by Morning- / and untouched by noon'.[19] And just as in Sigourney's poem, in the first version of the Dickinson poem, the flutterings and buzzings of anthropomorphized bees and birds prompt speculation as to why natural things endure while human virtue must perish:

> Light laughs the breeze
> In her Castle above them
> Babbles the Bee in a stolid ear
> Pipe the Sweet Birds in ignorant cadence
> Ah, what sagacity perished here!

Although the scene is Mrs. Sigourney's, these lines are already disturbed by an ambiguity, a 'slantness' running against the grain of Christian consolatory poetry. Mordant, this last stanza of the poem seems to express wonderment at the giddiness of nature indifferent to the saints below. It may be that 'what sagacity perished here' confers on the interred saints a superiority, a gravity lacking in the natural world. But it is unsettling that their wisdom has perished, and the 'here' may just as well refer to the scene itself, the 'Safe' graveside topos as a little too safe, a dubious destination for true sagacity.

The second version looks past Christian redemption entirely, flying outside and above the Christian cosmos, to find one more alien, modern and strange:

> Grand go the Years,
> In the Crescent above them -
> Worlds scoop their Arcs -
> And Firmaments - row -
> Diadems - drop -
> And Doges - surrender -
> Soundless as Dots,
> On a Disc of Snow.

Instead of a universe organized along the vertical Protestant axis—Heaven Above, Humans below—now the cosmos above the buried saints is made of Time itself, or of SpaceTime, whose broad and turbulent motions unsettle local historical norms and cultural meanings. The 'Diadems' and 'Doges', so imposing, so powerful in one historical time, are rendered grandiose, archaic, dated by the next (a development Dickinson's trademark use of capital letters presents to great effect). There are, it seems, forces even larger than history, in relation to which the Meek Members in their upholstered coffins seem more than mannered. Thus Dickinson situates her Christian Victorian culture within a larger Universe governed by astronomical and physical motions, by forces whose power to nullify is far more disinterested, and thus sublime, than the force of Christian judgement. The last line, 'Soundless as Dots, / On a Disc of Snow' finds Dickinson's imagination ranging far beyond Victorian death as it is conventionalized in satin-lined crypts and white marble monuments. True, the effaced letters of gravestones, the blanketings of snow on a grave are still discernible, but whereas convention uses these images as code for mutability, here it is convention itself losing definition, Victorian death practices, effaced, blanked out. 'Soundless as Dots, / On a Disc of Snow'—almost Cubist in its crossed registers, its abstracted geometries, its search for essential forms—takes the poem far beyond the world of sentimental feeling. And it takes the poem far beyond the world where smallness has a claim on largeness, beyond all the topoi and mechanisms of a world governed by Protestant Christianity.

As Dickinson writes in a slightly later poem that begins 'A Clock stopped' (a poem in which Calvin's Providential God and the Deist's Watchmaker God, in which biological time and historical time, sacred time, and mechanical time all stop turning, all stop ticking), the real answer to our fussy chronometers and our obsession with small motions is 'cool-concernless No'.[20]

Coolness itself may be Dickinson's most radical contribution to the poetry of the Victorian period. An interest in abstraction and analysis sets her apart from nearly every Victorian peer, and most particularly from the woman poets who reserved deepest feelings for: feeling itself. An irony of the ethos of sentimentalism is how little variety, despite much intensity, was permitted the feelings, and how incurious about the emotional element in which they lived authoresses were expected to be: a world that assigned men and woman separate spheres also sharply delimited the scope, even the number, of the emotions. If nineteenth-century American sentimentalism provides for the processing and resolution of identifiable feelings, feelings in Dickinson are part of more irregular economies, processed more eccentrically, and are the subject of inquiries more intellectual than sentimental. Instead of rousing or quickening feelings, and more than laying claim to unfeminine ones, Dickinson breaks them down to their constituent parts. She stands outside emotional norms, as if she were a scholar, a scientist (if also an experimental subject) of affect. She treats feelings not as wholes (and certainly not as virtues or vices) but as complex compounds, like elements on a periodic table.

If Dickinson's culture reserves highest esteem for grief, treating sorrow as a humour producing uniform symptoms or effects, grief in Dickinson is far more unpredictable. The speaker of Dickinson's 'The first Day's Night had come' encounters grief, not as a given of emotional life to be felt, but as a sort of duct or peephole into the organization of the inner life, and, in particular, into Time's irregular and variable operations within the psyche:

> The first Day's Night had come -
> And grateful that a thing
> So terrible - had been endured -
> I told my Soul to sing-[21]

As the Night now belongs to the day, the lightsome spiritual faculty that might have been expected to lift the sufferer's burden is damaged too, and grief is now borne down by helplessness. 'Inner resources' here merely swell the ranks of psychic dependants, or antagonists. Soul is not a firming resource but a dissociating force—not a reliable virtue but another care, an imp personified, but one subject herself to alien forces:

> She said her strings were snapt -
> Her Bow - to atoms blown -
> And so to mend her - gave me work
> Until another Morn -

Endurance had got the speaker to the end of the day, but now it too is on her hands, helpless, as her soul is. In this account of inner life, contending faculties of inner life press the membranes. Grief is where duration lodges, where time becomes a sort of surplus sensate organ, its throbbing localized within the sufferer. And while pain is diffused, time finds yet more punishing avenues of access, new ways to combine and deliver impact.

> And then - a Day as huge
> As Yesterdays in pairs,
> Unrolled it's horror in my face -
> Until it blocked my eyes -

These lines show time fracturing within the psyche, slicing familiar forms of affect into new and sharper-edged slivers of feeling, and they show, too, Christian consolations unequal to the task of mending a soul so aware of its own motions. Intellectual apprehension turns out to lend its own intensifications. Intellect turns the screw of feeling.

Nor are 'positive' feelings in Dickinson any less complex, any less palpable and dynamic. As she represents grief as a complex spatiotemporal zone, so joy too is an unstable element, compounded of forces to which selves are subject. Consider the instability of joy in the poem beginning 'I can wade Grief'. In lines of four beats each, no spondee out of place, the speaker boasts 'I can wade Grief- / Whole pools of it- / I'm used to that-':

> But the least push of Joy
> Breaks up my feet -
> And I tip - drunken -
> Let no Pebble - smile -
> 'Twas the New Liquor -
> That was all! [22]

Grief thigh-high: no problem. The poem's speaker habituates to this. But Joy creeps only to her feet before she begins to lose her balance, and the tippiness of the verse shows it. The enjambment that pivots 'Joy' to 'Breaks' is, on the 'heels' of two such fast anapaests, too fast, and so it sends the speaker grasping for the spondee, grief's dour biorhythm, its stolid forcefulness. An amplitude pressed, brimming and vibrant, inside the lines now substitutes for an external thickness the speaker, empty, stood in. Once she was a density, with motion but without play. Now she is a tipping container—hyphenate, joint-loosened, limpid and flowing. As fascinating as the loosening of the metres is, yet more fascinating is Dickinson's account of the psychic conversions her metrical texture mimes:

> Power is only Pain -
> Stranded - thro' Discipline,
> Till Weights - will Hang -
> Give Balm - to Giants -
> And they'll wilt, like Men -

Had the dynamics of repression and sublimation, the mechanisms of habit, the effects of adrenalin, ever found such expression in a poem before? Certainly not in the poetry of any American woman. In the lines above, Dickinson gives an account of the emotional life that seems to intuit twentieth-century understandings of the psyche's compensatory motions, its susceptibilities in quiet moments and its stress-activated faculties. Had he had the chance to read her, Freud would have recognized well this account of the psyche's economy.

He might well too, had he ever read Walt Whitman, have recognized why, despite entreaties, and at significant cost, Whitman insisted on leaving in his poems the sexual content his contemporaries begged him to excise. Emily Dickinson, when asked had she read him, famously replied that she had not as 'she'd heard he was disgraceful',[23] and such was the common view. Emerson's bedazzled delight on receiving Whitman's hand-printed edition of *Leaves of Grass* did not keep him, in 1859, from trying to persuade the bumptious New Yorker that the tremendous impropriety of some of his lyrics would surely impede his broader acceptance. Across the Atlantic, bohemian disrupters of the bourgeois pieties were themselves taken aback by Whitman's frankness. William Rossetti, Pre-Raphaelite editor of the first English edition of *Leaves of Grass* in 1868, perforce explained in his introduction to that work why he had decided to 'omit entirely every poem which could with any tolerable fairness be deemed offensive to the feelings of morals or propriety in this peculiarly nervous age'. Indeed, this first English edition of *Leaves of Grass* omitted not only the homoerotic and baldly phallic images of 'Children of Adam' and 'Calamus' but 'Song of Myself' (which he refers to as 'Walt Whitman') itself. Of this poem Rossetti writes 'it was clearly impossible that the book, with its audacities of topic and expression included, should retain the same chance of justice, and of circulation through refined minds and hands, which possibly may be accorded it after the rejection of all such peccant poems'.[24]

The real importance and contribution of Whitman's poetry was, however, vitally linked to such peccancy, and so whenever he could, he declined to countenance bowdlerizations, remaining apparently serene that he primarily appealed to readers 'ever so many ages hence'. And if posterity would possess, he may have reckoned, greater resources to appreciate him, perhaps those of his time who dared read him might (however glancingly) tap, touch, encounter parts of themselves the present found unable. *Leaves of Grass* in this sense is a proudly, deliberately closeted work, a work that reaches for parts of a self not present at all moments, not decent at many moments, a work willing to go where few poems had gone before: into the privacies and mysteries, the concealments, and revelatory instants of ordinary selves ready—and unready—fully to be themselves.

'Song of Myself', the flagship poem of *Leaves of Grass*, illustrates the problem Whitman's contemporary sponsors faced in endeavouring to present him, as well as the full scope of what Whitman endeavoured to achieve. The poem describes the sexual nature of human beings in terms so frank as to make reading them awkward in a mixed gathering, even now. Consider these lines, which a reader encounters within twenty minutes of beginning 'Song of Myself':

> Twenty-eight young men bathe by the shore,
> Twenty-eight young men and all so friendly;
> Twenty-eight years of womanly life and all so lonesome.
>
> She owns the fine house by the rise of the bank,
> She hides handsome and richly drest aft the blinds of the window.
>
> Which of the young men does she like the best?
> Ah the homeliest of them is beautiful to her.
>
> Where are you off to, lady? for I see you,
> You splash in the water there, yet stay stock still in your room.
>
> Dancing and laughing along the beach came the twenty-ninth bather,
> The rest did not see her, but she saw them and loved them.
>
> The beards of the young men glisten'd with wet, it ran from their long hair,
> Little streams pass'd over their bodies.
>
> An unseen hand also pass'd over their bodies,
> It descended trembling from their temples and ribs.
>
> The young men float on their backs, their white bellies bulge to the sun,
> they do not ask who seizes fast to them,
> They do not know who puffs and declines with pendant and bending arch,
> They do not think whom they souse with spray [25]

The radical power of the lines is in the way they mix and interimplicate imagination and fantasy, as if double-exposing one picture so as to disclose both its artistic and lubricious elements. In the lines above, the male form is exhibited both nude and naked. The almost classical sculpting of masculine musculature, the linear rendering of sinews and locks, is disturbed by the more prurient 'white bellies bulge', an image that, in turn, is complicated as well by the formal devices arrogated to its evocation. Note what careful deployment of alliteration and assonance, what metrical deliberateness, lifts the 'bulge' of those bellies and the rest of the sexual choreography ('pendant and bending'; 'descended trembling'; 'souse with spray'). The very waters that would cleanse the sexual instincts seem instead to quicken them.

The poem's evocation of the (imagined) few seconds before orgasm—perhaps male, perhaps female, perhaps both—does not in fact happen. Is it better or worse, less or more disgraceful, then, for being a product of imagination, for being the fantasy of a peeping sexual agent, a woman, who is herself part of the fantasy of the poem's speaker—and who herself is featured within the erotic scene blooming within the reader's imagination, via print, via these lines of poetry? The scene's most radical aspects are not in fact confined to the tableau of same sex eroticism, or voyeurism. Far more discomposing is the way sexuality is liberated from male–female, person-to-person, contact. The lines show desire as it may be quickened by the motion of water and sun on flesh, or by eyes over an actual scene, or within the theatre of mind itself, or as eyes move over a page. Reading itself is revealed as a kind of stroking here, not innocent, not separate from other bodily activities.

Far from denying the power of the sexual imagination, Whitman rather functionalizes, naturalizes, and universalizes these. The number twenty-eight is the key. Twenty-eight men makes an orgy, but it also measures a biological clock, the cycles of the moons and tides, and, especially, the menses. The number reminds us that the sexual throb and the continuity of life itself are married, and that sexual desire and the continuity of the world depend on each other as men and women do, as mind and body do, as tides and moon do. What goes on behind the curtains, the private hidden thing, in fact, the most universal thing, as every human scene under the sun, has its origin in sex.

That is, Whitman draws—indeed must draw—this same line of sexual tension through his whole poem, his whole *oeuvre*, for it is sex that gives his poetry line and duree, continuity and connection. Attraction is everything; coition is primary. 'Loafe with me on the grass' invites the poet in the first few lines of 'Song of Myself'. The loafing is the wellspring, the origin. Once on the grass, soul and body may engage in a species of 'oral'—which is simultaneously a kind of musical—sex. Proneness, the horizontal gradient, the stretch at full length, are key here, not mere narrative details, for they orient the poem to that substrate of experience cradling and running through all the discrete activities of men and culture, toward that desire extending itself towards tension, and then relaxation and release. Poetry runs from the same unclogged stream as sex, along this same horizontal axis, the axis of *langue* not *parole* ('Not words, not music or rhyme I want...not custom or lecture, not even...the best / Only the hum I like the hum of your valved voice'), the axis of the poetic line that works by laving and flowing—and by touching now this part to the quick and now that, rarely all parts (or all persons) at once. Thus soul 'reaches' for the body's 'feet' and the bodies 'beard', for all the metonymic parts of the self untended by ordinary poems.

Here, then, is the most foundational shift achieved by Whitman's poetics—the dissemination of the line of tension and attraction throughout all things:

> Urge and urge and urge, always the procreant urge of the world
> Out of the dimness opposite equals advance, always substance and increase, always sex,
> Always a knit of identity...always distinction...always a breed of life

As the horizontal supports the vertical, as sleep and sex support waking and culture, the 'always' of asserted continuity finds expression and the most literal representation in the Whitmanian line.

Whitman's line brings to light a set of poetic problems, in particular certain potentialities of the lyric, not hitherto tapped. Robert Louis Stevenson understood the full scope of the problem to which Whitman committed himself. 'How', Stevenson asked in his essay on Whitman, 'is the poet to convince like nature, not like books' when 'One brief impression obliterates another' and 'it is only on rare provocations that we can rise to take an outlook beyond daily concerns'.[26] How is any entity, any 'self', to find full representation when experience is, in fact, as continuous and unjointed as it is. To find a poetry adequate to the copiousness of each self's many attachments; a book expressive not only of its own but every book's wisdom; a bearing on human experience including more than the cramped perspective of one speaker islanded in one moment of time—these are hard challenges. And then to liberate language in its permeable and penetrating aspect, language in its most many-vectored and freely copulative aspect, as pure line of communication, as medium of ductile capacity—this is harder still.

What Stevenson saw in Whitman was the same quality William James eventually loved in him (a quality he admired in Stevenson himself). Whitman's poetry, for James, simply described the 'stream' in which substantives are secondary, in which the point is flow. Wider than a page-width, liberated from literary history, from syntactic exigencies and from burden of closure, Whitman's line gives graphic and aural presence to the vibrant hum of attraction, that urge that runs through all scenes and particulars. Certain particularly human activities—the opera, the sex act, the journey, war, and certain constants of the natural and built environment (oceans and rivers, birdsong, grass, the 'populous city')—are resonant conductors of the 'always'. The job of the poet is to make these sensible—on the ear, in the mind, and on the body's pulses. The Whitmanian line—supple, elastic—casts long and suspends itself across discrete phenomena, declaring itself in and of many places, of many persons, at once. As Whitman ends 'Song of Myself' his line continues on: It 'stops somewhere, waiting for you'.

Walt Whitman's approach to the congestion and stress of his times was to invent a line so elastic, a voice so transpersonal and a theory of the art so capacious that no phenomenon was too fearsome or immense to find its place. In Whitman, not even the Civil War, for all its horror, could interrupt the rhythmic, urgent hum of the 'always' this poet made it the particular office of his line to transmit. Like sex and music, war always was, Whitman reminds us. In his book, *Drum Taps*, war thus functions to reveal to her citizens their own deepest commitments, their own passions—those recurrent, rhythmic elements of themselves, not contingent but essential. In this modern war, as in ancient ones, America finds its rhythms (the taps of drums), its colours (of flags and uniforms), its unique forms and rituals (parades, marches, funerals, greetings, leavetakings) and its truest feelings (love, sorrow, fear, comradeship). War discovers for the nation those tones and cadences by which it will know, and sing, itself. In Whitman, the Civil War, an event that brings the nation into modernity, delivers America beyond its time into all time.

History plays a vastly different role in the work of Herman Melville. Born in New York in 1819, the same year as Whitman was, and dying within a year of him, in 1891, Melville lived through the exact century Whitman did, but he bore his violent times more heavily, and he let his poetry bear and augur the encroaching roughness of an increasingly modern world, one that had, over the mere five years of the Civil War, lost all its innocence. The rhythms of seasonal renewal and church on Sunday, of national destiny and youth coming to manhood, of reason's sway and America's certain destiny, of consciousness complacent within sense of self or soul, of action directed and governed by religious faith—all these rhythms and norms become, in Melville's poetry, dated, out of sync, as poetry itself is revealed out of sync; its engineering quaint, archaic. Rather like the iron-clad ship of which Melville writes in 'A Utilitarian View of the Monitor's Fight' Melville's verse has a stiff and carapaced feel, a gait often 'more ponderous',[27] as he admits, 'than nimble'. Whitman's verse—though coincident with the Victorian period and owing to English Victorians its dissemination in Europe—remains largely unaltered by historicism, largely unexercised by psychology, and largely shock-proof. Melville makes his verse, like his fiction, accommodate all the intellectual developments of his day. In this it is fair to say that while Whitman was probably the greater poet, Melville was the truer Victorian.

Indeed, as compared to Melville, Whitman—and perhaps every other poet of the day—seems provincial. As a writer of romances, novels, novellas, and magazine sketches, Melville admitted into his fiction all the turbulent currents of his day: nationalism, trans-nationalism, colonialism and war, migration, immigration, slavery and the labour question; the crowding of cities, the pitilessness of wilderness and the indifference of the machine; the depredations of imperial tyrants, of bureaucracies, of the state. He made his fiction absorb and reckon with all of these, and as the verb 'made' implies, he let his writing be the register of force applied. Indeed, force is Melville's primary theme, and he writes a poetry stressed, fractured, by force. Melville is a formalist, if a curious and revolutionary kind of formalist, the kind who lets poetic forms exhibit their own weakening. Their technical apparatus strained to the utmost, Melville's poems are all overloaded, swamped; his syntaxes buckle, and metre that is liquid one moment is, in the next, crammed. Materials—whether the poetic materials of diction and rhythm or the discordant materials of nineteenth-century life—clash and contend, and there is nothing to protect soft flesh from hard metal, music from noise, past romance from present pain.

All calmnesses of surface—whether of picturesque vista or of picture plane, of social form or facial politesse—will crack. And so poetry will too, subject to modern stress. Nature and its vaunted beauties might still soothe those poets with means and leisure to admire their Cambridge gardens. But Melville anticipates Hardy in a far darker vision of nature's succours. Nature is not only nodding daffodils—it is the Maldive shark with his 'port of serrated teeth'[28] and its feast of 'horrible meat'. Nature is the swift little pilot fish guiding the shark to his prey and then dining off the leavings. If, moreover, war and nature had customarily been conjoined, in such poems from *Battle-Pieces and Aspects of the War* as 'The March into Virginia', 'Reverie at Ball's Bluff', and 'Shiloh', Melville lets traditional poetic metres and stanzas represent normative poetic expectations that align natural growth and human heroism. Had it seemed only natural, only right, to see 'Young soldiers marching lustily' in 'the breezy summer time'?[29] Had nature lent her powers to human will, as pentameter verse lent its form to human hope—'They moved like Juny morning on the wave'—as effects would follow causes? 'All they feel is this: tis glory' and 'So they gayly go to fight'.[30] All wrong. Modern war renders such integrations (of men and weather, and of metre and stanza) false, gives the lie to sequences, gives the lie to the fit between what we feel and what is. Place itself is displaced as war dissolves topoi, dissociates objects, and alienates names from erstwhile significances. Thus in 'Shiloh', the

log-built church organizing a woodland settlement turns out to mean something different than it once did: now 'Shiloh' names where rain fell on the groaning dead; where a
bloody bivouac interrupted the natural cycle. Site, place, natural context provide none of
the stability Romantics found. 'What like a bullet undeceives',[31] Melville writes in 'Shiloh',
letting the torque in the syntax rebuke expectations, rebuke romance.

    Nor, even away from the battlefield or frontier, does Melville permit quiescence.
Republican democracy is a Darwinian business, the individual pitted always against
those hungrier than he. In his fictions of the mid-1850s, an exhausted Melville, writing from his Pittsfield, Massachusetts piazza, had represented country life as dirty and
gruelling. Rural life meant ague and crop rot and pitching the barn; it meant women
dying in childrbirth; men drowning conscience with drink; the restive young off to the
cities where the factories were, where young country girls gave their youth to the mills
or turned to prostitution, where young rubes struggled for livelihoods next to despised
blacks desperate for work, both pitted against despised immigrants. Populations once
buffered within distinct regional cultures lived cheek by jowl in volatile mixes. Thus
Melville's 'The Housetop: A Night Piece' of 1863, treats the city as a jungle where the
heat rises 'making apt for ravage' and where 'The Town is taken by its rats'. It is every one
for himself, even in New York, where competition banishes 'civil charms' to reveal 'man
rebound[ing] whole aeons back in nature'.[32] Progress—whether political or industrial,
commercial or economic—is regress in Melville. As a young man, he had witnessed at
sea the realities of industrial production. Whale ships were not romantic fishing boats
but floating, fiery, filthy factories, the ocean on which they floated a teeming commercial
freeway and arena for the contest of nations. At sea as on land, the valour, the skill, the
'pomp' of a more classic age were all now casualties of history. In 'A Utilitarian View', the
'strife of fleets heroic' gives way to mechanized battle: 'No passion. All went on by crank,
/ Pivot and screw, / And calculations of caloric'.[33] Once it had been—and here Melville is
close to Whitman—that war was a human art form, its paint representative, expressive.
No longer. Now 'war-paint shows the streaks of weather / War yet shall be, but warriors /
Are now but operatives'.

    In Melville's poems, disillusionment and reversal are primary and functional
forces: correction takes the place of inspiration. Thus in 'The Apparition', a poem based
on an incident of an explosion set off by Northerners who'd tunnelled under Confederate
lines, the new world of Force not only assaults bodies, but also consciousness. 'But ere
the eye could take it in, Or mind could comprehension win, / It sunk! And at our feet'.[34]
The 'It' in 'It sunk' is the ground itself, but also philosophical grounding, foundation,
these lost all in an instant shorter than perception can measure. It is not, that is, the
explosion per se that does the most damage. Worse is the way it seems to damage the
time-sense, ushering in new arrhythmias of time, new prospects of impermanence; a
nervousness now haunts even the past 'where the field / Long slept in pastoral green'. The
memorable last stanza of the poem make clear how an event in history—this one explosion or, as Melville implies, the long detonating chain of them that is the Civil War—
ramifies down the decades. For even as the field of war has become a field of knowledge,
cleared for the assertion of a new logic ('So, then, Solidity's a crust / The core of fire

below'), it is also broken off, syllogisms now become self-immolating, no shelf or vantage point from which to survey destruction.

The hard truths Melville devotes *Battle-Pieces* to limning have their counterpart in Hardy, and in the work of World War I poets who bring the Victorian age to an end. Dissociation of sensibility was Eliot's word for what the First World War ushered in, but this dissociation was already the keynote of the post Civil War world in which he came of age in St. Louis, the poetry of the period precociously dissociated, still arrested in the post-traumatic stress Melville renders in the 1860s. There are only two major poets to emerge before 1901—Stephen Crane, who publishes *Black Riders* in 1895 and Arlington Robinson who publishes *The Children of the Night* in the 1897. Both are connoisseurs of dissociation. In the astonishing 1895 book, *Black Riders*, published entirely in small caps, Crane presents little cells, little bunkers of poems, their typography and their narratives importunate, the pursuit of truth overrun by the forms, conventions of truth-seeking:

> I SAW A MAN PURSUING THE HORIZON;
> ROUND AND ROUND THEY SPED.
> I WAS DISTURBED AT THIS.
> I ACCOSTED THE MAN
> "IT IS FUTILE," I SAID,
> "YOU CAN NEVER—
>
> "YOU LIE," HE CRIED,
> AND RAN ON.[35]

In such poems the topos of quest, the conventions of philosophical dialogue, the prestige of human effort are all rendered ironic. Just so, in the poems of Edwin Arlington Robinson, the pursuit of 'Truth' and meaning are as if locked in specious caps. Robinson lets poetry's own rhythms, its own carefully controlled motions, represent a people going through the motions, living for form's sake. As Melville allowed poetry to discredit itself, Robinson writes masterpieces of forced music, of rationalization sheltering within convention and persons living in suspended animation. Whether it is his 'Eben Flood', who lives in a sodden state of romantic bad faith, or the trapped wife of 'Eros Turranos', whose marital torture goes on and on in cascading stanzas (enjambments pouring decade into decade over the line breaks), or 'Richard Cory' who puts himself through 'glittering' motions and dies formally impeccable, a suicide, Robinson's subjects exhaust the resources of grace and are punished by lyric susceptibilities.

The Civil War cuts the middle out of the America's Victorian era. What William Buckler called the 'high-Parnassian torpor of the 1860s'[36] had, in America, no counterpart: in the United States, the world in pieces had to be reconstructed, and the work was not pretty. In America there is an early, and a late, but no mid-Victorian period, though in this absent centre, there are the three great poets—Dickinson, Whitman, and Melville—whose importance would not begin to be discovered until well after Victoria's reign was over. Because of them, the years 1837–1901 were, nonetheless as rich and important a period of poetry productivity as America had yet seen, providing the United States with that literary history that, prior to Victoria's reign, had not yet commenced.

NOTES

1. Saul K. Padover, *The Karl Marx Library. Vol 1.* (New York: McGraw Hill, 1971), 83.
2. Ralph Waldo Emerson, *Essays First and Second Series* (New York: Library of America, 1990), 219.
3. Alexis de Toqueville, *Democracy in America*, trans. Alex Goldhammer (New York: Library of America, 2004), 556.
4. F. O. Matthiessen, *American Renaissance: Art and Expression in the Age of Emerson and Whitman* (Oxford: Oxford University Press, 1968), 526.
5. Geoffrey Tillotson, *A View of Victorian Literature* (Oxford: Oxford University Press, 1978), 319.
6. Henry Wadsworth Longfellow, *The Poetical Works of Longfellow*, no ed. given (Boston: Houghton Mifflin, 1975), xxvii.
7. Longfellow, 'The Landlord's Tale: Paul Revere's Ride', in *Poetical Works*, 207.
8. Philip Davis, *Why Victorian Literature Still Matters* (West Sussex: Wiley Blackwell, 2008), 39.
9. Longfellow, 'The Bridge', in *Poetical Works*, 63.
10. Davis, *Victorian Literature*, 29.
11. Longfellow, 'The Fire of Driftwood', in *Poetical Works*, 107.
12. Longfellow, 'The Cross of Snow', *Poetical Works*, 323.
13. Richard B. Sewall, *The Life of Emily Dickinson* (New York: Farrar, Straus & Giroux, 1974), 556.
14. Emily Dickinson, *The Poems of Emily Dickinson: Reading Edition*, ed. Ralph Franklin (Cambridge and London: The Belknap Press of Harvard University Press, 1998), 390.
15. Dickinson, 'On a Columnar Self', in *Poems*, 330.
16. Lydia Sigourney, *The Lady's Pearl: A Monthly Magazine Volume 2* (1842), 273.
17. Dickinson, 'I'm the little "Heart's Ease"', in *Poems*, 81.
18. Dickinson, 'I'll tell you how the Sun rose', in *Poems*, 204.
19. Dickinson, 'Safe in their Alabaster Chambers', in *Poems*, 64.
20. Dickinson, 'A Clock Stopped', in *Poems*, 116.
21. Dickinson 'The first Day's Night had come', in *Poems*, 195.
22. Dickinson, 'I Can Wade Grief', in *Poems*, 139.
23. Dickinson, *Emily Dickinson: Selected Letters*, ed. Thomas H. Johnson (Cambridge, Mass: The Belknap Press of Harvard University Press, 1986), 173.
24. William Rossetti in *Poems by Walt Whitman*, ed. William Rossetti (Chatto and Windus: Piccadilly, 1886), 22.
25. Walt Whitman, 'Song of Myself', in *American Poetry: The Nineteenth Century. Vol. 1*, ed. John Hollander (New York: Library of America, 1993), 720.
26. Robert Louis Stevenson and Elbert Hubbard, *The Essay on Walt Whitman; with A Little Journey to the Home of Whitman* (London: Roycroft, 1900), 36.
27. Herman Melville, 'A Utilitarian View of the Monitor's Fight', in *Battle-Pieces and Aspects of the War* (Amherst: Prometheus Books, 2001), 89.
28. Melville, 'The Maldive Shark', in *American Poetry: The Nineteenth Century. Vol. 2*, ed. John Hollander (New York: Library of America, 1993), 30.
29. Melville, 'Ball's Bluff: A Reverie', in *Battle-Pieces*, 28.
30. Melville, 'The March into Virginia', in *Battle-Pieces*, 22.
31. Melville, 'Shiloh', in *Battle-Pieces*, 63

32. Melville, 'The Housetop: A Night Piece', in *Battle-Pieces*, 86.
33. Melville, 'A Utilitarian View', in *Battle-Pieces*, 89.
34. Melville, 'The Apparition', in *Battle-Pieces*, 155.
35. Stephen Crane, *American Poetry: The Nineteenth Century. Vol. 2*, ed. John Hollander (New York: Library of America, 1993), 601.
36. William E. Buckler, *The Victorian Imagination: Essays in Aesthetic Exploration* (New York: New York University Press, 1980), 256.

SELECT BIBLIOGRAPHY

Adams, James Eli, *A History of Victorian Literature* (New York: Wiley Blackwell, 2012).

Buckler, William E., *The Victorian Imagination: Essays in Aesthetic Exploration* (New York: New York University Press, 1980).

Davis, Philip, *Why Victorian Literature Still Matters* (West Sussex: Wiley Blackwell, 2008).

Dickinson, Emily, *The Poems of Emily Dickinson: Reading Edition*, ed. Ralph Franklin (Cambridge, Mass: The Belknap Press of Harvard University Press, 1998).

Emerson, Ralph Waldo, *Essays First and Second Series* (New York, Library of America, 1990).

Gibbon, Charles, *The Casquet of Literature, Being a Selection in Poetry and Prose from the Works of the Most Admired Authors, Volume. 6* (London: Blackie and Son, Old Bailey EC).

Graham's American Monthly Magazine of Literature and Art, 33 (1848).

Hollander, John, *American Poetry: The Nineteenth Century, Volume 2: Melville to Stickney, American Indian Poetry, Folk Songs and Spirituals* (New York: Library of America, 1993).

Longfellow, Henry Wadsworth, *The Poetical Works of Longfellow* (Boston: Houghton Mifflin, 1975).

Marx, K. *On Revolution*, The Karl Marx Library, Volume 1, ed. and trans., S. Padover (New York: McGraw Hill, 1971).

Melville, Herman, *Battle-Pieces and Aspects of the War* (New York: Prometheus Books, 2001).

Stevenson, Robert Louis and Hubbard, Elbert, *The Essay on Walt Whitman; with A Little Journey to the Home of Whitman* (London: Roycroft, 1900).

Toqueville, Alexis de, *Democracy in America*, trans. Alex Goldhammer (New York: Library of America, 2004).

Tillotson, Geoffrey, *A View of Victorian Literature* (Oxford: Oxford University Press, 1978).

Whitman, Walt, *Poems by Walt Whitman*, ed. William Rossetti (Chatto and Windus: Piccadilly, 1886).

CHAPTER 15

THE POETRY OF MODERN LIFE: ON THE PAVEMENT

PETER ROBINSON

INSPIRATION struck W. B. Yeats in 1888 when, walking down Fleet Street, London, and hearing the sound of water from a fountain in a shop window, 'The Lake Isle of Innisfree' began to form: 'While I stand on the roadway, or on the pavements grey, / I hear it in the deep heart's core'.[1] The contrast of 'lake water lapping' and 'sounds by the shore' with the unmentioned street noises upon which his lyric closes sets the poet's heart at odds with road and pavement. It was not a new idea. In 1797 Coleridge evoked his 'gentle-hearted Charles' Lamb who had 'hungered after Nature, many a year, / In the great City pent'[2] and, the following February, he echoed and described himself as 'reared in the great city, pent 'mid cloisters dim'.[3] Wordsworth made contrast of sounds explicit when he pictured a child sitting 'While oaths, indecent speech, and ribaldry / Were rife about him as are songs of birds / In springtime after showers'.[4] Though unfair to say 'Wordsworth's eyes avert their ken / From half of human fate' here, his lines are figured on a contrast encouraging such an averting towards a more 'tranquil world'.[5] This essay is premised on objections to city life in the Romantic poets, and how, though presented as an index of urbanized alienation, the countryside and pastoral served to blank from representation material and themes that exercised, more frequently, the novelists. Seen in this light, one strand in Victorian poetry represents an attempt, mostly by indirect means, to regain access to the experience of modern life as it shaped the lives of many pent in expanding cities. One theme in this strand involves poetry written about the 'dissolute men / And shameless women'[6] that Wordsworth sees around the child 'Upon a Board' in the 'Residence in London' book of *The Prelude*—that's to say, poetry about prostitution and those plying their trade 'on the pavements grey'.

Among reasons making prostitution symbolic of modern life is its being an acute form of the wage slavery ubiquitous in orders below the polite—exacerbated by the

categorization of prostitutes as among those 'who will not work'.[7] Thomas Hardy dramatizes the idea in 'The Ruined Maid' from *Poems of Past and Present* (1902), but dated to
Westbourne Park Villas in 1866:

> Your hands were like paws then, your face blue and bleak
> But now I'm bewitched by your delicate cheek,
> And your little gloves fit as on any la-dy!—
> 'We never do work when we're ruined,' said she.[8]

Hardy doesn't endorse this view of prostitution, vocalizing a pigeonhole enshrined in
Mayhew's study of London populations through his dialogic lyric, embodying that attitude in the voice of its victim. The shared urban experience of wage slaves and prostitutes is that they sell the time of their lives to continue its existence, and are engaged in
forms of timed piecework. While there was rural prostitution, the image of the prostitute reaching poetry is in its urban manifestations. The poets concentrated on its lower
levels, because it intersected with the pavement, with artifice, the man-made, contrasted
with the natural in 'The Ruined Maid', and thus focused down on the acute humiliations
of the economically driven modern. Making a living by writing is timed piecework too,
the analogy with the oldest profession not lost on Joseph Conrad in a letter to J. B. Pinker
of 8 January 1902: 'I am no sort of airy R. L. Stevenson who considered his art a prostitute and the artists as no better than one. I dare say he was punctual—but I don't envy
him'.[9] Stevenson, unenviably dead eight years before, had asked in 'The Vagabond' for no
more than 'heaven above, / And the road below me'.[10]

'Any where, any where / Out of the world'[11]

Thomas Hood's 'The Bridge of Sighs' was first published in May 1844, its title one of
the poet's puns. Having nothing to do with Venice, it concerns the suicide of a woman
from one of London's bridges. In their notes, Susan J. Wolfson and Peter J. Manning
draw attention to the poem's origin in the case of a seamstress who attempts to drown
herself and her infant son in the Regent's Canal in March 1844, associating it thus with
'The Song of the Shirt'. Hood had, though, referred to a suicide from Waterloo Bridge
in the postscript to a 27 January 1844 letter to Charles MacKay in which he asks 'Did
you kill Mrs. Donally?' A note informs us: 'Mrs E. Donally, "an inveterate drunkard",
committed suicide by jumping off Waterloo Bridge on 23 January 1844 (*The Times* 27
January: 7). This event took place after her husband had threatened that because of her
ways he would kill himself'.[12] The poem's location, its themes, and suicide, not specifically associated with seamstresses, had recently passed through the poet's mind. By 10
April 1844, he could write to Fredrick Oldfield Ward that he had 'all but done a poem
on "the Bridge of Sighs"—ie Waterloo, and its Suicides'.[13] Wolfson and Manning list the

differences between the Regent's Canal case and the poem: 'Hood romantically converts several details: the suicide is solitary (no infanticide) and it succeeds; its victim is not middle-aged but young; its locale is the Thames's Waterloo Bridge (in one of London's poorer districts, a favourite of suicides, rather than a canal).'[14] However, they also observe that 'The sin to which Hood refers is the woman's suicide, a mortal sin'.[15] This puts readers off the thought that the poem may touch on prostitution, and in doing so echoes its absent presence in nineteenth-century culture. Details point to the situation of the young woman and the reasons for her act. Editing out the child, her middle age, and her profession as a seamstress, points readers, still needing an explanation for her act, to the situation of the young woman and implied reasons for jumping.[16] They will jump to their own conclusion, especially if allowed, despite Wolfson and Manning's single 'sin', to ponder what John Clubbe calls her 'unidentified "stains" or "slips"':[17]

> Touch her not scornfully;
> Think of her mournfully,
> Gently and humanly;
> Not of the stains of her,
> All that remains of her
> Now is pure womanly.

Though 'the stains of her' include being fished out of the filthy Thames, like a corpse in *Our Mutual Friend*, it occasions that contrast with the 'pure womanly', a phrase equivocating between 'just like a woman' and 'a spotless woman'—as the subtitle to Hardy's 1891 novel about a fallen country girl, *A Pure Woman*, would underline. Though Hood's girl has 'stains' in the plural, she is now 'pure', and the sexual frisson of her dead remains being 'pure' starts further thoughts about purity, deathliness, and sexual attraction in 'The Bridge of Sighs'. Yet her plural 'stains' return when she is first 'past all dishonour', then taken back to the Fall:

> Still for all slips of hers,
> One of Eve's family—
> Wipe those poor lips of hers
> Oozing so clammily.

This slip of a girl's 'slips' are associated with Eve, then with 'lips', a suggestive internal rhyme; while Hood, for his aesthetic, moral, and economic reasons, doesn't say she's a prostitute.

Wolfson and Manning's notes are again evasive, if not misleading, when they cite from the postscript of a 15 April 1844 letter of Hood's: 'I have done a poem for the Mag some say beats "The Shirt"', he wrote to J. T. J. Hewlett, adding, 'If the moneyed man does take to it we will have a capital campaign'.[18] Their interruption effaces a comically contrary authorial view: 'I have done a poem for the Mag some say beats "The Shirt", but I don't think it. If the moneyed man does take to it we will have a capital campaign.'[19] What's more, the letter contains a punning contextualization of that 'capital campaign' when, discussing the finances of his eponymous magazine, he writes: 'If Flight is insolvent now, he must have been so when he began the things.—On what grounds was he to be the proprietor, but as Capitalist paying all?'[20] How apt to be pursuing a debt-laden sponsor with the Dickensian name of Flight!

'The Bridge of Sighs' has a necrophilia-inflected image of a woman that men with money could 'take to', the poem a bit of piecework or self-selling, shifting attention from seamstress to hinted-at prostitute, which, if it works, will produce a capital amount of capital. To this end, Hood, freelance rhyming to make ends meet, gives his gentlemen investors an object for their sympathy, imagination, and cash. The clearest reason offered for her suicide is that 'Near a whole city full, / Home she had none' and, though one of 'Eve's family', lacks family and more:

> Had she a brother?
> Or was there a dearer one
> Still, and a nearer one
> Yet, than all other?

Where Wolfson and Manning subsume all her 'evil behaviour' into the one act of self-murder, Hood concludes with her leaving 'Her sins to her Saviour!' True, she might have been generally sinful, as who shall cast the first stone, and her only represented and specified sin is her mode of death; but her sexualized description between corruption and purity, and the allusion to Eve's family, allows the possibility that Hood had other specific sins to insinuate. The editors' endnote silently honours the discretion of Hood's poem, which at no point states that she has either been driven towards prostitution by her lacks of home and family, or has avoided it by committing suicide, or that she is doing so out of shame at having succumbed and, despite the stains, its not having relieved her from destitution. This may be reading in; but it is reading in invited by his incidental plurals. That Hood was using this poetic evocation of a pathetic situation to support and house a family is not irrelevant to its penumbra of implications either.

What might initially disturb, or even put off, a reader of 'The Bridge of Sighs' is the combination of this pathetically melancholy and sombre tale with the rhymes that jingle like change in a pocket. Edgar Allan Poe cites the whole of this 'universally appreciated' poem in 'The Poetic Principle' and remarks that the 'vigor of this poem is no less remarkable than its pathos. The versification, although carrying the fanciful to the very verge of the fantastic, is nevertheless admirably adapted to the wild insanity which is the thesis of the poem'.[21] The woman's state of mind is raised by the epigraph 'Drown'd! drown'd'—Gertrude's words in *Hamlet* (IV. vii. 184). Hood alludes not only to Ophelia and her mode of death, but also to her contextually provoked madness expressed in sexual *double entendres*. 'The Bridge of Sighs' glances by the mental state Poe takes as 'the thesis of the poem':

> Perishing gloomily,
> Spurr'd by contumely,
> Cold inhumanity,
> Burning insanity,

> Into her rest.—
> Cross her hands humbly,
> As if praying dumbly,
> Over her breast!

Conceiving of the poem as if it were 'The Raven', constructed upon a thesis,[22] Poe latches on to the mental disturbance to explain her suicide and colour its circumstances. Rhyming with 'inhumanity', and contrasted with the command to place her hands as if 'praying dumbly', the introduction of 'insanity' mitigates her deed and asks for the Christian burial of unhinged suicides. Unsound mind pleas mute social protest, and, like 'The Song of the Shirt', this poem's energy is focused on the woman's fate as a protest at the more general failure of culture and care.

Baudelaire's translation of the poem, a work he perhaps encountered through his reading of Poe, faithfully reports these details concerning her relation to the family of Eve and her plural sins. In the stanza with 'la famille d'Ève' he renders 'slips' as 'erreurs':

> Cependant à cause de toutes ses erreurs,
> Car elle était de la famille d'Ève,
> Essuie ses pauvres lèvres
> Suintant si visqueusement.[23]

In Baudelaire's version, the words for 'Eve' and 'lips' (lèvres) form a near rhyme. His editor notes, apropos of 'Le pont des soupirs', 'la resonance que ces vers ont dû avoir dans la pensée de Baudelaire, sensible comme un théologien à l'impureté de la Femme' [the resonance that these lines must have had on Baudelaire's thought, sensitive as a theologian to the impurity of Woman].[24] Underlining a sexualized interpretation of the poem, Baudelaire's editor doesn't clarify whether Hood's lines chastened this syphilitic flâneur's theological view of woman's impurity (he dictated the translation at Brussels in 1865) or confirm it.

Why did Baudelaire translate this poem of Hood's? In 'Le Peintre de la vie moderne' he writes of the artist's duty to the shifting surfaces of '*modernité*':

> Cet element transitoire, fugitif, dont les metamorphoses sont si fréquentes, vous n'avez pas le droit de le mépriser ou de vous en passer. En le supprimant, vous tombez forcément dans le vide d'une beauté abstraite et indéfinissable, comme celle de l'unique femme avant le premier péché [This transitory, fugitive element, whose metamorphoses are so frequent, you do not have the right to discount or let pass you by. In suppressing it, you inevitably fall into the void of an abstract and indefinable beauty, like that of the one woman before the original sin].[25]

With his vision of present-day artists suppressing the transitory and the fugitive who then fall into the void of an abstract beauty like that of Eve before the first sin, Baudelaire might have been echoing Hood's poem—for the young woman in 'The Bridge of Sighs', denied house-room in contemporary life, described by Hood as 'one of Eve's family', also falls 'forcément dans le vide' of a watery grave in the Thames at Waterloo. Exemplifying the suppression of the modern, Baudelaire imagines the case of a painter, significantly unlike the Manet of the 'Olympia': 'Si un peintre patient et minutieux, mais d'une imagination médiocre, ayant à peindre une courtesane du temps présent, *s'inspire* (c'est le mot consacré) d'une courtesane de Titien ou de Raphaël, il est infiniment probable qu'il fera une œuvre fausse, ambiguë et obscure' [If a patient and precise painter, but of mediocre imagination, having to paint a courtesan of the present day, *is inspired* (it's the time-honoured word) by a courtesan of Titian or of Raphael, it's infinitely probable that he will make a false, ambiguous and obscure work].[26] The shock of Manet's 'Olympia' resided in its being both a portrait of a real girl (his model Victorine Meurent) in a real place, and its alluding to works by Titian and Raphael. Unlike Manet, the painter whom Baudelaire imagines aping the Italian masters by suppressing the present circumstances falls, like Hood's young woman, into 'le vide'.

Yet a further insight implicit in Baudelaire's complex perception of real art coming from the eternalizing of the transitory (though not by way of its suppression as a short cut to an already historically consecrated eternal) is that there exists a perpetually present void at the heart of the transitory, the present, one to which Hood's poem also points: 'any where, any where / Out of the world!'[27] Thus Baudelaire too underlines the paradoxical condition of the prostitute in the art of modern life, its absent-presence. Hood's poem catches the larger ramification of this paradox in that, being on a suicide, it too is about absent-presence, the abyss at the heart of the modern, the real: 'Manet, rather than Monet, might have gone to La Grenouillère in knowing search of "the insignificant": those who "failed to signify"—the prostitutes, the bar maids—because they have no established place in the representational codes, the language, of the bourgeois social world'.[28] The deaths of prostitutes in literature are figurations of this failure to signify, protesting against it by succumbing to its consequence, just as the homelessness of the woman is not only her having to sleep rough, but her being un-housed in the social order.

'AH, POOR JENNY'S CASE'[29]

Robert Buchanan's pseudonymous article, 'The Fleshly School of Poetry: Mr. D. G. Rossetti', published in the *Contemporary Review* (Oct 1871), has proved his most enduring contribution to literature. Among its qualities, the piece opens by sketching what would become the scenario for *Rosencrantz and Guildenstern are Dead*.[30] Publishing it under the name 'Thomas Maitland' allowed the critic to make two references to his own poetic reputation: first, when casting the Victorian poets for roles in *Hamlet* (Tennyson and Browning playing the male lead on alternate nights), he modestly gives 'Mr. Buchanan that of Cornelius',[31] and then, more damagingly, when accusing Rossetti of plagiarizing his own work for

> 'Jenny', in some respects the finest poem in the volume, and in all respects the poem best indicative of the true quality of the writer's humanity. It is a production which

bears signs of having been suggested by Mr. Buchanan's quasi-lyrical poems, which it copies in the style of title, and particularly by 'Artist and Model'; but certainly Mr. Rossetti cannot be accused, as the Scottish writer has been accused, of maudlin sentiment and affected tenderness.[32]

'Artist and Model: A Love Poem' had appeared in *London Poems* (1866), a volume which includes both 'Liz' and 'Nell', evidence of a titular indebtedness for Buchanan.[33] Being unable to include out his own poetry and reputation, his having been accused of 'maudlin sentiment and affected tenderness', and worse, writing himself in under cover of a pseudonym, proved, once reconfirmed, what Rossetti in his reply called a 'strategic *fiasco*'.[34] As for Buchanan's sentiment and tenderness, 'The Little Milliner; or, Love in an Attic' versifies on her 'plain stuff-gown and collar white as snow, / And sweet red petticoat that peeps below', noting that

> She pats the pavement with her fairy feet,
> With fearless eyes she charms the crowded street;
> And in her pocket lie, in lieu of gold,
> A lucky sixpence and a thimble old.[35]

The accusation of 'plagiarism from that very poetic self of his which the tutelary prose does but enshroud for the moment' was rebutted by the author of 'Jenny', reporting that his poem had been written in 1857,[36] thirteen years before first publication, and explicitly by noting that this 'question can, fortunately, be settled with ease by those who have read my critic's poems; and thus I need the less regret that, not happening myself to be in that position, I must be content to rank myself with those who cannot pretend to an opinion on the subject'.[37] They couldn't have influenced Rossetti, he asserts, because he couldn't have read Buchanan's poems when he first wrote 'Jenny' (though revising it after 1866), and hadn't read them since.

Yet Buchanan was evidently in two minds about Rossetti's poem, seeing his own work in it, after all. He remarks that the 'first two lines' ('Lazy laughing languid Jenny, / Fond of a kiss and fond of a guinea')[38] 'are perfect'; yet, while thinking well of that couplet rhyme with its association of personal intimacy and payment, he can't say the same for the 'wretched pun' in lines wondering what occupies her head asleep on the speaker's lap: 'Whose person or whose purse may be / The lodestar of your reverie?' A third couplet, exclamation added, recalling Buchanan's milliner's petticoat ('Have seen your lifted silken skirt / Advertise dainties through the dirt!'), and said to illustrate 'the common stock of the walking gentlemen of the fleshly school', on the pavement themselves, most spurred Rossetti to defence of 'Jenny': 'Neither some thirteen years ago, when I wrote this poem, nor last year when I published it, did I fail to foresee impending charges of recklessness and aggressiveness, or to perceive that even some among those who could really read the poem and acquit me on those grounds, might still hold that the thought in it had better have dispensed with the situation which serves it for framework'.[39] But thought occasioned by situation is its deep heart's core:

> Jenny, you know the city now.
> A child can tell the tale there, how
> Some things which are not yet enroll'd
> In market-lists are bought and sold
> Even till the early Sunday light,
> When Saturday night is market-night
> Everywhere, be it dry or wet,
> And market-night in the Haymarket.
> Our learned London children know,
> Poor Jenny, all your pride and woe;
> Have seen your lifted silken skirt
> Advertise dainties through the dirt;
> Have seen your coach-wheels splash rebuke
> On virtue; and have learned your look
> When, wealth and health slipped past, you stare
> Along the street alone, and there,
> Round the long park, across the bridge,
> The cold lamps at the pavement's edge
> Wind on together and apart,
> A fiery serpent for your heart.[40]

In the eyes of those 'learned London children' the figure of 'Jenny' becomes generically the prostitute, and the speaker foresees what will become of her when she's lost her 'wealth and health'. Rossetti's rhyme of 'bridge' and 'pavement edge' might even be a tacit homage to 'The Bridge of Sighs'. However, after imagining the thought of the poem without its 'situation', Rossetti defends his decision to include it by reminding readers that 'Jenny' is a dramatic monologue, spoken by 'a young and thoughtful man of the world' whose 'many half-cynical revulsions of feeling and reverie, and a recurrent presence of the impressions of beauty (however artificial) which first brought him within such a circle of influence, would be inevitable features of the dramatic relation portrayed'.[41] Buchanan noted the 'soliloquy is long', admitting a 'suspicion that we are listening to an emasculated Mr. Browning', and Rossetti is neither speaker, that 'man of the world', nor subject, the sleeping Jenny herself.[42]

However, Buchanan discounts this formal detachment of the poet from guilt by association, pressing thus his 'fleshly' case: 'but "Jenny"', he writes, 'though distinguished by less special viciousness of thought and style' than 'The Blessed Damozel', 'Song of the Bower', and the love-sonnets, 'fairly made us lose patience' for we 'detect its fleshliness at a glance; we perceive that the scene was fascinating less through its human tenderness than because it, like all the others, possessed an inherent quality of animalism'. Buchanan then extends this quality to 'the kind of women whom it seems the unhappy lot of these gentlemen to encounter':

Females who bite, scratch, scream, bubble, munch, sweat, writhe, twist, wriggle, foam, and in a general way slaver over their lovers, must surely possess some extraordinary qualities to counteract their otherwise most offensive mode of conducting themselves. It appears, however, on examination, that their poet-lovers conduct themselves in a similar manner. They, too, bite, scratch, scream, bubble, munch, sweat, writhe, twist, wriggle, foam, and slaver, in a style frightful to hear of.⁴³

His writing, vividly exercised in its moralizing distortion, is a backhanded tribute to the power of 'Jenny' and acts as an overheated thermometer for the reality that Rossetti's poem acknowledges. Buchanan, who calls his *London Poems* 'quasi-lyrical', finds the same genre-ambiguity in Rossetti, discounting any supposed speaker of the soliloquy in favour of an identification of lubricious poet with lubricious situation.⁴⁴ Yet he adds gender ambiguity to that of genre, in his objection to the 'fleshly gentlemen', accusing them of believing 'that the poet, properly to develop his poetic faculty, must be an intellectual hermaphrodite'. Yet even here, the critic is unclear which tail he wants to pin on which donkey, in a pointed pastiche of Walter Pater's prose on the Mona Lisa, first published in the *Fortnightly Review* (1869):

> Whether he is writing of the holy Damozel, or of the Virgin herself, or of Lilith, or Helen, or of Dante, or of Jenny the street-walker, he is fleshly all over, from the roots of his hair to the tip of his toes; never a true lover merging his identity into that of the beloved one; never spiritual, never tender; always self-conscious and aesthetic.⁴⁵

The poet is synonymous with subjects and personas, a synonymy tacitly admired, for the true lover is said to be one 'merging his identity into that of the beloved'; but Rossetti doesn't do it in the approved way, because 'always self-conscious and aesthetic'. He is damned for identifying with, and being identifiable with, his subject-matter, and damned for being detached from it: '"Vengeance of Jenny's case", indeed!—when such a poet as this comes fawning over her, with tender compassion in one eye and aesthetic enjoyment in the other!'⁴⁶ Buchanan cites Rossetti's Shakespearean epigraph (another thing this poem has in common with Hood's 'The Bridge of Sighs'), namely Mrs. Quickly's words from *The Merry Wives of Windsor* (IV. ii. 57–8): 'Vengeance of Jenny's case! Fie on her! Never name her, child!'⁴⁷ Rossetti and Buchanan take positions around the epigraph, as to whether 'Jenny' should be mentioned or not. For where Mistress Quickly hears a 'whore' where there isn't one, in the 'Genitive—*horum, harum, horum*' (IV. ii. 56), the thrust of Buchanan's case is that we shouldn't hear of one where there is.

In the Fitzwilliam manuscript, Rossetti has adjusted the citation to delete the last five words of the full phrase: 'Never name her, child, if she be a whore!' He moves the exclamation mark forward without adding an ellipsis, as if symptomatically not mentioning the crucial fact about her. Yet his poem tells us clearly that she *is* a whore and affirms that she should be mentioned. Buchanan's being, retrospectively speaking, on the discredited side of this argument, doesn't lessen the significance of his article, issued as an enlarged pamphlet in May 1872, which suggestively identifies the poet with the prostitute, treats equally forms of male and female sexual behaviour, and even suggests a connection between the detachment of commercialized sexual relations and those of aesthetic contemplation and enjoyment. These characteristics of Buchanan's words may derive from 'person' and 'purse' in the literary marketplace, in reputation, and sales. He remarks disparagingly of the *Athenaeum*'s announcing that 'Mr. Swinburne's songs have already reached a second edition' or 'Good poetry seems to be in demand; the first edition of Mr. O'Shaughnessy's poems is exhausted',[48] while Ford Madox Brown traced the bile in 'The Fleshly School of Poetry' back to Buchanan's being called a 'poor and pretentious poetaster' in the same journal by William Michael Rossetti in 1865.[49]

'I DARE SAY HE WAS PUNCTUAL'[50]

John Davidson described Hood's 'The Song of the Shirt' as 'the most important English poem of the nineteenth century' and explained that

> Only a high heart and strong brain broken on the wheel of life, but master of its own pain and anguish, able to jest in the jaws of death, could have sung this song, of which every single stanza wrings the heart. Poetry passed by on the other side. It could not endure the woman in unwomanly rags.[51]

Davidson's prose suggests how this was done in his rhyme-like echo of 'single' in 'wrings'. Hood's rhyming combines being 'broken' and 'master of its own pain and anguish', his chimes entrapping his subjects in their fates and releasing both reader and subject from them. Such a combining of effort and constraint wrings with wrongs at the close of Hood's poem:

> With fingers weary and worn,
>   With eyelids heavy and red,
> A Woman sate in unwomanly rags,
>   Plying her needle and thread—
>   Stitch! stitch! stitch!
>   In poverty, hunger, and dirt,
> And still with a voice of dolorous pitch,
> Would that its tone could reach the Rich!
>   She sang this 'Song of the Shirt!'[52]

Like 'The Song of the Shirt', Davidson's 'Thirty Bob a Week' is a poem in which every stanza 'wrings the heart' with its own integrations of 'pitch' and 'tone':

> But I don't allow it's luck and all a toss;
>   There's no such thing as being starred and crossed;
> It's just the power of some to be the boss,
>   And the bally power of others to be bossed:
> I face the music, sir; you bet I ain't a cur;
>   Strike me lucky if you don't believe I'm lost![53]

In his essay 'On Poetry', Davidson writes decidedly against rhyme. He believes that blank verse forms the height of poetic achievement, and that rhyme is a sign of decadence.

Nevertheless, taking the example of Shakespeare's Sonnet 73, he cites the four lines ending 'Bare ruin'd choirs, where late the sweet birds sang' and notes: 'The rhymes of this quatrain toll like a death bell' in which 'there is a feeling of effort, as of a thing achieved and it is the rhyme that achieves', Davidson admitting that it is 'beautiful, it is poignant'.[54] The effort, and the tolling of a dead bell, can both be heard in the 'Thirty Bob a Week' stanza's music. It too sings a song of constriction, figuring the effort required to repeat it, assimilating and reliving the effort to continue that it shapes from the clerk's predicament. The second stanza, cited above, not only has the three entrapping rhymes culminating with 'lost!' but also rhymes on the same sound without its terminal consonant in 'boss' and 'toss'. There is, as it says, no question of luck in finding the rhymes here: the stanza is a model of the power that traps some and frees others. Its penultimate line, with the internal rhyme on 'sir' and 'cur' accelerates the financial constriction, yet also promises, in the new end rhyme, a development—but one crushed by the final line's discovery of a third, enclosing rhyme word. Just as Hood identified his fate with his poetic effects coming off, so too the clerk in Davidson's poem will 'face the music', and behind his speaker, also standing by his rhythm and rhyme, is the poet himself. This is the music of economic necessity, and someone else is calling the tune, compelling them to face it.

Yet both speaker and poet gain stature in the reader's eyes by recognizing it as such and still pressing his case within the musical form of his oppression. This is, then, a poem about the need to maintain independence even when you are near the bread line. The independence sounds within the poem's diction, a colloquial speech defended in the poem itself, though with an aside that might be thought out of character and situation: 'I ain't blaspheming, Mr. Silver-tongue; / I'm saying things a bit beyond your art'. Davidson is taking a swipe at Yeats, with whom he had quarrelled,[55] here in the last lines of stanza six, which finesses its criticism by alluding to the literary man's occult enthusiasms and the first sonnet in Sir Philip Sidney's *Astrophil and Stella*: 'With your science and your books and your the'ries about spooks, / Did you ever hear of looking in your heart?' Yet this momentary identification of clerk's, and poet's situations, is inseparably part of the poem's subject, embedded thematically in its technique. Davidson's next verse opens with a reaffirmation of the speaker's pride in independence. He isn't begging for a handout here: 'I didn't mean your pocket, Mr., no'.[56] Davidson's dislike of rhyme, and his masterful use of it in 'Thirty Bob a Week' to dramatize enduring necessity, shows in the penultimate stanza, where the clerk knows he was not consigned by nature or God to live that life; rather, his society conveniently underlines that the place he knows is destined and defined. His only hope is to accept outwardly and inwardly resist. He must generate his own dignity and yet still show subservience: 'And the difficultest job a man can do, / Is to come it brave and meek with thirty bob a week, / And feel that that's the proper thing for you'.[57]

Richard Le Gallienne recalled that Davidson 'found, as many another poet has done, that fame was more cry than wool, and that earning his livelihood continued as difficult as ever', noting a superficial paradox in his both registering and yet resisting 'reality':

> In this he was really no worse off than several of his famous contemporaries, but he had no bend in him, would not, or could not, stoop to journalism. A poet

who insisted on reality in his work, he was incapable of adapting himself to those materialistic conditions with which the most inspired poet must compromise if he is to continue to exist.[58]

In 1894, seven days before he published his best-known poem, Davidson complained to the publisher John Lane that his 'average income from all sources for the last month or two had been at the rate of 35/—a week'.[59] He received a Civil List pension of £100 per annum in 1906, but in March 1909, seemingly because on top of his economic difficulties he found himself to be suffering from cancer, committed suicide by drowning in the sea off Penzance. T. S. Eliot, a one-time clerk in financial difficulties, wrote of Davidson's poem:

> I am sure that I found inspiration in the content of the poem, and in the complete fitness of content and idiom: for I also had a good many dingy urban images to reveal. Davidson had a great theme, and also found an idiom which elicited the greatness of the theme, which endowed this thirty-bob-a-week clerk with a dignity that would not have appeared if a more conventional poetic diction had been employed. The personage that Davidson created in this poem has haunted me all my life, and the poem is to me a great poem for ever.[60]

Though Thomas Hood was in debt to the tune of between £200 and £300, obliging him to go into a five-year economic exile in 1835, his grafting of popular song rhythms into English verse left other poets, such as Poe, and many more readers besides, indebted to his melody. In April 1837, Hood wrote three letters for the *Athanaeum* called 'Copyright and Copywrong' in support of Talfourd's unsuccessful sixty-year protection bill. Clubbe points out that 'If copyright protection had given him a fair share of the income from the American sales of his books, his financial position would have been greatly relieved'.[61] But the debts of posterity are never, and never can be, repaid in cash. John Davidson's candour, his speaking out against 'Mr. Silver-Tongue', rings the changes for twentieth-century poetry, it being in the century following the death of Victoria that poetry went off, and stayed off, the gold standard.

'THE POET IS IN THE STREET'[62]

Late in 1894, Davidson wrote an anonymous report for John Lane at the Bodley Head on *London Nights*, Arthur Symons's third collections of poems. Though he recommended publication in an edition of 300 copies, his description of the volume is thought to have contributed to its rejection by this publisher. After being turned down by Heinemann, it appeared from Leonard Smithers in 1895, the year of the Wilde trials, and the response to Hardy's *Jude the Obscure*. Davidson had described the book as one in which 'the whole universe appears an embodiment of... utterly loveless and unimpassioned—mere and sheer libidinous desire', one in which the 'indecencies, impudences, and trivialities of harlotry are very deftly treated'.[63] 'Ten years ago', he added, 'I suppose it would have been to risk a sojourn in Holloway to publish "To One in Alienation", "Leves Amores", "White Heliotrope"'.[64] Karl Beckson observes that Lane's memory of the attacks on Symons's 'Stella Maris', published in the first number of *The Yellow Book* (April, 1894), combined with mention of Holloway prison to prompt Lane's decision.

Symons's 'Nora on the Pavement', also in *London Nights*, describes a music-hall ballet dancer, not on stage, but somewhere outside the theatre:

> As Nora on the pavement
> Dances, and she entrances the grey hour
> Into the laughing circle of her power,
> The magic circle of her glances,
> As Nora dances on the midnight pavement; [65]

The speaker has seen her on stage and recalls his feelings when looking at her dance once more on the street: 'Petulant and bewildered, / Thronging desires and longing looks recur' from his 'footlight fancy, petulant and bewildered'. Beckson observes that the poem is a portrait of one 'liberated from the demands of the stage but not from the spirit and form of the dance'; yet its closing stanzas, in freeing the dancer from the 'bewildered' feelings of the narrator, tacitly underlines the dynamic of attraction to the innocent, those remaining so in however unpromising circumstances, that is the poem's emotional theme:

> It is the very soul of Nora;
> Child, and most blithe, and wild as any elf,
> And innocently spendthrift of herself,
> And guileless and most unbeguiled,
> Herself at last, leaps free the very Nora.
>
> It is the soul of Nora,
> Living at last, and giving forth to the night,
> Bird-like, the burden of its own delight,
> All its desire, and all the joy of living,
> In that blithe madness of the soul of Nora.

Beckson provides a context on the page following his brief remarks about 'Nora on the Pavement'. On 15 October 1894 Symons wrote a public letter to the Editor of the *Pall Mall Gazette* attempting to defend The Empire Theatre, Leicester Square, and its promenade from accusations made to the Licensing Committee of the London County Council that it was being used for soliciting. He countered that 'I have visited the Empire on an average about once a week for the last year or two in my function as critic for several newspapers, and I must say that whenever I have had occasion to stand on the promenade I have never in a single instance been accosted by a woman', but in the course of doing so admits that 'vice, unfortunately, cannot be suppressed' and making an example of The Empire and 'driving these poor women onto the open streets' would be 'a grave injustice'.[66] Though 'Nora on the Pavement' is not about a dancer supplementing thus her income, the language of its arguing for the innocence of her dancing alludes to assumptions about the relationship between 'footlight fancies' on seeing such dancing, also accused of intending to 'excite impure thought and passion', and prostitution. When Symons writes that Nora is 'innocently spendthrift of herself', while contrasting her child-like soul with those who may be less innocently inviting others to spend money so as to spend themselves, his terms evoke the thought they fend off. Evoking prostitution, the poets are also on the pavement, and were selling such representations into a market too.

Le Gallienne recalled of the century's last decade a 'cult of London and its varied life, from costers to courtesans', linking this 'revival of interest in the town and urban things' to Buchanan's *London Poems*, and adding that 'of greater influence was Rossetti's "Jenny", which, 'doubtless, in addition to his Paris affiliations, had its influence on Mr. Arthur Symons with his celebration of the music hall, and his Noras of the Pavement'.[67] His plural again turns this innocent Nora into a more compromised generic term. Two further poems clearly associate the street and prostitution that Symons's verses skirt. 'Papillons du Pavé' by Vincent O'Sullivan vaunts its cross-Channel risk in a French title. Like the oft thought but ne'er expressed, the poetry of the 1890s flourishes with poems about street-walkers and pavements:

> A butterfly, a queer red thing,
> Comes drifting idly down the street:
> Ah, do not now the cool leaves swing,
> That you must brave the city's heat?
>
> A butterfly, a poet vain,
> Whose life is weeping in his mind,
> And all the dreaming of his brain
> Is blighted by the dusty wind.
>
> A painted butterfly sits there,
> Who sickens of the café chaff;
> And down the sultry evening air
> She flings her sullen weary laugh.[68]

The image of the soul, in a summer butterfly strayed onto a city street, a pavement butterfly, bifurcates into doubled and associated emblems: the blighted poet, whose romantic inspirations (also naturally in nature) are thwarted by the desiccated urban wind; and the artifice-enhanced butterfly, a young woman who lives by frequenting the cafés with their 'chaff' of harvest discards, one whose 'weary laugh' rhymes (or half-rhymes, depending on social class or regional accent) with the men of whom she has sickened. If there is protest in the associations with the butterfly, there is also solidarity—the 'chaff', we might imagine, equally dismissive of poet and prostitute, each, again linked to a marketplace in which both may be differently taken up and dropped.

Ernest Rhys' poem 'October: The Philosophy of the Pavement' is unambiguously about a Welsh girl on the London streets, caught up in its trade: 'What if my virtue's frail, she said: / Since life gets duller and duller, / Let it go fast and faster, till I'm dead!'—

> And if I die so soon, she said,
>   Far better dead and buried,
> Than living this wild life, she said,
>   Where women are so wearied,
> Upon the endless pavement that they tread.[69]

Like the ruined maid in Hardy's poem, Rhys's Mari is a woman come up to the capital and corrupted—just such a story, drawn from Mayhew's *London Labour and the London Poor*, as would inspire Philip Larkin's 'Deceptions' as late as 1950.[70] Rhys's poem voices the prostitute's desire for un-commercial relationships with the opposite sex: 'But if we had our way, she said, / With men,—then we would love them', not with pavements but 'flowers below, to dress the day':

> Then hardest hearted men, she said,
>   Would only love for kindness;
> And all sad women then, she said,
>   Should end their tears and blindness;
> And Christ save Mari Magdalen! she said. [71]

With those speech attributions, that 'said' and 'dead' rhyme, and 'wearied' echoing back to Tennyson's 'Mariana', Mari preserves the hopeful waiting for an un-commercialized love within her defensive self-esteem, her poem inwardly torn between 'don't care' and 'do care' stances. Thus, while Rhys has Mari retain the hope of a redeemed love, the gesture is compromised by its context, and has recourse to the stock biblical analogy for moralized images of repentant prostitutes in the period.[72]

W. E. Henley's 1877 'To W. R.', echoing Rossetti's 'Jenny' whose speaker speculates: 'perhaps you're merely glad / That I'm not drunk or ruffianly',[73] provided Joe Orton with his title *The Ruffian on the Stair*. In its allegory, we addressees are a girl's clients whom her pimp must kill, perhaps by means of such sexually transmitted diseases as had done for Baudelaire:

> Madam Life's a piece in bloom
>   Death goes dogging everywhere:
> She's the tenant of the room,
>   He's the ruffian on the stair.
>
> You shall see her as a friend,
>   You shall bilk him once and twice;
> But he'll trap you in the end,
>   And he'll stick you for her price.

> With his kneebones on your chest,
>   And his knuckles in your throat,
> You would reason—plead—protest!
>   Clutching at her petticoat;
>
> But she's heard it all before,
>   Well she knows you've had your fun,
> Gingerly she gains the door,
>   And your little job is done.[74]

The inevitability of its end offers an epitaph for this essay, one that would have its reverberations in both modernist poetry and Larkin's reaction against it, for it's hard to believe that when 'the young man carbuncular' in T. S. Eliot's *The Waste Land* 'Bestows one final patronising kiss, / And gropes his way, finding the stairs unlit…' and the typist 'Paces about her room again, alone'[75], its author didn't have Henley's 'meaning / Death'[76] allegory near the back of his mind. The poetry of modern life required the acknowledgement of such connections between sexuality, subjectivity, and the 'impressionistic' experience of cities—the penetration of exchange value and commercialized image into all social relationships, including, of course, those between poets and the highly competitive and ever more materially unrewarding market for their piecework.

Notes

1. W. B. Yeats, 'The Lake Isle of Innisfree', in *The Collected Poems*, 2nd edn., ed. Richard J. Finneran (Basingstoke: Macmillan, 1991), 39.

2. S. T. Coleridge, 'This Lime-Tree Bower My Prison', in *The Complete Poems*, ed. William Keach (Harmondsworth: Penguin Books, 1997), 139.

3. S. T. Coleridge, 'Frost at Midnight', in *The Complete Poems*, 232.

4. William Wordsworth, *The Prelude: The Four Texts (1798, 1799, 1805, 1850)*, ed. Jonathan Wordsworth (Harmondsworth: Penguin Books, 1995), vii. 270 (1805).

5. Matthew Arnold, 'Stanzas in Memory of the Author of "Obermann"', in *Poetical Works* (London: Macmillan, 1901), 327.

6. Wordsworth, *The Prelude* (1805), 270.

7. See Bracebridge Hemyng, 'Prostitution in London', Henry Mayhew, *London Labour and the London Poor; A Cyclopedia of the Condition and Earnings of Those that* Will Work, *Those that* Cannot Work, *and Those that* Will Not Work, *vol. 4, Those That Will Not Work by Several Contributors* (London: Charles Griffin and Company, 1861), 241.

8. Thomas Hardy, 'The Ruined Maid', in *The Complete Poetical Works of Thomas Hardy*, ed. Samuel Hynes, 5 vols. (Oxford: Oxford University Press, 1982–1995), i, 198.

9. Joseph Conrad, *The Collected Letters* 9 vols., ed. Fredrick R. Karl and Laurence Davies et al. (Cambridge: Cambridge University Press, 1983–2008), ii, 371. See Mary Ann Gillies, *The Professional Literary Agent in Britain 1880–1920* (Toronto: University of Toronto Press, 2007), 161.

10. R. L. Stevenson, 'The Vagabond', in *The Collected Poems*, ed. Roger C. Lewis (Edinburgh: Edinburgh University Press, 2003), 171.

11. Thomas Hood, 'The Bridge of Sighs', in *Selected Poems of Hood, Praed and Beddoes*, eds. Susan J. Wolfson and Peter J. Manning (Harmondsworth: Penguin Books, 2000), 147–150 for this and subsequence citations of the poem.

12. *The Letters of Thomas Hood* ed. Peter F. Morgan (Edinburgh: Oliver and Boyd, 1973), 592.

13. Hood, *The Letters of Thomas Hood*, 600.

14. *Selected Poems of Hood, Praed and Beddoes*, 343.

15. *Selected Poems of Hood, Praed and Beddoes*, 342.

16. Three excluded fragments published in *The Works of Thomas Hood* 10 vols. eds. his Son and Daughter (London: Moxon, 1869–73), ix, 208, preserve the child-murdering sin, commented on in John Clubbe, *Victorian Forerunner: The Later Career of Thomas Hood* (Durham, NC: Duke University Press, 1968), 174.

17. *The Works of Thomas Hood*, 173.

18. *Selected Poems of Hood, Praed and Beddoes*, 342.

19. Hood, *The Letters of Thomas Hood*, 604.

20. Hood, *The Letters of Thomas Hood*, 603.

21. Edgar Allan Poe, 'The Poetic Principle', in *The Complete Tales and Poems* (Harmondsworth: Penguin, 1982), 901, 904.

22. See Edgar Allan Poe, 'The Philosophy of Composition', in *The Complete Tales and Poems* (Harmondsworth: Penguin, 1982), 480–492.

23. Charles Baudelaire, translation of 'The Bridge of Sighs', ll. 27–30 in *Œuvres complètes* 2 vols., ed. Claude Pichois (Paris: Gallimard, 1975), i, 269.

24. Baudelaire, *Œuvres complètes*, i, 1292. This and the following translations are mine.

25. Baudelaire, *Œuvres complètes*, ii, 695.

26. Baudelaire, *Œuvres complètes*, ii, 696.

27. See 'Any where out of the world', in *Le spleen de Paris*, Baudelaire, *Œuvres complètes*, i, 356–357.

28. *Modernity and Modernism: French Painting in the Nineteenth Century*, ed. Francis Frascina et al. (New Haven and London: Yale University Press, 1993; rev. 1994), 178.

29. Ezra Pound, 'Hugh Selwyn Mauberley', in *Early Writings: Poetry and Prose*, ed. Ira B. Nadel (London: Penguin Books, 2005), 131.

30. See Robert Buchanan, 'The Fleshly School of Poetry: Mr. D. G. Rossetti', in *The Broadview Anthology of Victorian Poetry and Poetic Theory*, eds. Thomas J. Collins and Vivienne J. Rundle (Peterborough, Ontario: Broadview Press, 1999), 1329.

31. Buchanan, 'The Fleshly School of Poetry'.

32. Buchanan, 'The Fleshly School of Poetry, 1336.

33. Robert Buchanan, *London Poems* (London: Alexander Strahan, 1866). An enlarged gathering dated 1866–70 appears in Robert Buchanan, *The Poetical Works* (London: Chatto & Windus, 1884), 113–186. 'Artist and Model' is the song of a 'poor figure-painter' and 'the lady he loves', who, though they do 'wander / In town on Saturday night' have no connection with commercial sex, for 'people will buy my pictures, / And you will gather the gold' (147, 149).

34. Dante Gabriel Rossetti, *Collected Poetry and Prose*, ed. Jerome McGann (New Haven and London: Yale University Press, 2003), 335. For a chronology of the affair, and its effects on Rossetti's health, see Appendix 8 and 9, *The Correspondence of Dante Gabriel Rossetti*, 7 vols. eds. William E. Fredeman et al. (Cambridge: D. S. Brewer, 2002–8), v. 404–460.

35. Buchanan, 'The Little Milliner; or, Love in an Attic', in *The Poetical Works*, 115.

36. McGann notes it was 'composed in 1847–48; completely reworked in 1859–60 into a dramatic monologue; buried in 1862 with his other poems in his wife's coffin. Rossetti recovered it in 1869 and reworked it again for printing in 1870 *Poems*'. Rossetti, *Collected Poetry and Prose*, 381.

37. Rossetti, *Collected Poetry and Prose*, 338.

38. Rossetti, 'Jenny' in *Collected Poetry and Prose*, 60.

39. Rossetti, 'The Stealthy School of Criticism', in *Collected Poetry and Prose*, 337.

40. Rossetti, 'Jenny', in *Collected Poetry and Prose*, 63–64.

41. Rossetti, 'The Stealthy School of Criticism', *Collected Poetry and Prose*, 338.

42. For a Browningesque dramatic monologue spoken by the prostitute herself, see Augusta Webster, 'A Castaway', in *Portraits and Other Poems*, ed. Christine Sutphin (Toronto: Broadview, 2000), 192–213.

43. Buchanan, 'The Fleshly School', 1335.

44. McGann acknowledges Buchanan's point, without its *parti pris*, when noting that his '*inner* standing-point' allowed Rossetti to 'include his own subjectivity in the poem under the mask of the speaker', Rossetti, *Collected Poetry and Prose*, 381.

45. Buchanan, 'The Fleshly School of Poetry', 1336.

46. Buchanan, 'The Fleshly School of Poetry', 1337. See 'The Complete Writings and Pictures of Dante Gabriel Rossetti' at <http://www.rossettiarchive.org/docs/3-1848.fizdgrms.rad.html> (accessed 6 February 2012). McGann edits out the exclamation mark in his edition. See, Rossetti, 'Jenny', in *Collected Poetry and Prose*, 60.

48. Buchanan, 'The Fleshly School of Poetry', in *The Broadview Anthology of Victorian Poetry and Poetic Theory*, 1330, and see Andrew Nash, 'Robert Buchanan and Chatto & Windus: Reputation, Authorship, and Fiction as Capital in the late Nineteenth Century', *Publishing History*, 46 (1999), 5–33.

49. See Appendix 8, *The Correspondence of Dante Gabriel Rossetti*, v. 406.

50. Joseph Conrad, *The Collected Letters*, ii. 371.

51. John Davidson, 'Pre-Shakespeareanism', in *The Man Forbid and Other Essays* (Boston: The Ball Publishing Company, 1910), 36. It was first published in *The Speaker* 19 (28 Jan 1899), 107–108.

52. Hood, 'The Song of the Shirt', in *Selected Poems of Hood, Praed and Beddoes*, 144.

53. Davidson, *The Poems of John Davidson* 2 vols., ed. Andrew Turnbull (Edinburgh and London: Scottish Academic Press, 1973), i. 63.

54. Davidson, 'On Poetry' (1906), in *The Poems of John Davidson*, ii. 531–32.

55. See John Sloan, *John Davidson, First of the Moderns: A Literary Biography* (Oxford: Oxford University Press, 1995), 59–63.

56. Davidson, 'Thirty Bob a Week', in *The Poems of John Davidson*, i. 64.

57. Davidson, 'Thirty Bob a Week', 65.

58. Richard Le Gallienne, *The Romantic '90s* (London and New York: G. P. Putnam's Sons, 1926), 147–48.

59. Cited from Sloan, *John Davidson, First of the Moderns*, 112.

60. T. S. Eliot, Preface to *John Davidson: A Selection of his Poems*, ed. Maurice Linday (London: Hutchinson, 1961), also cited in *Poetry of the 'Nineties*, ed. R. K. R. Thoronton (Harmondsworth: Penguin Books, 1970), 78.

61. Clubbe, *Victorian Forerunner: The Later Career of Thomas Hood*, 58.

62. Davidson, 'Pre-Shakespeareanism', in *The Man Forbid and Other Essays*, 34.

63. Bodleian Library manuscript, cited from Karl Beckman, *Arthur Symons: A Life* (Oxford: Oxford University Press, 1987), 112.
64. Bodleian Library manuscript, cited from Sloan, *John Davidson, First of the Moderns*, 115.
65. Arthur Symons, *Poems: Volume One* (London: Martin Secker, 1924), 173.
66. Beckman, *Arthur Symons: A Life*, 110–11.
67. Le Gallienne, *The Romantic '90s*, 154.
68. Vincent O'Sullivan, 'Papillons du Pavé', in *Poetry of the 'Nineties*, 89–90.
69. Ernest Rhys, 'October: The Philosophy of the Pavement', in *Poetry of the 'Nineties*, 91.
70. See Peter Robinson, '"Readings will grow erratic", in Philip Larkin's "Deceptions"', *Cambridge Quarterly*, 38 (2009), 277–305.
71. Rhys, 'October: The Philosophy of the Pavement', in *Poetry of the 'Nineties*, 92.
72. See, for example, Amy Levy, 'Magdalene', in *Out of Borrowed Books: Poems by Augusta Webster, Mathilde Blind and Amy Levy*, ed. Judith Willson (Manchester: Carcanet Press, 2006), 212–14.
73. Rossetti, 'Jenny', in *Collected Poetry and Prose*, 61.
74. W. E. Henley, 'To W. R.', in *The New Oxford Book of Victorian Verse*, ed. Christopher Ricks (Oxford: Oxford University Press, 1987), 506–7.
75. T. S. Eliot, 'The Waste Land', in *Collected Poems 1909–1962* (London: Faber & Faber, 1963), 72.
76. T. S. Eliot, 'Marina', in *Collected Poems 1909–1962*, 115.

SELECT BIBLIOGRAPHY

Blyth, Caroline (ed.), *Decadent Verse: An Anthology of Late Victorian Poetry 1872–1900* (London and New York: Anthem Press, 2009).
Clark, T. J., *The Painting of Modern Life: Paris in the Art of Manet and his Followers* (London: Thames & Hudson, 1984; rev. ed. 1999).
Ford, Mark (ed.), *London: A History in Verse* (Cambridge, MA and London: Harvard University Press, 2012).
Fried, Michael, *Manet's Modernism: or, The Face of Painting in the 1860s* (Chicago: University of Chicago Press, 1998).
—— *Menzel's Realism: Art and Embodiment in Nineteenth-Century Berlin* (New Haven and London: Yale University Press, 2002).
Jackson, Kevin (ed.), *The Oxford Book of Money* (Oxford: Oxford University Press, 1995).
Leighton, Angela, and Reynolds, Margaret (ed.), *Victorian Women Poets: An Anthology* (Oxford: Blackwell, 1995).
Mayhew, Henry, *London Labour and the London Poor*, ed. Robert Douglas-Fairhurst (Oxford: Oxford University Press, 2010).
Rodensky, Liza (ed.), *Decadent Poetry from Wilde to Naidu* (London: Penguin Books, 2006).
Swinburne, Algernon Charles, *Major Poems and Selected Prose* ed. Jerome McGann and Charles L. Sligh (New Haven and London: Yale University Press, 2004).

CHAPTER 16

....

MODERNIST VICTORIANISM

....

ADAM PIETTE

HIGH Modernism is such a radical break from Victorianism that it might seem perverse to argue otherwise. Pound's mantra 'Make it new' was designed to help modernist avant-garde poets discard outmoded Victorian styles, values, stifling Victorian cant and culture. Wyndham Lewis, with *Blast*, blasts the years 1837–1900 to allow for a Nietzschean art-energy liberated from Victorian nostrums. Yeats divests himself of his floatier *fin-de-siècle* rhetoric to discover a hard plain speech both properly twentieth century and pre-nineteenth century. The women of the modernist *cénacles* in London stab the Angel in the House through the heart, and remove the Victorian matriarch from their hearts and minds. Modernist writing deploys a range of comic techniques to exorcize Victorian modes of feeling from the imagination: brutal satires like *Tarr*, knowingly superior essays like *Eminent Victorians*, novels such as *A Good Soldier* signalling the end of the Victorian family, shockingly frank displays of sexual depths with work by D. H. Lawrence. The movement espouses almost any other culture as long as it is not Victorian: there are strains of Romanticism in Yeats, attachment to French, German, and Russian writing in Bloomsbury generally, exploration of Chinese, Buddhist, classical, and medieval cultural moments with Pound and Eliot, and a return to ancient folkloric roots with the Irish Revival. Victorian writing is toxic, must be scorched from the memory bank. And it is with the poets that the anti-Victorian sentiment is most radical: from T.E. Hulme's assault on the nineteenth century for its fatuous attachment to democracy, progress, and emotionalism to the Imagist manifesto and Pound's bellowing against the sloppiness of Victorian idealizing.

Yet faintly one hears Victorian strains echoing within modernist poems. At the heart of the modernist project is the artist's Nietzschean life and death struggle with a post-Victorian environment, enacted most clearly with Wyndham Lewis's play *Enemy of the Stars*, printed in the launch issue of *Blast*. Arghol and Hanp are the two wrestling energies of the divided modernist mind, one the liberated artist, the other a parasite throwback to late Victorian *fin-de-siècle* posturing. The play features Arghol attempting to rid himself of his Victorian twin, this ape of god, this fake decadent pseudo-artist. But the ape is part of the artist, cannot be exorcized without self-destruction: the two fight and gnaw and bite, locked together like Ugolino and Ruggiero in the ninth circle. But the dialectic must end in death. The modernist artist, such a dyed-in-the-wool enemy of the Victorian artist within, is shaped at unconscious levels by the enemy he hates. The struggle can only lead to catastrophe: the artist is a snarling Timon, but has the smile of the Victorian parasite: there as a tic on his face too.[1] *Blast* may blast the years 1837 to 1900, but it also blesses forces from the Victorian era ('Bless England, industrial island machine').[2] Just as Freud was teaching modernists that it is impossible to kill one's parents for they occupy the unconscious as superego voices and romances, so is there a recognition of the enduring presence of Victorian culture as modernism's superego enemy: witness the care with which Virginia Woolf treats the spirit and example of her mother in *To the Lighthouse*, for instance. 'Victorian' is written through modernist poems like Brighton rock, but let us say cut short at 'Victor' to signal a male reaction against the overly feminized nineteenth century. Still the Victorian strain persists as a ghostly voice of the thing most despised, as a father and mother memory for the twentieth-century orphan-artist. This essay will be looking at work of modernist poets, particularly Pound and Eliot, to register that 'Victor/Victorian' signal on the higher frequencies.

V IS FOR VORTICISM

If Victorianism is the enemy, then it must shape the poetry written against its influence. This is a Hegelian truism, but perhaps it can be tested, and should only be tested, with the most rigorously un-Victorian of poems, the Vorticist poetry associated with *Blast*. Riding on the back of Marinetti's Futurist manifesto and its fusion of technology, militarism, misogyny, and revolutionary destruction of all institutions, the Vorticist movement allies Pound's hard-nosed historical sense (use the 'clean' male poetry of other languages, other periods to de-Victorianize the tribe) with Lewis's Nietzschean assault on all the pieties. It is distinct from Futurism because it finds Marinetti's worship of modern technology risible, and Marinetti himself a *fin-de-siècle* parasite-creature. Nevertheless, it is clear that the brute revolutionary posturing and headline shoutiness of the Futurists is to the Vorticist taste, for it helps rouse the energy needed to blast the Victorian establishment and its poetasting ways. The vortex is a whirlwind force that is a sexual, predatory energy within the warrior artist that needs to be released. And it is a collective force like revolutionary action, binding artist and public together in a riot of Victorian-destructive passions.

That vortex has its analogue, in poetic terms, in Pound's rugged satire: the poems in the first issue of *Blast* include comminations against the Victorian-Edwardian public, like 'Salutation the Third' ('I will laugh at you and mock you, / And I will offer you consolations in irony, / O fools, detesters of beauty');[3] bitter little mock translations from the classics, such as 'Come My Cantilations', staging a rejection of bourgeois London ('Let me be free of pavements') and favouring a Nietzschean elite ('Let come the gay of manner, the insolent and the exulting'), based on a toughening up of art as rejection of the mushiness of Victorian poetry: 'We speak of burnished lakes, / And of dry air, as clear as metal'.[4] Note the neo-futurist note in 'clear as metal', and the self-reflexive allusion to the poem's own irony in 'dry air'. And yet all three strategies, commination, mock translation, and elite 'hard' aesthetics are not unlike some versions of late Victorian aestheticism, a Paterian art idolatry combined with *poète maudit* braggadocio. Even what seems to be the trademark timbre of Pound's Vorticism, the dry ironies and savage satirical display, owe a deal to Whistler's jocular framing of Swinburne's criticism of his *Ten O'Clock Lecture* in *The Gentle Art of Making Enemies*. Or, indeed, to the parodies which Arthur Symons admired, particularly Landor's parodies and William Aytoun's parody of the Spasmodic School, 'Firmilian'.[5] The 'burnished lakes' is more cliché than proto-imagist, recalling Edgar Fawcett of all people, in the line from the 1891 *Songs of Doubt and Dream*: 'Shadows hung dense on the burnished lake'.[6] Pound's Vorticism has taproots, then, back into 1890s aestheticism and late Victorian parody and pastiche. Pound acknowledges the link in his *Blast* essay 'Vortex', where he quotes Whistler and Pater in order to help define Vorticist formalism.[7] He does so under the subtitle 'Ancestry': its ancestry in Victorian aestheticism haunts the modernist project, just as images of parents flit into the manifesto *sans vouloir*. 'Picasso, Kandinski', Pound tells us in the same section, are 'father and mother, classicism and romanticism of the movement'. It is as though the burly comedy and ferocious attitudinizing that went into Vorticism's formalist, anarchist, and revolutionary energies mask an orphaned state, an unconscious longing for ancestry, for the Victorian mother and father being rejected.

I IS FOR IMAGISM

It is the Imagists who campaign most sharply against Victorian rhetoric—reproducing the *Lyrical Ballads* moment of disjunction from eighteenth-century poetic diction. The manifesto identifies nineteenth-century poetic diction as its foil. In the list of Don'ts published in *Poetry* in 1913, Pound had zeroed in on what he calls 'abstraction': 'Don't use such an expression as "dim lands *of peace*". It dulls the image. It mixes an abstraction with the concrete. It comes from the writer's not realizing that the natural object is always the *adequate* symbol'.[8] The target is what Pound elsewhere names as the 'mushiness' and 'slop' of Victorian allegorizing—it reads like a line out of Frederick Ward ('I bathe within the founts that flow / From the dim lands of Long-ago'),[9] but is actually closer to home, taking a line from Ford Madox Ford's 1904 poem 'On a Marsh Road': 'The eternal silences; dim lands of peace'.[10] The joke is mischievous, since it was partly Ford who had made Pound see that abstraction and loose diction needed to be countered by a prose-like concreteness of treatment. But it does set the tone: contemporaries must be taught, through parodic play, how to divest themselves of Victorian habits.

The move against rhetoric cannot be so simply labelled modernist, however. Pound acknowledges that 1890s poetry made the first move: Whistler's statement in *Gentle Art* on line and colour quoted in *Blast* inaugurates the modernism Pound identified with Imagism:

The minute you have admitted that, you let in the jungle, you let in nature and truth and abundance and cubism and Kandinsky. Whistler and Kandinsky and some cubists were getting extraneous matter out of their art: they were ousting literary values. The Flaubertians talk a good deal about 'constatation'. The 'nineties' saw a movement against rhetoric. I think all these things move together.[11]

We can register more clearly the ways Imagist poems act as arenas where the 1890s anti-rhetorical movement ousts mid-Victorian poetic diction if we look to the poems of H. D. which Pound championed as exemplary.

In *Blast*, it is her poem 'Oread' which exemplifies the Vorticist image:

> Whirl up sea—
> Whirl your pointed pines,
> Splash your great pines
> On our rocks,
> Hurl your green over us,
> Cover us with your pools of fir.[12]

The image, according to Pound, fuses an emotion with a concrete object, and here we have H. D. combining a Lear-like invocation of storm with a relish of violence captured in the resemblance of peaking waves to pines. There is no attempt to state what the pines 'mean', or to allegorize the whirling sea. This is a poetry purged of fake Victorian abstraction by a Japanese discipline of image. Nevertheless, what Pound's advocacy obscures is how involved H. D. is in a battle with Victorian poetry. The opening line 'Whirl up sea' is odd enough to read as some kind of quotation, and it does allude back to the Bostonian poet William Wetmore Story's long 1844 poem 'Nature and Art', 'In passionate sobs the forest grieves, / The water-spouts whirl up to heaven'; a poem which also has lines about pine trees ('through sighing pines, / The spirit moaneth').[13] H. D.'s poem is locked in battle with the sanctimonious emotionalism of Story's poem, aiming the pointed barbs of her lines at his 'passionate', moaning self-indulgence. Poetasters such as Story, who have lent Nature 'a reverent ear', and read the 'restless sea' and other natural phenomena as Christian allegory, and who construct cliché-ridden odes to Art and the artist, are the enemy whom she dreams her modernist sea will engulf in apocalypse. It is in the spirit of radical feminism too: this is an invocation of an Oread, and not Story's masculine artist and God. Her pagan Aeschylean sea will hurl on 'our rocks', which include the 'Faith, calm, enduring as the silent rocks' of Story's unctuous rhapsody.

C IS FOR CITY

If modernist verse is free as much because it parodies bad Victorian verse as because of new techniques, then that owes a great deal to the French prose poem, and specifically Baudelaire's scathing Parisian satires. The modern battleground is the city, not the country or seashore. Baudelaire moves his language into the city as part of the post-Romantic predicament tormenting his generation: the city might release hostile energies in the anti-bourgeois artist if the imagination catches the larger forces running the metropolis, or identifies with the marginal dogs, tramps, and *saltimbanques* of the streets. The great poems of modernism in English, *The Waste Land* and *Hugh Selwyn Mauberley*, are set in London to signal Baudelaire's ancestry. Baudelaire's dandy and *flâneur* are masks worn by the designers of the broken shards of modernist poetics. Yet, again, the target and ancestry is more nuanced. If the 'Unreal city' of *The Waste Land* is indebted to Baudelaire's 'Fourmillante cité, cité pleine de rêves', then it is also inflected by the 1890s city poetics inspired by Baudelaire and the *symbolistes*, poems such as John Davidson's *Fleet Street Eclogues*, the pattern of which—four voices of city writers (journalists but sounding like the chattering dead) commenting on the passing of the seasons and on city corruption, sights, and sounds—is reworked by Eliot. His ballads were admired by Eliot,[14] and Davidson adopts the voices of Londoners to script the city as necropolis in ways that look forward to Eliot's work. 'A Loafer' has these lines that strike the *Waste Land* note:

> I move from eastern wretchedness
> Through Fleet Street and the Strand;
> And as the pleasant people press
> I touch them softly with my hand,
> Perhaps to know that still I go
> Alive about a living land.[15]

James Thomson's *The City of Dreadful Night* (with an epigraph from Dante) reads London as a necropolis too, of sleepwalking spirits, as a desert of dark forces ('some enormous things / Swooped past with savage cries and clanking wings'),[16] sinister, sexual, supernatural: elements reprised in Eliot's poem.

And the London poems of the 1890s point back, too, to the bleak vision of the city in poems like *In Memoriam* with its haunted mourner wandering the bald unlovely streets, or to *Maud* and the hooves beating above the grave of the mad I-voice. The city for Eliot is a spectral dream of clashing voices, prefiguring their own damnation, struck down by the age's faithlessness, war-dead hauntedness, spiritual desolation. The darkness of that vision owes much to Victorian post-Romantic exploration of the industrial metropolis.

T IS FOR THEATRICALITY

The idea of the city as a theatre of spectral voices confirmed modernists in their greatest debt to Victorian poetry, the theatricalizing of the lyric voice as performed in the dramatic monologue. Pound was trained by Browning in the uses of dramatic monologue as a genre capable of fusing political and personal animus with daring readings of culture and history. His mask-identities mimic Browning's *dramatis personae*; Pound was a Browning acolyte through and through, and proud to display his filiation: 'Überhaupt ich stamm aus Browning. Pourquoi nier son père.'[17] Derived from Browning, as son from father: the dramatic monologue, as well as the concept of epic ('Hang it all, Robert Browning, / there can be but one "Sordello"', runs the second of his *Cantos*)[18] are in his blood. As Eliot remarked in a review of Pound's *Quia Pauper Amavi*, Pound's historical method was 'a conscious and consistent application of a procedure suggested by Browning', a method which entailed conveying historical knowledge 'through historical masks'; and, since it is a *historical* method, 'the poet imposes upon himself, necessarily, the condition of continually changing his mask'.[19]

It is Browning's historical guises which are reprised in the personae of Pound's early poems: Bertrans de Born in 'Sestina: Altaforte', and other troubadour alter egos ('Guido Invites You Thus', 'Pierre Vidal Old'). Browning, Pound explained in a letter to Henry Ware Eliot, 'in his *Dramatis Personae* and in his *Men and Women* developed a form of poem which had laid dormant since Ovid's *Heroides* or since Theocritus',[20] and one can hear Browning's rough-hewn theatricality in the opening line of 'Sestina': 'Damn it all! All this our South stinks peace.'[21]

Browning also provided the core inspiration for the experiment in modernist epic, the *Cantos*: the first three written during the war were consciously modelled on *Sordello*, envious of Browning's power of technical innovation. The dramatic monologue is turned inside out, with Pound now his own persona, the silent interlocutor Browning himself:

> And you had a background,
> Watched 'the soul', Sordello's soul,
> And saw it lap up life, and swell and burst—
> 'Into the empyrean?'
> So you worked out new form, the meditative,
> Semi-dramatic, semi-epic story.
> And we will say: 'What's left for me to do?'[22]

As Forrest Read has argued, 'the choice of Browning reflected his belief in 1915 that *Sordello* was the last great poetic narrative, itself Browning's version of the "personal epic", the post-romantic autobiographical poem which at the same time sought the objective validity of actual history'.[23] By 1922, Pound lost confidence in this Browningesque experiment, removed the Browning cantos, and replaced them with mock translation of Homeric epic. Traces still remain in the opening of Canto II and elsewhere, but to all intents and purposes, Pound had decided to conceal the traces of his Victorian forebear, and to channel his energies into rivalling classical and medieval epic.[24]

Nevertheless, as poems like the 1913 'Mesmerism' show, Browning's ability to inhabit any mind and to speak from that vantage with such odd, cantankerous, glinting energy would remain part of Pound's repertoire. 'You wheeze as a head-cold long-tonsilled Calliope', he says in the poem, already reading Browning as muse of both epic and dramatic monologue.[25] Pound salutes the convoluted energy and power of the voice ('Eagled and thundered as Jupiter Pluvius'), the 'Mad as a hatter' eccentricity, the strange manic rhythmical force ('Old Hoppity-Hop o' the accents'), the clairvoyant dissection of culture and person ('what a sight you ha' got o' our in'ards / . . . crafty dissector'). As precursor, Browning leaves Pound with little to do but adapt, Americanize, and make extreme the epic/dramatic solutions Browning had found for post-Romantic poetry.

As Pound explained to Eliot's father, he tried to accommodate Browning's dramatizing techniques, by removing 'Browning's talk *about* this, that and the other, to confine my words strictly to what might have been the emotional speech of the character under such and such a crisis'.[26] And he had also chosen a different historical analogue to explore:

> Browning had cast his poems mostly in Renaissance Italy, I cast mine in mediaeval Provence, which was a change without any essential difference. T.S.E. has gone farther and begun with the much more difficult job of setting his 'personae' in modern life, with the discouragingly 'unpoetic' modern surroundings.[27]

It is with *Hugh Selwyn Mauberley*, however, that Pound discovers a more Eliotic use for Browning. The sequence is set in modern London in 1919, the London of salons, museums, libraries. And it deploys a dry, brittle, intellectual voice to articulate the death of 1890s aestheticism. Pound uses Browning's dramatic monologue technique to divest himself of late Victorian tics. Its form, a loose sequence of poems dwelling on the demise of art idolatry consequent on the radical break of the First World War, borrows the scheme of *Dramatis Personae* whilst creating a particular mind and style of address through the persona of Mauberley and his alter-ego, the *fin-de-siècle* Pound.

Browning haunts the sequence as father to the style, yet without the pastichy mimickry of 'Mesmerism'; for Pound is also parodying the Paterian-Yeastian-Swinburnian nether regions of 1890s poetics, with extraordinarily controlled satire. The opening poem 'E.P. Ode pour l'election de son sepulchre', dramatizes the death of the late Victorian Pound:

> His true Penelope was Flaubert,
> He fished by obstinate isles;
> Observed the elegance of Circe's hair
> Rather than the mottoes on sun-dials.[28]

The lines mock poems like Dante Gabriel Rossetti's 'Dis Manibus', an elegy on Flaubert which addresses him as 'scribe to Nero's soul';[29] Andrew Lang's 'Circe's Isle Revisited' ('No light of laughing eyes, or floating hair', the voice laments);[30] and Lang's 'François Villon': 'The new suns melt from off the sundial'.[31] They also style Pound's own aesthete self as creature of Ford's Flaubert fanaticism, the classicism and Francophilia of the Imagists, Eliot's contemporary way with the dramatic monologue, and Joyce's *Ulysses*: it mocks the modernists, in other words, as sepulchral ghosts of late Victorian aestheticism.

And yet, as the last poem of *Mauberley* demonstrates, there was still something to the Victorian ideal of art, at once chillingly dead and yet alive with Browningesque menace. In 'Medallion', obsession with inhuman art turns on the beholder, on Mauberley's dream of an art object world, transfixing the loved one as nightmare fossil of another age:

> The face-oval beneath the glaze,
> Bright in its suave bounding-line, as,
> Beneath half-watt rays,
> The eyes turn topaz.[32]

The Swinburnian richness of the sound texture ('glaze', 'as', 'rays', 'eyes', 'topaz') is belied by the shock of the art-petrification of the woman's eyes, and the sinister technological illumination as though for dissection or commodifying display. Pound returns to Browning's questioning of the collusion of aesthetic pleasure and sexual desire in so many of his dramatic monologues, 'My Last Duchess', 'Porphyria's Lover', 'Andrea del Sarto'. The end of the line of the post-Victorian artist in post-war London is a strange return to the boldest dramatic monologues of the nineteenth century.

If Eliot set his 'personae' in modern life, as Pound argued, this is partly to do with the influence of Tennyson's dramatic monologues, in particular *Maud: A Monodrama*, 'Tithonus', and 'Locksley Hall Sixty Years After'. For Eliot, Victorian culture had inaugurated a feverish and 'modern' sense of time: 'Tennyson lived in a time which was already acutely time-conscious', harried as it was by new technology and industrialism:

> [The time] had, for the most part, no hold on permanent things, on permanent truths about man and God and life and death. The surface of Tennyson stirred about with his time: and he had nothing to which to hold fast except his unique and unerring feeling for the sounds of words.[33]

In this same essay, Eliot takes Tennyson to task for mixing the lyric and dramatic: 'A poet can express his feelings as fully through a dramatic, as through a lyrical form'. But *Maud* is 'shrill rather than deep' because it is 'neither one thing or another'.[34] Yet Eliot's own dramatic monologues are similarly mixed, and seek out the 'feeble violence' of a work like *Maud*. If Tennyson's predicament was only to have the sounds of words in a time of destruction and impermanence, then the modernist moment, constructed as it was upon the ruins of the First World War, looks back to Victorian time-consciousness as a dramatic-lyric solution to the problem of expression. Eliot's lines are continually seeking out Tennysonian rhythms and sounds, in a time-conscious manner which Tennyson himself had perfected: 'Forward then, but still remember how the course of Time will swerve, / Crook and turn upon itself in many a backward streaming curve'.[35]

Eliot's early poetry is saturated with Tennyson reminiscences. Christopher Ricks has tracked the Tennyson allusions in his edition of the early poems, and found well over sixty. 'Tithonus' sings behind 'Hidden under the heron's wing'; *Maud* is alluded to several times in 'A Burnt Dancer'; and the 'Suite clownesque' series glances at *Enoch Arden* and *The Princess*.[36] What the poems do to Tennyson is to take the Victorianism and play a Laforguian highball cruel comedy off its surfaces: so 'Suite Clownesque I' uses the *In Memoriam* stanza, and situates itself in what seems a Victorian country house in opening lines that allude to Tennyson, only to throw onto the set Laforgue's clown, 'A self-embodied role, his soul / Concentrated in his vest and nose'.[37] The effect is intended to burlesque Tennysonian Victorianism, and yet this is not quite right. The clown appears 'Leaning across the orchestra', interrogating the audience with his red nose: the poem has shifted focus and theatricalized the Victorian setting. The 'painted collonades', 'potted palms', and 'lawns' are props and backdrops in a music hall, a Victorian–Edwardian music hall. The true effect of the poem is not to pitch Laforgue against Tennyson in a modernizing gesture, but to fuse the two separate spheres of Victorian high art (poetry) and Victorian popular entertainment (music-hall), to bring poet laureate and comedian into contact.

'The Love Song of J. Alfred Prufrock' achieves a similar double play with its source relationship with the previous century. It takes the Victorian dramatic monologues which are most anguished about poetry as vocation and as zone of post-Romantic morbidity and adds an annihilating sardonic humour to the expression. If Tennyson's 'Lotus-Eaters' and 'Tithonus' worry away at the belatedness of the Victorian poet, at the superannuation and ivory-tower inwardness felt to be the poet's only post-Romantic role, then Eliot plays it as a harsh vision of the poet as seedy clown, subject to nerves, paranoia, febrile anxieties, fear of women, crippling self-consciousness. Prufrock's move from hopeless rhetorical questions ('And how should I presume?') to the dream of 'sea-girls wreathed with seaweed red and brown' in 'the chambers of the sea' at the close of the reverie is telling.[38] It confesses the Tennysonian nature of the poetic gift as male desire with its allusion to 'The Mermaid': Eliot's disconcerting repetitions in the final six lines particularly of 'sea' recall the obsessive 'me'-'sea' rhymes of Tennyson's poem; the allusion picks up, too, on the mermaid's rhetorical questions ('And still as I comb'd I would sing and say, / "Who is it loves me? who loves not me?"').[39] 'The Mermaid' refuses to be kissed by the mermen, and the accompanying poem 'The Merman' has a delusional merman dreaming of the same kisses.[40] 'Prufrock' takes the little dramas and stages that failure anew. Eliot's persona is obsessed by the society hostesses running London and by the mermaids of his dreams, and that double desiring and failing fails and desires according to a Tennysonian formula.

O IS FOR OVERMAN

If the filiations linking Pound to Browning and Eliot to Tennyson are centred on the dramatic monologue, this implies that the post-Romantic dilemma had not been properly settled. The migratory theatricality of selfhood as historical method that Pound takes from Browning signals a concern with the ways subjectivity is shaped by power, culture, language, and uncontrollable desire. The fact Eliot takes on dissentient identities like Tennyson's 'Locksley Hall' voice as type of the multiple selving of the poet in modern times implies a similar perplexity about identity. But in both cases, the post-Romantic dilemma—what is now to be done with the poetic roles of bard, prophet, and legislator of the loving imagination rendered obsolete by Victorian industrial culture?—becomes a satirical and comic question. There is broad comedy in Browning, and there is much to be said for the approach to Tennyson that is sensitive to the wit of the poetry; nevertheless, the comedic imperative that is motivating Eliot and Pound has its source elsewhere. Partly it derives from the sardonic, self-stylizing manoeuvres of French poetry: for Eliot from Laforgue and Corbière encountered in Arthur Symons's *The Symbolist Movement in Literature*; for Pound in the tough intellectual wit of the troubadours. But importantly it derives also from the influence of Nietzsche, whose *Die fröhliche Wissenschaft* (*The Gay Science*) invited its readers to savour the *gai saber* of those same troubadours: the Christian Godhead is dead, selves are fictions that eternally recur throughout history, and the only response is to resurrect the free spirit of the poet as knight of a pseudo-Provençal culture.

Nietzsche included his own poems at the end of the volume, imitations of Provençal lyrics praising the merry, hedonistic, joyful energy of the South, whilst mocking the sombre gravitas of most nineteenth-century poetry. The free spirit is comedic, satirical, parodic, as Nietzsche insists in the preface to the second edition:

> it is not only on the poets and their fine 'lyrical sentiments' that this reconvalescent must vent his malignity: who knows what kind of victim he seeks, what kind of monster of material for parody will allure him ere long? [41]

Nietzschean comedy is subversive and consciously wicked. In a post-Darwinian environment, what preserves the species, he argues, is a martial spirit of taboo-destroying comedy. And most of all, the strong, free man celebrated by Nietzsche treats all others as subordinate selves to be taken up and discarded: 'they now use the visionaries, now the experts, now the brooders, now the pedants in their neighbourhood, as their actual selves for the time; but very soon they do not need them any longer!' The parodic poet-intellectual takes up these identities as though his subjectivity were a city:

> And thus while their environment and outside die off continually, everything seems to crowd into this environment, and wants to become a 'character' of it; they are like great cities in this respect. [42]

Nietzsche gave new impetus to the post-Romantic dramatic monologue, enabling it to become the parodic playground of the 'city'-poet as Overman. Browning's and Tennyson's theatricality is transvalued to become a means towards a martial arrogance and self-savouring wit for the sake of the artist as radical individualist.

The Nietzsche craze of the 1910s in London centred round Orage's *The New Age*, and the neo-Nietzscheans such as Oscar Levy included intellectuals who would later become key figures in the British fascism of the interwar years. [43] It also lies behind the posturing of the more 'paramilitary' of the avant-garde groups, especially Marinetti's Futurists. Mina Loy was closely involved with the Italian Futurists before evolving into a modernist feminist, and her poems are another test case for the absolute novelty of modernist writing. Her most Futurist poem, 'The Costa San Giorgio' from the *Italian Pictures* sequence, written whilst she was still in contact with Marinetti, finds verbal analogues for the contemporaneity of the movement. These lines give a flavour of the collage of objects, patches of thing seen, and body parts glimpsed on a walk through the city:

> Fluidic blots of sky
> Shift among roofs
> Between bandy legs
> Jerk patches of street
>
> Interrupted by clacking
> Of all the green shutters
> From which
> Bits of bodies
> Variously leaning
> Mingle eyes with the commotion [44]

A patchwork-selective, jerky camera eye is mimicked and alluded to in the pun on shutters, the futurist poet a machine for recording the sights and sounds of the day, identifying the artist with the chaotic desiring eyes of the Italians at their windows. To 'mingle eyes with the commotion' is to move the I-voice of lyric onto a collective plane, the eyes of a city, the commotion of the streets. This *flânerie*-dreamy emotional-visionary impulse is Nietzschean: 'It suffices to love, to hate, to desire, and in general to feel,—immediately the spirit and the power of the dream come over us … —we the night-walkers by day! We artists!' [45]

And yet there had been an earlier Nietzschean moment in the 1890s, when poets took up Nietzsche's call. John Davidson was a committed Nietzschean writing in the burly self-aggrandizing manner that Nietzsche advocated for the artist: 'Henceforth I shall be God: for consciousness / Is God'. [46] The first English translations appeared between 1896 and 1899 and were devoured by the poet. He took on an imperialist form of the elect strong man: 'the Englishman *is* the "overman"'. [47] He absorbed Nietzsche's apotheosis of the creative free spirit as atheist, materialist, joyful, elect. His London poems provide a fruitful intertext to Loy's Futurist poetry. Loy's 'blots of sky' recall Davidson's 'The Thames Embankment' where the 'sagging sky' contains 'blots of faintest bronze'. Loy's chaotic *flânerie* was also a Davidson technique: 'There are doubtless many ways of seeing, but for the Londoner … perhaps the best method is the least methodical'. [48] And that wandering gaze on the city features in 'November': 'Deep delight in volume, sound, and mass, / Shadow, colour, movement, multitudes, / Murmurs, cries, the traffic's rolling bass— / Subtle city of a thousand moods!' [49] The collective inclusivity of the gaze is there in Davidson's 'London':

> A rumour broke through the thin smoke
>   Enwreathing abbey, tower, and palace,
> The parks, the squares, the thoroughfares,
>   The million-peopled lanes and alleys,
> An ever-muttering prisoned storm,
> The heart of London beating warm. [50]

There is nothing as radical here as the cross-cutting, deliberately jerky and fusional, fluid poetics of Loy's poem. Still, the core Nietzschean freedom to acquire a city's worth of fleeting identities is shared by Davidson and Loy. The Futurist form of *flânerie* is founded on the Nietzschean premises of the 1890s and 1900s.

Loy was soon to rid herself of Futurism once she registered its misogyny and war-mongering. Marinetti had glorified war and contempt of women in his manifesto, and the proto-fascist politics of his Nietzscheanism came through once the First World War broke. The war gave material and lethal expression to the martial polemics of the London avant-garde. Marinetti had screamed out his war epic 'Zang-tumb-tumb' to a startled London audience in 1913 'with the help of the English artist C. R. W. Nevinson, who banged drums offstage to simulate the noise of battle'.[51] Loy was to purge Marinetti from her work through parody and direct confrontation of the misogyny written into militarism. 'One O'Clock at Night' from the *Three Moments in Paris* sequence is addressed to Marinetti and uses Nietzschean comedy to pillory his 'pugilist' assumptions and 'indisputable male voice' through sarcasm:

> Beautiful halfhour of being a mere woman
> The animal woman
> Understanding nothing of man
> But mastery and the security of imparted physical heat
> Indifferent to cerebral gymnastics
> Or regarding them as the self-indulgent play of children
> Or the thunder of alien gods [52]

The technique is close to Elizabeth Barrett Browning in *Aurora Leigh*: to address the male with an articulation of the kind of subjection expected by patriarchy. Aurora falls into this mode often, even when 'alone'. Loy's 'a mere woman' recalls 'Why what a pettish, petty thing I grow,—/ A mere mere woman, a mere flaccid nerve'.[53] The assumption that women cannot think or talk of intellectual matters recalls Romney's give-away proposal:

> you, Aurora, with the large live brow
> And steady eyelids, cannot condescend
> To play at art, as children play at swords,
> To show a pretty spirit, chiefly admired
> Because true action is impossible.[54]

Romney's condescension is masked behind his ideal of noble womanhood (picturesque merely, with those 'steady eyelids'), just as Marinetti's scorn for women as animal machines dresses its own misogyny up in a fiction of women as beautifully indifferent.

R IS FOR REVOLUTION

Loy's turn against Marinetti signals the emergence of the first twentieth-century wave of feminism after the New Woman movement. It is the sexual revolution of early

modernism which is so starkly different from Victorian prudery, idealism, and reticence. The relations between men and women were to develop in radically new ways,
incorporating experiments in different kinds of bond beyond the heterosexual couple
(think of the two couples of *Women in Love*, with male–male, female–female alliances
consolidating and challenging the male–female); rethinking of sexual identity in the
light of psychoanalysis and human biology (Woolf's espousal of androgyny, group and
collective forms of unconscious union in *The Waves*); advocacy of same-sex relations
(Edward Carpenter, Radclyffe Hall); the challenging of legal censorship of sexual content (Joyce, Lawrence); and the exploration of sexual fantasies, drives, and desires as
triggered by the sexologists such as Havelock Ellis (Joyce's 'Circe' and Molly Bloom's
monologue). The coincidence of this revolution with the emergence of militant feminism with the Suffragettes, birth control campaigning by Marie Stopes, and women's
new experiences of the world of work in the First World War make gender the key and
core object of analysis in modernist writing.

The poetry taking sexual relationships as its subject is contradictory, and it is in the
fissure between two kinds of treatment that the abiding presence of Victorian poetry can
be sensed. D. H. Lawrence's so-called 'poetry of the present' is frankly autobiographical,
a diary-form of writing which follows the feelings and sensations of Lawrence and his
partner through their marriage and beyond. The experiment aimed to capture the full
flow of sensations as they occur, with the Lawrences as exemplars of the new sexual and
emotional freedoms of the new era. Eliot's *The Waste Land* adopts a more sombre, reactionary stance: the new sexual freedom entails loveless, automatic, impermanent union,
desolate sex in soulless cities triggering a spiritual waste land across Europe. The distinction between the two men is not as stark as this might imply. Lawrence embraces the
powers given women by the feminist movements; however, the novels stage the genders
as polarized, with mastery by the male sexual impulse still implicit in the new arrangements. Eliot's poem is hysterically fearful of powerful women and their sexual assertiveness, yet at the same time there is a curious identification with women through the
Tiresias persona, and by way of the bonds structurally set up between the shell-shocked
male voices and the lonely, abused women of the metropolis.

Revolutions will entail reactions, and the feminist movements struck deep into the
imaginations of the male modernist generation. The reactions, though, may be subtler than the rampant misogyny of the avant-garde, or the arrogant powerplay of the
Nietzschean supermen-artists. In Eliot's case the rise of the women's movement drew
him towards a nostalgic music of the seventeenth century, as though to a *nostos* of
more ceremonial relations between men and women. It drew him too back towards the
Victorian era: in lines and poems which summon Victorian women as lost partners and
blood-relatives. The haunting line from 'What the Thunder Said', 'And voices singing
out of empty cisterns and exhausted wells', sings with memory of Victorian verse.[55] Alice
Cary's 'Longings', for instance, speaks of waste places and dream of rain. She longs 'to
make the waste places o'erflow with my strains, / As the meadows' green cisterns o'erflow
with the rains'.[56] 'Marina' accepts the nostalgic pull back to a more innocent womanhood with the I-voice dreaming of his lost daughter, and the poem moves deep in the

'unknowing, half conscious, unknown' backwaters of the mind, back to childhood along the shores of America, back to a garden of child boy and child girl: 'Whispers and small laughter between leaves and hurrying feet / Under sleep, where all the waters meet'.[57] Sentimental verse meets Eliot's in the deep act of nostalgic reminiscence, these lines from New England poet Elizabeth Akers Allen:

> A busy crowd flows through the noisy street,— …
> And crisp snow crackles under hurrying feet.
> Children are hastening school-ward, brisk and gay,
> Young laughing girls, and boyhood rude and bold.[58]

And the lines recall Thomas Moore, 'The Meeting of the Waters' and the rapt nostalgia for the 'Sweet vale of Avoca!'. 'Marina' is about dying feelings for this world as for a lost home, a lost daughter, and the allusion to Moore knits into the emotional texture Moore's Irish melancholy, the regret for 'that vale in whose bosom the bright waters meet' confessed as longing for a lost female body and its vales, 'the belov'd of my bosom'. 'Oh! the last rays of feeling and life must depart', sings Moore, 'Ere the bloom of that valley shall fade from my heart'.[59] Bosomed into Eliot's song is regret for Victorian sentimentality, for the lost simplicities of 'Young laughing girls, and boyhood rude and bold', for the last rays of feeling within a child's dream of girls and boys.

If Eliot allows Victorian verse in to register the gravitational pull back to the sweet childishness of Victorian gender roles, and finds a 'home' in nineteenth-century American women's singing voices, then Lawrence abjures the past, settles on the energies and flows of desire of the moment, of the present day:

> Give me the still, white seething, the incandescence and the coldness of the incarnate moment: the moment, the quick of all change and haste and opposition: the moment, the immediate present, the Now.[60]

The immediacy of the writing is threefold: it entails a notation of the everyday real, a poet's diary, a lover's notebook; also a compositional act of meditation, clearing the mind of everything but the time to hand; and a technical freedom from the past through the adoption of free verse, designed to capture fleeting impression, unshackled by the forms of the past. 'Free verse does *not* have the same nature as restricted verse. It is not of the nature of reminiscence … in free verse we look for the insurgent naked throb of the instant moment'.[61] Yet the poetry Lawrence writes is not quite free of the past. It is a creature of the nineteenth century too, for the poetry of the present and the free verse form that Lawrence identifies as properly 'insurgent' is Whitman's: 'This is the unrestful, ungraspable poetry of the sheer present, poetry whose very permanency lies in its wind-like transit. Whitman's is the best poetry of this kind.' If Whitman's poetry is a wind that acts as *afflatus* for Lawrence, it is because it is sexual, embodied, of the moment in terms of desire; it speaks from 'the *pulsating, carnal self*, mysterious and palpable'.[62] And the poems Lawrence published as exemplary of the poetry of the present summon Whitman's inspiring breath. 'Seven Seals' stages the male lover seeking to seal his loved one's body up with kisses, and begins with an 'insurgent naked throb' which eroticizes the Petrarchan conceit:

> I kiss your mouth. Ah, love,
> Could I but seal its ruddy, shining spring
> Of passion, parch it up, destroy, remove
> Its softly-stirring, crimson welling-up
> Of kisses! Oh, help me, God![63]

But as it progresses, the poem's menace grows, the male will to dominate asserts itself, the seven seals plugging up all her orifices with pornographic/Rosicrucian desire ('Full mid-between the champaign of your breast / I place a great and burning seal of love / Like a dark rose')—climaxing in a fantasy of 'iron kisses' that will encase her in the martial metal of the Nietzschean knight-at-arms:

> So you shall feel
> Ensheathed invulnerable with me, with seven
> Great seals upon your outgoings, and woven
> Chain of my mystic will wrapped perfectly
> Upon you, wrapped in indomitable me.

This creepiness he learned from Browning, but also from Whitman, the Whitman of the excessive love of citizen, soldier, woman, and reader:

> Here to put your lips upon mine I permit you,
> With the comrade's long-dwelling kiss, or the new husband's kiss,
> For I am the new husband, and I am the comrade.
>
> Or if you will, thrusting me beneath your clothing,
> Where I may feel the throbs of your heart or rest upon your hip,
> Carry me when you go forth over land or sea;
> For thus merely touching you is enough, is best,
> And thus touching you would I silently sleep and be carried
>   eternally.[64]

The sexual revolution of modernism caused this radical split in the male modernists' desiring imagination, between the self-infantilizing nostalgia for Victorian domestic ideology and a Nietzschean fiction of indomitable will, touched by Whitmanian eroticism, thrusting the text beneath the clothing of the reader like a dirty secret. In so doing they attempted to seal up the potential of the free women around them and in their mermaid dreams, turning Victoria into Victor, for a time, for a single incarnate moment.

Modernism remembered its Victorian enemy in more ways then I have had time to address. Yeats and the Irish Revival never cut away the bonds that held them to the radical and sentimental poetry of Moore and Mangan. Pound learned as much from Landor, perhaps, as from Browning. H. D.'s poetics sucked deep from the translating traditions of the nineteenth century. The Nietzschean comedy in modernist practices is always tempered by other forms of comedy, music hall as we have seen, but also by Lear and Carroll, by the radical nonsense of the Victorian parlour-room, and by the comic operas of Gilbert and Sullivan. There is an imperial strain too to early modernism, the draw to India and Buddhist writing, derived from the antiquarian and anthropological work of Victorian colonial scholars, and supplemented by Kipling in particular. And a great deal could have been said about the influence of Swinburne, Pater, and Symons on the modernist poets, proving again how all the waters meet at the border between *fin-de-siècle* and the twentieth century. The 'Victor' I have traced stalking the male modernists could also have been more energetically challenged by poets like Hope Mirrlees and her city poems with their take on the *flâneur*. Nevertheless, I hope I have gone some way to demonstrate that Victorianism, as 'forgotten' mother and father to the modernist text, is there as silent partner to the lines, haunting the modernist bodies and stage routines with lost intimacies: 'merely touching you is enough'.

NOTES

1. Wyndham Lewis, 'Enemy of the Stars', *Blast* 1 (1914), 51–87.
2. *Blast*, 23.
3. Ezra Pound, 'Salutation the Third', in *Blast*, 45.
4. Pound, 'Come My Cantilations', in *Blast*, 46.
5. William Aytoun, 'Firmilian', in *A Book of Parodies*, ed. Arthur Symons (London: Blackie & Son, 1908), 289–303.
6. Edgar Fawcett, *Songs of Doubt and Dream* (New York: Funk and Wagnalls, 1891), 226.
7. Pound, 'Vortex', in *Blast*, 154.
8. Pound, 'A Few Don't's by an Imagiste', *Poetry* (1913), 200–06 (201).
9. Frederick Ward, 'A Sea-Shell', in *English Roses* (London: Simpkin, Marshall, Hamilton, Kent, 1899), 371–2.
10. Ford Madox Ford, 'On a Marsh Road', in *The Face of the Night* (London: John McQueen, 1904), 69.
11. Pound, *Gaudier-Brzeska: A Memoir* (New Directions, 1974), 85.
12. Quoted by Pound, *Blast* 1, 154.
13. William Wetmore Story, *Nature and Art* (Boston: Little & Brown, 1844), 14.
14. cf. T. S. Eliot's preface to *John Davidson: A Selection of his Poems* (London: Hutchinson, 1961).
15. Eliot, 'A Loafer', in *Ballads and Songs* (London: John Lane, 1985), 89.
16. James Thomson, *The City of Dreadful Night* (Whitefish, Montana: Kessinger, 2004; 1st pub. 1874), 10.
17. 'I am above all derived from Browning. Why deny one's father?', *The Letters of Ezra Pound, 1907–1941*, ed. D. D. Paige (New York: Harvest, 1950), 218.
18. Pound, *The Cantos of Ezra Pound* (London: Faber and Faber, 1964), 10.
19. Eliot, 'The Method of Mr. Pound', *Athenaeum* (1919), 1065.
20. Pound, letter to Henry Ware Eliot, 28 June 1915, in *The Letters of T.S. Eliot*, vol. 1 (1898–1922), ed. Valerie Eliot (New York: Harcourt Brace Jovanovich, 1988), 100.
21. Pound, 'Sestina: Altaforte', in *Collected Shorter Poems* (London: Faber & Faber, 1984), 28.
22. Pound, 'Three Cantos' no. 1, *Poetry* 10 (1917), 117.
23. Forrest Read, 'Pound, Joyce, and Flaubert: The Odysseans', *New Approaches to Ezra Pound*, ed. Eva Hesse (Berkeley: University of California Press, 1969), 125.

24. The Three Cantos were written as a quest for the most fruitful cultural substitute for Browning's Renaissance, ending with Homer.

25. Pound, 'Mesmerism', *Collected Shorter Poems*, 13.

26. Pound, letter to Henry Ware Eliot, *The Letters of Ezra Pound, 1907–1941*, 100.

27. Pound, letter to Henry Ware Eliot, *The Letters of Ezra Pound, 1907–1941*, 100–1.

28. Pound, 'E.P. Ode pour l'election de son sepulchre', in *Collected Shorter Poems*, 187.

29. Dante Gabriel Rossetti, 'Dis Manibus', in *The Works of Dante Gabriel Rossetti*, ed. William M. Rossetti (London: Elllis, 1911), 246.

30. Andrew Lang, 'Circe's Isle Revisited', in *The Poetical Works of Andrew Lang* (London: Longmans, 1923), 102.

31. Lang, 'François Villon', in *The Poetical Works of Andrew Lang*, 48.

32. Pound, 'Medallion', *Collected Shorter Poems*, 204.

33. Eliot in '*In Memoriam*', *Selected Essays* (London: Faber & Faber, 1951), 328–38 (337).

34. Eliot in '*In Memoriam*' 322.

35. Alfred Tennyson, 'Locksley Hall Sixty Years After', in *Poems of Tennyson*, ed. Christopher Rocks, 2nd ed. (London: Longman, 1987), iii. 158.

36. Eliot, *Inventions of the March Hare: Poems 1909–1917*, ed. Christopher Ricks (London: Faber & Faber, 1996). Cf. Pound's own Tennyson parodies, 'Poems of Alfred Venison', in *Collected Shorter Poems*, 257–68.

37. Eliot, 'Suite Clownesque I', in *Inventions of the March Hare*, 32.

38. Eliot, 'The Love Song of J. Alfred Prufrock', in *The Complete Poems and Plays* (London: Faber & Faber, 1969), 17.

39. Tennyson, 'The Mermaid', in *Poems of Tennyson* i, 214.

40. Tennyson, 'The Merman', in *Poems of Tennyson* i, 213.

41. Friedrich Nietzsche, *The Joyful Wisdom*, trans. Oscar Levy (1910) (New York: Macmillan, 1924), 2.

42. Nietzsche, *Joyful Wisdom*, 71.

43. Dan Stone, *Breeding Superman: Nietzsche, Race and Eugenics in Edwardian and Interwar Britain* (Liverpool: Liverpool University Press, 2002).

44. Mina Loy, 'The Costa San Giorgio', in *The Lost Lunar Baedeker*, ed. Roger L. Coover (New York: Farrar, Straus & Giroux, 1996), 11–12.

45. Nietzsche, *Joyful Wisdom*, 98.

46. John Davidson, 'Ballad in Blank Verse of the Making of a Poet', in *Ballads and Songs* (London: 1895), 22. See John A. Lester, 'Friedrich Nietzsche and John Davidson: A Study in Influence', *Journal of the History of Ideas* 18 (1957), 411–429.

47. Davidson, 'A Poetic Disciple of Nietszche', *Daily Chronicle*, 23 May 1902, 3.

48. Davidson, *Sentences and Paragraphs* (London: Lawrence and Bullen, 1893), 88.

49. Davidson, 'November', in *Holiday and Other Poems* (London: Grant Richards, 1906), 32.

50. Davidson, 'London', in *Ballads & Songs* (London: John Lane, The Bodley Head, 1894), 87.

51. Carolyn Burke, *Becoming Modern: The Life of Mina Loy* (Berkeley: University of Califormia Press, 1997), 168.

52. Loy, 'One O'Clock at Night', in *The Lost Lunar Baedeker*, 15.

53. Elizabeth Barrett Browning, *Aurora Leigh* (iii. 36–37), in *Aurora Leigh, and other poems*, ed. Cora Kaplan (London: The Women's Press, 1978), 115. Aurora is echoing Romney's 'Mere women' (ii. 221).

54. Barrett Browning, *Aurora Leigh* (ii. 227–31), in *Aurora Leigh, and other poems*, ed. Cora Kaplan (London: The Women's Press, 1978), 81.

55. Eliot, *The Waste Land*, in *The Waste Land, Complete Poems and Plays*, 73.

56. Alice Cary, 'Longings', in *Early and Late Poems of Alice and Phoebe Cary* (New York: Houghton, Mifflin, 1887), 168.

57. Eliot, 'Marina', in *Complete Poems and Plays*, 109.

58. Elizabeth Akers Allen, 'February', in *Forest Buds, from the woods of Maine* (Boston: Brown, Bazin & Co., 1856), 189.

59. Thomas Moore, 'The Meeting of the Waters', in *The Poetical Works of Thomas Moore*, 10 vols. (London: Longman, 1840–41), vol. 4, 239.

60. D. H. Lawrence, 'Preface' to *New Poems*, in *The Complete Poems of D. H. Lawrence*, ed. Vivian de Sola Pinto and Warren Roberts (London: Penguin, 1971), 183.

61. Lawrence, 'Preface' to *New Poems*, 184–5.

62. Lawrence, 'Preface' to *New Poems*, 183.

63. Lawrence, 'Seven Seals', in *The Complete Poems*, 153.

64. Walt Whitman, 'Whoever You Are Holding Me Now in Hand', in *Leaves of Grass*, ed. Sculley Bradley and Harold Blodgett (New York: Norton, 1973), 116.

SELECT BIBLIOGRAPHY

Christ, Carol T., 'T. S. Eliot and the Victorians', *Modern Philology* 79(2) (1981), 157–165.

—— *Victorian and Modern Poetics* (Chicago: Chicago University Press, 1984).

Feldman, Jessica R., *Victorian Modernism: Pragmatism and the Varieties of Aesthetic Experience* (Cambridge: Cambridge University Press, 2002).

Joyce, Simon, *The Victorians in the Rearview Mirror* (Athens, OH: Ohio University Press, 2007).

Korg, Jacob, 'The Music of Lost Dynasties: Browning, Pound and History', *ELH* 39(3) (Sep., 1972), 420–440.

Laity, Cassandra, *H. D. and the Victorian Fin de Siècle: Gender, Modernism, Decadence* (Cambridge: Cambridge University Press, 1996).

Perkins, David, *A History of Modern Poetry: From the 1890s to the High Modernist Mode* (Harvard, Mass,: Harvard University Press, 1980).

Pound, Ezra, Review of *Prufrock and Other Observations* by T. S. Eliot, *Poetry* 10(5) (1917), 264–271.

Strachey, Lytton, *Eminent Victorians*, ed. John Sutherland (Oxford: Oxford University Press, 2003; 1st pub. 1918).

Taylor, Miles & Michael Wolff (eds.), *The Victorians since 1901: Histories, Representations and Revisions* (Manchester: Manchester University Press, 2004).

Weatherby, H. L., 'Vanishing Victorians', *The Sewanee Review* 98(1) (Winter, 1990), 96–103.

....

'DISPATCHED DARK REGIONS FAR AFIELD AND FARTHER': CONTEMPORARY POETRY AND VICTORIANISM

....

DAVID WHEATLEY

READERS of Samuel Beckett's poetry who also knew their Victorians would have been puzzled, opening the 2002 edition of his *Poems 1930–1989*, to read a previously unpublished text beginning 'One who never turned her back but / marched breast forward'.[1] The poem was not by Beckett, but a stanza from Browning's 'Epilogue to Asolando' which Beckett had copied to a notebook, whence an unsuspecting researcher had plucked it for inclusion in the Beckett canon. The unBeckettian tenor of Browning's sentiments ('we fall to rise, are baffled to fight better') might have raised suspicions, but the idea of a Victorian poet writing Beckett by proxy is not, in itself, as preposterous as all that. Nine years previously, Christopher Ricks's study, *Beckett's Dying Words*, contained a long extract from a curiously Beckettian poem by the Irish Victorian James Henry, 'So father Adam was his own born son', whose superabundant and complicated genealogy Ricks compares to the 'poor old lousy old earth' passage of Arsene's speech in *Watt*.[2] Another poem of Henry's included in Ricks's *New Oxford Book of Victorian Verse* was strikingly similar to Beckett's 'they come / different and the same' ('Another and another and another / And still another sunset and sunrise, / The same yet different, different yet the same').[3] Again like Beckett, Henry was a ferocious atheist. His complete absence from print other than under Ricks's sponsorship suggested the possibility of a scholarly hoax, but no: in 2002 Ricks's edition of the *Selected Poems of James Henry* pulled off the near-unprecedented feat of introducing a newly canonical poet over a century after his death, and one of whose 'precursors' (to be Borgesian about it, in the counterfactual style of the short story 'Kafka and his Precursors') appeared to be Samuel Beckett. His rediscovery reminds us that influence is more than a one-way-street from past to present, that the Victorians continue to 'read' us too, and repay our readings accordingly, remaining more deeply our contemporaries than we might imagine.

To F. R. Leavis, in his *New Bearings in English Poetry* (1932), it was a matter of urgency that the Victorians *not* be seen as our contemporaries. 'Nineteenth-century poetry, we realize, was characteristically preoccupied with the creation of a dream world,' he declares,[4] testing Tennyson, Arnold, and O'Shaughnessy against the waking reality of the twentieth century and finding them wanting. The unique deficiency of Victorian poetry was to have inherited an enfeebled, daydream version of Romanticism, allowing no protest against the world but that of withdrawal, without having found a new language in which to communicate this *malaise*. Instead, English poetry bobbed along on a sea of post-Victorian froth whose principal merit was to supply Ezra Pound with satirical targets in *Hugh Selwyn Mauberley*. The non-publication of Hopkins' work until 1918 underwrites Leavis's insistence on reading him, not as representative of an alternative strain in Victorian poetry, but as scarcely a Victorian at all. Like Eliot's dissociation of sensibility, Leavis's revisionism rests on any number of untested generalizations, our dissent from which can signify only culpable antiquarianism, as when a bewildered Thomas Hardy protested to Robert Graves that '*vers libre* could come to nothing in England...all we can do is write on the old themes in the old styles.'[5] For the contradictions and blind spots in Leavis's literary history, he need have looked no further than one of the poets praised in *New Bearings*, Ezra Pound, the second of whose *Cantos* opens with a theatrical 'Hang it all, Robert Browning, / there can be but the one "Sordello".'[6] Try as Leavis might to distance the mature Pound from the 'stale cream puffs'[7] of his early work, the continuity between Browning's mid-Victorian monologues and Pound's sprawling epic bodes ill for any attempt to draw a *cordon sanitaire* around post-modernist poetry in English as a Victorian-free zone.

If the past is another country, the nineteenth century is a territory to which the contemporary imagination has usually felt it has automatic rights of access. Andrew Davies' television adaptations of Dickens, George Eliot, and others follow a well-worn route of costume drama and sexing-up, but Victorian poetry has proved less amenable to popularization. The great exception is A. S. Byatt's *Possession* (1990), in which the relationship between Victorian poets Randolph Henry Ash and Christabel LaMotte is discovered by two contemporary academics. As the story unfolds, the poets' work moves more to the foreground of the narration, and what might have seemed an exercise in sophisticated parody (perhaps the most skilfully done in all contemporary fiction) becomes a site of coded revelation. The parallelism between the poets' and the academics' relationship obeys an implicit teleological drive: the impasse reached by the poets can be successfully resolved by their present-day interpreters. Brian Moore's *The Mangan Inheritance* (1979) is a more pessimistic novel about cultural inheritance. Here the poet is real, the Irish Victorian *poète maudit* James Clarence Mangan, but the attempt to reconnect with his patrimony by a latter-day Canadian descendant of the poet implicates him in dark tales of incest and madness. Past and present are locked in a struggle of wills, and while the narrative sets the present the task of completing and resolving the past, Moore reminds us that the present can just as easily be capsized by ill-judged meddling in buried histories we disturb at our peril.

Poetic conversations across centuries will always involve an unsettling of the contemporary voice, if the modern poet is not to lapse into the realm of kitsch Victoriana. Anthony Hecht deploys a muscular contemporary vernacular for 'The Dover Bitch', revisiting Arnold's 'Dover Beach' and subjecting the Victorian sage to some 'Criticism of Life' from his wife on the couple's underwhelming French honeymoon. She resents being thought of 'As a sort of mournful cosmic last resort', the speaker explains, who then outlines in less high-flown terms their alternative arrangements for sweetness and light ('She's really all right. I still see her once in a while / And she always treats me right').[8] The transgressive comedy leans heavily on stereotypes of Victorian prudishness, our amusement at which is not perhaps without a tinge of self-congratulation. The Victorians too faced risks in gazing across the centuries, as Hardy did in his poem '1967', written a century before that date. Belying his usual caution, the poet looked forward to 'A century, which, if not sublime, / Will show, I doubt not, at its prime, / A scope above this blinkered time'.[9] By the time he came to write 'Christmas: 1924', this meliorism was a thing of the past and Hardy conceded that humanity had learned nothing ('After two thousand years of mass / We've got as far as poison-gas').[10] Four years after 1967, meanwhile, Philip Larkin was looking back on Victorian 'fools in old-style hats and coats' in 'This Be the Verse', laughable perhaps but cocooned in the dubious 'innocence' of a former age, as captured in his 1960 poem 'MCMXIV'.[11] Lines of influence between present and past cross and tangle, and inform the contemporary poem on any number of levels. Our belated Victorian Ezra Pound divided poetry into three classes, melopoeia ('wherein the words are charged, over and above their plain meaning, with some musical property'), phanopoeia ('throwing a visual image on the mind') and logopoeia ('the dance of the intellect among words and ideas'),[12] and the work of modern poets who have revisited the Victorian era can be broadly grouped under these headings.

When Tom Paulin champions the anti-Tennysonian prosody of Hopkins, Christina Rossetti and Arthur Hugh Clough, he does so in the interests of a revived non-conformist Victorian melopoeia, which he has grafted in his own work onto his passion for non-standard vernacular English. Phanapoeia more closely characterizes the work of Mick Imlah, whose poems have prosodic engagements of their own with the work of Browning and Tennyson, but are most explicitly concerned with dramatic reanimations of their Victorian settings. Logopoeia is a more difficult concept, but with Geoffrey Hill we find a poet writing modernist sequences which simultaneously reimagine and renew the Victorian inheritance in ways that honour Pound's criteria. More rarely again, a writer will combine two or even all three of these categories. In his 2010 sequence *Oraclau/Oracles,* Hill explores his Victorian family history through, among other things, an engagement with Hopkins' time in Wales, where his study of *cynghanedd* influenced his developing theories of sprung rhythm. Some of the sequence's stanzas are headed 'Welsh apocalypse', and for many readers there will be something apocalyptic about Hill's writing too, in its syncretic condensation of historical vistas, metrical ingenuity, and dialogue with the great departed, in unit after unit of the poem's nine-line stanzas: poetry as *Gesamtkunstwerk.* Here is Hill apostrophizing Hopkins at St Beuno's:

> Spiritual rhetor,
> High Tory hiraeth, *seldomer heartsore*;
> But knew his own mind, minding the ploughshare;
> Knew his flinched heart hooked by the brute hebog;
> Flint under the flensing beat, the havoc.[13]

'Hiraeth' is a grief-struck homesickness and 'hebog' is a hawk. 'Poetry is the plough that turns up time', declared Osip Mandelstam,[14] and with his echoing of Hopkins' imagery in another poem about a hawk, 'The Windhover', Hill too is wringing uncanny harvests from the turned-up soil of the Victorian past. For a writer who has always insisted on poetry as a public rather than private discourse, Hill stands his ground impatiently against labellings of his work as difficult or obscure, with their implied verdict that the pasts convoked by his poetry no longer speak to us today. The corollary of this is the demanding texture of Hill's language, and its bravura displays of wrenching the medium free of the cant and jargon of the day, the degradations 'the age demanded', in *Mauberley*'s reiterated formulation. In 2011 Hill denounced the assumption that Carol Ann Duffy's colloquial style represents a more 'democratic' use of language and not, in his withering description, 'cast-off bits of oligarchical commodity English', the sealed-in idiolect of a language divorced from history.[15] Conversely, when Duffy writes of an anthology of soldier poetry that, for a poet today, it is 'humbling, allowing the voices of those who have been changed by war to speak through us', her use of 'allowing' perfectly epitomizes the present-centred amnesia that causes Hill such dismay.[16]

Not all revisitings of the past can operate at such a pitch of artistic integration as Hill's, however, and most often (not least for Hill himself) there is a painful reckoning with cultural loss to be negotiated before such moments of epiphanic connection. The opening poem of Oliver Reynolds' 1987 collection *Skevington's Daughter* is titled 'Victoriana'; its non-descript title fails to prepare us for its drama of shocking violence. The poem is decked out in the familiar props and bric-a-brac of the era—*The Times*, a train, beards, a brougham and driver, and gentlemen scholars—but something disturbing is lurking beneath the plush period décor. Dr Murray, first editor of the *OED*, is travelling to meet one of his most prolific contributors, W. C. Minor, who gives his address in correspondence as 'Broadmoor, Crowthorne, Berkshire', but omits to mention that he resides at the criminal lunatic asylum there. Serving in the American Civil War as a surgeon-captain Minor had branded a deserter, and on his discharge and emigration to Britain he suffered persecution mania, which led him to murder, as obliquely described in Reynolds' poem; when his condition worsened, in Broadmoor, he cut off his penis. Minor's encounter with Murray goes off awkwardly enough but without incident, and as Murray returns on the train he unpacks the edition of Ovid Minor has given him as a gift, finding 'pages / Dotted with globules of dried glue: / Braille tracks healing the torn paper'.[17] Torn pages can be healed, those 'braille tracks' signs of a loving attention denied the parchment of the similarly scarred deserter's skin. But the deepest wounds of all, to Minor's psyche, will rise to the surface, and out.

Minor returned in old age to the United States, where he was a patient at St Elizabeth's Hospital, where several decades later the young Elizabeth Bishop would visit another mad old man lost in a fantasy world of his own, the disgraced Ezra Pound. Leavis judged the Victorian predilection for fantasy evidence of a fragmented worldview, going down easily in the face of the dissociation of sensibility, but for modern poets, fantasy has often been an attractive entry point into Victorian culture, a revealing fault-line between public and private, the permissible and the taboo. Born a decade after the Victorian era closed, Elizabeth Bishop fills her work with backward glances at the nineteenth century. A youthful infatuation with Hopkins produced the baroque pastiche of 'Hymn to the Virgin'; 'Casabianca' recycles Felicia Heman's single deathless line ('The boy stood on the burning deck'); 'From Trollope's Journal' describes a visit by the novelist to the United States in 1861; and in 'The Gentleman of Shalott' Bishop dramatizes its speaker's unique hinge perspective between the Victorian and modern eras. In exploring her cloistered subject's condition Bishop drew on another painful experience of confinement, that of her mother, Gertrude Bishop, who was institutionalized in Nova Scotia Hospital in 1916, where she remained until her death. For James Joyce, the 'cracked lookingglass of a servant' was the fitting symbol of Irish art, suggesting that nineteenth-century realism would founder on a reality that was itself distorted and elliptic,[18] but for the Gentleman of Shalott alienation has become an intimately physical condition. Where the Lady of Shalott endures a classic Victorian sequestration from the outside world, her male counterpart's situation is more unusual, with the mirror in Bishop's poem appearing to run down his spine. He cannot be sure where reality ends and representation begins:

> He felt in modesty
> his person was
> half looking-glass,
> for why should he
> be doubled?[19]

The question of why images are reversed in mirrors has long preoccupied thinkers, from Plato and Lucretius to Kant and Martin Gardner. One answer lies in the unconscious aspect of our perspective: in holding a book up to a mirror we invert it along its horizontal axis, so that the text reads from right to left. What we assume to be a distortion is in fact a true representation. The Gentleman of Shalott, however, has clearly projected (appropriate verb) responsibility for his identity onto his image ('If the glass slips / he's in a fix—/ only one leg, etc.'). In an inversion of Plato's allegory of the cave, even when he looks at reality he sees only projections. Unlike the Lady of Shalott, trapped in her living death, the Gentleman has reached a state of coexistence with his specular self. His last word on the subject may be '"Half is enough"' but in (distorted) reality he has managed to double his options, just as Bishop does with her Victorian renovation of the modernist lyric.

The fantasy element in the Gentleman of Shalott's self-image is reflected in Bishop's attitude to the past in the monologue 'Crusoe in England', whose eighteenth-century speaker anachronistically quotes from Wordsworth's 'Daffodils'. Even allowing for modernist liberties with chronology, the poem reminds us of the worm holes waiting to swallow the voices of the past and the imaginative effort involved in their retrieval.

The Gentleman of Shalott inhabits a closed-in world, but one over which he can at least exercise some control, whereas the wider world of Victorian poverty and squalor presents a daunting tableau of buried narratives and chaos. Philip Larkin takes one such narrative, a description of a 'ruined' girl in Mayhew's *London Labour and the London Poor*, as the epigraph for 'Deceptions', and Tony Harrison extrapolates one of his 'School of Eloquence' sonnets from the only surviving words of a paperhanger, 'W. Martin', scratched behind a shutter in Dove Cottage (*'our heads will be happen cold when this is found'*).[20] No sooner does Larkin introduce his victim in 'Deceptions', however, than he tactfully backs off ('I would not dare / Console you if I could'),[21] unwilling to appropriate her suffering afresh. How to guarantee the integrity of the latter-day witness? We confront the dilemma-cum-opportunity identified by Christopher Ricks, with Keats in mind, of the 'fundamental double truth... that we are not other people, and so should never think that we can fully imagine their feelings, and yet that we can imagine others' feelings'.[22] In 'The Memres of Alfred Stoker', from *In the Echoey Tunnel* (1991), Christopher Reid incorporates the difficulties of cultural retrieval into the poem itself, the putative life-story of a centenarian still mentally inhabiting the Victorian world of his childhood, two external signs of which are his religious mania and semi-literate delivery. Stoker's extreme old age adds a comic quality to his observations of contemporary life ('its all rite / pece full / ixep the Tee vie / rubige'),[23] reminding us of the fallibility of even authentic testimony.

With the tricks of memory comes guilt, a quality intimately woven into Tony Harrison's negotiations with history, and nowhere more so than in his 1985 poem 'v.'. It is, without question, among the most powerful attempts in contemporary poetry to find a lyric style answerable to the weight of the past, even if the poem is finally unable to settle its differences with history as effectively as it might wish. Inspired by the miners' strike, 'v.' initially situates itself in a line of graveyard elegy traceable back to Gray, but its vision of departed certainties and trades passed on from one generation to the next is solidly Victorian, as is the coal industry that once underwrote the prosperity of West Yorkshire. The past is hierarchical and reassuring: 'Wordsworth built church organs, Byron tanned / luggage cowhide in the age of steam, / and knew their place of rest before the land / caves in on the lowest worked-out seam'.[24] Visiting his parents' grave, the poet is horrified to find it covered in racist graffiti, the handiwork of an unemployed skinhead, whom he then interrogates indignantly. When a film of 'v.' was broadcast on Channel 4 it was greeted with fury by the Conservative press, who saw no difference in Harrison repeating the skinhead's swear words and the offensiveness of this language per se.[25] This is a crass reduction of the poem's dramatic structure, but 'v.' is not without a peculiar reductiveness of its own. Harrison identifies strongly with the radical tradition, and when 'v.' begins in Beeston Cemetery by assigning the dead the names of Romantic poets, we might assume that Harrison bridles at the annexation of radical poetic energy to *bürgerlich* respectability, a decline that matches that of the young Romantic Wordsworth into the Victorian laureate who wrote sonnets in favour of the death penalty. In his ignorance, mistaking the poet's French (*'cri de coeur'*) for Greek, the skinhead cannot be expected to see past the assumption that culture is the property of the moneyed classes (the same assumption that licenses a teacher's interruption of Harrison's Yorkshire-accented reading of 'Cockney Keats' in 'Them and [uz]', ingrained Victorian respectability trumping the Romantic poet's non-standard accent).[26] Setting up a series of warring opposites ('Hindu/Sikh, soul/body, heart v. mind, /East/West, male/female'),[27] Harrison exposes the patronizing irony of any desire he might feel to speak for the skinhead: the skinhead, he reveals, is Harrison himself, or what he would have become had he remained in Leeds, festering in poverty. With this blow to Harrison's self-image the poem strikes a blow against the premature aestheticization of painful experience, and its reduction to an object of cultural consumption.

Yet this is not quite the conclusion reached by 'v.'. Having unveiled the skinhead's shock identity, the poem effectively dismisses him, fudging rather than resolving the uncomfortable questions he has raised, such as the overlap between his aggressive racism and the folksier version of the same prejudice displayed by the poet's father. When the poet engages with the skinhead and turns his swear words back on him the linguistic convergence is striking, but self-dramatization comes at the expense of wider social critique. The 'je' of Harrison's skinhead is henceforth insufficiently 'autre', to abuse the line of Rimbaud parroted by the poet in 'v.', and the poem's focus begins to contract. As the poet makes his way home one opposition, that of man and wife, is made to do duty for the entirety of the oppositions explored by the poem ('Home, home to my woman, where the fire's lit'),[28] imposing a resolution on the poem that duplicates the Victorian aestheticization of poverty and suffering which the poem seemed at such pains to reject. In the act of probing and denouncing the aesthetic ideology that drained the radical force of Romanticism, Harrison inexplicably succumbs to it too, producing a piece of Victoriana in the culpable sense of that term. In amidst its sound and fury, the poem makes its peace with funereal respectability more easily than it imagines, and the burden of history remains unlifted.

The pull of kitsch Victoriana will always be strong, but it too has enabled moments of genuine inspiration such as Seamus Heaney's 'The Biretta', where the genre scene depicted in Matthew Lawless's painting 'The Sick Call' is 'all / Solid, pathetic and Irish Victorian'.[29] *Station Island* confers a Victorian gloss on Heaney's Ulster childhood in 'The Railway Children', while 'The Birthplace' transfers his usual vocabulary of *lares* and *penates* to Thomas Hardy's Dorset ('Everywhere being nowhere, / who can prove / one place more than another?').[30] Heaney returns to Victoriana in the first of the sonnets in 'Clearances', when the story of his Protestant-born great-grandmother being abused in the street is rendered as '"The Convert", "The Exogamous Bridge" / ...a genre piece'.[31] A potent ingredient in Irish Victorian kitsch is Celticism of the Arnoldian kind, where scenes of peasant life are made to pass through the filtering sensibility of the foreign observer, if British, or auto-exoticizing observer if Irish. One such Irishman was the Tyrone-born William Carleton (1794–1869), a Protestant convert who enjoyed popular success with his *Traits and Stories of Irish Peasantry*. Heaney encounters his shade in the long poem 'Station Island' and is treated to another collection of generic Victoriana: Ribbonmen, St Patrick's Day parades, 'flax-pullings, dances, summer crossroads chat'[32] (not that the kitsch versions of these things did not precede and outlive Victorian times). Heaney has long been adept at moving between worlds, but to a sceptical critic such as David Lloyd this is evidence, not of skill but of complicity: Lloyd speaks of 'the seeming coherence' of Heaney's success and 'a discourse whose most canonical proponent argued for Celtic literature as a means to the integration of Ireland with Anglo-Saxon industrial civilization'.[33] This is harsh, but serves as a reminder of the political sensitivities surrounding Irish Victorianism (James Clarence Mangan owed his iconic nationalist status in Ireland to the blocking by his editors of any perceived affinity with his English contemporaries). The career of the young W. B. Yeats is the perfect example: even as the Countess Cathleen of his 1892 play makes the ultimate sacrifice to prevent the selling of the Celtic soul among her starving tenants, Yeats himself was marketing the Celtic soul as a literary curiosity to the jaded palettes of Victorian Britain. Where Harrison or Hill place their Victorian subjects in querulous juxtaposition with the contemporary, Heaney's is a more valedictory vision, but if this is nostalgia it is as much warning as wish-fulfilment. Cultural memory comforts and imprisons us at once, rendering up less the past in itself than the motley in which it takes refuge, a melancholy index of lostness, the Victorian priest 'Sad for his worthy life and fit for it'.[34]

Another Irish poet who has powerfully revisited the Victorian age is Ciaran Carson. Its imperial legacy is built into the fabric of Carson's Belfast: 'Balaclava, Raglan, Inkerman, Odessa Street', runs a list of street names in 'Belfast Confetti'. 'John Ruskin in Belfast' is a brilliant meditation on art and history, and among the outstanding contemporary poems on the nineteenth century. For Ruskin, passionate aesthete and scourge of Victorian philistinism, an industrial city such as Belfast was a battleground. As he approaches the city, 'the storm-cloud of the Nineteenth Century / Began to wheel', and Ruskin compares himself to Turner strapped to the mast of the *Ariel*. Ruskin is not without his own moments of Celticism in *The Mystery of Life and Its Arts*, as when he suggests that the 'kind Irish hearts' of his Irish listeners will be better disposed towards 'the truthful expression of a personal feeling than to the exposition of an abstract principle'.[35] Later in his lecture he contrasts two pieces of early artwork, one progressive in tendency and the other flawed, a 'corrigible Eve, and an incorrigible Angel', but, as he adds, 'I grieve to say, that the incorrigible Angel was also an Irish Angel!'[36] This is the passage incorporated into his poem by Carson, as Ruskin condemns the artist's *naïveté* ('*the missal-painter draws his angel / With no sense of failure, as a child might draw an angel*'), but with an implied justification in the childlike and excessively 'generous-hearted' nature of the Irish character, whether in the nineteenth century or a thousand years before.[37] Most tellingly of all, the artist has omitted to give the angel a mouth. In Carson's hands, however, this silence acquires a painful eloquence. The possibility of giving a voice to the voiceless dead is one that has exercised many contemporary Irish poets, including Seamus Heaney (most notoriously in the bog poems of *North*), or Eavan Boland in her consideration of the famine and its legacy, 'Achill Woman', but Carson's achievement here is to grant the angel powers of historical witness without putting words in its (absent) mouth:

That blank mouth, like the memory of a disappointed smile,
   comes back to haunt me.
That calm terror, closed against the smog and murk of Belfast:
   Let it not open
That it might condemn me. Let it remain inviolate.[38]

Turner's 'The Dawn of Christianity' hangs in the Ulster Museum in Belfast, and for Carson's Ruskin it becomes an agent of reconciliation between the 'opalescent mirror' of art and the violence of the imperial project, whether British or Roman. Ruskin ponders the holy family's flight into Egypt and the 'Massacre of Innocents, the mutilated hands and knees of children', lines that resonate deeply with the symbology of Ulster's Red Hand as the poem transforms itself into a *Kindertotenlied* for the child victims of the Northern Irish Troubles. The angel is an unlikely witness to the nightmare of history, but Ruskin too addresses us across an obstacle-fraught divide. Where David Lloyd condemned Seamus Heaney for lingering traces of Victorian Celticism, Carson feels no need to disinfect Ruskin's discourse of its (to our mind) simplifications and stereotypes. If anything, the poem is all the more powerful for implicating its speaker in the same imperial discourse it sets out to condemn.

Carson's 2003 collection *Breaking News* contains a sequence, 'The War Correspondent', devoted to the Crimean War and the work of the Belfast-born reporter for *The Times,* William Howard Russell.[39] Much of the poem is near-verbatim recycling of Russell's words. Victorianism need not exclude modernist or postmodernist experiment: Pound's feelings about the Victorians may have been ambivalent, but as he showed in *Mauberley,* a satirical return to the Victorian past can end up disarming even the most implacable avant-gardist. Peter Reading is hardly that, but throughout his career combined collage techniques and daring postmodernist narratives with a vein of anarchic Tory despair that make him an obvious inheritor of one Victorian at least for whom Pound had nothing but contempt—A. E. Housman. The early poem 'New Year Letter' inspects Housman's grave in Ludlow churchyard while noting the absence of his poems from the local library. It is not through recognition or readers that Housman lives on, but a desperate underclass of prisoners, drunks, and the homeless. Tom Paulin has painted Reading as a critic of the injustices of modern Britain (and even as an enemy of the 'reactionary preciosity' of Geoffrey Hill),[40] but much of the power of Reading's political poems comes from a blunt refusal to analyze or explain, preferring the simpler pleasures of execration. 'Shropshire Lads', from *Ob.,* begins with a sound bite of Tony Blair's ('Clear Beggars from Streets, says Blair'), before noting the cider-swilling Shropshire lads queuing to buy their booze from the local supermarkets: 'Oh yes, even in Salop, they are there, / anathemas of Tony fucking Blair'.[41] Pound suspected a high degree of sublimated masochism in Housman's doomed young men, and again *contra* Paulin, the reader will sometimes feel a perverse glee on Reading's part as his violent drunks assault a granny tottering to the shops. Drinking in Reading is not just the preserve of violent street gangs, and when the poet salutes a vintage wine, often in mock-Oriental style, we are close to the spirit of Edmund Fitzgerald. 'I drank wine and wept', cries a Chinese soldier returning from the wars to find his house in ruins and his wife long fled. In epigrammatic poems such as this ('From the Chinese', from *Work in Regress*; there are dozens like it),[42] Reading triangulates classical Chinese poems or those of the Greek anthology with the wine-bibbing wisdom of Fitzgerald's Rubáiyát, to moving and elegiac effect, for all the panoramas of violence and death that form their backdrop.

Reading's love of the classics has led him to experiment with quantitative metres in English, allying him to Robert Bridges rather than Housman. The subtlety of the results has not always been appreciated, as when one of the judges of the Whitbread Prize complained that Reading's *Stet,* which won the prize in 1986, 'doesn't even scan'.[43] The combination of foregrounded squalor in his subject matter and archly behind-the-scenes erudition is typical Reading, but when his work breaks down into a series of wordless metrical annotations he comes close to the spirit of Pound's parody of Housman in 'Mr Housman at Little Bethel' ('Come, tumtum Greek, Ulysses, come').[44] The nineteenth century also features in his 1988 sequence *Final Demands,* whose narrator presents a series of family papers discovered in a house-clearance. Reading reproduces rambling, inane poems in mock-copperplate font ('The Trees in Ashbourne Park are Green / The Flowers are really Glowing'),[45] interspersing these with a series of letters from the Second World War that culminate in a grim report of a soldier's death. The Victorian enigma of an old man and a hieroglyphic manuscript remains unexplained, 'conceal[ing] some strange sad mystery'.[46] The book ends with one of Reading's signature reversions to holograph, as the 'rustle of old gratuitous scrivenings' unravels into (once again) crossed-out prosodic notation. One of the last words in the sequence is 'papyrus', which may call to mind Pound's poem of that name from *Lustra,* in which a Sapphic fragment is presented amid ellipses as a strange and resonant *objet trouvé* from antiquity.[47] Here though, as Isabel Martin observes, 'Nothing survives—not words, not letters, not poetry books'.[48] Yet as cultural apocalypses go, Reading's remains deeply informed by the Victorian legacy that ends up reduced to dust in *Final Demands*. Paradoxically, decay too can number among the ways in which the past perpetuates itself.

As a poem about memory and its vanishing point, *Final Demands* could be described as an elegy for elegy, that most Victorian of genres. Tennyson's *In Memoriam* was a best-seller in its day, and a favourite of Queen Victoria's, and elegy has featured disproportionately on the few occasions when contemporary poetry has reconnected with a mass readership: three of the five poetry volumes to have been awarded the Whitbread/ Costa Book Award have been series of elegies for a spouse: Douglas Dunn's *Elegies,* Ted Hughes' *Birthday Letters,* and Christopher Reid's *A Scattering* (a fourth, Jo Shapcott's *Of Mutability,* was on the quasi-auto-elegiac subject of recovery from cancer). Nostalgia for elegy is also nostalgia for the poet's lost public status since Tennysonian times: directed by the Oxford Professor of Poetry at the Poet Laureate, Hill's attack on Carol Ann Duffy is a latter-day attempt to assert a public role for poetry in the life of the nation. Yet, as the Victorians themselves knew very well, returns to the past are not without inherent risk. In 'The Zoologist's Bath', Mick Imlah introduces us to the Victorian zoologist Arthur William Woolmer, who argued that land species would 'strive to return to their original element', culminating in a rebirth of the merman.[49] Savouring these anti-Darwinian regressive fantasies in his bath, Imlah's monologuist confidently expects that 'Before the hour, I shall have a fin'.[50] The skill with which Imlah teases the reader (Arthur William Woolmer is sadly fictional) while simultaneously renovating the Browningesque monologue is a masterly exercise in, and critique of, neo-Victorian engagements with the past. Much of the best contemporary poetry in a neo-Victorian vein combines homage and subversion in this knowing way. Lewis Carroll's nonsense verse depends on a subtle balance between anarchy and formality which has eluded many of his would-be successors, but in Frank Kuppner he has found a worthy contemporary inheritor, specializing in madcap scholar figures and learned parodies, notably in *Second Best Moments in Chinese History* and *A God's Breakfast*. Roy Fisher grafts modernist forms onto Victorian cityscapes in the sequences *City* and *A Furnace,* and in 'Eclogue' Michael Hofmann pithily juxtaposes contemporary decline with Victorian self-belief by way of underpinning classical myth. In 'Dante Gabriel Rossetti, *The Orchard Pit*', Peter McDonald offers a contemporary rewriting of the Victorian poet's dark visions of necrophilic love. His Rossetti is a 'man who been close to death', reporting back from the furthest reaches of the imagination, but placing himself at mortal risk to do so.[51]

I began by positing variously fragmented levels of response to the Victorian past in contemporary poetry, while suggesting Geoffrey Hill as a writer in whom the closest approximation to a fully integrated response occurs. No other modern poet has grappled longer or more rewardingly with his Victorian inheritance: in the *Collected Poems* of 1985 there are poems on the Pre-Raphaelites and John Bacchus Dykes, the narrator's 'brooding' on Ruskin's *Fors Clavigera* in *Mercian Hymns,* and poems on British India and 'The Idylls of the King' in the sonnet sequence 'An Apology for the Revival of Christian Architecture in England'. How alive is Hill's revivalism, and how much a matter of literary taxidermy? In interview Hill likes to emphasize the radical dimension of his conservative allegiances, but among his critics there have always been readers unconvinced by his ability to 'distinguish...a literary pastiche from a poem which can honour its influences', in the words of Tom Paulin, for whom the rhetoric of (Hill's) 'Idylls of the King' is 'straightforwardly Tennysonian', that is, fustily reactionary.[52] There is a luxuriance to Hill's Victorian visions, but never without a countermanding impulse to probe and hold to account; if the 'warheads of mushrooms' on which 'Idylls of the King' closes are nuclear warheads, the poem's preceding sylvan idyll too becomes retrospectively compromised and contaminated.[53] In 'A Pre-Raphaelite Notebook', Hill presents the fleshiness of Pre-Raphaelite art as a response to lost Romantic innocence or grace, but the pleasures quickly cloy and sicken: 'The God-ejected Word / resorts to flesh, procures carrion'.[54] Decadence becomes artistic auto-cannibalism, condemned to devour and regurgitate itself, 'Salvation's travesty' a 'stale head / sauced in original blood'.[55]

Paulin has championed the work of marginal or dissident Victorians, but misfit though he was, Hopkins's style of radicalism was closer to Hill's than Paulin allows; and by extension the Hill who has claimed kinship with not just Hopkins but Richard Oastler and William Cobbett as a 'Tory radical' is a more complex political figure than we might assume from Paulin's negative verdict. Paulin disapproves too of the epigraph to 'An Apology for the Revival of Christian Architecture in England' from Coleridge's

Anima Poetae, 'the spiritual, Platonic old England...', perhaps seeing in it a forerunner of the Powellite nationalism Hill echoes in *Mercian Hymns* XVIII. While Coleridge declined from youthful radicalism into a Conservative old age, Paulin prejudges the tone of both the epigraph and Hill's attitude to it. Coleridge did not quite survive into the Victorian period, but the fate of the radical Romantic legacy as the century progressed deeply preoccupies Hill. In 'The Death of Shelley', from the sequence 'Of Commerce and Society', the poet is swept away by the tide of history while the stolid carvings with 'unchanging features / Of commerce' remain in place. Romantic radicals give way to high-minded Victorian improvers such as John Bacchus Dykes and Ruskin, and the burdens of poverty and injustice, which by now begin to shade into memories of the poet's own family, take on an appearance of tragic immutability, as in *Mercian Hymns* XXV ('Brooding on the eightieth letter of *Fors Clavigera*, I speak this in memory of my grandmother, whose childhood and prime womanhood were spent in the nailer's darg').[56]

Hill's radicalism has come increasingly to the fore since *Collected Poems,* in his prose as well as his poetry; his dialogue with Hopkins in particular has been one of the animating passions of his recent work. Hopkins is one of only two nineteenth-century poets to whom Hill devotes whole essays in his *Collected Critical Writings* (the other is Whitman). Hill seizes on Hopkins' concept of 'bidding', by which he means 'the art or virtue of saying everything right *to* or *at* the hearer...and of discarding everything that does not bid, does not tell'.[57] As a precept of forceful communication, this is comparable to the letter to Dixon in which Hopkins compares Browning to a man 'bouncing up from table with his mouth full of bread and cheese and saying that he meant to stand no blasted nonsense'.[58] Both examples privilege the emotive, conative, and phatic elements of communication, in Roman Jakobson's terms (examples might include: 'Yuck!', 'Hey there!' and 'Can you hear me?' respectively) over any accompanying message. In line with his shift away from the symbolist *richesse* of his early work, the later Yeats was fond of signalling the rhetorical devices at work in his poems ('Another emblem there!'), and there is a strongly self-dramatizing, phatic vein in late Hill too, as in the square-bracketed hecklings of *The Triumph of Love,* which we might derive from Hill's love of Ken Dodd and Frankie Howerd and the Victorian music-hall tradition behind them.

One context in which abrupt emotive utterances might be called for is the delivery of judicial verdicts, a subject on which Hill has had much to say in connection with poetry and politics, in particular as centred on the figure of Ezra Pound. Writing on Pound's fascist disgrace, Hill notes that modern poetry often 'yearns for this sense of identity between saying and doing...but to Pound's embarrassment and ours it discovers itself to possess no equivalent for "hereby"'.[59] As Maximilian de Gaynesford has noted, Hill too has moments of nostalgia for such exercitive privileges, as in *The Triumph of Love* ('They have conceded me /—I think, beyond question—/ power of determination but without / force of edict'[60]—while at other times dismissing such ambitions for his work with impatience and derision. The only consolation (poetry is a 'sad / and angry consolation', Hill insisted in *The Triumph of Love*),[61] would be the successful raising of poetry to the level of performative utterance, honouring the bond of its word. I began with F. R. Leavis's hopes for a modernist poetics that would exchange the defeatism and interiority of the Victorians for a new vigour and engagement, but for Hill even Leavis's lodestar T. S. Eliot failed to escape as easily as all that from the dissociation of sensibility he had diagnosed. In 'Dividing Legacies' Hill argues for the difference in Eliot's work between the 'pitch' of the early Eliot and the inferior 'tone' that supplants it by the time of *Four Quartets,* a style of self-assured jadedness comparable to the 'Parnassian' side of Tennyson diagnosed by Hopkins.[62]

This accusation has not gone unchallenged: writing on Hill 'under the sign of Eliot and Pound' in *True Friendship,* Christopher Ricks disputes the justice of so tidy a division ('I am unable to fathom just what Hill means by "pitch"')[63]. In any case, the concertedness of Hill's onslaught on Eliot risks overstating the case or suggesting motives closer to home, in a desire not to surrender his own late work to any recognizable 'tone', to be diagnosed and attacked in turn by a future disciple of Hill's keen to come into his or her own by symbolically overturning Hill's authority. Hill engages in 'Dividing Legacies', but with no obvious or juridically binding outcome. Paradoxically then, this poet in whom the Victorian legacy and its modernist aftermath are most thrillingly alive is also the poet in whom they remain most warringly divided. Like the soldier in the final poem of 'Funeral Music' 'Crying to the end "I have not finished"',[64] Hill refuses anything as falsifying as a resolution in this epochal skirmish. As we have seen, Hill's 2010 sequence *Oraclau/Oracles* explores the poet's Welsh background through the figure of a great-grandfather, but uses Hopkins' residence at St Beuno's to further ponder the Victorian condition. The worlds of chapel and industry are bridged in Hill's sober hymns to the wonders of Victorian engineering:

> Thrust from the Avon's gorge
> The mathematics of Brunel emerge
> Into light's buffeting, the winds at large;
> Those who do well engaging grief and grace
> As grand suspensions meeting in mid-space.[65]

The contemporary poets who have engaged both the 'grief' and the 'grace' of the Victorian legacy engineer 'suspensions meeting in mid-space', across which commerce and traffic are possible but with pratfalls and plummets also possible at any time. Nevertheless, it is to this hazardous journey across the centuries that we are indebted for the accounts we find in *Oraclau/Oracles* and elsewhere of the Victorian age's 'Dispatched dark regions far afield and farther'.[66]

Notes

1. Samuel Beckett, 'Cimetière St. André', in *Poems 1930–1989* (London: John Calder, 2002), 45. The erroneous title derives from a French poem of Beckett's of the 1970s.
2. Christopher Ricks, *Beckett's Dying Words* (Oxford: Clarendon Press, 1993), 185–186.

3. James Henry, 'Another and Another and Another', in Christopher Ricks, ed., *The New Oxford Book of Victorian Verse* (Oxford: Oxford UP, 1987), 331.
4. F. R. Leavis, *New Bearings in English Poetry* (London: Pelican, 1972; 1st pub. 1932), 14.
5. Robert Graves, *Goodbye to All That* (London: Jonathan Cape, 1929), 377.
6. Ezra Pound, *The Cantos* (London: Faber and Faber, 1986), 6.
7. Ezra Pound, 'Foreword', *A Lume Spento and Other Poems* (New York: New Directions, 1965), 7.
8. Anthony Hecht, 'The Dover Bitch', *Collected Earlier Poems* (Oxford: Oxford University Press, 1991), 17.
9. Thomas Hardy, '1967', in *The Complete Poems*, ed. James Gibson (London: Macmillan, 1976), 220.
10. Hardy, 'Christmas: 1924', *Complete Poems*, 914.
11. Philip Larkin, 'This Be the Verse' and 'MCMXIV', in *Complete Poems*, ed. Archie Burnett (London: Faber and Faber, 2012), 88, 60–61.
12. Ezra Pound, 'How to Read', in *Literary Essays of Ezra Pound*, ed. T. S. Eliot (London: Faber and Faber, 1954), 25.
13. Geoffrey Hill, *Oraclau/Oracles* (Thame: Clutag Press, 2010), 5.
14. Osip Mandelstam, 'Word and Culture', in *The Collected Critical Prose and Letters*, trans. Jane Gary Harris and Constance Link (London: Harvill, 1991), 113.
15. Geoffrey Hill, 'Poetry, Policing and Public Order', lecture delivered in Oxford, 29 November 2011. See also Alison Flood, 'Carol Ann Duffy is "Wrong" About Poetry, Says Geoffrey Hill', *The Guardian*, 31 January 2012.
16. Carol Ann Duffy quoted in Nick Duerden, 'War Poetry Is As Alive As It Ever Was', *The Independent*, 28 October 2011. I am indebted to Tim Kendall for this point.
17. Oliver Reynolds, 'Victoriana', in *Skevington's Daughter* (London: Faber and Faber, 1985), 19.
18. James Joyce, *Ulysses*, ed. Declan Kiberd (London: Penguin, 1992), 6.
19. Elizabeth Bishop, 'The Gentleman of Shalott', in *Poems, Prose, and Letters*, ed. Robert Giroux and Lloyd Schwartz (New York: Library of America, 2008), 7.
20. Tony Harrison, 'Remains', in *Selected Poems* (London: Penguin, 1984), 180.
21. Larkin, 'Deceptions', in *Complete Poems*, 41.
22. Christopher Ricks, *Keats and Embarrassment* (London: Oxford University Press, 1976), 117.
23. Christopher Reid, 'The Memres of Alfred Stoker', in *In The Echoey Tunnel* (London: Faber and Faber, 1991), 52.
24. Tony Harrison, 'v.', in *Selected Poems* (London: Penguin, 1984), 236.
25. See Harrison, *v.* (Newcastle: Bloodaxe, 2000).
26. Harrison, 'Them and [uz]', in *Selected Poems*, 122.
27. Harrison, *Selected Poems*, 238.
28. Harrison, 'v.', in *Selected Poems*, 247.
29. Seamus Heaney, 'The Biretta', in *Seeing Things* (London: Faber and Faber, 1991), 27.
30. Heaney, 'The Birthplace', in *Station Island* (London: Faber and Faber, 1984), 35.
31. Heaney, 'Clearances', in *The Haw Lantern* (London: Faber and Faber, 1987), 25.
32. Heaney, *Station Island*, 66.
33. David Lloyd, *Anomalous States: Irish Writing and the Post-Colonial Moment* (Dublin: Lilliput Press, 1993), 37.
34. Heaney, 'The Biretta', in *Seeing Things*, 27.

35. John Ruskin, *The Mystery of Life and Its Arts* (New York: John Wiley & Son, 1869), 5.

36. Ruskin, *The Mystery of Life and Its Arts*, 29.

37. Ruskin, *The Mystery of Life and Its Arts*, 29.

38. Carson, *Belfast Confetti* (Oldcastle: Gallery Press, 1989), 98.

39. For more on Carson's depiction of Russell, see my '"Pushed Next to Nothing": Ciaran Carson's *Breaking News*', in Elmer Kennedy-Andrews, ed., *The Poetry of Ciaran Carson* (Dublin: Four Courts Press, 2009), 45–65.

40. Tom Paulin, 'Junk Britain: Peter Reading', in *Minotaur: Poetry and the Nation State* (London: Faber and Faber, 1992), 290.

41. Peter Reading, 'Shropshire Lads', in *Collected Poems 3: Poems 1997–2003* (Tarset: Bloodaxe, 2003), 62.

42. Reading, 'From the Chinese', in *Collected Poems 3*, 38.

43. Quoted in Isabel Martin, *Reading Peter Reading* (Newcastle: Bloodaxe, 2000), 158.

44. Ezra Pound, 'Mr Housman at Little Bethel', in *Literary Essays of Ezra Pound*, ed. T.S. Eliot (London: Faber and Faber, 1954), 64.

45. Peter Reading, *Final Demands* in *Collected Poems 2: Poems 1985–1996* (Newcastle: Bloodaxe Books, 1996), 140.

46. Peter Reading, *Final Demands* in *Collected Poems 2*, 121.

47. Ezra Pound, 'Papyrus', in *Selected Poems and Translations*, ed. Richard Sieburth (London: Faber and Faber, 2010), 44.

48. Isabel Martin, *Reading Peter Reading*, 186.

49. Mick Imlah, 'The Zoologist's Bath', in *Birthmarks* (London: Chatto & Windus, 1988), 57.

50. Imlah, *Birthmarks*, 61.

51. Peter McDonald, 'D. G. Rossetti, The Orchard Pit', in *Adam's Dream* (Newcastle: Bloodaxe, 1996), 44.

52. Tom Paulin, 'A Visionary Nationalist: Geoffrey Hill', in *Minotaur: Poetry and the Nation State* (London: Faber and Faber, 1992), 281.

53. Hill, 'Idylls of the King', in *Collected Poems* (London: Penguin, 1990), 162.

54. Hill, 'A Pre-Raphaelite Notebook', in *Collected Poems*, 167.

55. Hill, 'A Pre-Raphaelite Notebook', in *Collected Poems*, 167.

56. Hill, *Mercian Hymns* XXV, in *Collected Poems*, 129.

57. Gerard Manley Hopkins, *The Letters of Gerard Manley Hopkins to Robert Bridges*, ed. Claude Colleer Abbott (London: Oxford University Press, 1955), 160.

58. Hopkins, *The Correspondence of Gerard Manley Hopkins and Richard Watson Dixon*, ed. Claude Colleer Abbott (London: Oxford University Press, 1955), 74.

59. Hill, 'Our Word is Our Bond', in *Collected Critical Writings*, 163.

60. Hill, *The Triumph of Love*, 3; cf. Maximilian de Gaynesford, 'The Seriousness of Poetry', *Essays in Criticism* 59 (1), 2009, 1–21.

61. Hill, *The Triumph of Love* (London: Penguin, 1998), 82.

62. Hill, 'Dividing Legacies', in *Collected Critical Writings*, ed. Kenneth Haynes (Oxford: Oxford University Press, 2008), 366–379 (377–9).

63. Christopher Ricks, *True Friendship: Geoffrey Hill, Anthony Hecht, and Robert Lowell Under the Sign of Eliot and Pound* (New Haven: Yale University Press, 2010), 33.

64. Hill, 'Funeral Music', in *Collected Poems*, 77.

65. Hill, *Oraclau/Oracles*, 16.

66. Hill, *Oraclau/Oracles*, 17.

SELECT BIBLIOGRAPHY

Carson, Ciaran, *Belfast Confetti* (Oldcastle: Gallery Press, 1989).

Harrison, Tony, *Selected Poems* (London: Penguin, 1984).

Hill, Geoffrey, *Collected Poems* (London: Penguin, 1990).

——*Collected Critical Writings*, ed. Kenneth Haynes (Oxford: Oxford University Press, 2008).

——*Oraclau/Oracles* (Thame: Clutag Press, 2010).

Imlah, Mick, *Birthmarks* (London: Chatto & Windus, 1988).

Larkin, Philip Larkin, *Complete Poems*, ed. Archie Burnett (London: Faber and Faber, 2012).

Pound, Ezra, *Literary Essays of Ezra Pound*, ed. T. S. Eliot (London: Faber and Faber, 1954).

——*A Lume Spento and Other Poems* (New York: New Directions, 1965).

——*The Cantos* (London: Faber and Faber, 1986).

——*Selected Poems and Translations*, ed. Richard Sieburth (London: Faber and Faber, 2010).

Reading, Peter, *Collected Poems 2: Poems 1985–1996* (Newcastle: Bloodaxe Books, 1996).

——*Collected Poems 3: Poems 1997-2003* (Tarset: Bloodaxe, 2003).

PART III

READINGS

CHAPTER 18

RHYME, RHYTHM, VIOLENCE: ELIZABETH BARRETT BROWNING ON SLAVERY

CAROLINE LEVINE

POETRY is a craft of repetition-and-difference. Rhythm and rhyme organize words according to repeated patterns that poise us between past and future, establishing relationships of recurrence and setting up expectations for echoes and resonances to come. They unite words through shared sounds and tempos, but they also relentlessly differentiate, as rhymed words echo one another without becoming identical, and tempos mark transformation or disjunction over time as well as periodic recurrence. Poetry is thus an art of iterability and pace, of resonance and reverberation. For this reason, poetic thinking is often not reducible—or even translatable—into other kinds of argument.[1] But I want to suggest here that there are certain political thoughts that poetry is particularly adept at thinking. In the readings that follow, I will show how Elizabeth Barrett Browning theorizes political violence, using patterns of poetic form to afford a precise and rigorous understanding of the unjust workings of slavery.

I have argued elsewhere that politics, like poetry, is a matter of form. I define politics as the organizing, shaping forces that arrange experience, imposing categories and distinctions, and thus putting us in our places. Political forms can range from shapes (the panopticon or separate spheres) to rhythms (the patterns of industrial labour) to hierarchies (racism and bureaucracy).[2] Barrett Browning uses her art's practices of unity and division, repetition and substitution, to think through the patterns which politics and poetry share, and to draw from her knowledge of poetic forms some powerful and surprising political conclusions.

This essay will begin with a reading of the first of Barrett Browning's antislavery poems, 'The Runaway Slave at Pilgrim's Point' (1848), a dramatic monologue in the voice of an American slave who has murdered her child. She speaks as white pursuers close in on her. The poem has been both condemned and praised for its raw intensity, its strong diction, and willingness to confront violence.[3] In recent years, scholars have paid close attention to its publication in the US abolitionist periodical, *The Liberty Bell*.[4] But I wish to shift attention here from the usual focus on the poem's emotional power and its contexts to consider its structuring principles, both poetic and political. The metrical and rhyme schemes of the poem are irregular, unfamiliar, sometimes even off-kilter. Barrett Browning certainly knew how to abide by strict forms, and she handled traditional metres with ease and fluency, from the skilful blank verse of *Aurora Leigh* to Petrarchan sonnets. Why, then, does she opt for such an idiosyncratic set of patterns for her first poem about slavery? I will argue here that she is deliberately working against the conventional aesthetic goals of unity and harmony because she is thinking through the problem of divided political communities, riven with violence and hypocritical in their rhetoric. The last part of this essay will turn to Barrett Browning's two other poems on slavery, 'Hiram Powers' Greek Slave' (1850) and then, much more briefly, 'A Curse for a Nation' (1856). Recognizing that forms reverberate across time and space, the poet urges her readers to refuse local and specific loyalties and identifications in order to register the terrifying portability of unjust political forms across the world.

POETIC FORM, POLITICAL FORM

'The Runaway Slave at Pilgrim's Point' opens with a complex and extended meditation on sameness and difference. The slave bends her knee on a mark where centuries before pilgrims had arrived and thanked God for their freedom. An 'act of historical repetition'[5] begins, as the slave puts herself in the place of the pilgrims, who themselves changed identities on the same spot: 'Where exile turned to ancestor'.[6] A third substitution then takes place:

> O pilgrims, I have gasped and run
> All night long from the whips of one
>   Who in your names works sin and woe!
>
> (12–14)

Suddenly it is not only the slave but also the slaveholder who takes the place of the pilgrims, as the violent whips operate 'in the name of' the pilgrims. The substitutions of the opening stanzas (exile turns into ancestor turns into master *and* slave) thus produce a horrific discord: both the slave and the master can claim to be substitutions of the first pilgrims, but one echoes them as 'exile', desperately hungry for freedom, while the other echoes them as 'ancestor', possessing a national sovereignty that legitimates violence.

As if this were not complex enough, a fourth kind of repetition and substitution turns out to be at work in these early lines. 'I have run through the night; my skin is as dark' (5) the slave explains, positing an equivalence between the darkness of the night and the

darkness of her skin. Now God and nature join national history as patterns of relationship which the slave struggles to understand:

> I am black, I am black.
>   And yet God made me, they say:
> But if He did so, smiling back
>   He must have cast his work away
> Under the feet of his white creatures,
> With a look of scorn, that the dusky features
> Might be trodden again to clay.
>
> (22–8)

There is a hint of the infanticide to come, here, as the slave imagines the dark creature
violently pressed into the ground, but there is also a pattern of return: the dusky-fea-
tured slave is 'trodden again to clay', as if becoming one with an original medium. Barrett
Browning offers us a stark repetition ('I am black, I am black'), but also an impossible
division: if God made black people, he must also have sacrificed his own creatures, feeling the very un-godlike emotion of scorn.

> And yet, He has made dark things
>   To be glad and merry as light:
> There's a little dark bird sits and sings,
>   There's a dark stream ripples out of sight,
> And the dark frogs chant in the safe morass,
>   And the sweetest stars are made to pass
> O'er the face of the darkest night.
>
> (29–35)

The first 'And yet' in line 23 marked God's scorn, while the second, in line 29, marks his
love. And out of this double negative, this contradiction of a contradiction, emerges
another equivalence: now the skin colour of the slave does not set her side by side, unfavourably, with white-skinned people, but equates her with all dark things, and here a
new possibility emerges—perhaps God has intended black people to be 'glad and merry
as light'. A set of similarities echoing across the natural world holds out the promise
of God's love. The logic of race slavery, then, works through repetition, substitution,
equivalence, and division. The slave is like the exiled pilgrims, like the dark night, like
the clay underfoot, and like the beautiful things of nature. But crucially, each repetition,
each equation, also ends in dissonance: a contradictory legacy of the pilgrims (exile–
ancestor), a divided God (scorning–loving), and a split nature (ugly–beautiful).

   If patterns of repetition and division structure the poem's understanding of slavery
in these early stanzas, we can see how the poetic forms of rhythm and rhyme organize
experience in comparable ways. Rhythm, Derek Attridge writes, moves 'through *time*,
recalling what has happened (by repetition) and projecting itself into the future (by setting up expectations)'.[7] Barrett Browning's stanzas each have seven lines—an odd number in that it is both unusual and uneven. Rhyme royale, a seven-line stanza form that

had been mostly out of use since the Renaissance, is the closest model here, but this poem breaks rhyme royale's usual patterns, following an ababccb pattern that is not at all common in English poetry.[8] Metrically, the poem does not follow a strictly familiar pattern, either: it is a loose iambic tetrameter with numerous 'extra' syllables.[9] Barrett Browning's rhythm marks time in an uncomfortable, uneven way: there is enough regularity of beat here to feel some rhythmic recurrence, but it is also repeatedly excessive, enacting a tempo that is at once repetitive and dissonant. And if Barrett Browning's metre refuses to settle into an easy transmission from past to future, her rhyme scheme enacts another set of complex relations of similarity and difference. Rhymes begin with different sounds and end with identical ones. It is a form of equivalence that is never identity. And rhyming produces an experience of distance and connectedness across two registers, sound and time: on the one hand, the phonic experience of two rhyming words in their near-identity, and on the other, the pace at which rhymes happen—the number of beats that separate the rhymed sounds from each other. In 'The Runaway Slave at Pilgrim's Point', Barrett Browning structures each stanza as an opening quatrain, followed by a couplet, and then a single line that links back to the second and fourth rhymed lines. Every line bears a relation to another line; some are closer than others, but all are linked through repetition as well as difference. At some moments the similarities move close together; at others they are distant reverberations. There are many degrees of closeness in rhyme, not a single, stark opposition between sameness and difference.

How should we read the relations between the political forms explored in the poem and its poetic forms? In the past two decades, literary critics have tended to read literary forms as reflections or expressions of historical ones.[10] Suggestive echoes certainly invite a comparison between them. Barrett Browning's uneven rhythms give us an experience of time that is like the dissonant legacy of the pilgrims. And race, like rhyme, emerges as a structuring of sameness and difference, where slaves are both equivalent to free people and disconnected from the dominant white majority, both identical and crucially separated. Sometimes the likeness feels close, promising equality across persons; at other times a vast gap yawns, as the slave feels like dirt trodden underfoot by upright persons.

But I want to propose turning our usual reading habits upside down, and thinking of the poetic forms as primary, the rhythms and rhymes of poetry training us to grasp and understand the patternings of the social world. Barrett Browning points us to repetitive forms that shape experience across registers, from slavery to religion to poetic metre; in this respect, each is itself a kind of repetition of the others, national divisions echoing divided poetic forms resonating with the split patterns of race. None emerges as the basis or origin of the others. Rather than reading poetic form as an expression of politics, then, I want to suggest instead that for the poet, at least, rhythm and rhyme might come first: poetic patterns of repetition and difference offer Barrett Browning models for thinking through the political patterning of national history and racial hierarchy. As an accomplished thinker in and through rhyme, Barrett Browning immediately grasps the problem of racial violence as a political structure of echoes, equivalences, and differences.

NUMERICAL PATTERNS

The section that follows the poem's opening is a story, as the slave recounts the events that have led her to Pilgrim's Point. She tells of her love for another slave; the lover is killed; the narrator is raped, and she then kills the child born from the rape. The middle section of the text shifts the shape of its political forms somewhat, moving from forms of equivalence and substitution to patterns of pairs and unities. Throughout the poem, Barrett Browning focuses on repetitions and divisions, but the middle of the text casts political forms as particular numerical patterns: twos and ones. And at the end of the poem she structures our understanding of politics through multiple numerical orders, all overlaid on top of one another.

First, the two slaves in love believe that there is power in pairing: 'Oh, strong enough, since we were two, / To conquer the world, we thought' (66–67); 'We were two to love and two to pray' (86). But a second, dramatically different pair follows: 'moaning, child and mother / One to another, one to another' (110–11). Far from the sentimental attachment a reader might expect between mother and child, Barrett Browning offers us a stark division: 'A child and mother / Do wrong to look at one another / When one is black and one is fair' (138–40).

Both pairs end in violence. The first couple is destroyed by the slaveholders, who forbid the pleasure and power threatened by the slaves' love and so destroy the lover. The other pair, the mother and child, begins in division, but the poem's second act of violence, the death of the child, paradoxically reunites the two. 'All, changed to black earth,—nothing white,—A dark child in the dark! . . . And thus we were reconciled, / The white child and the black mother, thus' (185–86, 190–91). Both pairs, in the end, become one rather than two. The first concludes with the solitude of the slave who has lost her lover—'And now I cry who am but one' (90). The second ends in the supposed harmony that reconciles child and mother through violent death. Thus Barrett Browning makes clear that both pairings and unities enact a whole range of possibilities: coupling can bring like things close, such as the two slave lovers, or they can keep close things linked but horrifyingly separate, like the black mother with her white child. Oneness can mean a desperate solitude, or it can mean the power that might come from joining forces. There is no easy, straightforward correlation between certain forms of organization, like pairs, and their political implications: no form can lay claim to a single politics. But at the same time, Barrett Browning suggests, one cannot think the violence of slavery without such forms as pairs and unities. Thus the poet's rigorous and subtle kind of formalist thinking tracks the plural potentialities of social forms.

The concluding stanzas of the poem bring together the repetitions and substitutions of the opening with the couples and unities of the middle. The divisions now take shape on a different scale: not the intimate ties between two lovers, but the nation as a whole:

Whips, curses, these must answer those!
 For in this UNION you have set
Two kinds of men in adverse rows,
 Each loathing each; and all forget
The seven wounds in Christ's body fair,
 While HE sees gaping everywhere
Our countless wounds that pay no debt.
                                                      (232–38)

The nation pretends to be one—'this UNION'—but is in fact divided into two kinds of men, who forget Christ's seven wounds, a number which divides even further, into 'countless wounds'. The poem descends into a kind of infinite division and dissolution.

A poem that has been dealing with pairs and unities ends by dividing into multiple numerical patterns. Perhaps it is not surprising that the poet of 'How do I love thee? Let me count the ways' should be fascinated by numbers, a synonym for metre, a way to apprehend love, and here, a formal principle for grasping political relationships. Ones and twos—unions and divisions—structure political experience in complex ways. The United States is only hypocritically united, pretending to be one while actually being divided into two warring groups. Union can mean power—the joining together of like and unlike into a single harmonious whole—but it can also be used as a weapon to cover over deep division. Christ's sacrifice is a complex experience of numbers, too, in that it represents an exchange—seven wounds for the sake of all humanity—only to be echoed by an infinite mockery of this seven-fold sacrifice, as slaves are forced to exchange more for less, suffering uncountable wounds for precisely nothing in return.

The numbers invoked in this late stanza find immediate corollaries in the poetic structure. Each seven-line stanza could be said to repeat Christ's seven wounds, and each one ends with a single line that, like the solitary slave, claims only a distant echo of its fellows. The slave's willingness to repeat certain words and phrases twice over ('I am black, I am black!'; 'I will tell you low, low...') and the couplets that make up the fifth and sixth lines of each stanza draw insistent attention to pairing at the level of poetic form. The 'adverse rows' in the third line call up the poetic lines themselves, whose rhyming relation can be connective and divisive at the same time, like the nation. And with the capitalized word 'UNION', Barrett Browning's metre compresses three syllables into two, just like the nation, which pretends to be one, covering over its internal conflict and plurality. The poem's refusal of a familiar formal harmony—the jolting off-rhythms and the seven-line rhyme scheme—offer up an insistent feeling of difference rather than a balanced, concordant oneness. Like the nation, the poet seems to suggest, poetry itself is divisible by multiple and contending numerical orders that do not add up to a neat single whole but rather structure the poem according to numerous overlaid patterns: the couplet, the quatrain, the loose four-beat metre, the seven-line stanza, the solitary concluding line.

In this embrace of division over harmony, Barrett Browning recoils from one of the most traditional aims of aesthetic form. From Aristotle to Cleanth Brooks, the goal of art has often been seen as the achievement of a complex unity, triumphing over 'the apparently contradictory and conflicting elements of experience by unifying them into a new pattern'.[11] By contrast, Barrett Browning offers various numerical patterns, both poetic and political, all organizing her material at the same time: ones both solitary and divided, pairs both at war and at one, quatrains and tetrameter, sevens, and uncountable acts of violence. No single pattern unifies or dominates all of the others; there is no over-arching wholeness that can assimilate such difference. And neither politics nor poetry is primary here: both operate according to multiple principles of organization which echo and resonate with one another without any one ever becoming simply an index or reflection of the other.

And yet, on reading the poem through to the end, we might be tempted to conclude that there is one pattern that has been structuring the text all along: the relationship of return. The slave comes back to the site of the nation's origin, wonders whether God has cast black people back to their original clay, and returns her infant to herself by burying it in the dark earth—both separating and connecting the pair. The last line of each seven-line stanza resonates with the second and fourth lines above, offering a feeling of return. There is another kind of return at work across the content of the poem too—patterns of exchange. The slave trades looks with her lover, 'And from that hour our spirits grew / As if unsold, unbought' (64–65). Christ's exchange and the slaves' sacrifice for no return in stanza 34 are in this sense a repetition of a form that subtly shapes experience across different regis-ters in the poem: return as equivalence. What is the proper return for a slave's sacrifice—what is its equivalent? The poem has also asked: what is the equivalent of a pilgrim—the master or the slave? And is the slave equivalent to a material, a colour, a white woman, a martyr? The political aspiration to racial equality also of course takes shape here as a return—a movement back from imposed inequality to rightful equivalence.

In formal terms, return, exchange, and equivalence are all patterns of movement in two directions—away into difference and back into sameness—and as such they are structured like rhyme and rhythm. In keeping with the pairs and unities of the poem's middle, return involves processes of dividing and rejoining. Could we see return, then, as an overarching structuring principle for the poem? Yes, I think so but, crucially, this is not the same as saying that the poem resolves itself in or through this form. After all, some returns to oneness cover over division—the hypocritical union that pretends to join its people; some pairs are not split but joined—the slave lovers; and some pairs are both joined and divided—the slave mother and her dead child. In short, Barrett Browning does not treat any of the myriad returns that structure the poem as successful achievements of oneness or sameness. For the slave, return remains always dependent on internal division, and sometimes, as in the impossible exchange for the slaves' count-less sacrifices, fails altogether. In this poem, return always confronts degrees of distance and difference as much as it links and compares.

In fact, return is not really a single form at all but a way to think about patterns of dif-ferent kinds that structure the poem's form and its politics—recurrence and repetition, exchange and equivalence, substitution and origin, reverberation and delay. The pattern of return does not invite us to think a single thought. It is, rather, Barrett Browning's way of recognizing how pervasively our experience is structured according to sameness and difference, including racial division and the aspiration to equality, communities and rights, temporal intervals and inheritances, justice and union, history and inheritance. The form of the return takes shape disparately as discordant metre, lopsided rhyme, divided legacies, unequal exchanges, imposed inequality, and uneven grades of distance and difference. It is a common principle of politics and poetry. And I want to suggest that this is exactly why the poet is well placed to theorize political violence: it is a lifetime spent thinking about rhyme and rhythm that trains the poet to grasp the powerful, painful, omnipresent pattern of uneven return as a structure of political life.

Travelling form

If 'The Runaway Slave at Pilgrim's Point' invites us to look for patterns of recurrence that reverberate across registers of experience, Barrett Browning's later poems about slavery, 'Hiram Powers' Greek Slave' (1850) and 'A Curse for a Nation' (1856) push her insights about repetitive form to an ambitious new conclusion. Writing against the assumption that each of us has a primary responsibility to our own community or nation, Barrett Browning makes the case that political responsibility travels because political forms themselves return—patterns of sameness-and-difference repeating across time and space. In recent years, many literary and cultural critics have urged a move away from formalism precisely because form is too abstract and generalizing. Stuart Hall, for example, writes scathingly that formalism 'over-generalizes...so as to decontextualize and flatten out all the significant differences between the experiences of people in different situations, who are members of differing social and cultural groups, with access to different forms and quantities of economic and cultural capital'.[12] But if Barrett Browning is right, to insist on understanding political situations as radically distinct from one another—singular rather than repetitive—allows one to miss the ways that unjust forms organize social experience across time and space.

In the late 1840s, an American sculptor named Hiram Powers exhibited a work called 'The Greek Slave' in the US and Britain. The sculpture was a huge success wherever it went: New York, Washington, New Orleans, the Crystal Palace in London. The sculpture is crafted in white marble, suggesting a debt to ancient art. But in fact Powers' work had a closer referent: the Greek War of Independence from the Ottoman Empire that had taken place through the 1820s. Reports alleged that the Ottomans had sold Greek Christian women as slaves. Audiences praised the sculptor for conveying the dignity of a woman stripped to nakedness except for her Christian cross, rising above the shame of her condition with purity and faith.[13]

But there was something brazenly missing in these admiring reports. With the exception of a few abolitionist periodicals and a famous satirical cartoon in *Punch*, almost no one—including the visitors in New Orleans—bothered to connect Hiram Powers' 'Greek Slave' to North American slavery. With its conspicuous whiteness, its Christian cross, and its stylistic evocation of ancient Greece, Powers' work allowed visitors to express their horror at Greek enslavement while blithely ignoring a slavery that was closer at hand. In response, Elizabeth Barrett Browning wrote a sonnet that insists that we notice injustice wherever it appears:

> They say Ideal beauty cannot enter
> The house of anguish. On the threshold stands
> An alien Image with enshackled hands,
> Called the Greek Slave! as if the artist meant her
> (That passionless perfection which he lent her,
> Shadowed not darkened where the sill expands)
> To so confront man's crimes in different lands
> With man's ideal sense. Pierce to the centre,
> Art's fiery finger! and break up ere long
> The serfdom of this world. Appeal, fair stone,
> From God's pure heights of beauty against man's wrong!
> Catch up in thy divine face, not alone
> East griefs but West, and strike and shame the strong,
> By thunders of white silence, overthrown.[14]

The poem begins by reporting conventional wisdom: ideal beauty and suffering cannot inhabit the same space. Immediately, however, the poet complicates this claim: on the threshold of the house of anguish stands a figure that should not be there, does not belong—'an alien image with enshackled hands / Called the Greek Slave'. A figure that gestures *both* to aesthetic beauty *and* to human suffering, the Greek Slave explodes the distinction between art and anguish, standing in a space between the two.

If the sculpture here gestures in two directions—both to art and to suffering—line 7 points in multiple directions: 'As if the artist meant her / To so confront man's crimes in different lands'. This sudden move to different lands probably comes as a bit of a surprise. Only three lines earlier the figure is 'Called the Greek Slave', and there is no mention of anywhere other than Greece so far in the poem. But the end of this sentence calls the act of 'calling' into question. She may be *called* the Greek Slave, but it is as if the artist meant her to confront people in many lands. In other words, if we thought that the artist called the sculpture the Greek slave because he intended to represent a Greek slave, his intention takes a global detour: the title pointing to Greece but the sculpture itself pointing around the world. And in fact the rhyming patterns of the sonnet have been steadily moving us outward: the still sculpture, which 'stands', resonates with the opening out of the house of anguish, which 'expands', inviting us to turn our attention to 'different lands'. Rhyme, here, allows the still, single, particular art work to reverberate with a sprawling otherness, the inescapable similarity of the words binding them together despite their difference.

Line 8 brings another unsettling dislocation: 'Pierce to the centre, art's fiery finger', exhorts the poet. The centre of what, exactly? We have just been in different lands, and it is not possible to find the centre of a scattering. It is intriguing, too, that the word centre comes at the turn, or volta, of the sonnet. This is not the exact middle of the poem, which would be one line above. *Volta* in Italian means turn, a moving centre or pivot. In this particular sonnet the volta is also thoroughly dynamic, since it is enjambed. If art is to pierce to a centre, then, it is a location in the middle of a global scattering, and at the shifting, pivoting turn of the poem's form. Of course, one plausible reading is that the centre refers back to the beginning of the poem: back to the house of anguish, where art had been poised on the threshold. Now it is time to pierce to the centre, to find the hub or heart of human suffering—but the inside of the house of anguish has also expanded suddenly here to become the serfdom of 'this world'. The centre, then, is the centre of a globe which has no centre, the moving centre of suffering that is housed everywhere.

As the poem reaches its final three lines, the sculpture, which has been frustrating and multiplying its referents, is asked to move in opposing directions. The poet exhorts the sculpture to catch suffering upward and to throw strength down; it is asked to address 'not alone / East griefs but West'—presumably, that is, not only Ottoman, but also US, slavery. Even the famous and paradoxically thunderous 'white silence' of the last line points in two opposing directions: both toward the whiteness of the marble sculpture and toward the white audiences who refuse to speak out against slavery.

The title of Barrett Browning's poem might seem to point in one direction, then, toward a sculpture by Hiram Powers. But the sculpture in turn points to Greek slavery, which then points us not only east to Turkey but also west, to US slavery, and then, ultimately leads us to the 'serfdom of this world'. Up and down, east and west, the political power of art is to point away from itself in multiple directions. If we understand powerful social institutions and hierarchies as forms, as Barrett Browning does in 'The Runaway Slave at Pilgrim's Point', then this insistence on a dispersed indexicality begins to make sense. To point to one place and one place only is to miss the fact that the violent form of slavery repeats itself in at least two contexts: modern Greece and the United States. Slavery is, after all, a pattern of relations, a model for organizing society and labour—a form: sorting humans into owners and objects, and entitling possessors to legal and economic power over their objects; it is a portable kind of organization, capable of imposing itself on experience across centuries and continents. In 'The Runaway Slave', Barrett Browning worked through resemblances among multiple kinds of social and aesthetic organization, making sense of the violent, contradictory, divisive patterns of US slavery through patterns of echoing similarity and difference. In 'Hiram Powers' Greek Slave', she follows this formal insight to a frightening new recognition: as a formal patterning of sameness and difference, slavery itself can reverberate across the world.

At the same time that Barrett Browning is urging attention to the form of slavery as it travels around the world, she is writing in a poetic form that also travels, organizing experience across time and space: the fourteen-line sonnet. Barrett Browning opts for the Petrarchan form, which ends in a sestet rather than a couplet. Notably, her rhyme scheme here is even more repetitive than many sonnets in this Italian tradition: the concluding sestet, which usually rhymes two three-line pairs (cde cde), here rhymes the first, third, fourth, and sixth lines (cdc cdc), producing a relentless, uncompromising echo effect, and drawing the already repetitive rhymes close in an extra couplet (lines 10–11) that is not a routine feature of Italian sonnets. At the same time, the poem is highly enjambed, and its syntactical complexity makes it almost impossible to read in a steady forward fashion. If a reader needs to double back to make sense of the poem's meaning, it becomes difficult to hear the rhyme, no matter how repetitive it might be. Formally, then, Barrett Browning seems to point in multiple and even opposing directions, just as she does politically: she gives us a highly traditional poetic form, and points the reader both toward that form *and* away from it, both toward the resonating patterns of the rhymed words and away from them. Fascinated by patterns of repetition and difference, the coupling of rhymes that can be both pulled close together and pushed surprisingly far apart, Barrett Browning thinks through the political impulse towards separation in a form that relentlessly joins as much as it distinguishes.

This interest in sameness and difference is again important for understanding slavery. It is crucial to recognize that slavery is not exactly the same from place to place. It is repeated with differences, like rhymed words—echoing but not identical. In the Greek context, for example, slavery does not sort people by colour, as it does in the United States' context. But Barrett Browning suggests that to allow the particularity of Greek slavery to hide from us its likeness to African slavery is itself the gravest of mistakes. To understand white slaves as fundamentally different from black ones frees us to care about the one and to ignore the other. If we insist on feelings of difference, we miss the kinships that take shape on the level of form.

I have noted that the sonnet form, like slavery, travels and repeats, structuring experience according to its strict form across contexts. This may sound like a trivializing of slavery, but Barrett Browning's example suggests instead that a habit of thinking through repetitive, portable aesthetic patternings may help us to see how political violence, too, is patterned and transportable. Like slavery, the sonnet form inhibits and confines. Like slavery, it can have many contents—beauty and suffering, blackness and whiteness. And like slavery, it is not a natural or a necessary form but an artificial one, a crafted pattern of relationships. Unlike the slave, the sonneteer has the freedom to move in and out of her form's constraints, and in this case she resists confinement as much as she embraces it, expanding the form beyond its focus on a single moment to point to all of the world's suffering. But like the slaveholder or citizen, the poet makes—and therefore has the power to remake—relationships. Literary critics interested in politics have tended to think of social and political life as the 'real', set against the carefully crafted artifices of literary art. But if we consider the panopticon or the timetable or slavery as forms of social organization, we can see that our usual distinctions between real social forms and unreal aesthetic ones does not hold. Both literary forms and social formations are equally real in their capacity to organize experience, and both are equally *un*real in being artificial, contingent constraints that can be remade. Thus the portable, repetitive patterns of rhyme, rhythm, and the sonnet offer crucial insights into slavery without collapsing all experience into a single, flattened, unthinking sameness. And Barrett Browning suggests that an attention to reverberating formal similarity, which goes in all directions, produces a better, more responsible political and poetic thinking than a rigid embrace of local particularity.

Travelling responsibility

Not everyone realized that Barrett Browning's poem 'A Curse for a Nation' (1856) was also a poem about US slavery. Written in Italy, and sent 'over the Western sea,'[15] it took the form of a curse, indicting an unnamed nation for cruelty and hypocrisy. Some saw the main target as Britain and accused Barrett Browning of unpatriotic feeling.[16] I want to glance quickly at this poem here by way of a conclusion to suggest that it is no accident that readers could not decide on the poem's referents: it builds on the logic developed in 'The Runaway Slave' and 'Hiram Powers' Greek Slave' to reveal patterns of repetitive form and reverberating responsibility.

The poem opens with an angel who calls on the poet to 'Write a Nation's curse for me / And send it over the western sea'. The poet tries to shirk the task. She does not want to condemn the United States because of a double kinship with Americans: on the one hand, she is connected to them by blood and feeling, 'brothers . . . across the sea, / Who stretch out kindly hands to me' (11–12); on the other hand, she feels the corruptions and wrongdoings of her own nation so powerfully that it seems hypocritical to blame another: 'Evermore/ My heart is sore / For my own land's sins'. But it is precisely 'Because thou hast strength to see and hate / A foul thing done within thy gate', the angel declares, that she is the one who must write the curse. Alike hypocritical, the two nations are paradoxically linked by their internal division, echoing one another in splitting apart, and the poet must risk splitting apart herself, in cursing her brothers, for the very reason that she recognizes the resonance between them. The poem, here, becomes like a political echo chamber. Divisions also echo across registers in the poem: the poem has two parts: the command to curse and the curse itself; it begins with two voices, moving back and forth between the exacting angel and the shrinking, reluctant poet; it switches between two nations, as the poet constantly compares her homeland to the slaveholding United States. The final word of each stanza of the curse, '"Write"', also points in multiple directions, as Katherine Montweiler writes: 'Is the directive to "write" the antidote to the curse? Or is it a command to the poet herself to continue her divine labour? "Write" is also a pun on "right".'[17]

In the end, there is no end to the directions responsibility must travel: it must 'Go, wherever ill deeds shall be done'. And this is Barrett Browning's political, as well as her poetic, conclusion. Poetry and slavery, nations and stanzas: none of these are reducible to each other, but the poet allows their forms to resonate against each other, using poetry's patterns of likeness and difference to think through constraint and resistance, national union and racial difference, hypocrisy and responsibility. Since poetic forms, like political ones, travel and repeat, they can train us to respond to the unjust forms that shape experience, alarmingly, everywhere.

NOTES

1. Denis Donaghue makes this argument in 'Teaching Literature: The Force of Form', *New Literary History*, 30 (1999), 7.

2. Caroline Levine, 'Strategic Formalism: Toward a New Method in Cultural Studies', *Victorian Studies*, 48 (2006), 625–657.

3. See Melissa Schaub, 'The Margins of the Dramatic Monologue', *Victorian Poetry* 49 (2011), 557–568, and Tricia Lootens, 'Publishing and Reading "Our EBB"', *Victorian Poetry*, 44 (2006), 487–506.

4. See, for example, Majorie Stone, 'Elizabeth Barrett Browning and the Garrisonians', in Alison Chapman, ed., *Victorian Women Poets* (Woodbridge: Brewer, 2003), 33–56.

5. E. Warwick Slinn, *Victorian Poetry As Cultural Critique: The Politics of Performative Language* (Charlottesville: University of Virginia Press, 2003), 57.

6. Elizabeth Barrett Browning, 'The Runaway Slave at Pilgrim's Point', in *The Complete Poetical Works* (Cambridge: Riverside Press, 1900), 192.

7. Derek Attridge, *Poetic Rhythm: An Introduction* (Cambridge: Cambridge University Press, 1995), 4.

8. One early example is George Herbert's 'The Flower' (1633). Among Victorian poets, Algernon Charles Swinburne uses it in his poem 'Before the Mirror', inscribed to the painter Whistler, in 1866; James Thomson follows it in *The City of Dreadful Night* (1874), as does Robert Bridges in *Eros and Psyche* (1894) and Thomas Hardy in 'The Going' (1912).

9. See Nigel Fabb, *Language and Literary Structure* (Cambridge: Cambridge University Press, 2002), 121–122.

10. Herbert F. Tucker, for example, reads the unusual prosody of Barrett Browning's 'Cry of the Children' as revealing the uncomfortable disjuncture between the embodied time of human life and the jolting experience of factory labour. 'Of Moments and Monuments: Spacetime in Nineteenth-Century Poetry', *MLQ*, 58 (1997), 289. Similarly, Ivan Kreilkamp suggests that Victorian poetry could be read as offering up metrical experiences of social 'shock…mobility, acceleration, discontinuity, the transitory, the elusive and the ephemeral'—'Victorian Poetry's Modernity', *Victorian Poetry*, 41 (2003), 609.

11. Cleanth Brooks, *The Well Wrought Urn* (New York: Harcourt, 1942), 195.

12. David Morley and Kuan-Hsing Chen, *Stuart Hall: Critical Dialogues in Cultural Studies* (London: Routledge, 1996), 327.

13. For the sculpture's context, **see** Jennifer DeVere Brody, *Impossible Purities: Blackness, Femininity, and Victorian Culture* (Durham and London: Duke University Press, 1998), 67–70.

14. Barrett Browning, 'Hiram Powers' Greek Slave', in *Complete Poetical Works*, 198.

15. Barrett Browning, 'A Curse for a Nation', in *Complete Poetical Works*, 423.

16. See Dorothy Mermin, *Elizabeth Barrett Browning: The Origins of a New Poetry* (Chicago: University of Chicago Press, 1989), 234–35.

17. Katherine Montwieler, 'Domestic Politics: Gender, Protest, and Barrett Browning's Poems before Congress', *Tulsa Studies in Women's Literature*, 24 (2005), 311.

SELECT BIBLIOGRAPHY

Brody, Jennifer DeVere, *Impossible Purities: Blackness, Femininity, and Victorian Culture* (Durham and London: Duke University Press, 1998).

Brophy, Sarah, 'Elizabeth Barrett Browning's "The Runaway Slave at Pilgrim's Point" and the Politics of Interpretation', *Victorian Poetry*, 36 (1998), 273–288.

Levine, Caroline, 'Strategic Formalism: Toward a New Method in Cultural Studies', *Victorian Studies*, 48 (2006), 625–657.

Lootens, Tricia, 'Publishing and Reading "Our EBB": Editorial Pedagogy, Contemporary Culture, and "The Runaway Slave at Pilgrim's Point"', *Victorian Poetry*, 44 (2006), 487–506.

Mermin, Dorothy, *Elizabeth Barrett Browning: The Origins of a New Poetry* (Chicago: University of Chicago Press, 1989).

Montwieler, Katherine, 'Domestic Politics: Gender, Protest, and Barrett Browning's *Poems before Congress*', *Tulsa Studies in Women's Literature*, 24 (2005), 291–317.

Schaub, Melissa, 'The Margins of the Dramatic Monologue: Teaching Elizabeth Barrett Browning's "The Runaway Slave at Pilgrim's Point"', *Victorian Poetry*, 49 (2011), 557–568.

Slinn, E. Warwick, *Victorian Poetry as Cultural Critique: The Politics of Performative Language* (Charlottesville: University of Virginia Press, 2003).

Stone, Marjorie, 'Cursing as one of the Fine Arts: Elizabeth Barrett Browning's Political Poems', *Dalhousie Review*, 66 (1986), 155–173.

—— 'Elizabeth Barrett Browning and the Garrisonians', in Alison Chapman, ed., *Victorian Women Poets* (Woodbridge: Brewer, 2003), 33–56.

Tucker, Herbert F., 'An Ebbigrammar of Motives; or, Ba for Short', *Victorian Poetry*, 44 (2006), 445–465.

CHAPTER 19

....

TENNYSON: ECHO AND HARMONY, MUSIC AND THOUGHT

....

RUTH PADEL

TENNYSON knew little about music but his musicality came out when the greatest violin-ist of the age gave him a private performance. Joseph Joachim played, and Tennyson said he liked 'the poetry of the bowing'.[1] It is very unusual for a non-player to realize that it is the bow-arm, not the left hand with its showy vibrato and swoops up the fingerboard, which determines the sound. Like breathing for a singer, bowing creates tone, colour, phrasing, pause, tension and release, and above all connective energy. Tennyson spotted what Joachim's art depended on and called it 'poetry' because his depended on it too.

We often describe sonic imagination in terms of the ear, which stresses responsive-ness to sound. But how poets put words together is also conditioned by their experience of vocalizing, the physical use of their voice. Tennyson's mastery of sound drew on his early and continued practice of saying poems aloud.[2] The resonance of his own voice stirred him ('The first poetry that moved me was my own at five years old') and made him famous in his family, who thought he would be an actor; then among undergradu-ates (he read Keats, Milton, and Wordsworth as well as his own poems to Cambridge friends); and then throughout society, caricatured by Beerbohm's cartoon of Tennyson reading to the Queen. After reading *Maud* to one listener he said that, though many men may have written as well as that, no one had ever written anything that sounded so well.[3]

What 'voice' comes down to in a poem or song is vowels. Edward Fitzgerald described Tennyson's as 'very deep, and deep-chested,...murmuring like the sound of a far Sea or of a Pine-wood'.[4] You can't sing consonants (except L and R) or murmur them like pine-woods. They do what their name implies, 'sound *with*'. What powers speech is breathing, and consonants are sounds in which breath is stopped. They define a word, but what moves it forward are vowels. And as 'foot' reminds us, poetry too is movement. In Hebrew the word for 'movement' (*tenu'ah*, an anapaest with accent on the last syllable whose shape enacts its own movement) even means 'vowel'. Vowels are more personal than consonants. They come from within us, made by our breath. In Semitic languages, readers contribute vowels as they read.[5] In English, *I* is a vowel. Vowels can also change as you say them,[6] and are more individual than consonants. They express accent (maybe Tennyson was particularly sensitive to vowels because of his Lincolnshire accent), and populations change how they pronounce them.[7] Vowels are therefore emotive: from the sixteenth century onwards, ferocity about rhyming in English ('rhyming wars' never entirely go away) has been driven by the subjectivity of vowels, by a feeling that what matters for poetry in an uninflected language is the exact relating of vowels. They drive emotion as well as motion. Consonants can colour a poem emotionally too but, just as the sound of a violin is driven by the bow, so the emotion of most poems is driven by vowels.

'Tennyson knew his magician's business', said Aldous Huxley,[8] and part of that business was the way he uses and times the vowels. 'The Lotos-Eaters', for instance, is about a journey slowing and stopping, and one sonic image of that is the way the short A of 'land', goal word of the first line, is held up and lengthened through the poem. The poem begins with effort and 'land' is in the strong position at the first line's end. '"Courage", he said, and pointed towards the land'.[9] 'Land' sounds strong and energetic here but becomes increasingly wound around with seeming and dreaming. This land is where time 'seemèd always afternoon.' It is a 'land of streams' (which evokes the echoes 'seems' and 'dreams'). By its third appearance, 'land' has 'inner' in front of it. Then a 'dale' (a long A) appears, 'far inland'. The language is drawing readers 'in' just as the land draws 'in' the mariners. It is 'a land where all things always seem'd the same'—as, increasingly, do many of the rhymes, especially long ones likes 'streams' and 'gleams'. Then 'land', when they taste lotos, turns into 'island' and by the fourth stanza they are sitting on a beach dreaming of 'Fatherland' and have lost all connection to energy and effort. The rhythms, as an early commentator remarked, take 'the formative impulse of the feeling',[10] and the first line's energy has vanished. 'Our island home', they sing, 'Is far beyond the wave'. It no longer matters if this means Ithaca or this new island;[11] 'here' is now an I-land, where a self-administered narcotic embodied in song has displaced painful feelings onto the 'far far away'. Only the 'wave' is mourning. And only on 'alien shores'.

This is where they begin the 'Choric Song'.[12] The stanzas (which Tennyson expanded when he rewrote the poem) are numbered as if they were separate poems in a sequence. Like astrophic lyric monodies in Greek tragedy, each is a separate different string of lyric patterns. The first begins like the preceding Spenserian stanzas but then loosens, freeing itself, intensifying the languor, repeating end-rhymes as if it is too much trouble to think of new sounds. The first four lines start out *abab*:

> There is sweet music here that softer falls
> Than petals from blown roses on the grass
> Or night-dews on still waters between walls
> Of shadowy granite in a gleaming pass.

The long E of 'sweet' is echoed in 'between', 'gleaming' (with its shadow-implication, 'dreaming'), and 'sleep'. The U in repeated 'music' is echoed in 'dews', the O of 'blown' and 'roses' in 'shadowy', the OR of 'falls' and 'walls' in 'or'. Instead of following *bcbcc*, as in the introductory section, the singers enter new but also more repetitive territory, slowing up as lotos takes hold. The new lines have only one rhyme, *ccc*, two four-beat lines ('Music that gentlier on the spirit lies / Than tired eyelids on tired eyes'), followed by a six-beat line whose heart is five long slow monosyllables. 'Music that brings *sweet sleep down* from the blissful skies'. The long I *of* 'lies', repeated in 'tired', 'tired' and 'eyelids' (*I* am tired, as well as *eyes*) and then in two more end-rhymes, echoes the *I* they added to 'land' to make 'island'. Maybe the repetitions and self-referential harmonies sum up the 'strange charm' Tennyson said he associated with the words 'far far away'.

After three lines ending with the same rhyme, we have four ending with another, *dddd*:

> Here are cool mosses deep,
> And through the moss the ivies creep,
> And in the stream the long-leaved flowers weep,
> And from the craggy ledge the poppy hangs in sleep.

Short vowels are interwoven with related long ones, the short O of 'mosses' and 'moss' close to the OO of 'cool' and 'through'; the short I of 'in' following the long then short I of 'ivies'. The first vowel, the EE of the diphthong in 'here', is echoed in 'stream' and 'leaves'. The related short E is held back until 'ledge' in the fourth line, but long EE is the end of all four lines, as if this is the only possible rhyme now and we may never get out of it. The first line of this is three beats, the second four, the third five and the last six. With a beat added to each line and all ending with the same rhyme,[13] the rhythms as well as vowels provide an acoustic image for what the song is about: the lotos's hold on the speakers. The lengthening embodies their increasingly drugged inaction, and so do the rhymes. The slight journey from 'deep' through 'creep' to 'sleep'[14] reminds the listener that these speakers, who have journeyed so far, so painfully absent from home, are no longer aware of any reason to 'weep'. That wave is mourning on alien shores and on this one the long-leaved flowers are doing their grieving for them. This is the mariners' voice, but also the voice of a young poet mastering the art of impersonation. Just as Dickens's characterization was catalyzed by his experience of acting, so Tennyson's persona-poems spring in complicated ways from reading poems *to* people: from his powerful need for response.

Response is the resounding absence in three early poems enacting tension between the isolation of creativity, on one hand, and a longing to reach outside the place of making. The first sounds heard in Mariana's grange are made by animals outside at night, the night-fowl, cock, oxen, and shrill winds. Inside the 'dreamy' house are noises made by things small, hidden, or ghostly: creaky doors, a mouse (shrieking 'Behind the mouldering wainscot'), a fly singing 'in the pane' (which after 'shriek'd' rather than 'squeaked' suggests suppressed pain), sparrows on the roof, a ticking clock, 'old' footsteps, and voices.[15] Alongside these come her echoing words—'dreary', 'weary', 'said', and 'dead'. In *The Palace of Art*, the 'long-sounding corridors', and 'hollow shades' which the soul encounters, 'enclosing hearts of flame', are created out of Tennyson's sense that delight in what you make can isolate.[16]

> No nightingale delighteth to prolong
>   Her low preamble all alone
> More than my soul to hear her echo'd song
>   Throb through the ribbèd stone.

There is a tug of war between the remoteness of creativity and longing to connect, to reach across the moat. Tennyson's friend Trench told him at Cambridge, 'Tennyson, we cannot live in Art'.[17] The palace or tower can slice you off from real relationship. In Shalott, the Lady is making a 'magic web with colours gay' which represents a world she sees only in the mirror.[18] Set on a 'silent isle', this poem seems to turn on looking; but sound plays a vital role too. She 'has heard a whisper' of a curse. Outside the tower there is colourful traffic bustling towards a place she never sees, but for whose name her silent isle and grey towers make a shadowed rhyme and echo: 'many-towered Camelot'. In Part I her song 'echoes cheerly' but the only people who hear it are reapers, and the only words said are hers. She is 'half sick of shadows'. Then Lancelot flashes into her mirror—and with him, sound. He carries a bugle, his bridle rings 'merrily'; so does his 'Tirra lira' (echoed immediately in 'by the river'). After this, through 'noises of the night' she floats away singing a different song: 'A carol, mournful, holy, / Chanted loudly, chanted lowly'. She dies 'singing in her song', arrives 'silent into Camelot' and brings silence there too. In 'the lighted palace' the 'sound of royal cheer' dies. Lancelot's sounds called her out of an otherwise silent world of making. She lived 'singing'; she dies 'in her song'. The soul in *The Palace of Art* meets similar self-deadening. Her beautiful echoes turn to shrieks:

> 'No voice,' she shrieked in that lone hall,
>   'No voice breaks through the stillness of this world:
> One deep, deep silence all.'

Tennyson's ambivalence about architectural containment, the beautiful, evocative but isolating precinct, reflects not only his sense of what it is to be a poet but also his relation to form. You need the building blocks. Form is your fortification, your four grey towers. 'I dread', he said, 'the losing hold of forms'.[19] His readings made metrical patterns clear, giving 'noble value and emphasis to the metrical structure and pulses', said William Rossetti.[20] But you mustn't let form become a prison. Tennyson kept inventing new metrical and formal shapes,[21] and was able to do so partly because form is where he started. Also, perhaps, because his early formal training was associated with companionship. The future author of *In Memoriam* associated poetry's technicalities, especially metre, with older male family members. His favourite poem when he was 10 was Pope's *Iliad*. He composed hundreds of lines, and improvised, in Popeian metre. 'So could my two elder brothers, for my father was a poet and could write regular metre very skilfully'.[22] When he was eight, and too ill one Sunday to go to church, one brother gave him a slate and told him to compose poetry about flowers. By the time church was over, both sides were covered in lines in the style of James Thompson's *The Seasons*.[23] These boys and their father were not confined to metrics in one language: they had three to play with. Classical metrics were discussed at table. Aged 12, Alfred was translating Greek and Roman poets into English heroic couplets. When he was 19 his first published work appeared in *Poems by Two Brothers*. In fact three of them were involved: it was written with his brothers Charles and Frederick.[24]

But turn the crystal of poetry and beside the universal you get the particular, beside shared you get individual, and along with the rules of metrics there is the specificity of physical voice. Tennyson's passionate experience of voice was not that of his brothers and father, and it developed throughout his life. Voice, says a famous Royal Shakespeare Company coach, is the physical expression of the inner self,[25] and Tennyson's voice seems to have been the place where he felt most ease. He was more at home in the inward than the outward. He had a large shambly body, was very short-sighted, and felt easier in the self of the voice than his social self. Dante Gabriel Rossetti's sketch of him reading to Elizabeth Barrett Browning shows a torso turned to his listener, open book close to his eyes, spare hand clutching his lower leg: everything contained and tense, pouring into his voice. (Which was 'Like an organ', said Barrett Browning afterwards.) The awkward-ness which socially never left him vanished when he read.[26] There could be awkwardness *around* his readings—so many listeners so innocently unprepared for two or three hours of non-stop poetry, as tears streamed down his cheeks; he did not realize when it was too much or inappropriate—but not in them. Some people felt the music of his reading obscured the sense. Even Mrs Tennyson, who heard more readings than most, wrote in her journal when tackling a new poem: 'It is well to read things to oneself without the glamour of his reading, which may beguile one.'[27]

His need for the vocative, to read poems *to*, and early power of vocalization,[28] is back-ground to the way he uses 'voice', 'answer', 'return', 'echo', and echo's ambivalent accom-paniment, 'hollow': a word sometimes used to describe Tennyson's own vowels as we hear him on recordings 'mouthing out his hollow oes and aes'.[29] Echo is sound darting from a starting-point to somewhere else; and maybe returning. As on a violin the bow returns up after a down-stroke and down after the up, so echoes in poems comfort and delight by returning the sound. It is a response. To get it physically you need a hollow resonator, like the body of a violin, which is provided by the enclosures like the Palace of Art, or castle walls in 'The Splendour Falls'. But echo is also the basis of rhyme, a key principle in most poems, even apparently unrhymed ones, and a common metaphor for 'voice' in the work of Tennyson's poetic father-figure, Wordsworth.[30] The splendour falls on castle walls and 'Our echoes roll from soul to soul'. Seamus Heaney suggests that poets become 'classically empowered' when they discover 'the poetry of relation', like Wordsworth's 'boy' who calls to owls and hears them call back.[31] Echo is both inside and outside; yours and not yours; an invisible Muse who may or may not exist; a source of inspiration in the to and fro of ear and voice; a relationship in which you as first voice are in charge while as listener you enjoy the response as if it comes from someone else.[32]

For Tennyson, 'poetry of relation' seems to have been bound up with the masculine. Like Wordsworth, he found empowerment in his own voice very young. But he associ-ated it, not with owls, but with wind. 'Before I could read, I was in the habit on a stormy day of spreading my arms…and crying out, "I hear a voice that's speaking in the wind", and the words "far, far away" had always a strange charm for me'.[33] In his essay, 'On Some of the Characteristics of Modern Poetry, and on the Lyrical Poems of Alfred Tennyson', Arthur Hallam said Tennyson's poetry was marked by 'a return of the mind upon itself'.[34] A sense of voice, too, bouncing back, and of words returning from a long way off, seems part of Tennyson's delight in repetition; his awareness of power thrusting forward then falling back. As Excalibur returns to the lake, so 'human things' return 'on themselves' in 'The Golden Year', and in the last line of 'Tithonus', Dawn 'returns' on her 'silver wheels'.[35] Long afterwards, Tennyson returned in a notebook to the distancing repetition in that phrase 'far far away': 'Far—far away. / That weird soul-phrase of something half-divine / In earliest youth, in latest age is mine'.[36] In 'The Lotos-Eaters' the phrase speaks to the distancing of pain. After a sailor has tasted lotos, 'To him the gushing of the wave / Far far away did seem to mourn and rave / On alien shores'. Five decades later, Tennyson echoed that last half-line when writing about the death of his son Lionel on, precisely, an alien shore. For this poem he brought back the *In Memoriam* stanza with its *abba* rhythm of grief which wants to go on but also back. He had used it for seventeen years in writing about his beloved friend. Now he used it for his son, whose burial had happened far away, 'under a hard Arabian moon / And alien stars'.[37]

Tension between containment and adventure, reaching out into the world like the Lady of Shalott and flinching back from it, is expressed, not only in the *abba* form, but also in the ebb and flow of returning vowel sounds. While Merlin is being seduced by Vivien in 'Idylls of the King', he half-foresees that this will end in his own imprisonment:[38]

> So dark a forethought rolled about his brain,
> As on a dull day in an Ocean cave
> The blind wave feeling round his long sea-hall
> In silence.

The OR of 'fore' is immediately echoed in 'thought'; the long O of 'So' in 'rolled' and 'Ocean'; the long O followed by double L is semi-echoed also in 'dull' and 'hall'; the OW of 'about' is echoed in 'round'. 'Feeling' is echoed in 'sea-hall', the long I of 'blind' in 'silence'. But the main vowel-print of the passage is the long AY of 'brain' (which sums up wise Merlin) echoed in 'day', 'cave', and 'wave'. Rolling round was part of Tennyson's way of working. At Cambridge, composing in his head, he liked 'to roll around' the poem aloud before writing it down (Hallam is said to have transcribed 'The Lotos-Eaters' from behind Tennyson's chair as he did just that),[39] and here the vowels thrown up by these rollings-round reappear in the summing up: 'In silence'. Only someone who had spent a lifetime alert to repetition could have made that patterning part of the thought. Merlin's 'brain', 'blind' to what Vivien is doing, is rolling round in the 'cave' and 'hall' of itself, imprisoned in the very act of fore-imagining. The thought and the imprisoning both are and are not Merlin's.

Doubleness, the sound and the thought that both is and is not yours (as with words which 'like Nature, half reveal / And half conceal the Soul within', *In Memoriam* v. 3–4),[40] empowered Tennyson's persona poems too. *Persona,* Latin for 'dramatic character', translated the Greek *prosōpon,* 'face', but originally meant 'mask': from *per-sonare,* 'to sound through'. As with Echo, the voice that 'comes through' a persona both is and is not yours. In writing *Maud,* Tennyson was at last (having married and having published *In Memoriam,* sharing his life with a companion and his grief with the whole world) free to look freely at his old self, exorcize its misery, and use the myth which confronts the whole idea of mine and not-mine. Behind *Maud* stand Echo, Narcissus and their mutual blurring of real or imagined, self and other, male face and unseen voice. But having used personae and their doubleness powerfully in other well-received poems, Tennyson was taken aback by readers' reception of his speaker. He insisted this was non-autobiographical, the speaker was not-me, and then found himself identified with him. He wondered bitterly why people could not see that the speaker was mad.[41]

Maud's first words are 'I hate the dreadful hollow' (*Maud* Part I, i. 1). The hollow is where the speaker's father died, a 'ghastly pit' (image for the speaker's neurotic self-absorption) where 'a body was found' (Maud Part I, ii. 1) and where Echo, 'Whatever is asked her, answers Death' (*Maud* Part I, i. 4).[42] It is a quarry: a source, like the father who gave him 'life', of the fabric with which the civilization has been built, against which he rants until he reaches the word 'home' and worries that he is echoing his father's 'mood' and may echo his fate, too. 'What? Am I raging along as my father raged in his mood? / Must *I* too creep to the hollow and dash myself down and die…?' Is he his father's echo? Tennyson is drawing on his lifelong worries (up to now) about inheriting from his father 'the black blood of the Tennysons'. The speaker is terrified of 'The blot upon the brain, / That *will* show itself without.'[43] The father's image is the real entrapping hollow. Maybe he should flee, 'from the place and the pit and the fear'. This hollow from which stone came echoes like the ribbed stone in the Palace of Art. But though it is man-made, it is also on a moor and part of nature. Just as metrics were the building blocks and rules associated with father and brothers, whereas voice was individual freedom (and both were essential to his craft), so nature's echoey hollows were freer and more open-ended than architectural spaces. They were pliant with plants, streams, growth, and flow, a more fluid image for the containment of words in a poem.

Tennyson's islands draw on the *Odyssey's* sequence of dangerously captivating islands, to which in 'Ulysses' he added the home 'isle' of Ithaca.[44] They are alive and growing but damagingly isolating, like the 'hollow Lotos-land'. But in 1831, with Arthur Hallam, Tennyson found the ideal landscape of natural containment which was echoey but not cut off and potently creative. The streams, lush hollows, waterfalls and winding paths in the valley of Cauteretz, hallowed by Hallam's companionship but also reminiscent of the 'watery vale' and 'glimmering lake' of Wordsworth's *Prelude* when 'the boy' first discovers the power of voice, became his lifelong inspiration: this is the beautiful valley which echoes through his work.[45] It is the 'vale of Ida' in 'Oenone', which he began writing there. It is seen dimly though the drifting spray of the Lotos-Eaters' island and is also, perhaps, the 'valley of death' in 'The Charge of the Light Brigade' which evokes the soul-landscape of green pastures and still waters in Psalm 23.[46] In 'Come Down O Maid', what is 'of the valley' is love.[47] The valley was a freer image for a poem than a palace. Still intricately woven;[48] but natural, with waterfalls and streams expressing the freedom of the voice to find new forms. Because words themselves, he said, could 'flow / From form to form' (*In Memoriam* ii. 443.5).

This valley reappeared when he re-visited the actual valley thirty-one years later, in 'The Valley of Cauteretz':

> All along the valley, stream that flashest white,
> Deepening thy voice with the deepening of the night,
> All along the valley, where thy waters flow,
> I walked with one I loved two and thirty years ago.
> All along the valley, while I walked today,
> The two and thirty years were a mist that rolls away;
> For all along the valley, down thy rocky bed,
> Thy living voice to me was as the voice of the dead,
> And all along the valley, by rock and cave and tree,
> The voice of the dead was a living voice to me.[49]

The couplet form stresses the theme of relationship. Everything is in twos: 'I' and landscape, 'I' and the absent 'you'. The stream, the voice, is the fluid connection between them. The two components of the eighth line, 'living voice to me' and 'voice of the dead', return inverted in the last line, mirroring the 'I' and unsaid 'you'.

The vowels of 'I' and 'me' ('white', 'night', 'thy', 'I', 'I', 'thy', 'thy'; 'stream', 'deepening', 'deepening', 'me', 'tree', 'me'), counterpoint the unheard 'you' evoked by the repeated 'two' of 'two and thirty'. It was actually only thirty-one years since he had visited that valley with Hallam, but twoness is what the poem is about. 'Thirty-one' would have lost that: it would have lost the unconscious echo of the unsaid 'you'.[50]

The European journey with Hallam gave Tennyson a landscape-image for creative containment, just as Hallam's death (colouring his life with a desolation whose inwardness he knew in himself from the start) ultimately led to the creative valley of death which was *In Memoriam*. Tennyson was sometimes critical of his own rush to creativity when Hallam died. Writing poetry was a 'sad mechanic exercise' for 'the unquiet heart and brain' (*In Memoriam* v. 5). But this turning to creativity had been an early impulse, in a childhood he did not want to acknowledge had been unhappy, to transmute the pain of his father's angry destructiveness into creatively consoling words which, unlike personalities in the family, sounded good together.[51] From the start he found comfort in three things a poet needs: skill in 'measured language', delight in his own voice, and a sense that recovering from loss entails making words sound good together. 'He is a deep-mouthed hound', said a friend after hearing him read, 'and the sound of it is very grand; but I rather need to know by heart what he is reading for otherwise I find sense to be lost, from time to time, in sounds'. Being 'lost in sounds'—but not lost entirely because the sounds harmonize inside their boundary—is a hallmark of Tennyson's work. The safety of pattern, form, and 'measured language' was the best of his father (who 'could write regular metre very skilfully') but what was his own was his musicality, and his way with vowels. One friend remembered quoting one of Tennyson's lines and

Tennyson saying 'You don't say it properly'. Tennyson repeated it, 'lingering with solemn sweetness on every vowel sound'.[52] His innate musicality made him unusually alert, perhaps, to the musical power of a vowel. Partly through all that reading aloud, he learned how to turn the soft breath and inwardness of words into a family romance of sonic relationships: to harmony.

In music, harmony is a combination of simultaneously heard notes which sounds stable and satisfying. But a single note carries harmonic properties itself, and its overtones build up in sequence after it first sounds. If you play low C on the piano, other notes emerge and blend with it, so the full note actually contains them. The overtones grow fainter as they get higher, because the vibrating string (or in wind instruments a column of air in a pipe) vibrates not only through its length but also, simultaneously, in fractions of its length. First half, then third, quarter, fifth, and so on, smaller and smaller. The full-length vibration sounds the fundamental note, the fractional vibrations give the overtones, or 'harmonics'. The role of these overtones governed the way Western composers created chords. The ancient Greeks gave us the word *harmonia,* but as far as we know only sang in octaves. The chords which mark Western music, which Western composers and listeners gradually came to feel were satisfying and meaningful, took time to build. After the octave, the fifth appeared (around the ninth century), then the fourth and thirds, major and minor. Then the intervals decreased; Debussy makes chords with the second; then come semi-tones. So the way the West widened its concept of consonance exactly paralleled the sequence of overtones heard when a single note is played: the history of harmony follows the physics of a vibrating string.[53]

Tennyson treats vowels as a composer treats notes, alert to their harmonics. His listeners noticed him letting them resonate, taking his time to say them. You absorb the full sound of one of his lines only if you pause in the middle and the end to hear the vowels' harmonic resonances and cumulative effect, as in a musical chord.[54] In music, when notes are played in sequence, the interval between them becomes an emotive force. In Western solfege, the rising and falling intervals, third, fourth, fifth, sixth, and seventh, all acquired their own emotional colouring. I suspect that Tennyson intuited a similar colouring, which felt satisfying and stable to his contemporaries, in the sequential relations of different vowels, long O followed by long E, for instance; and that he used this to create a poem's emotional timbre. In the first line of 'Tears, Idle Tears', for instance, he maps the whole poem's emotional ground through the relation of repeated vowels, which he later replays:

> Tears, idle tears, I know not what they mean.
> Tears from the depth of some divine despair
> Rise in the heart, and gather to the eyes,
> In looking on the happy Autumn-fields,
> And thinking of the days that are no more.
>
> Fresh as the first beam glittering on a sail,
> That brings our friends up from the underworld,
> Sad as the last which reddens over one

That sinks with all we love below the verge;
So sad, so fresh, the days that are no more.

   Ah, sad and strange as in dark summer dawns
The earliest pipe of half-awakened birds
To dying ears, when unto dying eyes
The casement slowly grows a glimmering square;
So sad, so strange, the days that are no more.

   Dear as remembered kisses after death,
And sweet as those by hopeless fancy feigned
On lips that are for others; deep as love,
Deep as first love, and wild with all regret;
O Death in Life, the days that are no more. [55]

The first half of the first line intertwines repeated EAR with repeated long I. That is the first relationship—or in music's terms, first interval. The long O of 'knows' (which will be repeated in 'no more' in the last line of this and every stanza) and AY (which becomes an important sound but appears first in the unstressed, seemingly unimportant 'they') wrap round the repeated short vowel of 'not what'. EE (the first element in the EAR diphthong) is repeated in 'fields', the long I of 'idle' and 'I' echoes in 'divine', 'rise', and 'eyes'. The second line repeats EAR again, echoes it in its end-word 'despair', repeats the subsidiary short O of 'not what' in 'from' (and its own half-echo 'some') and 'of', and wraps the long vowels round a key new short vowel in 'depth'. This will echo through the poem in stress positions: in the second verse, in 'fresh…fresh' centred round 'friends'; in the last, in 'death…death' centred round 'regret'. Establishing long EE in stress-position at the end of the first line (echoed in 'fields' in the same position), the first verse sets up a chord-like sequence of vowels related to long E and A—EE, I, AIR, and AR. These are gathered together in the last line—which finally produces (after four lines evoking unconscious or sensory feeling, with heart and eyes, looking and not knowing) an object of conscious thought: 'days'. Its AY (echoing the surprise word 'sail') will emerge in the third verse ('in strange') as the vowel which replaces the word prepared for by 'depth': the second verse's 'fresh' (which itself prepares for 'death'). It will be repeated in 'awakened' and 'feigned'. This third verse reworks the first stanza's sequential chord of AH, OR, EAR, long I, AIR, and AY in a different order: 'Ah', 'dark', 'dawns', 'pipe', 'dying', 'dying', 'eyes', 'square'.

This just scratches the surface of the poem's sonorities. But all the chords, both these more obvious ones and littler more hidden ones, add up to a key point made by Ricks: that this poem, which evokes loss and absence, gives a powerful impression of rhyming while being in fact unrhymed; and that the absence of rhyme incarnates an emotional, human absence.[56] Like Mariana's grange, the poem is full of noises from an absent or unseen presence. As echo is the semblance of relationship, so the harmonies here are the ghost of rhyme. The physical interaction of sounds and silence are also the intellectual and emotional point of the poem. Tennyson's music was always inseparable, it seems, from his intellect as well as his imagination. Metrics, harmony, and voice—his music both embodies and is the thought.[57]

NOTES

1. Tennyson quoted in R. B. Martin, *Tennyson: The Unquiet Heart* (New York: Oxford University Press 1980), 522.
2. See Francis Berry, *Poetry and the Physical Voice* (London: Routledge & Kegan Paul, 1962), 36, 47–65.
3. Tennyson quoted in Christopher Ricks, *Tennyson* (London: Macmillan Press 1972), 13; Martin, *Tennyson: The Unquiet Heart*, 556.
4. Edward Fitzgerald quoted in Martin, *Tennyson: The Unquiet Heart*, 199.
5. Semitic scripts like Phoenician, Arabic, and Hebrew are consonantal alphabets. At first in Hebrew, vowels weren't marked at all: readers supplied the relevant vowel. Later, Hebrew and Arabic developed vowel marks near the consonant to indicate a spoken vowel but most practised readers do not use them.
6. Some vowel sounds, monophthongs like the I in 'dim', are pure and stable and don't change while you say them. Diphthongs mutate to another sound, like the AR in 'tears'; or to more than one like the triphthong in *flower: FLA- OO -ER.*
7. Vowels shifted forwards and up in the mouth in the Great Vowel Shift of English in the fifteenth and early sixteenth centuries, which separates Middle from Modern English.
8. Aldous Huxley, *Texts and Pretexts* (London: Chatto & Windus 1932), 232.
9. Tennyson, 'The Lotos-Eaters', in *Tennyson: A Selected Edition*, ed. Christopher Ricks. (Berkeley and Los Angeles: University of California Press 1989), 71.
10. George Brimley, 'Alfred Tennyson's Poems', in *Cambridge Essays* (London: J. W. Parker & Sons 1855), 237.
11. See Angela Leighton, *On Form: Poetry, Aestheticism and the Legacy of a Word* (Oxford: Oxford University Press, 2007), 72.
12. Tennyson, 'The Lotos-Eaters', in *Tennyson: A Selected Edition*, 73.
13. Ricks, in *Tennyson: A Selected Edition*, 73, suggests that Tennyson is echoing both rhyme and theme from the last four lines of Marvell's *Thyrsis and Dorinda*: 'Then let us give Carillo charge o' the Sheep. / And thou and I'le pick poppies and them steep / In wine, and drink on't even till we weep, / So shall we smoothly pass away in sleep'.
14. He had used these in a sea context in his previous collection. In 'The Kraken' (Ricks, *Tennyson: A Selected Edition*, 17–18) he moves from 'deep' to 'sleep', then from 'sleep' to 'deep', until the Kraken roars, wakes, and dies.
15. Tennyson, 'Mariana', in *Tennyson: A Selected Edition*, 3–6.
16. Tennyson, *The Palace of Art*, in *Tennyson: A Selected Edition*, 52–70. See Leighton, *On Form*, 57.
17. Quoted in Martin, *Tennyson: Unquiet Heart*, 147.
18. Tennyson, 'The Lady of Shalott', in *Tennyson: A Selected Edition*, 22.
19. Tennyson, quoted in J. C. C Mays, '*In Memoriam*: An Aspect of Form', *University of Toronto Quarterly*, 35(1965), 22; Leighton, *On Form*, 62.
20. William Rossetti quoted in Martin, *Tennyson: Unquiet Heart*, 394.
21. See T. S. Eliot, 'In Memoriam', in *Essays Ancient and Modern* (London: Faber & Faber, 1936), 175–190, describes how Tennyson extended the variety of metrical forms.
22. Tennyson quoted in J. B. Stearne, *Tennyson* (London: Evans Brothers Ltd, 1966), 16.
23. Martin, *Tennyson: Unquiet Heart*, 21.
24. *Tennyson: A Selected Edition*, 20.
25. Berry, *Poetry and the Physical Voice* (London: Routledge & Kegan Paul, 1962) 7.

26. Martin, *Tennyson: Unquiet Heart*, 199.

27. Emily Tennyson quoted in Martin, *Tennyson: Unquiet Heart*, 425.

28. See Martin, *Tennyson: Unquiet Heart*, 21, 35, 55, 148, 393; Stearne, *Tennyson*, 32.

29. These are Tennyson's words for his fictitious poet who burns his Arthurian epic but agrees to read the one book of it saved from the hearth ('The Epic'). But this poet is himself in porcelain-thin disguise (see Ricks, *Tennyson*, 140) and the phrase fits his own voice perfectly.

30. Tennyson was initially wary about meeting Wordsworth: see Martin, *Tennyson: Unquiet Heart*, 126.

31. Seamus Heaney, *The Government of the Tongue* (London: Faber & Faber, 1989), 153–159, see below note 47.

32. See Ruth Padel, *Silent Letters of the Alphabet*, (Newcastle: Bloodaxe Books, 2010), 49, 30, 51, 53.

33. Tennyson, quoted in Martin, *Tennyson: Unquiet Heart*, 21.

34. Arthur Hallam, 'On Some of the Characteristics of Modern Poetry, and on the Lyrical Poems of Alfred Tennyson', in *The Poems of A. H. Hallam, together with his Essay on the Lyrical Poems of Alfred Tennyson*, ed. R. Le Gallienne (London: The British Library, 2010), 129.

35. Tennyson, 'The Golden Year' and 'Tithonus', in *Tennyson: A Selected Edition*, 590, 245.

36. Tennyson quoted in Stearne, *Tennyson*, 17. Towards the end of his life he wrote a short poem for music called 'Far-Far-Away' in which the repeated phrase mimes its own distancing effect. Leighton, *On Form*, 71 compares *In Memoriam* ii. 326.9: 'he is not here, but far away.'

37. Tennyson, 'To the Marquis of Dufferin and Ava', in *Tennyson: A Selected Edition*, 661.

38. Tennyson, 'Idylls of the King', in *Tennyson: A Selected Edition*, 814.

39. Martin, *Tennyson: Unquiet Heart*, 92.

40. Tennyson, *In Memoriam*, in *Tennyson: A Selected Edition*, 348–9.

41. *Tennyson: A Selected Edition*, 514.

42. Ricks, *Selected*, 516.

43. Ricks, *Tennyson*, 38, 247; Ralph Wilson Rader, *Tennyson's Maud: The Biographical Genesis* (Berkeley: University of California Press, 1963), 96.

44. Tennyson, 'Ulysses', in *Tennyson: A Selected Edition*, 141–3. See Leighton, *On Form* 56–7 and also 62 where she points out that Tennyson's islands influenced Yeats's idea of islands where 'beauty, certain forms of sensuous loveliness were separated from all the general purposes of life'. Enoch Arden's island (*Tennyson: A Selected Edition*, 60–67) is described in a 28-line sentence which has no voice but the poem's voice. It feels, Ricks comments (*Tennyson*, 280), like a prison sentence.

45. Beneath the trees, or by the glimmering Lake...
    Blew mimic hootings to the silent owls
    That they might answer him.—And they would shout
    Across the watery Vale, and shout again,
    Responsive to his call... *The Prelude*, V, 364–97.

46. Tennyson, 'The Charge of the Light Brigade', in *Tennyson: A Selected Edition*, 509. See Martin, *Tennyson: Unquiet Heart*, 119–120. See Auden's idea, in his 'Elegy for W. B. Yeats', that poetry survives 'in the valley of its making'.

47. Tennyson, 'Come Down O Maid', in *Tennyson: A Selected Edition*, 320.

48. As an image for a poem, wovenness or tapestry (like the Lady of Shalott's magic web) is halfway between built stone and live, inter-wreathing nature. In *The Devil and the Lady*, a Jonsonian verse play Tennyson wrote at 14 (see Stearne, *Tennyson*, 18–21), a necromancer describes the 'dark reverse' to 'Life's fair tapestry':

> The intertwinings and rough wanderings
> Of random threads and wayward colourings—
> A melée and confusion of all hues,
> Disorder of a system which seemed Order.

49. Tennyson, 'In the Valley of Cauteretz', in *Tennyson: A Selected Edition,* 590.

50. In 1892, re-printing the poem, he was 'vexed' that he had written 'two', because he 'hated inaccuracy' and wanted to change this to 'one' but was persuaded not to—see *Tennyson: A Selected Edition,* 591.

51. See Ricks, *Tennyson,* 8, 14–16, and Martin, *Tennyson: Unquiet Heart,* 184.

52. See Peter McDonald, 'Tennyson's Dying Fall', in Robert Douglas-Fairhurst and Seamus Perry, eds., *Tennyson Among the Poets* (Oxford: Oxford University Press, 2009), 17, 23.

53. Paul Steinitz and Stella Sterman, *Harmony In Context: a New Approach to Understanding Harmony Without Conventional Exercises* (London, Belwin-Mills: 1976), 1–3.

54. See Berry, *Physical Voice,* 50 and 58; McDonald, 'Tennyson's Dying Fall', in *Tennyson Among the Poets,* 17, 23.

55. Tennyson, 'Tears, Idle Tears', in *Tennyson: A Selected Edition,* 266–67.

56. Ricks, *Tennyson,* 199. 'Now Sleeps the Crimson Petal' (*Tennyson: A Selected Edition,* 318–19) also feels rhymed but is not. The only rhyme (repeated five times) is 'me', from a speaker who urges the beloved to incorporate herself in him. 'Be lost in me'.

57. Leighton, *On Form,* 25, 170.

SELECT BIBLIOGRAPHY

Berry, F. *Poetry and the Physical Voice* (London: Routledge & Kegan Paul, 1962).

Brimley, G. 'Alfred Tennyson's Poems', in *Cambridge Essays* (Cambridge: Cambridge University Press, 1855).

Douglas-Fairhurst, R. and Perry, S. eds. *Tennyson Among the Poets: Bicentenary Essays,* (Oxford: Oxford University Press, 2009).

Eliot, T. S. 'In Memoriam', in *Essays Ancient and Modern,* (London: Faber & Faber, 1936), 175–190.

Frye, N. ed., *Romanticism Reconsidered* (New York: Columbia University Press, 1963).

Griffiths, E. 'On Lines and Grooves from Shakespeare to Tennyson', in R. Douglas-Fairhurst and S. Perry, eds., *Tennyson Among the Poets* (Oxford: Oxford University Press, 2009), 133–159.

Hallam, Arthur, *The Poems of A. H. Hallam, together with his Essay on the Lyrical Poems of Alfred Tennyson,* ed. R. Le Gallienne (London: British Library 2010).

Heaney, Seamus. *The Government of the Tongue* (London: Faber & Faber, 1989).

Leighton, A. *On Form: Poetry, Aestheticism and the Legacy of a Word* (Oxford: Oxford University Press, 2007).

—— 'Tennyson, By Ear', in R. Douglas-Fairhurst and S. Perry, eds., *Tennyson Among the Poets* (New York and Oxford: Oxford University Press, 2009), 337–355.

MacDonald, P. 'Tennyson's Dying Fall', in R. Douglas-Fairhurst and S. Perry, eds., *Tennyson Among the Poets* (New York and Oxford: Oxford University Press, 2009), 14–39.

Martin, R. B. *Tennyson: The Unquiet Heart* (New York: Oxford University Press 1980).

Rader, R. W. *Tennyson's Maud: The Biographical Genesis* (Berkeley, Los Angeles and London: University of California Press, 1963).

Ricks, C. *Tennyson* (London: Macmillan Press, 1972).

—— *Tennyson, A Selected Edition* (Berkeley and Los Angeles: University of California Press, 1989).

Stearne, J. B. *Tennyson* (Literature in Perspective) (London: Evans Brothers Ltd, 1966).

Steinitz, Paul, and Sterman, Stella, *Harmony in Context: A New Approach to Understanding Harmony Without Conventional Exercises (2)* (London: Belwin-Mills, 1976).

CHAPTER 20

BROWNING'S
BALANCING ACTS

ROSS WILSON

OUTLINING in 1885 some of the 'general characteristics' of Browning's work, the poet's friend and biographer, Mrs Sutherland Orr, made the following remark about the relation between 'his choice and treatment of subject' and his 'versification':

> With all his love for music, Mr. Browning is more susceptible to sense than to sound. He values thought more than expression; matter, more than form; and, judging him from a strictly poetic point of view, he has lost his balance in this direction, as so many have lost it in the opposite one.[1]

Adopting a 'strictly poetic point of view', Mrs Orr is sure where she stands. Browning, by contrast, is cast not merely as taking the opposite point of view, but rather as having 'lost his balance'. Many readers have been anxious that, in entering Browning's terrain, they might, along with him, lose their footing. In an important letter, John Ruskin, for instance, complained to Browning that 'You are worse than the worst Alpine Glacier I ever crossed. Bright, & deep enough truly, but so full of Clefts that half the journey has to be done with ladder & hatchet'.[2] Similarly, in a still noteworthy treatment of Browning's versification, Harlan Hatcher claimed of Browning that '[h]e did compose with great rapidity, two steps at a time, as if he were rushing up the steps of the Casa Guidi'—and as if he might, in his hurry, trip on one of the steps he skips over and go crashing through one of that Casa's famous windows.[3]

Browning was keen to respond to this kind of assessment of the alleged imbalances in his poetry—but not by simply insisting, against his critics, on the fundamental stability, so to speak, of his work. Replying to Ruskin, for example, Browning did not attempt to show that his correspondent could have kept his feet perfectly well without his ladder and hatchet, but argued instead that the glaciers and clefts of his poetry require more strenuous exertion and defter footwork than Ruskin appears to be ready for. 'You ought, I think,' he counselled, 'to keep pace with the thought tripping from ledge to ledge of my "glaciers", as you call them; not stand poking your alpenstock into the holes, demonstrating that no foot could have stood there;—suppose it sprang over there?'[4] Daring leaps 'from ledge to ledge' are rewarded by new scenes and, as the beginning of Browning's *La Saisiaz* (1877) has it, dramatic shifts in perspective: 'Ledge by ledge, out broke new marvels, now minute and now immense'.[5]

I wish, in this essay, to take these various reflections on the characteristic imbalances of Browning's poetry (which, as we have just seen, he himself hardly disavows) as the guiding thread, or, perhaps, critical handrail, for thinking about *The Ring and the Book* (1868–69). That poem is itself an extended and various reflection on the difficulty of achieving the balance of evidence and argument requisite to just judgement, and so this essay investigates Browning's moral, rhetorical, and rhythmical handling of balance throughout *The Ring and the Book*. When he discovered the 'square old yellow Book' on the Florentine market-stall,[6] Browning sought to weigh its competing accounts—an endeavour that the Old Yellow Book (hereafter: OYB) itself, for all its rich, meticulous recording of details, could never fully determine. It is this, sometimes apparently reluctant but never refused openness to judgement that is essential to *The Ring and the Book* itself.

Browning's initial reading of the OYB is conducted in a manner that would appear to put him ostentatiously in danger of 'tripping from ledge to ledge':

> I leaned a little and overlooked my prize
> By the low railing round the fountain-source
> Close to the statue, where a step descends:
> While clinked the cans of copper, as stooped and rose
> Thick-ankled girls who brimmed them, and made place
> For marketmen glad to pitch basket down,
> Dip a broad melon-leaf that holds the wet,
> And whisk their faded fresh. And on I read
> Presently, though my path grew perilous
> Between the outspread straw-work, piles of plait
> Soon to be flapping, each o'er two black eyes
> And swathe of Tuscan hair, on festas fine:
> Through fire-irons, tribes of tongs, shovels of sheaves,
> Skeleton bedsteads, wardrobe-drawers agape,
> Rows of tall slim brass lamps with dangling gear,—
> And worse, cast clothes a-sweetening in the sun:
> None of them took my eye from off my prize.
> Still I read on, from written title-page
> To written index, on, through street and street,
> At the Strozzi, at the Pillar, at the Bridge;

(i. 93–112)

A. K. Cook's assurance that 'Browning's walk home to Casa Guidi from the Piazza San Lorenzo may be followed on the map' is precisely out of place in its recourse to cartographic abstraction from the bustle, noise, and stench through which the purchaser of the OYB finds his way home.[7] Whereas his forebear Shelley apparently preferred to read standing up, Browning reads as he walks, negotiating the hazards of the Florentine streets.[8] It might be thought that the poet himself is simply oblivious to the trip hazards that lie in his way, since, he tells us, he did not take his 'eye' from his 'prize'. Of course, those of us not victims of some unfortunate accident have two eyes, as we are reminded when the poet describes 'piles of plait / Soon to be flapping, each o'er *two* black eyes / And swathe of Tuscan hair' (my emphasis). Perhaps, then, it is revealing that it is only a singular 'eye' that is not distracted from the OYB, since the thickly textured description of the walk from Piazza Lorenzo to Casa Guidi must surely be the work of at least one eye.

Later in the opening book of the poem, eye and foot are more completely harmonized when both together are metaphorically recast once Browning has completed the initial perusal of his purchase. Laying aside the OYB and stepping out onto the 'narrow terrace' of the Casa Guidi, where he encounters 'A busy human sense beneath [his] feet' (i. 493), he casts his eye to the end of the street and thence in imagination to the distant scenes where the action of the Franceschini case is laid. Thus 'Step by step, missing none and marking all, / Till Rome itself, the ghastly goal, I reached', and thus

> I saw with my own eyes
> In Florence as I trod the terrace, breathed
> The beauty and the fearfulness of night,
> How it had run, this round from Rome to Rome—
>
> (i. 523–26)

The poet's real feet treading the terrace and real eyes looking to the end of the street are sublimed, as it were, and operate in concert in his imaginary journey to Rome.

In that journey, the poet's feet follow his eye, whereas, as we have seen, in his journey from the Piazza Lorenzo to his home, we are somewhat less certain either that the poet is looking where he is going or, indeed, that he is fully engaged with the contents of the OYB. Walking from the marketplace, the poet keeps his feet, but only at the (deliberately run) risk of imbalance. One way of viewing Browning's side-stepping of the distractions and obstacles on his route home might, as I intimated above, emphasize the importance that he ascribes to the OYB. Although he may trip, he will hold his new treasure fast. But even if Browning was initially determined to keep the book securely in his grasp, his handling of it becomes distinctly cavalier: 'Do you see this square old yellow Book', he asks, 'I toss / I' the air, and catch again, and twirl about / By the crumpled vellum covers [...]?' (i. 33–35); 'Here it is, this I toss and take again; / Small-quarto size, part print part manuscript' (i. 84–85); and, even after the poem has been developed out of this invaluable tome, it is yet 'The yellow thing I take and toss once more' (xii. 226). In her important essay on the prolixity of Browning's poem, Isobel Armstrong comments that, unlike poems of *The Ring and the Book*'s length, '[a] short poem is like an object, a thing which one can, as it were, roll about in the palm of one's hand, easily perceiving it as an entity, easily accepting the experience we have as an instantaneous "whole".'[9] Long poems, the implication is, are not so easily handled. However, Browning's tossing and taking of the collection of documents on which the certainly lengthy *The Ring and the Book* is based suggests, if anything, a much freer hand than Armstrong envisages as weighing the pleasingly tactile short poem. We saw with Browning's walk from the Piazza Lorenzo to the Casa Guidi that the poet seems at least partly neglectful of the hazards that lie in his way; likewise, he repeatedly tosses the book in the air, letting it, even if momentarily, out of his control. That momentary lack of control might be especially risky in this case, since the book is a compilation of printed text and manuscript, and thus might not be bound together as securely as might be desired.[10] But even if the pages do not come loose mid-air, the poet cannot perfectly determine which way up or round the book will be when he catches it again—and even if he could, he immediately sets about 'twirling' it once he has caught it. Browning's casual, even careless, handling of the OYB is thus in stark contrast to the firmness of the 'Hand, / Always above my shoulder' (i. 40–41) responsible for steering him 'Toward Baccio's marble' (i. 45) where he found his purchase. The contrast is significant because it suggests that Browning's poetic (and human) intentions for the OYB are not quite so safely in hand as those of the divinely predestining power that brings him to it in the first place.

I want to return to Browning's claim that his discovery of the OYB is predestined later, but I have emphasized here the mildly treacherous character of Browning's walk from the marketplace to his house, and the vigorous and repeated revolutions he inflicts on the OYB, because I have wanted to draw out the characteristic disturbances to steadfast balance and firm handling that Browning's poetry performs. Many attempts have been made to ground *The Ring and the Book* by adducing from among its competing voices a central authority or morally uncompromised speaker.[11] 'Little Pompilia' (iii. 2), for instance, is one attractive candidate for the focus of Browning's sympathy. She also bears some striking similarities to the OYB itself, though, as we have seen, that object is at once both treasured and roughly handled by the poet. The child of 'A woman who professed the wanton's trade' (ii. 561), discovered by the childless, ageing, but respectable Violante, the infant Pompilia was, like the OYB turned up amongst damaged and counterfeit goods, 'a find i' the filth-heap' (ii. 558). Indeed, the account of 'The Other Half-Rome'—which emphasizes Pompilia's saintly endurance, in contrast to her meretricious parentage pruriently stressed by 'Half-Rome'—nevertheless likewise sees Pompilia as an object found among surrounding detritus: 'Another day finds her living yet, […]' opens Book III, 'Alive i' the ruins' (iii. 1, 7). The opening of 'The Other Half-Rome's account, though, also intimates another important aspect of Pompilia's characterization. Unlike the OYB itself, or, certainly, unlike its predestined discovery as initially presented by Browning, her very existence is remarkably accidental. Guido's venomous description of Pompilia as 'bye-blow bastard-babe / Of a nameless strumpet' (v. 770–71) is, in fact, echoed by Pompilia herself, albeit in less vituperative terms:

> My father,—he was no one, any one,—
> The worse, the likelier,—call him,—he who came,
> Was wicked for his pleasure, went his way,
> And left no trace to track by; there remained
> Nothing but me, the unnecessary life,
> To catch up or let fall,—
>
> (vii. 293–98)

Like the OYB, taken and tossed and twirled about, Pompilia is there 'To catch up or let fall'. But Pompilia's history is either, unlike the facts documented in Browning's market-stall purchase, unrecorded altogether—her father 'left no trace to track by'—or unreliable—she is made by Guido merely to trace the account that would convict her of adultery. Pompilia's ascribed identity is nevertheless inscribed for all—apart from the illiterate, to whose number she belongs—to read in the registration of her baptism: 'all my names / At length, so many names for one poor child, /—Francesca Camilla Vittoria Angela / Pompilia Comparini,—laughable!' (vii. 4–7). Thus, she is, from the start of her recorded life, excessively—laughably, even—overwritten, a fact that her own illiteracy only serves to reinforce, since the very inscription of that excess of names is itself more than she can master. The record of her existence, she hopes on her deathbed, will not be altogether the work of others, however. Hoping that the birth of her own child will be recorded in the parish register wherein her (to her at least) risible flight of names appears, she remarks that 'they will add, I hope, / When they insert my death, a word or two,— / Omitting all about the mode of death' (vii. 9–11). Though slightly later on she regrets her own inability to write because she is thus incapable of writing what her 'son should read in time' (vii. 83), her attempt to influence what is written about her focuses rather on the suppression of certain facts. Pompilia's commitment to the open communication of truth, on which the image of her as guileless victim depends, is not, therefore, as straightforward as it might seem.

Pompilia's tendentious self-representation is matched by the fact that insofar as the sympathies of the poem lie with her, they are evidence, not of its secure grounding on a firm basis, but of its bias.[12] As the focus of the poem's negotiation of competing rights to representation and self-representation, Pompilia is at the centre of its concern with the political upheavals of its own day. Isobel Armstrong rightly noted that, in its proliferated concern with whose speech may be credited, '*The Ring and the Book* must be seen as Browning's contribution to the debate on representation'.[13] That debate, at least as it was conducted between the Reform Acts of 1832 and 1867, frequently focused on the status and power of the class deemed to be at the middle of society (and who did the deeming was, of course, a central bone of contention). The middle of society in *The Ring and the Book*—as Pompilia, born 'mid Rome's worst rankness' (v. 769), adopted by exemplars of the middling sort, and married off to the scion of a declining aristocracy, learns to her cost—is neither a comfortable nor a secure place to be, despite comfort and security being the putatively defining characteristics of middle class existence. Pompilia's adoption by Violante and Pietro seems, at first glance, to ensure her a respectably definable position in society, in contrast to her own untraceable origins. Violante and Pietro are described by the broadly sympathetic 'The Other Half-Rome' thus:

> What could they be but happy?—balanced so,
> Nor low i' the social scale nor yet too high,
> Nor poor nor richer than comports with ease,
> Nor bright and envied, nor obscure and scorned,
> Nor so young that their pleasures fell too thick,

> Nor old past catching pleasure when it fell,
> Nothing above, below the just degree,
> All at the mean where joy's components mix.
>
> (iii. 119–26)

If the lines are reminiscent of the early eighteenth-century portrayal by John Pomfret ('a Person of Quality') of a bourgeois idyll ('I'd have a Clear and Competent Estate, / That I might live Genteelly, but not Great'), then they at the same time also evoke Matthew Prior's later parody of the modest lives lived out in such snug settings:

> Nor Good, nor Bad, nor Fools, nor Wise;
> They wou'd not learn, nor cou'd advise;
> Without Love, Hatred, Joy, or Fear,
> They led—a kind of—as it were:
> Nor Wish'd, nor Car'd, nor Laugh'd, nor Cry'd:
> And so They liv'd; and so They dy'd.[14]

To the extent that they are seen, at least by 'The Other Half-Rome' as inhabiting a centre ground untainted by the polymorphous extremes of society, the Comparini are set apart quite markedly from the 'people' at large, amongst whom extremes are abundant. The Pope, for example, quoting the tale of the bizarre 'cadaver synod', which took place eight hundred years prior to his own election, tells of how the body of the exhumed and condemned Formosus was thrown into the Tiber at Pope Stephen's command: "'The people, crowded on the banks to see, / Were loud or mute, wept or laughed, cursed or jeered, / According as the deed addressed their sense;'" (x. 97–99). The combination of plural possessive adjective and singular noun in 'their sense' is apt: though congregated as one, the people is multitudinous and contradictory, and hence unpredictable. Browning, as is well known, begins the poem sure of the British public's dislike for him and ends it in the tentative hope that he might, still, gain the favour of that changeable mass: 'British Public, ye who like me not' (i. 1379–80); 'British Public, who may like me yet' (xii. 835). It is as if Browning has engaged here, across the whole massive edifice of *The Ring and the Book*, in the lover's attempt to divine the affections of his or her paramour by plucking off the petals of a flower ('he loves me, he loves me not')—though he starts, pessimistically enough, with 'the British Public loves me not', and only then alternates to the hardly emphatic 'the British Public loves me (perhaps)'.

The game of 'he loves me, he loves me not' is a pertinent figure for *The Ring and the Book* for it is deeply concerned with the circulating of alternatives, with the apparent equality and opposition of reactions to actions. Indeed, this concern is evident in the process of Browning's arrival at the title for the poem. Writing to his publisher George Smith, Browning gave his reasons for demurring from the latter's suggestion of 'The Book and the Ring' as a title:

> I have been thinking over the 'name' of the Poem, as you desired,—but do not, nor apparently shall, come to anything better than 'The Franceschini'; that includes

everybody in the piece, inasmuch as every one is for either Franceschini or his wife, a Franceschini also. I think 'the Book & the Ring' is too pretty-fairy-story-like. Suppose you say 'The Franceschini' therefore. Good luck to it!'[15]

Eventually, poet and publisher reached a compromise with 'The Ring and the Book', which Browning, presumably, did not find 'too pretty-fairy-story-like' (although, of course, 'The Book and the Ring' is preserved in the title, significantly, of the poem's final book). This titular transposition is illustrative because it brings out the degree to which a swap in position of two otherwise unchanged elements makes (at least, here, to Browning) all the difference. No element of 'The Book and the Ring' is altered in 'The Ring and the Book', other than its position—but one is a fairy-story, the other the account of a sexually charged murder.

The differences made by this kind of chiastic inversion are a key focus of *The Ring and the Book*'s consideration of justice. The example of chiasmus given in Richard A. Lanham's *A Handlist of Rhetorical Terms* emphasizes the epigrammatic concision achieved by this rhetorical figure as wit turns on its victim: 'Your manuscript is both good and original; but the part that is good is not original, and the part that is original is not good'.[16] The examples of chiasmus in *The Ring and the Book* are not, however, the piquant expressions of apt judgement, but rather they question the administration of justice, both human and, strikingly, divine. It is fitting that 'the world come to judgment' in Book I should gather 'on Rome's cross-roads' (i. 640, 642), for 'There prattled they, discoursed the right and wrong, / Turned wrong to right, proved wolves sheep and sheep wolves, / So that you scarce distinguished fell from fleece' (i. 645–47). Even when recourse is had to chiasmus in order to express, not the too-easy inversion of the foundations of justice, but rather to show the causation at work in a particular sequence of events, the validity of what is presented as an ineluctable process is starkly brought into question. Imagining the life that Pompilia would have led had she not been rescued from it by Violante, Tertium Quid—the 'third thing' that speaks, out of kilter, in the poem's fourth book—plots a course predictable from the alike rigorous bases of the fallen world and Christian doctrine: 'some fourteen years of squalid youth, / And then libertinage, disease, the grave—/ Hell in life here, hereafter life in hell' (iv. 251–53). A poet who could ask 'All that I am now, all I hope to be,— / Whence comes it save from fortune setting free / Body and soul the purpose to pursue, / God traced for both?', might suspect that life in hell is punishment unfit for crimes that, because unfreely committed, are not crimes, but which themselves are hell in life.[17] Balancing the scales of justice in this case issues in the grossest perpetuation of injustice.

Elsewhere, and in holier company than that into which Pompilia was born, chiasmus inverts elements which, in the first place, do not observe a natural order. Rummaging through the books on offer on the market-stall, Browning comes across a couple of weighty devotional tomes: 'The Life, Death, Miracles of Saint Somebody, / Saint Somebody Else, his Miracles, Death and Life' (i. 80–81). The saints of the Roman Catholic Church are expected to conduct miracles after their deaths, but what Browning's chiastic inversion of 'Life, Death, Miracles' into 'Miracles, Death, and Life' hints at is not so much a faithful acceptance that miracles, or, indeed, life, may come after death, but rather a worldly scepticism at such a curious sequence. The order of 'Life, Death, Miracles' is a matter of crucial import, that is, for the determination of sainthood, but here that order is caught up in the mundane turmoil of the market-stall, as if the pages of the books containing the records of the saints have become disordered. Indeed, it is worth noting that the pagination of the OYB itself hardly follows an orderly sequence: in their bibliographical account of it, Hawlin and Burnett note that the pamphlets which constitute the book are not bound in chronological order, and that, moreover, since the order of the items as they appear in the book does not correspond to that given in the hand-written index, it is likely 'either that the volume was originally misbound or that it was rebound at some stage.'[18]

The possibility that the OYB might have been 'originally misbound', and thus imperfectly arranged even in its conception, signals its kinship with the suspect originals that proliferate both in the Florentine marketplace and, so it is claimed, in the great museums of Europe: 'a Lionard going cheap / If it should prove, as promised, that Joconde / Whereof a copy contents the Louvre!' (i. 72–74)[19] In this context, it is vital to remember that Browning casts himself as guided to the treasured book amongst the proliferation of trash by an originating force, the predestining 'Hand, / Always above my shoulder' (i. 40–41):

> I found this book,
> Gave a *lira* for it, eightpence English just,
> (Mark the predestination!) when a Hand,
> Always above my shoulder, pushed me once,
> One day still fierce 'mid many a day struck calm ...
>
> (i. 38–42)

The time of this event ('One day still fierce 'mid many a day struck calm') calls to mind the time of the finding of the 'Etrurian circlets' with which the poem opens ('found, some happy morn, / After a dropping April'), since, for one thing, both fierce day and happy morn are meteorologically distinct from the days around them. But there is a still closer, verbal resemblance between the account of the predestined discovery of the book and the elaboration a few lines earlier of the ring metaphor. Coming to the end of his description of the manufacture of rings to match the Etrurian circlets whose discovery anticipates that of the book, Browning exclaims: 'But this work ended, once the thing a ring, / Oh, there's repristination!' (i. 22–23). The echo of 'Oh, there's repristination!' seventeen lines later in '(Mark the predestination!)' is itself no accident, even if it serves to draw into question the simplicity of the scheme of predestined calling (rather than accidental happenstance) that Browning seems to be outlining. Occupying similar places and serving similar functions in the courses of the larger descriptions to which they belong, as well as taking a comparable semantic form, both 'Oh, there's repristination!' and '(Mark the predestination!)' appeal to the reader at crucial junctures to attend to particular qualities and also offer her an explicit evaluation of those qualities. But moreover, the close verbal echo of 'repristination' in 'predestination', the near intercalation of the letters and sounds of the one in the other, implicitly enacts the repristination that Browning explicitly describes in the opening of the poem.

Yet that, of course, is an awkward claim to make in connection with the apparent investment in both repristination and predestination here. First, the verbal echo, while extremely close, is not perfect: not quite all of the elements of 'repristination' are re-formed in 'predestination', and others have also found their way in. Second, the fact that the apogee of anticipation, 'predestination', is itself anticipated complicates the contention that it is the privileged originating power at work prior to and in the poem. What is more, 'predestination' is anticipated in its minute sonic and graphic materials, and thus the claim that it is what steers a course through the particular, teeming materials of the marketplace is, in this way, qualified by its own immersion in the materials of the poem itself.

This interchange between repristination and predestination is another example of the poem's complexly imbalanced balancing act. But it has a particular significance for the fate, so to speak, of the poem itself. The pairing might well be taken to characterize the relation between poet and reader, insofar as poet predestines a reading on the part of the reader that will then serve as repristination of that original intention. Such a schema of the relation between poet and reader has long, of course, been subject to sustained critique. It is unnecessary to rehearse that critique here, but I do wish to offer now an account of the specific challenges that the predestining author and repristinating reader encounter when immersed in the details of this poem. And I want to begin to do this by examining closely the poem's opening.

The famous opening line, divided around the empty space in which the ring, it is hoped, magically appears in the mind's eye (for it certainly does not appear in the body's) appeals for what Herbert Tucker has called 'the reader's collaborating fancy'.[20] Perhaps by the time we are presented with the ring again in line 30, now as the result of the process of its manufacture rather than of its conjuring out of nothing, we are indeed prepared to collaborate—but at that point we are told that all of this has been 'a figure, a symbol, say; / A thing's sign' (i. 31), by which it is strongly implied that the 'ring' is not even a 'thing' after all. This is disorientating, for we have been asked to assist in the imaginative fabrication of an object over the course of the poem's opening thirty lines, only to be told that that object is to be subordinated as a mere sign to 'the thing signified'. In their thick description and densely interwoven verbal music, and through the demands they make on sight and internal hearing (on, that is, reading), those lines have themselves become something like a non-fungible, qualitatively unique object, the exchange of which for something else we might wish to resist.

Indeed, the poem's interrogation of forms of equivalence stretches from its refusal to view the discrepant versions of the same events advanced by its different speakers as being of equal weight, to the relation between its two opening lines. Browning's earlier long poem, *Sordello* (1840), which had earned him the dislike of the British public, was written in heroic couplets: 'Who will, may hear Sordello's story told: / His story? Who believes me shall behold / The man...'.[21] *The Ring and the Book* is, of course, in blank verse, yet a couplet faintly haunts the poem's opening two lines, themselves concerned with the matching of one thing to another. It is perhaps not possible to hear quite so much as a half-rhyme in 'Do you see this Ring? 'Tis Rome-work, made to match / (By Castellani's imitative craft)', but the resemblance between 'match' and 'craft' is close enough to render the initiation of this reading slightly uncertain that this verse is, so to speak, entirely blank.

This is significant because the poem, from this point onwards, is both minutely and extensively concerned with the possibility or impossibility of, the occasion for, or frustration of balance predicated upon equivalence. Yet the slight uncertainty that characterizes the very reading of these opening lines—an uncertainty that affects not just whether we might (be willing to imagine that we) see 'this Ring', but also our hearing of these lines—also evinces the importance of the role of the reader of (and in) *The Ring and the Book*. I cited above Herbert Tucker's characterization of Browning's need for 'the reader's collaborating fancy', but, as Tucker goes on to emphasize, that collaboration is hardly made easy. 'In its thick totality', Tucker states, '*The Ring and the Book* is a work to be not cumulatively understood but locally transacted with, by a reader whose negotiations replicate the acts of partial accommodation, under difficulties, that the various speakers perform in their turn'.[22] Those local transactions indeed frequently involve partial accommodation under difficulties just in order to read the poem's words and lines. The peculiar character of Browning's diction, for instance, has long been a central topic for commentary on his work. Bernard Groom, for example, drew attention to Browning's predilection for compound words, and provided lists of examples of differently formed compound words occurring in Browning's poetry, which, he claimed, 'do something to suggest the vast range of the vocabulary which is needed when a mind so rapid, subtle, and original expresses itself in metrical form'.[23]

This account implies that, in view of the rapidity of Browning's mind, the concision of compound words offers a number of verbal shortcuts. Yet it could hardly be said of 'lily-flowers' or 'ring-thing', in the opening lines of *The Ring and the Book*, that the second terms really add any new information at all, let alone in conveniently abbreviated form. A further implication of Groom's assessment is that the expression of 'mind' in 'metrical form' is aided by recourse to sometimes outlandishly formed compounds which, somehow, enable the mind in question to speed ahead without repeating a diminutive set of basic terms. But metrical form is itself hardly unaffected by the use of compound words, since one criterion for the identification of them is the placement of stress in the elements from which they are formed (the classic example being the difference between the phrase 'black bird' and the compound 'blackbird'). Despite the general tendency for stress in a compound word to shift to the first of the elements comprising that word, it has been insightfully said that a 'degree of unease' attaches to compound words, since a compound word seems to demand 'some degree of rhythmic independence for each of its components'.[24] The line 'Spark-like 'mid unearthed slope-side figtree-roots' (i. 6), for example, might be straightforwardly accounted for as a heroic line with an initial inverted foot. Yet even if that account is granted, it requires considerable qualification. First, the least remarkable of the compounds here, 'unearthed', turns out to be an especially nice rhythmical case. When used as a past participle, the second syllable of 'unearthed', not the first, is stressed (for example: 'The horde was unearthed in a field in Somerset'), whereas here, when it serves as an attributive adjective, the first syllable (in keeping with the tendency of compounds) is stressed. Thus, one strong possibility for the enunciation of this word must be foregone, another adopted. Of course, this is the case with a large (even overwhelming) number of words deployed in metrical composition, but the point here is that the hovering of another possibility for the rhythmical realization of the words of the line is emphasized by the fact of the line's constitution from compounds.[25] 'Spark-like' and 'slope-side' are indeed forestressed, yet it would be wrong to say that 'like' and, especially, 'side' are altogether unstressed. This is still more the case with 'figtree-roots', since this is a compound whose first element is itself a compound, and thus the demand here for 'a degree of rhythmic independence for each of its elements' (to use Attridge's description again) is particularly clamorous.

I have emphasized Browning's use of compound words in the opening lines of this poem in order to emphasize that the difficult negotiations that the reader of *The Ring and the Book* must enter into are conducted as much on the level of the line and, indeed, word, as on that of its overall organization. The reader's decisions about the balance of a line, as of the balance of the scales of justice in the trial of the Franceschini case, are crucial to both the judgement and also, in a vital sense, the realization of the poem itself. If Browning's characteristic verse practice—which many of his contemporary critics thought merely unbalanced, or prosaic—makes it difficult for his reader to find her feet, it nevertheless keeps her on her toes. Opinions of the reader or comparable figures change in *The Ring and the Book* at least as frequently as the poem's speakers. On the one hand, the reader is, like the Pope in Arcangeli's plea to him in Book VIII, the judge minutely attentive to earthly details above which he is nevertheless decidedly elevated:

> Oh thou, who vigilantly dost attend
> To even the few, the ineffectual words
> Which rise from this our low and mundane sphere
> Up to thy region out of smoke and noise
>
> (viii. 1436–49)

But even here, there is the hint that, were the Pope once to descend into the smoke and noise, then he might attend to many, effectual words. Indeed, this hint is reinforced by the intimation of ritual observance gone wrong: the 'smoke and noise' beneath the Pope's 'region' are like secular versions of the incense and music offered in praise to God, and thus the fact that the Pope is incommunicably above them entails that his interaction with his plenipotentiaries is far less successful than that (assumed, hopefully, to obtain) between celebrants of the Mass and God Himself.[26]

Yet immersion in the all-too-worldly details of the Franceschini case cannot, on the other hand, simply be taken for granted, even on the part of less exalted personages than the Pope, such as the poem's readers. The speaker at the beginning of the poem's final book merely supposes that the reader he is addressing has judged what has been laid before her. Declaring of Guido to the reader that 'you have seen his act, / By my power—may-be, judged it by your own,—' (xii. 9–12), the speaker cannot be sure of the exact character of readerly activity, even after more than 15,000 lines, and thus the trial of sup-position, estimated judgement, and competing powers is the fate of the poem, as well as of the speakers in it.

Such a fate is as little predestined by the poet's power as the reader's judgement is a mere repristination of the works of that power. The mage who declares that "'I can detach from me, commission forth / Half of my soul'" (i. 749–50) to reanimate some "'Rag of flesh, scrap of bone in dim disuse'" (i. 753) begs the question as to why only half his soul seems to be required to bring to life the fragments he chances upon. If, by anal-ogy, one half of the soul for making 'the dead alive once more' (i. 779) in *The Ring and the Book* is the poet's, then the other is the reader's, but since the poet may himself discern 'no voice, no hearing' (i. 762) of that reader as he commissions forth his portion of soul, then reader's voice and hearing is something for which he may only hope.

Notes

1. Alexandra Orr, *A Handbook to the Works of Robert Browning*, 6th edn. (London: Bell and Sons, 1892; first publ. 1885), 9–10.
2. John Ruskin to Robert Browning, 2 December 1855, in Adam Roberts, ed., *Robert Browning* (Oxford: Oxford University Press, 1997), 690.
3. Harlan Hatcher, *The Versification of Robert Browning* (Columbus: Ohio State University, 1928), 3.
4. Browning to Ruskin, 10 December 1855, in *Robert Browning*, 691. For readings of Ruskin's complaints (and Browning's response to them), see Robert Preyer, 'Two Styles in the Verse of Robert Browning', *ELH*, 32 (1965), 62–84, and Yopie Prins, 'Robert Browning: Transported by Meter', in Meredith L. McGill, ed., *The Traffic in Poems: Nineteenth-Century Poetry and Transatlantic Exchange* (New Brunswick, NJ: Rutgers University Press, 2008), 205–230.
5. Browning, *La Saisiaz*, in *Robert Browning: The Poems*, 2 vols., ed. John Pettigrew and Thomas J. Collins (Harmondsworth: Penguin, 1981), ii. 505.
6. Browning, *The Ring and the Book*, in *The Poetical Works of Robert Browning*, ed. Ian Jack et al. (Oxford: Clarendon Press, 1983–), VIII–X: *The Ring and the Book*, ed. Stefan Hawlin and T. A. J. Burnett (1998), vii. 8. References to *The Ring and the Book* by book and by line-number will be to this edition and will be given in the text.
7. A. K. Cook, *A Commentary Upon Browning's 'The Ring and the Book'* (Hamden, CT: Archon, 1966), 8–9.
8. According to Edward Trelawny, Shelley 'always read standing if possible'—see *Records of Shelley, Byron, and the Author* (New York: New York Review of Books, 2000; 1st pub. 1887), 70.
9. Isobel Armstrong, '*The Ring and the Book*: The Uses of Prolixity', in Armstrong, ed., *The Major Victorian Poets: Reconsiderations* (London: Routledge & Kegan Paul, 1969), 179.
10. According to Cook in *A Commentary Upon Browning's 'The Ring and the Book'*, Browning's description of 'this book, / Print three-fifths, written supplement the rest' (i. 118–19) is a 'very strange inaccuracy; of the 262 pages of the Yellow Book not more than 14 are written' (9).
11. For critiques of these attempts, see Morse Peckham, 'Historiography and "The Ring and the Book"', *VP*, 6 (1968), 243–257; Adam Potkay, 'The Problem of Identity and the Grounds

for Judgment in "The Ring and the Book"', *Victorian Poetry*, 25 (1987), 143–157; and Britta Martens, *Browning, Victorian Poetics and the Romantic Legacy: Challenging the Personal Voice* (Farnham: Ashgate, 2011), 167–207.

12. See William Walker, '"Pompilia" and Pompilia', *Victorian Poetry*, 22 (1984), 47–63.

13. Armstrong, *Victorian Poetry: Poetry, Poetics and Politics* (London: Routledge, 1993), 317. See also G.K. Chesterton's earlier assessment of *The Ring and the Book* as 'the epic of free speech' in *Robert Browning* (London: Macmillan, 1903), 173. *The Ring and the Book* is the 'epic of free speech', not because there is lots of it in it, but because speech's freedom is epically contested throughout it.

14. Matthew Prior, 'An Epitaph' in *Poems on Several Occasions* (London, 1718), 283. John Pomfret's lines are quoted from *The Choice. A Poem*, 4th edn. (London, 1701), 4.

15. Browning to George Smith, 30 July 1868, Brit. Mus. Add. 43485, quoted in Betty Miller, *Robert Browning: A Portrait* (London: John Murray, 1952), 233.

16. Richard A. Lanham, *A Handlist of Rhetorical Terms*, 2nd edn. (Berkeley: University of California Press, 1991), 33.

17. The question cited is asked in Browning's sonnet 'Why I Am a Liberal', first published in Andrew Reid, ed., *Why I Am a Liberal, Being Definitions by the Best Minds of the Liberal Party* (London: Cassell, 1885).

18. Hawlin and Burnett, 'Appendix A: The Old Yellow Book', in *Poetical Works*, vii. 298.

19. Germane to the question of the relation between original and copy is Browning's handling of the transitions between the different languages of the OYB, the Florentine marketplace, and his poem, on which, see Matthew Reynolds's 'Browning and Translationese', *Essays in Criticism*, 53 (2003) 97–128 (especially 114–116).

20. Herbert F. Tucker, *Epic: Britain's Heroic Muse, 1790–1910* (Oxford: Oxford University Press, 2008), 439.

21. Browning, *Sordello* i. 1–3 in *Poetical Works*. For an account of Browning's couplets in *Sordello* in the context of the history of English verse practice, see Simon Jarvis, 'Archaist-Innovators: The Couplet from Churchill to Browning', in Charles Mahoney, ed., *A Companion to Romantic Poetry* (Oxford: Blackwell, 2011), 25–43.

22. Tucker, *Epic*, 442.

23. Bernard Groom, *On the Diction of Tennyson, Browning and Arnold* (Hamden, CT: Archon, 1970; 1st pub. 1939), 28.

24. Derek Attridge, *The Rhythms of English Poetry* (London: Longman, 1982), 277. I have commented on the use of compound words in Browning (largely in *Sordello* and *The Agamemnon of Aeschylus*) elsewhere: see 'Robert Browning's Compounds', *Literature Compass*, 6 (2009), 524–531. On the difficulties posed by Browning's versification more generally, see Park Honan, 'The Iron String in the Victorian Lyre: Browning's Lyric Versification', in Clarence Tracy, ed., *Browning's Mind and Art* (Edinburgh: Oliver and Boyd, 1968), 82–99, and Russell Astley, 'Browning's Logaoedic Measures', *Victorian Poetry*, 16 (1978), 357–368.

25. Apart, of course, from one word, "mid', which is, contrastingly, truncated. C. S. Calverley captures Browning's compulsive compounding and truncating well in his 'The Cock and the Bull': 'You see this pebble-stone? It's a thing I bought / Of a bit of a chit of a boy i' the mid o' the day—/ I like to dock the smaller parts-'o-speech'. See Simon Brett, ed., *The Faber Book of Parodies* (London: Faber and Faber, 1984; repr. 1987), 72.

26. Cf. the speaker of 'The Bishop Orders His Tomb at Saint Praxed's Church' imagining how, entombed, he will 'taste / Good strong thick stupefying incense-smoke!'

Select Bibliography

Armstrong, Isobel, 'The Ring and the Book: The Uses of Prolixity', in Armstrong, ed., The Major Victorian Poets: Reconsiderations (London: Routledge & Kegan Paul, 1969), 177–197.

—— Victorian Poetry: Poetry, Poetics and Politics (London: Routledge, 1993).

Astley, Russell, 'Browning's Logaoedic Measures', Victorian Poetry, 16 (1978), 357–368.

Cook, A. K., A Commentary Upon Browning's 'The Ring and the Book' (Hamden, CT: Archon, 1966).

Hatcher, Harlan Henthorne, The Versification of Robert Browning (Columbus: Ohio State University, 1928).

Hawlin, Stefan, Robert Browning (London: Routledge, 2002).

Honan, Park, 'The Iron String in the Victorian Lyre: Browning's Lyric Versification', in Clarence Tracy, ed., Browning's Mind and Art (Edinburgh: Oliver and Boyd, 1968), 82–99.

Martens, Britta, Browning, Victorian Poetics and the Romantic Legacy: Challenging the Personal Voice (Farnham: Ashgate, 2011).

Peckham, Morse, 'Historiography and "The Ring and the Book"', Victorian Poetry, 6 (1968), 243–257.

Potkay, Adam, 'The Problem of Identity and the Grounds for Judgment in "The Ring and the Book"', Victorian Poetry, 25 (1987), 143–157.

Preyer, Robert, 'Two Styles in the Verse of Robert Browning', ELH, 32 (1965), 62–84.

Prins, Yopie, 'Robert Browning: Transported by Meter', in Meredith L. McGill, ed., The Traffic in Poems: Nineteenth-Century Poetry and Transatlantic Exchange (New Brunswick, NJ: Rutgers University Press, 2008), 205–230.

Tucker, Herbert F., Epic: Britain's Heroic Muse, 1790–1910 (Oxford: Oxford University Press, 2008), 436–446.

....

CHAPTER 21

EDWARD LEAR AND 'THE FIDDLEDIDDLETY OF REPRESENTATION'

....

HUGH HAUGHTON

1 NONSENSE AND MUSIC

....

T. S. Eliot observes that if the music of poetry exists 'apart from the meaning', there would be 'poetry of great musical beauty which made no sense', but 'I have never come across such poetry'. Counter-intuitively perhaps, he takes Edward Lear as an 'apparently extreme example' of the importance of 'sense', declaring that 'his non-sense is not vacuity of sense: it is a parody of sense, and that is the sense of it'.[1] In poems like *The Jumblies* and *The Dong with the Luminous Nose*, Eliot says, 'We enjoy the music, which is of a high order, and we enjoy the feeling of irresponsibility towards the sense.' In his criticism Eliot was generally resistant to Victorian poetry, apart from Tennyson's, and his remarks about Lear as 'an extreme case' (alongside William Morris and Mallarmé) offer a convenient point of entry into the 'musical beauty' of the great nonsense poet. In this essay I want to identify some of the formal features of Lear's lyrics, which, though they include elements of parody, generate uniquely anomalous forms of their own.

Some of Lear's earliest poems are actual parodies, including 'Eclogue', a pastiche of one of Collins's Oriental Odes, and 'Journal' (1829), a makeover of Thomas Moore's *Fudge Family in Paris*, while a later letter includes a brilliant *spoof* of Clough's *Amours de Voyages* ('Breakfast of tea, bread and butter, at nine o-clock in the morning, / Sending my carpetbag onward I reached Twickenham station').[2] Unlike Carroll who remained structurally dependent on parody as a stimulus to his nonsense poetry, Lear devised a medium with its own logic. G. K. Chesterton argued that the 'best proof' of 'adventurous growth in the nineteenth-century' was not to be found in 'its portentous science and philosophy' but in 'the rhymes of Mr Edward Lear and the literature of nonsense', saying 'The Dong with the Luminous Nose' was 'original, as the first ship and the first plough were original'.³ Chesterton's metaphors of 'ship' and 'plough'—a vehicle of travel and instrument for transforming the ground for new growth—are characteristically apt for a poet so invested in travel and new botanical species. In fact Lear's nonsense lyrics are as formally inventive as Browning's dramatic monologues, Hopkins' stressful metrical experiments, or Dante Gabriel Rossetti's Bach-like explorations of sonnet form. That said, Lear's lyric narratives, with their 'irresponsibility' towards 'sense', find their formal incarnations far from what Matthew Campbell calls 'the strenuous difficulty' of the Victorian poetry of the will.⁴

Matthew Bevis remarks that Tennyson's *Poems* (1842) are full of 'characters who can be seen as parodies...of their author', and the same is true of Lear's longer lyrics.⁵ By profession Lear was a 'Dirty Landscape Painter' and prolific travel writer, and his nonsense translates topographical art and travel writing into a nonsensical key. Lear's letters turn anomaly to comedy. They overflow with verbally and graphically exuberant self-portraits of the artist as a comically spherical, bearded, bespectacled, peripatetic misfit. What the poems do is find a comparably exuberant medium for the same sense of anomaly. A poet of *amours de voyages*, Lear writes limericks about misfits defined by or confined by places, as well as longer lyrics about anomalous characters who look like parodies of their author wandering in foreign countries. The travellers in his poems are not landscape artists like Lear, or well-connected English tourists like his friends and patrons, but nonsense refugees driven by imperatives such as illicit love (the Owl and the Pussy-Cat), desire for exploration (the Jumblies), the need to escape social restrictions (Mr Daddy Long-legs and Mr Floppy Fly), and amorous regret (the Dong and Mr Yonghy-Bonghy Bò).

When set beside his fellow Victorian poets, Lear, like Carroll, still tends to be treated as something of an anomaly, operating on the nonsensical outer fringes of poetic tradition. Nevertheless he has much in common with his contemporaries. Like so many, he is primarily a narrative poet and indeed a biographical one. His poems, like Browning's 'Fra Lippo Lippi', Tennyson's 'The Lady of Shalott' or Morris's 'Defence of Guenevere', revolve around proper names: people and places, biography and geography. Like other Victorian narrative and dramatic poems, they tend to be set in far-away places and turn on crises of individual subjectivity and mis-alignments between self and circumstance. Like Dante Gabriel Rossetti and William Morris, Lear is a simultaneously pictorial and textual artist, and indeed we could view him as a Pre-Raphaelite who turns not to the Middle Ages but to childhood and foreign travel for inspiration.

Like the Pre-Raphaelites and his great poetic contemporaries, Lear is always acutely aware of his medium. In a letter of November 1858 to Chichester Fortescue, he speaks of showing some travel sketches to Arthur Stanley and others, and being 'pleased by their praise of their fiddlediddlety of representation'.⁶ Though he notes they didn't agree about 'the beauty of Palestine', he declares that '"there is beauty in everything" is a better principle than "look for conventional beauty, & failing that don't see any"'.⁷ In invoking the 'fiddlediddlety of representation', Lear is talking about the painstaking 'fidelity' of his topographical paintings, which were notoriously 'fiddly' to do. However, 'fiddlediddlety' also suggests the nonsense-world of nursery rhymes like 'Hey-diddle-diddle, the cat and the fiddle', a poem he illustrated a number of times. It reminds us that his nonsense poems are also exercises in unconventional beauty and involve their own 'fiddlediddlety of representation', as I hope to show.

In *The Field of Nonsense* Elizabeth Sewell argues convincingly that nonsense verse, far from being more disordered than other kinds, has a greater investment in principles of order: not only logic, as in Lewis Carroll, but in number, rhyme, syntax, grammar, and serial taxonomies such as the alphabet.[8] If Lear is pictorial, he is also, as Eliot noted, profoundly musical, and I want to extend Sewell's argument by exploring Lear's intricate musical inventiveness. The nonce-word 'Fiddlediddlety' encloses a vernacular violin (a 'fiddle'), reminding us that Lear composed and sang tunes for Tennyson lyrics, and that his 'longer lyrics' often invoke music and song. The Owl sings to 'a small guitar', the Dong plays a 'pipe', Mr Daddy Long-legs is renowned for 'mumbian' melodies, and Uncle Arly (who used to be 'one of the singers' but is now 'one of the dumms') is always accompanied by a cricket who sings a 'cheerious measure'.[9] 'Cheerious measure' suggests a song that is 'cheerful' but also metrical measures that are 'serious' and/or 'curious'. Lear's anomalous musical measures offer reasons to be cheerful, but they are also more curious (and indeed serious) than first meets the eye.

2 LIMERICKS, TEAPOTS AND QUAILS

If Lear is associated with any single form, it is the limerick, though the term did not come into circulation until after his death. The form seems to have been first launched around 1822 with the anonymous *Anecdotes and Adventures of Fifteen Gentlemen* which included 'There was an old man of Tobago', which Lear says gave him the cue for this own poetry:

> There was an old man of Tobago,
> Who lived on rice, gruel and sago,
>   Till, much to his bliss,
>   His physician said this—
> To a leg, sir, of mutton you may go.[10]

Introducing *The Book of Nonsense* in 1846 Lear says its metre was 'suggested to me by a valued friend as a form of verse lending itself to limitless variety for Rhymes and Pictures'.[11] By this account, 'Rhymes and Pictures' are twinned from the outset and it was the 'form' which provided their inspiration. What the sonnet was to Rossetti, the limerick was to Lear.

Like 'There was an old man of Tobago', Lear's limericks are typically triggered by a place-name, identifying their protagonist in terms of their place of origin. The form offers him a tightly enclosed medium for dramatizing spatial, topographical, social, or

temperamental restriction, as well as the impulse to escape from it. It embodies the pressure to conform to your place as well as the imperative to resist it in whatever idiosyncratic way you can, like the Young Person of Kew who, 'with blameable haste . . . devoured
some hot paste', or the old Person of Skye 'who waltzed with a Bluebottle fly', or the 'Old
Man of Cape Horn / Who wished he had never been born / So he sat on a chair, / Till he
died of Despair, that dolorous old Man of Cape Horn'.[12]

The limerick, for all its generative restrictions, offers Lear a peculiar formal ambiguity.
Pairing and despairing are Lear's great subjects, while formal pairing in terms of rhyme
and rhythm provides the motor of his verse. A limerick may be arranged in either 4 or
5 lines but, despite that, is neither wholly a quatrain nor a cinquain. In fact, in the original manuscript of *The Book of Nonsense* Lear dashed them off in three lines, as in the
following:

> There was an old man of *Coblenz*, The length of whose legs was *immense:*
> He went with one prance, from Turkey to France,
> This surprising old man of Coblenz.[13]

In this form, the lines are also relatively immense, with the rhyme of 'Coblenz' and
'immense' spanned within the first (a hexameter), and the leap from 'prance' to
France enacted in the second (a tetrameter). Even when printed as four lines, the
limerick is never a quatrain in terms of rhyme (with its *aaba* structure of end-rhymes
disguising the internal rhyme in the third). Printed as five lines in *aabba* form it
looks a conventional cinquain, but the shorter metrical force of the *bb* couplet syn-
copates and complicates the trajectory, while Lear's insistence on the repetition of
the first rhyme word in the last line turns it into a self-rhyme, a return to a point
of origin with only the mildest variation. This means that, whether cast in three,
four, or five lines, limericks revolve ambiguously around two pairs of asymmetrical
rhymed pairs.

'There was an old man with a beard' is untypically untopographical, though the beard
itself becomes almost topographical. The poem sets up a series of ambiguous singles
and pairs:

> There was an old man with a beard,
> Who said, 'It is just as I feared!—
> Two Owls and a Hen, four Larks and a Wren,
> Have all built their nests in my beard!'[14]

The comedy depends as much on the man's belated recognition of the ornithological
multi-occupation of his facial hair as the sheer fact of it. As usual in the arithmetical
world of nonsense, counting counts. One man plays host to eight birds—two singletons,
the Hen and Wren (who are, however, paired through rhyme), a couple of owls, and four
larks (which may or may not be in two pairs). The poem emphasizes nest-building and
makes us think about the ways its limited space also becomes a nest for the incongruous
winged cast.

More geographically typical is the man of Apulia:

> There was an old Man of Apulia,
> Whose conduct was very peculiar;
> He fed twenty sons, upon nothing but buns,
> That whimsical Man of Apulia.[15]

The Old Man must have (or have had) a wife, given the twenty sons, but he is left to his 'peculiar' singular existence. The poem revolves neutrally around the difference between that first 'peculiar' and the final 'whimsical'. The mention of 'twenty' suggests symmetry as well as multiplication (a doubling of ten), and the poem's first two and last lines are all ten syllables long, while the third has only fractionally more with eleven. The opposition of 'twenty' and 'nothing' in 'nothing but', and the not implausible but still odd-seeming rhyme of 'sons' and 'buns', generates a sense of disproportion, albeit a measured one. The full one-syllable rhyme of 'sons' and 'buns' contrasts nicely with the *Don Juan*-like rhyme of 'Apulia' and 'peculiar', playing up the difference between Italian and English, which Lear, like the equally well-travelled Byron, clearly relishes. So, formally, the poem revolves around a pair of pairs, suggests the missing wife (as part of the original couple), and leaves us with a strange insistence on a single staple diet (food being one of the defining occupations or pre-occupations of the protagonists of the limericks).

We might think of the limerick as the archetypal Lear poem, with the longer verse offering more elaborated versions of poems constructed around names and places, departing and returning. All Lear's poems come in series, however. This is not only true of the biographical Baedekers that are his limericks but the A to Zs of his numerous verse alphabets. Of his serial forms, the one-off 'Ribands and Pigs' (or 'Teapots and Snails') is particularly beautiful. The form has much in common with the limericks, and like them and the Alphabets depends on the mirroring of texts and pictures: 'Ribands & pigs, / Helmets & Figs, / Set him a jigging & see how he jigs'.[16] The verse depends on a series (or rather pair) of pairings of disparate objects, here 'Ribands and pigs' followed by 'Helmets and figs'. The plural items might be any number, but in nearly all cases the accompanying illustrations offer two. Here the illustration shows two ribbons, two pigs, two helmets, and (unusually) three figs, as well as the single figure of a man dancing a jig. The paired items don't have anything obvious in common, indeed their incongruity provides much of the vitality of the form. Nevertheless, the illustrations set up curious analogies between the curly ribbons, the curled tails of the pigs, the plumes of the two helmets and the stalky stems of the figs—an analogy strengthened by the wobbling feather in the jigging man's hat. Each dimeter line of the triplet rhymes with all the others, though the last is double the length of the first pair of lines, and also includes a kind of grammatical rhyme, where 'jigging' and 'jigs' offer different forms of the same verb, the present participle and third-person singular. The overall form, in other words, consists of a pair of lines consisting of paired nouns, followed by a single line that pairs two forms of the same verb as well as two other verbs, here 'set' (the first word of the last line for the whole set of 28) and 'see' (which, varied occasionally with 'hark' and 'hear', also runs through the whole set). The four-verb syncopated final tetrameter generates an energetic dance for the anonymous 'him' who the illustration reveals to be a dancing sailor, set jigging by the incongruous pairings of items.

Pears figure in another pair in the set: 'Eagles & pears, / Slippers & Bears, / Set him a staring & see how he stares!'[17] In terms of form, rhyme, metre, the poem is identical. The illustrations show pairs of eagles, pears, slippers, and bears, beside a tiny-bodied, big-headed, owl-eyed man who stares at them in happy amazement. As before, the pairings are inherently incongruous, though the illustration has the eagles on a branch and the pears with leaves, connecting both pairs to trees, while the slippers and bears are clearly designed for walking on the ground. The singular homunculus-like man is poised bird-like between ground and air, as if either alighting or landing, caught between the domain of the eagles and pears and that of slippers and bears.

All twenty-eight poems use this extremely tight, Webern-like form, generating some memorable and unlikely pairings. These include 'Poodles and pumps', 'Cutlets & eyes', 'Lobsters and mops', 'Volumes & Pigs', 'Camels & Keys', 'Steamboats & Eggs', while the singular anonymous figures animated by these pairings include a bee, a boat, a peacock, a dog, a frog, a kangaroo, a kite, and even a ball, as in 'Thistles & Moles, / Crumpets & Soles—/ Set it a rolling & see how it rolls' (the illustration showing a billiard-ball rolling down a line with an extremely steep gradient).[18] In this last example, 'Thistles & Moles', while pairing vegetables and animals, are both connected to the ground, while 'Crumpets & Soles', though of vegetable and animal origin, are connected via *cuisine*. We have a sense of the disparate being incongruously united, as in Dr Johnson's account of 'metaphysical poetry' where 'The most heterogeneous ideas are yoked by violence together'.[19] The illustrated poem gives us a powerful sense of an incongruously inter-animated world, where unusually paired things generate powerful reactions in apparently unrelated individuals. This is even true of the last poem in the series, which includes the only singular item in the first pair of lines and only generates boredom: 'Gruel & prawns, / Bracelets & Thorns, / Set him a yawning & see how he yawns!'[20] That final 'yawn' is so forceful it almost tears the yawner's face apart, confirming the energetic reactive logic of the series. 'Bracelets & Thorns' suggest things that are attractive and repulsive respectively, and their pairing, though it sets the man in the illustration yawning, gets the reader smiling.

3 LONGER LYRICAL FORMS

Though Lear's longer lyrics are more architecturally complex, they too depend on unlikely pairings and couplings. 'The Duck and the Kangaroo', for example, reports how a Duck, impressed by a hopping Kangaroo, says 'My life is a bore in this nasty pond, / And I long to go out in the world beyond' and is taken for a ride.[21] The pair 'hop the whole world three times round', prompting the poet to ask: 'And who so happy,—O who, / As the Duck and the Kangaroo?' In the text the gender of the incongruous world-travelling couple is unclear, while the illustrations show a large-tailed pouchless marsupial and a diminutive mallard smoking a cigar. The form of the poem is bouncy and regular, but not as symmetrical as it looks. In fact, each octave is made up of two differently formed quatrains. Starting with a neat *abab* pattern, the first octave then modulates to a rhymed couplet, followed by another which returns to the opening 'oo' rhyme, so that 'Kangaroo' is not only the last word of the first line but of the stanza. Later stanzas don't return to the initial rhyme in the same way, but use similar octaves, made up of an *abab* quatrain and a *ccdd* one. So, a poem about incongruous pairing works by eight-line units built out of a pair of contrasted quatrains.

'The Owl and the Pussy-cat' has a comparably triumphant finale, with the marriage dance of an almost equally gender-neutral couple. The Owl, serenading the Pussy, says 'What a beautiful Pussy you are!', which might suggest the beautiful cat was female (though it could go either way), while the Pussy calls the bird, 'You elegant fowl!', which might suggest a male (but again could go either way).[22] It is the Pussy, however, who takes the initiative by proposing to the owl ('O let us be married! too long we have tarried!') and steers the pea-green boat en route to the land where the Bong tree grows. In the illustrations, the cat looks protectively towards the bashful-looking owl during their negotiations with the Pig about the ring, but nothing in this tale of exotic elopement and romance between an impossible couple seems completely straightforward in terms of gender or other roles. The key agents in the wedding ceremony, the Pig and Turkey, are more usually thought of as paired items of food at a Christmas banquet rather than providers of a wedding ring and officiating Priest.

As a nonsense epithalamium for a biologically impossible couple, 'The Owl and the Pussy-cat' is refreshingly down-to-earth. The 'honey' suggests romantic sweetness, and even perhaps a honey-moon, but is accompanied by 'plenty of money, / Wrapped up in a five-pound note' (with honey wrapped in money a neat shorthand for Victorian marriage). The details give the Owl's starlight serenade a pragmatic dimension, like the wedding ring acquired from a pig where the bride and groom's 'I will' in the ceremony is transferred to a financial transaction in which a pig agrees to sell it 'for one shilling'. This is a world of decorum—caught in the lovers' idiom, 'You elegant fowl', 'How charmingly sweet you sing', 'Too long we have tarried' and so on—but also of measure in many senses. In addition to the 'one shilling', there are references to 'a five-pound note', 'a year and a day', and 'slices of quince' (slices, not segments or pieces), which are eaten with a 'runcible spoon' (not any old spoon, but a *runcible* one, a word that contrarily suggests both 'risible' and 'sensible', with a faint whiff of 'dunce' taken up in the final 'dance').

'The Owl and the Pussy-cat' is itself measured, with the melodic structure of its eleven-line stanzas as clean in outline as anything by Ezra Pound.[23] It is full of formal pairings and looks completely regular, but its rhymes are not always or necessarily at the end of lines, and the second and third stanzas are more intricately threaded and differently shaped to the first, though based on its template:

> The Owl and the Pussy-cat went to sea
>   In a beautiful pea-green boat,
> They took some honey, and plenty of money,
>   Wrapped up in a five-pound note.

> The Owl looked up to the stars above,
>   And sang to a small guitar,
> 'O lovely Pussy! O Pussy, my love,
>   What a beautiful Pussy you are,
>   You are,
>   You are!
>   What a beautiful Pussy you are!'

The poem launches with a decisive narrative statement, bracketing the protagonists firmly together: 'The Owl and the Pussy-cat went to sea'. The 'sea' is immediately echoed in the next line with the internal rhyme of 'pea' in the 'pea-green boat' (it might have been sea-green) and then the off-rhyme of 'money' in the next. In fact 'money' is the first of many lines which have no paired end-rhyme, though internally rhymed with 'honey'. The following two stanzas use the same doubling in their third lines ('married / tarried!', 'away / day'), but are also paired with an internally rhymed first line ('Pussy said to the *Owl*, "You elegant *fowl*!"', 'Dear Pig, are you *willing* to sell for one *shilling*'). This clarifies the fact that the first and third lines don't actually rhyme with each other, though they do rhyme internally. Again, this suggests a certain ambiguity or asymmetry in the stanza form itself, which sounds as if it is built around end-rhymes, but actually depends on internally rhymed fifth and seventh lines in the second and third stanzas: 'They sailed *away* for a year and a *day*', 'And there in a *wood* a Piggy-wig *stood*', 'They dined on *mince* and slices of *quince*'. This differentiates the later stanzas from the first, with an intensification of the already highly developed pairing principle. Indeed the final 'And hand in hand, on the edge of the sand' sets up a pair of lovers' hands within a triple rhyme that includes 'sand', a fact that completely overrides any sense we might have of 'sand' not being involved in any end-rhyme. Pairing is everywhere, but not in the expected forms or places.

This is a poem that insists on decorum, with its 'elegant' idiom, quoted romantic love-song, island wedding ceremony complete with ring, polite address to the pig ('Dear Pig, are you willing?') and the final feast and dance by the light of the moon.[24] It also, however, takes place in an elemental setting, the initial invocation of 'sea' and 'stars' followed by a voyage to 'the land where the Bong tree grows', and a final tableau which includes a 'hill', 'the edge of the sand', and 'moon' (returning to the 'stars above' of the first stanza). 'The land where the Bong-tree grows' suggests arboreal growth as its defining feature, and is a nonsense variant of the romantic formula made famous by Goethe's 'Kennst du das Land, wo die Zitronen blühn?', and Byron's *Bride of Abydos*, 'Know you the land where the cypress and myrtle / Are emblems of deeds which are done in their clime?'[25] 'The land where the Bong tree grows' gives the appeal of the exotic a touch of nonsense botany via the nonce-word 'Bong'. The fact that another manuscript has a 'Palm tree' and another 'Phloss' only underlies the felicity of the coinage.[26] The *OED* gives no historical use prior to Lear's poem (though the Australian 'billabong' was already current), and here it suggests geographically far-away fauna of the kind Lear was always drawing and painting, a tree that's definitely not English but has a certain booming English resonance (to go with 'Ding-Dong' or a booming dinner 'Gong').[27]

The poem's final 'moon' in quadruplicate plays out the resonance of 'Bong' in a related key, reminding us that, for all its sophisticated music, this is a poem built almost entirely around monosyllabic words and simple names.

Metrically each stanza is cast in a version of ballad measure, with alternating iambic tetrameters and trimeters disposed in a mainly alternating rhyme-scheme. The octave of the first stanza follows a basic *abcbdede* pattern (with an internally rhymed third line), while the second and third are paired together by the use of an *abcbdefe* pattern (with internal rhymes in lines one, three, five, and seven). At the end of each octave, the final two words of the eighth line are repeated in the subsequent pair of lines, followed by a quasi-choric reprieve of the entire line in the last.

The cantabile reprise of the Owl's barcarolle to guitar accompaniment in the last three lines complicates the shape. Taken as a whole we could construe this as an eleven-line stanza, though the two foreshortened repeated lines ('You are / You are') sandwiched between the full exclamatory line (or lines) 'What a beautiful Pussy you are!' could suggest either a ten-line stanza or an eleven-liner. This is a poem that thrives on repetition and different kinds of pairing. Within the song within the song, 'Pussy' is repeated four times, as is 'you are'. Within the first stanza, in addition to the repeated 'Pussy' at the end, the seventh line offers the chiasmic inversion of 'O lovely Pussy! O Pussy, my love', confirming the presence of Pre-Raphaelite patterning at every level.

Lear's epithalamium is a strange blend of urbane cantabile and romantic exoticism, and its immaculate decorum combines with a sense of subliminal transgression. There are few patently 'nonsensical' elements—apart from the nonce-words 'Bong tree' and 'runcible'—but the marital pair make a biologically impossible couple, a marriage of fur and feathers, mammalian quadruped and bird. The nonsense surface is a sign of a more radical oddity. The transgressive dimension of the marriage is brought out in two sequels, 'The Later History of the Owl and the Pussy-cat' narrated in a letter of 1884, and a poem called 'The Children of the Owl and the Pussy-cat', which opens:

> Our mother was the Pussy-Cat, our father was the Owl,
> And so we're partly little beasts and partly little fowl,
> The brothers of our family have feathers and they hoot,
> While all the sisters dress in fur and have long tails to boot.
> We all believe that little mice,
> For food are singularly nice.[28]

The rest of the unfinished manuscript tells of the death of their mother, who died 'long years ago', falling from a tree in Calabria, mentions their exile from the Gromboolian plains, and their father's tendency 'when he sees a star' to sing as before to his guitar, while taking 'no interest in the politix of the day'.[29] The sequel clarifies the gender of the originally enigmatic protagonists (the Owl male, the Pussy-cat female) but also spells out Lear's embrace of the marriage of flesh and fur, of 'beast' and 'fowl'. Though incongruous, cats and owls have a lot in common; they are nocturnal, have big eyes and hunt mice. Lear's Owl and Pussy-cat are appropriately nocturnal, with the Owl serenading the cat under the stars in the opening, and the two dancing by the light of the moon at the end. The final stanza of the original also imagines a banquet, but not on the food their children think 'singularly nice'. The sequel insists on their shared appetite, not for 'mince and slices of quince', but 'little mice' (reminding us that the word 'mice' is actually in 'mince' and suggesting they could have 'dined on mice, and helpings of rice', if Lear's sense of decorum had not been so sure-footed). It is part of the poem's underlying realism, however, that it implicitly recognizes the shared appetite of this pair of impossible lovers.

'The Daddy Long-legs and the Fly' is another poem about the romantic escape of an unlikely and apparently ill-matched pair. In this case both are winged insects and male, offering a zoomorphic version of Lear's life-long commitment to male friendship. It begins with a meeting on another sea-shore:

> Once Mr Daddy Long-legs,
>   Dressed in brown and gray,
> Walked about upon the sands
>   Upon a summer's day;
> And there among the pebbles,
>   When the wind was rather cold,
> He met with Mr Floppy Fly,
>   All dressed in blue and gold.
> And as it was too late to dine,
> They drank some Periwinkle-wine,
> And played an hour or two, or more,
> At battlecock and shuttledore.[30]

The well-dressed insects are very much Victorian gentlemen of leisure, and their relationship is played out in a shared drink of wine ('Periwinkle-wine' is more marine than usual vintages but manages to sound refined and sparkling) followed by a variant on battledore and shuttlecock (the precursor of badminton, which began to replace it in the 1850s). The elegantly elongated stanza of twelve lines is, as usual, crystalline in its metrical and narrative articulation. Again, however, it is less symmetrical than it looks. Divided into two parts, the octave has alternately rhymed and unrhymed lines (*abcb-defe*), in alternating tetrameters and trimeters, while the last four lines consist of a pair of rhymed tetrameter couplets. Constructed around the two protagonists, who are named in one line with their clothing described in the following one, the first six lines are given over to Mr Daddy Long-legs, named in the first line, while the last six include Mr Floppy Fly, named in the middle of the poem in the sixth line. The final, slightly metrically expanded and more closely rhymed quatrain, is given over to their shared time and space. The move towards this shared space defines the trajectory of the stanza and then the narrative as a whole. The nonsensically jumbled 'battlecock and shuttledore' gives them a game of their own, turning what might have been a battle or a cock-fight into a ceremonial equivalent of the dance enjoyed by the owl and pussy-cat.

As the eclogue-like conversation between the winged bachelors develops, it becomes increasingly and symmetrically mournful. The Fly reveals he no longer goes to court because he's ashamed of his short legs, while the Daddy Long-legs is no longer able to sing the kind of 'mumbian melody' the Fly enjoyed in the past, because his legs 'are grown too long'. This brings about a Dover Beach-style revelation of the tragic condition of the world on the sea-shore:

> They said, 'This is a dreadful thing!
>   The world has all gone wrong,
> Since one has legs too short by half,
>   The other much too long!...'

This has something of the awful symmetry of Beckett's *Endgame*, where Clov says 'I can't sit', and Hamm says 'And I can't stand', leading to the mordant reply, 'Every man his speciality'.[31] Unlike *Endgame*, however, Lear's poem imagines a triumphant exilic finale, in which the couple leave the court and society completely behind:

> Then Mr Daddy Long-legs
>   And Mr Floppy Fly
> Rushed downward to the foamy sea
>   With one sponge-taneous cry;
> And there they found a little boat,
>   Whose sails were pink and gray;
> And off they sailed among the waves,
>   Far, and far away.
> They sailed across the silent main,
> And reached the great Gromboolian plain;
> And there they play for evermore
> At battlecock and shuttledore.

Their journey recapitulates that of the Owl and Pussy-cat, the 'pink and gray' sails reminding us of the parti-coloured 'brown and gray' and 'blue and gold' coats of the protagonists as well as the 'pea-green boat' of their predecessors. The nonce-word 'spongetaneous' gives their spontaneity an appealing receptivity to water, and the end-words 'sea', 'waves', and 'silent main' evoke their maritime journey 'Far, and far away' to the 'great Gromboolian plain' (this being the first appearance of Lear's haunting geographical adjective.)

'The Jumblies' is the most triumphant of Lear's many escape stories, an account of a romantic sea-voyage in a sieve that is also a celebration of group solidarity in the face of group disapproval. Though 'everyone cried, "You'll all be drowned!", the 'Jumblies' chorus defiantly, 'But we don't care a button! we don't care a fig!/In a Sieve we'll go to sea!'[32] The paired 'button' and 'fig' hark back to 'Teapots and Quails', but 'The Jumblies' is unusual in Lear's poems in recounting a genuinely communal venture rather than setting an isolated individual or incongruous pair against what Auden called the 'legions of cruel inquisitive They'. Though Lear's green-headed travellers set off on a journey of exploration like those invoked in 'Ulysses' and Carroll's *The Hunting of the Snark*, they don't have a leader like Tennyson's oratorical Ulysses or Carroll's dyspraxic Bellman. The name 'Jumblies' clarifies Lear's interest in this particular crew. It derives from the noun 'jumble' and the associated adjective 'jumbled'. *OED* defines this as 'A confused or disorderly mixture or assemblage, a medley; also, disorder, muddle', quoting Cudworth in 1678 referring to 'a confused Jumble of Created, and Uncreated Beings' and Lady Wortley Montague's 'I have the oddest jumble of disagreeable things in my head'. The dictionary gives another equally relevant colloquial sense, meaning 'A shock, shaking, or jolting', exemplified by Fanny Burney in 1823 speaking of 'brisk jumbles in a carriage' and J. Colquoun in 1851 saying 'the jumble of the sea made shooting uncertain'. Lear's etymological coinage brilliantly evokes both a 'disorderly mixture or assemblage' and the percussive travel motion enthusiastically embraced by the Jumblies, who proclaim 'we never can think we were rash or wrong, / While round in our Sieve we spin!'

With its itemized record of discoveries and purchases ('And they bought a Pig, and some green Jack-daws, / And a lovely Monkey with lollipop paws, / And forty bottles of Ring-Bo-Ree, / And no end of Stilton Cheese'), the poem parodies accounts of contemporary geographical expeditions like Darwin's *Voyage of the Beagle* (though the 'Stilton Cheese' suggests that their itinerary must have included a visit to Britain as well as more exotic places). Its comic buoyancy depends on Lear's mastery of different measures (or scales). The Lilliputian boat has a 'pea-green veil', a 'riband by way of a sail', a 'tobacco pipe mast', and 'crockery-jar' shelter, but it sails on an epic journey through 'moonlight pale' to 'the Western Sea', recalling Tennyson's Ulysses, who determines 'To sail beyond the sunset, and the baths / Of all the western stars'.[33] The poem sets neatly prosaic and utile values ('a useful Cart, / And a pound of Rice') against Romantic ones, as when they 'whistled and warbled a moony song / To the echoing sound of a coppery gong, / In the shade of the mountains brown'. They bring back both 'a hive of silvery bees' and 'forty bottles of Ring-Bo-Ree', reminding us that in Lear's nonsense (as in Tennyson) counting matters, metrically and numerically. At the end we hear that 'In twenty years they all came back', only to find this qualified mysteriously to 'In twenty years or more'. Nothing is wholly predictable in Lear's metrical universe, however, and it is surprising to find the stanza enumerating the spoils of their voyage weighs in at one line short (nine lines plus the chorus rather than the usual ten). This reminds us that the poem is about the Jumblies defying restrictive social anathema ('And happen what may, it's extremely wrong/ In a Sieve to sail so fast!'), and resisting the apparently sensible admonitions of their elders against a long maritime journey in a vessel full of holes. The youthful sailors return triumphantly after an Odyssean voyage that takes them 'to the Western Sea', 'the Lakes', the 'Torrible Zone', and the 'hills of the Chankly Bore', regions informed by Lear's traveller's pictorial sensibility and etymological flair; the 'Torrible Zone' offering a 'horrible' or 'terrible' version of a 'Tropical Zone' and the 'Chankly Bore' a crankier version of the Severn Bore, defined by the *OED* as 'a violent encounter of two tides coming in'. The poem itself is about potentially violent encounters between different scales of value, but manages to keep them equably in balance as it sails calmly on.

Its form, like its cast, is essentially choric, and depends on repetition. The same choric refrain provides the final quatrain of all six 14-line stanzas, so that the last line of each echoes the opening 'They went to sea in a Sieve'. That initial nonsensical proposition involving an impossible vessel defined by its own leakiness rings through the entire poem, establishing its fugue-like motif and time-signature. It is notionally repeated in the first line itself ('They went to sea in a sieve, *they did*'), recurs in the second (as if the poem began as well as ended with a chorus), before being repeated another three times in the first stanza alone (making five times in all). However absurd, the declaration has clear shape and motor power. With two strong iambs followed by an anapaest (sandwiched by another iamb), it generates a dynamic momentum. The psalmist speaks of 'They that go down to the sea in ships', but the Jumblies' 'sieve' alliterates with 'sea' and subliminally sifts the sound of 'sea' within it. As the phrase recurs across each stanza, it expands, with the initial iambic beat ('They went to sea') modifying at the end of each stanza into an anapaestic one ('And they went to sea in a sieve'). Here the nonsense vessel which enables us as readers to experience the escapist journey of discovery is like a paradigm of nonsense poetry itself. Not only does the narrative come full circle at the close, with the Jumblies' triumphant return to the land they left at the outset, but the poem's choric last line ('And they went to sea in a sieve') returns upon its first.

The poem's Chorus provides the girder for its chaconne-like structure:

> Far and few, far and few,
>> Are the lands where the Jumblies live;
> Their heads are green, and their hands are blue,
> And they went to sea in a sieve.

On the face of it 'Far and few / Are the lands where the Jumblies live' is an understatement, since blue and green humans are farrer and fewer than is implied, and given the absence of any evidence of their geographical reality. Nevertheless the insistence on their distance and fewness lessens our sense of their non-existence, underlining the blithely Utopian status of the narrative. The chorus is characteristically shapely, with the alliterative phrase 'Far and few' repeated symmetrically within the bi-partite first line, setting up a strong trochaic counter-beat, with four stresses packed in its six words. The following two lines locate the protagonists in numerically small but nonetheless plural countries and offer a chromatic description that transcends our normal racial categories (they are 'blue' and 'green' rather than 'black' or 'white'). The lines shift between metrical categories too, with the second a bi-partite anapaestic line ('Are the lands where the Jumblies live'), the third a regular iambic tetrameter with a medial anapaest, and the last an anapaest sandwiched between iambs.

Metrical analysis makes heavy weather of a marvellously light vessel, but underlines the complexity of Lear's vehicles of metaphorical transport. 'The Courtship of the Yonghy-Bonghy-Bò' is a sadder romantic travel poem, but its form is even more intricate. A tragic-comic narrative of disappointed love, it dramatizes an unsuccessful marriage proposal made by the diminutive and nationally indeterminate 'Mr Yonghy-Bonghy-Bò' to the clearly English Lady Jingly Jones. Set on the exotic 'Coast of Coromandel' in Southern India, Lady Jones is first found 'talking / To some milk-white hens of Dorking' on 'a little heap of stones'.[34] Mr Bò's 'worldly goods', when itemized, amount only to 'Two old chairs, and half a candle,—/One old jug without a handle', but in making his romantic proposal, he offers them all to her, at the same time combining them with a picturesque but pragmatically enriched view of the sea:

> 'On the Coast of Coromandel
>   Shrimps and watercresses glow,
> Prawns are plentiful and cheap,'
>   Said the Yonghy-Bonghy-Bò.
> 'You shall have my chairs and candle,
> And my jug without a handle!
>   Gaze upon the rolling deep
>   (Fish is plentiful and cheap;)
>   As the sea, my love is deep!'
> Said the Yonghy-Bonghy-Bò,
> Said the Yonghy-Bonghy-Bò.

The romantic setting of the Indian coast, with a view over 'the rolling deep', and the touching love-song note of 'As the sea, my love is deep', are combined with a characteristically practical insistence on food and cost, as he insists that both prawns and fish are 'plentiful and cheap'. It turns out that the almost propertyless Mr Bò has no chance, since the aristocratic lady declines his offer, saying 'In England I've a mate!', before giving her husband's full name as 'Mr Jones—(his name is Handel),—/Handel-Jones, Esquire & Co'. Before the full panoply of Victorian bourgeois marriage suggested by the mercantile name 'Handel-Jones, Esquire & Co' (absurdly combining gentility and trade in one double-barrel), Mr Bò's modest proposal understandably falls flat. He sets off on Turtle-back 'With a sad primaeval motion / Towards the sunset isles of Boshen', leaving Lady Jingly Jones upon her 'heap of stones', where in his 'jug without a handle' she 'mourns' and 'moans / for the Yonghy-Bonghy-Bò'. In a poem caught between the irreconcilable values of 'The Coast of Coromandel' and 'Dorking', of 'Mr Bò' and 'Lady Jingly Jones', the 'sunset isles of Boshen' echo the biblical 'Land of Goshen' while internally incorporating the nonsense word 'Bosh' and Mr Bò's own name.

This poignantly absurd story of unconsummated extra-marital love is told in ten stanzas, with an elaborately Rossetti-like rhyme-scheme repeated religiously across the entire poem. The first four lines of each stanza take an easy *abcb* pattern, suggesting a ballad form of alternating rhymed and unrhymed lines, but both *b* and *c* rhyme-words are later woven into a fixed, absolutely *sui generis* scheme of rhymed triplets and couplets within a fixed *abcbaacccbb* structure (as in the stanza just quoted). This gives an eleven-line musical frame, built out of the end-rhymes of the first three lines (three *a*-rhymes, four *b*-rhymes, and four *c*-rhymes which include one triple-rhyme). This robust but syncopated and asymmetrical stanza form grounds the poem's comically poignant narrative and generates an effect that is both extravagantly Baroque and playfully *cantabile*. It also enables Lear to play around with knockabout rhymes ('gladly' and 'madly', 'Handel' and 'handle', 'Bay of Gurtle' and 'lively Turtle'). The most outrageous is the triple-rhyme of 'body', 'Hoddy Doddy', and 'modi- / Fy', where the last breaks the line and modifies the poem's decorum in a cheeky Byronic style that counters the story's otherwise 'sad primaeval motion'.

Lear's late poem 'The Dong with a Luminous Nose' is once again set on a Tennysonian 'great Gromboolian plain' and is full of self-conscious echoes and allusions to his earlier narrative poems—particularly 'The Jumblies', whose haunting refrain it quotes twice ('Far and few, far and few / Are the lands where the Jumblies live'). The protagonist is a comic incarnation of a Romantic wanderer, smitten with love for a departed 'Jumbly Girl', and presented stalking through a picturesque landscape complete with 'rocky shore', 'towering heights', and 'angry breakers', where he is viewed by 'those who watch at that midnight hour / From Hall or Terrace or lofty Tower'.[35] The Dong hails from the love-torn world of Schubert and Schumann, Byron and Keats, as well as specifically recalling Tennyson's 'The Lady of Shalott', where 'Under tower and balcony, / By garden-wall and gallery, / A gleaming shape she floated by'.[36]

Formally speaking the poem's own 'gleaming shape' is one of Lear's most elaborate and rhapsodically irregular. Rather like a Pindaric ode, the stanzas expand and contract in terms of line-length and indentation. The first two stanzas, though differently lineated, are each seven lines long with the same interlaced rhyme-scheme of *aabccbc*. They are followed, however, by an eleven-line stanza, which is composed of four rhymed couplets which modulate into four lines in an alternating rhyme-scheme, giving a pattern of *aabbccddbdb*. Thereafter, the stanzas are of even-numbered but different numbers of lines (fourteen, twenty, ten, sixteen, and eighteen respectively). These take various forms, with two incorporating the chorus from the Jumblies, and the last eighteen-line stanza ending with a reprise of the metre of the finale of 'The Owl and the Pussy-Cat' in a melancholy minor key:

> 'Yonder—over the plain he goes;
>   He goes!
>   He goes;
> The Dong with a luminous Nose!'

The Dong is defined by an elaborate nasal prosthesis, constructed to enable him to see where he is going in his demented search through the darkness for his lost 'Jumbly Girl':

> He gathered the bark of the Twangum Tree
>   On the flowery plain that grows.
>   And he wove him a wondrous Nose,—
>   A Nose as strange as a Nose could be!
> Of Vast proportions and painted red,
> And tied with cords to the back of his head.

The Dong's nose provides a suggestive figure for Lear's therapeutic art, an elaborate comic construction, 'as strange' as it can be, that is designed to cast light in the darkness, and offer a reassuring point of reference for the audience on 'Hall or Terrace or lofty Tower'. The nose is made from natural ingredients, drawn from the healing bark of the musical-sounding 'Twangum Tree', a relative of the 'Bong-tree' which grows in his territory as on the Owl and Pussycat's honeymoon island. However, it has to be 'woven' into its wondrous shape, as a text or tapestry is woven, and tied with 'cords' that are both structural and musical. The Dong's music, however melancholy its psychological origins, is associated with light, a search for consolation, and recognition from others. His

elaborately constructed nose gives comic expression to Lear's sense of absurdity, enabling him to give voice to grief in memorably misfitting lyric form.

4. Self-Portraits in Convex Mirrors

Lear's late retrospective verse is his most avowedly autobiographical. If this is implicitly the case with 'The Dong with a Luminous Nose', it is openly so in 'How Pleasant to
Know Mr Lear' and 'Some Incidents in the Life of my Uncle Arly' (with its inclusion
of Lear's own name in 'UncLE ARly'). 'How Pleasant' is a brilliant self-portrait of the
author in the third person, accompanied by a luminous pen drawing (labelled 'from a
photograph'). As befits a relatively formal portrait of a man whose 'mind is concrete and
fastidious', and in contrast to the longer lyrical narratives, it is written in neatly rhymed
trimeter quatrains. Some of these are relatively normative:

> He has ears, and two eyes, and ten fingers,—
> (Leastways if you reckon two thumbs;)
> Long ago he was one of the singers,
> But now he is one of the dumms.[37]

Here, the precise and fastidious metrical as well as visual imagination of the poet
engages in the counting games he loves, using two rhymes, and a combination of iambic
and anapaestic metres, which play off prosaic anatomical enumeration (though the pair
of eyes is enumerated, and the pair of ears not) against the opposition between being
formerly '*one* of the singers' and now '*one* of the dumms', an opposition central to the
musical form of the verse. Later we hear 'His body is perfectly spherical', and this absurd
visual self-portrait is reflected in the circular, if not necessarily spherical, shape of the
poem, which ends as it begins with the phrase 'How pleasant to know Mr Lear!'

In a letter Lear described 'My aged uncle Arly' as 'the last nonsense poem I will ever
write'.[38] In another he introduced it by saying, 'I shall send you a few lines just to let you
know how your aged friend goes on' before quoting the first stanza:[39]

> O my agèd Uncle Arly!—
> Sitting on a heap of Barley
>   All the silent hours of night,—
> Close beside a leafy thicket:—
> On his nose there was a Cricket,—
> In his hat a Railway Ticket;—
> (But his shoes were far too tight).[40]

The letter sets up a transparent equation between Lear and Arly, an equation intensified
when Lear complains of being 'frightfully pulled down by my illness—with swollen feet;
and unable to walk'. Like the limerick, the poem suggests a form of constriction ('But
his shoes were far too tight'). It is relatively conventional in shape, consisting of seven

regular but asymmetrical seven-line stanzas rhymed *aabcccb*. Each stanza consists of one, stretched, often self-interrupted sentence, giving a sense of a complex biography encapsulated in a confined space, like the shoes that are far too tight. Shoes contain feet, of course, and feet suggest metre, and this brief life of a traveller is cast in a basically four-beat metre, though it is regularly caught between trochaic tetrameters and ana-paestic dimeters (as in the opening line, which can be read 'O my ăgèd Uncle Ărly', or the last which can be read 'But his shŏes are far too tĭght'). Arly's companionable cricket is described as 'Chirping with a cheerious measure', and 'measure' as always is important, as when we hear he has been walking for 'three-and-forty winters'.

As in limericks, the heap of Barley seems determined by the need to rhyme (here with 'Arly'), yet it sets the protagonist on a measurable 'heap', suggesting a measure of his accu-mulated years (or ears). Barley is associated with beer and bread-making, but according to the *OED* barleycorns were also used as units of measurement and associated with the rites of Demeter, who some scholars take to mean 'Barley-mother'. The name 'Uncle Arly', as well as being an anagram of Lear, is a nonce one.[41] Though it looks like the adjective 'early' with a missing 'e', it is also a suffix, as in 'regularly' or 'singularly'. Lear's nonsense lyricism, as so often, moves between the expansive and reductive, the 'Timskoop Hills afar' and the 'Railway Ticket'. Like a later version of the Yonghy-Bonghy-Bó, the exiled Arly, with this nose, Cricket, hat, and ticket, is reduced to a minimum of props. However, he is also compared to the 'Ancient Medes and Persians', a phrase echoing the Book of Daniel's 'law of the Medes and Persians which altereth not', and he makes his living 'at intervals by selling / Propter's Nicodemus Pills', medicine that with its association to the New Testament Nicodemus (who visited Jesus by night), might be designed to improve night vision. The phrase about the tight shoes has a choric ring, occurring at the end of the fifth stanza, as well as the first and last, each time enclosed tightly in brackets. After his many years of wandering, Arly returns to 'Borly-Melling, / Near his old ancestral dwell-ing', a convincing English place-name which is an anagram of 'Merely Boring', resonates with the name 'Arly' and takes up the earlier rhymes of 'spelling', 'yelling', and 'selling'.

The poem, as so often in Lear, comes full circle, with the death of Arly on his heap of Barley. The opening rhymes are reversed ('On a little heap of Barley / Died my agèd Uncle Arly'), as are the later ones of 'Ticket' and 'Cricket'. Nevertheless the rhyme-words are the same, so that it ends with the odd post-mortem parenthetical comment '(But his shoes were far too tight')', reminding us that the always mobile traveller's life was marked throughout by pedestrian pains caused by inappropriate footwear. A compulsive wan-derer and exile like the poet, Arly is caught in a form that constricts his movement, a fact the tightly bound poem comically mirrors yet triumphs over. Like the Dong's 'wondrous nose', Arly's shoes are a resource and a limitation, a symbol of confinement and mobil-ity, restriction and travel. In these respects they are an apt emblem of Lear's resilient formal imagination. Though the tight shoes cause pain, Arly never thinks of jettisoning them. Keats, reflecting self-consciously on the 'pained loveliness' of the elaborately fet-tered sonnet, imagined 'Sandals more interwoven and complete / To fit the naked foot of Poesy'.[42] Arly's constricted shoes, like the Dong's elaborately constructed nose, can be read as a reflex of Lear's investment in tight metrical forms and the choreography of feet in motion. This in turn is a sign of his commitment in his nonsense art to the 'fiddlediddlety of representation' he valued in his painting. Arly's shoes may cause pain, but their anomalous tightness gives the poem the quirky gait and comic buoyancy characteristic of Lear's immaculately 'cheerious' lyrics.

NOTES

1. T. S. Eliot, 'The Music of Poetry' (1942), in *On Poetry and Poets* (London: Faber & Faber, 1957), 29.
2. Edward Lear, 'Eclogue', 'Journal', and verse-letter, in *Complete Verse and Other Nonsense,* ed. Vivien Noakes (London: Penguin, 2001), 3–5, 10–13, and 153–4.
3. G. K. Chesterton, 'A Defence of Nonsense', in *The Defendant* (London: Dent, 1901), 68.
4. Matthew Campbell, *Rhythm and Will in Victorian Poetry* (Cambridge: Cambridge University Press, 1999), 11.
5. Matthew Bevis, 'Tennyson's Humour', in Seamus Perry and Robert Douglas-Fairhurst, eds., *Tennyson Among the Poets* (Oxford: Oxford University Press, 2009), 243.
6. *Letters of Edward Lear to Chichester Fortescue*, ed. Lady Strachey (London: T. Fisher Unwin, 1909), 116.
7. *Letters of Edward Lear to Chichester Fortescue,* 116.
8. Elizabeth Sewell, *The Field of Nonsense* (London: Chatto & Windus, 1952).
9. Lear, various poems in *Complete Verse,* 238, 424, 247, 457.
10. Anonymous, 'There was an old man of Tobago', in *Chatto Book of Nonsense Poetry,* ed. Hugh Haughton (London: Chatto & Windus, 1988), 208.
11. Edward Lear, 'Introduction' to *A Book of Nonsense* (1844) quoted in *Lear in the Original,* ed. Herbert Liebert (London: Oxford University Press, 1975), 17.
12. Lear, various poems in *Complete Verse,* 337, 360, 377, 97.
13. Lear, manuscript poem quoted in *Lear in the Original,* 74.
14. Lear, 'There was an old man with a beard', in *Complete Verse,* 157.
15. Lear, 'There was an old man of Apulia', in *Complete Verse,* 95.
16. Lear, 'Ribands and Pigs', in *Complete Verse,* 135.
17. Lear, *Complete Verse,* 137.
18. Lear, *Complete Verse,* 148.
19. Samuel Johnson, *Lives of the Poets,* Vol. 1 (London: Oxford University Press, 1968), 14.
20. Samuel Johnson, *Lives of the Poets, Vol. 1,* 14.
21. Lear, 'The Duck and the Kangaroo', in *Complete Verse,* 207.
22. Lear, 'The Owl and the Pussy-cat', in *Complete Verse,* 238.
23. Karl Shapiro and Robert Beum note that stanzas of ten or more lines are harder 'to feel and grasp as a unit', *A Prosody Handbook* (New York: Harper & Row, 1965), 126. This is certainly not the case in Lear.
24. Christina Rossetti has a poem 'If a Pig Wore a Wig': 'If a pig wore a wig / What could we say? / Treat him as a gentleman, / And say 'Good Day'. / If his tail chanced to fail/ What could we do?/ Send him to the tailoress/ To get one new.' Lear's pig is also treated as a gentleman.
25. Johann Wolfgang Goethe, *Selected Verse,* ed. David Luke (London: Penguin Books, 1964), 85; George Gordon, Lord Byron, *The Bride of Abydos in Poetical Works* (Oxford: Oxford University Press, 1975), 264.
26. Manuscript of 'The Owl and the Pussy-cat', in *Complete Verse,* 507.

27. Vivien Noakes suggests, without any evidence, that it may derive from an ash tree near some cottages called 'the Little Bongs' near Knowsley. She also records variants on 'Bong' in other manuscripts, 'Phloss tree' and 'Palm Tree'. *Complete Verse*, 507.

28. Lear, 'The Children of the Owl and the Pussy-cat', in *Complete Verse*, 450, 541.

29. MS, David Attenborough; *Complete Verse*, 341–2.

30. Lear, 'The Daddy Long-legs and the Fly', in *Complete Verse*, 246.

31. Samuel Beckett, *Endgame, in The Complete Dramatic Works* (London: Faber and Faber, 1986) 97.

32. Lear, 'The Jumblies', in *Complete Verse*, 254.

33. Alfred Tennyson, 'Ulysses', in *Poems of Tennyson*, 3 vols., ed. Christopher Ricks (London: Longmans, 1969), i. 565.

34. Lear, 'Coast of Coromandel', in *Complete Verse*, 324.

35. Lear, 'The Dong with a Luminous Nose', in *Complete Verse*, 422.

36. Tennyson, 'The Lady of Shalott', in *Poems of Tennyson*, i. 360–1.

37. Lear, 'How Pleasant to Know Mr Lear', in *Complete Verse*, 428.

38. Lear, letter to the wife of his doctor, 1 March 1886, quoted in *Complete Verse*, 546.

39. Lear, letter to Chichester Fortescue of 4 June 1884, *Later Letters of Edward Lear*, ed. Lady Strachey (London: T. Fisher Unwin, 1911), 309.

40. Lear, 'My aged uncle Arly', in *Complete Verse*, 456.

41. Thomas Byrom, *Nonsense and Wonder: The Poems and Cartoons of Edward Lear* (New York: Dutton, 1977), 213.

42. John Keats, 'On the Sonnet', in *The Complete Poems*, ed. John Barnard (London: Penguin, 1977), 340.

SELECT BIBLIOGRAPHY

Auden, W. H., Introduction to *Oxford Book of Light Verse* (Oxford: Clarendon Press, 1938)

Byrom, T., *Nonsense and Wonder: The Poems and Cartoons of Edward Lear* (New York: E. P. Dutton, 1977).

Colley, Ann C., 'Edward Lear's Limericks and the Reversals of Nonsense', in *Victorian Poetry* 26.3 (1988). Special Edition 'In Honor of Edward Lear' ed. Ina Rae Hark, 285–299.

Chesterton, G. K., 'A Defence of Nonsense', in *The Defendant* (London: Dent, 1901).

Eliot, T. S., 'The Music of Poetry', in *On Poetry and Poets* (London: Faber, 1957).

Freud, Sigmund, *The Joke and its Relation to the Unconscious*, translated by Joyce Crick, with an introduction by John Carey (London: Penguin, 2003).

Haughton, Hugh ed., *Chatto Book of Nonsense Poetry* (London: Chatto & Windus, 1988).

Lecercle, Jean-Jacques, *The Philosophy of Nonsense* (London: Routledge, 1994).

Noakes, Vivien, *Edward Lear: The Life of a Wanderer* (London: Collins, 1968).

Sewell, Elizabeth, *The Field of Nonsense* (London: Chatto & Windus, 1952).

Stewart, Susan, *Nonsense: Aspects of Intertextuality in Folklore and Literature* (Baltimore: Johns Hopkins University Press, 1979).

CHAPTER 22

CRIME AND CONJECTURE: EMILY BRONTË'S POEMS

MICHAEL WOOD

I

AT the beginning of *Wuthering Heights*, Lockwood, the narrator, makes a series of mannered mistakes that would be patently funny if the context permitted anything resembling laughter. He thinks a bunch of dead rabbits on a cushion is a cat kept as a household pet; he assumes Catherine Heathcliff is Heathcliff's youthful wife; and he supposes that Hareton Earnshaw must be Heathcliff's son. On the last of these occasions, Heathcliff says, 'Unhappy in your conjectures, sir', and I want to pause over some of the implications of the very possibility of this splendid utterance.

The pause itself may remove us a little from many familiar conceptions of Emily Brontë and her writing: as rough, rude, unbending, gifted but savage, for example. Even Charlotte Brontë, the well-meaning source of a good deal of this mythology, reports Emily as smiling at a reading of an anxious review of *Wuthering Heights*. Emily is Ellis Bell in this account, and not a writer of indeterminate sex but clearly a woman mockingly disguised as a man: Charlotte is describing a she and saying 'he'. 'It is not his wont to laugh', Charlotte remarks, 'but he smiled half-amused and half in scorn as he listened'.[1] She could be talking about Heathcliff in the scene I have just evoked.

Really? What about Heathcliff the raw and evil figure who returns to civilization only to wreck it, the character Charlotte Brontë thought it might not be 'right or advisable' to create? Scornful, yes; but half-amused? Surely he can't be half anything, and is never amused. This is what Lockwood thinks, once he has got over his impression that Heathcliff is 'a capital fellow'. But Lockwood can report things he fails to understand, and it is notable that he says 'Heathcliff smiled again', when so far he has not described Heathcliff as smiling at all. He has told us about a grimace of hatred directed at Catherine, and 'an almost diabolical sneer' at Lockwood's second mistake—Heathcliff isn't present for the first.[2] So what does 'again' mean? I take it as a recognition of the smile in Heathcliff's tone, a blurred, belated indication that Heathcliff, for all his grimness, has plenty of style and wit; and perhaps as an oblique invitation (from a prescient Emily Brontë) to watch our own mythologizing, especially if we have seen too many movies, and thought too much about the moors without going there.

Heathcliff's response to Lockwood is carefully crafted to adapt and counter his tenant's affectations. When the man takes Catherine for Heathcliff's wife, he is both making small talk and trying to cheer everyone up ('They could not every day sit so grim and taciturn; and it was impossible, however ill-tempered they might be, that the universal scowl they wore was their every-day countenance'[3]). The way he goes about it is this:

> It is strange how custom can mould our tastes and ideas: many could not imagine the existence of happiness in a life of such complete exile from the world as you spend, Mr. Heathcliff; yet, I'll venture to say, that, surrounded by your family, and with your amiable lady as the presiding genius over your home and heart—[4]

Heathcliff interrupts at this point with his sneer to wonder where Lockwood thinks his amiable lady is. Lockwood explains that he means Heathcliff's wife, as if this rude northerner might not quite understand periphrasis, and Heathcliff instead of exploding or grunting, pretends to take him at his word: 'Well, yes—Oh! you would intimate that her spirit has taken the post of ministering angel, and guards the fortunes of Wuthering Heights, even when her body is gone. Is that it?' It's true that neither Lockwood nor the first-time reader knows anything of the novel's story yet, but given the intensity of Heathcliff's hatred for Isabella, this is both a cool and an elaborate reply, full of what we must take to be private amusement and scorn, as in the scene in Charlotte's letter. And when Lockwood moves to his third mistake, it is again through a bit of fancy wording, namely his suggestion that Hareton, as Heathcliff's son, must be the 'favoured possessor of the beneficent fairy'—that is Catherine, the erstwhile erroneously placed amiable lady. Hareton doesn't say anything, just looks furious and mutters a curse, and Heathcliff says, 'Unhappy in your conjectures, sir'.[5]

The beauty of the phrase—surely a reason for admiring Heathcliff's style, however much we may disapprove of his hatreds—lies both in its understatement (Lockwood is not just wrong but wildly and unkindly wrong) and its simple truth (Lockwood is unfortunate, his reading of the appearances is not implausible, and Catherine is indeed a Mrs Heathcliff). There are riches of meaning in both the adjective and the noun: 'unhappy' mainly means 'unlucky' in this context, but then think of all the other things it means, including the sense of domestic happiness evoked in Lockwood's speech; and 'conjectures' discreetly puts Lockwood's curiosity and its façade of sociability in their proper place as intrusive, snooping guesswork.

We find just this tone in some of Brontë's French exercises, again often taken as revealing a dark, untamed nature, rather than a person trying to get a little self-entertainment out of her homework. Surely her brilliant performance in a letter of apology from a music teacher, concluding with the writer's anticipated relief in not having to hear her wretched

pupil play ('je n'aurais pas la mortification d'être témoin du mauvais succès de mon tra-
vail…car je crains que votre exécution ne soit un peu trop remarquable'), belongs in the
latter category.[6] 'A little too remarkable' has just the same feel as Heathcliff's 'unhappy'.
It suggests someone adapted to the ways of the world and quite skilful in them—deft at
understatement and indirection—yet whose relation to that world is mocking at best,
consistently informed by half-portions of scorn and amusement.

But the moment in the exercises that most helps us with Brontë's voicing of this relation—and points us irresistibly towards the poems—is when Intemperance, leading the
candidates for the newly created post as Death's prime minister (the other runners are
Anger, Vengeance, Envy, Treason, Famine, Plague, Ambition, and Fanaticism), makes
her friend an important part of her campaign. 'J'ai une amie', she says in not entirely idiomatic French, 'devant laquelle toute cette assemblée sera forcée à succomber'.[7] Every
century will increase this friend's power, and she will see off ambition and anger, fanaticism, and famine, and all the rest. As Janet Gezari reminds us, this particular friend
doesn't appear in Charlotte's version of the same test, although Intemperance still carries
the day as in the model the young women were given, Jean-Pierre Florian's *Fables*.[8] The
friend's name is Civilization.

II

Emily Brontë became famous as a poet—well, two or three of her poems became mod-
erately famous—without being intensely read or deeply studied, and when her themes
and preoccupations turned out not quite to be those that 1980s' and 1990s' feminism
was looking for, she suffered a sort of unintentional neglect, almost becoming, as Gezari
finely puts it, 'inconsiderable again'.[9] And yet her best poems often place women in positions of extraordinary authority and power, and could even be thought of as inhabiting something like Julia Kristeva's third stage of women's time, where gender differences
would not disappear but cease to play most of their earlier roles. Whether such a stage
can be arrived at historically, outside of theory and poems, is of course another question.

This ignoring or resituating of gender is also relevant to the distinction (made by
Brontë herself and pounced on by critics and biographers) between Gondal poems and
others, since it is inevitably part of any story we construct around any particular set of
lines. I think Gezari is right to call this distinction 'specious', but it's worth spelling out
what 'specious' means in this context. It's not that there is no difference between the two
sets of poems, either in Brontë's mind or on the page, or both, only that the difference
won't do the work it is supposed to do. It won't supply or get rid of narrative, it won't help
us to separate what is personal from what is performed, or what is lyric from what is
dramatic.

Long ago, Fannie Ratchford made a bold and counterintuitive claim along these lines.
She thought the distinction was not specious but non-existent, since 'many, perhaps all'
of Brontë's poems belonged to the Gondal sequence, that is, 'were actually units in a

flaming epic of a purely imaginary world and its people'. Later in the same book she revised this claim to represent a 'conviction that all of Emily's verse, as we have it, falls within the Gondal context'. This was as we had it in 1955, but all the poems in the most recent editions had been published by then. Ratchford was 'convinced' that even the well-known 'No coward soul is mine', notoriously recited at Emily Dickinson's funeral, 'was spoken by a Gondalan facing a crisis incident to the Republican-Royalist conflict'.[10]

The attraction of this view is not its accuracy, since we know Brontë herself separated her Gondal poems from the others, but a sort of metaphorical critical truth. When Ratchford writes that not until a certain poem 'is reached in the reading does one become thoroughly aware of the compact unity of the group and feel intense conviction of the Gondal world', she is claiming more for Gondal than it will sustain, either in its fragmentary or reconstructed forms.[11] But it is the case, I think, that when one reaches the poem in question, 'The Death of A. G. A.', which Brontë worked on in January 1841 and May 1844, number 148 out of 181 in Gezari's edition, one registers a clear and urgent sense of Brontë's poetic project and what it required, whether one had such a sense before or not. The project required not so much a plot and an imaginary world as a moral occasion, fictional or actual, that would collect otherwise floating passions, and show us what was at stake beside loneliness, hopelessness, and mortality, which so many of the early poems insist on tunefully but vaguely, with an inordinate use of the word 'drear'. I'm not suggesting that Brontë's poems need a narrative, located in Gondal or elsewhere, only that to arrive at their strongest form they need to animate persons to whom damage can accrue or has accrued, and who can speak about their condition, or rather, who can play out their condition in their speech, rather than just mention it. This need is met in many poems, both those identified as belonging to the Gondal sequence, and those found in the other notebook.

'The Death of A. G. A.' is Brontë's longest poem and was not published until 1902—that is, it did not appear in *Poems by Currer, Ellis and Acton Bell* in 1846, or with the reprint of *Wuthering Heights and Agnes Grey* in 1850. It can't therefore, for early readers, have been the best way into the intensities of Brontë's verse, but it is a good place to start all the same. There is a certain amount of conventional diction here, taking the easy way into what feels like 'poetry' ('a weapon dire', 'features rare', 'bathed in gore', 'dreary doom', 'unweeting'), but the shifts of rhyme-scheme and timely reversals of stress are inventive; and the anger and violence of the characters and their world certainly find memorable expression. 'Were they shepherds', the poem begins, 'who sat all day / On that brown mountainside?' Of course they weren't and the speaker is scarcely pretending to ask, just evoking an innocence that will vanish immediately: a feigned conjecture, so to speak. They have long hair, and they are armed—a little later we learn that they are outlaws, a 'hunted band'. One of them looks like a princess, but an angry one, and the speaker remarks that it is 'well' that she has 'no subject land to sway': 'Fear might have made her vassals yield / But Love had been far away—'.[12] Love for her subjects, that is, because, in a sudden switch entirely characteristic of Brontë's writing, love in the shape of a man professing his passion for her is 'even at her feet'. He is Douglas, a 'wanderer' all his life, who has been tortured by 'men and laws' and spilt 'guiltless blood', but still loves this woman with the purity of an angel's devotion. She is Angelica, and she has other things in mind than Douglas' suit:

> I've known a hundred kinds of love [she says]
> All made the loved one rue;
> And what is thine, that it should prove
> Than other love, more true?

But today she has a new idea, or a new energy to pursue an old idea. She tells him of a childhood friend who was her 'all sufficing light', but who betrayed her by taking from her (and then abandoning) the man who was her 'dearer self'. This treacherous woman

> Laid my best affections low—
> Then mocked my grief and scorned my prayers
> And drowned my bloom of youth in tears—
> Warning, reproaches, both were vain;
> What recked she of another's pain?

Angelica then recounts an extraordinary scene, brilliantly adapted from *Hamlet*, where the prince spares Claudius because he is praying ('And now I'll do't. And so he goes to heaven... Why, this is hire and salary, not revenge!'). She found her enemy alone and in the open, she says, 'unarmed, as helpless as a child / She slumbered on a sunny lea'. Angelica got close enough to kill her, had her knife in her hand and her arm raised, but then the woman awoke and 'uttered such a dreary sigh' that Angelica, arriving at Hamlet's result by a reverse reason, decided 'she should not die / Since living was such misery'. But now she's ready 'to send [her] to hell', and asks for Douglas's help.

The next two sections of the poem show first the death of the still unnamed woman's two friends, Surry and Lesley, presumably fatally stabbed by the eager Douglas, and then Douglas and Angelica as they lie in wait for the woman we now learn is called Augusta—those are her initials in the title of the poem, of course. She arrives at the scene, and pauses to drink from a well. Then she turns to meet what the poem calls 'the Murderer's gaze', a sort of metonymy for something much more violent, since her hair and face are immediately streaming with blood. A long fight follows, in which gender seems to be ignored, and in a masterly double-take we see Augusta lying 'alone' on a green bank by the stream, only to learn in the next stanza that Douglas is dead too, and that Angelica, who appears to have been watching this mutual slaughter, has chosen to 'turn in mockery' from her suitor's 'last hopeless agony... And leave the hungry hawk to be / Sole watcher of the dead'. There follows an extraordinary sequence describing the dead Augusta, where the rhymes in three of the stanzas almost become repetitions of a single phoneme (swoon, gone, moon, stone; fell, pale, well, tale), and in one case offer a perfect visual echo as well as a proximity in sound: breath, heath, beneath, Death. It's as if the bones of language itself have been called upon to make a highly formalized funeral frieze. The last section of the poem records the meditation of one Lord Eldred over Augusta's body. He sounds a bit like Charlotte Brontë imagining Emily would have mellowed with age ('Had she but lived, her mind would of itself have grown like a strong tree, loftier, straighter, wider-spreading') and it's entertaining to think of Emily herself giving expression to this thought—if quite hard to believe she actually subscribed to it:

> For what thou wert, I would not grieve,
> But much, for what thou wert to be...
> Thy passionate youth was nearly past
> The opening sea seemed smooth at last
> Yet vainly flowed the calmer wave...

Gezari reminds us that the last phrase comes from Milton, and discreetly lets us discover for ourselves that it names the location where Satan finds 'ease' after his rough passage through the realm of Chaos and Night. Not such a quiet time ahead after all. The allusion perfectly fits Gezari's own sense that Brontë loves to unfinish what she seems to have completed.

III

Many of Brontë's poems—more than a third even by the most conservative count—depict the conspiracies and passions of the Gondal world, but two in particular show to a marked degree how a childhood game, while retaining the stark and extreme sense of crisis of the initial mode (when Brontë mentions Gondal in letters or notes, there always seems to an invasion going on), could modulate into an exploration of intricate and inward moral questions. In 'Why ask to know the date—the clime?', a mercenary fighting in an alien civil war takes on the manners of the place and period:

> I grew hard—I learnt to wear
> An iron front to terror's prayer;
> I learnt to turn my ears away
> From torture's groans, as well as they.
> By force I learnt—what power had I?
> To say the conquered should not die?[13]

Terror here, we perhaps now need to add, means fear not terrorism. But for all his talk, this man is not without conscience or compassion—'I was not to the centre, steel'—even if his qualms, in a very Brontëan move, at first make him behave worse not better. Mocking a dying prisoner, the leader of the enemy forces, was 'hard', he admits, meaning cruel, but immediately and trivially adds that the situation was tough for him too, since he had to keep himself awake somehow: 'twas hard my lids to keep / Through this long night, estranged from sleep'. This is self-entertainment in its negative mode, as when Lockwood, in the scene we have looked at, makes faces at the dogs in the living room of Wuthering Heights, and is attacked because the animals know even better than humans when they are being laughed at. The speaker continues with his 'cold insults o'er a dying bed', but understands now in memory that his sin is not violence or bloodshed but 'stifling mercy's voice within'. He learns this when his own son is taken by the enemy, and the dying prisoner, larger in spirit than his tormentor, refusing to cause 'equal woe', signs an order that no children are to be harmed. The speaker has already stabbed the prisoner's child four times before her father's eyes, but she survives, and the speaker guiltily looks after her. Here is how the poem ends:

> I could not rescue him his child
> I found alive and tended well
> But she was full of anguish wild
> And hated me like we hate hell
> And weary with her savage woe
> One moonless light I let her go

Even the absence of punctuation strikes a desolate note, as if no pause was possible in this harsh sequence. It's hard to imagine a stronger representation of what the unforgivable feels like to its perpetrator—especially when it's unforgiven.

   Brontë started a second version of this poem in May 1848, seven months before she died. The stance is more militant, more bluntly critical of 'our humanity' and the 'self-cursers avid of distress' who compose it. This is to say that the opening question—in this version 'Why ask to know what date what clime'—is manifestly rhetorical, since all dates and climes will undoubtedly reveal the same terrible behaviour. But then it's impossible to know where the poem is going, since it breaks off with the introduction of the mercenary, who is 'doubly cursed on foreign sod', and fighting 'neither for my home nor God'. The earlier version is lighter and faster, and not coincidentally, more lethal in its attack. The question is not entirely rhetorical. Time and place do make a difference, but not enough, and not in habits that matter:

> Why ask to know the date—the clime?
> More than mere words they cannot be:
> Men knelt to God and worshipped crime,
> And crushed the helpless even as we—
> But, they had learnt, from length of strife—
> Of civil war and anarchy
> To laugh at death and look on life
> With somewhat lighter sympathy.[14]

The terrible story of the two men and their children follows as an indication of what a lighter sympathy might look like. The unmentioned time and place could be anywhere but is somewhere; we are invited to supply alternatives if we can think of them, to make the words more than mere words. Is there a place and time where men have not knelt to God and worshipped crime? Done one and not the other, perhaps? And is this a God of crime, demanding worship, or is the 'and' a marker of hypocrisy: men knelt to a just God in supposed piety when all the while they were really worshipping crime. The interruption after 'we' allows us to be the crushers or the crushed, and the line break at 'life' has the wonderful effect of suggesting a complete and in its way admirable mentality: the ability to laugh at death and look on life, surely better than the other way round. Then we continue to read: no, they look on life with somewhat lighter sympathy. Only somewhat. The speed and obliquity of these lines, the amount of commentary implied without full statement, are amazing, almost Brechtian. I think of the remark in *Mother Courage* about the possibility of paying the enemy to let a prisoner go: 'They're human and after money like the rest of us. They're not wolves'.[15] They're human: they worship crime.

The second Brontë poem that so strongly shows how far the Gondal world can reach into complexity also exists in two versions. The text published in *Poems by Currer, Ellis and Acton Bell* was called 'The Prisoner (A Fragment)', and recounted a man's casual visit to his own dungeons, accompanied by an appropriately grim jailer. He seems surprised to find his 'guests' so 'darkly lodged', but—rather like the speaker of 'Why ask to know the date'—he cheers himself up by scoffing, in this case at the person who appears to be his sole prisoner, or at least the only one he has a conversation with: 'Art thou so much to fear, / That we must bind thee down and clench thy fetters here?'[16] This is an unpleasant bit of taunting tourism, but the man himself does draw our attention to his 'careless tongue', and his lack of concern for 'the lives wasting there away'. Then he sees the woman:

> The captive raised her face, it was as soft and mild
> As sculptured marble saint, or slumbering unwean'd child;
> It was so soft and mild, it was so sweet and fair,
> Pain could not trace a line, nor grief a shadow there.

She is indeed in chains, the woman says, but she will not be a prisoner for long. The jailer thinks she means someone is going to let her out, and seeks to disillusion her about any possible kindness in him or his master, but this only produces 'a smile almost of scorn', a combination we have seen before. She explains that no one can restore to her the life of her family or indeed her own life, so she has nothing to plead for. What she has is a firm expectation that death will soon set her free from prison and everything else. She expresses this expectation in lines which many critics regard as Brontë's finest, and which focus not on death but on its messenger:

> He comes with western winds, with evening's wandering airs,
> With that clear dusk of heaven that brings the thickest stars,
> Winds take a pensive tone, and stars a tender fire,
> And visions rise, and change, that kill me with desire.

The messenger brings an intuition of peace, 'mute music', 'unuttered harmony', the dawning of 'the Invisible': 'the Unseen its truth reveals'. But then the messenger departs; leaving only the mortal desire for his return, or rather for the final transfer to his world, since it is 'agony' to be back in the mortal body, 'When the ear begins to hear, and the eye begins to see; / When the pulse begins to throb, the brain to think again, / The soul to feel the flesh, and the flesh to feel the chain'. Then follows a stanza that completes the logic of the prisoner's thought—if death is a mystical union with the truth of the Unseen, who would not long for it?—while subtly shifting its ground: the longing is for death whatever it brings. The vision is also now curiously placed on this side of death rather than beyond; as if there were only a messenger, no place of origin for the message.

> Yet would I lose no sting, would wish no torture less,
> The more that anguish racks, the earlier it will bless;
> And robed in fires of hell, or bright with heavenly shine,
> If it but herald death, the vision is divine!

Brontë can't have known of Baudelaire's poem 'Le Voyage', but she has found its imagery and final movement, its indifference to the options of heaven and hell. Death is the captain of the ship that will take us elsewhere:

> Ô Mort, vieux capitaine, il est temps! levons l'ancre!
> Ce pays nous ennuie, ô Mort! Appareillons!
> Si le ciel et la mer sont noirs comme de l'encre,
> Nos coeurs que tu connais sont remplis de rayons!
>
> Verse-nous ton poison pour qu'il nous réconforte!
> Nous voulons, tant ce feu nous brûle le cerveau,
> Plonger au fond du gouffre, Enfer ou Ciel, qu'importe?
> Au fond de l'Inconnu pour trouver du *nouveau*![17]

Except that Baudelaire is saying that death will be worth it if it produces something new, and Brontë's prisoner is saying anything will be worth it as long as it produces death.

In this version the poem ends in the next stanza, with speaker and the jailer turning away, convinced they have 'no further power to work the captive woe', and not thinking of doing anything else for her. Gezari says 'the feminine endings in the last couplet have a destabilizing effect'—which is to say they can't close the question that has just been opened—death as promise or death as pure release—and perhaps are not trying to.[18] In the longer poem from which Brontë made this excerpt for the 1846 volume, we see why. This work is called 'Julian M. and A.G Rochelle'. It is a Gondal poem, not published in full until 1938, and these characters don't appear in any other. It also is written in four-line stanzas, but there are three stanzas before the line that opens 'The Prisoner' ('In the dungeon crypts, idly did I stray'). The stanza about working no further woe begins in the same way ('She ceased to speak') but continues differently; and is followed by fourteen more stanzas recounting the prisoner's release, and the slow romance that develops between her and the speaker.

The opening stanzas evoke a silent house, a snowy landscape, and a lamp lit to guide a 'Wanderer' to this place. The Wanderer's identity is not to be revealed, although the speaker makes no secret of the secret:

> Frown, my haughty sire, chide, my angry Dame;
> Set your slaves to spy, threaten me with shame;
> But neither sire nor dame, nor prying serf shall know
> What angel nightly tracks that waste of winter snow—[19]

Not being sire or dame or serf, at least not in the world of the poem, the reader draws from the later stanzas the inference that the angel is the prisoner we have yet to meet.

There are also five new (old) stanzas after the prisoner's response to the jailer and before her song about her evening visitor. She addresses Julian by name as an old playmate, now an enemy obviously, but perhaps less of a stranger to her than her friends:

> I cannot wonder now at aught the world will do
> And insult and contempt I lightly brook from you,
> Since those, who vowed away their souls to win my love
> Around this living grave like utter strangers move!

Julian stays in the dungeon after the jailer leaves ('my duty will not let me linger here all day'), and catches a look in the prisoner's eye that he interprets as a 'flash of longing quelled by fear', and a sign that 'Earth's hope was not so dead, heaven's home was not so dear'. He himself is confused, the scoffer now has a 'heart all newly taught to pity and adore', and thinks the prisoner will leave him if he sets her free. He risks it, though, and manages a rather grand line while doing it: 'Rochelle, the dungeons teem with foes to gorge our hate—/ Thou art too young to die by such a bitter fate!' She is duly grateful, he takes her away, hides her and (presumably) receives her at night, neglecting all his war-related duties and earning fulsome accusations of sloth and cowardice from his companions. And in the end, because he has dared the opinion of the world, it seems— 'by the patient strength that could that world defy'—he earns from Rochelle a love equal to his own for her.

The close of the poem is a little tame, if only because what Margaret Homans calls Julian's 'obnoxiousness' is too recent for us to see him as anything other than a rather undeserving romantic lead, and it is striking, as Homans also says, that Rochelle 'never speaks again after finishing her inspired description of the vision of death'.[20] We hear only of her 'warm unasked embrace' and her 'smile of grateful joy'. But her return to earth and hope is very moving, and completes rather than undoes her magnificent, ambiguous declaration. She did long for death, for whichever of the reasons on offer, and would have welcomed it if it had come. She believed in and was totally taken by the unheard sound and unseen visions her visitor brought her. But when she sees she may live, she chooses life.

IV

'Remembrance' is a Gondal poem of 1845, much admired by F. R. Leavis, and in the story intimated by the title in the manuscript ('R. Alcona to J. Brenzaida') is spoken by a grieving woman. The poem alone doesn't indicate a gender for the speaker, though, and belongs more to its own lyrical moment than to any narrative except that of quite generalizable time and loss. Its argument is closely related to the movement of thought in 'Julian M. and A.G Rochelle', except that the choice of life was made fifteen years previously, and made against the temptations of sorrow rather than in the wake of a release from prison. 'Have I forgot', the poem asks the corpse of an 'only Love', 'to love thee, /

Severed at last by Time's all-severing wave?' As so often in Brontë an apparently rhetorical question ('of course I haven't forgotten, would I be thinking so painfully about you and your grave if I had?') turns into an actual, rather complicated one. The answer is in part yes, 'the world's tide' has carried the speaker away, 'other desires and hopes' have beset him or her. But then the answer is also no, since

> No later light has lightened up my heaven,
> No second morn has ever shone for me;
> All my life's bliss from thy dear life was given,
> All my life's bliss is in the grave with thee.[21]

And yet—this is the true complication of the question—if one doesn't die of the greatest grief imaginable, then one hasn't merely survived, one has learned 'how existence could be cherished, / Strengthened, and fed without the aid of joy'. One has forgotten happiness, so to speak, but not the loved one. The poem ends with a beautiful, extraordinarily intricate argument that says, if I read it correctly, that even now I must treat my wish to die as the worst kind of risk, not because I am afraid of death or do not long to join you in the grave, but because if I failed (again) to die I would not know what to do with the half-life that would be left to me.

> Then did I check the tears of useless passion—
> Weaned my young soul from yearning after thine;
> Sternly denied its burning wish to hasten
> Down to that tomb already more than mine.
>
> And, even yet, I dare not let it languish,
> Dare not indulge in memory's rapturous pain;
> Once drinking deep of that divinest anguish,
> How could I seek the empty world again?

This is not so much a choice of life, as in the prisoner poem, and scarcely even a refusal of death. It is a recognition of the empty world's claim: an acknowledgement that it can be joylessly cherished, and perhaps needs to be cherished in this way. Pointing to the metre of the poem—'basically a pentameter . . . pulled out of the ordinary' by stress, caesura, and feminine endings—Cecil Day Lewis emphasizes its 'dragging effect'. 'It is the slowest rhythm I know in English poetry'.[22] This slowness completes the suggestion that there is nowhere to go except back to the world, even if there is apparently another, more romantic option, especially appealing, one would have thought, within the frame of a dramatic fiction.

Brontë's poem 'To Imagination' addresses just this assumption, although in a way which perhaps quietens the equivocation too quickly, as her best writing never does. The arc of thought in the poem asserts the consolations of the 'kind voice' coming from the imagination's world, 'the world within'. The speaker opens with gratitude and ends with a renewed 'welcome' of the 'Sure solacer of human cares, / And sweeter hope, when hope despairs'.[23] Stanzas four and five (out of six) evoke the necessary doubts. Reason reminds the speaker that 'cherished dreams' are different from 'Nature's sad reality', 'And Truth may rudely trample down / The flowers of Fancy, newly-blown'. Still, the imagination is always there, and it whispers, 'with a voice divine, / Of real worlds'. If these worlds are real too, then the stage seems set for a rescue of the imagination as a genuine counterpart to truth and reason, not just an escape from their glum pragmatism, but this is not where Brontë goes. Her speaker says she doesn't trust the imagination—'I trust not to thy phantom bliss'—but accepts it as a friend, a sort of supreme fiction in the manner of Wallace Stevens. This, I think, is what the 'sweeter hope' means. Not a false hope, an empty consolation; and not a real hope either: just what we have, if we are lucky, when hope is gone. If we are unlucky, we shall have nothing, or sheer despair. The imagination becomes the faculty that recognizes what we might call the unacceptability of reality—of a reality that is also undeniable.

This perception plays both ways in the poems. It asserts the unacceptability of what can't be denied; it shows that what can't be denied happens all the time. Two very moving poems in particular demonstrate such thoughts in action. One performs a version of 'Remembrance', except that the speaker is watching over the grieving person, a man who has lost a loved one and is now 'tracking farther day by day / The desert of Despair'. The speaker hears 'a thousand sounds of happiness' in the world, but 'one hardly uttered groan' is enough to make him or her 'think that misery / Rules in our world alone'. The man is 'too truly agonized to weep', although his sighs are 'anguish' to the speaker's ear. The poem's question is not about unhappiness in the world generally but about death's choosing to make this exceptionally happy person miserable: about why it decided to 'smite the loved the blest / The ardent and the happy breast'. No answer appears to be expected. Instead the poem pleads on the man's behalf for the release that is refused or unavailable in other texts, because despair, described as 'Life's conscious Death', is worse than anything, 'it tortures worse than thee'. The wished-for peace is eloquently evoked—'Enough of storms have bowed his head'—but of course the perversely selective Death of this poem is not likely to listen to anyone's prayer except to unravel it.[24]

The poem simply called 'Lines' is perhaps the most lyrical and desperate of the works that contemplate human chances in the unredeemed world. Again there is a speaker thinking about an unspeaking figure, but he is an 'iron man', caught up in sin and hell rather than sorrow. The poem evokes an idyllic sunny day and thoughts of childhood. 'Remembrance' is a preoccupation again, and appears as a sort of rhetorical inevitability: as what has to and does not occur. Surely the man must remember his past as 'an ardent boy', his mother, his gathering flowers for her, at least 'one lingering joy' or 'one sweet dream':

> Though storms untold his mind have tossed
> He cannot utterly have lost
> Remembrance of his early home
> So lost that not a gleam may come.[25]

'He cannot'. This is the speaker's poignant sense of the impossible. He or she thinks the man may now be at peace, or rescued from sin by remorse: 'Perhaps this is the destined hour / When hell shall lose its fatal power'. None of these hopes is anywhere near the truth, and the poem makes clear that the very entertaining of them was a helpless fantasy:

> One glance revealed how little care
> He felt for all the beauty there
>
> Oh crime can make the heart grow old
> Sooner than years of wearing woe
> Can turn the warmest bosom cold
> As winter wind or polar snow.

The beauty of this poem lies not in the plausibility or the failure of the speaker's hopes—although the eloquent, suspenseful evocation of them is important—but in the sustained surprise at their return and disappointment. 'Oh crime can make the heart grow old'—the line stands alone, without need of complement. An old heart is one that can't remember, or that can't be moved by its memories. An old heart belongs to a person who has cancelled his childhood. We knew that, and so did the speaker. And yet we need to hear it again, we need to be distressed by this terrible non-event, the heart's immobility. The chance of change is life itself; we can't abandon the thought of it. And of course the line doesn't stand alone, the thought continues. If we have imagined that the freezing effect of sorrow is among fate's worst gifts, we now learn that the force of crime on the criminal's heart is, if not stronger, at least faster-working. We are also likely to feel that an old heart is an even more desolate prospect than a cold one.

V

The poems we have looked at have led us through the scenery and performance of betrayal and revenge and unreconciled emotions: worlds of crime and torture that are nevertheless unmistakably 'civilized'. A young woman chooses life when she seems already to have chosen death. Another figure chooses life while seeming to continue to prefer death. The imagination is a way of rejecting these choices, indeed of rejecting the world, but it is not to be trusted, can only be treated as a liveable version of despair. Despair itself without imagination can scarcely be contemplated, and if redemption is a recurring human fantasy—a divine promise that perhaps has its longest and most varied life as a human fantasy—the unredeemed really do exist, there is no way around them, no way of building a world without them. Adorno said, 'The only philosophy which can be responsibly practised in face of despair is the attempt to contemplate all things as they would present themselves from the standpoint of redemption.'[26] Brontë knew this, but she also knew that one standpoint was never going to be enough. This is what Heathcliff's wit, and her own, suggest: a sense of occasion and an eye for discrepancy. The amusement may fade; scorn may no longer be in question. But all conjectures are unhappy in one way or another; and in Emily Brontë's poems conjecture itself is the revision of our simplifications, the responsible practice of remembering whatever our own aspirations most strongly invite us to forget.

NOTES

1. Charlotte Brontë, letter to W S Williams, quoted in Janet Gezari, *Last Things* (New York: Oxford University Press, 2007), 127.

2. Emily Brontë, *Wuthering Heights* (London: Penguin, 2003), 4, 14, 13.

3. Brontë, *Wuthering Heights*, 12–13.

4. Brontë, *Wuthering Heights*, 13.

5. Brontë, *Wuthering Heights*, 13, 14.

6. Charlotte Brontë and Emily Brontë, *The Belgian Essays*, trans. and ed. Sue Lonoff (New Haven: Yale University Press, 1996), 143. A literal English version would read 'I shall not have the mortification of witnessing the poor results of my work…for I am afraid your performance may be a little too remarkable.'

7. Brontës, *The Belgian Essays*, 229—'I have a friend before whom this entire assembly will be forced to succomb.'

8. Gezari, *Last Things*, 123.

9. Gezari, *Last Things*, 11.

10. Emily Brontë, *Gondal's Queen*, ed. Fannie Ratchford (Austin: University of Texas Press, 1955), 20, 32, 173.

11. Ratchford in *Gondal's Queen*, 24.

12. Emily Brontë, 'The Death of A. G. A.', in *The Complete Poems*, ed. Janet Gezari (London: Penguin, 1992), 158.

13. Brontë, 'Why ask to know the date—the clime?' in *The Complete Poems*, 184.

14. Brontë, 'Why ask to know the date—the clime?' (May 1848 version) in *The Complete Poems*, 183.

15. Bertolt Brecht, *Mother Courage and Her Children*, trans. David Hare (Madison, Wisconsin: Arcade Publishers, 1996), 44.

16. Brontë, 'The Prisoner (A Fragment)', in *The Complete Poems*, 14.

17. Charles Baudelaire, *Les Fleurs du mal*, trans. Richard Howard (Jaffrey, NH: David R Godine, 1982), 334. Howard's translation, 156–157, reads:

> Death, old admiral, up anchor now,
> this country wearies us. Put out to sea!
> What if the waves and wind are black as ink,
> our hearts are filled with light, you know our hearts!
>
> Pour us your poison, let us be comforted!
> Once we have burned our brains out, we can plunge
> to Hell or Heaven—any abyss will do—
> deep in the Unknown to find the *new*!

18. Gezari, *Last Things*, 74.

19. Brontë, 'Julian M. and A.G Rochelle', in *The Complete Poems*, 177.

20. Margaret Homans, *Women Writers and Poetic Identity* (Princeton: Princeton University Press, 1980), 117, 119.

21. Brontë, 'Remembrance', in *The Complete Poems*, 9.

22. Cecil Day Lewis, *Notable Images of Virtue* (Toronto: Ryerson Press, 1954), 13.

23. Brontë, 'To Imagination', in *The Complete Poems*, 20.

24. *The Complete Poems*, 172.
25. Brontë, 'Lines', in *The Complete Poems*, 97.
26. Theodor Adorno, *Minima Moralia*, trans. Edmund Jephcott (London: Verso Books, 2005), 247.

Select Bibliography

Armstrong, Isobel, *Victorian Poetry* (London: Routledge, 1993).

Attridge, Derek, *Poetic Rhythm* (Cambridge: Cambridge University Press, 1995).

Bataille, Georges, *La littérature et le mal* (Paris: Gallimard, 1957).

Blondel, Jacques, *Emily Brontë* (Paris: Presses universitaires de France, 1956).

Bristow, Joseph, *Victorian Women Poets* (London: Palgrave, 1995).

Gezari, Janet, *Last Things* (Oxford: Oxford University Press, 2007).

Homans, Margaret, *Women Writers and Poetic Identity* (Princeton: Princeton University Press, 1983).

Jacobs, Carol, *Uncontainable Romanticism* (Baltimore: Johns Hopkins University Press, 1989).

Leighton, Angela, *Victorian Women Poets: Writing against the Heart* (New York: Harvester, 1992).

Miller, J. Hillis, *The Disappearance of God* (Cambridge, Mass: Harvard University Press, 1963).

Moon, Michael, 'No Coward Soul', in Meredith McGill, ed., *The Traffic in Poems* (New Brunswick: Rutgers University Press, 2008).

Ratchford, Fannie, *Gondal's Queen* (Austin: University of Texas, 1955).

Tayler, Irene, *Holy Ghosts* (New York: Columbia University Press, 1993)

....

CHAPTER 23

ARTHUR HUGH CLOUGH: THE RECEPTION AND CONCEPTION OF *AMOURS DE VOYAGE*

....

ADAM PHILLIPS

Where are the great whom thou would'st wish should praise thee?
Arthur Hugh Clough, *Dipsychus and the Spirit*[1]

THERE is a consensus among critics of the last century that Clough is a poet consistently underrated and insistently misplaced. He is a greater poet than we have been able to acknowledge, and more a modern (or even modernist) poet than we take him to be. And it has been around *Amours de Voyage*—a contentious work from its initial publication in the *Atlantic Monthly* of February-May 1858—that the claims have been made. 'To speak of Clough's modernity', Barbara Hardy wrote, 'is understandable but misleading. Perhaps no other Victorian writer is so visibly imprisoned in his Victorianism'.[2] Hardy overstates the case as though the case won't be properly made both for Clough as sufficiently confined, and for Clough as a man of his time. And there may be forms of imprisonment that force a broaching of the future. Isobel Armstrong sees Clough, and particularly *Amours de Voyage*, as both a sign of the times and of the times to come. Once again, as in the poem itself—which is so concerned to distinguish the imprisonings that are self-imprisonings from the imprisonings that are not—openness is the issue. '*Amours de Voyage*', she writes, 'approaches the condition of a modernist poem, a self-reflexive poem without closure, dwelling on its self-reflexivity. It has often been compared in this respect with T. S. Eliot's *The Love Song of J. Alfred Prufrock*.'[3] We are being warned that Clough's apparent modernity helps and hinders our reading, that the poet and the hero of his poem are caught in something—are in some way stuck as representative men of their time, or of our time—and that we are likely to get the poetry wrong if we don't read it as resolutely mid-Victorian and ineluctably modernist.

If what Philip Davis calls Clough's 'strange new realism'—'By a strange new realism, the poetry reproduces, with honest unease, a disorientating sense of incongruously confused categories and languages and voices'[4]—makes *Amours de Voyage* sound rather more like *The Waste Land* than *Empedocles on Etna* or *Maud*, it is because the poem seems to have been clarified by modernist poetics rather more than by the poetry (and the criticism) of its own time, as though it is a poem that has made more sense as time has gone on. And yet this has at once relegated its status, and relegated it to the status of influential precursor. 'Clough has been given a good deal of attention in recent years', John Goode wrote in what is still the best essay on the poem, ' but most of it seems to be of the wrong kind...if Clough does foreshadow Eliot...this really entitles him to no more than a paragraph in a history of Eng. Lit'.[5] All good roads lead to Eliot, which is one way of diminishing *Amours de Voyage* (and not only *Amours de Voyage*), and one of Eliot's contributions to the history of Eng. Lit. was famously to diminish the Victorians. The Victorian nineteenth century, Eliot wrote in a grand, dismissive sweep, 'was a time busy in keeping up to date. It had, for the most part, no hold on permanent truths about man and God, and life and death'.[6] Leavis was to be the academic consolidator of Eliot's charge that the 'Victorian poetic tradition' was nugatory ('It was Mr Eliot who made us fully conscious', Leavis wrote, 'of the weakness of that tradition').[7] If *Amours de Voyage* has been, as Goode intimates, one of the casualties of what became a certain Lit. Crit. orthodoxy, it is also very much a poem about the difficulty of making claims, of knowing what to value and how to value it, of what the whole process of evaluation involves us in, and reveals us as. Which is why its reception—the language in which it has been redescribed and revalued—is peculiarly important.

When evaluation, and especially the self-evaluation of its hero, are a poem's abiding preoccupations—and *Amours de Voyage* is a series of inconclusive self-evaluations by Claude, the sound of whose name intimates someone being got at—the reader veers between being an antagonist and an accomplice (as one does with oneself). We need to take to heart, in other words, Clough's epigraphs to *Amours de Voyage*, and perhaps particularly the first one from *Twelfth Night*, 'Oh, you are sick of self-love, Malvolio / And taste with a distempered appetite'.[8] One can be sick of self-love in two senses, and one sense can entail the other. Claude is sick of the way he loves himself—which seems to preclude loving anything and anybody else, and, indeed, of loving some of the things that might matter to him most—and sick because he loves himself. And what is being intimated is that something was wrong with the way contemporary people valued themselves—both with what they chose to value about themselves, and how they did it, how they cultivated and enacted such value as they had. This, as the letters and the biographical information we have confirm, seems to have been the abiding preoccupation of Clough's adult life. In *Amours de Voyage*, Clough dramatizes the bathos and pathos of (modern) self-doubt; of the self imprisoned by the way it evaluates itself; of self-doubt as a kind of passionate and enervating self-love. The *OED*'s first cited instances in the language for 'bearableness', 'be-maddening', and 'untraitored' are in Clough's poetry (as are 'busy-ish' and 'poeticism', not unrelated to the narcissism of distraction). Claude can only be a modern master of defeatedness by finding ways of never quite knowing what matters to him.

Amours de Voyage is a poem about what became known as the value of value—a theme, so to speak, that links the Victorians with the so-called great modernists. And there is a paradoxical sense in which the claims made for the poem, both for and against, are of a piece with the preoccupations the poem explores. It is a poem, all of its critics insist in their different ways, that we are likely to get wrong, both as to its genealogy and its value. Indeed, the relationship between genealogy and value emerging in the nineteenth century was encountered as an essential perplexity. 'The claim that must be made for *Amours de Voyage*', Goode suggests, 'is not just that it is a masterpiece, but a major masterpiece...the major masterpiece of high Victorian poetry'.[9] When masterpieces have to be distinguished from major masterpieces, and major masterpieces distinguished from *the* major masterpiece, evaluation has become fraught.

We can place the writing of *Amours de Voyage* with some historical accuracy—the poem was begun in 1849 and worked on intermittently until its publication in 1858—but it has been, as we can see, a poem otherwise notoriously difficult to place. And this was also true for its contemporary readers and reviewers, and especially for Clough's friends, friendship having been the mainstay of Clough's life until his late marriage in 1854 ('Clough', Palgrave wrote in a memoir of his friend, 'might be said not so much to trust his friends, as to trust himself to them').[10] When his friends were not despairing—'I would cast it behind me and the spirit from which it emanates', Clough's friend John Shairp wrote to him, 'and to higher, more healthful, more hopeful things purely aspire...on the whole I regard Les Amours as your nature ridding itself of long-gathered bile'[11]—they were baffled and dismayed. And yet in their misgivings they are strikingly engaged in the poem even when they are not engaged by it. As though it was the effect of the poem to inspire pertinent doubt in its readers, doubt about what became known as the foundations of knowledge and belief, in which it is newly assumed that nothing is but naming makes it so, or as Claude writes, in ironic allusion, 'that which I name them they are' (I. vii). As though convictions are replaced by impressions, and appearances can only be compared with each other, and not with anything beneath them or beyond them. In a straightforward unrhymed couplet—about how shadows no longer have anything to rhyme with—Claude makes an ordinary language dismissal of Platonism and Christianity: 'What our shadows seem, forsooth, we will ourselves be. / Do I look like that? you think me that: then I AM that' (I. iv). 'Forsooth', for the Victorians an antiquated term, a faux medievalism, is an affectation about speaking truly. The correspondence theory of truth, in which words are suited to reality, is the first casualty of this poem that takes the form of a correspondence. But the astounding verbal precision of this poem about failure, narrated by someone who, in his own words, has 'always failed' (I. xi), failed two of Clough's closest friends, Matthew Arnold and Ralph Waldo Emerson, in the most revealing of ways. For both men the poem lacked substance.

Arnold was famously dismissive of *Amours de Voyage* in a letter to Clough, though his misgivings about Clough's poem were only known, of course, after the publication in

1932 of *The Letters of Mathew Arnold to Arthur Hugh Clough*. 'We will not discuss what is past anymore', Arnold writes, 'as to the Italian poem, if I forbore to comment it was that I had nothing special to say—what is to be said when a thing does not suit you—suiting and not suiting is a subjective affair and only time determines, by the colour a thing takes with years, whether it ought to have suited or no'.[12] How long does it take before we know whether we value something? We know things and people can come, in time, to matter to us, but how can we include this acknowledgement in our judgements? This is worth wondering about, and worth wondering about a poem so troubled by deferral as at once a necessity, an alibi, and a failing. Being unengaged is recognition of a kind—to disidentify with something (or someone) is to have first identified something—but what Arnold doesn't have to say about 'the Italian poem' is remarkable in the eloquence of its equivocations. We do not know now what the past is that Arnold doesn't want to discuss in the letter, but we do know just how much being in Rome makes Claude wonder what about the past is worth discussing, and what we might be doing by discussing the past— what Nietzsche was to call in the 1870s the question of 'History in the service and the disservice of life',[13] and what Claude poses as a slightly camp demand, 'Utter, O someone, the word that will reconcile ancient and modern' (I. x). As Clough and Arnold as accomplished classicists would know, the 'calling together' of ancient and modern that is the Latin origin of 'reconcile' was not going to be the work of a word, or the Word.

The poem is not in Italian—'the Italian poem'—and you can't help but hear the bore in Arnold's 'forbore'. It is, though, very much a poem about Italy and what Italy, and especially Rome and Roman republicanism, had become to the English by the mid-nineteenth century. 'If I forbore to comment' keeps Arnold's options open—and he does go on to comment—but to forbore is to 'tolerate, endure...do without...to part with or from...to avoid, shun...abstain or desist from'(*OED*), and these are the very things that Claude, the hero of the poem, does both to Rome and to the woman he desires, and indeed to his own desires. And then there is the reiterated 'suiting', a word Arnold picks up, wittingly or unwittingly, from the beginning and the end of Clough's poem. In the first section of the first canto Claude sets what will become the distinctive tone of the poem, and of his own voice within it: 'Rome disappoints me much; I hardly as yet understand but / *Rubbishy* seems the word that most exactly would suit it' (I. i). *Amours de Voyage* is a poem in which nothing really works for Claude (it 'seems' the word but it may not be; and suits have seams that hold them together). But finding the word that suits at least reveals why Rome doesn't suit him. Clough is interested, among many other things, in how it might suit Claude to see Rome as 'rubbishy'—full of the rubbish of the past, full of the least beautiful things that need to be got rid of—and why Rome doesn't suit him, and won't. 'Rome will not suit me', Claude begins his last letter in the poem, '...the priests and soldiers possess it' (V. x). Whether things and people are defined by who possesses them will also exercise Claude—as will the cumulative disappointment he is heir to as *Amours de Voyage* becomes an elegy for the modern self's quest for an accuracy about itself. That exacting modern self-consciousness seems to produce no more than a vaunted sense of failure, one that is endlessly ashamed of feeling such shame. 'I am ashamed my own self' (I. xi), Claude declares, and the odd syntax breathes shock and disbelief. Rome, that will all too briefly liberate Claude—'for the first time in life I am living and moving with freedom' (I. xi)—will expose his shamefully inadequate sense of who he is, and what he might be capable of wanting. It is pointedly not his life he refers to but life, and the wording suggests that living with freedom—as an idea in one's mind?—is not enough. One must move with it as well.

Rome 'not suiting' more obliquely refers also, at least for contemporary readers of the poem, to the Oxford Movement that Clough flirted briefly with at Oxford, and to Newman's ultimately finding that Roman Catholicism suited him. Once again in this context, the word is used, allusively, to ironize certain gravities. Claude, like his author it seems, is a character for whom conversion, to anything, would be part of the problem rather than part of the solution. When, in 1842, Clough had to subscribe to the Thirty Nine Articles of the Church of England in order to take up his fellowship at Oriel (where Newman was one of his colleagues) he wrote to his friend John Gell, 'It is not so much from any objection to this or that point as general dislike to [sic] subscription and strong feeling of its being after all . . . a bondage and a very heavy one, and one that may cramp one and cripple one for life'.[14] In the 1840s Clough was progressively subscribing to the idea that he must not subscribe to anything or to anyone, and to wondering what kind of success this might be, and what kind of failure. If the moral (and professional) life organizes itself around states of conviction, and states of conviction are a bondage, a cramping and a crippling for life, what kind of violence or violation is belief, religious or otherwise? *Amours de Voyage*, that is to say, is a mid-nineteenth century poem with what turned out to be startlingly modern preoccupations. Is some form of belief to be found, or is what William James called the will to believe itself the problem? *Amours de Voyage* was to be a poem vexed by subscription and its terrors—subscription that is itself a form of writing that is also a form of commitment, a self-declaration that is also a form of assent.

The poem tells a story of thwarted commitments, of a failed love affair between Claude and Mary Trevellyn, and of Claude's unplanned witnessing of the failed defence by Mazzini and Garibaldi of a new Roman republic. It is very much about the difficulty Claude has in finding or knowing what suits him—socially or politically, as a tourist or as a lover—and of being able to act on such knowledge (whether the words suit the things, and whether the words and the things suit the people). Claude is the suitor who is never quite sure what will suit him. As Arnold implicitly acknowledges in his letter, the word itself, in all it entails—in its multiple and significant contemporary meanings—requires a certain forebearance, partly because it juxtaposes, to use another of the poem's keywords, the overlapping preoccupations of Clough's capacious poem itself, which pays attention to evolution and to manners, to marriage, and to miracles. The *OED* has for the verb 'suit': 'To pay court to a woman . . . to set in due order, sort out . . . To make appropriate or agreeable to; to adapt or accommodate in style or manner . . . to be agreeable or convenient to . . . To be good for, to agree with'—all things Claude tries and fails to do and is confounded by in the poem.

Amours de Voyage is a poem about the hero's inconclusive attempts to love, to be politically engaged, to be 'open' to what is going on around and inside him; but it also houses a more radical uncertainty about what it would be to change, and to change for the better. The poem is riddled with images and vocabularies of change—and disclaimers: 'let us not talk of growth' (III. ii)—but with Clough leaving us feeling that Claude has travelled without knowing, or indeed finding out, and what it would be to arrive. R. H. Hutton wrote of Clough: 'the stronger the desire, he teaches, the greater is the danger of illegitimately satisfying the desire by persuading ourselves that what we wish to believe is true'.[15] In a melancholic parody of a quest romance, the traditional theme of the self defined by its dissatisfaction with itself—with its search for something essential that is missing—is replaced by a sense of the insufficiency of the self's desire, and the insufficiency of its objects of desire. All that is left for Claude is the pursuit of a rather nebulous knowledge. By the end of the poem Claude has neither solved nor resolved any of his problems; he has not answered his questions, nor clarified them; he has not taken refuge in paradox or irony or the delights of indeterminacy, in the modern way. He has dispensed with Love, Scripture, Faith, and Art ('I have no heart, however, for any marble or fresco', the line wanting us to hear the 'art' in 'heart'; V. x). The only thing he believes in now is the quest for Knowledge, something we were told in the second canto of the poem that women, and indeed Claude himself, have no appetite for: 'woman', he writes to Eustace, 'has no heart for the timid, the sensitive soul; and for knowledge,—/ Knowledge, O ye Gods!—when did they appreciate knowledge? / Wherefore should they, either? I am sure I do not desire it' (II. xiv). Neither women, nor the Gods—and the phrasing makes them indistinguishable—nor Claude 'desire' it, so what is it for? Is it merely a refuge from the real objects of desire, from the essential aspirations? The only real knowledge Claude has so far acquired from what the poem has told us—and if what the drama of the poem tells us is anything to go by—seems to be the knowledge that he is not suited to his life; or, if Claude is taken to be one kind of representative Victorian man, 'we' are not suited to our lives as we have thus far conceived of them: the dawning realization that haunted the nineteenth century. But the knowledge Claude seeks, if not actually redemptive, will bring some kind of value to his life—though he makes a characteristically rather vague assertion, a conclusion in which little is concluded. It has a rousing and resounding blandness in its half-hearted and clichéd description of the conventionally rigorous life: 'Let us seek knowledge;—the rest may come and go as it happens. / Knowledge is hard to seek, and harder yet to adhere to. / Knowledge is painful often; and yet when we know we are happy' (V. x). Claude notably doesn't tell us what we should seek knowledge of but that, perhaps ominously, he is going to seek it 'Eastward' in Egypt (not, in other words, in the West: as though the West no longer had the knowledge he needed). But he does tell us, oddly, that this knowledge is the only thing that can make us happy. We are not convinced by this invoking, at the last minute, of the great utilitarian term, nor by this vague Orientalism—is it the antiquarian, the scholarly, the mystical, the scientific that Claude is now promoting?—and we are not supposed to be. It was this that made Clough's other friend Ralph Waldo Emerson take against the poem in yet another letter.

For Emerson in 'Self-Reliance'—and Clough was a keen reader of Emerson's essays—'Power...resides in the moment of transition...in the darting to an aim'.[16] *Amours de*

Voyage, Emerson intimated, seemed (like Claude, like Rome) to be going somewhere—the paramount transcendentalist and pragmatic criterion—and then it misfired. Perhaps it even betrayed itself, and its readers. Just as Arnold did, Emerson takes in the poem, takes on the poem, by voicing his disappointment; as though the poem about things not really working or working out works, in an uncanny way, by not working for people. It seems to be about the way it disappoints, or fails to engage, or confounds, while being itself a poem about a character who disappoints and is disappointed, and fails to engage, and is confounded by himself. It is as though the poem is somehow contagious: it can't ultimately be celebrated because it doubts celebration. It can't ultimately succeed because success has become an unknown quantity. It can't aim because it doesn't have a target—as though Claude (and Clough's) failure was that they had no picture of their satisfaction. This, at least, is what Emerson suggests in his letter of 1858. 'When we began to build securely on the triumph of our poet over all gainsayers', Emerson writes,

> suddenly his wings flag, or his whim appears, and he plunges to a conclusion, like the ending of the Chancery suit in Bleak House, or like the denouement of Tennyson's Princess. How can you waste such power on a broken dream? Why lead us up to the tower to tumble us down? There is a statute of Parnassus, that the author shall keep faith with the reader; but you choose to trifle with him. It is true a few persons compassionately tell me, that the piece is all right, and that they like this veracity of much preparation to no result. But I hold tis bad enough in life and inadmissible in poetry. And I think you owe us a retribution of music, and to a musical argument.[17]

We should perhaps remember that Emerson would write 'Whim' on the lintel of his study, being a great believer in having the confidence of one's whims and one's genius ('I shun mother and father and wife and brother, when my genius calls me. I would write on the lintels of the door-post, *Whim*').[18] And we should also note that there is another 'suit' referred to here, in the context of a discussion—and Emerson allows the alternative view in—about how well suited the end of the poem is to the gist of the poem. The images are of failed agreements, broken promises, misleadings, tantalizations, and violent punishment. Something has gone badly wrong in a poem about things going badly wrong. 'He may be right and I wrong', Clough commented in a letter on Emerson's verdict, sounding rather like Claude, 'and all my defence can only be that I always meant it to be so and began it with the full intention of its ending so—but very likely I was wrong all the same'.[19] Right but wrong, wrong but right; both of them. That intentions are incommensurate with consequences is another thing that exercises Claude in *Amours de Voyage*. And also how wrong he is always likely to be, and the shame of not being able to be right. What are the cultural conditions, what are the inherited traditions that might have created this peculiarly modern kind of shame, and that might make knowledge, or the seeking of knowledge, seem like the self-cure? Claude describes the Christian faith in the first canto as involving 'Aspirations from something most shameful here upon earth' (I. iv), and shame, as we have seen, is a keyword in the poem. Emerson wanted Claude's travails to have inspired him, transformed him, given him more life, more self-reliance. But all he has gained are losses, loss of love and loss of confidence in love, loss of religious faith and loss of that belief in culture that Arnold hoped would replace and better the religious faith of previous generations.

Arnold was not, he claimed, disappointed by the poem (as if he had had no expectations of it); he just had 'nothing special to say' because the poem didn't suit him. This sets aside the rivalry that is everywhere in Arnold's engaged disengagement with 'the Italian poem' (it is an interesting principle that when a poem works for a reader he has something special to say about it, something that seems special if only to himself). Emerson, though, felt betrayed, at least by the end of the poem, and felt that Clough had betrayed himself by concluding the poem in the way he did. And the parallels that come to mind are Dickens in *Bleak House* and Tennyson in *The Princess*. For Emerson, that is to say, the poem is evasive, and about evasion (another key word in *Amours de Voyage*), about spurious resolutions and failures of nerve. For Arnold, it is about something not suiting. It is easy to feel that there is something evasive in Arnold's insistent reiteration of 'suiting' as the suitable word, and in his question that is not entirely a question because it doesn't have a question mark to identify it—'what is to be said when a thing does not suit you' (*Amours de Voyage* is what might be said, or rather written, when a thing doesn't suit you: the poem is, in this sense, an answer to his question). And it is not difficult to feel that, for Clough, in *Amours de Voyage* the satisfactions sought by Emerson were no longer possible, neither availing nor available. And that this too was the subject of the poem.

When Clough wrote to Mathew Arnold's brother Tom, in 1848, about Emerson he was, in a sense, setting out his own project in *Amours de Voyage*; and giving us an important clue about the civilization and its discontents that he was to explore in the poem. 'He is much less Emersonian than his Essays,' Clough wrote. 'There is no dogmatism, or arbitrariness or positiveness about him.'[20] Clough wanted to write in the way Emerson performed himself when he was not writing (Emerson's essays are dogmatic, arbitrary, and positive, and it is part of their artful originality, as Clough knew, to reveal the links between these terms). He wanted to find out if there was a form of virtue, a version of the religious, or the political, or the moral life—and a style, a kind of writing—that was neither dogmatic, nor arbitrary nor speciously optimistic. So if, as has often been noted, Goethe's *Roman Elegies* are in ironic juxtaposition to Clough's *Amours* in their unequivocal commitment to sexual love—in their positive worship of Eros and the Priapic— Emerson's *Essays* are the writings that *Amours de Voyage* most corresponds and argues with. *Amours de Voyage* is, among many other things, a counter-life to the life proposed and supposed by Emerson's *Essays*—the counter-life of a poetry that, as Clough wrote in a review of recent English poetry in 1853, need not 'content itself merely with talking of what may be better elsewhere, but seek also to deal with what IS here'.[21]

What is there for Claude in Rome is the accumulated past of Paganism and Christianity that he sees, in his casual dismissal of Western culture, as 'rubbishy': 'All the incongruous things of past incompatible ages / Seem to be treasured up here to make fools of present and future'(I. i). It was, of course, Emerson's view that we must not let the past diminish the present and the future, or not use it to do so; and that, as he wrote in his essay 'The Poet', it was the poet's vocation to 'ensure' his 'fidelity to his office of announcement and affirming'.[22] But through Claude, Clough announces the difficulty he has in affirming anything, and the difficulties inherent in affirmation itself (fidel-ity to an office of affirming is possibly what Clough meant by Emerson's 'positivism'). One of the difficulties inherent in affirmation is that it requires something to affirm; and *Amours de Voyage* begins by doubting what it proposes, by inviting us to go on a journey while warning us that travel is futile. *Amours de Voyage*, in its quest to deal with what is here, begins by wondering where here should be, so it begins with an urge to travel that is at the same time a scepticism about the lure of travel:

> *Come, let us go; though withal a voice whisper, 'The world that we live in,*
> *Withersoever we turn, still is the same narrow crib;*
> *'Tis but to prove limitation, and measure a cord, that we travel;*
> *Let who would 'scape and be free go to his chamber and think;*
> *'Tis but to change idle fancies for memories wilfully falser;*
> *'Tis but to go and have been'.*

(I)

In 'Come, let us go' we hear the beginning of *Prufrock*. But there also may be an allusion in this prologue to *Macbeth* in his 'fit', before the banquet, referring to himself as 'cabined, cribbed, confined, bound in / To saucy doubts and fear'.[23] Macbeth has suffered from his ambition for change, and for changing places; and Claude will suffer from saucy doubts and fear (the *OED* has for saucy, 'insolent towards superiors...smart, stylish'). But there is a stronger echo—not unrelated to this moment in *Macbeth* when the consequences of decisive actions begin to be fully felt—in Emerson's essay 'Self-Reliance', in which we are being encouraged to stay put if we want to get anywhere, and being grandly reassured that there is more to life than either idle fancies or memories wilfully falser. It is integral to the drama of the poem that at the very outset the enemy of promise—the voice that whispers, not unlike Milton's Satan in *Paradise Lost*, and insinuates that the only free-dom is freedom of thought—invokes the always promising Emerson:

> It is for want of self-culture that the Superstition of Travelling, whose idols are Italy, England and Egypt, retains its fascination for all educated Americans. They who made England, Italy or Greece venerable in the imagination did so by sticking fast where they were, like an axis of the earth. The soul is no traveller, the wise man stays at home...He who travels to be amused, or to get somewhat which he doesn't carry, travels away from himself, and grows old even in youth among old things...He carries ruins to ruins.[24]

Italy has been Claude's destination after leaving England, and Egypt is to be his next destination. 'Rubbishy' is Claude's word for the ruins, and Clough shows us the ruins Claude brings to these ruins: the ruination of a mid-nineteenth century scepticism in which everything can be doubted because nothing can be affirmed, and in which an obsession with failure is the secret sharer of the age of Empire and progress. What Emerson's Transcendentalism can't or won't quite countenance—and this is part of its strength as well of its weakness—is that a person (or a culture) might actually *be* ruined. What Millicent Bell calls 'the transcendentalist illusion that the disengaged spirit can keep itself free from constraining conditions, free from a design of life dictated by causes outside the sovereign self'[25] is the illusion, or the true belief, that Claude can neither sustain nor wholly dispense with. *Amours de Voyage* was Clough's attempt to straddle, or failing that to explore, this contradiction between Emerson's infinitely self-reliant self, and the self conditioned by circumstance, situated by its history.

For Emerson in 'Self-Reliance' the risk of travel is imitation; the engaged travelling spirit simply has more to imitate. 'What is imitation but the travelling mind?' Emerson asks. 'Insist on yourself, never imitate.'[26] And Claude, significantly, is in two minds in *Amours de Voyage* about his seemingly infinite capacity for imitation which he sees, characteristically, as both an escape and a return: 'I can be and become anything that I meet with or look at' (III. vii). And yet, Claude feels, there is something evasive, or regressive about this 'faint . . . but faithful assurance' that he can lose himself in anything:

> E'en from the stones of the street, as from rocks or trees of the forest,
> Something of kindred, a common, though latent vitality, greet me;
> And, to escape from our strivings, mistakings, misgrowths, and perversions,
> Fain could demand to return to that perfect and primitive silence,
> Fain be enfolded and fixed, as of old, in their rigid embraces.

(III. vii)

Claude, taking Emerson's injunction to its logical conclusion, as it were, sees his ability to imitate and identify with others—the non-human and, by implication, the human— as a death wish. But he sees as the alternative to this death-wish—in an implicit critique of Emerson's injunction—'strivings, mistakings, misgrowths, and perversions'. We should hear the two misses in the line, and the dread of desire and aspiration. At the end of the poem Claude's quest is to rationalize his fear of wanting a woman. In his distress in the final canto at having lost Mary, Claude speaks a line that sounds rehearsed, and sounds like Prufrock, 'I have had pain, it is true: I have wept; and so have the actors' (V. viii). Imitation, and invoking the imitators, is now the only way. Claude began by apparently insisting on himself—which means asserting a mixture of Oxford-educated intellectual doubts and upper middle class English prejudices—but concludes by imitating. Apart from his grief he imitates (and by imitating attempts to affirm) a pale version of pagan belief. There is nothing else but imitation, it seems, and yet we can only imitate the past, that which already exists and is available to be imitated. These are Claude's tacit conclusions, and they are, whatever else they are, an argument with Emerson and his Transcendentalist conceptions that opened up the future by not revering the past, that wanted the future to be an open invitation.

For Claude, in the first two cantos of the poem, falling in love and political engagement are forms of imitation, conventions he can disdain and do without. His questions are always—and they could be lines from one of Emerson's essays—'Is it an idol I bow to, or is it a God that I worship? / Do I sink back on the old or do I soar from the mean?' (I. Epilogue). If we can't tell the difference there may not be one. One answer to the first question is that an idol won't tell us, and a God won't need to. But if Gods and idols are similar, then we are never quite sure what we are valuing, and worship may be merely servility (and perhaps it is our abasement, our servility that matters most to us?). Claude is all too conscious that how we value what we value exposes us, and that uncertainty about values is radically depleting: 'but guessing is tiresome, very. / Weary of wondering, watching and guessing, and gossiping idly, / Down I go…' (II. v). The half-rhymes of 'very' and 'weary' and 'idly' and 'I go' make the necessary links. Clough is clearly worrying away here about liberalism, about whether we can have beliefs without believing in them too much, and if we can't what we can do instead of believe, or have instead of beliefs. As Claude falls for the appropriately named Mary, and begins to be moved and involved by the republican struggle in Rome—that is, stops guessing, wondering, watching and gossiping—he gains not, as Emerson would have wished, a renewed sense of power, but suffers further disillusionment. 'The Fates, it is clear, are against us', he concludes, but with a marvellous phrase of blighted resignation, 'I will go where I am led, and will not dictate to the chances' (V. viii). Claude's question has always been: what will I have to submit to? Marriage and family, political commitment, the class mobility of liberal democracy, art, learning, religious faith. And now he knows (Mary will find out what she has to submit to at the very end of the poem). If the Fates are against us then our projects count for nothing in the world as it is.

And yet, 'Do I sink back on the old, or do I soar from the mean?' is Emerson's question—his continual warning about the tyranny of the past, about our regressive wearying drive to imitate the past, our using the past to diminish and disqualify ourselves. The pun on 'mean' reinforces the point, and by knowingly referring us back to Aristotle's 'mean' in the *Nichomachean Ethics*, it is another sinking back on the old. Soaring is what Satan does in *Paradise Lost*, and the old as the mean—that which has become average, the costive, and ungenerous—is an Emersonian affirmation (whether or not Milton was of the Devil's party, Emerson certainly was). For Emerson we believe simply by imitating believers. And as Claude (and Clough) knew, to submit to The Fates is to sink back on the old, to endorse (i.e. imitate) an ancient belief about the cosmos. The Bible may be what Claude at one point in the poem calls, in another arch archaism, 'the olden-time inspiration' (III. iv), but so, from Emerson's point of view, is the wisdom of the ancients. 'And when we begin to build securely on the triumph of our poet over all gainsayers', Emerson wrote, 'suddenly his wing flags…and he plunges to a conclusion'.[27] The end of *Amours de Voyage* was not uplifting in the Emerson way. It was not a journey with an unexpected, desirable outcome.

Just as Claude and Mary fail to rendezvous—keep, in both senses, missing each other—so Emerson too, like many of Clough's contemporary readers, has a missed encounter with *Amours de Voyage*. He misreads Clough as having taken flight in the wrong sense. He sees the poem as, finally, a failure of nerve on Clough's part, when the poem is rather a study of a man's failure of nerve. Clough was speaking up in *Amours de Voyage*—as he was in many of his finest poems, most notably in *Adam and Eve*, *Dipsychus and The Spirit*, and some of the shorter lyrics—for the impossibility of whole-heartedness and the implications of this for relations between the sexes and for political engagement. New forms of self-division were appearing—new pictures of what was dividing the self, and of what it was divided into—and the sign of these self-divisions was a haunting sense of uncompleted or uncompletable actions, of desires spoiled by the conflicts they entailed, of beliefs undone by what the will to believe exposed.

What Claude articulates in *Amours de Voyage* is the narcissism of self-doubt, scepticism as a form of self-obsession. But this narcissism, this self-obsession, is the province of a certain kind of man, wherever he travels, and whenever he advises against it. It is this that makes Claude's incredible ignorance about women in *Amours de Voyage* such an essential part of the poem. Claude is at his least convincing—is, that is to say, at his most starkly defensive—in his pronouncements upon women and what they want, and this too is something about the poem that has become more legible over time. Claude's object of desire is his own unconvincing self; he is fascinated by his own gloomy uncertainty. Unlike Goethe's *Roman Elegies*, with their spell-bound erotic attentiveness to the loved and desired woman, *Amours de Voyage* is an elegy for a love affair that never happened—and, on a larger scale, an elegy for a culture's failed love affair with love itself. Claude, Clough wants us to see— like Goethe, but in a quite different way, an opposite way—couldn't make the woman he desired real enough for long enough. And so, Clough suggests, he couldn't make his desires real enough to himself. His own failings were more alluring than Mary was.

Incredible ignorance about women presumes, of course, a credible knowledge elsewhere. But I think Clough was impressing upon us, wittingly or unwittingly, both by his inclusion of women's voices in the poem, notably minimized by Claude's volubility—and through Claude's clichéd musings about women—a picture of Victorian masculinity, one version of it, in which an obsessive, cultivated (in both senses) self-preoccupation is organized to preclude exchange with women. Cultural ideals may be self-obsession by other means. It is not incidental that after the first two sections of Canto I in which Claude pontificates interestingly but in rather self-important ways about Rome, Christianity, and the history of the West—what it was and what it should have been—the first words in the poem by a woman are Georgina Trevellyn's to Louisa, 'At last' (I. iii); at last, an opportunity to speak (write), and at last, the reader might feel, a different kind of voice, a voice more exactly the kind of poetic voice that Clough was promoting in his review quoted earlier, a voice dealing with 'what is here', and not with what is, in the abstract, better and elsewhere. Claude writes of Roman history; Georgina writes of the practical actualities of travelling and family life.

We first hear Mary's voice in a postscript to one of Georgina's letters at the very end of Canto I in which we are given a description of Claude that is easy to assent to, both in its subtlety and its straightforwardness: 'I do not like him much, though I do not dislike being with him. / He is what people call, I suppose, a superior man, and / Certainly seems so to me; but I think he is terribly selfish' (I. xiii). The first line is what the reader tends to feel about Claude, but it is the casual suggestion that superiority in men is just a form of terrible selfishness that is arresting. It had been a culture of superior men that Clough had grown up in (though he notably devoted the last years of his life to a superior woman, Florence Nightingale). And it was as a critique of the idea of the superior man that he wrote *Amours de Voyage*. The second epigraph to the poem, from an unspecified but pointedly 'French Novel', 'Il doutait de tout, même de l'amour', is implicitly revised if not reversed by the end of the poem that has 'amour' in its title—to doubt love is to doubt everything.

Because Claude can't deal with the obstacles to love—with love as an obstacle-course, in which resistance is the point and not the problem—he cannot love, and Mary sees this clearly. The women in the poem, as Clough surely intended, are more clear-sighted though less 'cultured' than the men: more clear-sighted, that is to say, as Clough intimates, by being less cultured, less educated in the masculine way. As though the men, and particularly the superior men, have been hugely distracted—and in Claude's case paralyzed—by an education in self-love. Mary, Clough wants us to see, is much more exact, and therefore less speciously exacting than Claude. 'Oh, and you see I know so exactly how he would take it,' she writes,

> Finding the chances prevail against meeting again, he would banish
> Forthwith every thought of the poor little possible hope, which
> I myself could not help, perhaps, thinking only too much of;
> He would resign himself and go. I see it exactly.
> So I also submit, although in a different manner.
>
> (V. xi)

'Banish', with its Shakesperean echoes—the word is used most often in *Romeo and Juliet*—is what the man does, to thought and possibility and hope, all implicitly linked. Claude's resignation is a self-banishing, a refuge from his desire for Mary. Both Claude and Mary have to submit to the vagaries of Claude's character but, as Mary writes, in a different manner.

In a review of Clough's poetry in the *Atlantic Monthly* in April 1862, Clough's friend Charles Eliot Norton wrote of *Amours de Voyage* that it was 'at once established in the admiration of readers capable of appreciating its rare and refined excellence. The spirit of the poem is thoroughly characteristic of its author, and the speculative, analytic turn of his mind is represented in many passages of the letters of the imaginary hero'.[28] There were, we are reminded, readers not capable of such appreciation. And the speculative, analytic turn of the imaginary hero is taken, by his author, to be at best a mixed (and ironized) blessing. But there was another part of the author's mind represented by his imaginary heroine, and she would have seen exactly the force of her author's final epigraph to the poem, from Horace, about Anacreon—that is, about Claude—who 'in simple metres deplored his love' (to deplore being to grieve and to disparage). Or perhaps even more she would have known so exactly the truth of Thucydides, who provided an epigraph to *Amours de Voyage* from *The Peloponnesian War* that Clough ultimately discarded. Though it is, perhaps, a final word about Claude and, indeed, something Mary herself might have said: 'What you are looking for all the time is something that is, I should say, outside the range of ordinary experience, and yet you cannot even think straight about the facts of life that are before you.'

Notes

1. Arthur Hugh Clough, *Dipsychus and the Spirit in Clough: Selected Poems*, ed. J. P. Phelan (London and New York: Longman, 1995), 181.
2. Barbara Hardy, 'Clough's Self-Consciousness', in Isobel Armstrong, ed., *The Major Victorian Poets: Reconsiderations* (London: Routledge and Kegan Paul, 1969), 253.

3. Isobel Armstrong, *Victorian Poetry: Poetry, Poetics and Politics* (London: Routledge, 1993), 199.
4. Philip Davis, *The Victorians* (Oxford: Oxford University Press, 2002), 470.
5. John Goode, '*Amours de Voyage*: The Aqueous Poem', in *Major Victorian Poets*, 275.
6. T. S. Eliot, quoted in Christopher Ricks, ed., *The New Oxford Book of Victorian Verse* (Oxford: Oxford University Press, 1987), xxvii.
7. F. R. Leavis, quoted in Ricks, *Victorian Verse*, xxviii.
8. Clough, *Amours de Voyage*, in *Clough: Selected Poems*, 77. All subsequent references give Canto and Letter number in the main text.
9. Goode, '*Amours de Voyage*', 276.
10. F. T. Palgrave, *The Poetical Works of Clough* (London: Lawrence and Bullen, 1906), xxiv.
11. John Shairp quoted in Michael Thorpe, ed., *Clough: The Critical Heritage* (London: Routledge and Kegan Paul, 1972), 122.
12. Matthew Arnold, *The Letters of Mathew Arnold, Volume 1: 1829–1859*, ed. Cecil Y. Lang (Charlottesville, VA: University of Virginia Press, 1996), 259.
13. Friedrich Nietzsche, *Unmodern Observations*, ed. William Arrowsmith (New Haven: Yale University Press, 1990), 73–146.
14. Clough, *The Correspondence of Arthur Hugh Clough*, 2 vols., ed. Frederick L. Mulhauser (Oxford: Clarendon Press, 1957), i. 124.
15. R. H. Hutton, quoted in *Clough: Selected Poems*, 3.
16. Ralph Waldo Emerson, 'Self-Reliance', in *Essays: First Series* (Boston: Phillips and Samson, 1850), 61.
17. Emerson quoted in *Clough: The Critical Heritage*, 124.
18. Emerson, 'Self-Reliance', 45.
19. Clough, quoted in *Clough: The Critical Heritage*, 124.
20. Clough, *Correspondence*, i. 216.
21. Clough, review in *The North American* (July 1853), cited in James Insley Osborne, *Arthur Hugh Clough* (London: Constable, 1920), 164.
22. Emerson, 'The Poet', *Essays: Second Series*, in *The Collected Works of Ralph Waldo Emerson*, 9 vols., ed. Joseph Slater et al. (Harvard, Mass: Harvard University Press, 1971–), ii. 8.
23. *Macbeth*, III. iv. 24.
24. Emerson, 'Self-Reliance', 70–71.
25. Millicent Bell, ed., *The Wings of the Dove* (London: Penguin, 2008), xxx.
26. Emerson, 'Self-Reliance', 73.
27. Emerson quoted in Thorpe, *Clough: The Critical Heritage*, 124.
28. Charles Eliot Norton quoted in Thorpe, *Clough: The Critical Heritage*, 128.

Select Bibliography

Armstrong, Isobel, ed., *The Major Victorian Poets: Reconsiderations* (London: Routledge and Kegan Paul, 1969).
—— *Victorian Poetry: Poetry, Poetics and Politics* (London: Routledge, 1993).
Arnold, Matthew, *The Letters of Mathew Arnold, Volume 1: 1829–1859*, ed. Cecil Y. Lang (Charlottesville, VA: University of Virginia Press, 1996).
Clough, Arthur Hugh, *The Correspondence of Arthur Hugh Clough*, ed. Frederick L. Mulhauser, 2 vols. (Oxford: Clarendon Press, 1957).

——*Clough: Selected Poems*, ed. J. P. Phelan (London and New York: Longman, 1995).

Davis, Philips, *The Victorians* (Oxford: Oxford University Press, 2002).

Thorpe, Michael, ed., *Clough: The Critical Heritage* (London: Routledge and Kegan Paul, 1972).

Emerson, Ralph Waldo, *Essays: First Series* (Boston, MA: Phillips and Samson, 1850).

—— *Essays: Second Series*, in Joseph Slater et al, eds., *The Collected Works of Ralph Waldo Emerson*, vol. ii (Harvard, MA: Harvard University Press, 1971–).

CHAPTER 24

··

MATTHEW ARNOLD, OUT OF TIME

··

JANE WRIGHT

'[W]E are growing old, and advancing towards the deviceless darkness: it would be well not to reach it till we had tried at least *some* of the things men consider desirable'.[1] When Arnold wrote these regretful, elderly-sounding words to Arthur Hugh Clough, it was 1851 and he was 28. Arnold was fascinated by time. This has long been acknowledged in critical responses to the elegiac and late-Romantic voice of his poems, and, in recent decades, literary criticism (an activity that still owes much to Arnold) has shown signs of a reflected fascination, in its attempts to assess Arnold's cultural timeliness.[2] This essay reflects on some of the ways in which Arnold's poems harbour the feeling of being out of time, historically, metrically, and, especially, personally.[3] Many of Arnold's poems have time explicitly in mind. From his first published, 'Alaric at Rome' (1840), written in a shortened form of the Spenserian stanza, to 'Kaiser Dead' (1887), his last poem (an elegy to one of his dogs), Arnold was drawn to subjects or poetic forms which foreground not only losses, historical and personal, but an essential quality of poetry and the experience of reading: its temporality. Many of his best-known poems, including 'Mycerinus', 'The Sick King in Bokhara', 'Empedocles on Etna', 'Sohrab and Rustum', and 'Balder Dead', have ancient or mythical settings (they invoke a world outside the present time), and are also concerned with the end of a life (with running out of time). Others, including 'Resignation', 'Dover Beach', 'The Youth of Man', 'The Scholar-Gipsy', and 'Thyrsis', dwell on the forms of personal loss time brings. And many have in another sense sounded out of time to readers, as awkward metrically as their subject-matter can be historically or emotionally. When, in 1872, Henry Coleridge saw Arnold for the first time in years he thought him more youthful-looking than he had imagined: Arnold, quoting Coleridge in a letter, records: 'he said—"Matt!!—I expected to see a white-headed old man". I said that my white hairs were all internal'.[4] The sense of temporal disjunction is important as a characteristic of both the man and his work. And in his poetry this disjunction accentuates a vital quality of the experience of reading literature, one which Arnold (still

thinking of time) believed was important to 'the instinct of self-preservation in humanity': the combined experience of historical separation and imaginative presence.[5]

The questions in 'A Question. To Fausta', from Arnold's first volume, *The Strayed
Reveller, and Other Poems* (1849), grow out of the speaker's contemplation of time, and
are left to the reader at the end of the poem:

> Joy comes and goes, hope ebbs and flows
> >   Like the wave;
> Change doth unknit the tranquil strength of men.
> >   Love lends life a little grace,
> >   A few sad smiles; and then,
> >   Both are laid in one cold place,
> >   In the grave.
>
> Dreams dawn and fly, friends smile and die
> >   Like spring flowers;
> Our vaunted life is one long funeral.
> >   Men dig graves with bitter tears
> >   For their dead hopes; and all,
> >   Mazed with doubts and sick with fears,
> >   Count the hours.
>
> We count the hours! These dreams of ours,
> >   False and hollow,
> Do we go hence and find they are not dead?
> >   Joys we dimly apprehend,
> >   Faces that smiled and fled,
> >   Hopes born here, and born to end,
> >   Shall we follow?[6]

The 'hours' in the final stanza, which we are told with urgency ('!') we count, feel too
hastily met by 'dreams of ours'; the internal rhymes in the first line of each of this poem's
stanzas (and the other internal echoes—here 'count', 'hours', 'ours'; 'We', 'these', 'dreams')
restrain temporal extension and seem to pre-empt, and so cut short, the 'Joy' and 'hope'
which might attend the longer delays and clearer satisfactions of steadier verse forms.
The second line is abrupt, not only in its brevity: a shift in rhythm also imparts the
speaker's worry about the shifty nature of our experiences of time. And in each stanza
the latest sound of that line colludes in the shiftiness when it gets dragged into the third
line, and continues to echo (as in 'w*a*ve; / Ch*a*nge', 'l*ai*d', in the first stanza; 'fl*ow*ers; /
*Ou*r', 'd*ou*bts', in the second; 'h*o*ll*ow*, / D*o* we g*o*', 'H*o*pes', in the last). The feeling of pre-
cipitancy imparted by these echoes is partially compensated for by the note of continuation they also sound, and the result is a kind of rhetoric of sound effect. After so much
recurrence it feels especially hard, in spite of everything sorrowful that has been said,
and in spite of the warning contained in the name 'Fausta', to answer 'No' to the question
'Shall we follow?' The rhetoric of the poem is both linguistic and formal, and is poised to
make us feel that although 'Hopes' are 'born to end', still to deny our 'dreams' would be to
give up too soon. Arnold's poems are often wistful and resolute in this way.

Amid the turbulence of the modern world and against the fleeting nature of life, literature itself was the stay that Arnold championed in his later prose writing. His earlier poetry, though, had already begun to express his fascination with literature's power against the sadness of time-bound existence. 'The Strayed Reveller' begins with a 'Youth', who has entered the portico of Circe's palace, demanding:

> Faster, faster,
> O Circe, Goddess,
> Let the wild, thronging train,
> The bright procession
> Of eddying forms,
> Sweep through my soul![7]

Like the Youth's first words, Circe's first response concerns time. She asks: 'Whence art thou, sleeper?', and he (not merely 'a' but 'The Youth') responds that he is 'When the white dawn first / ... Came breaking', by which he must mean that he exists at the beginning of the world, or some time after Milton: a 'bright procession' follows God as he prepares to create the world in *Paradise Lost* (vii. 222), just before the first dawn (vii. 243–9).[8] Set in a mythical literary world where time has its own symbolic logic, The Youth is at a perpetual beginning. That befits not only his age but also the fact that he is a figure of Arnold's written into a setting borrowed from Homer's *Odyssey*—a figure 'making it new'—and, in turn, his final words (which are the final lines of the poem) reinforce that sense of timelessness by repeating exactly the opening lines, above. This poem, set outside of the poet's own time, one ancient mythical 'Evening', is an early instance of Arnold's preoccupation with literature's capacity to offer readers an experience that is both in and out of time, its capacity to be both passionately engaged and safely removed, like this unharmed Youth, whom Circe neither punishes nor transforms.[9]

Kenneth Allott, following Lionel Trilling, writes that 'The Strayed Reveller' is at odds with the sentiment of 'Resignation. To Fausta', published in the same volume.[10] If one accepts that the strayed Youth is himself a figure of the poet, however, intoxicated by a mythical Muse and (unlike those 'bards' who must suffer old age) 'Looking over the valley, ... Without pain', a shared fantasy emerges. Though they envision him by different means, both poems idealize a figure of the poet who is in some way outside of Time's prison.[11] Great poetry, for Arnold, was poetry in touch with deep feeling, yet also detached from it. The true poet cannot engage in life directly if he is to convey passion successfully in writing, says the speaker of 'Resignation', but instead 'Bears to admire uncravingly':

> Before him he sees life unroll,
> A placid and continuous whole—
> That general life, which does not cease,
> Whose secret is not joy, but peace.[12]

This assumes the note of a personal creed when one considers that many of Arnold's poems invoke worlds from the ancient or mythical past in which great emotional events take place. In *The Strayed Reveller*, the title poem and 'Resignation. To Fausta' are both poems concerned with the relation of poetry to passion, and they express that concern through different kinds of temporal disjunction.

Arnold could take against poets or poems he felt were agitating to read. And what he considered agitating was ill-controlled passion, undue analysis, and the contemporary world.[13] His criticisms of Clough in the letters can be severe. The age, he warned, was 'not unprofound, not ungrand, not unmoving:—but unpoetical', and not, therefore, a suitable subject for poetry. On reading Clough's long vacation pastoral, *The Bothie of Toper-na-Fuosich*, with its contemporary setting and concern for current education and class politics, he wrote to Clough:

> I have been at Oxford the last two days and hearing Sellar and the rest of that clique who know neither life nor themselves rave about your poem gave me a strong almost bitter feeling with respect to them, the age, the poem, even you. Yes I said to myself something tells me I can, if need be, at least dispense with them all, even him: better that, than be sucked for an hour even into the Time Stream in which they plunge and bellow. I became calm in spirit, but uncompromising, . . . and took up Obermann, and refuged myself with him in his forest against your Zeit Geist.[14]

To keep out of the present time, safe in a forest of literature, was preferable. A year later his frustration with the times sounds even more pervasive. Referring to their 'untoward generation', he lamented again: 'My dearest Clough these are damned times—everything is against one—the height to which knowledge has come, the spread of luxury, our physical enervation, the absence of great natures, the unavoidable contact with millions of small ones, newspapers, cities, light profligate friends, moral desperadoes like Carlyle, our own selves'.[15] It became a concern of his later essays to explain the importance of the epoch in which a writer lives. 'Gray', he writes, 'a born poet, fell upon an age of prose' and so was sometimes silenced by it.[16] Worse than that, Arnold explained in the 'Preface' to *Essays in Criticism* (1865), the present time was 'an epoch of dissolution and transformation' in which 'ties, and associations are inevitably broken up' and 'the shortcomings, errors, heats, disputes' of individuals 'are brought into greater prominence'.[17] That was why poetry should avoid the present age, but why, in turn, the literary critic must be careful to understand the epoch in which a writer lived and the demands which that epoch made upon him.[18]

Arnold wrote, then, about the fleeting nature of life and time, and tested his ideas about the power of poetry in poems that were set in other (ancient or mythical) times, or which mythologized memory and a personal past. Such thought-experiments with old subjects, and commitment to classical literature, led to a third way in which his poems can characteristically seem out of time. Marian Evans Lewes (later George Eliot) was among the first to observe that 'Mr Arnold's grand defect is his want of rhythm—we mean of that rhythm which is music to an English ear'; Yvor Winters thought him 'capable, although not invariably guilty, of very crude rhythm'; and T. S. Eliot, in a tone indebted to Arnold's own prose voice, equivocated: 'I am not sure that he was highly sensitive to the musical qualities of verse'.[19] The sonnet 'To a Friend' (1849) (probably Clough) begins with a line often quoted when a critic wishes to remark the unevenness of Arnold's versification:

> Who prop, thou ask'st, in these bad days, my mind?
> He much, the old man, who, clearest-souled of men,
> Saw The Wide Prospect, and the Asian Fen,
> And Tmolus hill, and Smyrna bay, though blind.
>
> Much he, whose friendship I not long since won,
> That halting slave, who in Nicopolis
> Taught Arrian, when Vespasian's brutal son
> Cleared Rome of what most shamed him. But be his
>
> My special thanks, whose even-balanced soul,
> From first youth tested up to extreme old age,
> Business could not make dull, nor passion wild;
>
> Who saw life steadily, and saw it whole;
> The mellow glory of the Attic stage,
> Singer of sweet Colonus, and its child.[20]

The poem is about the literature of the past and its effect on a present-day reader. The sense of the last two lines is that Sophocles is Athens' great playwright and is from Colonus, but there are ambiguities that have time in mind. Sophocles is the glory of the Attic theatre, and also of the Attic period, different kinds of 'stage'. He was born in Colonus, and his play *Oedipus Colonus* was his last work, written just before his death. Sophocles is singer of Colonus in both these senses, defined by his place of birth and by his last work. And at the end of his long life he remains the 'child' of at once his time, place, and art. Arnold's poem indulges in the fantasy of seeing life 'steadily' and seeing it 'whole' which Sophocles' life and work appear to offer; the poem begins with an 'old man' (Homer) and ends with Sophocles, 'child' of his time and art. The shifts in the poem's metre betray the fears that encourage such fantasy. Following the tumultuous opening lines, the verse becomes more harmonious as Arnold looks back across Sophocles' life. The effects of the metre can still be felt; the idea of getting 'up to extreme old age', for instance, is made palpable as the implicit elision ('t'extreme old age') imparts rapidity to the movement from 'first youth' to 'old age'. But Park Honan suggests that the 'verse cacophony' of the opening lines, and comparable lines of Arnold, 'is emblematic for the "bad days" that it treats. The discord of the age is heard in the verse'.[21] When thinking of the present Arnold's poem feels out of time metrically; looking out of his own era to the past, by contrast, brings it back into rhythm. The verse is at once in and out of time, in one way or another.

Honan makes this point (about cacophony and the present) in relation to Arnold's sense of his present day, the dreaded *Zeitgeist*. The same is true, though, in poems that speak of an unspecified or generic idea of the present, such as 'The Youth of Man' (1852), in which rhythmic awkwardness is partly generated by a jostling of metrical principles which themselves represent different eras in thinking about prosody: quantity (Greek and Roman metres) and accent (the modern measure).[22] A number of the poems written between 1850 and 1857 are Pindaric (lines typically contain three stresses, but between six and nine syllables). Honan calls the metre of these poems 'dactylic trimeter catalectic', and so finds the lines 'rugged'. But Arnold called them 'Pindaric' with good reason; the terms of neo-classical prosody (such as 'dactylic trimeter cataletic') cannot comfortably do descriptive justice to such lines of Arnold's, any more than they can to parts of Hopkins's 'Sprung Rhythm'. Like Hopkins's rhythms, the variations in Arnold's lines are partly accountable by comparison to time-signature in music. Take, as an example of Pindaric, 'The Youth of Man', in which the principle of quantity can be felt through the pace of the lines:

> We, O Nature, depart,
> Thou survivest us! this,
> This, I know, is the law.
> Yes! but more than this,
> Thou who seest us die
> Seest us change while we live;
> Seest our dreams, one by one,
> Seest our errors depart;
> Watchest us, Nature! throughout,
> Mild and inscrutably calm.[23]

The poem imagines an ageing couple standing on the balustrade of a castle, hearing their children playing below, and gazing out 'To the dim horizon'. Later, the speaker exclaims:

> Well I know what they feel!
> They gaze, and the evening wind
> Plays on their faces; they gaze—
> Airs from the Eden of youth
> Awake and stir in their soul;
> The past returns—they feel
> What they are, alas! what they were.
> They, not Nature, are changed.
> Well I know what they feel.

The couple can watch what is happening, but Nature has the real agency: they 'gaze', it 'Plays'. The phrase 'The past returns' has a touch of literal truth when followed by the words 'they feel', which themselves return, though now without exclamation. The fleeting possibility that the second 'feel' in this passage could be intransitive (created by the enjambment of 'The past returns—they feel / What they are') turns out to be a cruel trick that models the bathetic movement of the sense. Before the line break, it seems that the ability to feel is connected to the past in a positive way (the past returns and so the couple can feel again), but in fact the past is only a reminder of what has been lost (they feel what they are now by way of a sad comparison with what they were). Having addressed

'Nature' at the start, the poem closes with its only metrically extended line, a battle-cry
to the young to 'Yearn to the greatness of Nature; / Rally the good in the depths of thyself!' Reference to what is of 'thyself' finds the poem out of time metrically and actually.
Being in the present is uncomfortable. The temporal extension of the final line expresses
the discomfort of an older speaker who is himself yearning to the greatness of Nature as
he sees it embodied in the young.

The Scholar-Gipsy '[has] not felt that lapse of hours' partly because he is 'exempt
from age / . . . living as thou liv'st on Glanvil's page', partly because he '[had] *one* aim,
one business, *one* desire' which carried him through life unscathed, and partly because,
more sinisterly, he in fact '[has] not lived' at all.[24] By leaving mainstream society, the
Scholar-Gipsy has magically disentangled himself from the divisions inherent in a modern, post-Hegelian world. This is a particularly strong Arnoldian fantasy: there must
be a way to be free of the sense of temporal pressure and degradation that attaches to
'modern' society. It is a fantasy equally imbued, though, with a distinctly Arnoldian realism: the only way to be so free is either to die (like Empedocles or Sohrab) or to be the
stuff of story or legend (like the Merman, the Neckan, or the Scholar-Gipsy).

> But fly our paths, our feverish contact fly!
>   For strong the infection of our mental strife,
>   Which, though it gives no bliss, yet spoils for rest;
>   And we should win thee from thy own fair life,
>   Like us distracted, and like us unblest.
>   Soon, soon thy cheer would die,
>   Thy hopes grow timorous, and unfixed thy powers,
>   And thy clear aims be crossed and shifting made;
>   And then thy glad perennial youth would fade,
> Fade, and grow old at last, and die like ours.

'We' would exert, inadvertently, a power over the Scholar-Gipsy that is in some ways akin
to the power he seeks to learn from the Gypsies themselves: to 'rule . . . / The workings of
men's brains'. The difference is that the power 'we' would exert is the result of 'infection' rather than 'will'; what is missing in 'our' case is direct and controllable 'desire'. The
line 'Like us distracted, and like us unblest' sounds a brief note of eighteenth-century
balance, but in so doing sets form against content, or at any rate announces a kind of
balance that nobody wants. It is as though the pressures of the contemporary moment
sap Arnold's poetic speaker of a positive sense of desire, or of the ability to know where
desire originates. When it is most in touch with his times, the world of Arnold's poems
is a modern one in which 'we' risk being drained of desire by the inexorable nature of the
world's demands. The Scholar-Gipsy remains, in this sense, a figure for our educational
times—the eternal ideal undergraduate, always already a myth, but not for that reason
less at risk of being swept away completely (as the poem worries) by the misplaced values of modernity.[25]

Anyone who admires Clough's poetry may find it hard to forgive Arnold on first
reading 'Thyrsis' (subtitled 'A Monody, *to commemorate the author's friend*, ARTHUR

HUGH CLOUGH, *who died at Florence*, 1861').[26] Some experiences of grief contain bitter reproaches, and it can feel as though, in 'Thyrsis', Arnold could not find quite enough of the tact he so esteemed in critical prose finally to quell the irritation he felt with Clough, even for dying. The fifth stanza of 'Thyrsis':

> It irked him to be here, he could not rest.
>   He loved each simple joy the country yields,
>   He loved his mates; but yet he could not keep,
>   For that a shadow loured on the fields,
>   Here with the shepherds and the silly sheep.
>   Some life of men unblest
>   He knew, which made him droop, and filled his head.
>   He went; his piping took a troubled sound
>   Of storms that rage outside our happy ground;
>   He could not wait their passage, he is dead.

That some of these lines read like free indirect speech (not a quality common to the poem as a whole) has the effect of bringing the speaker and his dead friend into an awkward union. When we are told 'It irked him to be here, he could not rest'—especially when the irksomeness is so plainly a failing—we suspect the speaker of being irked just as much; enough at least that he feels the need to say so in an elegy. Was Thyrsis really so grumpy? Were there 'storms' only 'outside' Oxford ('our happy ground') when Clough and Arnold were there in the 1840s (those years when the Tractarians were troubling so many, and debates about educational reform in the two ancient universities were underway)? By the last line of this stanza, the words 'he is dead' jar against the previous possibility of the free indirect style. The speaker seems to imply, with a kind of subterranean crossness (there is a touch of 'and so' about that comma), that it was Thyrsis' own impatience that killed him. Arnold's phrase, 'Too quick despairer' (which in literal terms in the poem describes a cuckoo), came to define one long-lasting critical view of Clough, as well as of the relative attitudes and poetics of the two.[27] The subtleties of voice and tone of 'Thyrsis', however, are a means for the speaker to mourn himself in relation to Thyrsis—to mourn a friendship as much a friend. *If* Arnold may be seen as Corydon (the singer who conquers Thyrsis in the competition described in Virgil's *Eclogues*), to say that 'Time, not Corydon, hath conquered thee!' is as humble and tender about that relationship as it may be critical of Thyrsis' 'troubled' song.[28]

Having compared Thyrsis to the cuckoo, as one who departs 'When the year's primal burst of bloom is o'er', the speaker ventriloquizes his friend through the cuckoo's imagined cry, and so ascribes to him still more directly an instinctive rejection of his 'happy' surroundings (and implicitly of life): '*The bloom is gone, and with the bloom go I!*' None of this seems as vague or as admiring of his friend's qualities as a traditional elegy should be. Arnold sounds a note of elegiac self-interest and sustained criticism that would come to be seen as more characteristic of twentieth-century elegy.[29] Past forms can be fictions of belonging. Here, as elsewhere, Arnold has an idealized fiction of the past. But though he has the opportunity to sustain a past form (in this case the traditional elegy) finds that he is less at home there than he thought.[30] The sense that there is more going on in 'Thyrsis' than is ostensibly being said, more going on perhaps than the speaker fully owns, is unsettling. But, insofar as the poem, formally, puts us in a position to notice that, it is also unsettlingly honest. As with reading Hardy's poems, it can feel cleaner to accept at face value what Arnold's speakers tell us, than to try to tune in to the tremors of the buried life that shudder through tone and syntax and timings and mannered exclamations; cleaner, but also unsatisfying, and unconvincing.[31] This is one reason for the long-standing characterization of Arnold as an academic's poet. G. H. Lewes was among the first to remark: 'His poems will delight scholars'.[32]

Echoing Milton's lament for his university friend, Arnold later asks:

> Where are the mowers, who, as the tiny swell
> Of our boat passing heaved the river-grass,
> Stood with suspended scythe to see us pass?
> They all are gone, and thou art gone as well!
>
> Yes, thou art gone! and round me too the night
> In ever-nearing circles weaves her shade.

In 'Lycidas' Milton had written: 'But O the heavy change, now thou art gone, / Now thou art gone, and never must return!' and asked questions, not as Arnold does to create a retrospective frame, but to interrogate the world for his loss: 'Where were ye nymphs when the remorseless deep / Closed o'er the head of your loved Lycidas?'[33] That is, where Milton's speaker uses his questions to begin to conquer time, challenging the mythologised past in order to begin to reconcile himself with the present, Arnold uses this comparable moment to accentuate further his temporal alienation. The mowers 'with suspended scythe' are apt figures for the time before Thyrsis' death, but also recall Marvell's mowers, in 'Upon Appleton House' and the mower poems, and so renew allusively the ambivalence of those works regarding, on the one hand, the efficacy of retreat from the contemporary political world, and, on the other, active engagement with it.

The next time Arnold echoes 'thou art gone', as though still stuck in the early shock of grief, the poem is drawing to an end, and the speaker declares that 'me thou leavest here / Sole in these fields! yet will I not despair. / Despair I will not'. His attempt to claim his difference from Thyrsis catches on the repeated words. A ghostly trace of the question 'will I not despair[?]' and answer 'Despair I will' haunts these claims and makes them sound, if not despairing, desperate. The case is only worsened when the speaker continues with the following lament and question which together harbour Arnold's characteristic mix of gravity and levity, assertion and open uncertainty:

> Still, still these slopes, 'tis clear,
> Our Gipsy-Scholar haunts, outliving thee!
> Fields where soft sheep from cages pull the hay,
> Woods with anemones in flower till May,
> Know him a wanderer still; then why not me?

The exclamation, 'outliving thee!', sounds a lament, but is also a criticism, and almost a taunt. In context, the question 'then why not me?' is not a rhetorical appeal but the expression of a compound anxiety. The speaker wonders whether there is a problem with his own perception or that of others (the question might be paraphrased 'the fields know that the Scholar-Gipsy is still out there, so why don't I know it?' or, alternatively, 'the fields witness that the Scholar-Gipsy is still a wanderer, so why don't they recognize that I have successfully remained a wanderer too?': 'is there a problem with my view of the world, or with the world's view of me?'). The speaker of 'Thyrsis' wants to declare himself more settled and stable than his dead friend ever was. He also wants to declare that he has managed to remain a wanderer without faltering, and while he cannot quite reconcile the two emotionally, he can merge them in the expressive discomfort of the poem.

The poetic persona of Milton's 'Lycidas' detaches himself from the grieving voice of the first 185 lines of the poem when, at the end, he steps back and retrospectively frames that voice with the words 'Thus sang the uncouth swain to the oaks and rills, / While the still morn went out with sandals grey'. Milton's 'still morn' (a new and calmer beginning) is on the move, stepping out; in Arnold's elegy what is 'still'—the lasting 'slopes' and perpetual 'wanderer'—draws the speaker back to the past, just as the internal echoes 'Still, still', 'till', 'still', pull against the slow progress of the end-rhymes. Arnold's 'still' is both a clinging to the past and an entrapment in the present, not the adjective of newly achieved calm it is for Milton. Arnold's poem also ends with a shift in voice, but it is to the imagined voice of Thyrsis, offering comfort. The consolation is fantasized:

> Why faintest thou? I wandered till I died.
>   Roam on! The light we sought is shining still,
>   Dost thou ask proof? Our tree yet crowns the hill,
> Our Scholar travels yet the loved hill-side.

The last three stanzas of 'Thyrsis' may have been added late in the day, when Arnold, about to publish, had for the first time read the volume of Clough's *Letters and Remains* collected and edited by his wife, Blanche.[34] Arnold takes Thyrsis' voice out of time (speaking as it does from beyond the grave), and may have felt himself out of time to reassess. The endings of Arnold's poems can feel unsatisfying or abrupt in this way. Unlike the suggestively open-ended, inconclusive, or unresolved endings of Tennyson's or Browning's poems, Arnold's often finish in a way which at first feels incongruous, so that the reader is left with a dismaying feeling of being taken back to the beginning of the problem, or of having an unexpected aspect of a problem suddenly introduced. At these moments, the reader may be left with a sense of having run out of time, of having been unprepared for the final event or thought. One response is to go back to the start of the poem.[35] Arnold's poems are very good at encouraging that.

The poem 'Growing Old' has been thought to echo, respond to, or argue with, poets including Shakespeare, Wordsworth, Tennyson, and Browning.[36] But most of all Arnold echoes and argues with himself:

> What is it to grow old?
> Is it to lose the glory of the form,
> The lustre of the eye?
> Is it for beauty to forgo her wreath?
> —Yes, but not this alone.
>
> Is it to feel our strength—
> Not our bloom only, but our strength—decay?
> Is it to feel each limb
> Grow stiffer, every function less exact,
> Each nerve more loosely strung?
>
> Yes, this, and more; but not
> Ah, 'tis not what in youth we dreamed 'twould be!
> 'Tis not to have our life
> Mellowed and softened as with sunset-glow,
> A golden day's decline.
>
> 'Tis not to see the world
> As from a height, with rapt prophetic eyes,
> And heart profoundly stirred;
> And weep, and feel the fullness of the past,
> The years that are no more.
>
> It is to spend long days
> And not once feel that we were ever young;
> It is to add, immured
> In the hot prison of the present, month
> To month with weary pain.
>
> It is to suffer this,
> And feel but half, and feebly, what we feel.
> Deep in our hidden heart
> Festers the dull remembrance of a change,
> But no emotion—none.
>
> It is—last stage of all—
> When we are frozen up within, and quite
> The phantom of ourselves,
> To hear the world applaud the hollow ghost
> Which blamed the living man.

'And feel but half, and feebly, what we feel' is a line more insistent on the relation between feeling and feebleness, than on immediate clarity. The insistent present tense seems particularly incongruent with personal existence here: what is 'what we feel' under these circumstances? Is it what we feel in the present tense of old age, or what we feel in the present tense of an experience in memory? Does the line say that 'old age is to feel in a weaker way what we used to feel when we were young' or that 'in old age whatever we feel we feel it only weakly'? The word 'feel' is entangled in the word 'feebly', as though the line taunts the reader by playing the senses (sight and sound) off sense. This is less a poem about being out of time, than one which dwells painfully on what it is to be stuck in time and its horrible fluctuations.

Throughout the volume in which this poem appeared, *New Poems* (1867)—a volume in which (as Trilling notes) 'Nearly all the poems...touch upon death', and which was published at a time when Arnold had lost father, brother, friend, and son (two more sons would die in 1868)—the poet-speaker is a man trapped in ongoing time, 'immured / In the hot prison of the present', while those who are the subjects of other poems in the volume—Empedocles (the poem was re-printed at Browning's urging), Rachel (the French tragedienne Arnold admired, who died at 36), Dr. and William Arnold, Thyrsis (Clough)—all pass away.[37] It has been suggested that its title identifies 'Growing Old' as a bitter response to the opening lines of Browning's 'Rabbi Ben Ezra' (1864): 'Grow old along with me / The best is yet to be, / The last of life, for which the first was made'.[38] To that suggestion, it has been countered that the poem (in lines 19–20 especially) shows more verbal affiliation with Tennyson's 'Tears, Idle Tears' (Arnold, advancing on Tennyson's 'days', laments 'The years that are no more'), but also that Arnold rejects the emotional fullness of Tennyson's 'passion of the past' as much as he rejects the *joie de vivre* of Browning's Rabbi.[39] 'Growing Old', though, also echoes both the words and sentiment of the 28-year-old Arnold, to Clough, in the letter I quoted at the start of this essay: 'we are growing old, and advancing towards the deviceless darkness'. Frequent movement between the present participle and infinitive verb forms is common in Arnold's poems, and holds the reader in a strangely heightened or abstracted present. In 'Growing Old', the progressive tense of the present participle presides over a horrible world of infinitives in which the speaker, who sets aside the comforting fantasies which shape conceptions of the past and future, is trapped ('to grow', 'to lose', 'to forgo', 'to feel', 'to suffer', 'To hear the world applaud the hollow ghost / Which blamed the living man').

Arnold's fantasy of Sophocles, 'Who saw life steadily, and saw it whole', was a fantasy about Sophocles' abilities in 'first youth' and 'old age' alike. In this late poem, growing old means losing 'the glory of the form', yet not finding 'life / Mellowed and softened as with sunset-glow'. The earlier poem ends with celebratory reference to a dead man who is yet figured as an eternal 'child', this one with a 'hollow ghost' applauded where the 'living man' was 'blamed'. In an early review of Arnold's work, G. H. Lewes began by noting that 'with individuals as with nations, the baffled turbulence of Youth subsides into the calm acquiescence of Age, but in both the ideal is placed beyond the Present'.[40] It is in this fantasy, that either youth or old age was or will be better, that the atmosphere of Arnold's poetry comes closest to the force of his prose, especially where the latter is concerned with literature and culture. In the prose, his arguments explicitly rely on a combination of historical assessment and ahistorical principle which has seemed to some readers unsystematic, and has opened Arnold to criticism.[41] That, too, though, is a practice perfectly adequate to the nature of literature and the process, as Arnold saw it, of reading it attentively.

When Arnold's poems are so often, rightly, discussed as elegiac and late-Romantic (as self-consciously belated, in either case), it can be easy to overlook the powerful fantasy they offer the reader of the possibility of making time; not of taking or redeeming time, but actually gaining more of it. In one sense, most creative literature might be said to do this. In the act of reading we are both in and out of time, in another century, in another temporal order which has its own narrative capacities and temporal dimensions. By persistently looking back, however, or seeming to pause or abstract time for the sake of contemplation, and with the cacophonous or recitative timing of his poems' metres, Arnold generates an accentuated experience of the temporal conditions of reading. The world of his poems is forever on the brink of something (a death, a shoreline, a precipice, a city). Often the speaker focuses on another time, inhabiting a present moment which feels paused, anxious for the future, or perpetually sensing an ending. From the privileged vantage of that pause the reader is invited to sustain, with the speaker, a fragile fantasy of atemporality.

The late twentieth-century tendency to re-assess Arnold for our times, which I mentioned at the start, was partly an assessment of the extent to which his views keep up with or may be said to continue to set the pace of the present. A late quatrain, 'The Persistency of Poetry' (1867), expresses the view of the later criticism, and captures a hope about the place and function of poetry, in history and education:

> Though the Muse be gone away,
> Though she move not earth to-day,
> Souls, erewhile who caught her word,
> Ah! still harp on what they heard.[42]

'Though the Muse be gone away', we are made to feel that she is also detained here, keeping company with the sound of this verse about her lack of agency (as 'move' echoes 'Muse'). We feel that, though 'gone', her work may be carried 'on', even if only as an after-effect or matter of form. And then it turns out that, though we may not have 'her word' directly, we yet have word of her—she is Ophelia, and the poem demonstrates the persistency of Shakespeare by echoing Polonius's words regarding Hamlet, 'Still harping on my daughter' (II.ii.188–9).[43] T. S. Eliot wrote of Arnold (as much of the critic as the poet) that he 'represents a period of stasis; of relative and precarious stability,...a brief halt in the endless march of humanity...he marks a period of time, as do Dryden and Johnson before him'.[44] Such 'relative and precarious stability' is something the reader of Arnold's poems is encouraged to feel as a primary experience of reading and thinking through literature. A 'brief halt' and 'mark[ing of] a period of time' is one thing the act of reading may offer, and it is also what Arnold's poems are most often about (both in their content, and their self-conscious affect). E. M. Forster, finding Arnold 'of all the Victorians most to my taste', considered him 'a great poet, a civilized citizen, and a prophet who has managed to project himself into our present troubles, so that when we read him now, he seems to be in the room'.[45] In their broad outlines, Arnold's poems can feel time-bound to readers now (late-Romantic and mannered), yet they turn their anxiety about time and the present into presence of this kind, a presence felt not only in but *as* the significance of the act of reading. It is in heightening this sense of being out of time, suspended, in the present, in the complex activity of relating to other times, that Arnold's poems may be said best to remain, still, in step with the modern world.

Notes

1. Matthew Arnold, letter dated Saturday [shortly after December 19, 1851] in *The Letters of Matthew Arnold to Arthur Hugh Clough*, ed. Howard Foster Lowry (Oxford: Clarendon Press, 1932), 118. (The date was probably 20 December, which was a Saturday.) This is the first instance of 'deviceless' given in the *OED*. Arnold is also credited with the first instances of the time-related terms 'calendarial' (1867) and 'Zeit Geist' (1848).

2. See Eugene Goodheart, 'Arnold at the Present Time', *Critical Inquiry*, 9 (1983), 451–468; John Willinsky, 'Matthew Arnold's Legacy: The Powers of Literature', *Research in the Teaching of English*, 24 (1990), 343–361; Timothy Peltason, 'The Function of Matthew Arnold at the Present Time', *College English*, 56 (1994), 749–765; Bruce Novak, 'Humanizing Democracy: Matthew Arnold's Nineteenth-Century Call for a Common, Higher, Educative Pursuit of Happiness and Its Relevance to Twenty-First-Century Democratic Life', *American Educational Research Journal*, 39 (2002), 593–637.

3. Two good introductions relate Arnold's life to his writing: Stefan Collini, *Matthew Arnold: A Critical Portrait* (Oxford: Clarendon Press, 1988) and Ian Hamilton, *A Gift Imprisoned: The Poetic Life of Matthew Arnold* (London: Bloomsbury, 1998).

4. Arnold to his Mother, 23 December 1872, *Letters of Matthew Arnold, 1848–1888*, ed. George W. E. Russell, 2 vols. (London: Macmillan, 1895), ii. 90.

5. Arnold, 'The Study of Poetry' (1880), in *The Complete Prose Works*, 11 vols., ed. R. H. Super (Ann Arbor: University of Michigan Press, 1960-77), ix. 188.

6. Arnold, 'A Question. To Fausta' (?1844), in *The Complete Poems*, ed. Kenneth Allott, 2nd edn. (London: Longman, 1979), 38.

7. Arnold, 'The Strayed Reveller', in *Complete Poems*, 67. The magical goddess Circe is daughter of Helios (god of the sun) and Perse (an Oceanid).

8. John Milton, *Paradise Lost*, ed. Alastair Fowler, 2nd edn. (London: Longman, 1998).

9. In *The Odyssey* X, 261-268, Circe turns Odysseus' men into swine. Homer, *The Odyssey*, trans. Robert Fagles, intro. Bernard Knox (Harmondsworth: Penguin, 1996), 237–238.

10. Allott in Arnold, *Complete Poems*, 76n; and Lionel Trilling, *Matthew Arnold* (London: Harcourt, 1939), 100.

11. In 'Resignation' the speaker addresses Fausta as 'Time's chafing prisoner'—Arnold, *Complete Poems*, 88.

12. The 'two offices of Poetry', he told Clough, were 'one to add to one's store of thoughts and feelings—another to compose and elevate the mind by a sustained tone, numerous allusion, and a grand style' (about 1 March 1849, *Letters*, 100).

13. See his comments on Keats, Browning, and Tennyson (after September 1848–9, *Letters*, 96–7) and on Clough's poems (early part of February 1849, *Letters*, 98–99).

14. Arnold, letter dated November 1848 in *Letters*, 95. Cp. 'The World and the Quietist. To Critias' (1849), *Complete Poems*, 106.

15. Arnold, 23 September 1849, in *Letters*, 109, 111.

16. Arnold, 'Thomas Gray' (1880), in *Prose* ix. 200.

17. Arnold, 'Preface' to *Essays in Criticism* (1865), in *Prose* iii. 288.

18. See Arnold, 'The Function of Criticism at the Present Time' (1864), in *Prose* iii. 258–285.

19. George Eliot, unsigned review, *Westminster Review* (July 1855), in Carl Dawson, ed., *Matthew Arnold: The Poetry. The Critical Heritage* (London: Routledge and Kegan Paul, 1973), 130; Winters, *Forms of Discovery* (Alan Swallow, 1967), 183, quoted in Christopher Ricks, *Allusion to the Poets* (Oxford: Oxford University Press, 2004), 308; T. S. Eliot, 'Matthew Arnold', in *The Use of Poetry and the Use of Criticism* (London: Faber and Faber Ltd, 1933), 118.

20. Arnold, 'To a Friend', in *Complete Poems*, 110.

21. Park Honan, 'Matthew Arnold and Cacophony', *Victorian Poetry* 1 (1963), 118.

22. See Arnold's poised discussion of quantity and accent in 'On Translating Homer' and 'Last Words'; also Joseph Phelan, *The Music of Verse: Metrical Experiment in Nineteenth-Century Poetry* (Basingstoke: Palgrave, 2012), 77–87.

23. Arnold, 'The Youth of Man', in *Complete Poems*, 265.

24. Arnold, 'The Scholar-Gipsy', in *Complete Poems*, 355.

25. For discussion of Arnold and education, see Dinah Birch, *Our Victorian Education* (Oxford: Blackwell Publishing, 2008). See also G. Wilson Knight, *Neglected Powers: Essays on Nineteenth and Twentieth Century Literature* (London: Routledge and Kegan Paul, 1971), 234–235.

26. Arnold, 'Thyrsis', in *Complete Poems*, 537.

27. David Williams, *Too Quick Despairer: The Life of Arthur Hugh Clough* (London: Rupert Hart-Davis, 1969) is one obvious instance of what for a while became a standard response to Clough's life and work.

28. Virgil, *Eclogues* vii, *The Eclogues. The Georgics*, trans. C. Day Lewis, intro. R. O. A. M. Lyne (Oxford: Oxford University Press, 1983), 29–32. See also Michael Timko, 'Corydon had a Rival', *Victorian Newsletter* 19 (1961), 5–11; and Jerome L. Mazzaro, 'Corydon in Matthew Arnold's "Thyrsis"', *Victorian Poetry* 1 (1963), 304–306.

29. See Jahan Ramazani, *Poetry of Mourning: The Modern Elegy from Hardy to Heaney* (Chicago: University of Chicago Press, 1994).

30. The clearest example of this is 'Dover Beach', which may be read as three incomplete, or eroded, sonnets. See Ruth Pitman, 'On Dover Beach', *Essays in Criticism* 23 (1973), 109–136.

31. For further discussion (not including 'Thyrsis'), see William E. Buckler, 'Victorian Modernism: The Arnold-Hardy Succession', *Browning Institute Studies*, 11 (1983), 9–21.

32. 'Schools of Poetry, Arnold's Poems', Leader (1853), in *Critical Heritage*, 83.

33. John Milton, 'Lycidas' in *Complete Shorter Poems*, ed. John Carey, 2nd edn. (London: Longman, 1997), 246.

34. David J. DeLaura, 'Arnold, Clough, Dr. Arnold, and "Thyrsis"', *Victorian Poetry* 7 (1969), 191–202, suggests that on reading the *Remains* 'Arnold added three more stanzas [to "Thyrsis"], the reason being an apparently abrupt decision to reassociate Clough somehow with the poet's quest' (198).

35. Francis O'Gorman, 'Matthew Arnold and Rereading', *Cambridge Quarterly* 41 (2012), 245–261, writes that in his prose Arnold 'described texts that, if read properly, were excluded from temporality' (246), whereas his poetry offers 'ways in which the reader might apprehend themselves rereading', as the poems perform the 'task of returning and perceiving afresh' (258).

36. Arnold, 'Growing Old', in *Complete Poems*, 582, and 583–584nn.

37. Trilling, *Matthew Arnold*, 296–7.

38. Conrad A. Balliet, '"Growing Old" along with "Rabbi Ben Ezra"', *Victorian Poetry* 1 (1963), 300–301.

39. John Huebenthal, '"Growing Old", "Rabbi Ben Ezra", and "Tears, idle tears"', *Victorian Poetry* 3 (1965), 61–63.

40. 'Schools of Poetry, Arnold's Poems', Leader (1853), in *Critical Heritage*, 77.

41. The criticism began early. Arnold described himself defensively as an 'unsystematic writer' in *Culture and Anarchy* (1867–9); *Culture and Anarchy and other writings*, ed. Stefan Collini (Cambridge: Cambridge University Press, 1993), 102 (cp. 57).

42. Arnold, 'The Persistency of Poetry', in *Complete Poems*, 578.

43. William Shakespeare, *The Complete Works*, ed. Stanley Wells, Gary Taylor, John Jowett, and William Montgomery (Oxford: Clarendon Press, 1988).

44. T. S. Eliot, 'Matthew Arnold', in *The Use of Poetry and the Use of Criticism* (London: Faber and Faber, 1933), 103.

45. E. M. Forster, *Two Cheers for Democracy* (London: Edward Arnold and Co., 1951), 202.

SELECT BIBLIOGRAPHY

Arnold, Matthew, *The Complete Poems*, ed. Kenneth Allott, 2nd edn. (London: Longman, 1979).

—— *The Complete Prose Works*, 11 vols., ed. R. H. Super (Ann Arbor: University of Michigan Press, 1960–77).

Collini, Stefan, *Matthew Arnold: A Critical Portrait* (Oxford: Clarendon Press, 1988).

Dawson, Carl, ed., *Matthew Arnold: The Poetry. The Critical Heritage* (London: Routledge and Kegan Paul, 1973).

Hamilton, Ian, *A Gift Imprisoned: The Poetic Life of Matthew Arnold* (London: Bloomsbury, 1998).

Lowry, Howard Foster, ed., *The Letters of Matthew Arnold to Arthur Hugh Clough* (Oxford: Clarendon Press, 1932).

Russell, George W. E., ed., *Letters of Matthew Arnold, 1848–1888*, 2 vols. (London: Macmillan, 1895).

Trilling, Lionel, *Matthew Arnold* (London: Harcourt, 1939).

CHAPTER 25

MODERN MEN AND WOMEN: MEREDITH'S CHALLENGE TO BROWNING

ANDREW ELFENBEIN

GEORGE Meredith's sonnet sequence *Modern Love* dwarfs his other poems in reputation and influence.[1] Traces of it crop up from Edwin Arlington Robinson and Edna St. Vincent Millay to Rosamond Lehman's pioneering lesbian novel, *Dusty Answer* (1927) (from 'Ah, what a dusty answer gets the soul') and possibly even Hollywood's *Casablanca* (1942), when Meredith's 'A kiss is but a kiss now!' seems to become 'A kiss is just a kiss'.[2] Although the fame of *Modern Love* may have left Meredith's other poetry in undeserved obscurity, I follow the critical trend by concentrating on it as his major poem.

For someone reading Meredith's poetry in Phyllis Bartlett's definitive edition, *Modern Love* comes as a jolt. It's in his 1862 volume, his second, and looks so little like the poems in his first volume of 1851 that it seems to have come from a different person. His first volume thoroughly, even strenuously, embraces convention. Technically impressive, it fits into a tradition of lyric poetry stemming from the early nineteenth-century amalgam of Keats, Shelley, Felicia Hemans, and Letitia Elizabeth Landon. Different as these poets are, they contribute to a set of clichés that Meredith eagerly imitates, as in the opening of his 'Song':

> Love within the lover's breast
> Burns like Hesper in the west,
> O'er the ashes of the sun,
> Till the day and night are done;
> Then when dawn drives up her car—
> Lo! it is the morning star.[3]

Here, his perfect, monosyllabic rhymes, pulsing trochees, and clean, end-stopped couplets make his poetry hypnotically facile. The poem reads like a technical exercise in poetic minimalism, as if someone had made Meredith write poetry by working within a restrictive set of rules. The result is dazzling and forgettable.

Modern Love changes the rules of the game:

> By this he knew she wept with waking eyes:
> That, at his hand's light quiver by her head,
> The strange low sobs that shook their common bed,
> Were called into her with a sharp surprise,
> And strangely mute, like little gaping snakes,
> Dreadfully venomous to him. (i. 1–6)

Whereas 'Song' hurtles ahead, as if its lines could not wait to reach the end, *Modern Love* crowds its pentameters with obstacles. Most obviously, the syntax resists decoding. The first line throws out three pronouns, 'this', 'he' and 'she', with no antecedents. We might guess that 'he' and 'she' are the couple representing 'modern love', but 'this' is puzzling. Rather than referring to a specific noun, 'this' broadens out to describe a catastrophic breakdown between the couple, but this semantic expansion is not comprehensible until after several lines. In addition, Meredith's syntax features weird adjective–noun combinations, such as 'waking eyes'. The progressive participle 'waking' describes eyes in the process of awakening, but the situation suggests that the wife is already awake. Her eyes are awake and 'waking' at the same time, leaving her suspended between a completed action and one in progress. Moreover, Meredith uses the passive voice to describe how the woman stops crying: her 'strange low sobs' are 'called into her'. To have sobs 'called into' a person is not the same as stopping crying: the sobs are still there, just dragged back into the self, waiting to be let loose again. The passive voice avoids attributing direct agency to her, as if the narrator wanted to signal that he gives us an external impression rather than her actual thoughts. Her sobs are 'strangely mute', present even after they have stopped. Overall, Meredith's syntax asks the reader to labour over each phrase, unlike the honed simplicities of 'Song'.

Commentators attribute Meredith's changed style to his unhappy marriage to Mary Ellen Nichols. As Margaret Harris explains, the melancholy 'occasioned by the death of Mary before long assumed powerful shape in the poem sequence *Modern Love*'.[4] Although the poem is not directly autobiographical (for example, the wife in *Modern Love* does not run away with her lover, as Nichols did), reading Meredith's tragedy as the source for his poem creates a compelling story: heartbreak wounded a mediocre poet into genius. Yet, at the risk of spoiling a good story, I want to argue that *Modern Love* did not arise from life alone. It ironizes the traditional sonnet sequence, and much of the best scholarship on it examines its devastating revision of Petrarchanism, the general English sonnet tradition, and the prior history of the nineteenth-century sonnet.[5] If Meredith's first volume demonstrated how skilfully he could follow established conventions, *Modern Love* showed how to shatter them.

Nineteenth-century readers also noticed that Meredith was not simply autobiographical, but they were most struck, not by his revision of the sonnet tradition, but by his relation to a contemporary Victorian poet, Robert Browning. Speaking of Browning, Oscar

Wilde wrote in *The Critic As Artist*, 'The only man who can touch the hem of his garment is George Meredith. Meredith is a prose Browning, and so is Browning. He used poetry as a medium for writing in prose.'[6] Wilde's comment is so witty, and so well phrased, that it has substituted for critical discussion of the relationship between the two poets. Yet in *Modern Love*, Browning is a more seductive presence for Meredith than either the wife or the 'Lady', the woman whom the husband takes as a mistress. *Modern Love* differs from Meredith's first volume, not only because of his bad marriage, but also because Browning's masterpiece, *Men and Women* (1855), changed for Meredith what it meant to be a poet.

Browning taught Meredith how to create what Eric Griffiths calls a 'printed voice', a poetic voice that uses the resources of punctuation (rhetorical questions, dashes, parenthesis, periods in the middle of lines) to draw attention to an imitation of the voice speaking in poetry.[7] Paradoxically, the harder poetry works to recreate aurality, the more it draws attention to its punctuated writtenness, as in Browning's 'Demand / The reason why—"'tis but a word"—object—"A gesture"' ('An Epistle...of Karshish' 165–67), or Meredith's 'Her wrists / I catch: she faltering, as she half resists / "You love...? love...? love...?" all on an indrawn breath' (xlii. 16).[8] Yet even as Browning and Meredith create the impression of a voice speaking through print, they give their speakers syntax far removed from ordinary language use. Their speakers unweave the conventional fabric of grammar to force readers to follow quick changes of thought and make counterintuitive inferential leaps.

Beyond stylistic similarities, both poets probe the psyche under stress. Their poems mimic psychological case studies that step back from standard frames of reference to see another mind on its own terms. Moreover, these are minds *in extremis*, pushed by circumstance into painful, sometimes almost unbearable, situations. In many cases, the source of this stress is love, and especially modern love, or, as in Browning's historical monologues, a nineteenth-century sense of love projected into the past. For both poets, past models of heterosexuality no longer fit the worlds they describe. Whereas Tennyson addressed the issues of modern love with *The Princess*, an odd, even wacky fable, Browning and Meredith refuse Tennyson's moralizing to explore uncertain terrain on which modern men and women meet.

Browning seems like a bad choice to inspire an autobiographical poem because he is best known for dramatic monologues, whose speakers are understood to be not Robert Browning. *Men and Women* is famous for poems like 'Andrea del Sarto', 'Fra Lippo Lippi', 'Bishop Blougram's Apology', and 'Cleon', which show us the confessions, subterfuges, unwitting self-disclosures, and tricky power plays of one character after another, some actual historical figures, some inspired by historical figures, and others purely fictional. Yet more important for *Modern Love* was a different side of *Men and Women*, its love poems. *Men and Women* has several happy love poems, such as 'My Star', but the volume ranges from the bliss of 'By the Fire-Side' to the bitter self-questioning of 'A Light Woman'. Across varying tonalities, Browning's treatments of love have a constant: the belief that love can lead to self-transcendence by presenting a secular salvation. Even characters who have lost love still cling to its transcendent possibility. They prefer to retain love as an illusion than to face a world without it.

Meredith in *Modern Love* knows what Browning's characters never admit, the possibility that love, far from leading to transcendence, opens a path to hell. Transcendent love like that of Browning's characters appears in *Modern Love* as a crippling ideal degrading those who strive for it: as the husband notes, 'In Love's deep woods/I dreamt of loyal Life: the offence is there!' (x. 7–8). The 'loyal Life' for which he has striven has led to shipwreck, although, as other sonnets reveal, the husband has hardly been as loyal as he here claims. Meredith's poem is particularly chilling because trust between husband and wife has died, but the relationship has not. Not quite able to separate, they stay together in a game that Meredith calls 'Hiding the Skeleton' (xvii. 7). They linger in a twilight world of surmises, partial revelations, mutual betrayal, frustration, and self-loathing that takes them far from even Browning's bitterest speakers. While Browning's speakers elaborate the great, good moment of epiphany, Meredith's sonnets are so baffled that at times the speaker does not know what he is talking about: he ends sonnet 31 asking, 'What's my drift?' (xxxi. 16).

The contrast between Browning's 'By the Fire-Side' and Meredith's sonnet 16 reveals in miniature Meredith's larger revision of Browning. In 'By the Fire-Side' the speaker begins with a cosy domestic scene as he and his wife Leonor sit at the fire; he imagines how he will go back in memory to the moment when they first declared their love:

> With me, youth led...I will speak now,
> No longer watch you as you sit
> Reading by fire-light, that great brow
> And the spirit-small hand propping it
> Mutely, my heart knows how—
>
> When, if I think but deep enough,
> You are wont to answer, prompt as rhyme;
> And you, too, find without a rebuff
> Response your soul seeks many a time
> Piercing its fine flesh-stuff.[9]

Rather than speaking, husband and wife have found a spiritual conversation so deep that they speak silently. Although the wife's 'spirit-small hand' props her head 'mutely', the husband can talk to her merely by thinking 'deep enough': she then answers 'prompt as rhyme'. Likewise, he claims, Leonor has easy access to him, since in him she finds the 'response' that her 'soul seeks'. At least according to him, they achieve a communion of souls, each able to pierce its 'fine flesh-stuff' as if the body were a thin curtain, a secularized and domesticated piercing of an apocalyptic veil.

The speaker remembers the epiphanic moment when Leonor confessed her love for him, a moment that has expanded to fill his entire life. In retrospect, he thanks her for not toying with him to prove his dedication to her, but for simply declaring her love:

> But you spared me this, like the heart you are,
> And filled my empty heart at a word.
> If you join two lives, there is oft a scar,
> They are one and one, with a shadowy third;
> One near one is too far.

> A moment after, and hands unseen
> Were hanging the night around us fast;
> But we knew that a bar was broken between
> Life and life; we were mixed at last
> In spite of the mortal screen.[10]

Heterosexual union usually comes with strings attached because there is 'oft a scar', presumably the memory of a former lover who forms a 'shadowy third' and makes 'one near one' lack complete unity. But the speaker believes that between him and his wife 'a bar was broken between / Life and life': they have 'mixed at last / In spite of mortal screen'. Browning's formal arrangement of his lines carefully reinforces this spiritual union. He enjambs the line 'broken between / Life and life', so the ability of the stanza to break a line becomes a metaphor for the breaking of the barrier between 'life and life', which then occupy the next line together. Likewise, he uses the shrinkage from tetrameter to trimeter lines in the last line of the stanza to figure a spiritual condensation, as if the line's need for fewer syllables imaged the couple's ability to meet without the barrier of 'mortal screen'.

In Sonnet 16 of *Modern Love*, Meredith devastatingly rewrites 'By the Fire-Side':

> In our old shipwrecked days there was an hour,
> When in the firelight steadily aglow,
> Joined slackly, we beheld the red chasm grow
> Among the clicking coals. Our library-bower
> That eve was left to us; and hushed we sat
> As lovers to whom Time is whispering.
> From sudden-opened doors we heard them sing:
> The nodding elders mixed good wine with chat.
> Well knew we that Life's greatest treasure lay
> With us, and of it was our talk. 'Ah, yes!
> Love dies!' I said; I never thought it less.
> She yearned to me that sentence to unsay.
> Then when the fire domed blackening, I found
> Her cheek was salt against my kiss, and swift
> Up the sharp scale of sobs her breast did lift:—
> Now am I haunted by that taste! that sound!

(xvi. 1–16)

As in Browning, two lovers sit by the fireside and remember their past love; as in Browning, one particular moment haunts the speaker. But Meredith's poem hollows out the victories of Browning's. Even at the beginning of the poem, the fact that the lovers are 'joined slackly' predicts future divisions, as does the fire's 'red chasm'. Whereas Browning's fireside was an emblem of domesticity and an external sign of inner warmth, Meredith's is an image of impending extinction. On the page, Meredith's poem even looks grimmer than Browning's: the undulating lines of Browning's stanza give way to the wall-like block of Meredith's sonnet.

Seemingly out of the blue, Meredith's speaker comments tactlessly, 'Love dies!' and follows it with the cryptic line, 'I never thought it less', which could mean 'I never thought the less of love, even though it dies'; or 'I never thought love could do otherwise than die'; or 'I mentioned the idea that love dies, even though I never thought less about it'. Whatever his clause means, it reverses Leonor's 'word' that fills the speaker's heart in 'By the Fire-Side': Leonor's word guarantees her love, while the husband's comment shatters his wife's trust. In an echo of the sequence's traumatic opening, she responds with a 'sharp scale of sobs'. Remembering his great, good moment with Leonor, Browning's speaker recalls 'the sights we saw and the sounds we heard, / The lights and the shades made up a spell'. The magical union of sight and sound in Browning becomes the harrowing linking of texture and sound in Meredith's 'sharp scale of sobs', in which 'sharp' floats between its musical meaning, describing pitch, and its more familiar tactile sense. Rather than being haunted by the memory of an infinite moment shared with a beloved, Meredith's speaker is instead haunted by the bad spell of his wife's tears: 'Now am I haunted by that taste! that sound!' The master-stroke is the final adverb 'now', with which the speaker switches from past to present. It has the force of 'only now', as if he realizes at last, in the moment of uttering the sonnet, what his wife's sobbing meant, a realization that drives home his previous blindness to her suffering.

Yet for all the misery of Meredith's lovers, they do something that Browning's do not: they talk to each other. Looking back at 'By the Fire-Side' after reading Meredith, it seems the speaker's happiness has a cost. Although he spends several stanzas retracing a long walk he took with Leonor, it is not initially clear from his description that she was even part of the walk, and he does not name her until one hundred lines into the poem. Even after he does, she remains completely silent, and he twice draws attention to her 'spirit-small hand' propping up her head 'mutely'. She is doubly silenced: not only does she not say anything, but even her body, which one might presume to be silent anyway, is as mute as Porphyria's. While Browning sometimes indicates when speakers, such as Fra Lippo Lippi, respond to actual or implied responses from their interlocutors, we have no such hints about Leonor. She is utterly silent. Although the husband imagines the communion of souls, he speaks for both.

Within the frame of Browning's poem, nothing suggests that Leonor is unhappy with her marriage or her husband. But Meredith rewrites Browning's poem as if to unsettle its speaker's confidence that one can speak for two. When the speaker in Sonnet 16 throws out his idea that love can die, he notes about his wife, 'She yearned to me that sentence to unsay'. Although how 'yearning to' translates into a speech act is not clear, he recognizes that she possesses a will different from, and in opposition to his. Yet he indicts himself in the act of trying to describe her. His verb for her, 'yearned', gently accuses her of wilful self-delusion, as if she wants him to deny what she has already thought. The delusion draws out the implicit pun in 'that sentence': whereas the speaker refers to a syntactic unit, his wife hears it as a juridical sentence, a proclamation of doom on their marriage.

The couple in *Modern Love* has a dysfunctional relationship, packed with lies, self-deception, casual brutality, and uncertainty, but Meredith makes this relationship, strained as it is, look at least like an actual relationship. Betrayal is hardly a new topic in love poetry, but Meredith uses the wife's betrayal (and the husband's betrayal of her) to criticize a one-sided poetic tradition of heterosexuality. Even as he keeps the husband at the centre, his perspective never ignores or assumes that he fully understands the wife: her words and actions are always present, along with obsessive attempts to gauge her motives.

To move from this particular sonnet to Meredith's sequence as a whole, Meredith writes as if *Men and Women* pretended to be about men *and* women, but was really about men *or* women. It's as if, from Meredith's point of view, Browning has fifty chances to get it right, but never quite pulls off what he promises. Meredith inverts Browning's universe by presenting, not fifty different speakers, but one speaker trying fifty times to tackle the relation between two people (the matching of fifty speakers with fifty sonnets may be Meredith's most explicit hint at his debt to Browning). Whereas Browning brags to Elizabeth Barrett Browning, 'Love, you saw me gather men and women / Live or dead or fashioned by my fancy / Enter each and all' ('One Word More' 741), Meredith substitutes a minimalist hell for Browning's plenitude. Repeatedly, we confront the same characters: the husband, his wife, the 'Lady' whom he takes as a lover, yet never loves, and the shadowy man with whom his wife has supposedly been unfaithful. Instead of Browning's endless novelty, Meredith traps us within a repetitive net of deceit and recriminations; although several critics have attempted to discern a sequential plot, the most salient impression is of a richly textured stasis.

Formally, Meredith's sixteen-line sonnet has a complex relation to Browning. Although Browning used blank verse for ambitious dramatic monologues, his love poems that are Meredith's most immediate preoccupation are metrical experiments in peculiar, sometimes virtuosic, verse forms. In a strange trade-off, Meredith's sixteen-line pentameter sonnets look on the page more like excerpts from Browning's blank verse monologues, while his actual dramatic monologues (grouped together as 'Roadside Philosophers' in the 1862 volume) look, metrically, more like Browning's love lyrics. Meredith manipulates, not only his lines, but also the traditional sonnet's complex rhyme scheme, as if to draw it closer to blank verse. His sonnets rhyme *abbacddceffeghhg*, four quatrains with embracing rhymes. Virtuosic as this rhyme scheme may look on its own, it is a letdown in the context of the larger sonnet tradition. Meredith's four quatrains destroy both the punch of the Shakespearean sonnet, with its drive to an epigrammatic couplet, and the *volta* of the Italian sonnet tradition, in which the octave's *abbaabba* gives way to a new mood and a newly unsteady combination of *c*, *d*, and *e* rhymes. *Modern Love*'s pile-up of four quatrains with the same rhyme scheme takes away not only the variations of the traditional sonnet's rhymes but also rhyme as cue to structure. Meredith's sequence looks comparatively more blank, as if the guideposts of the traditional sonnet had become obsolete.

Instead, Meredith, like Browning, treats poetic structure as something located as much at the level of the line as of the stanza or entire poem. Although Elizabeth Helsinger has argued for the importance of visual representation to the poetic practice of Pre-Raphaelite poets, for Meredith and Browning, sound matters more than sight.[11] They both write as if the aural possibilities of poetry had not yet been fully explored, and foreground syntactic markers as much to create new sounds as to convey new meanings. For example, Browning's 'A Lover's Quarrel' features one of his favourite poetic devices, the rhetorical question:

> What of a hasty word?
> Is the fleshly heart not stirred
>   By a worm's pin-prick
>   Where its roots are quick?
> See the eye, by a fly's foot blurred—
>   Ear, when a straw is heard
> Scratch the brain's coat of curd![12]

Browning experiments with what happens to the poetic line when it ends with a question mark. His short lines lighten the weight of the speaker's questions, as does the coincidence of questions with line-endings that fit neatly in the stanza. The speaker here has lost his beloved over what he views, in retrospect, as a 'hasty word'. His rhetorical questions justify himself: he asks 'What of a hasty word?' because he wants his hasty word to be disregarded as a momentary lapse. His next question has a similar tone: the fleshly heart feels the 'worm's pin-prick' at its roots, even if only for a brief moment, like the eye blurred by a fly, or the ear irritated by the sound of straw. Browning lets the fleetness of his speaker's rhetorical questions indict his own glibness.

Meredith, like Browning, fills his poems with interrogatives: his speaker constantly questions himself. Yet questions function differently in *Modern Love* than in Browning's love poetry. In sonnet 35, the speaker broods as usual on his wife's motives:

> What is she doing? What does she demand
> From Providence or me? She is not one
> Long to endure this torpidly, and shun
> The drugs that crowd about a woman's hand.
> At Forfeits during snow we played, and I
> Must kiss her. 'Well performed!' I said: then she:
> ''Tis hardly worth the money, you agree?'
> Save her? What for? To act this wedded lie!
>
> (xxxv. 9–16)

The rhetorical questions of Browning's confident speaker have dwindled into the bafflement of Meredith's. At the beginning of this quotation, Meredith writes as if the speaker can hardly be bothered to keep the metre: whereas Browning's question marks neatly coincide with line endings, Meredith's shred the line. Meredith creates a rhetoric of anti-rhetoricity, as if these questions burst from a speaker no longer able to contain himself. Yet he quickly recovers his controlled self-loathing when he describes the winter game of Forfeits that he plays with his wife. Although infidelity overdetermines the game's name, in the game itself players put some personal item or sum (a 'forfeit') in a tray, which they earn back by performing some action.[13] In the case of *Modern Love*, the speaker has had to kiss his wife. Looking back on their charade of marital intimacy, he bursts out again with questions: 'Save her? What for? To act this wedded lie!' His anger appears in response not to his own self-certainty, as in Browning, but to his wife's question, ''Tis hardly worth the money, you agree?' She takes his agreement as a given, in response to which he explodes. His anger arises, either because he does not agree and

resents her assuming that he would, or because he does agree, but resents her for matching him in disillusion. His final questions, unlike his earlier ones, presume the answer
that saving her is pointless. Yet even his need to question suggests that he is not as certain as he wishes to appear. The issue is not whether he can save his wife, but whether he
can save himself. The serene confidence of Browning's lover becomes the grim movement in Meredith from uncertainty and bafflement to angry disgust.

Beyond rhetorical questions, Meredith also imitates, but revises, Browning's obsessive exploration of how to stop poetic lines in their tracks, as in this excerpt from 'Andrea
del Sarto':

> It saves a model. So! keep looking so—
> My serpentining beauty, rounds on rounds!
> —How could you ever prick those perfect ears,
> Even to put the pearl there! oh, so sweet—
> My face, my moon, my everybody's moon.
> Which everybody looks on and calls his,
> And, I suppose, is looked on by in turn,
> While she looks—no one's: very dear, no less.[14]

Andrea here speaks to Lucrezia, his unfaithful wife and model. The starts and stops of
his speech enact a drama of shifting moods; he moves from barking orders ('So! Keep
looking so—') to sighing over her beauty ('oh, so sweet') to rhapsodizing ironically
about her universal promiscuity ('My face, my moon, my everybody's moon'). Yet he
brings himself up short when he admits that her availability guarantees that she is no
one man's possession. Browning parallels the syntactic interruption with a metrical one
that signals Andrea's limited control over his wife: 'While she looks—no one's'. The verb
'looks' can mean both 'views' and 'appears as': in the previous lines, Andrea has used it
to mean 'views', and leads us to expect that it will have the same meaning in 'she looks'.
The line should continue by describing how Lucrezia looks at something or someone.
Instead, during the caesura represented by the dash, Andrea switches the meaning of
'look' from 'views' to 'appears as', to underscore that she looks 'no one's'. Andrea calls
her not 'everybody's moon,' but 'my everybody's moon', paradoxically underscoring his
simultaneous ownership and estrangement.

Meredith, too, addresses his unfaithful wife with Browning-like broken lines, but
with none of Andrea's ironic resignation:

> Madam, 'tis understood
> When women play upon their womanhood;
> It means, a Season gone. And yet I doubt
> But I am duped. That nun-like look waylays
> My fancy. Oh! I do but wait a sign!
> Pluck out the eyes of pride! thy mouth to mine!
> Never! though I die thirsting. Go thy ways!
>
> (xxiv. 10–16)

Whereas Andrea's mood-shifts all remain within his overall framework of self-protecting resignation, Meredith's speaker shuttles between trust and suspicion, all signalled by internal line breaks. The occasional misalignments of line and syntax breaks make the speaker's hesitations seem even more hesitant: the poetic line works against the definitiveness of any given mood. As soon as the husband rejects his wife, claiming that the 'season' for forgiveness is gone, he reverses direction, with 'And yet I doubt' hanging as an enjambment, undercutting his previous sternness. He then in turn undercuts his own doubts, and admits that his wife's innocent appearance 'waylays' his fancy: whatever her actual guilt or innocence may be, he imagines her innocent appearance attacking him. Finally recoiling in disgust at his perceived weakness, he turns the hope of forgiveness hinted at in his recognition of his wife's 'nun-like' appearance into an opportunity to play Hamlet ranting at Ophelia, as he quotes 'Go thy ways to a nunnery'.[15] Yet the melodrama of his hammy 'Go thy ways!' suggests less a final revulsion from his wife than revulsion from his own continued longing for her.

Meredith's most dramatic revision of Browning occurs, not in an individual sonnet or in particular poetic devices, but at the end of his sonnet sequence, when he confronts Browning's poetics of transcendent love. As I have noted, all Browning's lovers at least imagine the possibility of a moment when, as the speaker of 'By the Fire-Side' puts it, the bar is broken between life and life. Meredith, too, describes a breakthrough moment for his couple, but a far darker one than in Browning. In Sonnet 48, we learn that the wife has at last left to allow the husband to pursue his mistress, who has appeared throughout the poem as an inadequate substitute. Yet in Sonnet 49, she reappears and at last asks for him to come to her:

> About the middle of the night her call
> Was heard, and he came wondering to the bed.
> 'Now kiss me, dear! it may be, now!' she said.
> Lethe had passed those lips, and he knew all.
>
> (xlix. 12–16)

Meredith again uses the odd passive voice as in the first sonnet, when the wife's 'call / Was heard'. The enjambment after 'her call' momentarily suspends the line to open up possibilities about the effects of her call, which the weak passive voice in the next line, 'was heard', quickly diminishes. The husband does not even have enough agency to hear his wife's voice; her 'call' spreads amorphously, hardy even directed to the husband. The larger point about the call is that the two are so estranged that they no longer sleep together, unlike in the first sonnet, where he hears her sobs in bed. Now, he must come as a guest, one so surprised that Meredith describes him as 'wondering'. Like the enjambed 'her call', the word 'wondering' hovers on the brink of hopeful possibilities. He may wonder why she calls for him, perhaps with the glimmer of hope that she still cares about him. Yet Meredith raises this wondering hope only to dash it.

The sonnet's final two lines are Meredith at his most cryptic: '"Now kiss me, dear! it may be, now!" she said. / Lethe had passed those lips, and he knew all'. The 'he knew all' turns the conclusion into a revelation, the epiphany loved by Browning's lovers.

Yet we remain in the dark about the epiphany's content. As often in Meredith, the problem is pronouns, the wife's 'it' and the narrator's 'all'. Houghton and Stange, in their anthology of Victorian poetry, claim that the lines 'suggest that the wife, having decided to kill herself, and feeling death near, forgets their estrangement and remembers only their original love'.[16] The gloss provides a satisfying end, far more satisfying than what Meredith actually wrote. While the reference in the last line to 'Lethe' hints at the wife's suicide by poison, her death sentence is ambiguous. The clause 'it may be, now' leaves unanswered what the 'it' is that at last 'may be'. She may refer specifically to their kiss, as if, on her deathbed, she can at last kiss him without fear of the rivalries that have plagued them. But 'it' has other possible references: forgiveness between them; an end to their hostility; an authentic emotion; a satisfying future for him, freed from her; a satisfying death for her, freed from him. Even her modal verb 'may be' has both the double sense of permission and of a conditional possibility. What persists through these ambiguities is the urgency of her appeal, with its twice repeated 'now': the great good moment that Browning prizes in his love poems becomes the desperate plea for a kiss.

Similarly ambiguous but even more grim is the sonnet's concluding 'he knew all'. In Browning, such a phrase would be a triumphant moment, the secular revelation of love. In Meredith, it is not. 'All' cries out for a modifying phrase to give it substance, but Meredith brilliantly leaves it bare. Does 'all' mean all about her suicide, all about her motivation in leaving him, all about the relations between them, or all about his own failures in their relationship? Usually when writers leave a word like 'all' undefined, they let unspoken possibilities enrich the aura around the word. Yet in Meredith, the plenitude of possible meanings around 'all' has the opposite effect. It diminishes the word by giving it an absolute finality. Not knowing exactly what 'all' describes produces a final spondaic foot with the grimness of a death-knell.

When Meredith published *Modern Love* in 1862, Browning was still a little known poet who received scant respect from critics. Yet Meredith revealed himself to be Browning's most perceptive early reader, not through critical commentary on Browning, but in *Modern Love*'s reworking of Browning's philosophy and poetics of love. *Modern Love*, which received mostly negative reviews on its first appearance, would in time be recognized as a classic. After it, the amalgam of Keats, Shelley, Hemans, and Landon that had inspired Meredith's early poetry looked obsolete, even childish. Moreover, Meredith's poem staked out a place for poetry that distinguished it from the novel. Many Victorian novels feature unhappy couples, usually between secondary characters: no matter how miserable married couples may be, Victorian novels feature courtship plots that drive toward a presumably happy heterosexual union. *Modern Love*, in contrast, puts marital unhappiness front and centre, and avoids the temptation to give readers an 'out', to provide some contrast to the misery it presents. Meredith proves that poetry could explore the dark side of love more deeply than novels ever could. In crafting his response to *Men and Women*, Meredith unsettled familiar assumptions about how men and women were supposed to relate to each other and about how Victorian love poetry ought to look, sound, and mean.

Notes

1. On Meredith's American reception, for example, see Adela Pinch, 'Transatlantic Modern Love' in Meredith McGill, ed., *The Traffic in Poems: Nineteenth-Century Poetry and Transatlantic Exchange* (New Brunswick, NJ: Rutgers University Press, 2008), 160–82.
2. George Meredith, *Modern Love*, in The *Poems of George Meredith*, 2 vols., ed. Phyllis B. Bartlett (New Haven: Yale University Press, 1978), i. 145, 134.
3. Meredith, 'Song', in *Poems*, i. 7.
4. Margaret Harris, 'Meredith, George (1828–1909)', in *Oxford Dictionary of National Biography* (Oxford: Oxford University Press, 2004). Online edition available at: <http://www.oxforddnb.com.ezp2.lib.umn.edu/view/article/34991>.
5. For examples, see Marianne Van Remoortel, *Lives of the Sonnet, 1787–1895: Genre, Gender and Criticism* (Farnham, Surrey: Ashgate Publishing, Ltd., 2011); Kenneth Crowell, '*Modern Love* and the Sonetto Caudato: Comedic Intervention through the Satiric Sonnet Form', *Victorian Poetry*, 48 (2010), 539–557; John Holmes, 'Darwinism, Feminism, and the Sonnet Sequence: Meredith's *Modern Love*', *Victorian Poetry*, 48 (2010), 523–538; and Arline Golden, '"The Game of Sentiment": Tradition and Innovation in Meredith's *Modern Love*', *ELH*, 40 (1973), 264–84.
6. Oscar Wilde, 'The Critic As Artist', in *The Soul of Man Under Socialism and Selected Critical Prose*, ed. Linda Dowling (Harmondsworth, Middlesex: Penguin, 2001), 218.
7. Eric Griffiths, *The Printed Voice of Victorian Poetry* (Oxford: Oxford University Press, 1989).
8. Robert Browning, 'An Epistle…of Karshish', in *Robert Browning: The Poems*, 2 vols., ed. John Pettigrew and Thomas J. Collins (New Haven: Yale University Press, 1981); i. 569.
9. Browning, 'By the Fire-Side', in *Robert Browning: The Poems*, i. 556.
10. Browning, 'By the Fire-Side' i. 560.
11. Elizabeth K. Helsinger, *Poetry and the Pre-Raphaelite Arts: Dante Gabriel Rossetti and William Morris* (New Haven: Yale University Press, 2008), 3–9.
12. Browning, 'A Lover's Quarrel', in *Robert Browning: The Poems*, i. 532–33.
13. Alice Bertha Gomme, *The Traditional Games of England, Scotland, and Ireland*, 2 vols. (London: David Nutt, 1894), i. 137–38.
14. Browning, 'Andrea del Sarto', in *Robert Browning: The Poems*, i. 644.
15. William Shakespeare, *Hamlet*, III. i. 131, in *The Complete Works of William Shakespeare*, ed. David Bevington, 4th edn. (New York: HarperCollins, 1992), 1088.
16. Walter E. Houghton and G. Robert Stange, eds., *Victorian Poetry and Poetics*, 2nd edn. (Boston: Houghton Mifflin, 1968), n.646.

Select Bibliography

Comstock, Cathy, '"Speak, and I See the Side-Lie of a Truth": The Problematics of Truth in Meredith's *Modern Love*', *Victorian Poetry*, 25 (1987), 129–141.

Crowell, Kenneth, '*Modern Love* and the Sonetto Caudato: Comedic Intervention through the Satiric Sonnet Form', *Victorian Poetry*, 48 (2010), 539–557.

Golden, Arline, '"The Game of Sentiment": Tradition and Innovation in Meredith's *Modern Love*', *ELH*, 40 (1973), 264–84.

Holmes, John, 'Darwinism, Feminism, and the Sonnet Sequence: Meredith's *Modern Love*', *Victorian Poetry*, 48 (2010), 523–538.

Lucas, John, 'Meredith as Poet', in Ian Fletcher, ed., *Meredith Now: Some Critical Essays* (London: Routledge & Kegan Paul, 1971), 14–33.

Mermin, Dorothy M., 'Poetry as Fiction: Meredith's *Modern Love*', *ELH*, 43 (1976): 100–19.

Pinch, Adela, 'Transatlantic Modern Love', in Meredith McGill, ed., *The Traffic in Poems: Nineteenth-Century Poetry and Transatlantic Exchange* (New Brunswick, New Jersey: Rutgers University Press, 2008), 160–82.

Van Remoortel, Marianne, *Lives of the Sonnet, 1787–1895: Genre, Gender and Criticism* (Farnham, Surrey: Ashgate Publishing, Ltd., 2011).

Watt, Stephen, 'Neurotic Responses to a Failed Marriage: George Meredith's *Modern Love*', *Mosaic: A Journal for the Interdisciplinary Study of Literature*, 17 (1984), 49–63.

CHAPTER 26

RAISING THE DEAD: DANTE GABRIEL ROSSETTI'S 'WILLOWWOOD' SONNETS

J. B. BULLEN

By general consent, the four sonnets that go to make up the 'Willowwood' sequence are fundamental to the structure of Dante Gabriel Rossetti's *House of Life* and central to his mediation between painting and poetry. It has often been pointed out that these sonnets, written in mid December 1868, mark his return to poetry after a period of six years of almost complete silence. 'Willowwood' held singular importance for him, and thereafter, when he arranged and rearranged *The House of Life*, it remained at its heart.[1] There is also general agreement about the power of the sequence and on the broad nature of its themes, themes dealing with loss, parting, death, and melancholy. At this point, however, critical opinion diverges. There is no consensus, for example, about the nature of the loss or parting. We know that the sonnets were written at an identifiable moment when powerful emotions came into violent conflict in Rossetti's life, and the imagery leaves the reader in no doubt that Rossetti was working through a strong sentimental nexus. But what was the cause? Some critics have suggested that the sentiments were directed at Rossetti's involvement with Jane Morris,[2] a few that the feelings arose primarily from the death of Elizabeth Siddal, while a third group feels that the beloved of the poems is 'not a person at all',[3] but that Rossetti was 'haunted' by the platonic idea of the inaccessible woman.[4] As for the concluding 'secret' imparted by the personification of Love, some believe this brings comfort, 'hope'[5] or at least 'catharsis',[6] whereas others claim that it offers no resolution or closure.[7]

Part of the reason for the critical uncertainty lies in the hallucinatory nature of the sequence. As Joan Rees pointed out, the fluid, dissolving, and shifting imagery produces 'a remarkable blend of the surrealistic with a kind of factual dispassionateness'.[8] The uncertainty created by this 'precise imprecision' has led, in turn, to disagreement as to whether the group as a whole signifies 'the pangs of severance', 'love and the hope of fulfilment', the 'obsessive nature of the desire for unity', or the 'homoerotic potential of love'.[9] Rossetti's original title was 'A Dream'.[10] The first sonnet of 'Willowwood', he said, was 'a dream or trance of divided love, momentarily re-united by longing fancy'.[11] Though dreams may be open to multiple interpretation they have their own internal symbolic logic. 'Willowwood' is no exception.

The circumstances of the production of 'Willowwood' provide a clue to its hallucinatory quality. The year 1868 was marked by a number of crises in Rossetti's life. Since the summer of the previous year he had been suffering from serious insomnia and worrying symptoms of mental disturbance. Worst of all his eyesight had been intermittently failing and he was threatened with the possibility of blindness. His doctors (and he consulted many of them) were unanimous that he had nothing organically wrong with him. The problem, they said, was psychic not physical, but this did not help. By August 1868 he was regularly afflicted with 'whirling and flickering and something like approaching apoplexy'.[12] With weakening eyesight and worsening insomnia he began to sink into serious depression or melancholia, so on 23 September he decided to escape from London and join his close friend William Bell Scott who was with Alice Boyd at her country home, Penkill Castle, in Scotland. He stayed until 2 November.

In spite of his deteriorating health Rossetti had managed two major pictures in that year. Both featured Jane Morris. The first, *La Pia de' Tolomei*, was begun in January and depicted the unhappy Pia from the *Purgatorio* imprisoned by her cruel husband in the Maremma.[13] A second immediately followed. This was *Portrait of Mrs William Morris* often known as 'The Blue Silk Dress'. Both works were responses to Rossetti's increasing and passionate obsession with Morris's wife and were completed while Jane periodically stayed with Rossetti in his house in Cheyne Walk, sometimes in the company of William Morris but often alone. By July 1868 their affair was almost certainly consummated.[14]

At Penkill, Rossetti confessed his state of mind to William Bell Scott and spoke darkly of self-destruction during their long walks together. He admitted his guilty passion for Jane Morris but spoke of an even greater anxiety. This second preoccupation, Scott reported, was like the 'Spartan Fox', a wound tearing at his entrails, but about which he was forced to remain silent.[15] It was the guilt he felt about Elizabeth Siddal and her death. Looking back over his life with Elizabeth Siddal, Rossetti admitted that he had 'much to reproach [himself] with'[16] and when Siddal died he attempted to make amends with a dramatic funeral gesture in which he placed the manuscript of his poems in her coffin. Since the poetry had been already advertised for publication he was consigning to the grave not only his work but his reputation as a poet. But even this did not salve his conscience and he continued to worry whether he would ever be found 'worthy to meet her again'.[17] Worthy or not, the possibility of a reunion played on his mind since the circumstances of Siddal's death offered him no closure. In the years that followed she was, according to his brother, 'constantly present to him'.[18] Rossetti, he said, was 'haunted by memories [and] hounded by thoughts and fantasies'[19] where the only hope of coming to terms with the 'painful associations' of her death would be in a second meeting when 'some secret might be wrested from the grave'.[20]

At Penkhill Scott, realizing that Rossetti desperately needed a diversion, suggested he might abandon painting, break his silence, and turn back to poetry. He had already attempted two sonnets, 'Newborn Death 1 and 2', and when he returned to London he took up Scott's idea of writing something more substantial. By mid December he had completed the 'Willowwood' quartet, which, his brother claimed, was 'about the finest thing he has done'.[21]

Just as Rossetti felt that were he to meet Lizzie again some secret might be revealed, so in the first sonnet of 'Willowwood' a reunion between speaker and beloved is managed by the personification of Love who possesses a 'certain secret thing he had to tell'. The mystery of that secret is not revealed until the third sonnet, but since it lies at the heart of the whole sequence, it was undoubtedly something that preoccupied Rossetti. Two events from the closing months of 1868 might throw some light on the mystery. The first in October was a seemingly inconsequential letter from the influential critic Henry Buxton Forman (whom Rossetti had never met) enquiring about the volume of poems advertised in 1861.[22] Unknown to Buxton Forman, publication was impossible because those poems now lay in Highgate Cemetery with Elizabeth Siddal's corpse. The second event was almost certainly related to the first. Sometime in December Rossetti's friend, Charles Augustus Howell, made a terrifying suggestion. Given that Rossetti was once on the point of publication, might the poems not be exhumed from Lizzie's grave? We have only Rossetti's startled reply, saying that he would think about the idea and thanking Howell for 'such a mark of friendship'.[23] The letter of appreciation to Howell was dated 17 December. On the following day, 18 December, William Michael announced that 'Willowwood' was finished.[24]

'Willowwood' involves three characters and a resurrection: the speaker of the poem, the figure of Love who, when the poem opens, sits silently with him on the side of the well, and the phantom woman conjured from the depths of the water:

> I sat with Love upon a woodside well,
> Leaning across the water, I and he;
> Nor ever did he speak nor looked at me,
> But touched his lute wherein was audible
> The certain secret thing he had to tell:
> Only our mirrored eyes met silently
> In the low wave; and that sound came to be
> The passionate voice I knew; and my tears fell.
> And at their fall, his eyes beneath grew hers;
> And with his foot and with his wing-feathers
> He swept the spring that watered my heart's drouth.
> Then the dark ripples spread to waving hair,
> And as I stooped, her own lips rising there
> Bubbled with brimming kisses at my mouth.[25]

In a close and attentive reading of the sequence, Isobel Armstrong draws attention to the insistent presence of the consonant 'l' in this first stanza. The initial letter of Love, she says, 'saturates every line, as if the poem is afloat in the medium of these liquid sounds' and is interrupted only when Love touches the surface of the water.[26] Liquidity has two points of origin here, the well water and the tears of the speaker. The first is a source of emotional sustenance, the second a form of emotional expression. In the first sonnet of 'Willowwood' the well water quenches the speaker's 'heart's drouth', and in the last sonnet it provides him with 'a long draught' as the beloved sinks away. Then there are the tears. When the speaker's tears fall and mingle with the well water, the eyes of the beloved are invoked from beneath the reflected eyes of Love. The speaker's tears fall because he believes he hears the voice of the lost beloved in the music of Love's lute. The figure of Love literally, and the emotion of 'love' metaphorically, generate tenderness that in turn gives rise to tears of mourning, tears that initiate a sequence of events through the four sonnets. 'Mourning' is the crucial word here. 'Willowwood' is not an elegy in the sense that Tennyson's 'In Memoriam' or Swinburne's 'Ave Atque Vale' are elegies, but some critics have suggested that the poems possess elegiac elements.[27] Developing this idea, I want to suggest that, by mapping these elements against Freud's famous analysis of what he called, 'the work of mourning', it is possible to interpret the group in terms of Rossetti's need to come to terms with the death of his wife. In Rossetti's case the process of mourning was complicated by his involvement with Jane Morris. This, as reported by Bell Scott, had reached scandalous proportions by December 1868,[28] yet Rossetti was still haunted by memories of Elizabeth Siddal. Suddenly the need for closure with Lizzie was given unexpected urgency by Howell's suggestion of reopening her grave.

As the tears of mourning from the eyes of the speaker conjure up the eyes of the beloved, Love simultaneously draws with his foot and his wing feathers on the surface of the water. If the powerful emotions of the speaker prompt the ghostly appearance of the beloved, her materialization is facilitated by the angelic figure of Love. In other words, through Love's agency the speaker momentarily penetrates the fluid membrane dividing the human world from the spirit world. Though Rossetti is employing an elaborate form of *prosopopeia* in this scene, we know that he had a long-standing fascination with this kind of spiritual communication. 'Everything that appertained to the mystic', wrote his assistant Henry Treffry Dunn, 'had a strange fascination for him',[29] and in 1868 the need to cure the gnawing wound of the 'Spartan Fox' took him deeper into the realms of mystical experience.

Rossetti's interest in the spirit world was probably first awakened by the artist Anna Mary Howitt and her parents William and Mary. In the late 1840s Anna had been a fellow pupil with Rossetti at Sass's art school. In 1854 she had extended her friendship to Elizabeth Siddal, drew her portrait, and when Lizzie fell ill recommended she consult the spiritualist doctor, Garth Wilkinson.[30] Between 1856 and 1858 Rossetti, probably accompanied by Elizabeth Siddal, participated in séances at the Highgate home of the Howitts. In 1857, Anna Mary turned exclusively to automatic writing and spirit-drawing and in 1859 she received further encouragement by her marriage to the committed spiritualist, Alaric Alfred Watts. By 1866 she had become, according to William Michael Rossetti, 'an extraordinary spirit-drawing medium'.[31]

Rossetti's attitude to supernatural phenomena grew more serious after his wife's death. For the next two years, so his doctor recorded, he saw her nightly at the foot of his bed.[32] Whether he tried to communicate with her we do not know, but in 1864, always 'anxious to get some message',[33] he began to attend public spiritualist sessions staged by the Davenport brothers. Though these were little more than a form of popular entertainment, Rossetti took them seriously enough to discuss their implications with his sister, Christina. He was reintroduced to private séances by Whistler's mistress, Jo Hiffernan, and though initially he found the experience disturbing,[34] it was not long, according to Dunn, before 'he went to all the private séances to which he happened to be invited'.[35] In 1865 he began to organize sessions of his own in the studio at 19 Cheyne Walk with the specific intention, Helen Rossetti Angeli claimed, of coming 'into communication...with his wife's spirit'.[36] Rossetti's brother was originally sceptical about the occult appearances, but by October of that year William Bell Scott was astonished to learn that William Michael had been converted to communication with the dead, telling Scott that Elizabeth Siddal was 'constantly appearing...at the séances at Cheyne Walk'.[37] Between 1865 and 1868 Rossetti's brother scrupulously recorded those séances, and though not all involved Rossetti and many did not invoke Lizzie, her spirit, nevertheless, was often summoned from the grave.[38]

In the first sonnet of 'Willowwood' the beloved materializes from the dead through drawing. 'With his foot and with his wing feathers' the figure of Love etches the surface of the water to create the waving hair of the beloved. This strongly resembles spirit-drawing and Rossetti must have been fully aware of Anna Howitt's accomplishment in this field. In 1865 she sent Rossetti communications from Lizzie in the spirit world[39] and on at least one occasion her husband, Alaric Watts, attended séances with Rossetti.[40] Contemporary mediums frequently employed automatic drawings of this kind. William Michael records several in his diary, [41] and in 1868 Holman Hunt was present at one where the medium produced images of a crane, an angel, and a griffin.[42] Rossetti too was attempting a kind of spirit-drawing. His justifiably famous *Beata Beatrix* (fig. 26.1) was a triumph of occult art that evoked the spirit of Elizabeth Siddal in the context of the death of Beatrice Portinari. It was begun in earnest in 1865 and while he was slowly working on the canvas it hung on the wall of the very studio in which many séances took place.

In 1866, Georgiana and William Cowper saw the painting and immediately offered to buy it when it was finished. Georgiana, like many of her contemporaries had become a passionate spiritualist in a time of mourning. Her mother had died in 1861, and on the advice of William and Mary Howitt (Anna Mary's parents) had turned to séances.[43] By the time they persuaded Ruskin to join their circle at Broadlands in 1864 they were mixing with some of the best-known mediums. These included the famous Daniel Home (Browning's 'Mr Sludge'), and Mrs Mary Marshall who presided over many of the sessions in the Rossetti circle and who regularly produced spirit-drawings. Undoubtedly the Cowpers identified *Beata Beatrix* as a supernatural work and later in 1866 asked Ruskin to visit Rossetti to confirm their decision. Though relations between Rossetti and Ruskin were lukewarm, he called at Cheyne Walk and 'expressed great admiration' for '*Beatrice in a Death-trance*'.[44] But for Rossetti letting go of both the painting and what it symbolized was very hard and it took another five years before the Cowpers were able to take delivery of the canvas.

FIGURE 26.1 *Beata Beatrix*, c. 1864–70, Dante Gabriel Rossetti 1828–1882, © Tate, London 2013

Beata Beatrix possesses many elements that link it to the 'Willowwood' sonnets. Both poem and picture involve three figures if in slightly different spatial relations. In the middle distance of *Beata Beatrix* stands the personification of Love with an aureole and carrying a flaming heart. To the right Dante observes the scene. In the foreground sits the dead or dying figure of Elizabeth Siddal/Beatrice in a trance. Rossetti said that 'Willowwood' was 'a dream or trance', while *Beata Beatrix,* was intended, he claimed, to symbolize death 'under the semblance of a trance'.[45] Both 'Willowwood' and *Beata Beatrix* set up a relay between the living and the dead in supernatural terms, a relay that was not uncommon in the period when the cult of supposed communication with the dead was extremely widespread. But however tempting spiritualism might have been, it must have inhibited what more recent psychiatric studies call 'healthy mourning'. From Freud onwards, through to the writing of Melanie Klein and Julia Kristeva, analysts agree that in 'healthy mourning' the mind has to come, often painfully and reluctantly, to the conclusion that the dead have vanished for ever.[46] In this way, the mind has to abandon its emotional attachment and let go. But ever since 1865 Rossetti, by actively pursuing this route to Lizzie Siddal, had been inhibiting the process. The advent of Jane Morris, however, changed things, and her renewed presence in Rossetti's life created a compelling need to shift from the old love to the new one. Finally, when in December 1868, this exigency was strengthened by the suggestion that his poems might be wrested from Elizabeth Siddal's grave, 'giving up' became, for Rossetti, even more imperative.

The climax of the first sonnet involves a meeting, the very meeting of which Rossetti once wondered if he were 'worthy'. In an excitedly tactile moment the couple engage in a greeting that resembles a champagne toast: 'And as I stooped, her own lips rising there / Bubbled with brimming kisses at my mouth'. The idea of the speaker stooping over water that holds the image of a human face provides a trope from an important controlling myth in this sequence. In book three of Ovid's *Metamorphoses,* Narcissus, disdaining the affection of Echo, fell in love with the beauty of his own reflection in a pool (believing it to be another's), remained forever unsatisfied, and finally pined to death. 'The tale of Narcissus', writes Marina Warner, 'illuminates the perplexing, alluring, and perilous status of a self that can appear in every way real and yet lacks embodiment'. 'It tells a literal story', she says, 'about reflexion in a way that bears on reflexivity, the foundation of self-hood'.[47]

In the sonnet, the speaker, as he stoops towards the surface of the water to engage with the face of the beloved, comes perilously close to encountering something that might actually be his own reflection. It has often been noticed that Rossetti's representation of women was self-reflexive. 'He seems', writes Helene E. Roberts, 'to define himself [and] his identity in terms of women',[48] and his stories and poetry often explore this particular symbiosis.[49] The moment in 'Willowwood', however, is a complex one. Both Catherine Maxwell and Isobel Armstrong point out the centrality in these poems of this ambiguously narcissistic moment. Maxwell skilfully relates the conjunction of speaker and image to Rossetti's anxiety about the potentially destructive power of the mirror,[50] while Armstrong points out that the speaker and beloved are both the 'poet's self and not himself, Narcissus and not Narcissus'.[51] The kiss in 'Willowwood' represents a moment where the self fleetingly confronts something that might or might not be its own image. It is a moment that hovers between independence and identification, but when Narcissus in the myth identified with his own reflection, the effect was catastrophic.

The story of Narcissus was famously invoked by Freud. In 1914 he published 'On Narcissism: an Introduction' and in his paper 'Mourning and Melancholia' (1915) he wrote of how important is the management of narcissism in 'the work of mourning' and how its negotiation completes the relinquishing of the love-object.[52] Narcissism, he explained took two forms, primary and secondary. The first represents the infant's love directed to its own identity. This is essential for self-preservation and guarantees the continued coherence of the ego. In normal circumstances, according to Freud, ego-libido is superseded by object-libido, the psychic force that governs our attachment to others. In maturity, self-love appears to yield to object-love and gives rise to an image of the self mediated by the external world. As Freud describes it, object-love, or the love of another person remains essentially narcissistic but in a disguised form. Love of another he claims, 'displays the marked sexual overvaluaton which is doubtless derived from the child's original narcissism and thus corresponds to a transference of that narcissism to the sexual object'.[53] Given Rossetti's tendency to identify the self with the female other, the encounter between speaker and beloved is, therefore, potentially narcissistic, and the loss of the love-object brings about a disruption of this cathexis. Such a loss, Freud suggests, precipitates the subject into a struggle between life and death, between a desire to live that entails abandoning the other, and desire to die that entails clinging to and following the other into death. In healthy mourning the mourner 'is persuaded by the sum of the narcissistic satisfactions it derives from being alive to sever its attachment to the object that has been abolished'.[54] If it fails to make this break the subject sinks into the secondary narcissism of Narcissus, and the free libidinal energy that might have been drawn back and then directed at a new object is destructively redirected at the self and the subject moves from mourning into potentially suicidal melancholia.

In the second sonnet of 'Willowwood' the lover's kiss is accompanied by Love's song. Through art, Love has facilitated the apparition of the beloved; now music prepares for the communication of the 'secret'. In this sonnet the speaker fails as yet to understand the exact meaning of the song, but he grasps its nature.

> ...his was such a song,
> So meshed with half-remembrance hard to free,
> As souls disused in death's sterility
> May sing when the new birthday tarries long.

This music, sung by those lingering in some transitional state of 'soul sleep' and awaiting their final translation, has the effect of expanding the consciousness of the speaker. He becomes aware of something beyond the woman and beyond the well.

> And I was made aware of a dumb throng
> That stood aloof, one form by every tree,
> All mournful forms, for each was I or she,
> The shades of those our days that had no tongue.
> They looked on us, and knew us and were known.

Alistair Grieve accurately notices the correspondence between this image and Rossetti's, occult, *How They Met Themselves* (fig. 26.2).[55] Rossetti called this a 'bogie picture'. It was a sinister doppelganger drawing completed in Paris during his honeymoon in 1860, and dated with the full extent of his acquaintance with Elizabeth Siddal, '1851–1860'. Two lovers, in a scene of awed amazement, pause beside trees in a dense wood where they meet their ghostly counterparts. In 1864 Rossetti produced two watercolour replicas, but the picture was on his mind in May 1868 when he asked Howell to try and buy one of the replicas back so that he could re-work it.[56] In the poem the figures are multiplied many times to become a 'dumb throng' of memories, possibly William Michael's 'painful associations' from the past.

Memory, says Freud, plays a central part in the work of mourning. In order to gain release from the lost object 'each single one of the memories...in which the libido is bound to the object is brought up and hypercathected and the detachment of the libido is accomplished in respect of it'.[57] The critic Tammy Clewell comments: 'The work of mourning, as Freud describes it, entails a kind of hyperremembering, a process of obsessive recollection during which the survivor resuscitates the existence of the lost other...replacing an actual absence with an imaginary presence'.[58] The appearance of the 'shades' or ghosts suggests symbiotic narcissism, 'for each was I or she', and their mournfulness is perhaps connected with the joint life of speaker and beloved. Then as

FIGURE 26.2 *How They Met Themselves*, c.1850/60, Rossetti, Dante Charles Gabriel (1828–82) / Fitzwilliam Museum, University of Cambridge, UK / The Bridgeman Art Library

the gaze of these ghostly counterparts falls on the embrace of speaker and lover, a dramatic change of perspective takes place.

> While fast together, alive from the abyss,
> Clung the soul-wrung implacable close kiss;
> And pity of self through all made broken moan
> Which said, "For once, for once, for once alone!"
> And still Love sang, and what he sang was this:—

The attractive, effervescent meeting of lips of the first sonnet has become an impersonal 'implacable close kiss' between the speaker and what has become an almost sinister being, risen 'alive from the abyss'. Originally narcissistically attached to the image of the beloved, the speaker, encouraged by the words of Love's song, now seems to be initiating the process of detachment. It is evident that the 'work of mourning' has begun in earnest.

Those same words now provide an insight into the inhabitants of Willowwood, the kind of place that Willowwood represents and the importance of not lingering there:

> O ye, all ye that walk in Willowwood,
> That walk with hollow faces burning white;
> What fathom-depth of soul-struck widowhood,
> What long, what longer hours, one lifelong night,

> Ere ye again, who so in vain have wooed
> Your last hope lost, who so in vain invite
> Your lips to that their unforgotten food,
> Ere ye, ere ye again shall see the light!

The song, performed against the 'implacable close kiss' of the two lovers, seems to be addressed to both of them locked as they are, in their emotionally famished embrace. The speaker's personal thirst for contact in the first sonnet now extends to the emotional starvation of all denizens of this dark place of tears ('weeping-willow' wood) and mutual bereavement (widowhood). Both speaker and beloved have lost hope, yet they still retain the memory of physical intimacy, and both will have to endure a long separation before they are permitted to rise to the light.

Love's song then offers an account of the physical environment of Willowwood:

> Alas! the bitter banks in Willowwood,
> With tear-spurge wan, with blood-wort burning red:
> Alas! if ever such a pillow could
> Steep deep the soul in sleep till she were dead,—
> Better all life forget her than this thing,
> That Willowwood should hold her wandering!

Jerome McGann is surely right to see in Willowwood the countertype of the medieval *locus amoenus,* the paradisal garden of chivalric literature.[59] Guillaume de Lorris's *Le Roman de la Rose,* also a dream vision, involves a part wild, part cultivated garden: 'Along the brooks and banks', ran 'clear, lively fountains' from which 'sprang...thick, short grass'. Sleep here is so delightful that on these banks 'one could couch his mistress as though on a feather bed'. In the grass are 'beautiful violets, fresh young periwinkles...with flowers of various colour and sweetest perfumes'.[60] In sharp contrast to the medieval *locus amoenus* the banks of Willowwood sport spurge and wort, natural if poisonous plants made artificial by the addition of their visceral body-fluid pre-fixes, tears and blood. In *Le Roman de la Rose* the dreamer discovers a 'fountain under a pine', the equivalent of Rossetti's 'woodside well'. It stands 'within a marble stone' where 'on the border of the upper side', we are told were 'cut small letters saying there fair Narcissus died'.[61] At first Guilluame's dreamer fears that his fate would be that of Narcissus, but gaining courage he peers into the water. Immediately he is trapped, not by his own reflection, but by 'the simple will to love'. He is transfixed by the vision of a female rose, 'with a colour as red and as pure as the best that Nature can produce'.[62]

But the final words of Love's song contain the core of the secret that Rossetti was seeking. The 'painful thoughts' of his wife's death, said his brother, generated such fantasies in his mind that he 'long turned on the unrestful bed'.[63] Rossetti who was living in the state of Willowwood had come to realize that he could never 'couch' himself or his mistress on the banks of this place and that the only salvation for both speaker and beloved lay in separation and detachment. To complete the mourning process Freud emphasized that the subject had to first establish the reality that the love-object no longer existed and 'all libido shall be withdrawn from its attachments to the object'. This, he said, usually meets with opposition as the subject clings 'to the object through the medium of a hallucinatory wishful psychosis'.[64] 'Willowwood' begins with such a wishful psychosis, but as Love's song progresses so detachment between speaker and beloved is slowly if reluctantly enacted.

> So sang he: and as meeting rose and rose
> Together cling through the wind's wellaway
> Nor change at once, yet near the end of day
> The leaves drop loosened where the heart-stain glows,—
> So when the song died did the kiss unclose;

Mortality and severance are reintroduced into the poem through the simultaneous dying of the song and the parting of the lovers, and that parting brings back the spirit-drawing of the first sonnet: 'And her face fell back drowned, and was as grey / As its grey eyes; and if it ever may / Meet mine again I know not if Love knows'. Anne Mary Howitt described her own experience of spirit-drawing at the moment when 'the hand of the medium feels itself impelled...to rapidly outline with a pencil, or colour, the form of the spirit picture on the paper'. 'The 'spirit-picture', she said, was 'of the nature of dissolving views'.[65] The 'dissolving view' was a form of Victorian entertainment that produced the illusion of one image merging fluidly with another by using two lantern slides in an alternate sequence. The aquatic image of the beloved in 'Willowwood', like Rossetti's *Beata Beatrix* shares something of that same fluidity. They combine precise detail, the grey eyes of the beloved in the poem and the symbolist details in the painting, with elements that are mysterious, misty and out of focus. The dissolving view was closely related to the nineteenth-century phantasmagoria, and the phantasmagoria was able to produce images that not only merged, but ones that advanced and retreated, creating the illusion of pictures rising to a surface then falling back beneath it.[66] In Rossetti's case, the persistent hallucinatory swirling shapes produced by his ophthalmic problems, combined with his experience of phantasmagoric animation and the creation of spirit-drawing, can help to explain the peculiar quality of the rising and falling image of 'Willowwood'. Rossetti used the effect of the hallucinatory, dissolving-view to create an emblem of the process of psychic attachment and detachment in terms that appeared to be supernatural.

In the final sonnet of 'Willowwood', the retreating and fading image changes the mythopoetic underpinning of the sequence. Here the story of Narcissus gives way to the legend of Orpheus and Eurydice. The speaker, once again facilitated by the medium of Love, is no longer trapped in the narcissistic 'implacable kiss' of the first embrace. Now, like Orpheus who looked behind and had to leave his wife in Hades, he allows the phantom to return to the spirit world. In Freudian terms, the necessary, if difficult, process of the libidinal withdrawal is taking place. But will the couple meet again? The speaker confesses that Love, even if he has the knowledge, is unable to tell him, and the spirit of Elizabeth Siddal herself concurs. In the last of Rossetti's recorded séance conversations with her, she, too, was unsure about a further reunion. The session took place on

14 August 1868, three months before Rossetti wrote 'Willowwood'. He was in the studio with his brother, his assistant Treffry Dunn, and Fanny Cornforth. 'Elizabeth Rossetti' was named and Rossetti questioned her. 'Are you my wife?' he asked. 'Yes'. 'Are you now happy?' 'Yes.' 'Happier than on earth?' Once again, 'Yes'. 'If I were to join you would I be happy?' 'Yes.' 'Should I see you at once?' 'No.' 'Quite soon?' 'No.'[67]

Though both Lizzie and the angel of Love are uncertain about the future, the speaker's release of the image into the water is nonetheless a positive development in the mourning process. The water, once essential to slake his 'heart's drouth' now acts as the symbolic alternative for potentially destructive symbiosis: 'Only I know that I leaned low and drank / A long draught from the water where she sank, / Her breath and all her tears and all her soul'. The fading of the phantasmagoric image of the beloved, and its replacement by a symbolic essence is then blessed by the angel of Love: 'And as I leaned, I know I felt Love's face / Pressed on my neck with moan of pity and grace, / Till both our heads were in his aureole'. The tactile experience of the lips of the beloved in the first sonnet is replaced by the pressure of Love's face on the speaker's neck in this last one. The living and the dead are now separated and the mourning process advanced to its conclusion. The beloved is not forgotten, but detached. The grey face beneath the water is not dismissed, but is included in the act of benediction where, together with the face of the speaker, it is caught in the halo that surrounds Love's head.

In spite of the absence of critical consensus, 'Willowwood' appears valedictory and elegiac rather celebratory. Thanatos takes precedence over Eros in a necromantic ritual enacted by what Rossetti called a 'lively band of bogies'.[68] Without being too determinedly biographical, the sense of loss and parting in occult circumstances points to feelings associated with Elizabeth Siddal rather than Jane Morris. The process of abandonment and mourning, however, might not be confined to his dead wife. It is also possible to read it as directed to his important, if temporary, turn from visual art to poetry and the consequent effects on his own personality. Whatever the truth, 'Willowwood' represents a hope rather than an achievement, a desire rather than a fulfilment. Three years later in the wake of Robert Buchanan's cruel references to the ghost of Rossetti's marriage, his melancholia returned. He succumbed to mania and attempted to join Elizabeth Siddal in the grave.

Notes

1. This was established by Douglas J. Robillard in 'Rossetti's "Willowwood" Sonnets and the Structure of the *House of Life*', *Victorian Newsletter*, 22 (1962), 5–9 and has been broadly accepted ever since.

2. William Michael Rossetti, *Dante Gabriel Rossetti as Designer and Writer* (London: Cassell, 1889), 216, and Oswald Doughty, *A Victorian Romantic: Dante Gabriel Rossetti* (London: Oxford University Press, 1960), 384–385.

3. Jerome McGann, 'Scholarly Commentary to "Willowwood"', in *The Rossetti Archive*—<http://www.rossettiarchive.org/docs/14-1869.raw.html> (accessed 8 February 2013).

4. Catherine Maxwell, 'It Once Should Save as Well as Kill: D.G Rossetti and the Feminine', in David Clifford and Laurence Roussillon, eds., *Outsiders Looking In: The Rossettis Then and Now* (London: Anthem Press, 2004), 229.

5. David G. Riede, *Dante Gabriel Rossetti and the Limits of Victorian Vision* (Ithaca: Cornell University Press, 1983), 147.

6. Paull Franklin Baum, *The House of Life* (Cambridge, Mass: Harvard University Press, 1928), 143.

7. E. Warwick Slinn, 'Rossetti's Elegy for Masculine Desire: Seduction and Loss in the *House of Life*', in David Latham, ed., *Haunted Texts: Studies in Pre-Raphaelitism: In Honour of William E. Fredeman* (Toronto; London: University of Toronto Press, 2003), 63.

8. Joan Rees, *The Poetry of Dante Gabriel Rossetti: Modes of Self-Expression* (Cambridge: Cambridge University Press, 1981), 85.

9. Rossetti, *Dante Gabriel Rossetti as Designer and Writer,* 216; Stephen J. Spector, 'Love, Unity, and Desire in the Poetry of Dante Gabriel Rossetti', *ELH*, 38 (1971), 456; John Holmes, *Dante Gabriel Rossetti and the Late Victorian Sonnet Sequence: Sexuality, Belief and the Self* (Aldershot: Ashgate, 2005), 69

10. See <http://www.rossettiarchive.org/docs/14-1869.unionms.rad.html> (accessed 8 February 2013).

11. Rossetti, 'The Stealthy School of Criticism', *Athenaeum*, 2303, 16 Dec. 1871, 793.

12. DGR to Charles Augustus Howell, 21 Aug. 1868, in *The Correspondence of Dante Gabriel Rossetti*, ed. William E. Fredeman, Antony H. Harrison, Roger C. Lewis and Jane Cowan (Woodbridge: D. S. Brewer, 2002–), 68.127.

13. See J. B. Bullen, *Rossetti: Painter and Poet* (London: Frances Lincoln, 2011), 194–196, where both *La Pia* and 'The Blue Silk Dress' are illustrated.

14. Both Jan Marsh and I agree that the evidence points to a date in April 1868. See Marsh, *Dante Gabriel Rossetti: Painter and Poet* (London: Weidenfeld & Nicolson, 1999), 338, and Bullen, *Rossetti,* 148.

15. William Bell Scott, *Autobiographical Notes*, 2 vols. (London: James R. Osgood, McIlvaine & Co, 1892), ii. 65–66. The 'Spartan Fox' is a reference to a Spartan boy who stole a live fox and concealed it under his shirt. When challenged about it he maintained complete silence though the fox was chewing into his stomach.

16. DGR to William Michael Rossetti, 17 Apr. 1860—Rossetti, *Correspondence,* 60.8.

17. DGR to Ann Gilchrist, 2 Mar. 1862—Rossetti, *Correspondence,* 62.18.

18. William Michael Rossetti in *Family Letters,* i. 255.

19. William Michael Rossetti, *Dante Gabriel Rossetti: His Family Letters* (London: Ellis and Elvey, 1895), i. 256.

20. Rossetti, *Family Letters,* i. 255.

21. William Michael Rossetti, *Rossetti Papers, 1862 to 1870* (London: Sands & Co., 1903), 339.

22. DGR to Henry Buxton Forman, 13 Oct, 1868—*Correspondence,* 68.145.

23. DGR to Charles Augustus Howell, 17 Dec. 1868—*Correspondence,* 68.167.

24. *Rossetti Papers,* 339.

25. Dante Gabriel Rossetti, 'Willowwood' in *The House of Life: A Sonnet Sequence*, ed. Roger C. Lewis (Woodbridge: Boydell & Brewer, 2007), 119–128.

26. Isobel Armstrong, 'D. G. Rossetti and Christina Rossetti as Sonnet Writers', *Victorian Poetry*, 48 (2010), 466.

27. Slinn, 'Rossetti's Elegy for Masculine Desire', 60; William E. Fredeman, 'Rossetti's 'in Memoriam': An Elegiac Reading of *The House of Life*', *Bulletin of the John Rylands Library, Manchester*, 47 (1965), 298–341.

28. William E. Fredeman, 'The Letters of Pictor Ignotus: William Bell Scott's Correspondence with Alice Boyd, 1859–1884', *Bulletin of the John Rylands Library*, 58 (1975), 101–102.

29. Henry Treffry Dunn, *Recollections of Dante Gabriel Rossetti and His Circle* (London: Elkin Mathews, 1904), 55.

30. Some years later in 1863 Rossetti read Garth Wilkinson's collection of 'bogie' poems, *Improvisation from the Spirit* (1857), as he called them, written in automatic writing. See Rossetti, *Correspondence*, 63.17.

31. W. M. Rossetti, *Rossetti Papers*, 218.

32. Shonfield, Zuzanna, *The Precariously Privileged: A Professional Family in Victorian London* (Oxford: Oxford University Press, 1987), 112.

33. Helen Rossetti Angeli, *Dante Gabriel Rossetti: His Friends and Enemies.* (London: Hamish Hamilton, 1949), 206.

34. Luke Ionides, *Memories* (Ludlow: Dog Rose, 1996), 12.

35. Dunn, *Recollections*, 55.

36. Angeli, *Rossetti*, 208.

37. Fredeman, 'The Letters of Pictor Ignotus', 92, and Scott, *Autobiographical Notes*, ii. 66.

38. William Michael Rossetti's unpublished séance diary in Rare Books and Special Collections, Angeli-Dennis Collection, University of British Columbia. There are some twenty sessions recorded between 1865 and 1868, though internal evidence suggests that there were others that went unrecorded. Angela Thirlwell in *William and Lucy: The Other Rossettis* (New Haven, Conn ; London: Yale University Press, 2003), 98–104, gives an account of some of these.

39. Carl Ray Woodring, *Victorian Samplers: William and Mary Howitt* (Lawrence: University of Kansas Press, 1952), 205.

40. Rossetti, Séance Diary, 24 Apr. 1868.

41. William Michael in *Rossetti Papers*, 156–7 and 213.

42. Marsh, *Rossetti*, 337.

43. See Van Akin Burd, *Ruskin, Lady Mount-Temple and the Spiritualists: An Episode in Broadlands History* (London: Brentham Press for the Guild of St. George, 1982).

44. Rossetti, *Rossetti Papers*, 199.

45. DGR to Mrs. William Cowper-Temple, 26 Mar. 1871—*Correspondence*, 71.43.

46. Sigmund Freud, 'Mourning and Melancholia', in *The Standard Edition of the Complete Psychological Works of Sigmund Freud, 14 (1914–1916), on the History of the Psycho-Analytic Movement, Papers on Metapsychology and Other Works*, ed. by James Strachey and Anna Freud (London: Vintage, 2001), 244; Melanie Klein, 'Mourning and its Relation to Manic-Depressive States', in *Love, Guilt, Reparation and other works, 1921–1945* (London: Hogarth Press, 1975), 344; Julia Kristeva, *Melanie Klein*, trans. Ross Guberman (New York: Columbia University Press, 2000), 79–80.

47. Marina Warner, *Phantasmagoria: Spirit Visions, Metaphors, and Media into the Twenty-First Century* (Oxford: Oxford University Press, 2006), 169.

48. Helene E. Roberts, 'The Dream World of Dante Gabriel Rossetti', *Victorian Studies*, 17 (1974), 386.

49. See Bullen, *Rossetti*, 6–9.

50. Maxwell, 'D. G Rossetti and the Feminine', 230.

51. Isobel Armstrong, *Victorian Poetry: Poetry, Poetics and Politics* (New York ; London: Routledge, 1993), 255.

52. Freud, 'Mourning and Melancholia', 249.

53. Sigmund Freud, 'On Narcissism: An Introduction', in *The Standard Edition of the Complete Psychological Works of Sigmund Freud, 14 (1914–1916)*, 88.

54. Freud, 'Mourning and Melancholia', 255.

55. Alistair Grieve, 'Dante Gabriel Rossetti: How They Met Themselves', in *The Pre-Raphaelites* (London: Tate Gallery, 1984), 254.

56. DGR to Charles Augustus Howell, *c*.4 May, 1868—*Correspondence*, 68.76.

57. Freud, 'Mourning and Melancholia', 245.

58. Tammy Clewell, 'Mourning Beyond Melancholia: Freud's Psychoanalysis of Loss', *Journal of the American Psychoanalytic Association*, **52** (2004), 43.

59. McGann, <rossettiarchive.org/docs/14-1869.raw.html> (accessed 9 February 2013).

60. Guillaume de Lorris and Jean de Meun, *The Romance of the Rose*, trans. Charles Dahlberg (Princeton: Princeton University Press, 1971), 49.

61. Lorris, *Romance of the Rose*, 50.

62. Lorris, *Romance of the Rose*, 53.

63. Rossetti, *Family Letters*, i. 256.

64. Freud, 'Mourning and Melancholia', 244.

65. Anna Mary Howitt, 'Thoughts Concerning the Mystical Death of the Insane: No. VI', *The Psychological Review*, 5 Aug. 1882, 133.

66. Both the phantasmagoria and the séance specialized in supernatural phenomenon. Both were hugely popular in the 1860s, but their relationship was problematic. The foremost British practitioner of the phantasmagoria, John Henry Pepper, scorned the way in which mediums seemed to be creating effects by occult means of exactly the kind he brought about by optical ones. See Mervyn Heard, *Phantasmagoria: The Secret Life of the Magic Lantern* (Hastings: Projection Box, 2006), 224–225. Isobel Armstrong, in *Victorian Glassworlds: Glass Culture and the Imagination 1830–1880* (Oxford: Oxford University Press, 2008), 264–265 also writes interestingly about this phenomenon.

67. Rossetti, *Séance Diary*, 14 August 1868.

68. DGR to Frances Mary Lavinia Rossetti, 1 Mar. 1869—*Correspondence*, 69.20.

Select Bibliography

Angeli, Helen Rossetti, *Dante Gabriel Rossetti: His Friends and Enemies* (London: Hamish Hamilton, 1949).

Armstrong, Isobel, *Victorian Poetry: Poetry, Poetics and Politics* (London: Routledge, 1993).

—— 'D. G. Rossetti and Christina Rossetti as Sonnet Writers', *Victorian Poetry*, 48 (2010), 461–471.

Bullen, J. B., *Rossetti: Painter and Poet* (London: Frances Lincoln, 2011).

Dunn, Henry Treffry, *Recollections of Dante Gabriel Rossetti and His Circle* (London: Elkin Mathews London, 1904).

Freud, Sigmund, 'Mourning and Melancholia', in *The Standard Edition of the Complete Psychological Works of Sigmund Freud. Volume XIV, (1914–1916), on the History of the Psycho-Analytic Movement, Papers on Metapsychology and Other Works*, ed. James Strachey and Anna Freud (London: Vintage, 2001), 239–258.

McGann, Jerome, *Rossetti Archive*: <http://www.rossettiarchive.org/> (accessed 8 February 2013).

Marsh, Jan, *Dante Gabriel Rossetti: Painter and Poet* (London: Weidenfeld & Nicolson, 1999).

Maxwell, Catherine, 'It Once Should Save as Well as Kill: D. G Rossetti and the Feminine' in Clifford, David and Roussillon, Laurence, eds., *Outsiders Looking In: The Rossettis Then and Now* (London: Anthem Press, 2004), 223–236.

Rossetti, Dante Gabriel, Fredeman, William E., Harrison, Antony H., Lewis, Roger C., and Cowan, Jane, *The Correspondence of Dante Gabriel Rossetti* (Woodbridge: D. S. Brewer, 2002–).

—— and Lewis, Roger C., *The House of Life: A Sonnet Sequence* (Woodbridge: Boydell & Brewer, 2007).

Rossetti, William Michael, *Dante Gabriel Rossetti as Designer and Writer* (London: Cassell, 1889).

——*Dante Gabriel Rossetti: His Family-Letters*, 2 vols. (London: Ellis and Elvey, 1895).

——*Rossetti Papers, 1862 to 1870* (London: Sands & Co., 1903).

—— Unpublished séance diary in Rare Books and Special Collections, Angeli-Dennis Collection, University of British Columbia.

Scott, William Bell, *Autobiographical Notes... 1830–1882* (London: James R. Osgood, McIlvaine & Co, 1892).

CHAPTER 27

CHRISTINA ROSSETTI: RAVENS, COCKATOOS, AND RANGE

CONSTANCE W. HASSETT

I THE 'UNEMPHATIC' AND 'DEEPLY UNPARAPHRASABLE' LYRICS

VETERAN Rossettians know the pleasure of drifting through her *Complete Poems*, but perhaps the continuing vitality of her reputation as a lyric poet is in the spread of a handful of exquisite favourites to less weighty venues—anthologies, hymnals, children's collections, and even videos on YouTube, where one finds Helen Mirren reading 'Up-Hill' and a girl's choir from Phoenix singing 'Windflowers'.[1] The late Philip Larkin kept her work at his desk, and the recent American Laureate Mark Strand tells of returning again and again to her 'dark' lyrics.[2] Similarly even those of her contemporaries unfamiliar with her collections—*Goblin Market and Other Poems* (1862), *The Prince's Progress and Other Poems* (1866), *Sing-Song: A Nursery Rhyme Book* (1872), *A Pageant and Other Poems* (1881), and *Verses* (1893)—would have come upon 'Up-Hill', 'A Birthday', and twenty-one other titles in *Macmillan's Magazine* throughout the 1860s.[3] There too they would have found 'The Bourne', later singled out by a young Arthur Symons in a glowing review of 'Miss Rossetti's Poetry'. Symons introduces the poem by saying that Rossetti 'can also, like Keats, be "half in love with easeful death", and in such a mood she can sing of nothing so sweetly, so peacefully, with such desire and sympathy, as the narrow grave that takes us and covers us over at last'. He then cites the poem in full:

> Underneath the growing grass,
> > Underneath the living flowers,
> > Deeper than the sound of showers:
> > There we shall not count the hours
> By the shadows as they pass.
>
> Youth and health will be but vain,
> > Beauty reckoned of no worth:
> > There a very little girth
> > Can hold round what once the earth
> Seemed too narrow to contain.[4]

Though this essay will largely concern itself with acknowledging Rossetti's range, her periphery, it might be best to begin by amplifying Symons's compelling appreciation of this typically and *centrally* Rossettian piece. As in the well-known 'Dream-Land', Rossetti's negations create an impression of acute sentience: the phrase 'deeper than the sound' remembers what it denies. As in the much anthologized 'After Death', the inability to 'see' summons up the faintly palpable touch of passing shadows. The lovely voweling of 'underneath', 'underneath', and 'deeper' builds a crooning momentum that gently expands into the poignant blankness of a shifter, 'there'.[5] The alternating rhythm conveys increasing emotional distress as the phrase 'a very little girth' pushes softly across the line break (like inevitability itself) into the stress-full phrase, 'Cán hóld róund'.[6] The monumentally tactful 'whát' and the retrospective 'ónce' quietly admit that every cherished one of us becomes an anonymous 'what' that 'once' lived. The poem ends in understatement. The final line, with the verb 'seemed' positioned at its front, calmly emphasizes the word we resist, 'contain'. Quite delicately and without ever using the word 'grave' or 'coffin', it tells us that regardless of disproportionate affections and aspirations, our existence, like the poem's own, is contained within a 'very little girth'.[7] 'The Bourne' might also be said, with respect to its genre, to self-reflexively use its own 'small girth' to remark the universally mortal condition 'we' suffer, although it acknowledges no specifiable occasion and addresses no one in particular. It aspires, in other words, to the condition of pure lyric. Symons describes Rossetti's overall style as 'unemphatic', which is his label for the reticent quality that, as Angela Leighton puts it, makes the poems 'deeply unparaphrasable'.[8] His sense of 'Miss Rossetti's genius' accords well with modern criticism's. Anne Jamison, for example, extols the Rossettian evasiveness that leaves causes of pain 'unspecified, unexplained, and unnamed', while Isobel Armstrong points to inexplicitness as the means to 'potent under-meanings'.[9]

II BALKED NARRATIVE AND DISABLED KNOWINGNESS

I want to expand our sense of Rossetti's centre beyond the fine tact of 'Remember', the ghostly restraint of 'At Home' and, the bleak sorrow of 'A Pause of Thought' and 'Mirage'.[10] The discussion that follows considers a less familiar Rossetti, the poet whose enjoyment of grotesquerie, turbulent rhythms, and comically undignified scenarios was well known to Victorian readers but remains largely overlooked in recent discussion of her aesthetic. *This* Rossetti wrote tales of new-born crocodiles ('My Dream'), punning revenants ('The Ghost's Petition'), scrappy siblings ('Noble Sisters')[11], and two especially quirky bird poems that have slipped from modern notice: 'A Bird's Eye View' and 'Freaks of Fashion'.[12] These are fine poems in themselves, but they also serve to remind us that the riddling silliness of *Sing-Song*, with its chattering magpies and growling boys, and the rambunctious cacophony of 'Goblin Market' are not one-off or isolated effects in her oeuvre.[13]

'A Bird's-Eye View' was known to Rossetti's contemporaries from its appearance in *Macmillan's* soon after the success of *Goblin Market*, while 'Freaks of Fashion' was included in her *Pageant* collection and singled out by Symons who delightedly mis-praised it as a 'child's jingle about birds and their costumes' and thought it 'laughably true to Nature'.[14] Neither poem is a song or sonnet; neither fits the received 'understanding of "lyric" as the mode of subjectivity…in which a solitary "I" is overheard in meditation or conversation with an unnamed other'.[15] Both deal in what might be called fabulous narrative, offering absolutely fresh stories with talking birds who ponder variations on the mutability topos. The poems' formal panache as they combine unusual physical perspectives, the one aerial and the other hedge-bound, with respectively dour and hilarious pronouncements, supplies a prime opportunity to rethink Rossetti's poetic range.

'A Bird's-Eye View' draws its inspiration from a constellation of materials, including 'The Twa Corbies', that grisly ballad of corvine predation and female disloyalty that Scott's *Minstrelsy* brought to the Pre-Raphaelites' attention, and Edgar Allan Poe's 'The Raven'. The Rossettis were so avidly interested in their American contemporary that Christina, on first reading 'Annabel Lee', thought Gabriel might have written it as 'an imitation of Poe'.[16] Gabriel himself drew illustrations for 'The Raven' and claimed that 'The Blessed Damozel', which gives 'utterance to the yearning of the loved one in heaven', was conceived as a 'reversal' of Poe's depiction of male grief.[17] Christina's 'A Bird's-Eye View' provides a reversal as well, but one that is torqued on a different axis. Rather than depicting permanent sorrow on earth or in heaven, her narrative—in a development more in keeping with the pessimism of 'The Twa Corbies'—eliminates the lover's grief altogether by having *her* ravens watch a male lover take 'another mate'.[18]

'A Bird's-Eye View' opens onomatopoetically with the 'Croak, croak, croak' of a raven with 'ominous eye'. Perched on a 'crooked tree', this 'fatal black bird' apostrophizes a ship carrying a Bride to her Bridegroom:

> 'O ship upon the high seas,
> Freighted with lives and spices,
> Sink, O ship,' croaked the Raven:
> 'Let the Bride mount to heaven.'

The raven's off-rhyme on 'high seas' and 'spices' grates a bit with an acoustic warping of the kind that reviewer Robert Buchanan, in a fiercely unpleasant attempt to regulate aesthetic taste, would later censure as one of Gabriel's disfiguring affectations. But

Christina, instead of resisting distorted sound as 'mere fiddlededeeing', values the nagging mismatch as a way of enforcing the faint irony of bird's speech per se.[19] Perhaps, too, the ambiguity of his verb 'let'—its opposite meanings as an imperative 'make it so' or a concessive 'allow it to happen'—register for later re-consideration. Warned, however, to 'shun' and 'fear' this creature, the insufficiently wary reader endows the bird with preternatural hostility.

The story moves tensely forward as Rossetti deploys an array of voices and moods to anticipate what is miserably inevitable. Regretful kinfolk yearn to 'clasp' the sea-faring Bride; the raven emits 'chuckling and choking' (possibly drowning) sounds; the Bridegroom's people complain that the ship 'tarries'. Then at exactly mid-poem (and at the precise top of the paired columns on *Macmillan's* printed page) the raven makes a startling disclosure about a second bird at the journey's and presumably the narrative's end: 'But I have a sable brother: / He sees where ocean flows to, / And he knows what he knows too'. This wry hint at possible connivance seems (but only seems) validated by a *post hoc, propter hoc* logic in the next stanza's report that the ship 'never / Hove in sight'.

Tellingly, what occurs in the remaining stanzas is less an event *in* the story than something that happens *to* the story. Rossetti lets the ballad itself balk at reporting the shipwreck and its disturbing aftermath, specifically, that the Bridegroom recovers from loss, loves anew, and leaves the all-seeing ravens to be the Bride's only mourners. Three patently evasive stanzas attend to the crowd's mounting 'dread', their ignorance of how the Bride 'perished', and the second raven's taciturnity. In refusing to tell the harm that befalls the Bride, the poem virtually protests its role in delivering the narrative. 'A Bird's-Eye View' as such seems to want a different ending, perhaps an epithalamium on 'marriage mirth' as in 'Maiden Song' or a celebratory refrain—'my love is come to me'— as in 'A Birthday'.[20]

By now, the reader yearns for the facts that come so abruptly in the poem's last stanza. The Bride's loss at sea is followed by a second vanishing, her erasure from the Bridegroom's shallow memory. Seizing ironically on the phrase 'a year and a day', the legal archaism for specifying limited obligations, Rossetti fast-forwards to the Bridegroom's wedding. This is the event that warrants her version of the pathetic fallacy, that is, her ravens' wearied melancholy:

> After a year and a day
> The Bridegroom is brave and gay:
> Love is sound, faith is rotten;
> The old Bride is forgotten:—
> Two ominous Ravens only
> Remember, black and lonely.

The impression of a rushed conclusion carries a forceful inference about the behaviour it reports. The 'respite and nepenthe' that Poe denies his raven-beleaguered survivor is here conferred as a *fait accompli*![21] Instead of a midnight message for a dreary lover, there's a new understanding for the poem's reader. The raven cries in Rossetti's ballad are a legitimately dolorous lament, an avian 'O tempora o mores'. Hardly menacing, the opening 'croak, croak, croak' now strikes the reader—and this is the poem's revisionary surprise—as a prophetically helpless alarm-note, an expression of misgiving about human infidelity. It's an open question whether or how strenuously the poem is making a specifically feminist objection to nineteenth-century gender relations and marriage ratios. Memory's erosions and the heart's defections are, after all, among Rossetti's paramount themes, and in one of the spectre poems, 'The Hour and the Ghost', it is the woman whose acceptance of new love brings on a supernatural visit from the deceased husband.[22] Even the beautiful sonnet sequence 'Monna Innominata' grieves the disruption of a love that 'now can never be'.[23]

As attention finally turns in 'A Bird's-Eye View' from the Bridegroom to the ravens themselves, the pair become emblems of ontological loneliness and perhaps, too, of an elegiac poiesis. Afflicted with an ethically attuned eye, these ravens endure a disabled knowingness that neither foments nor hinders human forgetfulness but, like a true elegist's, can only lament the reality of damped and faded human affection. As threnodists who 'remember', they are as fated to sorrowfulness as the rhyme that so perfectly enfolds 'only' within an inevitable 'lonely'. Situated at opposite ends of a narrated calamity, they embody the lyric principle of return and repetition, lastingly desolate, while the Bridegroom, a denizen of narrative, moves on toward an untroubled future.

III COMIC CHATTER AND VICTORIAN FASHION SENSE

In a later narrative, Rossetti slides along the rhetorical continuum from pathetic fallacy, with ravens more human than humans, to fully fledged anthropomorphism, with birds who talk as if they are humans. Solemnity gives way to comical chatter about the era's voguish 'Freaks of Fashion'.

When it comes to fashion, Christina Rossetti is legendary, thanks to Max Beerbohm's nostalgically affectionate drawing in *Rossetti and His Circle*, for having no more sense of style than a dreary 'pew-opener'.[24] But the jest should not be taken literally. As contemporary photographs show, Rossetti adapted her style to the occasion and times, going from pagoda-sleeves and voluminous skirt in the 1863 family groups taken by Mr. Dodgson (Lewis Carroll) to a tightly corseted, double-skirted dress for a formal author-photo in 1877.[25] In the interval, Rossetti saw the 'rapid succession of styles' that attracted the *Punch* cartoonists' satire, from the enormous crinolines of the 1860s to the tied back skirts, draped bustles, and implausible trains of the 1870s.[26] That she had a spectator's interest in the newest *toilette de promenade* is clear from her holiday report of spending several 'amused' hours on the Parade watching the 'costumes that pass before us in a brisk panorama!'[27] A second-hand connection with the fashion elite emerges in a discussion of the ball gown worn by her friend Ellen Heaton for the festivities occasioned in 1873 by a state visit from the Shah of Iran. Curious about the 'assembly at Guildhall' with 'royal personages' and the 'unique travelled Shah', Rossetti wants to know if Heaton's gown 'did not look very nice after all', supposing her 'dressmaker found time to finish it with a beautiful sash'. She also inquires whether 'the Caesarevena' is 'as pretty as the Princess of Wales?'[28] Had Rossetti cared to, she might have consulted *The Illustrated London News* for sketches of Princess Alexandra's and her sister's bustled and trained dresses.[29]

While this particular silhouette fell out of style the next year, the bustle was to make a comeback soon after Rossetti's witty appropriation of the term for its homonymic hint of unruliness: 'Such a bustle and squeak!'[30] 'Freaks of Fashion' opens emphatically with the narrator's consternation over a noisy scene of instruction as parental birds take their nestlings 'under the wing' in an attempt to cultivate the naked ones' in-born fashion sense:

> Such a hubbub in the nests,
>   Such a bustle and squeak!
> Nestlings, guiltless of a feather,
>   Learning just to speak,
> Ask—'And how about the fashions?'
>   From a cavernous beak.

The exclamatory rhythm lands emphatically on 'guiltless', anticipating with its pun the guilty pleasures of plumage. That the ludicrous query comes from 'cavernous' beaks suggests the nestlings' vacuous receptivity to fashion trends and the likely frivolousness of the advice to come. That they are just learning to speak implies that news of 'the fashions' is a childish discourse, but as Rossetti well knows, it is also, incontrovertibly, the professional discourse driving the late-century surge in fashion journalism, the era's proliferation of etiquette manuals, and, as we shall see, some baleful editorializing.

The parent generation includes domestic and tropical birds whose heterogeneity anticipates the helter-skelter quality of their counsel:

> Perched on bushes, perched on hedges,
>   Perched on firm hahas,
> Perched on anything that holds them,
>   Gay papas and grave mammas
> Teach the knowledge-thirsty nestlings:
>   Hear the gay papas.

The quadrupling of 'perched' underscores the birds' conspicuous proliferation, while the pun on 'hahas' (garden borders and laughter) signals Rossetti's comic intent. By having the parents alight indiscriminately on 'anything that holds them', she suggests the shakiness of their knowledge-base while at the same time gently mocking the pupils with the faux-solemn epithet 'knowledge-thirsty'. (At the end, when the nestlings begin to feel hungry, the issue of taste in clothes yields to hearty interest in the taste of 'breakfast'.) Such a gathering of miscellaneous birds is, of course, utterly unnatural, a literary *mise-en-scene* descended from Chaucer's *Parliament of Fowls* (with an avian council that fails to reach accord). Promiscuous mixing is otherwise a human project, as in the Regent's Park aviary where Christina liked to 'Zoological Gardenize' or at Gabriel's Cheyne Walk menagerie where a 'talking grey parrot' and 'raven' consorted with 'peacocks, wood-owls, Virginian owls, Chinese horned owls, a jackdaw, laughing jackasses (Australian kingfishers)' and 'undulated grassparrakeets'.[31] The poem's joke, obvious but not trivial, is that the papas' and mammas' fashion preferences align with their natural species markers. The transparent complacency of recommending their own plumage allows Rossetti to take genial aim at everyday narcissism and didactic posturing. Inevitably the birds' self-admiration activates fashion's etymological link with 'faction', and the elders' disagreements shape the poem's trajectory.

The first presenter is a robin redbreast who, conceding the follies of courtship, affirms the appeal of 'a scarlet waistcoat' when it's time 'to plume and pair'. Rossetti's own pairing of male display with ornithological fact light-heartedly satirizes what is sometimes idealized as the 'visual, physical, erotic self'.[32] Next up is a female Jackdaw with a forward-looking fashion sense. Given her naturally gray nape, she predicts that 'Neat gray hoods will be in vogue'; and in keeping with her species' reputation for loquacity, she rambles on about her headgear:

> 'Glossy gray
> Setting close, yet setting easy,
>   Nothing fly-away;
> Suited to our misty mornings,
>   À la negligée.'

The 'close' repetition of 'setting' produces her dictum's 'easy' fit within the poetic line, thus neatly enacting its own message. Such self-referential mimicry is a staple feature of the poem, one that is both cause and result of Rossetti's constantly varied syntax within otherwise matched sexains. Each pronouncement is shaped to its speaker's taste and temperament. This particular stanza's playfulness is conspicuously heightened by the bi-lingual rhyme chain. With rising syllable counts and differing morphologies ('gray', 'fly-away', 'negligée'), the phrasing echoes Victorian fashion writers' over-reliance on 'à la' for its Parisian colouring.[33] Dresses have sleeves à la Bédouin or waist bands à la paysanne, and voguish items are generically 'à la mode'. The very essence of fashion, that is to say, is imitation. In this instance, Rossetti's use of 'à la negligée' carries a slightly deflating hint that the Jackdaw is over-concerned with a neglig-ible costume accessory.

At least, that's the opinion of the high-toned Cockatoos, who condescendingly demur that 'Hoods may do for mornings' but, invoking the decorum that defines nineteenth-century dressiness, recommend modified crowns for high-society 'evenings'. They coolly add that 'High head-dresses, curved like crescents' are what 'well-bred' ladies choose. Unaware that their 'salmon' and 'sulphur' crests are literally 'freaks of fashion'— received meanings of that term ranging from streaks of colour to whimsical oddities— the cockatoos regard their tufts as unambiguous signs of wealth, status, and privileged upbringing. Rossetti's timing of this bit of species snobbishness during breeding season makes the cockatoos' claim to social superiority patently absurd. Their discourtesy, in any case, belies the professed link between a perfect costume and actual refinement. To clinch this point, Rossetti brings on an ill-bred, well-dressed Peacock. Perhaps recalling the nuisance-quality of her brother's peacocks which, according to legend caused their interdiction ever after in Cheyne Walk leasing agreements,[34] she allows this gorgeously rude creature to scream that 'a train or tail' is 'essential' to one's self-display: 'Not too stiff, and not too frail; / These are best which rearrange as / Fans, and spread or trail'. Using a pair of intensifiers (tóo, tóo) to stiffen this injunction about stiffness, Rossetti arranges for the line's enjambment to trail mimetically into a fanned-out array of verbs: 'rear-range', 'spread', 'trail'. The ostentatious trains that entail such careful manipulation are indeed a feature of high fashion attire (and a mandated essential for certain occasions). At the same time the lines' carefully managed behaviour provides a subterranean hint that social position, like fashionable self-presentation, is a studied performance.

After treating their plumage as so many accent pieces (waistcoats, hoods, headdresses, trains), the birds discuss their colouration (white, yellow, peach, and black) with a naïve advocacy that Rossetti reduces to comedy. First comes a swan with 'An inimitable neck' and a smoothly extended syntax:

> 'After all, there's nothing sweeter
>   For the lawn or lake
> Than simple white, if fine and flaky
>   And absolutely free from speck.'

Rossetti has fun with this sweet fashion specialist, her graceful neck an illustrator's cliché and perhaps a whimsical allusion to the 'round reared neck' of the beloved in Gabriel's 'The House of Life'.[35] Mild flippancy is evident, too. The phrase 'fine and flaky', ordinarily associated with crumbling pie-crusts, serves as a light-hearted reminder of how quickly fine white muslin, batiste or 'lawn' fabrics become spotted, and how unreasonable it is to expect otherwise. Indeed, Rossetti's treatment of the speck-free ideal, delivered with a trio of conspicuously imperfect rhymes ('lake', 'flaky', 'speck'), provides acoustic resist-ance to the swan's notion of immaculate perfection. Nothing stays pristine.

Nonetheless, whether the garment is a white gown or, as Alexander Pope would have it, a 'new brocade', Victorian social critics invoked the zeugma structure that stains a woman's attire and her respectability. The more acidulous commentators like Eliza Lynn Linton, protected by anonymity, freely insinuated that a woman in a soiled gown might be assumed 'perhaps not quite without reason, to have lost something more than the mere perception of technical taste'.[36] Linton's opinions on fashion and the fashionable caused widespread consternation, especially her piece on 'The Girl of the Period' with its bitter characterization of the English girl's clothes-consciousness as evidence of a depraved fascination with the French *demi-monde*.[37] Rossetti's correspondence with women friends shows her discussing Linton's essays and assuming the author was a clergyman.[38] She would not, however, believe that the girls of her acquaintance—specif-ically 'the Madox Brown girls', one of whom would someday become her sister-in-law—were sullied by their stylishness.[39] Assurances on this matter came from none other than Ellen Heaton (the future attendee at the Guildhall fête for the Shah of Iran).[40] Spiteful and overweening condemnation of tempted innocence is hardly a sentiment Rossetti endorses. She is, after all, the author of *Goblin Market*, a poem deemed objectionable by some contemporaries for its tolerance of symbolically dishevelled clothing. As modern readers know, when Laura, a maiden as innocently lovely as 'a rush-imbedded swan', succumbs to goblin wiles, Rossetti does not punish her with absolute ruin.[41] She is saved by the self-sacrificing Lizzie, whose goblin violators, as the poem's illustrators since Housman all show, 'tore her gown and soiled her stocking'.[42] If one admits Linton's fashion essays into the deep background for 'Freaks of Fashion', it is possible to see the poem as an equally tempered rejection of editorializing virulence, a response that pushes Linton's brutal attitude and tonality 'securely into the past'.[43]

The swan's demure advocacy of 'simple' white elicits a flurry of counter-assertions, with the hilarious result that the colloquium itself, a living embodiment of fashion's 'rapid succession of styles', seems likely to yield only a rapid succession of opinions. The momentum speeds up as two species recommend their own colouration, once again trimming their phrases with French:

> 'Yellow,' hinted a Canary,
> 'Warmer, not less *distingué*.'
> 'Peach colour,' put in a Lory,
> 'Cannot look *outré*.'

The acoustic surprise of the '*distingué*' / '*outré*' rhyme captures the *outré* quality of fashion itself, while its chiming becomes a sound-figure for the birds' temporary agreement, their achieved harmony as they warm to the topic of their mutually bright tints. To demonstrate how (and how speedily) fads spread, Rossetti immediately shows the particoloured parrots parroting the others' colour-endorsements: "'All the colours are in fashion, / And are right," the Parrots say'.

Such indiscriminateness will not serve, however, and the Blackbird, a sternly elegant male, attempts a definitive 'lesson' by suggesting his beak's contrastive principle as the gold standard for fashion. Rossetti awards him a rare and pride-full Latin-based polysyllable (a specimen of what an earlier century might have labelled 'aureate diction'), and her poem's most extravagant rhyme:

> 'Very well. But do contrast
> Tints harmonious,'
> Piped a Blackbird, justly proud
> Of bill aurigerous;
> 'Half the world may learn a lesson
> As to that from us.'

Rossetti inflates the Blackbird's rigorous prescriptiveness with ramped-up alliteration ('piped', 'blackbird', 'proud', ' bill') of the kind that Symons—setting up a stylistic contrast between the Rossetti poets—associates with the 'polysyllabic and consonanted harmonies' of Gabriel Rossetti's verse.[44] The aural exuberance here, along with the varied mimicry throughout 'Freaks of Fashion', tells us how thoroughly Rossetti enjoys her own prosodic skill.

With the Blackbird's explicit bid for instructional stature, the poem threatens to become a male-to-male debate. His narcissistic 'lesson' is blatantly ignored by a long-legged Stork who attempts to provide the last word on the subject. In his view, stature (as opposed to vesture) is the crucial feature in male self-presentation:

> 'Aim at height and *chic*:
> Not high heels, they're common; somehow,
> Stilted legs, not thick,
> Nor yet thin:' he just glanced downward
> And snapped to his beak.

Irked and also poorly coordinated, he relies on mimetically choppy syntax to prohibit 'high heels' and clumsily 'stilted' phrasing to recommend his own 'somehow, / Stilted legs'. (Compare his off-kilter 'not thick, / Nor yet thin' with a smooth alternative, 'not thick / Not thin'.) Resentful that his stature can be counterfeited by 'common' emulators, he inadvertently exposes his anxiety about class blurrings. He's as haughty as the top-knotted Cockatoos but lacks the females' smug confidence in their breeding. In effect, Rossetti positions these would-be fashion elites as binary opposites: the females assume that the elegance of their attire effectively excludes imitators, but the male fears that a well-heeled interloper can pass for a gentleman. In touching on the possibility of convincing mimicry, these arbiters come inadvertently close, as did the Peacock, to exposing the 'performative nature of both dress and class'.[45] There's the additional irony that the Stork, while sneering at the common (presumably affordable) styles adopted by his social inferiors, is conducting *himself* in deplorably snappish fashion.

Indeed, watching this self-appointed arbiter of the 'common' behave so 'belligeratingly' (as Rossetti might have said),[46] the assembled mammas fear that he might become explicitly insulting. Discomposed at the likelihood of incivility, they become

> anxious
> Lest the next thing said
> Might prove less than quite judicious,
> Or even underbred.

Resorting to indirect discourse, Rossetti provides a delicately evasive subjunctive, 'might prove less than quite judicious'. (Blunter alternatives would have fit the metre, for example 'might prove shockingly malicious'.) Imagining these birds as too lady-like to condemn the Stork's deportment as bad form, but compelled to smooth over this moment of social *awk*wardness, Rossetti indulges in a deliciously improbable pun. She lets 'a mother auk' resume 'the broken thread of speech' with a placidly banal set of etiquette-writer's instructions:

> 'The main points, as it seems to me,
> We mothers have to teach,
>
> 'Are form and texture, elegance,
> An air reserved, sublime;

> The mode of wearing what we wear
>   With due regard to month and clime,
> But now, let's all compose ourselves,
>   It's almost breakfast-time.'

Such parodic summation, with its vapid generalization about 'form' (a term that can be 'promiscuously adapted to a multitude of meanings') and its inflated reference to the 'sublime' undermines the opinionatedness that has preceded it.[47] Although the auk intends to prevent disagreement and sweetly avoids Linton-esque disapproval, her feather-brained insipidity summons up Victorian ornithologist Richard Bowdler Sharpe's description of the Great Auk, as 'stupidly tame in its disposition'.[48] There's an inspired silliness in choosing an auk, a bird reported in the Victorian press to be extinct since 1844, to mediate a discussion of *la dernière mode* and permitting her the fashion writers' voguish word 'compose'. (Elegant costumes were invariably said to be 'composed' of satin *poult de soie* or some other luxury fabric.) The term is a reminder as well of Rossetti's own need at this juncture to compose a suitable conclusion that will sustain her poem's hilarity.

This she achieves by awarding the poem's last exuberant words to the nestlings:

> A hubbub, a squeak, a bustle!
>   Who cares to chatter or sing
> With delightful breakfast coming?
>   Yet they whisper under the wing:
> 'So we may wear whatever we like,
>   Anything, everything!'

The prominently re-iterated 'bustle!' signifies insouciant disregard of superabundant advice. Echoing the 'anything' that initially refers to the parents' perches, the *dernier cri* of the featherless young is giddy self-permission to wear 'Anything, everything' they please. Mild chaos is a familiar Rossettian topos. One of the *Sing-Song* nursery rhymes excitedly anticipates the toppling of a 'house of cards', while others, much like 'Goblin Market', propose a cautiously detached view of 'adult knowingness'.[49] Since 'Freaks of Fashion' depends on Rossetti's own alertness to the gloss of textures, the flutter of fabric, and the vibrancy of colour, it's pleasing to find her now bequeathing these pleasures (along with 'delightful breakfast') to her unfledged nestlings.

Considered as a pair, 'A Bird's-Eye View' and 'Freaks of Fashion' exhibit Rossetti's keen interest in the figure of the commentator, whether as bleak seer or opinionated expert. While neither poem relies on a sole party's interiority, the generic feature usually thought to make lyric poetry *lyric*, these arguably peripheral narratives engage in vigorous dialogue with the lyric core of Rossetti's oeuvre. 'A Bird's-Eye View', on the one hand, gives eccentric access to the mode Symons describes as 'essentially sombre', the mode Rossetti facetiously owns up to in 'The Months' when the 'youngest sister' arrives 'looking dim / And grim / With dismal ways'.[50] 'A Bird's-Eye View' metamorphoses this 'sister' into a raven who embodies Rossetti's lyric grimness and speaks against the poem's narrative drive into a future free of the past. 'Freaks of Fashion', on the other hand, engages in gleeful meta-poetic critique. With its *outré* rhyming, formal mimicry, and the auk's endorsement of 'reserve', the poem puts the birds' unchangeable 'nature' in tension with the playful quirkiness of art. Their colouration is genetic, to be sure, but their confusing it with the freedom of fashion provides a lively reminder that literary styles—including Rossetti's—are always a matter of choice. Even a poem like 'The Bourne', with its centrally Rossettian reticence and delicacy, depends on formally unobtrusive fashioning to achieve the quietness that is more than *mere* quietness. Together and in the full Rossettian context, 'A Bird's-Eye View' and 'Freaks of Fashion' suggest a cohesive aesthetic that allows 'unadorned' lyrics and flamboyant narratives to comment on each other.[51] Not only do these new-made bird stories extend the rambunctious legacy of 'Goblin Market', they encourage the use of 'quirky', 'cacophonous', and 'parodic' along with 'tactful', 'understated', and 'self-poised' in future treatments of Rossetti's range of style.

Notes

1. For 'Windflowers', see 'Twist me a crown of wind-flowers', in Christina Rossetti, *The Complete Poems of Christina Rossetti*, ed. R. W. Crump (London: Penguin, 2001), 235.
2. Jonathan Aaron, 'About Mark Strand', *Ploughshares* 21 (1995), 205.
3. George J. Worth, 'Poetry in *Macmillan's Magazine*: A Preliminary Report', *Victorian Periodicals Review* 23 (1990), 56–60.
4. Anonymous [Arthur Symons], 'Miss Rossetti's Poetry', *The London Quarterly Review* 136 (1887), 343; Rossetti, 'The Bourne', in *The Complete Poems of Christina Rossetti*, 136.
5. Anne Ferry, *By Design: Intention in Poetry* (Stanford: Stanford University Press, 2008) discusses function words with 'no inherent signifying capacity' (22).
6. James Longenbach, *The Resistance to Poetry* (Chicago: University of Chicago Press, 2004) theorizes line endings as 'a means of annotating syntax' (21).
7. Antony H. Harrison, *Christina Rossetti in Context* (Chapel Hill: University of North Carolina Press, 1988), examines the ten stanzas Rossetti excised from 'The Bourne' manuscript (9–10).
8. Symons, 'Miss Rossetti's Poetry', 338; Angela Leighton, 'On "the hearing ear": Some Sonnets of the Rossettis', *Victorian Poetry* 47 (2009), 506.
9. Anne Jamison, *Poetics en passant: Redefining the Relationship Between Victorian and Modern Poetry* (New York: Palgrave, 2009), 198; Isobel Armstrong, 'D. G. Rossetti and Christina Rossetti as Sonnet Writers', *Victorian Poetry* 48 (2010), 472.
10. Rossetti, various poems in *The Complete Poems of Christina Rossetti*, 31, 22, 45, 49.
11. Rossetti, various poems in *The Complete Poems of Christina Rossetti*, 33, 139, 27.
12. Rossetti, various poems in *The Complete Poems of Christina Rossetti*, 128, 321.
13. Rossetti, 'What does the donkey bray about?', in *The Complete Poems of Christina Rossetti*, 241; Rossetti, 'Hop-o'-my-thumb and little Jack Horner', in *The Complete Poems of Christina Rossetti*, 230.
14. Symons, 'Miss Rossetti's Poetry', 346; Rossetti, 'Freaks of Fashion', in *The Complete Poems of Christina Rossetti*, 321, previously appeared in Routledge's *Every Girl's Annual* (1878),

326–28, cited in Alison Chapman and Joanna Meacock, *A Rossetti Family Chronology* (New York: Palgrave: 2007), 299.

15. *The Sound of Poetry/The Poetry of Sound*, eds. Marjorie Perloff and Craig Dworkin (Chicago: University of Chicago Press, 2009), 2.

16. Rossetti, *The Letters of Christina Rossetti*, 4 vols., ed. Antony H. Harrison (Charlottesville: University of Virginia Press, 1997–2004), i. 31.

17. Jerome McGann, 'Literary History and Editorial Method: Poe and Antebellum America', *New Literary History* 40 (2009), 840; T. Hall Caine, *Recollections of Dante Gabriel Rossetti* (London: 1882), 284.

18. Maureen McLane, *Balladeering, Minstrelsy, and the Making of British Romantic Poetry* (Cambridge: Cambridge University Press, 2008), notes how sardonically 'The Twa Corbies' plays on the 'human susceptibility to the pathetic fallacy' (265).

19. Thomas Maitland [Robert Buchanan], 'The Fleshly School of Poetry: Mr. D. G. Rossetti', *Contemporary Review* 18 (1871), 346.

20. Rossetti, various poems in *The Complete Poems of Christina Rossetti*, 110, 30.

21. Edgar Allan Poe, 'The Raven', in *The Collected Tales and Poems of Edgar Allan Poe* (New York: Modern Library, 1992), 945.

22. Rossetti, 'The Hour and the Ghost', in *The Complete Poems of Christina Rossetti*, 34.

23. Rossetti, 'Monna Innominata 9', in *The Complete Poems of Christina Rossetti*, 298.

24. *Rossetti and His Circle* (London: Heinemann, 1922), plate 12.

25. For Rossetti's photos, see *Letters*, i. 176 and iii. frontispiece. Rossetti's 1863 gown is similar to that worn by the Princess of Wales in an 1862 carte-de-visite at the National Portrait Gallery, which can be seen online: <tinyurl.com/3ltx98v> (accessed 23 January 2012).

26. Christina Walkley, *The Way to Wear 'em: 150 Years of Punch on Fashion* (London: Owen 1985), 11.

27. Rossetti, *Letters*, ii. 236.

28. Rossetti, *Letters*, i. 432. Princess Alexandra's sister Dagmar was married to the future Tsar, Alexander III. Ellen Heaton was an early collector of Dante Gabriel Rossetti's work, including a half dozen watercolours now at the Tate Britain.

29. 'The Shah of Persia', *Illustrated London News*, 5 July 1873, 4.

30. See C. Willett Cunnington, *English Women's Clothing in the Nineteenth Century* (New York: Dover, 1990; 1st pub. 1937), 308, 321.

31. Rossetti, *Letters*, i. 70; William Michael Rossetti, *Dante Gabriel Rossetti; His Family Letters*, 2 vols. (London: Ellis, 1895), i. 251.

32. Brent Shannon, *The Cut of his Coat: Men, Dress, and Consumer Culture in Britain, 1860–1914* (Athens, Ohio: Ohio University Press, 2006), 54.

33. Rossetti makes no use of the tailoring idiom sometimes called 'dressmaker's French' (Cunnington, *English Women's Clothing*, 5). See *Punch*'s 1848 recommendation that 'Gowns…be of the elegant shape called trousseaux, or looped with attaché', quoted in Walkley, *The Way to Wear 'em*, 18.

34. William Michael Rossetti, *Dante Gabriel Rossetti*, i. 254.

35. Dante Gabriel Rossetti, Sonnet XXXI, in *Collected Poetry and Prose: Dante Gabriel Rossetti*, ed. Jerome McGann (New Haven: Yale University Press, 2003), 141.

36. Anon. [Elizabeth Lynn Linton], 'Pinchbeck', *The Saturday Review* 25 (1868), 676.

37. Linton, 'The Girl of the Period', *The Saturday Review* 25 (1868), 339–40. On the controversy Linton provoked, see Hilary Fraser, Stephanie Green, and Judith Johnston, *Gender and the Victorian Periodical* (Cambridge: Cambridge University Press, 2003), 21, 26–27.

38. Rossetti, *Letters*, i. 313.
39. Lucy Madox Brown married William Michael Rossetti in 1874.
40. *Letters*, i. 312.
41. Rossetti, *Goblin Market, in The Complete Poems of Christina Rossetti*, 7. On Laura's rescue, see Jill Rappaport, 'The Price of Redemption in "Goblin Market"', *Studies in English Literature 1500–1900* vol. 50 (2010), 853–875.
42. For Lawrence Housman's illustration, see Lorraine Janzen Kooistra, *Christina Rossetti and Illustration: A Publishing History* (Athens, Ohio: Ohio University Press, 2002), 89.
43. Carolyn Williams, *Gilbert and Sullivan: Gender, Genre, Parody* (New York: Columbia University Press, 2011), xiv, and general principles of parody (6–7).
44. Symons, 'Miss Rossetti's Poetry', 338.
45. Shannon, *Cut,* 159.
46. Rossetti, *Letters*, ii. 283.
47. Angela Leighton, *On Form: Poetry, Aestheticism, and the Legacy of a Word* (Oxford: Oxford University Press, 2007), 243.
48. Richard Bowdler Sharpe, the ornithologist for the British Museum, believed that the Great Auk's disposition 'alone account[ed] for its rapid extermination'; see his *A Hand-book to the Birds of Great Britain*, 4 vols. (London, Allen, 1894), iv. 113, or online at [archive.org/details/handbookgbbirds04sharrich]
49. Constance W. Hassett, *Christina Rossetti: The Patience of Style* (Charlottesville, University of Virginia Press, 2005), 128–29, 135.
50. Symons, 'Miss Rossetti's Poetry', 341; Rossetti, 'The Months: A Pageant', in The *Complete Poems of Christina Rossetti*, 280.
51. Symons, 'Miss Rossetti's Poetry', 338.

SELECT BIBLIOGRAPHY

Chapman, Alison, and Meacock, Joanna, *A Rossetti Family Chronology* (New York: Palgrave: 2007).
Ferry, Anne, *By Design: Intention in Poetry* (Stanford: Stanford University Press, 2008).
Harrison, Antony H., *Christina Rossetti in Context* (Chapel Hill: University of North Carolina Press, 1988).
Hassett, Constance W., *Christina Rossetti: The Patience of Style* (Charlottesville: University of Virginia Press, 2005).
Jamison, Anne, *Poetics en passant: Redefining the Relationship Between Victorian and Modern Poetry* (New York: Palgrave, 2009).
Kooistra, Lorraine Janzen, *Christina Rossetti and Illustration: A Publishing History* (Athens: Ohio University Press, 2002).
Leighton, Angela, *On Form: Poetry, Aestheticism, and the Legacy of a Word* (Oxford: Oxford University Press, 2007).
Longenbach, James, *The Resistance to Poetry* (Chicago: University of Chicago Press, 2004).
McLane, Maureen N., *Balladeering, Minstrelsy, and the Making of British Romantic Poetry* (Cambridge: Cambridge University Press, 2008).
Perloff, Marjorie, and Dworkin, Craig (eds.), *The Sound of Poetry/The Poetry of Sound* (Chicago: University of Chicago Press, 2009).

Rossetti, Christina, *The Complete Poems of Christina Rossetti*, ed. R. W. Crump (London: Penguin, 2001).

Rossetti, Christina, *The Letters of Christina Rossetti*, 4 vols., ed. Antony H. Harrison, (Charlottesville: University of Virginia Press, 1997–2004).

Rossetti, Dante Gabriel, *Collected Poetry and Prose: Dante Gabriel Rossetti*, ed. Jerome McGann (New Haven: Yale University Press, 2003).

Williams, Carolyn, *Gilbert and Sullivan: Gender, Genre, Parody* (New York: Columbia University Press, 2011).

CHAPTER 28

WILLIAM BARNES: VIEWS OF FIELD LABOUR IN *POEMS OF RURAL LIFE*

MARCUS WAITHE

WITH the exception of Christopher Ricks, who counts William Barnes among those Victorian poets who possessed 'true voices of feeling', modern critics have responded nervously to the emotional strain in *Poems of Rural Life*.[1] Andrew Motion admits that Barnes is 'a poet who needs some apologies', explaining that 'His religious conviction, for instance, can seem sentimental and smug'.[2] In the early years of revived interest in Barnes, Paul Zeitlow complained that his 'idealized countryside often becomes sentimental',[3] citing the objection that Barnes never 'views rural life from the vantage ground of urban sophistication on which both he and his audience live'.[4] I shall return to the second half of this observation, especially as it concerns an absence of 'contrast *within the poem*';[5] but Zeitlow's claim is at variance with the 'feeling' of several poems collected in the first edition of *Poems of Rural Life in the Dorset Dialect* (1844).[6] 'Eclogue:—The Common A-took In' wastes no time in confronting the 'ideal' with a vivid evocation of the social harm wrought by enclosure.[7] Even when the harvest is taken in, the customs described bear the imprint, or folk memory, of what might go wrong. 'A Zong ov Harvest Huome' sings gratitude to the harvesters, but also musters the insurance of a charm against crop failure.[8] And while that generic past of 'Fat beef an' puddèn' known as 'merry England' is never far away, Barnes's poetry can be markedly unsentimental.[9] In 'Vellen the Tree', the practical and realist outlook of the phlegmatic countryman overcomes any maundering feeling for severed roots, for the loss of a place 'Wher the mowers did goo to ther drink, an' did lie'.[10] Zeitlow's analysis makes more sense if we restrict its scope to one crucial feature of these rural poems: their insistent idealization of the lived experience of labour in the fields. It is with this particular variety of rural 'feeling' that my essay is concerned.

While Zeitlow's emphasis on idyllic conditions applies more accurately to the representation of field labour, it does not follow that the scope for comparison with 'urban sophistication' is diminished. A lack of 'contrast' *within* the poem need not preclude 'vantage ground'. Comparison can be generated just as well at the point of composition or reception. Barnes's poems are peculiarly adapted to the generation of such 'implied' discrepancies. This is because they celebrate a form of labour that is qualitatively distinct from the poetic effort that brought them into being. There is a biographical context for this 'discrepancy' in the remark of Barnes's daughter that, 'much as he loved the country and country-folk he did not see in it the proper sphere of his life's labour'.[11] I will explore the awkward implication of these facts for a man who published an extended treatise on the meaning of work in *Views of Labour and Gold* (1859),[12] and queried the notion 'that every change from the plough towards the desk…is an onward step', but did not supply an accompanying explanation of literary labour, or explain how an idealization of reaping and threshing might reflect on those whose labours and lots were unrelated to the rural economy.[13] This awkwardness applies especially to the 'views' afforded by Barnes's poetry, which validate the spectacle of field labour, yet grant no defensible 'viewing position' from which poet or audience can contemplate the scene without actually joining the working party.

* * *

Barnes's thinking about labour did not develop in isolation. The period's 'gospel of work' informs a conventional message about constancy of vocation in all weathers, in 'The Shep'erd Buoy'.[14] In 'Work and Wait', the Calvinist spirit of deferred satisfaction is the guiding force: '"work and wait"', we are told, 'will win the day'.[15] Unthinking 'busyness' is the dominant spirit in other poems. Barnes promotes an analogy between human industry and the 'work' of nature, such that Skimpolian taunts about obtrusive animal 'confectioners' are a distant prospect.[16] In 'The Woodlands' attention is directed to 'The twitt'ren birds a-buildèn roun'.[17] In 'The Sky A-Clearèn', there are 'busy birds upon the wing',[18] and in 'Night A-Zettèn In', a contrast is set up between the well-earned leisure of the evening, and the 'spiders, roun' the flower-stä'ks', that 'Ha' cobwebs eet to spin, O'.[19] Although derived from Virgil,[20] the more immediate source for this motif was the world of seventeenth-century Dissent: notably, Isaac Watts's homily to the 'busy bee' in *Divine Songs* (1715).[21] In Barnes's poems, such sentiments complement another great legacy of the revival in Puritan literature: the world-making rationale of *Robinson Crusoe* (1719), in which habitable reality is constituted from a series of manual tasks that confer sovereignty on the worker-owner. The 'husband' in 'Work and Wait' boasts accordingly: 'My new-built house's brick-red side / A few years since was clay unfound; / My reeden roof, outslanting wide, / Was yet in seed, unsprung from ground'. The legitimacy of this home is directly linked to the effort expended in its fashioning.

The difference between such visions and those of Watts is that Barnes identifies no inertia or sloth to overcome, and no environmental rift: the human and animal inhabitants of this landscape feel the pull of work as a natural impulse, and the working goes together with the singing. While the house is built and 'found' by human acts, its provenance is organic: its origin is in 'seed' and vegetable growth. Barnes is not guilty of displacing labour from the rural scene, but the work that takes centre stage is itself idealized, such that a figure resembling Holman Hunt's *Hireling Shepherd*—listless, morally dubious, and disenfranchised—is inconceivable.[22] In its more radical forms, Barnes's 'cottage economy'[23] sets him against 'excessive division of labour'.[24] He is equally critical of the genteel prejudice that encourages the privileged classes to shun labour as something inherently demeaning. Reporting the case of the country bred 'young lady' who declared in fine weather, "'I know nothing of haymaking:'", he laments an 'affecting ignorance of what has been the main wealth of England from the time of the old Britons to our own'.[25] The obvious source for Barnes's objection to 'a truly idle class' is Carlyle.[26] There are signs, too, of Ruskinian influence in his 'Greek' emphasis on combining agriculture with statecraft.[27] Apart from praising Homer, Socrates, and Hesiod, Barnes stakes out more singular cultural preferences by praising 'a Saxon dialogue' that granted farming 'the headship of all worldly crafts'.[28]

It is possible in this way to trace the moral content of Barnes's work to a broad arena of Victorian thought about 'work ethics'. What is less familiar, and what warrants special attention, is Barnes's approach to dramatizing and adapting these ideas in his poetry. He does not belong to that neo-Classical school of pastoralism that idealizes labour by removing it from the landscape.[29] Nor is it true that Barnes's labourers are 'the upper class in lower-class drag', as Barry Reay has claimed of 'George Stubbs's late eighteenth-century imagery of *Haymakers* ... and *Reapers*'.[30] Barnes's field workers are not simple proxies for the desires of an audience. Rather, the idealization lies with the labour component. A Pelagian theology holds temporary sway, such that labour is a guarantor and source of happiness.

The centrality of field labour to this society is determined by its isolation from the rest of the world. It is a 'folkloric' existence, in which the pattern of life is determined by the shape of the year.[31] The resulting 'seasons of labour' dictate wealth and priorities, to the exclusion of alternatives that rely on commerce with strangers. The poems' focus on proximity and circularity is a token of this existence. In 'Vellen the Tree', we are told familiarly that the object of the day's labour was 'the girt elem tree out in little huome groun'. Its close, relational, quality guarantees the unalienating nature of the task. Ground is the place of work, and the root of sustenance,[32] but it is also 'huome', a quasi-mystical site of belonging and fellowship. When the eponymous heroine of 'The Milk-Mâid o' the Farm' tells us, 'I be so happy out in groun', she expresses a kind of earth-belonging that binds labour and the immediate outside of 'groun' into an experience of well-being normally reserved for the comforts of the hearth-place.[33] Just as the milkmaid gathers the benefits of self-sufficiency through happiness, so the speaker of 'The Shepherd o' the Farm' fuses wholesome pride with a symbol of his labour in the phrase: 'An' be so proud a-rovèn round / Wi' my long crook'.[34] Barnes believed that this kind of self-contained, rural society, fostered self-respect and independence: '"You can't take a pride in a thing which you don't make," he said.'[35] The milkmaid acts accordingly in processing the yield of her work as cheese. A monarchical appendage is in several cases the sign of an overbrimming work-pride: the 'long whip' of 'The Carter' is likened, with Chaucerian descriptive mischief, to 'a sceptre',[36] and in the 'Milk-Mâid' and 'Shepherd' poems, the speakers conjure a crown. 'The Best Man in the Vield' offers a variation on this scenario. In that poem, the same work-pride is discussed, but it is infused with a competitive spirit,[37] such that the actors exchange rival accounts of their individual working prowess: 'Ya grinnèn fool! I warnd I'd zet thee blowèn, / If thee wast wi' me var a dae a-mowèn.'[38] Working becomes a kind of fighting in the challenge, 'Come on then, Samel, let's jist have oone bout'. And yet we are never left in any doubt that the yields of this activity are communal, and that the forms of pride are rooted in self-respect rather than 'mammon-worship'.[39]

These poems indulge the conceit that they are occasional, that the changing seasons provide a natural premise for poetic expression, whether working or festive. The first collection derives its structural logic from those poetic 'cycles of the year' that reach back through Keble's *The Christian Year* (1827), Thomson's *The Seasons* (1730), and Spenser's *The Shepheardes Calendar* (1579). Poems devoted to festivals and seasonal tasks are arranged according to their association with 'Spring', 'Summer', 'Fall', or 'Winter'. In 'Summer', Barnes answers the challenge of John Clare's 'Haymaking',[40] with 'Hây-Miakèn'[41] and 'Hây-Carrèn', two poems dedicated to the combination of sociality and seasonality represented by that task.[42] They are joined by 'The Meäd A-Mow'd'[43] and 'Thatchèn O' the Rick',[44] each of them formally related to the genre of the work-song. In Fall, 'A Zong Ov Harvest Huome' installs the relation between labour and season as a functional absence: 'The groun' is clear', the poet writes, 'Ther's nar a ear / O' stannen carn a-left out now'. And in 'Out A-Nuttèn', a poem redolent of Clare and Wordsworth, a rural voice tells how 'Laste wik, when we'd a-hal'd the crops, / We went a-nuttèn out in copse'.[45] The priority of the action over the intent is signalled by the careful notation of equipment and process: 'Wi' nuttèn-bags to bring huome vull, / An beaky nuttèn-crooks to pull / The bushes down'. The same kind of detail accumulates in 'Tiakèn in Apples': 'We took the apples in laste wik, / An' got zome proper yachèn backs, / A-stoopèn down al day to pick / 'Em al up into mäens an' zacks'.[46] 'Keepèn up o' Chris'mas' reminds us that 'Winter' is devoted to festive activity;[47] but Barnes ensures that the work of the season is represented by 'The Carter', who tells us 'I da bring in vuzz vrom down, / An' I da goo var wood to copse'.

Barnes happily combines this stress on customary duration with temporal precision. Within the scope of one title, 'Wik's End in Zummer, in the Wold Vo'ke's Time', three separate measures of time are invoked: the week, the season, and a mythic yesteryear.[48] The information that a particular task was performed 'Laste wik' ('Out A-Nuttèn') supplies a feeling of immediacy, but that sense is augmented by a definite, stage-by-stage detailing of the labour that goes beyond the compass of one moment. Barnes details the tools used, and the effects on the body, revealing the materiality and texture of the task. Amidst the recurrence of labour and season, there emerges a quality of stability, the sense of a 'steady-state' world, consisting of eternal types who enlarge, as they live within, its poetic time-scheme. A curious routine of self-identification reinforces the effect: 'I BE the milk-mâid o' the farm' declares Barnes's untroubled Tess; 'I BE the Shepherd o' the farm:', proclaims his carefree Gabriel Oak. While the Dorsetshire form of the verb emphasizes the sense that this is a question not of employment, but of *being* in a role and an environment, the combination of definite article and occupation evokes a pointed universal. There will always be such a person, we infer. And yet there is humane specificity in the timing, in the first-person voice, and the insistence on 'the farm', rather than 'a farm'.

The impression of dependable human presences is reinforced by our sudden immersion in the naming economy of 'the farm'. Characters are not introduced, but referred to familiarly by first names, such as 'Sam' or 'Poll', or more intimately still, as familial relations, such as 'uncle'.[49] Just as the poems reverse the de-skilling lamented by William Cobbett in *Cottage Economy* (1821), so they re-integrate the rural community he feared was becoming atomized as farmers ceased to entertain their labourers at table.[50] The poetry, in other words, is not simply a dramatization of Barnes's discursive 'view', but in itself a process of restoration, a 'showing' as well as a 'telling'. This is a working world small enough to make spare use of first names. Working parties do not consist of strangers: they are bound, instead, by relationships that precede contractual employment.

* * *

These recommendations of labour as a source of joy, to be executed manually, communally, and within the limits of season and diurnal span, prompt the difficult question of where this leaves the reader who lives elsewhere, and the poet, whose labour is not represented. The query would be less pressing were it not for the fact that Barnes's poems carry the assumption that anyone listening must be a villager of some sort. At best, the reader becomes an honorary or an accidental insider. At worst, we are imposters, and the misplaced familiarity is merely a polite mechanism for keeping the intruder at bay. The poetic world of Dorsetshire not only avoids the outside view, but hardly registers the possibility of 'an elsewhere' from which alien goods, processes, or ideas, might come. We develop the sense of an enclosed and exclusive community that avoids any outward transaction with the reader.

In his analysis of Wordsworth's 'The Solitary Reaper', J. H. Prynne alludes to the 'georgic' 'subtype' of pastoral.[51] This, he suggests, relies on 'a recognised gap between viewer and viewed (in complexity of consciousness, urban/rural origins and status, social class and occupational difference)'.[52] It is remarkable that Barnes offers no such proxy for the reader in the artificial persona of poet or external observer, nor any textual mechanism for gaining a purchase on this poetic world. The lack of a Wordsworthian poet in the landscape heightens the sense that these labours are sufficient to themselves. To borrow Zeitlow's terms, there is no 'radical discontinuity experienced by the speaker' in Barnes's work.[53] His mowers and haymakers are not conscious of being viewed: they are simply going about their business, and the only voices we hear are those enrolled in the task. There is no-one to ask them questions, no-one to deliver an official report on their prowess or to dispense condescension. Nor are they framed as poignant symbols of a fading ideal. This contrasts with better-known versions of pastoral, such as Marvell's or Arnold's. In the work of both poets, the figure of the mower assumes a symbolic quality that depends on the sense of being viewed from without, and of being looked back upon.[54] Barnes's poetry realizes the self-sufficiency and narrative of seasonal labour so fully that we lose the longer view. His poetic folk inhabit 'a natural scheme benignly supportive of primal tillage and husbandry', but there is no gap *within* the poem that needs to be stabilized.[55]

Annihilation of the poetic self is the dominant effect, producing a series of views on labour without any defined sense of a 'viewer' who is not part of the community being observed. The result is a kind of participant admiration, typified by the rapt account of working prowess and strength in 'Hây-Carrèn'. A voice, which must be present in the scene, dwells on how 'The luoaders, strong o' yarm, da stan'', and how they are equipped 'Wi' skill to build the luoad upright'. Such viewing is itself transformed into activity. This is evident first in the action of emotion: the sight, we are told, 'da stir my heart'. That, in turn, builds capacity, in 'My blood da rin so brisk an' warm, / An' put sich strangth it*hin* my yarm', and finally desire, expressed in the confession 'That I da long to toss a pick / A-pitchèn ar a-miakèn rick'. Even amidst the passive reverie of a landscape piece, such as 'Carn A-Turnèn Yoller', a peculiar kind of looking is repeated across the stanzas—'Let I look down upon a groun''[56]—that becomes a memory and a warm fantasy of action in the thought that ''Tis merry when the brawny men / Da come to reap it down'.[57]

As the gap between admiration and personal involvement narrows, the sense of mediation between audiences and kinds of work is lost. Even 'The 'Lotments', which so vividly evokes the grim prospect of stone-breaking, subsides into a restorative fantasy of the family harmony conferred by wholesome labour relations with 'groun', 'what wi' dungèn, diggèn up, an' zeedèn'.[58] In those poems that afford 'views' of communal labour, there is no mechanism for admitting the world-weary perspective of the audience. When intrusion occurs, the effect is to immunize rather than to violate the workings of the rural world. The snake in the grass is known as a menace, but its casual slaying is more diversion than trial: 'Wher Sam da zee the spekled sniake / An' try to kill en wi' his riake'.[59] The effect in many poems is one of total immersion in an ideal existence, where mundane acts of labour acquire an Edenic glow, and where the attendant voices, whether narrative or dramatic, are those of the labourers themselves.

If the lack of a 'place to stand' puts the audience in an awkward position, the predicament of the poet is more challenging still. Sue Edney has recently suggested that Barnes's intense concern with locality was 'a means of dealing with the pressures of *not* being any of the characters he portrays'.[60] This pressure of '*not* being' had its basis, not in Barnes's childhood—he came from a farming family and grew up in the Vale of Blackmore—but in the professional circumstances of his adult life. When Barnes evoked the life of the field labourer, he was looking back into his family history, not peering across an intractable class barrier. As Motion notes, 'his father John described himself in a Population Return compiled during the year of William's birth as a "labourer in husbandry"'.[61] It would be equally mistaken to categorize Barnes as a 'peasant poet'.[62] Clare's reputation and compositional procedure relied on a link between 'books' and 'toiling in the fields';[63] in Barnes, that link is severed. Though the language of his poems drew stubborn authenticity from his 'native speech', no equivalent competency underwrote his poetic views of reaping and threshing. The education and connections fostered by his career as a schoolmaster, and then as a parish priest, meant that he was no longer a 'native' in the occupational sense. He replaced participation in field labour with sympathetic views of it, or with the recreational, or synthetic, labour of threshing in his schoolyard garden.[64]

And yet Edney's reference to 'pressures' suggests a position more exposed than simple yearning or nostalgia. Barnes's mother worried that her small and delicate child had hands that 'were quite unfitted for the manual labour of a farm'.[65] This dark presage was accompanied by an indication of providential exemption: 'The village oracles', we learn, 'comforted her' with the prophecy that '"he'll get his living by learning-books and such like"'.[66] The reassurance in this case is complicated. Hands 'unfitted' in this way entail exile from the farming 'home place'. They signify an expulsion, or at least an anecdotal rationalization of those inclinations recorded by Baxter's observation that 'The office work at Mr. Dashwood's was on the whole more congenial to him than the labour of the farm'.[67] Though Barnes's poems are remarkable for the extent to which they avoid this disjunction, an important exception is 'The Young Rhymer Snubbed'.[68] In that short work, we glimpse the predicament of one whose 'small hands' neither qualify him for farm work, nor yield the income of professional employment. Published in the *Dorset County Chronicle* in 1859, and then added to the third collection of *Poems of Rural Life in the Dorset Dialect* in its second edition (1864), the poem offers a rare challenge to the impression that Barnes felt no tension between the celebration of rural labours and rural pleasures. 'To meäke up rhymes' is first presented as a habit of mind, an uncontroversial pastime. A 'snub' follows that indicates several kinds of concern about the dubious status of rhyming as working, and perhaps also the feigning or fibbing associated with rhetorical fabrication. Crucially, such complaints issue from inside the very rural idyll that the poems celebrate. A first sardonic echo, '"You meäke up rhyme!"', quibbles with the claims of the creative faculty, and is uttered by the generalized voice of 'vo'k'. The word refers both to 'the people I know' and 'the people in my world', the rural folk whose horizons are limited by the imperatives of subsistence farming. The subsequent stanzas include other figures of homely defiance: the father of no great 'learnèn', who 'Zaid rhymèn wer a treäde but vew got fat in', and the mother who 'zaid she'd sooner hear me stammer / Than gauk about a-gabblèn rhymes an' Latin'. The 'vo'k' of the first stanza resume their case: there may be a market in the larger world, but 'Could you write fine enough to please a squire?' At the end of the stanza, the reduction of the gratuitous to the ruinous culminates in the pathological: there is no 'cure' for rhyming, the poet admits. He thereby accepts the logic of the criticism, allowing himself only a mildly satiric flourish, in the assurance that if there were a cure, 'I'm sure I'd try it'. His defence, such as it is, resides in a reassertion of the gratuitous. The 'bleäme' comes from family and 'vo'k', but also from within, through an internalization of arguments yoked to the thought that rhyme 'do keep me poor'.

Barnes was not then oblivious to the conflict between the kind of 'making' recognized by the people of the countryside, and the poet's way of 'meäkèn rhymes'. That conflict is all the keener because the poet-speaker describes his predicament in dialect. Dialect forms both the fabric of the poetry and a generalized cultural imprint for what 'vo'k zaid'. The 'losèn geäme' of poetry has much in common with the 'losèn geäme' of local speech, but here the two causes seem to be opposed. This goes to the heart of Barnes's dilemma. As a dialect poet, he is a literary alien at home, and the epitome of the culture that rejects him abroad. He cannot step away, into the world of the squire; but neither is he free to lend a hand in the fields.

Barnes relieves this almost unbearable pressure by closing the gap between the labour he portrays and the position of the poet and audience. One method operates on the level of language, and applies to the forms of alienation experienced by readers unfamiliar with Dorsetshire speech. Barnes eventually heeded calls for him to write in standard English; but he also revised the dialect poems across successive editions, choosing words and spellings that he believed would improve comprehension.[69] The result in one poem is a striking mitigation of his original insistence on a voice sealed off from exterior description. 'I be the Milk-Mâid o' the Farm' becomes 'O Poll's the milk-maïd o' the farm!'[70] It is not that the audience suddenly has somewhere to stand—the problems of labour and the naming community still apply—but it is striking that revisions aimed at increasing intelligibility should entail a substitution of direct speech for third-person narrative. It is tempting to think that the pressure to supply a vantage point became overwhelming, and that Barnes succumbed to it by installing a descriptive voice, a source of authority not grammatically bounded by the rural environment.

It might be argued that Barnes responded to anxieties about the role of poetry in portraying labour by casting the poet as a co-worker. Kurt Heinzelman suggests a source for this conceit in Dryden's sleight of hand as a translator of Virgil's *Georgics*: Dryden, he argues, converts a textually ambiguous appeal to Caesar's concern for 'rustics' into an affirmation of 'the vital link between farmer and writer'.[71] Barnes conflated 'the Poet's and the Ploughman's Cares' by healing the rift between poetic language and the sealed rural economy of work.[72] His poetry comes not from the mouth of the poet, or by licence of the muse, but from within the rural community and indeed the working process itself. Work-songs achieve this by casting poetry and labour as mutually sustaining enterprises. Instead of an apostrophizing device, the repeated 'O', in 'Wheat',[73] and 'The Meäd A-Mow'd', marks time in the manner of an unaccompanied folksong or shanty: 'Droo hày in cock, O; / We al da vlock, O, / Along our road vrom the meäd a-mow'd'.[74] This is not just a poem about field work; its rhythms set time for the swishing action of the scythe, and so it becomes a practical action in its own right. A similar marking effect is achieved by Barnes's many strong end-rhymed couplets. All the while, as Prynne notes, a capacity for song indicates 'having breath to spare', a settling into work not 'totally subdued by its demands on stamina'.[75] Song acquires an association with necessity through this employment in 'work', and such work transcends mere subsistence through its generation of a tuneful 'surplus'.

The tradition of pastoral poetry contains a precedent for the reconciliation of work and poetry. Just as the shepherds of that genre perform their parts in 'singing' matches, so Barnes adds a Blakean touch in 'Thatchèn o' the Rick' when he describes how a symbol of the pastoral scene is transformed into an instrument of song:[76] 'Ar zot a-cuttèn, wi' a knife, / Dry eltrot roots to miake a fife'.[77] The reverie of contentment to which this transformation leads is repeated in 'The Shepherd o' the Farm', whose speaker develops the rhythm of a repeated conjunction:

> An' wi' my zong, an wi' my fife,
> An' wi' my hut o' turf an' hurdles,
> I wou'den channge my shepherd's life
> To be a-maide a king o' wordless.

'Zong' becomes an integral part of the 'shepherd's life', more a channel for acts than a setting for speech.

Dialect, apart from presenting an analogy with the lost cause of field labour, promises a coming to terms with the very qualities of manual exertion that Barnes's mother found lacking in his small hands. Much of the Anglo-Saxon vocabulary that Barnes substituted for Latinate forms entailed a withdrawal from abstraction into a manual register. For instance, the standard term 'language' finds its earthy equivalent in 'speech-craft'.[78] In *Views of Labour and Gold*, Barnes notes that the book began as a course of lectures, but since then he had 'wrought it up into a rather fuller and more exact shape'.[79] Evidently, this is not simply a translation from one idiom into another: it deals also with values, with a restoration of language to the realm of craft, as a 'wrought' form that is also a shape in the world. Such effects do not operate only at the level of diction. Barnes considered the West Saxon of Dorsetshire a 'purer' relic than anything in the linguistic cargo of standard English.[80] In 'The Milk-Mâid o' the Farm', the modal forms of the dialect infuse verbs of action with an insistent 'doing'. While the milkmaid 'Da skim' the yellow cream, the shepherd reports that 'zome / da catch the sheep, and zome / Da mark ther zides wi' miaster's mark'. Barnes also employs 'syllabic augment' in the perfect participle of verbs, explained in his 'Dissertation' as the remnant of the '*ge*' in German, and in Anglo-Saxon, the '*ge* or *a*'.[81] One interpretation of such 'remnants' is that they are by definition obsolete. But Barnes restores them to functionality by suspending them in a medium of rhythmic utterance:

> I BE the Shepherd o' the farm:
> An' be so proud a-rovèn round
> Wi' my long crook a-*thi*rt my yarm,
> As ef I wer a king a-crown'd.

The 'obsolete' prefixes in 'a-rovèn', 'a-*thirt*' and 'a-crowned' are redeemed by their role within the iambic patterning. Song, and dialect, become an integrated doing, and poetry stakes its claim to a working role in the rural world.

Barnes prepares the ground for this kind of experiment, but he stops short of William Morris's re-description of the poet as a craftsman, and Gerard Manley Hopkins's resolution to hammer the language of revived Saxonism in a 'random grim forge'.[82] Though Hopkins was an admirer of Barnes, the older poet's work was less susceptible to favourable comparison with the skill of artisanship or the 'honest' toil of field labour.[83] Even when an affinity emerges between mowing or thatching and 'song' in Barnes's work, one wonders whether it actually improves the position of the modern 'clever head' or deracinated poet when the conditions are so specific and so devoid of outward application.[84] Efforts to synthesize the linguistic process of the poem with its working content do not fully integrate the poet, because they only ever re-describe the poetic function in terms amenable to the world of Dorsetshire. When, in 'Hây-Maikèn', we hear of how 'Ther tongues da rin wi' joke an' tiale', the narrative impulse seems, like these views on labour, sealed off from external reference.[85] The effect, potentially, is to rob the modern poet of a role. Rural labours are made to 'speak for themselves', and no attempt is made to account for the gap between subject matter and the literary process of production.

* * *

This incommensurability is not all encompassing. We feel none of the paranoia of Clare's snipe, about whose rural peace 'fear encamps', and certainly the poems are equipped to transmit an infectious joy.[86] But I want to suggest that Zeitlow is wrong to highlight an absence of 'contrast'. While a sealed and self-referential quality is indeed a feature of the scenes and scenarios that Barnes conjures, this does not entail a 'sentimental' shutting down of conflict. Rather, the arena of conflict is displaced away from the viewed labour process, so that it is felt instead at the point of reception. Readers confront in these poems differences of dialect and action; but the experience does not, and cannot, confer citizenship of the fields. Far from being compromised by sentimentality, or by the idealized field-labour that generates their cyclical and self-enclosed time-scheme, Barnes's rural poems depend for effect on their vulnerability. When confronted with the spectacle of a joyful, liberating, and communal pursuit, the unlicensed viewer is liable to feel anxious yearning for a defensible place to stand and admire, either within the world of the poem, or from without.

Denying this to the viewer—and denying the poetic persona an equivalently official position—induces anxiety in proportion to the extent that joy and community are projected internally. This paucity of reference to the exterior world is the active consequence of the poems' uncompromising passivity. To the extent that they enact a contrast of the kind Zeitlow finds lacking, it is the poet and the reader who perpetrate an unregistered intrusion. Reading these poems resembles a sacrificial act. When we assume a viewing position on a world that will not admit us, the effect is not neutral. The world we know, and the author-function of the poet, are obliterated in favour of the poem-world's integrity of time and season and work. With no mediator of happiness to absorb the pressure of the unhappy contrast, we take that burden on ourselves.

In utopian fiction, a proxy for the reader is usually expelled from the 'good place' at the close of the narrative. The resulting frustration may prompt a resolution to close the gap between utopian happiness and the imperfect world beyond.[87] For the reader of pastoral poetry, the course of action is less obvious. We may be able to discharge our anxieties by blaming the corrupt or cynical observer; we might even believe that, given the chance, we would integrate more fully with this rural way of life. But Barnes neither expels us nor lets us in; he neither represents our world, nor recommends the poetic Dorsetshire as an alternative. It is the very vulnerability of this gentle haven that determines its uncompromising strength. Because it has not entered into self-consciousness, it does not know what is coming. It is the reader who bears the weight of that knowledge, and the reader who puzzles over the predicament of a viewer who is afforded no position from which to view.

NOTES

1. Christopher Ricks in *The New Oxford Anthology of Victorian Verse*, ed. Christopher Ricks (Oxford: Oxford University Press, 1987), xxx.
2. Andrew Motion, 'Introduction' to *William Barnes: Poems Selected by Andrew Motion* (London: Faber and Faber, 2007), xix.
3. Paul Zeitlow, 'Thomas Hardy and William Barnes: Two Dorset Poets', *PMLA*, 84 (1969), 295.
4. Zeitlow, 'Thomas Hardy and William Barnes', 294.
5. Zeitlow, 'Thomas Hardy and William Barnes', 294.
6. William Barnes, *Poems of Rural Life, in the Dorset Dialect: with a Dissertation and Glossary* (London: John Russell Smith, 1844). All quotations are from the first edition, unless otherwise stated.
7. Barnes, 'Eclogue:—The Common A-took In', in *Poems of Rural Life*, 172–175. Cf. land clearance and pitiless labour in 'a-cracken stuones / Upon the road', in 'Eclogue. The 'Lotments', *Poems of Rural Life*, 74.
8. Barnes, 'A Zong ov Harvest Huome', in *Poems of Rural Life*, 148: 'An' mid noo harm o' vire ar starm / Beval the farmer ar his carn;'
9. Barnes, 'Harvest Home. *The Vust Piart. The Supper*', in *Poems of Rural Life*, 144.
10. '[T]he girt elem tree', we are blankly informed, 'Wer a-stannen this marnen, an' now's a-cut down', Barnes, *Poems of Rural Life*, 58.
11. Lucy Baxter, *The Life of William Barnes: Poet and Philologist* (London: Macmillan, 1887), 13.
12. William Barnes, 'Views of Labour and Gold' (1859), in William Barnes: *Collected Prose Works* (London: Routledge / Thommes Press, 1996).
13. Barnes, 'A Dissertation on the Dorset Dialect of the English Language', in *Poems of Rural Life*, 36.
14. Barnes, 'The Shep'erd Buoy', in *Poems of Rural Life*, 237. See Walter Houghton, *The Victorian Frame of Mind*, *1830–1870* (New Haven: Yale University Press, 1957), 242–262; Asa Briggs, *Victorian People: A Reassessment of Persons and Themes 1851–67* (Harmondsworth: Penguin Books, 1971), 124–147; John Barringer, *Men at Work: Art and Labour in Victorian Britain* (New Haven: Yale University Press, 2005), 242–262.
15. Barnes, 'Work and Wait' in *Poems of Rural Life in Common English* (London: Macmillan, 1868), 84.
16. Mr Skimpole refuses the 'model' of 'the busy Bee', labelling him an egotistical 'confectioner'; Charles Dickens, *Bleak House*, ed. Stephen Gill (Oxford: Oxford University Press, 1996), 106.
17. Barnes, 'The Woodlands', in *Poems of Rural Life*, 143.
18. Barnes, 'The Sky A-Clearèn', in *Poems of Rural Life*, 119.
19. Barnes, 'Night A-Zettèn In', in *Poems of Rural Life*, 172.
20. In Book IV of *Georgics*, Virgil reports from the hive: 'All aglow is the work', *Virgil Eclogues Georgics Aenied I–VI* (Cambridge, Mass: Harvard University Press, 1998), 209.
21. Isaac Watts, 'Song XX Against Idleness and Mischief', in *Divine Songs, Attempted in Easy Language, for the Use of Children* (Derby: Thomas Richardson, Friar-Gate, 1829), 38.
22. William Holman Hunt, 'The Hireling Shepherd', oil, Manchester Art Gallery, 1851.
23. William Cobbett encouraged the revival of home brewing, bread making, and bee keeping, in *Cottage Economy* (1821) (London: C. Clement, 1822), 11–48; 49–78; 170–174.
24. William Barnes, *Views of Labour*, 3.
25. Barnes, *Views of Labour*, 94.

26. Barnes, *Views of Labour*, 173. Carlyle condemned 'idle aristocracy' in *Past and Present*, ed. H. D. Traill, *The Centenary Edition of the Works of Thomas Carlyle*, 30 vols (London: Chapman and Hall, 1897), x. 173.

27. Ruskin defended the political virtue of agriculture in *Fors Claverigera: Letters to the Workmen and Labourers of Great Britain* (1871–1884) and founded The Guild of St George to practise it.

28. Barnes, *Views of Labour*, 98.

29. Cf. Barry Reay's description of that 'deep England' where 'the workers…are almost invisible', *Rural Englands: Labouring Lives in the Nineteenth Century* (Palgrave Macmillan, 2004), 172.

30. Reay, *Rural Englands*, 173.

31. I borrow the term 'folkloric' from M. M. Bakhtin's 'Forms of Time and Chronotope in the Novel', in *The Dialogic Imagination: Four Essays*, trans. Caryl Emerson and Michael Holquist, ed. Michael Holquist (Austin: University of Texas Press, 1981), 84–258.

32. In 'Wik's End in Zummer, in the Wold Vo'ke's Time', similarly, 'The hâymiakers did come vrom groun', / An' al zit down, wi' weary buones', 115.

33. Barnes, 'The Milk-Mâid o' the Farm', in *Poems of Rural Life*, 54.

34. Barnes, 'The Shepherd o' the Farm', in *Poems of Rural Life*, 86.

35. Baxter, *The Life of William Barnes*, 204.

36. Barnes, 'The Carter', in *Poems of Rural Life*, 199.

37. cf. the rural contest of 'haymaking as boon work', rewarded by meals and ale; see Christopher Dyer, 'Work Ethics in the Fourteenth Century', in James Bothwell, P. J. P. Goldberg and W. M. Ormrod, eds., *The Problem of Labour in Fourteenth-Century England* (Cambridge: Boydell & Brewer, 2000), 23.

38. Barnes, 'The Best Man in the Vield', in *Poems of Rural Life*, 112.

39. Barnes, *Views of Labour*, 27.

40. John Clare, 'Haymaking', in *The Later Poems of John Clare 1837–1864*, 2 vols, ed. Eric Robinson and David Powell (Oxford: Clarendon Press, 1984), i. 281–282.

41. Barnes, 'Hây-Miakèn', in *Poems of Rural Life*, 106.

42. Barnes, 'Hây-Carrèn', in *Poems of Rural Life*, 107.

43. Barnes, 'The Meäd A-Mow'd', in *Poems of Rural Life*, 118.

44. Barnes, 'Thatchèn O' the Rick', in *Poems of Rural Life*, 128–130.

45. Barnes, 'Out A-Nuttèn', in *Poems of Rural Life*, 159–160. See John Clare, 'Nutting', in *John Clare: Major Works*, ed. Eric Robinson and David Powell (Oxford: Oxford University Press, 2004), 131. See William Wordsworth, 'Nutting', in *The Poetical Works of William Wordsworth*, ed. Ernest de Selincourt, 5 vols (Oxford: Clarendon Press, 1944), ii. 211–212.

46. Barnes, 'Tiakèn in Apples', in *Poems of Rural Life*, 161.

47. Barnes, 'Keepèn up o' Chris'mas', in *Poems of Rural Life*, 202–203.

48. Barnes, 'Wik's End in Zummer, in the Wold Vo'ke's Time', in *Poems of Rural Life*, 115.

49. Barnes, 'Hây-Miakèn', in *Poems of Rural Life*, 106; Barnes, 'Thatchèn o' the Rick', in *Poems of Rural Life*, 130.

50. See 'The Shepherd o' the Farm': 'when the shearèn's al a-done, / Then we da eat, an' drink, an' zing / In miaster's kitchen', in Barnes, *Poems of Rural Life*, 86.

51. J. H. Prynne, *Field Notes: 'The Solitary Reaper' and Others* (Cambridge: Barque Press, 2007), 4.

52. Prynne, *Field Notes*, 4.

53. According to Zeitlow, Barnes's lack of 'obstruction' to kindly feelings 'allows no room for the sorts of painful memories which so often rise to haunt the speakers of Hardy's poems'— 'Thomas Hardy and William Barnes: Two Dorset Poets', 295.

54. The pain of love is the intrusive force in Marvell's 'Damon the Mower': 'How happy might I still have mowed, / Had not Love here his thistles sowed!'—*The Poems of Andrew Marvell*, ed. Nigel Smith (Harlow: Longman, 2003), 138. In Arnold's 'Thyrsis', the 'mowers' vanish at the first hint of personal loss—*The Poems of Matthew Arnold*, ed. Miriam Allott, 2nd edn. (London: Longman, 1979), 544–545.

55. Prynne, *Field Notes*, 4.

56. Barnes, 'Carn A-Turnèn Yoller', in *Poems of Rural Life*, 141.

57. Barnes, 'Carn A-Turnèn Yoller', in *Poems of Rural Life*, 142.

58. Barnes, 'The 'Lotments', in *Poems of Rural Life*, 74.

59. Barnes, 'Hây-Miakèn', in *Poems of Rural Life*, 106.

60. Sue Edney, '"Times Be Badish Vor the Poor": William Barnes and His Dialect of Disturbance in the Dorset "Eclogues"', *English*, 58 (2009), 213.

61. Motion, 'Introduction' to *William Barnes*, x.

62. Clare's poems were introduced as 'the genuine productions of a young Peasant, a day-labourer in husbandry', in *Poems Descriptive of Rural Life and Scenery by John Clare, A Northamptonshire Peasant*, 2nd edn. (London: Taylor and Hessey, and E. Drury, 1820), i.

63. See Clare, 'Labour's Leisure', in *John Clare: Major Works*, 194.

64. Baxter notes that 'The lawn was always mowed by his busy scythe' and that 'A frequent entry in the Italian diary is the word "*Zappando*" (digging)' in *The Life of William Barnes*, 27.

65. *The Life of William Barnes*, 10.

66. *The Life of William Barnes*, 10.

67. *The Life of William Barnes*, 12.

68. Barnes, 'The Young Rhymer Snubbed', in *Poems of Rural Life*, 2nd edn. (1864), 139–140.

69. See T. L. Burton, 'What William Barnes Done: Dilution of the Dialect in Later Versions of "Poems of Rural Life"', *The Review of English Studies*, 58 (2007), 338–363.

70. Barnes, 'The Milk-Maïd o' the Farm', in *Poems of Rural Life in the Dorset Dialect* (London: Kegan Paul, Trench, Trübner, 1905), 13.

71. Kurt Heinzelman, 'The Uneducated Imagination: Romantic Representations of Labor', in Mary Favret and Nicola Watson, eds., *At the Limits of Romanticism* (Bloomington, IN: Indiana University Press, 1994), 107.

72. Dryden wrote: 'But thou, propitious *Caesar*, guide my Course, / And to my bold Endeavours add thy Force. / Pity the Poet's and the Ploughman's Cares, / Int'rest thy Greatness in our mean Affairs' (I.60–63), *Virgil's Georgics*, in *The Poems of John Dryden*, 4 vols., ed. James Kinsley (Oxford: Clarendon Press, 1958), ii. 920.

73. Barnes, 'Wheat', in *Poems of Rural Life in the Dorset Dialect*, 2nd edn. (London: John Russell, 1863), 178–180.

74. Barnes, 'Wheat', in *Poems of Rural Life*, 118.

75. Prynne, *Field Notes*, 13. Prynne discusses 'the exertion of a field-worker … who *also* sings, as a comfortable discharge of customary practice' (11–20).

76. William Blake, 'Introduction' to Songs of Innocence and of Experience, in *William Blake: The Complete Poems*, ed. Alicia Ostriker (Harmondsworth: Penguin Books, 1977), 104.

77. Barnes, 'Thatchèn o' the Rick', in *Poems of Rural Life*, 128.

78. Barnes, *An Outline of English Speech-craft* (London: Kegan Paul, 1878).

79. Barnes, Preface, *Views of Labour*, n.p.

80. Barnes, 'A Dissertation on the Dorset Dialect of the English Language', 37.

81. Barnes, 'A Dissertation on the Dorset Dialect of the English Language', 29; Barnes offers the Dorsetshire example, 'He've a*lost* his hatchet'.

82. Gerard Manley Hopkins, 'Felix Randal' in *The Poetical Works of Gerard Manley Hopkins*, ed. N. H. MacKenzie (Oxford: Oxford University Press, 1990), 165.

83. John Burnett notes that 'farm labouring was regarded as unskilled', *Useful Toil: Autobiographies of Working People from the 1820s to the 1920s* (London: John Burnett, 1974), 23.

84. Barnes wrote that 'the thatch of the cottage shelters many a clever head which only wants an opportunity', *Views of Labour*, 127.

85. Barnes, 'Hây-Maikèn', in *Poems of Rural Life*, 106.

86. John Clare, 'To the Snipe', in *John Clare: Major Works*, 207.

87. See William Morris's *News from Nowhere* (1890), in *Collected Works of William Morris*, 24 vols., ed. May Morris (London: Longmans, 1910–15), xvi. 1–211.

SELECT BIBLIOGRAPHY

Bakhtin, Mikhail, *The Dialogic Imagination: Four Essays*, trans. Caryl Emerson and Michael Holquist, ed. Michael Holquist (Austin: University of Texas Press, 1981).

Barrell, John, *The Dark Side of the Landscape: The Rural Poor in English Paintings, 1730–1840* (Cambridge: Cambridge University Press, 1980).

Baxter, Lucy, *The Life of William Barnes: Poet and Philologist* (London: Macmillan and Co., 1887).

Briggs, Asa, *Victorian People: A Reassessment of Persons and Themes 1851–67* (Harmondsworth: Penguin Books, 1971; 1st pub. 1955), 124–147.

Burnett, John, *Useful Toil: Autobiographies of Working People from the 1820s to the 1920s* (London: John Burnett, 1974).

Burton, T. L., 'What William Barnes Done: Dilution of the Dialect in Later Versions of "Poems of Rural Life"', *The Review of English Studies*, 58 (2007), 338–363.

——'Dialect Poetry, William Barnes and the Literary Canon', *ELH*, 76 (2009), 309–341.

Campbell, Matthew, *Rhythm and Will in Victorian Poetry* (Cambridge: Cambridge University Press, 1999).

Edney, Sue, '"Times Be Badish Vor the Poor": William Barnes and His Dialect of Disturbance in the Dorset "Eclogues"', *English*, 58 (2009), 206–229.

——'William Barnes's Place and Dialects of Connection', in Kirstie Blair and Mina Gorji, eds, *Class and the Canon: Constructing Labouring-Class Poetry and Poetics, 1780–1900* (Basingstoke: Palgrave Macmillan, 2012), pp. 191–210.

Forsyth, R. A., 'The Conserving Myth of William Barnes', *Victorian Studies*, 6 (1963), 325–354.

Heinzelman, Kurt, 'The Uneducated Imagination: Romantic Representations of Labor', in Mary Favret and Nicola Watson, eds., *At the Limits of Romanticism* (Bloomington: Indiana University Press, 1994), 101–124.

Hertz, Alan, 'The Hallowed Pleäces of William Barnes', *Victorian Poetry*, 23 (1985), 109–124.

Hess, Scott, 'William Wordsworth and Photographic Subjectivity', *Nineteenth-Century Literature* 63 (2008), 283–320.

Houghton, Walter, *The Victorian Frame of Mind, 1830–1870* (New Haven: Yale University Press, 1957).

Janowitz, Anne, *Lyric and Labour in the Romantic Tradition* (Cambridge: Cambridge University Press, 2005).

Keith, W. J., 'Thomas Hardy's Edition of William Barnes', *Victorian Poetry* 15 (July, 1977), 121–131.

Loughrey, Bryan, *The Pastoral Mode: A Casebook* (London: Macmillan, 1984).

Marinelli, P. V., *Pastoral* (London: Methuen, 1971).

Prynne, Jeremy, *Field Notes* (Cambridge: Barque Press, 2007).

Reay, Barry, *Rural Englands: Labouring Lives in the Nineteenth Century* (Basingstoke: Palgrave Macmillan, 2004).

Ricks, Christopher, ed., *The New Oxford Anthology of Victorian Verse* (Oxford: Oxford University Press, 1987).

Robinson, Solveig, 'Of "Haymakers" and "City Artisans": The Chartist Poetics of Eliza Cook's *Songs of Labor*', *Victorian Poetry*, 39 (2001), 229–254.

Schur, Owen, *Victorian Pastoral: Tennyson, Hardy, and the Subversion of Forms* (Columbus: Ohio State University Press, 1990).

Williams, Raymond, *The Country and the City* (London: Chatto and Windus, 1973).

Zeitlow, Paul, 'Thomas Hardy and William Barnes: Two Dorset Poets', *PMLA*, 84 (1969), 291–303.

CHAPTER 29

....

DREAMING REALITY: THE POETRY OF WILLIAM MORRIS

....

CLIVE WILMER

'Who...would guess from his poetry', wrote F. R. Leavis in 1932, 'that William Morris was one of the most versatile, energetic and original men of his time, a force that impinged decisively in the world of practice? He reserved poetry for his day-dreams'.[1] William Morris (1834–96) was indeed an active man: craftsman and designer, businessman, environmental and political activist. He was also prolific as a writer in verse and prose. Leavis was not wrong to associate his poetry with dream. Morris affirmed as much in a letter of 1856: 'I can't enter into politico-social subjects with any interest, for on the whole I see things are in a muddle, and I have no power or vocation to set them right in ever so little a degree. My work is the embodiment of dreams in one form or another.'[2] This conscious evasion of the issues that by the 1880s were to take him over anticipates the strategy of his long poem *The Earthly Paradise* (1868–70). As he puts it in the 'Apology':

> Dreamer of dreams, born out of my due time,
> Why should I strive to set the crooked straight?
> Let it suffice me that my murmuring rhyme
> Beats with light wing against the ivory gate,
> Telling a tale not too importunate
> To those who in the sleepy region stay,
> Lulled by the singer of an empty day.
>
> Folk say, a wizard to a northern king
> At Christmas-tide such wondrous things did show,
> That through one window men beheld the spring,
> And through another saw the summer glow,
> And through a third the fruited vines a-row,

While still, unheard, but in its wonted way,
Piped the drear wind of that December day.

So with this Earthly Paradise it is,
If ye will read aright, and pardon me,
Who strive to build a shadowy isle of bliss
Midmost the beating of the steely sea,
Where tossed about all hearts of men must be;
Whose ravening monsters mighty men shall slay,
Not the poor singer of an empty day.[3]

The manner and tone of this are characteristic of Morris's middle period—roughly 1867–72. The gentle irony in the self-characterization, the Keatsian loveliness and the melancholy are all marks of the incipient Aesthetic Movement. Indeed the lyric, as its singer frankly avows, is a wizard-poet's apology for escapism, but it is too simple to say (as Leavis does) that the real world is disregarded. The speaker is explicit that, behind the appearances of spring, summer, and fruitful autumn, the bleak fact of winter is not to be wished away. If the younger Morris was anxious to avoid politico-social subjects, it was not merely to indulge in fantasy. For one thing, the emergence of psychoanalysis in Morris's old age and Leavis's childhood is evidence of the ways in which, for some thinkers of the late nineteenth century, the quest for 'reality' began in dreams and the depths of the psyche, but it was also through such dreaming that Morris was enabled to discover his own political vision and authority. Throughout his life, responding to the tradition of dream poetry in the Middle Ages—a tradition including Dante, Chaucer, and Langland—Morris was inclined to draw on his dreams as paradigms for action and models for transformations of society. As he says in the last sentence of his prose narrative *News from Nowhere,* 'if others can see it as I have seen it, then it may be called a vision rather than a dream'.[4]

Long before the days of his political activism, Morris had been conscious that dreams could provide vivid alternatives, if not always attractive ones, to the dullness of bourgeois life. How else could he have come to write his earlier work, collected in *The Defence of Guenevere and Other Poems* (1858)? What he tries to do there, drawing on medieval art and literature, is dream the reality of medieval life. This is not a paradox. To imagine another social order, another economic system, a different scale of priorities—as Morris had to do if he was to write convincingly of the Middle Ages—is to go some way towards questioning the inevitability of the order in which one lives. It is one thing to say that Morris dreams of the Middle Ages, another that he refuses to idealize or moralize them—that, on the contrary, he seeks to imagine a life that could really have been. In the view of his political biographer, 'The intensity of the feelings in these poems comes, not from the Middle Ages, but from William Morris... it is a measure of the intensity of his own revolt against the impoverished relationships of his own society'.[5]

But, dreams aside, the most damaging criticism of Morris's poetry has been that it is not altogether serious: that poetic skill came easily to him, that he surrendered to his facility and used the poetry to soothe his audience rather than, as he might have done, to challenge it. A number of critics have made the obvious comparison of his poems to the decorative arts he practised as a craftsman: 'he wove his poems like tapestries, limiting his vocabulary like the colour range of his wool, conventionalizing and symbolizing his subject matter to meet the limitations of his material—limitations which in *The Earthly Paradise* were not inherent but imposed, and coarsened its quality'.[6] Since one of the purposes of beautiful patterns, as Morris in his lectures often insists, is to provide rest for the eyes in a living-space, such readings are not without substance or even attractiveness. The question is whether the pursuit of fantasy or literary excitement might not serve a social function as valuable as the insights of social realism. Certainly in the prose romances he wrote in his last years, he was thinking of fantasy as a form of political refreshment, much like the importance of holiday to work.[7] The Prologue to *The Earthly Paradise* broods on these issues:

> Forget six counties overhung with smoke,
> Forget the snorting steam and piston stroke,
> Forget the spreading of the hideous town;
> Think rather of the pack-horse on the down,
> And dream of London, small and white and clean,
> The clear Thames bordered by its gardens green.[8]

This is *paralipsis*: the rhetorical figure whereby a writer, by seeming to dismiss a topic, draws it to our attention. Instructed to forget the smoke, we call it to mind and, with it, the squalor and misery of industrial London in a bleakly competitive era. What is more, though at the start of *The Earthly Paradise* it is easy for the reader to escape London, much as the wanderers of Morris's poem flee from the Black Death, it remains impossible to escape the harshest fact of existence—that we must die—and the failed attempt of the wanderers to do so is soon to be set before us as the poem's central concern. It is indeed possible to argue that Morris's poetry, quite as much as Tennyson's or Arnold's, is motivated by the mid-nineteenth-century 'crisis of faith' and the loss of a belief in eternal life. This was to be an issue for Morris the Socialist as well as for Morris the aesthete: if there is no heaven, can we find or create a heaven on this earth?

Nevertheless, can it be said that 'the idle poet' sells his vocation short? In 1855, when Morris's Oxford friends were stunned by his first adult poem, he is supposed to have said: 'Well, if this is poetry, it is very easy to write'.[9] He was later to repudiate Romantic ideas of inspiration: 'There is no such thing. It's a matter of mere craftsmanship'.[10] And yet, as David Latham has shown in an article on Morris's manuscripts, there is ample evidence that he worked on his poetry as carefully as he worked at anything.[11] Neither work nor craftsmanship was ever for Morris an insignificant matter. 'The lesson which Ruskin here teaches us', he wrote in his Preface to Ruskin's *The Nature of Gothic*, 'is that art is the expression of man's pleasure in labour'.[12] He only appears to disparage Romantic ideals of poetry because he disliked the suggestion that making poems was fundamentally different from making carpets or furniture. Art and work, for Morris, were synonyms. What he was reacting against—and doing so long before he recognized it—was a bourgeois notion of art as self-expression. What interested him was the role which art might play in a society of equals. *The Earthly Paradise* is concerned with a society brought into existence, and then sustained, by the arts of poetry and storytelling.

THE DEFENCE OF GUENEVERE

The Defence of Guenevere, and Other Poems has its roots in a great deal of deep and passionate reading and much brooding on medieval art. Yet the book's *effect* is not in the least bookish. It is, on the contrary, one of starkly dramatic realism. This is where Morris differs from his medievalizing contemporaries—from Rossetti quite as much as from Tennyson. It was undoubtedly a poetry of dream, but Morris's writing is rarely 'dreamy'. He is interested in imagining a possible reality. *Pace* Paul Thompson, we are not at all in the tapestry world of 'The Lady of Shalott', but in a world of violence, guile, passion, betrayal, and irrational courage. The intensely visualized images are designed to make the narratives and characters credible and vividly present to us. The imprisoned protagonist of 'Sir Peter Harpdon's End', for instance, talks of his thought as 'alive / Like any curling snake within my brain',[13] and one is struck by ferocious images of sex, death, and violence—as in 'Concerning Geffray Teste Noire': 'I saw you kissing once, like a curved sword / That bites with all its edge, did your lips lie',[14] or in 'The Haystack in the Floods' when the ambushed Sir Robert is dragged away from his wife by his enemy Godmar, stabbed and thrown to Godmar's mercenaries:

> the blow told well,
> Right backward the knight Robert fell,
> And moan'd as dogs do, being half dead,
> Unwitting, as I deem : so then
> Godmar turn'd grinning to his men,
> Who ran, some five or six, and beat
> His head to pieces at their feet.[15]

It is clear that a key source of Morris's realism is Pre-Raphaelite painting, particularly the brightly coloured, closely observed, hallucinatory observations of nature one finds in the early work of J. E. Millais, William Holman Hunt, and Arthur Hughes. Visual art and craft are broadly significant too, from the unsurprising emphasis on architecture and design to medieval painting, about which Paul Thompson makes an acute comparison: 'He used none of the underlying technique of a plot, with its hints, connections, and surprises; instead he presented a series of vivid visual scenes, like a medieval fresco painter or illuminator'.[16] This combination of hyper-realism with discontinuity makes the poems feel startlingly modern at times, their narratives disrupted by intense particulars.

The sources of this originality, once noticed, seem obvious. The Tennyson of 'The Lady of Shalott' and 'Morte d'Arthur' suggested a way of handling medieval subject matter. Like Tennyson, Morris looks to Sir Thomas Malory as a narrative source, but the use he makes of him could hardly be more different. It was not Tennyson's purpose to deliver a convincing picture of medieval life. So Morris, in effect, combines Tennysonian matter with the manner of Robert Browning. The abrupt dramatic energy of the poems, their urgently unpredictable rhythms and the unconventional force of their imagery are all learnt from Browning. Still more important are the medieval sources. Malory is certainly there, but he is not the timeless dreamer he was for Tennyson. He is very much the soldier who fought in the Wars of the Roses, and Morris blends his influence with that of the fourteenth-century chronicler Jean Froissart, whose *Chroniques* record events in England and France at the time of the Hundred Years' War. Morris was helped in absorbing Froissart by the splendid late medieval translation of John Bourchier, Lord Berners (1523–25). Froissart, as Berners renders him, is a writer with no illusions about our potential for cruelty or capacity for self-deception, while remaining a gentleman possessed by the ideals and splendours of chivalry. A significant number of the poems in *Guenevere* are inspired by Malory, but the harsher pieces have their roots in Froissart: 'The Haystack in the Floods', 'Concerning Geffray Teste Noire', 'The Judgement of God', 'Sir Peter Harpdon's End', and so on.

Nikolaus Pevsner, writing in praise of Morris's stained glass, perceptively observed that he 'looked on the Middle Ages rather for guidance than for actual paradigms'.[17] Inspired though Morris was by medieval craftsmanship, it is impossible to confuse his designs with medieval ones, or even to mistake them for poor imitations. The secret of his art lies in its modernity—and medieval art, unrestored and unreconstructed, had a non-canonical freshness in the nineteenth century that made it appear modern. Morris in all his activities blends that freshness with methods unambiguously modern. Take the opening of his title poem, 'The Defence of Guenevere':

> But, knowing now that they would have her speak,
> She threw her wet hair backward from her brow,
> Her hand close to her mouth touching her cheek,
>
> As though she had had there a shameful blow,
> And feeling it shameful to feel ought but shame
> All through her heart, yet felt her cheek burned so,
>
> She must a little touch it; like one lame
> She walked away from Gauwaine, with her head
> Still lifted up; and on her cheek of flame
>
> The tears dried quick; she stopped at last and said:
> "O knights and lords, it seems but little skill
> To talk of well-known things past now and dead.
>
> "God wot I ought to say, I have done ill,
> And pray you all forgiveness heartily!
> Because you must be right, such great lords; still
>
> "Listen, suppose your time were come to die,
> And you were quite alone and very weak;
> Yea, laid a dying while very mightily

"The wind was ruffling up the narrow streak
Of river through your broad lands running well:
Suppose a hush should come, then some one speak:

" 'One of these cloths is heaven, and one is hell,
Now choose one cloth for ever; which they be,
I will not tell you, you must somehow tell

" 'Of your own strength and mightiness; here, see!'
Yea, yea, my lord, and you to ope your eyes,
At foot of your familiar bed to see

"A great God's angel standing, with such dyes,
Not known on earth, on his great wings, and hands,
Held out two ways, light from the inner skies

"Showing him well, and making his commands
Seem to be God's commands, moreover, too,
Holding within his hands the cloths on wands;

"And one of these strange choosing cloths was blue,
Wavy and long, and one cut short and red;
No man could tell the better of the two.

"After a shivering half-hour you said:
'God help! heaven's colour, the blue;' and he said, 'hell.'
Perhaps you then would roll upon your bed..." [18]

Like Tennyson, Morris filters his narrative through a female persona. Tennyson's model here was Ovid's *Heroides*: poems in which female protagonists reflect on the heroes of epic poetry, converting the central interest of the poem from the martial and external to the internal and domestic. Despite the innovation, however, the powerfully symbolic frame of Tennyson's *Idylls of the King* (1859) is weakened by moralizing. Morris's interest, by contrast, is in the Queen's *emotion*: not in the rights or wrongs of it but in its depth, and in the incapacity of others to legislate for it. 'The poem', as Walter Pater put it, 'is a thing tormented and awry with passion, like the body of Guenevere defending herself from the charge of adultery, and the accent falls in strange, unwonted places with the effect of a great cry'.[19] Morris's sympathy for women's feelings is even more striking in 'The Haystack in the Floods', where Jehane, rather than submit to Godmar's desires, in effect consents to the murder of her husband. Neither poem conforms to the dramatic conventions established by Browning in his dramatic monologues, though it is undoubtedly his *Men and Women* (1856) that provided Morris with the device he needed: the creation of a voice that encourages us, though it does not oblige us, to sympathize with the heroine's point of view.[20] This is a matter of tone, the adaptation of speech to metre and, in the case of 'Guenevere', the convention of the silent interlocutor. I do not know if Pater's use of the word 'accent' alludes specifically to the versification, but it is undoubtedly the case that much of the poem's feeling derives from the high degree of tension between speech rhythm and prosodic order, syntax and lineation. At its best this provides a movement exceptional in intensity of feeling and emotional variety, as in 'Her hand close to her mouth touching her cheek, // As though she had had there a shameful blow', the second line of which, as Paul Thompson has said, sounds 'like stammering direct speech'.[21] At its worst, the rhythm Morris heard is barely recoverable—as in the line '"God help! heaven's colour, the blue;" and he said, "hell."'

But good or bad, the method is avant-garde. Within that method, though, there is a consciousness depicted that strikes one as medieval, or at any rate wholly foreign to the outlook of the nineteenth-century Protestant bourgeoisie. Morris's characters are the opposite of Tennyson's 'King Arthur, like a modern gentleman'.[22] Guenevere's 'cloths on wands', which offer heaven or hell, are, like her angel with dazzling wings, medieval conceptions, startling in their oddity. The curious arbitrariness of the offer is at once medieval in its fatalism and modern in its intuition of a darkly meaningless universe—one in which human feelings and attachments provide the only light. What we have here, as so often in Morris, is a composite of ancient and modern. The voice of Guenevere, like the voices in Browning, is that of an individual as understood in the post-Romantic era: the 'I' of Wordsworth or Shelley transferred, as it is in Browning and Tennyson, to a persona, characteristically (as usually in Tennyson) standing as the contrary of the poet's overt self—here female rather than male. But this elaboration of bourgeois individualism was not to satisfy Morris for long, and the story of his subsequent poetry becomes his endeavour to restore the poetic voice to a role in the community—like blind Homer, maker of songs, or the bard who intoned *Beowulf* to the harp.

THE EARTHLY PARADISE

In 1886, Morris was asked to produce a list of his favourite books. He began with what Giuseppe Mazzini called 'Bibles': the Hebrew Bible itself, Homer, Hesiod, the Edda, and the other old Norse poems, *Beowulf*, the *Kalevala*, the *Shahnameh*, the *Mahabharata*, the traditional poems of the Welsh and Irish peoples, and 'folk tale collections headed by Grimm and the Norse ones'. Such works, he wrote, 'cannot always be measured by a literary standard, but to me are far more important than any literature. They are in no sense the work of individuals, but have grown up from the very hearts of the *people*'.[23] The Morris who wrote that had for three years been an active Socialist, so it is hardly surprising to find him speaking for a popular conception of literary culture. What he says, however, is consistent with all his original motives as an artist. As early as 1853 Morris had been gripped by Ruskin's 'The Nature of Gothic' because it depicted an alternative to nineteenth-century modes of production. The stone-carver working on a Gothic cathedral, Ruskin argued, was accorded a kind of creative freedom quite foreign to the industrial system, in which labour is divided and the alienated workman no better than 'a machine...an animated tool'. In recognizing 'the individual value of every soul' the Gothic culture assumed a kind of creativity that is both individual and collaborative.[24] But it was not only the workmen on the building site who collaborated: Gothic buildings are historical artefacts, and different *ages* have collaborated in their making, much as the *Iliad*, say, far from being the creation of an individual called Homer, is probably a compendium of inherited traditions.

Morris's own modes of production were not as collaborative as he might have wished. He was, in many respects, a benign autocrat. No doubt he realized this, recognizing that artists in industrial societies are isolated individuals. He was also conscious that in cultures much older than ours there are works of art, directly related to Mazzini's 'Bibles', which are plainly the work of individuals too. The classic example is Virgil's *Aeneid*. In drawing on the structure of Homer's epics, and imitating certain of their incidents—the catalogue, the invocation, the journey to the underworld—Virgil created the conventions of epic poetry, to be borrowed in their turn by later poets. In 1876, Morris translated the *Aeneid*, and, mindful of these complexities, turned it into a different sort of poem: not, as it might have been, a modernized version of the poem, but something more like a sixteenth-century romance.[25] When he translated the *Völsunga Saga* from Icelandic in 1870 he delighted in the work's all-too-evident inconsistencies, which are testimony to its piecemeal construction over the ages.[26]

It was no doubt sentimental of him, but Morris lamented the fact that he lived in a culture like Virgil's rather than Homer's. Yet Virgil could provide a middle path. So too could Chaucer and Boccaccio, both of whom feature on Morris's list, though their work is something different again. They are essentially collectors of popular and traditional tales, who orchestrate their collections into complex wholes. *The Canterbury Tales* and *The Decameron* provide the obvious model for Morris's own compendium of legends, *The Earthly Paradise*, which is inescapably a post-Romantic poem, though it has sources as diverse as Persian, Icelandic, and Greek. But there is an important difference: the post-Romantic sensibility must be taken to include the historical consciousness and so, paradoxically, Morris's modernity is most clearly seen in his deliberate and strategic archaism, as in his version of Virgil.

This archaism is one of many features that have told against the poem in modern times. Others include its unmanageable length—at 42,000 lines it is very nearly the longest poem in English—and the soporific smoothness of both metre and narrative, which is in contrast to the jaggedly disruptive manner of his first book. In recent years, however, a number of critics, mostly in the United States, have sought to revalue the poem, attributing its neglect to our intellectual laziness: a passive acceptance of the modernist reaction against Victorian monuments.[27]

The objections, nevertheless, are worth considering. Although it draws on Chaucer and Boccaccio, the poem has nothing of their earthiness to balance the Romantic elements; it has none of their humour either, or their skill in creating character. Though Morris is strikingly candid about physical desire, including female desire, he is anxious and slightly coy about actual sex. He is also inclined to pull his punches in his handling of violent scenes—in remarkable contrast to *The Defence of Guenevere*. All these flaws may be seen as concessions to Victorian prudery, though, conscious that folk tales contain much gratuitous violence, Morris may have modified his sources to focus on their humanity. But most of the tales, particularly the classical ones with their soothing, idealized, Golden Age atmosphere, tend to merge into each other. It is not that Morris is boring: he was, as his daughters testified, a marvellous storyteller, and some of these stories, read separately, are hard to put down. But his failure to prune, condense, vary the tone and harden particular details, leads to a kind of slackness, so that one's very pleasure in his skill and fluency turns in the end to weariness.

On the other hand, there is much in the poem that a reader of modern poetry might turn to with confident pleasure: the casual blending of history and myth, the eclectic plunder of a range of cultures, juxtaposing them and conflating one with another, Morris's knack of calling real things to mind simply by naming them. There are several passages such as the following:

> Think, listener, that I had the luck to stand
> Awhile ago within a flowery land
> Fair beyond words; that thence I brought away
> Some blossoms that before my footsteps lay,
> Not plucked by me, not over-fresh or bright;
> Yet, since they minded me of that delight,
> Within the pages of this book I laid
> Their tender petals, there in peace to fade.
> Dry are they now, and void of all their scent
> And lovely colour, yet what once was meant
> By these dull stains, some men may yet descry
> As dead upon the quivering leaves they lie.
> Behold them here, and mock me if you will,
> But yet believe no scorn of men can kill
> My love of that fair land wherefrom they came,
> Where midst the grass their petals once did flame.[28]

It is not difficult to see how the virtues of this passage—its fluency, the flawless and seemingly effortless rhyming couplets, the sweetness of its melancholy—might come in time to seem anodyne. But coming, as it does, early on in the poem, its impact is considerable. Florence S. Boos has argued that much in Morris's historicism—with its large element of fantasy, its intertextuality, its plurality of genres and so on—should appeal to devotees of the post-modern. She also mentions its reflexiveness, which is undoubtedly at work here. Flowers, of course, are traditionally poems, and leaves are also pages. The stain of colour left on the page by a pressed flower is the residue of emotion that words carry. The flowery land is paradise; it is also the past; it is also what Keats called 'the realms of gold', the country of literature. Moreover, these flowers and leaves, like poetry and the emotions it records, are strictly speaking dead. Yet it is an unusual kind of death. For looking at the flowers, like reading and re-reading the words, revives the emotion, calls it back to life. The frame narrative of *The Earthly Paradise* concerns a group of Nordic wanderers who have embarked on a long and apparently fruitless quest for the earthly paradise. This passage subtly suggests that, unknowingly and at the end of their lives, they have stumbled upon it by chance. It is that thing called poetry, in which beauty lives forever; it is not simply a *paradis artificiel,* for it depends on an experience of life, and the sense of life is renewed in a new relationship, that between the reader and the writer or, in the terms of Morris's fable, between the narrator and his audience. All of which brings into consideration the part played by the reader in the making of literature.

The passage in question is part of the frame narrative, which begins with the Prologue and tells the story of the wanderers, who, living in the fourteenth century, have put to sea to escape from the Black Death—an idea clearly lifted from Boccaccio. They decide to sail in quest of the earthly paradise, which they have heard of as an island wholly free of age and death. What 'paradise' means, however—perhaps what death means too—goes through many transformations before the last of Morris's lines. Each landfall they make at first appears paradisal but leads in time to conflict, so that the wanderers are forced to set out again in quest of their goal. As the years pass and their journeys wear them out, they turn into disappointed old men and eventually, after the most disastrous of their encounters, just twelve survivors set sail again for Europe and the acceptance of mortality. Their fortune is to reach one of the 'happy isles' of legend. It is inhabited by a people descended from the classical Greeks but cut off from the subsequent course of European history. Significantly, both the wanderers and their new hosts are dislocated peoples, connected to their past through language and the stories they have inherited from their cultures. The twelve wanderers are welcomed by twelve elders of the city; the two groups of elderly men become friends and every month they celebrate their meeting in an exchange of stories. So each month, beginning in March and the infancy of the year, one elder relates a classical myth and one wanderer a medieval tale. As in *The Canterbury Tales,* there are link passages, such as the one I have quoted, which bind the stories together, though there are no characters. As a result, we have a collection of twenty-four stories and two seasonal cycles. This is the length of the Homeric epic, but significantly, like Tennyson's *Idylls of the King* with its twelve Virgilian books, it recalls epic qualities while explicitly rejecting the epic range or posture. However Chaucerian the poem may be, it is also modern in its implied conviction that the full heroic arc is beyond the reach of a contradictory and fragmented age—something which Morris apparently changed his mind about when in the mid 1870s he embarked on an actual epic, *Sigurd the Volsung.*

In describing this frame, I have missed out one major element. Each month begins with a Romantic lyric in the voice of 'the idle singer'. These lyrics are outstandingly beautiful in the way that the best of Keats is. They also appear to supply the primary motives for the poem in Morris's personal life: the breakdown of his marriage to Jane Morris and his loss of religious faith. At any rate, his singer is obsessed with the impermanence of love, which alone gives meaning to life, and the inevitability of meaningless death. It was this that made E. P. Thompson dismiss *The Earthly Paradise* as 'The Poetry of Despair', though he ought perhaps to have picked up from it a foretaste of Morris's Socialism.[29] We realize, as we read each tale, that each is about a quest for love and fulfilment, and that all of them are actually or implicitly haunted by the necessity of failure. But as we move from spring to winter, and the depth of failure becomes more painful, a range of consolations begins to be present to us. One of them, as the passage I have quoted starts to suggest, is provided by the pursuit of art, though there is also a suggestion, perhaps not fully realized by Morris himself, that the partial transfer of identity from self to com-munity—the experience, in fact, of the elders and wanderers—could rescue the modern bourgeois from the pointlessness of existence. It is a nice irony that the poem praised by Walter Pater as typifying 'Aesthetic Poetry' foreshadows Morris's Socialism and a cri-tique that places 'Bibles' above the literature of subjective feeling.

It is possible with hindsight to disagree with Pater's emphasis, but the acuteness of his criticism of Morris has never been equalled, and modern assessments of *The Earthly Paradise* seem to be moving back in his direction. In particular, his understanding of how modernity responds to the pastness of the past helps us to see why the poem has to be so self-conscious and reflexive—why 'the tale of the tribe' (to borrow Kipling's phrase) requires an innocence in both poet and audience that modern society sim-ply cannot possess. Like Pevsner, he notices that Morris does not mimic the past: 'The poetry is neither a reproduction of Greek or mediæval life or poetry, nor a disguised reflex of modern sentiment…Like some strange flowering after date, it renews on a more delicate type the poetry of a past age, but must not be confounded with it'.[30]

What Pater fails to notice, however, is the presence late in *The Earthly Paradise* of a poem that seems to indicate a route out of reflexivity. This is 'The Lovers of Gudrun', which, derived from the Icelandic *Laxdaela Saga,* depicts with immense vigour, blunt-ness, and emotional frankness the un-ideal vagaries of one young woman's complex and—from a Victorian point of view—possibly shocking love-life. It has been noticed that Morris, even before the breakdown of his marriage, was preoccupied with emo-tional triangles—Launcelot and Guenevere, Tristram and Iseult, Helen and Paris and, eventually, Sigurd and Brynhild. 'The Lovers of Gudrun' must have been written as he suffered the pangs of his own crisis and his capacity to express emotional complexities seems to have gained from it—as in the following passage. Gudrun, thinking herself abandoned by Kiartan, whom she loves, takes revenge on him by marrying Bodli. When Kiartan unexpectedly returns, she is worse than disconcerted:

> she forgot those eyes
> What they were now, all dulled with miseries;
> And she forgot the sorrow of the heart
> That fate and time from hers had thrust apart.
> Still wrong bred wrong within her; day by day
> Some little speck of kindness fell away,
> Till in her heart naked desire alone
> Was left, the one thing not to be undone.
> Then would the jealous flame in some wise burn
> Within her, that to Bodli she would turn,
> And madden him with fond caressing touch
> And tender word…[31]

This would, as Amanda Hodgson says, 'be totally out of place in any of the other poems in *The Earthly Paradise*'.[32] The tension between syntax and lineation here gives an energy to the couplets, which mirrors what seems an honesty of feeling in the narrative. This hardly suggests escapism. 'Realism' is rather the word that comes to mind.

SIGURD THE VOLSUNG

'The Lovers of Gudrun' represents a change of direction in Morris's work, as also in his life. In 1868 he befriended the Icelandic scholar Eiríkr Magnússon. He had long been interested in the literature and mythology of the north, and Magnússon's friendship provided him with the opportunity to try translating the Icelandic sagas. It was also Magnússon who persuaded him to turn his poetic talents to Norse themes, the first result being 'The Lovers of Gudrun' itself. During the early 1870s Morris worked on the translations with characteristic energy, developing a kind of pseudo-archaic English to represent more sympathetically the expression of what might be thought a barbarous era.[33] He visited Iceland twice, wrote a splendid journal of his travels and eventually dared against what he had thought his better judgement to compose an epic of his own. *Sigurd the Volsung* (1876) is based on the greatest of the sagas, the *Völsunga Saga,* which he had translated in 1870. It is Morris's last important achievement as a poet and for several of his readers perhaps the best, combining the narrative fluency of *The Earthly Paradise* with the passion and forcefulness of *Guenevere.*

I have mentioned the personal anguish expressed in the monthly lyrics of *The Earthly Paradise.* In some unpublished lyrics of the same period, Morris dealt more frankly and fully with his feelings, though still with a touch of reticence.[34] It is clear that he had resolved not to interfere in his wife's emotions and that he was helped in this by his reading of the sagas. There is evidence that their laconic stoicism provided him with an example of how to live a life free of regret. In letters of the period he writes of what he calls 'the religion of the Northman', namely 'the worship of Courage',[35] and there can be no doubt that *Sigurd the Volsung* is partly based on an implied analogy between the martial values of a simpler age and the moral courage called for by the full emotional life. In a similar spirit he sought to make up for the disappointments of his marriage with commitment to political struggle and the hope of creating a genuine community.

Morris was increasingly sceptical of the value of recreating the past for the modern age. In 1877, for example, he was to launch the Society for the Protection of Ancient Buildings, designed to resist the Victorian custom of reconstructing medieval buildings in the name of 'restoration', and soon after the Society's foundation, he withdrew from the business of furnishing ancient churches with his company's stained glass. It was only, therefore, under pressure from Magnússon that he allowed himself to re-tell the story of Sigurd and, in doing so, quite consciously to compromise the standards he had set himself. He must therefore have thought that at all costs he had to avoid pastiche, while at the same time eschewing that 'transfusion of modern sentiment into an ancient story' he had come to dislike in Tennyson.[36]

He also had to deny himself the accoutrements of 'civilized' discourse. There was, at the time, a great deal of interest in the Germanic roots of English and even in the possibility of an English without Latinisms. Morris was never a purist in these matters, but in *Sigurd* he did attempt a much more Germanic English and coined a good many words of his own to bring his poem closer to Icelandic usages. Metre was fundamental to the process. Like many other late Victorian poets, Morris seems to have become dissatisfied with the iambic pentameter as practised by Arnold and Tennyson. He might have been expected to attempt a revival of Old English alliterative verse, but he must have been warned off by the danger of pastiche. What in the event he chose was a hexameter made up mainly of anapaests—hardly a traditional form, but with heavy alliteration and a generous use of polysyndeton and parataxis, it does succeed in calling to mind the poetry of a heroic age, without any danger of mimicry. It is the sort of metre we now associate with the battle poems read to schoolboys in the imperial era: Tennyson's 'The Revenge', Chesterton's 'Lepanto', and several of Kipling's poems, certain of which are clearly indebted to *Sigurd*. Given those associations, it is extraordinary that Morris achieves a long narrative of such relentless energy, so sombre with feelings of doom and tragic grandeur. There is no preaching. The moral force of the poem is in the sense it gives of a past era's nobility, suggesting, indeed, how barbarism might provide a nobler manner of life than the bourgeois civilization that Morris so despised. Moreover, there are some modern messages. As in 'The Lovers of Gudrun', the masculine values of the poem are balanced by the presence of female perspectives, and the evident analogy between, on the one hand, the manly endurance of the Volsung patriarch Sigmund, and on the other, the anguish of Brynhild, afflicted by desire and jealousy. Overshadowing all these sorrows is the Norse conception of fate. By way of example, let us consider the striking passage in which Sigmund meets his doom in the person of Odin, the one-eyed father of the gods. The scene is his last battle and the Branstock is Sigmund's sword, first given to him by Odin as a mark of his ascendancy.

> White went his hair on the wind like the ragged drift of the cloud,
> And his dust-driven, blood-beaten harness was the death-storm's angry shroud
> When the summer sun is departing in the first of the night of wrack;
> And his sword was the cleaving lightning, that smites and is hurried aback
> Ere the hand may rise against it; and his voice was the following thunder.
>
> Then cold grew the battle before him, dead-chilled with the fear and the wonder...
> ....
>
> But lo, through the hedge of the war-shafts a mighty man there came,
> One-eyed and seeming ancient, but his visage shone like flame:
> Gleaming-grey was his kirtle, and his hood was cloudy blue;
> And he bore a mighty twi-bill, as he waded the fight-sheaves through,
> And stood face to face with Sigmund, and upheaved the bill to smite.
> Once more round the head of the Volsung fierce glittered the Branstock's light,
> The sword that came from Odin; and Sigmund's cry once more
> Rang out to the very heavens above the din of war.
> Then clashed the meeting edges with Sigmund's latest stroke,
> And in shivering shards fell earthward that fear of worldly folk.
> But changed were the eyes of Sigmund, and the war-wrath left his face;
> For that grey-clad mighty helper was gone, and in his place
> Drave on the unbroken spear-wood 'gainst the Volsung's empty hands:
> And there they smote down Sigmund, the wonder of all lands,
> On the foemen, on the death-heap his deeds had piled that day.[37]

Morris's achievement here is to hand the legend over to the reader without irony or literary self-consciousness. The drive of the metre and the freshness of the similes are intoxicating. At the same time, there is nothing simplistic about the poem. The life it evokes and the outlook are wholly adult, and the emergence of Odin 'through the hedge of war-shafts' is a magnificent image of the limits of human aspiration, which contrasts with the feeling in the saga as translated by Morris and Magnússon: 'But now whenas the battle had dured a while, there came a man into the fight clad in a blue cloak, and with a slouched hat on his head, one-eyed he was, and bare a bill in his hand'.[38]

And yet in some sense the poem *is* self-conscious, *does* represent a sophisticated kind of literary artifice. The subject of the poem is not so much Sigurd, his exploits and his tragedy, as the very existence of the tale itself in the form of the saga. The poem can be read as alluding to the narrative's survival as a structure of accretions built up over several centuries and oftentimes conflicting with one another. As Paul Thompson puts it, 'The saga had been...committed to writing in the later Middle Ages, after generations of embellishment and divergent versions had reduced it to a noble ruin rather than a coherent story'.[39] Morris gives to this fragmentation a formulaic structure: four distinct books which develop from myth and symbol to something like modern realism. The earlier parts of the story, which tell of the hero's ancestry, belong to a primitive era of magic and revenge. The early legends of Sigurd, his fight with the dragon Fafnir and his first meeting with Brynhild, are similarly fantastical but with something of the fabulous attaching to them. The tragic involvement of the mature Sigurd with the House of the Niblungs is the newest part of the story and seems to have abandoned the timelessness of myth. Its concerns are primarily human and social rather than supernatural or heroic, though the latter categories naturally play their instrumental part. The last book follows on from Sigurd's tragedy, but the record is fragmentary and incomplete.

It was this 'curious entanglement of the ages' in the *Völsunga Saga* that attracted Morris so profoundly:[40] the feeling that not only was this a sequence of legends and myths at the root of northern culture but that in its own imperfect structure and condition it embodied the history that had created it. The saga was a kind of composite created by the collaborations of the ages, much like a Gothic cathedral. In the four books of *Sigurd the Volsung,* he gives a rational shape to the layers of accretion. He does not seek, as Pound or Eliot might have, to mimic the ruinous structure of his source, but we do nonetheless experience the poem as a process of cultural growth. The first book belongs in the same world as *Beowulf.* The third book, which charts the conflict between the woman Sigurd loves and the wife he has been cheated into marrying, would not be out of place in a nineteenth-century novel.

Sigurd the Volsung provides the climax for Morris's prolific but intermittent poetic career. There *are* subsequent poems, most of them collected in his *Poems by the Way* (1891),[41] but in the last twenty years of his life his literary skills mostly sought prose outlets. *Sigurd* is not a throwback, not a wilful piece of nostalgia, though its matter is partly Morris's impassioned relationship with the people of past ages and their art. In the article 'How I became a Socialist' (1894), Morris wrote: 'Apart from the desire to produce beautiful things, the leading passion of my life has been and is hatred of modern civilization'.[42] He was not yet a Socialist when he wrote *Sigurd*, but in this evocation of what his contemporaries would have thought the barbarous beginnings of our race, he comes closer than anywhere to giving that hatred expression and justifying it with the depth of his attachments.

NOTES

1. F. R. Leavis, *New Bearings in English Poetry: A Study of the Contemporary Situation*, 2nd edn. (London: Chatto, 1950), 21.
2. William Morris, *The Collected Letters of William Morris*, 4 vols., ed. Norman Kelvin (Princeton: Princeton University Press, 1984–96), i. 28.
3. Morris, 'Apology' for *The Earthly Paradise*, in *The Collected Works of William Morris*, 24 vols., ed. May Morris (London: Longman, 1910–15), iii. 1–2.
4. Morris, *News from Nowhere* in *Works*, xvi. 211.
5. E. P. Thompson, *William Morris: Romantic to Revolutionary*, 2nd edn. (London: Merlin, 1977), 71.
6. Paul Thompson, *The Work of William Morris* (London: Heinemann, 1967), 194.
7. Note the subtitle of his utopian romance, *News from Nowhere; or, An Epoch of Rest* (1891), in Morris, *Works*, xvi. 1.
8. Morris, 'Prologue' to *The Earthly Paradise* in *Works*, iii. 3.
9. J. W. Mackail, *The Life of William Morris*, 2 vols. (London: Longman, 1899), i. 52.
10. Mackail, *Life*, i. 186.
11. David Latham, '"A Matter of Craftsmanship": William Morris's manuscripts'—accessible online at <http://www.morrissociety.org/publications/JWMS/SU85.6.3.Latham.pdf> (accessed 7 February 2013).
12. Morris, 'Preface' to John Ruskin, *The Nature of Gothic: A Chapter from 'The Stones of Venice'* (London: George Allen, 1899), vii.
13. Morris, 'Sir Peter Harpdon's End', in *Works*, i. 54.
14. Morris, 'Concerning Geffray Teste Noire', in *Works*, i. 80.
15. Morris, 'The Haystack in the Floods', in *Works*, i. 128.
16. Paul Thompson, *The Work of William Morris*, 186.
17. Nikolaus Pevsner, *The Buildings of England: Cambridgeshire*, 2nd edn. (Harmondsworth: Penguin, 1970), 86.
18. Morris, 'The Defence of Guenevere', in *Works*, i. 1–2.
19. Walter Pater, 'Aesthetic Poetry' (1868), in *William Morris: The Critical Heritage*, ed. Peter Faulkner (London: Routledge, 1973), 80.
20. Morris reviewed *Men and Women*, in the *Oxford and Cambridge Magazine* in 1856 (*Works*, i. 326–48).
21. Paul Thompson, *The Work of William Morris*, 183.
22. Alfred Tennyson, 'The Epic', in *The Poems of Tennyson*, 3 vols., ed. Christopher Ricks, 2nd edn. (Harlow: Longman, 1987), ii. 19.
23. Morris, *Collected Letters of William Morris*, ed. Norman Kelvin, 4 vols. (Princeton, NJ: Princeton University Press, 1984–96), ii. 514–17.
24. Ruskin, *The Works of John Ruskin*, 39 vols., ed. E. T. Cook and Alexander Wedderburn (London: George Allen, 1903–12) x. 192, 190.
25. Morris, *The Aeneids of Virgil Done into English*, repr. in *Works*, 11.

26. Anon., *Völsunga Saga: The Story of the Volsungs and Niblungs, with Certain Songs from the Elder Edda*, trans. Morris and Eiríkr Magnússon, repr. in *Works*, 7.
27. See Blue Calhoun, *The Pastoral Vision of William Morris' 'The Earthly Paradise'* (Atlanta: University of Georgia, 1975) and Florence S. Boos, *The Design of William Morris' 'The Earthly Paradise'* (Lewiston: Edwin Mellen, 1990).
28. Morris, *The Earthly Paradise,* in Works, iii. 81.
29. E.P. Thompson, *William Morris: Romantic to Revolutionary*, 110–50. Morris became a Socialist in 1883.
30. Pater, 'Aesthetic Poetry', 79–92.
31. Morris, 'The Lovers of Gudrun', in *Works*, v. 337.
32. Amanda Hodgson, *The Romances of William Morris* (Cambridge: Cambridge University Press, 1987), 87.
33. For the word 'barbarous' I am indebted to Simon Dentith, 'Sigurd the Volsung: Heroic Poetry in an Unheroic Age', in Peter Faulkner and Peter Preston, eds., *William Morris: Centenary Essays* (Exeter: University of Exeter Press, 1999), 60–70. Dentith is one of a few contemporary scholars who have written well on *Sigurd*. See also his 'The Matter of Britain and the Search for a National Epic', in *Epic and Empire in Nineteenth-Century Britain* (Cambridge: Cambridge University Press, 2006), 64–83. In addition, see Herbert Tucker, *Epic: Britain's Heroic Muse, 1790–1810* (Oxford: Oxford University Press, 2008) and Amanda Hodgson, 'The Troy Connection: Myth and History in *Sigurd the Volsung*' in Faulkner and Preston, eds., *William Morris*, 71–79.
34. Morris, 'Poems of "The Earthly Paradise" time', *Works*, xxiv. 87–366.
35. Mackail, *Life*, i. 334, 335.
36. Mackail, *Life*, i. 299.
37. Morris, *Sigurd*, in *Works*, xii. 53–54.
38. Morris, *Völsunga Saga*, in *Works*, vii. 314.
39. Paul Thompson, *The Work of William Morris*, 199.
40. *William Morris: Artist, Writer, Socialist*, 2 vols., ed. May Morris (Oxford: Basil Blackwell, 1936), i. 475.
41. Morris, *Poems by the Way*, in *Works*, xxiv.
42. Morris, 'How I became a Socialist', in *Works*, xxiii. 279.

SELECT BIBLIOGRAPHY

Armstrong, Isobel, *Victorian Poetry: Poetry, Poetics, Politics* (London: Routledge, 1993).
Boos, Florence S., *The Design of William Morris' 'The Earthly Paradise'* (Lewiston: Edwin Mellen, 1990).
Calhoun, Blue, *The Pastoral Vision of William Morris: 'The Earthly Paradise'* (Atlanta: University of Georgia, 1975).
Chandler, Alice, *A Dream of Order* (London: Routledge, 1971).
Faulkner, Peter, *Against the Age: An Introduction to William Morris* (Allen and Unwin: London, 1980).
Hoare, Dorothy M., *The Works of Morris and Yeats in Relation to Early Saga Literature* (Cambridge: Cambridge University Press, 1937).
Hodgson, Amanda, *The Romances of William Morris* (Cambridge: Cambridge University Press, 1987).

Latham, David, *Writing on the Image: Reading William Morris* (Toronto: University of Toronto Press, 2007).

MacCarthy, Fiona, *William Morris: A Life for our Time* (London: Faber, 1995).

Mackail, J. W., *The Life of William Morris*, 2 vols (Longmans: London, 1899).

Morris, May, *The Introductions to the Collected Works of William Morris*, 2 vols. (New York: Oriole, 1977).

Noyes, Alfred, *William Morris* (London: Macmillan, 1908).

Thompson, E. P., *William Morris: Romantic to Revolutionary*, 2nd edn. rev. (London: Merlin, 1977).

Thompson, Paul, *The Work of William Morris* (London: Heinemann, 1967).

Tompkins, J. M. S., *William Morris: An Approach to the Poetry* (London: Cecil Woolf, 1988).

Waithe, Marcus, *William Morris's Utopia of Strangers: Victorian Medievalism and the Ideal of Hospitality* (Cambridge: D. S. Brewer, 2006).

....

CHAPTER 30

CITY OF PAIN: THE POETRY OF JAMES THOMSON

....

MARK FORD

In the last year of his life, James Thomson (1834–1882) composed a pair of contrasting poems on the theme of sleep. The first, 'The Sleeper', for which he was paid four guineas by the *Cornhill* magazine, where it appeared in March of 1882, describes a young woman drifting into a peaceful doze in a warm, comfortable parlour. 'The fire is in a steadfast glow', it opens,

> The curtains drawn against the night;
> Upon the red couch soft and low
> Between the fire and lamp alight
> She rests half-sitting, half-reclining,
> Encompassed by the cosy shining,
> Her ruby dress with lace trimmed white.[1]

The poet watches, fascinated, as the young woman's eyelids slowly close, and as her hand slips languidly from her chin and throat to her breast; sensual, quasi-erotic details ('The little pink-shell ear-rim flushes / With her young blood's translucent blushes, / Nestling in tresses warm as fur') are countered by an insistence on the absolute innocence of the girl and the scene: 'Her brown and blue-veined temple gleaming / Beneath the dusk of hair back-streaming / Are as a virgin's marble shrine'. He observes the effect of a dream on her sleeping features, 'fluttering o'er the lips', stirring 'the eyelids in their rest', troubling her breathing 'like a ripple on a river'. What sort of dream is she having, he wonders; the smile it evokes allows him to deduce it concerns 'A pleasant not a passionate theme, / A little love, a little guile'. She doesn't, fortunately, talk in her sleep, and thus reveal to him 'the secret of some maiden feeling' he has no right to hear. The dream passes, and he watches her as she settles into 'deep sleep', 'sweet sleep', 'pure sleep from which she will awaken / Refreshed as one who hath partaken / New strength, new hope, new love, new faith'.

By the time 'The Sleeper' had appeared in the *Cornhill*, Thomson had drafted most of 'Insomnia', which he completed on 8 March 1882. (Thomson's poetic manuscripts are all carefully dated.) 'Insomnia' appeared in the first posthumous collection of Thomson's poems, *A Voice from the Nile and Other Poems*, edited by Bertram Dobell and published in 1884. It opens at midnight. Everyone else in the house where the poet is staying has gone to bed, confident of a good night's rest:

> But I with infinite weariness outworn,
>   Haggard with endless nights unblessed by sleep,
>   Ravaged by thoughts unutterably forlorn,
>   Plunged in despairs unfathomably deep,
>   Went cold and pale and trembling with affright
>   Into the desert vastitude of Night,
>   Arid and wild and black;
>   Foreboding no oasis of sweet slumber,
>   Counting beforehand all the countless number
> Of sands that are its minutes on my desolate track.[2]

And in this foreboding he is, inevitably, proved right. While the others enjoy sleep's 'divine oblivion and repose', the poet suffers a particularly agonizing *nuit blanche*, for at the striking of each hour, a figure appears in his room. That of the hour from one to two is shrouded and sombre and has folded wings; he begs this figure, whose sex is not revealed, to unfurl them and fan slumber through his brain, only to learn that if he wants to be carried aloft on the figure's strong 'pinions' over the 'hollow night' and into morning's 'golden springs', he must fall asleep first.

This, of course, he cannot do. 'That which I ask of you', he complains, 'you ask of me'— the insomniac's Catch 22. Instead, he must cross, alone and on foot, the hour, which he figures as a deep and precipitous ravine: he must work his way down, as best he can, its steep sides, 'Staggering, stumbling, sinking depths unseen, / Shaken and bruised and gashed by stub and stone', then flounder across its furious, foaming, icy torrent-brook, and then ascend the opposite ridge, an 'awful scarp',

> Clinging to tangled root and rock-jut sharp;
>   Perspiring with faint chills instead of heat,
>   Trembling, and bleeding hands and knees and feet;
>   Falling to rise anew;
>   Until, with lamentable toil and travel
>   Upon the ridge of arid sand and gravel
> I lay supine half-dead and heard the bells chime Two.

Each new 'Watcher', as he calls them, is more terrifying and implacable than the one before, and when four o'clock strikes he can bear it no longer. He dresses and leaves the house, wandering the deserted streets of the city until dawn. The immeasurable distance he feels between himself and the rest of humanity is vividly captured as the city begins to stir: 'When some stray workmen half-asleep but lusty / Passed urgent through the rain-pour wild and gusty, / I felt a ghost already, planted watching there'.

One has to reach across the Channel for a term that can adequately characterize the poet of 'Insomnia' and 'The City of Dreadful Night', or poems such as 'In the Room', or 'A Real Vision of Sin', or 'To Our Ladies of Death': the Thomson of these poems is that rare thing in mid-Victorian verse, an authentic *poète maudit*, beyond consolation, condemned to record in lurid gothic 'the ghastly hours of all the timeless Hells' he lived through, and yet conscious that his words can do but feeble justice to the depths and intensity of the despair to which he was prone: 'I look back on the words already written, / And writhe by cold rage stung, by self-scorn smitten, / They are so weak and vain and infinitely inane', he observes miserably towards the end of 'Insomnia'.

Thomson's masterpiece, 'The City of Dreadful Night', was composed at more or less exactly the same time as Arthur Rimbaud's *A Season in Hell*, in the early 1870s, but rather than creating a poetic language that was '*absolument moderne*', it demonstrated—much to the profit of that great Thomson enthusiast, T. S. Eliot[3]—how Dante's *Inferno* might serve as a model for a poet looking to describe a contemporary urban dystopia. '*Je parvins à faire s'évanouir dans mon esprit toute l'espérance humaine. Sur toute joie pour l'étrangler j'ai fait le bond sourd de la bête féroce*' (I succeeded in driving all hope from my mind. With the stealth of beasts, I leapt on every happiness and wrung its neck),[4] declared Rimbaud unambiguously at the opening of *A Season in Hell*. The young seer's ability to see through and cast off the belief-systems of his day resulted in the creation of an extraordinary new poetic idiom. Thomson never aspired to be a revolutionary of this kind, and his exclusion from the bourgeois comforts of hearth and home so poignantly hymned in 'The Sleeper' was involuntary and undesired, rather than deliberate and defiant. Anne Ridler perhaps rather overstates the case when she asserts in her introduction to her 1963 edition of Thomson's poems and letters that 'it is no use looking to him for freshness of diction, for subtleties of metrical variation',[5] but it is certainly true that Thomson delivered his unnervingly bleak vision of life after God in terms that derive, rather than secede from, his major English-language influences—Shelley, Poe, and Browning.

It is this *maudit* strand in Thomson's poetry that has most often awakened the interest of later generations of readers—though, in truth, that interest has been flickering rather than constant—and that proved influential on later poets such as Eliot or, more recently, Mick Imlah, whose section on B. V. (Thomson's pen-name, short for Bysshe Vanolis [an anagram of Novalis]) in his 'Afterlives of the Poets' brilliantly recreates the poet's last days in the grip of his twin related demons, insomnia and alcohol.[6] The part played by Thomson's dipsomania in the division between the *maudit* and the bourgeois in both his life and his work can hardly be overstated. It allies him with the split personalities depicted in various nineteenth-century explorations of the *doppelgänger*, the likes of Stevenson's Jekyll and Hyde, Poe's William Wilson, and James Hogg's Robert Wringhim in *The Private Memoirs and Confessions of a Justified Sinner*. For just as an unfathomable gulf yawns between poems such as 'The Sleeper' and its dark antithesis, 'Insomnia', or the jaunty lyrics of 'Sunday Up the River' and the unsparing 'The City of Dreadful Night', so it could sometimes seem there were two James Thomsons. A telling instance of this is related by J. W. Barrs to Thomson's first biographer, Henry Salt:

> His absolute abandonment during these attacks was sufficient to attest their nature, and no more pregnant illustration of the metamorphosis he underwent could well be found than the remark made by his landlord's children on one such occasion. Thomson was naturally very loving with children, and children invariably returned his affection. Once, when he came back to his rooms in Huntley Street in the fullness of the change wrought by his excesses, the children went to the door to admit him, but closed it again and went to their father, telling him that 'Mr Thomson's wicked brother was at the door,' and for some time they could not recognise 'our Mr Thomson' in the figure of the dipsomaniac claiming his name.[7]

Another friend, G. W. Foote, left this account of Thomson's alcoholism:

> He was not a toper; on the contrary, he was a remarkably temperate man, both in eating and drinking. His intemperate fits came on periodically, like other forms of madness; and naturally as he grew older and weaker they lasted longer, and the lucid intervals became shorter. The fits were invariably preceded by several days of melancholy, which deepened and deepened until intolerable. Then he flew to the alcohol, so naturally and unconsciously that when he returned to sanity he could seldom remember the circumstances of his collapse.[8]

Foote also records Thomson once telling a friend that alcoholism ran in his family, and indeed that 'nearly all the members of it who "had brains", especially a gifted aunt of his, fell victim to its power'.[9] Whatever its origins, Thomson's 'constitutional melencholia' (Foote's term), and the drinking sprees to which it impelled him, eventually separated him from all but the most steadfast of his friends; and it transformed London, in his imagination, into a phantasmagoric simulacrum of a city, a nocturnal urban wilderness inhabited only by ghosts and damaged, desperate exiles,

> Each adding poison to the poisoned air;
> Infections of unutterable sadness,
> Infections of unutterable madness,
> Infections of incurable despair.[10]

'The City of Dreadful Night' stands apart from other long poems of the Victorian era that wrestle directly with theological and philosophical issues—poems such as *In Memoriam*, 'Dipsychus', or 'Empedocles on Etna'—in that, unlike Tennyson or Clough or Arnold, Thomson, by this stage of his life, had no faith to lose, and he knew it. Its introductory section states explicitly that the poem will be comprehensible only to those in a similarly faithless condition: 'pious spirits' who believe in God or hopeful 'sages who foresee a heaven on earth', Thomson trenchantly declares, 'For none of these I write, and none of these / Could read the writing if they deigned to try.'[11] His aim, instead, is to reach out to others as metaphysically destitute as himself and let them know they're not alone, a motivation that allies the poem with numerous twentieth-century explorations of disillusionment and suffering:

> Yes, here and there some weary wanderer
>   In that same city of tremendous night,
> Will understand the speech, and feel a stir
>   Of fellowship in all-disastrous fight;
> 'I suffer mute and lonely, yet another
> Uplifts his voice to let me know a brother
>   Travels the same paths though out of sight.'
>
> (Proem, 29–35)

Compare with this, say, Philip Larkin's 'Sympathy in White Major', in which Larkin expresses the hope that his poetry will allow all those who believe they've missed out on life at least to feel part of a group of like-minded failures.

Like so much of Thomson's writing in both verse and prose, 'The City of Dreadful Night' originally appeared in the secularist magazine *The National Reformer*, edited by the militant atheist and political activist Charles Bradlaugh. Bradlaugh and Thomson first met in 1852, when both were stationed in army barracks in Ballincollig in Ireland. It was only gradually that Thomson, who had been raised an Irvingite Evangelical by his devout Scottish mother, found his beliefs being eroded, not only by Bradlaugh, but by the publications of such as Darwin and Huxley and Spenser and Lyell in the late 1850s and early 1860s. 'The City of Dreadful Night''s precursor, 'The Doom of a City' of 1857, is as lurid and, in some parts, as striking as the later poem, but in the end delivers a fairly orthodox Christian message: come the end of the world, the sinful will be punished, or at least pulverized, while an elect few will be translated to heaven, where Thomson even imagines them singing and playing harps in a 'radiant quire'.[12] He began, however, contributing to *The National Reformer* soon after it was founded by Bradlaugh in 1860, and his numerous articles for it that decade, all signed B.V., trace an increasingly deepening scepticism that seems to have culminated in a personal crisis in 1869. On 4 November of that year he recorded in his diary 'Burned all my old papers, manuscripts, and letters', further noting that the process took him five hours: 'But after this terrible year, I could do no less than consume the past. I can now better face the future, come in what guise it may.'[13] No one has ever discovered exactly what made the preceding year so terrible, but shortly after this conflagration Thomson began work on the first sections of a poem that so squarely faces the future that Edmund Blunden declared it, in 1932, 'the most anticipative poem'[14] of its time.

It consists of a Proem of six seven-line stanzas, and of twenty-one sections; the odd-numbered sections are written, like the Proem, in seven-line stanzas rhyming *ababccb*, while the even-numbered sections are predominantly in six-line stanzas rhyming *ababcc*, but these even-numbered sections also contain set-piece speeches by various characters composed in a range of stanza forms and rhyme schemes. As a whole the sequence is at once exquisitely shaped and beautifully varied; Thomson clearly devoted much time to the mathematical aspects of the poem, and even alerts us in a footnote to the significance of the poem's having twenty-one sections. He has just been describing, in Section II, how he followed the passage of a denizen of the city to three sites of traumatic significance: a church ('Here Faith died, poisoned by this charnel air'), a villa

('Here Love died, stabbed by its own worshipped pair'), and a squalid house ('Here Hope died, starved out in its utmost lair'). Like one of Dante's damned, this pilgrim seems condemned to repeat his triangular journey over and over, and when asked by the poet why, answers 'coldly' with a brilliantly effective metaphor:

> Take a watch, erase
> The signs and figures of the circling hours,
>   Detach the hands, remove the dial-face;
> The works proceed until run down; although
> Bereft of purpose, void of use, still go.

(II, 32–36)

Take a man's seventy years, Thomson then instructs us in a footnote, divide them by the 'persistent three' of dead Faith, dead Love, and dead Hope, and you get this equation: LXX ÷ 333 =.210 recurring, that is the 21 sections of the poem and the 0 of the Proem repeated for ever. Further, as the poet Edwin Morgan pointed out in his excellent introduction to an edition of the poem published in 1993, the triple rhyme of section I's opening stanza is deliberately repeated in section XXI's closing stanza, with one pointed, crucial difference: there / air / fair becomes air / there / despair.[15]

In general the odd, seven-line stanza sections are devoted to meditation and description, while in the even sections Thomson presents vignettes of despair like that of the traumatized pilgrim of section II, or the character in section IV who recounts, in an idiom heavily influenced by Browning's 'Childe Roland', his journey across a nightmarish desert; he fronts its horrors boldly enough, the birds with 'savage cries and clanking wings' swooping past him, the 'fleshless fingers cold' that pluck at him, the 'Serpents, heaped pell-mell / For Devil's roll-call and some *fête* of Hell' hissing at him, until he arrives at the sea; there he meets a woman holding in her hand a red lamp that horrifyingly turns out to be her own 'burning heart' trickling blood. Appalled by this, the narrator then somehow divides himself into two: one of him stands apart and watches, while the other sinks into a swoon, and has blood dripped onto his forehead by the woman holding her lamp-heart, blood she then wipes away with her tears and hair. Eventually both swooning self and woman are washed out to sea, and the other self is left to tell his tale, Ancient Mariner-style, to anyone in the city of dreadful night who'll listen.

In their extravagance and intensity such narratives are closer to Poe, or Poe's admirer and translator, Baudelaire, than to anything in Victorian poetry, delivered though they are in a language that borrows heavily from the Gothic side of Shelley and Browning. While it would take the genius of Eliot to find a way of fusing Thomson's Dantescan vision of the urban inferno with realistic details of modern London in the manner that makes *The Waste Land* so startling, Thomson's poem is not devoid of glimpses of the nocturnal city that the poet paced in the throes of his insomnia: street-lamps burn, the moonlight silvers empty squares, the dark shrouds 'countless lanes and close retreats'. While it's often signalled that the poem's city is a city of the mind ('How he arrives there none can clearly know'), at one point its silence is shattered by the 'booming and jar of ponderous wheels' and the 'trampling clash of heavy ironshod feet'; a vast dray pulled by a team of snorting horses arrives, as if we were in the middle of a bit of London scene-setting by Dickens. And the poem's river can't help but evoke the Thames:

> I sat forlornly by the river-side,
>   And watched the bridge-lamps glow like golden stars
> Above the blackness of the swelling tide,
>   Down which they struck rough gold in ruddier bars;
> And heard the heave and plashing of the flow
> Against the wall a dozen feet below.
> Large elm trees stood along the river-walk...
>
> (VI, 1–7)

It's during his sojourn on this river-walk that he overhears a couple propound what might be described as Thomson's own brand of secularist doctrine, one that significantly lacks Bradlaugh's hope that the dissemination of atheism might relieve mankind from its mind-forged manacles and enable the creation of a better society:

> 'The world rolls round for ever like a mill;
> It grinds out death and life and good and ill;
> It has no purpose, heart or mind or will.
>
> 'While air of Space and Time's full river flow
> The mill must blindly whirl unresting so:
> It may be wearing out, but who can know?'
>
> (VIII, 36–41)

The most comforting thing a secularist sermonizer can find to say to a 'gloom-arrayed' congregation in section XIV is that at least loss of belief in the afterlife means that, when you eventually feel you've had enough, you can kill yourself without fear of retribution: 'But if you would not this poor life fulfil, / Lo, you are free to end it when you will, / Without the fear of waking after death' (XIV, 82–85). It was such sentiments that earned Thomson the sobriquet, bestowed by Bertram Dobell, of 'the laureate of pessimism'.[16]

The 'anticipative' aspect of the poem is particularly strong in section XVIII, in which the protagonist wanders into a suburb in the north of the city. There he comes across a creature crawling painfully down a lane, only to realize that this creature is in fact a man, or what 'had been a man', his 'Long grey unreverend locks befouled with mire'. Like so many of the maimed compulsives of Samuel Beckett's fiction and theatre, he is pursuing a hopeless quest, convinced he is on the point of discovering the 'long-lost broken golden thread' that will lead him from the unendurable present, this 'accursed night without a morn', back through 'vast wastes of horror-haunted time' to his earliest infancy, thus enabling him to revert to the state of a baby 'cradled on its mother's knee'. The unillusioned poet can only wonder at this perverse longing to 'seek oblivion through the far-off gate / Of birth, when that of death is close at hand!'

Yet, however futile the poem acknowledges all human endeavour to be, it concludes with an admiring description of a vast bronze statue erected on an 'upland bleak and bare' above the city. This statue is of the 'wingèd Woman' depicted in Albrecht Dürer's 1514 engraving *Melencolia I* (see Figure 30.1).

FIGURE 30.1 The 'wingèd Woman' depicted in Albrecht Dürer's 1514 engraving *Melencolia I*

For Thomson she is a figure, not only of melancholy, but also of all the ingenious means with which humanity has striven against the forces of chaos and darkness. These are precisely itemized in the poem ('a pair of compasses... The instruments of carpentry and science... Scales, hour-glass, bell...'). Her wings, like those of the first Watcher in 'Insomnia', are furled, but Thomson still allows himself to derive a measure of uplift from her powers of stoical endurance in face of the naked truth of our condition (and surely he must have hoped his own poem might function in an analogous way):

> Thus has the artist copied her, and thus
> > Surrounded to expound her form sublime,
> Her fate heroic and calamitous;
> > Fronting the dreadful mysteries of Time,
> Unvanquished in defeat and desolation,
> Undaunted in the hopeless conflagration
> > Of the day setting on her baffled prime.
>
> > > (XXI, 43–49)

Thomson goes on to commend her 'indomitable will', and even to suggest that, however 'baffled', her creativity will prove unstoppable: 'The hands shall fashion and the brain shall pore, / And all her sorrow shall be turned to labour'. Yet while a number of the more positive terms deployed in high romanticism's encounters with the infinite manage to infiltrate Thomson's vocabulary in this final section—'sublime', 'mighty', 'passionate', 'solemn'—the knowledge with which Dürer's wingèd woman is invested is more a summation of, than a contradiction of, the poem's 'anticipative' philosophical premises. There is nothing meaningful out there:

> The sense that every struggle brings defeat
>> Because Fate holds no prize to crown success;
> That all the oracles are dumb or cheat
>> Because they have no secret to express;
> That none can pierce the vast black veil uncertain
> Because there is no light beyond the curtain;
>> That all is vanity and nothingness.
>
> (XXI, 64–70)

'Behind the veil, behind the veil', exclaimed Tennyson in LVI of *In Memoriam* when confronted with the notion that life is 'futile' as well as 'frail'.[17] Thomson sternly dismisses this specious comfort: none can pierce the veil because there's nothing behind it. Although the woman's ability to persist in the face of endless defeat allows her to seem, in the opening lines of the poem's final stanza, a late descendant of romanticism's various figures of intellectual beauty, and even as engaged in some kind of ambivalent dialogue with the natural sublime, this proves momentary, indeed almost elegiac, for the poem's conclusion firmly indicates that the only consolation that she, and by extension art, can truly offer, is the one he promised in the Proem, to which this circular poem is about to return us: a sense of solidarity in suffering:

> The moving moon and stars from east to west
>> Circle before her in the sea of air;
> Shadows and gleams glide round her solemn rest.
>> Her subjects often gaze up to her there:
> The strong to drink new strength of iron endurance,
> The weak new terrors; all, renewed assurance
>> And confirmation of the old despair.
>
> (XXI, 78–84)

In his autobiography *Something of Myself* (1937), Rudyard Kipling recalls that he read Thomson's poem in his schooldays, and that it 'shook me to my unformed core'.[18] (He in turn composed a short story, first published in 1887, called 'The City of Dreadful Night', which describes an insomniac's ramble around the streets of Lahore, and makes numerous allusions to Thomson's poem.) The poem's power to shake its readers derives in no small measure from the repetitive, hypnotic rhythms in which it presents its relentless series of disillusionments and losses. Matthew Arnold, in 'Stanzas from the Grand Chartreuse' (a poem that inspired a poetic response in kind from Thomson, 'Suggested by Matthew Arnold's *Grande Chartreuse*', composed in 1855), described himself as 'Wandering between two worlds, one dead, / The other powerless to be born, / With nowhere yet to rest my head'[19]: 'The City of Dreadful Night' makes brilliant use of Dante to create a mid-Victorian limbo in which Arnold's sense of metaphysical homelessness is shared by all, and dramatically illustrated by both a diverse cast of characters and by Thomson's wide-ranging philosophical speculations. The latter at times take us into very murky waters indeed. In Section VII, for instance, Thomson reports that 'some say' there are phantoms abroad in the city who 'mingle freely with sparse mankind'. This mingling seems to have a sexual element, and is again 'anticipative', in this case of Bram Stoker's vampires haunting nocturnal London in his novel *Dracula* of 1897. Thomson's phantoms do not, however, feed on the blood of mankind, instead appearing to be sort of phantom-flashers:

> The phantoms have no reticence at all;
> The nudity of flesh will blush though tameless,
> The extreme nudity of bone grins shameless,
> The unsexed skeleton mocks shroud and pall.
>
> (VII, 11–14)

The distinction between mankind's 'nudity of flesh' which, however unbridled the sexual appetite, can still give rise to feelings of shame, and the 'shameless' 'nudity of bone' of the phantoms is a dizzying one, and seems again to prefigure some of the ways in which Eliot recast late Victorian Gothic into something more radically unsettling, as in a poem such as 'Whispers of Immortality', with its weirdly eroticized corpses: 'And breastless creatures under ground / Leaned backwards with a lipless grin'.[20]

And yet, however outlandish or bewildering the poem's speculations and cast, it never seeks to break free from its overarching formal framework or its stately poetic diction. The liminal world it describes is movingly implicit in this disjunction between the daring of Thomson's thought and the conventionality of the poem's forms and language; its full, indeed often thumping, rhymes and insistent use of repetitions can make the poem hover somewhere between the incantatory and the imprisoning. If the poem's city is a place of radical homelessness, its style yet communicates an inability to jettison the poetic conventions Thomson inherited, leaving it effectively stranded between two worlds, to adapt Arnold's phrase, with nowhere to rest its head.

It would, however, in time find a significant and admiring readership, though six years elapsed between the appearance of the poem in four instalments in the *National Reformer* in the spring of 1874, and its publication in a volume, *The City of Dreadful Night and Other Poems*: those other poems included 'In the Room' (which is spoken by the furniture in a room in which a man has just committed suicide), 'To Our Ladies of Death' (which imagines, Hamlet-like, the dispersal of the poet's own corpse: 'One part of me shall feed a little worm, / And it a bird on which a man may feed'[21]), as well as a number of more cheerful sequences such as the wonderful 'Sunday at Hampstead' and the frolicsome 'Sunday Up the River'. If this book didn't quite make Thomson famous, it sold well enough to make viable the publication of a second collection, *Vane's Story, Weddah and Om-El-Bonain, and Other Poems* shortly after, and then a volume of prose pieces, *Essays and Phantasies*, the following year, 1881. But the flurry of attention garnered by the appearance of these titles occurred just when the poet was beginning to lose in earnest his battle against his own melancholy, and the dreadful nights to which it drove him. It was only in these last couple of years that he managed to earn any money from his poetry, money he fast squandered: the four guineas, for instance, that he received from the *Cornhill* for 'The Sleeper' was likely to prove, Barrs wearily noted, the occasion for another 'sad, sad spree'.[22]

Thomson's letters of contrition on recovery from such 'sprees' are often both eloquent and unsparing: to Barrs on April 22 of 1882 he confessed:

> I scarcely know how to write to you after my atrocious and disgusting return for the wonderful hospitality and kindness of yourself and Miss Barrs. I can only say that I was mad. In one fit of frenzy I have not only lost more than I yet know, and half murdered myself (were it not for my debts I sincerely wish it had been wholly), but justly alienated my best and firmest friends, old and new, both in London and Leicester.
>
> As, unfortunately for myself at least, I am left alive, it only remains for me to endeavour my utmost by hard and persistent struggling to repay my money debts, for my debts of kindness can never be repaid. If I fail, as very probably I shall fail, the failure will but irresistibly prove what I have long thoroughly believed, that for myself and others I am much better dead than alive.
>
> As apologies would be worse than useless, I will conclude by simply expressing my deep gratitude for your astonishing undeserved goodness to myself, and my best wishes for the welfare of you and yours.[23]

To his credit, Barrs himself seems to have viewed Thomson's excesses more as a malady than a weakness. In his statement to Salt he declared: 'No mortal ever strove against an overpowering disease more grimly than Thomson, and when friends were to be pained by his succumbing to the mania it was always combated and repulsed to the last moment'.[24] Over the years, critics and biographers have pointed to this or that event in Thomson's life as the decisively formative catalyst of his ruinous addiction. The death, at the age of 14, of one Matilda Weller, whom he got to know in Ireland in the early 1850s, was popular with a number of those who wrote memoirs of the poet in the years immediately following his death. Bradlaugh, however, was scornful of all such attempts to attribute his friend's views and problems to this early loss, though he did allow that in his morbid moments Thomson was himself prone to building a 'poetical romance about her memory'.[25]

It's perhaps also worth pointing out that many of Thomson's friends recall him as not at all a gloomy companion. 'His light feet and merry tongue', remembers Bradlaugh's daughter, Hypatia, made him, when it came to ballroom dancing, 'one of the most desirable partners'.[26] He was popular in a wide circle of friends, regularly engaging in all sorts of outdoor activity, from boating to grouse-shooting, from tennis to horse-riding, and he was passionately fond of music, and in particular of the works of Mozart and Beethoven.

In literary matters as well as in musical ones Thomson had excellent taste, championing Blake, Whitman, Melville, and Flaubert, translating Leopardi, Heine, and Gautier (having taught himself Italian, German, and French), and praising Baudelaire's *Les*

Paradis Artificiels. During his two decades as a literary, political, and cultural journalist for a series of secularist magazines and papers, Thomson published hundreds of reviews and essays on topics ranging from 'Religion in the Rocky Mountains' (following a trip he made to Colorado in 1872 as the Secretary of the Champion Gold and Silver Mines Company) to the curse of British Philistinism ('Bumble, Bumbledom, Bumbleism' (1865)). A number of his attacks on social injustice and on the institutions of the era, in particular on the crown and on religion, became well known in Victorian free-thinking circles. The most wittily barbed of these is 'A Famous Old Jewish Firm', which figures Jah as an irascible Jewish merchant, and reads the Bible as an account of his business dealings with Abraham and Jacob and their heirs. At length, rather like Dickens's Dombey, feeling his age and the need of a successor, Jah expands the firm into Father, Son and Co., much to the displeasure of his erstwhile partners. The Co. remains a shadowy figure, but the Son, 'with that eccentricity which has ever abundantly characterized [Jah]'s proceedings' is brought up 'as a poor Jewish youth, apparently the child of a carpenter called Joseph, and his wife Mary':

> Joseph has little or no influence with the firm, and we scarcely hear of transaction done through him, but Mary had made the most profitable use of her old *liaison* with Jah, and the majority of those who do business with the firm seek her good offices, and pay her very liberal commissions. Those who do not think so highly of her influence, deal with the house chiefly through the son, and thus it has come to pass that poor Jah is virtually ousted from his own business. He and the third partner are little more than sleeping partners, while his mistress and her son manage every affair of importance.[27]

This new business hierarchy proves instantly successful, and the product is soon being exported all around the world. Jonathan Swift, as the above makes clear, was the dominant influence on Thomson's satirical prose style, though it must be confessed he rarely achieves the devastating verbal precision and wit of Swift at his best. His versatility as a journalist was most fully tested after he finally cut all ties with Bradlaugh and *The National Reformer* in 1875, the year after it published 'The City of Dreadful Night'; Thomson found himself reduced to writing for the trade magazine *Cope's Tobacco Plant*, a Liverpool-based journal sponsored by a tobacco company. This meant channelling his literary enthusiasms through topics related, however tangentially, to the production and consumption of tobacco, a challenge to which he often rose triumphantly. Though his critical prose is not much read these days, it's nearly always shrewd and sprightly, while his more poetic prose pieces, which he called Phantasies, such as the stately, symphonic 'A Lady of Sorrow' or 'In Our Forest of the Past', stand comparison with the best of De Quincey (a powerful influence on their conception and cadences) or the more speculative, symbolic side of Poe. The Lady of Sorrow in the latter strongly resembles the figure of the wingèd Woman at the end of 'The City of Dreadful Night', eloquently propounding a stoical atheism ('whatever is born in Time must decay and perish in Time'[28]), and hymning the comforts and release of death. At the Phantasy's end her 'thin weird voice' dies away 'in the dense blackness subterranean, as a star-speck dwindles in the formless night; and the gloom, so deep and crushing in the revelation of her voice, grows deeper still and yet more awful in the following utter silence'.[29]

'Dense blackness…formless night…gloom…utter silence…': if it was Thomson's pessimism that lay behind his appeal to such as the young Kipling and the adolescent Eliot, the 'less deceived' aspect of his work was, in many ways, thrust upon him, rather than being the result of a determined questing after the new. His drinking put the tempting comforts of bourgeois life beyond his reach, and converted him from a poet one might ally with Coventry Patmore into one who anticipated the despairs and disjunctions of a later century. Given the fact that Thomson often worked in the British Library, how tempting it is to imagine him in May of 1873 sitting across from the 18-year old Rimbaud (readers were supposed to be over 21 but the *enfant terrible* had brazenly lied on his application for a reader's pass), both furiously scribbling away at their nightmarish long poems. Like *A Season in Hell*, 'The City of Dreadful Night' articulates a radical isolation and disconnection that marks a new stage in imaginings of the modern metropolis. The first of its epigraphs is from Dante: 'Per me si va nella città dolente' (Through me is the way into the city of pain). This was probably the first line of Dante's that Eliot ever read, and Thomson's city of pain lies, like its own 'Great ruins of an unremembered past', buried somewhere beneath Eliot's 'Unreal city', the earlier poet's roaming phantoms haunting 'shadowy streets' transformed by Eliot into zombie-like commuters flowing through fog over London Bridge.

The many dreadful nights that Thomson lived through in his last drink-addled months culminated in a binge that led to a spell in prison, and then, on 1 June, to an intestinal haemorrhage from which he died two days later in University College Hospital. His last words, according to a friend who was present at his death, were too desperate ever to be repeated.

Notes

1. James Thomson, 'The Sleeper', in *Poems and Some Letters of James Thomson*, ed. Anne Ridler (Carbondale: Southern University Press, 1963), 214.
2. Thomson, 'Insomnia', in *Poems and Some Letters of James Thomson*, 226.
3. For a full account of Thomson's influence on Eliot, see Robert Crawford, *The Savage and the City in the Work of T.S. Eliot* (Oxford: Clarendon Press, 1987), 36–53. In his Preface to *John Davidson: A Selection of His Poems*, ed. Maurice Lindsay (London: Hutchinson, 1961), Eliot reveals that he read Thomson in his 'formative years between the ages of sixteen and twenty', and that Thomson's work 'impressed [him] deeply'.
4. Arthur Rimbaud, *A Season in Hell in Selected Poems and Letters*, trans. and ed. John Sturrock and Jeremy Harding (London: Penguin, 2004), 138.
5. Anne Ridler in *Poems and Some Letters of James Thomson*, xliv.
6. Mick Imlah, *The Lost Leader* (London: Faber and Faber, 2008), 117–124.
7. *Poems and Some Letters of James Thomson*, xv.
8. *Poems and Some Letters of James Thomson*, xv.

9. Thomson quoted in Tom Leonard, *Places of the Mind: The Life and Work of James Thomson* (London: Chatto & Windus, 1993), 307.

10. Thomson, *The City of Dreadful Night,* in *Poems and Some Letters of James Thomson,* 197.

11. Thomson, *The City of Dreadful Night,* 177.

12. Thomson, 'The Doom of a City', in *Poems and Some Letters of James Thomson,* 41.

13. Thomson quoted in Leonard, *Places of the Mind,* 144.

14. Edward Blunden, quoted by Edward Morgan in his Introduction to his edition of *The City of Dreadful Night* (Edinburgh: Canongate, 1993), 7.

15. Morgan, 'Introduction', 16.

16. Dobell's biography of Thomson of 1910 is entitled *The Laureate of Pessimism: A Sketch of the Life and Character of James Thomson ('B. V.').*

17. Alfred Tennyson, *In Memoriam in Poems of Tennyson,* 3 vols., ed. Christopher Ricks (London: Longman, 1987), ii. 374.

18. Rudyard Kipling, *Something of Myself,* ed. Robert Hampson (London: Penguin, 1987), 52.

19. Matthew Arnold, 'Stanzas from the Grand Chartreuse', in *Selected Poems and Prose,* ed. Miriam Allott (London: Everyman, 1978), 102.

20. T. S. Eliot, 'Whispers of Immortality', in *Collected Poems, 1909–1962* (London: Faber and Faber, 1974), 55.

21. Thomson, 'To Our Ladies of Death', in *Poems and Some Letters of James Thomson,* 73.

22. John Barrs quoted in *Poems and Some Letters of James Thomson,* 275.

23. Thomson quoted in Leonard, *Places of the Mind,* 295.

24. Barrs quoted in *Poems and Some Letters of James Thomson,* xv.

25. Charles Bradlaugh quoted in Leonard, *Places of the Mind,* 313.

26. Hypatia Bradlaugh quoted in *Poems and Some Letters of James Thomson,* xvi.

27. Thomson, 'A Famous Old Jewish Firm', in *The Speedy Extinction of Evil and Misery: Selected Prose of James Thomson,* ed. William David Schaefer (Berkeley and Los Angeles: University of California Press, 1967), 47.

28. Thomson, 'A Lady of Sorrow', in *Selected Prose of James Thomson,* 335.

29. Thomson, 'A Lady of Sorrow', 341.

SELECT BIBLIOGRAPHY

Dobell, Bertram, *The Laureate of Pessimism: A Sketch of the Life and Character of James Thomson ('B. V.')* (London: Bertram Dobell, 1910).

Leonard, Tom, *Places of the Mind: The Life and Work of James Thomson* (London: Chatto & Windus, 1993).

Pawley, Richard, *Secret City: The Emotional Life of the Victorian Poet James Thomson (BV)* (Lanham: University Press of America, 2001).

Salt, Henry S., *The Life of James Thomson* (London: Watts & Co., 1914).

Schaefer, William David, *James Thomson, B.V.: Beyond 'The City'* (Berkeley and Los Angeles: University of California Press, 1965).

Thomson, James, *The City of Dreadful Night and Other Poems* (London: Reeves and Turner, 1880).

—— *Vane's Story, Weddah and Om-El-Bonain, and Other Poems* (London: Reeves and Turner, dated 1881).

—— *Essays and Phantasies* (London: Reeves and Turner, 1881).

—— *A Voice from the Nile and Other Poems* (London: Reeves and Turner, 1884).

—— *Poems, Essays and Fragments*, ed. J. M. Robertson (London: A and H. B. Bonner, 1892).

—— *The Poetical Works of James Thomson*, 2 vols. (London: Reeves and Turner and Bertram Dobell, 1895).

—— *Poems and Some Letters of James Thomson*, ed. Anne Ridler (Carbondale: Southern University Press, 1963).

—— *The Speedy Extinction of Evil and Misery: Selected Prose of James Thomson*, ed. William David Schaefer (Berkeley and Los Angeles: University of California Press, 1967).

—— *The City of Dreadful Night*, ed. Edwin Morgan (Edinburgh: Canongate, 1993).

CHAPTER 31

....

AUGUSTA WEBSTER: TIME
AND THE LYRIC IDEAL

....

EMILY HARRINGTON

'There remains
The day that is to come,' Tse-Ky replied.

'Yea!' said Yu-Pe-Ya, 'by and by is wide
To halt the traveler who asks for now.'

'And yet,' the other said, 'men scarce allow
Now's self so clearly theirs as by and by:
To-day is always gone, to-morrow nigh.'

Augusta Webster, 'Yu-Pe-Ya's Lute'[1]

IN this passage from Augusta Webster's *Yu-Pe-Ya's Lute*, two friends who must part, but plan to meet again a year later, discuss how to think about time. Thinking about the future can mitigate the pain of the present, they suggest, but at the same time a focus on what is to come deprives them of a full experience of 'now'. Yu-Pe-Ya asserts that thoughts of 'by and by' arrest progress for someone eager to focus on the present. This problem animates much of Augusta Webster's poetry both thematically and formally. Some poems, such as 'The Snow Waste' and 'With the Dead' represent the torture of an interminably intermediate state as murderers contemplate their sins in purgatorial places, while others, such as 'Circe' and 'A Woman Sold' depict two women's impatience for a relationship with a man. In Webster's posthumously published sonnet sequence, *Mother and Daughter*, a mother desires both to stop time and to move it forward, knowing that as her daughter grows up they must become increasingly separate: as they gain the future, they lose the past. These poems, as well as others, depict the pleasures and pains of anticipating the new and the agony and ecstasy of waiting. Patricia Rigg notes that the lyrics collected in *A Book of Rhyme* especially focus on themes of transience and impermanence.[2] *Yu-Pe-Ya's Lute*, a narrative poem in heroic couplets interrupted by the songs of its title character, epitomizes Webster's use of a formal hybrid to explore the dynamics of stasis and progress. These dynamics, she suggests, affect readers' expectations of poetry, the creation of memories, the formation of relationships, and the attempt to preserve what is lost with the passage of time.

In her own day as well as in our own, Augusta Webster has been best known for her dramatic poetry, and she has frequently been compared to Robert Browning on the basis of this work.[3] Poems such as 'A Castaway', in the voice of a kept woman, 'A Woman Sold,' about a woman who marries for money rather than love, as well as her monologues in the voices of Medea and Circe all showcase both Webster's formal poetic prowess as well as the complex social demands of middle-class women in the latter half of the nineteenth century. All of these poems demonstrate the dangers of women's necessary reliance on the emotional and financial support of men. These poems correlate with the politics of her prose essays from *The Examiner*, collected in *A Housewife's Opinions*, as well as with Webster's activism: she was a member of the London School Board and agitated on behalf of women's suffrage. In his 1907 anthology introduction to Webster, Mackenzie Bell notes these facts in the first paragraph, following them with a discussion of the 'virility' and 'strength' of her verse. Bell dubs her genius 'dramatic' and hardly discusses her lyrics at all.[4] In his obituary for Webster, Theodore Watts predicts that her reputation will rest on her 1870 volume *Portraits*, and this projection has largely been borne out, even as scholars in the last few decades began to recover her work.[5] Much scholarship of recent decades focuses on Webster's dramatic monologues, which Patricia Rigg has argued might more accurately be called monodramas.[6] Yet, as Rigg has also noted, during the last two decades of her life, Webster turned her focus to lyric poetry, and in her career overall dramatic poetry does not constitute the majority of her work.[7] Her reputation notwithstanding, Webster wrote many forms in addition to the dramatic, including sonnets, rispetti, and other lyric poems, as well as a novel, translations from Greek, and *Yu-Pe-Ya's Lute*.[8] Although Webster has most often been compared to Browning, a reading of *Yu-Pe-Ya's Lute* shows her to be in dialogue with Keats and Tennyson, inserting herself into the conversation about nineteenth-century lyric.

Poetic forms that drew on both lyric and narrative proliferated in the nineteenth century, as Monique Morgan has noted, because the lyric had a critical and aesthetic prestige while the novel was enormously popular. Webster contributes to what Morgan calls 'a heightened sense of the tension between lyric and narrative' by giving Yu-Pe-Ya's songs narrative elements that only his friend and perfect audience Tse-Ky can apprehend, while at the same time writing a narrative that consistently circles back on itself, in a refusal to progress.[9] The title character, for instance, must say farewell, over and over, with each new episode of the story, and yet the tale begins with a journey that ultimately situates him right back where he started. This kind of generic experimentation is important in Webster's career because it embodies the conflicting temporal desires that animate so much of her work. The problem of how to think about time is for her a poetic problem as well as a psychological one.

Before I go on to examine several passages of *Yu-Pe-Ya's Lute*, it will help to understand the contours of the story. Yu-Pe-Ya has returned to his homeland as a representative from a foreign kingdom, where he is a wealthy diplomat and also known as a master minstrel. When it is time for him to return to his king, he realizes that he may never see his homeland again, so he requests to make the trip by riverboat, rather than on the roads, so that he may sear images of the land into his mind during the slow journey. When he reaches the border between the two kingdoms, a storm forces his crew to anchor his boat at the edge of the river overnight. Unable to sleep, Yu-Pe-Ya takes out his lute and begins to play. As he plays, a string breaks, a sign that a fellow master minstrel lurks in the vicinity. Thinking it unlikely that an educated musician would be in such a remote location, he wonders aloud whether robbers might be marauding nearby. An invisible voice tells him that no one is threatening, that it is only a humble woodman who stopped to judge the music. Yu-Pe-Ya takes offence at the word 'judge' and his men go after the woodman and bring him back to the boat. There, Yu-Pe-Ya puts him through a series of tests, upon which the woodman, Tse-Ky, proves that he knows the lore of the lute, produces the words to tunes that Yu-Pe-Ya plays, and most importantly, perfectly articulates the sentiment of a song that Yu-Pe-Ya had only composed that day. This last ability proves Tse-Ky to be the most intimate type of friend to Yu-Pe-Ya, one who crosses class boundaries and who knows his friend's heart better than he knows it himself.

The two friends spend the night deep in conversation. As dawn approaches, Yu-Pe-Ya implores Tse-Ky to continue with him on his journey and to come to the king's court. Tse-Ky, however, must stay in his rural village to care for his aging parents, who have no other children. Unable to convince him to stay with him for even one more day, Yu-Pe-Ya promises to return to the same place a year later. Tse-Ky agrees to meet him there. Before leaving, Yu-Pe-Ya gives Tse-Ky some gold coins. When he returns a year later, Yu-Pe-Ya does not see Tse-Ky waiting for him in the designated place. After waiting and speculating about the reason, he resolves to find him in his village. On the way there, he asks directions of an old man who turns out to be Tse-Ky's father. He reveals that Tse-Ky recently died of exhaustion, having purchased many books with the gold his friend had given him, and having stayed up many nights reading after long days of manual labour. Yu-Pe-Ya goes with Tse-Ky's father to his grave, near the place on the river where they were to have met. After singing two laments, he smashes his lute there, asserting that it is no good any more, since his most important audience is no longer alive to hear it. The poem closes with Yu-Pe-Ya's promise to return to take care of Tse-Ky's elderly parents, because Yu-Pe-Ya declares that the two friends were like brothers.

Webster takes the story from Théodore Pavie's 'Le Lute Brisé', which appears in a collection of stories translated from Chinese into French.[10] The outline of the story above correlates almost entirely with the French source, but Webster's adaptation makes some crucial changes. Its attention to the way time passes—to the slowness of the boat trip, to the intensity of the friends' brief time together, to Yu-Pe-Ya's uncertain wait to be reunited, and to the way in which Tse-Ky's death deprives him of emotions of anticipation—is all Webster's. This attention to timing appears in her versification as well (the French story is almost entirely in prose), particularly in her use of open heroic couplets. The matter of metre and poetry divides the two friends, for while Tse-Ky will speak the words of the tunes that Yu-Pe-Ya plays, he refuses to sing them himself; for the most

part, Tse-Ky speaks in the heroic couplets of the narrative, while the stanzaic verses of
the songs come from Yu-Pe-Ya. Another important difference lies in Webster's presentation of the lute itself as a friend-figure, one that has a will of its own. 'Le Lute Brisé'
enumerates the circumstances in which one must not play the lute, such as 'when one
first learns of a death' or 'when one is not accompanied by a friend who knows music'.[11]
Webster leaves out the list, which also includes requirements for burning the right perfumes and wearing ceremonial clothes, but in her version the lute itself enforces its
own rules, its string breaking when first in the presence of Tse-Ky and playing only
'one long wail' when Yu-Pe-Ya returns and attempts to summon his friend with music.
Webster may have chosen to adapt this story because it resonates so keenly with the
lyric traits that Elizabeth Helsinger has identified in other Victorian narrative poems
with embedded songs: 'the otherness of song, that is its refigurings of time, space, and
powers of mind and language; song's potential social and formal generativity; and its
lyrically confounding multiplicity of voice'.[12] In addition to using song in this story to
'refigure time', Webster amplifies the original story's idea that song forms the basis for
intimate connections; Yu-Pe-Ya attempts to rely on vocal multiplicity for the song to be
the meeting-place for friends who cannot be together.[13]

Before he meets Tse-Ky, Yu-Pe-Ya's closest relationship is with the lute itself, which
seems to understand him better than he knows himself:

> And then he took his lute, that second heart
> Which seemed to share his pulses and be part
> Of the pent heart within him and expound
> In living rhythms and sweet articulate sound
> Its mute dim longings and to himself reveal
> Some secret of himself he could not feel
> Until the music spoke it.
>
> (107–113)

Although the lute is only 'part' of his 'pent heart', Yu-Pe-Ya cannot feel his own emotions until the lute gives them expression. The 'longings' that belong to the lute 'reveal',
but also form, Yu-Pe-Ya's emotional secrets. The instrument, rather than the musician,
is the articulate one. The figure of the lute situates poetry's agency outside of the poet.
By presenting the lute as a friend with its own will, one that tells the singer what to feel
and what to sing, Webster declares poetry to be functionally dialogic, happening as an
exchange rather than as a soliloquy.

The dialogue within the poem is manifest in Webster's use of heroic rhyme. In the
passage below, Webster tells us explicitly that singing also is an act of listening, positing poetry as responsive as well as expressive. At the same time, the poem performs
that responsiveness by repeating rhymes with the word 'reveal'. In the passage above,
the sense of 'reveal' resonates with 'feel', suggesting that the emotions are not so much
uncovered fully formed, but that the process of revelation arouses the feelings themselves. Below, by rhyming 'reveal' with its opposite, 'conceal', Webster shows us how
poetry can do two things at once:

He took his priceless lute and listening sang
A tender song that like a farewell rang.
And yet, because a sorrow or a bliss
Will scarcely speak itself the thing it is,
But shapes its truth into a half disguise
And, like some painter who will make the eyes,
The smile, he lives by, in an altered face,
Or like the lapwing flitting past the place
She has no thought to leave, will part conceal
The thing it tells, part what it hides reveal,
No farewell trembled on his tongue at all,
He sang but of the summer and its fall.

(133–144)

Webster uses open heroic couplets, the subject of intense political and poetic debate less than a century before. Eighteenth-century poets, particularly Pope, tended to favour closed heroic couplets, in which the syntax aligns with the rhyme so that lines close out grammatically and aurally at once. In his *Poems* of 1817 and in *Endymion*, Keats enjambed his heroic lines and Tory critics faulted the looseness of his versification, along with the liberal politics they indicated.[14] Christine Sutphin describes *Yu-Pe-Ya's Lute* as a story about masculine friendship across class lines, a theme that aligns with Webster's activism as well as open couplets' association via Keats with ideas of social and political freedoms across the class spectrum.[15] Yet the effect of the couplets also highlights how Webster uses poetic form to play with time. Her syntax seems deliberately drawn out at times in order to conflict with the anticipated conclusion of every couplet. In the passage above, the sequence of similes keeps the reader from pausing at the end of a rhyme and pushes the reader on past the point where she would otherwise be inclined to stop a while. The deceptive lapwing usefully figures the way that these couplets work: a new simile opens the second line of the couplet and flies right past its stopping point on the word 'place', where the versification invites us to pause, while the continuing syntax of 'she has no thought to leave' propels us forward into the next couplet. Similarly, at this point in the poem Yu-Pe-Ya wants to pause in his homeland, but his duties to his king (and the current of the river) force him onward. After meeting Tse-Ky, he wants to stop even more fervently, but must still continue on. Webster's use of open heroic couplets, then, as well as her mix of narrative and lyric verse reflects Yu-Pe-Ya's temporal and spatial conflict: he wants to pause and stay, yet feels compelled to continue forward.

If these heroic couplets take their formal cues from Keats' narrative verse, then the song that follows must remind readers of his ode 'To Autumn'. Here are the last two stanzas of Yu-Pe-Ya's song that rings but does not sing 'farewell':

'Too soon so rich, ripe summer,
For autumn tracks thee fast;
Lo death-marks on the leaf!
Sweet summer, and my grief;
For summer come is summer past.

Too soon, too soon, lost summer;
Some hours and thou art o'er.
Ah! Death is part of birth:
Summer leaves not the earth,
But last year's summer lives no more.'

(155–164)

This song was anthologized, by Webster in *A Book of Rhyme*, as well as in A. H. Miles'
The Poems and the Poetry of the Nineteenth Century, where Bell's introduction calls it
'lovely'.[16] On its own, it performs within standard lyric tropes lamenting the passage
of time. While Keats' ode celebrates the waning ripeness of the last fruits to precede the
frost, elevating the diminished music of the season, Yu-Pe-Ya's song reduces summer to
time past, reminding readers that the name of the season sounds like the passage of time
itself: 'Some hours'. Far from being able to accept charms that might be considered lesser,
Yu-Pe-Ya's insistence on the present and fear of the waning future are so intense that,
ironically, he cannot appreciate the present moment because he insists on mourning it.

That difference between Keats' ode and Yu-Pe-Ya's lament forms the grounds of
Tse-Ky's ability to understand the song as a final farewell. Within the longer narrative,
readers understand the interpretive difficulty of the song. Because 'a sorrow or a bliss
/ Will scarcely speak the thing it is', full understanding of both emotions and poems
requires a fine-tuned sensibility. Tse-Ky demonstrates this sensibility when he interprets
this song, exposing its subterranean 'farewell'. In order to give Tse-Ky a final test to prove
his poetic sensitivity, in addition to his knowledge of all the finer points of master minstrelsy, of the 'answering rhythms, the complex harmonies', Yu-Pe-Ya plays the tune for
this song on his lute. Tse-Ky responds with a complete understanding of the song:

'And I heard the voice
Of summer birds, leaves merry on their trees,
Bright waters rippling; and yet under these
Dim whispers of farewell. And the sweet pain
Of present ecstasy, knowing it must wane.'

(459–463)

In this moment, Tse-Ky reveals himself to be both Yu-Pe-Ya's ideal audience and most
intimate friend. Tse-Ky perfectly understands Yu-Pe-Ya's temporal conflict, identifying
the 'farewell' that Yu-Pe-Ya meant but did not utter. Tse-Ky shows an uncanny ability to
read Yu-Pe-Ya's story within his lyric, demonstrating his power to see past lyric conventions and to give them specificity. As Tse-Ky interprets the song, he also understands
the singer, and this forms the basis for an intimate friendship that develops over the
course of their intense night together. Yet how do we understand the way Tse-Ky, as
the ideal audience, reads Yu-Pe-Ya's story in a lyric in the context of Webster's injuc-
tion against biographical readings in her essay 'Poets and Personal Pronouns'? Webster
writes 'We look to the poet for feelings, thoughts, actions if need be, represented in a
way which shall affect us as the manifest expression of what our very selves must have
felt and thought and done if we had been those he puts before us and in their cases.' In
other words, poems generate emotions rather than merely passively representing them.

Webster's essay continues by arguing that even the poets we think of as writing most bio-graphically or confessionally lead lives inspired by their poetry: 'Byron's most Byronic heroes were certainly less a portrait of him than he of them; he made them and then imi-tated them.'[17] Tse-Ky's reading of Yu-Pe-Ya's story creates that story, rather than merely passively interpreting it.

Yu-Pe-Ya's Lute bears out the idea that poems produce emotions as much if not more so than people do. Yu-Pe-Ya asserts that in addition to being an ideal audience, Tse-Ky can be a source for both feeling and verse, even if he never says or sings a word. After Tse-Ky demonstrates his mastery by identifying the 'farewell' in the summer song, Yu-Pe-Ya asks him to play a song on his lute, a testament to the intimacy and trust he feels for Tse-Ky. Tse-Ky refuses, however, casting himself as a listener rather than a singer:

> '. . . my tongueless mind
> Within the secret silences of thought
> Accepts the urging voices ever brought
> To him who listens in this world of ours . . .
> Knows them, and has no answer save to know.'
>
> (621–625)

Tse-Ky's silence is receptive without being passive. His finely tuned ear and insistence on silence remind the reader of the importance of listening, and reading. Tse-Ky's reply here suggests that the consumption of art requires just as much skill as its production. Yu-Pe-Ya, however, cannot bear for Tse-Ky's brilliance not to have a part in the circula-tion of minstrelsy. Webster recalls Keats again in Yu-Pe-Ya's response, remembering the 'unheard melodies' of his 'Ode on a Grecian Urn': 'The heart that sings not has the sweeter songs.' Yu-Pe-Ya reads Tse-Ky's silence as a force that works through the songs of others:

> 'Nay, and shall one like thee indeed not speak,
> If he keep silence, yet in many a voice
> Of minstrel men who in his strength rejoice
> As the blossoms in the root's strength where it lies
> Deep under earth, and they shine in the skies—
> Of minstrel men beside him who declare
> (He and themselves aware or unaware)
> His thought by theirs, and most repeat him then
> When most they are themselves?'
>
> (637–45)

If Tse-Ky will not utter his thoughts himself, Yu-Pe-Ya avers, other songsters will trans-pose his thoughts into their verses, whether or not they even know it. These minstrels will then find their own identities by repeating the products of Tse-Ky's 'tongueless mind'. Yu-Pe-Ya accepts Tse-Ky's silence on these terms but asks him when he will bring his 'root strength' down from the rural mountains to influence the poets of the plains. Webster presents in the voice of Yu-Pe-Ya her own idea that poets themselves imitate poems; future poets will be 'most themselves' when they 'most repeat' Tse-Ky's thoughts, which Yu-Pe-Ya has cast as the root of poetry. But if he is silent and refuses to travel with Yu-Pe-Ya out of his rural village, how will these future poets access Tse-Ky's thoughts?

At this point, Tse-Ky defers to the future, in the passage with which I began this essay. Yu-Pe-Ya then sings a song about waiting, but after singing two stanzas, he says 'Is the strain mine or thine?' Yu-Pe-Ya finds solace in the idea that the friends meet not only in person but also in song, and that in song their thoughts and feelings become indistinguishable. Indeed, after Tse-Ky says 'There remains / The day that is to come', Yu-Pe-Ya sings 'Waiting, waiting. 'Tis so far / To the day that is to come', repeating Tse-Ky's words (648–9, 656–7). Yet the repetition is a response that transforms the forbearance that Tse-Ky asks for into impatience: from it 'remains' to it is 'so far'. Yu-Pe-Ya has put Tse-Ky's words into song, but has altered his thought. As readers of this narrative poem can see, Yu-Pe-Ya's ideal of pure poetic identification is impossible to sustain, not only because Tse-Ky is inaccessible but because the strains of poetry and thought multiply rather than unify.

The temporal problem reaches its peak at this point in the poem, proving that their friendship, their perfect poetic mutual understanding, can only exist in the passing moment, in intermediate space and time, between past and present, between kingdoms, between social classes. Tse-Ky's steadfast refusals, to sing, to accompany Yu-Pe-Ya, halt the narrative just where it might be beginning and enforce a stasis on what might be the progress of the poem. Yu-Pe-Ya's final song to Tse-Ky while he is alive begins as one about waiting, suggesting that in anticipating the future, one has neither the present nor the future. Faced with the loss of his friend, Yu-Pe-Ya sings to preserve Tse-Ky's presence (and the present) in Yu-Pe-Ya's own voice, imagining that the relationship between the friends lives on in song. This song figures Yu-Pe-Ya as a bird, representative of singing and expressiveness, and Tse-Ky as a flower whose perfume is a silent sweetness that imbues the bird's songs with beauty. In the penultimate stanza of the song, the flower addresses the bird:

> 'Bird who art dew-drops and flame, bird who art rapture and song,
>> Sweetest of sweet,
> Lo, there's a voice part mine, songs that to me too belong,
> Songs that grew of my growth, voice that has breathed my breath.
> Bird that while I sit mute singest beside on the tree,
> Hast thou ever a song taking no perfume of me?
> Give forth my sweetness in song; bird, thou art singing for both,
> Singing our hearts to heaven, singing to earth at our feet;
>> My voice in thee.'
>
> (685–93)

Ventriloquizing Tse-Ky, animating him with his own words and voice, Yu-Pe-Ya undermines Tse-Ky's insistence on his position as a silent listener. Whereas Tse-Ky, as we saw in the passage above, 'has no answer save to know', valuing listening above all else, Yu-Pe-Ya puts his own thoughts into Tse-Ky's voice, via the flower figure, rather than articulating Tse-Ky's ideas. By insisting that his friend must want him to give voice to his thoughts, he actually reverses his ideal by giving his own ideas his friend's voice. Yu-Pe-Ya's strategy to hold on to his friend and to stop time must, of course, fail. This song attempts to collapse multiple moments into one, as it unifies multiple voices, linking the absent voice of lyric to the genre's elusive present. Yu-Pe-Ya's inability to be the singing surrogate for his friend marks his new friend as lost from the moment they meet. The irreproducibility of his thoughts in his friend's voice, as much as any reason given in the plot—Tse-Ky's duty to care for his parents—signals the onward march of time that destroys Yu-Pe-Ya's fantasies of lyric stasis.

True to the social critiques characteristic of her other poems, Webster asserts that class inequality remains another important impediment to the lyric ideal that Yu-Pe-Ya articulates. Tse-Ky's death from too much reading implies that literature, far from lifting him out of poverty, exacerbates, rather than ameliorates, his position among the rural working class. This idea complicates the lesson that Yu-Pe-Ya learns when he admits how wrong he was to assume that a rural working man would be incapable of recognizing the aesthetic subtlety of a master minstrel. Yet Webster insists on the difficulty of finding a place for the arts in the lives of the poor. When Yu-Pe-Ya plays a lament on his lute for his deceased friend, the villagers begin to dance around him. Shocked, Yu-Pe-Ya asks Tse-Ky's father why they would rejoice, and his father responds that they never hear music, so when they do, they cannot try to understand it, they can only delight in hearing any music at all. While this scene points to a problem with access to the arts for the poor, Tse-Ky's death from exhaustion, having to do manual labour all day and only being able to read at night, suggests that workers need not only access, but leisure time in which to enjoy the arts and to read. In this narrative poem about the give-and-take of lyric poetry and whether and how poetry can affect the sensation of time passing, Webster raises, if obliquely, the problems with aesthetic philanthropy. She also addresses the conflict between practical and intellectual and aesthetic needs in 'In an Almshouse', which depicts an elderly man, poor, blind and sick, who lived as a scholar but hesitated to take his place among the clergy, and in his old age misses 'Where books are read and written, my world once'.[18] Although I do not have space to dwell on this idea here, it is important to point out that in what is arguably Webster's most aestheticist work, *Yu-Pe-Ya's Lute*, she is compelled to address the social implications of aesthetic ideals.

This awareness of the inaccessibility to so many of the pleasures and bittersweet pains of an elevated style of music and poetry may well have been one of Webster's motivations to critique the lyric ideals of the nineteenth century. This critique appears in the contrast between *Yu-Pe-Ya's Lute* and Tennyson's *In Memoriam A.H.H.* It is impossible to read a poem about a poet whose friend and ideal audience dies too young without thinking of Tennyson's grief at the loss of Arthur Hallam, whose review 'On Some Characteristics of Modern Poetry' helped to launch Tennyson's career. In the inevitable comparison, Webster stakes a place in the lineage of the poets of sensation, typified by Keats and Shelley, established by Hallam in his famous review. By the time that Webster wrote *Yu-Pe-Ya's Lute*, she was already known for her dramatic monologues and thereby associated with Robert Browning. In this poem, therefore, she deliberately attempts to place herself within a lyric tradition. Rather than celebrating lyric's powers, however, she articulates its problems, contrasting Yu-Pe-Ya's desire for song to stop time and to unite him with his friend with his inability to do so. In *In Memoriam*, Tennyson resolves his mourning by feeling Hallam's spiritual presence:

> Far off thou art, but ever nigh;
> I have thee still, and I rejoice;
> I prosper, circled with thy voice;
> I shall not lose thee though I die.[19]

Voice here is not a product of a human body but a force of nature, a lasting metaphysical presence. In contrast, Yu-Pe-Ya's declaration that he will give voice to Tse-Ky's thoughts compensates for Tse-Ky's silence, but not for his absence or for his death. Whereas Tennyson can incorporate the memory of Hallam into his concept of his poetic practice, Yu-Pe-Ya can no longer imagine producing songs when his most important audience member is gone. This shift in attitude marks not only a spiritual and religious scepticism—a stance consistent with Webster's monologues in the voices of nuns, priests, and potential clergy—but an uncertainty about poetry's potential to maintain a sense of connection across such otherwise insuperable divides.

Yu-Pe-Ya's dirge for Tse-Ky recalls Section II of *In Memoriam*, where the old yew tree represents the permanence of death, in contrast with the flowers, which can be renewed each season. Webster, however, insists on Tse-Ky's death as his own loss of the experience of anticipation, rather than renewal and repetition:

> 'Dead, my beloved! This small purple weed
> That grows upon thy grave shall have its time
> To ripen and to wane, to bloom and seed;
> But thou, strong doer, might'st not wait thy deed,
> But thou, oh noblest, might'st not wait thy meed:
> Dead in thy prime!'
>
>   (1188–93)

This dirge presents living itself as a process of waiting. Although Yu-Pe-Ya earlier regretted summer's presence because it held the certainty of its own end, he now recognizes that to develop and even to 'wane' is part of life. Yu-Pe-Ya now recognizes that waiting, which earlier he bemoaned, is the privilege of the living.

The dirge also recapitulates the narrative of the friends' first meeting, but this time casts the scene as static vacancy, rather than as a moment of possibility:

> 'Gone, my beloved! I that held thine hand
> Left sudden in a joyless waste alone!
> I tossing on life's sea, and thou to stand
> Hidden in the shadows of the silent strand.
> Thou seeing me from where I may not land!
> Gone from me, gone!'
>
>   (1194–9)

Yu-Pe-Ya's depiction of his mourning state is curiously similar to the scene in which he met Tse-Ky, when he was in an anchored boat avoiding the storm-tossed river current, while Tse-Ky heard his songs from a hiding place in the bushes on the shore. Echoes of the narrative that appear in Yu-Pe-Ya's songs emphasize that the lyric cannot be perfectly atemporal, nor is the aesthetic preservation it offers sufficient to counter the loss of his friend. Consequently, Yu-Pe-Ya rejects song altogether, destroying his lute at Tse-Ky's gravesite.

In destroying the lute, Yu-Pe-Ya also rejects possibilities for new friendship. Ever attempting to unify with his friend, he takes over his role caring for his elderly parents. He addresses the lute:

> '...he is not who could tell
> The thing thou wouldst have said; lie in his grave.
> Farewell, I need thee not; I will not have
> A friend except him dead, not even thee.'
>   (1207–10)

Yu-Pe-Ya smashes the lute because he can no longer perform the public function of song that will be required of him if he returns to his king's court. Yet song's function has also become too intensely private. His encounter with Tse-Ky solidifies his idea of song as an intimate exchange, an occasion for perfect mutual understanding. Tse-Ky's death convinces him that if he can no longer have the audience who will capture the nuances of his music more perfectly than he can himself, then there is no point in making music any more. But just as Webster questioned the intensity of Yu-Pe-Ya's fantasy of poetic union, his idea that he can express his friend's thoughts in music, she also casts doubt on his decision to destroy the lute. Tse-Ky's father replies with 'The pity of it! The pity of it, though!', giving voice to regret (1219). Webster questions the necessity of giving up music altogether, suggesting that in having so fully given himself over to the fantasy of poetic union, and of lyric stasis, Yu-Pe-Ya cannot see his way to a poetry that embraces ambivalence and ambiguity about its own status. Rigg argues that Yu-Pe-Ya's destruction of the lute marks his transformation from a self-centred man to one devoted to the care of others. She reads the 'violent' gesture as in fact a peaceful one, since it will allow Yu-Pe-Ya to live a quiet life taking care of Tse-Ky's parents, one that embodies his love for his friend.[20] However, Yu-Pe-Ya's rejection of song is not Webster's. The father's call of 'The pity of it' asks for some balance between Yu-Pe-Ya's disappointment and his fantasy of poetic ecstasy upon meeting Tse-Ky. This balance requires an acceptance of the ways in which lyric and narrative impinge on each other, and the temporal problems that suggest that neither genre can entirely be free of the other.

The final verse paragraph, especially in the last lines, reveals that the temporal problem that dogged Yu-Pe-Ya at the beginning of the poem remains, and the conclusion is as much about the status of poetry as it is about the selflessness of love. Before he can spend his life caring for Tse-Ky's parents, Yu-Pe-Ya must be released from his obligations to his king. The poem ends with his farewell to Tse-Ky's parents, with Tse-Ky's father repeating 'The pity of it', and finally with a vision of the boat that will take Yu-Pe-Ya back to the king:

> Presently came a ship and glided on
> Adown the river, motionless and swift,
> Like a strong swan taking the current's drift.
>   (1264–6)

Yu-Pe-Ya remains trapped in a conflict between motion and stasis, temporal progress and dwelling on the present moment. Narrative here, and in the poem's other repetitions, tends towards the lyric; by repeating and recasting previous images, it remains trapped in a loop, unable to progress. As much as Yu-Pe-Ya has tried to destroy song, he cannot completely eliminate repetition, so characteristic of lyric, from the narrative of his life.

Yu-Pe-Ya's Lute typifies the consistent lyric-narrative hybridity of Webster's *oeuvre*. Her dramatic monologues tell as well as interrupt stories as they meditate from a singular point of view. Her lyrics, as in *Mother and Daughter* and in the 'English Rispetti', frequently appear in sequences that give narrative contours to lyric reflections. Although Webster uses different forms throughout her career, most of her experiments contain this hybridity. It exemplifies her concern for the experience of the passage of time, which is a reminder of lyric's attempt to overcome absence by stopping time and the generic assertion that the beloved that was here or will be here can be made present through poetry. Yu-Pe-Ya believes in the genre's capacity to fulfil this promise, yet is also disappointed. In the contrast between his hope for Tse-Ky to be part of his song and Tse-Ky's resolute insistence on his own silence, listening, and rural life, Webster shows Yu-Pe-Ya's ideals to be unattainable. Instead, Webster suggests that readers must find a middle ground between these two characters' experiences of their art. If Yu-Pe-Ya too readily imposes his ideas on Tse-Ky, Tse Ky is too passive. Webster argues for poetry as a powerfully shaping force—it can describe our feelings before we know them ourselves—but she also asserts that we must read and write through disappointment and loss, to allow our experience of life and of poetry to be both 'motionless and swift'.

Notes

1. In *Portraits and Other Poems*, ed. Christine Sutphin (Peterborough, ON: Broadview Press, 2000), 305.
2. Patricia Rigg, *Julia Augusta Webster: Victorian Aestheticism and the Woman Writer* (Madison, N.J.: Fairleigh Dickinson University Press, 2009), 205.
3. The late-Victorian anthologist Eric Roberston writes, 'Mrs. Augusta Webster is the one poetess who resembles Robert Browning in her style of thought...but her powers are distinct and original'—*English Poetesses* (London: Cassell, 1883), 354. In her seminal text reigniting interest in Victorian women poets, Angela Leighton also makes the comparison, *Victorian Women Poets: Writing Against the Heart* (Charlottesville: University of Virginia Press, 1992), 177–178. Robert Fletcher discusses Webster's monologues of 'monomaniacal masculinity' as inspired by, but more ambivalent than, Browning's explorations of the same themes—'The Perverse Secrets of Masculinity in Augusta Webster's Dramatic Poetry', in Albert D. Pionke and Denise Teschler Millstein, eds., *Victorian Secrecy* (Aldershot: Ashgate, 2010), 149.
4. Mackenzie Bell, 'Augusta Webster', in Alfred H. Miles, ed., *The Poets and the Poetry of the Century* (London: George Routledge & Sons, 1907), 106, 111.

5. Theodore Watts, 'Mrs. Augusta Webster', *Athenaeum*, 15 Sept. 1894, 355.

6. Patricia Rigg, 'Augusta Webster: The Social Politics of Monodrama', *Victorian Review*, 26 (2000), 75–107. Rigg prefers this term because, unlike dramatic monologues which critique the individualized speaker with irony, Webster's monodramas comment on social and political problems by using a more generalizable character.

7. Patricia Rigg, 'Augusta Webster and the Lyric Muse: The Athenaeum and Webster's Poetics', *Victorian Poetry*, 42 (2004), 135–164.

8. The focus on Webster's dramatic poetry has turned around in recent years with a number of articles on her sonnet sequence *Mother and Daughter*. See Nicole M. Fluhr, '"Telling What's O'er": Remaking the Sonnet Cycle in Augusta Webster's Mother and Daughter', *Victorian Poetry*, 49 (2011), 53–81; Melissa Valiska Gregory, 'Augusta Webster Writing Motherhood in the Dramatic Monologue and the Sonnet Sequence', *Victorian Poetry*, 49 (2011), 27–51; Marianne Van Remoortel, 'Metaphor and Maternity: Dante Gabriel Rossetti's House of Life and Augusta Webster's Mother and Daughter', *Victorian Poetry*, 46 (2008), 467–486; Emily Harrington '"Appraise Love and Divide": Measuring Love in Augusta Webster's Mother and Daughter', *Victorian Poetry*, 50 (2012), 259–278.

9. Monique Morgan, *Narrative Means, Lyric Ends: Temporality in the Nineteenth-Century British Long Poem* (Columbus: The Ohio State University Press, 2009), 3.

10. Théodore Pavie, *Choix de Contes et Nouvelles, Traduits du Chinois* (Paris: Benjamin Duprat, 1839).

11. The translations are my own, from the following: 'quand on apprend une nouvelle de mort' and 'quand on ne se trouve pas à portée d'un ami qui connait la musique'. Pavie, *Choix de Contes*, 274–5.

12. Elizabeth Helsinger, 'Song's Fictions', *The Yearbook of English Studies*, 40 (2010), 144.

13. Although a full exploration of the topic does not lie within the purview of this essay, it is important to acknowledge the significance of Webster's use of a Chinese tale to critique and revise nineteenth-century British poetic ideals. Views of the Chinese were increasingly negative in nineteenth-century Britain, as David Porter notes in *Ideographia: The Chinese Cipher in Early Modern Europe* (Palo Alto: Stanford University Press, 2001). The Opium Wars in particular contributed to a view in this period of the Chinese as 'lawless', 'lazy', and 'conceited'—Catherine Pagani, 'Chinese Material Culture and British Perceptions of China in the Mid-Nineteenth Century', in Tim Barringer, ed., *Colonialism and the Object: Empire, Material Culture and the Museum* (London: Routledge, 1998), 28. For more on British and American appropriations of Chinese figures to articulate ideas about sympathy, see Eric Hayot, *The Hypothetical Mandarin: Sympathy, Modernity and Chinese Pain* (Oxford: Oxford University Press, 2009).

14. William Keach, 'Cockney Couplets: Keats and the Politics of Style', *Studies in Romanticism*, 25 (1986), 182.

15. Christine Sutphin, 'Introduction' and ed., *Portraits and Other Poems* by Augusta Webster, 14.

16. Webster, *A Book of Rhyme*, 50; Miles, *The Poems and Poets*, 112.

17. Augusta Webster, 'Poets and Personal Pronouns', in *Portraits and Other Poems*, 367, 370.

18. Webster, 'In an Almshouse', in *Portraits and Other Poems*, 245.

19. Alfred Tennyson, 'In Memoriam A.H.H.', in *Poems of Tennyson*, volume 2, ed. Christopher Ricks, 2nd edn. (London: Longman, 1987), CXXX, 13–16.

20. Rigg, *Julia Augusta Webster*, 167.

Select Bibliography

Gregory, Melissa Valiska, 'Augusta Webster Writing Motherhood in the Dramatic Monologue and the Sonnet Sequence', *Victorian Poetry*, 49 (2011), 27–51.

Harrington, Emily, '"Appraise Love and Divide": Measuring Love in Augusta Webster's *Mother and Daughter*', *Victorian Poetry*, 50 (2012), 259–278.

Helsinger, Elizabeth, 'Song's Fictions', *The Yearbook of English Studies*, 40 (2010), 141–159.

Leighton, Angela, *Victorian Women Poets: Writing Against the Heart* (Charlottesville: University of Virginia Press, 1992).

Morgan, Monique, *Narrative Means, Lyric Ends: Temporality in the Nineteenth-Century British Long Poem* (Columbus: Ohio State University Press, 2009).

Pavie, Théodore, *Choix de Contes et Nouvelles, Traduits du Chinois* (Paris: Benjamin Duprat, 1839).

Rigg, Patricia, *Julia Augusta Webster: Victorian Aestheticism and the Woman Writer* (Madison, NJ: Fairleigh Dickinson University Press, 2009).

—— 'Augusta Webster and the Lyric Muse: The Athenaeum and Webster's Poetics', *Victorian Poetry*, 42 (2004), 135–164.

Webster, Augusta, *Portraits and other Poems*, ed. Christine Sutphin (Peterborough, ON: Broadview Press, 2000).

CHAPTER 32

··

SWINBURNE: THE
INSUPERABLE SEA

··

SIMON JARVIS

SWINBURNE has long been celebrated, among other things, as the poet of the sea. But A. E. Housman was not persuaded that Swinburne's celebrated love for the ocean amounted to very much: 'The sea is a natural object; and Swinburne had no eye for nature and no talent for describing it.'[1] Later in the same lecture Housman developed this theme. He denies both that the sea is a fertile topic for poetry, and that Swinburne's poetry 'about' the sea could be valued even as a good treatment of this unpromising area: 'The sea, to be sure, is a large department; and that is how it succeeded in attracting Swinburne's attention; for he seldom noticed any object of external nature unless it was very large, very brilliant, or very violently coloured.'[2] The sea, in other words, was so big that even Swinburne could not miss it. As these sentences suggest, Housman is dissatisfied with the imprecision of what he calls Swinburne's 'descriptions' of the sea: they 'might have been written by a man who had never been outside Warwickshire.'[3] Housman is not alone in having felt Swinburne to lack descriptive particularity. His complaint is closely connected to his ambivalence towards Swinburne's virtuosity in versification. Its mastery risks unthinking automatism: at one point Housman calls Swinburne's verse 'a sausage-machine'.[4] The man who does not hear its melody 'must be deaf', yet Swinburne's is not the best kind of verse melody. Like Pope's, Housman thinks, the music of Swinburne's verse is addressed to 'the external ear' alone. It does not, like Blake's or like Milton's, find out 'the inner chambers of the sense of hearing...the junction between the ear and the brain'.[5]

Housman's remarks touch a nerve which remains raw for Swinburnophiles today. Because Swinburne has so frequently been disparaged for *mere* virtuosity, his admirers have sometimes felt it necessary to respond by insisting (irrelevantly) on his sincerity. A recent essay by Jerome McGann, however, indicates a way out of this blockage. Claiming, correctly, that '[t]he great prosodic scholar George Saintsbury was one of the last to have a clear grasp of what Swinburne's work involved',[6] McGann understands Swinburne's verse as 'poetry in the condition of music'. He suggests that the emptying-out of semantic reference which is so often complained of by Swinburne's critics might be just what makes possible what we might think of as the poet's prosodic intelligence.[7]

McGann's emphasis falls on the evacuation of semantic reference and syntactic logic in favour of a verse art aspiring to the condition of music. But how is verse as 'music' figured, here? Primarily, it seems, as what would lack not only semantic reference or grammatically controlled logic, but as the realm of metapoeticality or autoreferentiality themselves. Of the passage in *Anactoria* around which the practical part of McGann's article revolves, he writes that it 'is, in a sense, a personification of the idea of the poem, just as the poem is, in a sense, a personification of the idea of poetry as such'.[8] My account proceeds, instead, from the hypothesis that no art is really about itself.[9] Even where the usual means by which a poem might seem referentially to lay hands on the world itself are relegated or mutilated or disarranged, this does not mean that the poem can only, or must even primarily, be about itself or even about poetry itself. In this essay I gratefully follow McGann's cue as to the centrality of rhyme—its centrality, however, to what I take, precisely, to be Swinburne's prosodic thinking. I shall concentrate on what I consider to be Swinburne's greatest long poem, his couplet narrative *Tristram of Lyonesse* (1882).

SWINBURNE IMMERSED

'A natural *object*'—and so, in a way, the sea is, except in so far as that word almost implies that it might be possible to walk round it; 'a large *department*'—this it hardly, except for the convenience of Housman's irony, could be called. When Swinburne writes about the sea, he is not usually gazing at it, but swimming in it. Even when he is on dry land, his writing about the sea is continuously kinetic: writing to Mary Gordon of the harbour at Boscastle, he illustrated its unusual shape by a diagram, remarking on how 'the sea swings to and fro beneath the cliffs, foams and swells, beats and baffles itself against the steep faces of rock...it was very queer, dark grey swollen water, caught as it were in a trap, and heaving with rage against both sides at once, edged with long panting lines of incessant foam that swung and lapped along the deep steep cliffs without breaking, and had not room to roll at ease'.[10] Swinburne's interest in rendering the sea's dynamic force breaks out in copious verbal alternative ('swung and lapped') and prose rhyme ('deep steep'). Still more striking are his powerful projections of affect: his sea pants, rages, has no room for ease.

These deep feelings are not chance appearances. As Rikky Rooksby has pointed out, Swinburne's own relationship to the sea appears to have been powerfully masochistic.[11] A good deal of his correspondence with Richard Monckton Milnes concerns their shared interest in de Sade. The tortures of the sea are enough to give a corpse an erection, Swinburne thinks, and it is a pity, from a purely erotic point of view, that de Sade did not think to include these cruelties with all the others.[12] This unexpected erotic association recurs often in Swinburne's letters. On reading an article on Walt Whitman, what especially delighted him was the report of Whitman's 'amorous embrace of the sea in bathing': 'I would give something to have a dip in the rough water with him'.[13]

The cadaver in Swinburne's letter to Milnes, though, brings out a doubleness of register even here. The *supplices de mer* are not only exquisitely sexual: they are also resuscitators, fit to bring a corpse back to life. Swinburne was also capable of linking marine delights with those of his own *métier*: one letter of enthusiastic praise for his poetry brought an acknowledgement that 'I don't myself know any pleasure physical or spiritual (except what comes of the sea) comparable to that which comes of verse in its higher moods...'.[14] Mrs. Gosse delighted Swinburne by telling him that 'the sound of the sea on the black rocks of the Cornish coast had reminded her of *The Triumph of Time*'.[15] This circle of associations is closed when we recall how often, as Yopie Prins has emphasized, Swinburne made connections between punishment and verse in his letters and prose fiction. Verse 'hurts horribly', one character tells another in *Lesbia Brandon*.[16] Sea:pain, sea:verse, and verse:pain are closely connected in the textual remnants of Swinburne's psyche.

In few of Swinburne's poems does his hunger for the sea crash and beat so powerfully as in *Tristram of Lyonesse*. The action rarely leaves it for long. The first and last books are titled for two sea-voyages, the sailings of the Swallow and the Swan; where the poem's actors are not diving into, swimming in, or sailing calmly across the sea: they are generally looking out over it, or at least somewhere close to it; even where the actors are not themselves immersed in the sea or gazing at it, the sea still furnishes an apparently inexhaustible supply of metaphors for everything else which they might think, feel, and experience. 'Sea' is the very last word of the poem, as it had been the very last word of Swinburne's collection *Poems and Ballads* ('Dedication. 1865': 'Night sinks on the sea'), as it had been the last word of Swinburne's tragedy *Erechtheus* ('And friendship and fame of the sea'), as it was to be the last word of his later long lyric 'Off Shore' ('But thou art the God, and thy kingdom is heaven, and thy shrine is the sea'), and as it had been the very last word of Swinburne's earlier *tour de force* in couplets, *Anactoria*.[17] There we find: 'And shed around and over and under me / Thick darkness and the insuperable sea'.[18] In *Tristram*: 'And over them, while life and death shall be, / The light and sound and darkness of the sea'. In neither poem does the choice of 'sea' as the very last word of the poem feel accidental. It is hard to believe that Swinburne was not acutely aware, as he conceived the close of *Tristram*, of echoing, lexically and rhetorically, that of *Anactoria*.

Clearly there is something like a compulsion at work here. Swinburne could hardly have failed to notice his own fondness for placing the same word at the end of many extended verse-compositions, yet gave in to it none the less. Any long poem in rhyme has something like a hierarchy of endings in it. Rhymes are recognizable as rhymes, on one way of accounting for them, by appearing at the ends of lines. A rhyme which closes a sentence, a rhyme which closes a verse-paragraph, a rhyme which closes a canto or book, a rhyme which closes an entire long poem—each of these may take on a correspondingly more powerful sense of finality, of destination, especially when, as may readily happen, we grow intimate with Swinburne's authorship, we become alert to the possibility that the endings of his poems may be echoing or even rhyming with each other.

Sea is something like the ending of endings for Swinburne, and it is surely not accidental that it outranks, in his work, another familiar candidate for that role, *death*. Both the ending of 'Anactoria' and that of *Tristram* are sea-deaths, of kinds. In 'Anactoria' the formula-rhyme 'death / breath' has already been sounded a number of times. 'Death' and 'sea', in fact, each appear nine times in 'Anactoria', and of these nine appearances, in each case fully six are as rhyme-words. In 'death's' case, 'breath' is, naturally, on each occasion the rhyme-partner. But in each of these cases, Swinburne conspicuously meets the criterion that where the rhyme itself is worn smooth, something about the thought must be pointed—most spectacularly in the justly celebrated couplet: 'Relapse and reluctation of the breath, / Dumb tunes and shuddering semi-tones of death'.[19]

Here the powerfully strange conversion of death into a musical instrument by the attribution to it of 'semitones', the resonant obscurity of the word 'reluctation', the sharp oxymoron 'dumb tunes', as well as the insistent assonance on $| \Lambda |$, pushing against the $| e |$ of the rhyme, all produce a compressed difficulty, a dark wit, so that, after this, the great familiarity of the death/breath rhyme is a kind of release, something into which we may compliantly subside. That this rhyme has occurred so many times in a compara-tively short poem makes it, when we consider too what Sappho is made to say, almost a pointed refusal that Swinburne will not end the poem with it. The whole poem moves towards the affective colouration now given its final word. *Sea*, after this poem, is that in which absolutely everything whatever, not only this individual, but also what would otherwise be supposed immortal, like the gods, or everlasting, like time, is to come to an end. Sea's final rhyme subsumes the death/breath rhyme which has proximately pre-ceded it. The sea, not death, is this poem's absolute master, and it is partly by Swinburne's closely felt compositional economy with this verse-word that his poetry comes to escape the risk of a merely abstract negation of meaning.

At the end of *Tristram of Lyonesse* the order of events and the mode of narration are different. Tristram and Iseult have already achieved their love-death,[20] in an identical rhyme (therefore, a failed or half-rhyme) which offers perhaps the poem's single most directly affecting moment:

> And ere her ear might hear her heart had heard
> Nor sought she sign for witness of the word;
> But came and stood above him newly dead,
> And felt his death upon her: and her head
> Bowed, as to reach the spring that slakes all drouth;
> And their four lips became one silent mouth.[21]

This last line is the closing line of the poem's narration proper: a few lines of white space are left before the poem's epilogue. These closing lines of the body of 'The Sailing of the Swan' recall the closing lines of the poem's first book, 'The Sailing of the Swallow'; the kiss of death is paired with the first kiss.

> each on each
> Hung with strange eyes and hovered as a bird
> Wounded, and each mouth trembled for a word;
> Their heads neared, and their hands were drawn in one,
> And they saw dark, though still the unsunken sun
> Far through fine rain shot fire into the south;
> And their four lips became one burning mouth.
>
> (40)

The effect relies on the idea that readers will remember a single line several thousands of lines ago. The poet is confident of the memorability of this earlier line, because it concentrates at an especially hierarchically marked place in the printed structure (the end of the book) and in the erotic narrative structure (the point where Tristram and Iseult become lovers) the strangest of images for eros, where not two but four become one, as though this lovers' union were at the same time a union of seasons or of quarters of the earth. 'Mouth' is not an easy word to rhyme, but Swinburne is determined to have it at the end of this book of this poem, and his brilliant display of verbal fireworks in the penultimate line lets its potentially awkward rhyme-partner 'south' pass as a given: the concatenation of stresses in the middle of the line, along with the little plays and echoes among the syllables so stressed—*fine rain shot fire*—take all our attention away from it (why into the south, particularly, rather than the west, we might otherwise ask) and softens us up for the erotic killer punch of the final line. It is perhaps the single most memorable line of the early part of the poem, and that it then recurs in this almost exact echo—with only the substitution of 'silent' for 'burning'—seems to bring that feeling which has hitherto been allowed to ebb and flow with the tidal movements of Swinburne's verse to a single point of breaking. Playing against the willed enough immediate rhyme of 'drouth', is this forlorn long-distance repetition: 'mouth: mouth'.

A DROWNED LYRIC

Tristram, then, alerts us to the possibilities of long-distance rhyming. It is not compulsory for a rhyme to be adjacent to its partner, nor even relatively close to it. The criterion of rhyme is memorability: must, might, or can the first rhyme-partner still be in a reader's mind when its pair turns up? Rhyming verse can thus have prominently built into its architecture, even for an epoch such as our own in which unprecedentedly little verse is known by heart, verse's ineliminable association with technologies of remembering. So far, the kinds of instances I have been concentrating on, with one or two exceptions, have been what are probably examples of verse-thinking at the instant of composition, the poet's stock of rhymes handled resourcefully and alertly with continuous vigilance for their mutual semantic and affective resonances and relations. But Swinburne is also willing to do something much more baroque. He consciously plans, that is, an entire, now celebrated, 'antiphon'[22] of matching rhymes to come at the beginning and end of his poem.

It is not certain whether, when he first composed his 'Prelude. Tristram and Iseult' to *Tristram of Lyonesse*, Swinburne had already planned his set-piece. The 'Prelude' first appeared as 'Tristram and Iseult. Prelude of an Unfinished Poem' in *Pleasure: A Holiday Book of Prose and Verse* (1871). It opens with a simple and radical solution to one perceived difficulty with the couplet form. The first forty-four lines constitute a single extended sentence, beginning thus: 'Love, that is first and last of all things made, / The light that has the living world for shade...' The sentence opened by 'Love' is kept open by a catalogue of love's attributes, continually but irregularly returning to the word 'love', which begins eleven of the lines making up the sentence. Its power comes, not only from Swinburne's universally admitted strength of incantation, but also from the way in which it mobilizes from the very start of the poem a generic ambivalence which is central to its life. Herbert Tucker, in his matchless account of *Tristram*, seizes this at once: 'The distinctive success of the poem as published in 1882 arose from its solution of a real and historically representative problem that its author's astonishing lyric gift entrained.... How might a poetics of momentaneousness be dilated to epic proportions, or conversely how might a verse narrative of book length be maintained at the pitch of intensity to which his imagination resonated?'[23] Swinburne's 'Prelude' had already in 1871 provided an indication of the centrality of this problem. It sounds to the reader directly lyric in the most immediate sense. It sounds, that is, as though it is must be an apostrophe to love. The poet is addressing love, enumerating its powers and glories, and then he is going to ask it for something. Yet in the event the sentence, at long last, turns aside from this, turns, but only at its last gasp, into narrative: 'Led these twain to the life of tears and fire...'[24] The poem as a whole does not attempt a mingling of lyric and narrative modes at this formal level of its mode of narration and address, although interpolated songs and direct speeches of the actors provide many opportunities for lyric. The underlying framework is unambiguously narrative, even if, at the level of its verse texture, that narrative is conducted in a medium which is clearly driven by, rather than just using as an instrument, techniques which have generally been thought of as lyric ones—above all, intensely worked verbal instrumentation (see the section titled 'The Storm of rhythms'). But because of this opening, the entire poem is as it were stood over by a phantom lyric which has been raised, but not laid.

This is why, I think, that what Swinburne then does in the last book of the poem—to begin it with an exact echo of the invocation of Love, which, this time, invokes instead Fate, and each of whose rhyme-words, with the exception of 'above / love', which now becomes 'fate / hate', is precisely the same as the rhyme-words in the invocation of Love—becomes more than a willed feat of virtuosity. The crucial point about it is that, by this point, the reader knows for certain that the poem is not lyric, but narrative. The mingled relief and disappointment which can be felt when the opening invocation to Love turns out not to be a hymn but only the start of a story is now fully confirmed here, in Fate's fateful ratification of desire as something to be buried. As in the case of the later 'mouth: mouth' echo, these rhymes have a double character: full and exact within the couplets, over the entirety of the poem they are only identical rhymes. Fate's narrative does not rhyme with the vanishing lyric address to Love, but blanks it with a story.

THE UNASSIMILABLE NAME

There is a central respect, indeed, in which this poem's very structure characterizes narrative itself as the unrhymeable, as an element destined to be at war with rhyme (remembering that 'rhyme' is also a synecdoche for 'verse'). Both the lovers have, in the story, a matching protagonist bearing the very same name as them. Iseult's is Iseult 'of Brittany', or 'of the White Hands', whom Tristram weds in an unconsummated marriage after the lovers are discovered; Tristram's, another knight named Tristram who asks for the hero's help.[25] Swinburne develops the Tristram/Tristram relation much less than he does the contrast among the two Iseults—partly, perhaps, because the male relation is organized around prowess in battle, something in which Swinburne is perhaps less interested than any other Arthurian poet before or since. The Iseult/Iseult relation, on the other hand, is not merely developed, but developed quite explicitly around the point that Tristram's lover and his virgin wife both have the same name—the only thing about her which awakens his desire:

> And when between strange words her name would fall
> Suddenly straightway to that lure's recall
> Back would his heart bound as the falconer's bird
> And tremble and bow down before the word.
> 'Iseult'—and all the cloudlike world grew flame,
> And all his heart flashed lightning at her name;
> 'Iseult'—and all the wan waste weary skies
> Shone as his queen's own love-enkindled eyes.
>
> (71)

Iseult of the white hands notices the power which her name in particular has, guessing correctly that it is not for her sake that the name induces this response in her husband, but guessing incorrectly that it is for the sake of 'one long dead, / Some sister that he loved'. Iseult's name is a 'lure'. It keeps the predator domesticated.

The erotic power of a name is an especially sensitive spot for a poem like this to narrate—a poem which is itself one in which the most powerful feelings have come to dwell, not in whole words alone, but even (as we shall see) in little phonemic and printed scraps. It is an instance of fetishism: the name, which has no signification, nevertheless contains, for the lover, irresistible power. The perplexity as to why and how this peculiar combination of syllables should come to possess such power is not unlike the perplexity as to why and how rhymes, or any form of verse phonemic patterning, should be capable of capturing and releasing powerful emotion. It is no accident that Swinburne here connects and distinguishes the two. Iseult's name is not a 'rhyme', but a 'burden', a refrain and a weight borne: the participial adjective 'reverberate', meanwhile, could qualify either 'rhyme' or 'burden' here.

Just this connection and contrast between 'rhyme' and 'burden' is precisely what Swinburne then develops, for he gives us the very song in which this is supposed to happen:

'Stars know not how we call them, nor may flowers
Know by what happy name the hovering hours
Baptize their new-born heads with dew and flame:
And Love, adored of all time as of ours,
Iseult, knew nought for ages of his name.

'With many tongues men called on him, but he
Wist not which word of all might worthiest be
To sound for ever in his ear the same,
Till heart of man might hear and soul might see,
Iseult, the radiance ringing from thy name.

'By many names men called him, as the night
By many a name calls many a starry light,
Her several sovereigns of dividual fame;
But day by one name only calls aright,
Iseult, the sun that bids men praise his name.

'In many a name of man his name soared high
And song shone round it soaring, till the sky
Rang rapture, and the world's fast-founded frame
Trembled with sense of triumph, even as I,
Iseult, with sense of worship at thy name.

'In many a name of woman smiled his power
Incarnate, as all summer in a flower,
Till winter bring forgetfulness or shame:
But thine, the keystone of his topless tower,
Iseult, is one with Love's own lordliest name.

'Iseult my love, Iseult my queen twice crowned,
In thee my death, in thee my life lies bound:
Names are there yet that all men's hearts acclaim,
But Love's own heart rings answer to the sound,
Iseult, that bids it bow before thy name.'

(72–73)

This lyric, I want to suggest, is the sacrificial victim of the poem's defence of what it itself calls 'love's rekindling rhyme' (126). Iseult's name is in every sense a 'burden', of course, because there are two Iseults, whose names can never be made to rhyme with each other, but only to face off against each other, to reprise each other. This poem, from one point of view, rhymes the word 'name' as copiously as could be wished. Every stanza finishes with the word 'name', and its rhyme-partner differs each time: 'flame', 'same', 'fame', 'frame', 'shame', 'acclaim'. Yet this same structure produces, from another point of view, an insistent unrhymed repetition. At the same time as the word 'name' is being so fully rhymed with, it is also just being repeated at the end of every stanza. Meanwhile, the word also appears in the main body of every stanza as well, in a poem which is itself a (fanciful enough) discussion of naming. The sound of the word 'name', by the end of the lyric, has become less assimilable than ever: its last repetition does not carry the pleasurable relinquishment into an expected return which is one of the possibilities given by rhyme, but rather sticks out insistently.

It is a real question whether the interpolation of this lyric is a success. The lyric is even ugly. If so, its ugliness lies not only, perhaps, in disgust at the lie which the lyric represents (since Iseult of the white hands is actually present, Tristram can hardly pretend to be surprised if she takes herself to be its addressee), but in our sense of an arbitrary tear in the poem's fabric. It is the only occasion on which Tristram appears calculating, designing a deception. More shocking than the deception is the deliberation. Tristram is a hero of radical passivity. Even when he is leaping into the sea and swimming vigorously through it, the emphasis lies on his being buffetted, submerged, and borne up, carried along by the sea. The scenes in which he dispatches rival knights feel, chiefly for this reason, a little like a calque of unassimilated subject matter. Above all, this unease lies in the very artfulness of the lyric given to Tristram. The waves of couplet rhyme in the poem proper do not only bear Tristram, but also Swinburne's poetic thinking, along with them; here, however, they are diverted into a series of rills, pipes, and fountains.

Tucker justly remarks that *Tristram of Lyonesse* has no real villain.[26] But Iseult of the white hands, by its close, has certainly come to concentrate any available negativity, since 'hatred thrilled her to the hands and feet' (156). Even though Iseult of the white hands is the addressee of this song, not its singer, the discordant note of that pleasure in hating is, in the poem, first anticipated here, not explicitly, but in the kind of speech-act which this song represents: an attempt to channel, train, and deploy rhyme, whose failure is manifested in the identical repetition of 'name' six times at the last word of every stanza. The lyric cheats not only the Breton, but the Irish Iseult too, because it loves only her name. Feigning to be a love-lyric, the song's concealed aggression nevertheless leaks out in its harping on the 'name'. Rhyme, for *Tristram of Lyonesse*, is to be oceanic, in the sense adumbrated above: it is to be that medium which bears poetic thinking up, not that tool to which instrumental thinking helps itself to in order to secure some effect. Accordingly, the poem's most conspicuous attempt to put rhyme into the service of a purpose fails to serve that purpose—and also fails properly to rhyme.

Towards the end of *Tristram of Lyonesse*, the identity of the two heroines' names plays a critical narrative role. Tristram is waiting for his lover Iseult to arrive, and momentarily mistakes Iseult of the white hands for her: '"Iseult?" and like a death-bell faint and clear / The virgin voice rang answer—'I am here' (163). Although Tristram soon realizes his mistake, the comparison of Breton Iseult's voice to a death-bell links this mistake with what happens two pages later, when she kills Tristram by returning lie for lie: Iseult of the white hands tells Tristram that the sail on the Swan is black (meaning that Irish Iseult is not aboard), even though it is in fact 'snowbright' white (165). Tristram expires instantly. The story is sewn up, then, with this failed rhyme, with the repetition of the name Iseult, even as rhyme itself insuperably continues to wash around and over and under it.

The Storm of Rhythms

Thus far we have mainly been concerned with the crucial role which rhyme plays in the poem's larger architecture. But that architecture is by no means the most prominent feature of the poem as it is actually experienced at sea level, by a reader. The story is difficult to keep one's eye on. But this is not, as with Browning's *Sordello*, because it is so complicated, but because of the relative weightings which are given to incident, and to affective exploration, respectively. Critical plot points often pass by in a mere couplet or turn of phrase, while the precise tonality of a feeling of desire or fear may be explored for pages together. What Tucker calls the 'incessant phonic-semantic crisscross'[27] at the level of Swinburne's line, couplet, and verse paragraph cannot really be understood as a form of timbral colour, set in the service of illustrating and developing the narrative. It threatens, rather, to engulf that narrative. The sequence of the story is set in competition—rather than only in helpful co-operation—with another set of sequencings and patterning. It is this other series which produces the texture of Swinburne's poem, its oceanic element:

> So for an hour they fought the storm out still,
> And the shorn foam spun from the blades, and high
> The keel sprang from the wave-ridge, and the sky
> Glared at them for a breath's space through the rain;
> Then the bows with a sharp shock plunged again
> Down, and the sea clashed on them, and so rose
> The bright stem like one panting from swift blows,
> And as a swimmer's joyous beaten head
> Rears itself laughing, so in that sharp stead
> The light ship lifted her long quivering bows
> As might the man his buffeted strong brows
> Out of the wave-breach; for with one stroke yet
> Went all men's oars together, strongly set
> As to loud music, and with hearts uplift
> They smote their strong way through the drench and drift.
> Till the keen hour had chafed itself to death
> And the east wind fell fitfully, breath by breath,
> Tired; and across the thin and slackening rain
> Sprang the face southward of the sun again.

(36–37)

No English poet had done anything quite like this before. Nor was Swinburne's manner to prove readily continuable. Ezra Pound asked in his *ABC Of Reading*, '[d]id the "90s" add anything to English poetry, or did they merely prune Swinburne?'[28] The verse is not to be pruned, however, without producing something quite different. What needs pruning would be something rambling, overgrown, or 'diffuse', but this would be a mistaken characterization, not so much because, as Eliot claimed, Swinburne's 'diffuseness is one of his glories', but because, on the contrary, such characterizations miss the propulsive complexity of Swinburne's verse, produced by the clashing and coinciding forces of syntax, metre, and rhythm, semantics, instrumentation, and rhyme.[29]

Rhyme's force here, as everywhere, can hardly be disclosed without considering its interactions with everything else. It is essential, first of all, to consider Swinburne's bravura handling of rhythm, and its relation to syntax, in a passage of this kind. It is full of crests and eddies, because Swinburne so often packs clusters of stresses together: 'shorn foam spun'; 'sharp shock plunged'; 'that sharp stead'; 'light ship lif[ted]'; 'one stroke yet'; 'all men's oars'. Such triple successions of stress are familiar in the English heroic line, of course; they do not, by themselves, dislocate it.[30] Here, however, they come together with a much more dislocated pattern, that of two stresses followed or preceded by two unstressed syllables ('breath's space through the'; 'bright stem like one'; 'strong way through the'). You can see the effect of this in a line like 'Down, and the sea clashed on them, and so rose'. 'On' would not ordinarily carry a stress, but the metrical pull to give it one here is extraordinarily powerful, because otherwise the line seems as though it might founder altogether: it already takes a great gulp of air after its first syllable, and its two pairs of stressed syllables—'sea clashed' and 'so rose'—leaving a lurch of unstressed syllables for the metrical pattern to get across, like a boat coming off a tall wave into what would momentarily feel like thin air.

In this context of exacerbated metrico-rhythmic peaks and troughs, rhyme's site at line-end becomes even more than usually prominent. Swinburne's handling of this metrical place in this passage is violent. It is not so much the infrequency of any punctuation at line-end here as the sharpness with which the breaks cut into clauses which produces this effect. The cut falls several times between subject or object and verb: 'the sky / Glared'; 'head / Reared'; 'rain / Sprang'. More often than not the first syllable of these lines is stressed, but in a number of instances there is a quite particular way of foregrounding the collision of line-final with line-initial stress: Swinburne repeats the vowel of the rhyme-word immediately preceding it in the first word of the next. So 'bows' and 'brows' gains as it were an over-rhyme: 'Out', and this echo-technique is then itself immediately echoed: 'yet / Went'; and again, at the close of the next couplet: 'lift...drift / Till'. It is as though Swinburne had temporarily and locally added, to the existing line-final rhyme-canon, a line-initial one of assonance. We begin to look out for assonances which chime with rhymes at the beginning of lines.

There are very many other patterns of echoing and chiming at work in this passage. None of them, however, is primarily amplifying or decorating any semantic or thematic point. They form, instead, a crucial part of Swinburne's verse manner of perfectly-judged near-overload. The entire set of phonological relations in this one passage would take a chapter to describe, but the experience of reading the sequence is over in a few seconds. The impossibility of noticing all this consciously is its point. This passage is also full of alliterations (in particular a whole series of twists on consonantal combinations with s-: sp-, st-, str-, sw-, and so on) but unless one is reading only with the eye, rather than chiefly with the mind's ear, one hardly notices them, because there is so much else going on. Readers' brains are to be overtaxed as much as possible while still observing certain fixed and retained constraints of rhyme and metre. The verse's virtuosity partly consists in its calling forth an answering readerly virtuosity, as though Swinburne were challenging the reader to see if they can keep afloat in all this.

VERSE THINKING AT THE LIMITS
OF MASOCHISM

Let us return to the contrast between what I described as the 'oceanic' quality of rhyming in the body of *Tristram of Lyonesse* and the way in which rhyme is used in Tristram's song on Iseult's name. It is hardly possible to miss the ringing of the changes, there, on the rhymes for 'name', and the repetition of that word at the end of each stanza. Therefore it is marked in just the opposite way to the kind of effect I was considering in relation to the nautical passage above: it is picked out for explicit interpretation, not for inexplicit absorption. It is, in fact, the phonemic illustration or instrumentation of a fantasy: a fantasy about the power of Irish Iseult's name, which Tristram cruelly or unthinkingly or duplicitously delivers to Breton Iseult. But the effects which I have just been talking about—Swinburne's systematic overtaxings or overloadings of a reader's mental ears—are, precisely, inoperable for fantasy, because they cannot be made sufficiently symbolic.

It is at this point that I should like to return to the theme of Swinburne's masochism. This has played a central part in recent interpretation, not merely of his life, but also of his poetry—and with what looks like good reason, because of the explicit connections which a number of his prose texts make between verse and pain. Swinburne's letter to Richard Monckton Milnes, recalling the punishments administered by one of his masters at school, has taken an especially prominent place. It has become, de facto, a more centrally canonical text than many of Swinburne's poems:[31]

> Once, before giving me a swishing that I had the marks of for more than a month (so fellows declared that I went to swim with), he let me saturate my face with eau-de-Cologne. I conjecture now, on looking back to that 'rosy hour' with eyes 'purged by the euphrasy and rue' of the Marquis de Sade and his philosophy, that, counting on the pungency of the perfume and its power over the nerves, he meant to stimulate and excite the senses by that preliminary pleasure so as to inflict the acuter pain afterwards on their awakened and intensified susceptibility. If he did, I am still gratified to reflect that I beat him; the poor dear old beggar overreached himself, for the pleasure of smell is so excessive and intense with me that even if the smart of birching had been unmixed pain, I could have borne it all the better for that previous indulgence. Perhaps he had no such idea, and I, grown over-wise through perusal of Justine and Juliette, now do him more than justice; but he was a stunning tutor; his one other pet subject was *metre*, and I firmly believe that my ear for verses made me rather a favourite. I can boast that of all the swishings I ever had up to seventeen and over, I never had one for a false quantity in my life. (Can you say the same? I should imagine you *metrical* as a boy.) One comfort is, I make up for it in

arithmetic, so my tutor never wanted reasons for making rhymes between his birch and my body.

You must excuse my scribbling at this rate when I once begin, for the sake of that autobiographical fact about perfume and pain, which you can now vouch for as the experience of a real live boy. I always wanted to know if other fellows shared the feeling. Conceive trying it in a grove of budding birch-trees scented all over with the green spring. Ah-h-h![32]

The letter is startling in its confirmation of the close link in Swinburne's mind, not merely between poetry and pain, but between *verse* and pain. As Yopie Prins comments, 'through rhythmic beating Swinburne learns to internalize the beat of poetry'.[33] Although Swinburne, of course, boasts just the opposite here, that his command of metre was so secure that he never needed to be beaten, the beatings for poor maths (even supposing Swinburne's account of his own metrical precocity to be literally honest) still stand behind his experience of verse numbers. And these mathematical beatings themselves then bring on a metaphor from verse: this (literally!) 'stunning' tutor makes 'rhymes between his birch and my body'.

It is tempting to take a letter such as this as a key to the affective power of rhyme for its author, and perhaps even to the meaning of the way in which rhyme is deployed in his poetry. Rhyme would be the pleasure extracted from pain: the repeated metrical 'blows' of line end—a metaphor which is by no means unique to Swinburne—coinciding with a sweetness extracted in the echo of like sounds. Before we do that, though, we need to think a little about how this letter reads. Swinburne's scribbling is part of a fantasy he is sharing with Milnes. He wants Milnes to share in his feelings ('I always wanted to know if other fellows shared the feeling'), and co-operating in imagining scenarios still more exquisitely degrading ('Conceive trying it...!') is an important part of this. In fact, he sometimes appears to have had trouble in getting Milnes interested in some corners of his erotic life: the insistence with which Swinburne returns to the sexual excitement produced by being buffetted by the sea rather suggests a failure to arouse any interest in his oceanophilia on his correspondent's part. Swinburne's final 'Ah-h-h!', in this letter, shares some of this insistence: it manages to sound less like a spontaneous expression of pleasure than like a moment of defiant self-applause and hectoring instruction to feel likewise.

The handling of rhyme in Swinburne's *Tristram*, I want to suggest, is something like the *opposite* of the way in which it is treated in this letter. Tempting as it might be, that is, to understand Swinburne's handling of rhyme as the deliberate fantasized extension of a masochistic pleasure in pain of all kinds, including the pain inflicted by the sea, the true case might be the reverse: that Swinburne's rhyming could in his writing about the sea be made to release those oceanic feelings which his masochism otherwise contained, controlled, and domesticated. That this could happen has to do partly with the new kind of couplet deployed in *Tristram of Lyonesse*: a couplet drawing on that developed in 'Anactoria', certainly, but dropping a certain Restoration quality of the couplet-writing in that early masterpiece in favour of much more sustained propulsion at the level of the verse-paragraph. *Tristram of Lyonesse* achieves something hardly foreseen in what the poet himself said *about* verse: a mode which, instead of adumbrating and then illustrating or instrumentating a fantasy, permits a fidelity to the *shape* of erotic experience. The currents and eddies of verse open up in Swinburne thoughts and feelings to which his own prose could not reach.

Notes

1. A. E. Housman, 'Swinburne', *The American Scholar*, 39 (1969–70), 64. Note, however, that Housman wished these lectures, including that on Swinburne, to be destroyed. He did not consider them suitable for publication.
2. Housman, 'Swinburne', 74.
3. Housman, 'Swinburne', 74.
4. Housman, 'Swinburne', 76.
5. Housman, 'Swinburne', 66.
6. Jerome McGann, 'Wagner, Baudelaire, Swinburne: Poetry in the Condition of Music', in *'A Hundred Sleeping Years Ago': In Commemoration of Algernon Charles Swinburne, April 5, 1837—April 10, 1909*, special issue of *Victorian Poetry*, eds. Terry L. Meyers and Rikky Rooksby, 47 (2009), 620.
7. McGann, 'Wagner, Baudelaire, Swinburne', 628.
8. McGann, 'Wagner, Baudelaire, Swinburne', 628.
9. For a more extended discussion of some of the reasons for this belief, see my discussion of T. W. Adorno's *Ästhetische Theorie* (Frankfurt am Main: Suhrkamp, 1970), in Simon Jarvis, *Adorno: A Critical Introduction* (Cambridge: Polity Press, 1998).
10. Swinburne to Mary Gordon, 2 Sept. 1864, in *The Swinburne Letters*, 6 vols., ed. Cecil Y. Lang (New Haven: Yale University Press, 1959–62), i. 106.
11. Rikky Rooksby, *A. C. Swinburne: A Poet's Life* (Aldershot: Scolar Press, 1997), 8.
12. Swinburne to Richard Monckton Milnes, 27 Dec. 1862, in *Letters*, i. 66–67.
13. Swinburne to M. D. Conway, 7 Nov. 1866, in *Letters*, i. 208.
14. Swinburne to J. C. Collins, 27 March 1876, in *Letters*, iii. 160.
15. Edmund Gosse, quoted in Lang, *Letters*, iv. 106n.
16. Swinburne, *Lesbia Brandon*, ed. Randolph Hughes (London: Falcon Press, 1952), 148. See Yopie Prins, *Victorian Sappho* (Princeton: Princeton University Press, 1991), 124; Catherine Maxwell, *Swinburne* (Tavistock: Northcote House, 2006), 20.
17. Swinburne, various poems, in *Poems and Ballads* (London: John Camden Hotten, 1866), 344; *Erectheus: A Tragedy* (London: Chatto and Windus, 1876), 105; *Poems*, 6 vols. (London: Chatto and Windus, 1904), v. 54; *Tristram of Lyonesse and Other Poems* (London: Chatto and Windus, 1882), 169.
18. Swinburne, 'Anactoria', in *Poems and Ballads*, 76.
19. Swinburne, 'Anactoria', 66.
20. For Swinburne and Wagner see, in addition to McGann, S. J. Sillars, 'Tristan and Tristram: Resemblance or Influence?', *Victorian Poetry*, 19 (1981), 81–6.
21. Swinburne, *Tristram of Lyonesse*, 165.
22. The term is Rikky Rooksby's: see Rooksby, 'The Algernonicon, or Thirteen Ways of Looking at *Tristram of Lyonesse*', in Rooksby and Nicholas Shrimpton, eds., *The Whole Music of Passion: New Essays on Swinburne* (Aldershot: Scolar Press, 1993), 75.

23. Herbert Tucker, *Epic: Britain's Heroic Muse 1790–1910* (Oxford: Oxford University Press, 2008), 523.

24. Swinburne, 'Tristram and Iseult. Prelude of an Unfinished Poem', in *Pleasure: A Holiday Book of Prose and Verse* (London, 1871), 46; 'Tristram of Lyonesse', 4.

25. 'Tristram of Lyonesse', 59–83; 138–45.

26. Tucker, *Epic*, 532.

27. Tucker, *Epic*, 523.

28. Ezra Pound quoted in Maxwell, *Swinburne*, 4.

29. T. S. Eliot, 'Swinburne As Poet', in *Selected Essays* (London: Faber and Faber, 1951), 324.

30. Derek Attridge, *The Rhythms of English Poetry* (London: Longman, 1982), 248–56.

31. Yopie Prins leads the way here: Prins, *Victorian Sappho*, 124.

32. Swinburne to Richard Monckton Milnes, 10 Feb. 1863 in *Letters*, i. 78.

33. Prins, *Victorian Sappho*, 122.

SELECT BIBLIOGRAPHY

No fully satisfactory complete edition of Swinburne's verse yet exists. Jerome McGann and Charles L. Sligh, eds., *Swinburne: The Major Poems and Selected Prose* (New Haven: Yale University Press, 2005) is a useful and generous selection. The attractively typeset 'Golden Pines' editions are still widely and inexpensively available secondhand. Swinburne's letters are edited by Cecil Y. Lang (New Haven: Yale University Press, 1959-62, 6 vols.); these are now supplemented by a further three volumes of *Uncollected Letters* (London: Pickering and Chatto, 2005, 3 vols.) edited by Terry L. Meyers.

Hyder, Clyde K., *Algernon Swinburne: The Critical Heritage* (London: Routledge Kegan Paul, 1970).

McGann, Jerome, *Swinburne: An Experiment in Criticism* (Chicago: University of Chicago Press, 1972).

Maxwell, Catherine, *Swinburne* (Tavistock: Northcote House, 2006).

Meyers, Terry L., and Rooksby, Rikky, "'A Hundred Sleeping Years Ago": In Commemoration of Algernon Charles Swinburne, April 5, 1837 – April 10, 1909', special issue of *Victorian Poetry*, ed. Terry L. Meyers and Rikky Rooksby, 47 (2009).

Prins, Yopie, *Victorian Sappho* (Princeton: Princeton University Press, 1991).

Rooksby, Rikky, *A.C. Swinburne: A Poet's Life* (Aldershot: Scolar Press, 1997).

—— and Nicholas Shrimpton, eds., *The Whole Music of Passion: New Essays on Swinburne* (Aldershot: Scolar Press, 1993).

Saintsbury, George, *A History of English Prosody* (London: Macmillan, 1923), 3 vols.

Tucker, Herbert, *Epic: Britain's Heroic Muse 1790–1910* (Oxford: Oxford University Press, 2008).

CHAPTER 33

··

HARDY'S IMPERFECTIONS

··

SEAMUS PERRY

HARDY's first volume of verse, *Wessex Poems*, which appeared in 1898 when he was 59, marked an abrupt close to his career as a novelist. In the *Life* that Hardy cast in the third person and published under his wife's name, he associated the abandonment of fiction with the bloody reception that the critics had given *Jude the Obscure* (1895); but he said, at the same time, that the move to verse, long meditated, constituted less of a new start than it did a homecoming: for it was poetry which, he claimed, 'had always been more instinctive with him, and which he had just been able to keep alive from his early years, half in secrecy'.[1] '[W]rote verses 1865-68; gave up verse for prose, 1868-70; but resumed it later':[2] the thumbnail sketch of a writing life that Hardy supplied for *Who's Who* suggests a 'later' poetic voice arising out of some relationship with story-telling.

Lytton Strachey once opined that '[t]he originality of his poetry lies in the fact that it bears everywhere upon it the impress of a master of prose fiction', and the remark, no doubt obvious enough, nevertheless contains a genuine and important truth.[3] Whether Strachey's attribution of 'mastery', with its implication of impressive authorial command and formal polish, hits quite the right note is another matter though, given that Hardy's novels have seemed to most readers anything *but* masterly: 'he gave you the impression of writing with the stub of a blunt pencil', as Somerset Maugham observed of a character based, in part, on Hardy.[4] The novels certainly have a quality quite unlike, say, that of something by James, a fundamental difference in modes of proceeding of which the Master himself was spikily aware: *Tess of the D'Urbervilles* was, James said, 'chock-full of faults and falsity and yet has a singular beauty and charm'.[5] (Hardy recognized James no less clearly as 'the antithesis of myself'.[6]) It was in a roughly Jamesian spirit, then, that David Lodge once called Hardy an '"in-spite-of" novelist': that is to say, a great one to be sure, but only '"in spite of" gross defects' including 'his capacity for writing badly', which puts it baldly enough.[7] But, looking at the same phenomenon in a more sympathetic way, the hallmark unevenness of Hardy's prose, even the moments of 'writing badly', can appear part of a more inclusive and wholly individual sort of literary experience. Of the critics tuned to that wavelength, John Bayley has written most memorably

about the effect. 'Hardy's words and sentences give the impression of continuing instability,' says Bayley, 'while reading we are waiting for something unexpected, good or bad,
to happen to them': he is not a writer who finds 'safety in style'.[8] (The poet Thom Gunn
made a good connection between this highly idiosyncratic kind of writing and Hardy's
admiration for his own Tess: 'It was the touch of the imperfect upon the intended perfect
that gave the sweetness, because it was that which gave the humanity'.[9]) Some reviewers
lamented his switch to verse: 'He is not at home, he does not move easily in it', said *The
Spectator*.[10] But then, not being easily 'at home' was always the characteristic of authorial
presence in everything Hardy wrote. That was something he intuited himself. The secret
of a 'living style' in prose, he noted, lay in 'not having too much style—being, in fact,
a little careless, or rather seeming to be, here and there'.[11] It is not a sentiment you can
easily imagine James seriously entertaining, any more than you can picture him endorsing Randall Jarrell's definition of a novel as 'a prose narrative of some length that has
something wrong with it';[12] but Hardy might well have appreciated the drollness of the
remark.

As Bayley says, there is a subdued wit and even a kind of propriety about imperfec-
tions occurring in an account of the Hardy universe of all places, which is also a thing
of some length which emphatically has something wrong with it.[13] Eliot thought Hardy
wrote 'always very carelessly; at times his style touches sublimity without ever having
passed through the stage of being good'.[14] But Empson saw its appropriateness: 'it might
be called a certain clumsiness that fits his grim scenery'.[15] 'Is not this incompleteness a
characteristic of all phenomena, of the universe at large?' Hardy once enquired of an
interviewer. 'It often seems to me like a half-expressed, an ill-expressed idea.'[16] And if
the move from novels to poetry was, as Hardy insisted, 'not so great as it seemed', then
that was in part because common to both modes was an abiding interest in what Hardy
once called 'the FAILURE of THINGS to be what they are meant to be'—a failure which,
he added, 'lends them, in place of the intended interest, a new and greater interest of an
unintended kind'.[17] In the novels Hardy had mapped and chronicled an entire province
of pervasive misfortune, a region characterized by tragicomic misalignments and bad
timing. The turn back to poetry offered a different repertoire of formal effect with which
he could continue the business of imagining imperfection.

The early masterpiece, 'Neutral Tones', written before any of the novels, anticipates a
lifetime of such accomplishments. Like many Hardy poems, it is a retrospect upon a love
affair that went wrong, and the poem articulates the feeling of getting wrong-footed by
life chiefly through the deft wrong-footing of its own verse:

> We stood by a pond that winter day,
> And the sun was white, as though chidden of God,
> And a few leaves lay on the starving sod;
> —They had fallen from an ash, and were gray.[18]

The basic stanza here is three lines of four feet, and a concluding line with three, and the
poem quickly establishes a complex but rhythmically assured interplay of iambs and
dactyls.[19] But then the last line of the stanza stages a marvellously approximate stab at

a line of anapaests, 'fallen' cumbrously refusing to be the poetic syllable ('fall'n') which such a metre would properly require. The last line of the poem builds on that rhythmical venture to make a greater disappointment: 'And a pond edged with grayish leaves', a finely imponderable line metrically speaking, as though it were choosing to hold true to the unsatisfactory contours of actual experience ('ish') rather than fulfilling a more simply literary design. Dennis Taylor has written superbly of this sort of hallmark line in Hardy: 'We try to read it slowly according to its natural accents, but the rhythm strains to impose its pattern. The difficulty is functional for Hardy dramatises how his language and rhythm are being influenced by forces outside his control'.[20] Hardy himself analyzed the effect in his master, William Barnes: 'by a felicitous instinct he does at times break into sudden irregularities in the midst of his subtle rhythms and measures, as if feeling rebelled against further drill. Then his self-consciousness ends, and his naturalness is saved'.[21] An overpowering impression of honesty, which is so often what we are moved by in Hardy, is frequently the work of an inspired maladroitness in that way—'fallings from…fair beginnings' into 'fearful unfulfilments', as Hardy put it in 'The Lacking Sense'.[22] But then 'fearful' might rule out the curious affectionate complicity that such effects can elicit from their sympathetic reader, which is what his friend Gosse was no doubt getting at when he identified 'a gaiety not quite consistent in the most pessimistic of poets':[23] the whole paradox of Hardy's art, and the secret of its comedy, lies in his willingness and ability to turn 'Unsuccesses to success'.[24]

Unhappy memories in Hardy, especially of love affairs that never start or get nowhere, are never properly laid to rest: his poetry is consequently honour-bound not to end too assuredly with things done and dusted. 'No man's poetry can be truly judged till its last line is written', Hardy once wrote, trying to cheer himself up after some bad reviews.[25] And what is true of a career may hold true, too, of an individual poem. A later poem, 'The Caged Goldfinch', shows the power of ending well by not ending finally:

> Within a churchyard, on a recent grave,
>   I saw a little cage
> That jailed a goldfinch. All was silence save
>   Its hops from stage to stage.
>
> There was inquiry in its wistful eye,
>   And once it tried to sing;
> Of him or her who placed it there, and why,
>   No one knew anything.[26]

The last line, which thanks to its enjambment momentarily rises into a rueful motto about life at large, hesitates between three beats and two: among the things about which the poem must confess ignorance is the rhythm of its own concluding line. In one way, the verses are a highly literary joke: Hardy is self-consciously bringing up to date the marmoreal graveyard thoughts of someone like Thomas Parnell or Thomas Gray. But there are more complicated matters at work here too, not least in the unstated but unmistakable identification between the confined bird and the modern poet, whose lyricism is evidently unable to attain anything in the old high style. It is one of the poems that shows the continuity between verse-writer and novelist that Strachey noticed; but the novelist makes his appearance here only to be disappointed by a more inconsequential kind of genius. That is not true of the first appearance of the poem, as it happens, which ended with a third stanza:

> True, a woman was found drowned the day ensuing,
>   And some at times averred
> The grave to be her false one's, who when wooing
>   Gave her the bird.[27]

But this is the ending of a minor poem, and its limitation is down to more than a distracting and irrelevant coincidence with the expression 'to give someone the bird'. It ties the poem up neatly with the narrative finality of a jilted lover plot, where the abbreviated poem wins a new greatness by leaving everything wide open—not least by arranging for the sonic latitude by which 'sing' fails singingly to chime with 'anything'. (You could hardly mispronounce it 'any*thing*' merely to rise to the demands of the rhyme, yet enunciating it as '*any*thing' leaves the rhyme syllable to a dying fall.)

It is nice to learn that Hardy had a recurrent dream which generally ended 'by my falling down the turret stairs of an old church due to steps being missing':[28] his verse repeatedly catches you short as you set out to take an anticipated step. 'The Thing Unplanned', a highly characteristic poem if not a great one, nicely captures Hardy's abiding fascination in things that occur without contemplation, and articulates the errant moment in an unscheduled change of verse form. It sets out with the scene-setting of a good narrative artist, and then abruptly discovers a quite different sort of interest, as though an incipient novel had been thrown away on a whim:

> The white winter sun struck its stroke on the bridge,
>   The meadow-rills rippled and gleamed
> As I left the thatched post-office, just by the ridge,
> And dropped in my pocket her long tender letter,
> With: 'This must be snapped! it is more than it seemed;
>   And now is the opportune time!'
>
> But against what I willed worked the surging sublime
> Of the thing that I did—the thing better! [29]

Unpredicted endings of one kind and another feature across the wide territory of the *Complete Poems*. 'Snow in the Suburbs', say, after two lovely stanzas of description, changes its formal tack completely:

> The steps are a blanched slope,
>   Up which, with feeble hope,
> A black cat comes, wide-eyed and thin;
>   And we take him in.[30]

The last line demonstrates that purposeful irresolution with which Taylor characterizes the Hardy line, somewhere between the rhythm of speech (here, two feet) and the rhythm of metre (three). There is a whole-hearted but entirely un-self-congratulatory sort of generosity in letting the cat into the poem, as well as into the house. And there is a superbly judged lyrical minimalism altogether about the close, to which the rhythmical lassitude contributes, as though verse were on winter rations; the rhyme 'thin'/'in' is about as thin as a rhyme can get. In 'The Rift' Hardy imagines 'true tones—of span so brief—/ That met my beats of joy, of grief, / As rhyme meets rhyme';[31] and his own rhymes usually meet surely enough, whatever the wandering thoughts entertained by his rhythms; but he can deploy rhymes that do not meet with tremendous effect too. The stanza of 'Where They Lived' has an unrhymed fifth line built in, which rises in its last iteration to the brilliance of:

> And where were hills of blue,
> Blind drifts of vapour blow,
> And the names of former dwellers few,
> If any, people know,
> And instead of a voice that called, 'Come in, Dears,'
> Time calls, 'Pass below!'[32]

The unrhymed phrase, amid the stanza's otherwise close rhymes, is the phrase that is itself no longer spoken, as though the whole idea of that which is *dear* has become sadly out of tune in this new dispensation.

Hardy would sometimes speak about his sense of the world in ways which felt like a piece of ambitious metaphysics: his critics often referred to his philosophical 'pessimism', as Hardy complained in the 'General Preface' to his works—or, as one wag preferred, 'Tessimism'.[33] Hardy's protests at being misunderstood were perhaps not entirely ingenuous, for his philosophical pretensions, winningly homespun and frequently the object of self-deprecation, were evidently close to his heart. The problem with modern literature, he told *The Guardian* in 1904, was 'the absence of a philosophic standpoint'. The standpoint he had in mind was necessitarianism, which is to say a denial of human freedom and agency:[34] it was within the spirit of the age, he thought, to accept 'the Monistic theory of the Universe'.[35] Generally, abstraction does not do his poetry much good. A poem such as 'In a London Flat', say, certainly does not evade the taking of 'a philosophical standpoint'; but in that poem Hardy chooses to juxtapose his metaphysical idiom with the voice of anecdote, and it proves an unforgiving sort of juxtaposition as there is no question which works better.[36] The poem opens with all the gripping immediacy of a short story: '"You look like a widower," she said / Through the folding-doors with a laugh from the bed', and by the end of the poem that is (of course) what he has indeed become:

> He, watched by those Phantoms, again sat there,
> And gazed, as if gazing on far faint-shores,
> At the empty bed through the folding-doors
> As he remembered her words; and wept
> That she had forgotten them where she slept.

The tenderness of the thing stems partly from the poem's own sympathetic act of echoic self-remembrance, and also in the way that the domestic ordinariness of the setting yet possesses something of the sad romanticism of Keats gazing through magic casements towards 'fairy-lands forlorn'. The middle stanza, by abrupt contrast, has the camera zooming out startlingly, and the tone gone all wrong, as though some tough-minded part of Hardy felt obliged to rubbish his own disposition to pity: '"Let's get him made so—just for a whim!" / Said the Phantom Ironic. " 'Twould serve her right / If we coaxed the Will to do it some night"'.

The swerve, which does not come across as remotely unwitting, is oddly ugly, not stylistically but in a moral way. The distinguished critic R. P. Blackmur, who found such thoughts especially repellent, once accused Hardy of deploying his monistic ideas as 'rigid frames to limit experience as far as possible': Hardy was, Blackmur wrote in 1940, an example of 'the absolutist, doctrinaire, as we now call it totalitarian, frame of mind'.[37] And it is true that the lesser poems do picture a world of all-too-predictable misfortune, a very lumpish kind of 'irony'. 'Must it not go amiss?' asks the momentarily contented speaker in 'He Fears His Good Fortune',

> [']Well . . . let the end foreseen
> Come duly!—I am serene'.
> —And it came.[38]

'And it always *does* come in Hardy', as Samuel Hynes says in his excellent study.[39] When, in 'The Curate's Kindness', a well-meaning parson goes the extra mile to ensure that an elderly couple will not be separated once they enter the workhouse, you can guess that his wife's company is the last thing the old man wants: '"To get freed of her there was the one thing / Had made the change welcome to me"'.[40] Well, it is a good joke of the *Punch* kind, as D. J. Enright once observed;[41] and its unsentimental satire on assumptions, both humanitarian and literary, is slickly done. But elsewhere, and especially when encountered repeatedly, the theme of cosmic come-uppance can become a bit samey. You know that a poem that begins with a description of lovely fuschias hanging over a garden-path has something coming: 'But when her funeral had to pass / They cut back all the flowery mass / In the morning'.[42]

But the best of Hardy's poems enjoy a much more glancing or elusive relationship with narrative expectation. 'The Darkling Thrush', for instance, a public poem produced to usher in a new century, embarks on what feels like a well-worn course: in the depths of winter, the speaker is suddenly surprised by the resilient song of the bird, 'a full-hearted evensong / Of joy illimited'.[43] Everything is set for an improving encounter, of a roughly Wordsworthian kind, in which momentary despondency is corrected by an example of stoic affirmation set by nature. But then (as indeed is often the case in Wordsworth too) the poem comes to its close suspended within a net of beautifully poised negative constructions, Hardy reflecting

> That I could think there trembled through
> His happy good-night air
> Some blessed Hope, whereof he knew
> And I was unaware.

Up-beat endings can rarely have kept their good cheer more tightly under wraps: the thought is presented only as a possibility that might have been pursued ('I *could*'), as it might have in a less emotionally circumspect sort of poem. And Hardy's own ignorance of any such 'blessed hope' is presented with a darkly jocular ambiguity: it is either a gap to be made good by the education that, thanks to the exemplary thrush, he can now begin to acquire, or, more mordantly, a firmly held personal conviction which is not to be swayed by the heedless performance of a bird at dusk.

Wordsworthian encounters often gain meaning by being cast as somehow intended to happen, as though by providence—'peculiar grace, / A leading from above, a something given', as Wordsworth says in 'Resolution and Independence'. Hardy's universe feels much less intended. When he referred to the 'Monism' of modern thought, I suppose he must have had in mind the post-Hegelian Idealism of T. H. Green and others, then at the height of intellectual fashion; but if so the comparison only brings into disarming relief how quirky Hardy's version of Monism really was. He would refer impressively on occasion to 'the all-immanent Will'[44] that animated everything, from Wessex lovers to Napoleon. But in practice the Will that drives history in the Hardy universe is not a purposeful and shaping omnific agency, but rather 'some Vast Imbecility'[45] that proceeds without a clue. The Hardy God, practitioner of 'forethoughtless modes', quite lacks prescience, and seems as much at sea in his cosmos as everyone else is:[46]

> *Thus doth the Great Foresightless mechanize*
> *In blank entrancement now as evermore*
> *Its ceaseless artistries in Circumstance*
> *Of curious stuff and braid,*

as Hardy put it at the close of *The Dynasts* (III, 'After Scene'). The Romantics, as Hardy well knew, were fond of likening the figure of the poet to God, something which worked well to aggrandize the making of verses; but the force of the analogy works for Hardy in a different way. Divine artistry in Hardy is only ever imperfectly in control: in 'By the Earth's Corpse', God apologetically admits that lots of wrong things got into Creation somehow '[w]hich my too oft unconscious hand / Let enter undesigned'.[47] Contingency, not 'Monism', is really the animating principle of the Hardy world, and that is what the poems work to incorporate into their textures and structures. 'Chance rules Hardy's universe, and often it seems to determine his style as well', Hynes says, describing the complex interplay of purpose and inadvertence that seems to make up the verbal life of a Hardy poem: 'Why *not* make poems out of clashing incongruities, since this is the way the world is?'[48]

Less metaphysically, Hardy sometimes thought about such matters in terms supplied by Gothic architecture, a habit shared with many of his contemporaries, though his own architectural education gave the analogies a sharper edge. 'He knew that in architecture cunning irregularity is of enormous worth', Hardy observed of himself in the third-person *Life*: 'it is obvious that he carried on into his verse, perhaps in part unconsciously, the Gothic art-principle in which he had been trained—the principle of spontaneity, found in mouldings, tracery, and such like—resulting in the "unforeseen" (as it has been called) character of his metres and stanzas'.[49] The outcome of his lesser poems can seem all too 'foreseen', enjoyable though we may certainly find the glum jokes that result. But the best of Hardy imagines the 'forethoughtless modes' of human life in ways more memorable and moving. The impression repeatedly given by the great poetry is less of individuals haplessly caught up in an implacable narrative that they cannot master, and more a matter of existing in a place where you find yourself caught out by an accident that you could never have known was coming—'Life' as a 'thwarted purposing'.[50]

Hardy was always moved by the poignancy of unawareness—of being 'The Impercipient', as one of his earlier poems is entitled. His touching sympathy for the plight of animals, like Auden's, stems from this: he imagines game-birds perplexed that the creatures who cared for them so attentively should now have begun to shoot at them ('The Puzzled Game-Birds'). And his beautifully judged poem, 'Bags of Meat', pictures a bewildered beast at a cattle auction, in a tone which uncannily anticipates Larkin:

> Each beast, when driven in,
> Looks round at the ring of bidders there
> With a much-amazed reproachful stare,
>   As at unnatural kin,
> For bringing him to a sinister scene
> So strange, unhomelike, hungry, mean . . .[51]

And the lot of the Hardy animal is not so unlike that of the human. In the lovely Boer war elegy, Hodges remains forever sadly incorporated into an 'unknown plain' that he would not have recognized.[52] In a more whimsical spirit, the bodily remains of Shelley's skylark lie exemplarily unheeded, 'A pinch of unseen, unguarded dust'. But the fascination with people and things unknown and unregarded is ubiquitous, and comes in different tempers: 'Nobody took any notice of her as she stood on the causey kerb', he begins one poem inimitably;[53] and in 'In a Cathedral City' he is touchingly struck by 'The spot's unconsciousness of you!'[54] More momentously, no one could have guessed what would happen to the Titanic and its iceberg: 'No mortal eye could see / The intimate welding of their later history'.[55] Nor is one any more likely to take notice of one's self, or to notice what, in retrospect, stands revealed as what really mattered all along: 'we were looking away!'[56] 'No prelude did I there perceive / To a drama at all, / Or foreshadow what fortune might weave / From beginnings so small'.[57] Hindsight is the stuff of his poetry, and it is rarely much of a benefit: '"If you had known"'.[58] '*If*—to what a degree that brief diminishing limiting vocable is important in his poems', Geoffrey Grigson once observed: '*if* life was so and so, *if* I had dared, *if* you had loved me or *if* love had continued, *if* you were here and not elsewhere and hadn't broken the appointment, *if* you were not dead'.[59] Hardy's people inhabit a present tense of 'all unknowing',[60] only ever coming to knowledge belatedly: 'And no one knew, unless it was God'.[61] So, no-one then. Not knowing matters so much for Hardy that he strove to invent verbs that portrayed ignorance as though it somehow possessed all the qualities of an act, instead of being merely a gap in awareness: the world at large is not just oblivious to the lost loveliness of the 'careworn wife' in 'Wives in the Sere', but somehow positively 'unknows' it.[62]

The poems written in the aftermath of his wife's death are among his finest works because they draw so deeply and tellingly, not just on all the emotions of retrospect, but on a bereavement that was wholly unexpected—'No soul foreseeing'[63]—something, as Hardy said afterwards, 'so unforeseen that I can scarcely realize it at times even now'.[64] The poems are about the unforeseen, and they experience unforeseen trajectories of their own, as in 'The Voice', with its remarkable, audacious last verse, which suddenly forgets the stanzaic occasion of its existence and speaks with a new voice:

> Woman much missed, how you call to me, call to me,
> Saying that now you are not as you were
> When you had changed from the one who was all to me,
> But as at first, when our day was fair.
>
> Can it be you that I hear? Let me view you, then,
> Standing as when I drew near to the town
> Where you would wait for me: yes, as I knew you then,
> Even to the original air-blue gown!
>
> Or is it only the breeze, in its listlessness
> Travelling across the wet mead to me here,
> You being ever dissolved to existlessness,
> Heard no more again far or near?
>
> Thus I; faltering forward,
> Leaves around me falling,
> Wind oozing thin through the thorn from norward,
> And the woman calling.[65]

The poem is great in many ways: in the enactment of recollection brilliantly caught in a sudden sharpness of detail ('the original air-blue gown'); in the terrible poignancy of the address, its neediness and yet confessed fictiveness; in the extraordinary stretching-out of the verbal imagination under duress to 'existlessness'. (So much better, that, than the more decorous 'wan wistlessness' to which Hardy revised the line in later editions.) 'The Voice' is a poem about an imaginary voice, and also a poem that itself imagines a voice 'faltering forward', lapsing from the dactylic sway established by the opening line to the crumbling lines of the last verse, collapsing ('falling' retrospectively discovers a 'fall' in 'faltering') into the metrical attenuation of the last line, which seems to stand quite free of any metrical duty altogether. It is a poem all about feeling lost, and it loses its own way with a sympathetic creativity, capturing what F. R. Leavis, otherwise no unquestioning admirer of Hardy, discerned as 'the recognition of utter loss'.[66]

The poems to his dead wife are at the heart of Hardy's achievement as a poet, but their greatness stems from virtues that are on show elsewhere too. One of the pleasures of

Hardy, as Philip Larkin once said, is the sheer amount of it, and the way that you can repeatedly find unremembered treasures.[67] Take, for example, 'At the Railway Station, Upway':

> 'There is not much that I can do,
> For I've no money that's quite my own!'
>   Spoke up the pitying child—
> A little boy with a violin
> At the station before the train came in,—
> 'But I can play my fiddle to you,
> And a nice one 'tis, and good in tone!'
>
>   The man in the handcuffs smiled;
> The constable looked, and he smiled, too,
>   As the fiddle began to twang;
> And the man in the handcuffs suddenly sang
>   With grimful glee:
>   'This life so free
>   Is the thing for me!'
> And the constable smiled, and said no word,
> As if unconscious of what he heard;
> And so they went on till the train came in—
> The convict, and boy with the violin.[68]

The experience related here is wonderfully present yet wholly imponderable; it connects up with no larger structures of explanation, let alone moralization or reflection: its vividness is a product of its inconsequentiality. The metrical desultoriness of its last line (how nicely it contrasts with the purposeful dance of iambs and the central anapaest in 'A little boy with a violin') emulates the pitch of a voice concluding nothing very affirmatively. The tone throughout is impressively unsentimentalizing: Hardy includes all the ingredients necessary for a contrast between childish innocence and criminal experience, or between freedom and constraint, and pointedly chooses to pursue none of them. The incident stands almost as a self-justifying curiosity, as inscrutable as something you would see from a passing railway carriage (a location of which Hardy was fond). Its power stems not from an expansion of sympathy nor an insightful exercise of imagination, but, paradoxically, from a refusal to indulge either beyond what is known: the authorial attitude here is at once deeply humane and quite uninvolved, an emulation of the 'nonchalant universe' that Hardy saw at large.[69] It is a minor poem but a fine one, and like all of Hardy, while possessing none of the artfully cultivated difficulty of his younger modernist contemporaries, its complexities are real and in a way the more powerful for arising within a manner that initially comes across as homely and even amateur. As Leonard Woolf remarked of the man, the impression was one of simplicity, but also 'of something which is almost the opposite of simplicity'.[70]

Notes

1. Florence Emily Hardy, *The Life of Thomas Hardy 1840–1928* (London: Macmillan, 1966; 1983), 291.
2. Thomas Hardy quoted in Samuel Hynes, *The Pattern of Hardy's Poetry* (Chapel Hill: University of North Carolina Press, 1956; 1961), 133.
3. Lytton Strachey, 'Mr Hardy's New Poems' (1914), in *Literary Essays* (London: Chatto and Windus, 1948), 220.
4. W. Somerset Maugham, *Cakes and Ale, or, The Skeleton in the Cupboard* (London: Heinemann, 1930), 185.
5. Henry James, *The Critical Muse: Selected Critical Writings*, ed. Roger Gard (Harmondsworth: Penguin, 1987), 305.
6. Reported by Frank Hedgcock, from a visit to Hardy in 1910: Gibson, James, ed., *Thomas Hardy: Interviews and Recollections* (Basingstoke: Macmillan, 1999), 95.
7. David Lodge, *The Language of Fiction: Essays in Criticism and Verbal Analysis of the English Novel* (London: Routledge and Kegan Paul, 1966), 164.
8. John Bayley, *An Essay on Hardy* (Cambridge: Cambridge University Press, 1978), 2, 3.
9. Thom Gunn, 'Hardy and the Ballads', in *The Occasions of Poetry: Essays in Criticism and Autobiography*, ed. Clive Wilmer (London: Faber, 1982) 99.
10. Quoted in Hynes, 57.
11. Hardy, *Life*, 105.
12. Randall Jarrell, 'An Unread Book', in *No Other Book: Selected Essays*, ed. Brad Leithauser ([n.p.]: Harper Collins, 1999), 362.
13. 'The quality of disappointment we taste in our experience of his text may seem to be a formalisation of disappointment as a bulky ingredient in life—certainly in life as he presents it', Bayley, *Essay*, 10–11.
14. T. S. Eliot, *After Strange Gods: A Primer of Modern Heresy* (London: Faber, 1934), 54–55.
15. William Empson, 'Selected Poems of Thomas Hardy', in *Argufying: Essays on Literature and Culture*, ed. John Haffenden (London: Chatto and Windus, 1987), 422.
16. Hardy quoted in *Real Conversations Recorded by William Archer* (London: Heinemann, 1904), 45.
17. Hardy, *Life*, 291, 124.
18. Hardy, 'Neutral Tones', in *The Complete Poems of Thomas Hardy*, ed. James Gibson (New Wessex edition; London: Macmillan, 1976), 12.
19. cp. Dennis Taylor, *Hardy's Metres and Victorian Prosody* (Oxford: Clarendon Press, 1988), 261.
20. Dennis Taylor, *Hardy's Poetry 1860–1928* (London: Macmillan, 1981), 4.
21. Hardy, 'Preface' to *Select Poems of William Barnes: Thomas Hardy's Personal Writings*, ed. Harold Orel (London: Macmillan, 1967) 76–82, 80–81.
22. Hardy, 'The Lacking Sense', in *Poems*, 117.
23. Edmund Blunden, *Thomas Hardy* (London: Macmillan, 1941), 173.
24. Hardy, 'Friends Beyond', in *Poems*, 60.
25. Hardy, *Life*, 302.
26. Hardy, 'The Caged Goldfinch', in *Poems*, 491.
27. Hardy, earlier version of 'The Caged Goldfinch', in *Poems*, 963.
28. *Friends of a Lifetime. Letters to Sydney Carlyle Cockerell*, ed. Viola Meynell (London: Jonathan Cape, 1940), 287.
29. Hardy, 'The Thing Unplanned', in *Poems*, 789.

30. Hardy, 'Snow in the Suburbs', in *Poems*, 733.

31. Hardy, 'The Rift', in *Poems*, 623.

32. Hardy, Where They Lived', in *Poems*, 463.

33. Hardy suspected Andrew Lang to be responsible for the term: see Michael Millgate, *Thomas Hardy. A Biography* (Oxford: Oxford University Press, 1982), 321.

34. Gibson, *Interviews and Recollections*, 75.

35. Hardy, 'Preface' to *The Dynasts: An Epic-Drama* (London, Macmillan, 1978), 4.

36. Hardy, 'In a London Flat', in *Poems*, 689–90.

37. R. P. Blackmur, 'The Shorter Poems of Thomas Hardy', Southern Review 6 (1940), 20–48.

38. Hardy, 'He Fears His Good Fortune', in *Poems*, 510.

39. Hynes, *Pattern*, 51.

40. Hardy, 'The Curate's Kindness', in *Poems*, 208–9.

41. D. J. Enright, *The Alluring Problem. An Essay on Irony* (Oxford: Oxford University Press, 1986), 87.

42. Hardy, 'The Lodging House Fuchsias', in *Poems*, 855.

43. Hardy, 'The Darkling Thrush', in *Poems*, 150.

44. Hardy, 'The Unborn', in *Poems*, 287.

45. Hardy, 'Nature's Questioning', in *Poems*, 66.

46. Hardy, 'An Inquiry', in *Poems*, 758.

47. Hardy, 'By the Earth's Corpse', in *Poems*, 126.

48. Hynes, *Pattern*, 63.

49. Hardy, *Life*, 301.

50. Hardy, 'Yell'ham Wood's Story', in *Poems*, 298.

51. Hardy, 'The Puzzled Game-Birds', in *Poems*, 808.

52. Hardy, 'Drummer Hodge', in *Poems*, 90–1.

53. Hardy, 'The Market Girl', in *Poems*, 240.

54. Hardy, 'In a Cathedral City', in *Poems*, 222.

55. Hardy, 'The Convergence of the Twain', in *Poems*, 307.

56. Hardy, 'The Self-Unseeing', in *Poems*, 167.

57. Hardy, 'At the Word "Farewell"', in *Poems*, 432.

58. Hardy, 'What might have moved you?', in *Poems*, 633.

59. Geoffrey Grigson, 'The Poet who did not Care for Life' in *The Contrary View. Glimpses of Fudge and Gold* (London: Macmillan, 1974), 193.

60. Hardy, 'The Pine Planters', in *Poems*, 273.

61. Hardy, 'A Poor Man and a Lady', in *Poems*, 793.

62. Hardy, 'Wives in the Sere', in *Poems*, 143.

63. Hardy, 'The Going', in *Poems*, 339.

64. Hardy to Pearce Edgcumbe, 26 December 1912 (a month after Emma's death): *The Collected Letters of Thomas Hardy*, ed. Richard Little Purdy and Michael Millgate, 7 vols. (Oxford: Clarendon Press, 1978–1988), iv. 251.

65. Hardy, 'The Voice', in *Poems*, 346.

66. F. R. Leavis, 'Hardy as Poet', in *The Critic as Anti-Philosopher. Essays and Papers*, ed. G. Singh (London: Chatto and Windus, 1982), 103.

67. Philip Larkin, 'The Poetry of Hardy' in *Required Writing. Miscellaneous Pieces 1955–1982* (London: Faber, 1983), 176.

68. Hardy, 'At the Railway Station, Upway', in *Poems*, 607.

69. Hardy, *Life*, 378.

70. Leonard Woolf, *The Nation*, 21 Jan. 1928 in Gibson, *Interviews and Recollections*, 121.

SELECT BIBLIOGRAPHY

EDITIONS

The important editions of the poems are: Gibson, James, ed., *The Complete Poems of Thomas Hardy*, (New Wessex edition, London: Macmillan, 1976); Gibson, James, ed., *The Variorum Edition of the Complete Poems of Thomas Hardy* (Basingstoke: Macmillan, 1979); Hynes, Samuel, ed., *The Complete Poetical Works of Thomas Hardy*, 5 vols. Oxford: Clarendon Press, 1982–1995). Hardy's surviving notebooks have been published: Björk, Lennart A., ed., *The Literary Notebooks of Thomas Hardy*, 2 vols. (London: Macmillan, 1985); Pamela Dalziel, and Michael Millgate, eds., *Thomas Hardy's 'Studies, Specimens &c.' Notebook* (Oxford: Clarendon Press, 1994); Greenslade, William, *Thomas Hardy's 'Facts' Notebook: A Critical Edition* (Aldershot: Ashgate, 2004); Pamela Dalziel and Michael Millgate, eds., *Thomas Hardy's 'Poetical Matter' Notebook* (Oxford: Oxford University Press, 2009). His autobiography in disguise originally appeared in two volumes under the declared authorship of Florence Emily Hardy: *The Early Life of Thomas Hardy, 1840–1891* (London: Macmillan, 1928) and *The Later Years of Thomas Hardy, 1892–1928* (London: Macmillan, 1930); they were collected together as *The Life of Thomas Hardy, 1840–1928* (London: Macmillan, 1962). The recovered original text is presented in Michael Millgate, ed., *The Life and Work of Thomas Hardy* (London: Macmillan, 1984).

SECONDARY READING

Bayley, John, *An Essay on Hardy* (Cambridge: Cambridge University Press, 1978).
Cox, R. G., ed., *Thomas Hardy: The Critical Heritage* (London: Routledge and Kegan Paul, 1970).
Davie, Donald, *With the Grain: Essays on Thomas Hardy and Modern British Poetry*, ed. Clive Wilmer (Manchester: Carcanet, 1998).
Hynes, Samuel, *The Pattern of Hardy's Poetry* (Chapel Hill: University of North Carolina Press, 1961).
Mallett, Philip, ed., *Palgrave Advances in Thomas Hardy Studies* (Basingstoke, Palgrave Macmillan, 2004).
Millgate, Michael, *Thomas Hardy: A Biography* (Oxford: Oxford University Press, 1982). Revised and expanded as *Thomas Hardy: A Biography Revisited* (Oxford: Oxford University Press, 2004).
Paulin, Tom, *Thomas Hardy: The Poetry of Perception* (London: Macmillan, 1975).
Pite, Ralph, *Thomas Hardy: The Guarded Life* (London: Picador, 2006).
——'Hardy and Mew', in O'Neill, Michael, ed., *The Cambridge History of English Poetry* (Cambridge: Cambridge University Press, 2010).
Riquelme, John Paul, 'The Modernity of Thomas Hardy's Poetry', in Dale Kramer, ed., *The Cambridge Companion to Thomas Hardy* (Cambridge: Cambridge University Press, 1999).
Taylor, Dennis, *Hardy's Literary Language and Victorian Philology* (Oxford: Clarendon Press, 1993).
—— *Hardy's Metres and Victorian Prosody, with a Metrical Appendix of Hardy's Stanza Forms* (Oxford: Clarendon Press, 1988).
—— *Hardy's Poetry, 1860–1928* (London: Macmillan, 1981).
—— 'Hardy as a Nineteenth-Century Poet', in Dale Kramer, ed., *The Cambridge Companion to Thomas Hardy* (Cambridge: Cambridge University Press, 1999).

CHAPTER 34

···

HOPKINS'S BEAUTY

···

MARTIN DUBOIS

THE song of the Leaden Echo in Hopkins's 'The Leaden Echo and the Golden Echo' (1882) opens with a question: 'How to keep—is there ány any, is there none such, nowhere known some, bow or brooch or braid or brace, lace, latch or catch or key to keep / Back beauty, keep it, beauty, beauty, beauty, . . . from vanishing away?'[1] The scramble for purchase begins even before the word 'beauty' appears, perhaps in anticipation of the likelihood that its very mention will impel the movement out of reach. By way of answer, the Golden Echo offers a redirection: 'Give beauty back, beauty, beauty, beauty, back to God beauty's self and beauty's giver'. In the word's reverberation, this too traces beauty's propensity to fleet and vanish. But if the repetitions have 'beauty' fading just as it is on the point of return, the contrasting unmelodiousness of 'back' secures it for God: '*Back* is not pretty', Hopkins commented of the poem, 'but it gives that feeling of physical constraint which I want'.[2]

Hopkins's poetry can often seem to constrain beauty, in order that its appreciation might serve as a means of spiritual dedication. The poet, according to his early critical champion, F. R. Leavis, had 'a habit of seeing things as charged with significance; "significance" here being, not a romantic vagueness, but a matter of explicit and ordered conceptions regarding the relations between God, man and nature'.[3] It is a view of Hopkins's distinctiveness to which later studies have largely held. According to Hilary Fraser, 'Hopkins' awareness of Christ as the divine archetype of created beauty. . .enabled him to merge his love of beauty and poetic creativity with his religious commitment'.[4] As Hopkins's poetry comes to be regarded as performing ordering work, integrating aesthetic and spiritual impulses, it tends to be scrutinized according to a single measure: the explicitness with which it is able to restore beauty 'back to God beauty's self and beauty's giver'. Faced with the convoluted density of his later poetry, it can appear (as Fraser also observes) that 'the synthesis did not always hold up for him in practice'.[5] Yet the notion that Hopkins's poetry was a consistent project needs to be reconsidered. This priest-poet rarely saw the composition of poetry as amounting to a function of priesthood, instead recognizing other, more effective means of fulfilling the spiritual duties he saw as his life's major task; the absence of a stable objective for his writing is reflected in the variousness of its spiritual perspectives and commitments. Rather than try to encompass Hopkins's writing within a linear framework, we would do better to find in diversity one of its riches. Hopkins's encounter with beauty is an obvious place to start.

'Dappled Things'

Cleaning out water-closets in the Jesuit novitiate, Hopkins apprehended a winter beauty: 'The slate slabs of the urinals even', he noted in his journal, 'are frosted in graceful sprays.'[6] The stubbornly factual cast of this observation is characteristic. The sight of a dying sheep in 1873 found equally unflinching record: 'there ran slowly from his nostril a thick flesh-coloured ooze, scarlet in places, coiling and roping its way down, so thick that it looked like fat'.[7] 'Pied Beauty' (1877) gives this manner of visual perception explicitly religious direction and force:

> Glory be to God for dappled things—
>   For skies of couple-colour as a brinded cow;
>   For rose-moles all in stipple upon trout that swim;
>   Fresh-firecoal chestnut-falls; finches' wings;
> Landscape plotted and pieced—fold, fallow, and plough;
>   And áll trades, their gear and tackle and trim.
>
> All things counter, original, spáre, strange;
>   Whatever is fickle, frecklèd (who knows how?)
>   With swíft, slów; sweet, sóur; adázzle, dím;
>   He fathers-forth whose beauty is pást change:
>   Práise hím.[8]

Hopkins had ambitions to be a painter-poet before he decided upon becoming a priest; his sketch-books and journals of the early- and mid-1860s show him methodically training his sketching eye according to the principles laid out in John Ruskin's *Elements of Drawing* (1857). 'Pied Beauty' reveals how thoroughly Hopkins had assimilated Ruskin's precept to discern general laws of existence from the minute scrutiny of nature's true particulars. The poem fashions its final unity out of a potentially cacophonous variety. It is composed in 'stipple', arrested by dots of natural detail, yet at the same time lent an overall cohesiveness by virtue of its formal design. Impelled by the back-weighted syntax, 'All things' of the second stanza gather to the God 'whose beauty is pást change', and thence to the emphatic decree with which the poem ends, this last a special effect of Hopkins's reworking of the sonnet form ('Pied Beauty' is a 'curtal' sonnet, a sonnet whose dimensions are proportionally shrunk in relation to its Petrarchan original).

More than to any other form, Hopkins was attracted to the sonnet, and 1877 was his year of sonnet epiphany, yielding (in addition to 'Pied Beauty') 'God's Grandeur', 'The Starlight Night', 'As kingfishers catch fire', 'The Windhover', and 'Hurrahing in

Harvest', among others. All this came in succession to 'The Wreck of the Deutschland', the extraordinary first product of Hopkins's creative maturity, completed the previous summer. Hopkins was at the time undertaking theological studies in North Wales. The fertile richness of the Welsh countryside drew from him joyous admiration. In 'Pied Beauty', true to the Ruskinian bearings of Hopkins's visual imagination, this admiration is accompanied by a determination to see afresh, forsaking conventionalizing impressions. So Hopkins couples skies and cows, and—as if to ensure that a stanza which utters a general truth is not itself complacently generalizing—jolts out of the alliterative stride of 'swíft, slów; sweet, sóur' with 'adázzle, dím', a pairing which bears a hallmark of Hopkins's way with words, involving an aggressive shift of lexical class (a verb—'dazzle'—coined into an adjective—'adázzle').

Thinking of Hopkins, Marianne Moore remarks that 'precision is a thing of the imagination; and it is a matter of diction, of diction that is virile because galvanized against inertia'.[9] The gain Hopkins's diction makes from the frequent manipulation of word class is one of precision. His manner of pressing verbs out of their habitual grammatical usage was part of his commitment to the exact realization of nature's 'state of perpetual variation', as Ruskin described it in Modern Painters, I (1843).[10] '[A]dázzle' is traced with the motion of the verb from which it is derived; 'dím' is more familiar an adjective, but here too a measure of action inheres in description. Such virility in diction was additionally the product of an imagination galvanized by knowledge of contemporary scientific debates, especially in energy physics. Hopkins's early critical advocates liked to think of him as an accidental Victorian, modern in all but his dates. In few other areas as science has it been so comprehensively proven by recent critics that our earlier impression of Hopkins as a poet segregated from the intellectual currents of his time was a Leavisite fancy.[11] With his characteristically rangy curiosity, Hopkins was aware of new theories which implied both the dynamism of energy flows and the potential for energy to dissipate (the process known as 'entropy'); these provided a spur to poetry which is at once stimulated by material change and anxious about the potential for a very specific kind of inertia—the inertia of physical waste.

The latter part of 'Pied Beauty' is an act of praise doubling as a piece of deductive logic. It is a sonnet of intense cogency; imperatives stand guard at either end of the poem, channelling the celebration of nature's variety into its proper course. Hopkins's poems of this period are often emphatic in their turn from admiration to praise. 'Part the First' of 'The Wreck of the Deutschland' is similarly bookended, opening with an acknowledgment of God as 'giver of breath and bread', and closing with an entreaty to 'Make mercy in all of us, out of us all / Mastery, but be adored, but be adored King'.[12] In one sense this forcibility is the counterpart to the novelty of Hopkins's insight. The formal theological teaching Hopkins received claimed a strict division between the divine and the natural order. He had to turn elsewhere to find corroboration for his distinctive realization of nature as grace-filled. Much has been written about the sway the medieval philosopher Duns Scotus held over Hopkins, most especially in relation to the part Scotus's ideas played in crystallizing what Hopkins intended by his private terminology of 'inscape' and 'instress'.[13] What has not been sufficiently remarked is how little of Scotus's work

Hopkins actually encountered. Hopkins's formal studies comprised a narrow diet of baroque scholasticism to which Scotus would have been a marginal presence, likely to feature only in the capacity of minor deviant from the major creed. Happening upon Scotus's commentary on the *Sentences* of Peter Lombard in the library at Stonyhurst in the early 1870s, Hopkins found himself 'flush with a new stroke of enthusiasm'.[14] But since the Stonyhurst copy was a sixteenth-century edition, the interpretation of which would have required good palaeographical skills, the precise nature of that excitement must remain elusive.[15] As important as what Hopkins took from Scotus may be what advocacy of Scotus represented for him: a flag to wave in opposition to the dominant mode of Catholic theology at the time, a rigidified Thomism which ran contrary to Hopkins's instinct for discerning God's animating touch in nature's diversity as in human uniqueness. If Hopkins's poetry of this period is more often expository than exploratory, that is partly because the absence of firm support from his formal studies for a spiritual comprehension of nature's variety lent particular urgency to the task of declaring that 'The world is charged with the grandeur of God'—'charged' here suggesting not only God's vivifying presence in creation, but also human responsibility for that which is held in divine trust.[16]

The first mention of 'inscape' and 'instress', terms of Hopkins's invention which have framed much critical discussion of his poetry, arrived before Hopkins had likely heard of Scotus, appearing in notes on Greek philosophy made subsequently to the completion of his undergraduate studies at Oxford. A range of definitions has been offered in critical commentary as to their meaning, partly in recognition of the fact that this meaning was not secure. In a fashion typical of Hopkins, 'inscape' originated as a noun but was also before long used as a verb ('to inscape'). Usually understood to signify the inner or distinctive quality of a thing or scene, 'inscape' can also correspond in Hopkins's writing to the accidental form of the whole (hence Hopkins's note on his observation of a moonlit landscape: 'I read a broad careless inscape flowing throughout').[17] There is the added complication that Hopkins on occasion implied that 'inscape' was not a fixed quality: 'The Horned violet is a pretty thing, gracefully lashed. Even in withering the flower ran through beautiful inscapes by the screwing up of petals into straight little barrels or tubes'.[18] 'Instress' is, if anything, more slippery, being at once the force which sustains the 'inscape' and the impact of perceiving the 'inscape' on the beholder.

The diverse resonance of these terms for Hopkins's writing was partly the result of changes in his thought across a long period. It also attests to the fact that Hopkins's inclination for theorizing was not often attended by the kind of systematic conceptualization which leads to consistent application. That most discussion of 'inscape' and 'instress' occurred in private notes meant that Hopkins was rarely required to expound their meaning to others. The circular phrasing of an oft-cited reference to 'inscape' in Hopkins's letters is in this sense revealing: 'as air, melody, is what strikes me most of all in music and design in painting, so design, pattern or what I am in the habit of calling "inscape" is what I above all aim at in poetry'.[19] '[W]hat I am in the habit of calling "inscape"': if 'habit' can for Hopkins sometimes denote practised discipline—witness his early sonnet 'The Habit of Perfection' (1865)—here it provides the pretext for Hopkins at once to mention his favoured term and glide over the specific details of its meaning. The haziness of the relation implied by the conjunction ('design, pattern *or*...') is accounted for by means of Hopkins's gesture towards a personal and customary idiom. That idiom holds an extreme importance for Hopkins's poetry, but it is allowed to remain, as a matter of private 'habit', only partially elaborated.

One of the few explicit references to either 'inscape' or 'instress' in the poems comes in 'The Wreck of the Deutschland': 'His mýstery múst be instréssed, stressed', the poet declares at one point, stipulating the need for what Terry Eagleton calls a 'strenuously subjective, realizing response' to God's presence in the world.[20] It is a response which engages a characteristic shift of lexical class ('instréssed'). The line is the more strenuous for Hopkins's refusal of the expected lilt of 'instressed, stressed' in order to remain concentrated on 'stress', a word with almost as many shades of implication as 'inscape' in Hopkins's personal lexicon, oscillating (though not collapsing the difference) between prosodic, emotional, and philosophical categories.

Hopkins was only persuaded to break a seven-year, self-imposed, and near-complete poetic silence to begin work on 'The Wreck of the Deutschland' by his rector's remark that such was the poignancy of the *Deutschland* tragedy 'that he wished someone would write a poem on the subject.'[21] What resulted may as a consequence be more inflected with the ultramontane spirit dominant among his Jesuit contemporaries than is 'Pied Beauty', a poem differently attuned, but 'The Wreck of the Deutschland' nonetheless belongs with the 1877 nature sonnets for the deliberateness with which the poet applies his energies in vindication of the divine mystery. Discussion of prosodic 'stress' in 'The Wreck of the Deutschland', the poem which saw the first full realization of Hopkins's sprung rhythm, has been bedevilled by a desire on the part of critics to smooth out the creases in the poet's differing and various explanations of its nature. This has most often manifested itself in a willingness to ordain Hopkins's so-called 'Author's Preface' the definitive statement of sprung rhythm's workings, when it was in fact written with the express intention of overcoming Coventry Patmore's resistance to Hopkins's innovation. Presumably Hopkins believed Patmore would appreciate the clarity of knowing that sprung rhythm was always a falling rhythm, but it is far from apparent that this is what Hopkins held generally.[22] What is important to register in the context of 'The Wreck of the Deutschland' is what sprung rhythm enables: a forcibility that ensures 'The Wreck of the Deutschland' comes close to 'Pied Beauty' in singleness of vision. Hopkins once explained to Robert Bridges that he employed sprung rhythm for its combination of 'markedness of rhythm... and naturalness of expression'; one of the best recent accounts of the measure likewise proposes that it is 'the very springiness of sprung rhythm that allows Hopkins such range, which he realises through the juxtaposition of stress with looser, smoother, more delicate sound patterns.'[23] Yet that it is 'markedness' which is to the fore at the close of 'The Wreck of the Deutschland' in the poem's emphatically possessive final line, can be taken as a sign of Hopkins's determination to conduct the poem's theodicy on absolute terms: 'Our héart's charity's héarth's fíre, our thóughts' chivalry's thróng's Lórd'. Just as the quality Hopkins admires in his maker is that of mastery, of the authority of the 'master of the tides', so too the impression left by the poet himself is of bold assertiveness, of an effort to subdue all to the imperative given in 'Pied Beauty': 'Práise hím'.

WORDS AND BODIES

Expanding upon the question posed in the poem's title, the opening lines of 'To what serves Mortal Beauty?' (1885) are diverted by sensation: 'To what serves mortal beauty— dangerous; does set danc- / Ing blood'.[24] The echo here of an earlier letter suggests where Hopkins most often located this hazard: 'I think…no one can admire beauty of the body more than I do, and it is of course a comfort to find beauty in a friend or a friend in beauty. But this kind of beauty is dangerous'.[25] The letter goes on to allot a higher significance to 'beauty of mind' and 'beauty of character', recognizing an order of value to which Hopkins's poems do not always submit. The 'lovely manly mould' of the 'sea-corpse' washed to shore in 'The Loss of the Eurydice' (1878), and thus 'strained to beauty', is one of several male bodies to have set the poet's blood dancing—bodies of men who, as Simon Humphries has noticed, are disturbingly all silent, seemingly unable or unwilling to speak.[26] The homoeroticism latent in such moments has been a persistent focus of recent commentary on Hopkins.[27] In 'To what serves Mortal Beauty?', the English slaves so admired by Pope Gregory that he sent a mission to their native land are evidence for the spiritual good of physical attractiveness:

> To what serves mortal beauty—| dangerous; does set danc-
> Ing blood—the O-seal-that-so | feature, flung prouder form
> Than Purcell tune lets tread to? | See: it does this: keeps warm
> Men's wit to the things that are; | to what good means—where a glance
> Master more may than gaze, | gaze out of countenance.
> Those lovely lads once, wet-fresh | windfalls of war's storm,
> How then should Gregory, a father, | have gleanèd else from swarm-
> Èd Rome? But God to a nation | dealt that day's dear chance.
> To man, that once would worship | block or barren stone,
> Our law says / love what are | love's worthiest, were all known;
> World's loveliest—men's selves. Self | flashes off frame and face.
> What do then? how meet beauty? | Merely meet it; own,
> Home at heart, heaven's sweet gift; | then leave, let that alone.
> Yea, wish that though, wish all, | God's better beauty, grace.

Managing the bulkiness of the alexandrine requires that each line be split in two, a fact which, combined with multiple dislocations of syntax, lends the poem a stiff, staccato-like air: opportunities to linger over (rather than 'Merely meet') beauty are in appropriately short supply. Yet the account of Pope Gregory's admiration of the English slaves departs from this more general abruptness. There is the imprecision of 'lovely' (an adjective, as Josephine Miles observes, variously applied in Hopkins's poetry to 'Death,

Providence, weeds, fire, behaviour, woods, manly mould, Christ, dale, lads, mile, men's selves').[28] And in the succession of 'wet-fresh' by 'windfalls of war's storm', the alliterative chime pursued across the caesura, there is a hint that the aural might here be shaping the moral as well as being shaped by it (compare the more directly pious wordplay attributed by Bede's *Ecclesiastical History* to Gregory: the English [*Angli*] slaves 'have the face of angels [*angelicam*], and such men should be fellow-heirs of the angels [*angelorum*] in heaven').[29] Prisoners of war are not normally 'wet-fresh', even if, as Gregory marvelled, they are fair-haired, violence here bearing captivatingly tender fruit.

Imprecision might seem a rare quality in Hopkins. His style more obviously tends towards an extreme conspicuousness, as with the novelty of 'adázzle' in 'Pied Beauty', a word whose very newness renders a series of concrete adjectives ('swíft, slów; sweet, sóur'; adázzle, dím') additionally concrete. Hopkins himself once proposed that 'We may think of words as heavy bodies, as indoor or out of door objects of nature or man's art', as though words could be solid masses, imbued with the physicality of what they signify.[30] Elsewhere, though, he suggested that verse might also be 'speech wholly or partially repeating some kind of figure which is over and above meaning, at least the grammatical, historical, and logical meaning'.[31] That which is 'over and above meaning' comes further to the fore in Hopkins's own writing after 1877, in poetry composed in brief moments of respite from a life of priestly service of 'ginger-bread permanence', as he once called it, spent shuttled between postings.[32] Take the 'downdolfinry and bell-bright bodies' encountered by the 'stranger' in the late poem 'Epithalamion' (1888):

> Careless these in coloured wisp
> All lie tumbled-to; then with loop-locks
> Forward falling, forehead frowning, lips crisp
> Over fingerteasing task, his twiny boots
> Fast he opens, last he off wrings
> Till walk the world he can with bare his feet
> And come where lies a coffer, burly all of blocks
> Built of chancequarrièd, selfquainèd, hoar-huskèd rocks
> And the water warbles over into, filleted | with glassy grassy
>   quicksilvery shivès and shoots
> And with heavenfallen freshness down from moorland still brims,
> Dark or daylight on and on. Here he will then, here he will the fleet
> Flinty kindcold element let break across his limbs
> Long. Where we leave him, froliclavish, while he looks about him, laughs, swims.[33]

The preponderance of distinctively Hopkinsian epithets—'chancequarrièd, selfquainèd, hoar-huskèd'; 'froliclavish'—gives a very different impression to the bathing which takes place in Hopkins's early poem 'A Vision of the Mermaids' (1862), in which the sea-creatures bask in recognizably Keatsian light, 'spurr'd and ray'd/With spikèd quills all of intensest hue'.[34] 'A Vision of the Mermaids' aspires to more languorous motion than 'Epithalamion', as some among the mermaids 'plash / The languent smooth with dimpling drops', while others, 'diving merrily, downward drove, and gleam'd/With arm and fin'. The movement of the later poem is less mellifluous and we would do well not to take its airiness entirely casually. Yet the language of the poem still appears more driven by surface than depth, the sequence of *y*-ending adjectives ('glassy grassy quick-silvery') trying for alliterative sparkle rather than descriptive precision. The swimmers 'lie tumbled-to', a haphazardness reflected in the poem's acoustic leaps, as words tumble into each other, 'Forward falling' finding 'forehead frowning', 'lips' shading into 'crisp', 'water' into 'warbles'.

This is the sort of poem that might frustrate unsympathetic readers of Hopkins. T. S. Eliot considered that Hopkins's 'innovations…sometimes come near to being purely *verbal*, in that a whole poem will give us *more* of the same thing, an accumulation, rather than a real development of thought or feeling'.[35] W. B. Yeats, deigning against his better instinct to include Hopkins in *The Oxford Book of Modern Verse* (1936), found the Victorian poet 'typical of his generation where most opposed to mine': 'His meaning is like some faint sound that strains the ear, comes out of words, passes to and fro between them, goes back into words, his manner a last development of poetical diction'.[36] Yeats's hostility was bound up with dislike of the strain of English Catholicism he took Hopkins to represent; the curious substance of Eliot's complaint was that he found Hopkins no bulwark in 'the struggle…against Liberalism'.[37] Even so, the choice to focus antagonism on the poet's supposed verbalism is striking given how habituated subsequent Hopkins criticism has become to just the opposite realization: the suggestion that for Hopkins, as J. Hillis Miller asserts, 'Words are the dynamic internalization of the world'.[38] From Miller's claim it is only a short leap to comprehending that Hopkins placed an absolute value on the capacity of words to incarnate meaning, in the manner of Hopkins's notes on Greek philosophy of 1868: 'All words mean either things or relations of things: you may also say then substances or attributes or again wholes or parts'.[39] It has often been said that Hopkins desired always to collapse the distance between word and thing—an assertion which usually leans heavily upon the perception that Hopkins's notes on Greek philosophy provide a prospectus to the subsequent two decades of his poetry.[40] Whether the notes should be accorded this status is doubtful. Certainly it is a mistake to restrict his poetry to a single mode. One of the loveliest lines in Hopkins—'Though worlds of wanwood leafmeal lie'—is also among the most fragile, its verbal echoes all the fainter for being played to the metrical score (the accent on the vowel in 'worlds' lost to its echo in 'wanwood', a similar fading occurring across '*leafmeal*').[41] This is a gentler, sadder response to mortal beauty than is demanded in the later poem of that name: 'Merely meet it; own, / Home at heart, heaven's sweet gift; | then leave, let that alone'. The idea that all of Hopkins's poetry strives to attribute words with bodily weight will not get us far here.

Hard Truths

Hopkins has never been short of detractors. Kingsley Amis, in one of his swaggering letters to Philip Larkin, gave a notably blunt rendition of what many others have also felt:

About Hopkins: I find him a bad poet—all this how to keép is there ány any stuff strikes me as a bit unnecessary—and so his defence of his work to Bridges, in spite of Bridges being a bumblock of the first order, seems arrogant to me: You must be wrong when you don't like my stuff, d'you see, because *I know* my stuff's good, d'you see? And his silly private language annoys me—'what I am in the habit of calling *inscape*' well *getoutofthehabitthen*. I had another go at his poetry the other day, and confirmed my previous impression of it as *going after the wrong thing*, trying to treat words as if they were music. They aren't, are they? If his verse can't be read properly without key-signatures and sharps and flats, *so much the worse for it*. And as for this bitch batch bum come cock cork fork fuck stuff; *what is the point of it?* Eh? Outrider— aaaaaagh; counterpointed rhythm—uuuuuuuth, and you can't *have* counterpointed *rhythm*. I'm sorry to go on like this, but I do feel it.[42]

Along with echoes of Eliot's and Yeats's censure of Hopkins ('trying to treat words as if they were music'), there is here a more familiar objection: an objection to the wantonness of Hopkins's difficulty. In this Amis was in agreement with his alleged 'bumblock', Robert Bridges, who—in the edition of Hopkins Bridges published in 1918—famously offered a disclaimer in respect of Hopkins's method: 'there are definite faults of style which a reader must have courage to face, and must in some measure condone before he can discover the great beauties...It was an idiosyncrasy of this student's mind to push everything to its logical extreme, and take pleasure in a paradoxical result'.[43] Even Hopkins's best advocates recognize that his difficulty can be rebarbative. Elizabeth Bishop notices that 'At times the obscurity of [Hopkins's] thought, the bulk of his poetic idea seems too heavy to be lifted and dispersed into flying members by his words; the words and the sense quarrel with each other and the stanzas seem to push against the reader, like coiled springs against the hand.'[44]

Unwieldiness is a strong characteristic of the poetry Hopkins wrote in Ireland from 1884. Hopkins admitted to R. W. Dixon that his 1887 sonnets 'Tom's Garland' and 'Harry Ploughman' were 'works of infinite, of over great contrivance, I am afraid, to the annulling in the end of the right effect'.[45] One need not entirely accept the self-critique to see the truth about 'Tom's Garland' that it contains:

Tom's Garland:

upon the Unemployed

Tom—garlanded with squat and surly steel
Tom; then Tom's fallowbootfellow piles pick
By him and rips out rockfire homeforth—sturdy Dick;
Tom Heart-at-ease, Tom Navvy: he is all for his meal
Sure, 's bed now. Low be it: lustily he his low lot (feel
That ne'er need hunger, Tom; Tom seldom sick,
Seldomer heartsóre; that treads through, prickproof, thick
Thousands of thorns, thoughts) swings though. Commonweal
Little Í reck ho! lacklevel in, if all had bread:
What! Country is honour enough in all us—lordly head,
With heaven's lights high hung round, or, mother-ground

That mammocks, mighty foot. But nŏ way sped,
Nor mind nor mainstrength; gold go garlanded
With, perilous, O nó; nor yet plod safe shod sound;
    Undenizened, beyond bound
Of earth's glory, earth's ease, all; no-one, nowhere,
In wide the world's weal; rare gold, bold steel, bare
    In both; care, but share care —
This, by Despair, bred Hangdog dull; by Rage,
Manwolf, worse; and their packs infest the age.[46]

The poem better conveys the density of Hopkins's feeling than its cause. Even the 'Garland' of the title proves hard to place, having at once to do with instruments of labour (the hobnails on a labourer's boots and the pick he carries over his shoulder) and, later, with aspects of wealth ('gold go garlanded / With, perilous, O nó'). Observing Hopkins's recourse to codas, the curious elisions in lines five and six, and a succession of impenetrable conjunctions and repetitions, John Sutherland aptly remarks that 'Tom's Garland' is 'so thickly enfolded in its own technique as to be almost strangled by it'.[47] Asking for Bridges's advice on appending codas to the sonnet, Hopkins acknowledged that 'It is the only time I have felt forced to exceed the beaten bounds.'[48] If the excess is perhaps a little less knotted than the bulk, the final two lines especially, we are far from the fluent progression and intense logicality of Hopkins's earlier nature sonnets. These last would be qualities out of place in confronting what is stubborn and unmalleable in the world and in personal experience—the burden of 'Tom's Garland' as of the greater part of Hopkins's later poetry. 'Tom's Garland' attends to malfunction, to the 'packs' doing harm to the communal body, and the tangle of its words implies, according to Geoffrey Hill, 'that, because the men cannot work, therefore the poem itself cannot'.[49] The problem for Hopkins's reader comes when the nature of the obstruction can hardly be known for the poem so entirely taking on its aspect.

As the difficulty of Hopkins's poetry increases, its trade with beauty appears to lessen. The clunking internal rhyme of the war-song, 'What shall I do for the land that bred me', provides about the most notable instance of the word 'beauty' in Hopkins's poetry after 1884: 'Immortal beauty is death with duty, / If under her banner I fall for her honour'.[50] It is apt that part of this war-song should have been composed during an afternoon spent in Phoenix Park, scene of a notorious double-murder of British officials by a Fenian splinter group a few years earlier, for Hopkins in Ireland frequently felt himself to be trapped fighting under the wrong banner, the unhappy grind of his teaching at University College, Dublin, performed under the direction of an Irish episcopate set upon—as he saw it—undermining the land that bred him, and its control over Irish affairs. Contrary to the vague hope of his superiors that the change of work would suit his peculiar temperament, Hopkins felt severally estranged in Ireland—'at a thírd / Remove', according to one of a series of anguished poems written in around 1885–6, poems known collectively as the 'terrible' sonnets.[51]

These were years for Hopkins of spiritual as well as political dislocation. Critics disagree over whether the 'terrible' sonnets were a means to purgation or, alternatively, whether they in fact reveal collapsing belief. It is perhaps too easy to interpret them as the unhappy climax of Hopkins's poetry. What comes after—for Hopkins continued to write poetry until his death in 1889—is no less effortful in expression, but it is better able to make sense of personal struggle within the divine plan. In the same year that he wrote 'What shall I do for the land that bred me', Hopkins contemplated a different path to immortality, this time opened not by sacrifice for one's country, but by Christ himself:

> Enough! the Resurrection,
> A heart's-clarion! Away grief's gasping, | joyless days, dejection.
> Across my foundering deck shone
> A beacon, an eternal beam. | Flesh fade, and mortal trash
> Fáll to the residuary worm; | world's wildfire, leave but ash:
> In a flash, at a trumpet crash,
> I am all at once what Christ is, | since he is what I am, and
> This Jack, joke, poor potsherd, | patch, matchwood, immortal diamond,
> Is immortal diamond.[52]

'That Nature is a Heraclitean Fire' is a highly personal Everyman poem. The 'poor Jackself' of the 'terrible' sonnet 'My own heart let me more have pity on' is now more evidently a Jack of all trades, patching holes, a splinter to light fires with.[53] Saddest here is 'joke', for it has the ring of personal knowledge, given that Hopkins's 'strange innocent seriousness'—as Katherine Tynan once named it—continually left him open to misconception and ridicule (Tynan's report of Hopkins's complaint at his mistreatment by his Dublin students is a hammed-up version of what was a likely sentiment: "'I do not object to their being rude to me personally," he said, "but I do object to their being rude to their professor and a priest'").[54] The lines toil, progressing from 'residuary worm', an unlovely legalism, to the harsh interchange between 'ash', 'flash', and 'crash'. In its pairing with 'diamond', 'I am, and' provides about the most heavy-handed of all Hopkins's rhymes.

Considered as part of a continuous poetic project, as one element in a systematic venture, Hopkins's spiritual vision is here run ragged, the codas to the sonnet providing less a synthesis of thought than a last-ditch rescue from the Heraclitean pyre. Seen more flexibly, it may be that Hopkins's insight is of a different order. The manner of religious apprehension has altered, not simply the contexts for Hopkins's assertion of faith. If 'That Nature is a Heraclitean Fire' lacks the poise of Hopkins's earlier location of divine beauty in the play of natural forms, that is perhaps because Hopkins here does not seek for poise. Difficulty might instead be essential to the poem's truth. For it allows a hard beauty to emerge—the beauty of the 'immortal diamond' unearthed, sourced from obscure depths, a rough jewel obtained from shards of broken pottery and scraps of wood.

NOTES

1. Gerard Manley Hopkins, 'The Leaden and the Golden Echo', in *Gerard Manley Hopkins: The Major Works*, ed. Catherine Phillips (Oxford: Oxford University Press, 2002), 155–6.

2. Hopkins, *The Letters of Gerard Manley Hopkins to Robert Bridges*, ed. Claude Colleer Abbott (London: Oxford University Press, 1955), 162.

3. F. R. Leavis, *The Common Pursuit* (Harmondsworth: Penguin, 1969; 1st pub. 1952), 51–2.

4. Hilary Fraser, *Beauty and Belief: Aesthetics and Religion in Victorian Literature* (Cambridge: Cambridge University Press, 1986), 70.

5. Fraser, *Beauty and Belief*, 104.

6. Hopkins, *The Journals and Papers of Gerard Manley Hopkins*, ed. Humphry House and completed by Graham Storey (London: Oxford University Press, 1959), 196.

7. Hopkins, *Journals and Papers*, 230.

8. Hopkins, 'Pied Beauty', in *Major Works*, 132–3.

9. Marianne Moore, 'Feeling and Precision', *The Sewanee Review*, 52 (1944), 500.

10. John Ruskin, *The Works of John Ruskin*, 39 vols., eds. E. T. Cook and Alexander Wedderburn (London: G. Allen, 1903-12), iii. 294.

11. See among others Gillian Beer, 'Helmholtz, Tyndall, Gerard Manley Hopkins: Leaps of the Prepared Imagination', in *Open Fields: Science in Cultural Encounter* (Oxford: Clarendon Press, 1996), 242–72, and Daniel Brown, *Hopkins' Idealism: Philosophy, Physics, Poetry* (Oxford: Clarendon Press, 1997).

12. Hopkins, 'The Wreck of the Deutschland', in *Major Works*, 110–19.

13. See e.g. Christopher Devlin, S. J., 'Hopkins and Duns Scotus', in Margaret Bottrall, ed., *Gerard Manley Hopkins: Poems: A Casebook* (London: Macmillan, 1975), 113–16, and Thomas Doyle, S.J., '"What I do is me": Scotist Elements in the Poetry of Gerard Manley Hopkins', *Hopkins Quarterly*, 20 (1993), 3–21.

14. Hopkins, *Journals and Papers*, 221.

15. The Stonyhurst copy is now held by Heythrop College Library, London. My thanks to Philip Endean for this information.

16. Hopkins, 'God's Grandeur', in *Major Works*, 128.

17. Hopkins, *Journals and Papers*, 218.

18. Hopkins, *Journals and Papers*, 211. See Dennis Sobolev, 'Inscape Revisited', *English*, 51 (2002), 219–34.

19. Hopkins, *Letters to Bridges*, 66.

20. Terry Eagleton, 'Nature and the Fall in Hopkins: A Reading of "God's Grandeur"', *Essays in Criticism*, 23 (1973), 72.

21. Gerard Manley Hopkins, *The Correspondence of Gerard Manley Hopkins and Richard Watson Dixon*, ed. Claude Colleer Abbott (London: Oxford University Press, 1955), 14.

22. See Michael D. Hurley, 'Darkening the Subject of Hopkins' Prosody', *Victorian Poetry*, 43 (2005), 485–96.

23. Michael D. Hurley, 'What Sprung Rhythm Really Is NOT', *Hopkins Quarterly*, 23 (2006), 89.

24. Hopkins, 'To what serves Mortal Beauty?' in *Major Works*, 167.

25. Hopkins, *Letters to Bridges*, 95.

26. Hopkins, 'The Loss of the Eurydice' in *Major Works*, 135–8; Simon Humphries, 'Hopkins's Silent Men', *ELH*, 77 (2010), 447–76.

27. See Julia F. Saville, *A Queer Chivalry: The Homoerotic Asceticism of Gerard Manley Hopkins* (Charlottesville: University Press of Virginia, 2000). For a contrasting view of the body and touch in Hopkins, see Duc Dau, *Touching God: Hopkins and Love* (London: Anthem, 2012).

28. Josephine Miles, 'The Sweet and Lovely Language', *Kenyon Review*, 6 (1944), 356.

29. *The Ecclesiastical History of the English People*, ed. Judith McClure and Roger Collins (Oxford: Oxford University Press, 1999), 70.

30. Hopkins, *Journals and Papers*, 269.

31. Hopkins, *Journals and Papers*, 289.

32. Hopkins, *Letters to Bridges*, 55.

33. Hopkins, 'Epithalamion', in *Major Works*, 179–80.

34. Hopkins, 'A Vision of the Mermaids' in *Major Works*, 11–15.

35. T.S. Eliot, *After Strange Gods: A Primer of Modern Heresy* (London: Faber and Faber, 1934), 47.

36. W. B. Yeats, *The Oxford Book of Modern Verse, 1892–1935* (Oxford: Clarendon Press, 1936), xxxix.

37. Eliot, *After Strange Gods*, 48.

38. J. Hillis Miller, *The Disappearance of God: Five Nineteenth-Century Writers* (Cambridge, Mass: Harvard University Press, 1963), 285.

39. Hopkins, *Journals and Papers*, 125.

40. e.g. Isobel Armstrong, *Victorian Poetry: Poetry, Poetics and Politics* (London: Routledge, 1996): 'He searches for the least abstract and most physically immediate word so that it becomes solidified into sensuous being, behaving as what it designates' (428).

41. Hopkins, 'Spring and Fall', in *Major Works*, 152.

42. Kingsley Amis, *The Letters of Kingsley Amis*, ed. Zachary Leader (London: HarperCollins, 2000), 232–33.

43. Robert Bridges, 'Editor's Preface to Notes', in *Poems of Gerard Manley Hopkins* (London: Oxford University Press, 1918), 99.

44. Elizabeth Bishop, 'Gerard Manley Hopkins: Notes on Timing in His Poetry' (1934), repr. in *Prose*, ed. Lloyd Schwartz (London: Chatto & Windus, 2011), 474.

45. Hopkins, *Correspondence of Hopkins and Dixon*, 153.

46. Hopkins, 'Tom's Garland', in *Major Works*, 178.

47. John Sutherland, '"Tom's Garland": Hopkins' Political Poem', *Victorian Poetry*, 10 (1972), 113.

48. Hopkins, *Letters to Bridges*, 263.

49. Geoffrey Hill, *The Lords of Limit* (1984), repr. in *Collected Critical Writings*, ed. Kenneth Haynes (Oxford: Oxford University Press, 2008), 102.

50. Hopkins, 'What shall I do for the land that bred me', in *Major Works*, 181–2.

51. Hopkins, 'To seem the stranger' in *Major Works*, 166.

52. Hopkins, 'That Nature is a Heraclitean Fire and of the comfort of the Resurrection', in *Major Works*, 180–1.

53. Hopkins, 'My own heart let me more have pity on', in *Major Works*, 170.

54. Katharine Tynan, *Memories* (London: Eveleigh Nash & Grayson, 1924), 156.

SELECT BIBLIOGRAPHY

Armstrong, Isobel, *Victorian Poetry: Poetry, Poetics, and Politics* (London: Routledge, 1993).

Beer, Gillian, *Open Fields: Science in Cultural Encounter* (Oxford: Clarendon Press, 1996).

Brown, Daniel, *Hopkins' Idealism: Philosophy, Physics, Poetry* (Oxford: Clarendon Press, 1997).

Campbell, Matthew, *Rhythm and Will in Victorian Poetry* (Cambridge: Cambridge University Press, 1999).

Cotter, James Finn, *Inscape: The Christology and Poetry of Gerard Manley Hopkins* (Pittsburgh: University of Pittsburgh Press, 1972).

Endean, Philip, S. J., 'The Spirituality of Gerard Manley Hopkins', *Hopkins Quarterly*, 8 (1981), 107–29.

Fennell, Francis L., ed., *Rereading Hopkins: Selected New Essays* (Victoria: University of Victoria Press, 1996).

Griffiths, Eric, *The Printed Voice of Victorian Poetry* (Oxford: Clarendon Press, 1989).

Groves, Peter, 'Hopkins and Tractarianism', *Victorian Poetry*, 44 (2006), 105–12.

Martin, Robert Bernard, *Gerard Manley Hopkins: A Very Private Life* (London: Harper Collins, 1991).

Milroy, James, *The Language of Gerard Manley Hopkins* (London: André Deutsch, 1977).

Nixon, Jude V., *Gerard Manley Hopkins and His Contemporaries: Liddon, Newman, Darwin, and Pater* (New York: Garland, 1994).

Phillips, Catherine, *Gerard Manley Hopkins and the Victorian Visual World* (Oxford: Oxford University Press, 2007).

Saville, Julia F., *A Queer Chivalry: The Homoerotic Asceticism of Gerard Manley Hopkins* (Charlottesville: University of Virginia Press, 2000).

White, Norman, *Hopkins: A Literary Biography* (Oxford: Clarendon Press, 1992).

CHAPTER 35

MICHAEL FIELD (KATHARINE BRADLEY AND EDITH COOPER): *SIGHT AND SONG* AND SIGNIFICANT FORM

LINDA K. HUGHES

IF more prolific as a playwright, Michael Field is best known today for queering the fin-de-siècle lyric.[1] Not only did aunt and niece Katharine Bradley (1846–1914) and Edith Cooper (1862–1913) consider themselves '*closer married*' than the Brownings, but their successful collaboration on lyrics also decentered expressive models of poetry and the poet, calling into question Wordsworth's characterization of poetry as the 'spontaneous overflow of powerful feelings'.[2] Michael Field's eight volumes of lyrics characteristically gesture toward multiplicities underlying their singular poetic 'voice' in announcing their poems' interdependence with extratextual sources, so that a single volume embraces more than one artistic expression. *Long Ago* (1889) affixes Greek epigraphs from Henry Wharton's 1885 edition of Sappho to each lyric and plays upon Sapphic themes.[3] The poems in *Sight and Song* (1892) are named after old master paintings and identify the artworks' painters and galleries housing them in subtitles. The title of *Underneath the Bough* (1893) comes from *The Rubáiyát of Omar Khayyám*, itself a blend of Edward FitzGerald's translation and poetic invention.

Sight and Song asked readers to immerse themselves in lyric expression yet also to bring knowledge of art galleries or art reproductions to the reading process, as well as art criticism. As Rachel Teukolsky observes, 'The three major artforms of aestheticism...were poetry, painting, and aesthetic criticism.'[4] Central to that criticism, Teukolsky demonstrates, was an unresolved, persistent tension between 'visual formalism' that became dominant in modernist art—an emphasis on perceiving 'shape, color, line, facture [the painter's execution of the work's surface], or composition'—versus subjective response that found a narrative in a painting or created one in responding to it.[5]

Like earlier scholars I investigate Michael Field's represented modes of seeing paintings in *Sight and Song*. But rather than emphasizing their response to visual art in terms of gender and sexuality, or their negotiation of the impasse between art's static spatiality and language's temporality,[6] I place the poems in relation to the pull between visual formalism and subjective responses to art that Teukolsky traces among nineteenth-century and twentieth-century art critics. W. B. Yeats claimed that in *Sight and Song* Michael Field subordinated their lyric gift to 'the studious and interpretive side of the mind', and that they preferred to 'write a guide-book to the picture galleries of Europe'.[7] Michael Field did provide a guide of sorts, but principally to diverse ways of seeing paintings. *Sight and Song* is thus an exemplary fin-de-siècle volume insofar as it looks back to Romantic and Victorian practices yet also anticipates the aesthetic premises and modes of vision of modernism.

Like Teukolsky, Linda Shires has recently examined the close intersection of nineteenth-century literature and visuality and pushed back the date of experimentalism in aesthetic modes of seeing to the early and mid-nineteenth century, emphasizing that "'visual culture is always contested and . . . no one way of seeing is ever wholly accepted in a particular historical moment'".[8] The preface to *Sight and Song* confirms these assertions. The volume's poems, it contends, aim 'to translate into verse what the lines and colours of certain chosen pictures sing in themselves; to express not so much what these pictures are to the poet, but rather what poetry they objectively incarnate', a task for which 'patient, continuous sight' is essential. In keeping with their rejection of 'mere subjective enjoyment', they quote Gustave Flaubert's 'Correspondence': 'Il faut, par un effort d'esprit, se transporter dans les personages et non les attirer à soi' ('One must, through mental effort, be carried inside the characters, not attract them to oneself'). Only they substitute 'paintings' for 'characters' to identify their stance.[9]

Immediately recognizable as an avant-garde statement akin to modernist impersonality,[10] the preface at once invokes and departs from several precursors. The Kantian terms 'objective' and 'subjective' were familiar to readers from S. T. Coleridge's *Biographia Literaria* (1817) or Robert Browning's 'Essay on Shelley' (1852). Julia Saville traces Michael Field's citation of Flaubert to their attendance at Walter Pater's 1890 lecture on Prosper Mérimée, but Pater had refused the term 'translation' in his 1878 essay 'The School of Giorgione': 'the sensuous material of each art brings with it a special phase or quality of beauty, untranslateable into the forms of any other'.[11] Nonetheless, they follow Pater's turn towards visual formalism, his distancing of visual art from narrative content, and insistence that art is 'always striving to be independent of the mere intelligence, to become a matter of pure perception'.[12] Both Pater's tenets were to become axiomatic to Bernard Berenson, with whom Bradley and Cooper discussed paintings while writing *Sight and Song*, and modernist theorist Clive Bell.[13] Berenson and Bell alike repudiate art as 'illustration', and Bell insists instead on art's 'significant form' rendered through line and the relations among lines, planes, and (so long as it functions as form rather than decoration) colour.[14] This visual focus was essential in creating a responsive twentieth-century audience for 'primitive' and abstract art, and promoted viewers' ability to see paintings' surfaces simultaneously with their representations of three-dimensionality.[15]

For all its bold movement toward visual formalism, the preface nonetheless turns back toward subjectivity in closing, as Ana Vadillo and others have noted: 'When such [impersonal] effort has been made, honestly and with persistence, even then the inevitable force of individuality must still have play and a temperament mould the purified impression' (vi). Not surprisingly, given such unsteady allegiance to visual formalism, the lyrics of *Sight and Song* range eclectically in their modes of seeing, from conventional Victorian attempts to find a story in a painting or even journalistic description of paintings' contents to fin-de-siècle subjective impressions.[16] Key poems, however, achieve the avant-garde aim of the preface and, moreover, represent the act of seeing 'significant form' in paintings even while calling attention to verbal art's distinctive qualities. In its theoretical underpinnings, modes of vision, imaginings of ekphrasis—a 'verbal representation of visual representation'[17]—and poetic forms and themes, *Sight and Song* thus encompasses early and late nineteenth-century and proto-modernist practices, sometimes within a single poem.

The volume is most overtly aligned with aestheticism, not least in making art its subject and inspiration. Nicholas Frankel also points out the volume's aesthetic materialization as a visual object in its title page and layout.[18] Michael Field's concern to fashion an objet d'art from poetic texts is also clear from the deliberate placement of poems to create rhythms, echoes, contrasts, and shapes. The volume begins and ends, for example, with lyrics inspired by two Antoine Watteau paintings found in the Louvre, 'L'Indifférent' and 'L'Embarquement Pour Cythère'; the last even echoes the opening lines of the first—'He dances on a toe / As light as Mercury's'[19]—in noting how one lover is 'raised on tip-toe' to address 'his lofty dame'.[20] Several juxtaposed lyrics also call attention to the shaping poet behind formal groupings, as when 'The Rescue', inspired by Tintoretto's painting in which a warmly responsive nude woman lowers herself into the arms of a virile rescuer clad in dark armour, is countered by the succeeding 'Venus and Mars', a response to the Botticelli painting in which the gazing female figure is fully clothed while naked Mars, stripped of his armour, lies deep in vacuous post-coital sleep.

If Michael Field's aestheticism is most conspicuous in *Sight and Song*, the much-discussed poem entitled 'A Portrait' demonstrates their aesthetic eclecticism. Based on Bartolommeo Veneto's painting housed in the Städelsche Institut, Frankfurt, which depicts a woman with bared left breast wearing a headdress wreathed in box-tree leaves, the painting is sometimes identified as *Flora* or *Portrait of a Young Lady* but is listed as *Portrait of a Courtesan* in Berenson's book on Venetian art.[21] Michael Field occludes Berenson's full title but not his typecasting. Their treatment is resolutely Victorian insofar as they imagine a story behind the painting, which then becomes an illustration of a courtesan's determined will to preserve her beauty: 'She will be painted, she who is so strong / In loveliness, so fugitive in years'.[22] One of the volume's epigraphs comes from John Keats's 'Ode to Psyche', 'I see and sing, by my own eyes inspired', and 'Portrait' itself alludes to 'Ode on a Grecian Urn', Keats's famous meditation on visual art's capture of fleeting beauty and time. If Keats's urn is a 'Cold Pastoral' or 'foster-child of silence and slow time' that depicts a maiden who 'cannot fade',[23] the courtesan possesses 'cold' beauty and 'slow-fostered graces', and her painted box-tree wreath 'with the year's waste will not fade'. Closely identifying the courtesan with the urn, Michael Field simultaneously pays tribute to a Romantic forebear and underscores the woman's already-accomplished transformation into art. The poem also adopts mid-Victorian flower language and the iconography of the fallen woman in comparing the courtesan's 'crinkled locks' to the 'yellow snakes' of a Medusa and having her select 'violet larkspur' (associated with haughtiness) and the 'columbine' (indicative of folly) for her portrait.[24] Yet 'Portrait' is also a Swinburnean and decadent poem insofar as its courtesan is a phallic, perverse woman[25] who follows her 'strange, emphatic insight true' in deciding to bare her breast, and relies not on passion but on reason to achieve her will: '[she] planned / To give her fragile shapeliness to art, whose reason spanned / Her doom, who bade her beauty in its cold / And vacant eminence persist for all men to behold!' She thus 'conquer[s] death' not through faith or memory but art.

The poem's narrative impetus, however, is called into question by a counter tendency to represent the painting as an image without meaning or message, as in the opening lines:

> A crystal, flawless beauty on the brows
> Where neither love nor time has conquered space
> On which to live; her leftward smile endows
> The gazer with no tidings from the face . . .

Insofar as the poem at once implies a narrative behind a painting and sees the image as 'a fair, blank form, unverified by life', the poem puts Victorian realism and decadent artifice in play and destabilizes both. Given its scant attention to visual formalism, however, 'A Portrait' remains emphatically fin-de-siècle, looking back to Romantic and Victorian modes, participating in aestheticism and decadence, yet going no further.

Two other poems adopt mid-Victorian techniques while paying homage to Michael Field's former mentor, Robert Browning, and registering the feminist art criticism of Anna Jameson. The grotesque, as Isobel Armstrong notes, was associated with struggle, distortion, abnormality, and above all with the poetry of Robert Browning after Walter Bagehot's 1864 essay on 'Wordsworth, Tennyson, and Browning; or, Pure, Ornate, and Grotesque Art in English Poetry'.[26] Relative to conventional representations of the Madonna and Victorian motherhood, the opening stanza of 'A Pietà', inspired by the Carlo Crivelli painting of Mary, John, and Mary Magdalen with the dead Christ (formerly in the Dudley Gallery, now in the Metropolitan Museum of Art), is strikingly grotesque:

> A mother bent on the body of her Son,
> > Fierce tears and wrinkles around her eyes,—
> > > She has open, stiffened lips
> > > And an almost lolling tongue,
> > > > But her face is full of cries:
> > Almost it seems that the dead has done her wrong,
> > > Almost it seems in her strife
> > > Of passion she would shake the dead to life.[27]

Stanzas 2, 3, and 5 likewise detail grotesque elements derived from close observation of Crivelli's painting: the 'fine tips' of the 'thorns on his brow' that 'Through the forehead [are] forcing room'; the dead Christ's 'hirsute nipple' beneath which flesh 'flaccid and dragged from the strain / Of the cross' is visible; the disciple 'John's wailing face' and the Magdalen's 'Wonder' at 'the hole' in Christ's hand 'Scooped by the large, round nail'. Possibly the poem's unusual thirteen-line stanzas in which some lines find no answering rhyme are a formal poetic response to grotesque painterly details, since the stanzas distort by foreshortening sonnet length and the sonnet's harmonies of rhyme. The poem slides from the grotesque to the exhilaration of beauty, however; for as in 'A Portrait', the body's degradation is offset by redemption through art: 'Yet there is such subtle intercourse between / the hues'; 'how [Mary's] sleeve of peach/That crosses the corpse's grimy gold/Gives it luster!' Diverting the gaze from religious iconography to a pictorial colour scheme and its effects, and from narrative to form, the poem seizes upon the defining line that shapes the Magdalen's head ('O glorious spring of the brow, simple arch / Of the head') to celebrate, not the woman herself, but her painterly, formal representation:

> O solemn, dun-crimson mass
> Of hair, on the indigo
> Of the bodice that in curling wave doth pass!
> How exquisite, set between
> This blue and a vest of translucent green,
> The glimpse of scarlet belt;
> Or the glow, the almost emerald line,
> Round the neck where the hood bends over
> Such faint reds of the mantle . . .

After reporting this experience of seeing form in the painting's surface, the poem nonetheless reverts to narrative (even a message), when it concludes by recalling that the Magdalen rather than the Virgin Mary first sees 'Christ new-born from the tomb'. Michael Field's pietà is less about maternal grief than the superior love, 'reticence', and 'hard patience' of an aesthetically redeemed, formally enhanced Magdalen.

This treatment of the Magdalen is indebted to Anna Jameson's *Sacred and Legendary Art* (1845–1864), which Katharine Bradley had read.[28] As Judith Johnston remarks, 'For Jameson, the image of the Magdalen is the site on which she most forcibly contests [the binary of whore and Madonna], locating not the aggressive carnal prostitute, but rather an already redeemed woman, chosen as the first penitent, chosen as the first to recognise the risen Christ', who has agency outside the home and thus effectively contrasts 'the passive domesticated image of the Madonna'.[29] *Sight and Song*, like Jameson's art commentaries, adopts ekphrasis to represent female power, though Michael Field tends to favour pagan rather than Christian subjects for this purpose. 'Marriage of Bacchus and Ariadne', a response to Tintoretto's painting in the Ducal Palace at Venice, is a particularly clear instance, since it intervenes in the reception of a painting of immense prestige among Victorian and late-Victorian connoisseurs. Ruskin pronounced it one of the 'noblest pictures in the world', Pater a depiction of 'glorious bodily presences', John

Addington Symonds 'if not the greatest, at any rate the most beautiful, oil picture in existence', a 'most perfect lyric of the sensuous fancy from which sensuality is absent'.[30]

Michael Field resituates the painting by turning it into an image of female agency and a male deity's submission to the human condition. In an early draft in Cooper's hand, lines describe Theseus' desertion of Ariadne and her sudden volte face from Theseus to Bacchus:

> Ariadne had been left
> Voiceless, of her prince bereft, . . .
>
> Theseus went: now some one came
> From the waste & bowed like flame
> Toward herself in his desire;
> Life was in her blood like fire.[31]

Here she is both powerless and fickle. The final version deletes the passage and renders Ariadne as 'Queenly' rather than 'Voiceless' as she 'on the samphire rock / . . . sits'.[32] Moreover, she submits less to Bacchus than to Love: 'Love entreats the hand to wed, / Gently loosening out the cold / Fingers toward that hoop of gold'. Above all, Michael Field imparts agency to Ariadne by rendering Bacchus as her 'patient' supplicant: 'In his eyes there is the pain / Shy, dumb passions can attain / In the valley'. Indeed, he is more vulnerable than Ariadne:

> Is he not a mendicant
> Who has almost died of want?
> Through far countries he has roved,
> Blessing, blessing, unbeloved;
> Therefore is he come in weed
> Of a mortal bowed by need,
> With the bunches of the grape
> As sole glory round his shape:
> For there is no god that can
> Taste of pleasure save as man.

In stressing the suffering of Bacchus and thus his potential parallels with Christ ('blessing, blessing, unbeloved'), Michael Field most likely glances toward the figure of Dionysius Zagreus, the hunter exiled from Olympus and torn apart by humans who do not recognize his divinity, described by Pater in two 1876 essays and 'Denys L'Auxerrois'.[33] Altogether, Bacchus's pain, pleading, and submission to human form diminish his masculine, divine power (especially relative to late-Victorian commentaries on the painting) in favour of the 'Queenly' Ariadne, who draws him to her. The effect is intensified by another of the volume's textual juxtapositions, since this lyric immediately follows 'A Pen-Drawing of Leda', in which Leda is not a passive victim of rape but a woman who controls a god: 'Although his hectoring bill / Gapes toward her tresses, / She draws the fondled creature to her will'.[34] In its focus on subject matter rather than form, the poem is nonetheless as mid-Victorian in its mode of vision as in its feminism.

The sequential representation of deities begun in 'A Pen-Drawing of Leda' contin-ues with 'Figure of Venus in "Spring"', two poems in conversation with late-Victorian discourses, and a third that anticipates modernist formalism. 'Apollo and Marsyas', a response to Perugino's painting in the Louvre, confronts readers with a shocking turn into racialized discourse and elitism. The satyr Marsyas, who challenged Apollo, god of music and poetry, to a musical contest and was afterward skinned alive by Apollo, is a familiar subject in Renaissance art and Victorian mythography. In *Queen of the Air* (1869) Ruskin identifies Apollo with 'intellectual', Marsyas with 'brutal, or meaning-less music'.[35] Michael Field incorporates Ruskin's judgement and additional elements of Victorian anthropology into 'Apollo and Marsyas'. The poem's aesthetics seem as con-servative as its content; like much journalism devoted to gallery shows, the poem's ekph-rasis rarely goes beyond narrating a depicted situation, pointing out principal visual details, and elaborating upon the implied message or meaning of the image.

Apollo, supremely beautiful and confident, stands 'Magnanimous' in a pastoral land-scape, as Marsyas, playing his 'brutish notes',[36] emerges as a racial inferior:

> Unapprehending,
> Absorbed, the brown, inferior man,
>   On his tune spending
> All honest power, believes he can
> Put the young shepherd-god to shame.
>   Scrutinise and hate
> His spiritless brows, the red down on his pate,
>   The diligent eyes that scan
>   His fingers as they grate!

Marsyas, whom readers are invited to despise, is a primitive so low on the evolutionary scale that he has residual fur on his 'pate', in contrast to the idealized figure of Apollo with his 'Breeze-haunted tresses'. Pointing out the 'uncouth limbs' and 'abhorred / Strains' of the 'Painstaking herdsman at his task', Michael Field adjudges Marsyas a poetic plodder and seems to endorse his impending torture as a means of protecting the charmed circle of inspired poets:

> Shame and displeasure—
> The god of inspiration set
>   To hear a measure
> Of halting pace! But he will whet
> A knife and without comment flay
>   The immodest faun,
> Fearing poets should, indifferent through scorn,
>   License all that hinds beget
>   Or zealots feeble-born.

Such calm acceptance of torture to preserve aesthetic privilege is deeply disturbing. But the racist elitism of 'Apollo and Marsyas' acquires a new significance in relation to the succeeding lyric. 'The Blood of the Redeemer', based on Giovanni Bellini's painting in the National Gallery, offers a Swinburnean critique of Christians who, to save them-selves (rather than poetry, as with Apollo) emerge as more cruel and barbaric than the pagan god. Michael Field's point of departure for 'Redeemer' is a perception of the painting's formal disjunction between the wan, crucified Christ who dominates the foreground and the exuberant decorative art and dawn sky behind. The visual incongru-ity is paralleled by the lyric's language allocated to Christ versus insatiable Christians.

Of the pallid Christ's stigmata and Cross Michael Field asserts, 'Those transverse beams / Of yon high cross' that Christ balances in the crook of his arm 'confine Him not; it seems / Simply a token'.[37] Their Christ 'has paced onward and holds forth / Indifferent His pierced palm'. The lyric then abruptly shifts from third to second-person to ventrilo-quize and critique Christian insistence on Christ's suffering:

> O Life, O Clay,
> Our fears allay!
>
> But to the people wert Thou crucified;
> To eyes that see, behold, Thou dost abide
> Dying for ever. Thus Thine Eastertide
>   Breaks over Thee,—the crown of thorn
> Laid by, but the whole breaking heart in quick
>   Sorrow and sick.

To underscore Christians' insatiable demands that Christ keep dying, the point is repeated in the tenth stanza:

> Once crucified and once given to the crowd,
> But to Thy Church for aye a Victim vowed,
> Thou dost not die, Thy head is never bowed
>   In death: we must be born again;
> Thus dying by our side from day to day
>   Thou art the Way.

Hostility is here directed to the Church, not to Christ, who stands apart from this use of his story as he stands aloof from his setting in the painting. While the closing stanza may seem pious, its irony would have been clear to readers accustomed to A. C. Swinburne's critique of Christians' celebration of death rather than sensuous life in 'Hymn to Proserpine':

> There is no light athwart these eastern skies
> For us, no joy it is that Thou dost rise—
> Our hope, our strength is in Thy sacrifice:
>   To-day, to-morrow must Thou die,
> For ever drawing all men to Thy feet,
>   O Love most sweet!

To contest selfish preoccupation with Christ's sacrifice, the lyric dwells upon the paint-ing's low wall incised with classical figures. Possibly inspired by Keats's 'Ode on a Grecian

Urn' ('Who are these coming to the sacrifice?'), Michael Field contrasts pagans who joy-
ously oversee sacrifices with Christians who delegate sacrifice to their God:

> Blithe Pagan youths sculptured behind Thee go
> Processional to sacrifice; some blow
> A horn, some feed the censer, none can know
> What he should do; but Thou dost give
> Thyself and consecrate their rites, how vain,
> O Lamb fresh slain!

The artfully ambiguous 'how vain' may characterize pagan rites or Christ's ever-renewed
sacrifice. The visual delight of the painting's dandiacal angel garbed in 'yellow sleeves /
And robe of lovely, limpid blue' or 'bright, scarlet shoes, / Plumes lit by the jay's piercing
blue', likewise contrasts the suffering Christ drained of life. 'Apollo and Marsyas' and
'The Blood of the Redeemer' thus both treat the theme of cruelty and divinity; but while
the disjunctions in 'Redeemer' are propelled by formal visual analysis, ekphrasis here
goes no further than invoking beautiful colours, shapes, and light.

'The Sleeping Venus', which succeeds them, offers a powerful alternative: a
self-pleasuring deity who is neither cruel nor elicits cruelty, who is intimately
connected to the earth on which she lies rather than alienated from it, and who
assumes beauteous female rather than male form. Inspired by Giorgione's painting in the Dresden Gallery, this lyric devoted to the goddess of love is a sequence of
sonnet-length stanzas that play upon Shakespearean sonnet rhyme but forego iambic
pentameter in favour of a more fluid, variant pulse.[38] Read in terms of shifting aesthetic theory and modes of vision, the poem is most important for its attention to
significant form and innovative poetic techniques that convey both visual form and
the act of seeing it.

To be sure, the lyric reports with fair accuracy the landscape details in Giorgione, just
as Michael Field had included conventional ekphrasis in 'Apollo and Marsyas':

> Wolds, that half-withered by the heat o'erhead,
> Press up to a little town
> Of castle, archway, roof and shed,
> Then slope in grave continuance down:
>> On their border, in a group,
>> Trees of brooding foliage droop
>> Sidelong; and a single tree
>> Springs with bright simplicity,
>> Central from the sunlit plain.[39]

Most scholars find Michael Field's ekphrastic rendering of transgressive sexuality and
gender especially notable. The poem asserts that Venus is 'Pure as are the things that
man / Needs for life and using can / Never violate nor spot', yet it also celebrates Venus's
self-pleasuring with the hand that falls quite literally upon her mons veneris in the
painting:

> Her hand the thigh's tense surface leaves,
> Falling inward. Not even sleep
> Dare invalidate the deep,
> Universal pleasure sex
> Must unto itself annex—
> Even the stillest sleep; at peace,
> More profound with rest's increase,
> She enjoys the good
> Of delicious womanhood.

Vadillo and Ehnenn also note that despite Michael Field's avowed aim to produce poetry that paintings 'objectively incarnate', 'The Sleeping Venus' explicitly represents gendered spectators who look at the painting in the following lines: 'while we gaze it seems as though / She had lain thus the solemn glebes among / In the ages far ago'.[40]

But 'The Sleeping Venus' is also propelled by Giorgione's interplay of line, colour, and mass that interconnects the slopes and mounds of the luminous Venus to those of the darker landscape surrounding her. Thus the poem opens, 'Here is Venus by our homes / And resting on the verdant swell / Of a soft country flanked with mountain domes'. As I remark elsewhere, 'Flanks and domes are of course precisely what we gaze upon in Giorgione's Venus'.[41] If the 'sympathy between / Her and Earth' becomes one of the lyric's principal themes, the poem more strikingly represents both what the perceiving poet sees *in* the painting through perspective's illusion of three-dimensionality[42] and *at* the painting's two-dimensional surface. The former is ekphrastically rendered by foreground and background detail amidst commentary on Venus as divinity and sexed woman. But Venus is also a two-dimensional visual shape fashioned from distinctive lines and curves:

> And her body has the curves,
> The same extensive smoothness seen
> In yonder breadths of pasture, in the swerves
> Of the grassy mountain-green
> That for her propping pillow serves:
> …
> And from the elbow raised aloft
> Down to the crossing knees a line descends
> Unimpeachable and soft
> As the adjacent slope that ends
> In chequered plain of hedge and croft.

As stanza three continues, Venus's breasts are simultaneously eroticized sites of physicality and geometric shapes that echo the shape of hills in the background, a representation that likewise synthesizes three- and two-dimensional acts of seeing:

> Circular as lovely knolls,
> Up to which a landscape rolls
> With desirous sway, each breast
> Rises from the level chest,

> One in contour, one in round—
> Either exquisite, low mound
> Firm in shape and given
> To the August warmth of heaven.

'The Sleeping Venus' is thus a record of seeing as much as a description of a pictorial scene, and lyric devices extend the attention to form. Michael Field 'translates' the painting's mirrored forms in figure and landscape into metrical terms, for example, by crafting numerous paired lines in which the same number of feet are given first in a trochaic, then an iambic pattern. This reversed (hence mirroring) sonic pattern can be seen in lines 1–2 and 4–8 of the opening stanza, though it recurs throughout:

> Hére is Vénus bý our hómes
> And résting ón the vérdant swéll
> Of a soft country flanked with mountain domes:
> Shé has léft her árchèd shéll,
> Has léft the bárren wáve that fóams,
> Amíd earth's frúitful tílths to dwéll.
> Nóbly líghted whíle she sléeps
> As swárd-lands ór the córn-field swéeps.

Michael Field also 'translates' the act of seeing into poetry by creating metaphors of visual elements, as in the passage rendering the interplay of line and shadow in Venus's ankle, knee, and lined eyelids:

> the line
> Of her left leg stretching shows
> Against the turf direct and fine,
> Dissimilar in grace to those
> Little bays that in and out
> By the ankle wind about;
> Or that shallow bend, the right
> Curled-up knee has brought to sight
> Underneath its bossy rise,
> Where the loveliest shadow lies!
>
> ...
>
> Eyelids underneath the day
> Wrinkle as full buds that stay,
> Through the tranquil, summer hours,
> Closed although they might be flowers.

Lines are lines in the painting; in the poem they become bays, a bend, and wrinkled surfaces that recall flowers. By such means, Michael Field resolutely insists on techniques specific to poetry—metrics, sonic effects, metaphor—in the act of verbally representing both the painting's formal features and subject matter. The dynamic oscillation between looking into and at Giorgione's canvas not only plays out uneven allegiances in fin-de-siècle aesthetic theory and poetry but also dramatizes a mode of vision.

Nor is 'The Sleeping Venus' the sole lyric in which Michael Field invents new ekphrastic technique to represent visual form. 'Saint Sebastian', inspired by Antonello da Messina's painting in an adjacent hall in Dresden, appears earlier in *Sight and Sound* and, like 'The Sleeping Venus', is often read in terms of same-sex desire.[43] But the lyric also registers the poet's apprehension of significant vertical forms that shape and unify the painting, not only the upright saint bound to a soaring tree but also the echoing 'Arch and chimney' that 'rise aloft into the air' and 'shafts of sandy-coloured tone' in the background.[44] Their proliferation of terms ('trunk', 'shaft', 'column', 'pillar') for verticality form a counterpart to the painting's visual verticals. Their handling of verticals also renders the lyric startlingly proto-Freudian. For in linking verticality to rigidity and rising motion, they also imply phallic tumescence, as in the opening lines:

> Young Sebastian stands beside a lofty tree,
> Rigid by the rigid trunk that branchlessly
>   Lifts its column on the blue
>   Of a heaven that takes
>   Hyacinthine hue
>   From a storm that wellnigh breaks.

The troping of body as rising, rigid tree is enforced by 'trunk', which names a corporeal as well as arboreal form. A subsequent simile comparing Sebastian's body to sculpture, 'Naked, almost firm as sculpture, is his form', likewise underscores rigidity, even as his face shining 'as olive marble that reflects the mere / Radiance it receives upon a surface clear' echoes the 'marble of the courtyard' noted earlier.[45]

The significance of these phallic forms becomes overt in the lyric's eleventh and thirteenth sestets, which contend that Sebastian's martyrdom consists not in sacrificing his life for God but in sacrificing the pleasure of sex, as indicated by the 'shattered' pillar—another vertical—at his feet:

> Captive, stricken through by darts, yet armed with power
> That resents the coming on of its last hour,
>   Sound in muscle is the boy,
>   Whom his manhood fills
>   With an acrid joy,
>   Whom its violent pressure thrills.
> . . .
> At his feet a mighty pillar lies reversed;
> So the virtue of his sex is shattered, cursed:
>   Here is martyrdom and not
>   In the arrows' sting;
>   This is the bitter lot
>   His soul is questioning.

Daringly direct in its phallic imagery and action, the poem is also transgressive against Christianity in its representation of a saint who resents his God, as indicated by lips set 'In a pained, protesting curve' and eyes that 'have met / God within the darkening sky / And dispute His will'. Like 'The Sleeping Venus', 'Saint Sebastian' also synthesizes a record of simultaneously viewing both three- and two-dimensionality in painting; in addition to the painting's verticals, for example, the lyric points out with exactness an elliptical line on Sebastian's face created by shadow: 'Shadow, circling chin and cheek, / Their ellipse defines'.

Sight and Song is certainly one of Michael Field's most intriguing volumes in relation to gender, sexuality, aestheticism, and the interchange between Bradley and Cooper's poetry and life-writing in their journal (in which they took notes on paintings and penned initial drafts). But the volume acquires greater significance when placed amidst shifting aesthetic theories and modes of vision that looked back to narrative approaches to visual art even while apprehending an emergent visual formalism. In responding poetically not just to old master paintings but also to competing aesthetic theories, Michael Field produced a volume important to Victorian poetry itself, serving variously as an echo chamber and fore-glimpse of Romantic and Victorian precursors or modernist poets, and demonstrating through inventive stanzaic forms and lyric versatility why Michael Field has emerged from obscurity and invites ongoing scholarly attention.

Notes

1. Jill Ehnenn, *Women's Literary Collaboration, Queerness, and Late-Victorian Culture* (Aldershot: Ashgate, 2008), 14–17, 25–57. Like Marion Thain, I use 'Michael Field' to designate the joint poetic persona of Bradley and Cooper (albeit a plural pronoun to refer back to them); see Thain, *'Michael Field': Poetry, Aestheticism and the Fin de Siècle* (Cambridge: Cambridge University Press, 2007), 4–5.

2. Michael Field, *Works and Days. From the Journal of Michael Field*, ed. T. and D. C. Sturge Moore (London: John Murray,1933), 16; William Wordsworth, 'Preface' to *Lyrical Ballads* in *Wordsworth: Poetical Works*, ed. Thomas Hutchinson and Ernest de Selincourt (Oxford: Oxford University Press, 1936), 735.

3. Yopie Prins, *Victorian Sappho* (Princeton: Princeton University Press, 1999), 74.

4. Rachel Teukolsky, *The Literate Eye: Victorian Art Writing and Modernist Aesthetics* (Oxford: Oxford University Press, 2009), 108.

5. Teukolsky, *The Literate Eye*, 8.

6. For discussion of the gendered gaze, sexuality, and erotic agency, see Ana I. Parejo Vadillo, '*Sight and Song*: Transparent Translations and a Manifesto for the Observer', *Victorian Poetry*, 38 (2000), 15–34; Julia F. Saville, 'The Poetic Imaging of Michael Field', in Joseph Bristow, ed., *The Fin-de-Siècle Poem: English Literary Culture and the 1890s* (Athens: Ohio University Press, 2005), 178–206; Hilary Fraser, 'A Visual Field: Michael Field and the Gaze', *Victorian Literature and Culture*, 34 (2006), 553–71; and Ehnenn, *Women's Literary Collaboration*, 25–57. Vadillo, Saville, and Thain (*'Michael Field'* 4, 16, 67) all note the importance of Pater and Bernard Berenson to the volume. Vadillo's essay explores its 'translation' of paintings as a two-step process that begins in formal perception and culminates in personal response. Thain focuses on Michael Field's 'ekphrastic agency' in

negotiating spatiality and temporality and sees each poem enacting the desires of ekphrasis to merge painting and poetry; the project's inherent contradictions, she contends, are most productively mediated through synaesthesia (66–71).

7. W. B. Yeats, review of *Sight and Song*, *The Bookman* 2 (July 1892), 116.

8. Linda M. Shires, *Perspectives: Modes of Viewing and Knowing in Nineteenth-Century England* (Columbus: Ohio State University Press, 2009), 2–5, 10. Shires specifically investigates 'experimentation with classical linear perspective and realist point of view' (3). Her quotation about contested visual culture comes from Nicholas Mirzoeff, *An Introduction to Visual Culture* (New York: Routledge, 1999), 44.

9. Michael Field, *Sight and Song* (London: Elkin Mathews and John Lane, 1892), v. The literal translation of Flaubert is provided by Sharon Fairchild.

10. Nicholas Frankel, *Masking the Text: Essays on Literature & Mediation in the 1890s* (High Wycombe, The Rivendale Press, 2009), 64, 71.

11. Saville, 'The Poetic Imaging of Michael Field', 180; Walter Pater, 'The School of Giorgione', *Fortnightly Review*, 22 (October 1877), 526–27.

12. Pater, 'The School of Giorgione', 530. As Teukolsky observes (*The Literate Eye*, 123), Pater himself nonetheless reverted to paintings' 'subject matter', hence narrative context, in discussing actual paintings in the essay.

13. Saville, 'The Poetic Imaging of Michael Field', 182–83; see also Marion Thain and Ana Parejo Vadillo, eds., *Michael Field, The Poet: Published and Manuscript Materials* (Peterborough, Canada: Broadview Press, 2009), 29, 315–16. I rely more on Clive Bell's formalist theory, spelled out in detail in 1914, than Teukolsky, who focuses on Roger Fry's essays in *Vision and Design* (1924).

14. Bernard Berenson, *The Florentine Painters of the Renaissance* (1896; 3rd edn.: Boston, 1909), 8–9; Clive Bell, *Art* (London: Chatto & Windus, 1949; 1st pub. 1914), 8, 17, 236.

15. Teukolsky notes that twentieth-century art critic Clement Greenberg, the 'most influential art writer promoting abstract impressionism' who praises 'abstract painting for its emphasis on the flatness of the canvas', cited Pater's 1878 essay in his 1940 article, 'Toward a New Laocoön' (Teukolsky, *The Literate Eye*, 242n.6, 102). For more on 'primitive art' and visual modernism, see Bell, *Art*, 22–25, 122–23, and Teukolsky, 192–233.

16. As Pater famously asked in the preface to *Studies in the History of the Renaissance* (London: Macmillan and Co., 1873), 'What is this song or picture . . . to *me*?' (viii).

17. W. J. T. Mitchell, *Picture Theory* (Chicago: University of Chicago Press, 1994), 152.

18. Frankel, *Masking the Text*, 65–71.

19. Field, 'L'Indifférent', in *Sight and Song* (London: Elkin Mathews and John Lane, 1892), 1.

20. Field, 'L'Embarquement Pour Cythère', in *Sight and Song*, 121.

21. Berenson, *The Venetian Painters of the Renaissance*, 3rd ed. (London: G. P. Putnam's Sons, 1894), 81. The German title for the painting is *Weibliches Idealbildnis*, indicating an idealized or imaginary portrait of a woman.

22. Field, 'A Portrait' in *Sight and Song*, 28.

23. John Keats, 'Ode on a Grecian Urn' in *John Keats*, ed. Elizabeth Cook (Oxford: Oxford University Press, 1990), 288–89.

24. Margaret Pickston, *The Language of Flowers* (London: Michael Joseph Ltd., 1968), n.p.

25. For discussion of the phallic woman, who appropriates masculine power or induces male anxiety that she may possess a phallus, see Glen O. Gabbard and Kim Gabbard, 'The Phallic Woman in Contemporary Cinema', *American Imago*, 50 (1993), 421–39. Cf. Saville, 'The Poetic Imaging of Michael Field', 195, and Fraser, 'A Visual Field', 568.

26. Isobel Armstrong, *Victorian Poetry: Poetry, Poetics and Politics* (London: Routledge, 1993), 285–86. Bagehot's article appeared in *National Review* 1 (November 1864), 27–67.

27. Field, 'A Pietà' in *Sight and Song*, 106.

28. Bradley mentions Jameson's expertise on sacred art in a letter of 9 September 1880 to Cooper; see *The Fowl and the Pussycat: Love Letters of Michael Field, 1876–1909*, ed. Sharon Bickle (Charlottesville: University of Virginia Press, 2008), 28, 30n.5.

29. Judith Johnston, *Anna Jameson: Victorian, Feminist, Woman of Letters* (Aldershot: Scolar Press, 1997), 184.

30. John Ruskin, Venetian Index in *The Stones of Venice*, *The Works of John Ruskin*, 39 vols., ed. E. T. Cook and Alexander Wedderburn (London: George Allen, 1903–12), xi. 375; Pater, 'A Study of Dionysius', *Fortnightly Review*, 19 (December 1876), 758; John Addington Symonds, *Renaissance in Italy: The Fine Arts* (London: Smith, Elder, & Co., 1898), 276, 276n.3. Bradley was at one time a disciple of Ruskin and joined the Guild of St. George (see, e.g. Bickle, *The Fowl and the Pussycat*, xviii–xix).

31. BL Additional MS 46778, f. 55v, 56r. Quoted by permission of Charmian O'Neil and Leonie Sturge-Moore.

32. Field, 'Marriage of Bacchus and Ariadne', in *Sight and Song*, 83.

33. Pater, 'The Myth of Demeter and Persephone', *Fortnightly Review*, 19 (February 1876), 265; 'A Study of Dionysius', 768, 770–71; and 'Denys l'Auxerrois', *Macmillan's Magazine* 54 (October 1886), 413–23. See Stefano Evangelista, '"A Revolting Mistake": Walter Pater's Iconography of Dionysus', *Victorian Review*, 34 (2008), 210–13.

34. Field, 'A Pen-Drawing of Leda', in *Sight and Song*, 81.

35. Ruskin, *The Works of John Ruskin*, xix. 342–43.

36. Field, 'Apollo and Marsyas', in *Sight and Song*, 87–88.

37. Field, 'The Blood of the Redeemer', in *Sight and Song*, 94.

38. Erik Gray terms each stanza an 'inverted and attenuated sonnet' and notes the formal play upon Venus's autoeroticism in the fifth stanza's enjambment between sestet and octave, 'hand and thigh crossing from one half of the stanza to the other', in 'A Bounded Field: Situating Victorian Poetry in the Literary Landscape', *Victorian Poetry* 41 (2003), 467.

39. Field, 'The Sleeping Venus', in *Sight and Song*, 104.

40. Vadillo, '*Sight and Song*', 24–25; Ehnenn, *Women's Literary Collaboration*, 86–88. Michael Field was not the first to assert the purity of Giorgione's Venus. As Julia M. Ady remarked in 1889, 'By the side of this sleeping form in her exquisite purity and refinement, all other nude goddesses pale'; see 'The Art of Giorgione. II.', *Portfolio*, 20 (January, 1889), 212.

41. Linda K. Hughes, 'Reluctant Lions: Michael Field and the Transatlantic Literary Salon of Louise Chandler Moulton', in Margaret D. Stetz and Cheryl A. Wilson, eds., *Michael Field and Their World* (High Wycombe: Rivendale Press, 2007), 121.

42. Fraser terms this 'binocular three-dimensionality' since two women gaze ('A Visual Field', 554).

43. See, e.g. Vadillo, '*Sight and Song*', 30; Saville, 'The Poetic Imaging of Michael Field', 192–93; Ehnenn, *Women's Literary Collaboration*, 92–93.

44. Field, 'Saint Sebastian', in *Sight and Song*, 70–71.

45. Significantly, according to Teukolsky, Pater himself turned to classical statuary rather than music in the essay 'Winckelmann' (1867) to identify 'pure form' (Teukolsky, *The Literate Eye*, 108).

SELECT BIBLIOGRAPHY

Bell, Clive, *Art* (London: Chatto & Windus, 1949; 1st pub. 1914).

Bickle, Sharon, ed. *The Fowl and the Pussycat: Love Letters of Michael Field, 1876–1909* (Charlottesville: University of Virginia Press, 2008).

Ehnenn, Jill, *Women's Literary Collaboration, Queerness, and Late-Victorian Culture* (Aldershot: Ashgate, 2008).

Field, Michael, *Works and Days. From the Journal of Michael Field*, ed. T. and D. C. Sturge Moore (London: John Murray,1933).

Frankel, Nicholas, *Masking the Text: Essays on Literature & Mediation in the 1890s* (High Wycombe, The Rivendale Press, 2009).

Fraser, Hilary, 'A Visual Field: Michael Field and the Gaze', *Victorian Literature and Culture*, 34 (2006), 553–71.

Pater, Walter, 'The School of Giorgione', *Fortnightly Review*, 22 (October 1877), 526–38.

Saville, Julia F., 'The Poetic Imaging of Michael Field', in Joseph Bristow, ed., *The Fin-de-Siècle Poem: English Literary Culture and the 1890s* (Athens: Ohio University Press, 2005), 178–206.

Stetz, Margaret D., and Cheryl A. Wilson, eds., *Michael Field and Their World* (High Wycombe: Rivendale Press, 2007).

Teukolsky, Rachel, *The Literate Eye: Victorian Art Writing and Modernist Aesthetics* (Oxford: Oxford University Press, 2009).

Thain, Marion, *'Michael Field': Poetry, Aestheticism and the Fin de Siècle* (Cambridge: Cambridge University Press, 2007).

Thain, Marion, and Ana Parejo Vadillo, eds., *Michael Field, The Poet: Published and Manuscript Materials* (Peterborough, Canada: Broadview Press, 2009).

Vadillo, Ana I. Parejo, '*Sight and Song*: Transparent Translations and a Manifesto for the Observer', *Victorian Poetry*, 38 (2000), 15–34.

CHAPTER 36

·····································

ALICE MEYNELL, AGAIN AND AGAIN

·····································

MEREDITH MARTIN

ALICE Meynell's life spanned the end of the Victorian era and the beginning of the twentieth century but we think of her as a Victorian poet. She has seldom been described as a modern poet, and most readers would be surprised to learn that her last book of poems was published the same year as T. S. Eliot's *The Waste Land*. Talia Schaffer's critical assessment of her essays expertly shows how Meynell looks forward towards the twentieth century in her aestheticized prose, experimenting and pushing the boundaries of the personal essay, bringing a fin-de-siècle sensibility to the burgeoning and quickly changing field of literary and cultural criticism. Yopie Prins argues that her poetic rhythms remain fixed to a particular prosodic past, though that past springs from the 'new prosody' of Coventry Patmore.[1] Her prosody of pauses, Prins argues, makes material the figure of metre and realizes her wish to find the spiritual and poetic meted out in strict laws against which her carefully chosen silences—and repetitions—expressively press. She is perfectly placed in the transitional period when changing ideas about Victorian, Edwardian, and Georgian poetics at once overshadowed and provided a brilliant foil to the movements associated with the rise of experimental modernism. However, her poetic experiments, her steadfast Catholic faith, her public persona as a popular essayist whose authority sometimes springs from the fact that she was, first, naturally, and at a young age, a poet, also complicates any simple reading of her as an ageing Victorian along the lines of Arthur Symons, Robert Bridges, and Thomas Hardy. Like Symons, Bridges, and Hardy, Meynell outlived the era that shaped her early writing. Accidents of publication have largely shaped the early twentieth-century assessment of her poetics: that is, after her star as a journalist had risen high enough, her early poems were reprinted to great acclaim at the turn of the century. And now, in the early twenty-first century, it is difficult to read her poems apart from her poetic essays, apart from her writing on metre, and apart from our own changed thinking about women and the market of, and for, modern and modernist poetry. Indeed, reading Meynell's poems now, she seems presciently looking backward and forward, and, in doing so, re-assuring us—somewhat like a doting mother—that we will come back to poets like her who believed so firmly in the spiritual properties and possibilities of poetry at the moment of modern disillusionment. I want to look first at her reception both today and at the beginning of the twentieth century to help me read one of her own poems about 'modern poetry'. Then I want to build on Prins's reading of Meynell's prosodic silence with a brief look at two nostalgic poems which reveal a lingering anxiety that perhaps we would not, in this day and age, have the ability to read Meynell's poetry as expertly as she may have hoped, despite her seemingly intuitive belief that we would keep trying, again and again.

In her 1916 introduction to Elizabeth Barrett Browning's 'The Art of Scansion' Meynell writes: 'It is interesting to see Elizabeth Barrett eager over the dead languages. In her own living language she was modern in her day, more modern than any contemporary except the poet whom, nearly twenty years after this letter was written and the controversy closed, she married. It was modern to write poetry as she wrote, with an emphatic use of modern prose words.'[2] Meynell emphasizes Elizabeth Barrett's modernity—careful to use Elizabeth Barrett Browning's maiden name, as if to prove that it was not her marriage to Robert Browning, that oft-cited proto-modernist, which influenced Elizabeth Barrett's diction but rather that her poetess predecessor could, as Yopie Prins has argued, understand the 'bonds of verse' to be flexible enough to fit modern prose words without the modernizing influence of a man. The gender of most of her poetic predecessors was an issue that shadowed much of Meynell's writing, and reviews of her work seldom described her in terms other than diminutive. Meynell may have been thinking about what was and was not modern (or bold, daring, and, in some way, masculine) in 1916 because that engine of 'new' poetry, Harriett Monroe's *Poetry* magazine, published in Chicago, had just reviewed Meynell's *Poems* two years earlier, in an aggressively diminishing tone:

> White, pure, cool, delicate, shy—such adjectives as these greet this small volume of collected poems which partly express thirty years' emotional experience of high and sensitive spirit. One might wish that the poet were less reserved, less austere...there is no mystical rapture or ritualistic color in her poems. Their tone is silvery, and the religious motive often present is of an early Protestant severity.[3]

Monroe's own prose here ('silvery', 'severity') contradicts itself—the 'emotional experience' that the small volume ostensibly collects is not available to the reader because the poet is too reserved, too austere. As Schaffer notes, this aesthetic withholding works for her prose but not, in Monroe's opinion, for her poetry.

Though Meynell herself was seldom described as modern, her poem 'A Modern Poet' became, along with 'Renunciation', one of her most often reprinted pieces. The poem first appeared in her slim volume titled *Preludes* in 1875 as 'A Song of Derivations' in a longer suite of poems dedicated to different views of the poet. In her essay on *Preludes*, Linda Peterson notes that reading Meynell's early verses and her disavowal of these verses helps us to understand her ambivalence about women's poetry in 1875 more broadly—whether Meynell's poems are 'best read with a women's tradition of Sapphic verse' or 'de-segregated and read alongside the work of her male contemporaries'.[4] That the poem 'A Modern Poet' first appears in 1875 under the title 'Song of Derivations' not only shows us her ambivalence about women's poetry but about her own reception as a poet of the nineteenth or of the twentieth century. From whom is her own particular verse derived? From what is English poetry derived? And how can one read a poem about derivation over one hundred years after its composition? From 'Derivation' to 'Modern', the poem itself shifts from being always already old or always already new, depending on how we encounter it.

The title is first changed in two major anthologies: Alfred Miles's *Poetry of the Century* (1898) and Edmund Clarence Stedman's *A Victorian Anthology* (1895). The nineteenth century, Meynell's poem announces in Miles's anthology, is already modern. Miles re-positions 'The Modern Poet', not as an early poem (these are 'preludes' in Miles's book, just like the title of her early book), but as a 'miscellaneous poem' along with 'My Heart shall be Thy Garden' and 'Renouncement'—ostensibly Meynell's most famous sonnet. 'The Modern Poet' is detached, then, from the early poems and, like 'Renouncement', begins its circulation as a meditation that will follow Meynell into the twentieth century, guaranteeing that she might be seen as someone burdened by the very pressure to be, herself, a modern poet. 'The Modern Poet' augers her arrival in Stedman's American anthology while it appears as almost an afterthought—a 'miscellaneous' modern poem appended to the more easily classified poetess poems of the rest of Miles's collection. Stedman's *Victorian Anthology*, the companion to his 1875 *Victorian Poets*, places Meynell among the 'recent poets of Great Britain' and 'The Modern Poet' is the first of five poems to appear there—both 'Modern', 'recent' and, as Michael Cohen has argued, newly 'Victorian'.[5] In her first widely circulated appearance in print, then, Meynell was poised as the Victorian modern.

However, the poem itself, 'The Modern Poet' looks firmly to the past. A 'song' about derivation and origin, the poem attempts to tie Meynell's poet to no origin and all origins at once. The poem begins:

> I come from nothing: but from where
> Come the undying thoughts I bear?
>   Down through long links of deaths and births
>   From the past poets of the earth.
> My immortality is there.[6]

Her thoughts are both 'from nothing' and 'undying' and, like the maternal poetess she would grow into, she 'bears' these undying thoughts 'down'—through 'deaths and births'. Her own immortality is in these undying thoughts she bears, pens, writes down on the page.

Meynell's enjambment and phrasing pace out the line in pauses and silences. Her prosody sets up the rhythm and syntactic patterning for the rest of the poem: internal rhyme ('come', 'from', 'come') and alliteration ('long links', 'past poets') help the stanza hover between sequence of choppy smaller statements 'I come from nothing' (pause) 'but from where' (pause) / 'Come the undying (pause) thoughts I bear' in the second and third lines, to the longer, enjambed flow of the fourth and fifth line, ending with an authoritative statement 'My immortality is there.' But there is no 'there'—just a long cast gaze into the past, to look at the past poets who have achieved immortality and to think, optimistically, about the immortality she herself will achieve. The poem continues:

> I am like the blossom of an hour;
> But long long vanished sun and shower
>   Awoke my breath in the young world's air.
>   I track the past back everywhere,
> Through seed and flower, and seed and flower.

Tracking the 'past back everywhere' does not give us much of a location or origin, just an undying, universal, and naturalized sense that this 'modern' poet is only modern insomuch as she is derivative—taking those undying thoughts from the past poets of the earth and making sure they are reiterated, renewed, and periodically re-appearing like flowers in the 'young' and modern world. Here, too, her own reiterations and renewals continue. This second stanza employs what becomes a signature Meynell device: *plôce* ('long long' and 'seed and flower, and seed and flower'). The controlled pace and reiteration here expresses not only that the seeds become flowers again and again and that poets will write poems again and again, but that Meynell's past-tracking also means she embraces this derivation—sings it, and uses this device to coo at us, as if rocking the reader into a sort of lull or slumber. The poems are her children but so, her repetition seems to insist, are we her readers.

The third stanza abandons the image of the ever-renewing flower to the other common figure of posterity, the river that flows from past to present—'Or I am like a stream that flows / Full of the cold springs that arose / In morning lands, in distant hills; / And down the plain my channel fills / With melting of forgotten snows'. The past is traced for us, already, in the figure of the river progressing from the earliest days (morning lands) to the modern era. The poem ends:

> Voices I have not heard possessed
> My own fresh songs; my thoughts are blessed
>   With relics of the far unknown;
>   And, mixed with memories not my own,
> The sweet streams throng into my breast.
>
> Before this life began to be,
> The happy songs that wake in me
>   Woke long ago and far apart.
>   Heavily on this little heart
> Presses this immortality.

Thinking of her own diminished status as a female poet ('this little heart'), Meynell draws power and strength from a nascent, natural urge to write poetry in a great tradition ('memories not my own') both ancient and modern ('relics of the far unknown'). But tracking the past back is a task that haunts Meynell, as England's poetic past is being tracked and traced in the late nineteenth century quite differently from one trained in classical metres may have imagined. Is every poem a song of derivation? And how, for Meynell, does English metre figure into the idea of tradition and innovation?

In her 1893 essay 'Decivilised,' Meynell troubles over the word derivation; 'nothing can be much sadder' she writes, than 'the failure of derivation'. She continues:

> [E]vidently we cannot choose our posterity. Reversing the steps of time, we may, indeed, choose backwards. We may give our thoughts noble forefathers. Well begotten, well born our fancies must be; they shall be also well derived. We have a voice in decreeing our inheritance, and not our inheritance only, but our heredity. Our minds may trace upwards and follow their ways to the best well-heads of the arts. The very habit of our thoughts may be persuaded one way unawares by their antenatal history. Their companions must be lovely, but need be no lovelier than their ancestors: and being so fathered and so husbanded, our thoughts may be entrusted to keep the counsels of literature.[7]

This 'antenatal history' is paternal—forefathers, fathers, husbands—and with this we are advised to keep counsel. Meynell tries to 'trace upwards' these masculine 'well-heads' of the arts, but the tracks she traces in this poem seem to be both her own footsteps and the masculine steps of poets past. Though here she mixes the metaphors of streams, steps, and voices, those footsteps of the past—in the form of prosodic feet, laws of verse, and English metres—will become her main symbol for negotiating the old and the new in the early twentieth century.

Indeed, this negotiation is present in her own selection of poems for posterity, a small anthology titled *The Flower of the Mind* which she selected in 1897. Including only one poem by Aphra Behn and another by Anna Letitia Barbauld, Meynell's anthology defends her choice of poetic predecessors by the poetic forms they employ. She includes many Scottish ballads but writes passionately of a kind of 'decivilization' of English metre:

> It is to be noted that the modern, or comparatively modern, additions to old songs full of quantitative metre…full of long notes, rests, and interlinear pauses, are almost always written in anapaests. The later writer has slipped away from the fine, various, and subtle metre of the older. Assuredly the popularity of the metre which, for want of a term suiting the English rules of verse, must be called anapaestic, has done more than any other thing to vulgarise the national sense of rhythm and to silence finer rhythms. Anapaests came quite suddenly into English poetry and brought coarseness, glibness, volubility, dapper and fatuous effects. A master may use it well, but as a popular measure it has been disastrous.[8]

As a practitioner, herself, of these finer rhythms, Meynell uses this discursive introduction to justify her choice of the 'greatest' poems and to show that it is possible, in her own writing, to revive those 'long notes, rests, and interlinear pauses', a project that, though hearkening back to a different metrical past, nonetheless makes her poetic language more flexible than the many popular, martial measures that proliferated in the Edwardian and Georgian periods.

Meynell's main forefather in the concept of embodied poetic rhythm was Coventry Patmore. In her essay 'Patmore's Law, Meynell's Rhythm', Yopie Prins argues that 'although she outlived the fin de siècle, her poetry recalls the past century as a period when prosody was regularly used for the regulation of thought. To imagine meter as a living, embodied form thus became Meynell's poetic calling.'[9] She reads Meynell's letters, journals, poems, and the essays 'Coventry Patmore's Odes' and 'The Rhythm of Life' especially, to show how, for Meynell, 'nature is best understood as a metrical phenomenon'.[10] Prins rightly sees Meynell's poetry as part of the 'long history in nineteenth-century women's verse, in which Victorian poetesses measure the pulse of their poetry by the quickening of blood and breath. The impulse, or aspiration, to give new life to the rhythms of poetry is articulated', Prins reminds us, 'by Aurora Leigh, the prototype for the poetess in Elizabeth Barrett Browning's novel-poem.'[11] In addition to her use of Barrett Browning as poetic prototype, Prins takes us to Meynell's careful reading—and re-writing, in her poetry—of Coventry Patmore:

> 'Law...should be the poet's only subject'; the poet should demonstrate how 'the music of verse arises, not from infraction but from inflection of the law of the set metre...in correspondence with feelings and passions'. Indeed, it is the inflection of meter that produces passion, as 'law puts a strain upon feeling, and feeling responds with a strain upon law' (151). This mutual restraint defines the lyric strains of Meynell's poetry, bending the bonds of verse without breaking them, creating inflection without infraction.[12]

The living, embodied form of metre is as present in Meynell's poetry as her essays. These steps, traced back through time in 'The Modern Poet', are fetishized as metrical feet in Meynell's essays in *The Spirit of Place* (which was dedicated to Patmore). Published in 1898, this collection of essays deepens her engagement with metre as an embodied form and poetry as a readable allegory nearly everywhere in nature. In her essay 'The Foot' she writes:

> We shall not praise the 'simple, sweet' and 'earth-confiding feet' enough without thanks for the rule of verse and for the time of song. If Poetry was first divided by the march, and next varied by the dance, then to the rule of the foot are to be ascribed the thought, the instruction, and the dream that could not speak by prose. Out of that little physical law, then, grew a spiritual law which is one of the greatest things we know; and from the test of the foot came the ultimate test of the thinker: 'Is it accepted of Song?'[13]

The physical, spiritual law slides into Song, into poetry, so that Meynell moves, next, to a discussion of her own art in prose and verse: 'Lesser virtues may flower in daily liberty and may flourish in prose; but infinite virtues and greatness are compelled to the measure of poetry, and obey the constraint of an hourly convent bell. It is no wonder that every poet worthy of the name has had a passion for metre, for the very verse. To him the difficult fetter is the condition of an interior range immeasurable'.[14] The metrical foot tracks the past back and it is unnatural, here, in many ways, when she moves her metrical material to the figure of the repeating convent bell. All paths lead back to original constraints, all bells echo with the sound of other poetic prede-cessors, and metre is a form that means both the visual track of these past poems and the heard echo of the prior poet's words, but this is a man-made sound, notably, and unlike other constraints, this manufactured music needs to reach a reader trained to respond to it.

Even more importantly, the echo of the bell may fade. At the end of her essay 'Decivilized' Meynell worries: 'of a sequel, which of us is sure? Which of us is secured against the dangers of subsequent depreciation?'[15] If her currency is a poetic tradition that is changing, and a poetic form that has fewer and fewer readers, in the twentieth century, who will be able to read and understand it, what will become of her poetic and metrical project? These issues concerned Meynell more and more toward the end of her life, when by the time of her death in 1922, the place of poetry as a spiritual guide—and the poetess as prophetess—seemed less and less likely. Toward the end of her poetic career, then, the 'modern' poet turned away from allegorizing poetic form, and formal predecessors, as parts of the natural world and began to address English metre directly. In two poems published posthumously and written the year before her death, 'The Laws of Verse' and 'The English Metres', Meynell anticipates the obsolescence of the particular derivations she found most modern.

> The Laws of Verse
>
> Dear laws, come to my breast!
>   Take all my frame, and make your close arms meet
> Around me; and so ruled, so warmed, so pressed,
>   I breathe, aware; I feel my wild heart beat.
>
> Dear laws, be wings to me!
>   The feather merely floats. O be it heard
> Through weight of life—the skylark's gravity—
>   That I am not a feather, but a bird.[16]

Meynell addresses the laws of English metre as 'dears', as if they are not part of her past but her progeny, her particular future. Prins reads this poem as an invocation of Meynell's poetic spacing, 'a mental apprehension of metre in the mind's eye and the mind's ear'.[17] This 'passionate attachment to form itself' is, for Prins, a 'formalization rather than a personalization of passion'. And, indeed, whereas the 'dear laws' seem like little children, we see that she uses them to assert, at the end of the poem, that she not only watches over them but uses them to elevate herself to the position of the bird / bard who can understand and display them.

In the companion poem to this one, 'The English Metres', Meynell again addresses poetic form directly and positions herself among those who believe that classical feet are laudable as representatives of the measure of English poetry. Meynell does not bother to justify her terminology—she writes as if the Greek words for metrical feet are not only appropriate but as if they have become a crucial part of an English landscape. Despite her adoption and naturalization of these terms, this is a subtle elegy, a concern about depreciation. Meynell asserts that 'English metres' exist and have characteristics that align them with the nation, with all that is right and good about English, and yet there is a meta-metrical narrative at work in this poem as well, in which the poem mourns its own inability to be understood as a metrical allegory.

> The rooted liberty of flowers in the breeze
>   Is theirs, by national luck impulsive, terse,
> Tethered, uncaptured, rules obeyed 'at ease'
>   Time-strengthened laws of verse.
>
> Or they are like our seasons that admit
>   Inflexion, not infraction: Autumn hoar,
> Winter more tender than our thoughts of it,
>   But a year's steadfast four.
>
> Redundant syllables of Summer rain,
>   And displaced accents of authentic Spring;
> Spondaic clouds above a gusty plain
>   With dactyls on the wing.
>
> Not Common Law, but Equity, is theirs—
>   Our metres; play and agile foot askance,
> And distance, beckoning, blithely rhyming pairs,
>   Unknown to classic France;
>
> Unknown to Italy. Ay, count, collate,
>   Latins! With eye foreseeing on the time
> And numbered fingers, and approaching fate
>   On the appropriate rhyme.
>
> Nay, nobly our grave measures are decreed:
>   Heroic, Alexandrine with the stay,
> Deliberate; or else like him whose speed
>   Did outrun Peter, urgent in the break of day.[18]

Notice that the vulgar anapaest gets no mention here. The poem is rooted in Edwardian concepts of metrical freedom and wartime conceptions of poetic form. For instance, the first stanza calls English metre 'by national luck impulsive, terse, / Tethered, uncaptured, / rules obeyed 'at ease' / Time-strengthened laws of verse'. Metre itself is like a soldier 'at ease', still serving the country, but not bound to perform any duty. English laws of verse are 'rooted' in history, but this history has taught them to strive toward freedom. Her own diction is 'terse' and 'tethered' here, as it describes the 'impulsive' and 'uncaptured' laws of verse, demonstrating that her practice shows that she admits to adhering to some sort of law, though she also admits that this law has not been 'captured' by any adequate description. The English laws of verse are always rooted in England, but they are still 'at liberty', though 'by national luck' they have been strengthened and codified somewhat by the passage of time.

Meynell measures time by metrical seasons ('a year's steadfast four') and, like metre, the four seasons 'admit inflexion, not infraction'. Just like metre, the seasons might be different from our expectations of them, 'winter more tender than our thoughts of it'. Her own four beat lines are as inevitable as the seasons but nonetheless subtler than any description. In the third stanza, nature is allegorized into metre: 'redundant syllables of Summer rain, / And displaced accents of authentic Spring'. The metrical feet, rather than taking on the characteristics of actual feet, sprout wings and fly: spondees are clouds, dactyls are 'on the wing'. Rather than reference the standard iamb and trochee, Meynell inserts the most controversial metrical feet (the spondee and dactyl) as if to show how natural these have become—an inevitable part of the English landscape. The 'bird' as inspiration has become the metrical foot itself: not the poet or the poem, but that term with which we describe the poem is 'on the wing'.

Nor does Meynell adhere to a strict iambic metre. The poem welcomes dactyls and spondees, and it is not, though it seems like it almost should be, a lesson in expressive reading. Unlike Coleridge's 'Lesson for a Boy', Meynell does not employ dactylic feet in the line 'with dactyls on the wing', nor are there spondees in the line 'spondaic clouds above a gusty plain'. Authentic spring, in Meynell's metrical allegory, is not configured in the line through displaced accents, and even the amphibrach and dactyl of 'redundant syllables' seem altogether necessary. There is no stanza in which the form, actual or allegorical, imposes itself; the three lines of pentameter followed by one of trimeter never succumb to a strict iambic except in the playful line in stanza four: 'Our metres; play and agile foot askance'. In Meynell's poem, agile feet of English metre can play without fear of reproach.

And yet, the fourth stanza alludes to the Common Law versus Equity, thus referring to a legal, rather than natural, origin of 'our metres'. Rather than 'Common Law', in which metrical form would be decided solely on precedent and custom (despite how they are rooted in history), English metres have 'Equity'. By using this legal terminology, Meynell alludes to the British and American system of ethical modification to the rule of law. Modification based on fairness is the rule to which Meynell refers here, and this flexible interpretation of the laws of verse is 'unknown to classic France', and 'unknown to Italy' (in stanza five). Though the English metres are natural, their modification—indeed, codification—might be seen as unnatural or external. The English metres are defined in opposition to their continental counterparts. Even the Latins are seen as too strict, 'with eye foreseeing on the time / And numbered fingers, and approaching fate, / On the appropriate rhyme', their verses leading inevitably and predictably to a conclusion we can count on.

'Nay nobly our grave measures are decreed': she refers to the history of English verse in this final stanza—the heroic couplet, (those 'distant, beckoning, blithely rhyming pairs') and the Alexandrine, but again, 'decreed' and 'stay' have a slightly legal tone to them. English metres have all the freedom they want in 1923, and yet unless the English metres are 'decreed' noble, deliberate, they might take on too much speed. John (20:1–9) outruns Peter 'urgent in the break of day' to see the resurrected Christ. Here, the poem favours the nobility, the heroism, and the deliberation of the national metres, fearing that without a lawful decree, without the 'rooted liberty', verse might be too young, too eager, to quick to discard the careful wisdom of the past. Because both John and Peter are disciples to a 'higher law', their reticence to let go of the laws of English metre and the freedom they entail, coupled with the eagerness to rush into a new poetic era, are written into this final stanza.

Alice Meynell herself celebrated periodicity. Her well-known essay 'The Rhythm of Life' begins 'if life is not always poetical, it is at least metrical;'[19] and the essay ends by citing the 'law that commands all things—a sun's revolutions and the rhythmic pangs of maternity',[20] gesturing to a career-long project of spiritualizing literature—especially poetry—and feminizing poetic form. She was a Victorian poetess who many scholars recognize as an idealization of Coventry Patmore's 'angel in the house', a Catholic convert who had eight children, a public figure celebrated for reticence, silence, and privacy, the object of a number of literary statesmen's crushes (Patmore, John Ruskin, and George Meredith, notably), a suffragette, a prosodic experimenter and virtuoso, and an essayist whose poetic prose pushed the boundaries of 'criticism'. Of her prose, Schaffer writes, 'obsessed with the notion of self-revelation, yet deeply wedded to the idea of self-concealment, Meynell artfully promised perpetual exposure, which she perpetually and pleasurably deferred'.[21] The perpetual and pleasurable deferment of exposure took form in her essays and poems, but she did reveal an ongoing concern with how she would be read in the future.

Meynell was one of a handful of complex literary figures who attempted, but eventually failed, to weather the transitional period between the fin-de-siècle and the advent of high modernism, with its ambivalent and, at times, aggressive relationship to women in the literary marketplace. T. S. Eliot dismissed her essays in a review of *Hearts of Controversy* in 1918, as 'what a University Extension audience would like; but it is not criticism'.[22] If we expand Meynell's own belief in the powerful pathos that emerges when a (woman) writer strains against the 'bonds of verse' and the constraints of criticism to address her reception in the twentieth and twenty-first centuries, we see that she herself was aware of how her own reputation and reception would change depending on the lens through which she was viewed. In this way, Meynell anticipated the complicated reception of the fin-de-siècle 'poet' at the border of the nineteenth and twentieth centuries, and her poetry, concerned with itself as poetry (as opposed to a poetic essay, for instance) argues for a spiritual, natural 'essence' that is at once reliant on past forms and is cautious about striking a chord that is too altogether new. She sometimes names her poetic predecessors and sometimes abstracts 'poetry' into the wind, bird song, and various figures in the natural world. But she also thinks about poetic forms as a student of them—as an avid reader of Patmore's poetic theory, as a metrist whose concern is with poetic feet, and with English metre and an anthropological, natural past for this metre she imagines in her essays. In this way, Meynell wants her feet on the ground, as it were, but rather than looking towards other natural figures to think through poetic metre, she makes English metre such a natural, constraining, and necessary idealization that it is hard to see beyond its purview.

NOTES

1. See Talia Schaffer, 'Writing a Public Self: Alice Meynell's "Unstable Equilibrium"', in *Women's Experience of Modernity 1875–1945* (Baltimore: Johns Hopkins University Press, 2002): 'Alice Meynell's complicated work confirms the need to remap the period. Her particular contribution: bringing the late Victorian conventions of aestheticism to bear on political issues around gender' (14). See also 'The Angel in Hyde Park: Alice Meynell's "Unstable Equilibrium"', in Schaffer, *The Forgotten Female Aesthetes: Literary Culture in Late-Victorian England* (Charlottesville: University of Virginia Press, 2000), and Ana Parejo Vadilo, 'Alice Meynell: An Impressionist in Kensington', in *Woman Poets and Urban Aestheticism: Passengers of Modernity* (London: Palgrave Macmillan, 2005) for Meynell's prose; for Meynell's prosodic form, see Yopie Prins, 'Patmore's Law, Meynell's Rhythm', in *The Fin-de-Siècle Poem: English Literary Culture in the 1890s*, ed. Joseph Bristow (Athens: Ohio University Press, 2005), 261–284.
2. Alice Meynell, *The Art of Scansion* (London: privately printed by Clement Shorter, 1916), viii.
3. Harriet Monroe, 'Alice Meynell', *Poetry*, 4 (1914), 70–71.
4. Linda H. Peterson, 'Alice Meynell's *Preludes*, or Preludes to What Future Poetry?', *Victorian Literature and Culture* 34 (2006), 405–426.
5. Michael Cohen, 'E. C. Stedman and the Invention of Victorian Poetry', *Victorian Poetry*, 43 (2005), 165–189.
6. Meynell, 'The Modern Poet', in *The Collected Poems of Alice Meynell* (London: Burns and Oates, 1913), 114.
7. Meynell, 'Decivilized', in *The Rhythm of Life, and Other Essays* (London: Elkin Matthews & John Lane, 1893), 9.
8. Meynell, *The Flower of the Mind* (London: Grant Richards, 1897), x.
9. Prins, 'Patmore's Law, Meynell's Rhythm', 268.
10. Prins, 'Patmore's Law', 269.
11. Prins, 'Patmore's Law', 271.
12. Prins, 'Patmore's Law', 275. Here Prins is quoting from Coventry Patmore, *Essay on English Metrical Law: A Critical Edition with a Commentary*, ed. Mary Roth (Washington: Catholic University of America Press, 1961).
13. Meynell, 'The Foot', in *The Spirit of Place and Other Essays* (New York and London: John Lane Company, 1898), 47.
14. Meynell, 'The Foot', 44–45.
15. Meynell, 'Decivilized', in *The Rhythm of Life, and Other Essays*, 10.
16. Meynell, 'The Laws of Verse', in *The Complete Poems of Alice Meynell* (London: Burns, Oates & Co, 1923), 130.
17. Prins, 'Patmore's Law, Meynell's Rhythm', 275.
18. Meynell, 'The English Metres', in *Complete Poems*, 133.
19. Meynell, *The Rhythm of Life, and Other Essays*, 1.
20. Meynell, *The Rhythm of Life*, 6.
21. Schaffer, 'Writing a Public Self', 14.
22. T. S. Eliot, 'Review of Alice Meynell's *Hearts of Controversy*', *Egoist* (1918), 50. Quoted in Jonathan Rose, *The Intellectual Life of the British Working Classes* (New Haven: Yale University Press, 2003), 435.

SELECT BIBLIOGRAPHY

Aherne, John, 'Alice Meynell: A Sybil Smoking a Cigarette', in *Serendipity: Essays on Six Catholic Authors* (North Andover: Merrimack College Press, 1985), 26–41.

Alexander, Calvert, 'Alice Meynell', in *Catholic Revival* (Milwaukee: The Bruce, 1935), 113–128.

Anderson, Kathleen, '"I make the whole world answer to my art": Alice Meynell's Poetic Identity', *Victorian Poetry* 41 (2003), 259–275.

Badeni, June, *The Slender Tree: A Life of Alice Meynell* (Padstow: Tabb House, 1981).

Chesterson, G. K., 'Alice Meynell', *Dublin Review* 172 (1923), 1–12.

Frawley, Maria, '"The Tides of the Mind": Alice Meynell's Poetry of Perception', *Victorian Poetry* 38 (2000), 62–76.

Leighton, Angela, *Victorian Women Poets: Writing Against the Heart* (Charlottesville: University Press of Virginia, 1992).

Meynell, Alice, *Poems* (London: Elkin Matthews and John Lane, 1893).

—— *The Rhythm of Life, and Other Essays* (London: Elkin Matthews & John Lane, 1893).

—— *The Spirit of Place and Other Essays* (London: John Lane, 1898).

—— *Later Poems* (London: John Lane, 1902).

—— *The Collected Poems of Alice Meynell* (London: Burns and Oates, 1913).

—— *Last Poems* (London: Burns, Oates & Washbourne, 1923).

Meynell, Viola, *Alice Meynell, A Memoir* (London: Jonathan Cape, 1929).

Noble, James Ashcroft, 'Alice Meynell', in *The Poets and Poetry of the Century*. Volume 8 ed. Alfred Miles (London: Hutchison, 1898), 421–422.

Patmore, Coventry, 'Mrs. Meynell', in *Religio Poetae* (London: George Bell and Sons, 1893), 199–212.

Peterson, Linda H., 'Transforming the Poet: Alice Meynell as Fin-de-Siècle Englishwoman of Letters', in *Becoming a Woman of Letters: Myths of Authorship and Facts of the Victorian Market* (Princeton: Princeton University Press, 2009), 171–296.

Prins, Yopie, 'Patmore's Law, Meynell's Rhythm', in *The Fin-de-Siècle Poem: English Literary Culture in the 1890s*, ed. Joseph Bristow (Athens: Ohio University Press, 2005), 261–284.

Schaffer, Talia, *The Forgotten Female Aesthetes: Literary Culture in Late Victorian England* (Charlottesville: University Press of Virginia, 2000).

—— 'A Tethered Angel: The Martyrology of Alice Meynell', *Victorian Poetry* 38 (2000), 49–61.

Tuell, Anna Kimball, *Mrs. Meynell and Her Literary Generation* (New York: E. P. Dutton, 1925).

Tynan, Katherine, 'Mrs. Meynell and Her Poetry', *Catholic World* 1907 (1913), 668–678.

Vadilo, Ana Parejo, *Women Poets and Urban Aestheticism: Passengers of Modernity* (Basingstoke: Palgrave Macmillan, 2005).

Wilde, Oscar, 'English Poetesses', in *The Queen in The Uncollected Oscar Wilde*, ed. John Wyse Jackson (London: Fourth Estate, 1991; 1st pub. 1888), 59–66.

CHAPTER 37

···

HOUSMAN'S DIFFICULTY

···

JANET GEZARI

In 1928, A. E. Housman politely declined to give A. J. A. Symons permission to include poems from *A Shropshire Lad* in an anthology of nineties' verse and cited his 'invariable rule'.[1] The rule was simple: 'I do not allow poems from *A Shropshire Lad* to be reprinted.'[2] In 1935, about a year before his death, he just as politely refused W. B. Yeats's request to reprint poems from *Last Poems* in another anthology. He changed his mind a few days later, and happily agreed to the publication of 'the five pieces you specify'. In his previous letter to Yeats, Housman's account of his reasons for declining such invitations had been extensive enough for him to apologize for offering it. His body of published work is slight (only sixty-three poems in *A Shropshire Lad* and only forty-one in *Last Poems*); 'there are far too many anthologies in the world already'; and finally, he is 'unwilling to countenance an anthology which by its very conception allots so much importance to Hopkins, not chiefly because I myself regard him as a moth blundering round a candle but from a craven fear of being some day made to look foolish if, for instance, posterity decides that Doughty was the epoch maker'.[3] That would be Charles Montagu Doughty, the now forgotten author of a six-volume epic, *The Dawn in Britain*, published in 1906. The facetious worry about Doughty is in line with Housman's refusal of almost all of the honours he was offered because, A. S. F. Gow suggests, 'he mistrusted the judgment of his fellow men. "You should be welcome to praise me," he wrote in one of the prefaces, "if you did not praise one another."'[4]

Housman stood his ground with Symons, and both his opposition to anthologies in general and his suspicion of other people's judgements would have played parts in that refusal. In his letter to Grant Richards, who was acting as Symons' agent, he softened his obduracy with characteristically deadpan humour: 'He may be consoled, and also amused, if you tell him that to include me in an anthology of the Nineties would be just as technically correct, and just as essentially inappropriate, as to include Lot in a book about Sodomites.' (This is wittier than his postscript, which has its place among the many funny things Housman said, not all of which were vituperative: 'If Mr Symons ever feels sad, he ought to be able to cheer himself up by contemplating his handwriting.'[5])

Cast forth from Sodom, Lot is saved because he is righteous and specifically because he is not guilty of the sin of sodomy, which is a blazon of unrighteousness in the Genesis story. He offers his virgin daughters to the men of the town when they demand to *know* his house guests, who happen to be angels in disguise. Like Lot, then, Housman is the exceptional man, the one who doesn't share the habits and proclivities of the poets who are his contemporaries. Lot's wife is the central figure in one of the poems set aside by Housman but published posthumously by his brother in *More Poems*. The poet would have been sympathetic to the regard she had for her town and the company of the people she had grown up among. 'Lot's wife was salt and barren, because she was full of loss and mourning, and looked back,' as Marilynne Robinson puts it in *Housekeeping*.[6] Her looking back costs her her life in a way that would have been especially poignant to Housman, both because of salt's association with tears and because of the transformation of living, breathing flesh into something hard and fixed, like stone or bone. Who but Housman would have written a poem in which a visitor to the British Museum communes with a Greek statue, shares the marble's exile from the place of its making, and leaves feeling the weight of his own trouble lightened and his courage hardened? Like Housman's poem about Lot's wife, this poem, included in *A Shropshire Lad*, contains some of his most characteristic elements: geographical or temporal exile from 'a land of lost content', a brooding sense of 'heavy ill', and admiration for those who can be still in the presence of danger or violent emotion.[7] Even when being still means being dead, Housman's admiration is tinged with envy and longing:

> Loitering with a vacant eye
> Along the Grecian gallery,
> And brooding on my heavy ill,
> I met a statue standing still.
> Still in marble stone stood he,
> And stedfastly he looked at me.
> 'Well met,' I thought the look would say,
> 'We both were fashioned far away;
> We neither knew, when we were young,
> These Londoners we live among.'[8]

Lot's wife is the entry point for the poem published posthumously in *More Poems*, but Lot's own story is even more compelling for Housman. It provides exactly the kind of dramatic irony his poems, like and not like Hardy's, deal in. Lot escapes the fate of both Sodom and his wife, and yet, like Job, the biblical figure who more often haunts Housman's poems, he suffers the fate that has been reserved especially for him, and that puts an end to any comforting thought that he has been chosen by God to have his punishment remitted. For Housman knows, as Lot won't yet, that the loss of his wife is insidiously and inevitably connected to his daughters' decision to make him drunk and lie with him in order to generate the children who will continue his bloodline.

> Half-way, for one commandment broken,
>   The woman made her endless halt,
> And she today, a glistering token,
>   Stands in the wilderness of salt.
> Behind, the vats of judgment brewing
>   Thundered, and thick the brimstone snowed:
> He to the hill of his undoing
>   Pursued his road.[9]

The poem's alternating lines of iambic tetrameter and iambic trimeter and alternating masculine and feminine rhymes are common in Housman's verse, which knowingly evokes both ballads and hymns. The truncated last line is unusual for him and perfectly embodies the undoing awaiting Lot, cutting short his righteousness before his end. In *In Memoriam*, Tennyson wonders what hope there is for modern rhyme that 'turns a musing eye / On songs, and deeds, and lives, that lie / Foreshortened in the tract of time?'[10] Housman's poems often take their inspiration from foreshortened lives, and then go on to celebrate the foreshortening. The heroes of *A Shropshire Lad* are the 'lads that will die in their glory and never be old', the ones who are smart enough 'to slip betimes away / From fields where glory does not stay'.[11] Housman's description of Lot's wife as a 'glistering token' captures the keenness of his dedication to glory and its handmaiden, honour. Here *glistering* refuses any implication of a false or outward shining. Instead, it is the sign that death, which comes too late for Lot, has preserved Lot's wife as she was and will be, the still point of the turning world, no longer forced to see her neighbours burning behind her and not yet able to see her husband's dishonour ahead. Housman's world wasn't turning the way T. S. Eliot's was. It was likely to be turning worse and worse.

Opinions about Housman's relation to his period diverge as widely as opinions about the merit or meretriciousness of the poems themselves. Critics have offered briefs on Housman's affiliation with the Georgians, the Romantics, the Pre-Raphaelites, the mid-Victorians, and the Decadents. The nineties, in particular, were rife with poetry. Swinburne's *Astrophel and Other Poems* appeared in 1894, followed by *The Tale of Balen* in 1896, and both Yeats and Lionel Johnson published books of poems in 1895. There were first books of poems by John Gray (*Silverpoints*, 1893), Ernest Dowson (*Verses*, 1896), Alfred Douglas (*Poems*, 1896), and Thomas Hardy (*Wessex Poems*, 1898). If we define Victorian poems as poems published during the Victorian period, only the sixty-three poems published in 1896 as *A Shropshire Lad* count Housman in. The forty-one poems in *Last Poems* share their publication date—1922—with *The Waste Land*, the poem that did more than any other to define modern poetry in a way that left Housman behind. The style of the poems published by Housman in *Last Poems* or published after his death by his brother Laurence—forty-eight as *More Poems* in 1936 and twenty-three as *Additional Poems* in 1937—does not differ from the style of the poems in *A Shropshire Lad*. Many were written well before their publication and usually before 1910. The poem about Lot has a composition date that puts it solidly in the company of the poems in *A Shropshire Lad*.

The humour of the conceit in which Housman associates himself with Lot is layered. Housman wasn't a sodomite, and couldn't, like Wilde, have been accused of posing as one. We know nothing about his sex-life, if he had a sex-life as an adult, and only a little about his love-life, but lad-love is one of his poems' animating emotions. Auden, who had the benefit of being able to read Housman's posthumous poems as well as his brother's memoir about him, saw a divided man: 'Jehovah Housman lived the virginal life of a don; Satan Housman thought a good deal about stolen waters and the bed.'[12] The phrase 'stolen waters', which appears in *More Poems* xxii, has as its two clearest sources Proverbs 9:17 ('Stolen water is sweet; food eaten in secret is delicious'), cited in Burnett,[13] and Lewis Carroll's poem, 'Stolen Waters', oddly not cited in Burnett, but a likely influence. Housman's relation to his homosexuality didn't meet Auden's standards and isn't likely to meet those of contemporary gay activists. There was much about which Housman preferred to remain silent: 'Others have held their tongues, and so can I.'[14]

There's more disdain than sympathy in Auden's deprecation of Housman's choices. His poem 'A. E. Housman' says that Housman was 'Heart-injured in North London' and implies, questionably, that disappointed love hurt him into Latin scholarship.

> Deliberately he chose the dry-as-dust,
> Kept tears like dirty postcards in a drawer;
> Food was his public love, his private lust
> Something to do with violence and the poor.[15]

Peter Howarth admires Auden's 'inspired guess' in his recent consideration of Housman's substantial library of pornographic, erotic, and sexological books, probably collected between 1895 and 1922.[16] Although it was Laurence Housman who gave a substantial portion of the collection to Cambridge University Library after his brother's death, Housman had not kept his interest in such matters a secret. In 1932, he offered his copy of the *Bibliotheca Germanorum Erotica et Curiosa* to Trinity College,[17] and Howarth quotes his unembarrassed and light-hearted reference to his collection, in a letter to Edmund Gosse, as 'sadly incomplete, and not at all worth leaving to the British Museum when I die'.[18] According to Howarth, the medical sexology in the collection emphasizes homosexuality, but the pornography is wide-ranging and inclusive. Howarth argues that 'the strong bias in this collection toward exclusively flagellatory and sadomasochistic material, particularly in the pseudo-medical category, suggests that Housman found here something he recognized in himself'.[19]

F. W. Bateson refers to Housman's homosexuality as an 'aspect of the Housman problem', but *problem* is wrong, and *difficulty* is better, since Housman's homosexuality wasn't open to solution.[20] Bateson quotes the first stanza of *More Poems* xxxi ('Because I liked you better') and asserts that 'a critic's first concern is with the poems as poems and not with the neurosis of his poet'. We can note the ease of the diagnosis—not exactly Housman's own but not unrelated to it—as well as the assumption that a 'concern with the poems as poems' would not have to take in, though not necessarily take up, the poet's homosexuality. There is, to begin with, the matter of occasion, and the poem's probably owing its inspiration to some exchange with Moses Jackson, Housman's 'greatest friend'.[21] According to *The American Heritage Dictionary of the English Language*, the term *neurosis* is no longer used in psychiatric diagnosis, but Bateson's turn from it obscures the extent to which Housman's awareness of himself as homosexual both shaped, and matters, to his poems, as Elizabeth Barrett Browning's awareness of herself as a woman or Yeats's Irishness matter to theirs. The charge of neurosis registers a psychological reading of the poems as compensatory, as well as a view of homosexuality no longer current or acceptable. This reading of Housman's poems was alive in 1936, when Bateson was writing, and is still potent today. It is related to Eliot's remark about Ruskin, which Burnett quotes in his essay on 'Allusion in Housman' and applies to Housman's savage quarrels with classical scholars: 'the emotional intensity … is partly a deflection of something that was baffled in life'.[22]

This is especially true for some kinds of poetry. Composing a lyric poem, Northrop Frye writes, is a 'displaced activity, as when a chimpanzee crossed in love starts digging holes in the ground instead'.[23] But 'it takes more than a broken heart' to make a true poet.[24] Housman's heart was broken under particular circumstances that included a refusal grounded in sexual preference, Moses Jackson's for women and Housman's for men (or lads), and it was moreover a heart belonging to a particular man. In addition to being a kind of love that was unacceptable to society and punishable, as Oscar Wilde's arrest, trial, and conviction demonstrated in 1895, Housman's love for Moses Jackson was singular, and its not being requited was the most important thing that happened to and for him. Philip Larkin gets this right: 'If unhappiness was the key to poetry, the key to unhappiness was Moses Jackson. It would be tempting to call this neurosis, but there is a shorter word. For as Housman himself said, anyone who thinks he has loved more than one person has simply never really loved at all.'[25] Love is just a four-letter word. One of Housman's achievements as a poet was to connect his private unhappiness to other, related kinds of unhappiness and then to a common unhappiness surpassing his own thwarting and suffering. The general idea is easily travestied, as it is in the first stanza of Ezra Pound's 'Mr. Housman's Message': 'Woeful is this human lot. / *Woe! woe, etcetera*…'.[26] If Pound's poem shows how little can be made of the message he distils from Housman's poetry, Randall Jarrell's inspired readings of 'Crossing alone the nighted ferry' and 'It nods and curtseys and recovers' show how much can be made of the way in which Housman's generalizations emerge from the particularities of his best poems.[27] It is this difficulty in Housman's poems that saves them from being careless, adolescent in mood and thought, and hopelessly romantic and sentimental—all charges frequently levelled against them—and that interests me in this account of them.

I want to return to *More Poems* xxxi and to the poem that immediately precedes it in order to address some of their particularities as poems. Both have been read as patently autobiographical, grounded in Housman's parting from Moses Jackson when Jackson sailed for India in 1887, and Housman's reasons for not publishing these poems almost certainly included a wish to protect his privacy and Jackson's. The earliest surviving draft of *More Poems* xxxi is dated February 1893 to August 1894, six or seven years after Jackson's departure. There is no complete draft, and Burnett relies on Housman's latest versions for his text:

Because I liked you better
    Than suits a man to say,
It irked you and I promised
    I'd throw the thought away.

To put the world between us
    We parted stiff and dry:
'Farewell,' said you, 'forget me.'
    'Fare well, I will,' said I.

If e'er, where clover whitens
    The dead man's knoll, you pass,
And no tall flower to meet you
    Starts in the trefoiled grass,

Halt by the headstone shading
    The heart you have not stirred,
And say the lad that loved you
    Was one that kept his word.

Like many of Housman's poems, this one sounds like a ballad. Housman's innovation here is to take the traditional stuff of ballads—the focus on a crucial episode, the use of dialogue, and the themes of betrayed love and the parting of lovers by death—and to truncate the narrative and alter the usual story in fundamental ways. Wordsworth anticipated him in the first innovation, notably in his Lucy poems, but Housman's changes to the story are uniquely his own. The first two stanzas recount a parting in the past, which is explained unusually: one man liked another 'better / Than suits a man to say'. Jarrell's assumption that the speaker is addressing a woman in 'Crossing alone the nighted ferry' does no harm to his analysis, and, apart from those of Housman's poems that explicitly specify a woman, there are some in which the sex of a character doesn't matter. It matters to this poem, not because of the poem's biographical sources but because of the way the two parties to this transaction are described and positioned. An earlier draft had 'Than friends in liking may,' and Carol Efrati points out that Housman's revision emphasizes social conventions rather than morality, so that the later version 'reveal[s] something of Housman's own deepening understanding—and acceptance—of his own feelings'.[28] The feelings are, I think, more complicated than this suggests. Housman's own view of suitability was stern and strenuous, as is the view of the speaker of 'Shot? so quick, so clean an ending?'. This poem was inspired by, and praises, the suicide of a gentleman cadet at the Royal Military Academy, Woolwich, whose suicide note cited his motives as 'utter cowardice and despair' and a determination not to 'morally' injure anyone else: 'Oh that was right, lad, that was brave'.[29]

'Because I liked you better' lets the question of why the degree of liking is unsuitable hang in the poem's air. It is unsuitable because social conventions disallow it, or because the law prohibits it, or because the love is unrequited. The feeling is manly enough in both versions of the line; the final version says that expressing it is not. What constitutes the happiness of one friend tires, disgusts, bores, and burdens the other. By now, we're

well outside the territory of traditional ballads and beginning to recognize a more modern mindscape. The better liking is merely a 'thought'. The word is generous because it
inoculates the friend. The parallelism of the two remedies proposed by the poem—forgetting his love for his friend and putting the world between them—is more explicit in
a cancelled draft of line 4 in which 'To' replaces 'I'd.' Line 5 can be read as a poetic way of
describing a literal fact and as a biographical reference—India is far from England—or
as another acknowledgment of the worldly conventions that prohibit a better liking, but
its simple language invites us to see something infinitely larger in the promised separation, what Housman calls 'the sum of things' in another poem.[30] The parting words of
these friends need not sound different when spoken, so that the difference of meaning between 'Farewell' and 'Fare well' belongs primarily to the page, where it serves to
undermine the preceding line's heavily loaded assertion that they parted 'stiff and dry'.
Or, the speaker's parting words keep back the truth that, even in parting, these friends
don't agree. There's also, I think, a hint of what remains unspoken by one of them: 'Fare
you well, for ill fare I'.[31]

The final two stanzas imagine a scene in the future, when the speaker will be dead
and buried and the friend he loved may visit his grave. There's something odd to
begin with about a *siste viator* poem that addresses one reader only. There has been
a lot of discussion of line 14, which Housman's drafts show he laboured over. Variant
readings include 'The heart by nothing stirred', 'The heart that is not stirred', and
'The heart no longer stirred'. All of them say that the speaker's heart is stock-still
because he is dead, and any of them would have been clearer in its meaning than the
line Housman settled on: 'The heart you have not stirred'. The change in the tense
of the verb to past perfect tells the same truth (no dead man's heart can be stirred)
but also pushes the line in the direction of a lie: my heart never was 'stirred' by you.
The lie is the one his friend wants to hear and the one that keeps the promise the
speaker made all those years ago. Like the good soldiers in *A Shropshire Lad*, he does
the brave thing because he has engaged to do it. Kenneth Millard reads the poem as
'a drama which tells of not telling',[32] but a better point is surely that the poem does
its telling for those who have ears to hear, which may not include the friend being
addressed. The last stanza presents a good example of having your cake and eating it
too. The speaker denies his love for his friend but also directs the friend to remember him as 'the lad that loved you'.

Housman would have had Tennyson's *Maud* in mind when he wrote his last stanza,
although the reminiscence of Tennyson may not rise to the level of an allusion:

> She is coming, my own, my sweet;
> > Were it ever so airy a tread,
> My heart would hear her and beat,
> > Were it earth in an earthy bed;
> My dust would hear her and beat,
> > Had I lain for a century dead;
> Would start and tremble under her feet,
> > And blossom in purple and red.[33]

The most obvious contrast is between Tennyson's mad lover's confidence that his love survives death and Housman's speaker's view that death puts an end to life, a view his poems express with tenacious consistency. Housman's speaker is morbid yet sane, and thwarted yet resigned. In 'The Name and Nature of Poetry' Housman declined to define poetry but named 'the class of things to which it belongs': 'I should call it a secretion; whether a natural secretion, like turpentine in the fir, or a morbid secretion, like the pearl in the oyster'.[34]

The poem I have been examining is a morbid secretion, a pearl. One of the other poems produced by the same irritation is 'The New Mistress', a poem in which a woman's rejection of her lover propels him to enlist:

> 'Oh, sick I am to see you, will you never let me be?
> You may be good for something but you are not good for me.
> Oh go where you are wanted, for you are not wanted here.
> And that was all the farewell when I parted from my dear.'[35]

Here, the woman and her lover play roles analogous to, but quite distinct from, those played by the friends in 'Because I liked you better'. 'The New Mistress' will not yield much to a reader in search of biographical information, but it can serve to remind us that while Housman's parting from Moses Jackson supplied an irritation, the achievement of his poems required and reveals considerable detachment from both his own feelings and his own experience.

I want to look at the less well known and also less successful poem that immediately precedes 'Because I liked you better' in *More Poems*. It was also composed at around the same time, that is, the time when Housman was writing the poems published in *A Shropshire Lad*.

> Shake hands, we shall never be friends; give over:
>   I only vex you the more I try.
> All's wrong that ever I've done and said,
> And nought to help it in this dull head:
>   Shake hands, goodnight, goodbye.
>
> But if you come to a road where danger
>   Or guilt or anguish or shame's to share,
> Be good to the lad that loves you true
> And the soul that was born to die for you,
>   And whistle and I'll be there.[36]

Although no one actually speaks in this poem, two voices with distinctively different tones inhabit it. The first voice belongs to the poem's speaker, who is talking to himself ('give over') as much as to his friend ('I only vex you the more I try'). The second belongs to the speaker as well, but it is a voice tuned so as to mimic the voice of the friend he is addressing. This is a voice that has affinities with the voices of the poems in *A Shropshire Lad*, not Housman's but Terence's or another character's, and it is a voice readers have either loved or hated. It has a range of tones, some of which have reminded readers of Rudyard Kipling's *Barrack-Room Ballads* (1892). In 'Shake hands, we shall never be friends; give over' the solemn constraint of one voice yields to the tired language and pat cadences of the other in the last line of the first stanza. The tone of 'Shake hands, goodnight, goodbye'—the only line in the poem with a good swat on every other syllable—is a false tone, much too glib and chipper to express the stupid ('dull') condition of someone whose love is unrequited and who yet stands waiting to be called into service. The plot is the same as the plot of Michael Drayton's poem 'Since there's no help, come let us kiss and part'. So: a first stanza in which one man says farewell to another, and a second in which he reveals that their parting can always be rescinded and that his love endures and is always available for recovery. We can anticipate the sense of the second stanza, at least as soon as we hear the 'But' with which it begins. The only reward this speaker can imagine for himself is that his friend will turn to him in a future time of trouble, and this hope is open to the charge of sentimentality as well as to the suspicion that it is tainted by Schadenfreude. Yet although the speaker submits to the conditions of the friendship or refusal of friendship forced upon him by sinking the tones of his own voice in those of his friend, the poem bears witness to the violence of his capitulation. These two speakers are worlds apart, and the poem knows it.

Except in his light verse, Housman rarely writes regularly anapaestic verse. He understood the dangers for serious poetry of its 'simple and rather shallow music',[37] and he uses anapaests knowingly in his poems. In 'Oh, who is that young sinner with the handcuffs on his wrists?'—one of the poems inspired by the spectacle of Oscar Wilde's trial in 1895—the anapaestic first foot doesn't appear until the fourth line of the first stanza. Thereafter, lines begin with the anapaest much more regularly than with the iamb. One effect of the regular iambs in the first feet of the poem's first three lines is to emphasize the who, what, and wherefore of the scene these lines describe:

> O who is that young sinner with the handcuffs on his wrists?
> And what has he been after that they groan and shake their fists?
> And wherefore is he wearing such a conscience-stricken air?
> Oh they're taking him to prison for the colour of his hair.[38]

In taking 'the measure of the poem's *saeva indignatio*', a reader will be helped not only by some knowledge of the precedents with respect to hair colour and the prejudices against it,[39] but also by the anapaests that introduce almost every line of the poem as soon as the speaker stops asking questions and starts vilifying the prisoner and savouring the punishments awaiting him. The momentum of the anapaestic opening perfectly suits the banal brutality of these ideas and feelings. It's a rhythm that seems made to sing the speaker's romping delight in pain inflicted arbitrarily and grotesquely:

> 'Tis a shame to human nature, such a head of hair as his;
> In the good old time 'twas hanging for the colour that it is;
> Though hanging isn't bad enough and flaying would be fair
> For the nameless and abominable colour of his hair.

In the long lines of this poem, as in those of 'The New Mistress', Housman's metre may be best described as dipodic. These lines can be scanned as iambic, but when they are read aloud, the stresses in them are regular but not equally strong. In performance, four strong stresses alternate with four weaker stresses. The driving rhythm of these poems connects them to ballads as well as to drinking and marching songs. The same metre, complete with initial anapaests, is an unsurprising choice for the Mock Turtle's song to accompany the Lobster-Quadrille in *Alice in Wonderland*.

Housman's metrical technique has more often been harshly criticized than admired, and notably by Pound, who said it was formed predominately on the system of '*ti Tum ti Tum ti Tum*'.[40] Yet Housman's metres, like his drafts, show how intensely he laboured over some of his poems in order to achieve a wide range of very precise effects. This is an aspect of his poems' difficulty that he was himself fully aware of. Consider the Laura Matilda stanza, so called because it is the stanza of 'Drury's Dirge', a poem attributed to 'Laura Matilda' and published in Horace and James Smith's popular book of parody poems, *Rejected Addresses* (1812). 'I believe I am too fond of the Laura Matilda stanza, which I think the most beautiful and the most difficult in English,' Housman wrote in a letter to J. W. Mackail.[41] The Laura Matilda stanza is a quatrain made up of four-beat lines, with alternating feminine and masculine rhymes. In *The Cambridge History of English Poetry*, Nicholas Shrimpton describes it as made up of 'trochaic tetrameters, rhymed abab, with the second and fourth lines truncated to give masculine rhymes'.[42] In Pound's notation, we could describe it as *Tum ti Tum ti Tum ti Tum* (or *Tum ti Tum ti Tum ti Tum ti* in lines where there are feminine endings). Housman used this stanza rarely—twice in *A Shropshire Lad* and once in both *Last Poems* and *Additional Poems*—but he used features of it in a great many poems, especially alternating masculine and feminine rhymes and stresses on the first syllable of a line. 'Reveille' is one of the two poems in *A Shropshire Lad* written in Laura Matilda stanzas. It was also one of Housman's poems selected for *The Times Broadsheets* and distributed to soldiers and sailors on active duty in 1915:

Reveille

Wake: the silver dusk returning
　Up the beach of darkness brims,
And the ship of sunrise burning
　Strands upon the eastern rims.

Wake: the vaulted shadow shatters,
　Trampled to the floor it spanned,
And the tent of night in tatters
　Straws the sky-pavilioned land.

Up, lad, up, 'tis late for lying:
　Hear the drums of morning play;
Hark, the empty highways crying
　'Who'll beyond the hills away?'

> Towns and countries woo together,
>   Forelands beacon, belfries call;
> Never lad that trod on leather
>   Lived to feast his heart with all.
>
> Up, lad: thews that lie and cumber
>   Sunlit pallets never thrive;
> Morns abed and daylight slumber
>   Were not meant for man alive.
>
> Clay lies still, but blood's a rover;
>   Breath's a ware that will not keep.
> Up, lad: when the journey's over
>   There'll be time enough to sleep.[43]

What is it that made the Laura Matilda stanza, in Housman's view, 'the most beautiful and the most difficult in English'? The difficulty of the stanza and its beauty are of a piece. One is surprised to see it done at all, and then more surprised to see it done well and done in a poem that is neither light nor satiric. Trochaic metres in general are far less common than iambic metres in English verse, including Housman's, although they are a feature of many songs and nursery rhymes. 'There is a widespread perception among poets and prosodists that trochaic meters are in some way more rigid, more brittle, "more difficult to maintain" (Hascall) than iambic ones'.[44] The still greater brittleness of the Laura Matilda stanza, its exclusion of variant feet, and particularly of anapaests, increases its difficulty. So does the requirement that fully 20 per cent of the poem's syllables participate in its rhymes. That every other line of the stanza has more stresses than slacks adds to its difference from ordinary English speech and to the demands it makes on the poet.

Housman's title calls attention to his poem's metre because it is, wittily, a dactyl: 'reveille', with its French etymology and its English pronunciation, is a word that Scott writes as 'reveillie' in *Old Mortality*, and Kipling as 'Revelly' in *Barrack-Room Ballads*. Other features of 'Reveille', especially its diction, also emphasize its Englishness. Some of the poem's most memorable lines are composed entirely of words that encode a native English language history: 'Clay lies still, but blood's a rover; / Breath's a ware that will not keep'. I doubt that many soldiers would have understood 'thews that lie and cumber / Sunlit pallets'. 'Thews' is an Anglo-Saxon word, and 'cumber' a Middle-English one that was obsolete when Housman composed his poem. The lines that follow in the quatrain provide a gloss: 'Morns abed and daylight slumber / Were not meant for man alive'. Another feature of this poem is the kind of alliteration that recalls an Anglo-Saxon poem, binding together the first and second halves of a line divided by a strong caesura. 'Forelands beacon, belfries call' is a good example of such a line, and it is also made up entirely of native words. These formal elements of the poem—diction, alliteration, and metre—work together to supply the sense of history that rides on the surface of a poem like *ASL*, xxxi ('On Wenlock Edge the wood's in trouble'), also selected for distribution to British troops. 'Reveille''s progress from its first word ('Wake') to its last ('sleep') repeats the progress of many of Housman's poems, but peace, darkness, and sound sleep are not the rewards this poem promises. Housman or Housman's poems—the distinction is not always clear—have often been accused of rejecting life, but the world of 'Reveille' is full of more satisfactions than any man can hope to enjoy. The poem celebrates the lures to action and the pursuit of pleasure and adventure. Housman took considerable pains with this poem, and it must have given him considerable pleasure to write it.

This was not the kind of difficulty that T. S. Eliot had in mind when he stipulated difficulty as the condition for modern poetry. The straightjacket of the Laura Matilda stanza is an extreme example of the dislocation of language generated by rhyme and metre, a dislocation from speech which Pound decried and which Housman both celebrates and uses all of his resources to combat. The play of voices in Housman's poems supplies their most compelling difficulty and distinguishes them from the poems of his contemporaries, but it does not make them modern poems. His poems look backwards, not forwards, seeking 'something in man which is obscure and latent, something older than the present organization of his nature, like the patches of fen which still linger here and there in the drained lands of Cambridgeshire'.[45] J. M. Coetzee glosses 'fens' in his Nobel Prize address: 'Fens are tracts of wetland. There are tracts of wetland all over Europe, all over the world, but they are not named fens, *fen* is an English word, it will not migrate'.[46] Housman's poems are as English as bubble and squeak. They contain too much that is foreign even to an American reader to travel lightly. It is an irony of poetry's history that Housman's claim here, which includes his reaching out to those in the past, especially the Roman past of England, was also Eliot's claim, the claim of a man who chose to become English.

Notes

1. A. E. Housman, *The Letters of A. E. Housman*, 2 vols., ed. Archie Burnett (Oxford: Clarendon Press, 2007), ii. 93.
2. Housman, *Letters*, ii. 252.
3. Housman, *Letters*, ii. 499, 501.
4. A. S. F. Gow, *A. E. Housman: A Sketch* (Cambridge: Cambridge University Press, 1936), 52.
5. Housman, *Letters*, ii. 93.
6. Marilynne Robinson, *Housekeeping* (New York: Bantam Books, 1982), 153.
7. A. E. Housman, *A Shropshire Lad* xl and li in *The Poems of A. E. Housman*, ed. Archie Burnett (Oxford: Oxford University Press, 1997).
8. Housman, *ASL*, li in *Poems*.
9. Housman, *More Poems*, xxxv in *Poems*.
10. Alfred Tennyson, *The Poems of Tennyson*, 3 vols, ed. Christopher Ricks (London: Longman, 1969, rpt. 1987), ii. 390.
11. Housman, ASL xxiii and xix in *Poems*.
12. W. H. Auden, 'Jehovah Housman and Satan Housman', in Christopher Ricks, ed., *A. E. Housman: A Collection of Critical Essays* (Englewood Cliffs: Prentice-Hall, 1968), 33.
13. Housman, *More Poems* xxii, in *Poems*, 439.
14. Housman, *Additional Poems,* vi in *Poems*.
15. Auden, 'A. E. Housman', in *Critical Essays*, 11.

16. Peter Howarth, 'Housman's Dirty Postcards: Poetry, Modernism, and Masochism', *PMLA*, 124 (2009), 769.
17. Housman, *Letters*, ii. 308.
18. Howarth, 'Housman's Dirty Postcards', 766; Housman, *Letters*, i. 378.
19. Howarth, 'Housman's Dirty Postcards', 767–9.
20. F. W. Bateson, 'The Poetry of Emphasis', in *Critical Essays*, 130–1.
21. *Poems*, 446.
22. Archie Burnett, 'Silence and Allusion in Housman', *Essays in Criticism*, 53 (2003), 162.
23. Northrop Frye, 'Approaching the Lyric', in Chaviva Hosek and Patricia Parker, eds., *Lyric Poetry Beyond New Criticism* (Ithaca: Cornell University Press, 1985), 32.
24. Norman Page, *A.E. Housman: A Critical Biography* (New York: Schocken Books, 1983), 6.
25. Philip Larkin, 'All Right When You Knew Him', in *Required Writing* (New York: Farrar Straus Giroux, 1982), 265.
26. Ezra Pound, 'Mr. Housman's Message', in *Critical Essays*, 12.
27. Randall Jarrell, 'Texts from Housman', in *Critical Essays*, 51–61.
28. Carol Efrati, *The Road of Danger, Guilt, and Shame* (Madison, NJ: Associated University Presses, 2002), 320.
29. Housman, *ASL* xliv and n.353 in *Poems*.
30. Housman, *ASL* xxxvii in *Poems*.
31. Housman, *ASL* xlvii in *Poems*.
32. Kenneth Millard quoted in Burnett, 'Silence and Allusion', 162.
33. Tennyson, *Maud*, in *Poems of Tennyson*, ii. 565.
34. Housman, 'The Name and Nature of Poetry', in Christopher Ricks, ed., *A. E. Housman: Collected Poems and Selected Prose* (London: Penguin, 1988), 370.
35. Housman, *ASL* xxxiv in *Poems*.
36. Housman, *More Poems* xxx in *Poems*.
37. Housman, 'Swinburne' in *Ricks, A. E. Housman: Collected Poems and Selected Prose*, 283.
38. Housman, *AP* xviii in *Poems*.
39. Ricks, 'A.E. Housman and "the colour of his hair"', *Essays in Criticism*, 47 (1997), 240–55.
40. Pound, 'Mr Housman at Little Bethel', in *Polite Essays* (London: Faber and Faber, 1937), 27.
41. Housman quoted in *Poems*, 322.
42. Nicholas Shrimpton, 'Later Victorian Voices', in Michael O'Neill, ed., *The Cambridge History of English Poetry* (Cambridge: Cambridge University Press, 2010), 696.
43. Housman, *ASL* iv in *Poems*.
44. Alex Preminger and T. V. F. Brogan, eds., *The New Princeton Encyclopedia of Poetry and Poetics* (Princeton: Princeton University Press, 1993), 1309.
45. Housman, 'The Name and Nature of Poetry', in *A. E. Housman: Collected Poems and Selected Prose*, 369.
46. J. M. Coetzee, 'He and His Man'—accessible online at <http://www.nobelprize.org/nobel_prizes/literature/laureates/2003/coetzee-lecture-e.html>

Select Bibliography

Bayley, John, *Housman's Poems* (Oxford: Clarendon Press, 1992).
Burnett, Archie, 'Silence and Allusion in Housman', *Essays in Criticism*, 53 (2003), 151–173.
Douglas-Fairhurst, Robert, in P. J. Marshall, ed., 'A. E. Housman's Rejected Addresses', *Proceedings of the British Academy* (Oxford: Oxford University Press, 2007), 83–111.

Efrati, Carol, *The Road of Danger, Guilt, and Shame* (Madison, NJ: Associated University Presses, 2002).

Gow, A. S. F., *A. E. Housman: A Sketch* (Cambridge: Cambridge University Press, 1936).

Housman, A. E., *The Letters of A. E. Housman*, 2 vols., ed. Archie Burnett (Oxford: Clarendon Press, 2007).

—— *The Poems of A. E. Housman*, ed. Archie Burnett (Oxford: Oxford University Press, 1997).

Howarth, Peter, 'Housman's Dirty Postcards: Poetry, Modernism, and Masochism', *PMLA*, 124 (2009), 764–81.

Page, Norman, *A. E. Housman: A Critical Biography* (New York: Schocken Books, 1983).

Reckford, Kenneth, 'Stoppard's Housman', *Arion*, 9 (2001), 108–49.

Ricks, Christopher, ed., *A. E. Housman: A Collection of Critical Essays* (Englewood Cliffs: Prentice-Hall, 1968).

—— ed., *A. E. Housman: Collected Poems and Selected Prose* (London: Penguin, 1988).

—— 'A. E. Housman and "the Colour of his Hair"', *Essays in Criticism*, 47 (1997), 240–55.

Stallman, Robert W., 'Annotated Bibliography of A. E. Housman: A Critical Study', *PMLA*, 60 (1945), 463–502.

....

CHAPTER 38

RUDYARD KIPLING PLAYS THE EMPIRE

....

PETER HOWARTH

'I AM not a poet and never shall be,' admitted Kipling to his future wife Carrie in 1889, 'but only a writer who varies fiction with verse.'[1] Many of Kipling's best readers have feared something similar. Writing 'verse' to vary the fiction implies that the fiction was the real interest; 'the value of writing English verse', Kipling later advised, 'is that it makes you handier in writing prose—gives you more words and better command over 'em'.[2] And the assumption that 'verse' is a kind of artistic Sandhurst suggests Kipling's interest was more in enforcing obedience than developing a poet's sensibility. 'Kipling was not trying to write poetry at all', T. S. Eliot warned, if we mean by poetry the lyric's concentrated expression of interior feeling:

> We expect to have to defend a poet against the charge of obscurity: we have to defend Kipling against the charge of excessive lucidity…We expect a poet to be ridiculed because his verse does not appear to scan: we must defend Kipling against the charge of writing jingles.[3]

Kipling's obviousness, Eliot proposes, stems from his un-modern conception of how poems should be made. His own method was to balance conscious intention with the unconscious suggestions of meaning offered by the music of the form. Kipling began with a meaning and used his form to drive it home; he had, as a younger and more hostile Eliot put it, 'an idea to impose', and he imposed it 'in the public speaker's way, by turning the idea into sound, and iterating the sound'.[4] Being a 'public speaker' meant Kipling also denied the cardinal modern principle that a true poem can have no obvious persuasive design on its reader. To be the free experience unique to proper art, poems should allow the reader to enter a state of balanced impulses with no one of them predominating.[5] For E. M. Forster, the difference between Kipling's prose and his verse was just this difference in mental and political attitude:

> His stories in prose…are strung together on a thread of criticism; both sides of the question are given us, and we are not informed which is the right side. His stories in verse are compacted of passion: one side only is given, nor while we read do we remember that another may exist. It is this that gives the Narrative poems their magic.[6]

The criticism is concealed within the praise, for though Kipling is real poetry, 'magic' implies a manipulative force directed against the reader's will, sapping our power to criticize. To Auden, Kipling's verse-form was the 'esthetic corollary' of his militaristic imperialism, which entailed the suspension of democracy under a state of emergency:

> His virtuosity with language is not unlike that of one of his sergeants with an awkward squad…Under his will, the vulgarest words learn to wash behind their ears and to execute complicated movements at the word of command, but they can hardly be said to think for themselves.[7]

Kipling himself meant the distinction between poet and versifier a little differently, though. His fiancée had been thinking about what a shared life with this successful, volcanic, suspicious young genius might mean for her. Whatever she imagined being a writer's wife would mean, exploded Kipling, it wasn't that:

> You wrote, Mademoiselle, some stuff—not to put too fine a point upon it—some ABJECT DRIVELLING ROT—LUNACY—BOSH—!—on the subject of *All in A Garden Fair* and your views about poets and sympathy, culled from the pages of Walter Besant…Heart's heart, that sort of thinking about sympathy to be given to me, is like the letting in of waters. In the first place I am not a poet and never shall be—but only a writer who varies fiction with verse.[8]

Besant's novel is about the growth of a poet's mind as he becomes a professional writer, and it had been Kipling's own inspiration to quit his Indian newspaper job and come to London to make his name three months previously. But Besant's plot turns on the heroine's realization that she can never marry the poet, because poets are so perpetually needy: 'He wants continually the encouragement, praise and sympathy which a woman looks for from her husband. Without this support, he would droop, and fall into melancholy and distrust.'[9] Kipling had melancholy and distrust aplenty, but clearly felt that the sympathy of a woman who 'will enter into your thoughts, and understand your work, the manner and meaning and *technique* of it', would sink him.[10] And if not being a poet meant refusing anyone's sympathy, it also meant refusing the division built into Besant's plot between the poet Allen and his high-minded circle, all followers of Art, and the practical man, Will, who eventually returns from overseas to marry the heroine:

> Allen's eyes had, more than ever, the far-off expectant look of one who lives in imagination. Will's more than ever the steady, watchful look of one who works. His

eyes were like the eyes of a pilot for trusty watch and ward. For him, the world was full of work to be done, and it was no place for dreams.[11]

To be a writer and not a poet, for Kipling, meant doing Will's work in Allen's form, refusing the division between a free but rarified high art and the unimaginative practical life of the many. It meant being guarded, not expressive, and guarding oneself, kept awake by a sense of continuing threat largely unnoticed by the majority. No coincidence that as he was writing this letter to Carrie, he was putting together the first parts of *Barrack-Room Ballads*.

The distinctiveness of that famous volume for Kipling's poetics, though, is not just in its innovative use of 'vulgar' language, or its sympathy towards the ordinary private, or its use of various ballad forms to make the poems easily taken up by people who would never normally think poetry had anything for them. In a letter written the same day as the one to Carrie, Kipling remarked to Addington Symonds that 'if you see Macmillan's you may find that Yussuf has been writing Border Ballads', in this case, 'The Ballad of East and West'.[12] The first line of the refrain, 'East is East, and West is West, and never the twain shall meet' has unfortunately become a shorthand summary of the imperial racism that Kipling's poetics supposedly promote: the line was made into an entire justification for British colonialism by no less than Lionel Dunsterville, the original of 'Stalky', in his address to the Kipling Society.[13] But the tale of the hard-fought duel between the border-thief Kamal and the gallant British Colonel's son was meant to say the opposite: '*But there is neither East nor West, Border, nor Breed, nor Birth, / When two strong men stand face to face, though they come from the ends of the earth!*'[14] The equality between fighting men is Kipling's version of universal brotherhood, and its echo of Jesus's warning to the chosen in Matthew 8:11 ('and I say to you that many will come from East and West, and take their places at the feast') rebukes British assumptions that they alone were a new chosen race. By signing it 'Yussuf', the Islamic version of his own first Christian name 'Joseph', Kipling was signifying to the readers of *Macmillan's* that they might not be able to tell quite whose side the newly arrived writer of this ballad was taking, either. 'One View of the Question', a story he was at work on at the same time, takes the point of view of a Muslim spy to make criticisms of English degeneration which are indistinguishable from Kipling's own view of the case. Such prickly ambivalence is a hallmark of *Barrack-Room Ballads*, and of so much of Kipling's verse before and after it. Civilization is threatened and must be guarded, but to be one of the guards often means identifying more with your opponent than with 'home'. This is the counterpart of the frontier mentality of the Anglo-Indian world Kipling had just come from, always dismissive of Indian moves towards self-rule, but equally fearful that the home country which underwrote their superiority was about to betray them, and needed stiffening up. Attacking both sides often makes Kipling's message less than obvious, as the prophet of Empire who frequently hated England itself.

And though the verse form still seems to drill its words into compliance, as Auden complained, the way its forms ask to be performed frames those commands rather differently. Kipling never took the stance of the lyric poet writing in solitude whose internal authenticity is preserved because his readers merely overhear him, and he had little interest in the publishing model which backs up this story, the slim volume issued in small quantities which hopes one day to be recognized by the discerning few. Coming from a more threatened location, within or without, Kipling's poetry was always written to stir, and he needed more immediate forms of distribution for it, publishing in newspapers, pamphlets, and broadsides, and encouraging oral retransmission by using music hall, comic-song and hymn-settings, duly taken up by composers, churches, and the organizers of military parades.[15] Critics of the fiction have often noticed the tension between Kipling's would-be dominant frame narrator and the ungovernable, inflected, and dissonant voices within the tales, and found there evidence of his unconscious sympathy with the colonized which the official part of him is resisting.[16] That tension between character and narrator is not nearly so present in the poems, which is perhaps why they seemed more one-dimensional to Forster, and colonial propaganda to many others. But the formal tension of Kipling's poems opens up instead in the gap between the group solidarity suggested by the form's intended performance situation, and the discomforting attitude of the words themselves, pitting performers against audience, and audience against each other. If Kipling's poems frequently try to unite the nation by identifying an enemy, their manner of performance just as quickly suggests that the 'They' being blamed also exist here, now, among 'Us'. The baffling diversity of perspective Kipling's speakers employ has led both David Bromwich and Jan Montefiore to call him a modernist-in-waiting.[17] But no matter whose voice he is adopting, that sense of challenge to friend and foe remains a constant.

From the start, writing had been for Kipling an affair of attack and defence. In *Something of Myself*, he relates how the perpetual interrogations of the rabidly evangelical 'Aunty' with whom he had been sent to board in England made reading an act of self-preservation, and talking an act of self-preservation under threat. Her one aim was to catch him out; his lifelong revenge on her was to really *become* the liar she accused him of being, a tale-teller and inventor of fictions.[18] Rescued from the boarding-house, Kipling was much happier at the United Services College celebrated in *Stalky & Co.*, but being sensitive, clumsy, and myopic, he could never be one of the strong, practical boys for whom the school was designed, the offspring of service families all destined for military careers of their own.[19] Through the merciless sarcasm of his Classics and English teacher, on the other hand:

> I came to feel that words could be used as weapons...and our year-in year-out bickerings gave us both something to play with. One learns more from a good scholar in a rage than from a score of lucid and laborious drudges...I discovered, also, that personal and well-pointed limericks on my companions worked well, and I and a red-nosed boy of uncertain temper exploited the idea—not without dust and heat.[20]

Battle and India are both proverbially the places of dust and heat, and the resonances of the final phrase suggests that writing verse satire was Kipling's way of joining his fellows on the frontier. A 1912 address to schoolboys preparing for military career extended the analogy between writing and fighting. 'Many of you are going to enter what is called the

the life of action, in which you will discover that you will have to think harder, closer and quicker than the bulk of men who take up what is so kindly called 'the intellectual life', Kipling remarks, apparently in self-criticism. But in fact, literature turns out to be the best training of all:

> You will have to guess... at what is going on behind the next hill... and you will have to think what is in the mind of the man who is opposed to you. And you must do that in life as well as in the Service... We can pick up from Literature a few general and fundamental ideas as to how the great game of Life has been played by the best players.[21]

If Life itself is a battle won by those who can second-guess their opponents, Kipling implies, then an ability to pick up the smallest hint of the plot, or sympathize with an elusive character will be vital for success. And the echo of *Kim* in the final sentence continues the suggestive analogy between imperial spycraft and the game Kipling saw his own writing playing. Thinking of life as a game makes everything in it a manoeuvre. What you see is never indifferent or 'natural', but always a sequence of potentially important signs—though these signs may have been put there deliberately to trick you. (In that respect, the spy's world has a similar effect to the charged atmosphere of Kipling's ghost stories, where there are no unobserved observers.) The writer-spy's reward is to see through the ordinary events of life and detect the hidden nets tightening, an insight which gave continual impetus to Kipling's securocratic politics. The price is living in a world of permanent threat, either from opponents without or from your own desires giving themselves away. Yet if Kim is a figure for the artist, the implication is that the reader is, temporarily, his opponent, the enemy-double necessary for the game to continue. The obscurities of Kipling's fiction, then, are practice in learning to play the game. One soon learns that friends are not to be believed, that obvious action is a feint, and that each innocent event will need to be re-read to perceive its real significance for the plot. Kipling may have felt drawn to the idea of writing as spy-game, not only because it reflected his guarded emotional life and his politics, but because it requires his reader to adopt the same alert, suspicious point of view.

Though they are not about spying as such, the feeling of move, bluff, and counter-move permeates Kipling's first volume of poems, the *Departmental Ditties*. Written for circulation among the soldiers and civil servants of Anglo-India, they not only reveal, of course, that Indians only ever intrigue to their own advantage ('A Legend of the Foreign Office', 'What Happened'), but also that the upholders of civilization and fair play are more interested in status battles than they are in governing well. In this world of favouritism, the chance of promotion outweighs truthfulness ('The Man Who Could Write'), promises ('The Post That Fitted'), and love ('Study of an Elevation', 'Pink Dominoes'). This is true even at the top: 'One Viceroy Resigns' counsels the incomer that since governing India is all guesswork, his priority should be his own reputation: 'accept on trust and work in darkness, strike / At venture, stumble forward, make your mark, / (It's chalk on granite)'.[22] Unsurprisingly, the Simla government had brought the ordinary Indian very little either. 'The Masque of Plenty' turns their official reports into scenes from a courtly masque, those entertainments which took place in the seats of power to make a play out of the works of good governance. But in Kipling's version, even the 'HIRED BAND' sing off-key:

> God bless the Squire
> And all his rich relations
> Who teach us poor people
> We eat our proper rations—
> We eat our proper rations,
> In spite of inundations,
> Malarial exhalations,
> And casual starvations[23]

Not only does this implicitly recognize that the Empire is the feudal system writ new, the word 'rations' also makes the peasants into soldiers, meaning the poor are not hungry because of the Indian climate, but because the Empire itself has taken their labour and failed to feed them enough. In 'What the People Said', the same peasant is indifferent to the coming of all Empires:

> Mogul, Mahratta and *Mlech* from the North,
> And White Queen over the Seas—
> God raiseth them up and driveth them forth
> As the dust of the ploughshare flies in the breeze[24]

The missing 'the' before 'White' is both a tic of Indian English and a deft piece of indifference: what does it matter who or what she or they are, if the Empire will in turn be ploughed over? No wonder these verses displeased the higher latitudes of the Simla administration, who thought them bad for morale.[25]

But the remarkable thing is that Kipling managed to please so many of the middle-ranking civil servants, while suggesting that they also do nothing but intrigue, and that their work will come to nothing. Only in Death will the truly incorruptible civil service finally be established, in 'The Last Department':

> When leave, long overdue, none can deny;
> When idleness of all Eternity
>   Becomes our furlough, and the marigold
> Our thriftless, bullion-minting Treasury[26]

It's a curious message; first, you had better put up with the frustrations of corrupt management because it's better than being dead, but second, carrying on means knowing that your own survival is of no particular value to the system. 'Trust me, Today's Most Indispensables, / Five hundred men can take your place or mine', it concludes, and the perfectly regular form amplifies that sense of everything coming in replaceable units. The satires on love present another version of the same two-sided attitude. Since women are usually playing a double game in some way ('Delilah', 'The Story of Uriah'), the natural response of the Departmental man is wariness ('Certain Maxims of Hafiz'). Yet the bachelor speaker of 'The Betrothed', famously sure that 'a woman is only a woman, but a good Cigar is a Smoke', is not really one of us either.[27] Unlike white women, he reflects, cigars demand 'nought in return / With only a *Suttee's* passion—to do their duty and burn'. Since the banning of suttee had been one of the most symbolic markers of British justice and its right to rule, the voice of the cynical Anglo-Indian bachelor is now closer to Hindu patriarchy than to his own side.

Most of the *Departmental Ditties* were first published in the pages of the Lahore *Civil and Military Gazette*—some of them were direct responses to the news itself elsewhere in the paper—and their satirical accounts of sexual intrigue, political in-fighting and government incompetence are all well-tried journalistic means for working up the readers' interest by putting them in the know and in the right.[28] But when put side by side, not all their perspectives are compatible, and the volume's original readers must at some point have experienced themselves betraying the values of the implied audience (the hard-working middle-rankers fed up with poor management) to pass as a member of another (the doubter of British justice, the worldling who knows life is only a game). In fact, this pleasurable sense of keeping an internal, interior difference from one's own side was designed into the book's format. Kipling's account suggests he wanted to publish it after soldiers told him it was being 'sung to banjoes around camp fires, and...had run as far down the coast as Rangoon and Moulmein, and up to Mandalay'.[29] But when Kipling put the volume together, the binding and cover took it far from the campfire ethos. The book was:

> A lean oblong docket, wire-stitched, to imitate a D. O. Government envelope printed on one side only, bound in brown paper, and secure with red tape. It was addressed to all heads of department and all government officials, and among a pile of papers would have deceived a clerk of twenty years' service.[30]

Apparently hand-written, the envelope actually read 'To All Heads of Department and all Anglo-Indians'. Somewhere between the underground school magazine and an official government report into corruption, these were poems to be illicitly enjoyed at work, under the noses of one's more dutiful, or unwary, colleagues.

KIPLING AND THE MUSIC HALL

'Nov 15th...Dined at the Italian restaurant and after dinner concluded to go to Gatti's Music Hall. This opened a new world to me and filled me with fresh thoughts—surely the people of London require a poet of the Music Halls.'[31] Why did the music halls so catch Kipling's imagination, following his move to London? After all, it was a substantial jump from the Anglo-Indian insiderism of *Departmental Ditties* to verse adapting the comic monologues and catchy choruses of what was the biggest-selling and most spectacular form of entertainment in the world at the time. A simple answer is that the music halls were the ideal place to make art out of soldiers. Following the shambles of the Crimea, the Victorian army had undertaken a comprehensive reformation of its organization and its reputation. Turning the soldier into a figure of public respect required a new public visibility through parades, pageants, and ceremonies like trooping the colour, or by making drill a form of public entertainment using recently professionalized military bands playing music-hall tunes. In search of a bit of respectability itself, the music hall returned the favour by making the soldier a regular feature on the bill, either in song, or in person, transforming his image from ruffian to loveable rogue, and soon the epitome of national strength through self-discipline and self-sacrifice. Of course, music hall's taste for melodrama worked well with accounts of brave soldiers confronting evil foes, and the swords, uniforms, and explosions of battle-scenes provided ample fare to satisfy the halls' taste for the spectacular. But it was not uncommon to bring real soldiers on stage to perform drill, either, or to trade on public sympathy by involving decorated veterans of the colonial wars in Afghanistan, Sudan, and later, South Africa, the real Empire starring at the Empires, as it were.[32] Though the halls had been by now transformed from home-made entertainment of the working classes to luxurious, mixed-class entertainment venues, the older tradition of raising support for deserving cases continued, and the comic-tragic monologues about veterans in hard times provided ample material for sympathy, sometimes becoming fund-raising opportunities themselves. This was the situation for which Kipling's astonishingly popular song, 'The Absent-Minded Beggar', was written, raising money for the families of men fighting in the Boer War. A precursor of today's charity pop-song spectacular, Kipling and Sullivan's royalties were waived in favour of donations to the *Daily Mail*'s fund, allowing the song to be taken up by every current star who would sing it to encore after encore. During its rollicking chorus of 'pay—pay—pay!', the hats were passed round, ensuring shame on everyone who didn't publicly contribute, and an opportunity to star for anyone who gave something obviously big.[33]

That song's unsubtle manipulation of theatrical situation to support an imperial war cemented the connection in many people's minds between Kipling's music hall-inspired forms, his popularity, and his coercion. Many early reviews had called him 'vulgar', with implications of swagger and poor taste: the 'cheap effects' of *Barrack-Room Ballads*, said one, come because Kipling 'has the true contagion of the best Music-hall patter song of the hour'.[34] To Orwell, worried about groupthink, it was more sinister: reading Kipling 'gives one the same sensation as one gets from watching a third-rate Music-hall performer', a crude, compulsive vitality leaving the individual feeling 'seduced by something spurious, yet unquestionably seduced'.[35] Even the historian of music hall, Peter Bailey, describes it as Kipling's 'perfect bully-pulpit', because its 'ritual antiphony of posture and response, inherited from melodrama with its hagio-demonology of heroes and villains' encouraged tribalistic patriotism, 'a form of incantatory collective self-admiration among audiences flushed with enthusiasm for themselves'.[36]

But it is just this ebullient atmosphere which would be instantly punctured by a singalong to many of the *Barrack-Room Ballads*. Imagine the families of servicemen catching the final verse of 'The Young British Soldier':

> When you're wounded and left on Afghanistan's plains
> And the women come out to cut up what remains,
> Jest roll to your rifle and blow out your brains
> An' go to your Gawd like a soldier.[37]

The cheerful horror makes this an initiation song for the mess-room, not the music hall, the fellowship of those tough enough to admit things inadmissible in public—except, of course, it is being published so the public can eavesdrop. Indeed, 'Snarleyow' was candid enough about the mercy killing of the wounded to draw criticism from the doughtiest of Boer War opponents, W. T. Stead. It was Stead who first called the Boer War a 'Music-hall' war, and blamed Kipling for encouraging it.[38] An early number of his campaign paper, *War against War,* printed the following verses:

> But chain up your Kipling roarer,
> And muzzle your swaggering Joe,
> And chain up your mad Press prophets,
> Your gamblers cocksure 'in the know'.
>
> Your hypocrites yelling and clapping,
> With their iron, and fire, and cant,
> Their Bibles, and bullets explosive,
> Their Music-hall conquering rant![39]

But the news of Kipling's journey to South Africa and the success of 'that miserable production, the "absent-minded beggar" ' spurred him to protest against Kipling for *slandering* the troops:

> Mr Kipling's 'gin-nosed muse' has created the 'most vulgar of all our modern rhymesters'...He pursues Tommy into all his weaknesses and vices, and makes jingling rhymes about them all. According to Kipling, the British soldier is an insensate debauchee, a drunkard, and a mere human machine, to be moved about and destroyed at will by a Government that treats him like 'a little whipped dog'. The picture is disgusting and disheartening did not many of us happily know it to be utterly untrue.[40]

If even Stead could find Kipling's attitude insulting, then the Ballads were clearly not ideal fodder for music-hall jingoism.

In truth, Kipling's attraction to the music hall stemmed as much for its possibilities for creative antagonism than for national unity. Becoming a 'poet of the Music-halls' meant cocking a snook at the Oxbridge-educated and Wildean aesthetic circles in which he had been received on his arrival in London, and whom he cordially hated. Though he was already socially and artistically well connected thanks to his Burne-Jones cousins, the letters of 1889–90 show him always isolating himself, taking the part of the trade artist facing down a world of arrogant coterie theorists and rip-off publishers, or the hard-headed colonial who knows that the art and leisure of the society he is being entertained by depends on the very colonies they wished to jettison.[41] And he reported back to his Indian readership that, despite the music hall's vulgar reputation, the audience are perfectly respectable, 'no better and no worse than folk who require fifty girls very much undressed, and a setting of music, or pictures that won't let themselves be seen on account of their age and varnish, or statues and coins'.[42] High Art, classical antiquity, cheap titillation, and the music-hall song are all equally forms of look-but-don't-touch entertainment, purchased to transport their viewers into regions normally unattainable. The gratifications offered by the halls were the honest truth behind drawing-room pre-tentions to disinterested leisure, and their scorn of the vulgar and obvious.

But if music hall meant taking the people's side against the elite, it equally meant the performers squaring up against their own audience. In 'My Great and Only', the story of his own attempts to write a music-hall hit, Kipling concludes with the hope that some-day, someone will write songs that are 'coarse, but clear-sighted, hard but infinitely and tenderly humorous, speaking the people's tongue, and telling them in swinging, urging, dinging verse what it is that their inarticulate lips would express'.[43] The fear underneath this manifesto is magnified by the military and hunting metaphors which structure the story's climax:

> Through the roar in my ears I fancied I could catch a responsive hoofbeat in the gallery. The next four lines held the house to attention. Then came the chorus and the borrowed refrain. It took—it went home with a crisp click. My Great and Only saw his chance. Superbly waving his hand to embrace the whole audience, he invited them to join in... I had my house hooked—gaffed under the gills, netted, speared, shot behind the shoulder—anything you please. That was pure joy![44]

This is an audience not quite realizing they are being *baited*: the 'crisp click' of success might imply a gate-key, a trigger, or a rifle-bolt, but it is not the tone of being all pals at the Palace.

Making music-hall dynamics the animating poetic of *Barrack Room Ballads*, then, meant making songs which incite their audience against the respectable, only to then make them something of a target too. Aesthetes are taken into the mess-room to hear songs which relish their offences against good taste ('"Birds of Prey" March', 'The Widow's Party') as a way of admitting the real horror of fighting life. Experiencing their performance, read or heard, then becomes one of the unpleasant initation rites Kipling's fiction is so fond of. A would-be patriotic audience, on the other hand, hear soldiers who are either reprobates, angry, or unconsolable, and often thoroughly fed up with the England listening to them. And this sense of discomfort between the soldiers on stage and their audience opens up an essential dimension of what the songs are about: the feeling of army privates that they are more menaced by those on their own side than the enemy. Take a song like 'Screw-Guns', whose chorus is a singalong:

> For you all love the screw-guns—the screw-guns they all love you!
> So when we call round with a few guns, o' course you will know what to
>   do—hoo! hoo!
> Jest send in your Chief an' surrender—it's worse if you fights or you runs:
> You can go where you please, you can skid up the trees, but you don't get
>   away from the guns![45]

The brisk triple rhythm brings audience and screw-gunners swaying in unison together against the other side. But by verse three, the 'you' has shifted, and the guns have turned on their own:

> If a man doesn't work, why, we drills 'im an' teaches 'im 'ow to behave.
> If a beggar can't march, why, we kills 'im and rattles 'im into 'is grave.
> You've got to stand up to our business an' spring without snatching or fuss.
> D'you say that you sweat with the field-guns? By God, you must lather
>   with us—'Tss! 'Tss!

The big drum beating the footsoldiers along in 'Route Marchin'' is at first telling everyone else on the Grand Trunk Road to get out of the way. But its pidgin-Hindustani phrase also picks up the privates' scarcely suppressed resentment at the army itself, forcing them on and on with 'every bloomin' campin'-ground exactly like the last'.[46] Kipling's translation of '*Kiko kissywarsti* don't you *hamsher argy jow*?' was not 'why don't you get out of the way?' but 'why don't you get on?' which makes its question directed at the soldier as much as the civilian: no wonder they hear it half in the language of the colonized.

One significance of calling these poems 'Ballads' is that by adopting the even, relentless pace of the ballad forms for stories of contemporary soldiers, Kipling makes the relentless work of army duty take the place of the inexorable fates that drive the older ballad heroes to fight and die. Nothing can halt the advance of the guns in 'Snarleyow', not even injured soldiers they run over, nothing will wait decently for the maiden to mourn in 'Soldier, Soldier', and nothing can stop the regiment from hanging Danny Deever. Adopting the ballad's question-and-answer form between the sergeant and the men during drill so draws out the eventual revelation of *why* the sergeant 'looks so white' that the delay becomes the emotional crux of the poem:

> They are hangin' Danny Deever, you must mark 'im to 'is place,
> For 'e shot a comrade sleepin'—you must look 'im in the face;
> Nine 'undred of 'is county an' the Regiment's disgrace,
> While they're hangin' Danny Deever in the mornin'.[47]

The ambiguous 'you' of the second line suggests the men are being forced to look Danny in the face because he wouldn't shoot face-to-face himself. Eyes front, they must watch him choking, 'black against the sun', not spared the results of their own justice, and the rhythmic performance of the ballad in time to the marching forces the audience to pay attention at someone else's pace as well. And if the Private-to-Sergeant questions of the song are patterned on the Maiden-to-Sailor mess-room bawdy of 'Barnacle Bill the Sailor', as Carrington believed, then an unstated equation is being made between the soldiers being forced to watch the execution, and the maiden being raped.[48] The same trick is pulled in 'Ford o' Kabul River', where the up-and-at-'em tune of 'Tramp, Tramp, Tramp, The Boys are Marching' echoes ironically through the chorus as the singer tries not to think about the men being swept away like his friend:

> Ford, ford, ford o' Kabul river,
> Ford o' Kabul river in the dark!
> There's the river up an brimmin', an' there's 'arf a squadron swimmin'
> 'Cross the ford o' Kabul river in the dark.[49]

Forster felt that the comic rhyme between 'brimmin'' and 'swimmin'' rang a false note here, for Kipling's appeal to his audience overwhelmed what a private soldier would ever really say.[50] But as the marching rhythm is in deliberate contrast to the men who have lost their pace and their footing, so the incongruous rhymes are someone trying to cheer himself up, and cheer an audience up. By being sung to this tune, as it is meant to, the song is flagging its unsuitability for the public performance it is currently receiving.

This audience-needling in Kipling's performances also extends to one of the most infamous ballads, 'Loot', with its advice to 'treat a nigger to a dose of cleanin'-rod' in order 'to pay yourself for fightin' overtime'. Orwell thought there was no sign in Kipling's work that he disapproved of the sentiment, but bearing in mind Kipling's incandescent fury at the piracy of his fiction copyrights at the time this song went to press, surely it is the scripted stage-directions of the final chorus which lend the edge:

> (*Chorus*) Yes, the loot,
>   Bloomin' loot!
> In the tunic an' the mess-tin an' the boot!
>   It's the same with dogs and men,
>   If you'd make 'em come again
> (*fff*) Whoop 'em forward with a Loo! loo! Lulu! Loot! loot! loot!
> Heeya! Sick 'im, puppy! Loo! loo! Lulu! Loot! loot! loot![51]

If you take the soldier's side and sing along, you become one of the 'dogs and men' in the process of being carefully whooped forward with the prospect of 'Loo! loo! Lulu!': pack hounds, whose safety is in numbers. The mixture of nastiness and jollity in these poems is not meant to stop the English identifying with their soldiers, then, but it makes the identification happen through fear as much as sympathy, taking the audience into unsafe territory.

As Kipling's vision of Empire as moral regeneration became predominant, his fear of inner collapse grew stronger. The enemy were not only at the gate ('For All We Have and Are') but already within, stirred up by German spies, Irish traitors, suffragettes, and socialists, and the later poems continue to search out that threat by testing the permanent battle-readiness of every reader. 'Recessional' turns its attack on the Diamond Jubilee celebrants, and their trust in weapons, 'Captains and Kings'.[52] But though the poem counsels repentance for one's faith in weapons and armies, and was used in a peace service at Westminster Abbey, its real purpose was not to turn from militarism, but to strike renewed fear into Kipling's own nation. Even its publication in *The Times* was a coup, compared by one correspondent to a poker game: 'you have let the others show their hand... and then when the last grand stand came down, and the "incident was closed", you came out with your four aces'.[53] The ulcerated 'Epitaphs of the War' were meant to be another unanswerable challenge, rounding not only on cowards, statesmen, and stay-at-homes, but on those who presume to stop and shed a tear as well. The uncharacteristic, almost Imagist brevity of 'An Only Son', for instance, is designed to leave the passerby with nothing to say which would not be presumptuous: 'I have slain none except my Mother. She / (Blessing her slayer) died of grief for me.'[54] Even in 'The White Man's Burden' of 20 years before, the British had offered the United States no actual triumph, only the 'thankless' task, 'the blame of those ye better, / The hate of those ye guard'.[55] If that poem has 'Stand Up, Stand Up for Jesus' under its breath, as Mattinson suspects, then the note of bitterness grows stronger still, for the hymn promises cheerfully that 'the fight shall not be long', whereas Kipling's empire heroes can only warn that 'when your goal is nearest', you must 'Watch Sloth and heathen Folly / Bring all your hope to naught'. There can be no end to the fight in Kipling—perpetual wakefulness is, perhaps, the trouble with belonging to the Empire on which the sun never sets—and never more than at the moment of triumph.

'If' is, of course, the most famous version of this perpetual struggle, with its unresolvable tension between the competitive appetite of the whole poem, and the indifference to Triumph and Disaster, success and obscurity counselled by the parts. Just when you think you have succeeded in life, the poem guarantees you will be failing again by not being indifferent to triumph, disaster, and so forth. But something of the same trap is sprung on Kipling's critics in the much more liberal-sounding 'We and They'. Its Stevensonian nursery-rhyme tone pokes fun at the British for not realizing they are a tribe like any other, with peculiar customs of dress and food:

> But if you cross over the sea,
> Instead of over the way,
> You may end by (think of it!) looking on We
> As only a sort of They![56]

Here, the Empire will end up by alienating its own centre. How true, thinks the good critic, and why could Kipling not realize how much his hostility to Indians and Africans, his pumped-up imperial manliness, his dread of women and the unconscious, were driven by the same need to reinforce a 'They' against a 'We'? And instantly, the poem has provoked another We and They, those who understand its ironies, opposed to the unwitting They who don't, the stance celebrated by the 'Ballad of East and West' as fellowship through combat. Kipling's cunning is that, even in opposing him, you may find yourself playing his game.

Notes

1. *The Letters of Rudyard Kipling*, ed. by Thomas Pinney, 6 vols (London: Macmillan, 1990–2004), I: *1872–89* (1990), 379.
2. Kipling, *Writings on Writing*, eds. Sandra Kemp and Lisa Lewis (Cambridge: Cambridge University Press, 1996), 98.
3. T. S. Eliot, 'Rudyard Kipling', *A Choice of Kipling's Verse* [1941] (London: Faber and Faber, 1963), 8 ('Kipling'), 6 ('We expect...').

4. T. S. Eliot, 'Kipling Redivivus' [1919], *Rudyard Kipling: The Critical Heritage*, ed. by Roger Lancelyn Green (London: Routledge and Kegan Paul, 1971), 323.

5. A Coleridgean principle crystallized in I. A. Richards, *Science and Poetry* (London: Kegan Paul, Trench, Trübner, 1926), 34.

6. E. M. Forster, 'Kipling's Poems' [1909], ed. by Michael Lackey, *Journal of Modern Literature* 30:3 (2007), 12–30 (15).

7. W. H. Auden, 'A Poet of the Encirclement' [1943], *Prose*, II: *1939–48*, ed. by Edward Mendelson (London: Faber, 2002), 202.

8. *Letters*, I, 379.

9. Walter Besant, *All in a Garden Fair*, new edn. (London: Chatto and Windus, 1890), 303.

10. Besant, *All in a Garden Fair*, 306.

11. Besant, *All in a Garden Fair*, 277.

12. *Letters*, I, 380.

13. Lionel Dunsterville, 'Kipling's India', *Critical Heritage*, 373.

14. Rudyard Kipling, 'The Ballad of East and West', *Complete Verse: The Definitive Edition* (London: Hodder and Stoughton, 1989), 233.

15. For evidence of the variety of Kipling's publishing formats, see David Alan Richards, *Rudyard Kipling, A Bibliography* (New Castle, Delaware: Oak Knoll and The British Library, 2010), especially the checklist of musical settings by Brian Mattinson (E4, 691–726). For parades, see Ann Parry, *The Poetry of Rudyard Kipling* (Buckingham: Open University Press, 1992), 79.

16. e.g. Zohreh T. Sullivan, *Narratives of Empire: The Fictions of Rudyard Kipling* (Cambridge: Cambridge University Press, 1993), 33–37.

17. David Bromwich, 'Kipling's Jest', *A Choice of Inheritance* (Cambridge, MA: Harvard University Press, 1989), 186. Jan Montefiore, *Rudyard Kipling* (Tavistock: Northcote House, 2007), 113.

18. Andrew Lycett, *Rudyard Kipling* (London: Weidenfeld and Nicolson, 1999), 50.

19. See Charles Allen, *Kipling Sahib: India and the Making of Rudyard Kipling* (London: Little, Brown, 2007), 96–107.

20. Kipling, *Something of Myself* (London: Macmillan, 1937), 32–33.

21. 'The Uses of Reading', *Writings on Writing*, 66–67.

22. Kipling, *Complete Verse*, 69.

23. Kipling, *Complete Verse*, 37.

24. Kipling, *Complete Verse*, 66.

25. Allen, *Kipling Sahib*, 269.

26. Kipling, *Complete Verse*, 21.

27. Kipling, *Complete Verse*, 49.

28. Andrew Rutherford, 'News and the Muse: Press Sources for Some of Kipling's Early Verses', in *Kipling 86*, ed. Angus Ross (Brighton: University of Sussex Library, 1987), 38–56.

29. 'My First Book', *McClure's Magazine* 3: 6 (November 1894), 564.

30. 'My First Book', 564.

31. *Letters*, I: 366.

32. See Dave Russell, '"We carved our way to glory": the British soldier in music hall song and sketch, c. 1880–1914', in *Popular Imperialism and the Military, 1850–1950*, ed. J. M. MacKenzie (London: Macmillan, 1992), 50–79. The Moss Empires were the largest chain of Music-halls in Britain at the time.

33. John Lee, 'Following Kipling's "The Absent-Minded Beggar"', *Kipling Journal* 85:341 (April 2011), 6–26.
34. Francis Adams, 'Mr Rudyard Kipling's Verse', *Fortnightly Review* 54:283 (November 1893), 590–603 (596–97).
35. 'Rudyard Kipling', in Elliott Gilbert, ed., *Kipling and the Critics* (London: Peter Owen, 1965), 85.
36. Peter Bailey, 'Kipling's Bully Pulpit: Patriotism, Performance and Publicity in the Victorian Music Hall', *Kipling Journal* 85:341 (April 2011), 28–41 (37).
37. Kipling, *Complete Verse*, 416.
38. Bailey, 'Kipling's Bully Pulpit', 31.
39. Ouida, 'To England', *War Against War*, Friday 3 November, 1899, 33.
40. 'The Gin-Nosed Muse of Kipling', *War against War*, 26 January 1900, 235. Stead is quoting an unnamed correspondent: 'little whipped dog' is from the refrain of 'Snarleyow'.
41. See the bitter 'Letters on Leave', *Abaft the Funnel* (New York: Doubleday, Page, 1909), 203–04.
42. 'My Great and Only', *Abaft The Funnel*, 265–266.
43. 'My Great and Only', 273.
44. 'My Great and Only', 269–270.
45. Kipling, *Complete Verse*, 416.
46. Kipling, *Complete Verse*, 423.
47. Kipling, *Complete Verse*, 396.
48. *The Complete Barrack-Room Ballads of Rudyard Kipling*, ed. by Charles Carrington (London: Methuen, 1973), 161.
49. Kipling, *Complete Verse*, 420.
50. Forster, 'Rudyard Kipling', 19–20.
51. Kipling, *Complete Verse*, 409.
52. Kipling, *Complete Verse*, 327.
53. Letter from Richard Harding Davies, 16 July 1897, Kipling Papers, Wimpole Archive, University of Sussex Special Collections SxMs38/2/2/2/3/5/23.
54. Kipling, *Complete Verse*, 385.
55. Kipling, *Complete Verse*, 323.
56. Kipling, *Complete Verse*, 769.

Select Bibliography

Charles Allen, *Kipling Sahib: India and the Making of Rudyard Kipling* (London: Little, Brown, 2007)
Peter Bailey, 'Kipling's Bully Pulpit: Patriotism, Performance and Publicity in the Victorian Music Hall', *Kipling Journal* 85:341 (April 2011), 28–41.
Baucom, Ian, *Out of Place: Englishness, Empire and the Locations of Identity* (Princeton, NJ: Princeton University Press, 1999).
Bratton, J. S., ed., *Music-hall: Performance and Style* (Milton Keynes: Open University Press, 1986)
Bromwich, David, 'Kipling's Jest', *A Choice of Inheritance* (Cambridge, MA: Harvard University Press, 1989), 170–196.

Carrington, Charles, ed., *The Complete Barrack-Room Ballads of Rudyard Kipling* (London: Methuen, 1973)

Gilbert, Elliott, ed., *Kipling and the Critics* (London: Peter Owen, 1965), particularly essays by Lewis, Orwell, Trilling, and Jarrell.

Kipling, Rudyard, *Writings on Writing*, ed. by Sandra Kemp and Lisa Lewis (Cambridge: Cambridge University Press, 1996)

Lootens, Tricia, 'Victorian Poetry and Patriotism', in *The Cambridge Companion to Victorian Poetry*, ed. by Joseph Bristow (Cambridge: Cambridge University Press, 2000), 255–280.

Lycett, Andrew, *Rudyard Kipling* (London: Weidenfeld and Nicolson, 1996).

Mackenzie, J., ed., *Popular Imperialism and the Military, 1850–1950* (Manchester: Manchester University Press, 1992)

Martin, Meredith, *The Rise and Fall of Meter: English Poetry and National Culture, 1860–1930* (Princeton, NJ: Princeton University Press, 2012)

Montefiore, Jan, *Rudyard Kipling* (Tavistock: Northcote House, 2007).

Parry, Ann, *The Poetry of Rudyard Kipling* (Buckingham: Open University Press, 1992).

CHAPTER 39

....

VICTORIAN YEATS

....

PETER MCDONALD

IN 1933, the young Irish poet Austin Clarke kept an appointment with his senior contemporary, W.B. Yeats, in order to discuss undertaking a Life of the by then famous writer. Clarke's project came to nothing; or rather, what it came to eventually was a poem rather than a biography, for thirty-five years later he published 'In the Savile Club', where conversation between the younger and the older man goes from awkwardness to chill:

> I groped around the Nineties.
>   'Mr Yeats,
> In order—as it were—to understand
> *The Wind among the Reeds*, those exquisite
> Love lyrics, can I venture to ask what is—
> If I may say so—their actual basis in
> Reality?'
>   How could I know a married
> Woman had loosened her cadent hair, taken him,
> All candlestick, into her arms?
>   A stern
> Victorian replied:
>   'Sir, do you seek
> To pry into my private affairs?'[1]

Clarke's anecdote (though it is also something more than that) serves as a reminder that W. B. Yeats did not just stop being a Victorian when the 'Victorian' period of history or literature came to an end. There is an important sense in which the poet was a Victorian all along. In that, Yeats was hardly unusual, and Clarke's conversational blunder might have been committed with scores of other celebrated people at that time. It is an understandable blunder for all kinds of reasons—not least, because Yeats's love poetry from the 1890s seems to accommodate a moderate degree of biographical curiosity from its readers. In the twentieth century, too, the poet had by this point proved himself a prolific autobiographer, and one whose subject was especially the life he had lived in the last Victorian decades. Clarke's 'I groped around the Nineties' makes a poetic felicity out of an infelicitous moment: there is no groping, assuredly, in *The Wind Among the Reeds* (1899), for those particular 'love-lyrics' are as determinedly 'exquisite' about what exactly they reveal of 'private affairs' as they are exquisitely erotic in their intense evocations of the love (and loves) from which they arise. 'I groped' is painfully awkward in that context—wonderfully so, as though it were a planned faux pas. Nobody knows where to look.

To look at W.B. Yeats and see a Victorian poet—or at any rate, to see a Victorian— is inevitably a little unsettling. In terms of the conventional literary-historical categories, it is also rather lacking in glamour: there is none of the exciting glare and flash of Modernism, which demands a certain dullness in its Victorian background for the brightness of its own lustre. The poet of 'Coole Park and Ballylee, 1931' did not, after all, announce of his generation, 'We were the last Victorians.'[2] A chronological perspective on all this is clear enough: born in 1865, Yeats lived for almost half his days in the reign of Queen Victoria (and as her subject, moreover); he was publishing his own poetry at the same time as new volumes were appearing from Tennyson and Swinburne, Patmore and Morris. By the beginning of the twentieth century, books of his like *Poems* (1895 and 1899) and *The Wind Among the Reeds*, along with collections of folklore (such as *The Celtic Twilight* (1893)) and short fiction (*The Secret Rose* (1897)) and plays including *The Land of Heart's Desire* (1894), as well as a multitude of critical essays and reviews, had made Yeats a fairly well-known writer on the contemporary scene. At the time, his 'Victorianism' was an obvious matter, if an utterly unremarkable one; later on, it was subjected by the poet himself to a series of radical switches of critical perspective.

Yeats's many retrospectives on his earlier years were in the service of creative ambitions that demanded a great gulf to exist between Victorian and modern civilization, in Ireland as in Britain. The series of substantial autobiographical writings that begins with *Reveries over Childhood and Youth* (1916) paints a vivid picture of a culturally distant world, from which the poet would seem to have made his escape. By the time of his *Oxford Book of Modern Verse* Introduction, just a couple of years after the interview with Clarke, Yeats felt able to look down on Victorianism from a very great height, identifying himself and his generation of artists with what he called the 'revolt' against it:

> The revolt against Victorianism meant to the young poet a revolt against irrelevant descriptions of nature, the scientific and moral discursiveness of *In Memoriam*—'When he should have been broken-hearted', said Verlaine, 'he had many reminiscences'— the political eloquence of Swinburne, the psychological curiosity of Browning, and the poetical diction of everybody: Poets said to one another over their black coffee—a recently imported fashion—'We must purify poetry of all that is not poetry'...Poetry was a tradition like religion and liable to corruption, and it seemed that they could best restore it by writing lyrics technically perfect, their emotion pitched high, and as Pater offered instead of moral earnestness life lived as 'a hard gem-like flame' all accepted him for master.[3]

Aestheticism as the form of anti-Victorian 'revolt' is in significant part a useful interpretation of Yeats's own, for by the 1930s, the poet needed to divide himself not just
from the Victorian period but from his own generation, which he cast as (in one autobiographical title) *The Tragic Generation*, and from whose dangers and artistic beliefs, it
seemed, Yeats alone had escaped. As the Introduction puts it: 'Then in 1900 everybody
got down off his stilts; henceforth nobody drank absinthe with his black coffee; nobody
went mad; nobody committed suicide; nobody joined the Catholic church; or if they did
I have forgotten.'[4]

This particular retrospective, with its sweeping—and foreshortening—comedy of
prejudice, is justly celebrated. But the writing's manners are not by any means those of
1936: there is a certain irony in the (unmistakeable) presence behind the prose-style
here of Yeats's non-surviving Victorian acquaintance, Oscar Wilde. And it's worth comparing that Paterian flame with the kinds of poetic lighting Yeats himself saw fit to recommend in the 1880s and 1890s: 'Modern writers', he wrote in 1892, 'have been heavily
handicapped by being born in a lyrical age, and thereby compelled for the most part to
break up their inspiration into many glints and glimmers, instead of letting it burn in
one steady flame.'[5] If that flame is lit directly from Pater's *The Renaissance*, it is also fed
from the one that burns behind the poetry of Shelley: in Yeats's far from scholarly essay
'The Philosophy of Shelley's Poetry' (1900) he wrote:

> I think too that as he knelt before an altar, where a thin flame burnt in a lamp made
> of green agate, a single vision would have come to him again and again...and
> that this one image, if he would but brood over it his life long, would lead his soul,
> disentangled from unmeaning circumstance and the ebb and flow of the world,
> into that far household, where the undying gods await all whose souls have become
> simple as flame, whose bodies have become quiet as an agate lamp.[6]

Yeats's prose style here, it might be thought, carries more than a hint of absinthe and
black coffee. But 'the ebb and flow of the world' is acknowledged, even as it is accommodated to the burning of that 'thin flame'; 'unmeaning circumstance', too, is a concept that has to be grasped before it can be dismissed. Undoubtedly, the young Yeats
was aware of the modernity of the times in which he lived, and the lamp of agate which
he wanted to light is part of a rejection of a contemporary Victorian world of other,
more garish, lights. At the end of an 1891 review, Yeats acknowledged 'the body and
pressure of time' which 'has brought us the last degradation and mingled us with
the dust', and offered a peroration (against one unfortunate Mr. Leland, an offend-
ing author), the Victorianism of which—in condemnation of the Victorian age—is
impeccable:

> Because we hurry over the ground at sixty miles an hour, and may some day do so
> at a hundred and sixty, with a penny comic paper in our hands and our nerves awry
> from the crush at the ticket-office, we are not proved, in spite of Mr. Leland, wholly
> to over-top Merlin, or to be wise as Faustus or the Centaur Chiron or he that met his
> image walking in a garden. We are made great not by the things we do or have done
> to us but by the thing we are in ourselves.[7]

The sentiments, like the world being reported upon, are closely aligned to the main-stream of mid- and late nineteenth-century social and cultural critique, and could easily belong to William Morris or, only a little further back, Matthew Arnold, John Ruskin, or Thomas Carlyle. Merlin and the rest make for a less familiar company in this respect, though; and their presence alongside a high-speed rail link, the 'penny comic paper', and the jostle for tickets is meant to disconcert. 'He [*sic*: Yeats's syntax here evidently defeated *The National Observer*'s sub-editor] that met his image walking in the garden' is not exactly someone to be encountered in a Victorian ticket-office: as Yeats knows, and as he is aware that only some of his readers will know, he is Shelley's Magus Zoroaster, from *Prometheus Unbound*.[8] If 'the thing we are in ourselves' retains a faintly Arnoldian ring, its context is radically altered by elements such as these.

'The thing we are', for Yeats, is always in some measure a secret thing. By the 1890s, Yeats's writing was becoming ever more visibly an inscription of various kinds of *arcana*—folkloric, mythological, magical, and personal—but in idioms that declared the most profoundly traditional of allegiances. This is as true of Yeats's poems as of his other work. In a poem that first appeared in *The Countess Kathleen and Various Legends and Lyrics* (1892), Yeats famously invokes three Irish nineteenth-century predecessors; but he goes on to align them with visions far removed from anything which they them-selves could ever be imagined to have seen:

> *Nor may I less be counted one*
> *With Davis, Mangan, Ferguson,*
> *Because to him who ponders well*
> *My rhymes more than their rhyming tell*
> *Of the dim wisdoms old and deep,*
> *That God gives unto man in sleep.*
> *For round about my table go*
> *The magical powers to and fro.*
> *In flood and fire and clay and wind,*
> *They huddle from man's pondering mind,*
> *Yet he who treads in austere ways*
> *Must surely meet their ancient gaze.*[9]

Thomas Davis, James Clarence Mangan, and Sir Samuel Ferguson have little in com-mon other than their being Irish: it is very hard to conceive of a poetic taste which would find the radically differing styles of all three to its liking. And not Yeats's taste, either, for his difficulty in appreciating the mechanical (if patriotic) versifying of Davis made that poet's 'Young Ireland' propaganda (of the 1840s) a sometimes awkward issue in the Irish cultural circles of Yeats's early years. Mangan, by whom Yeats was fascinated, and whose verse had an influence on his own lyric forms, was long dead, and little known outside Ireland; Ferguson (best-known in Victorian Britain for his strenuous early poem 'The Forging of the Anchor', but most important for the young Yeats as the author of epics drawing upon Irish mythological materials, such as *Congal* and *Conary*) made an important exemplar for the young poet, but was a poetic influence which he rap-idly outgrew.[10] For all that, what Yeats's poem is doing here with Irish poetic history is a good example of his way of bringing a common tradition into contact with something much more individual and esoteric: in doing so, he creates a kind of two-way traffic, and this is as true of his relation to Victorian poetry generally as it is to his three chosen Irish poets. In the case of this poem, the reader is asked to look from the familiar names to the stranger 'magical powers' and 'dim wisdom' that 'Round about my table go'. Once looked at, these will prove to be looking in the reader's direction (as in Yeats's) already: 'he who treads in austere ways / Must surely meet their ancient gaze'. Any young man's poem will often have the implicit message, 'Look at me'; that is no less true here, but Yeats cultivates attention as well as simply courting it, and is training it to see the unknown behind the known. A contemporary vision is the means of asserting a timeless—or 'ancient'—visionary capacity, in which Irish distinctiveness from the metropolitan bustle of Victorian Britain is absolutely necessary. As Yeats puts it in the dedication to his collection of stories, *The Secret Rose* (1897): 'So far...as this book is visionary it is Irish...no shining candelabra have prevented us from looking into the darkness, and when one looks into the darkness there is always something there.'[11]

In terms of his own perspective on Victorian poetry, Yeats was not always so unequivocally in revolt as his later accounts would suggest. The ability to see things in the darkness, for example, by turning the eyes of the imagination away from the glaring lights of modernity, was something which Yeats's early journalism was ready to accord to senior as well as junior contemporaries. It may be a surprise to those who know best the later Yeats to learn that in 1892 he named as 'the greatest romantic poem of the century' Tennyson's *Idylls of the King*.[12] That was to a British audience just after Tennyson's death, but even while the Laureate was still alive Yeats could write of him just as approvingly in an American publication, making him seem a natural recruit to the Celtic supernaturalist cause:

> The Irish peasant believes the whole world to be full of spirits, but then the most distinguished men have thought not otherwise. Newspapers have lately assured us that Lord Tennyson believes the soul may leave the body, for a time, and communicate with the spirits of the dead. The Irish peasant and the most serene of Englishmen are at one. Tradition is always the same. The earliest poet of India and the Irish peasant in his hovel nod to each other across the ages, and are in perfect agreement.[13]

The fanciful picture is nevertheless an interesting one: modern rationalism is merely something that blocks the view, and the most famous modern poet is able to regard and to be regarded by the world's believers in 'tradition' in the most equable fashion. Ireland was offered by Yeats as a portal to the past—'westward', he wrote in 1890, 'the second century is nearer than the nineteenth';[14] and Tennyson himself might be said to have passed through this particular gateway, in his poem 'The Voyage of Maeldune', published in 1880 and an influence on the young Yeats. 'The earliest poet of India' was not, in fact, a creature wholly of the youthful Yeats's imagination—at least, not necessarily more so than was 'the Irish peasant in his hovel': both were important cultural accessories for a new writer seeking to make good his niche in the Victorian literary marketplace. *The Wanderings of Oisin and Other Poems* (1889) contains 'An Indian Song', the dialogue

'Jealousy' set in '*A little Indian temple in the Golden Age*', 'Kanva on Himself', and 'Kanva, the Indian, on God'—this last a poem in rhymed alexandrines that seem to aspire to a faintly Tennysonian grandeur of movement, though not in the event achieving this in any very convincing way. The poem's climactic conclusion might just—though only just—escape bathos:

> I passed a little further and I heard a peacock say:—
> 'Who made the grass and made the worms and made my feathers gay,
> He is a monstrous peacock, and He waveth all the night
> His languid tail above us, lit with myriad spots of light.'[15]

The average Irish peasant would have had to come quite a long way out of his hovel, and get as far as the gardens of the nearest Big House, to recognize this: but Yeats's intention, at any rate, is to get Eastern and Western poetic images in sight of one another, with Victoria's Laureate, too, somewhere within nodding distance.

Such moments of poetic intensity in Yeats's early work may sometimes seem a little too dazzling. To go no further than decorative wildfowl, even the peacock's 'myriad spots of light' might have rendered the poet fatally inattentive, as an early ill-wisher (probably the Irish political journalist and orator J. F. Taylor) pointed out apropos of 'An Indian Song', where 'on each lea / The pea-hens dance', by saying that he was 'tempted to wish that [Yeats] would study the ways of poultry'.[16] Peacocks might (in a manner of speaking, at any rate) 'dance'; but not peahens—and telling a peacock from a peahen, even for the short-sighted, is not after all too difficult. Interestingly, Yeats's private response (to his mentor, the senior Fenian figure John O'Leary) made it clear that his peahens were Indian—'they dance throughout the whole of Indian poetry… The wild peahen dances or all Indian poets lie'.[17] This suggests that one answer to the question of how closely Yeats took notice of things he saw would be that he allowed—more or less deliberately—poetry to crowd his vision: in this case, he saw not peahens, but images from Indian poets.

It is reasonable to suppose that the one Indian Yeats actually knew in the late 1880s might have been more sympathetic to such views on poultry. Mohini Chatterjee, a Theosophical envoy sent in 1886 from the court of Madame Blavatsky to the small circle of Yeats's young acquaintances who were styling themselves the Dublin Theosophical Society, was to have a lifelong influence on Yeats, prompting tributes (in verse as well as in prose) into the 1930s. Chatterjee is the model for 'Kanva' in the early poems, and is accorded the first of his numerous retrospective portraits by the Victorian Yeats of 1900. Here 'the coming of a young Brahmin into Ireland' is read as a symbolic moment, but his accompanying luggage includes more than just Eastern wisdom: 'he came with a little bag in his hand and *Marius the Epicurean* in his pocket'. There is something Paterian about anyone who can, as Yeats puts it, 'hold that we lived too much to understand the truth or to live long', and something distinctively late-Victorian, too, about Chatterjee's insistence on the necessity of re-directing the attention from outward things:

> And once, when we questioned him of some event, he told us what he seemed to
> remember, but asked us not to give much weight to his memory, for he had found

that he observed carelessly. He said, 'We Easterns are taught to state a principle carefully, but we are not taught to observe and to remember and to describe a fact. Our sense of what truthfulness is is quite different from yours.' His principles were a part of his being, while our facts, though he was too polite to say it, were doubtless a part of that bodily life, which is, as he believed, an error.[18]

Here is a man who might be unreliable on the behaviour of peafowl; but unreliable on principles very similar to Yeats's own. The imperatives of 'observe...remember...describe' have no particular force in Yeats's poetic theories, and are closer to those forces against which his early art is in reaction. In Yeats's hands, a visionary poetry is not the same as a poetry of faithful observation, whether for good or ill.

'The Wanderings of Oisin', the narrative poem intended by Yeats as the kick-start for his poetic career, is pointedly not a work of any kind of realism, visual or otherwise. The story of Oisin's three centuries of time-out from the mortal world, and his sojourns (with Niamh, his lover from the world of Faery) on islands of dancing and happiness, feasting and fighting, and finally slumber and dreaming, is plainly an allegorical one, even though the allegory itself is not plain; yet the main point of Yeats's poem lies as much in its style as in its dark meaning (or meanings). The elements of that style are not wholly Yeats's own—Keats, Tennyson, Swinburne, and Morris, as well as the nearer to home Ferguson, are often here, but their combination is distinctively that of an original poet, capable of producing something simultaneously of its time and profoundly new. In this, the rejection of any realist aesthetic proves crucial.

Near the beginning of 'Oisin', Yeats sets out to describe the otherworldly Niamh—though the style of this description is itself not quite of the usual descriptive world:

> Her eyes were soft as dewdrops hanging
> Upon the grass-blades' bending tips,
> And like a sunset were her lips,
> A stormy sunset o'er doomed ships.
> Her hair was of a citron tincture,
> And gathered in a silver cincture;
> Down to her feet white vesture flowed
> And with the woven crimson glowed
> Of many a figured creature strange,
> And birds that on the seven seas range.
> For brooch 'twas bound with a bright sea-shell,
> And wavered like a summer rill,
> As her soft bosom rose and fell.[19]

The visual difficulty of this is hard to miss: the 'dew-drops' provide a visual image for something ('Her eyes') described initially as 'soft', but do not really tell us much about what 'soft' eyes would really look like—and if we were to stick stubbornly to visualization in our reading here, the detail of 'grass-blades' bending tips' would suggest that Niamh has eyes on stalks.[20] Instead, Yeats wants readers to receive images on top of other images, in turn, which provide not accounts of, or equivalents to, what Oisin can see, but a series of suggestions and impressions which, like moment coming upon moment, weave and unweave the picture. Niamh's lips, then, do not in any real sense resemble a 'sunset'—Yeats's word 'like' intends much more than this, for the picture in this case is one of storm and doom, with 'ships' again adding an image that is visually irrelevant, even though in itself strongly visual. So, what does 'like' mean, and do, in this context? In 1889, Yeats was still three years from publishing 'The Rose of the World', with its conjunction of lips and the destruction of Troy ('For these red lips, with all their mournful pride, / Mournful that no new wonder may betide, / Troy passed away in one high funeral gleam'), as well as 'The Sorrow of Love' ('And then you came with those red mournful lips, / And with you came the whole of the world's tears, / And all the sorrows of her labouring ships'), but the lines in 'Oisin', like these, are clearly a calling-up of Marlowe's Helen, and her 'face that launched a thousand ships / And burnt the topless towers of Ilium'.[21] The 'ships', of course, are summoned by rhyme also; and this 'lips'/ 'ships' rhyme had worked for Yeats even before 'Oisin', in his Arcadian drama of 1885, 'The Island of Statues', where the Trojan Aeneas is seen 'With all his ships' leaving Dido, 'Enamoured of the waves' impetuous lips'.[22] Almost at once, the speaker of the rhyme is told that 'The faery blossom lies upon thy lips'—a line that reveals some of the poetic *provenance* here, for it is in Tennyson's 'Oenone' (another Troy-haunted poem, echoed much in early Yeats) that 'He pressed the blossom of his lips to mine' occurs. The couplet in 'Oisin' allows the visual field to be crowded by poetry, so that as Niamh's fine clothes are brought into view, it is no surprise that they are themselves full of meaning, alive with shapes of birds and 'many a figured creature' over all that white and crimson. Whatever else could be said about the bosom that is rising and falling underneath this outfit, Yeats chooses to return exactly to his adjective for Niamh's eyes, 'soft'—here with a less abstract softness, perhaps. The effect of the whole is both sensual and disorienting: to be 'like' something, here, is not to be narrowly likened in the interests of accuracy, but to be brought into contact with a multiplying, teeming realm of symbolic (and poetic) matter.

Yeats was certain of the importance of 'Oisin', but unsure about how successfully its style was articulated. Even just after finishing the work, he could write to Katharine Tynan (an Irish poet of his own generation, at that point a rather more successful one), expressing his dissatisfaction:

> Some thing I had to say. Don't know that I have said it. All seems confused incoherent inarticulate. Yet this I know I am no idle poetaster. My life has been in my poems. To make them I have broken my life in a morter as it were . . . I have seen others enjoying while I stood alone with myself—commenting, commenting—a mere dead mirror on which things reflect themselves. I have buried my youth and raised over it a cairn—of clouds.[23]

This is unusually frank, and the fear of having been 'a mere dead mirror' lets slip something about the importance of a new poetic optics (so to speak) in the style Yeats was already trying to achieve. The 'mere dead mirror' wouldn't mistake peacocks for peahens, yet the danger in attempting a poetry of more actively visionary power is that it puts the poet's expressive abilities under breaking pressure. Already, in 1888, Yeats insists that his poetry contains his life, and not in any easy or pain-free sense of simply accommodating that life: 'I have broken my life in a morter'. The metaphor may owe something to alchemy, but it seems that Yeats hopes here for results more clear, and less clouded, than those he felt he had in fact achieved.[24]

'The Wanderings of Oisin' was to be extensively revised by Yeats for its appearance in his 1895 *Poems*, in line with a general intention to achieve a more definite vividness of expression and effect. In rewriting the lines quoted above, Yeats concentrated the impact of the 'sunset'/'doomed ships'/'lips' simile by cutting away other images, most importantly ridding the text of the awkward 'tincture'/'cincture' couplet, and allowing the colour of Niamh's hair to be tinged by the previous image, with the new 'gloomed' echoing (and so in some measure absorbing) the existing 'doomed':

> [We] found on the dove-gray edge of the sea
> A pearl-pale, high-born lady, who rode
> On a horse with bridle of findrinny;
> And like a sunset were her lips,
> A stormy sunset on doomed ships;
> A citron colour gloomed in her hair,
> But down to her feet white vesture flowed,
> And with the glimmering crimson glowed
> Of many a figured embroidery;
> And it was bound with a pearl-pale shell
> That wavered like the summer streams,
> As her soft bosom rose and fell.[25]

The introduction of 'findrinny' ('A kind of red bronze', according to Yeats's 1895 note) builds towards the 'stormy sunset', and it reddens the 'citron' that 'gloomed' in Niamh's hair, so that the climactic 'glimmering crimson' of clothes whose emblematic embroideries are no longer detailed in the verse now stands in strong contrast to the whites and off-whites of the 'dove-grey edge of the sea', the 'white vesture', and the new compound adjective 'pearl-pale', which takes the place of the previously repeated 'soft', and is used both of Niamh and the shell. Undoubtedly Yeats is aiming here for a more concerted (and perhaps more painterly) colour-composition, but he is doing so in the conviction that the symbols in his poetry—however unknown they may be to a reading audience—work more powerfully for being more clearly (and artfully) delineated.

The Yeats of the 1890s was, as is well known, a magician as well as a writer. By the end of the decade, these seemed to him less kindred aspects of his calling than competing callings in themselves. However much we may suspect Yeats's poetics of this time of a heavy reliance on smoke and mirrors—elaborately mysterious symbolism (as in 'The Rose' which features so prominently in a large number of pieces, and goes on to give itself as a group title to many of them in the poet's later *Collected* arrangements), incantatory rhythms and repetitions, and out-of-the-way occultism and myth—Yeats does get rid of those visionary clouds which, in 'Oisin' and elsewhere, had (it seemed to him) managed only to obstruct the view. His poetry of the 1890s is an occultist's poetry, certainly, and the knowledge by which it is powered is often in the nature of secret knowledge; but that poetry's work is much more definitely conceived by Yeats, and its personal and public bearings are much more effectively brought into conjunction, than anything he had been able to achieve in the 1880s. For Yeats himself, this was a movement away from Victorianism—explicitly, in his later accounts, an artistic escape from it—towards an idiom at once symbolic, personal, and culturally dynamic (in relation to Irish nationalism). In terms of favoured precursors, the likes of Tennyson were to fade into the background, along with Morris and Swinburne, and it was the symbolically clear-sighted William Blake (on whom Yeats laboured, with Edwin J. Ellis, long and hard to produce a weighty edition and commentary in 1893) who replaced Shelley: 'Most of us feel, I think', Yeats could now write, 'no matter how greatly we admire him, that there is something of over-much cloud and rainbow in the poetry of Shelley, and is not this simply because he lacked the true symbols and types and stories to express his intense subjective inspiration?'[26]

Throughout the 1890s, Yeats felt himself to be hot on the trail of 'true symbols' in poetry. 'The Two Trees', which first appeared in *The Countess Kathleen and Various Legends and Lyrics*, set for the poet a lyric agenda with symbolic clarity at its heart. The poem is very carefully shaped into two twenty-line stanzas, which correspond to each other metrically, in diction, and in the repetition of particular motifs. The two trees, each occupying a stanza, carry detailed symbolic meanings, but those meanings are not, so to speak, the business of the poem itself, for the verse is designed to deliver symbols powerfully, and not to interpret them. For this, visual definiteness is important; and 'The Two Trees' is governed by the instruction (to the 'Beloved') to 'gaze':

> Beloved, gaze in thine own heart,
> The holy tree is growing there;
> From joy the holy branches start,
> And all the trembling flowers they bear.[27]

Tree, branches, and flowers are designedly simple elements; what is not simple is seeing a tree growing in the heart, and deciding on the import of a word that is simple at first sight— 'holy'. Much of the effect depends, in fact, on Yeats's use of the definite article: 'A holy tree is growing there' would do more than just risk bathos—a holy tree, and a couple of pious shrubs to go with it, perhaps?—but 'The holy tree' strikes immediately a note of unperturbed seriousness: not just any tree that might be declared 'holy', but this one, with which (the definite article unfussily intimates) both the speaker and the 'Beloved' are familiar enough to be able to recognize without further description. 'Holy'—a word so suddenly repeated here—might usually suggest no more than the platitudinous adjectival arsenal of a hymnal's off-the-peg poetic diction, yet in Yeats's hands it feels different: again, there is a sense here of familiarity, even if it is (as often in Yeats's other lyrics of the time) the familiarity of wonders. It's not wrong to hear Blake in 'holy', for this poem as a whole is indebted profoundly to him, but neither is it necessary to give the word the force of an allusion, still less to read it as obliging us to examine its allusive force: like symbols, allusions for Yeats can be efficacious without requiring specific recognition. This is true, too, of more arcane symbolic content: the most that can be said for the significance of this—of the two aspects of the Kabbala's mystic tree of being, the *Sephiroth* (benign) and the *Qlippoth* (malign) —was said by Richard Ellmann: 'Although the poem is comprehensible without the esoteric source, the source helps to explain how it came to be written.'[28] And this seems entirely in line with the poet's hopes for symbolism in his poetry at the time, for Yeats's art guarded alike the ancient secrecies and the personal privacies by which it was fed.

'The Two Trees', then, is able to accommodate its own esoteric sources as parts of a wholly natural lyric expression and arrangement: its roots, in this sense, are not visible. Of course, it is also a poem committed deeply to roots, and to thinking about life in terms of roots: 'The surety of its hidden root, / Has planted quiet in the night'. The 'Beloved', planted thus in 'quiet', is in a good position to observe 'through bewildered branches' 'Winged Loves borne on in gentle strife, / Tossing and tossing to and fro / The flaming circle of our life'. This transformation of life—and in particular, of a love-life—into a kind of rococo firework display is part of an insistence on the positive potential of the inward gaze:

> When looking on their shaken hair,
>   And dreaming how they dance and dart,
> Thine eyes grow full of tender care:—
>   Beloved, gaze in thine own heart.

The first stanza commends the kind of 'gaze' which is receptive to the heart's displays, as a way of cultivating that 'tender care' which the speaker of the poem both commends and solicits. It is with the second, symmetrically answering stanza that Yeats allows his tree metaphor to show its darker side. Blake's 'vegetable glass of nature', in which the physical world mistakes its own reflections for the beginning and the end of reality, contributes to Yeats's more intense—because, perhaps, more privately pained—'bitter glass':

> Gaze no more in the bitter glass
>   The demons with their subtle guile
> Lift up before us when they pass,
>   Or only gaze a little while;
> For there a fatal image grows,
>   With broken boughs and blackened leaves
> And roots half hidden under snows
>   Driven by a storm that ever grieves.
> For all things turn to barrenness
>   In the dim glass the demons hold—
> The glass of outer weariness,
>   Made when God slept in times of old.[29]

'The bitter glass' (whose consonants warp into the phrase 'their subtle guile' in the next line) may well stand here for all of the realist aesthetics (and ethics) which Yeats associated with the nineteenth century—'a mere dead mirror on which things reflect themselves', in his words of 1889. But there is nothing 'mere' about this: the 'fatal' image which grows in the mirror is that of a ramifying 'barrenness', and now the image of an 'outer weariness' threatens to spread to the beholder, with terrible consequences:

> There, through the broken branches, go
>   The ravens of unresting thought;
> Peering and flying to and fro,
>   To see men's souls bartered and bought.
> When they are heard upon the wind,
>   And when they shake their wings—alas!
> Thy tender eyes grow all unkind:—
>   Gaze no more in the bitter glass.

These 'ravens' are given an unexpected appellation in 'of unresting thought' (it takes some nerve, indeed, to produce ravens of any kind after Edgar Allan Poe): 'thought' is more usually to be valued, and all the more for its capacity not to tire. This 'thought', however, is tireless only in bringing about 'outer weariness'—a world of scientific certainty, we might hazard, and modern objectivity. Souls being 'bartered and bought' (this, in a volume which has the play *The Countess Kathleen* as its centrepiece) is the language of mainstream Victorian cultural critique, of Carlyle and Ruskin at their most unreconciled to the contemporary world. For Yeats, this is not the worst thing, and it is not the climactic thing in his poem: 'Thy tender eyes grow all unkind' is the most catastrophic consequence which the lyric can imagine, since it faces the possibility that the 'Beloved' could give herself over to a form of reality beyond the poem's embracing symbolic reach. The 'Beloved', and not the way of the world, is the overriding concern of 'The Two Trees', and her importance is never allowed to go out of focus. In this poem about gazing, eyes that grow full of 'tender care' can barter that tenderness for what renders them 'unkind'. Since 'The Two Trees' is shaped very clearly as a poem that is able—in formal terms—to look at itself, the redundancy (and danger) of 'the bitter glass' is something to be observed in action.

This shows Yeats coming into the full strength of his symbolist writing, a strength which was to be tested through the 1890s, reaching its crisis-point in *The Wind Among the Reeds* and the highly-wrought fictions of *Rosa Alchemica*, *The Adoration of the Magi*, and *The Tables of the Law* (1897). In ridding himself of the cloudier manifestations of Celtic romance, Yeats learned how to treat Irish mythic material with a sharpness of visual realization (and a ruthless cutting-away of narrative redundancies) which rendered it as immediate as it was symbolically loaded. Throughout, the intention was to drive towards the kind of definite, ordered, symbolic suggestion which might have the force of revelation rather than observation. Yeats's friendship with Arthur Symons allowed him glimpses (if little more) of contemporary French *symboliste* poetry and theory, but this was for him more in the nature of corroboration than inspiration, and his own pains over Blake had taught him already a great deal about symbolic meaning and aesthetics. In 1896, Yeats felt able to identify Blake as 'certainly the first great *symboliste* of modern times', and this conversion of Blake into a late-Victorian contemporary is suggestive.[30] (Blake was in any case something of a Victorian discovery, and Yeats was well aware that he was carrying on from Dante Gabriel Rossetti in fostering the poet's reputation.) In describing and promoting Blake, Yeats describes and promotes his own art too:

> William Blake was the first writer of modern times to preach the indissoluble marriage of all great art with symbol. There had been allegorists and teachers of allegory in plenty, but the symbolic imagination, or, as Blake preferred to call it, 'vision', is not allegory, being 'a representation of what actually exists really and unchangeably.' A symbol is indeed the only possible expression of some invisible essence, a transparent lamp about a spiritual flame; while allegory is one of many possible representations of an embodied thing, or familiar principle, and belongs to fancy and not to imagination: the one is a revelation, the other an amusement.[31]

In accounting for—as well as accounting to—the world's reality, it is symbolic art which is supremely capable of seeing what is really there. Blake's word, 'vision', is the word that really counts for Yeats as he attempts to define symbolism. As well as putting symbolism at a decisive distance from allegory (the two had often been easy enough to confuse in 'The Wanderings of Oisin'), Yeats insists on revelatory rather than reflective light (the 'transparent lamp about a spiritual flame' takes over from the 'thin flame' that burned in 'a lamp of green agate' for Shelley, even though it still owes much to Pater's 'hard, gem-like flame'). Coleridge's distinction between fancy and imagination comes ready to hand, but it is something of a blunt instrument here: 'vision', in making the 'invisible' real and present in symbolic art, allows Yeats to proclaim an aesthetic allegiance far removed from any Arnoldian 'criticism of life'.[32] In dealing with art and symbol, as with life and that symbolic art, Yeats in the 1890s wants nothing less than an 'indissoluble marriage'.

The phrase is not without ironies in the context of Yeats's life at the time. Maud Gonne would not consent to his marriage proposals (although, confusingly and frustratingly, she repeatedly spoke to Yeats of an out-of-body, 'astral' marriage between the two of them), while Olivia Shakespeare (who was Yeats's lover in 1896–7, and was eventually to become one of the closest of his friends) was married already, all too indissolubly. It might be said that *The Wind Among the Reeds* (the best part of its decade in the writing) celebrates the marriage of art and symbol for want of other, more mundane, nuptials to celebrate. This would be misleading, though, if it were taken to imply that Yeats's book is really a kind of displacement activity. Instead, the volume is the most intense, and most deliberately wrought, of his early works; it marks, also, the high-point of his maturity as a Victorian poet. Barely a shred of the poet's tattered romantic life is biographically identifiable in the book (especially given its original assignment of different lyrics to speakers such as 'Aedh', 'Michael Robartes', 'Hanrahan', and 'Mongan'), but the young Austin Clarke was forgivably eager, all those decades later, to think the torn pieces worth groping after. We might say (as Clarke could not) that poems to two women create in *The Wind Among the Reeds* a certain mirroring effect, so that those addressed to Maud, and those to Olivia, face each other in melancholy relation. When 'Aedh Laments the Loss of Love', for example, the title requires more than just Yeats's many pages of endnotes to deflect our curiosity:

> Pale brows, still hands and dim hair,
> I had a beautiful friend
> And dreamed that the old despair
> Would end in love in the end:
> She looked in my heart one day
> And saw your image was there;
> She has gone weeping away.[33]

This beloved would have been well advised to keep her gaze fixed on her own heart, and not on that of the poem's speaker. The poem's bareness is of a piece with its depressed finality: no symbols come to the speaker's aid, or in any way serve to redeem the situation. Instead, it is the presence of an 'image' in the heart which precipitates the end of things, recalling the very different mood of the ninth poem preceding this (published originally six years before it), 'Aedh tells of the Rose in his Heart', where:

> The wrong of unshapely things is a wrong too great to be told;
> I hunger to build them anew and sit on a green knoll apart,
> With the earth and the sky and the water, remade, like a casket of gold
> For my dreams of your image that blossoms a rose in the deeps of my heart.[34]

'Unshapely things' may be an affront to Yeats's deepest artistic ambitions, but the perfection of a blossoming image proves to be not without its cost.

Yeats's principal symbol in these years, that of the Rose, is perhaps asked to do rather too much work: it is sexual, mystical, and nationalist at once (not to speak of its Blakean elements), and it gives Yeats a lot of poetic trouble to keep this symbol from slipping into the registers of ritual magic, and thus into that second-best imaginative world of 'allegory'. The powerful sensuality of *The Wind Among the Reeds*—the poems' breathlessly heightened perceptions of hair being unloosened, and falling over the ardent lover, of 'cloud-pale eyelids, dream-dimmed eyes', of 'that pale breast and lingering hand', and of women who can rejoice that 'My heart upon his warm heart lies, / My breath is mixed into his breath'—is not entirely (or even primarily) a symbolic matter; but in artistic terms, it steals the show from the Rose.[35]

All of this makes Yeats more of a Victorian than many attributions of 'symbolist' to his poetic style tend to suggest. The sensuality owes much to poetry, as well as to the senses: to Swinburne (and especially the Swinburne of *Tristram in Lyonesse* (1882)), to Dante Gabriel Rossetti, and perhaps to Meredith, as well as others. Where Yeats departs from such exemplars is in the force of revelation—indeed, of apocalyptic change—which he tries to yoke to the senses' most pained and exquisite evidence. 'Certainly', Yeats announced in 1895, 'a belief in a supersensual world is at hand again'.[36] Yet even 'supersensual' comes to Yeats by way of Tennyson, whose *Merlin and Vivien* (1847) speaks of 'Such a supersensual sensual bond'.[37] In the poem Yeats placed last in *The Wind Among the Reeds*, 'Mongan Thinks of his Past Greatness', the totality of perceptible existence—'all things'—is not enough to exhaust or to satisfy desire; but desire has to go unsatisfied, all the same:

> I have drunk ale from the Country of the Young
> And weep because I know all things now:
> I have been a hazel tree and they hung
> The Pilot Star and the crooked Plough
> Among my leaves in times out of mind:
> I became a rush that horses tread:
> I became a man, a hater of the wind,
> Knowing one, of all things, alone, that his head
> Would not lie on the breast or his lips on the hair
> Of the woman that he loves, until he dies;
> Although the rushes and the fowl of the air
> Cry of his love with their pitiful cries. [38]

The success of this poem makes good the failure of a poem published ten years before, 'Kanva on Himself', and certainly recalls the conversation in Dublin of Mohini Chatterjee in 1886. Mongan—'a famous wizard and king who remembers his passed lives', according to Yeats in 1898,[39] but tempting the eye, at the same time, to mistake him for James Clarence Mangan—has made Oisin's visit to the 'Country of the Young', as well as experiencing existence at all its levels. Where for 'Kanva' this might be a state of fulfilment, for Mongan it is anything but. The terrible and torturing knowledge of the impossibility of consummating 'his love' could not be convincingly addressed by 'Kanva''s reflections: 'Hast thou not sat of yore upon the knees / Of myriads of beloveds, and on thine / Have not a myriad swayed beneath strange trees / In other lives?'[40] For Mongan, there is finally only the knowledge that 'the rushes and the fowl of the air / Cry of his love with their pitiful cries': related as these may be to the 'ravens of unresting thought', they can do just as little as their less 'pitiful' relatives to alleviate the situation. *The Wind Among the Reeds* begins with anticipation of an otherworldly apocalypse, and Niamh—Oisin's Niamh—'calling *Away, come Away*';[41] but it ends in the repeating and ineffectual cries which are parts of, and not apart from, a suffering world.

In his relation to the work of the major Victorian poets, Yeats does represent a change: it is a change of means, and possibly to some extent also a change of direction. Where mid-nineteenth-century verse had been expansive, in both length and intellectual scope, Yeats's poetry learned to be concentrated, its formal concentration adding to the intensity of its vision. The lyric forms and expression in Yeats are not ornamental, or matters of elegant accompaniment to the meaning of literary work; in fact, they are the essence of that work, and the dynamics in their shapes are where it most begins and ends. In the 1890s, Yeats had a lot invested in 'vision' as poetry's business, but his writing handled in effect two different conceptions of what that 'vision' might be. On the one hand, there were the properties of symbolic art, those symbols into which the poet ploughed so much arcane learning and research; on the other, there were the possibilities opened by the increasing concentration and power of the lyrics themselves. Both conceptions were to do with 'revelation' rather than the observation and reflection which Yeats thought so typical of realist nineteenth-century art, but the symbols merely promised one kind of 'revelation', while the lyrics actually delivered another.

Reviewing his friend Arthur Symons in 1897, Yeats gives an account of contemporary poetry which is of relevance to the question of what he thought was happening to 'Victorian' literature:[42]

> It seems to me that the poetry which found its greatest expression in Tennyson and Browning pushed its limits as far as possible, tried to absorb into itself the science and philosophy and morality of its time, and to speak through the mouths of as many as might be of the great persons of history; and that there has been a revolt—a gradual, half-perceptible revolt, as is the fashion of English as contrasted with French revolts—and that poetry has been for two generations slowly contracting its limits and becoming more and more purely personal and lyrical in its spirit.[43]

The roll-call of poets Yeats then produces is extensive—as well as Symons, there are Arthur Lang, Austin Dobson, Edmund Gosse, Robert Bridges, Francis Thompson, W. E. Henley, Lionel Johnson, John Davidson, Lionel Johnson, Richard le Gallienne, and William Watson. The one poet who, by steady 'contraction' of 'limits' and by 'becoming more and more purely personal and lyrical', was at this point writing great poetry goes necessarily unnamed, and is Yeats himself. 'Personal and lyrical' goes to the heart of things, and what Yeats's poetry contains is not the gossip of 'my private affairs', but a self that discovers in lyric its own meaning and direction. The kinds of lyric concentration which Yeats was in the process of discovering were to have the most profound consequences for the poetry of the next century, including of course his own poetry in that century. For all that, they are distillations of Victorian poetry—Tennyson, Browning, and all—and their 'revolt' against it is properly a 'gradual' one. True, the Yeats of 1897 had ring-fenced this particular kind of 'revolt' from that much more definite and political form of revolt he believed imminent, and which he was working to bring about: this was neither English nor French, but Irish. Yet however little Yeats felt he owed as an Irishman to Queen Victoria, he knew how much he had absorbed from the poets of the Victorian age—a more honourable debt, and one that took an entire career to settle.

NOTES

1. Austin Clarke, 'In the Savile Club', in *Collected Poems* ed. R. Dardis Clarke (Manchester: Carcanet Press, 2008), 398.
2. Romantics had—and have—more of a shine to them: 'We were the last romantics— chose for theme / Traditional sanctity and loveliness': W. B. Yeats, 'Coole Park and Ballylee, 1931', in *The Variorum Poems of W.B. Yeats*, ed. Peter Allt and Russell K. Alspatch (London: Macmillan, 1956), 491.
3. Yeats, 'Introduction' to *The Oxford Book of Modern Verse* (1936) in *Later Essays*, ed. William H. O'Donnell with assistance from Elizabeth Bergmann Loiseaux (New York: Scribner, 1994), 183.
4. Yeats, 'Introduction' to *The Oxford Book of Modern Verse*, 185.
5. Yeats, 'The Death of Oenone' [review in *The Bookman*, December 1892 of Tennyson's new (and posthumous) *The Death of Oenone, Akbar's Dream, and Other Poems* (1892)], in *Early*

Articles and Reviews: Uncollected Articles and Reviews Written Between 1886 and 1900, ed. John Frayne and Medeleine Marchaterre (New York: Scribner, 2004), 189.

6. Yeats, *Early Essays*, eds. George Bornstein and Richard J. Finneran (New York: Scribner, 2007), 71–72.

7. Yeats, review of *Gypsy Sorcery and Fortune Telling* by Charles Leland, *The National Observer*, 18 April 1891, in *Early Articles and Reviews*, 130.

8. 'Ere Babylon was dust, / The Magus Zoroaster, my dead child, / Met his own image walking in the garden' (P. B. Shelley, *Prometheus Unbound* Act I, ll.191–193).

9. Yeats, 'Apologia Addressed to Ireland in the Coming Days': the poem's title became finally 'To Ireland in the Coming Times', and over years Yeats made numerous revisions to the text. The first printed version here (in which the italics are Yeats's) is reproduced in *The First Yeats: Poems by W.B. Yeats, 1889–1899*, ed. Edward Larrissy (Manchester: Carcanet Press, 2010), 129.

10. This is, of course, to compress a great deal of argument and detail on Yeats's relation to the three named predecessors. For a short introduction to the issues involved, see Philip L. Marcus, 'Nineteenth-Century Irish Poetry', in David Holdeman and Ben Levitas, eds., *W.B. Yeats in Context* (Cambridge: Cambridge University Press, 2010), 301–309. For an insightful reading of these writers against the background of Irish history, see R. F. Foster, *Words Alone: Yeats and his Inheritances* (Oxford: Oxford University Press, 2011).

11. Yeats, dedication 'To A.E.' [Yeats's friend George Russell], *The Secret Rose* (1897), repr. in *Short Fiction*, ed. G. J. Watson (London: Penguin, 1995), 79.

12. Yeats, letter published in *The Bookman*, November 1892—*The Collected Letters of W.B. Yeats* vol.1, ed. John Kelly and Eric Domville (Oxford: Clarendon Press, 1986), 326.

13. Yeats, 'Irish Wonders', *Providence Sunday Journal*, 7 July 1889, repr. *Letters to the New Island: A New Edition*, ed. George Bornstein and Hugh Witemeyer (Basingstoke: Macmillan, 1989), 97.

14. Yeats, 'Tales from the Twilight', *The Scots Observer*, 1 March 1890, repr. *Early Articles and Reviews*, 113.

15. Yeats, 'Kanva, the Indian, on God', in *The First Yeats*, 43. The poem was first published as 'From the Book of Kauri the Indian—/Section V. On the Nature of God' in the *Dublin University Review*, October 1886, and Yeats retained it in his canon after *The Wanderings of Oisin and Other Poems* (from 1895 onwards) as 'The Indian Upon God'.

16. Yeats, 'An Indian Song', in *The First Yeats*, 42; in 1895 and thereafter, the poem was retitled 'The Indian to his Love', and this phrase was revised into the full line 'The peahens dance on a smooth lawn'. The review of *The Wanderings of Oisin and Other Poems* in the *Freeman's Journal*, 1 Feb. 1889, is quoted and attributed to Taylor in *The Collected Letters of W. B. Yeats*, i. 139.

17. Yeats to John O'Leary, 3 Feb. 1889, *Collected Letters*, i. 138. Yeats's grand disdain here ('As to the poultry yards, with them I have no concern') stirred critical flurries many years later: for an account of Christopher Ricks's verdict that 'a high price is paid by a poetry which invokes poultry and at the same time declares that it has no concern with the poultry yards', see Peter McDonald, *Serious Poetry: Form and Authority from Yeats to Hill* (Oxford: Clarendon Press, 2002), 47, and Peter Robinson, *Poetry, Poets, Readers: Making Things Happen* (Oxford: Clarendon Press, 2002), 86–88. To all this, it may be added that Yeats was correct to assert that peafowl may be seen dancing in the works of the great fifth-century Sanskrit poet Kalidasa, but incorrect to think them peahens rather than peacocks: e.g. 'Pleased on each terrace, dancing with delight, / The friendly Peacock hails

thy graceful flight' (*The Megha Dúta Or Cloud Messenger*, trans. H. H. Wilson, 2nd edn. (London: Richard Watts, 1843), 33).

18. Yeats, 'The Way of Wisdom', *The Speaker*, 14 April 1900, a piece intended for his *Ideas of Good and Evil* (1903), but not included there, and revised as 'The Pathway' for vol. 8 of his *Collected Works* (1908): not repr. until *Early Essays*, 290.
19. Yeats, 'The Wanderings of Oisin' (1889 version), in *The First Yeats*, 4.
20. The dew-drop image occurs in Yeats's principal source, an eighteenth-century Gaelic poem by Michael Comyn, translated by Bryan O'Looney in *Transactions of the Ossianic Society, For the Year 1856*, 4 (1859), 237: 'Her eyes blue, clear, and cloudless, / Like a dew drop on the top of the grass'. This and other points of contact are detailed in Russell K. Alspach's indispensable, 'Some Sources of Yeats's *The Wanderings of Oisin*', *PMLA*, 28 (1943), 849–866.
21. Yeats, 'The Rose of the World' (1892), in *The Variorum Poems of W. B. Yeats*, 111; Yeats, 'The Sorrow of Love' (1892), in *The First Yeats*, 117, and *The Variorum Poems of W. B. Yeats*, 120; Christopher Marlowe, *Doctor Faustus* V.iii.
22. Yeats, 'The Island of Statues: An Arcadian Faery Tale—in Two Acts', in *The Variorum Poems of W. B. Yeats*, 677.
23. Yeats to Katharine Tynan, 6 Sept. 1888, in *Collected Letters*, i. 93–94.
24. cf. another letter from Yeats to Tynan on the same subject, a couple of weeks later (22–28 September 1888): 'Nothing anywhere has clear outline. Everywhere is cloud and foam … In the second part of Oisin under disguise of symbolism I have said several things, to which I only have the key. The romance is for my readers, they must not even know there is a symbol anywhere. They will not find out. If they did it would spoil the art. Yet the whole poem is full of symbols—if it be full of aught but clowds.' *Collected Letters*, i. 98.
25. Yeats, 'The Wanderings of Oisin', in *Poems* (London: Fisher Unwin, 1895), 6.
26. Yeats, 'The Message of the Folk-lorist', *The Speaker* 19 Aug. 1893, in *Early Articles and Reviews* 212.
27. Yeats, 'The Two Trees', in *The First Yeats*, 125–126; for later changes to the text, see *The Variorum Poems of W. B. Yeats*, 134–135.
28. Richard Ellmann, *The Identity of Yeats*, 2nd edn. (London: Faber and Faber, 1964), 76.
29. William Blake, 'A Vision of the Last Judgment', in W. B. Yeats and Edwin J. Ellis, eds., *The Works of William Blake: Poetic, Symbolic, and Critical*, 2 vols. (London: Quaritch, 1893), ii. 394.
30. Yeats, 'William Blake and His Illustrations to *The Divine Comedy*', in *Early Essays*, 378 [this portion of the article was later dropped by Yeats from the reprinting of his essay in *Ideas of Good and Evil* (1901)].
31. Yeats, 'William Blake and His Illustrations to *The Divine Comedy*', 88.
32. Matthew Arnold was, nevertheless, a crucially significant figure in Yeats's intellectual development, not least on account of his *On the Study of Celtic Literature* (1866). For an excellent account of Yeats's debts to Arnold, and the extent of his non-repayment of them, see George Watson, 'Yeats, Victorianism, and the 1890s', in Marjorie Howes and John Kelly, eds., *The Cambridge Companion to W. B. Yeats* (Cambridge: Cambridge University Press, 2006), 36–58.
33. Yeats, *The Wind Among the Reeds* (London: Elkin Mathews, 1899), 21; first published in 1898 as 'Aodh to Dectora'; in 1906, this became 'The Lover Mourns for the Loss of Love', in *The Variorum Poems of W. B. Yeats*, 152. Yeats's 'Notes', mainly on mythological and symbolic matters, occupy 43 of the 1899 volume's 108 pages.

34. Yeats, *The Wind Among the Reeds*, 6; *The Variorum Poems of W. B. Yeats*, 140. First published as 'The Rose in my Heart' in 1892.
35. Yeats, 'Aedh Tells of the Perfect Beauty', *The Wind Among the Reeds*, 42; Yeats, 'Michael Robartes Remembers Forgotten Beauty', *The Wind Among the Reeds*, 28; Yeats, 'The Heart of the Woman', *The Wind Among the Reeds*, 20.
36. Yeats, 'Irish National Literature, III', *The Bookman*, Sept. 1895, repr. as 'The Body of the Father Christian Rosencrux', in *Ideas of Good and Evil; Early Articles and Reviews*, 281.
37. Alfred Tennyson, *Merlin and Vivien* (1874), line 107 (translating a phrase from Goethe's *Faust*).
38. Yeats, 'Mongan Thinks of his Past Greatness', in *The Wind Among the Reeds*, 61–2.
39. Yeats, note to the poem on its first appearance in *The Dome*, Oct. 1898.
40. Yeats, 'Kanva on Himself', in *The First Yeats*, 44.
41. Yeats, 'The Hosting of the Sidhe', in *The Wind Among the Reeds*, 1.
42. Yeats, 'Mr. Arthur Symons' New Book', *The Bookman*, April 1897, repr. *Early Articles and Reviews*, 333.
43. Yeats, 'Mr. Arthur Symons' New Book'.

SELECT BIBLIOGRAPHY

Alspatch, Russell K. 'Some Sources of Yeats's *The Wanderings of Oisin*', *PMLA*, 28 (1943), 849–866.
Foster, R.F. *W.B. Yeats: A Life* vol.1 *The Apprentice Mage* (Oxford: Oxford University Press, 1997).
—— *Words Alone: Yeats and his Inheritances* (Oxford: Oxford University Press, 2011).
Kelly, John *A W.B. Yeats Chronology* (Basingstoke: Palgrave Macmillan, 2003).
Watson, George 'Yeats, Victorianism, and the 1890s' in Marjorie Howes and John Kelly, eds., *The Cambridge Companion to W. B. Yeats* (Cambridge: Cambridge University Press, 2006), 36–58.
Yeats, W.B. *Early Articles and Reviews: Uncollected Articles and Reviews Written Between 1886 and 1900* eds. John P. Frayne and Madeleine Marchaterre [*The Collected Works of W.B. Yeats* Vol. 9] (New York: Scribner, 2004).
—— *Early Essays*, eds. George Bornstein and Richard J. Finneran [*The Collected Works of W.B. Yeats* Vol. 4] (New York: Scribner, 2007).
—— *Mythologies* eds. Warwick Gould and Deirdre Toomey (Basingstoke: Palgrave Macmillan, 2005).
—— *The Collected Letters of W.B. Yeats* vol.1 ed. John Kelly and Eric Domville (Oxford: Clarendon Press, 1986).
—— *The Collected Letters of W.B. Yeats* vol.2 eds. Warwick Gould, John Kelly, and Deirdre Toomey (Oxford: Clarendon Press, 1997).
—— *The First Yeats: Poems by W.B. Yeats, 1889–1899* ed. Edward Larrissy (Manchester: Carcanet Press, 2010).
—— *The Variorum Edition of the Poems of W.B. Yeats* eds. Peter Allt and Russell K. Alspach (London: Macmillan, 1956).

CHAPTER 40

THE PASSION OF CHARLOTTE MEW

TIM KENDALL

Is Charlotte Mew a Victorian poet? Anthologists have stretched definitions in order to accommodate her work: Francis O'Gorman locates it 'in the very last moments of Victorian writing',[1] while Angela Leighton considers that it marks 'practically the end of the road of Victorian women's poetry'.[2] Mew herself failed to muster even a latecomer's sense of belonging: not simply late, she was *too* late. 'No change is like this change',[3] she acknowledged with bewilderment in 1901 as she elegized a Queen and an era. Her great poetry of the 1910s knows itself born out of time, divorced from temperamental kinships and finding few points of connection with contemporary writers.

Mew did, nevertheless, attract a handful of important admirers: Thomas Hardy, for example, called her 'far and away the best living woman poet'.[4] This is high praise, even if its exact altitude remains uncertain. But despite having also won the admiration of May Sinclair, Siegfried Sassoon, and Virginia Woolf, she remained virtually unknown during her lifetime. Her only book of poems, *The Farmer's Bride* (1916), proved hard to shift; Harold Monro wrote two months after publication with the bleak news that sales were 'going dead'.[5] Mew was not her own strongest advocate: shy, often reclusive, diminutive and doll-like according to reports, she could never easily be persuaded to give public readings. 'Are you Charlotte Mew?' she was asked on her first visit to Monro's Poetry Bookshop, and replied characteristically: 'I am sorry to say I am'.[6] Yet having finally agreed to perform for select audiences at a patron's home, she astonished the assembled guests:

> They sat facing the little collared and jacketed figure, with her typescripts and cigarettes, who would never begin until she felt like it. Once she got started (everyone agreed) Charlotte seemed possessed, and seemed not so much to be acting or reciting as a medium's body taken over by a distinct personality. She made slight gestures and used strange intonations at times, tones that were not in her usual speaking range.[7]

Favouring tobacco over laurel, this is otherwise a Pythian performance. The inspired poet speaks through her unprepossessing diurnal self, which must suffer the costs and consequences of oracularity. Afterwards, Mew asks her patron whether there will be 'a heavy bill for something [she] never much wanted to buy—i.e. the world's faint praise'.[8]

How improbable, then, that this mere acquaintance of celebrity should have addressed so urgently its temptations and perils. 'Fame', written in 1913 at the height of the literary *soirées*, casts a cold eye on the blandishments of the literary set as it seeks to clarify the troubled relationship between public, private, and inspired selves:

> Sometimes in the over-heated house, but not for long,
> >   Smirking and speaking rather loud,
> >   I see myself among the crowd,
> Where no one fits the singer to his song,
> Or sifts the unpainted from the painted faces
> Of the people who are always on my stair;
> They were not with me when I walked in heavenly places;
> >   But could I spare
> In the blind Earth's great silences and spaces,
> >   The din, the scuffle, the long stare
> >   If I went back and it was not there?
> Back to the old known things that are the new,
> The folded glory of the gorse, the sweet-briar air,
> To the larks that cannot praise us, knowing nothing of what we do
> >   And the divine, wise trees that do not care
> Yet, to leave Fame, still with such eyes and that bright hair!
> God! If I might! And before I go hence
> >   Take in her stead
> >   To our tossed bed,
> One little dream, no matter how small, how wild.
> Just now, I think I found it in a field, under a fence—
> A frail, dead, new-born lamb, ghostly and pitiful and white,
> >   A blot upon the night,
> >   The moon's dropped child![9]

Who is speaking? Another of Mew's poems, 'On the Road to the Sea', prompted Florence Hardy to enquire whether the speaker is a man or a woman.[10] Joseph Bristow describes the speaker of 'Fame' as 'implicitly (though not definitively) male',[11] but Mew fosters the uncertainty so that she can write with candour about same-sex passion. The dramatic quality of lyric, and the fantastic nature of an imagined affair with Fame, allow Mew to make full—if deniable—disclosure. Hers is a higher consciousness which spies disapprovingly on the smug *arriviste* at the literary event, but which also exists apart from the figure who has 'walked in heavenly places'. This is conspicuously *not* oracular poetry. Although it characterizes and incorporates both the inspired and the banal, the voice of 'Fame' originates in a place distinct from both.

The reasons for this fissure in Mew's creativity—between the self who walks in heavenly places, the self as public poet, and the self who *writes* poetry—have to do with a particular Victorian legacy. When Mew's persona imagines going back to the heavenly places of her past, she describes what may at first glance seem to be a generic natural paradise of gorse, and a sweet-briar air, and larks, and trees—and devoid of human companionship. No scholar has attempted an identification, but its whereabouts help explain the exile's longing which pervades her poetry. The 'sweet-briar air' comes with its own 'folded glory' out of Emily Brontë's 'Love and Friendship': 'The wild rose-briar is sweet in spring, / Its summer blossoms scent the air'.[12] (A rose-briar is a sweet-briar is a briar rose.) Although Mew evokes and resists a Latin pun in her reference to 'the larks that cannot praise us'—larks are *alauda* and so traditionally they represent the laudatory—once more her primary source is Emily Brontë, whose *Wuthering Heights* brings larks and trees together in a dispute over heavenly places:

> 'One time, however, we were near quarrelling. He said the pleasantest manner of spending a hot July day was lying from morning till evening on a bank of heath in the middle of the moors, with the bees humming dreamily about among the bloom, and the larks singing high up overhead, and the blue sky and bright sun shining steadily and cloudlessly. That was his most perfect idea of heaven's happiness: mine was rocking in a rustling green tree, with a west wind blowing, and bright white clouds flitting rapidly above; and not only larks, but throstles, and blackbirds, and linnets, and cuckoos pouring out music on every side, and the moors seen at a distance, broken into cool dusky dells; but close by great swells of long grass undulating in waves to the breeze; and woods and sounding water, and the whole world awake and wild with joy.'[13]

'Fame' folds together the glory of these competing visions to establish its heavenly places: old and known they may be, but they originate in Brontë's work. Mew cannot write out of them without subordinating her genius to a predecessor. So she must establish a separate vision, haunted by an ecstasy which it has shared but been obliged to abandon.

Brontë, according to Mew, wrote with a 'passion' which '[t]he two most prominent women poets of the century, Mrs Browning and Christina Rossetti...have never surpassed'.[14] If 'passion' is the measure of artistic achievement, what hope for Mew? Initially, 'Fame' meets the challenge by setting the passionate obscurity of Brontë's life against a rival and more ignoble passion for celebrity. Mew's persona has cast herself out of Brontë's lonely heaven, tempted by a sexual liaison with a personified Fame whose depiction owes much to Keats's sexually available 'wayward girl'.[15] The poem sketches the lineaments of gratified desire in that 'tossed bed': Mew's friend Alida Monro commented with misplaced assurance that 'Charlotte had no idea how a bed got tossed'.[16] The poet who writes with such erotic yearning for Fame's 'eyes' and 'bright hair' knows passionately how beds get tossed. (Compare the title poem of *The Farmer's Bride*—which immediately precedes 'Fame' in the collection—as it expresses an urgent erotic hunger for the eponymous 'maid': 'The soft young down of her, the brown, / The brown of her—her eyes, her hair, her hair!')[17] But despite this sexual allure, Fame may yet be 'bid adieu'— as Keats had advocated—along with the over-heated house and the bed's turbulence.

A remedy is promised by a return to the 'blind Earth's great silences and spaces'—'blind' so that it grants to the solitary spirit the liberty of going unobserved. Thank heavens that neither larks nor trees 'care' about human ambition.

Even though the appeal of disappearing back into Brontë's heaven is almost irresistible, 'Fame' *does* eventually resist, because while it fantasizes about that destination and starts the journey, it ends with a detour—a topographical *clinamen*—into another much stranger 'dream' which finds and brings to bed a 'frail, dead, new-born lamb'. This is no *agnus dei*, although it may evoke the biblical ideal of predator lying down peacefully with prey. Mew's ultimate allegiance to an unmourned animal miscarriage rebukes overheated fame and solipsistic heaven alike. It typifies a poetry populated by the abandoned, the fallen, the trapped, the mad, the grief-damaged, the newly dead. Mew's instinctive loyalties mark her apart from Emily Brontë, or at least from the Brontë described by Mew (in what is otherwise a high-pitched encomium) as having made a 'resolute rejection of human interest and sympathy'.[18] Both may be poets of solitude, but whereas Brontë exalts in its freedoms, Mew yearns for the warmth of fellow creatures and shares their suffering. The dream of 'Fame' is 'wild'—a word commonly associated with Brontë and her work: Mew herself expresses approval of Brontë's passion because it is 'wayward and wild as storm'.[19] But the 'frail' dead lamb which Mew's speaker hugs close is outside the ken of a poet such as Brontë whose elder sister famously described her as 'stronger than a man'.[20] Taking it to bed in place of Fame, Mew finds a touchingly bizarre image to convey her commitment—no less passionate for being entirely useless—to the downtrodden and dispossessed, and to the frail rather than the strong.

The peculiarities of 'Fame', and the poem's hard-won and contingent rejection of Brontë's 'heavenly places', do nothing to disguise its profound engagement with Victorian antecedents. Tensions between enclosed and open space seem familiar to any reader of *Wuthering Heights* and—for that matter—of Victorian literature *passim*. *The Farmer's Bride* is named after a madwoman in the attic, and across Mew's work can be found more than the requisite number of locks and graves and windows and narrow doors. 'I remember rooms that have had their part / In the steady slowing down of the heart',[21] 'Rooms' begins, the lyric's second line enacting the heart's slowing down towards the final and smallest room of all: the coffin which is variously a 'dustier quieter bed' ('Rooms') or the 'new-made narrow bed' of 'that dark room' in which the dead are'[s]hut' ('Exspecto Resurrectionem').[22] 'Shut' is one of Mew's most commonly used words, contributing to a lexicon of unprecedented claustrophobia—claustrophobic images claustrophobically repeated: 'Like the shut of a winter's day' ('The Farmer's Bride'); 'It is always shut this narrow door' ('The Narrow Door'); 'Someone has shut the shining eyes' ('Beside the Bed'); 'like a screen, / It shuts God out' ('Pécheresse'); 'The room is shut where Mother died' ('The Quiet House'); 'Shut with you in this grim garden' ('Jour des Morts'); 'Beyond the window that you shut to-night' ('The Forest Road'); 'Shut, scared eyes' ('The Forest Road');'Shut in to-night' ('Exspecto Resurrectionem'); 'From your reaped fields at the shut of day' ('On the Road to the Sea'); 'And what sunrise / When these are shut shall open their little eyes?' ('Do Dreams Lie Deeper?'); 'flung wide the door / Which will not shut again' ('The Call'); 'As shut as those / Your guarded heart' ('Absence'); 'My eyes are shut against the grass' ('Moorland Night'); 'And feel the darkness slowly shutting down' ('"There shall be no night there"').[23] This compulsive shutting in or out or down halts communication, trapping characters in the isolation of their unfulfilled desires. It is bleak preparation for the untossed bed which awaits us after death.

The defining drama of Mew's poetry is a war between such tropes of restraint, constraint, and confinement, and tropes of release and freedom. Mew's most conspicuous formal signature is her juxtaposing of varied line lengths to enact the conflict. The fourteen-syllable line in 'Fame' which incorporates 'heavenly places', for example, contrasts with the straitened confines of 'To our tossed bed': the tossed bed may seem to promise a wild freedom, but it turns out to be a suffocating trap. With a similar prosodic mimesis, the flight of the farmer's bride from her marriage is described by a hypermetric line which runs well past the poem's usual octosyllabics: 'So over seven-acre field and up-along across the down / We chased her'. And 'The Quiet House' breaks its pentameter to imitate what it describes: 'Thin shafts of sunlight, like the ghosts of reddened swords have struck our stair'.[24] Penelope Fitzgerald mistakenly refers to these poems' 'free rhyming verse',[25] but Mew is no Ogden Nash. Even poems with lines of more than twenty syllables stay within, and push against, the far limits of accentual-syllabic metre. Mew's greatest achievement, the long poem 'Madeleine in Church', ranges between four and twenty-eight. Madeleine speaks better than she knows in a tacit defence of Mew's prosodic practices:

> I think my body was my soul,
> And when we are made thus
> Who shall control
> Our hands, our eyes, the wandering passion of our feet.[26]

In its understanding of the relationship between body and soul, this owes something to Whitman; in diction, it owes more to the conclusion of *Paradise Lost* ('They hand in hand with wandering steps and slow, / Through *Eden* took thir solitarie way').[27] But Mew insists on 'feet', as Milton does not, because she wants a double meaning which commentates on her own metrical practices: her poetic feet are themselves liable to wander passionately and as if uncontrollably. Her rhythms become the rhythms of the body, fallen and unruly, and having their own agency they will not be confined. Rhythm is resistance. Mew seeks an effect as strikingly visual as it is aural: she variously indents the left-hand margin, and obliges Harold Monro to publish *The Farmer's Bride* in an 'unusually wide format' to manage what she calls 'the abnormal lines of "Madeleine" (which I am sure should not turn over)'.[28] To sanction the turning over of lines at the whim of publishers and their petty practicalities would be to allow the impression of restraint where there must be visible release.

No matter whither Mew's lines may wander, rhyme insists on return. So the 'frail, dead, new-born lamb, ghostly and pitiful and white', drawn out in adjectival agony, is tied to an unadorned annotation: 'A blot upon the night'. Rhyme answers Madeleine's question about control by exerting an authority which can, nevertheless, deliver unexpected liberation. The end-rhymes of 'Fame'—faces / stair / places / spare / spaces / stare / there—seem like habitual gestures until they are broken by a new rhyme word which is itself (literally) 'new'. After the breathlessness of a twelve-line sentence with intensive rhyming patterns, 'new' is a blast of oxygen in the poem's overheated house. A comparable overheating occurs during 'Madeleine in Church', when Madeleine addresses a crucifix with growing exasperation:

> Oh! quiet Christ who never knew
> The poisonous fangs that bite us through
> And make us do the things we do,
> See how we suffer and fight and die,
> How helpless and how low we lie,
> God holds You, and You hang so high,
> Though no one looking long at You,
> Can think you do not suffer too,
> But, up there, from your still, star-lighted tree
> What can You know, what can You really see
> Of this dark ditch, the soul of me!

Another of Madeleine's many rhetorical questions, this becomes accusatory and is punctuated to a crescendo: comma splicing allows little pause for breath amid the onrush of the complaint, and the exclamation mark indicates that there is no expectation of a reply. Madeleine's childlike sense of injustice is appropriately conveyed in the most unsophisticated of rhymes—knew / through / do / You / too. These are supported by internal rhymes and repetitions: 'You do not do', Madeleine very nearly tells Christ, and finger-jabbingly returns to the word 'You' as often as her successor in Sylvia Plath's 'Daddy'. The move away from 'You' and 'we', to 'You' and 'me', demonstrates her personal vulnerability to Christ's failure to 'know' and 'see' her.

The words 'see' and 'me' rhyme four times during 'Madeleine in Church', and the rhyme occurs on at least another dozen occasions throughout Mew's work. That frequency signals a preoccupation with concealing and revealing the self: Christ and readers alike have the opportunity to 'see' (or fail to see) the otherwise withheld secrets of Mew's personae. She explains to Sydney Cockerell about the 'cri de coeur' by which the writer of dramatic monologue 'either has or has not the person', and goes on to find exemplary cases in which the author has 'not only the cry but the gesture and the accent'.[29] Her own characters express themselves by means of what Auden would later call 'The elementary language of the heart'.[30] Words, images, rhymes recur as if Mew's poems were all one poem of a haptic longing felt so intensely that it incorporates agony and madness: 'A rose can stab you across the street / Deeper than any knife', the speaker of 'The Quiet House' puts it, unforgettably. Madeleine is the spokeswoman for characters whose sensory perceptions become overpowering:

> We are what we are: when I was half a child I could not sit
> Watching black shadows on green lawns and red carnations burning in the sun,
> Without paying so heavily for it
> That joy and pain, like any mother and her unborn child were almost one.
> I could hardly bear
> The dreams upon the eyes of white geraniums in the dusk,
> The thick, close voice of musk,
> The jessamine music on the thin night air,
> Or, sometimes, my own hands about me anywhere—
> The sight of my own face (for it was lovely then) even the scent of my own hair...

With her echo of God's enigmatic self-revelation—'I am that I am'—Madeleine claims a privilege which matches the divine and escapes its jurisdiction. She repeats the phrase later when discussing her namesake, Mary Magdalene: 'She was a sinner, we are what we are'. Made as we are, Madeleine argues, we cannot but sin; and the sinfulness which manifests itself in adulthood as sexual already seems latent in what she describes of her passionately synaesthetic childhood. If musk has a voice, music reciprocates with its jessamine scent. Or is it that the scent of jessamine seems like music on the night air? So exquisitely overwrought and blended are the senses that no safe distinction between the literal and the figurative can be drawn. Madeleine may fear that the years have dulled her intensity, but the child is mother of the woman: she still imagines drinking 'the golds and crimsons' of the church's lancet-window in order '[t]o know how jewels taste', and she reassures herself with the thought that 'they are not gone, yet, for me, the lights, the colours, the perfumes'. Madeleine's surreptitious allusion to Dowson's 'They are not long, the weeping and the laughter' represents her as a survivor of Decadence and a keeper of its flame. Dowson stresses the brevity of 'the days of wine and roses',[31] while Madeleine accepts their impermanence but finds that they linger: 'they are not gone, yet'.

Mew discards Victorian resolutions while sharing Victorian predilections. Most shocking of all about Madeleine—the literary descendent of countless Victorian fallen women—is her refusal to repent or die (or, better still, repent *and* die). This is one Decadent who will not be making the voluntary journey into the bosom of the Church: if Christianity disapproves of her, it must therefore be unnatural and inhumane. Madeleine vows to fight to the end, until in a severely abbreviated line of submission and entrapment, 'it is forced from us with our last breath / "Thy will be done"'. That may sound like defeat, but in this battle there are victories for both sides: Mew's description of the effect on Christ of the Magdalene's touch, and of 'her perfume cl[inging] to You from head to feet all through the day', is more scandalously concupiscent than a hothouse of Swinburnian exotica. Small wonder that the printer's compositor for *The Farmer's Bride* refused to set up 'Madeleine in Church' because he considered the poem to be blasphemous.

Mew's career-long fascination with the figure of the fallen woman must have been partly motivated by a sexuality which Church and State considered sinful. It is also a gesture of commitment to a bygone age. Early on, she had established her Decadent credentials with a short story, 'Passed', in the second volume of *The Yellow Book*, where it kept illustrious company with works by Henry James, Aubrey Beardsley, and John Davidson. 'Passed' is not much more than *fin de siècle* by numbers—replete with London slums, a 'notorious thoroughfare' in which the wares of the 'human mart' are sold, a Catholic church, a fallen woman (recently deceased), her newly fallen sister (not yet deceased), and an upper-class man who has betrayed one and will soon, no doubt, betray the other.[32] Apart from its conventional tropes and motifs, the story falters beside the best of Mew's poems because its narrator is a respectable woman who witnesses and judges, but never enters the psychology of the other protagonists: distance defeats sympathy. It takes a long time for Mew to solve that problem. Having fallen almost entirely silent after the persecution of Oscar Wilde, she returns as a visible writer (and makes her miraculous debut as a writer of extraordinary power) when in 1912 she belatedly discovers that greatest of Victorian poetic forms: the dramatic monologue. There was nothing inevitable about the form's longevity. One of the startling coincidences of modern literary history is that, independently and simultaneously, three major poets should have shaped and secured its post-Victorian future. *North of Boston* (1914), *The Farmer's Bride* (1916), and *Prufrock and Other Observations* (1917) have been responsible for ensuring the dramatic monologue's prominence through the twentieth century and beyond.

Not all Mew's dramatic monologues are spoken by fallen women; not all her poems about fallen women are dramatic monologues. Even so, the confluence of form and theme is a natural corollary of Mew's deep understanding of the dramatic monologue's opportunities. It takes a poet with Mew's gifts for prosody to capture those qualities of voice (and their bodily origins) which she extols to Sydney Cockerell: 'the cry…the gesture and the accent'. But it takes a poet with Mew's gift for drama to understand how the dramatic monologue's silent interlocutor presses against the *cri de coeur*; and how the reader might in turn be pressed to sympathize with a speaker whose viewpoint is the sole means of entry into the poem. Robert Langbaum has identified 'an effect peculiarly the genius of the dramatic monologue', that is, 'the effect created by the tension between sympathy and moral judgment'.[33] It is a consequence of the dramatic form that sympathy will always have the upper hand, even in the case of egregious villains discussed by Langbaum such as the speaker of Browning's 'My Last Duchess'. What Langbaum concedes about the Duke might serve equally for Madeleine: 'We suspend moral judgment because we prefer to participate in the duke's power and freedom, in his hard core of character fiercely loyal to itself. Moral judgement is in fact important as the thing to be suspended, as a measure of the price we pay for the privilege of appreciating to the full this extraordinary man.'[34] Madeleine's is the defiance of a character which remains 'fiercely loyal to itself'. Although the fallen woman had been given voice before in dramatic monologues, such as Greenwell's 'Christina' and Meynell's 'A Study', those personae legitimized, encouraged, and voiced moral judgements because they had already repented their previous lives. (The glorious exception is Augusta Webster's 'A Castaway', to which 'Madeleine in Church' is gratefully indebted.)[35] Repentance, as Langbaum implies, subtracts the drama from dramatic monologue. Even as Madeleine rampages through the Church's prohibitions, the reader puts on her knowledge with her power and never forgets the cost of rejecting Madeleine in favour of 'the tame, bloodless things'.

'Madeleine in Church' is a dramatic monologue which wants nothing better than to become a dialogue. Madeleine seeks sympathy—or meaningful interaction of any kind—not from the reader but from her silent interlocutor. (Imagine if Browning's 'Porphyria's Lover' had ended, not by reporting God's silence, but by addressing God directly: 'And yet You have not said a word.'). One of Mew's most brilliant innovations is to turn the issue of *address* into a drama of its own. To whom does she speak? How should the ensuing silence be heard and understood? She switches addressee and switches back, becoming by turns desperate, confiding, censorious, dismissive; and she is met with a silence which itself shifts meaning according to what is asked of it. Mew understands, better than any of her predecessors, the propensity for dramatic monologue to become an elegiac and even an eschatological form. Browning's Duke might have been answered by the envoy, and his Mr. Sludge encounters an interlocutor so physical that he may yet choke Sludge into immortal silence: 'Please, sir! your thumbs are through my windpipe, sir!'[36] But the silent interlocutors of Mew's monologues exist in a state beyond the realm of speech, incapable of any such intervention as they are cut off by madness ('The Forest Road') or death ('In Nunhead Cemetery', 'Beside the Bed', 'A Quoi Bon Dire'). Who better than the dead to serve as the addressees of one-sided conversations? Mew's speakers address the absences which keep them company.

In Mew's hands, dramatic monologue acknowledges a problematic indebtedness to another form: prayer. God would be the ultimate silent interlocutor, never answering but shaping speech with what may be a strong silence, or just the silence of the void. 'Exspecto Resurrectionem', the final poem in *The Farmer's Bride*, is a prayer to Christ as the 'King who hast the key / Of that dark room, / The last which prisons us but held not Thee'. Christ, if only he will act, can deliver the interred dead into an eternity of freedom from constraint; and the silence which is the end of the book is therefore also the silence of Christ's response. Prayer is always fraught in Mew's poetry, its efficacy deeply uncertain. 'The Fête', a fallen *man* poem (fallen teenage boy, to be precise), wants the safety of repentance for its traumatized initiate into the world of adult sexuality, yet his sudden apostrophe to the Virgin Mary announces the impossibility of supplication: 'Mother of Christ, no one has seen your eyes: how can men pray / Even unto you?'[37] The eyes are dangerous—this teenager insists as he struggles to transfer guilt—because 'Only the hair / Of any woman can belong to God'.

Madeleine would find nothing to dispute in that sentiment, ripped as she is by 'The poisonous fangs that bite us through'. Her monologue moves in and out of prayer, referring to Christ sometimes in the second person, sometimes in the third. Sometimes Christ is divine, sometimes he is dying on his cross, sometimes he is overcome with vulnerability to human passion. Always he is silent, as part of the 'utter silence and the empty world' which pain Madeleine in her loquacious despair. Faced with the loneliness of age and the greater loneliness of the grave, Madeleine turns blasphemy into prayer: 'There must be someone. Christ! there must, / Tell me there *will* be some one. Who? / If there were no one else, could it be You?' Christ, of course, will tell her no such thing: the irresistible force of her passion meets its immoveable object in a silence imposed by the dramatic monologue itself. The poem's final stanza accepts that Christ can never be reached:

I cannot bear to look at this divinely bent and gracious head:
When I was small I never quite believed that He was dead:
And at the Convent school I used to lie awake in bed
Thinking about His hands. It did not matter what they said,
He was alive to me, so hurt, so hurt! And most of all in Holy Week
When there was no one else to see
I used to think it would not hurt me too, so terribly,
If He had ever seemed to notice me
Or, if, for once, He would only speak.

No surprise that Madeleine should have dwelt so 'terribly' on the Passion of Christ. She shows no awareness of—or interest in—the resurrection story, and what sound like attempts to instruct Madeleine into a decent orthodoxy are instantly dismissed as beside the point: 'It did not matter what they said'. Madeleine's identification with Christ's life and suffering is more intensely realized than any of the anonymous believers can manage, and the worthlessness of their words stands in contrast to the value placed on the potential for Christ's utterance. But Madeleine in adulthood has given up hoping that Christ will notice her or speak. Hers is a tragedy of poetic form. Dramatic monologue is cruelly fitted to accommodate a life of passionate loneliness, religious doubt, and urgent but unanswered desperation.

Notes

1. Francis O'Gorman, ed., *Victorian Poetry: An Annotated Anthology* (Oxford: Blackwell, 2004), 682.
2. Angela Leighton, 'Charlotte Mew (1869–1928)', in Angela Leighton and Margaret Reynolds, eds., *Victorian Women Poets: An Anthology* (Oxford: Blackwell, 1995), 646.
3. Charlotte Mew, 'V. R. I.', in *Collected Poems & Prose*, ed. Val Warner (London: Virago, 1981), 59.
4. Thomas Hardy quoted by Penelope Fitzgerald, *Charlotte Mew and Her Friends* (London: Collins, 1984), 181.
5. Harold Monro quoted in Fitzgerald, *Charlotte Mew and Her Friends*, 165. *The Farmer's Bride* was reissued in an expanded edition in 1921. It appeared under the title *Saturday Market* in the United States. *The Rambling Sailor* was published posthumously in 1929.
6. Mew quoted by Alida Monro, 'Memoir' in Mew, *Collected Poems* (London: Duckworth, 1953), viii.
7. Fitzgerald, *Charlotte Mew and Her Friends*, 111.
8. Quoted by Fitzgerald, *Charlotte Mew and Her Friends*, 114.
9. Mew, *Collected Poems & Prose*, 2–3.
10. Florence Hardy quoted by John Newton in Mew, *Complete Poems*, ed. John Newton (London: Penguin, 2000), 116–117.
11. Joseph Bristow, 'Charlotte Mew's Aftereffects', *Modernism / Modernity*, 16 (2009), 258.
12. Emily Brontë, 'Love and Friendship' in *The Complete Poems*, ed. Janet Gezari (London: Penguin, 2002), 10.

13. Brontë, *Wuthering Heights* (London: J. M. Dent & Co., 1910), 271. This may be the edition most recently read by Mew when she wrote 'Fame'.
14. Mew, 'The Poems of Emily Brontë', *Collected Poems & Prose*, 365.
15. John Keats, 'On Fame', in *Poems by John Keats* (London: George Bell & Sons, 1897), 334.
16. Alida Monro quoted by Fitzgerald, *Charlotte Mew and Her Friends*, 160.
17. Mew, 'The Farmer's Bride', in *Collected Poems & Prose*, 2.
18. Mew, 'The Farmer's Bride', 368.
19. Mew, 'The Farmer's Bride', 363.
20. Charlotte Brontë, quoted by Mew, *Collected Poems & Prose*, 368.
21. Mew, 'Rooms' in *Collected Poems & Prose*, 38.
22. Mew, 'Exspecto Resurrectionem', in *Collected Poems & Prose*, 28.
23. Mew, various poems in *Collected Poems & Prose*, 1, 3, 8, 12, 19, 20, 20, 22, 28, 30, 40, 47, 47, 50, 58.
24. Mew, 'The Quiet House', in *Collected Poems & Prose*, 18.
25. Fitzgerald, *Charlotte Mew and Her Friends*, 124.
26. Mew, 'Madeleine in Church', in *Collected Poems & Prose*, 24.
27. John Milton, *Paradise Lost*, xii. 648–649.
28. Mew to Harold Monro, 9 February 1916, quoted by John Newton, 'Textual Notes', in *Complete Poems*, 131.
29. Mew to Sydney Cockerell, 10 July 1918—*Complete Poems*, 108.
30. W. H. Auden, 'In Time of War', in Auden and Christopher Isherwood, *Journey to a War* (London: Faber, 1939), 280.
31. Ernest Dowson, *'Vitae summa brevis spem nos vetat incohare longam'*, in *The Poems of Ernest Dowson* (London: John Lane, The Bodley Head, 1905), 2.
32. Mew, 'Passed', in *Collected Poems & Prose*, 65–78.
33. Robert Langbaum, *The Poetry of Experience: Dramatic Monologue in Modern Literary Tradition* (New York: Random House, 1957), 85.
34. Langbaum, *The Poetry of Experience*, 83.
35. For the connections between 'A Castaway' and 'Madeleine in Church', see Angela Leighton, *Victorian Women Poets: Writing Against the Heart* (London: Harvester Wheatsheaf, 1992), 285; and Newton, 'Textual Notes', in Mew, *Complete Poems*, 114–15.
36. Robert Browning, 'Mr Sludge, "The Medium"' in *Dramatis Personae* (London: Chapman and Hall, 1864), 172.
37. Mew, 'The Fête' in *Collected Poems & Prose*, 7.

SELECT BIBLIOGRAPHY

Bristow, Joseph, 'Charlotte Mew's Aftereffects', *Modernism / Modernity*, 16 (2009), 255–280.
Denisoff, Dennis, 'Grave Passions: Enclosure and Exposure in Charlotte Mew's Graveyard Poetry', *Victorian Poetry*, 38 (2000), 125–140.
Fitzgerald, Penelope, *Charlotte Mew and Her Friends* (London: Collins, 1984).
Langbaum, Robert, *The Poetry of Experience: Dramatic Monologue in Modern Literary Tradition* (New York: Random House, 1957).
Leighton, Angela, *Victorian Women Poets: Writing Against the Heart* (London: Harvester Wheatsheaf, 1992).

—— and Margaret Reynolds, eds., *Victorian Women Poets: An Anthology* (Oxford: Blackwell, 1995).

Mew, Charlotte, *Collected Poems & Prose*, ed. Val Warner (London: Virago, 1981).

——*Collected Poems*, with a memoir by Alida Monro (London: Duckworth, 1953).

——*Complete Poems*, ed. John Newton (London: Penguin, 2000).

O'Gorman, Francis, ed., *Victorian Poetry: An Annotated Anthology* (Oxford: Blackwell, 2004).

Walsh, Jessica, "'The Strangest Pain to Bear": Corporeality and Fear of Insanity in Charlotte Mew's Poetry', *Victorian Poetry*, 40 (2002), 217–240.

PART IV

THE PLACE OF POETRY

CHAPTER 41

....

MARKETPLACES

....

SAMANTHA MATTHEWS

Publication—is the Auction
Of the Mind of Man—[1]

[I] mechanically stopped before the window of a shop at which various
publications were exposed; it was that of the bookseller to whom I had
last applied in the hope of selling my ballads or Ab Gwilym, and who had
given me hopes that, in the event of my writing a decent novel, or a tale, he
would prove a purchaser.[2]

THE unnamed protagonist of George Borrow's autobiographical novel *Lavengro* (1851),
drawn back to the site of an earlier rejection, contemplates the aspiring Victorian poet's
typical quandary: he needs to sell his poetry; the bookseller wants to buy prose. The
poetry on offer here appears esoteric—English verse translations of Old Norse ballads
and of the medieval Welsh poet Dafydd ap Gwilym—but that is not the problem.[3] A sample is "'very pretty indeed, and very original; beats Scott hollow, and Percy too: but, sir,
the day for these things is gone by; nobody at present cares for Percy, nor for Scott, either,
save as a novelist'". As a veteran of 'many severe losses', the bookseller is risk-averse.

The nineteenth-century publishing industry is dominated by the growth of a mass readership, and defined by that readership's preference for prose fiction, religious literature
(Borrow's bookseller believes 'evangelical tales' are the next big thing), periodicals, and reference books. Publishers know they can make money from novels, whether in the standard three-volume format retailing at 31*s*.6*d*. (bought in bulk by circulating libraries such as
Mudie's and W. H. Smith), serialized in shilling monthly or weekly parts, or in magazines.
The new author who writes for a poetic taste 'gone by', or writes experimental dramatic or
lyric verse, is confronted by tough economic realities: he must either possess sufficient independent wealth to pay for publication, or make a living from another profession and reserve
poetry for leisure time. *Lavengro*'s protagonist does not remain for long out in the street
looking in: he follows the bookseller's advice, and becomes a hack-writer of marketable
prose. Consequently, 'to this day the public has never had an opportunity of doing justice

to the glowing fire of my ballad versification, and the alliterative euphony of my imitations of Ab Gwilym'.[4] The tone is wry, but the value attributed to formal craft and beauty contests the bookseller's estimate of poetry on purely economic grounds. Victorian poems move in more exchange economies than one: their success or failure can be measured in terms of sales figures, the profits and the loss, but also by cultural influence, critical esteem, public affection, and subjective interpretation. As material texts, poems can be seen as examples of what John Plotz calls 'portable property', as 'dually endowed' belongings: 'at once products of a cash market and, potentially, the rare fruits of a highly sentimentalized realm of value both domestic and spiritual, a realm defined by being anything but marketable'.[5]

There is ample evidence that Victorian poetry was, in the popular phrase, a drug on the market; indeed, Charlotte Brontë told correspondents that 'our book is found to be a drug', when the *Poems* (1846) of Currer, Ellis, and Acton Bell sold only two of its over-optimistic first edition of 1,000 copies in the first year.[6] When Eliza Acton proposed a new verse selection to Thomas Longman, the publisher's response was 'My dear madam, it is no good bringing me poetry; nobody wants poetry now. Bring me a cookery book, and we might come to terms': the result was *Modern Cookery for Private Families* (1845), so the commercial soundness of Longman's advice was vindicated.[7] Yet the 'nobody' invoked alike by Borrow's old-fashioned, small-scale publisher-bookseller, and Longman, head of a modern professional publishing company, is the bogeyman of a publishing industry struggling to adapt to a democratizing, demand-led readership. Germane here is Pierre Bourdieu's view of the field of production as based on an 'opposition between the *field of restricted production* as a system producing cultural goods...destined for a public of producers of cultural goods, and the *field of large-scale cultural production*, specifically organised with a view to the production of cultural goods destined for non-producers... "the public at large"'.[8] The Victorian publishing industry was increasingly oriented to large-scale cultural production, while the ethos and mechanisms of restricted production defined the poetry market, particularly for early-career poets. The tension between the two fields differently affected poets, publishers, printers, and readers; the numbers who did want poetry were a proportionately small but influential constituency for whom marginal status intensified commitment. Publishers had to factor symbolic value into their calculations, since having reputable poets on their books also maintained intellectual and moral credibility with readers.

It was not economically viable for the publishing sector to divide itself into small, devoted poetry specialists, and commercial behemoths publishing everything else. The period's most famous poetry-publisher Edward Moxon was, in Stephen Gill's words, 'poet-struck' and 'determined to build up a publishing house that would be worthy of the Muse'.[9] Moxon's list included Wordsworth and Tennyson, and his success was founded partly on sympathetic personal relationships with his authors. Yet as Gill concedes, '[e]conomics had to be paramount', and Moxon's poets were subsidized by steady sellers, such as *Haydn's Dictionary of Dates*. Economic considerations are paramount in Robert Browning's 1835 description of offering Moxon *Paracelsus*:

[N]o sooner was Mr Clarke's letter perused than the Moxonian visage loured exceedingly thereat—the Moxonian accent grew dolorous thereupon:—'Artevelde', has not paid expenses by about 30 & odd pounds: Tennyson's poetry is *'popular at Cambridge' & yet* of 800 copies which were printed of his last, some 300 only have gone off: Mr M. hardly knows whether he shall ever venture again, &c &c & in short begs to decline even inspecting &c &c.[10]

Moxon invokes Henry Taylor's verse drama *Philip Van Artevelde: A dramatic romance* (1834) and Alfred Tennyson's *Poems* (1833) as evidence of the publisher's conundrum. Public exposure and critical esteem are no guarantee of breaking even. Browning relishes the generic features of his rejection scene: archaism and hyperbole inscribe Moxon as a terrible god sitting in judgement, but his language exposes him as a man of business parroting clichés. Browning is also alert to the scenario's inherent absurdity: a poetry-publisher refuses even to read a new poem.[11] Browning laughed off the experience because he had a pre-existing relationship with a different publisher—though only a fortnight earlier, he had blamed Saunders & Otley for the failure of his debut, *Pauline* (1833): 'Several well-disposed folks actually sought copies & found none—& ... so exorbitant a price was affixed to a trifle of a few pages, as to keep it out of the hands of everybody but a critic intending to "show it up"'.[12] Browning went back to Saunders & Otley with *Paracelsus*, '& marvel of marvels, [I] do really think there is some chance of our coming to decent terms'.[13]

Coming to 'decent terms' with a publisher was fraught in a niche market further subdivided into coteries along lines of class, politics, and religion. Standard contractual terms required the poet to take on half profits and losses. Print-runs were small, 250 or 500 copies, and it was necessary to sell more than two-thirds of the run to break even. First-time authors, or those with poor sales records, had to subsidize heavily, or to fund entirely the production, distribution, and advertising costs of a new volume. Independently wealthy authors were at an advantage, while those without capital had to borrow or seek financial support from sponsors. In Browning's mordant summary: 'to present oneself to a bookseller piece in hand & purse in pocket ... [is] to insure the suppression of the verse & perdition of the purse'.[14] Working-class poets had particular difficulty getting into print.[15] Charles Kingsley's fictional tailor-poet Alton Locke succeeds in publishing his small octavo *Songs of the Highways*, but only with the help of an old-fashioned patron, subscribers, and at the moral cost of censoring 'passages of a strong political tendency'.[16] The poet's vocation became identified with bourgeois complacency: as Elizabeth Barrett noted in 1844, 'In the eyes of the living generation, the poet is at once a richer and poorer man than he used to be; he wears better broadcloth, but speaks no more oracles; and the evil of this social incrustation over a great idea is eating deeper and more fatally into our literature than either readers or writers may apprehend'.[17] Even for middle-class poets assisted by loans or gifts from family or friends, there was a price to be paid in kind. Browning's aunt, Christiana Silverthorne, gave him £30 to pay the costs of *Pauline*. Browning consequently had two sources of guilt: keeping the gift secret from his parents, and knowing that most of the money disappeared into advertising that never eventuated (the printing costs were only £6 5s). The resemblance between standard poetry-publishing contracts and what is now called vanity publishing meant that critics carped at the ease with which comfortably-off authors apparently bought their way into the literary world. Arthur Symons characterized A. Mary F. Robinson as 'the spoilt child of literature', who 'naturally signalized her coming of age by the publication of a volume of poems'; M. Lynda Ely qualifies this: Robinson's *A Handful of Honeysuckle* (1878) 'was published by Kegan Paul at her parents' expense expressly in lieu of a coming-out ball'.[18]

In such unpropitious trade conditions, poets' hopes that fame and fortune could be made from publishing appears delusional. Yet within a generation poetry had been big business. Walter Scott's phenomenally popular verse romances were expensive books that sold in bulk. *Marmion* (1808), priced at 31s.6d., sold '13,000 in the first six months, and six editions by the end of the year'; *The Lady of the Lake* (1810) retailed at a formidable 2 guineas, yet sold more than 30,000 copies in its first year.[19] By the time he was negotiating a contract for *Rokeby* (1815), Scott could secure an unprecedented £2,000 advance on the volume's sales. A few other Romantic poets benefited from this popular enthusiasm; Byron's *The Corsair* (1814) 'sold ten thousand copies on its first day of publication in 1814 and twenty thousand in its first fortnight'.[20] Thomas Moore was paid £3,000 for the copyright of his oriental romance *Lalla Rookh* (1817).[21] Scott's success was a mixed blessing for the poetry industry as a whole. Readers of his narrative poetry changed their focus to the novels of 'the author of *Waverley*', and thereafter formed the foundation of the mass readership for Dickens and Thackeray.[22]

Early editions of Scott's poetry dominated the giftbook market, the main retail context for single-authored poetry selections. In the early 1820s, Rudolf Ackermann imported from Germany the literary annual, a periodical anthology of poetry and prose aimed at middle-class women readers and sold in the run-up to Christmas, in which modish steel-plate engravings of society beauties and sentimental landscapes were at least as important as the poetry. According to T. F. Dibdin, Ackermann's *Forget Me Not* was 'the parent of that numerous offspring of Annuals ... of which a good lusty impression of about 16,000 copies is regularly struck off'.[23] The annuals' heyday (1825–35) coincided with two serious trade-cycle depressions (1825–6, 1829–32), and the conservative morality and cautious business model of successful ventures, including *The Literary Souvenir*, *The Gem*, and *The Keepsake*, reflect those straitened times. Where editions of Scott cost over a guinea, Charles Heath's long-running *The Keepsake* (1828–57) retailed, in all its gilded, red watered-silk glory, at a comparatively affordable 13s. The first issue, *The Keepsake for 1828* (London: Hurst, Chance, & Co., 1828), sold out an edition of 15,000 copies. The annuals' editors and promoters knew that their goods had a limited shelf life, and strategically recruited high-profile artists and poets to signify quality and attract notice. The privileging of image over text—some poems were commissioned as pendants to pictures which could be separately purchased as art prints—deterred poets with a reputation to protect. The annuals were important for women poets such as Felicia Hemans and Letitia Landon ('L.E.L.', editor and sole contributor to *Fisher's Drawing-Room Scrap-Book*), and an additional source of income for poets who contributed single poems, reviews, and miscellaneous prose to the periodicals. However, as Lee Erickson notes, they also 'attracted the readers of new poetry and so significantly reduced the market for volumes of verse written by individual poets'.[24]

Moxon's disinclination to take on an intellectually serious poem like *Paracelsus* in 1835 is more explicable against a background in which pictorial anthologies with poetical illustrations held sway, and middle-class readers were buying fewer and cheaper books; of the depressed London book market in 1832 Dibdin remarked that 'men wished to get for *five*, what they knew they could not formerly obtain for *fifteen*, shillings'.[25] James Barnes argues that often 'adverse conditions, both economic and social... forced or enticed publishers and booksellers into new directions', and recurring trade depressions (1837–42 was another) stimulated the publishing industry to make the most of technological advances that reduced production costs, such as the steam-driven Fourdrinier paper-making machine.[26] Retrenching publishers looked to their backlists: the day for Scott and Byron might have gone by, but they took up more than their fair share of the early Victorian market. William St Clair notes that 'Already by the mid 1830s the minimum price of *Marmion* and *The Lady of the Lake* had fallen to a shilling, a tenth of the previous price, and it continued to fall'.[27] The unit cost of each copy of the 'People's Edition' of *Marmion* (Chambers, 1837), an initial edition of 3,130, was less than 6*d*. Stereotyping allowed publishers to print multiple editions from plates without the expense of keeping type standing, so follow-up editions made from the same plates were less than 3*d*. Where Byron's in-copyright *Poetical Works* (John Murray, 1819) cost 42*s*., the 1826 Galignani pirated *Complete Works* was 20*s*.; by the 1840s, Murray's collected Byrons were 12*s*., and still losing market share to out-of-copyright editions by Daly (7*s*. 6*d*.) and Bohn (5*s*.).[28]

With hard-pressed publishers hustling for any advantage, and siding with dead poets against the living, old contentions about copyright revived. Under the 1814 Copyright Act, the author held copyright for twenty-eight years after a work's publication, or the author's lifetime (whichever was longer). Where earlier poets had worked within the confines of patronage and subscription, poets of the 1830s were dealing with what Erickson memorably calls 'the maelstrom of the marketplace'.[29] Sergeant Thomas Noon Talfourd's parliamentary campaign to extend copyright to the term of the author's life plus sixty years, which coincided exactly with the 1837–42 economic depression, attracted celebrity supporters including Wordsworth and Dickens. The 1842 Copyright Act extended copyright to forty-two years during the author's life; posthumous rights were limited to seven years to appease the cheap reprint trade. How helpful the new legislation was for poets is a moot point. It gave some protection if the publisher was declared bankrupt (as many were), and was profitable for authors who retained their copyrights (though the vast majority could not find a buyer). As important was the symbolic affirmation of the transcendent value of poets and poetry. Analysing 'the literalmindedness of Wordsworth's attempts to make copyright answer, in terms of pounds, years, and legal obligations, questions about how much a book is worth, how long it will endure', Susan Eilenberg proposes that Wordsworth's 'real object... was to secure a refuge from oblivion, a means to enable writing to transcend itself': he had, after all, wanted not extended but perpetual copyright.[30] The 1842 Act was an unsatisfactory compromise, particularly regarding international rights; as Catherine Seville notes, 'For almost the whole of the nineteenth century America offered only informal protection to foreign copyright works.'[31] Negotiating the publication of *Aurora Leigh* in 1855, Robert Browning complained about the New York publisher C. S. Francis's 'unfair practice of declaring himself Elizabeth Barrett Browning's American publisher, warning off all other prospective candidates, simply by virtue of his having pirated her work so successfully for so long'.[32] Yet this unlicensed association also made it mutually advantageous for C. S. Francis to buy the poem (for £100), and the firm advertised its $1.00 edition of *Aurora Leigh* as published 'simultaneously with the London edition' on 15 November 1856.[33]

1842 marked the beginnings of a new confidence in poetry publishing. Wordsworth's poetry finally became profitable after he accepted the Laureateship in 1843. Moxon's patience was rewarded when Tennyson broke his ten years' silence with the well-received two-volume *Poems* (1842), followed by *The Princess* (1847), and the breakthrough year of 1850, when *In Memoriam* was closely followed by Tennyson's appointment as Poet Laureate. By November 1854, the reviewer of a new edition of the standard poets could assert that 'Poetry was long thought and called a drug in the market; but, just as in this unhealthy season there is a prodigious demand for drugs, so it is also in the literary world, and ... poetry, like opium, is at present a *drug in demand*.'[34] Even allowing for the laboured transformation of the stock 'drug in the market' formula, this is an equivocal celebration; implicitly, the 'literary world' too is in an 'unhealthy season'.

Flattered though he was by Prince Albert's advocacy, Tennyson came close to rejecting the public office as a threat to his privacy and artistic credibility. The dangers of popularity and publicity for a poet are age-old concerns, but they acquire peculiar force in the industrialized mid-Victorian market. Take the case of *In Memoriam A.H.H.* (1850), published in late May in a first edition of 1,500 copies at six shillings each; a second impression (also 1,500) was needed in mid-July; there was a third impression (2,000) by the end of August; and a fourth impression (3,000) at Christmas. Eight thousand copies of an anonymous elegy in six months, and earnings of £445 for Tennyson in the first year, justify the claim that *In Memoriam* 'secured both Tennyson's reputation and his income from literature'.[35] Yet if 'reputation' is glossed as 'critical repute', Tennyson's success conflicts with the received idea that poetic reputation and profit were incompatible, and that exposure in the market was fatal to poetic ideals. D. G. Rossetti's view of the deleterious effect of financial success on the quality of Tennyson's poetry influenced his decision not to publish a selected volume until *Poems* (1870): 'my verse, being unprofitable, has remained ... unprostituted'.[36] Tennyson had treated this trope in an early poem, 'The Walk at Midnight':

> The whispering leaves, the gushing stream,
> > Where trembles the uncertain moon,
> Suit more the poet's pensive dream,
> > Than all the jarring notes of noon.
> Then, to the thickly-crowded mart
> > The eager sons of interest press;
> Then, shine the tinsel works of art—
> > Now, all is Nature's loneliness![37]

Tennyson reverses expectation by claiming the nocturnal landscape and the 'poet's pensive dream' as the meaningful reality, belonging to a transcendent and eternal 'Now', as against the workaday world. The poet is aligned with Romantic obscurity against the 'eager sons of interest' confecting superficial commercial art. The poem's appearance in *Poems by Two Brothers* (Louth: J. & J. Jackson, 1827), an anonymous, modest volume from a provincial publisher-cum-stationer, is nevertheless an attempted engagement with the 'thickly-crowded mart'.[38] Do popularity and profit damage poetry's aesthetic, moral, intellectual, or emotional value, or is this view simply prejudice against a mass audience? Is the market always wrong?

Tennyson was not alone in meditating on these questions. In 'Thoughts on Poetry and its Varieties' (1833), John Stuart Mill seeks to reconcile his view that 'All poetry is of the nature of a soliloquy' with the necessity of engaging with the market in order to reach readers:

> It may be said that poetry which is printed on hot-pressed paper and sold at a bookseller's shop, is a soliloquy in full dress, and on the stage. It is so; but there is nothing absurd in the idea ... A poet may write poetry not only with the intention of printing it, but for the express purpose of being paid for it; that it should *be* poetry, being written under such influences, is less probable; not, however, impossible.[39]

Mill fair-mindedly elaborates on this possibility (or not impossibility), but his evocation of the lengths the poet must go to in order to avoid poetry degenerating into eloquence, expresses the conviction that poetry seldom survives its embodiment as commercial product. Such anxieties that the individualist imagination is obstructed or destroyed by the influence of the mass market are often articulated through the figure of the urban crowd:

> But it is no small evil that the avenues to fame should be blocked up by a swarm of noisy, pushing, elbowing pretenders, who, though they will not ultimately be able to make good their own entrance, hinder, in the mean time, those who have a right to enter. All who will not disgrace themselves by joining in the unseemly scuffle must expect to be at first hustled and shouldered back.[40]

Macaulay's description of a mass of second-rate poets (such as Robert Montgomery, the review's main target) blocking up the 'avenues to fame', and so obstructing the righteous progress of the gifted few, literalizes the complex dynamics of market competition into an 'unseemly' scrum. The passage was first published in the *Edinburgh Review* in 1830, but anticipates the language of competition associated with Darwinian evolutionary theory.[41] Macaulay still adheres to a principle of divine justice: the 'pretenders' will fail to 'make good their own entrance', and the true poet will achieve fame, eventually—as do Tennyson and Browning. The same trope articulates no such confidence in 1854: 'Not only are new poems pouring from the press ... but editions of old standard poets are running, sweating, jostling against each other in all our literary thoroughfares'.[42] Due to the suggestive power of the metonymic convention by which the name of the poet stands for his or her poetry, this passage both anthropomorphizes books and embodies 'old standard poets' uncannily forced back to life to make money for Victorian publishers.

Tennyson's ambivalence about his own works competing in the crowd was intensified by the steady stream of letters, manuscripts, and volumes of verse he as Poet Laureate received from aspiring poets. In 1883 he wrote to a working man who had sent a poem, that 'it is so much the habit of the age to try and express thought and feeling in verse each one for himself, that there are not I expect many listeners and therefore poetry is not generally profitable in a money point of view'.[43] The advice he gives in old age shortly before accepting a barony is consistent with that given in 'The Walk at Midnight': 'by all means write if you find solace in it but do not be in a hurry to publish. Poetry should be the flower and fruit of a man's life... to be a worthy offering to the world'.[44] Appealing as is Tennyson's adherence to the principles of restricted production that characterized his early career, it leaves out of the picture much of what his readership considered a 'worthy offering'. The 'Moxon Tennyson', the illustrated giftbook edition of Tennyson's *Poems* (1857), often cited as a prime example of an ambitious but financially ruinous Victorian publishing project, has been reassessed by Lorraine Janzen Kooistra alongside the 1860s' illustrated collections of such disregarded poets as Eliza Cook, Adelaide Anne Procter, and Jean Ingelow. These middlebrow women poets aimed squarely at a mass readership that loved 'Mariana' and 'The Lady of Shalott', but rejected the confusing 'mono-dramatic' form of *Maud*. Kooistra quotes an 1866 review of Procter in which Lucy Larcom claims that 'many so-called second-rate poets "have become a heart and home blessing to thousands" because they teach the mass readership to cultivate taste': as did Tennyson's poetry, whether he liked it or not.[45]

Poetry was 'not generally profitable', but in Tennyson's unique case it made a fortune: his wealth at death was £57,206 13s. 9d.[46] Tennyson's poetry earnings were a leitmotif of negative criticism of the later work, most notably Alfred Austin's spiteful 1869 attack, in which he reprises the old saw that the modern age's materialistic spirit is hostile to the creation of great art: 'For art is not like dry-goods.... Though the material and labour requisite for the production of art must be paid for somehow, all the money in the world cannot produce one stroke of art, any more than it can produce the notes of a nightingale.'[47] Tennyson was sensitive on the subject, complaining that the inclusion of images of his houses in the multi-volume Cabinet Edition (1874–81) 'Americanized and vulgarized' him. He was right to worry; the *Publishers' Circular* commented that Aldworth was 'far more grand than any poet's residence we remember'. Indeed, 'fit for a duke', it archly concluded: 'We rejoice to find the Laureate so well lodged. Literature seems, indeed, to be "going up" in the market.'[48]

The crunch point for estimations of Tennyson's worth was *Enoch Arden and Other Poems*, published by Edward Moxon & Co. in August 1864. On the day of publication 17,000 copies of the 6s. volume in green-cloth were sold. The collection's extraordinary popularity attracted immediate notice in *The Times*:

> In these times, when satirists tell us that poetry has died out, and that the most unsaleable of wares is a volume of poems, the Laureate issues a little book, which, although this is for publishers the dead season of the year, goes off like a prairie on fire. Thousands on thousands of copies of it are now in circulation all over England.[49]

In the first few weeks 40,000 went (Mudie's bought 2,500, a real endorsement when poetry was not the circulating library's stock-in-trade), and the first edition of 60,000 sold out by the end of the year. According to Patrick Scott, '*Enoch Arden* was the first of Tennyson's poems to make an impact on the whole of the reading public', and instant success modulated into lasting popular affection for the title poem, which went through at least twelve English editions before 1900. This is not the place to address the question of how exactly *Enoch Arden* 'fulfilled the unformulated wishes of the large majority of his countrymen'.⁵⁰ Rather, Tennyson's commodification is suggested by an eight-page catalogue for 'Messrs. Edward Moxon & Co., Dover Street. October, 1864', bound at the *front* of early copies.⁵¹ Instead of the title-page, the eager buyer found a pricelist of 'Works by the Poet Laureate' headed by 'Mr. Tennyson's New Volume. / ENOCH ARDEN, Etc.'. The temptation to buy other books to complete the set—each bibliographical description includes attractive attributes—obstructs access to the poem: *Idylls of the King* is in 'A New Edition./With a Dedication to the Memory of the/Prince Consort' (7s.); *An Index to "In Memoriam"* is advertised 'Price 2s. cloth limp, or 1s. 6d. sewed, for binding up with "In Memoriam"'. The works' popularity is impressionistically suggested: the one-volume *Poems* is in its sixteenth edition, *In Memoriam* its fifteenth. The use of untestable sales statistics, a standard Victorian promotional technique, can be frustrating for the publishing historian who, like the speaker of T. W. H. Crosland's 'To a Publisher', wants

> To know for a fact
> How many copies
> Mr. So-and-so, and Mr. So-and-so, and Mr. So-and-so
> Really do sell,
> And how many "A second large edition"
> And "Tenth impression"
> Really mean.⁵²

In Moxon & Company's catalogue what they seem to mean is that the purchaser should be inspired to emulate other customers. Success inspires imitation in buyers as well as makers of poetry, as in Browning's 'Popularity', where the 'true poet' gains nothing by his discoveries, while 'Hobbs, Nobbs, Stokes and Nokes' reap the financial and critical glory.⁵³

In *The Golden Treasury*, at least, popular success and critical esteem memorably coincided: it was the most famous of a flowering of anthologies in the second half of the century, many elaborately illustrated.⁵⁴ Anxious about how his selection would be received, F. T. Palgrave limited the July 1861 first edition to a modest 2,000 copies, but it was 'reprinted in October (1,200 copies), and again in November (3,800 copies, so 7,000 by then)'.⁵⁵ Already in October Palgrave felt confident that the sales were an indicator of higher ideals elevating readers, and wrote to Tennyson (the dedicatee): 'I hope you are really pleased with the "Treasury"—dedication included. It sells well, and seems not only to give pleasure, but to arouse thought and discussion about poetry, which I regard as the *causa finalis* of such a book.'⁵⁶ It was reprinted six times in the 1860s, and again in the 1870s, ten times in the 1880s, and another five times to 1897 (the year of Palgrave's death), when *The Golden Treasury: Second Series* (1897) was published. Although Victorian poems only make up a small proportion of the 1861 *Golden Treasury*, the book is a Victorian classic that survived the anti-Victorian backlash: 'Until the Second World War, sales then averaged over ten thousand a year'.[57]

Religious poetry outsold secular poetry until the 1870s, and the best-selling work in the sector was John Keble's *The Christian Year* (1827).[58] Keble's Oxford publisher, J. H. Parker & Co., recorded sales of 305,500 until copyright expired in 1873, but Simon Eliot and Andrew Nash query the claim that it was 'in its 57th edition by 1858 and its 122nd by 1869', arguing that these were simply new impressions, not distinct editions, and re-prints were modest print-runs (1-3,000 copies).[59] The downward adjustment of Parker's claims for the book's popularity is an empirical corrective to the company's self-promotion that also responds to the difficulty most modern readers have in understanding the poems' appeal; as Owen Chadwick put it, 'I confess that I can only understand, with a bare assent of the intellect, the influence exerted by *The Christian Year*'.[60] When a scholar of Tractarianism struggles to make that imaginative leap, the sales figures stand for an alienating otherness.[61] Feeling rather than intellect explains *The Christian Year*'s value to its Victorian readers. Favourite verses were transcribed in letters of condolence, and Keble's 'in part pietistic, in part romantic' approach to Christian devotion inspired intense gratitude in his public.[62] When George Cornish's daughter died of scarlet fever in the late 1830s, as Pat Jalland notes, Cornish wrote to Keble that 'The comfort which your dear Book gives would of itself make me eternally turn to you.' The retail value of Cornish's copy is an offensive irrelevance in this affective context.

Such evidence of private, anguished reading and re-reading during a time of trial, is diametrically opposed to Margaret Oliphant's view of *The Christian Year*'s later commodification. In *Salem Chapel* (1863), Nonconformist preacher Arthur Vincent loses his vocation after falling in love with an implausibly lovely young dowager. The fatal encounter occurs on her territory, a fashionable 'branch of the London Masters' bookshop; that Vincent shuns the local independent bookseller, a steady evangelical tradesman like the members of his own chapel, marks the beginnings of his religious and class betrayal. Immobilized by desire and fear, Vincent takes refuge at a side-table displaying 'all the varieties of the "Christian Year"'.[63] The priggish Nonconformist bends over 'the much-multiplied volume with a beating heart, poising in one hand a tiny miniature copy just made to slip within the pocket of an Anglican waistcoat, and in the other the big red-leaved and morocco-bound edition, as if weighing their respective merits'; the only merits of which he is really aware are the lady's. Before she notices his existence, the dowager needs the last item on her shopping-list, *The Christian Year*: '"Not the very smallest copy, Mr Masters, and not that solemn one with the red edges; something pretty, with a little ornament and gilding: they are for two little *protégées* of mine. Oh, here is exactly what I want!"'[64]

The scene is informative about publishers' strategies for extending the life of a lucrative poetic property, and also gives a warning against presuming that sales equate to reading experiences, popularity, and influence. The text is 'much-multiplied', packaged in various sizes, weights, appearances, and prices, to appeal to different market sectors.

The dowager is a discerning customer who seeks an optimal match between the giftbook and its recipient, so that the pill of Keble's religious verses is sugared with a pretty binding: there is no guarantee that the *protegées* will read their gifts. Vincent worships her as an angel from heaven, who casts the enchantment of poetry over the bookshop (when she leaves he returns 'to those prose regions which were his own lawful habitation'); the reader sees instead a customer who knows 'exactly what [she] want[s]'.[65] Plotz claims that poetry 'provoked fewer debates about the relationship between material embodiment and higher meaning' than the novel.[66] The example of *The Christian Year* suggests that the debates may be less directly articulated, but are just as resonant.

Most Victorian poems notable for high sales started selling well immediately or soon after publication. An instructive exception is Edward FitzGerald's *Rubáiyát of Omar Khayyám, the Astronomer-Poet of Persia*, which follows a dramatic, if delayed trajectory from restricted to large-scale production. The poem first appeared in 1859 as an anonymous shilling pamphlet published by the specialist bookseller Bernard Quaritch in a small edition (250). There was one review, one notice, and no sales. Judged according to the market, the *Rubáiyát* was an abject failure, but these criteria were not FitzGerald's. He paid for publication in order to control it (there was no contract or profit-sharing agreement), and to give a small number (40) to friends. FitzGerald's approach belongs to the field of restricted production: it resembles Tennyson's use of privately printed trial editions to test responses before formal publication, but was also consistent with FitzGerald's self-image as a gentleman amateur. Quaritch was given the rest to sell, if he could: FitzGerald had no interest in a financial return.[67] By 1861 the remaining copies were on the street in the 'penny box', waiting to become waste paper.[68] Instead, a Pre-Raphaelite associate bought one for D.G. Rossetti, who showed it to Swinburne: as the earlier cases of Keats and Blake show, Pre-Raphaelite endorsement could be priceless cultural capital. William Morris produced four calligraphic copies in the 1870s as gifts for friends, part of the revival of scribal publication associated with the Arts and Crafts movement. Morris gave one illuminated manuscript as a birthday present to Georgiana Burne-Jones in 1872, honouring the poem and its translator (whose name he did not then know), but also paying tribute to his close ties with the Burne-Joneses.[69]

The *Rubáiyát*'s public fortunes improved gradually, with small lifetime editions incorporating revisions in 1868, 1872, and 1879. By fits and starts, as Karlin observes, 'the *Rubáiyát* was changing from an eccentric and individual enterprise to a commercial "property" whose production and distribution lay in other hands than those of the author'.[70] When Quaritch priced the third edition (1872) at 7s.6d., FitzGerald grumbled, 'I suppose it is that he expects to sell only a few; and those few to a few who do not mind giving for one hundred such Quatrains what they might buy all Tennyson for'.[71] More likely, canny Quaritch anticipated that the *Rubáiyát*'s stock would rise further. FitzGerald did not make it easy for Quaritch to capitalize on public interest in the *Rubáiyát*, particularly in the United States. After Boston publisher James R. Osgood brought out a cheap edition in 1878, Quaritch reproached FitzGerald for throwing 'into the hand of American pirates the opportunity of reprinting and *misprinting at libitum*', and pleaded: 'Do let me reprint the Rubáiyát! I have so many inquiries for copies that it is painful to be unable to supply a want felt by that part of the public with which I desire to be in connexion.'[72] Only after FitzGerald's death in 1883 was Quaritch really able to make that 'connexion', as the *Rubáiyát* became a sensationally popular, 'much-multiplied' poem of the 1890s.[73]

Sales of single-authored poetry selections and collected editions have been the standard measures for evaluating Victorian poetry's status in the market. Yet '[C]ollected editions are not necessarily the best way of assessing the success of poetry publishing'.[74] As Eliot and Nash point out, poetry is a 'highly protean form' that could appear in small selections, as 'single poems in anthologies and textbooks—or in newspapers and magazines. A significant amount of the poetry the average reader would have been exposed to during this period would have taken the form of individual poems published in newspapers or gift-books or reproduced by copying into a reader's commonplace or autograph book.'[75] Eliot and Nash emphasize the momentum of transmission and reproduction, poems being 'published or republished', 'occur[ing] or reoccur[ing]' in diverse contexts—some directly controlled by the market, but others in the realm of domestic scribal publication, where the market's influence worked more subtly.

Poetry published in periodicals does not always conform to the stereotypical second-rateness of the newspapers' 'Poet's Corner'. Arthur Hugh Clough's *Amours de Voyage* was first published in the *Atlantic Monthly* (February–May 1858). Linda K. Hughes argues for the importance of serious poetry in defining the editorial policy of major periodicals, and their relationship with readers; when the illustrated *Cornhill Magazine* launched in 1860, contributions by household names including Arnold, Charlotte Brontë, Barrett Browning, and Tennyson 'enhance[d] the symbolic capital of their enterprise.'[76] With Tennyson's 'The Charge of the Light Brigade', first published in *The Examiner*, 9 December 1854 (attributed to 'A. T.'), the opportunity to reach readers quickly stimulated a fine integration of form with topicality. He revised the poem for *Maud and Other Poems* (1855), before it was printed on single sheets for soldiers in the Crimea. June Steffensen Hagen views these different methods of publication as Tennyson's response to his role as Poet Laureate, showing his 'newly acquired flexibility and increasing attention to appealing to a wider audience through diversity of media and greater topicality'.[77] Kathryn Ledbetter sees them as enabling the delayed victory of first, best instincts: the revisions 'confirm Tennyson's initial emotional inspiration: after making changes to tone down the poem, Tennyson reverted to the *Examiner* version for 2,000 quarto pamphlets...printed for distribution to soldiers at Sebastopol in August, 1855'.[78]

W. B. Yeats's 'The Lake Isle of Innisfree' has long transcended the context of its original periodical publication in W. E. Henley's *National Observer* (13 December 1890). Yeats revised it for his collection *The Countess Kathleen* (1892), and for his *Poems* (1895, 1899), but also allowed it to appear in four anthologies that indicate his 1890s' cultural and ideological influences: *The Book of the Rhymer's Club* (1892), the Religious Tract Society's *Leisure Hour* (August 1896), William and Elizabeth Sharp's anthology *Lyra Celtica* (1896), and Stopford Brooke and T. W. Rolleston's *A Treasury of Irish Poetry in the English Tongue* (1900).[79] Peter McDonald gives due prominence to the poem's authoritative appearance in *Poems* (1895), where Yeats 'had an extraordinary influence over its total design', and 'the complex, multi-voiced section entitled "The Rose"' asserts his 'poetic quest for "the Eternal Rose of Beauty and Peace"'.[80] Yet he knowingly surrendered control over the interpretative context of 'The Lake Isle' in the anthologies, where 'it began a rich public life in which Yeats's own designs were variously embellished, subverted, or effaced'. In tension with Yeatsian self-making is a willed suspension of the poet's ingrained mistrust of readers.

Knowing surrender to the public is turned to different ends in Rudyard Kipling's fund-raising poem 'The Absent-Minded Beggar', which presents a characteristically frank view of the transaction between poet, press, and public. The poem was first published in the *Daily Mail*, 31 October 1899, as part of the newspaper's patriotic campaign to raise money for the families of British soldiers fighting in the South African War. A large amount of revenue was generated from modest beginnings: Kipling offered the poem gratis on the condition that the paper's proprietor, Alfred Harmsworth, donated his author's fee to 'any one of the regularly ordained relief-funds, as a portion of your contribution . . . It's catchpenny verse and I want it to catch just as many pennies as it can.'[81] The poem raised directly from the public around £135,000, and indirectly probably another £165,000.[82] The poem's refrain 'Pass the hat for your credit's sake, and pay—pay—pay!' puns on economic and ethical value, leaving the public in no doubt of their debt and responsibility to the soldiers and their families.[83] 'The Absent-Minded Beggar' is effective 'catchpenny verse' that breaks the convention of masking the economic transaction between poet and publisher, instead using the poet's gift of his fee as a model for the public to follow in making their own donations to the relief fund.

Amongst the *Outlook Odes* (1902) written by the journalist, editor, and poet T. W. H. Crosland is an address 'To a Bookseller' voiced by a poet who attempts to buy 'a good edition of Shelley'. The bookseller, a fat youth in large boots, responds:

> "Ninepenceshillingnetoneandsixpencenethalfacrownnettwoandeightpencethree andninepencefiveshillingsnethalfaguineaaandkindlystepthisway."

Crosland's jocular 'ode' is comparatively formless, but the bookseller's patter, running-together prices from cheapest to dearest, descends further into the prosaic. When the poet tartly replies, "'Thank you, / But I want Shelley, / Not egg-whisks'", the bookseller recommends 'The best line in the market': 'A heavy volume, / Bound like a cheap purse', with 'stodgy running-titles' and a 'red-line border', at 2*s*. 8*d*.[84] The book exhibits the classic symptoms of a late-Victorian stereotype edition, a cheaply printed text embellished with a red border and pretentious binding. When the speaker looks disappointed, the bookseller 'told me that I could not expect / Kelmscott Press and tree-calf / At the money'. Crosland's poet identifies the fracture in the late-Victorian poetry market, where the customer is faced with a choice between ugly, affordable books churned out by steam-presses and distributed by rail, and beautiful, hand-printed small editions produced by private presses such as William Morris's Kelmscott Press. It was a sign of things to come.

Notes

1. Emily Dickinson, 'Publication—is the Auction' (c.1863), in *The Complete Poems of Emily Dickinson*, ed. Thomas H. Johnson (London: Faber and Faber, 1982), 348.

2. George Borrow, *Lavengro: the Scholar—the Gypsy—the Priest*, 3 vols. (London: John Murray, 1851), ii. 243.

3. The poems are 'translated by myself; with notes philological, critical, and historical'— Borrow, *Lavengro*, ii. 16.

4. Borrow, *Lavengro*, ii. 183.

5. John Plotz, *Portable Property: Victorian Culture on the Move* (Princeton: Princeton University Press, 2008), 2.

6. Charlotte Brontë, *The Letters of Charlotte Brontë: With a Selection of Letters by Family and Friends*, 3 vols., ed. Margaret Smith (Oxford: Clarendon Press, 2004), i. 531; quoted in Susan R. Bauman, 'In the Market for Fame: The Victorian Publication History of the Brontë Poems', *Victorian Review*, 30 (2004), 62. The origins of the phrase 'drug on/in the market' are disputed; the French 'drogue' was a pharmaceutical ingredient, but became a general term for a commodity that 'has lost its commercial value or has become unsaleable' ('drug, n.1', definition 3. *OED*, Third edition, September 2009; online version June 2012: <http://www.oed.com/view/Entry/57982> (accessed 29 January 2013)).

7. Thomas Longman quoted in F. A. Mumby, *Publishing and Bookselling: A History from the Earliest Times to the Present Day* (London: Jonathan Cape, 1954), 235.

8. Pierre Bourdieu, 'The Market of Symbolic Goods', in Randal Johnson, ed., *The Field of Cultural Production: Essays on Art and Literature* (New York: Columbia University Press, 1993), 115.

9. Stephen Gill, *William Wordsworth: A Life* (Oxford: Oxford University Press, 1989), 388.

10. Robert Browning to W. J. Fox, 16 April 1835, *The Brownings' Correspondence*, 20 vols. to date, eds. Philip Kelley and Ronald Hudson (Winfield, KS: Wedgestone Press, 1985), iii. 134.

11. Perhaps Moxon was saving up: only two years later he gave Wordsworth £1,000 for his poetical works.

12. Browning to W. J. Fox, 27 March 1835, *Brownings' Correspondence*, iii. 130.

13. Browning, *Brownings' Correspondence*, iii. 134. Saunders & Otley rejected *Paracelsus*, which Effingham Wilson accepted as a favour to W. J. Fox. Browning's father paid. See the headnote to 'Paracelsus' in *The Poems of Browning*, 4 vols., ed. John Woolford and Daniel Karlin (London: Longman, 1991–), i. 98.

14. Browning, *Brownings' Correspondence*, iii. 130.

15. See Mike Sanders, *The Poetry of Chartism: Aesthetics, Politics, History* (Cambridge: Cambridge University Press, 2009).

16. Charles Kingsley, *Alton Locke: Tailor and Poet. An Autobiography*, ed. Elizabeth F. Cripps (Oxford: Oxford University Press, 1983), 179.

17. Elizabeth Barrett Browning, 'Preface' to *Poems* (1844) in *The Poetical Works of Elizabeth Barrett Browning* (London: Smith, Elder & Co., 1897), xiii.

18. M. Lynda Ely, '"Not a Song to Sell": Re-presenting A. Mary F. Robinson', *Victorian Poetry*, 38 (2000), 95.

19. Richard D. Altick, 'Publishing', in *A Companion to Victorian Literature and Culture*, ed. Herbert F. Tucker (Oxford: Blackwell, 1999), 292.

20. Lee Erickson, *The Economy of Literary Form: English Literature and the Industrialization of Publishing, 1800–1850* (Baltimore: Johns Hopkins University Press, 1996), 23.

21. William St Clair, *The Reading Nation in the Romantic Period* (Cambridge: Cambridge University Press, 2004), 162.

22. Pragmatic alliances were forged between poetry and the novel: the Brontës' *Poems* (1846) failed, but Charlotte persuaded Smith, Elder and Company to 'repackage their novels with their verse' so that it partook of 'the growing fame of the Brontë novels' (Bauman, 'In the Market for Fame', 44). Narrative poetry was more marketable than lyric and dramatic verse, as evidenced by the mid-Victorian popularity of R. H. Barham's *The Ingoldsby Legends* (1840) and T. B. Macaulay's *The Lays of Ancient Rome* (1842).

23. [Thomas Frognall Dibdin], *Bibliophobia: Remarks on the present languid and depressed state of literature and the book trade, In the letter to the author of Bibliomania. By Mercurius Rusticus* (London: H. Bohn, 1832), 26.

24. Lee Erickson, 'The Market', in Richard Cronin, Alison Chapman and Antony H. Harrison, eds., *A Companion to Victorian Poetry* (Oxford: Blackwell, 2002), 346.

25. Dibdin, *Bibliophobia*, 31.

26. James Barnes, 'Depression and Innovation in the British and American Booktrade, 1819–1939' in Robin Myers and Michael Harris, eds., *Economics of the British Booktrade 1605–1939* (Cambridge: Chadwyck-Healey, 1985), 209.

27. St Clair, *Reading Nation*, 419.

28. St Clair, *Reading Nation*, 516, 519.

29. Erickson, *Economy of Literary Form*, 171.

30. Susan Eilenberg, 'Mortal Pages: Wordsworth and the Reform of Copyright', *ELH*, 56 (1989), 369–370.

31. The legislation only caught up with the complexities of international publishing relations with the 1911 Copyright Act. Catherine Seville, 'Copyright', in David McKitterick, ed., *The Cambridge History of the Book in Britain, vol. VI 1830–1914* (Cambridge: Cambridge University Press, 2009), 222.

32. Margaret Reynolds, 'Editorial Introduction', in *Aurora Leigh* (Athens, OH: Ohio University Press, 1992), 88.

33. Reynolds, 'Editorial Introduction', in *Aurora Leigh*, 94.

34. Anon., 'Poetry and the Drama: Parker's New Edition of the English Poets', *The Critic*, 13 (1 Nov. 1854), 589. British Periodicals Online, <http://search.proquest.com/docview/4871344?accountid=9730> (accessed 29 January 2013).

35. Simon Eliot and Andrew Nash, 'Mass Markets: Literature', in McKitterick, *Cambridge History of the Book in Britain*, 435.

36. Quoted in John Barclay, 'Consuming Artifacts: Dante Gabriel Rossetti's Aesthetic Economy', *Victorian Poetry*, 35 (1997), 1. While noting critics' counterview of Rossetti's complicity with the market, Barclay argues that 'the formal and thematic preoccupations of his work often…dramatize problems of consumption or aesthetic response in ways that…open critical perspectives on the commercial culture with which he was entangled.' (1)

37. Tennyson, 'The Walk at Midnight', in *Poems of Tennyson*, 3 vols., ed. Christopher Ricks, 2nd edn. (London: Longman, 1987), i. 137.

38. 'The Walk at Midnight' is one of several poems in this volume not reprinted in Tennyson's lifetime.

39. J. S. Mill, 'Thoughts on Poetry and its Varieties', *Monthly Repository*, Jan. 1833, in John F. Stasny, ed., *Victorian Poetry: A Collection of Essays from the Period* (New York: Garland: 1986), 71–72.

40. [T. B. Macaulay], 'Art. IX.-1. The Omnipresence of the Deity, a Poem', *Edinburgh Review*, 51 (April 1830), 200. The review's running header is 'Mr. Robert Montgomery's *Poems*, and the modern art of puffing'.

41. The review was collected in Macaulay's *Critical and Historical Essays: contributed to The Edinburgh Review*, 3 vols. (London: Longmans, 1843), ii. 649–50. The *Essays* went through several editions (1854, 1866).

42. Anon., 'Poetry and the Drama', 589.

43. Tennyson, *The Letters of Alfred, Lord Tennyson*, ed. Cecil Y. Lang and Edgar F. Shannon, Jr., 3 vols. (Oxford: Clarendon Press, 1982–93), iii. 247.

44. Tennyson, *Letters of Alfred Lord Tennyson*, iii. 247.

45. Lucy Larcom, 'Adelaide Anne Procter's Poems', *Arthur's Home Magazine* (June 1866), 379, quoted in Lorraine Janzen Kooistra, *Poetry, Pictures, and Popular Publishing: The Illustrated Gift Book and Victorian Visual Culture 1855–1875* (Athens, OH: Ohio University Press, 2011), 127.

46. Christopher Ricks, 'Tennyson, Alfred, first Baron Tennyson (1809–1892)', in *Oxford Dictionary of National Biography* (Oxford University Press, 2004); online edn. May 2006 <http://www.oxforddnb.com/view/article/27137> (accessed 29 January 2013).

47. Austin's requirements for making great art include 'spontaneity, simplicity, faith, unconscious earnestness, and manly concentration'. [Alfred Austin], 'The Poetry of the Period', *Temple Bar*, 28 (Dec. 1869), 35.

48. *Publisher's Circular*, 37 (1 Aug. 1874), 484. Tennyson quoted in *Letters of Alfred, Lord Tennyson*, iii. 83n.

49. 'Tennyson's New Poems', *The Times*, 17 Aug. 1864, 9, col. A, quoted in P. G. Scott, *Tennyson's Enoch Arden: A Victorian Best-Seller* (Lincoln: The Tennyson Society, 1970), 1.

50. Scott, *Tennyson's Enoch Arden*, 2. For a revisionary account of the poem's emotional contexts, see Kirstie Blair, '"Thousands of throbbing hearts": Sentimentality and Community in Popular Victorian Poetry: Longfellow's *Evangeline* and Tennyson's *Enoch Arden*', *19: Interdisciplinary Studies in the Long Nineteenth Century*, 4 (2007), <http://www.19.bbk.ac.uk> (accessed 29 January 2013).

51. Tennyson, *Enoch Arden and other poems* (London: Edward Moxon, 1864), my personal copy. This bold marketing strategy would not have been countenanced by Edward Moxon, (d. 1858); he preferred to generate publicity from reviews not advertising.

52. T. W. H. Crosland, 'To a Publisher', in *Outlook Odes* (London: At the Unicorn, 1902), 37.

53. Browning, 'Popularity', in *Poems of Browning*, iii. 380–85.

54. See Sabine Haas, 'Victorian Poetry Anthologies: Their Role and Success in the Nineteenth Century Book Market', *Publishing History*, 17 (1985), 51–64, and Kooistra, *Poetry, Pictures, and Popular Publishing*, chs. 1 and 3.

55. Christopher Ricks, 'The Making of the *Golden Treasury*', in Francis Turner Palgrave, *The Golden Treasury*, ed. Christopher Ricks (Penguin Books, 1991), 441.

56. Palgrave quoted in Ricks, 'The Making of the *Golden Treasury*', 442.

57. Ricks, 'The Making of the *Golden Treasury*', 444.

58. See Rosemary Scott, 'Pious Verse in the Mid-Victorian Market Place: Facts and Figures', *Publishing History*, 33 (1993), 37–58.

59. Eliot and Nash, 'Mass Markets: Literature', 433.

60. Owen Chadwick, 'Introduction', in *The Mind of the Oxford Movement* (London: A. & C. Black, 1963), 63.

61. For a more empathetic recent interpretation, see Marion Shaw, '*In Memoriam* and *The Christian Year*', in Kirstie Blair, ed., *John Keble in Context* (London: Anthem Press, 2004), 47–56.

62. See Pat Jalland, *Death in the Victorian Family* (Oxford: Oxford University Press, 1996), 282.

63. Margaret Oliphant, *Salem Chapel: Chronicles of Carlingford* (London: Virago, 1986), 61.

64. Oliphant, *Salem Chapel*, 62, 63.

65. Oliphant, *Salem Chapel*, 66, 63.

66. Plotz, *Portable Property*, 187n.

67. Information is from Daniel Karlin, 'Publication History', in Edward Fitzgerald, *Rubáiyát of Omar Khayyám: The Astronomer-Poet of Persia*, ed. Daniel Karlin (Oxford: Oxford University Press, 2009), lix–lvi.

68. The link between financially unviable poetry and recycling is often made; in 1850 Charlotte Brontë avers that 'nobody in Cornhill will … affirm that "poetry" has a value except for the trunkmakers' (Brontë, *Letters*, ii. 488).

69. The copy given to Georgiana Burne-Jones is British Library MS Add. 37832. See Michaela Braesel, 'William Morris, Edward Burne-Jones and "The Rubáiyát of Omar Khayyám"', *Apollo*, 159 (2004), 47–56.

70. Karlin, 'Publication History', lii.

71. Fitzgerald quoted in Karlin, 'Publication History', lii.

72. Bernard Quaritch quoted in Karlin, Publication History', liii.

73. See William H. Martin and Sandra Mason, *The Art of Omar Khayyam: Illustrating FitzGerald's Rubaiyat* (London: I. B. Tauris, 2007).

74. Eliot and Nash, 'Mass Markets: Literature', 433.

75. Eliot and Nash, 'Mass Markets: Literature', 433.

76. Linda K. Hughes, 'What the Wellesley Index Left Out: Why Poetry Matters to Periodical Studies', *Victorian Periodicals Review*, 40 (2007), 94.

77. June Steffenson Hagen, *Tennyson and His Publishers*, (University Park: Pennsylvania State University Press, 1979) 94.

78. Kathryn Ledbetter, *Tennyson and Victorian Periodicals: Commodities in Context* (Aldershot: Ashgate, 2007), 126.

79. Peter McDonald, 'A Poem for All Seasons: Yeats, Meaning, and the Publishing History of "The Lake Isle of Innisfree" in the 1890s', *Yearbook of English Studies*, 29 (1999), 204.

80. McDonald, 'A Poem for All Seasons', 229.

81. Rudyard Kipling to Alfred Harmsworth, 22 October 1899, unpublished letter, British Library. See John Lee, 'Following "The Absent-minded Beggar": A Case-History of a Fund-Raising Campaign of the South African War', Voluntary Action History podcasts, 22 November 2010, <https://historyspot.org.uk/podcasts/voluntary-action-history-seminars-podcast/following-absent-minded-beggar-case-history-fund> (45 min 32 sec, accessed 29 January 2013).

82. *The Daily Mail* also donated the substantial sum of £40,000, to make earnings of £340,000 for the poem. John Lee, 'Following Rudyard Kipling's "The Absent-Minded Beggar"', *Kipling Journal*, 85 (2011), 8.

83. Rudyard Kipling, 'The Absent-Minded Beggar', in *The Definitive Edition of Rudyard Kipling's Verse* (London: Hodder & Stoughton, 1989), 459.

84. Crosland, *Outlook Odes*, 67–8.

SELECT BIBLIOGRAPHY

Cruse, Amy, *The Victorians and their Books* (London: George Allen & Unwin, 1935).

Eliot, Simon, 'What Price Poetry? Selling Wordsworth, Tennyson and Longfellow in Nineteenth- and Early-Twentieth-century Britain', *Publications of the Bibliographical Society of America*, 100 (2006), 425–445.

Erickson, Lee, *The Economy of Literary Form: English Literature and the Industrialization of Publishing, 1800–1850* (Baltimore: Johns Hopkins University Press, 1996).

—— 'The Market', in Richard Cronin, Alison Chapman, and Antony H. Harrison, eds., *A Companion to Victorian Poetry* (Oxford: Blackwell, 2002), 345–360.

Faxon, Frederick W., *Literary Annuals and Gift Books: A Bibliography 1823–1903* (Pinner: Private Libraries Association, 1973).

Haas, Sabine, 'Victorian Poetry Anthologies: Their Role and Success in the Nineteenth Century Book Market', *Publishing History*, 17 (1985), 51–64.

Hagen, June Steffensen, *Tennyson and his Publishers* (University Park: Pennsylvania State University Press, 1979).

Hughes, Linda K., 'What the *Wellesley Index* Left Out: Why Poetry Matters to Periodical Studies', *Victorian Periodicals Review*, 40 (2007), 91–125.

Joseph, Gerhard, 'Commodifying Tennyson: The Historical Transformation of "Brand Loyalty"', *Victorian Poetry*, 34 (1996), 133–147.

Kooistra, Lorraine Janzen, *Poetry, Pictures, and Popular Publishing: The Illustrated Gift Book and Victorian Visual Culture 1855–1875* (Athens, OH: Ohio University Press, 2011).

Ledbetter, Kathryn, *Tennyson and Victorian Periodicals: Commodities in Context* (Aldershot: Ashgate, 2007).

McKitterick, David, ed., *The Cambridge History of the Book in Britain, vol. VI 1830–1914* (Cambridge: Cambridge University Press, 2009).

St Clair, William, 'The Romantic Poets in the Victorian Age', in *The Reading Nation in the Romantic Period* (Cambridge: Cambridge University Press, 2004), 413–432.

Scott, Rosemary, 'Pious Verse in the Mid-Victorian Market Place: Facts and Figures', *Publishing History*, 33 (1993), 37–58.

Vincent, David, *Literacy and Popular Culture: England 1750–1914* (Cambridge: Cambridge University Press, 1989).

Weedon, Alexis, *Victorian Publishing: The Economics of Book Production for a Mass Market, 1836–1916* (Aldershot: Ashgate, 2003).

CHAPTER 42

INNER SPACE: BODIES AND MINDS

STEPHANIE KUDUK WEINER

In his 1891 study *Browning as a Philosophical and Religious Teacher,* Sir Henry Jones argues that philosophers, poets, and scientists are united in a 'universal brotherhood'. Dispensing with 'the notion that philosophers occupy a transcendent region' and 'the view that scientific men are mere empirics', he aligns the 'inner movement' of both disciplines with a more widely accepted understanding of the work of the poet: 'All alike endeavour to interpret experience'.[1] Indeed, for many Victorians the poet stood between the philosopher and the scientist, interpreting experience by drawing on transcendent ideas and empirical observations. Many Victorian poems explore the ways in which acts of careful and eager perception involve both ideas and observations, engaging the mind and the body in numerous, complex, and intersecting ways. These poems also often portray in great detail the processes of memory, reflection, and abstraction that follow on and make sense of experience. Minds and bodies are continually and deliberately present in Victorian poetry. They are shown to interact on at least three levels: first, in immediate sensory experience; second, in a poem's recording, representation, and exploration of that experience and the knowledge it requires and produces; and finally in the experience a poem presents to its readers, which in its own turn addresses itself to readers' bodies and to their minds.

A fascination with the interaction of minds and bodies in real-life sensation and cognition, in works of art, and in our experience of them is pervasive in nineteenth-century British culture. In the visual arts, this fascination motivates a wide range of experiments, from the Pre-Raphaelite concern with naturalistic detail to the impressionism of James McNeill Whistler and the New English Art Club.[2] Writers of sensation fiction sought to send a tingle up the spines of readers, a vivid example of the more general allegiance of Victorian novelists to what Nicholas Dames has called 'physiological novel theory'.[3] Like the Enlightenment and Romantic traditions they extended, Victorian philosophy and psychology were centrally interested in questions of perception and cognition.

This interest can be traced through John Stuart Mill's *System of Logic* (1843), Herbert Spencer's *Principles of Psychology* (1855), and Alexander Bain's *The Senses and the Intellect* (1855) into the fin de siècle in reprints and new editions of these texts, as well as in new works such as F. H. Bradley's *Appearance and Reality* (1893). Conversations among these writers were also carried out in journals such as *Mind*, which Bain founded in the 1870s, and in the leading periodicals of the day, the *Westminster Review*, the *Contemporary Review*, and the *Fortnightly Review*.[4] Thus the public of generally educated readers had access to sustained discussions of apparently arcane questions, such as precisely how active a role the mind plays in sense perception (a problem at the centre of a dispute between Bain and James Ward in the 1880s).[5] Or, what should be the philosophical and linguistic foundations of a properly scientific epistemology (a topic addressed by Karl Pearson in *The Grammar of Science* in 1892)?[6] As scholars including Dames, George Levine, and Ian Small have shown, these writers exerted a prevailing influence on Victorian literature and the arts.[7]

This influence registers most clearly in the sophistication with which artists and authors treat sense experience and its relation to knowledge. Crucially, sensation was important to the Victorians, in large part because it was fraught with epistemological weight. In particular, much of the energy giving force to aesthetic treatments of sense experience came from the 'omnipresent debate' between empiricist and idealist theories of knowledge.[8] For empiricists, sensation was the foundation of all knowledge, whereas for idealists reality was mind-dependent. Yet both empiricists and idealists had long explored the interaction between sensation and intellect; both were interested in the ways in which sensation involves the mind and contributes to our store of facts and ideas. Moreover, many Victorian philosophers, not to mention most artists and intellectuals, were attracted to elements of both schools of thought. This meant that the 'omnipresent debate' was less a neatly two-sided contest than an enabling tension, a set of technically incompatible but practically complementary investigations of how cognition shapes perception and how sense experiences are built up into ideas.

Victorian poets seem to have found this tension especially productive. They inherited from their Romantic forbears a poetic form—the meditative lyric—that was at once highly prestigious and finely adapted to exploring the relation between the mind and the body. Both formally and thematically, the Romantic meditative lyric concentrates the generic tendency of all lyric poems to establish 'a reciprocal relation between mind and world... such that each determines the other'.[9] Wordsworth and Keats elevated the lyric to an eminent position in the hierarchy of literary modes by experimenting with the contours of this lyric reciprocity. For both Romantic poets and the implied readers of their poems, as Noel Jackson explains, 'the pleasures of the imagination are routinely located between the operation of the senses and of the intellect'. As such, aesthetic experience, whether of nature or of art, 'cuts across... body and mind, the empirically verifiable and the phenomenally pure', connecting 'the "lowest", most immediately embodied sense of touch' to 'the most exalted operations of the mind'.[10] Especially when infused with the natural theology that the Romantics embraced less ambivalently than their Victorian heirs would do, Romantic lyrics conveyed an abiding faith that physical sensations of the natural world were uniquely aligned with knowledge, even with truth and wisdom. Although certain Victorian poets sometimes lost that faith, they continued to view the meditative lyric, whether inflected autobiographically or dramatically, as a privileged site for investigating the interaction of mind and body in real-life experience and in art.

In addition, Victorian poetics tended to understand poetry as a principal nexus between the mind and the body. On the one hand, a dominant strain of Victorian poetic thought, stretching from Arthur Hallam in the 1830s to W. B. Yeats in the 1890s, argued that a poem invites readers to feel embodied sensations of its sounds and rhythms and, moreover, that this invitation is essential to what makes a poem a poem. Such arguments often take the form of assertions of the non-semantic powers of poetic language and form. Hallam thus writes that the 'poetry of sensation' exerts upon its readers 'a sort of magic, producing a number of impressions, too multiplied, too minute, and too diversified to allow of our tracing them to their causes'.[11] The Spasmodic poet Sydney Dobell, similarly, claims that 'Poetry...is actually in tune with our material flesh and blood', instructing the audience of a lecture he delivered in 1857 to 'forget...altogether the sense of the individual words and attend only to the effect of the rhythmic combination'.[12] Gerard Manley Hopkins says in his letters, 'sometimes one enjoys and admires the very lines one cannot understand', and he often notes of his own poetry that its 'life' is audible rather than legible: 'you must not slovenly read it with the eyes but with your ears...My verse is less to be read than heard'.[13] From Algernon Swinburne and Walter Pater to the aesthetic poets of the fin de siècle, the ideal of 'pure poetry' rested on a confidence in the power of musical language as against referential speech. Even an 'objective poet', according to Robert Browning, accesses the power of an 'auditory' that 'by means of his abstract, can forthwith pass to the reality it was made from'—in other words, as J. Hillis Miller has demonstrated, the movement, sounds, and textures of Browning's verse themselves convey the vital matter of its subject.

On the other hand, this attentiveness to readers' immediate, sensuous experience of poetry accompanied an interest in how a poem offers readers *mediated* experiences of the world it describes. Victorian poetics recurs frequently to discussions of how it is that poems prompt readers to imagine objects, places, and states of mind. Browning defines the objective poet in precisely these terms, as 'one whose endeavour has been to reproduce things external (whether the phenomena of the scenic universe, or the manifested action of the human heart and brain) with an immediate reference, in every case, to the common eye and apprehension of his fellow men, assumed capable of receiving and profiting by this reproduction' (1001).[14] Like Browning, the most trenchant theorists of the period attended to how poets' and readers' immediate and mediated experiences relate to one another. Pater, accordingly, begins 'The School of Giorgione' (1877)—the chapter of *The Renaissance* in which he famously asserts that '[a]ll art constantly aspires towards the condition of music', that is, towards its utter immediacy, its indifference to mediated ideas—by stating, 'art addresses not pure sense, still less the pure intellect, but the "imaginative reason" through the senses'.[15] The various 'impressions' the aesthetic critic works by 'analysing and reducing' to their 'elements' are to be found in 'a picture, a landscape... in life or in a book', which means that some of the impressions are conjured by the mind of a reader in ways that constitute powerful experiences in their own right as well as call up, combine, and refine sensory data drawn from past experiences.[16]

What results from these strains in Victorian poetics is, above all, an intensely experimental posture toward imagery and description. For all their important differences, Victorian poets were united by an enquiring approach to the ways in which poems can refer to, depict, and construct real and imagined worlds of sense experience—on the page and in the minds of readers. Poets from William Morris to Ernest Dowson made frequent use of primary colours, depicting scenes by arranging monochromatic shapes.[17] Others tested the limits of vertical and horizontal modes of sustained description, whether in Matthew Arnold's multi-sensory scene-setting in the opening stanzas of 'Dover Beach' (1867) and 'Stanzas from the Grande Chartreuse' (1855), in Arthur Symons's phantasmagoric sequence *Décor de Théâtre* (1895), or in Christina Rossetti's lists of similes in *Goblin Market* (1862):

> White and golden Lizzie stood,
> Like a lily in a flood,—
> Like a rock of blue-veined stone
> Lashed by tides obstreperously,—
> Like a beacon left alone
> In a hoary roaring sea,
> Sending up a golden fire,—
> Like a fruit-crowned orange-tree
> White with blossoms honey-sweet
> Sore beset by wasp and bee,—
> Like a royal virgin town
> Topped with gilded dome and spire...[18]

Indeed, a defining characteristic of many Victorian poets' craft is their handling of description. From Tennyson's early innovations in the pathetic fallacy to Browning's atomistic and grotesque particulars, from the painterly techniques of the Pre-Raphaelites to the impressionist cityscapes of the fin de siècle, we can often identify the work of a Victorian poet based solely on how images operate in a given poem. Two pairs of writers—Tennyson and Browning in the first half of the period, Hopkins and Swinburne in the second—suggest at once how the best poets of the era developed unique means of exploring the interaction of the mind and the body, and how much their approaches partook of shared concerns and parallel strategies. While they seem at first glance to present opposing models—the 'poetry of sensation' versus 'objective poetry', a Christian poetics of attention to God's creation versus an atheistic poetics of 'fleshly' aestheticism—on closer analysis their similarities and differences alike assume a more subtle cast.

Tennyson's early works give rise to a 'poetry of sensation' that ripples through the art and literature of the nineteenth century. The influence of poems such as 'Mariana' (1830) and 'The Lotos-Eaters' (1832, 1842) on Spasmodic writers, the 'fleshly school' of Swinburne and his Pre-Raphaelite compatriots, and fin-de-siècle aestheticism has led Jason R. Rudy to argue that 'the history of Victorian poetry is in no small part a history of the human body'.[19] But, as is evident both in Tennyson's poems of the 1830s and in the review by Hallam that applies the phrase 'poet of sensation' to him, Tennyson dwells not on embodied sensation alone but on its relation to the operations of the mind.

Throughout his essay, Hallam emphasizes the 'peculiar conditions of thought' and the 'elevated habits of thought' that are conveyed in the poetry of sensation through its 'luxuriance of imagination' and 'vivid, picturesque delineation of objects'.[20] Rather than communicating 'a mere notion in the understanding', the poet of sensation expresses a way of experiencing the world in which sensation and thought are united:

> Susceptible of the slightest impulse from external nature, their fine organs trembled into emotion at colours, and sounds, and movements, unperceived or unregarded by duller temperaments. Rich and clear were their perceptions of visible forms; full and deep their feelings of music. So vivid was the delight attending the simple exertions of eye and ear, that it became mingled more and more with their trains of active thought, and tended to absorb their whole being into the energy of sense.[21]

Hallam praises poets of sensation for their capacity fully to experience 'external nature' and the arts by means of a lively receptivity and responsiveness that 'mingle[s]' 'active thought' with an 'energy of sense'.

In Hallam's review and, as we shall see, in the poems it addresses, poets of sensation resolve the rift between empiricist and idealist epistemologies by stressing the activity of both the senses and the intellect in the experience of sensation and in the crafting of the poem on the page. As Donald S. Hair and Rudy show, Hallam drew on both epistemological traditions in his theory of sensation. By foregrounding processes of sensation and reflection, both as they are described in a poem and as they are experienced by readers, Hallam places Tennyson firmly within a trajectory stretching back to Locke and Berkeley.[22] In addition, Hallam and Tennyson had been students at Cambridge of William Whewell, whose 'antithetical epistemology' sought to 'combine empirical and a priori elements in an epistemology and scientific methodology'.[23] As Laura J. Snyder explains, his philosophy is '"antithetical" in that it expresses what Whewell called the Fundamental Antithesis, or dual nature, of knowledge[:] all knowledge involves an ideal, or subjective, element as well as an empirical, or objective, element'—that is, '*both* observation *and* pure reason'.[24] As he wrote in his *History of Scientific Ideas* (1858), 'Without our ideas, our sensations could have no connexion; without external impressions, our ideas would have no reality; and thus both ingredients of our knowledge must exist'.[25]

Tennyson's early poems explore this axiom, not as it operates in common or normal acts of perception but rather 'in states of extreme emotion, obsession, or hallucination'.[26] In 'Mariana', the protagonist's deranged state of mind causes her sensations to cohere in the shape of a uniform tissue of dreary decay, while the external impressions she receives confirm her conviction of the reality of her abandonment and her lonely existence at the moated grange. Consider the poem's final stanza:

> The sparrow's chirrup on the roof,
>   The slow clock ticking, and the sound
> Which to the wooing wind aloof
>   The poplar made, did all confound
> Her sense; but most she loathed the hour
>   When the thick-moted sunbeam lay
>   Athwart the chambers, and the day
> Was sloping toward his western bower.
> Then, said she, 'I am very dreary,
>   He will not come,' she said;
> She wept, 'I am aweary, aweary,
>   Oh God, that I were dead!'[27]

Confounded by signs of life and of time, and by hints of romance and of motion, she most 'loathed the hour' of sunset because unlike the graduated time of the clock and the sounds of nature's vitality, the close of day marks a definitive ending. She seizes on the diurnal evidence of her existential condition, but she can make no sense of sensory data that suggests other aspects of the external world. From the opening lines of the poem, Mariana's sensibility dictates which elements of her surroundings are noticeable and meaningful (the 'blackest moss,' the 'rusted nails'), but it is in the final stanza that the dynamic interplay of her mind and her body are most vividly presented. She can neither filter out the sparrow's chirp nor integrate it into her knowledge of the world— it simply 'confound[s] her sense'. Tennyson demonstrates that the interaction between her ideas and her impressions makes up her experience of the world and also that her experience is at once distorted and accurate, partial and true. The poem implies that these dynamics, which are readily understood in relation to Mariana's obsessive and melancholy encounters with the world, apply equally to quotidian sense experience.

Tennyson undertakes similar explorations in 'The Lady of Shallot' (1832). Here, the lady's curse obscurely involves being forbidden to look directly at the world outside her tower, yet her defiant act of immediate observation—'She saw the water-lily bloom, / She saw the helmet and the plume, / She looked down to Camelot'—leads to the creation of a new sort of art.[28] The lady inscribes her name (which is also the title of the poem) on the prow of her boat, sings her way into Camelot, and becomes an object of the villagers' uncomprehending gaze. The metapoetic meditation in this poem puzzles out the contrary, equally unsatisfying possibilities of an art based on observation and experience and one based solely on second-order impressions or ideas—'shadows of the world', the sole source of the lady's knowledge in the first phase of the story. Though she finds no reconciliation of the two modes, the poem itself seems to do so, if only by staging the conflict. In 'The Lotos-Eaters' the pleasures of a sensation divorced from intellect threaten to deprive the mariners, not only of thought, but of experience itself. In 'Ulysses' (1842), conversely, the eponymous speaker vows 'To follow knowledge like a sinking star, / Beyond the utmost bound of human thought'—that is, over the curve of the ocean into the unknown sea.[29]

In *In Memoriam, A. H. H.* (1850), sensation and knowledge are consistently allied, but also poised against a new third term, which at first is *death* but which over the course of the poem becomes *faith*. Hallam's death removes him from the sphere of Tennyson's sense experience and human knowledge into a merely conjectural afterlife lying entirely 'behind the veil, behind the veil'.[30] In the early poems of the sequence, Tennyson repeatedly notes Hallam's inaccessibility to all modes of human sense perception: 'My Arthur, whom I shall not see', 'A hand that can be clasped no more'; 'where warm hands have pressed and closed, / Silence, till I be silent too . . . A Spirit, not a breathing voice' (ix. 17, vii. 5, xiii. 7–8, 12). Death, 'the Shadow feared of man', 'spread his mantle dark and cold' and 'bore thee where I could not see' (xxii. 12, 14, 17). No voice to hear, no hand to clasp, no face to see: the lost friend is lost to earthly, physical experience. Moreover, after Hallam's death the world seems by turns to mock Tennyson with its continued 'noise of life' and to become as void as the mantle of death (vii. 10). When he visits Hallam's 'dark house' at dawn, for instance, Tennyson writes, 'ghastly through the drizzling rain / On the bald street breaks the blank day' (vii. 1, 11–12).

As the poem unfolds, these competing ways of depicting an empty world cohere in Tennyson's examination of the knowledge that can be yielded by empirical investigation of life on earth, most explicitly in science, but also in human experience and memory. 'Knowledge is of things we see', he writes in the unnumbered prologue that frames the whole poem, whereas faith pertains to what we 'have not seen'—Christ's face and, more broadly, the afterlife—and therefore 'cannot know' (xxii. 2, 21). Human beings engage in acts of 'believing where we cannot prove' (4). Unlike the early poems in which death is the enemy of sensation and knowledge, the prologue (which Tennyson wrote after the rest of *In Memoriam* was complete) presents faith as simply their opposite.

Yet Tennyson's concluding embrace of a faith characterized by its lack of direct experience is belied by the many ways in which *In Memoriam* links faith, knowledge, and sensation in networks of reciprocal exchange. What is unseen and unknown now may have been seen and known in the past, and thus still be available as memory, a mental faculty that after Wordsworth involves not only remembered sensations but new ones that for poets at any rate are remarkably vivid and substantial. Alternatively, what is unobserved and unknown may be imagined, conjectured, posited, or otherwise made an object of thought. Most important, it may be actually experienced as an absence, as a blankness or a lost presence, as when Tennyson reads Hallam's letters:

> So word by word, and line by line,
>   The dead man touched me from the past,
>   And all at once it seemed at last
> The living soul was flashed on mine,
>
> And mine in this was wound, and whirled
>   About empyreal heights of thought,
>   And came on that which is, and caught
> The deep pulsations of the world. (xcv. 33–40)

Hallam's touch is no mere metaphor here. It palpably registers on Tennyson's body and in his mind, sending him into 'heights of thought' that are 'empyreal'—that is, heavenly, but containing the 'real' within them, connecting him to 'that which is . . . the world'. By the final lyrics in the sequence, Tennyson describes Hallam as simultaneously 'known and unknown... loved deeplier, darklier understood', and he assumes responsibility for his own continued experience of Hallam's presence on earth: 'Behold, I dream a dream of good, / And mingle all the world with thee' (cxxix. 5, 10, 11–12).

What is true of the absent friend is also true of the divine, equally in times of faith and in passages of doubt. As T. S. Eliot said, the poem's 'doubt is a very intense experience'—for the poet and for the reader.[31] As the meditative lyrics that comprise *In Memoriam* move from landscape description to stories of Christmas celebrations, from poems about science to poems about language, always pivoting along an axis of inner and outer experience, they examine the limits that sense experience places upon what human beings can know, as well as how embodied sensations and mental acts nevertheless enable us to experience and imagine that which lies beyond earth and beyond mortal understanding.

In Browning's poetry, both bodies and minds are emphatically present. The starkly corporeal bodies of murdered women and dying bishops jostle for space with bodies that are very much alive: talking, eating, walking, riding in carriages, speeding along on sweaty horses, turning their heads ever so slightly. And Browning's men and women are always seeing, hearing, touching, and tasting the world. They even describe what Alexander Bain calls 'sensations of organic life': respiration, hunger, pain, muscular movements, and the 'appetite that brings the *Sexes* together'.[32] Concurrently, Browning's poems take as their central subject how the human mind works. As critics since Robert Langbaum have argued, Browning's dramatic monologues analyze the quick turns, the unwilling and unintentional confessions, the obliquely grasped motives, and the dubious self-justifications that characterize the mental lives of human beings throughout history and around the world. They also display the mind's faculties of imagination and memory and its capacity to generate genuine insight and compelling philosophy. For Browning's readers, moreover, his poems present worlds that are thickly crowded with sensory data and richly imbued with intellectual challenges.

To borrow the terms Browning uses in his essay on Shelley: he is an objective poet who 'reproduce[s] things external' to himself, 'this world', which 'is not to be learned and thrown aside, but reverted to and relearned' (1001, 1003). In his dramatic monologues, perhaps paradoxically, he is also a subjective poet, not in presenting his own inner life but in showing how individuals apprehend external reality 'with reference to their own individuality' (1003). Like Tennyson, thus, his work cuts across the 'omnipresent debate' and contributes to Victorian efforts to understand the world as apprehended, and the mind that is the agent of that apprehension. Browning's focus on depicting the 'keenness of the universe, nature and man, in their actual state' bespeaks an enduring concern with the sensory stuff that is shown to be at once the basis and the object of human knowledge (1005). 'This world's no blot for us / Nor blank', Fra Lippo Lippi says, 'it means intensely, and means good: / To find its meaning is my meat and drink'.[33]

Browning's poetics are also importantly shaped by theological questions and commitments, though the latter can be difficult to discern in the mosaic of statements made by his speakers, who are inevitably flawed even when they are wise. Most critics have agreed that the imperfection of this world seemed to Browning to indicate the possibility of a higher, more perfect plane of existence. He wrote in 'Abt Vogler' (1864), 'On the earth the broken arcs; in the heaven, a perfect round'.[34] Careful attention in an empiricist vein to 'this world', accordingly, implied ideas that bore a vexed, rich relation to human knowledge, for Browning as for Tennyson in *In Memoriam*. Moreover, as Donald S. Hair and Richard S. Kennedy write, Browning's interest in the mind was inextricable not only from his interest in the body but also from his interest in the soul: 'The mind, in his view, is the agent of the soul, and the senses are the agents of the mind—the five senses, in combination with the mind's awareness of its own actions, an awareness that Locke labelled "reflection"'. For Hair and Kennedy, Browning's experiments with the dramatic monologue convey his career-long effort to 'study the acts of the mind when they manifest themselves in conduct, and especially in speech, since every statement represents a judgment made by the mind, which in turn is acting for the soul, for which such acts are crucial... The soul "wakes / And grows" (in the words of Bishop Blougram) when the mind tries to make sense of experience'.[35] These intricately imbricated circles of cause and effect, agency and reaction, sensation and idea, generate a body of poetry that is correspondingly labyrinthine and tangled—and that constitutes one of the great literary statements about the mutual constitution of experience and intellect.

In 'How It Strikes a Contemporary' (1855), Browning presents the poet's mode of observation as intensely active, open-minded, and moral. Much of this poem consists of a list of things the poet sees and his manner of seeing them:

> He walked and tapped the pavement with his cane,
> Scenting the world, looking it full in face ...
> You'd come upon his scrutinizing hat,
> Making a peaked shade blacker than itself
> Against the single window spared some house
> Intact yet with its mouldered Moorish work,—
> Or else surprise the ferrel of his stick
> Trying the mortar's temper 'tween the chinks
> Of some new shop a-building, French and fine.
> He stood and watched the cobbler at his trade,
> The man who slices lemons into drink,
> The coffee-roaster's brazier, and the boys
> That volunteer to help him turn its winch.
> He glanced o'er books on stalls with half an eye...[36]

No passive recipient of external impressions, the poet instead probes with his eyes and with his cane. Like Tennyson's Mariana, he also shapes what he perceives. 'Scenting the world', he smells so forcefully he seems to endow his environment with fragrances. Even his hat conveys his 'scrutinizing' posture and 'mak[es] a peaked shade' against the window. Above all, he is curious: attentive to old and new buildings alike, as intrigued by the coffee-roaster's machine and the boys who share his fascination as he is by the cobbler. Importantly, his moral force inheres in the townspeople's reaction to his vigilant observation rather than in his own judgments. 'He took such cognizance of men and things, / If any beat a horse, you felt he saw; / If any cursed a woman, he took note', the speaker reports. Whether he sees the horse being beaten or not, 'you felt' that he did, projecting onto the poet the inner pangs of conscience. When they see themselves through the poet's eyes, the townspeople see themselves through a specifically moral lens. In this way, Browning brings to light the ethical function of the poet's activities of observing and recording the world. He also demonstrates the larger stakes of his poetry's sustained exploration of the act of observation in and of itself, suggesting the foundational significance he assigned to each particularist detail that appears in his many poems.

'Fra Lippo Lippi' (1855), too, abounds in particulars whose ethical import is made clear in the overt themes of the monologue. The stuff of everyday life in the gutters and churches of Renaissance Florence—the 'fig-skins, melon-parings, rinds and shucks, / Refuse and rubbish'; the 'good bellyful, / The warm serge and the rope that goes all round'—may be the most tactile details of this poem. But it is the faces that best exemplify Browning's method. From the poem's opening lines, when Lippo encounters the police at the alley's end, the human face is the master-image for combining empirical data with transcendent truth. Lippo calls attention to his own face in the third line, exclaiming 'You think you see a monk!' and he jokes about the characters he sees in the faces of the policemen: 'He's Judas to a title, that man is! / Just such a face!' At the end of the poem, he returns to his own 'blushing face', this time also in a painting, caught in the act of watching and painting in a glorious depiction of the 'Madonna and her babe, / Ringed by a bowery flowery angel-brood, / Lilies and vestments and white faces':

> Well, all these
> Secured at their devotion, up shall come
> Out of a corner when you least expect,
> As one by a dark stair into a great light,
> Music and talking, who but Lippo! I!—
> Mazed, motionless and moonstruck—I'm the man!
> Back I shrink—what is this I see and hear?
> I, caught up with my monk's-things by mistake,
> My old serge gown and rope that goes all round,
> I, in this presence, this pure company!

The white faces and Lippo's amazed and blushing face, the angels and the all-too human monk. The angels' faces demonstrate their pure devotion, while Lippo's face betrays his reaction to what he sees and hears. Like Tennyson's 'empyreal' thoughts, the painting Lippo imagines in his mind mingles the soul and the body, revealing the intimate connection between 'the value and significance of flesh' and the ineffable beauty of divinity and devotion.

Lippo's superiors object to this method. His first painting, which portrays 'every sort of monk' and parishioners from 'good old gossips' and 'little children' to a murderer, prompts the prior to instruct him to 'Make them forget there's such a thing as flesh'. 'Your business is to paint the souls of men', the prior says. 'Give us no more of body than shows soul!' Lippo's reply makes use of the double-meaning of the word 'sense', with its reference to both intelligence and bodily experience: 'Now, is this sense, I ask?' As he continues, he expresses a theory of realistic depiction thoroughly imbued with transcendent meaning, once again recurring to the image of the face:

> Take the prettiest face,
> The prior's niece … patron saint—is it so pretty
> You can't discover if it means hope, fear,
> Sorrow or joy? won't beauty go with these?
> Suppose I've made her eyes all right and blue,
> Can't I take breath and try to add life's flash,
> And then add soul and heighten them threefold?
> Or say there's beauty with no soul at all—
> (I never saw it—put the case the same—)
> If you get simple beauty and nought else,
> You get about the best thing God invents:
> That's somewhat: and you'll find the soul you have missed,
> Within yourself, when you return him thanks.

The mutuality of soul and flesh in this passage is supported by its thorough fusion of real-life observation and artistic representation. The painter who sees the patron saint in the prior's niece transfers that vision onto the canvas. When he takes a breath after accurately capturing her lovely eyes in blue paint, he puts that breath into her represented body: 'I … add life's flash' and 'add soul' to the image. Similarly, the passage assumes that the painting's viewers bring their own souls to the act of aesthetic contemplation. The spontaneous gratitude that wells up when they see the painting is the manifestation of their souls, brought to the fore if only by the 'simple beauty' of the canvas.

For all the ease with which Lippo renders the beauty he sees onto the canvas and with which his audience transfers the beauty of the image to a recognition of beauty in God's creation, the mediation involved in these transferences is important to the poem. Representation matters—it turns out to have powers that immediate sense experience lacks. 'We're made so that we love / First when we see them painted, things we have passed / Perhaps a hundred times nor cared to see', Lippo explains. 'And so they are better, painted—better to us, / Which is the same thing', he continues; 'Art was given for that; / God uses us to help each other so'. The more we learn to see aesthetically, the better viewers we are of the world of shared reality. 'You've seen the world /—The beauty and the wonder and the power', Lippo exclaims to his policeman interlocutor, 'The shapes of things, their colours, lights and shades, / Changes, surprises—and God made it all!' A capacity to see the formal composition of the world's continual succession of sights—'this fair town's face, yonder river's line, / The mountain round it and the sky above, / Much more the figures of man, woman, child'—is for Lippo a capacity to apprehend both its tactile reality and its spiritual meaning. Such a vision fully harmonizes the powers of the physical eye, the mind, and the soul, both in art and in life.

Like Tennyson and Browning, Hopkins also unites sustained attention to the outer world of nature and the inner realm of consciousness with a careful exploration of epistemological problems. As a student at Oxford in the 1860s, he read widely in empiricist and idealist philosophy, benefitting from the expansion of the curriculum and the charismatic, rigorous teaching that characterized the course in 'Greats'.[37] As Daniel Brown has shown, his thought was profoundly shaped by the post-Kantian philosophy of his tutor T. H. Green. Hopkins follows Green in viewing consciousness as the agency through which all sensation occurs and acquires meaning, and in understanding particular objects of experience as significant because they manifest transcendent ideas. 'The Idea is only given ... from the whole downwards to the parts,' Hopkins writes in his *Journal*.[38] For Hopkins, the crucial ideas of causality, time and space, and particularity and generality are all theological at their core. Thus both the objects of sense experience and the self-reflexive experience of consciousness equally evince and partake of the 'pure Being' of the divine, as Hopkins explains in 'Hurrahing in Harvest' (written 1877):

> Summer ends now; now, barbarous in beauty, the stooks rise
> Around; up above, what wind-walks! what lovely behaviour
> Of silk-sack clouds! has wilder, wilful-wavier
> Meal-drift moulded ever and melted across skies? ...
> These things, these things were here and but the beholder
> Wanting; which two when they once meet,
> The heart rears wings bold and bolder
> And hurls for him, O half hurls earth for him off under his feet.[39]

When the 'two'—world and beholder, things and mind—'meet', the heart flies up. In meeting, 'they become a single being or thought', Brown argues, 'radically destabiliz[ing] the discrete relations of the individual subject to its finite objects, the earth, and the infinite object of its aspirations, the pure Being of God'.[40]

Hopkins developed two concepts in his writings to capture such 'meetings' in life and in poetry: inscape and instress. Both prioritize the apprehending mind and its capacity to recognize the divinity as well as the individuality of objects of sensation. W. H. Gardner defines inscape as 'a name for that "individually-distinctive" form (made up of various sense-data) which constitutes the rich and revealing "oneness" of the natural object', a 'oneness' that simultaneously evinces the object's individuality and its continuity with God.[41] In 'Pied Beauty' (written 1877), accordingly, Hopkins celebrates 'all things counter, original, spare, strange ... swift, slow; sweet, sour; adazzle, dim' as manifestations of the infinite variety of God's creation: 'He fathers-forth whose beauty is past change: / Praise him'.[42] In 'As Kingfishers Catch Fire' (written 1877), the uniqueness of the flashes of light and peals of sound that 'Each moral thing ... Deals out' leads to a similar insight: 'Christ plays in ten thousand places, / Lovely in limbs, and lovely in eyes not his'.[43]

The vivid specificity of Hopkins's images thus record and propound a nuanced conception of how the mind makes meaning of sense experience and of how sensation lends concreteness and force to transcendent ideas. The sounds and syntax of his poetry also register his exploration of the interaction of the mind and body, both in the real-life experiences recorded and examined in his poems and in the experiences they offer readers. For instance, the attention to sound in 'As Kingfishers Catch Fire', where 'Stones ring;...each tucked string tells, [and] each hung bell's / Bow swung finds tongue', parallels the poem's attention to the power of the sounds of language.[44] The close association between the sounds of Hopkins's poems and the sounds he describes in them characterizes his entire *oeuvre,* and suggests how centrally it concerns itself with the interplay of immediate and mediated sensation, that is, of bodily and mental experience. 'Poetry is speech framed for contemplation of the mind', he wrote in his *Journal,* 'to be heard for its own sake and interest even over and above its interest of meaning...at least the grammatical, historical, and logical meaning'.[45] Here Hopkins thoroughly takes for granted that both mind and body participate in imagined sense experience. Precisely because it is framed for the mind, the poem is *heard* in ways that go beyond semantic meaning. Hopkins's syntax assumes a similar dynamic interaction. As Susan Chambers argues, his experiments with representing consciousness involve a 'kinesthetics of syntax' that generates effects both within the poem and for the reader, effects that are 'mental as well as auditory, muscular and musical, visceral and intellectual at once'.[46] By offering a mimesis of the rhythms of thought, with all its sudden epiphanies and anxious stretches of uncertainty, the syntax of Hopkins's poems continues the experiments of Tennyson and Browning in representing the movements and operations of the mind.

These experiments are also pursued by Swinburne. Since the publication of *Poems and Ballads, First Series* in 1866, he has been understood as the foremost practitioner of literary aestheticism, the leader of the so-called 'fleshly school' of poetry. Indeed, his poems present the human body in strikingly somatic, carnal terms. But the sensuality of his work has mistakenly led not only initial readers but later critics to misunderstand the stakes of his 'fleshly' poetics—stakes that are in fact thoroughly and rigorously philosophical.[47] Whereas Hopkins' poetics is shaped by the idealist philosophy of his teachers and the transcendentalism of his religious beliefs, Swinburne embraces an empiricism that sets itself against all claims for inborn ideas—but not against the powers of the mind. Indeed, reading Swinburne in conjunction with Hopkins demonstrates once again how much both empiricism and idealism intersected in the Victorian period in arguments about the ways the mind participates in acts of sensation and in the intellectual labour of reflection, memory, and imagination that follows on and makes use of it.

Swinburne's poetry is also important in extending Tennyson's exploration in *In Memoriam* of the ways in which the limits of sense experience trace a boundary to human knowledge. Unlike Tennyson, Swinburne refuses to speculate about what lies 'behind the veil': 'Who knows if haply the shadow of death / May be not the light of life?' he asks in 'Neap-Tide' (1889).[48] 'No sense that for ever the limits of sense engird, / No hearing or sight that is vassal to form or speech', he writes in 'The Seaboard' (1884), 'Learns ever.../ Hears ever.../ Sees ever.../ Clasps ever.../ The goal that is not, and ever again the goal'.[49] What lies beyond human sensory capacities, Swinburne argues throughout his poetry, lies beyond the scope of human knowledge.

Equally important, he draws on Tennyson in scrupulously marking the ways in which he invests immediate sensory experience with larger meanings. In early poems such as 'The Garden of Proserpine' (1866), the imaginary 'sleepy world' in which the poem is set is twice removed from 'the world' of shared reality and all its labours, temporal rhythms, and pains: 'Here…in doubtful dreams of dreams'.[50] In later descriptive poems such as 'By the North Sea' (1880) and 'The Lake of Gaube' (1904), the investment of meaning is linguistic and cognitive rather than fantastical. In 'The Mill Garden' (1884), Swinburne deconstructs the experientially instantaneous sight of the flowers in the garden into bits of raw sensory data, the names of everyday language, and the sense-making ideas of depth and height:

> Stately stand the sunflowers, glowing down the garden-side,
> Ranged in royal rank arow along the warm grey wall,
> Whence their deep disks burn at rich midnoon afire with pride,
> Even as though their beams indeed were sunbeams, and the tall
> Sceptral stems bore stars whose reign endures, not flowers that fall.[51]

Swinburne shows how the sunflowers present a 'glowing', fiery brightness of 'deep disks' vividly contrasting with the 'grey wall' behind them. They look like light arranged in lines and circles, but they are already cast in words that belong to quotidian existence and presented according to a specifically poetic syntax characterized by inversions and interruptions. By calling attention to itself, the simile in the fourth line emphasizes how visual stimuli, language, and cognition interact in the process of perception, as do the more subtle metaphors contained in words such as 'royal' and 'reign'. Throughout his work, Swinburne explores how the special resources of poetic language—figures, images, lines, syntax—can reveal the interchange of minds and bodies in real-life experience and in memory and imagination, on the page and in the mind of the reader. In so doing, he participates in an enquiry which lies at the very heart of Victorian poetry.

NOTES

1. Henry Jones, *Browning as a Philosophical and Religious Teacher* (New York: Macmillan and Co., 1891), 35.
2. For an overview, see Luke Herrmann, *Nineteenth Century British Painting* (London: Giles de la Mare, 2000). See also Elizabeth Prettejohn, *Art for Art's Sake: Aestheticism in Victorian Painting* (New Haven: Yale University Press for the Paul Mellon Center for Studies in British Art, 2007). On British impressionism, see Anna Greutzner Robins, *A Fragile Modernism: Whistler and His Impressionist Followers* (New Haven: Yale University Press for the Paul Mellon Center for Studies in British Art, 2007).
3. See Nicholas Dames, *The Physiology of the Novel: Reading, Neural Science, and the Form of Victorian Fiction* (Oxford: Oxford University Press, 2007).
4. See Ian Small, *Conditions for Criticism: Authority, Knowledge, and Literature in the Late Nineteenth Century* (Oxford: Clarendon Press, 1991), 65–70.
5. On this debate, see Small, *Conditions for Criticism*, 64–88.
6. On Pearson and this debate more generally, including its impact on the Victorian novel, see George Levine, *Dying to Know: Scientific Epistemology and Narrative in Victorian England* (Chicago: University of Chicago Press, 2002), 220–267.

7. See Dames, *Physiology of the Novel*; Levine, *Dying to Know*; Small, *Conditions for Criticism*, 64–88.

8. Wendell V. Harris, *The Omnipresent Debate: Empiricism and Transcendentalism in Nineteenth-Century English Prose* (DeKalb: Northern Illinois University Press, 1981).

9. William Elford Rogers, *The Three Genres and the Interpretation of Lyric* (Princeton: Princeton University Press, 1983), 68–69.

10. Noel Jackson, *Science and Sensation in Romantic Poetry* (Cambridge: Cambridge University Press, 2008), 12.

11. Arthur Henry Hallam, 'On Some of the Characteristics of Modern Poetry and on the Lyrical Poems of Alfred Tennyson,' *The Englishman's Magazine*, August, 1831, in Walter E. Houghton and G. Robert Stange, eds., *Victorian Poetry and Poetics*, 2nd edn. (Boston: Houghton Mifflin Co., 1968), 848–860, 850.

12. Sydney Dobell, 'Lecture on the 'Nature of Poetry' (1857), in *Thoughts on Art, Philosophy, and Religion* (London: Smith, Elder, & Co., 1876), 22, 55.

13. Gerard Manley Hopkins to Robert Bridges, May 13 1878, in Gerard Manley Hopkins, *Selected Letters*, ed. Catherine Phillips (Oxford: Clarendon Press, 1990), 95, 97, 97; Hopkins to Bridges, Aug. 21 1877, in *Selected Letters*, 91.

14. Robert Browning, 'Introductory Essay' ['Essay on Shelley'] [1852], in *Robert Browning: The Poems*, 2 vols., eds. John Pettigrew and Thomas J. Collins (New Haven: Yale University Press), i. 999–1013, 1001. J. Hillis Miller, *The Disappearance of God Five Nineteenth-Century Writers* (Cambridge: Belknap Press, 1963), 81–156.

15. Walter Pater, 'The School of Giorgione', in *The Renaissance; Studies in Art and Poetry*, ed. Adam Phillips (Oxford: Oxford University Press, 1986), 86, 83, italics in the original.

16. Pater, 'Preface' to *The Renaissance*, xxx.

17. On visual dynamics in the poetry of Morris, see Margaret A. Lourie, 'The Embodiment of Dreams: William Morris' 'Blue Closet' Group', *Victorian Poetry*, 15 (1977): 193–206; in Dowson, see Stephanie Kuduk Weiner, 'Sight and Sound in the Poetic World of Ernest Dowson', *Nineteenth-Century Literature*, 60 (2006), 481–509.

18. Christina Rossetti, 'Goblin Market', in *The Complete Poems of Christina Rossetti* (London: Penguin, 2001), 16. On Rossetti's use of lists, see Sean C. Grass, 'Nature's Perilous Variety in Rossetti's Goblin Market', *Nineteenth-Century Literature*, 51 (1996), 356–376. On description in Symons's decadent poetry, see Michael J. O'Neal, 'The Syntactic Style of Arthur Symons', *Language and Style*, 15 (1982), 208–218.

19. Jason R. Rudy, *Electric Meters: Victorian Physiological Poetics* (Athens: Ohio University Press, 2009), 2.

20. Hallam, 'On Some of the Characteristics of Modern Poetry', 851, 853.

21. Hallam, 'On Some of the Characteristics of Modern Poetry', 850.

22. Donald S. Hair, *Tennyson's Language* (Toronto: University of Toronto Press, 1991), 41–56.

23. Laura J. Snyder, *Reforming Philosophy: A Victorian Debate on Science and Society* (Chicago: University of Chicago Press, 2006), 37.

24. Snyder, *Reforming Philosophy*, 37–38, 39.

25. William Whewell, *History of Scientific Ideas, Being the First Part of the Philosophy of the Inductive Sciences*, 2 vols., 3rd edn. (London: John W. Parker and Son, 1858), i. 58.

26. Carol T. Christ, *The Finer Optic: The Aesthetic of Particularity in Victorian Poetry* (New Haven: Yale University Press, 1975), 26.

27. Tennyson, 'Mariana', in *Poems of Tennyson*, 3 vols., ed. Christopher Ricks (Berkeley: University of California Press, 1989), i. 209.

28. Tennyson, 'The Lady of Shallot', in *Poems of Tennyson*, i. 393.

29. Tennyson, 'Ulysses', in *Poems of Tennyson*, i. 618.

30. Tennyson, *In Memoriam*, in *Poems of Tennyson*, ii. 374.

31. T. S. Eliot, 'In Memoriam', in *Essays Ancient and Modern* (New York: Harcourt, Brace, 1936), 186–203, 201.

32. Alexander Bain, *The Senses and the Intellect*, 3rd edn. (London: Longmans, Green, and Co., 1868), facsimile reprint Elibron Classics (2005), 104, 244, italics in the original.

33. Browning, 'Fra Lippo Lippi', in *The Poetical Works of Robert Browning*, eds. Ian Jack et al. (Oxford: Oxford University Press, 1988-), v. 49.

34. Browning, 'Abt Vogler', in *Robert Browning: The Poems*, i. 780.

35. Richard S. Kennedy and Donald S. Hair, *The Dramatic Imagination of Robert Browning: A Literary Life* (Columbia: University of Missouri Press, 2007), 303.

36. Browning, 'How It Strikes a Contemporary', in *Poetical Works of Robert Browning*, v. 179–80.

37. See Daniel Brown, *Hopkins' Idealism: Philosophy, Physics, Poetry* (Oxford: Clarendon Press, 1997), 1–42, especially 7–9, 25–27.

38. Hopkins, *The Journals and Papers of Gerard Manley Hopkins*, eds. Humphrey House and Graham Storey (London: Oxford University Press, 1959), 120.

39. Hopkins, 'Hurrahing in Harvest', in *The Poetical Works of Gerard Manley Hopkins*, ed. Norman H. Mackenzie (Oxford: Clarendon Press, 1990), 148–49. I have removed Hopkins's diacritical marks.

40. Brown, *Hopkins' Idealism*, 186.

41. W. H. Gardner, 'Introduction' to *Poems and Prose of Gerard Manley Hopkins* (London: Penguin, 2008), xx.

42. Hopkins, 'Pied Beauty', in *Poetical Works of Gerard Manley Hopkins*, 144.

43. Hopkins, 'As Kingfishers Catch Fire', in *Poetical Works of Gerard Manley Hopkins*, 141.

44. James I. Wimsatt, *Hopkins's Poetics of Speech Sound: Sprung Rhythm, Lettering, Inscape* (Toronto: University of Toronto Press, 2006), 111, emphasizes that 'Hopkins's theories of language and poetry underwent important changes between his early university days and his late twenties', shifting from an interest in 'onomatopoetic evocation of lexical meanings' to a 'sensory and emotional inscape, particularly aided by verse's repetitions of the speech-sound figures.'

45. Hopkins, *Journals and Papers*, 289.

46. Susan Chambers, 'Gerard Manley Hopkins and the Kinesthetics of Conviction', *Victorian Studies*, 51 (2008), 7–35, 25.

47. I make this argument more fully in 'Knowledge and Sense Experience in Swinburne's Late Poetry', in Yisrael Levin, ed., *A. C. Swinburne and the Singing Word: New Perspectives on the Mature Work* (Farnham: Ashgate, 2010), 11–27.

48. Algernon Charles Swinburne, 'Neap-Tide', in *The Poems of Algernon Charles Swinburne*, 6 vols. (London: Chatto & Windus, 1904), iii. 240.

49. Swinburne, 'The Seaboard', in *A Midsummer Holiday, Poems of Algernon Charles Swinburne*, vi. 6.

50. Swinburne, 'The Garden of Proserpine', in *Poems of Algernon Charles Swinburne*, i. 169.

51. Swinburne, 'The Mill Garden', in *A Midsummer Holiday, Poems of Algernon Charles Swinburne*, vi. 11.

SELECT BIBLIOGRAPHY

Armstrong, Isobel. *Victorian Poetry: Poetry, Poetics, and Politics*. (London: Routledge, 1993).
Blair, Kirstie. *Victorian Poetry and the Culture of the Heart* (Oxford: Clarendon Press, 2006).
Brown, Daniel. *Hopkins' Idealism: Philosophy, Physics, Poetry* (Oxford: Clarendon Press, 1997).
Chambers, Susan. 'Gerard Manley Hopkins and the Kinesthetics of Conviction.' *Victorian Studies* 51 (2008), 7–35.
Christ, Carol T. *The Finer Optic: The Aesthetic of Particularity in Victorian Poetry* (New Haven: Yale University Press, 1975).
Dames, Nicholas. *The Physiology of the Novel: Reading, Neural Science, and the Form of Victorian Fiction* (Oxford: Oxford University Press, 2007).
Dowling, Linda. *Language and Decadence in the Victorian Fin de Siècle* (Princeton: Princeton University Press, 1986).
Hair, Donald S. *Tennyson's Language* (Toronto: University of Toronto Press, 1991).
Jackson, Noel. *Science and Sensation in Romantic Poetry* (Cambridge: Cambridge University Press, 2008).
Levine, George. *Dying to Know: Scientific Epistemology and Narrative in Victorian England* (Chicago: University of Chicago Press, 2002).
Rudy, Jason R. *Electric Meters: Victorian Physiological Poetics* (Athens: Ohio University Press, 2009).
Rylance, Rick. *Victorian Psychology and British Culture, 1850–1880* (Oxford: Oxford University Press, 2000).
Small, Ian. *Conditions for Criticism: Authority, Knowledge, and Literature in the Late Nineteenth Century* (Oxford: Clarendon Press, 1991).
Snyder, Laura J. *Reforming Philosophy: A Victorian Debate on Science and Society* (Chicago: University of Chicago Press, 2006).
Tucker, Herbert F. *Tennyson and the Doom of Romanticism* (Cambridge: Harvard University Press, 1988).

CHAPTER 43

....

OUTER SPACE: PHYSICAL SCIENCE

....

ANNA HENCHMAN

VICTORIAN poets and physical scientists were both driven by two impulses: the desire to identify connections between apparently disparate entities and the use of the imagination to do so. While in poetry, disputes about what characterized poetic imagination were plentiful, the use of the imagination itself was generally not seen to be problematic. In the context of the British physical sciences, by contrast, attitudes toward the scientific imagination involved a profound tension between exercising the imagination through the use of analogy, and reining in the imagination by foregrounding the importance of empirical observation.

This essay begins by discussing the ambivalence about the imagination that characterizes Victorian astronomy and physics—the longing to connect as well as growing fears about doing so. Victorian poets turned to physical science both because it enabled them to articulate a sense of patterns and forces behind the everyday appearance of things, and in order to explore the imaginative act of making connections itself. The second part of this essay explores three concrete preoccupations that we find in Victorian poetry and science: first, identifying shapes that recur throughout the universe in a wide range of scales (waves, orbs, and discs); second, breaking down distinctions between gaseous, liquid, and solid matter; and third, focusing on forces and substances (such as gravity and light) that manage *physically* to travel from outer space to the vicinity of the earth.

The physical sciences involve the study of inorganic matter—anything that is not considered to be alive. In the Victorian period, they included astronomy, geology, chemistry, and physics, each of which possessed subdivisions that often overlapped, and that shifted with the changing context of scientific knowledge. We can register many of these changes in the terms that had not yet been coined in 1830, but were familiar by the end of the century. In 1842, the Victorians became the first to refer to the astronomical universe as 'outer space'. Thermodynamics, astrophysics, spectroscopy, X-rays, and even the word 'scientist' itself are salient examples. William Whewell first suggested using 'scientist' as a term in lieu of natural philosopher at the third meeting of the British Association for the Advancement of Science in 1833.[1] Physics involved increasing intersections between a set of forces that had been known as the 'imponderables': entities such as electricity, heat, and magnetism which clearly had a physical existence but did not possess the qualities usually associated with matter, including weight, impenetrability, or extension.[2]

Early in the Victorian period, the known dimensions of the interstellar astronomical universe had increased dramatically. William Herschel's discovery of Uranus in 1781 had doubled the size of the solar system. Then, in 1838, F. M. Bessel was the first to use stellar parallax successfully to calculate the distance of a nearby star. He determined that a star in the Swan—one of earth's closest neighbours—was 10.4 light years, or more than sixty trillion miles, away. It was not yet clear how far other stars might be—but what was certain was that light might take thousands of years to reach from more distant stars to the earth. The solar system, it now seemed, was at the centre of neither the universe nor even the Milky Way. The question of whether separate 'island universes' (what we now call galaxies) existed outside of the Milky Way was a topic of debate until 1925.[3]

Paradoxically, perhaps, within this increasingly vast, possibly infinite universe, the physical sciences offered several ways in which to envision a connectedness between parts of the material world that otherwise seemed entirely inaccessible. Literal and figurative images of connection fuse into one another, as we can see in the title of Mary F. Somerville's masterful *On the Connexion of the Physical Sciences,* first published in 1834. Somerville's book emphasizes the growing sense that there are unified laws which link electricity to magnetism, sound, and light. These connections are imagined in a variety of ways that were themselves difficult to distinguish: as interconnected laws (in terms of physical forces that turn out to behave in the same way), and as temporal or material continuity (star dust turns to stars and planets, and out of that same matter biological life is born). These links appear in physical forms found throughout the material universe: waves, orbs, and swirling discs. Each of these models of connection becomes a metaphor for the ways that the mind can extend itself out into the universe: through the vision, the spirit, the intellect, and the imagination.

THE SCIENTIFIC IMAGINATION

In order to understand the relationship between poetic and scientific imaginings, we need to appreciate the centrality of analogy in the Victorian scientific method. The activities of categorizing and hierarchizing knowledge relied both on making distinctions and on discovering connections between apparently unlike things. In the 1830s there was a particularly powerful sense that extraordinary connections were on the verge of being discovered between entities that were called imponderables, such as electricity, magnetism, and heat.

These discoveries directly depended on analogic thinking. In the cases of both gravity and electromagnetism, huge steps forward in science had depended on recognizing that phenomena that seemed unrelated were in fact indissolubly linked. Although Isaac Newton's discovery that gravity was the force that held the solar system together dated back to 1686, it was still a subject of intense excitement among Victorian scientists and poets alike. George Meredith refers to gravity as 'The mystic link... / Whereby star holds on star'.[4] Mary Somerville writes that, 'Particle acts on particle according to the same law when at sensible distances from each other... The earth and a feather mutually attract each other in the proportion of the mass of the earth to the mass of the feather'.[5] The major breakthroughs in wave theories of light, sound, electricity, and magnetism gradually occurred over the course of the nineteenth century. In 1830 John Herschel praised Hans Oersted for 'pertinaciously adher[ing] to the idea of a necessary connection between [electricity and magnetism]... His perseverance was at length rewarded by the complete disclosure of the wonderful phenomena of electro-magnetism'.[6] Herschel goes on to emphasize that 'the whole history of this beautiful discovery may serve to teach us reliance on those general analogies and parallels between great branches of science by which one strongly reminds us of another, though no direct connection appears'.[7] The belief in hidden connections between natural laws only grew in ensuing decades, as Michael Faraday theorized that electricity and magnetism were one and the same thing, and James Clerk Maxwell went on to confirm those theories through experiment. By the end of the century a further set of related phenomena had been discovered, including radio waves, X-rays, and the electron.

But a fear of seeing connections that were not in fact there went hand in hand with the investment in analogic thinking. This is one reason why, as Lorraine Daston and Peter Galison show in *Objectivity*, scientists increasingly worried about restraining their imagination, feeling that knowing too much about a subject might become a bias rather than an asset.[8] We see this split in astronomy in the contrast between William Herschel's insistence that his discovery of Uranus in 1781 was no accident but *depended* on his hard-won familiarity with the skies. A century later, fears that the human mind expected to see what it wanted to see led to worries about 'the personal equation' in astronomy. These fears manifested themselves in hiring untrained observers, and embracing what Daston and Galison term 'mechanical objectivity' in which the human tendency to interpret as one observes became less of a problem. Many saw the emphasis on empiricism as a particularly British approach to studying the natural world, in the tradition of Francis Bacon and John Locke, in contrast to German idealism, or *Naturphilosophie*. But the desire completely to separate science from imaginative thinking would always remain an impossible task. As Richard Holmes writes in reference to Charles Babbage, 'Science must always be more than the simple observation of phenomena or data. It was simultaneously a subjective training in observational skills, self-criticism, and interpretation'.[9]

In his 1872 *Essays on Astronomy*, popular astronomer Richard A. Proctor reflects on the scientist's need to possess a lively imagination. Proctor notes the fluidity with which both astronomer William Herschel (1738–1822) and his son John Herschel (1792–1871) moved between meticulous empirical observation and a willingness to theorize connections that could not be determined by experiment or observation. Proctor writes:

> Another faculty which the theorist should possess in a high degree is a certain liveliness of imagination, whereby analogies may be traced between the relations of the subject on which he is theorising and those of objects not obviously associated with that subject.... It is obvious that the faculty is of extreme importance, though it is one which requires a judicious control, since if it be too readily indulged it may at times lead us astray.[10]

What is at stake in this balance between recognizing connections and stopping the imagination from going too far is a tension between empirical and deductive approaches that had dominated British scientific debates since Bacon's 1620 *Novum Organum*. That balance was the most important source of controversy in nineteenth-century science. In discussions of how scientists worked, imagination was always set against observation.

Proctor emphasizes both the importance of the imagination and its dangers, invoking the need for restraint on the part of the scientist. Proctor suggests that talented scientists share the ability to identify similarities between apparently unlike things. He notes 'Sir John Herschel's aptitude in tracing such analogies' and Herschel's 'singularly strong belief in the existence of analogies throughout the whole range of created matter'.[11] Proctor cites a letter he himself received from Herschel in which he discusses the prevalence of forms of swirling discs at all scales of the astronomical universe. 'If these forms belong to and form part and parcel of the galactic system, then *that system includes within itself miniatures of itself on an almost infinitely reduced scale*' (emphasis mine).[12]

The sense of a sharp methodological divide between the sciences and the humanities was infinitely less pronounced than it is today. In the realm of poetry, writers tended not to worry about the power of the imagination. The use of analogy, metaphor, and metonymy to link unlike things was the norm. Many of the new ideas found *within* science became powerful resources for a wide range of Victorian poets, including Gerard Manley Hopkins; Alfred, Lord Tennyson; Christina Rossetti; George Meredith; Thomas Hardy; and Matthew Arnold. While it is true that rumblings about the forthcoming disciplinary divisions between the arts and the sciences were audible in the 1820s (as in Thomas Carlyle's 1829 'Signs of the Times'), and that science itself would become increasingly professionalized, cultural literacy crucially involved *both* poetic and scientific literacy. Poets were steeped in science, and scientists steeped in poetry. The great poems and science writing of the day appeared side by side in periodicals such as *Nature* and *The Westminster Review*. We find Tennyson cited on astronomy in Proctor's *Essays on Astronomy* and Sir Robert Ball's 1885 *Story of the Heavens* (which is then in turn cited in James Joyce's *Ulysses*). Both Dante's and Lord Byron's words appear in Mary Somerville's 1834 *Connexion*. The extent to which poets incorporate explicit references to science differs by degrees—Tennyson is repeatedly hailed as the poet with the most serious knowledge of science, and was inducted into the Royal Society in 1865.

Poets were drawn to the physical sciences for a wide range of reasons. For many poets the astronomical universe was still deeply allied with the heavens inhabited by some form of divine presence. Physical science, and astronomy in particular, offered new models for thinking about old mysteries: the origins of the cosmos, the transition between birth, life, and death, divine omnipresence, and the relationship between body and soul. In the minds of writers such as Hopkins, Tennyson, and Rossetti, epistemological questions about how we know what we know were intimately linked to cosmic and spiritual questions.

The nineteenth century saw a growing sense of connection across this staggeringly huge cosmos. Hidden and unexpected similarities between earth and the stars appeared in stellar spectroscopy, which proved that the very same chemical elements found on earth existed millions of miles away. At the same time, there was a sense that laws were being found that might connect ideas that had seemed utterly unrelated for centuries or millennia: the magnetic pull of iron to a flash of lightning, the motion of waves to the shape of light. Underwater telegraph cables used electricity to unite continents, the sun behaved according to the same laws of conservation as a coal stove, and geologists posited that continents that now lay thousands of miles apart had once been a single mass of land. In the works of Meredith, Hopkins, and Rossetti, these mysterious facts and phenomena became powerful metaphors for the unseen.

The remainder of this essay turns to look at several models of connection that occur in both poetry and scientific treatises. Instead of focusing on the one-way influence of physical science on poetry, I would like to call attention to patterns we find in both disciplines: a fascination with recurring shapes and forms, an interest in physical connections between the earthly and the cosmic, and a desire to upset distinctions between matter and force.

FORMS THAT RECUR IN NATURE: WAVES, ORBS, SWIRLS

The nineteenth century was marked by a growing awareness of recurring forms in the physical and life sciences. Johann Wolfgang von Goethe, for instance, was fascinated by the similarity between a leaf's structure and that of a human skeleton. One of the great successes of analogical thinking in the physical sciences involved the increasingly accepted idea that sound, light, electricity, and magnetism all had the properties of waves. Although Isaac Newton had proposed that light consisted of particles, the undulatory (or wave) theory of light gained more and more traction in the early decades of the nineteenth century. By the middle decades of the Victorian period, the question of what light—or other forms of what we now call electromagnetic radiation—consisted of was still highly mysterious. As Isobel Armstrong writes, 'It was possible to hold different accounts of the unseen agency of light ... Clerk Maxwell's electromagnetic theory of light, though formulated by 1864, and theorized by Faraday in 1846, was fully integrated into accounts of light in popular treatises only at the end of the century.'[13] Faraday's model proposed that electricity and magnetism were not only related—which scientists had suspected for decades—but actually inseparable from each other. The larger category of electromagnetic radiation included a vast spectrum of waves, only some of which were discovered by the end of the Victorian period. Undularity was a universal form. As Ralph Waldo Emerson would remark in his 1836 essay 'The Humanity of Science': 'The phenomena of sound and light were observed to be strikingly similar. Both observed the same law of reflection, of radiation, of interference and harmony. That is, two rays of light meeting, cause darkness; two beats of sound meeting, cause silence'.[14]

Undularity had longstanding associations with rhythm and poetic metre, a fact noted by poets and scientists alike. Arnold's description of the 'cadence' of pebbles flung by ocean waves explicitly links music with waves in 'Dover Beach'. Many critics have noted how the uneven length of that poem's lines evokes the shapes of breaking waves, while the metre mimics the back and forth motion of the water:

> Listen! you hear the grating roar
> Of pebbles which the waves draw back, and fling,
> At their return, up the high strand,
> Begin, and cease, and then again begin,
> With tremulous cadence slow, and bring
> The eternal note of sadness in.[15]

Tennyson's 'Break, break, break' provides a grimmer version of the ocean's metre. He places grief-laden silence between each crashing wave. William Whewell's discussion of time in his 1840 *Philosophy of the Inductive Sciences* implicitly likens time to a wave. Time is like 'a line indefinitely extended both ways' that can be broken up into forms of 'rhythm' or 'recurrence', including that of alternation, 'as when we have alternate strong and slight syllables'.[16] He writes that 'the simplest of all forms of recurrence is that which has no variety;—in which a series of units, each considered as exactly similar to the rest, succeed each other, as *one, one, one*'.[17] Such were the forms of electromagnetic waves. These forms of regular undulation—often with no palpable physical existence—were increasingly ubiquitous.

Two fascinating aspects of wave-like energy such as light and sound were first, their immaterial nature, and second, the fact that they seemed to require a medium through which to travel. As early as the 1840s Faraday's concept of the field suggested that some waves could travel through a vacuum. But most people, including many scientists, believed that the universe was filled with a substance called ether. One of the results of this property of waves was the fact that it was very difficult to represent what waves were like in a verbal context. This was a problem for both scientists and poets. In a chapter on the undular nature of sound, for instance, Somerville compares air to a field of corn. This enables her to place waves vividly before her readers:

> the propagation of sound may be illustrated by a field of corn agitated by the wind. However irregular the motion of the corn may seem on a superficial view, it will be found if the intensity of the wind be constant, that the waves are all precisely similar and equal, and that all are separated by equal intervals and move in equal times...as their oscillations do not all commence at the same time, but successively, the ears will have a variety of positions at one instant.[18]

Sound requires the medium of air, which Somerville describes as 'a compressible and elastic fluid'.[19] Corn requires an external force to act upon it (the wind). Sound moves from particle to particle within the air: 'when one particle begins to oscillate, it communicates its vibrations to the surrounding particles, which transmit them to those adjacent, and so on continually'.[20] Much as poets found it hard to depict ineffable concepts such as loss, futility, or faith, scientists struggled to explain discoveries that elude sensory perception. The distinction between wave as a substance and wave as a disturbance of that substance was particularly difficult to convey.

Scientists faced similar challenges in trying to convince their audiences that light was composed of waves rather than particles. We can see a striking exploration of light's wavy nature in Thomas Hardy's poem 'At Rushy-Pond'. The poem is not *about* the idea that light is a wave; instead it explores a paradox typical of many of Hardy's speakers—a preference for the absent image of someone over her present self. But Hardy was fascinated by the behaviour of light—its reflection, refraction, and colour, and we can read this poem as invoking the strangeness of the ideas about light that theorists of optics were proposing during his lifetime. The speaker of 'At Rushy-Pond' attends to two competing versions of the moon, the 'substant Thing' that hangs in the sky and its reflection in the pond before him. The poem juxtaposes the real moon with a luminous form teased by the 'winged whiffs' of wind blowing across the water. The conflict at the heart of the lyric lies in the speaker's response to these two images, a conflict that is re-enacted on the part of the reader, whose ability to visualize each version of the moon is utterly dependent on the descriptions Hardy provides.

The moon first appears as a reflection on the surface of the pond: 'On the frigid face of the heath-hemmed pond / There shaped the half-grown moon'.[21] Even in these first two lines, the poem endows the lunar reflection with a vitality that the actual moon lacks. The reflection is given the qualities of a living thing, growth and mobility, the ability to 'shape' itself. By contrast, the pond lies 'frigid'. The vitality of the reflected moon grows exponentially in the second stanza, where the speaker describes the wind's manipulation of the bright, watery reflection:

> And the wind flapped the moon in its float on the pool,
>   And stretched it to oval form;
> Then corkscrewed it like a wriggling worm;
>   Then wanned it weariful.

This stanza takes the reader through several transformations of the moon's image, including flapping, stretching, and corkscrewing, each of which are performed on the water by the wind. The reflection dances before the speaker like something alive, thereby gaining a sensory salience that the actual moon lacks.[22] In the next stanza the speaker confesses, 'I cared not for conning the sky above / Where hung the substant Thing'. However illogical, his fascination with the wriggling form makes sense from a visual standpoint: the reflection's motion and proximity draw his eyes away from the actual moon down to the waving reflection. The combination of light, wind, and water allow Hardy plausibly, but surprisingly, to describe the reflection as 'corkscrewed', elongated and twisted round. In an even more rare formulation, he describes the moon as a wriggling worm: slender, linear, and organic, as opposed to fat, spherical, and rocky.[23]

If we think about the status of matter in this image of a reflected moon moving on a wind-blown pond, we start to gauge some of the distinctions in types of substance that interest both poets and physical scientists. Each of these substances possesses different properties. Wind is never visible except in its effects on other things. 'Who has seen the wind?' Christina Rossetti will ask.[24] Light lacks substance, but is radiant and warm, while water here is liquid, three-dimensional, and whiffed into visible waves. Then there is the solid moon—hanging there in the sky, with an actual diameter that is one-fourth as wide as the earth's, Somerville notes. It is a typical strategy of Hardy's to use the reflected light from celestial bodies to think about how one person fails to pay attention to the presence of another.

Orbs

Another fundamental form that seemed increasingly to populate the cosmos was the sphere. The science writer Robert Chambers describes 'mazy dances of vast families of orbs' that make up the newly observed stellar universe.[25] One of the abiding questions was whether galaxies equivalent to our own existed outside of the Milky Way. As Linda E. Marshall explains, Christina Rossetti was more prescient than many of her contemporaries in believing that multiple galaxies did indeed exist.[26] In 'All Thy Works Praise Thee, O Lord', subtitled 'a processional of creation', Rossetti has the 'Powers' recite the following lines: 'We Powers are powers because He makes us strong; / Wherefore we roll all rolling orbs along, / We move all moving things, and sing our song'.[27] Marshall aptly notes that 'For Rossetti, the new astronomy, like contemporary advances in science and technology generally, was an additional source of those [scriptural] parables and analogies which by means of the visible unearth the invisible'.[28]

Tennyson was particularly attached to the word 'orb' which he uses repeatedly, and in a variety of ways. The line 'Thine are these orbs of light and shade' in the prologue to *In Memoriam* refers most clearly to the moons and planets of the solar system, but with it he also invokes individual human beings who are both independent individuals, and part of a larger system.[29] In physical terms, this tension between self and system was explained by way of gravity: gravity held systems of stars and planets together, and likewise held particles of matter together in the form of spheres. 'A solid sphere...may be supposed to consist of an infinite number of concentric hollow spheres', writes Somerville.[30] Spheres are evident in the shape of the earth and of the sun, which Tennyson terms, respectively, 'This round of green, this orb of flame' (*In Memoriam*, section XXXIV). The roundness of the earth is rarely perceived directly, and both Hardy and Tennyson remark on the difficulty of reconciling the image of a perfectly rounded earth with the earth as they know it from its surface. In Hardy's 1866 poem 'At a Lunar Eclipse', the speaker follows the shadow of the earth as it 'steals along upon the Moon's meek shine'.[31] He watches the flawlessly circular shadow of the earth, cast by the sun, travel across the moon's luminous surface. The lunar eclipse offers a rare glimpse of the earth's actual shape and position in space, here poised between the sun and the moon. The speaker wonders what connection that tiny circular shadow has with the earth as he *ordinarily* experiences it: as large, flat, stationary, and packed with colours, smells, and sounds. 'How shall I link such sun-cast symmetry / With the torn troubled form I know as thine...?' he wonders, addressing the earth: 'Can immense Mortality but throw / So small a shade...?' He struggles to relate the 'moil and misery' found on the surface of the earth to that perfect shadow.

SWIRLS

Herschel's suggestion that the world contains miniatures of itself at every scale resonated strongly with the way that many poets envisioned the organizing structures of the material world. One of the most complex recurring shapes found throughout the universe was a flat swirling disc made up of smaller individual units, such as solid stars, luminous star dust, or the rocky matter out of which Saturn's rings were composed. Some of these took a spiral shape, a shape that is discernible in the structure of the Milky Way, in other star clusters, and even in the proposed origins of the solar system, in which star dust evolved into the system of a sun, planets, and satellites it consists of today. The first spiral nebula was discovered by Lord Rosse in 1845, offering an image of a star system in the process of forming and condensing into a more solid system of stars and satellites. In 1887 a photograph was taken of the nebula in Andromeda, and as a result of the photograph's extended exposure, that nebula was discovered to have the shape of a spiral. (Only later would it turn out to be a separate galaxy.)

Hardy and Tennyson follow Shelley in likening these extra-terrestrial swirls to swarms of bees. The image first appears in Shelley's 1820 'The Cloud'. A rent in the cloud reveals stars peering from behind the moon: 'And I laugh to see them whirl and flee, / Like a swarm of golden bees'.[32] Although Tennyson excised the following passages from the final version of his 1833 poem 'The Palace of Art', the lines became well known. Richard Proctor would even use them as an epigraph to *Essays on Astronomy*. The scene depicts a female astronomer watching the skies from a tower through a telescope:

> Hither, when all the deep unsounded skies
>   Shudder'd with silent stars, she clomb,
> And as with optic glasses her keen eyes
>   Pierced thro' the mystic dome,
> Regions of lucid matter taking forms,
>   Brushes of fire, hazy gleams,
> Clusters and beds of worlds, and bee-like swarms
>   Of suns, and starry streams.[33]

Tennyson refers to some of the most striking findings in late eighteenth- and nineteenth-century astronomy here, including the many star clusters William Herschel had
observed, and the evolutionary account of the world. Later in the century we see Hardy
taking up the same image. He owned Proctor's 1872 *Essays on Astronomy* and would
certainly have seen the Tennyson epigraph, even if he did not know Tennyson's lines
before. In any case, the likening of stars to bees appealed to Hardy's lifelong fascination
with the mind's ability rapidly to move from the tiny to the cosmic.

Such analogies can be found throughout Hardy's writing. He sees a miniature form
of a nebula, for instance in a swarm of bees in the 1874 *Far from the Madding Crowd*.
These bees actually undergo the process of condensing into a seemingly solid body, just
like the luminous celestial matter that forms itself into a star according to the nebular
hypothesis:

> Bathsheba's eyes, shaded by one hand, were following the ascending multitude
> against the unexplorable stretch of blue ... A process somewhat analogous to that of
> alleged formations of the universe, time and times ago, was observable. The bustling
> swarm had swept the sky in a scattered and uniform haze, which now thickened to a
> nebulous centre: this glided on to a bough and grew still denser, till it formed a solid
> black spot upon the light.[34]

A crucial aspect of Hardy's strategy as a writer is to find, at microscopic and macroscopic
levels, elements of the natural world that illuminate the human. These bees are just one
instance of the continuities he sees throughout the structure of the cosmos. Humboldt
too remarks the fact that 'Arabian astronomers' compare the appearance of thousands of
shooting stars in the sky to 'swarms of locusts'.[35] Analogies often occurred between the
stars that thickly populated the sky and groups of animate beings. Rossetti gives voice
to the 'Stars' in this way, describing them as a 'throng': 'We Star-hosts numerous, innu-
merous, / Throng space with energy untumultuous, / And work His Will Whose eye
beholdeth us'.[36]

PHYSICAL LINKS: GRAVITY, LIGHT, COMETS, AND METEORITES

Faced with accounts of increasingly vast stretches of interstellar space, many Victorians
searched for images of literal and figurative connection with those distant spaces.
Scientists and literary writers often focused on moments of actual physical contact
or connection between the earth and bodies at great distances. Two forms of contact
were the force of gravity and rays of light. The tension between the inaccessibility of
the stars and these tenuous forms of contact appears throughout Victorian literature.
Hardy describes the 'fragile line of sight' that links two observers in *Two on a Tower* with
'the remotest star visible'.[37] In his 1888 poem 'Meditation Under Stars', George Meredith

wonders whether there can be any connection whatsoever between the cold light of the stars and 'our blood-warm Earth'.[38] For Meredith vision is not enough; the stars are 'seen' but 'unrevealed'. He initially articulates a sense of deep disconnect between earth and outer space. Connection, when it does come, comes by way of the heart rather than the eye:

> What links are ours with orbs that are
>   So resolutely far:
> The solitary asks, and they
> Give radiance as from a shield:
>   Still at the death of day,
>   The seen, the unrevealed.
>   Implacable they shine
> To us who would of Life obtain
> An answer for the life we strain
>   To nourish with one sign.
> Nor can imagination throw
> The penetrative shaft...

Here the vision that extends into space is repelled; light bounces off the stars and fails to penetrate their relation to earthly life; the stars 'give radiance as from a shield' rather than insight. The speaker strains for 'one sign' but the stars shine 'implacable'. The 'penetrative shaft' imagination attempts to throw falls back to earth with a thud. The language of shields and shafts subtly suggests military attack, and the earthly speaker's campaign does not work. On its own, 'the ball of sight' gets him nowhere, and he cannot yet find a link between the stellar and the human.

As the poem develops, however, love, 'the beating heart behind the ball of sight' does find a source of connection, envisioned as 'the mystic link / Whereby star holds on star'. In physical terms that force is gravity, expressed here in terms of touch (hold) rather than vision. On a metaphorical level, that hold registers a mysterious sense of similitude that extends between the stars and the inhabitants of earth. Neither vision nor imagination is enough: 'To deeper than this ball of sight / Appeal the lustrous people of the night'. But once the heart recognizes the stars as warm and lifelike, the speaker is suddenly able 'to penetrate black midnight':

> To feel...
>   That there with toil Life climbs the self-same Tree,
> Whose roots enrichment have from ripeness dropped.
> So may we read and little find them cold:
> ...to penetrate black midnight; see,
> Hear, feel, outside the senses; even that we,
> The specks of dust upon a mound of mould,
> We who reflect those rays, though low our place,
>   To them are lastingly allied.

Once that feeling of connection is achieved, outer space suddenly takes on the qualities of organic life: the warmth and vitality of trees and roots. Trees simultaneously extend themselves up into space and down into earth as they grow. In this poem roots and branches stand in for gravity, and gravity represents an almost spiritual link between living beings and lifeless stars.

Many writers resemble Meredith in envisioning gravity, light, and heat, as entities that were privileged in being able to stretch across the universe and connect the earthly with inaccessible outer space. When Tennyson writes, 'Science reaches forth her arms / To feel from world to world' (*In Memoriam,* section XXI), he figures the telescope as an agent of touch, extending itself into space to gather rays of light. As Isobel Armstrong has shown, Richard Proctor pictured the earth as a giant projecting device, sending images out into the universe:

> Events have happened on our earth and been forgotten, which, nevertheless, are at this very instant of my writing visible from some one or other of the orbs which people space...and there is no event...visible from standpoints without the earth, which has not thus been rendered visible over and over again hereafter as light-messages conveying its history have passed beyond star after star.[39]

Somerville points out just how empty the cosmos now seems to be: 'The known quantity of matter bears a very small proportion to the immensity of space. Large as the bodies are, the distances which separate them are immeasurably greater'.[40] But she depicts those spaces as 'traversed in all directions by light, heat, [and] gravitation'.[41] She wonders if gravity itself is subject to time as light and sound are, whether there is such a thing as the speed of gravity.

In the first volume of his magisterial *Cosmos,* published in 1845, Alexander von Humboldt likewise identifies light, heat, and gravity as our only forms of contact with remote stretches of space. But then he pauses to consider another of his own statements, adding another 'mode of contact' to the list:

> Another and different kind of cosmical or rather material mode of contact, is, however, opened to us, if we admit falling stars and meteoric stones to be planetary asteroids...They acquire an actual material existence for us, reaching our atmosphere from the remote regions of universal space, and remaining on the earth itself...we may examine, weigh, and analyse bodies that appertain to the outer world. This awakens, by the power of the imagination, a meditative spiritual strain of thought.[42]

Humboldt writes with wonder about the idea of examining and weighing matter that comes from outside the earth's atmosphere. Once again, the distinction between the remoteness of vision and the intimacy of touch becomes important. Humboldt's excitement at the idea of being able to touch a piece of outer space registers the longing for access we find in much Victorian writing about interstellar space.

In poetry, comets take on a similarly uncanny status as visitors from elsewhere that come into the neighbourhood of our planet for a short time, and then return to space. Temporally and spatially, they exist outside human scales, but they visit our world for a time. Of Donati's comet, Hardy writes:

It bends far over Yell'ham Plain,
And we, from Yell'ham Height,
Stand and regard its fiery train,
So soon to swim from sight.

It will return long years hence, when
As now its strange swift shine
Will fall on Yell'ham; but not then
On that sweet form of thine.[43]

The brief feeling of contact is articulated in the way that the bodies momentarily strain towards one another. The comet 'bends' down while the two observers ascend to 'Yell'ham Height'. And yet the scale on which comet and human beings exists enables only one moment of contact. Next time it visits earth they will be dead. Its 'fiery train' appears tiny in comparison to its actual size, the extent of which Hardy would have known. Humboldt notes:

> their tails in several instances extend over many millions of miles. The cone of luminous vapour which radiates from them has been found, in some cases (as in 1680 and 1811) to equal the length of the earth's distance from the sun,... It is even probable that the vapour of the tails of comets mingled with our atmosphere in the years 1819 and 1823.[44]

The strange juxtaposition found in astronomy between intimacy (touch, shine, or mingling) and distance (in space and in time) fires the imagination of poets and scientists. We see them constantly trying to translate the universe into earthly terms, but then reeling at the actual distances involved.

Often the strangeness of unseen forces and alien visitors is used to explore the aspects of earthly life that most elude comprehension, like the passage from life to death. After seeing Tempel's comet in 1864, Gerard Manley Hopkins likened himself to 'a slip of comet... Come out of space':

... when she sights the sun she grows and sizes
And spins her skirts out, while her central star
Shakes its cocooning mists; and so she comes
To fields of light; millions of travelling rays
Pierce her; she hangs upon the flame-cased sun,
And sucks the light as full as Gideon's fleece:
But then her tether calls her; she falls off,
And as she dwindles shreds her smock of gold
Amidst the sistering planets, till she comes
To single Saturn, last and solitary;
And then goes out into the cavernous dark.
So I go out: my little sweet is done:
I have drawn heat from this contagious sun:
To not ungentle death now forth I run.[45]

The sun is 'contagious' in that it attracts the speaker's attention, radiating heat and light, keeping earth and the comet in tow through its gravitational pull. The comet is 'pierce[d]' by 'millions of travelling rays', and travels on a 'tether', the path of its orbit around the sun. Life is figured as the small section of a comet's orbit during which it passes into earthly view. But what is most mysterious about Hopkins's description of this celestial body is how she passes back 'out into the cavernous dark'. The poem reminds us that human lives are punctuated by dark—the absence of life and consciousness—on both sides, before birth, and after death.

GAS, SOLID, AND LIQUID: THE LIQUEFACTION OF EARTH AND AIR

Many of the findings of the Victorian physical sciences upset distinctions that seemed fundamental—between particles and waves, between matter and the immaterial, between centre and periphery, and between the organic and the inorganic. When we look at verbal representations of the vast reaches of outer space, we find both poets and scientists using a similar set of techniques to help their readers imagine phenomena that elude or directly contradict human sensory perception. Scientists and poets both upset the distinctions between conventional ways of thinking about matter—as gas, liquid, and solid—by depicting gaseous things as liquid or solid. Shelley's depiction of the 'solid atmosphere' of a cloud is a striking precedent.[46] Somerville depicts outer space as a place that is neither full nor quite empty. She presents the interspaces between the stars as a kind of crossroads filled with perpetual activity:

> The known quantity of matter bears a very small proportion to the immensity of space. Large as the bodies are, the distances which separate them are immeasurably greater...It is clear that space is not pervaded by atmospheric air, since its resistance would, long ere this, have destroyed the velocity of the planets; neither can we affirm it to be a void, since it seems to be replete with ether, and traversed in all directions by light, heat, gravitation, and possibly by influences whereof we can form no idea.[47]

One of the challenges Somerville faces is attempting to help her readers imagine the scope of the spaces that astronomy involves. The image of light, heat, and gravitation ceaselessly traversing space helps to carve out the space itself in this passage. In *Dreaming by the Book,* Elaine Scarry details a range of strategies involved in enabling readers to enact complex acts of picturing in their heads. She argues that the sensory power of words often depends on setting one kind of substance against another substance. Scarry gives several examples, including a 'passing of a filmy surface over another (by comparison, dense) surface', human beings skating across the ice, or light sparkling on a gold shield:

It is often the case that in enlisting us into the mental action of building images, writers often purposely require us to take a scrim of what can only be half-imagined and superimpose what can be fairly fully imagined; just as an even fainter scrim of what can only be one-eighth imagined will be superimposed on the sturdy surface of the half-imagined. This constant layering of unequally achievable images provides the basic scaffolding of the imagination.[48]

If we extend this idea of Scarry's to all sorts of levels of contrast between different kinds of matter, suddenly a number of problems inherent in Victorian physical science become visible. Physicists, astronomers, and geologists are frequently attempting to convince their readers to imagine distinctions between two levels of essentially immaterial matter.

In the passage above, Somerville creates several different layers of the barely there. These vary greatly in density. In this context, what we ordinarily think of as thin air comes to seem thick with matter, capable of slowing the trajectories of stars, planets, and moons down to a stop. Ether (which would eventually be proven not to exist in the early twentieth century) has a mysterious status in between air and utter void. It allows things like light and heat to pass through it without slowing them down as it goes. The 'void', utter emptiness, is the standard against which we are asked to measure other things that barely seem to exist (such as ether and gravity and heat). Ether is not only 'replete', but the site of constant activity, 'traversed in all directions' by forces that criss-cross from system to system.

Hopkins in his 'Blessed Virgin Compared to the Air We Breathe' provides a prime example of such confusions of state. He thickens the air, making it fat with energy. The confusion begins with the title, in which an iconic human figure is likened to a gas. The blue atmosphere behaves like a liquid, 'lapping' around the four fingergaps.[49] Air is a 'bath'.[50] The air itself can be filled with other things—sapphire-shot, charged, and steeped. It can be folded around someone like a blanket—and it is constantly juxtaposed with dense, sharp, heavy minerals in this poem. A wide range of critics, from Gillian Beer and Daniel Brown to Alice Jenkins and Barri Gold have emphasized the importance of Faraday's and Maxwell's revisions of a Newtonian view of matter in Victorian literature. Jenkins explains that while an atomistic Newtonian view of space and matter involved a rigid distinction between space and the bodies that exist in that space, the development of field theory in the mid-1840s challenged such a distinction. Jenkins writes:

> The traditional view sees objects as having 'a definite form and a certain limited size', but in Faraday's new theory, 'that which represents size may be considered as extending to any distance to which the lines of force of the particle extend.' ... The physical boundaries of a body, then, are not those perceptible to the eye or touch.[51]

It is not simply that 'forces pervade all space and all the bodies in it; instead space and matter alike *consist in* these forces'.[52] As a result space is 'full, but full of force rather than full of objects...Each atom extends...throughout the whole of the solar system'.[53] Increasingly, matter does not seem to hold steady, or to have outlines, or edges. This is not only an idea that appeals to many literary writers, but also an idea that the scientists themselves are trying to get their minds around by thinking in terms of the contrasts in density that Scarry describes as central to literary technique.

We see this revised attitude toward matter in the fluidity of forms that start to appear as literary writers imagine the movements of the earth over millions of years. Noting that a solid substance mimics a gaseous substance if time is sped up enough, Tennyson turns landmasses into clouds that constantly shift their form:

> The hills are shadows, and they flow
> From form to form, and nothing stands;
> They melt like mist, the solid lands,
> Like clouds they shape themselves and go.

> (*In Memoriam,* section CXXIII)

This dramatic speeding up of time is a technique that T. H. Huxley will take up in his 1870 lecture to working-class men, 'On a Piece of Chalk'. Huxley demonstrates that what is now the familiar English countryside was once 'an ancient sea-bottom.... The earth...has been the theatre of a series of changes as vast in their amount as they were slow in their progress.... Our great mountain ranges...have all been upheaved'.[54] The imperceptibility of momentous change inspires Tennyson to call both astronomy and geology 'terrible muses'. He alludes to an anxiety that arises when a thing can be known only by analogy, rather than by direct observation. Behind fears about analogical thinking is a worry about the leap one makes between observing phenomena and making sense of what one observes. In some cases, extraordinary connections lead to incredible breakthroughs in scientific thought: Newton's gravitational pull and Faraday's model of electromagnetism. But in other cases, analogic thinking threatens the legibility of the world, and the edges or distinctions by which we separate this from that.

A final way that science was mobilized by literature was to theorize about the actual process by which the human mind connects things: what we might term thinking about thinking itself. Browning, for instance, compares the reader's act of synthesis to the astronomer's in the preface to *Paracelsus*: 'were my scenes stars, it must be his cooperating fancy which, supplying all chasms, shall collect the scattered lights into one constellation—a Lyre or a Crown'.[55] This itself is a wonderful metaphor for the mysterious action that the mind engages in when turning apparently shapeless or meaningless phenomena into meaning-laden forms. The comparison works on many levels—the act of constellation-building involves grouping stars together in a Linnaean or geographical fashion—that star is connected to that and not to that. It also involves imposing shapes on a set of points of light that in turn evoke narratives—the hunter, the Swan. It has the effect of making stars easier to identify and remember—and it also hints at the desire human beings have to turn something inorganic into something alive and laden with meaning. Browning suggests that the work of interpretation—of identifying analogies and seeing connections—is an advantage rather than a danger where his work is concerned. With this comparison we get a hint at the kinds of artistic and intellectual impulses that attract Victorian poets to the vast, remote phenomena of the physical sciences.

NOTES

1. Richard Holmes, *The Age of Wonder: How the Romantics Discovered the Beauty and Terror of Science* (New York: Pantheon Books, 2008), 449.
2. Laura Saltz, 'The Magnetism of a Photograph: Margaret Fuller and Daguerrotype Portraiture', *English Language Notes*, 56 (2010), 110–112.
3. Michael J. Crowe, *Modern Theories of the Universe: From Herschel to Hubble* (New York: Dover Publications, 1994).
4. George Meredith, 'Meditation Under Stars', in *The Poems of George Meredith*, ed. Phyllis Bartlett (New Haven: Yale University Press, 1978), 528.
5. Mary. F. Somerville, *On the Connexion of the Physical Sciences* (London: John Murray, 1840), 6–7.
6. John F. W. Herschel, *A Preliminary Discourse on the Study of Natural Philosophy* (London: Longman, Rees, Orme, Brown, and Green, 1830), 340.
7. Herschel, *A Preliminary Discourse*, 340.
8. Lorraine Daston and Peter Galison, *Objectivity* (New York: Zone Books, 2007), 115–190.
9. Holmes, *The Age of Wonder*, 440.
10. Richard A. Proctor, *Essays on Astronomy* (London: Longmans, Green, and Co., 1872), 21.
11. Proctor, *Essays on Astronomy*, 21.
12. Proctor, *Essays on Astronomy*, 22.
13. Isobel Amstrong, *Victorian Glassworlds: Glass Culture and the Imagination 1830–1880* (Oxford: Oxford University Press, 2008), 283.
14. Cited in Laura Saltz, *Photography's Imponderables: American Romanticism and the Science of Light* (forthcoming book manuscript).
15. Matthew Arnold, 'Dover Beach', in *Selected Poems* (New York: Penguin Classics, 1995), 164.
16. William Whewell, *Philosophy of the Inductive Sciences, Founded upon their History* (London: John W. Parker, 1840), 126.
17. Whewell, *Philosophy of the Inductive Sciences*, 126.
18. Somerville, *Connexion*, 147.
19. Somerville, *Connexion*, 148.
20. Somerville, *Connexion*, 148.
21. Thomas Hardy, 'At Rushy-Pond', in *Thomas Hardy: The Complete Poems*, ed. James Gibson (Houndmills, Basingstoke: Palgrave, 2001), 713–714.
22. See Elaine Scarry's chapter 'Stretching, Folding, Tilting', in *Dreaming by the Book* (Princeton: Princeton University Press, 1999), 111–157.
23. See Elaine Scarry, *Dreaming by the Book*, 3–9.
24. Christina Rossetti, *Sing-Song: A Nursery Rhyme Book*, in *Christina Rossetti: The Complete Poems*, ed. R. W. Crump (New York: Penguin Books, 2005), 250.
25. Robert Chambers, *Vestiges of the Natural History of Creation* (London: John Churchill, 1846), 17.
26. Linda E. Marshall, 'Astronomy of the Invisible: Contexts for Christina Rossetti's Heavenly Parables', in *Women's Writing*, 2 (1995), 176–177.
27. Rossetti, 'All Thy Works Praise Thee, O Lord', in *Poems*, 338.
28. Marshall, 'Astronomy of The Invisible', 168.
29. Alfred, Lord Tennyson, 'Prologue' to *In Memoriam*, in *Tennyson: A Selected Edition*, ed. Christopher Ricks (Berkeley: University of California Press, 1989), 342.
30. Somerville, *Connexion*, 5.

31. Hardy, 'At a Lunar Eclipse', in *Poems*, 116.
32. P. B. Shelley, 'The Cloud', in *Shelley: Selected Poetry* (New York: Penguin, 1985), 181.
33. Tennyson, 'The Palace of Art', in *Poems*, 64.
34. Thomas Hardy, *Far from the Madding Crowd* (New York: Penguin Books, 2003), 156–157.
35. Humboldt, *Cosmos*, 124.
36. Rossetti, *Poems*, 338.
37. Thomas Hardy, *Two on a Tower* (Oxford: Oxford University Press, 1993), 32.
38. Meredith, 'Meditation Under Stars', in *Poems*, 538.
39. Quoted in Armstrong, *Glassworlds*, 255.
40. Somerville, *Connexion*, 429.
41. Somerville, *Connexion*, 429.
42. Alexander von Humboldt, *Cosmos: Sketch of a Physical Description of the Universe*, Vol. 1, trans. E. C. Otte (Baltimore: Johns Hopkins Press, 1849), 137.
43. Hardy, *Poems*, 151.
44. Humboldt, *Cosmos*, 100.
45. Gerard Manley Hopkins, *Selected Poetry* (Oxford: Oxford University Press, 1998), 39.
46. Shelley, *Selected Poetry*, 161.
47. Somerville, *Connexion*, 429.
48. Scarry, *Dreaming by the Book*, 76.
49. Hopkins, 'Blessed Virgin Compared to the Air We Breathe', in *Poetry*, 142.
50. Hopkins, 'Blessed Virgin', in *Poetry*, 142. See Daniel Brown, *Hopkins' Idealism: Philosophy, Physics, Poetry* (Oxford: Clarendon Press, 1997) 244–262.
51. Alice Jenkins, *Space and the 'March of Mind': Literature and the Physical Sciences in Britain 1815–1850* (Oxford: Oxford University Press, 2007), 200.
52. Jenkins, *Space and the 'March of Mind'*, 200.
53. Jenkins, *Space and the 'March of Mind'*, 201.
54. Thomas Henry Huxley, 'On a Piece of Chalk: A Lecture to Workingmen', in *Selections from Huxley* (Boston: Ginn and Company, 1911), 70–71.
55. Robert Browning, 'Preface' to *Paracelsus*, quoted in C. Willard Smith, *Browning's Star-Imagery: The Study of a Detail in Poetic Design* (Princeton: Princeton University Press, 1941), 3.

SELECT BIBLIOGRAPHY

Armstrong, Isobel, *Victorian Glassworlds: Glass Culture and the Imagination, 1830–1880* (Oxford: Oxford University Press, 2008).
Beer, Gillian, *Open Fields: Science in Cultural Encounter* (Oxford: Oxford University Press, 1996).
Brown, Daniel, *Hopkins' Idealism: Philosophy, Physics, Poetry* (Oxford: Oxford University Press, 1996).
Crowe, Michael J., *Modern Theories of the Universe: From Herschel to Hubble* (New York: Dover Publications, 1994).
Daston, Lorraine, and Galison, Peter, *Objectivity* (Cambridge, Mass.: Zone Books; Distributed by the MIT Press, 2007).
Gold, Barri J., *ThermoPoetics: Energy in Victorian Literature and Science* (London and Cambridge, Mass.: The MIT Press, 2010).

Gossin, Pamela, *Thomas Hardy's Novel Universe: Astronomy, Cosmology, and Gender in the Post-Darwinian World* (Aldershot: Ashgate, 2007).

Holmes, Richard, *The Age of Wonder: How the Romantic Generation Discovered the Beauty and Terror of Science* (New York: Pantheon Books, 2008).

Hunt, Bruce J., *Pursuing Light and Power: Technology and Physics from James Watt to Albert Einstein* (Baltimore: The Johns Hopkins University Press, 2010).

Jenkins, Alice, *Space and the 'March of Mind': Literature and the Physical Sciences in Britain, 1815–1850* (Oxford: Oxford University Press, 2007).

Korg, Jacob, 'Astronomical Imagery in Victorian Poetry', in James Paeadis and Thomas Postlewait, eds., *Victorian Science and Victorian Values: Literary Perspectives* (New Brunswick: Rutgers University Press, 1985), 137–158.

Lightman, Bernard, *Victorian Popularizers of Science: Designing Nature for New Audiences* (Chicago: University of Chicago Press, 2007).

Marshall, Linda E.. 'Astronomy of the Invisible: Contexts for Christina Rossetti's Heavenly Parables', in Mary Arseneau, Anthony Harrison, and Lorraine Janzen Kooistra, eds., *The Culture of Christina Rossetti: Female Poetics and Victorian Contexts* (Athens: Ohio University Press, 1999).

Millhauser, M., *Fire and Ice: the Influence of Science on Tennyson's Poetry*. Tennyson Society Monographs, 4 (Lincoln [Eng.]: Tennyson Society Tennyson Research Centre, 1971).

Otis, Laura, *Literature and Science in the Nineteenth Century: An Anthology* (Oxford: Oxford University Press, 2002).

CHAPTER 44

···

CITY AND STREET

···

ROLF P. LESSENICH

'LONDON—World City 1800–1840' was the subject of a rich exhibition of objects and texts in Essen's Villa Hügel in 1992. It illustrated London's growth during the period that saw the doubling of its population and the explosion of its industrialization, along with the demolition of its medieval wall and the building of new bridges. It signalled the beginning of scholarly interest in the role of the city during the Romantic period, so that scholars could no longer assume that the Victorian city was an innovative product of the reign of Queen Victoria. In the meantime, much research has been done on London as cosmopolis in the poetry, prose, and arts of the Romantic period, and it has become apparent that, contrary to the traditional assumption of a divide between country and city, the two spaces had begun to intersect. It was only after 1830, and more so after 1850 with the viaducts of the London railways above residential areas and the rapid increase of factories in the heart of London, that—as Philip Davis puts it—'the city, roofed in and smoked over, became almost literally a huge separate world of its own, sealed off spacially and historically'.[1]

Rural travellers like William Cobbett found traces of the city everywhere: canals, feeder roads, and other supply networks. Conversely, Londoners visiting the new fashionable panoramas in the Rotunda of Leicester Square and the Great Rooms in Spring Gardens, Robert Barker's panoramic *View of London* of 1791, and Thomas Girtin's *Eidometropolis* of 1802, surveyed their city from a vantage point in the country. These first panoramas made the visitors wander around a 360-degree view from sunlit gardens to smoky forges and factories. Barker's Rotunda, with its two panorama levels, remained a popular city experience for seventy years, well into the Victorian period. Later panoramas of London and Paris were simply too big in size to allow a view of the whole, and fragmentation of view, as well as of society, became a major theme in Victorian city poetry. New and popular magic lantern shows, which brought changing scenes of nature and the Gothic into London, had been initiated by the illusionist Philippe Jacques de Loutherbourg's *Eidophusicon* in Lisle Street near Leicester Square (1781), by Paul Philipsthal's *Phantasmagoria* at the illegitimate Lyceum Theatre in the Strand

(1801), as well as by Jacques Daguerre's *Diorama* imported from Paris to Regent's Park (1823).[2] Thus, Romantic perspectivism and subjectivism, which opened our eyes to the fact that we see the same scene differently in various lights and moods and with various pre-conceived expectations, stood at the beginning of the modern extension of actual by virtual sights, adding new alienated spaces to old familiar ones.[3]

London was quickly becoming a noisy city of multiplying popular visual attractions. Blake, Keats, and the whole 'Cockney School' were Londoners, and poets from the country such as Wordsworth and Coleridge were simultaneously repelled and fascinated by the whirl and speed of a rapidly expanding London. The formerly established contrast between Wordsworth's predominant fear of London and Walt Whitman's predominant enjoyment of New York is no longer tenable.[4] The Romantic poets visited the glaring shows and the illegitimate theatres of London, many of them in the poor quarters where a new 'low-class culture' now challenged the elitist culture of the classical tradition. Their acceptance of the city as a world of art and fanciful entertainment recurred in the Decadent neo-Romanticism of the Fin de Siècle, when the poetry of Frederick Locker-Lampton, Austin Dobson, and Laurence Binyon focussed on the pleasures while excluding the pains of London, and when Oscar Wilde and the early Decadent Arthur Symons replaced the Romantic joy in the city's remaining intersections with original nature by a praise of artificial nature and artificial luxury.[5] Unlike their Romantic predecessors such as Charles Lamb and William Hazlitt, however, they tended towards escapism in their fascination with London's pleasures and their disgust with London's poor.

Romanticism had begun to renegotiate the ugly and the ideal, revulsion and exaltation. The Romantic exploration of the unconscious unveiled man's love/hate relationship with the monstrous, the terrible, the haunting, the sublime—in short the Gothic, as the uncanny other which is but a projection of the self. As Alfred de Musset's portrait of Paris in his Byronic poem *Rolla* (1833) affirms, ugliness and corruption overshadowed the initial impression of beauty and health when entering the modern city from without: 'Thus, when you enter society, you find its sewers.'[6] On his first visit to London in 1820, John Clare saw an illuminated space in the night from afar and, on entering, was confused by 'the excess of novelty', meaning the gas light that was introduced in London in the century's first decade.[7] The country resident and sensitive artist who went to live in London could be driven to the brink of madness by London's sights and sounds. The theme of threatening city madness recurs again and again in Victorian city poetry, from Arthur Hugh Clough to William Sidney Walker and Mathilde Blind. In Victorian literature, this old order of the city's first splendid appearance and its subsequently revealed abject reality was frequently reversed.[8] Dickens's *Bleak House* (1852–3), for instance, begins with a memorable portrait of the fog and dirt and visual as well as social fragmentation of London, and *Our Mutual Friend* (1864–5) with the poverty and criminal scenes of London, before the city's fascination, beauty, and humanity are set in relief. Hippolyte Taine's *Notes sur l'Angleterre* (1871) further expands on the unnatural deformities of London, subsequently qualifying the sense of disgust by a strong fascination with the artificial sublime, the natural vitality of street life, and the natural beauties spreading over the repellent monstrosity. Nothing here is original: everything is transformed, violently changed, from the earth and man himself, to the very light and air. But the hugeness of the accumulation of man-made things takes off the attention from this deformity and this artifice: in default of a wholesome and noble beauty, there is life, teeming and grandiose. The gleam of brown river water, 'the scattering of light imprisoned in vapour', the white and rosy luminosity playing over all these colossal objects, spreads a kind of grace over the monstrous city, like a 'smile upon the face of a shaggy and blackened Cyclop'.[9]

From the Romantic to the Victorian period, the new, ever-changing and ever-maddening chaos of the rankly growing industrial cities stood in need of domestication and order, be it by mapping, planning, statistics, or art. The poet or painter could give chaos shape and prevent it from further fragmentation, as in Blake's *Jerusalem* (1805–20). Blake became a favourite poet with the late Victorian Rhymers' Club, and the journalist John Davidson may have remembered Blake's metaphysical vision when, in his own scientific and materialist vision, he imagined how Fleet Street, now a hectic noisy narrow thoroughfare disfigured by dirt and sewage, acceleration and inhumanity, was 'once a silence in the ether', 'Matter of infinite beauty and delight'.[10] Now, it is a fragment, a degenerate space where the natural rhythms of work by day and rest by night no longer exist, fallen out of the originally holistic universe in a postlapsarian state beyond salvation. Unlike Blake, therefore, Davidson found no lasting remedy in his artistic domestication of London's wrecking of men's nerves. His 'London' song of 1894 evokes a Romantic idyll, Wordsworth's sonnet 'Upon Westminster Bridge' (1802) in particular, only to subvert it in the final stanza: the beautiful fog turns out to be nothing but smog enclosing a noisy space that knows no rest.

Baudelaire's *Salon* of 1859, reviewing a city painting, echoes phrases from Wordsworth and Coleridge and thus confirms the truth of the observation that Baudelaire's strict form intended to give artistic form to the realities of chaos and deformity. What distinguishes Baudelaire from the Romantic Neoplatonists is his doubt of a world beyond, so that his vision is not one of truth and prophecy, but mere form-giving. In the poems of 'Tableaux parisiens' of *Les Fleurs du Mal* (1857) and in the characterization of the flâneur in *Le Peintre de la Vie Moderne* (1863), both well-known texts in Britain, the fragmentation of human society and the atavistic jungle-nature of the city are ultimate truth, which art can only make bearable. The heretical, neo-pagan nature of Baudelaire's concept of the aimless city wanderer becomes evident in 'Les foules' (posth. 1869). City wandering among street crowds is modern deracination, intensifying not only the Humean and Byronic loss of a fixed personal identity, but also involving an intoxicated and feverish bath orgy of insatiable excess, a remnant of pristine pre-ethical nature in modern artificiality so often observed in nineteenth-century city poetry:

It is not given to every man to take a bath of multitude; enjoying a crowd is an art; and only he can relish a debauch of vitality … on whom, in his cradle, a fairy has bestowed the love of masks and masquerading, the hate of home, and the passion for roaming … The poet enjoys the incomparable privilege of being able to be himself or someone else, as he chooses. Like those wandering souls who go looking for a body,

he enters as he likes into each man's personality... The man who loves to lose himself
in a crowd enjoys feverish delights... What men call love is a very small, restricted,
feeble thing compared with this ineffable orgy, this divine prostitution of the soul
giving itself entire... to the stranger as he passes.[11]

The Baudelairean city flâneur had two precursors in two works simultaneously published in the liberal *London Magazine*, Charles Lamb's series of essays entitled *Elia*
(1820–25) and Thomas De Quincey's *Confessions of an English Opium Eater* (1821). In a
letter to Wordsworth dated 30 January 1801, Lamb refused to accept Wordsworth's invitation to the Lake District on the ground of a Cockney Romantic artist's preference of a
live cityscape to a dead landscape. What the Radical Lamb here described was an early
form of Baudelaire's orgiastic *bain de multitude* with its aimlessness and disconnected-
ness, reflected in Lamb's, De Quincey's, and Hazlitt's rambling essay form. Romantic
philosophers, Coleridge and Emerson, aestheticized the non-aesthetic, as they understood beauty to lie in the imaginative eye of the beholder rather than in the object.
London, the 'Great Wen' of Cobbett's *Rural Rides* (1830), was not only conceived as a
diseased growth, but also as a beautiful space opening new possibilities for Romantic
wanderlust:[12]

> The Lighted shops of the Strand and Fleet Street, the innumerable trades, tradesmen
> and customers, coaches, waggons, playhouses, all the bustle and wickedness round
> about Covent Garden, the very women of the Town, the Watchmen, drunken scenes,
> rattles—life awake, if you awake, at all hours of the night, the impossibility of being
> dull in Fleet Street, the crowds, the very dirt and mud, the Sun shining upon houses
> and pavements, the print shops, the old book stalls, parsons cheap'ning books,
> coffee houses, steams of soups from kitchens, the pantomimes—London itself a
> pantomime and a masquerade,—all these things work themselves into my mind and
> feed me, without a power of satiating me. The wonder of these sights impells me into
> night-walks about her crowded streets, and I often shed tears in the motley Strand
> from fulness of joy at so much Life.[13]

Throughout the Victorian era, city poetry remained what it had been in the Romantic
period, a matter of changing visual selections and perspectives, as illustrated in both the
title and the contrastive structure of Arthur Symons's prose treatise *London: A Book of
Aspects* (1908). Streets and open spaces could be rendered either beautiful or infernal
by fog, night, artificial lights, rain showers, emptiness, crowds, or prostitutes. At the end
of the nineteenth century, Symons still alluded to Lamb's letter in order to illustrate his
own fascination with London, in which visions of beauty selected for Impressionistic
portraits of London's aesthetic and erotic potential alternate with visions of ugliness and
squalor selected for Symbolist portraits of London's destructive potential. If we compare
Symons's 'Nocturne' (1889), written before Symons's volte-face, to the position of W. B.
Yeats and the country-oriented Celtic Revival on the visual model of James McNeill
Whistler, with 'London: Midnight' (1896), the contrary aspects and artistic concepts
become obvious. 'Nocturne' features a speaker vividly remembering his brief encounter

with a prostitute after an entranced carriage ride through misty, glittering, gas-lit streets on a rainy day, in expectation of 'love without the pain'. 'London: Midnight', by contrast, features a hurried and isolated speaker in a nocturnal street, who hears nothing but the blended mechanical workings of his watch and his heart, with the cries and murmurs of the suffering multitude filtered far away. Time is as indifferent as are the speaker and the multitude. The references to Blake's 'London' (1789) show the fundamental difference. The Romantic speaker is compassionate and integrated, his heart beat is natural, and he hears first of all the anguished cries of others; the late Victorian speaker is blasé and ego-centric, his heart beat is mechanical like the dehumanizing mechanical city described in *London: A Book of Aspects*. Worse than the Baudelairean flâneur with his erotically associated bath in the multitude, he is sterile and cold like a fin-de-siècle dandy.

The Victorian city poet was confronted with an artificial sublime of gas lights, factory stink, excavated underground tunnels, overcrowded tram and train stations, railway noise and speed later rendered worse by the unnatural noises of cars and gramophones, and streets and spaces built into more and more immeasurable extensions. The city appears as an anthill with troglodytic associations, individuals regressing to prehistoric ape men or animals without an aim or control of their lives, 'seized as if in a gigantic grip'[14]—anticipating the representations of dehumanized soldiers in the trench poetry of the Great War. Alexander Smith's portrait of a howling train rushing into a dark tunnel in the direction of the ever-expanding giant Glasgow permanently lit by gaslight or ironworks visible from afar, threatening the countryside's formerly distinct identity, is haunting artificial Gothic, the aesthetics of deformity and denaturation.[15] This artificial sublime had gained so firm a grip of many speakers that they had been irreparably estranged from the natural sublime. By the middle of the nineteenth century, neither Smith in 'Glasgow' (1857) nor Baudelaire in 'Tableaux parisiens' (1861) could imagine a return to the natural and healthier countryside. The post-Baudelairean aestheticist dandy then cultivated a cool distance (especially to social and moral problems) and a preference for the artificial. Sociologically, the dandy has been explained as a result of the intelligent city dweller's and street walker's sensual overload, causing a crisis of the nerves to which he reacted with a pose of cold blasé indifference:[16] Arthur Symons's prologue to *Days and Nights* (1889), which seeks to exclude the city's infernal chaos with the solemn rhythmic pace of an *ars poetica*, would support this theory:

> go where cities pour
> Their turbid human stream flowing onward evermore
> Down to an unknown ocean,—there is Art.
>
> She stands amid the tumult, and is calm
> She reads the hearts self-closed against the light;
> She probes an ancient wound, yet brings no balm;
> She is ruthless, yet she doeth all things right.[17]

Coming from the country, like Wordsworth, Symons went to live in London and came intensely to enjoy the city, finally returning to his native countryside, like his Celtic Revival friend Yeats, to describe the repulsive speed, squalor, and stench of London, as well as its sickening gin palaces and *bohèmes*. But whatever was uppermost, there was always the admixture of the other, either in one and the same poem or in separate contradictory ones.

This division is also to be observed in the Paris poetry of Arthur Rimbaud or the French London poetry of Emile Verhaeren.[18] Externally, this mirrored the fact that mid-Victorian London underwent the most extensive building boom since its reconstruction after the Great Fire of 1666, with splendid new buildings and squares a contrast against slums and their dirty stinking streets. This gap widened in the years 1870–90, aggravated by shocking news from the Paris Commune of 1871, so that Coventry Patmore's and Gerard Manley Hopkins's city poetry was mainly concerned with the fear of a peaceful and speechless London multitude turning into a murderous and shrieking London mob. Anonymous crowds rolling through narrow streets or spit out by trains in railway stations could be either feared as a phalanx of potential rioters and assassins or as commiserated poor, de-individualized, and socially disconnected individuals in the sense of *magna civitas magna solitudo*. The national trauma of the French Revolution and its subsequent London riots was revived. This trauma was additionally fed by the Humean view of man's 'antithetically mixed' nature that came up with Romanticism's exploration of the unconscious and the rise of psychoanalysis.[19] Angst as a result of the loss of identity and sociability in the streets of a 'monstrous anthill', aptly described as 'citephobia',[20] could erupt in violence that caused angst to others: *territus terreo*. This double nature of London is central in Arthur Conan Doyle's Sherlock Holmes stories, where it reflects the protagonist's double nature of virtue and vice, bourgeoisie and underworld: London is both Holmes's dear city of beautiful streets and the 'great cesspool into which all the loungers and idlers of the Empire are irresistibly drained'.[21]

In Victorian city poetry, moreover, we experience an incessant conflict between the real and the ideal, *spleen et idéal*, with reminiscences of the 'beautiful city' of myth (Jerusalem, Camelot) evoked as corrective for the drab reality of filth and poverty, much like Victorian neo-Gothic. This resulted in an even more sharpened awareness of 'the condition of England problem'. William Ernest Henley's *London Voluntaries* (1893), for instance, gives a quickly moving panorama of London with changing seasons, changing lights, changing focuses, and changing moods marked by changing music (five voluntaries or organ solos). The streets of London are seen from a static point of view in the first part (*grave*), in a Romantic evening scene, whereas, in the second part (*andante con moto*), they are visualized from a quickly moving hansom while day is breaking, in a staccato succession of short abrupt sense impressions evoking symbolist associations. Evensong bells, loitering lovers, flickering gas lamps, blindfold rows of casements, barges, carriages, synaesthetically perceived in calm or haste, are but changing accidental details of one nature. Conservative backward-orientation and modernist forward acceleration, however, converge in Henley's anti-modernist concept of one unalterable circle of life, death, and regeneration. Every impression of London's streets is distinct in this impressionistic poem, yet together they compose a gestalt. Nature and artifice mix in ever changing ways in this urban version of Haydn's *Seasons*, with quick transformations echoed by sudden changes of sound orchestration, enjambments, and irregular lines and rhymes: 'Trafalgar Square (The fountains volleying golden glaze) / Shines like an angel market'.[22] The windows in the streets can glimmer like gold in the autumn morning sun, implying Blakean promises of Paradise Regained; or the streets can be dreary and littered by poor men and prostitutes moaning under the infection of the wind which carries suffocating smoke from the East End factories in winter; and spring can make the streets and buildings seem regenerated like nature, which is still omnipresent in the city, 'The laughing-places of the juvenile earth'.[23] In Henley's Christian vision, God has made one nature obeying one natural law. Pan is not dead, neither in the city nor in the country, symbolized by the Thames: 'The ancient River singing as he goes, / New-mailed in morning, to the ancient Sea'.[24]

Romantic and Victorian city poetry have many things in common: the intersection of city and country, the Janus-faced nature of the city, the vision of a better or worse urban future, the shaping and saving or the disillusioning imagination, the beauty or deformity of ugliness, and the subjectivity of the lyrical speaker's changing moods who, with Wordsworth, 'half creates and half perceives' the chronotopes of city scenes alternating with light and the seasons. Arthur Hugh Clough's *Dipsychus* (1850) features a tempted youth and his tempting spirit, both personae of the author, Tennysonian 'two voices' that leave the 'twin-souled' titular hero quite undecided whether to escape from the city back to more natural and moral scenes or to accept the city's revolting filth, stench, and anonymity together with its pleasures and temptations. Notwithstanding his call for a realistic treatment of the city, in his 1853 review of three Victorian city poets (Matthew Arnold, Alexander Smith, William Sidney Walker), Clough's *Dipsychus* (as well as his other city poems) vacillates between moods of acceptance and rejection.[25] As the title indicates, psychomachia and Romantic interiority dominate the long dramatic poem, which has almost no external plot.

Clough as well as the Chartist Saunders Mackaye in Charles Kingsley's *Alton Locke* (1850) and other mid-Victorian poetological voices, however, make a basic difference apparent that distinguishes Victorian from Romantic city poetry. Romantic city poets tended to focus on the city's exciting sights, pleasures, and sublimity, often exalting drab urban realities in mythical terms, as the descriptions of Babylon (versus Golgonooza) in Blake's *Jerusalem* (1804–20). Blake's 'London' is an exception only when read out of context. When Victorian city poets, by contrast, portrayed London through the lens of myth, Henley's El Dorado and Thomson's Inferno, they mostly did so for the purpose of a *descensus ad inferos*. Zanoni, the eponymous hero of Edward Bulwer-Lytton's historical novel of 1842, advises the young English artist Clarence Glyndon to quit visions of airy beauty and to descend into the dirty streets of Naples and Rome: 'True art finds beauty everywhere'.[26] This is also the feeling behind Robert Browning's dramatic monologue 'Fra Lippo Lippi' (1855), whose fifteenth-century speaker, a historical Carmelite friar and suggested prototype of a Victorian artist, does not disdain to seek models for his paintings in the most disreputable streets of Florence. Art must partake of religion and must, by consequence, paint the whole of life, for 'God made it all'.[27] The more earthbound vision of the Victorians, believers or sceptics or agnostics, concentrated on filthy streets polluted with soot and industrial smoke, overcrowding and fever epidemics and gin palaces, deafening and maddening noise, stench caused by open sewers and the intermixture of cowsheds and piggeries with dwelling-houses, prostitution and exploitation of workers, beggars and starving poverty, isolation of the individual in the mass, atheism, and suicide. This was recalcitrant material for the poet to work with, but Romanticism had provided the concept of the saving imagination. In his above-mentioned 1853 article in the *North American Review*, Clough asked: 'Could it [poetry] not attempt to convert into beauty and thankfulness, or at least into some form and shape... the actual, palpable things with which our everyday-life is concerned[?]'[28]

In Elizabeth Barrett Browning's *Aurora Leigh* (1857), the titular heroine's artistic imagination allows her to see beauty in the depressing fog that swallows the 'Spires, bridges, streets, and squares' as well as the river of London: 'Your city poets see such things / Not despicable'.[29] Poetry published for the benefit of mankind allows her to surmount all her distress in London. The concept is a psychoanalytical or therapeutic one (as elaborated, say, in the verse of the Romantic Paris poet Alfred de Musset). Suffering communicated in art makes life bearable, whereas silent suffering is death.[30] Robert Williams Buchanan, who had come to London from rural Scotland in 1860 to be a city poet and (in contrast to Musset) found consolation in meditation and religion, saw his role in giving a voice to the voiceless and weary and near-dead in the city crowd, including himself, singing and praying alone in the anonymity of London's 'streets of stone'.[31] In his *London Poems* (1866), he recalled passages from Wordsworth and Keats in order to contradict their Romantic Neoplatonism. The glory and the dream of childhood are not to be recovered; escape back to the country is no viable solution for a modern city dweller, because the city is addictive; art is hard work and no easy inspiration; and the modern poet is a spiritual Victorian *miles Christianus* who has a mission to the modern city dweller. Unlike the speaker of Keats's ode, who 'darkling' listens to the nightingale, the Victorian poet 'darkling' seeks to do his duty: 'Darkling, I long'd for utterance, whereby / Poor people might be holpen, gladden'd, cheer'd'.[32]

In 'The City Without God', which forms part of his later long epic poem *The City of Dream* (1888), Buchanan insistently warned against modern scientific attempts at making urban life bearable. A godless city, be it never so hygienic and organized, would become an inhuman nightmare, as it was later described in Aldous Huxley's and George Orwell's dystopias.[33] Retiring into what Matthew Arnold called 'the buried life' rather than to Bexhill or rural Scotland, the poet finds at times the rhythm and 'sweetness' to make the noise and anonymity of the streets bearable and 'the life of London musical'.[34] Overcoming Romantic illusions and escapism, the poet faces the bitterness much like Baudelaire, but with a religious faith to support him:

> For the sound of the city is awful,
>   As the people pass to and fro,
> And the friendless faces are dreadful,
>   As they come, and thrill through us, and go;[35]

Arnoldian 'sweetness and light' temper urban ugliness and urban spiritual drought as they temper the deformity of modern scientific writing, shoring culture against anarchy.

There is no Wordsworthian 'Oh joy that…!' in glory regained, but an acceptance of dread, sadness, error, and vulnerability in 'the unsung city's streets', which can, however, 'pass into sweetness and sound':

> And I murmur these songs of the city,
>   Its sorrow, its joy, and its sin;
> …
> I murmur these songs of the city,
>   And cast them as bread on the sea;
> And mine eyes are dim with the singing
>   That is all the world to me![36]

Religious consolation, artistic form-giving, rural retrospect, escape to the countryside, or withdrawal into city parks, theatres, panoramas, dioramas, museums, and concert rooms remained correctives or recreations for a dwindling number of city poets. These were no longer easy solutions for the socially committed Victorian poet who, unlike the aesthetes Arnold and Wilde in their retirements, lived exposed to the nauseous and noisy streets of the city. Walker, who chose to make a living as a city poet in London and whose city poems Clough reviewed seven years after Walker's tragic death in London in 1846, was driven almost to madness and physical breakdown by the commotion and noise of the streets that allowed his overstrained nerves no rest day and night. Walker's religious faith, which he had lost together with his university position, no longer provided help. Pouring his suffering into verse was meant to provide relief for himself and his readers through a creative imagination, which also enabled him to concentrate on small soothing things, isolated remnants of *rus in urbe* such as the flickering flame on the hearth or, as in Alexander Smith's 'Glasgow' (1857), a few flowers in a gloomy backyard or a solitary sunbeam shivering upon a church spire. The brutal realism of Walker's ''Tis Utter Night' is thus made bearable, even without visions of a better future in the city corresponding to a better past in the country.[37] The daily noise of the streets, which carries no Wordsworthian symbolism reconciling man to the imperfect world, still haunts the speaker in his quiet room at night:

> 'Tis utter night; over all Nature's works
> Silence and rest are spread; yet still the tramp
> Of busy feet, the roll of wheels, the hum
> Of passing tongues,—one endless din confused
> Of sounds, that have no meaning for the heart,—
> Marring the beauty of the tranquil hour,
> Press on my sleepless ear. Sole genial voice,
> Heard indistinctly through the tumult, soothes
> My soul with its companionable sound,
> And tales of other days. Thither I turn
> My weary sense for refuge[38]

Other examples of such artistically domesticated realism are the speakers' visions of the city and street in Alfred Lord Tennyson's *In Memoriam* (1850) and *Maud* (1855), ones tinctured by moods of mourning, despair, or madness. On the brink of madness, the morbid speaker of *Maud* imagines himself dead and buried below a busy street, where the city noise that unhinged his mind in his lifetime will pursue him in death and cheat him of the promise of *requiescat in pace*,—a mad scene marked by irregular metres, wild scansions, disrupted rhythms, staccato repetitions, breathless asyndeta, and lack of structured thought:

> And the hoofs of the horses beat, beat,
> The hoofs of the horses beat,
> Beat into my scalp and my brain,
> With never an end to the stream of passing feet,
> Driving, hurrying marrying, buying,
> Clamour and rumble, and ringing and clatter.[39]

In Tennyson's *Locksley Hall Sixty Years After* (1886) the old disillusioned speaker of his earlier, more optimistic *Locksley Hall* (1842) sees nothing but London's misery in his darkened mood, one, however, that is mitigated by strictly and beautifully elaborated scansions:

> There among the glooming alleys Progress halts on palsied feet,
> Crime and hunger cast our maidens by the thousand on the street.
>
> There the Master scrimps his haggard sempstress of her daily bread,
> There a single sordid attic holds the living and the dead.
> There the smouldering fire of fever creeps across the rotted floor,
> And the crowded couch of incest in the warrens of the poor.[40]

Whereas Tennyson's urban vision darkened over the course of his life, with depression leaving little room for positive prospects, Matthew Arnold's city poems continually wavered between outrage at the fever of modern city life and escape to rural retrospect, integrating visions of a more humane city. He accepted the city as unavoidable in the course of civilization, but saw its future positive potential, including more and more art, theatres, museums, and, above all, city parks in the sense of *rus in urbe*. He chimed in with the mass of Victorian writers in prose and poetry who, in the tradition of Cowper and Wordsworth, described a modern city without rural spaces, *urbs sine rure*, as hell on earth, 'unnatural' and 'wicked'.[41] Without rural retreats, there was neither calm nor community nor religion, human ties that made urban spaces urbane by preserving man's individuality in the mass. As man could find 'the buried life' within himself, so he could maintain rural calm in a Romantic intersection of city and country. '...on men's impious uproar hurled', he composed 'Lines written in Kensington Gardens' (1852) and 'The Future' (1852), his most typical city poems. In a pair of sonnets entitled 'East London' and 'West London' (1863), Arnold expressed his envy of the Reverend William Tyler's firm belief that he could overcome the depression caused by the 'squalid streets of Bethnal Green' by focusing on the expectation of a better world beyond, as well as by observing beggars crouching 'on the pavement close by Belgrave Square', whose dignity in poverty 'points us to a better world than ours'.[42] Faith has grown shaky, so that religion must be replaced by art, according to Arnold, and more radically in Nietzsche's formulation, the last stronghold of metaphysics in this world. In his vision of a better future on this side of the grave, Arnold took a step towards the city poetry of the Radical Socialist William Morris, who sought to embellish all objects of daily use from street to shop and cutlery. At the opposite end of the political spectrum, he also anticipated the city poetry of the Tory Roden Noel, Robert Buchanan's friend, who discovered the promising seeds of social virtues in the squalor of man-made London as well as in the God-made country.

Roden Noel's realistic depictions of the miseries of the monstrous city from the hellish gloom of its streets 'blotting out sweet heaven' to the weariness of its bestialized masses worn out by work and competition closely resembles Tennyson's *Locksley Hall Sixty Years After*, except in its non-mitigating broken rhythms. A dark mood sees nothing but dark streets and dark lumpen proletariat conspiracies, as if they were the decree of fate:

> This huge black whirlpool of the city sucks,
> And swallows, and encroaches evermore
> On vernal field, pure air, and wholesome heaven—
> A vast dim province, even under cloud,
> O'er whose immeasurable unloveliness
> His own foul breath broods sinister, like Fate.[43]

But the speaker's mood changes and his verse flows more easily when he remembers 'little, nameless, unremembered acts of kindness and of love' (Wordsworth) in this unwholesome and inhuman space. A boy dying from a street accident who, with his last breath, makes his father swear to no longer beat his mother, and a mother forgiving and nursing her wicked son on his deathbed, are promises of redemption. Then the Christian speaker remembers his poet's mission to remind those who suffer in the city of the religious promise of a better future with a healthier life and of re-established social connections across barriers of competition and class. Again, the Victorian poet remembers his Romantic predecessors in his imagery of *rus in urbe*:

> Therefore, dear birds, in leafy woods ye warble,
> And you, my children, by the rivulet
> Play, laughing merrily, because the world
> Is sound at heart, howe'er it seems to ail.[44]

By contrast, 'A March Day in London' (1889) by Amy Levy, possibly the first London literary flâneuse,[45] presents an almost hopeless vision of the city, in the tradition of Byron's Disillusionism rather than Arnold's Victorianism. The clear blue sky contrasts with the dark streets, and, conversely, the speaker's depression in daylight is temporarily relieved by calm and hope in darkness, when the ruby lights of hansom coaches flicker through the fog like fireflies. Intersections of city and countryside become visible in a Whistlerian or Wildean aestheticization of Dickens's 'sooty spectre' and Ruskin's 'storm-cloud'.[46] And yet, the promise of regeneration in a new day, suggested by the poor remnants of nature and its symbols in the city, is vain, moving in an absurd circle of paradise lost and paradise seemingly regained. The dialectical antithesis of the squalor and inhumanity of the city will have the last word without a final synthesis.

Darkness also dominates the city poetry of Mathilde Blind, whom Levy knew from the circle of women writers that she frequented in London. Depression, discrimination of women, discrimination of homoeroticism, and the Jewish experience of deracination darkened the mood of both poets. Blind's sonnet 'Manchester by Night' (1893) portrays an unnatural and inhuman city to which night can give no rest, disturbed by hustle and bustle and the noise of engines in the streets, and where the moon weeps over the turbulence and recklessness of man alienated from himself in the masses. The biblical sacrificial pillars of smoke joining earth and heaven now 'clime heavenward' from factories and have become monstrous sacrifices. Man is shut out from heaven by 'narrow cloudy bars'; former life has become life-in-death.[47] This is the mood of Byron's 'Darkness' (1816), though without Byron's apocalyptic hopelessness. Blind loved to read Byron and also edited his poems, letters, and journals, but she was an admirer of Percy Shelley and George Eliot as well as of Mazzini and Garibaldi, with whom she shared a melioristic belief in a better future for this world. If Levy stood in the tradition of Byron's Disillusionism, Blind, the daughter of a German revolutionary of 1848, rather followed Shelley's Neoplatonism. 'The Orange-Peel in the Gutter' (1867), a poem on a piece of refuse in a 'drear and darksome London street' with 'dusky houses' and 'grimy windows', isolated from the sky by fog and rain, concentrates on a Wordsworthian or Emersonian minimal symbol that recalls to the visionary speaker her prophetic mission to her readers, in rhymed Wordsworthian tetrameters reminiscent of church anthems:

> No cell, no garret, and no tomb,
> For which no flower of love doth bloom!
> No place so waste, so dark, so drear,
> But heavenly beauty lurketh there!
> And from these two will ever spring,
> As music from the harp's sweet string,
> As from the nest the lark soars high,
> As from the flame the live sparks fly,
> The fountain of great poesy,
> Will shine and flash, and flame and glow,
> Like to a million coloured bow
> Of hope and peace, a lovely sign,
> Flinging around that world of thine
> A glory that is all divine![48]

The social reformer and journalist George Robert Sims, well known for his literary attacks on almsgiving and workhouses, stood somewhere between Levy and Blind. With his revolting descriptions of London street life and the effects of London poverty he fought for a more humane city, though without Blind's visionary confidence. He gives an individualized portrait of the inhumanity of city life in a narrative dialogue between the speaker and a despairing woman sitting in a slum street near Drury Lane at night-time, 'Christmassing À La Mode De Slumopolis' (1883). Poverty allows her no chance to participate in pleasures of any sort, theatrical or religious; her husband beats her out of despair; her children have died. This is a socialist's visualization of unredeemed, though possibly redeemable misery where, as in Blind's 'Manchester by Night', religious ritual is perverted into infernal street scenes:

> I left the woman with a coin—it went, no doubt, in gin—
> And thought of how this time of joy is made a time of sin;
> How homes are ruined, limbs are maimed, and helpless children killed,
> While prison cells and workhouse wards with maddened fools are filled.
> I thought of Christ's sweet carnival to heathen rites 'demeaned',
> And Christmas made the harvest-time of Drink—hell's fiercest fiend.[49]

By contrast, James Thomson's 'City of Dreadful Night' (1880) again describes the irredeemable darkness of the city's spaces, streets and houses and churches, in the tradition of Byron's and Levy's Romantic Disillusionism. Thomson's imaginary modern city is an apocalyptic inferno dreamed in the manner of Dante Gabriel Rossetti's *à-rebours*-reading of Dante: sometimes a personal vision of dark streets and disconnected despairing individuals; at other times, a philosophical representation of the city as epitome of an absurd universe. Even where natural or artificial lights illuminate the streets and open spaces, the speaker's focus is on ultimately unconquerable darkness:

> Although lamps burn along the silent streets,
> Even when moonlight silvers empty squares
> The dark holds countless lanes and close retreats;
> But when the night its sphereless mantle wears
> The open spaces yawn with gloom abysmal,
> The sombre mansions loom immense and dismal,
> The lanes are black as subterranean lairs.[50]

Against the background of urban noise and speed that Thomson experienced as a tramp in London, the silence and languor of his city were not meant to be realistic. They form parts of a Poesque artificial landscape of the soul denoting man's cosmic desertion. After Thomson's death, in the 1890s, when the busy streets of cities were rendered additionally noisy and hectic by automobiles and when industrial pollution and social problems increased, there came Decadent and counter-Decadent poetic responses. John Davidson, like Thomson a Scottish expatriate, lamented 'London's storm and stress of trades' in realistically invective poems about London's railway stations and streets, where 'life's pace' is unnaturally 'set by automobilism'.[51] Influenced by Darwin and Nietzsche, harassed by the rush and bustle of his life as a journalist in London which eventually ended in depression and suicide in 1909, he described the monstrosity, deformity, hurry, and chaos of the Thames Embankment, Fleet Street, or London Bridge Railway Station as monstrous births of evolution. In these city poems, he condemned the increased speed of cars and trains that Henley accepted.[52] Instead of a neo-Gothic corrective or an aestheticist beautification, his Darwinian fancy led him back down the line of evolution, to a more natural time without chaotic and noisy streets, without machines speeding up life and reducing distances, without exploited anonymous masses, and without merely functional architectural deformities in the bedlam of streets and squares. His heroic couplets are broken and belie Pope's discovery of order in the world and progressivist optimism:

> Before the Atlantic race
> Developed turbined speed; before life's pace
> Was set by automobilism; before
> The furthest stars came thundering at the door
> To claim close kindred with the sons of men;
> Before the lettered keys outsped the pen;
> Ere poverty was deemed the only crime
> Or wireless news annihilated time,
> Divulged now by an earthquake in the night,
> This ancient terminus first saw the light.[53]

On the other hand, the early Symons, and even more so Wilde, excluded the seamy sides of London from their visions. Decadent neo-Romantics, admirers of James McNeill Whistler's London *Nocturnes* and 'Ten O'Clock' lecture of 1885, they created impressionistic poems celebrating artifice above nature. They imaginatively transformed smoke and prostitution in streets or in brothels, much as Moreau painted the beautifully tattooed but essentially evil Salome.

In contradistinction to this fin-de-siècle aestheticism, Early Modernism after the Great War again tended to foreground the negative sides of the city, following Davidson and Symons's later work. But the rural spaces in Georgian poetry are also troubled so as to discredit them as an easy alternative to urban spaces. In Imagist poetry, London is alienated by fragmentary glimpses so that no outsider would recognize it. After 1918, the negative effect of fragmentation was enhanced by glimpses of the social disaster, the crowds of crippled and unemployed soldiers as well as exploited workers that defaced the city's streets and squares.[54] It was the inhuman city of Fritz Lang's film *Metropolis* (1927) with its eclectic pastiche of quickly changing street scenes. T. S. Eliot's 'Unreal City, / Under the brown fog of a winter noon' in *The Waste Land* (1922), where anonymous crowds pour over London Bridge and where personal contacts are failures, owe much to Davidson, whose poetry the young Eliot admired.[55] D. H. Lawrence's equally negative poetical portrait of city-life may also have been inspired by the dark city poems of the German pre-War Expressionist Georg Heym as well as by the fatalism of Great War trench poetry. It envisaged the 'poor people' anonymously crowding the streets of 'the great cities' as shoals of 'fearful and corpse-like fishes' caught on iron hooks and pulled around in absurd circles on 'invisible wires of steel' by a malignant fate, 'hooked fishes of the factory world'.[56]

Notes

1. Philip Davies, *The Victorians, The Oxford English Literary History*, vol. 8 (Oxford: Oxford University Press, 2002), 28.

2. See James Chandler and Kevin Gilmartin, eds., *Romantic Metropolis: The Urban Scene of British Culture, 1780–1840* (Cambridge: Cambridge University Press, 2005).

3. See Peter Otto, *Multiplying Worlds: Romanticism, Modernity, and the Emergence of Virtual Reality* (Oxford: Oxford University Press, 2011).

4. Kristiaan Versluys, *The Poet in the City: Chapters in the Development of Urban Poetry in Europe and the United States (1800–1930)* (Tübingen: Narr, 1987), 24–74. The ambivalence of the city was already apparent in Neoclassicism, when Boileau, following Horace, enjoyed the city, yet found it the wrong place for creative writing.

5. William B. Thesing, *The London Muse: Victorian Poetic Responses to the City* (Athens, GA: University of Georgia Press, 1982), 155–169, 169–180.

6. Alfred de Musset, *Rolla*, ii. 43–44 in *Poésies complètes*, ed. Maurice Allem (Paris: Gallimard, 1957), 276: 'C'est ainsi qu'en entrant dans la société / On trouve ses égouts'.

7. Simon During, 'Regency London', in James Chandler, ed., *The Cambridge History of English Romantic Literature* (Cambridge: Cambridge University Press, 2009), 340–41.

8. Angelika Corbineau-Hoffmann, *Kleine Literaturgeschichte der Großstadt* (Darmstadt: Wissenschaftliche Buchgesellschaft, 2003), 14–21.

9. Hippolyte Taine, *Notes sur l'Angleterre*, 2nd edn. (Paris: Hachette, 1872), 9 (my translation).

10. John Davidson, 'Fleet Street', in *Selected Poems and Prose*, ed. John Sloan (Oxford: Clarendon Press, 1995), 127.

11. Charles Baudelaire, 'Les foules', in *Œuvres complètes,* ed. Y.-G. Le Dantec (Paris: Gallimard, 1961), 241–42 (my translation).

12. Simon P. Hull, *Charles Lamb, Elia and the London Magazine* (London: Pickering & Chatto, 2010), 87–119.

13. Charles Lamb, letter to Thomas Manning, 30 January 1801, in *The Letters of Charles Lamb, to which are added those of his sister Mary Lamb*, 3 vols., ed. E. V. Lucas (London: Methuen, 1935, repr. New York: AMS Press, 1968), i. 267.

14. Arthur Symons, *London: A Book of Aspects*, ed. Ian Fletcher and John Stokes (New York and London: Garland, 1984, repr. of 1909 version), 12.

15. Alexander Smith, 'Glasgow', in *City Poems* (Boston: Ticknor & Fields, 1857), 43–44.

16. Georg Simmel, *Die Großstädte und das Geistesleben* (Dresden: Zahn & Jaensch, 1903).

17. Symons, 'Prologue' to *Days and Nights* in *Collected Works*, 9 vols., (London: Secker, 1924), i. 3.

18. Elisabeth Frenzel, *Motive der Weltliteratur*, 4th edn. (Stuttgart: Kröner, 1992), 674.

19. Byron, Childe Harold's Pilgrimage, in *Poetical Works*, 7 vols., ed. J. J. McGann (Oxford: Clarendon Press, 1980-93), ii. 89, See also Bertrand Russell, *A History of Western Philosophy*, 'Byron and the Modern World', 2nd edn. (London: Allen & Unwin, 1971), 716–21.

20. Julian Wolfreys, *Writing London* (London: Palgrave, 1998–2007), i. 95–138.

21. Arthur Conan Doyle, 'A Study in Scarlet', ch.1 in *The Annotated Sherlock Holmes*, 2 vols., ed. W. S. Baring-Gould (London: John Murray, 1968), i. 145.

22. William Henley, *London Voluntaries*, ii. 47–9, in *Works*, 5 vols. (London: Macmillan, 1921), i. 197.

23. Henley, *London Voluntaries*, v. 64, in *Works*, i. 203. See Jerome Hamilton Buckley, *William Ernest Henley: A Study in the 'Counter-Decadence' of the Nineties* (Princeton: Princeton University Press, 1945), 183–92.

24. Jerome Hamilton Buckley, *William Ernest Henley*, 194–95.

25. Jerome Hamilton Buckley, *The Victorian Temper* (London: Yale University Press, 1951), 107–8, and William Thesing, *The London Muse*, 39–56.

26. Edward Bulwer-Lytton, *Zanoni* (1842), in *Novels and Romances*, 10 vols. (London: Routledge, Warne, and Routledge, 1863), vii. 89.

27. Robert Browning, 'Fra Lippo Lippi', in *Poetical Works*, 15 vols., eds. Ian Jack et al. (Oxford: Clarendon Press, 1988-), v. 48.

28. A. H. Clough in *North American Review*, 77 (1853), 3.

29. Elizabeth Barrett Browning, *Aurora Leigh*, ed. Margaret Reynolds (Athens, OH: Ohio University Press, 1992), iii. 182, 186–87.

30. Musset, 'Nuit d'Octobre', in *Poésies complètes,* ed. Maurice Allem (Paris: Gallimard, 1957), 320–28.

31. Robert Buchanan, 'Last Night', in *Complete Poetical Works*, 2 vols. (London: Chatto & Windus, 1901, repr. New York: AMS Press, 1976), ii. 340.

32. Buchanan, 'Bexhill, 1866', in *London Poems*, (London and New York: Alexander Strahan, 1866), 6.

33. R. A. Forsyth, 'Robert Buchanan and the Dilemma of the Brave New Victorian World', *Studies in English Literature*, 9 (1969), 647–57.

34. Buchanan, 'Bexhill, 1866', in *London Poems*, 8.

35. Buchanan, 'London, 1864', in *London Poems*, 192.

36. Buchanan, 'London, 1864', 194.

37. Thesing, *The London Muse*, 79.

38. William Sidney Walker, 'Tis Utter Night', in *The Poetical Remains of William Sidney Walker*, ed. J. Moultrie (London, 1852), 81.

39. Alfred Tennyson, *Maud*, ii. 246–51, in *Poems of Tennyson*, 3 vols., ed. Christopher Ricks, 2nd edn. (London: Longman, 1987), ii. 576–77.

40. Tennyson, *Locksley Hall Sixty Years After*, in *Poems of Tennyson*, iii. 157–58.

41. Jean-Paul Hulin, '"Rus in Urbe": A Key to Victorian Anti-Urbanism', in Jean-Paul Hulin and Pierre Coustillas, eds., *Victorian Writers and the City* (Lille: Publications de l'Université de Lille III, 1979), 11–40.

42. Matthew Arnold, 'East London' and 'West London', in *Poems*, ed. Kenneth Allott, 2nd edn. (London: Longman, 1979), 525–26.

43. Roden Noel, 'A Lay of Civilization, or London', in *Collected Poems*, ed. Victoria Buxton (London: Paul, Trench, Trübner & Co, 1902), 303.

44. Noel, 'A Lay of Civilization, or London', II. 839-42, ed. cit. 310.

45. Deborah Parsons, *Streetwalking the Metropolis: Women, the City, and Modernity* (Oxford: Oxford University Press, 2000), 92.

46. William Sharpe, 'London and Nineteenth-Century Poetry', in Lawrence Manley, ed., *The Cambridge Companion to the Literature of London* (Cambridge: Cambridge University Press, 2011), 134–36.

47. Mathilde Blind, 'Manchester by Night', in *The Victorians: An Anthology of Poetry and Poetics*, ed. Valentine Cunningham (London: Blackwell, 2009), 821.

48. Blind, 'The Orange-Peel in the Gutter', in *Poems by Claude Lake* (London: Alfred W. Bennett, 1867), 56–57.

49. George Robert Sims, 'Ballads and Poems', in Davies, *The Victorians*, 897.

50. James Thomson, 'The City of Dreadful Night', i. iii. 1–7, in *Poems and Some Letters*, ed. Anne Ridler (London: Centaur Press, 1963), 181.

51. Davidson, 'London Bridge', in *Fleet Street and Other Poems*, 114–16.

52. For a sociological analysis of this acceleration, see Hartmund Rosa, *Beschleunigung: Die Veränderung der Zeitstrukturen in der Moderne* (Frankfurt am Main: Suhrkamp, 2005).

53. Davidson, 'London Bridge', lines 31–40, 114.

54. Peter Barry, 'London in Poetry since 1900', in *The Cambridge Companion to the Literature of London*, 180–87.

55. T. S. Eliot, *The Waste Land*, in *Complete Poems and Plays* (London: Faber & Faber, 1969), 1970, 62, 68.

56. D. H. Lawrence, 'More Pansies', 'City-Life', posth. 1932, in *Complete Poems*, eds. Vivian de Sola Pinto and Warren Roberts (London: Heinemann, 1964), II. 632.

SELECT BIBLIOGRAPHY

Buckley, J. H., *The Victorian Temper* (London: Yale University Press, 1951).

Chandler, James and Gilmartin, Kevin, eds., *Romantic Metropolis: The Urban Scene of British Culture, 1780–1840* (Cambridge: Cambridge University Press, 2005).

Davis, Philip, *The Victorians. The Oxford English Literary History*, vol. 8 (Oxford: Oxford University Press, 2002).

Dyos, H. J. and Wolff, M., eds., *The Victorian City: Images and Realities*, 2 vols. (London: Routledge and Kegan Paul, 1973).

Hulin, Jean-Paul and Coustillas, Pierre, eds., *Victorian Writers and the City* (Lille: Publications de l'Université de Lille III, 1979).

Levebvre, Henri, *The Production of Space*, trans. D. Nicholson-Smith (Oxford: Blackwell, 1991).

Manley, Lawrence, ed., *The Cambridge Companion to the Literature of London* (Cambridge: Cambridge University Press, 2011).

Onego, S. and Stotesbury, J., eds., *London in Literature: Visionary Mappings of the Metropolis* (Heidelberg: Winter, 2002).

Parsons, Deborah, *Streetwalking the Metropolis: Women, the City, and Modernity* (Oxford: Oxford University Press, 2000).

Simmel, Georg, *Die Großstädte und das Geistesleben (The Metropolis and Mental Life)* (Dresden: Zahn & Jaensch, 1903).

Thesing, William, *The London Muse: Victorian Poetic Responses to the City* (Athens, GA: University of Georgia Press, 1982).

Versluys, Kristiaan, *The Poet in the City: Chapters in the Development of Urban Poetry in Europe and the United States (1800–1930)* (Tübingen: Narr, 1987).

Wolfreys, Julian, *Writing London*, 3 vols. (London: Palgrave, 1998-2007).

CHAPTER 45

··

IN THE ARTIST'S STUDIO

··

CATHERINE MAXWELL

> One face looks out from all his canvasses,
>   One selfsame figure sits or walks or leans;
>   We found her hidden just behind those screens...[1]

THE artist's studio, like the artworks produced within it, has both a private and public function. Christina Rossetti's famous sonnet describes exploring a studio that evokes the one belonging to her brother, Dante Gabriel. As a privileged viewer, the speaker has licence not only to view the paintings on display but also to investigate what is 'hidden just behind those screens'. Discovering the model who may have retired to change her dress or avoid inspection, the speaker, unlike the casual visitor, is able to muse on this female subject whose face has become the artist's obsession.[2] Yet her omnipresence in his paintings—'One face looks out from all his canvasses / One selfsame figure sits or walks or leans'—would, she implies, give any visitor pause for thought. The studio tantalizes and intrigues, even functions as a kind of open secret.

Elizabeth Barrett Browning's Aurora Leigh is another privileged studio visitor who penetrates a mystery. Writing to her of his recent engagement, the painter Vincent Carrington declares

> Remember what a pair of topaz eyes
> You once detected, turned against the wall,
> That morning in my London painting-room;
> The face half-sketched, and slurred; the eyes alone!
> But you... you caught them up with yours, and said
> 'Kate Ward's eyes, surely.'—Now I own the truth:
> I had so thrown them there to keep them safe from Jove,
> They would so naughtily find out their way
> To both the heads of both my Danaës
> Where just it made me mad to look at them.
> Such eyes! I could not paint or think of eyes
> But those,—and so I flung them into paint
> And turned them to the wall's care.[3]

Fighting an obsessive urge to give Kate's eyes to other female subjects, Carrington thinks to disburden himself in a private sketch, which is nonetheless unwittingly decoded by Aurora. Now acknowledging his love, Carrington makes a more public declaration of his passion that would be visible to any studio visitor. Forsaking mythological subjects, he has 'let out', as he says, Kate's eyes and by implication his secret, painting a 'half-length portrait' that shows her 'whole sweet face' (vii. 591–5).

Tempting though it is to think of the studio as a secluded space for self-communing creativity, for many of the most famous Victorian artists—Frederic Leighton, James McNeill Whistler, Dante Gabriel Rossetti, and Edward Burne-Jones—it frequently acted as a version of the gallery, displaying not only finished creations and works in progress, but also the artist himself, a celebrity who might provide a commentary on his own collection, answer questions, or have an assistant perform such tasks for him. The description given by Henry Treffry Dunn, Rossetti's assistant, of the studio he first saw at Cheyne Walk in 1863, makes it clear that this was no austere, paint-splashed workspace but

> a large and roomy apartment, well-lighted and liberally stocked with Chippendale chairs and lounges of various inviting form, whereon one might sit at ease and enjoy a survey of his pictures which stood about on easels. Several cabinets of English and Spanish design and workmanship filled up the odd nooks and corners of space that were left.

This luxurious, well-appointed room also housed 'a well-stocked Chippendale Bookcase', a large wardrobe containing costumes for the models, and an old Portuguese cabinet containing necklaces and 'knick-knacks of all kinds'—all this intimating that Rossetti's studio was as much about collecting, display, and exhibition as it was about creativity.[4] Indeed the art historian Charlotte Gere writes of the 'show studio', a place for possible 'convivial gatherings', 'parties', or musical entertainments that acted as 'a civilized way of showing off the pictures in the name of wider culture'.[5] As they acquired fame and money, leading Victorian artists invested in large properties that accommodated not only their studios but also their domestic lives, the house becoming an extension of the studio and decorated with beautiful artefacts in keeping with its aesthetic. Such properties showcased a carefully cultivated image of the artist and his work to a select audience of visitors: friends, acquaintances, other artists or celebrities, invited guests, approved applicants, and interviewers.

Although intended for an audience, such artists' homes bear a passing resemblance to the 'lordly pleasure-house' the speaker builds for his soul in Tennyson's 'The Palace of Art' (1832), a glamorous aesthetic space where, isolated from the pressing cares of the world, the soul can sing and delight in beauty. Tennyson carefully details the many artworks that decorate the palace—a collection that, as Jonah Siegel has suggested, anticipates the museum or public gallery. Significantly, when the soul, overcome by self-disgust, leaves the palace, she declares her hope to 'return with others there / When I have purged my guilt'.[6] While inaccessible to the masses, the 'palace of art' owned by the successful Victorian painter or sculptor, arguably bridges the gap between public and private art, opening up the studio to selected visitors eager to take advantage of an exclusive opportunity and gain insights into the process of artistic creation.

However, Rossetti's sonnet apart, very few Victorian poems are set in contemporary artists' studios. Indeed depictions of the physical act or process of artistic creation are relatively uncommon and, where these do occur, there is rarely direct reference to the studio. Tennyson's 'The Gardener's Daughter or, the Pictures' (1842) features a painter who relates how he came to woo the beautiful maiden who was his 'first, last love', and concludes with him unveiling her image, captured 'As I beheld her ere she knew my heart'.[7] But although lyrical descriptions of the woman and the garden support Arthur Hallam's belief that 'poetry cannot be too pictorial . . . it is the business of the poetic language to paint', there is scant reference to the act of painting.[8] Similarly, in spite of his own elaborate workspace, the studio barely figures in Dante Gabriel Rossetti's poems. In 'The Portrait' (1870), a poem that, like Tennyson's, figures a bereaved artist and his painting of his dead beloved, there is no indication where the speaker views the painting. Although he does briefly refer to the process of composition—'In painting her I shrined her face / Mid mystic trees, where light falls in/ Hardly at all'—it later turns out that this scene, which commemorates the realization of reciprocated love, is painted soon afterwards to capture the moment, and is not executed in the studio. [9]

However, though neither poem gives us the physical environment of the studio, both open up that private space in which the artist reveals his art and something of himself. In both, the act of painting is an act of devotion preserving a beloved image, which the painter then displays to a privileged viewer or the reader-as-viewer. Such poems can be regarded as occupying the studio space in which the painter, dilating on his life and art, chooses to display a work of deep personal significance and reveal the secret meaning behind it.

Though less personally charged, various of Dante Gabriel Rossetti's 'double works' (sonnets written to accompany his own artworks such as 'Lilith', 'Sybilla Palmifera', or 'Saint Luke the Painter') also read as the painter-poet treating the reader to a private studio view and providing privileged insights in the form of commentary. Alternatively poems written about artworks by the artist's friends represent the viewpoint of the appreciative studio visitor whose sensitive interpretation is offered in homage. Such poems might include the imaginative reveries in *The Defence of Guenevere* (1858) that William Morris wrote for Rossetti's watercolours 'The Blue Closet' (1865–7) and 'The Tune of Seven Towers' (1857);[10] Rossetti's own 'For *The Wine of Circe* by Edward Burne-Jones' (1870);[11] Swinburne's 'A Christmas Carol' (suggested by a Rossetti drawing) and his 'Before the Mirror (Verses Written Under a Picture)', inspired by Whistler's 'The Little White Girl (Symphony in White No. 2, 1864)'; [12] and Browning's 'Deaf and Dumb' commemorating a sculptural group by Thomas Woolner and 'Eurydice to Orpheus: A Picture by Leighton'.[13] Publication of these poems signifies the artist's implicit approval, which he might make manifest, like Leighton who included Browning's lyric in the catalogue entry for his painting at the Royal Academy exhibition of 1864, or Whistler who pasted Swinburne's verses printed on gold paper to the frame of his painting at the RA exhibition in 1865.

Artistic display of another kind occurs in Browning's light-hearted monologue, 'Youth and Art' (1864) which, although not set in the studio, provides a tantalizing glimpse of it. Kate Brown, a singer, reminisces nostalgically about her bohemian apprenticeship when she lodged across the way from Smith, an aspiring sculptor. Without reaching the top of their professions, both have done passably well in later life, but Kate feels they missed out by failing to act on a mutual attraction apparent at the time when they 'For fun watched each other's windows'.[14] No palace of art, Smith's studio was obviously a modest affair, yet for Kate it served the purpose of displaying the artist who, she recalls,

> lounged, like a boy of the South,
> Cap and blouse—nay, a bit of a beard too;
> Or you got it, rubbing your mouth
> With fingers the clay adhered to.

Smith was clearly of more interest to her than his sculptures: she remembers jealously taking notice 'When models arrived, some minx/Tripped up-stairs, she and her ankles.'

For Kate, Smith's studio showcases the artist not the art, her unembarrassed voyeurism matched by the sculptor's interest in her rather than her music. It is implied that each of these young artists performs for the other and enjoys attracting the other's attention and desire. Kate's frank appreciation reminds us of the complex erotic dynamics of the studio where the artist not only represents and exhibits his desires but might, in displaying himself, also become an object of desire. In Kate Brown, whose name signals the poet's sympathetic identification, Browning boldly endorses the female viewer's right to express her desire through both her voice and her gaze.

That daring is carried through into 'Beatrice Signorini', one of the few Victorian poems that features a female artist, in this case the Baroque Italian painter Artemisia Gentileschi (1593–1652), now celebrated by feminist art historians for her depictions of courageous assertive heroines.[15] Browning does not mention these, instead singling out for praise the nude study she painted for the Casa Buonarroti which he titles 'Desire', a stronger version of its usual name *Allegoria della Inclinazione* (*Allegory of the Inclination*). Artemisia's ability to recognize her own and others' desires is of prime importance when she attracts the attention of the artist Francesco Romanelli, who has left his wife behind in Viterbo while practising his trade in Rome. For Francesco, the studio or workshop is the site of conflicting erotic and professional impulses as, watching her paint, he realizes Artemisia's superiority but cannot admit it:

> Whereon, instead
> Of the checked love's utterance—why he said
> Leaning above her easel: 'Flesh is red'
> (Or some such just remark) 'by no means white
> As Guido's practice teaches: you are right'.[16]

Unlike his 'placid Beatrice-wife' who, he complacently thinks, regards him as above criticism, Artemisia, confident in her own ability, shows no submissive tendencies: 'What surprise / —Nay scorn, shoots black fire from those startled eyes! / She to be lessoned in design forsooth!' The object of Francesco's desirous gaze, Artemisia, unlike most women viewed in the studio, remains in control of her identity and power. Calling time on their relationship, she sends Francesco home with a painting, a gift for his wife, that acts like a cryptic communication between the two women, channelling some of her fierce intelligence and fiery passion into the passively acquiescent Beatrice, and transforming her from a docile 'consort with the milk for blood' into a spirited woman with independent powers of judgement. Artemisia's painting, a work that sparks desire, energizes both Francesco and Beatrice and ultimately reinvigorates their marriage for the better.[17]

While Browning's Renaissance painter poems have little to say about the studio per se, the place in which art is made is often a site of tension. The church, a major source of commissions, and a key location for making and displaying art, imposes constraints that can stifle the artist's impulses. Pictor Ignotus admits that 'at whiles/My heart sinks, as monotonous I paint / These endless cloisters and eternal aisles / With the same series';[18] Frà Lippo Lippi learns to draw in the convent on his 'copy-books' and 'On the wall, the bench, the door', his first proper design being a 'covered bit of cloister wall', but quickly finds his facility for vivid realist design checked by his superiors who want him to paint in a more idealist way.[19] Most of his works are frescoes commissioned for church walls; other commissions are for wealthy patrons like the 'saints and saints / And saints again' he has been painting for Cosimo de' Medici when he gets bored and decides to go out roistering. Frà Pandolf in 'My Last Duchess' seems to have painted his portrait of the Duchess in the ducal palace at Ferrara overseen by the coldly disapproving Duke who resents the polite compliments the painter pays his wife. Andrea del Sarto, in the 'melancholy little house' he shares with his wife Lucrezia, apparently lacks a studio, the seemingly uncomfortable doubling of domestic space with workspace an indicator of the tense relations of his art and married life. The reluctant Lucrezia 'must serve / For each of the five pictures we require—/ It saves a model'; to his chagrin, she is evidently uninterested in his art and the skill required 'to paint a little thing like that you smeared / Carelessly passing with your robes afloat'.[20]

Lucrezia, an unwilling subject, compensates by spending her husband's earnings and pursuing her own pleasures outside the marriage. Nonetheless she serves to reminds us that the studio can also be a site of tension for the female model, transformed into images over which she has no control. Various women poets intimate that the male artist's studio is the place where he transforms his model into his preferred type or types, or as Christina Rossetti puts it: 'Not as she is, but as she fills his dream'. In this sense, the studio looms large in May Probyn's late Victorian dramatic monologue 'The Model', which reflects on the unequal relationship between the male artist and his female sitter and the power wielded by him when representing her. Published before Rossetti's sonnet, this poem gives the illusion of responding to it, providing a more explicit critique of sexual politics and giving the model her own voice and point of view. Moreover, Probyn's male artist who evidently works in the Pre-Raphaelite style owes something to Dante Gabriel Rossetti, the original of the painter in Christina Rossetti's sonnet.

Probyn's nameless speaker tells how, seen by an artist in the street, she is summoned to pose for him as the infamous Herodias of the Gospels (Matthew 14. 3–12; Mark

6. 17–29), the adulterous queen who had her daughter Salome request the head of John the Baptist. Yet it transpires that the artist painted her three years previously as a young Virgin Mary, 'grave and innocent, / Sitting untroubled at a spinning-wheel'.[21] At this earlier time, like many male artists, he became sexually involved with his model, but when the relationship ended, abandoned her to her own devices. Now worldly-wise and disillusioned by hardship, she is so physically changed that he unwittingly selects her to pose as a voluptuous and sinister femme fatale—'Steeped to the brows in splendid shamelessness'—discovering her identity only when he asks her name.

This artist uses the studio to turn his model into images that obey the binary stereotype of woman as virgin or whore, leaving no room for the complexity of the actual woman. The Victorian female model was frequently regarded as little better than a prostitute—both being women who sell their bodies to accommodate male fantasy—and there is a dismal inevitability about the way that the once-virginal girl ends up resembling the queen John the Baptist condemned for her immorality. If, as implied here, the studio is a place of sexual exploitation, then the model may all too easily 'fall' from maiden to streetwalker, the street, an additional source of income when times are hard, being significantly where the cruising artist 'finds the face he needs'.

Second time around, the studio allows recognition which is also misrecognition; the artist realizing his model's former identity yet repressing his part in her transformation, insults her by denying that he ever loved her, implying that even then she was as hard and invulnerable as he now reads her to be. Affronted, she slaps his face and walks out, this heartening moment of retaliation a pyrrhic victory in that the episode makes her dwell on the crudely mismatched identity ascribed to her:

> I think that had he loved me in those days,
> Never so little, only for an hour,
> To-day, perhaps, I were not all I am—
> Perhaps Herodias had not worn my face.

Like other Victorian female poetic subjects who contemplate representations of themselves conferring social and sexual identity, Probyn's speaker simultaneously resists and accepts the images that constrain her sense of self.[22]

In their awareness of the limitations of male-authored fictive images of women, Rossetti and Probyn may be responding to an influential precursor. Barrett Browning's *Aurora Leigh*, dated 1857, was actually published on 15 November 1856, seven weeks before Rossetti penned her sonnet. Dante Gabriel, sent a presentation copy, was 'revelling' in it by late November, and is more than likely to have shared it with his sister, a huge admirer of Barrett Browning.[23] In a crucial early passage, Aurora relates how as a young child she would gaze at her dead mother's portrait.

> The painter drew it after she was dead;
> And when the face was finished, throat and hands,
> Her cameriera carried him, in hate
> Of the English-fashioned shroud, the last brocade
> She dressed in at the Pitti. 'He should paint

No sadder thing than that, she swore, 'to wrong
Her poor signora.' Therefore very strange
The effect was. I, a little child, would crouch
For hours upon the floor, with knees drawn up
And gaze across them, half in terror, half
In adoration, at the picture there,—
That swan-like supernatural white life,
Just sailing upward from the red stiff silk
Which seemed to have no part in it, nor power
To keep it from quite breaking out of bounds:
For hours I sate and stared.

(i. 128–43)

Painted to commemorate the once-living woman, the portrait, begun at the death-bed and finished in the studio, disturbingly only reinforces her decease. While the maid wants the painting to do justice to her mistress's vitality, the uncanny mismatch between the pallid mortuary image and the superimposed colourful silk gown makes the subject into an elusive spectre. The artist conveys not the essence of the living woman but her ghost, his failure perhaps indicative of a larger cultural failing to provide authentic images of women. As a girl, Aurora projects onto the painting the prevailing literary and cultural representations of women, the maternal portrait becoming a repository of crudely oppositional feminine archetypes.

And as I grew
In years, I mixed, confused, unconsciously,
Whatever I last read or heard or dreamed,
Abhorrent, admirable, beautiful,
Pathetical, or ghastly, or grotesque,
With still that face... which did not therefore change,
But kept the mystic level of all forms
And fears and admirations; was by turns
Ghost, fiend, and angel, fairy, witch, and sprite...

(i. 147–54)

Aurora signals the limited repertoire of available feminine representations, a macabre matrix of 'dead' or unreal images. Her subsequent development as a woman and literary artist challenges her culture's impoverished sense of female identity by providing an alternative set of positive, vital, and liberatory images.

Barrett Browning's belief in the politically and socially transformative power of art is expressed in her sonnet 'Hiram Powers' *Greek Slave*' (1850): 'Pierce to the centre, / Art's fiery finger!—and break up ere long / The serfdom of this world!'[24] A close friend of the American neo-Classical sculptor Hiram Powers (1805–73) whom she first met in May 1847, she saw his statue of the Greek slave towards the end of that month at his studio, a short walk from Casa Guidi, the Brownings' Florentine home.[25] Powers's statue depicts a naked Greek woman about to be sold into slavery by the Turks during the struggle for Greek independence (1821–32) but, as Barrett Browning indicates in her sonnet, was seen as an iconic protest against oppression in general, including American slavery:

> appeal, fair stone,
> From God's pure heights of beauty against man's wrong!
> Catch up in thy divine face, not alone
> East griefs but west,—and strike and shame the strong,
> By thunders of white silence, overthrown.

The statue, completed in 1843, was widely exhibited and admired though caused scandal in some quarters on account of its nudity. To modern eyes the image is problematic in other ways; the combination of the expressionless bland nude and the chains of bondage seems unpleasantly titillating. Yet to its Victorian defenders the Christian slave, stripped for sale though modestly trying to shield herself, was an emblem of Christ-like suffering and purity rising above degradation. The very lack of expression—'passionless perfection' as Barrett Browning calls it—confirmed the purity and ideal nature of the work. For Barrett Browning, Powers has succeeded in making the ideal not a thing apart but an active force for good. Noting that 'They say Ideal beauty cannot enter / The house of anguish', she counters with the observation that 'On the threshold stands / An alien Image with enshackled hands', seen as intended by the artist 'To, so, confront man's crimes in different lands / With man's ideal sense'. While the statue may be 'passionless', the sonnet is not. Barrett Browning's exclamatory tone, imperative apostrophes to Art and the 'fair stone', and vigorous advocacy, are emotionally charged and bespeak action and movement. If it seems strange that this fervid energy is generated by an 'ideal' sculpted figure that is more than usually passive, Barrett Browning's call to 'break up . . . / The serfdom of the world' arguably also breaks up the rigidities of the conventional sonnet form with a freewheeling rhetoric, strenuously worked syntax, and elastic enjambment.

The *Greek Slave* toured America in 1847–8 and appeared at the Crystal Palace Exhibition of 1851 where it was the centrepiece of the American section. The original marble, bought by an English purchaser, ended up at Raby Castle, County Durham, but Powers made five more full-size versions, three half-size versions, and numerous small versions and busts, thus maximizing the sculpture's display potential.[26] Although inspired by an artwork seen in the studio, the sonnet takes for granted and even emphasizes the statue's function as a polemical exhibition piece moving large audiences by its moral appeal, with a strong hint of a desired transformative effect on its American viewers.

This move into the gallery or exhibition space brings us into the domain of poetry that pays homage to famous artworks or the publicly displayed works of acclaimed artists. 1850, the year Barrett Browning published her sonnet on Powers's sculpture, also saw the publication in *The Germ* of Dante Gabriel Rossetti's original six 'Sonnets for Pictures', featuring paintings by Memling, Mantegna, Giorgione, and Ingres, seen in Bruges, the Louvre, and the Luxembourg Palace Museum during an 1849 trip to Paris and Belgium with Holman Hunt. In his *Poems* (1870) Rossetti replaced the Memling sonnets with 'For *Our Lady of the Rocks* by Leonardo da Vinci', which he wrote 'in front of the picture in the Brit: Inst: many years ago'.[27] The impulse to respond to artworks seen in galleries remained with him and, in 1880, towards the end of his life, he composed another sonnet celebrating Michelangelo's *Holy Family* in the National Gallery.

The sonnet, also used by Rossetti for his 'double works', is an ideal medium for the appreciation of an artwork, encapsulating in condensed form the salient details of the viewer's impression, whether documentary, meditative, or freely associative. In the 'Conclusion' to *Studies in the History of the Renaissance* (1873), Walter Pater proposed that the purpose of life was to seek out, savour, and treasure up peak moments of perceptual experience, with art an especially rich source of such moments. The commemorative and crystallizing capacity of the sonnet, its ability to act as a 'moment's monument' (to use Rossetti's words), makes it the perfect form to hold onto, preserve, and deliver again the transcendent or transformative instant that is the special gift of art.[28] Small wonder then that Pater should allude obliquely to Rossetti's sonnet 'For *A Venetian Pastoral* by Giorgione' in 'The School of Giorgione' (1877), an essay that enlarges on art's privileged relation with the epiphanic moment. Pater's perception that Giorgione's school typically depicts 'ideal instants...exquisite pauses in time, in which, arrested thus, we seem to be spectators of all the fullness of existence' accords well with Rossetti's summation that Giorgione's painting gives us 'Life touching lips with immortality'.[29]

Rossetti's use and development of the 'art sonnet' to commemorate both his own works and those of others would prove highly influential. A condensed, intricately structured form in which the sestet is a reflection on, response to, or resolution of a problem or complex matter posed in the octave, the Petrarchan sonnet is ideally suited to the exploration of contradiction, paradox, and enigma, qualities frequently associated with great works of art. Swinburne, for example, makes brilliant use of this sonnet form in his short sequence 'Hermaphroditus', a poem that teases out and dilates on the mysterious contradictions implicit in the celebrated antique statue of the Louvre hermaphrodite, viewed during a trip to Paris in March 1863. Ever fascinated by the meeting and mergence of opposites, Swinburne strengthened the sonnet's inherent capacity for paradox with his signature use of chiasmus as he mused on the hermaphrodite's ability to rouse in the spectator 'A strong desire begot on great despair, / A great despair cast out by strong desire'.[30] Like Barrett Browning, who in her polemical treatment of Powers' sculpture emphatically disrupts the classic formality of the sonnet, Swinburne skilfully makes form consonant with his vision. As his poem—contemplative rather than documentary—undoes the clear lines of classical sculpture, hazing and blurring what is seen, the wavering suggestive language and the fluid lyricism seductively soften and smooth down any sense of tightness, urgency, or constraint that might be associated with the rigorous discipline of the sonnet:

> To what strange end hath some strange god made fair
>   The double blossom of two fruitless flowers?
> Hid love in all the folds of all thy hair,
>   Fed thee on summers, watered thee with showers,
> Given all the gold that all the seasons wear
>   To thee that art a thing of barren hours?

As Stefano Evangelista has intimated, this poem, along with Swinburne's two famous essays, 'Notes on Designs of the Old Masters at Florence' and 'Notes on Some Pictures of

1868'—both published in 1868—show him as much at ease in the gallery as in the studio.[31] Two later Swinburne poems that suggest the gallery experience and commemorate paintings by the French artists Gustave Courbet and Henri Fantin-Latour can be found in his *A Century of Roundels* (1883). The roundel, which Swinburne adapted from the French rondeau and made his own, consists of eleven lines, with a refrain occurring in lines four and eleven that echoes the opening words of the first line. Using only two rhymes, it is a demanding compressed form that has an inherent circularity. Employed proficiently, it allows the poet to contemplate or consider a particular object, topic, or state of affairs from various angles, turning it round, as it were, or revisiting it to get a complete picture or refine a point of view. In 'A Landscape by Courbet' the speaker uses the first person plural, the 'we' of the poem representing admirers of the artist who might seek out his paintings in a gallery.[32] The roundel, opening with the words 'Low lies the mere', examines a peaceful lake scene that bears no trace of anything gloomy—'eye nor ear / Sees aught at all of dark, hears aught of shrill'—yet viewing the work in the light of the painter's recent death (Courbet had died in December 1877) confers a sense of despondency at odds with the painting's tranquillity.

> Strange, as we praise the dead man's might and skill,
> Strange that harsh thoughts should make such heavy cheer,
> While, clothed with peace by heaven's most gentle will,
>   Low lies the mere.

This apparently simple poem uses the repeated scanning of the painting signalled in the refrain to encapsulate art's paradox of sameness and difference. The speaker registers two things: first of all, that although human circumstances change, art remains the same (a version of the tension between art and life observed in Keats's 'On a Grecian Urn'); second, although art remains the same, we as individuals affected by change bring different emotions and ideas to it. On the one hand the landscape, captured in its summer serenity, can reflect only itself; separated from the artist that created it, it has no responsibility to anything other than itself, and there is a sense that the speaker admires and perhaps envies its undisturbed peace. On the other hand, for the knowing late Victorian viewer, Courbet's painting is now the work of a dead master and commemorates his skill; blithe though his landscape may be, it is hard to contemplate without sadness, feelings perhaps intensified by the thought of his premature death in virtual exile in Switzerland.

Courbet's pupil, Henri Fantin-Latour, famed for his flower paintings, is the subject of 'A Flower-Piece by Fantin'. Swinburne had met Fantin-Latour on his trip to Paris in 1863 and considered him a friend.[33] The painting under consideration, possibly *Still Life with Pansies* (1874), features a vase of pansies—flowers often known by the old-fashioned name 'heart's ease'—and the words 'Heart's ease or pansy' furnish the opening and refrain. The more familiar word 'pansy' derives from the French 'pensée' meaning 'thought', the flower so named because of its resemblance to a pensive human face. Playing on the two different meanings assigned to the flower, Swinburne's roundel opens with the question: 'Heart's ease or pansy, pleasure or thought, / Which would the picture give us of these?'[34] Yet although the initial meaning associated with 'Heart's ease' is 'pleasure', the repetitions of the name transform it into something more like 'consolation'. Speculating that 'Surely the heart that conceived it sought / Heart's ease', the speaker's intuition that the picture was intended as an anodyne for pain grows—'The hand impelling the heart that wrought / Wrought comfort here for a soul's disease'—leading to a final certainty that the 'Deep flowers…Lean and lend for a heart distraught / Heart's ease'.

If the previous roundel opened the question of what the viewer brings to the picture, this one takes it a step further. For the speaker this painting of flowers, a seemingly innocent and simple subject, addresses something deeper. There is a growing certainty that the artist intended his painting as a solace, but it is ambiguous whether the 'soul's disease' it is meant to soothe is his own or the spectator's. The speaker may initially understand the painter as relieving his own sorrow, but that consolation also comes to do duty for the spectator. The painting is as revelatory of the speaker's heart as it is of the painter's; indeed the attribution of motive or a particular emotional state to the painter looks like projection, indicating the speaker's own 'heart distraught' and need for comfort at the moment of viewing the picture. This personal need is partly disguised by the 'us' of line two. As in the previous roundel, the speaker uses a generalized first-person plural; but the sudden shift from a consideration of 'pleasure' to consolation, the intense probing of the painting's motivation, the focus on 'a heart distraught' and the flowers that in the present moment 'Lean and lend' their aid, all suggest that this is the response of an individual speaker intuitively responding to the leading questions posed by the Paterian 'aesthetic critic'—'What is this song or picture…to *me*? What effect does it really produce on me?'[35]

Pater's influence can also be felt in two sonnets by Eugene Lee-Hamilton that describe the painting of the Medusa in the Uffizi ascribed in the nineteenth century to Leonardo da Vinci. Poems about paintings often reference earlier poems about paintings whose ghostly lineaments can be glimpsed within the later works like buried old master images; both these sonnets clearly allude to Shelley's ekphrastic poem on the Uffizi picture, a poem that also informs Pater's description of the Medusa in his essay on Leonardo, though arguably what Pater brings to the scene is as important to Lee-Hamilton as Shelley. For Shelley, Pater, and Lee-Hamilton, the Medusa painting depicts a primal scene of aesthetic fascination (and one recalls that 'fascination' is properly the spellbinding effect of snakes on their prey.) Visible in Shelley's arrested enthralled 'gazer' and Pater's Leonardo, obsessed by the desire for an image that will unite his 'swarming fancies' as an 'interfusion of the extremes of beauty and terror', fascination is something compulsively repeated, a relay extending from the painting, through the texts that rearticulate it, to the readers who experience it refracted through the mirror of literary art.[36] Lee-Hamilton's sonnets intensify the decadent element in Pater's interpretation ('the fascination of corruption'); the Medusan beauty that counterpoints and partly alleviates terror in the essay disappears almost entirely, absorbed instead into the formal beauty of the sonnets themselves.

Published in *Imaginary Sonnets* (1888), the first of these two poems might be linked to the studio, if this is understood as the place of artistic inspiration. All the 'imaginary' sonnets replicate the voice of a mythological, legendary, or historical personage, envisaged at a particular and usually significant moment in time, each sonnet thus crystallizing or becoming a 'moment's monument'. 'Leonardo da Vinci on his Snakes (1480)' fixes the moment of imaginative conception in which Leonardo, fascinated by his snakes writhing on the floor, is inspired with the idea for his painting: 'What if I painted a Medusa's head…?'[37] Accomplished sonneteer that he is, Lee-Hamilton uses the Petrarchan form to dazzling effect: the octave portrays the immediate scene of Leonardo relishing the animated spectacle of his snakes' fluid 'undulation', while the sestet represents the projected future painting of the 'Fresh severed' Medusa head, the hair-snakes imagined as 'still writhing in a slow/Death-struggle'. Lee-Hamilton prepares beautifully for the volta which releases the moment of conception by having Leonardo observe of the sinuous wave of snakes in the preceding two lines: 'The live meander moves so soundlessly— / Inscrutable as magic's very core'. The phrase 'magic's very core', situated at the very heart of the poem, seems to tap into the magic core of Leonardo's own creativity, begetting in the thinking space that separates octave from sestet the image of the uncanny Medusa head, itself perhaps an analogue of or symbol for that Leonardesque creativity that holds us spellbound.

We shift from the studio to the gallery as Lee-Hamilton returns obsessively to the painting in a second sonnet, this a more straightforward ekphrasis, in a series of twelve poems about artworks titled 'Brush and Chisel' in *Sonnets of the Wingless Hours* (1894). In 'On Leonardo's Head of Medusa', octave and sestet are cleverly deployed to focus on the already deceased 'livid and unutterable head' as contrasted with the desperate terminal struggle of 'the dying vipers'.[38] The Uffizi was Lee-Hamilton's local gallery though it is doubtful whether he entered it during the period he composed these sonnets when stricken by the obscure 'cerebro-spinal' illness that left him virtually bed-bound for twenty years. For one whose poems frequently vent a nightmarish sense of entrapment, the prolonged living death of the Medusa or awareness of her paralysing power might have a personal application.[39] More than a decadent depiction of a scene or *homage* to its previous interpreters, this second Medusan sonnet also signals Lee-Hamilton as a Paterian observer with a unique investment in the painting.

Pater's legacy also informs *Sight and Song* (1892), a collection of thirty-one poems by Michael Field (Katharine Bradley and Edith Cooper) that, in the words of their recent editors, '"translated" into poetry the pictures the poets had seen in their strolls round various art galleries and museums both in London and in Continental Europe'.[40] Initially Bradley and Cooper look set to resist the Paterian imperative when they declare in their Preface that their aim is 'to express not so much what these pictures are to the poet, but rather to express what poetry they objectively incarnate'.[41] Yet, while they pay careful attention to colour, form, and composition, their own selective and interpretative viewpoint is everywhere apparent, particularly with regards to female subjects whom they read as in control of their desires. Their vision of the Mona Lisa, though obviously influenced by Pater's description, is more attentive to the detail of the painting, using this to project a calmly self-aware, seductive femme fatale. For them, Sodoma's drawing of Leda showing the swan her eggs instances confident assertion: 'Although his hectoring bill /

Gapes towards her tresses, / She draws the fondled creature to her will';[42] Giorgione's *Sleeping Venus* is no passive nude intended to gratify male eyes but a woman who enjoys her own sexuality:

> Her hand the thigh's tense surface leaves,
>   Falling inward. Not even sleep
>   Dare invalidate the deep
>   Universal pleasure sex
>   Must unto itself annex—[43]

Even when they read Bartolomeo Vento's *Portrait* as an arresting beautiful image that bears no trace of the subject's personality, the story they reconstruct of the sitter suggests a purposeful agency seemingly at odds with their verdict of a picture 'unverified by life'.[44] Their subject is no compliant artist's model but a courtesan who, dreading the inevitable loss of her beauty, resolves to commission a painted record of herself and carefully plans the costume, floral ornaments, and pose in which she will be immortalized. Too strong and determined a presence to be finally deemed 'a fair, blank form', the courtesan of the story intimates that once Bradley and Cooper consult the imagination, their creative instincts triumph over documentary intention.

Pater's insistence on knowing 'one's own impression as it really is' and realizing it 'distinctly' also pervades the final group of short lyrics explored here; these, like the sonnets already discussed, have the similar ability of capturing the moment. While, unlike the sonnets, they do not describe specific artworks, they arguably do recall paintings by one of the most important artists of late Victorian England, James McNeill Whistler, an American living in London, identified by British contemporaries as an 'impressionist'.[45] Whistler's colour-studies refuse subordination to narrative, a refusal made apparent through innovative musical titles such as 'Symphonies', 'Nocturnes', 'Harmonies', and 'Arrangements', which emphasize formal composition. Signalling the dominant colours of the work (*Symphony in White*, *Nocturne in Black and Gold*), these titles ask the viewer to relish art for artistry's sake, and not for any moral or message. Many of Whistler's paintings further this aestheticist project by taking a subject that might ordinarily be thought unprepossessing, an industrialized or drearily urban stretch of the Thames, for example, and transforming it into a scene of beauty. Thus works such as 'Nocturne: Blue and Silver—Chelsea' (Tate, 1871) and 'Nocturne: Blue and Gold—Old Battersea Bridge' (Tate, 1872–5) capture the instant 'when the evening mist clothes the riverside with poetry, as with a veil, and the poor buildings lose themselves in the dim sky, … and the whole city hangs in the heavens and fairyland is before us'.[46] Oscar Wilde, drawing attention to the way such painting made viewers into connoisseurs of hitherto unappreciated or disregarded natural effects, undoubtedly complimented Whistler when he wrote 'To whom, if not to [the Impressionists] and their master, do we owe the lovely silver mists that brood over our river, and turn to faint forms of fading grace curved bridge and swaying barge?'[47]

Wilde's lyric 'Symphony in Yellow' (1889) is an obvious nod to Whistler but goes one better by taking a Thameside view seen by daylight and making this apparently unpromising subject into an artfully composed impressionistic study. The banal signs of daily London life—the omnibus, the hay transported by barge for the horses that pull the city's carts and carriages, the 'thick fog' indicative of urban pollution—are harmonized into a study in yellow—a fashionable 'aesthetic' colour. True to the transformative principles of aestheticism, mundane objects are compared to and thus momentarily transformed into exotic or precious ones: the workaday omnibus becomes a yellow butterfly (the butterfly coincidentally being Whistler's painterly signature), the fog a 'silken scarf', and the Thames—probably 'pale green' with pollutant—'a rod of rippled jade'.[48]

The slight form of the late Victorian lyric, its short, simple stanzas and generally uncomplex diction, means it is especially good at suggesting the transience and ephemerality of the moment. While the more impressively 'monumental' structure of the sonnet makes it ideal for dwelling on and expanding the moment into a prolonged meditative pause, the lyric snatches at a quick but vivid impression. A harmony in blue, Mary Elizabeth Coleridge's 'L'Oiseau Bleu' (1897) is a lyric whose visual freeze-frame captures the image of the bluebird, traditionally associated with happiness and thus something fleeting:

> The lake lay blue below the hill.
> O'er it, as I looked, there flew
> Across its waters, cold and still,
> A bird whose wings were palest blue.
>
> The sky above was blue at last,
> The sky beneath me blue in blue.
> A moment, ere the bird had passed,
> It caught his image as he flew.[49]

Coleridge's poetic eye acts like a camera that takes coloured snapshots yet her poem, like Wilde's, is not a documentary photograph but an impression indelibly marked by subjectivity. The impressionistic lyric uses evocative detail sparingly in a fragmentary way, often allowing readers space to free-associate or use their imagination, as is the case in Arthur Symons's lyric 'Pastel' (1896) whose title indicates an impressionistic sketch:

> The light of our cigarettes
> Went and came in the gloom:
> It was dark in the little room.
>
> Dark, and then, in the dark,
> Sudden, a flash, a glow,
> And a hand and ring I know.
>
> And then, through the dark, a flash
> Ruddy and vague, the grace
> (A rose!) of her lyric face.[50]

The gloom of this locale, lit atmospherically only by cigarettes and two flashes of illumination—probably struck matches—allowing glimpses of a hand and a pretty woman's face, is a Whistlerian nocturne of black splashed with pink and gold. As tantalizingly as it hints at erotic excitement, it withholds as much as it reveals. Is this a smoky backroom in a pub or a club, or is it a bedroom? Is the woman a mistress, a wife—the speaker's own or someone else's—or a demi-mondaine? The poem's subtitle 'Masks and Faces', offering no clue as to how to distinguish between the two, teasingly reinforces ambiguity, but also suggests that to the sympathetic viewer, a mask, a persona, can sometimes become a face. Symons's carefully cultivated urban decadence characteristically allows him to discover poetry and beauty where others find squalor, and this poem perhaps discovers him in the transgressive act of conjuring the fallen woman into poetry as the romantic 'rose' of a 'lyric face', a sign of the ephemeral beauty that is the very hallmark of lyric.

As has been previously observed, Symons's lyric with its apparitional rose presages Pound's imagist poem 'In a Station of the Metro':

> The apparition of these faces in the crowd;
> Petals on a wet, black bough.[51]

Similarly Michael Field's 'Cyclamens' (1893), an arrangement in white whose treatment of the striking pallor and precision of the flowers has a strong sculptural element, anticipates the Imagism of H. D.'s flower poems:

> They are terribly white:
>> There is snow on the ground,
> And a moon on the snow at night;
> The sky is cut by the winter light;
> Yet I, who have all these things in ken,
> Am struck to the heart by the chiselled white
> Of this handful of cyclamen.[52]

Inspired by impressionistic works, these late Victorian lyrics use the 'Whistlerian' mode of aesthetic vision to capture subjects seen outside the studio or the gallery, corroborating Wilde's insight that influential ways of seeing filter into public consciousness and shape other kinds of perception. The instantaneous arrest of an image is also reminiscent of photography, itself becoming an art form at this time and increasingly ambitious outside the studio. Absorbing the lessons taught by art, such lyrics embrace the wider world, their artful simplicity a shaping force on the visual strategies of a generation of writers striving to reinvent themselves but unable to escape the aesthetic legacy of their Victorian poet-precursors.

Notes

1. Christina Rossetti, 'In an Artist's Studio', in *The Complete Poems*, ed. R. W. Crump (London: Penguin, 2001), 796. Apparently inspired by a visit to Dante Gabriel Rossetti's studio and his many portraits of Elizabeth Siddal, the poem, composed on 24 December 1856, first appeared in the posthumous *New Poems* (1896) edited by W. M. Rossetti.

2. I follow Alison Chapman, who reads l.3 as referring to the artist's model, although 'her' could equally refer to a 'hidden' painting (or paintings). Chapman notes the poem's 'refusal to distinguish between the model and her representation'. See *The Afterlives of Christina Rossetti* (London: Macmillan, 2000), 95, 94.

3. Elizabeth Barrett Browning, *Aurora Leigh*, vii. 578–90, ed. Margaret Reynolds (Ohio: Ohio University Press, 1992), 479.

4. Henry Treffry Dunn, *Recollections of Dante Gabriel Rossetti & His Circle or Cheyne Walk Life*, ed. Rosalie Mander (Westerham: Dalrymple Press, 1984), 15, 16, 18.

5. Charlotte Gere, *Artistic Circles: Design and Decoration in the Aesthetic Movement* (London: V&A Publishing, 2010), 55, 53.

6. Tennyson, 'The Palace of Art', in *The Poems of Tennyson*, 3 vols., ed. Christopher Ricks, 2nd edn. (Harlow: Longman, 1987), i. 456. Jonah Siegel, 'Display Time: Art, Disgust, and the Returns of the Crystal Palace', in *The Arts in Victorian Literature*, eds. Stefano Evangelista and Catherine Maxwell, *The Yearbook of English Studies* 40 (2010), 33–60; 35–7.

7. Tennyson, 'The Gardener's Daughter or, the Pictures', in *The Poems of Tennyson* ii. 569.

8. Arthur Henry Hallam to W. B. Donne (1831) in Hallam Tennyson, *Alfred Lord Tennyson: A Memoir*, 2 vols. (London: Macmillan & Co., 1897), i. 501.

9. Dante Gabriel Rossetti, 'The Portrait', in *The Works of Dante Gabriel Rossetti*, ed. William M. Rossetti (London: Ellis, 1911), 169. The poem, published in *Poems* (1870), was revised in 1869 from 'On Mary's Portrait' (1847).

10. See Rossetti's comment to William Allingham about Morris (18 December 1856): 'To one of my water-colours—called *The Blue Closet*, he has written a stunning poem.' *The Correspondence of Dante Gabriel Rossetti*, 9 vols., eds. William E. Fredeman et al., (Woodbridge: D. S. Brewer, 2002–), ii. 147.

11. Rossetti wrote the poem after *Circe* was exhibited, sending Burne-Jones a copy on 17 March 1870 (*The Correspondence of Dante Gabriel Rossetti*, iv. 397), but almost certainly would have first seen the painting in the studio.

12. Swinburne's poem and the drawing correspond to the Rossetti watercolour of this title (Fogg Musuem, 1857–8). A close friend, Swinburne often visited Whistler's studio, describing various unexhibited works in 'Notes on Some Paintings of 1868' (1868).

13. Woolner's sculpture, known as 'Constance and Arthur or Brother and Sister', was exhibited at the International Exhibition in South Kensington during May–November 1862. Browning, who knew Woolner well, gave him a copy of his poem on 24 April 1862. Leighton, a good friend of Browning's, designed Elizabeth Barrett Browning's tomb in Florence.

14. Robert Browning, 'Youth and Art', in *Robert Browning: The Poems*, 2 vols., eds. John Pettigrew and Thomas J. Collins, (Harmondsworth: Penguin), i. 16.

15. Included in *Asolando: Facts and Fancies* (1889), 'Beatrice Signorini' is now dated between 1853 and 1866.

16. Browning, 'Beatrice Signorini', in *The Poetical Works of Robert Browning*, 15 vols., eds. Ian Jack et al. (Oxford: Clarendon Press, 1983–), xv. 416.

17. See my fuller account of this communication in Catherine Maxwell, *The Female Sublime from Milton to Swinburne: Bearing Blindness* (Manchester: Manchester University Press, 2001), 172–4.

18. Browning, 'Pictor Ignotus', in *The Poetical Works of Robert Browning* iv. 29.

19. Browning, 'Frà Lippo Lippi', in *The Poetical Works of Robert Browning* v. 41.

20. Browning, 'Andrea del Sarto', in *The Poetical Works of Robert Browning* v. 264.

21. May Probyn, 'The Model', in *A Ballad of the Road and Other Poems* (London: W. Satchell, 1883), 37–40. The painting recalls Rossetti's 'The Girlhood of Mary Virgin' (Tate Britain, 1848–9), which depicts the young Virgin at her needlework. See also Rossetti's companion poem 'Mary's Girlhood', *Works*, 173.

22. See, for example, 'A Castaway' and 'Faded' in Augusta Webster, *Portraits and Other Poems*, ed. Christine Sutphin (Peterborough, ON: Broadview, 2000), 192–213; 213–18.

23. Rossetti to Ellen Heaton (*c*. 28 November 1856), in *The Correspondence of Dante Gabriel Rossetti* ii. 137.

24. Elizabeth Barrett Browning, 'Hiram Powers' Greek Slave', in *The Works of Elizabeth Barrett Browning*, 5 vols., ed. Sandra Donaldson et al. (London: Pickering & Chatto, 2010), ii. 150. The poem was first published in *Household Words* on 26 October 1850.

25. Powers called on the Brownings on 18 May 1847 shortly after their arrival in Florence. Barrett Browning was already familiar with his statue (probably through pictures). See *The Brownings' Correspondence*, ed. Philip Kelley et al., 17 vols. (Winfield, KS: The Wedgestone Press, 1984–), xiv. 208, 216.

26. Richard P. Wunder, *Hiram Powers, Vermont Sculptor 1805–1873*, 2 vols. (Newark and London: University of Delaware Press and Associated University Presses, 1991), ii. 157–77.

27. Rossetti to W. M. Rossetti (27 August 1869) in *Correspondence of Dante Gabriel Rossetti* iv.252.

28. Rossetti, introductory sonnet to *The House of Life*, *Works*, 74.

29. Walter Pater, 'The School of Giorgione', in *The Renaissance: Studies in Art and Poetry*, ed. Donald L. Hill (Berkeley: University of California Press, 1980), 118. Rossetti, 'For *A Venetian Pastoral* by Giorgone', in *Works*, 188; Pater's 'Giorgione' was collected in *The Renaissance* (3rd ed., 1878).

30. Algernon Charles Swinburne, 'Hermaphroditus', in *Poems and Ballads & Atalanta in Calydon*, ed. Kenneth Haynes (Harmondsworth: Penguin, 2000), 66. For an extended treatment, see Maxwell, *The Female Sublime from Milton to Swinburne*, 200–7.

31. Swinburne's two essays were published respectively in the *Fortnightly Review* (July 1868) and a pamphlet 'Notes on the Royal Academy Exhibition, 1868'. Both appeared subsequently in his *Essays and Studies* (1875). See Stefano Evangelista, 'Swinburne's Galleries', in *The Arts in Victorian Literature*, 160–79.

32. Swinburne, 'A Landscape by Courbet', in *The Poems of Algernon Charles Swinburne*, 6 vols. (London: Chatto & Windus, 1904), v. 176.

33. Swinburne, in *The Swinburne Letters*, ed. Cecil Y. Lang, 6 vols. (New Haven: Yale University Press, 1959–62), i. 164.

34. Swinburne, 'A Flower-Piece by Fantin', in *The Poems of Algernon Charles Swinburne*, v. 177.

35. Pater, 'Preface' to *The Renaissance*, xix–xx.

36. Percy Bysshe Shelley, 'On the Medusa of Leonardo da Vinci in the Florentine Gallery', in *Shelley: Poetical Works*, ed. Thomas Hutchinson (Oxford: Oxford University Press, 1970), 582; Pater, 'Leonardo da Vinci', 82, 83, 230. Pater omitted the reference to Shelley's poem in the fourth and final edition of *The Renaissance*, used as the basis for most subsequent editions.

37. Eugene Lee-Hamilton, 'Leonardo da Vinci on his Snakes (1480)', in *Imaginary Sonnets* (London: Elliot Stock, 1888), 25.

38. Lee-Hamilton, 'On Leonardo's Head of Medusa', in *Sonnets of the Wingless Hours* (London: Elliot Stock, 1894), 47.

39. The severed Medusa head, a classic Freudian castration image, might also communicate pervasive feelings of blight and lost potential.
40. *Michael Field: The Poet*, eds. Marion Thain and Ana Parejo Vadillo (Peterborough, ON: Broadview Press, 2009), 83.
41. Michael Field, 'Preface' to *Michael Field: The Poet*, 85.
42. Field, 'A Pen-Drawing of Leda', in *Michael Field: The Poet*, 102.
43. Field, 'The Sleeping Venus', in *Michael Field: The Poet*, 105. The imagery bears a coincidental resemblance to Swinburne's more sensational 'lesbian' reading of Titian's *Venus of Urbino*. See Evangelista, 'Swinburne's Galleries', 177.
44. Field, 'A Portrait', in *Michael Field: The Poet*, 94.
45. See my 'Whistlerian Impressionism and the Venetian Variations of Vernon Lee, John Addington Symonds, and Arthur Symons', in *The Arts in Victorian Literature*, 217–45.
46. James McNeill Whistler, 'Mr Whistler's Ten O'Clock Lecture' (1885), in *The Gentle Art of Making Enemies* (London: Heinemann, 1890; repr. 1994), 144.
47. Oscar Wilde, 'The Decay of Lying' (1889), in *Oscar Wilde: The Major Works*, ed. Isobel Murray (Oxford: Oxford University Press, 2000), 232.
48. Wilde, 'Symphony in Yellow', in *The Complete Works of Oscar Wilde*, 4 vols., ed. Russell Jackson and Ian Small et al. (Oxford: Oxford University Press, 2000–), i. 168.
49. Mary Elizabeth Coleridge, 'L'Oiseau Bleu', in *The Collected Poems of Mary Coleridge*, ed. Theresa Whistler (London: Rupert Hart-Davis, 1954), 163.
50. Arthur Symons, 'Pastel: Masks and Faces' from *Silhouettes* (2nd edn., 1896), in *Arthur Symons: Selected Writings*, ed. R. V. Holdsworth (Manchester: Carcanet Press, 1989), 30.
51. Hugh Kenner, *The Pound Era* (Berkeley and Los Angeles: University of California, Press, 1971), 183. Ezra Pound, 'In a Station of the Metro', in *Selected Poems 1908–1959* (London and Boston: Faber & Faber, 1977), 53.
52. Michael Field, 'Cyclamens', in *Underneath the Bough* (London: G. Bell & Sons, 1893), 108.

Select Bibliography

Bullen, J. B., *The Pre-Raphaelite Body: Fear and Desire in Painting, Poetry, and Criticism* (Oxford: Clarendon Press, 1997).
Evangelista, Stefano and Catherine Maxwell, eds., *The Arts in Victorian Literature: The Yearbook of English Studies* 40:1 and 40:2 (2010) (London: Modern Humanities Research Association).
Flint, Kate, *The Victorians and the Visual Imagination* (Cambridge: Cambridge University Press, 2000).
Helsinger, Elizabeth, *Poetry and the Pre-Raphaelite Arts: Dante Gabriel Rossetti and William Morris* (New Haven: Yale University Press, 2008).
Hollander, John, *The Gazer's Spirit: Poems Speaking to Silent Works of Art* (Chicago: University of Chicago Press, 1995).
Maxwell, Catherine, *Second Sight: The Visionary Imagination in Late Victorian Literature* (Manchester: Manchester University Press, 2008).
Østermark-Johansen, Lene, *Walter Pater and the Art of Sculpture* (Farnham and Burlington, VT: Ashgate, 2011).
Peters, Robert L., 'Whistler and the English Poets of the 1890s', *Modern Language Quarterly*, 18 (1957), 251–61.

Prettejohn, Elizabeth, *Art for Art's Sake: Aestheticism in Victorian Painting* (New Haven: Yale University Press, 2007).

Riede, G. David. *Dante Gabriel Rossetti and the Limits of Victorian Vision* (London: Cornell University Press, 1983).

Smith, Lindsay, *Victorian Photography, Painting and Poetry: The Enigma of Visibility in Ruskin, Morris and the Pre-Raphaelites* (Cambridge: Cambridge University Press, 1995).

Stein, Richard, *The Ritual of Interpretation: Literature and Art in Ruskin, Rossetti, and Pater* (Cambridge, MA: Harvard University Press, 1975).

Wagner, Jennifer Ann, *A Moment's Monument: Revisionary Poetics and the Nineteenth-Century English Sonnet* (London: Fairleigh Dickinson Presses and Associated University Presses, 1996).

CHAPTER 46

....

ON NOT HEARING: VICTORIAN POETRY AND MUSIC

....

FRANCIS O'GORMAN

VICTORIAN poets were surprisingly deaf to music. I do not, of course, mean they were deaf to the sound of poetry, or that they did not think or write about music. Tennyson famously, according to W. H. Auden, had the 'finest ear, perhaps, of any English poet'.[1] The 'perhaps' is a donnish affectation—perhaps. But it helps, at least, to make the line more rhythmically sophisticated. Tennyson's sensitivity to real music is, however, not something we know much about.[2] Certainly, he notices music as grand vibration, rather than as much else, in *In Memoriam* (1850): 'The storm their high-built organs make', he says in lyric LXXXVII, recounting his visit back to Cambridge, and to his old room, after Hallam's death: 'And thunder-music, rolling, shake / The prophet blazoned on the panes'.[3] The music the organist plays is pulsation: the sound disturbs the air and shakes the windows. Tennyson discerns nothing about form, harmony, counterpoint, and musical content, and offers no closer analysis of what he hears other than what sound waves do to glass (and the shaking prophet on the window is as much visual as audible). Perhaps Tennyson was thinking specifically of his own college, Trinity. Either the organ builders John Lincoln (1808) or Flight and Robson (1819) may have been the first to provide 16′ pedal pipes for the Trinity organ, an instrument originally built by 'Father' Smith in two phases (1693–5 and 1707–8), though the compass of the first pedal board is unknown. Nevertheless, we can be sure there were newish 16′ pedal pipes, which speak an octave below piano pitch at Trinity when Tennyson was there. The lowest notes of such a stop (probably either GG or CC), more of a boom than a pitch, might well have made windows rattle. But that fact tells us nothing about what, exactly, the organist was playing. Elsewhere, Tennyson was no more discerning. In *The Princess* (1847), the songs are important: they contribute to the generic medley as well as, perhaps, to the poem's cryptic meditation on the place of lyric in discursive poetry, the poetry of ideas. The songs are frequently anthologized, not least because they do seem able to stand alone, as if they belong to a different world than the dramatic action, and public debate, of the rest. "'Let some one sing to us"', says Ida in Part IV, before we hear the memorable song 'Tears, idle tears': "'lightlier move / The minutes fledged with music:" and a maid, / Of those beside her, smote her harp, and sang.'⁴ It is curious how the thought of music almost troubles the music of Tennyson's line: 'lightlier move / The minutes fledged with music' half-stumbles with that faintly awkward 'lightlier move', while no clear visual image springs to mind with the description of those 'minutes' as somehow growing stronger feathers out of fluffy juvenile down to the accompaniment of music. A harpist might well quietly wonder, too, whether harps are really at their best when 'smote', however much the line was a commonplace in the nineteenth century.⁵

Songs play a related role in Matthew Arnold's 'Empedocles on Etna' (1852), where Callicles' music contrasts the mental turmoil of Empedocles' ruminations of time out of joint in what Callicles calls his 'man-hating mood'.⁶ Music is a kind of distraction, an alternative. Indeed, according to Pausanias, Empedocles himself, Orpheus-like, used to heal with music, to 'Chain madmen by the music of his lyre' and 'Cleanse to sweet airs the breath of poisonous streams'.⁷ But those days are gone. Neither music nor words, neither reason nor feeling avails against Empedocles' oddly triumphant gloom now. The reader is only invited to understand something extremely general about the possible pleasures of song from 'Empedocles', the added force of music over words. But Arnold's consideration of the uses of music could hardly be said to be central to the poem. Music is his more explicit subject elsewhere. The 'Epilogue to Lessing's Laocoön' (1867) is not a well-known text, and falls into that category of a work that is not a poem of ideas but a poem about ideas. The 'Epilogue', nevertheless, is part of a well-known tradition: a discussion of the relative merits of the arts and, here, an attempt to define the specific genius of poetry. It resists Lessing's own sense, in his influential essay *Laokoon: Oder über die Grenzen der Malerei und Poesie* (1766), that the specific nature rather than hierarchy of each of the arts is the best concern of the critic. Music is credited by Arnold's companion, with whom he is arguing, with a healing power. A greater force to 'soothe our pains' is to be found in 'Mozart, Beethoven, Mendelssohn'⁸ than in the words of many poets. Music is balm, as it once was for Empedocles. But is there anything more exact revealed in this poem about the nature of music, and, in particular, about a specific *piece* of music, actually heard? The poet and his companion walk towards Westminster Abbey, and, observing its towers, hear the music coming from within the Abbey walls (a rehearsal, a concert? surely not a service⁹):

> [']While through their earth-moored nave below
> Another breath of wind doth blow,
> Sounds as of wandering breeze—but sound
> In laws by human artists bound.
> 'The world of music!' I exclaimed:—
> 'This breeze that rustles by, that famed
> Abbey recall it! what a sphere
> Large and profound, hath genius here!

The inspired musician what a range,
What power of passion, wealth of change!
Some source of feeling he must choose
And its locked fount of beauty use,
And through the stream of music tell
Its else unutterable spell;
To choose it rightly is his part,
And press into its inmost heart.

'*Miserere, Domine!*
The words are uttered, and they flee.
Deep is their penitential moan,
Mighty their pathos, but 'tis gone.
They have declared the spirit's sore,
Sore load, and words can do no more.
Beethoven takes them then—those two
Poor, bounded words—and makes them new;
Infinite makes them, makes them young;
Transplants them to another tongue,
Where they can now, without constraint,
Pour all the soul of their complaint,
And roll adown a channel large
The wealth divine they have in charge.
Page after page of music turn,
And still they live and still they burn,
Eternal, passion-fraught, and free—
Miserere, Domine!'[10]

Arnold's words are a concise compendium of many poets' assumptions about music as what might be called an emotional presence in the period. Over the expressive capacity of mere language, music, at this point in the poem's argument at any rate, is allowed the force of exceptional passion and a meaning beyond, but not without, emotion that cannot be caught in exact verbal terms. The composer—we learn that it is Beethoven—has changed language into an amalgam of experience, meaning, and feeling that is 'Eternal, passion-fraught, and free'. Made intimate, music lifts a listener into an acoustic eternity, charged with feeling.

Arnold's conception of music is an ancient one: a form of art that conjoins the heart and the mind, reason and feeling, and is more than the sum of those parts. 'To match and mate / Feeling with knowledge,—make as manifest / Soul's work as Mind's work',[11] was, as Robert Browning's 'With Charles Avison' from *Parleyings with Certain People of Importance in their Day* (1887) puts it, often recognized as the distinctive ambition of music in its highest power. The Victorian poets rarely challenged this assertion. But Arnold claims a lot for a piece heard from a distance while walking and talking: a lot for music that allegedly comes from Westminster Abbey and which is audible, apparently, from a bridge in Hyde Park. The distance perhaps accounts for why Arnold misheard the words. If the music was Beethoven's *Missa Solemnis* (1824)—probably given its first complete performance in England by the Royal Philharmonic Society only in 1846—presumably he was hearing the first part of the composer's almost clamorous setting of the final movement of the *Missa*, the *Agnus Dei*, with its petitionary words, 'miserere nobis'. Beethoven is, as Arnold thought, almost mighty in his pathos there. 'Miserere, Domine', certainly, appears neither in that mass nor in the Latin Ordinary anywhere. It is odd that Arnold should not have remembered the Ordinary, but not odd that he should have failed to discriminate what the Abbey choir was supposedly singing from Hyde Park. Music is primarily registered, dimly coming across central London, as emotional force, as a form of art uniquely probing and 'press[ing] into' the 'inmost heart' of words. It does not seem to matter that the details are lost, or if the unlikely episode was true anyway.

Tennyson heard music outside the building in which it was happening, as a disturbance of the air. Arnold, hearing through stonework, thought of air too: the wind brings the sound to him and links music to the atmosphere, as if in some way it is an exhalation of breath. Breathed music might suggest its naturalness, its unforced artlessness, as well as its intangibility, its existence diffused into the environment, like scent or light. Writing of more half-heard music, William Alexander (1824–1911), husband of the celebrated hymn writer Cecil Frances Alexander (1818–95), introduced more breath: '"Speak then no words"', Alexander has his speaker say, in 'Music or Words?', another Arnoldian poem of debate over their relative merits:

> but some soft air
> Play; as it scarcely ripples there,
> Or, rather say, as its true wing
> With silver over-shadowing
> Throbs—and no more—my soul beneath
> Shall pass without one troubled breath
> From sleep to dreams, from dreams to death.
>
> 'Wherefore be utter'd words kept far,
> Such as may that dim music mar,
> That exquisite vagueness finely brought,
> A gentle anodyne to thought—
> Speak me not any words, O friend!
> At least one moment at life's end
> I want to feel, not comprehend.'[12]

The speaker's pun is partly on 'air', as both an air of music (a song or melody) and the element in which music is apprehended, helping the speaker sleep 'without one troubled breath'. This is dim music too, an 'exquisite vagueness' that sounds like a characteristically Aesthetic Movement pleasure. We know almost nothing except its vague effects. Music is a 'gentle anodyne' to thought, a blessing because it enables one to feel but not know, to experience emotion but not to be troubled with analyzing it. Alexander's poem eventually places words as the superior form of communication: music is hardly more than a pleasing soporific: a dull narcotic, numbing pain. But the sense of music as something generalized and diffused through the ambiance, as an art form linked to exhalation and natural sound, and as an aesthetic creation seemingly for the expression of pure emotion, were all well established elements of Victorian poetry's conception of the idea of music.

If breath quietly linked music to the natural, Algernon Charles Swinburne was more explicit in hearing the sounds of the natural world as music. He imagined poetry as a form of such natural sound that infused the air long after the death of the poet. Music was, in this respect, like light in Swinburne's poetry: propagated through space, of no exact origin, it was both intangible and ineradicable. 'With chafe and change of surges chiming', Swinburne wrote in 'At a Month's End' from *Poems and Ballads, Second Series* (1878), 'The clashing channels rocked and rang / Large music, wave to wild wave timing, / And all the choral water sang'.[13] Hearing the sounds of the sea, Swinburne converted them into 'music' that the reader can never literally hear through the silent words on the page. Natural, authentic, wholly itself, this kind of natural sound flooded Swinburne's verse, always half-suggesting more-than-human powers animating the natural world of which, elsewhere, Swinburne was scornful. Caught between that which was 'merely' natural and that which was God-like or God-given, music's continuance in the atmosphere suggested the poet's more general ambivalence about the supernatural, but provided, at least, a ready trope for legacies. When, in 'Astrophel' from *Astrophel and Other Poems* (1894), Swinburne thought of Sir Philip Sidney set amid the 'music in heaven', he imagined that Sidney's 'One lyre...outsings and outlightens / The rapture of sunset'.[14] Sidney had become part of the music of the heavens that was—through the poet's characteristic synaesthesia—brighter than light. Sidney's art endures as a powerful wish, through a compelling though not entirely clear image, as Théophile Gautier endures, according to 'Memorial Verses' in *Poems and Ballads* II, as 'A new song mixed into the song supreme / Made of all souls of singers and their might'.[15] That was a secular version of the choir of angels, the *chorus angelorum*, of the Latin requiem (and Swinburne's coincidental admission into this line of 'all souls', the Christian commemoration of the dead the day after All Saints' Day, coyly suggests further the tug of Christian promise that the poem cannot more openly admit). Music's flow into the atmosphere offered Swinburne a figure of the endurance of human souls through art in time: as sound could not be seen or touched, music figured the penetration of the aesthetic into the environment among the living in a way that was as rhetorically persuasive as it was costive about the specifics of the posthumous bequest of art, and the theology of the human soul. Music's occupation of the air was the audible embodiment of a mysterious hope.

Paintings might endure long after an artist's death. John Ruskin thought of that frequently, remarking, in 1870, that the Florentine art of painting on ceramics produced something 'more permanent than the Pyramids'.[16] 'Music is gone', Ruskin said in an Oxford lecture in 1871, 'as soon as produced—marble discolours,—fresco fades,—glass darkens or decomposes—[oil] painting alone, well guarded, is practically everlasting'.[17] But there is no living performer behind that continuation in the visual arts. Writers may 'speak' to readers through their books, long after death too. But they do so only metaphorically. Yet music, before the invention of sound recording, always required a living musician, a player, to bring it into existence. There was always life literally involved.

And the living nature of performed music could well seem like the extended life of the composer, his (or her) continuing presence. '[Here's] your music all alive once more—', says Browning's speaker in 'With Charles Avison', his last important poem about music, 'As once it was alive, at least'.[18] In the long legacy of the Romantic debates about the life of art, which lasted far beyond the nineteenth century, the aptness of music as a vehicle of human survival was not inaudible. And music—or rather an idea of music—touched on more shadowy vitalities too. Swinburne limited his imaginings of world-music, the sounds that permeated and apparently originated from the natural world, as that which was without explicit Christian reference, even if his language was shaped by memories of the Christian liturgy and faith. Openly Christian meanings were derived elsewhere, however, from this putative music of nature—the remains, perhaps, of the ancient notion of the music of the spheres. Such music could be associated with continual worship, as if the generality of natural sound represented, without going too deeply into theology, the perpetual acclaim of God from the world He made. 'The earth is full of music pure and sweet', wrote the Anglican clergyman Charles Dent Bell (1819–98) in 'Music' from *Diana's Looking Glass and Other Poems* (1894): 'That rises like a sacred hymn to heav'n, / Or anthem perfect in its rhythmic beat / Sounding from early dawn till close of even'.[19] This is supposedly a 'pure music', a single intention uncorrupted by intrusion or sin, which rises in praise to God. And it is not so remote from Swinburne's ravished sense of the earthly and universal harmonies into which great souls might be absorbed. Pure, perhaps—but also confusing. The collective sound in Bell's ears is an anthem 'perfect in its rhythmic beat', yet that description is at once tautology and a puzzle. Bird song, the sounds of the wind in trees, the sounds of the sea are not 'perfect in [their] rhythmic beat', if 'perfect' means strict. What matters is not musical accuracy, but the impression of a great sound in acclamation. Music as a generalized, only partly heard, sonic experience was frequently apprehended by the poets in such terms, and it served the useful purpose of connecting human beings to the highest things without specific theology, and in a way that involved the fusion of emotion with thought. In this kind of listening was passion united with a sense of human elevation to the sacred; in it, too, was an awareness of pleasures beyond the quotidian and beyond, but not against, the rational. The transcendental was within human hearing. And one did not have to listen too hard.

Adelaide Anne Procter's 'The Lost Chord' (1858) has a special place within Victorian efforts to discern in music a revelation because its popularity was immense, and across classes. Easily accessible and narrating an engaging movement from the mundane to a vision of comfort, Procter's words assured the reader of the proximity of the marvellous, even as only a fleeting sensation. The poet hears a sound, seated one day at the organ, which can neither be described nor played again. Arthur Sullivan, setting the words to music in 1877 while his brother lay dying, did not, of course, propose the lost chord itself. And a sense of the lostness of that mysterious sound is peculiarly vivid in Procter's words that bring into sharp relief the silence of printed poetry against music that is described but cannot be heard.[20] It is not only the silence of print that is an impediment, for Procter throws up other barriers between the unheard sound and its empirical reality as a piece of documentable, and recreatable, music. We know that the chord was 'Like the sound of a Great Amen',[21] and if this might usefully suggest the hidden chorus of angels that spoke through the soul of the organ, it is still musically confusing. 'Amen' is two syllables, and there is only one chord; and 'Amen' for any musician means a plagal cadence, a progression of two chords (subdominant to tonic) that no single chord can imply. Procter's lost chord is *so* lost that we cannot even *wonder* what it was like.

Thomas Hardy, once dreaming of life as a cathedral organist[22] and knowledgeable about folk fiddle music, linked music with other spiritual powers, including the spectral musicians who sing in 'The Choirmaster's Burial' from *Moments of Vision* (1917). In a more earth-bound sense, music crossed from present experience to human memory in Hardy's poetry, sometimes with a distinctive sense of personal interiority, of individuality, and even of pleasure. Personal experience could be revived by sound; even by the *sight* of a musical instrument. 'To My Father's Violin', from *Moments of Vision*, ruminates on the usefulness of the Orpheus story for Hardy's now dead father who is without his musical instrument in the underworld. Yet it is not theology or myths that are the centre of the text but recollection. Hardy remembers his father's playing in a touchingly pleasurable retrospect: moments when, as the poet says to the violin, 'he made you speak his heart / As in dream'.[23] Here really had been the spontaneous overflow of powerful feelings, the unhindered transmission of self to sound. But could *poetry* ever be such an unmediated projection directly from the heart? Was there a hidden dream, or chastisement, for the lyric here?

Music was bound with the past more sorrowfully for Hardy elsewhere. In 'The Last Performance', also from *Moments of Vision*, music is an audible acknowledgement of the proximity of the grave and a final summing-up, so it seems, of the personal history that made an individual herself:

> 'I am playing my oldest tunes,' declared she,
>   'All the old tunes I know,—
> Those I learnt ever so long ago.'
> —Why she should think just then she'd play them
>   Silence cloaks like snow.
>
> When I returned from the town at nightfall
>   Notes continued to pour
> As when I had left two hours before:
> 'It's the very last time,' she said in closing;
>   'From now I play no more.'
>
> A few morns onward found her fading,
>   And, as her life outflew,
> I thought of her playing her tunes right through;
> And I felt she had known of what was coming,
>   And wondered how she knew.[24]

The recovered sound of the past becomes the past itself. The childhood of a dying woman lives for a moment again in music, but then, in turn, those sounds become a remembered epitaph, once heard by the living as if a mysterious indication of a woman's extraordinary, visionary knowledge of the approach of death. Hardy's poem—almost obtrusively at the end dwelling on a capital A, as if a starting note, the point of alphabetical and musical departure—recollects a moment of hearing. But the music that readers cannot hear teases us with an elegiac intensity, with the capacity of sound to express almost mystical knowledge that language on its own cannot articulate. The emotional and spiritual limits of the elegiac lyric are quietly exposed in a poem that silently yearns for the communicative power of the dying woman's music.

Many of the Victorian poets preferred, in general, to think of an idea of music, or what they thought were the ideas *in* music. The notion of music as an achieved form of art, with rules and decorum, with issues of interpretation and performance, slipped beyond their experience of listening. Certainly, music seemed largely to arise without any issues of a performer's interpretation, without any thorough sense of music *as* performance. Swinburnean world-music, for a start, was always already complete and was not subject to change: it was never available for a second performance with a different emphasis. Hearing the curve of a phrase, a sequence of musical intervals, a progression of chords, a set of distinct pitches, let alone the larger formal structures and genres—dance, sonata, passacaglia, concerto, rondo, symphony, march—was most often rejected in preference for sound that was more or less translatable into generalized verbal meaning involving both heart and head. Much recent writing by literary scholars on the topic of nineteenth-century music has followed the Victorians' own lead in studying the apparent meanings of music that can be expressed, however incompletely, in words. In dwelling on the musical 'event', on occasions of performance or that involve cultural meanings—a matrix of conflicting and multiple ideologies—contemporary analysts of music in literature have taken up the pervasive methodologies of cultural studies. An idea of music, with all its ideological implications, is the determining and determined object of investigation. For Phyllis Weliver's edited collection, *The Figure of Music in Nineteenth-Century British Poetry* (2005), 'figure' does the same work as 'idea'.[25] Such conceptions are far from what the music philosopher Peter Kivy thinks of as 'music alone', as he explores the significance of strictly *meaningless* (in the verbal and discursive sense) instrumental sounds that fascinate and reward.[26] It is not necessary in the contemporary cultural studies' analysis to consider listening to music at all, or even to be able to read music, but only to analyse wordable ideological meanings around the events of others' listening. There is a disconcerting silence at the heart of this investigation of sound. Angela Leighton has written beautifully of the way in which poetry, addressing the subject of sound, might invite us to think of reading as a kind of listening. 'It is not just that literature takes us by the ear,' she says, 'making us hear its rhythms, its pauses, its underground noises, and it is not just that the act of listening may be written in as part of the story; it is also that the text works by becoming a listening space, a hold which holds us attentive to words, especially words which have suffered the lovely deflection, estrangement and blockage of what we call the literary.'[27] Yet it is also part of Victorian poetry's engagement with music that it is a form of *not-listening*, of barely hearing at all.

The notion that one might speak of the pleasures of form without invoking 'content' might have been a commonplace of *l'art pour l'art*, as writers and artists encouraged their audience, for instance, to consider the beauties of writing even if its subject was suffering, violence, or pain. But that preference for form over content (I use this crude binary in full awareness of its inadequacy) struggled to make an impression in the mid-century on the business of listening of music. When Walter Pater famously said in the essay on 'The School of Giorgione' (1877) that all art aspired to the condition of music because it sought the union of form with content, the fusion of means with end, it is tempting to wonder what Pater knew of the *form* of music at all.[28] Oscar Wilde imitated Pater when he said in the 'Preface' (1891) to *The Picture of Dorian Gray* (1890/1) that 'From the point of view of form, the type of all the arts is the art of the musician.'[29] But around Wilde, as around Pater, literary writers were more ready to understand the union of form and content in music as, in practice, content swallowing up form. What really mattered was what could be said about music's effects, not about its patterning, its acoustic organization, its concordance with the rules of Western harmony. Darwin's meditation on the nature of music slipped, suggestively, between recognition of its distinctiveness as 'pure' sound, and a swift desire to encode it with translatable, verbalizable meaning that had unambiguous sense rooted in human feeling. Darwin thought music was the literal origin of verbal language, considering that the meaning of words was grounded in the earliest natural music and comprehensible within the general theory of selection in relation to sex. In *The Descent of Man* (1871), he said:

> that language owes its origin to the imitation and modification of various natural sounds, the voices of other animals, and man's own instinctive cries, aided by signs and gestures. When we treat of sexual selection we shall see that primeval man, or rather some early progenitor of man, probably first used his voice in producing true musical cadences, that is in singing, as do some of the gibbon-apes at the present day; and we may conclude from a widely-spread analogy, that this power would have been especially exerted during the courtship of the sexes,—would have expressed various emotions, such as love, jealousy, triumph,—and would have served as a challenge to rivals. It is, therefore, probable that the imitation of musical cries by articulate sounds may have given rise to words expressive of various complex emotions.[30]

Darwin flirts with a notion of 'true musical cadences'. But what are they? Certainly, he means by 'cadences' only the general sense of the rise and fall of sound, not the specifically musical sense of a final harmonic sequence. Yet, still, what is this 'true music'? Does Darwin mean that the sounds belonged within the Western diatonic scale or followed its harmonic logic? That they were rhythmic in a notatable way? Whatever he meant (and neither of those explanations seems likely), this 'music' in Darwin's retrospect becomes almost immediately associated with translatable sense and communication of willed meaning. This apparently pure music (perhaps it would be clearer if Darwin simply said 'animal sound') becomes unworded intention, expressing love, jealousy, and triumph before, in due course, becoming associated with more complex feelings in the birth of language. The primary purpose of the earliest 'music' is expressionist, though across Darwin's evolutionary narrative drifts for a moment a kind of content-free sound of 'true musical [cadence]', flitting unglossed and unanalyzed across the dimmest beginnings of human life on Earth.

Robert Browning considered, implicitly, such a Darwininan slippage to produce the most searching of all the nineteenth-century's poetic analyses of how to 'hear' the 'sense' of music. Browning's grasp of musical terminology—or his speakers' grasp, we can never decide—was not accurate. But he was intrigued by the persisting human efforts to make music comprehensible in language really used by men, and his dramatic monologues open up such efforts to view. Regarding them, the reader is delicately invited to wonder about the legitimacy of these interpretive moves, their basis in desire, the haunting sense of inevitable partiality and failure that may attend them, the lingering idea of something missed or misjudged. The speaker of 'A Toccata of Galuppi's' from *Men and Women* (1855) is keen to ascribe both visual images and verbal meaning, even actual dialogue, to what he understands a keyboard toccata is 'saying'. The movement is from perceived pitch to image, harmonic progression to verbal statement about eighteenth-century Venetian high society. Here he is in the middle of his analysis:

> What? Those lesser thirds so plaintive, sixths diminished, sigh on sigh,
> Told them something? Those suspensions, those solutions—'Must we die?'
> Those commiserating sevenths—'Life might last! we can but try!'
>
> 'Were you happy?'—'Yes.'—'And are you still as happy?'—'Yes. And you?'
> —'Then, more kisses!'—'Did *I* stop them, when a million seemed so few?'
> Hark, the dominant's persistence till it must be answered to![31]

Where Darwin thought 'music' was intimately related to expressions of human emotion fundamental to behaviour, Browning's speaker draws out startlingly exact propositions, even if they are only apparent to him: we do not know what other listeners think, just as we do not know which (if any) piece by the real composer Baldassare Galuppi (1706–85) he is hearing. The composer's apparent self-expression has been scattered into the voices and minds of others, as if the keyboard piece is an act of multiple ventriloquization of real speakers. Sound becomes visualized and verbalized sense (though we know that the speaker has never been to Venice and so what he 'sees' can only be the reproduction of what he has seen and read elsewhere). Browning's text offers a temptation: an invitation to think this is how music *can* be understood, but the poem cannot dispense with a silent question—the characteristic of Browning's dramatic monologues is that they hold up speech for scrutiny of assumptions and attitudes—about whether the speaker's imagination is all-too-active, all-too-verbal-and-visual in its reception of sound. Perhaps music should really be heard in quite a different way.

That process of interpretation is more suggestively uncertain for the organist-speaker of 'Master Hugues of Saxe-Gotha', from *Men and Women*. Browning's monologist endeavours, sitting at his instrument, to ascribe character to musical line while retaining a degree of abstraction. This is a text which, in the first place, admits of the existence of the performer's interpretation, and so, implicitly, of the potential differences between performances. That is sharply different from any Swinburnean notion of music as unchanging and unchangeable. When the poet and, as it happens, Swinburne scholar Theodore Wratislaw, wrote in 1896 to a pianist, 'Once more, once more, bid rise and swoon and ache / This song of Schumann's filled with tremulous pain,'[32] there was, characteristically for poets in the period, no active sense of performed music as interpretable. What we are about to hear is the same as we heard before. But Browning's text admits that music is subject to a performer's thoughts and abilities, and thus, implicitly, its 'meaning' may shift. The speaker of 'Master Hugues' makes an effort to describe the entries of Hugues' five-part fugue in words (this is music of exceptional abstraction in which the pleasures of form are concentrated). The player ascribes emotional characteristics to the fugue subject as it is developed, but does not collapse description into plain narrative in the manner of the listener to Galuppi:

> One says his say with a difference;
>   More of expounding, explaining!
> All now is wrangle, abuse, and vociferance;
>   Now there's a truce, all's subdued, self-restraining:
> Five, though, stands out all the stiffer hence.
>
> One is incisive, corrosive:
>   Two retorts, nettled, curt, crepitant;
> Three makes rejoinder, expansive, explosive;
>   Four overbears them all, strident and strepitant:
> Five...O Danaides, O Sieve![33]

Part of the player's challenge is to find out the 'meaning' of all this. Browning's speaker-player must wonder if the interweaving subjects and countersubjects of Hugues' fugue (Hugues of Saxe-Gotha is an imaginary composer) amount to a statement. 'Is it your moral of Life?', he asks with unusual frankness about the propositions of the aural, searching out what he thinks is the composer's intention. Yet at the same time, something bothers him about his own question. The organist wonders, if only for a moment, whether something more difficult to describe, something outside words, exists in this fugal complexity that so taxes the fingers: "'But where's music, the dickens?'"[34] The question hangs in the air, unanswered. And it would be hard to exaggerate what it might imply amid the poetic ruminations in the nineteenth century over how to write of a listener's response to music. What *is* music? and how should we listen to it? Does it convey 'meaning' or must we think differently about experiencing it? How can music become an object of criticism, of words at all? How can a listener interpret? How should poets retell their experience of music in their own art form? Is the composer's intention, particularly in instrumental music, discernible and narratable, however incompletely, in language? How might a poet recognize that musicians hear music differently from those who do not understand what it is they are hearing in any technical sense? Browning's speaker quickly prefers to moralize over the meaning of the fugue: readers, indeed, may well be invited to judge Master Hugues as a minor composer since he does not appear to have a clear sense of what he was 'saying' at all. Yet something else has been said, an unsettling thought about music *ohne Worte*, of sound as 'sense' outside words, of an art form that cannot entirely be rendered in the terms of another, of the uniqueness of music as an aural art uniquely dependent on a performer's technical competence and interpretive ability.

Music can work alongside words, of course, even entering a vital dialogue like that of the piano and voice in the Romantic song cycle. The Victorian poets' interest in ballads glanced to a closer cooperation of music with language, as did the hymn writers, from the authors of *The National Chartist Hymn Book* (1845)[35] to the hugely influential collection for the Church of England, *Hymns Ancient and Modern* (1861). Thomas Moore's *Irish Melodies* (from 1808) remain intimately connected with—melodies.[36] But the Victorian absorption with music as the unmediated expression of the heart, or as that which filled the biological world with sound, naturally most suited listeners to Richard Wagner (1813–83), the controversial experimenter with the new *Gesamtkunstwerk*, the total work of art. Wagner's experiments with musical expression, the startling harmonic developments emblematized by the music drama *Tristan und Isolde* (first performed in 1865), and the notion of *unendliche Melodie* where melody resisted the limitations of cadence, seem to have entranced Swinburne. Wagner's development proved an acoustic counterpart for the ambition of his poetry. 'From the depths of the sea', Swinburne wrote in 'The Death of Richard Wagner' from *A Century of Roundels* (1883) on the composer's demise that year:

> from the wellsprings of earth, from the wastes of the midmost night,
> From the fountains of darkness and tempest and thunder, from heights
>   where the soul would be,
> The spell of the mage of music evoked their sense, as an unknown light
>   From the depths of the sea.[37]

Connected to natural forces, giving voice to a spiritual–sensual apprehension of experience on a huge scale, Wagner in Swinburne's hands sounds not unlike Swinburne himself, even as his long lines half imitate the *unendliche Melodie*. Late Victorian poetry's interests in the erotics of music, 'soft throbbing music in the night',[38] as Arthur Symons put it in 'Music and Memory' from *Silhouettes* (1896), suggested a paler version of the erotics of Wagner at the *fin de siècle*.[39] For the Irish diarist and poet William Allingham, music likewise flooded landscapes, consuming spaces with the sound of desire, with music's 'strange amorous rapture passing fair'.[40] Love and passion: music was still what Charles Darwin had more or less thought it had been early on in the history of human language: an unmediated non-vocal expression of emotion like that which lay at the beginning of language's efforts to communicate.

Arnold proposed in 'Epilogue to Lessing's Laocoön' that poetry possessed greater power than music because it could, in the right hands, tell of more than a moment of a human life. The poet could narrate, and emotionally explore, 'The thread which binds it all in one, / And not its separate parts alone!'[41] That was not an easy argument to make in 1867, though, for Arnold had to brush to one side musical forms that explicitly endeavoured to narrate the movement of the mind and heart: most obviously at that point, the song cycle. This is all the odder because Arnold's *Switzerland* sequence[42] is close in spirit, following the emotional logic of the episodic narrative, to the great Romantic song cycles themselves: Schubert's *Die Schöne Müllerin* (1823, words by Wilhelm Müller) and *Winterreise* (1828, words also by Müller), Schumann's *Dichterliebe* (1840, words by

Heinrich Heine). Yet the more the Victorian poets meditated on the apparent 'meanings' of music, the more accidentally suggestive became their desire, I think, to reclaim one art form in the terms of another. Music swelled erotically around them; it cascaded from nature; it hymned the heavens and expressed the human experience of the transcendental; it was caught up, as in Tennyson's *Maud: A Monodrama* (1855), with national sentiment as Maud sings 'A passionate ballad gallant and gay, / A martial song like a trumpet's call!'[43] But in these efforts to bring music into a discursive field, to make sound (semi-) propositional, or to draw out its ideological force and render it, however generally, in words, the reader attentive to music as structured sound, and as more than simply these forms of meaning, discerns a curious invitation. In the poets' inattentiveness to the musical details of what is being heard, we sense, perhaps, an encouragement to attend more carefully to the specifics of art forms *in their own terms*. The musical reader may instinctively wish to hear more than the poets do in their experience of music. But obliquely such readers may sense too, as they acknowledge the absence of a thorough crossing-point between words and music, a desire to attend to *poetry's* distinctive way of being and meaning more carefully.

Of course, poetry is heard as well as seen. Its sounds can be part of its meaning or nature, and musical vocabulary may serve to reveal something about that. Swinburne could write of William Blake's 'vigorous harmonies of choral expression'[44] and urge that his readers paid attention to the 'sonorous and successive harmonies'[45] of Shakespeare's *Richard III* (c.1591), learned from Christopher Marlowe. Such language was commonplace, and it has never been confined to the Victorian period. But this language describes only in the most general terms the sound of poetry (what *kind* of harmonies?) and is hardly an exact vocabulary for the nature of rhythm or more detailed analysis of what implications rhyme or metre might or might not bear. Such musical language remains irresistible, though, and no other terminology has ever seemed quite so sufficient for descriptions of poetry's patterns of sound, its rhythmic variations, schemes of accentuation and their deviations, chiming of vowels and consonants, its verbal 'music' even in poetry that reaches for the intense emotional absorption of music itself. Symptomatically, George Saintsbury, writing his *A History of English Prosody from the 12th Century to the Present Day* (1906–10), could not dispense with musical vocabulary in trying to describe the effects of rhythm. The borders between poetry and music are not impermeable. Yet there is still a silence in what many of the Victorian poets heard. 'For music he had no gift nor appreciation', we learn of one great and 'harmonious' poet of the age of Queen Victoria, whose work was and is frequently spoken about in terms of music: 'Not to put too fine a point upon it, he was totally devoid of "ear," and to listen to a performance on any instrument drove him wild with petulance and impatience'.[46] It is a surprising scene. Poetic harmonies are one thing, but real musical ones another. The poet devoid of 'ear' is Algernon Charles Swinburne, poet of music, as remembered by his biographer Edmund Gosse in 1917. This is quite another ear, so to speak, from that which Auden half mischievously attributed to Alfred Tennyson. Poet of harmonies, Swinburne is a poet of verbal music, perhaps a poet of the 'whole music of passion'.[47] But he is not a poet of the art made from harmonious patterning of the twelve notes of the Western scale. He hears, and he does not.[48]

Reading about music in Victorian poetry confronts us with efforts to figure an art form in incomplete terms, with a struggle to hear something that is not poetry. That struggle—like trying to hear Beethoven through an abbey wall—may remind us most obviously of the significance of the sound of poetry, and what it might and might not mean. That struggle might encourage us to wonder about how, exactly, to write about the nature and experience of music too, a topic that continues to absorb aestheticians to the present day. That was Browning's interest, certainly. But most of all, that struggle, so easily missed in the current preference among cultural critics to attend to the 'event' of music and its verbalizable meanings, reminds us that poetry is not music, even if it can be heard when it is read aloud. Hardly aware of the differences, it seems, between word art and music (differences irreducible yet so tempting to hide), the Victorian poets implicitly ask us, as they meditate on the experience of sounds in words, to pay more careful attention to the specificities of their own art. For poetry, too, is a form of meaning and experience that cannot easily be converted into something else. What is to be found in reading about music in Victorian poetry is a strange, an unexpected, prompt to think harder about nothing less than the scope and responsibilities of criticism to the art it addresses. Writing on music, the Victorian poets are sometimes frustrating and sometimes infuriating. They do not hear music as a musician does. But they remind us eloquently of the limits of interpretation, and they hint at the significance and 'meanings' of all great art forms that go beyond our capacity for talking about them. In their forms of inattentiveness, in their energetic pursuit of the 'irreferent', to borrow Herbert F. Tucker's useful term,[49] the Victorian poets may allow us to discern what has been missed, what has been bundled into the terms of another art, in their half-apprehension of music and their efforts to render, often very generally, its 'sense' in words. We must listen to them not listening. And so doing, we have a chance of being reminded, I think, of the acutest forms of attention that really do need to be paid to any art form's particularities.

Notes

1. W.H. Auden, *Forewords and Afterwords* (London: Faber, 1973), 222. For useful discussion of Auden's view, see Seamus Perry, 'Are we there yet?', *London Review of Books*, 33 (20 January 2011), 13–16. My thanks to the late Percy M. Young for much early encouragement to think about music and literature. Thanks also to Matthew Bevis, Katherine Mullin, Stephen Farr, and Nicholas Thistlethwaite for reading earlier drafts of this essay. Remaining errors are my own.
2. In Hallam Tennyson's *Alfred Lord Tennyson: A Memoir*, 2 vols. (London: Macmillan, 1897), we learn that Tennyson 'had a love for the simple style of Mozart', and that he 'played himself a little on the flute, but only "cared for complicated music as suggesting echoes of winds and waves"' (i. 66). Later, we hear of Tennyson, recovering a lost voice, singing 'an octave to the piano' (ii. 395).
3. Alfred Tennyson, *In Memoriam*, in *Poems of Tennyson*, 3 vols., ed. Christopher Ricks, 2nd edn. (Harlow: Longman, 1987), ii. 403.
4. Tennyson, *The Princess*, in *Poems of Tennyson*, ii. 232.

5. See, for instance, William Sotheby, *Saul: A Poem in Two Parts* (Boston: West, 1808), 89; *The Poetical Works of Robert Browning*, 15 vols., eds. Ian Jack et al. (Oxford: Oxford University Press, 1988-), ix. 26 (*The Ring and the Book*); William Morris, *The Story of Sigurd the Volsung and the Fall of the Niblungs* (Boston: Roberts, 1891), 98.

6. Matthew Arnold, 'Empedocles on Etna', in *The Poems of Matthew Arnold*, eds. Kenneth Allott and Miriam Allott (Harlow: Longman, 1979), 160.

7. Matthew Arnold, 'Empedocles on Etna', 161.

8. Arnold, 'Epilogue to Lessing's Laocoön', in *The Poems of Matthew Arnold*, 551.

9. The *Missa Solemnis* has very limited use as a liturgical mass.

10. Arnold, 'Epilogue to Lessing's Laocoön', in *The Poems of Matthew Arnold*, 553–554.

11. Robert Browning, 'With Charles Avison', in *The Poetical Works of Robert Browning*, xv. 221.

12. William Alexander, 'Music or Words?', in *The Finding of the Book and Other Poems* (London: Hodder and Stoughton, 1900), 182.

13. Algernon Charles Swinburne, 'At a Month's End', in *Poems and Ballads (Second and Third Series)* (London: Heinemann, 1921), 29.

14. Algernon Charles Swinburne, 'Astophel', in *Astrophel and Other Poems* (London: Chatto & Windus, 1894), 1.

15. Swinburne, 'Memorial Verses', in *Poems and Ballads, Second Series*, 60.

16. John Ruskin, Lecture X in *Lectures on Art* in *The Library Edition of the Works of John Ruskin*, 39 vols., ed. E. T. Cook and Alexander Wedderburn (London: Allen, 1903–12), xx. 120.

17. Ruskin, 'The Relation Between Michael Angelo and Tintoret', in *The Library Edition of the Works of John Ruskin*, xxii. 93.

18. Browning, 'With Charles Avison', in *The Poetical Works of Robert Browning*, xv. 218.

19. Charles D. Bell, 'Music', in *Diana's Looking Glass and Other Poems* (London: Arnold, 1894), 19.

20. My argument may be contrasted with Eric Griffiths' in *The Printed Voice of Victorian Poetry* (Oxford: Clarendon, 1989) that Victorian poetry aspires more towards the condition of the audible voice.

21. Adelaide Procter, 'The Lost Chord', in *The Poems of Adelaide A. Procter* (Boston: Osgood, 1873), 119.

22. See Francis O'Gorman, ' "Blush, sad soul, what harmonies are these!" The Organ in Nineteenth-Century English Literature', *Yearbook of the Royal College of Organists*, (2003–4), 66–73.

23. Thomas Hardy, 'To My Father's Violin', in *The Complete Poems* (London: Macmillan, 1976), 451.

24. Hardy, 'The Last Performance', in *The Complete Poems*, 487.

25. See Phyllis Weliver, ed., *The Figure of Music in Nineteenth-Century British Poetry* (Aldershot: Ashgate, 2005).

26. See Peter Kivy, *Music Alone: Philosophical Reflections on the Purely Musical Experience* (Cornell: Cornell University Press, 1990).

27. Angela Leighton, 'Thresholds of Attention: On Listening in Literature', in Subha Mukherji, ed., *Thinking on Thresholds: The Poetics of Transitive Spaces* (London: Anthem, 2011), 210.

28. See Angela Leighton, 'Pater's Music', *Journal of Pre-Raphaelite Studies*, 14 (2005), 67–79.

29. Oscar Wilde, *The Picture of Dorian Gray* (Harmondsworth: Penguin, 1949), 5.

30. Charles Darwin, *The Descent of Man and Selection in Relation to Sex*, 2nd edn. (London: Murray, 1874), 87. See also Peter Kivy, 'Charles Darwin on Music', *Journal of the American Musicological Society*, 12 (1959), 42–48.

31. Browning, 'A Toccata of Galuppi's', in *The Poetical Works of Robert Browning*, v. 58–59.

32. Theodore Wratislaw, 'To a Pianist' from *Orchids: Poems* (London: Smithers, 1896), 87.
33. Browning, 'Master Hugues', in *Poetical Works of Robert Browning*, v. 200.
34. Browning, 'Master Hugues', v. 202.
35. For a digital version of the only known surviving copy, see <http://www.calderdale.gov.uk/wtw/search/controlservlet?PageId=Detail&DocId=102253> (accessed 31 January 2012).
36. On this topic, see most recently Siobhán Fitzpatrick, ed., *My Gentle Harp: Moore's Irish Melodies, 1808–2008* (Dublin: Royal Irish Academy, 2008).
37. Swinburne, 'The Death of Richard Wagner' from *Poems*, 6 vols. (London: Chatto & Windus, 1905), v. 136.
38. Arthur Symons, 'Music and Memory', in *Silhouettes: Second Edition, Revised and Enlarged* (London: Smithers, 1896), 46.
39. On Wagner in the *fin de siècle*, see Emma Sutton, *Aubrey Beardsley and British Wagnerism in the 1890s* (Oxford: Oxford University Press, 2002) and the same author's essay, '"The Music Spoke for Us": Music and Sexuality in *fin-de-siècle* Poetry', in Phyllis Weliver, ed., *The Figure of Music in Nineteenth-Century British Poetry* (Aldershot: Ashgate, 2005), 213–229.
40. William Allingham, 'Doth Music tickle ear, and that's the whole', in *Blackberries Picked Off Many Bushes* (London: Longman, 1893; 1st pub. 1884), 12.
41. Arnold, 'Epilogue to Lessing's Laocoön', in *The Poems of Matthew Arnold*, 555.
42. The collection of poems, including 'Isolation. To Marguerite' (1857) and 'To Marguerite Continued' (1852), which reached its final form in 1877.
43. Tennyson, *Maud,* in *Poems of Tennyson*, ii. 533. See Ayse Çelikkol, 'Dionysian Music, Patriotic Sentiment, and Tennyson's *Idylls of the King*', *Victorian Poetry*, 45 (2007), 239–256.
44. Swinburne, *William Blake: A Critical Essay* (London: Chatto & Windus, 1906), 282.
45. Swinburne, *A Study of Shakespeare*, 2nd edn. (London: Chatto & Windus, 1880), 44.
46. Edmund Gosse, *The Life of Algernon Charles Swinburne* (London: Macmillan 1917), 168.
47. See Rikky Rooksby and Nicholas Shrimpton, eds., *The Whole Music of Passion: New Essays on Swinburne* (Aldershot: Scolar, 1993).
48. Swinburne was notorious for his inability to hear music, and the readiness with which his imagination changed it to something else. Gosse tells another tale of Swinburne being tricked into thinking 'Three Blind Mice' was 'a very ancient Florentine ritornello' when it was mischievously played for him on the piano. See Edmund Gosse, *Portraits and Sketches* (London: Heinemann, 1913; 1st pub. 1912), 47.
49. In conversation with Professor Tucker.

Select Bibliography

Clapp-Itnyre, Alisa, 'The Contentious "Figure" of Music in the Poetry of Thomas Hardy', *Hardy Society Journal*, 22 (2006), 26–34.
Correa, Delia da Sousa, ed., *Phrase and Subject: Studies in Literature and Music* (Oxford: Legenda, 2006).
Eastham, Andrew, 'Walter Pater's Acoustic Space: "The School of Giorgione", Dionysian Anders-Streben, and the Politics of Soundscape', *The Yearbook of English Studies*, 40 (2010), 196–216.
Cumming, Naomi, *The Sonic Self: Musical Subjectivity and Signification* (Bloomington: Indiana University Press, 2001).

Hueffer, Francis, *Half a Century of Music in England, 1837–1887: Essays Towards a History* (London: Chapman and Hall, 1889).

Hughes, Linda K., 'From Parlor to Concert Hall: Arthur Somervell's Song-Cycle on Tennyson's "Maud"', *Victorian Studies*, 30 (1986), 113–129.

Kivy, Peter, *Music Alone: Philosophical Reflections on the Purely Musical Experience* (Cornell: Cornell University Press, 1990).

Leighton, Angela, 'On "the Hearing Ear": Some Sonnets of the Rossettis', *Victorian Poetry*, 47 (2009), 505–516.

Solie, Ruth A., 'Music', in Francis O'Gorman, ed., *The Cambridge Companion to Victorian Culture* (Cambridge: Cambridge University Press, 2010), 101–118.

Temperley, Nicholas, ed., *The Lost Chord: Essays on Victorian Music* (Bloomington: Indiana University Press, 1989).

Weliver, Phyllis, ed., *The Figure of Music in Nineteenth-Century British Poetry* (Aldershot: Ashgate, 2005).

——'A Score of Change: Twenty Years of Critical Musicology and Victorian Literature', *Literature Compass*, 8 (2011), 776–794 [online journal].

CHAPTER 47

CHURCH GOING

KIRSTIE BLAIR

THE assumption that the nineteenth century was a period in which religion was in crisis, and that some of the finest poetry of the period bore witness to this crisis, has been long-lasting and influential in readings of Victorian poetry and poetics, as well as Victorian religion. As the religious historian Timothy Larsen comments in *Crisis of Doubt*, 'Too often, the crisis of faith is presented as the most important thing to be said about religion and the Victorians, or even the only thing to be said'. Larsen notes that English or literary studies has been 'a major contributor to this distortion' of perspective.[1] In recent literary criticism, however, this view now seems, to a considerable degree, outdated. The many and diverse ways in which religion influenced Victorian poetry and poetics—not to mention the ways in which Victorian poetry helped to shape perceptions of Victorian religion—provide an exciting and varied field for new literary scholarship, exemplified in the work of critics such as William McKelvy, Charles LaPorte, Emma Mason, Mark Knight, F. E. Gray, and many others.[2] Their work serves to highlight, as Linda K. Hughes notes in a recent introduction to Victorian poetry, that while literary critics have conceptualized nineteenth-century poetry in secular terms, Victorian poets and their readers 'took for granted that poetry was intimately related to religious faith'.[3]

Three areas, or genres, have provided particularly fertile ground for revisionary studies of Victorian literature and religion. First, devotional poetry by women writers has received considerable attention, with a growing critical consensus, exemplified in work by Cynthia Scheinberg, Karen Dieleman, Mason, and Gray, that religion opened up possibilities for women writers rather than limiting them. The key individual here is, of course, Christina Rossetti, with at least four monographs in the last fifteen years and numerous articles and book chapters specifically dedicated to her religious poetry and prose.[4] Second, and often related in the sense that women's hymn-writing has been extensively discussed, the hymn has been re-evaluated as an important poetic genre.[5] Lastly, while critics such as G. B. Tennyson, W. David Shaw, and Stephen Prickett produced seminal works discussing Tractarian poetry and poetics—and in particular

Tractarian theories on reserve and symbolism—in the 1970s and 1980s, the first decade of the twenty-first century saw a renewed critical engagement with Tractarianism and its wider influence on Victorian poetry.[6] In addition to these large and overlapping fields, the last few years have seen significant studies of poetry and the higher criticism, poetry and theology, and Roman Catholic poetry and poetics, and a great many studies of individual authors, among whom Gerard Manley Hopkins continues to stand out as the single most-discussed religious poet of the period.

Christina Rossetti is a good example of a writer whose poetry was shaped not simply by devotion to God, but by devoted and regular churchgoing. Leaving aside those poets who were also ordained ministers, of whom Hopkins is the most important instance, relatively few of the 'canonical' Victorian poets fall into this category, though many evinced a deep and abiding affection for the forms and ceremonies of Christianity. Thomas Hardy, with his strong interests in church architecture, music, and liturgy, is indicative of an attitude that reverenced the church without necessarily believing in God. His poetry, in poems such as 'Afternoon Service at Mellstock', makes it clear that experiences of church, not simply religious or spiritual experience per se, are integral to his poetics.[7] Given the number of works produced in the nineteenth century that claimed the Bible and the Book of Common Prayer as poetry, not to mention the increasing use of hymns in worship, church was the location in which many Victorians, whether poets, readers of poetry, or otherwise, would have encountered poetry on a regular basis. The experience of churchgoing looms large in Victorian poetry because contemporary arguments about the efficacy of communal worship in creating and sustaining faith often bled into debates about the uses and ends of poetry: according to many commentators, participating in a service or privately reading devotional poetry involved submitting to an emotionally heightened experience dependent upon structured language and repetitive forms. Poets such as John Keble, whose *Christian Year* was the most influential example of Victorian religious verse, could use acts of private reading to reinsert the reader into the wider community of worshippers.

In the nineteenth century, this particular argument drew more force from Anglicanism than any other denomination. As Mason and Knight argue in their introduction to nineteenth-century literature and religion:

> [E]xpressions of faith outside the Church of England remained highly contingent on the Established Church. In many ways, the so-called secularization of religion in the latter part of the nineteenth century is best understood as a diminution of the power and reach of the Established Church rather than the decline of Christian ideas and culture.[8]

This essay largely agrees that even for those who would have described themselves as chapel-goers rather than churchgoers, or who deliberately eschewed any formal worship, the idea of the Church still loomed large. The same holds true for the small group of religious poets from denominations other than Christianity, though their work is not discussed here. Rather than concentrating on poets, poems, and genres that have already received considerable critical attention (in my own work as well as that of others), this essay focuses on churchgoing quite literally, discussing the fantasy of the church as refracted through popular religious verse by writers from very different religious backgrounds. Opening with a discussion of 'village church' poems, I will briefly consider how this genre, much beloved by minor Victorian poets, made its way into major Victorian poems, before turning to a selection of little-known poems that deliberately stage their rejection of churchgoing as part of an ongoing dissenting, radical political commitment.

Nineteenth-century Anglican poets had a particular investment in writing poems that reflected upon churchgoing, either by representing the experience of listening to and participating in religious services, or, even more commonly, by considering churches and churchgoing as an observer who was not, at that precise moment, actually attending church. Felicia Hemans's 'Sabbath Sonnet' is one of the most important and, given her fame, one of the most influential works in this genre:

> How many blessed groups this hour are bending,
> Thro' England's primrose meadow-paths, their way
> Towards spire and tower, midst shadowy elms ascending,
> Whence the sweet chimes proclaim the hallowed day!
> The halls from old heroic ages gray
> Pour their fair children forth; and hamlets low,
> With whose thick orchard-blooms the soft winds play,
> Send out their inmates in a happy flow,
> Like a freed vernal stream. I may not tread
> With them those pathways—to the feverish bed
> Of sickness bound; yet, O my God! I bless
> Thy mercy, that with Sabbath-peace hath filled
> My chastened heart, and all its throbbings stilled
> To one deep calm of lowliest thankfulness! [9]

'Sabbath Sonnet' epitomizes the concerns of this genre, which focuses heavily on the Anglican country church as a symbol for an English community unified across classes and generations by a shared past ('old heroic ages') most fitly exemplified in common religious worship. Halls and hamlets—which signify the class divide between the inhabitants of this village, and are implicitly older, traditional buildings—are the subject of the verbs 'pour' and 'send out', giving them a kind of active agency which perhaps suggests the continuity of Sunday worship across time and the extent to which it, as a tradition, is embedded in the historical, visible structures of English rural life. 'Sabbath Sonnet' also suggests that church is organically intertwined with the fruitfulness of the English countryside. 'Pour', 'flow', and 'freed vernal stream' indicate that worship is not compulsion or duty but a natural impulse, and both 'pour' and 'thick orchard-blooms' suggest fruitful abundance and excess. This is obviously a thriving and productive community.

Hemans's poem was first published posthumously in the *Poetical Remains* of 1836, where it is the final poem in the volume. In some editions the poem includes the date of composition, 26 April, 1835. Easter fell on April 19 in 1835, and this happy churchgoing scene perhaps had added resonance for Hemans (and for the alert reader) because the Sunday after Easter is traditionally known in the Catholic and Anglican churches as 'Low' Sunday, anticlimactic after the excitement of Easter week. 'Sabbath Sonnet' eschews the climax of the Church year for a quieter week, explicitly celebrating peace, lowliness, and a typical rather than an exceptional Sunday. Whether or not this date is specified, all editions include the headnote 'Composed by Mrs Hemans a few days before her death, and dictated to her brother'. 'Sabbath Sonnet' thereby acquires intense importance within Hemans's works as apparently her final composition, plus added emotional resonance because the headnote suggests that it was composed on her death-bed, and hence that the speaker in the sextet is the dying poet, too weak even to hold a pen. D. M. Moir's biographical introduction to the *Remains* emphasizes that 'Nothing can be more indicative' of Hemans's resigned Christian spirit in her final illness 'than the Sabbath Sonnet'.[10] This, then, is the poem that family and friends wanted Hemans to be remembered by, nicely combining her longstanding emphases on piety, patriotism, reverence for family (in 'blessed groups'), praise of Nature, and a focus on the suffering, emotional female poet. The poem gains pathos from the fact that Hemans herself is at a remove from the happy scene described, both physically unable to attend church, and, at the time of her death, in Ireland.

'Sabbath Sonnet' self-consciously represents an imagined rather than an actual scene of churchgoing. In doing so it deliberately introduces the idea that this act of imagination, or indeed an act of faith in assuming the continuance of Anglican tradition when the poet cannot herself witness it, has the same emotional affect as attending church: it makes the poet feel herself part of a national religious community that transcends time and place. Victorian poems, as this essay suggests, think a great deal about the charged moment when *other people* are attending religious services, such that the act of composing a poem instead of churchgoing—whether the poet cannot or will not attend church—is both a celebration of worship and a substitution for it. Communal worship in set forms of words is replaced by the individual's lyrical impulse in this genre, but the resulting poems might be considered as performative in that they frequently emphasize the individual's membership of the community described and the poem's contiguity with religious forms.

It is not a coincidence that Hemans's poem on the Sabbath took the shape of a sonnet. As Joseph Phelan has noted in a fine chapter on the nineteenth-century devotional sonnet, this form had particular significance in Victorian religious poetry.[11] Its associations with self-chosen constraint and submission, which fit well with the emphasis on chastening and calming in the close of 'Sabbath Sonnet', held special importance for the High Church Anglican and Roman Catholic traditions. Taking their cue at least in part from Wordsworth's *Ecclesiastical Sonnets*, first published in 1821–22 and an unabashed celebration of the history and culture of the Church of England, there are a great many religious sonnets that fall into the 'village churchgoing' category. Poems by Charles Dent Bell and Charles Turner Tennyson, both well-connected and literary Anglican ministers (Bell commemorates his friendship with the Arnold family in his Lake District poems) provide representative examples. Turner's 'An English Church' was first published in 1830 and given this title on republication in 1868:

The bells awake the sabbath's choral prime,
By breezes soften'd to a harp-like tone;
Lowly and sweetly from the distance thrown,
They greet the ear with jubilee and chime!
Follow the sound and it will lead thee on
Into an English church, the Home of prayer,
For who shall say she is not lovelier there
Than in all other fanes beneath the sun?
There, if thou doubtest, may it not impart
Fresh hope, to learn that others' hope is sure?
There, duly as the merchant to the mart,
Come aged men, whom daily death makes fewer:
There all the spirit of a Christian heart
Is bodied forth in gentle rites and pure! [12]

'Sweet' and 'lowly' are words that recur in Hemans's sonnet, and, as also in Bell's son-net below, suggest a high valuation of the English church as at least outwardly humble and unassuming. Although this sonnet addresses the reader, as opposed to Hemans's first-person perspective, it is similarly focused on the moment when the church bells sound on a Sunday morning, thus acting itself as a call to churchgoing as well as a cel-ebration of it. Turner, as Valentine Cunningham has recently argued, used the small space of the sonnet as a vehicle for his conservative nationalism in celebrating how a small country like England could achieve power above its size.[13] 'An English Church', more strongly than Hemans's 'Sabbath Sonnet', embraces the public, nationalistic rheto-ric of defenders of the Church of England as the purest branch of Christianity, though the questions in lines 7–8 and 9–10 sound a note of defensiveness, as the possibility of doubt is introduced. Turner's sonnet, indeed, might seem rather ambiguous in its com-parison of the church to the 'mart' and in the implicit suggestion that the congregation is elderly and dying off: this works to negate rather than support the powerful identi-fication of the church with the family and domestic life. 'Gentle' is a significant choice of adjective, because while it is linked to 'lowly', it has strong class implications. In the 1868 collection, these might be more noticeable because Turner included a sonnet on an outdoor dissenting meeting, 'Fanaticism, A Night-Scene in the Open Air', which in cen-suring the 'narrow-minded fancies, crude and mean' of the preacher and congregation, whose 'raving' and 'rant' can be heard even above a gale, invites comparison to the soft breezes and 'gentle rites' of the higher-class Anglican church.[14]

Bell's poem, published in 1877, is much more particular in emphasis, celebrating the church in which he was minister, St Mary's, Ambleside:

Sweet village church amidst the purple hills,
    That rise in grandeur from the emerald plain,
    Like loving guardians of thy holy fane,
Built within sound of two clear mountain rills,
Whose music all the peaceful silence fills.
    Dear house of God! Till life itself shall wane,

> Thy memories shall haunt both heart and brain,
> Never to fade till death these pulses still.
>   Oft in thy walls, so simple, yet so fair,
> I've felt the calm that breathed from place and hour,
> The softened light, the organ's mellow power,
>   Sweet hymn, and swelling psalm, and holy prayer;
> So rapt the spirit, and so deep the spell,
> If this were earth or heaven I could not tell.[15]

Although this sonnet is included in a set of poems seemingly written in the period when Bell lived in the Lake District, it positions itself within the discourse of nostalgia and memory as supports to faith. As in Hemans's poem, the power of the village church rests on its integration with the environment, so that the music of the streams and the music inside the church are implicitly at one. St Mary's is both a specific, named, village church and a liminal space between earth and heaven. The sonnet—like those by Turner and Hemans—derives its power from this tension between the 'sweet', 'simple' building and the concentrated emotional power of the worship within it, a power perceived as inescapable, haunting.

These three poems indicate the persistence of a nostalgic tradition within popular Victorian religious poetics, which tended to celebrate Anglican ritual through a particular focus on Sunday service in the village church and, as a subsection of this, on the sound of church bells as a call to worship. Such poems idealize a British Christian community, embodied in the natural and built environments, and generally located in a rural setting with its perceived values of simplicity, purity, organicism, and mutual affection and support. These tropes had extraordinary emotional resonance and wide circulation in Victorian literature and culture. The 'village church service', for instance, is also a staple scene in the novel, with George Eliot and Hardy taking particular enjoyment in playing with its established conventions. The sonnets by Hemans, Turner, and Bell might seem trite and unengaging compared with the Victorian religious poems that are classroom staples, poems such as Matthew Arnold's 'Dover Beach', Tennyson's *In Memoriam*, and Gerard Manley Hopkins's sonnets. But without appreciating the strata of religious verse that lie beneath these canonized works, it is difficult to appreciate how far these poets managed to break with, or conform to, convention. The standard 'churchgoing' poem is important, then, because it gives us insight into the rule, rather than the exception, in Victorian religious poetry.

The scenario imagined by Hemans often becomes shorthand for a nostalgia-fuelled leap of faith, as evident in Tennyson's 1842 poem 'The Two Voices'. After his bitter struggle with a voice urging despair and suicide, the speaker achieves a hard-won security, not by having the last word in the argument, but by seeing a family group on their way to Sunday service:

> I ceased, and sat as one forlorn.
> Then said the voice, in quiet scorn,
> 'Behold, it is the Sabbath morn.'

And I arose, and I released
The casement, and the light increased
With freshness in the dawning east.

Like softened airs that blowing steal,
When meres begin to uncongeal,
The sweet church bells began to peal.

On to God's house the people prest:
Passing the place where each must rest,
Each entered like a welcome guest.

One walked between his wife and child,
With measured footfall firm and mild,
And now and then he gravely smiled.

The prudent partner of his blood
Leaned on him, faithful, gentle, good,
Wearing the rose of womanhood.

And in their double love secure,
The little maiden walked demure,
Pacing with downward eyelids pure.

These three made unity so sweet,
My frozen heart began to beat,
Remembering its ancient heat.

I blest them, and they wandered on:
I spoke, but answer came there none:
The dull and bitter voice was gone.[16]

The initial scorn in the taunting voice might almost indicate an awareness of how cliché this scenario is. The soft breezes and sweet bells may come directly from Turner's sonnet, with 'sweet', definitely a key-word in this genre, appearing twice. The churchgoers the speaker sees are as eager to attend a church as those in 'Sabbath Sonnet', as 'prest' suggests, and the church democratically makes all welcome. The happy nuclear family are presented as typical churchgoers, offering a vision of sympathy and connection within the family, and in the integration of the family into the wider churchgoing community, that gives the speaker hope that his isolation and misery is not a necessary part of the human condition. Although he is still partly dwelling on death, the 'place where each must rest' is a euphemistic allusion, and the peaceful country churchyard suggests another kind of unity between the current and past churchgoers, rather than an image of decay and oblivion. The vernal imagery of Hemans's poem recurs in the implicit analogy of the speaker's heart to the 'mere' defrosting in the spring breezes, while the emphasis on the affective power of this scene on mind and body is also very similar to 'Sabbath Sonnet'. Formally, Tennyson could have been aware that several nineteenth-century religious poets used three-line rhyming stanzas with deliberate reference to the Trinity, as in Keble's 'Trinity Sunday' from *The Christian Year*. Indeed, the High Church *Christian*

Remembrancer commented in a major review of 'The Religious Poets of the Day' in 1841 that triplets were particularly suitable for religious verse: 'Their recurring rhymes, and, as it were, sombre monotony, are in true keeping with that subdued and awestruck feeling which is surely the native one of the saints, as seen in the restrained utterance of liturgies'.[17] The reviewer specifically references R. C. Trench's 'The Day of Death' as a successful use of this form, a poem with which Tennyson could well have been familiar given his friendship with Trench.[18] Certainly, whether or not Tennyson is consciously thinking about the religious implications of his chosen form and its measured pace, at this point the speaker of 'The Two Voices' also comes to value regularity, 'measur'd' and paced, as evident in the repetitive and ongoing nature of church services, above the feverish speculation of the poem up to this point.

The speaker in 'The Two Voices' is profoundly moved by the sight of churchgoers, but he does not rush down to join them. Tennyson's speakers always seem to experience church best from a distance. While *In Memoriam*, for instance, is doubtful about the efficacy of service and ritual in healing the speaker's grief, it does cycle towards a similar appreciation of the church in the sections on church bells, concluding with the unambiguously celebratory 'Ring out, wild bells, to the wild sky'.[19] In this section, Tennyson provided a major and oft-quoted contribution to the pre-existing body of poems that reflected upon church bells as signifiers of Anglican piety (change-ringing, which is what these writers had in mind, is a peculiarly British form of bell-ringing with a very distinctive sound) and that tended to use the healing music of the bells as indicative of the potential powers of religious poetry, as well as the lasting power of the Church. By the 1880s, so clichéd were church bells in Victorian verse that the satirical magazine *Judy* published a poem, 'Church Bells from Two Points of View', in which one half satirizes all the clichés ('My own church bell! How sweet its sound!), while the other represents a speaker humorously raging at the noise and disruption of 'That dashed church bell' and threatening to smash parson and bell alike.[20] That *In Memoriam* could be integrated easily into this existing tradition of village-church poetry, in which the sound of bells is ubiquitous, is evident from memorial poems such as H. D. Rawnsley's sonnet, 'Christmas Without the Laureate':

> Our old church bells
> Give back an echo of the songs he sung,
> But sadness sounds in every silver tongue[21]

Or George Douglas Campbell, Duke of Argyll's 'The Burial of Alfred, Lord Tennyson, in Westminster Abbey', which observes:

> The village church, embowered in trees,
>   With old grey tower or pointed spire,
> Calling to prayer, has woke from thee
>   The deepest measures of thy lyre.[22]

Obviously, many memorialists were strongly invested in claiming Tennyson as an orthodox defender of the faith. But it is worth noting both that his contemporaries felt they could legitimately read him as a superior representative of the village-church school, and that they regarded this school as the highest kind of poetry.

Tennyson might not have agreed with these assessments, but he certainly lent some measure of his strength to supporting the poetry of and about the Church. Other contemporaries had less sanguine relationships to this poetic tradition. In *Dipsychus and the Spirit*, for instance, Arthur Hugh Clough's speaker is haunted by bells, but rather than the soothing English church bells these are maddening:

> A bell rang in my head all night,
> Tinkling and tinkling first, and then
> Tolling; and tinkling; tolling again.
> So brisk and gay, and then so slow!
> O joy, and terror! mirth, and woe!
> Ting, ting, there is no God; ting, ting—
> Dong, there is no God; dong,
> There is no God; dong, dong! [23]

The lines that represent the ringing bell are deliberately unmetrical, in contrast to the self-conscious melodiousness of most church bell poems. To understand the force and black humour of Clough's passage we must recognize the disjunction between the bleak message that these imagined Italian bells hammer home and the usual message of faith and hope associated with the memory of English church bells. As a disaffected former member of the Church of England, who nonetheless felt more allegiance to it than to any other religious institution, Clough writes with a deliberate awareness of tradition and an ironic view of it. The same is true of many other Victorian poets. Dante Gabriel Rossetti, to take one other example from many, wrote a pair of sonnets dedicated to his sisters, 'The Church Porches', that play out his adherence to, yet rejection, of the values of High Church Anglicanism:

> Sister, first shake we off the dust we have
>   Upon our feet, lest it defile the stone
>   Inscriptured, covering their sacred bones
> Who lie i' the aisles which keep the names they gave,
> Their trust abiding round them in the grave;
>   Whom painters paint for visible orisons,
>   And to whom sculptors pray in stone and bronze;
> Their voices echo still like a spent wave.
>
> Without here, the church-bells are but a tune,
> And on the carven church-door this hot noon
>   Lays all its heavy sunshine here without:
> But having entered in, we shall find there
> Silence, and sudden dimness, and deep prayer,
>   And faces of crowned angels all about. [24]

This first sonnet is dedicated to 'M.F.R', Maria Rossetti, who would eventually enter an Anglican sisterhood. Written in 1853 (though the sonnets were not published together until 1911), 'The Church Porches' have been seen by David G. Riede as part of the process by which Rossetti 'acknowledged the attraction of an aesthetically beautiful religion but affirmed that it must be left behind', and Ernest Fontana agrees that 'the interior of the church is merely a provisional aesthetic, not permanent spiritual refuge from the heat and dust of the world'.[25] Yet if these poems conclude with the speaker literally leaving church, they also emphasize his familiarity with churchgoing. The first seven lines here echo the discourse of the High Church ecclesiologists, in seeing architecture, sculpture, ornamentation, art, and music as part of a combined, synaesthetic experience, contiguous with the language of prayer and song. But the reference to the 'spent wave' suggests less the excitement of the ongoing ecclesiological revival (very dear to the hearts of Maria and Christina Rossetti) and more a sense that the force of Anglicanism, or indeed Christianity, has been lost. The rhyme of 'wave' with 'grave' from line 5, where 'in the grave' is also ambiguous about whether this 'trust' is a living or dead power, contributes to this doubt, as does the double stress on 'spent wave', introducing a note of discordance in the rhythm. In the sestet, the speaker also implies that the church bells, rather than possessing powerful historical and religious associations, have no effect on those who are not already going to church. 'But' in line 12, however, does seem to counter some of this hesitation, particularly since the final line could be interpreted as an allusion to a cherished belief that angels were literally present during church worship (as in Keble's 'The Empty Church', 'And well we know bright angel throngs/Are by') while also permitting the interpretation that the praying worshippers themselves are like angels.[26]

The second sonnet, dedicated to 'C.G.R.', Christina Rossetti, shows the speaker and his sister about to depart after a service:

> Sister, arise: We have no more to sing
>   Or say. The priest abideth as is meet
>   To minister. Rise up out of thy seat,
> Though peradventure tis an irksome thing
> To cross again the threshold of our King
>   Where His doors stand against the evil street,
>   And let each step increase upon our feet
> The dust we shook from them on entering.
>
> Must we of very sooth go home? The air,
>   Whose heat outside makes mist that can be seen,
>   Is very clear and cool where we have been.
>   The priest abideth ministering, Lo!
> As he for service, why not we for prayer?
>   It is so bidden, sister, let us go.[27]

Like many of Christina Rossetti's religious poems, this apparently takes the form of a dialogue, in which the brother urges the necessity of leaving the security of the church for the perils of the outside world. This contrast of worldly-wise brother and more devotionally inclined (and conventional) sister was a commonplace in Victorian religious discourse, as with *In Memoriam*, 'Leave thou thy sister when she prays' (xxxiii. 8). The speaker here does not leave his sister to pray: indeed, he uses religious language to assume authority over her, though it is unclear in 'it is so bidden' whether the authority is that of God. Like the first sonnet, the second highlights the speaker's reverence for the Church, especially in '*our* King' and 'His doors'. 'Sing or say' is also a direct and knowing allusion to an ongoing controversy over this ambiguous phrase in the Book of Common Prayer (centring on the value or otherwise of chanting in Anglican worship), and the enjambment might even teasingly suggest that the speaker is in the pro-chanting camp before the second line adds the alternative. The sonnet to Maria, who worked directly within the Church, concludes inside it, whereas the second sonnet suggests that the work expected of Christina may lie in the outside world. It is not too much of a stretch to suggest that the power that bids them leave the church may be the force of art. Of course, 'let us go' does not necessarily mean that the speaker and his sister actually leave: we do not know whether this exhortation was obeyed. If this is a personal poem, in part about the religious allegiances of the Rossetti siblings, then Dante Gabriel would have known that Christina was unlikely, in art or life, to be persuaded away from the Church. His title and his sonnets, in form and content, signal that he operates within the same tradition as his sisters while adopting a liminal position—locating himself in the porch, not truly within the church—that allows both admiration and scepticism for faith as embodied in churchgoing.

Church poetry, whether it is as ambiguous in its stance as these sonnets or as partisan as those by Hemans, Turner, and Bell, should never simply be dismissed as conventional or minor verse, because this overlooks the historical context in which any and every poem on the Church of England was a salvo in ongoing religious disputes. These poems are not light-hearted celebrations of Anglicanism, but pointed, fierce, and intensely anxious. They celebrate churchgoing, and the Church of England in particular, not so much because its position was secure, but because it was generally perceived as under threat, both from within and without. Famously, the religious census of 1851, which attempted to measure the numbers of churchgoers on a particular Sunday, controversially concluded that only half the population attended Anglican services. Visions of the peaceful village church sounding out its ancient music to a willing community were perhaps less commemorations of something that was already happening than wishful thinking. In the field of poetry, highly educated Anglican poets still tended to dominate popular religious verse, but they would have been well aware that here, too, dissenting voices were making their mark. The best-known Victorian poets from dissenting backgrounds were Robert and Elizabeth Barrett Browning, who did write against the Church and support dissenting chapel-going to some extent, but usually, in their poetry at least, subtly and ambiguously.[28] Popular dissenting poetry entered the Victorian cultural imagination most strongly through the general adoption of hymns across denominations, but was also very important in terms of a substantial body of now-forgotten poems that were explicitly anti-Church, written to counter the kind of rhetoric used by Hemans, Turner, and others. Religion and politics were united in the work of radical (often Chartist) poets, who deliberately situated themselves as Christians (and as Christian poets) outside and in opposition to Anglican norms.[29]

For Chartist poets and their allies, to whom poetry was a vital tool in educating and rousing readers to political action, the Church of England was an old enemy. As Eileen Yeo observes in her seminal study of early Chartism and Christianity, 'The Anglican church held an established place in radical demonology as the immoral handmaiden of a corrupt political order' and rapidly 'became an armed battleground in the class war'.[30] Her reference is to the parish church demonstrations in 1839, in which a body of Chartists would march to their local church and occupy it during the Sunday service. While it seems that they usually listened relatively politely to the minister, the fact that they deliberately wore their working-clothes and occupied paid sittings within the church indicated their view of a Church which, from their perspective, preached doctrines of openness and equality while implicitly favouring the well-to-do. Anglican ministers felt deeply threatened. Some, like the always controversial Evangelical minister Francis Close, of Cheltenham, used their sermons to harangue the Chartists while ostensibly making a plea for the haunting historical and aesthetic appeal of Anglicanism:

> I trust that the sweet sounds of divine service, perhaps new to the ears of some of them, may have sunk into their hearts, and that they have found a beauty in the worship of the sanctuary, which they thought not of before.[31]

Close also objected vehemently to the fact that the Chartists had begun to design their own religious forms for use in political meetings, including a hymn book in which, he suggested, rampant infidelity was 'veiled by all the beauties of poetry'.[32] Eileen Groth Lyon convincingly argues that such adoption of religious forms by political agitators should be seen less as parody, subversion, or defiance of the established order and more as holding 'positive meaning for radicals among whom religion was in fact deeply important'.[33] As Mike Sanders discusses in a major article on the Chartist hymn, at least three established Chartist hymn books existed, though only one small pamphlet hymn book, recently located by Sanders, is known to have survived.[34] Individual poems published in Chartist periodicals and collections frequently used hymn-like stanzas or described themselves as hymns, often because they were designed to be sung at mass gatherings. Ernest Jones's celebration of one huge outdoor meeting, 'The Blackstone-Edge Gathering', first published in the leading Chartist periodical *The Northern Star* in its 'Songs for the People' series, gave a suggested tune for the poem under the title. The poem was thus constituted as a political song, but given the emphasis within it on mass singing as an act of worship, 'The Blackstone-Edge Gathering' also deliberately highlights its own ambiguous status as hymn:

> And up to heaven the descant ran,
> With no cold roof twixt God and man,
> To dash back from its frowning span,
>   A church prayer's listless mockery.[35]

Jones reverses Turner's negative contrast of the 'fanaticism' of an open-air religious meeting with the safety and security of the parish church by valuing the freedom of nature over the cold formality of the church.

For Anglican writers, both the ancient medieval cathedrals and parish churches and the new Gothic revival churches acted as powerful symbols of the survival and integrity of a particularly British religious and national identity. For political radicals and dissenting writers, these churches were rather symbols of the stranglehold that the political and religious establishment had on the land and its people. Gothic architecture in particular did not recall a time when happy artisans laboured in the service of God, but was a visible signifier of the persistence of feudalism in British culture. Thomas Cooper, one of the best-known Chartist poets and the author of their most ambitious work, *The Purgatory of Suicides* (1845), consistently returned to this theme. In the early poem 'Lincoln Cathedral' (1829) he describes the cathedral as 'Great sepulchre of haughty gloom and grandeur' and 'The tomb / Of regal priests who banqueted on joys / Wrung from the peasant's woes'.[36] Cooper's autobiography admits his nostalgic attachment to his Anglican parish church, 'associated with the happy feelings of boyhood', around this time, but as he found greater spiritual sustenance in Methodism and as an independent religious thinker, and as he became increasingly politically active, his anti-clericalism grew.[37] By the time he wrote *The Purgatory of Suicides* while imprisoned in Stafford gaol, anti-church rhetoric was a dominant note. His opening recollection of the speech that landed him in prison summarizes his argument as:

> Behold, in pomp, the purple prelate ride,
> And, on the beggar by his chariot's side
> Frown sullenly, although in rags and shame
> His brother cries for food! Up, swell the tide
> Of retribution, till ye end the game
> Long practised by sleek priests in old Religion's name.[38]

Bishops, who automatically gained seats in the House of Lords and were thus political as well as religious targets, were particularly subject to attack in Chartist discourse for their alleged corruption and vast incomes. Cooper's alliteration in the first line of the stanza, emphasizes, in its spat-out plosives, the vehemence and anger of his oral delivery of this message. As Stephanie Kuduk has shown, his use of the Spenserian stanza highlights his links to a national epic tradition, as well as emphasizing his literary credentials and associating *The Purgatory of Suicides* with the radical verse of Shelley's *The Revolt of Islam* and Byron's *Childe Harold*.[39] But it also has religious implications. On the one hand, in *The Faerie Queene* Spenser was an ardent defender of the Protestant church against the Roman Catholic, a stance that Cooper could happily support. On the other, he was defending the established order of Church and State, which meant that in the 1830s supporters of his work (and frequent users of the Spenserian stanza) included the well-known Tractarian poets, Keble and Isaac Williams. Cooper's use of this form is, in part, an act of appropriation and defiance.

On the dream-journey in *The Purgatory of Suicides*, the speaker encounters a fantastic cavern carved in stone, which provides the opportunity for five stanzas critiquing the politics of Gothic ecclesiastical architecture:

> Not, as with fashion of that twilight time
> When sky-born Truth, by priestly hands arrayed
> In vulgar vestments of the motley mime,
> Played conjurer in 'dim religious' shade,—
> And peasant thrall, by bell and book dismayed,
> Glanced tremblingly on corbel, niche and pane,
> Where imp, saint, angel, knight with battle-blade,
> Griffin, bat, owlet more befooled the swain,
> Till, when the incense fumed, round swum his wilder'd brain;
>
> Not, after pattern of old monkish mode;
> Not, as by wand of mitred magic hung,
> The rocky arch that mystic aisle bestrode,—[40]

Cooper had probably not read Williams' successful Tractarian volume *The Cathedral, or the Catholic and Apostolic Church in England* (1838) (both because of Williams' politics and because it would not have been available in an affordable edition), which takes its cues from George Herbert and Wordsworth, but he would have been well aware of the ongoing ecclesiological and architectural revival of the 1830s and 40s, for which works like *The Cathedral* were important advocates, and deliberately writes against it here. 'Dim religious' is a reference to Milton's 'Il Penseroso', which concludes with a paean to the Church and its services and was thus an influential work for defenders of Anglicanism in this period:

> But let my due feet never fail,
> To walk the studious cloister's pale,
> And love the high embowed roof,
> With antique pillars massy proof,
> And storied windows richly dight,
> Casting a dim religious light.[41]

Where Milton, in this famous passage, had 'light', Cooper has 'shade', using his rewriting to critique a poetic tradition for obfuscating the political implications of Anglican architecture and worship.

As the Chartist movement lost ground in the late 1840s and 1850s, anti-clericalism remained a vital rallying cry. Jones, whose fervour against the Established Church seems perhaps opportunistic given that, as Miles Taylor's recent biography notes, he was 'a fairly observant Anglican' prior to his conversion to Chartism, deployed vitriolic rhetoric against the Church as a tool to drum up support and readers for his periodical and other publications.[42] In the first volume of his self-authored periodical *Notes to the People* (1851), his article on 'The Bishops and their Doings' commented, characteristically, that 'blood, plunder and cruelty are their leading characteristics', while in the contemporary lecture series on church history bound up with this periodical he stated that 'the church in all ages has been the greatest curse with which humanity has been afflicted, and the greatest enemy religion has ever had'.[43] In the year of the 'Papal Aggression', such rhetoric was likely to be particularly popular. Jones's poetry in *Notes to the People* operated marginally more subtly, and perhaps success-fully, by mobilizing affect in the service of anti-Church rhetoric. His poem on 'St Coutts, or The Charity Church', for instance, gains pathos from the subtitle 'Composed in Westminster Prison, on hearing that Miss B. Coutts had built a church opposite its gate'. The poem implicitly contrasts the charity that spent money on a lavish church, with the Christian charity that should have been shown to a suffering prisoner: the 'holiness of flesh and blood' that is neglected in favour of 'the holiness of stone'. The new church can offer no spiritual comfort to Jones, and is instead a representation of the coldness, hardness and venality of supporters of the Establishment, as opposed to the equality offered by God:

> The seats in heaven are for the just
> And neither bought nor sold:
> God is not bribed with granite dust,
> As men are bribed with gold.[44]

This attack on the practice of renting pews to the wealthy was, incidentally, one area in which Jones and the High Church Rossetti sisters were in entire agreement.[45] 'Beldagon Church', also included in *Notes to the People*, seems like a deliberate reworking of nostal-gic representations of the trip to Sunday service. It opens with the church bells sounding on 'The Walk to Church':

> Loud the lofty belfry rung,
> Wide the massy portal swung—
> For Beldagon's Cathedral-fane
> A proud Assembly sought again.
>> High the fields are waving;
>> Orchard fruit is blest—
>> Summer's merry saving
>> For Winter's happy rest.
>> O'er the clover lea
>> The blossom-loving bee,
>> Neglectful of her Maker
>> Tho' 'tis Sunday-morn;
>> Little Sabbath-breaker:
>> Winds her humming horn,
>> Where lilybell and rose
>> No door denying close—
>> Asking neither price nor pay,
>> Wooing what may pass that way,
>> To be their sweets' partaker.[46]

This starts out very like Hemans, Tennyson, and others, but with 'proud' in line 4 it is clear that, rather than adhering to the genre, 'Beldagon Church' turns away from it. Nature is not an integral part of the Sabbath celebrations but a contrast to it. The flowers, unlike the Church, are democratically open to all comers. The lilies of the field do not seek economic gain, and the speaker is fondly indulgent towards the 'sabbath-breaker' bee. Like the speakers in positive representations of churchgoing, he is outside the church, but rather than wishing to be part of this community, or urging others to attend the service, he encourages his hearer to prefer nature over the Bishop of Beldagon's sermon and hymn:

> But ere you pass yon portal, stay!
> The bells have yet a space to chime—
> Then let them toll their sullen rhyme,
> And come away awhile with me
> To harvest-field and clover lea;
> Sit by Nature's side, and pray,
> And join her service for the day: [47]

Interestingly, part II of the poem, 'The Ritual of Nature', employs extremely varied and unpredictable line-lengths and metrical patterns, whereas when the speaker and auditor return to church for 'The Service' in part III, the form shifts to steady iambic tetrameter couplets, then long seven-beat iambic lines for the Bishop's sermon (IV), and a standard four-line stanza for his hymn (V). The conventionality of the church service is thus highlighted formally, as well as in the derivative language of the Bishop's threatening rhetoric of hellfire and damnation. Jones's poem is far more ideologically successful than his anti-clerical prose, because it leaves the Bishop's gloomy negativity, mirrored by the dark spaces of the church, to speak for itself, in sharp contrast to the sunny scenes of nature outside the church. 'Beldagon Church' is in the same tradition as Elizabeth Barrett's 'A Sabbath Morning at Sea', in which the speaker contrasts the formality of the church service with her own enjoyment of the pleasures of nature and experience of worship outside church. [48]

As these varied instances show, both the space of a church and the act of churchgoing were vital for Victorian poetry. Poems about churchgoing could act, through both form and content, as propaganda for or against the Church and everything it stood for. Aware that their readers would know the familiar tropes of this genre of poetry, Victorian poets could also use them to reflect implicitly upon the status of their poems as devotional works, as part of, or separate from, the experience of ritualized worship. The longevity of this poetic tradition, which for nineteenth-century writers stretched back to Herbert, Donne, and earlier, is also clear in its survival into the twentieth century in the writings of John Betjeman, and in Philip Larkin's well-known 'Church Going' (1954). Larkin's speaker in 'Church Going' assumes that the power of the Church has faded and he is uncomfortable, awkward, half-mocking, and patronizing in his attitude towards the old building, yet he also acknowledges its historical resonance and its power to draw him in without conscious intention, 'Yet stop I did, in fact I often do'. The final stanza's conclusion that 'A serious house on serious earth it is, / In whose blent air all our compulsions meet' again makes this particular church representative of English history and the wider survival of the religious impulse. [49] 'Church Going' is, like Rossetti's 'The Church Porches', a serious poem in the churchgoing tradition, even while it sets itself up as a possible critique of this tradition.

Larkin is thinking critically and affectionately about Betjeman's many poems about churchgoing here: as Kevin Gardner comments, Betjeman 'wrote unapologetically of his commitment to Anglicanism' from his conversion in 1939.[50] For Betjeman, Christianity was bound up with Englishness, and with his commitment to 'the old churches of England': 'They alone remain islands of calm in the seething roar of what we now call civilization. They are not backwaters...but strongholds.'[51] Gardner and Peter Lowe both discuss the constant presence in Betjeman's poems of churches and church bells, signifiers of the enduring presence of Anglicanism amidst a potentially threatening modernity, though without relating this to the religious poetry of the nineteenth century.[52] Yet Betjeman's poetry of faith clearly references, not only poets such as Hardy, but also a tradition of minor Victorian poetry with which he was very familiar—indeed, among his many interests in Victorian poetry, he edited a collection of Turner's sonnets and wrote a poem about the little-known Chartist poet Ebenezer Jones. Many of his poems deliberately celebrate, not just the Church, but the Victorian church, as in 'St. Saviour's, Aberdeen Park, Highbury, London, N.', the 'great red church of my parents':

> For over the waste of willow-herb, look at her, sailing clear,
> A great Victorian church, tall, unbroken and bright
> In a sun that's setting in Willesden and saturating us here.

'Great', repeated twice, is admiring and suggestive of awe, as well as referring to the imposing architectural presence of the church. These lines celebrate its survival—willow-herb grew abundantly on the bombed sites of post-war London—while also, in the setting sun, providing a suggestion that the church building may have endured only to witness the decline of the Church. Typically of Betjeman's churchgoing poems, in the final lines he contrasts the sounds of modernity to the enduring pulse of Christianity: 'Beyond the throb of the engines is the throbbing heart of all—/Christ, at this Highbury altar, I offer myself To Thee.'[53] For Betjeman, as for his nineteenth-century predecessors, churches are structures of feeling, connected across England and through history in a web of still-living faith. The 'courage and conviction of the Victorians' that he saw in their churches, he also saw in their belief in the importance of British poetry and religion as mutually affirming discourses, both, for Betjeman, under threat in the twentieth century, but both capable of survival.[54]

ACKNOWLEDGEMENT

I am grateful to the Armstrong Browning Library, Baylor University, for research leave funding that supported the completion of this essay.

NOTES

1. Timothy Larsen, *Crisis of Doubt: Honest Faith in Nineteenth-Century England* (Oxford: Oxford University Press, 2006), 1, 5.

2. William McKelvy, *The English Cult of Literature: Devoted Readers, 1770–1880* (Charlottesville: University of Virginia Press, 2007); Charles LaPorte, *Victorian Poets and the Changing Bible* (Charlottesville: University of Virginia Press, 2011); F. E. Gray, *Christian and Lyric Tradition in Victorian Women's Poetry* (New York: Routledge, 2010); Mark Knight and Emma Mason, *Nineteenth-Century Religion and Literature: An Introduction* (Oxford: Oxford University Press, 2006). Forthcoming studies of relevance include Joshua King, *Imagined Spiritual Communities in Britain's Age of Print*, in progress; Krista Lysack, *Daily Devotions: Victorian Devotional Books and Their Readers*, in progress. I am grateful to King and Lysack for sharing details of these projects.

3. Linda K. Hughes, *The Cambridge Introduction to Victorian Poetry* (Cambridge: Cambridge University Press, 2010), 140.

4. See Gray, *Christian and Lyric Tradition*, Karen Dieleman, *Religious Imaginaries: The Liturgical and Poetic Practices of Elizabeth Barrett Browning, Christina Rossetti and Adelaide Procter* (Athens: Ohio University Press, 2012), Cynthia Scheinberg, *Women's Poetry and Religion in Victorian England: Jewish Identity and Christian Culture* (Cambridge: Cambridge University Press, 2002), and Emma Mason, *Women Poets of the Nineteenth Century* (Tavistock: Northcote House, 2006). On Rossetti, monographs include Mary Arseneau, *Recovering Christina Rossetti: Female Community and Incarnational Poetics* (Houndmills: Palgrave, 2004); Diane D'Amico, *Christina Rossetti: Faith, Gender and Time* (Baton Rouge: Louisiana State University Press, 1999); Lynda Palazzo, *Christina Rossetti's Feminist Theology* (Houndmills: Palgrave, 2002) and Dinah Roe, *Christina Rossetti's Faithful Imagination* (Houndmills: Palgrave, 2006).

5. The seminal work on Victorian hymns is that of J. R. Watson, in *The English Hymn* (Oxford: Clarendon Press, 1997) and various essays. Recent studies of hymns by women writers include Nancy Cho, 'Gender and Authority in British Women Hymn-Writers' Use of Metre, 1760–1900', *Literature Compass*, 6 (2009), and essays by Susan R. Bauman and Sandra Hagan in Nastasha Duquette, ed., *Sublimer Aspects: Interfaces Between Literature, Aesthetics and Theology* (Newcastle: Cambridge Scholars, 2007).

6. Stephen Prickett, *Romanticism and Religion: The Tradition of Coleridge and Wordsworth in the Victorian Church* (Cambridge: Cambridge University Press, 1976); G. B. Tennyson, *Victorian Devotional Poetry: The Tractarian Mode* (Cambridge MA: Harvard University Press, 1981); W. David Shaw, *The Lucid Veil: Poetic Truth in the Victorian Age* (Madison: University of Wisconsin Press, 1987). For some recent work on Tractarian poetics, see *Victorian Poetry*, 44 (2006). See also Kirstie Blair, *Form and Faith in Victorian Poetry and Religion* (Oxford: Oxford University Press, 2012).

7. See Jan Jędrzejewski, *Thomas Hardy and the Church* (Houndmills: Macmillan, 1996). Hardy is discussed in more detail in Blair, *Form and Faith*, 114–121.

8. Knight and Mason, *Nineteenth-Century Religion and Literature*, 7.

9. Felicia Hemans, *Poetical Remains of the Late Mrs Hemans* (Edinburgh: William Blackwood, 1836), 321.

10. Hemans, *Poetical Remains*, vxxiii.

11. Joseph Phelan, *The Nineteenth-Century Sonnet* (Houndmills: Palgrave, 2005), 85–106.

12. Charles Tennyson, *Sonnets and Fugitive Pieces* (Cambridge: B. Bridges, 1830), 37.

13. Valentine Cunningham, 'Charles (Tennyson) Turner and the Power of the Small Poetic Thing', *Victorian Poetry*, 48 (2010), 509–21.

14. Charles Tennyson Turner, *Small Tableaux* (London: Macmillan, 1868), 71.

15. C. D. Bell, 'St Mary's Church, Ambleside', in *Voices from the Lakes* (London: James Nisbet, 1877), 13.

16. Alfred Tennyson, 'The Two Voices', in *The Poems of Tennyson*, 3 vols, ed. Christopher Ricks (Harlow: Longman, 1987), i. 591.

17. 'The Religious Poets of the Day', *Christian Remembrancer*, Sept. 1841, 167.

18. 'The Two Voices' was partly written in 1833, but not completed and published until 1842 (see Ricks in *The Poems of Tennyson*, i. 569). Trench's 'The Day of Death' first appeared in *Sabbation; Honor Neale; and Other Poems* (London: Edward Moxon, 1838). Marion Shaw briefly remarks on 'unmistakable' similarities between Trench's 1830s' poetry and Tennyson's in 'Friendship, Poetry and Insurrection: The Kemble Letters' in Robert Douglas-Fairhurst and Seamus Perry, eds., *Tennyson Among the Poets* (Oxford: Oxford University Press, 2009), 213–231, 218–19.

19. *In Memoriam*, CVI, in Ricks, *The Poems of Tennyson*, ii.427.

20. 'Church Bells From Two Points of View', *Judy, or the London Serio-Comic Journal*, June 22, 1887, 299.

21. Hardwicke Drummond Rawnsley, *Valete: Tennyson and Other Memorial Poems* (London: J. Maclehose, 1893), 32.

22. George Douglas Campbell Argyll, 'The Burial of Alfred, Lord Tennyson, in Westminster Abbey', in *The Burdens of Belief* (London: John Murray, 1894), 35.

23. Arthur Hugh Clough, *Dipsychus and the Spirit* (vi. 8–15), in *The Poems of Arthur Hugh Clough*, 2nd edn., ed. F. L. Mulhauser (Oxford: Clarendon Press, 1974), 247.

24. Dante Gabriel Rossetti, 'The Church Porches', in *The Works of Dante Gabriel Rossetti*, ed. William Michael Rossetti (London: Ellis, 1911), 198.

25. David G. Riede, *Dante Gabriel Rossetti and the Limits of Victorian Vision* (Ithaca: Cornell University Press, 1983), 53, and Ernest Fontana 'Exercitive Speech Acts in the Poetry of Dante Gabriel Rossetti', *Victorian Poetry*, 47 (2009), 451.

26. John Keble, 'The Empty Church', in *Lyra Innocentium: Thoughts in Verse on Christian Children, Their Ways and Their Privileges* (Oxford: J. H. Parker, 1846), 260.

27. Rossetti, 'The Church Porches' (ii), in *Works of Dante Gabriel Rossetti*, 198.

28. For a lengthy discussion of the Brownings' dissenting poetics, see Blair, *Form and Faith*, ch. 4.

29. The importance of religion in Chartist poetry has only recently been re-examined. Mike Sanders' seminal *The Poetry of Chartism: Aesthetics, Politics, History* (Cambridge: Cambridge University Press, 2006) includes commentary on the messianic impulse in Chartist verse. Two important articles that emphasize Chartist Christianity are Roy Vickers, 'Christian Election, Holy Communion and Psalmic Language in Chartist Poetry', *Journal of Victorian Culture*, 11 (2006), 59–83, and Pamela Gilbert, 'History and its Ends in Chartist Epic', *Victorian Literature and Culture*, 37 (2009), 27–42.

30. Eileen Yeo, 'Christianity in Chartist Struggle 1838–42', *Past and Present*, 91 (1981), 126, 137.

31. Rev. F. Close, *The Chartists' Visit to the Parish Church: A Sermon* (London: Hamilton, Adams, 1839), 17.

32. Close, *The Chartists' Visit*, 20.

33. Eileen Groth Lyon, *Politicians in the Pulpit: Christian Radicalism in Britain from the Fall of the Bastille to the Disintegration of Chartism* (Aldershot: Ashgate, 1999), 195–6.

34. Mike Sanders, '"God is our guide! our cause is just!": The National Chartist Hymn Book and Victorian Hymnody', *Victorian Studies*, 54 (2012), 679–705. I am grateful to the author for sharing this work in manuscript form.

35. Ernest Jones, 'The Blackstone-Edge Gathering', *The Northern Star*, 458 (22 August 1846), n.p.

36. Thomas Cooper, 'Lincoln Cathedral', in *The Poetical Works of Thomas Cooper* (London: Hodder & Stoughton, 1877), 439.

37. Cooper, *The Life of Thomas Cooper*, 2nd edn. 3 (London: Hodder & Stoughton, 1872), 77–8.

38. Cooper, *The Purgatory of Suicides. A Prison-Rhyme*, 3rd edn. (London: Chapman & Hall, 1853), 4.

39. Stephanie Kuduk, 'Sedition, Chartism and Epic Poetry in Thomas Cooper's *The Purgatory of Suicides*', *Victorian Poetry*, 39 (2001), 165–86.

40. Cooper, *The Purgatory of Suicides*, 13.

41. John Milton, 'Il Penseroso', in *Milton: Complete Shorter Poems*, ed. John Carey (London: Longman, 1971), 146.

42. Miles Taylor, *Ernest Jones, Chartism, and the Romance of Politics 1819–1869* (Oxford: Oxford University Press, 2003), 67.

43. Ernest Jones, 'The Bishops and Their Doings', *Notes to the People*, 1 (London: J. Pavey, 1851), 263; *Canterbury Versus Rome, and Christianity in Relation to Both* (n.pub: n.d), 52.

44. Jones, 'St Coutt's', *Notes to the People*, 1 (London: J. Pavey, 1851), 69.

45. See Mary Arseneau, 'Pews, Periodicals and Politics: The Rossetti Women as High Church Controversialists', in David Clifford and Laurence Roussillon, eds., *Outsiders Looking In: The Rossettis Then and Now* (London: Anthem, 2004), 97–114.

46. Jones, 'Beldagon Church', *Notes to the People*, 1, 22.

47. Jones, 'Beldagon Church', 23.

48. For a longer discussion of this poem, see Blair, *Form and Faith*, 135–7.

49. Philip Larkin, 'Church-Going', in *Philip Larkin: Collected Poems*, ed. Anthony Thwaite (London: Faber & Faber, 1990), 97–8.

50. Kevin J. Gardner, *Betjeman and the Anglican Imagination* (Waco: Baylor University Press, 2010), 2.

51. John Betjeman, 'How to Look at a Church' (1938), in *Trains and Buttered Toast*, ed. Stephen Games (London: John Murray, 2006), 234.

52. See Peter J. Lowe, 'The Church as a Building and the Church as a Community in the Work of John Betjeman', *Christianity and Literature*, 57 (2008), 559–81.

53. Betjeman, 'St Saviour's', in *John Betjeman: Collected Poems* (London: John Murray, 2006), 126.

54. Betjeman, 'From Lyndhurst' (1950), *Trains and Buttered Toast*, 274.

Select Bibliography

Blair, Kirstie, *Form and Faith in Victorian Poetry and Religion* (Oxford: Oxford University Press, 2012).

Dieleman, Karen, *Religious Imaginaries: The Liturgical and Poetic Practices of Elizabeth Barrett Browning, Christina Rossetti, and Adelaide Procter* (Athens: Ohio University Press, 2012).

Gray, F. E., *Christian and Lyric Tradition in Victorian Women's Poetry* (New York: Routledge, 2010).

Knight, Mark and Mason, Emma, *Nineteenth-Century Religion and Literature: An Introduction* (Oxford: Oxford University Press, 2006).

LaPorte, Charles, *Victorian Poets and the Changing Bible* (Charlottesville: University of Virginia Press, 2011).

Larsen, Timothy, *Crisis of Doubt: Honest Faith in Nineteenth-Century England* (Oxford: Oxford University Press, 2006).

McKelvy, William, *The English Cult of Literature: Devoted Readers, 1770–1880* (Charlottesville: University of Virginia Press, 2007).

Phelan, Joseph, *The Nineteenth-Century Sonnet* (Houndmills: Palgrave, 2005).

Prickett, Stephen, *Romanticism and Religion: The Tradition of Coleridge and Wordsworth in the Victorian Church* (Cambridge: Cambridge University Press, 1976).

Tennyson, G. B., *Victorian Devotional Poetry: The Tractarian Mode* (Cambridge, Mass: Harvard University Press, 1981).

Watson, J. R., *The English Hymn* (Oxford: Clarendon Press, 1997).

CHAPTER 48

IRISH POETRY IN THE VICTORIAN AGE

JUSTIN QUINN

WHEN Henry Wadsworth Longfellow's poem, *The Song of Hiawatha* was published in 1855, the *New York Times* was not impressed: 'Trespassing so closely in form and substance on the Norse mythology, as does the song of "Hiawatha," we doubt very much if Mr. LONGFELLOW has done the world of poesy any service by producing it.' It has some value, the reviewer continues, as 'an Indian saga, embalming pleasantly enough the monstrous traditions of an uninteresting and, one may almost say, a justly exterminated race, the Song of "Hiawatha" is entitled to commendation'. But the project is doomed, as 'there is no romance about the Indian'.[1] The poem became one of the runaway successes of America, selling 30,000 copies in the first six months, and enjoyed great popularity in England. In Europe, it was translated into many different languages. In the Victorian period it was difficult to say whether Tennyson's fame exceeded Longfellow's, but that uncertainty does not detract from our ironic enjoyment of the reviewer's statement that '"Hiawatha" we feel convinced will never add to Mr. LONGFELLOW's reputation as a poet'.[2]

A gifted translator, as well as gifted poet, Longfellow used trochaic tetrameter for his narrative poem, which he had encountered in the Finnish epic *Kalevala*. His experimental syncretism involved not only the adaptation of this form to English, but also the sentimentalization of Native American tribes, and the story of their extinction. His ambition was to produce a national epic for his country that would at once express continuity with European traditions and the novelty of American experience. Like many other poets of the Victorian period he was preoccupied with prosodic innovation, and as a professor of modern languages at Harvard College, he ranged widely in European literature in search of appropriate models. His choice of metre was criticized by the *New York Times* reviewer with acuity, but subsequent critics have been more sympathetic. Dana Gioia remarks that many of them have missed the poem's originality. He continues:

Longfellow tries to invent a medium in English to register the irreconcilably alien cultural material he presents... [The metre] is an overt distancing device, as was the incorporation of dozens of Ojibway words. These devices continuously remind the listener that *Hiawatha*'s mythic world is not our own.[3]

Longfellow drew on the research of Schoolcraft and Tanner for information about the Ojibwe people, and this use of exoticism replicates the procedures of Romantic poets such as Southey in *The Curse of Kehama* (1810) and Moore in *Lalla Rookh* (1817) that relied on printed sources for their tales of the Orient (Byron went East to see for himself). There is one important difference, however: Longfellow marks his material as autochthonous, as Virgil did for Rome and Malory for England, and as Tennyson had already started doing in the early 1840s. It also foreshadows the auto-exoticism that critics would later identify in W. B. Yeats, as he employed Irish folk tales and place names in his poetry about County Sligo.

The *New York Times* reviewer sees Ojibwe mythology as a closed chapter that has no connection with contemporary American civilization, but indulges in a little comparative anthropology. He deprecates the feats of one of the giants in *Hiawatha*, and then declares:

Contrast this with the slaying of the Nemean lion by Hercules, or his stealing of the golden apples from the garden of the Hesperides. Why, Fin Mac Cool, that big stupid Celtic mammoth, has a score of such adventures in his history; and there is still a stone shown somewhere in Scotland, that the great hulking fellow is said to have flung across from the Irish shore.[4]

The comments presume a hierarchy of mythological refinement that has Greece at the top, Celtic stories in the middle, and the Native American material near the bottom. The esteem for works such as Macaulay's *The Lays of Ancient Rome* (1842) or Tennyson's 'Ulysses' (1842) implied that England, and anglophone culture in general, inherited the best of the Classical world so that it could explain itself to itself. Other critics and scholars when considering the confrontation between the refined, civilized literature of their times and what they viewed as primitive materials, did not resort to hierarchy: for example, Samuel Ferguson and Aubrey de Vere believed that although England's culture had arrived at an advanced state by the end of the nineteenth century, it too had emerged from rough material, and so gave hope to Ireland. But what should be emphasized is that Victorian culture was setting for itself the task of confronting such primitive materials—raising ghosts, as it were. The more it sought refinement, the more the culture was haunted by such hulking mammoths out of mythology (or the working classes), and the more it experimented in order to accommodate them. (Also, it's not hard to see in the description of Finn McCool above the Irish men who were settling in areas such as the Five Points, and who by 1860 would make up a quarter of New York's population, terrorizing the city.)

These two interests of Longfellow—prosodic innovation and native mythology—help us understand the poetry of Ireland in this period. But they also help us to understand how the direction that Irish poetry took in the nineteenth century reflected more general movements in anglophone poetry.[5] Longfellow represents the refined, educated linguist and *literato* who must mediate between primitive materials and the tastes of a metropolitan centre, primarily London (also Dublin and Edinburgh for Irish poets). Irish figures from across the century such as J. J. Callanan, Aubrey de Vere, William Allingham, and Samuel Ferguson, and eventually Yeats, all play similar roles. These poets were often well educated in Classical and modern languages, but had varying degrees of competence with the language of the Irish material (from Callanan, who was a native speaker, to Yeats, who was entirely ignorant of it); and these variations (in some cases they occur across the decades of individual poets' lives, as they become more proficient in Irish, as is Ferguson's case) are integral to any study of Irish poetry in the nineteenth century.

The effort of some of these poets to expand the formal and thematic resources of poetry to include Irish elements places them, paradoxically, at the centre of English poetry. In this I follow the work of Matthew Campbell in his *Irish Poetry under the Union*, where he remarks that to read Victorian Irish verse

> involves reading against the grain, in many ways celebrating, if that were possible, its baggage as synthetic, forged, stolen or mere translation. Then again, what of *Tam O'Shanter*, 'The Rime of the Ancient Mariner' or 'The Lady of Shalott'? These are synthetic British products which were partly recovered mythic or oral tradition, but mostly invention.[6]

Campbell's study gives us new ways to understand Irish poetry of the period, at once acknowledging its strange and varied engagement with native materials, but calibrating its acoustic within the anglophone tradition. Such a critical approach on the one hand admits and interrogates Irish antecedents, and on the other allows us to begin exploring works by Irish poets that make no claim to a nationalist Irish pedigree, but rather proclaim their place within anglophone poetry more generally.

One Longfellow-esque figure is William Allingham (1824–1889), born and raised in Ballyshannon, a small coastal town in Donegal, fascinated by local Irish-language songs and poems, while at the same time building connections with the editors and luminaries of London's literary life (he would later be an intimate of Carlyle, Tennyson, and the Rossettis, among others, and edit *Fraser's* for a few years in the 1870s). Ballyshannon is both the boondocks and the location of the most advanced and sophisticated literary work that was going on in this period. It is like a hardship posting for a brilliant diplomat. Allingham is a necessary conduit through which flows new material, transforming the literary centre, even as that centre condescends to him, as Tennyson did in conversation with him, time after time. Just as the *New York Times* reviewer senses physical danger in Irish mythology that is possibly connected to the less well-lit parts of his city, so too does Allingham fret about the incendiary materials of the Irish folk tradition. Through his versions of local ballads, and his poetic narrative *Laurence Bloomfield in Ireland* (1864), he is fascinated by the elements of Irish culture and society that have historically resisted imperial integration, and he offers eirenic solutions in his poetry similar to Longfellow's smooth and peaceful transition from Native American culture to Christianity and subordination to European settlers. Politically, as a young man, Allingham stopped just short of Unionism and he was also an Irish patriot: such a combination was not unusual in the period, as he believed that Irish culture could find its most profound fulfilment guided by the hand of the Protestant Ascendancy in the country. In his diary, he refers to certain of his fellow Irishmen as 'natives', implying that he himself is not, although his family settled in Ireland during the reign of Elizabeth I.[7] He also writes there how he fears the Irish Catholics en masse, but not individually: on a personal level, there is only friendship.[8]

How to deal with Ireland for an English readership? In her study of Allingham's poetry, Wendy Mooney details the different ways that Allingham did this. In some poems the Irish countryside is anglicized, as Allingham writes about a generic Nature that bears no mark of Ballyshannon or its environs. Mooney also comments on the ways in which Allingham suppressed certain unpleasant political aspects of his Irish material.[9] At other times he introduces trace elements, but even these are readily comprehensible by an English reader. For instance, 'Among the Heather' is about the poet's encounter with a local girl:

> One evening walking out, I o'ertook a modest *colleen*,
> When the wind was blowing cool, and the harvest leaves were falling.
> 'Is our road, by chance, the same? Might we travel on together?'
> 'O, I keep the mountain side' (she replied), 'among the heather.'
>
> 'Your mountain air is sweet when the days are long and sunny,
> When the grass grows round the rocks, and the whin-bloom smells like honey;
> But the winter's coming fast, with its foggy, snowy weather,
> And you'll find it bleak and chill on your hill, among the heather.'
>
> She praised her mountain home: and I'll praise it too, with reason,
> For where Molly is, there's sunshine and flow'rs at every season.
> Be the moorland black or white, does it signify a feather,
> Now I know the way by heart, every part, among the heather?
>
> The sun goes down in haste, and the night falls thick and stormy;
> Yet I'd travel twenty miles to the welcome that's before me;
> Singing hi for Eskydun, in the teeth of wind and weather!
> Love'll warm me as I go through the snow, among the heather.[10]

The most obvious traces of Irishness are the *cailín* of the first line in English orthography, the name 'Molly', and the place-name 'Eskydun', but these elements do not disrupt the canons of English poetic taste. There may indeed be an Irish forebear for this poem—or Allingham, as was often his practice, may have written it in imitation of the Gaelic mode. What is more important, however, than such considerations is that the poem plays a variation on one of the best known English poems of the nineteenth century, Wordsworth's 'The Solitary Reaper', and also echoes his 'To the Highland Girl of Inversneyde', both to be made touchstones by Francis Palgrave in his *Golden Treasury* of 1861 (Allingham worked for the Golden Treasury series in the 1860s). Thus, Allingham's poem primarily moves within the English tradition, and carefully rations and restricts the Irish elements so that they are digestible for an English audience, much as a curry house in Croydon. In Wordsworth's poem, the reaper sings in Scots-Gaelic and he cannot understand her as a result; for Allingham, there is no language barrier, and yet there is a barrier of maidenly modesty (who knows what this gentleman wants?) and a cultural one also. The speaker after all is not a 'big stupid Celtic mammoth' but a polite, educated man with a different accent and a respectable job. The precise nature of the 'love' mentioned in the last line is left unclear, just as ultimately Allingham is unclear about his own status in Ireland, both culturally and politically.

When reviewing the poetry of Samuel Ferguson (1810–1886), Aubrey de Vere remarked that '[h]is Irish poetry is Irish, not, like a good deal which bears that name, *i.e.*, by dint of being bad English, while stuffed with but the vulgarer accidents, not the essential characteristics of Gaelic Ireland—not thus, but by having the genuine Gaelic spirit in it'.[11] After de Vere, there are few critics who have defended Ferguson's poetry; rather he is universally acknowledged as perhaps the most important explorer of Irish-language poetry in the Victorian period. He brought a philological seriousness to the research, lashing out at translations that were too conventionally mellifluous and failed to let the 'genuine Gaelic spirit' come through. Of course, each generation has had a different idea of the precise characteristics of that spirit, but without Ferguson's achievement Yeats would have had a significantly depleted palette. De Vere's remark also helps us to understand how such figures, when turning to Irish material, desire to expand the poetic idiom of English, just as Longfellow set out to do with his adaptation of a Finnish metre.

A further aspect is that they wish to prove that Gaelic culture can stand comparison with the likes of Homer. Here is de Vere again, in booster mode:

> Few can peruse these extracts without perceiving that novel to English readers as is such a poetic theme, and embarrassing as are a few of the Gaelic names, this work belongs to the 'great' style of poetry, that style which is characterised by simplicity, breadth of effect, a careless strength full of movement, but with nothing of the merely 'sensational' about it, and an entire absence of those unclassic tricks that belong to meaner verse. It has caught thoroughly that Epic character so remarkable in those Bardic Legends which were transmitted orally through ages when Homer must have been a name unknown in Ireland.[12]

Distinctly critical of England's policies for Ireland, he nonetheless wants his country to remain within the Union, and that a strong hand be used to extinguish separatist feeling.[13] In his cultural work, he wished to show that Ireland was worthy of such inclusion, that it had noble materials, although these were still in primitive forms (hence the occasional 'embarrassment' they cause). Also, he is anxious that there be no confusion over which 'great' characteristics are to be found in Gaelic culture—that is, none of the Paterian 'sensationalism' of the Aesthetic School, which he considered unmanly and immoral (he writes at tedious length about the improving aspects of literature),[14] but rather vigorous and heroic models of behaviour, that also can in places be dovetailed with Christianity. The contortions that such imaginative work entails are occluded from de Vere's own bland lines. (Geoffrey Taylor remarked that he 'remained unmarried which, considering the insipidity of his love poems, is not surprising';[15] that insipidity marks most of his *oeuvre*.) But what is important is that here is another version of the bone the *New York Times* reviewer picked with Longfellow: in what exact way are such primitive materials salient to modern civilization? What version of the past will help us construct the future? Raising ghosts is a perilous affair, as one can never be sure they will obey their necromancers to the letter. Certainly de Vere and Ferguson would have been appalled by the subsequent uses that the Irish material was put to.

Ferguson's work, as remarked above, brings Irish material into sharper focus, which was salutary, but it also marked the beginning of Irish poetic isolation. Reviewing the period which followed Ferguson, Patrick Crotty writes that one of the problems of the Revival poets 'who appear, from our contemporary perspective, to bob in Yeats's wash is that their very success in affecting the manner and/or pursuing the matter of Ireland cut them off from wider concerns'.[16] Critical narratives of Irish poetry still have not completely recovered from this isolation, which is evident in the reception of poetry by Henry, Synge, and Wilde, as we will later see.

An extreme example of the practices of forgery, theft, or 'mere translation' is James Clarence Mangan (1803–1849). He was the author of one of the most popular versions of the poem 'Roísín Dubh', beloved of nationalists, and he translated many other poems from Irish. But this 'mere translation' was part of a larger translation practice, often from languages he was unfamiliar with, and often producing versions in English that had no originals. Such a nomadic practice is glossed by Campbell:

> Importing the sensualism and transcendentalism of German interest in Persian, Ottoman or Coptic poetry into English, the eventual contact with Irish language poetry provided an odd synthetic encounter indeed. Mangan's Irish poetry sounds not just the Celtic but also the Teutonic, the gothic and the oriental, and frequently his English poetry achieves a stylistic originality which is outside any English-language comparison: 'It is not English poetry' Frank O'Connor said of Mangan's 1844 pseudo-Turkish translation, 'The Caramanian Exile'. Add in those moments of doubling as well as those of indirection and wilfully static non-conclusion ('Endure,—adore!'), and we have the often infuriating play with a poetry unable and unwilling to break free from its desire to remain in 'the monstrous condition of travelling without a purpose of terminating our journey.'[17]

David Wheatley also remarks on the way that nationalist critics, such as Thomas Kinsella, 'foreclose so decisively on Mangan's polyglot energies, binding him to the dyad of English and Irish which he had struggled so hard to evade'.[18] The nationalist desire for freedom—cultural and political—is, for Wheatley's generation of critics, transformed into a desire for poetry written in Ireland to be free of the label 'Irish':

> a nationalist canon that cannot accommodate Mangan has larger problems to solve than any amount of revisionist sniping. One immediate problem with the nationalist reluctance to go beyond the English-Irish dyad is how many more languages than Irish and English have been the vehicles of literary production in Ireland over the centuries.[19]

He then goes on to mention examples of literature in Ireland that were written in a variety of languages, concluding that 'Irish writing is and will be whatever people choose to write in that country, in whatever tongue'.[20] By attending to these 'polyglot energies'—the beguiling multiplicity of self and tongue that is at the heart of Mangan's poetic output—a further space is opened in Irish poetry: the drama of the self, which would become central to the *poètes maudits*, and later to Modernist practice. In the poem 'Neither One Thing Nor t'Other', Mangan presents this dilemma, and the consequent escape route:

> Oh, my love, see and pity
>   My desolate plight!
>   I am on the *shughraun*,—and the move,—day and night.
> I am hunted from country and city,
>   The Church, my own mother,
> Opines I must go to Old Nick for a home,
> For she vows that I'm neither for England nor Rome,
>   Neither One thing nor t'Other.[21]

Writers such as Melville, James, and Conrad demonstrated the aesthetic force of vagueness in literature: so, too, does Mangan show us a way out of the blind alley of cultural nationalism, no matter how sophisticated, whether it be of Thomas Davis or Seamus Deane. The end of the poem declares 'I am another', which Wheatley, in his introduction to his selection of Mangan's poetry, identifies as a precursor to Rimbaud's 'JE est un autre', three decades in advance.[22] Decades after the closing of Modernism, we are able to see many of the drawbacks of such a literature of the 'self'; nevertheless, this should not prevent us from registering such a counter-force in the aesthetic strategies of poetry written in Ireland during the Victorian period. Mangan's example, moreover, is instructive: by learning to read his work not purely for nationalist propaganda, other vistas open up, allowing us to relish the poetry of a fugitive figure like James Henry (1798–1876) who wrote epigrams, poetic travelogues, and lyrics. A physician and noted Virgilian scholar of independent means, he travelled extensively in Europe from library to library, publishing many of his books at his own expense. He thus flew under many radars until Christopher Ricks drew attention to his poetry.[23]

The poetic achievement of J. M. Synge (1871–1909), while small in extent, is forceful. In the preface to the first book of poems published a few days after his death, he named the poets who were important to him: François Villon, Robert Herrick, and Robert Burns; in the poem 'On a Birthday', he adds Pierre Ronsard, Thomas Nashe, and Francis Beaumont. The list is suggestive in several ways: first, there is no Irish poet; second, no nineteenth-century poet; third, there is a concentration of love poetry; fourth, Beaumont, like Synge himself was celebrated rather as a dramatist than poet.

He presents a problem for critical narratives of several persuasions. His poems clearly cannot be fitted into the same postcolonial story that serves his drama so well, as they neither avoid nor trumpet their Irish provenance. He does not try to de-Hibernicize nature for English consumption (as for instance Thomas Caulfield Irwin did), neither is he indulging in exoticism for that same audience. He knows that he belongs within the tradition of English poetry, but does not thematize this in the self-conscious manner of later poets like Derek Walcott and Seamus Heaney. Synge will casually mention Irish place names—from his native Wicklow on the east coast (the most anglicized part of the island) to the west coast, where he learnt Irish and found the material for his plays. Compare this with Heaney's poems like 'Anahorish' and 'Sruth' which replay the imperial story through poetic descriptions of the sounds of Irish words in English; or furthermore Heaney's introduction to Beowulf in which he claims the Old English poem as his birthright, even though he is Irish. This talks up the symbolism of the work, whereas Synge merely does the work. That Herrick and Beaumont are part of his inheritance requires no further comment from him, that is, apart from writing the poems that would confirm the ancestry.

At the same time, he disdains nationalism, as is clear from the cancelled fragment of one poem from 1907: 'For its better far to be a / _____ than patriot / Rhyming reems of bloody rot'.[24] As a fluent speaker of Irish at a time when many vocal Irish nationalists were English-speaking monoglots, and as someone who had spent extended periods on the Aran Islands in a community that was the subject of nationalist fantasy, Synge could pour such disdain with a rare authority. This is also suggestive for the way it sounds like the imperialist hauteur of the Englishman considering the upstart Irish. The word left blank—a trochee, along with the first stress of the next foot—leaves it for us to imagine what entity is so low that it is higher than a 'patriot'. And of course, there is the inspired rhyme of 'patriot/rot'. Despite these pleasing notes, we must remind ourselves that the passage was rejected by Synge. Ultimately, it was not even worth his while firing off a round at such 'patriots'.

After such housekeeping, we are left with a handful of poems—by my reckoning, ten to fifteen—that are an important achievement. They are noteworthy for their uncompromising treatment of human emotion, their avoidance of Victorian consolation of the kind that Tennyson often distributed to the doleful middle classes, their wit, and their sensuality. Yeats, in his preface to the first edition, praises Synge's poems also for their personal nature: 'The whole book is of a kind almost unknown in a time when lyricism has become abstract and impersonal'.[25] Yeats does not mean that Synge was voluble on the subject of himself—in the preface, he emphasizes Synge's reserved nature—rather that his poems are fuelled by personal experience and not by abstract values: 'Now and then in history some man will speak a few simple sentences which never die, because his life gives them energy and meaning'.[26] The poems are the arena of violent emotion, and Yeats elaborates:

> He could not have loved had he not hated, nor honoured had he not scorned; though his hatred and his scorn moved him but seldom, as I think, for his whole nature was lifted up into a vision of the world, where hatred played with the grotesque, and love became an ecstatic contemplation of the noble life.[27]

Such motions and counter-motions animate the following untitled poem:

I know the songs of the shower
Of thrush and pipit and wren
All the passionate flower
Of anguish in morbid men

Yet sweeter the sighs of your sighing
Three sighs half sighed for me
With lips that wrecked yet derided
The depth of my ecstasy.[28]

It reminds us of the poems Edward Thomas would write about a decade later. The opening is conventional enough in its description of fauna and weather, apart from the assertion of knowledge: this suggests that the 'songs' will be surpassed in some way in what
follows. Our attention is arrested to a greater degree by lines three and four, as they force
us to wonder what kind of songs anguished, morbid men might sing; there is also the
striking image of anguish as a flower inside men's bodies or minds. The *volta* comes with
the next stanza, the first two lines of which lead us to expect a conventional statement
about the sweetness of the lover's sighs. They might indeed be 'half sighs', but still they
are capable, as the last line will tell us, of bringing the speaker to ecstasy. The complication occurs in the penultimate line, as the lover derides the speaker at the intensest
moment of his ecstasy. (In my view the word 'wrecked' should rather be 'recked', meaning to take heed of or care for something.[29]) Yeats is correct: there is nothing 'abstract'
about this ecstasy. It is physical, but not exclusively so: it also catches the paradoxes of
the lovers' relationship. The enjambment of the final two lines has the effect of isolating
the ecstasy, but also undercutting it.

The poem 'In May' displays a comparable sensuality:

In a nook
That opened south,
You and I
Lay mouth to mouth.

A snowy gull
And sooty daw
Came and looked
With many a caw;

'Such,' I said,
'Are I and you,
When you've kissed me
Black and blue!'[30]

'South' is a particularly difficult word to find a rhyme for, and this difficulty is trebled,
as the line is three feet short of the more common measure in English poetry, iambic
pentameter. In the latter there is much room for syntactic rearrangements to make the
rhyme unexpected. But Synge chooses the harder way, even as he makes it look easy. The
breathtaking brass neck of the fourth line here, delivered with such casualness and flair,

brings in an image of utter physical intimacy. It is shocking that he has not held this back for later, and that he spurns all prudish paraphrase and circumlocution. One imagines the mouths open, as the lovers abandon themselves to their work (if they were not open, he would have written 'lips'). The third-last line inverts the polite order that our parents and teachers try to impress on us, in part for his final rhyme, but also as an inversion of the third line, where he lists the lover before himself. In the final two lines, we have once again an expression of physical intimacy that is both tender and shaded with violence. The lover is made ever whiter and snowier by the act of kissing, while the speaker is bruised by it. What seemed like equality, or unity, in the first quatrain, is marked by a counter-motion.

I remarked above Synge's acquisition of Irish, and also his disdain for the Irish nationalist agenda. During the course of the twentieth century, the Irish language has become hooked to nationalist ideology, but as in the cases of Ferguson and de Vere, this was not always so. Although the tourist industry of the Irish state uses the image of Synge for marketing purposes (his face is to be found on tea towels, and large panels in Dublin Airport), he is noteworthy for the ways that he found to deal with Irish experience outside, or rather without relation to, a nationalist cultural aesthetic. His slight poetic *oeuvre* displays a concentration on material that makes it irrelevant. For instance, 'Prelude' ends with a curious rhyme:

> Still south I went and west and south again,
> Through Wicklow from the morning till the night,
> And far from cities, and the sites of men,
> Lived with the sunshine and the moon's delight.
>
> I knew the stars, the flowers, and the birds,
> The grey and wintry sides of many glens,
> And did but half remember human words,
> In converse with the mountains, moors, and fens.[31]

The word 'fen' is from the Old English word *fęn*, and retains the original meaning of 'water meadow' or 'bog'. Although there is no shortage of such a geographical feature in the Irish landscape, the word is not used in the country. It thus invokes an English landscape, rather than an Irish one. Yet this word is rhymed with the word for another geographical feature: a mountain valley. The word 'glen' comes from *gleann* and pronounced in modern Irish to rhyme with 'brown'. According to the *OED*, the word entered the English language in 1489, and initially it was used only to refer to such valleys in Ireland and Scotland; examples of historical usage suggest it began to be used to describe valleys outside that area in the eighteenth century. Synge does not inflect the plural of this word in the Irish way (he has 'glens' not *gleannta*). From the mid-twentieth century, the use of rhyme is often considered a device by which the poet imposes his or her will on the materials, often in ways that go against their grain, and this is contrasted unfavourably with the more organic form of free verse. As a critical standpoint this is reductive; more particularly, in 'Prelude' we can see how Synge is led to the word 'fens' through the Irish 'glens', hardly by design, and yet once the thing is done, the pattern is pleasing on linguistic, poetic, and cultural levels. Something of the same pattern is present in the word 'Wicklow' also. Unlike many Irish place names, it is not a transliteration from Gaelic, but is rather of Viking, or Danish, origin; the Irish word for the county is Cill Mhantáin. The county was part of the Pale, the part of Ireland where the English influence was, and still is, the strongest. It is usually contrasted with the Western seaboard, which is supposed to be the repository of Gaelic identity.

The poem's cultural geography pushes on, however, to a further level, as the speaker drifts away from 'human words', whether they be in English or Irish, as he strikes up a conversation 'with the mountains, moors, and fens'. This reminds us of the first meaning of the word 'conversation', that is, the action of living in a particular place or among particular people (one of the *OED*'s examples is from *c.*1440: 'Where is his conuersacion but in the Empire of hevene?'). Synge's 'conversation' is in the county of Wicklow, where his family was from; and his conversation *with* the county brings him beyond the issues of cultural identity that have marked—in positive and negative ways—so much Irish literature since the nineteenth century. It is almost an impertinence to mention them at all, as they do not pertain to the poem: the poem's achievement is to make their distinctions and allegiances fade. Like 'I know the songs of the shower', this poem also makes a strong claim to knowledge, but it is a type of knowledge uncodified by language. The poem is set in Ireland and was written by an Irishman, but it is not simply an Irish poem: the pantheon of anglophone poetry is the first category for Synge's achievement.

Like Synge's poetry, Oscar Wilde's has been overlooked in favour of his dramatic works, as well as his ability to manipulate new media to create cultural celebrity. He will not stand comparison as a poet with either Hardy or Yeats but his achievement, though uneven, is not as negligible as several generations of critics would have it.[32] The obstacles to critical reconsideration are three-fold. First, a lot of his poetry is little more than *fin de siècle* decoration, an opulent rehash of Keats with added eroticism. It is difficult to continue reading a poem that begins thus: 'As oftentimes the too resplendent sun / Hurries the pallid and reluctant moon…'[33] This is like nothing so much as expensive, gilded wallpaper, of which he had endless rolls (as we see in a poem like 'Charmides', where we are curious only about when it will end). Second, his successful poems have nothing to do with the Irish narrative. It makes as much sense to call 'Impression du Matin' an Irish poem as it does to call 'Ulysses' a Lincolnshire poem. Even those critics who have adopted the complex protocols of postcolonialism view this type of poetry as effete and marginal, unconnected with the cultural work of 'inventing Ireland'. Third, there seems to be hardly any tonal, thematic, or formal continuity between the poetry and the prose. His most recent editors do not go as far as saying his poems were good, rather that it is possible to see them 'as an attempt to renegotiate the relationship between concepts such as originality and creativity, journalism and art'.[34] Yet this does Wilde and his readers a disservice, as there is a core of about thirty pages that are worthy of inclusion in any anthology of the period.

The first influences on his poetry were the classics and Walter Pater's aestheticism. Many of his early poems are translations from Greek written while he was at Trinity College, Dublin, and Magdalen College, and this preoccupation developed in the later poems on Italian subjects, such as 'By the Arno', 'Sonnet on Approaching Italy', and

'Urbs Sacra Æterna', among others. The title of 'Impression du Voyage' indicates its provenance in Charles Baudelaire and Théophile Gautier, and the poem also wends its way to Mediterranean climes, until in the final line, with exultation, he proclaims: 'I stood upon the soil of Greece at last!'[35] It was first published in 1877, when Wilde was three years into his time at Magdalen, and the same year in which he was rusticated for returning late in Easter term to Oxford from Greece. The poem's colour work is not overdone, and there is even a mention of a 'ripple of girls' laughter at the stern' suggesting 'manly' aspects that Pater's followers were often thought to lack. Although Wilde does not explain the meaning of Greece, it is clear that it is different from the understanding that prevailed in British educational institutions at the time. It is an immersion in the world of the senses that would have been impossible in England, but it also proposes a different meaning for Classical culture than it had within British educational institutions of the time, or for figures like de Vere and Ferguson, discussed above.

It was perhaps through the example of his friend, and later enemy, James Whistler, that Wilde learned to exult in the greys, browns, and very occasional golds of England and especially London. From the early 1860s, Whistler had painted impressionistic pictures, and then given them titles which undermined their figurative nature, for instance, 'Symphony in White, No.1: The White Girl' (1862), or 'Nocturne: Blue and Gold: Old Battersea Bridge' (1872). The gesture is complex, as the title indicates the artist's lack of interest in subject matter, in favour of a particular arrangement of colours and forms. Whistler wants us to know that he doesn't care where he finds this particular arrangement, even if it be in zones traditionally considered unsuitable for art, and thus probably in bad taste. And yet, to add a slight insult to injured taste, he lets us know that it is in fact a girl, or his mother, or a bridge, that is depicted. Such painting eschews the narrative possibilities of figurative art, replacing them with a provocative theoretical narrative of perception and the development of artistic taste. 'Impression du Matin' clearly proclaims its provenance in the first line's reference to a 'nocturne'. (In 1877, Whistler sued John Ruskin for derogatory remarks made about the American's Nocturne series of paintings, and the public notoriety of the case would have made Wilde's reference unambiguous for readers of *World: A Journal for Men and Women*, where the poem was first published in 1881.)

> The Thames nocturne of blue and gold
>   Changed to a Harmony in grey:
>   A barge with ochre-coloured hay
> Dropt from the wharf: and chill and cold
>
> The yellow fog came creeping down
>   The bridges, till the houses' walls
>   Seemed changed to shadows, and St. Paul's
> Loomed like a bubble o'er the town.
>
> Then suddenly arose the clang
>   Of waking life; the streets were stirred
>   With country waggons; and a bird
> Flew to the glistening roofs and sang.

> But one pale woman all alone,
>> The daylight kissing her wan hair,
>> Loitered beneath the gas lamps' flare,
>> With lips of flame and heart of stone.[36]

Wilde, like Whistler, pretends he is merely interested in the play of colour and form—a flaming red in the shape of lips, the particular movement of the yellow fog, etc.—but the poem's final words make clear that his intent is elsewhere: the 'heart of stone' of the prostitute is hidden within her ribcage and thus cannot be part of the play of sensory perception. Here Wilde steps beyond the painterly mode, proclaimed so loudly from the start with the capitalized 'Harmony', and gestures towards morality. Moreover, the aesthetic contemplation of the city that the poem so beautifully performs is consonant with most citizens' indifference to the prostitute. She is merely part of the urban backdrop. And yet Wilde sets up a counter-motion in the poem, emphasized all the more by its being withheld till the final phrase. It is a Parthian shot that transforms our view of the poem's imaginative work. If his earlier poems resemble luxuriant wallpaper, then 'Impression du Matin' is like a tiny Monet masterpiece resting upon their background.

'The Harlot's House' is a more discursive poem in this mode, and is equally evocative; however, it employs narrative to set up the counter motion. The lovers stand on the street regarding the shadow play of prostitutes and customers on the blinds of the house. But then the addressee leaves the speaker and 'Love passed into the house of Lust'.[37] This brings an end to the revelry that the poet witnessed in the house:

> Then suddenly the tune went false,
> The dancers wearied of the waltz,
> The shadows ceased to wheel and whirl,
>
> And down the long and silent street,
> The dawn with silver-sandalled feet,
> Crept like a frightened girl.

One appreciates the cliché of the dawn's 'silver-sandalled feet' because of the intense contrast with the unadorned urban scene. Wilde's poem draws on Gautier, especially on his 'Carnaval', from *Émaux et Camées* (1852), about the masques of Venice:

> Venise pour le bal s'habille.
> De paillettes tout étoilé,
> Scintille, fourmille et babille
> Le carnaval bariolé.[38]
>
> *(Venice dresses herself for the ball. / Its sequins starred, /
> its flurries, its talk—/ the motley carnival scintillates.)*

But Gautier's poem ends with a thrilled recognition of identity beneath the motley disguises ('carnaval bariolé'):

Ah! fine barbe de dentelle,
Que fait voler un souffle pur,
Cet arpège m'a dit: C'est elle!
Malgré tes réseaux, j'en suis sûr,

Et j'ai reconnu, rose et fraîche,
Sous l'affreux profil de carton,
Sa lèvre au fin duvet de pêche,
Et la mouche de son menton.

*(Ah! that fine beard of lace / a pure breath billows /
That arpeggio has told me: It's her! / Despite your nets,
I'm sure of it. // And I recognised her, rose and fresh, /
beneath the hellish paste-board mask / Her cushioned lip
of peach / And the dimple of her chin.)*

For Gautier, the mask is 'l'affreux profil', and when this is lifted away we gain access to the world of sensuous pleasure, attending to the smallest details of the woman's skin. Wilde inverts this, as the world is revealed as hideous at the end of his poem, but still we have the same play of carnival and fleshly pleasure. Gautier's manifesto of art for its own sake was influential on the early Wilde, but the Irishman was ultimately unable to embrace it; thus a profitable tension is set up in his work between his desire for it, and his moral scruples and suspicion of sensuality.

Poems like 'Impression du Matin' and 'The Harlot's House', by channelling French poetic exemplars and an American's images, also helped open the way for a poetry of the city in the English language. It difficult for us now not to see in Wilde's 'yellow fog' and other elements here the necessary precursors of Eliot's 'The Love Song of J. Alfred Prufrock'. Christopher Ricks documents many echoes of Wilde in Eliot's early poetry, mentioning especially 'The Harlot's House'.[39] They both drew from French sources, but Eliot was also aware of the ways in which Wilde had conveyed these in English, and his tone poems display several debts to his forebear.

The nationalist critical narrative of Irish poetry in the Victorian period provides us with much material that comes to fruition later. We are grateful to builders for constructing opera houses, but we don't ask them for an aria. Apart from a few scattered works by Mangan and Allingham, there is little of interest. When the nationalist frame is lifted away, the picture changes to admit primarily Synge and Wilde, yet the *oeuvres* of these figures are so fragmented or slight that they dissolve into the larger picture of English poetry in the period, indisputably minor, but brilliant nevertheless.

ACKNOWLEDGEMENT

I am grateful to Matthew Campbell, Wendy Mooney, and David Wheatley for sharing their work and insights with me during the writing of this essay.

NOTES

1. Anonymous, 'Longfellow's Poem', review of *The Song of Hiawatha*, by Henry Wadsworth Longfellow, *New York Times*, 28 Dec. 1855.
2. William St Clair gives Longfellow the lead in this. *The Reading Nation in the Romantic Period* (Cambridge: Cambridge University Press, 2004), 391.
3. Dana Gioia, 'Longfellow in the Aftermath of Modernism', in Jay Parini and Brett C. Millier, eds., *Columbia History of American Poetry* (New York: Columbia University Press, 1993), 88.
4. Anon., 'Longfellow's Poem', *New York Times*.
5. His work was also popular in Ireland, one index of which is chapter 4 of Charles Kickham's novel, *Knocknagow* (1873), most of which is taken up with a debate about one of Longfellow's poems.
6. Matthew Campbell, 'Introduction' to *Irish Poetry under the Union*, (Cambridge: Cambridge University Press [forthcoming]).
7. William Allingham, *Diary 1847–1889* (London: Centaur Press, 2000), 16, and note to page 7.
8. Allingham, *Diary 1847–1889*, 19.
9. Wendy Mooney, 'William Allingham in his Contexts', doctoral dissertation presented at Trinity College, Dublin (2011).
10. William Allingham, 'Among the Heather', in *Poems*, ed. Helen Allingham (London: Macmillan, 1912), 54–55.
11. Aubrey de Vere, *Essays Chiefly Literary & Ethical* (London: Macmillan, 1889), 124.
12. de Vere, *Essays*, 120. See also his introduction to his own poetry: 'It has been remarked that in the characters of Homer—so absolutely true are they to nature—the qualities which bear the same name are yet essentially different qualities; as, for example, courage as illustrated in Achilles and Ajax, in Diomed and in Hector. This mark of truthfulness strikes us at once in the Tain'—*The Foray of Queen Maeve* (London: Kegan Paul, Trench, 1882), x.
13. De Vere, 'A Policy for Ireland', in *Essays*, 151–61.
14. For instance, 'Literature in its Social Aspects', the first essay in *Essays Chiefly Literary & Ethical*.
15. Geoffrey Taylor, ed., *Irish Poets of the Nineteenth Century* (London: Routledge and Kegan Paul, 1951), 73.
16. Patrick Crotty, 'The Irish Renaissance: 1890–1940', in Margaret Kelleher and Philip O'Leary, eds., *Cambridge History of Irish Literature*, 2 vols. (Cambridge: Cambridge University Press, 2006), ii. 50.
17. Campbell, *Irish Poetry under the Union* [forthcoming].
18. David Wheatley, '"Fully Able /To Write in Any Language—I'm a Babel": James Clarence Mangan and the Task of the Translator' University of Aberdeen Research Institute [forthcoming].
19. Wheatley, '"Fully Able"' [forthcoming].
20. Wheatley, '"Fully Able"' [forthcoming].
21. James Clarence Mangan, 'Neither One Thing Nor t'Other', in *Poems*, ed. David Wheatley (Loughcrew: Gallery Press, 2003), 119.
22. Wheatley in *Poems*, ed. David Wheatley, 15.
23. See Christopher Ricks in *The New Oxford Book of Victorian Verse*, ed. Christopher Ricks (Oxford: Oxford University Press, 2002), 328–335, and in his edition of the *Selected Poems of James Henry* (New York: Handsel, 2002).

24. J. M. Synge, *Collected Works I: Poems*, ed. Robin Skelton (Gerrards Cross: Colin Smythe, 1982), note to page 38.
25. W. B. Yeats in Synge, *Collected Works I*, xxxiii.
26. W. B. Yeats in Synge, *Collected Works I*, xxxiii.
27. W. B. Yeats in Synge, *Collected Works I*, xxxiii.
28. W. B. Yeats in Synge, *Collected Works I*, 26.
29. The word 'wrecked' in the seventh line does not make sense in the context of the poem. It is possible that Synge wrote this instead of 'recked', and this error was repeated by the editor. Another possibility is that the line should have 'and' instead of 'yet'. Since the poem was neither published in Synge's lifetime nor did it appear in the Cuala edition of 1909 (the proofs of which Synge corrected), it is impossible to resolve this.
30. Synge, 'In May', in *Collected Works I*, 53.
31. Synge, 'Prelude', in *Collected Works I*, 32.
32. Geoffrey Taylor, the editor of one of the finest anthologies of nineteenth-century Irish poetry, omitted him, perhaps because his first poetry publication fell outside the nineteenth century —*Irish Poets of the Nineteenth Century* (London: Routledge and Kegan Paul, 1951). Patrick Crotty, in his survey of Irish poetry from 1890 and 1940 only discusses 'The Ballad of Reading Gaol', which, although Wilde's most famous poem, is not one of his finest—'The Irish Renaissance: 1890–1940', 64–65.
33. Oscar Wilde, *The Complete Works*, vol. 1, Bobby Fong and Karl Beckson, eds. (Oxford: Oxford University Press, 2000), 123.
34. Bobby Fong and Karl Beckson, eds., *The Complete Works*, i. x.
35. Wilde, 'Impression du Voyage', in *The Complete Works* i. 34.
36. Wilde, 'Impression du Matin', in *The Complete Works* i. 153.
37. Wilde, 'The Harlot's House', in *The Complete Works* i. 162.
38. Théophile Gautier, *Émaux et Camées*, ed. Claudine Gothot-Mersch (Paris: NRF-Gallimard, 1981), 39. Also see Lothar Hönnighausen, *The Symbolist Tradition in English Literature*, condensed and trans. Gisela Hönnighausen (Cambridge: Cambridge University Press, 1988).
39. See Ricks in T. S. Eliot, *The Inventions of the March Hare, Poems 1909–1917*, ed. Christopher Ricks (London: Faber and Faber, 1996), 150.

SELECT BIBLIOGRAPHY

Campbell, Matthew, 'Poetry in English, 1830–1890: From Catholic Emancipation to the Fall of Parnell', in Margaret Kelleher and Philip O'Leary, eds., *Cambridge History of Irish Literature. To 1890*, vol. 1 (Cambridge: Cambridge University Press, 2006), 500–43.
——*Irish Poetry under the Union*, Cambridge University Press [forthcoming].
Cronin, Michael, *Translating Ireland: Translations, Languages, Cultures* (Cork: Cork University Press, 1996).
Crotty, Patrick, 'The Irish Renaissance: 1890–1940', in Margaret Kelleher and Philip O'Leary, eds., *Cambridge History of Irish Literature To 1890*, vol. 2. (Cambridge: Cambridge University Press, 2006), 50–112.
Deane, Seamus et al., eds., *The Field Day Anthology of Irish Writing*, 5 vols. (Derry: Field Day Publications, 1991–2002).

Denman, Peter, *Samuel Ferguson: The Literary Achievement* (Gerrards Cross: Colin Smythe, 1990).

Graham, Colin, *Ideologies of Epic: Nation, Empire and Victorian Epic Poetry* (Edinburgh: Edinburgh University Press, 2001).

Ó Dúill, Gréagóir, *Samuel Ferguson: Beatha agus Saothar* (Dublin: An Clóchomhar Tta, 1993).

Patten, Eve, *Samuel Ferguson and the Culture of Nineteenth-Century Ireland* (Dublin: Four Courts Press, 2004).

Quinn, Justin, *Cambridge Introduction to Modern Irish Poetry 1800–2000* (Cambridge: Cambridge University Press, 2008).

Taylor, Geoffrey ed., *Irish Poets of the Nineteenth Century* (London: Routledge and Kegan Paul, 1951).

Welch, Robert, *A History of Verse Translation from the Irish 1789–1897* (Gerrards Cross: Colin Smythe, 1988).

CHAPTER 49

....

EMPIRE AND ORIENTALISMS

....

JOSEPH PHELAN

Oh, I see the crescent promise of my childhood hath not set.
Ancient founts of inspiration well through all my fancy yet.

(Tennyson, 'Locksley Hall')

THERE is, in these lines, a delicate pun on 'crescent' (in a poem not noted for its delicacy) which sums up Tennyson's ambivalent relation to the matter of the East. The 'Ancient founts of inspiration' which run through 'Locksley Hall' come, as Tennyson acknowledged, from Sir William Jones's translation of the Arabic *Mu'allakat*, and in particular from the first poem of the group, 'Amriolkais'; Christopher Ricks has persuasively argued that the long trochaic lines of 'Locksley Hall' might have been inspired by the incantatory rhythms into which Jones's prose translation naturally falls.[1] The benign idea of cultural interaction implied by these lines, however, sits oddly alongside the notorious fantasy of miscegenation which immediately precedes them. The narrator's dream of sexual conquest—'I will take some savage woman, she shall rear my dusky race'—provokes complex and contradictory feelings which he seems unable to control; it is first lingeringly indulged, and then angrily repudiated, resulting in a line which has often been seen as the embodiment of the Victorian period's intellectual and cultural arrogance: 'Better fifty years of Europe than a cycle of Cathay'.

These contradictory attitudes and violent mood swings highlight the complexities of the interaction between 'Orientalism', in its many forms, and the representation of Empire in Victorian poetry. Ever since the publication of Edward Said's hugely and deservedly influential *Orientalism* in 1978, these two 'discourses' have been seen as inextricably linked, with Orientalism twining itself around Imperialism like a vigorous and luxuriant creeper, both disguising and drawing strength from the power-relations of colonial rule. As 'Locksley Hall' indicates, though, these languages and ideas can be separated from and even opposed to one another. The non-progressive, hieratic 'Cathay' of the narrator's imagination is clearly not the same place as the source of the 'founts of inspiration' which renew and reinvigorate him; and both are distinct from the 'Summer isles of Eden' where the 'savage woman' lives, a place imagined as a dangerously enticing pre- or post-civilized world. The poem's exploration of these topics is made even more complex when we remember that he was born in 'yonder shining Orient', and that his father was killed in 'wild Mahratta-battle'—in one of the wars, that is to say, which helped to consolidate British control over its most lucrative and prized Oriental possession, India.[2] The Orient is, in this poem, both a destructive and a redemptive element, something which deprives the narrator of his father's protection, but also offers him some imaginative respite from disillusionment and despair.[3]

In tracing the relation between Orientalism and Empire across the poetry of the nineteenth century, it becomes apparent that what Said calls Romantic Orientalism—'that collection of dreams, images, and vocabularies available to anyone who has tried to talk about what lies east of the dividing line'—gradually comes under pressure from the systematic and scientific 'Orientalism' of imperial instruction and administration.[4] Tennyson, again, serves to illustrate this tendency: the intrusion of the language of Western racial and cultural supremacy into 'Locksley Hall' demonstrates how far he has travelled from his youthful infatuation with the *Arabian Nights*. The relation between these two 'Orientalisms' is not always an antagonistic one: as Daniel Karlin has recently demonstrated in his edition of Fitzgerald's *Rubáiyát of Omar Khayyám*, philological inquiry and textual scholarship could enable as well as inhibit the poetic imagination. For the most part, though, Victorian poets gravitated towards a more austere version of the Orient than their Romantic precursors (or French contemporaries), trying to find in the Arabic, Persian, or Sanskrit literature which was increasingly available to them elements that resisted the stereotypes of the luxurious, sensuous, and disorderly East.

This chastened Orientalism was, however, only occasionally and obliquely linked to explicit reflection on the contemporary political situation in the East. The relative scarcity of poems about Empire in the work of the most important poets is a striking feature of Victorian literature, given the centrality of Empire to our understanding of the period. For most of the nineteenth century, 'Empire' was, in the words of the historian J. R. Seeley, seen as 'too military and despotic' a term to suit the relation between Britain and its colonies: emperors were foreign opportunists and tyrants like France's Napoleon III, not constitutionally sanctioned British monarchs.[5] The reinvention of Queen Victoria as Empress of India in 1877—Disraeli's most audacious *coup de théâtre*—was perhaps the decisive moment in the rehabilitation of the notion of Empire, and spawned the alternately sentimental and bloodthirsty Imperialist poetry of the late Victorian and Edwardian periods. Even this poetry, though, in the hands of a Kipling or a Housman, could become a vehicle for some of the anxieties and ambivalences of the new age of Imperial expansion and self-confidence, especially in its effect on the ordinary soldiers and civilians who conquered and peopled the Empire.

The incipient conflict between the dream-like, fantastic Orient of the Romantic poets and the East of their relatively disenchanted Victorian successors is apparent in Louisa Stuart Costello's *The Rose Garden of Persia*, first published in 1845. Persian poetry has a special place in the history of Western Orientalism, as the site of a struggle between a vivid and sensual native tradition and what Costello, in the introduction to her edition, calls the '[bigotry] and ignorance' of the Islamic conquerors of the country.[6] The result is a poetry in which the 'legitimate magic' of the indigenous tradition is often forced to appear in the guise of religious mysticism, and in which a strand of mordant satire persists beneath or alongside the endorsement of officially sanctioned religious values. For the Romantics, the quintessential Persian poet was Hafiz, the Anacreon of the East, whose celebrations of the pleasures of living were the inspiration behind Goethe's *West-östlicher Diwan*.[7] Their Victorian successors, however, became more interested in those elements of Persian poetry which undermined the stereotype of the Oriental, and Hafiz was gradually supplanted by Firdusi as the principal focus of interest. Costello renders some of Firdusi's satirical verses, occasioned by the ingratitude of the monarch for whom he had written the national epic *Shahnameh*, in the accents of Pope or Johnson:

> In Mahmoud who shall hope to find
> One virtue to redeem his mind?
> A mind no gen'rous transports fill;
> To truth, to faith, to justice chill!
> Son of a slave!—His diadem
> In vain may glow with many a gem,
> Exalted high in power and place,
> Outbursts the meanness of his race! [8]

She also devotes several pages to 'Omar Khiam', whom she calls the 'Voltaire of Persia' because of his 'boldness in denouncing hypocrisy and intolerance', especially in his 'much celebrated' series of *Rubajat*.[9] These satirical elements by no means dominate Costello's volume: as her title suggests, much of it is given over to standard-issue Oriental verse of the kind described by Sir William Jones as 'rich in forcible expressions, in bold metaphors, in sentiments full of fire, and in descriptions animated with the most lively colouring'.[10] Indeed, she reinforces the luxurious and sensuous quality of the poetry with lavish and vividly coloured illustration, producing a book which is itself a kind of precious artefact. But her volume is an attempt to give some sense of the tonal variety and complexity of Persian poetry, and to hint at ways in which elements of this Oriental tradition might be used to reinvigorate English verse.

Costello's volume was the subject of a lengthy and largely positive notice in the *Westminster Review* for July 1847 by the Oriental scholar Edward Cowell, who saw in it an implicit rebuke to 'the mad partiality of Sir W. Jones and others, to whom Eastern literature was an El-Dorado of all that is beautiful'.[11] Cowell emphasizes the organic quality of Persian poetry, presenting its opulent and sometimes extravagant imagery as the natural outcome of the life and feelings of the Persian people. He notes the similarities between Firdusi's typically 'oriental' comparison of the Pleiades to a moth drawn to the lamp of the moon and Tennyson's description of them in 'Locksley Hall' as 'fire-flies tangled in a silver braid', but adds that the Persian poet's image has a resonance denied to Tennyson's because of its deep roots in national belief and mythology. In what must be, at least in part, a warning to those tempted to cherry-pick the 'beauties' of Oriental literature as ornaments for their own verse, he argues that literature produced by imitation of foreign models is 'at best a sickly exotic, with no innate vigour breathing through its leaves'.[12]

The difference between the popular conception of Oriental poetry and the reality available to scholars is, he suggests, most apparent in the figure of Firdusi, whose stern and Homeric stories of the Persian monarchy demonstrate to a sceptical public 'how simple and natural a Persian poet can be, after all that has been said of oriental extravagance and bombast'.[13] In his specimen translations from Firdusi, Cowell highlights this simplicity by replacing Costello's tediously formulaic heroic couplets with what he calls a 'literal prose version', designed to mimic the movement and imagery of the original poems as closely as possible:

> Her maidens rose from before her,
> They turned their faces to aid her in her despair.
> They decked themselves in robes of brocade,
> And adorned their hair with roses;
> And they went all five down to the stream,
> Full of colours and perfumes, like the glad spring.[14]

We would, of course, refer to this now not as prose but as free verse; translation was one of the engines of metrical innovation in nineteenth-century poetry, and there are resemblances between this verse form and the one used by Matthew Arnold in some of his 'Oriental' poems. There is also an unmistakeably biblical flavour to this and similar translations by Cowell, due to his use of the syntactic parallelism identified by Lowth as the key to the poetry of the Old Testament. The extent to which the Bible should be regarded as a specimen of Oriental poetry remained a profoundly sensitive topic throughout much of the nineteenth century, and became entangled, as we shall see later, with the emerging language of racial identity and classification.

The reassessment of Persian poetry apparent in the work of Costello and Cowell helps to explain Matthew Arnold's decision to turn to Firdusi when looking for a subject with which to illustrate his doctrine that poetry should aim at the representation of a single 'great action'.[15] *Sohrab and Rustum*, Arnold's most significant Oriental poem, is based on an episode of the *Shahnameh*, in which the father and son of the title engage in single combat, unaware of their relation to one another.[16] There is little or nothing of the stereotypically Oriental in Arnold's version of the story, which looks explicitly (and rather too self-consciously) to Homeric epic rather than to any Eastern sources for its inspiration. *Sohrab and Rustum* is, in this respect, typical of Arnold's extensive but rather oblique poetic engagement with the East. His early poetry, in particular, is full of the stock characters of Orientalism—the King, the Merchant, the Vizier—but the landscape they inhabit is a bleak and wintry one, always ruled over by despotism or the threat of war; he is particularly drawn to the northern extremes of the Oriental world, to Bokhara and the borders of Persia. This disenchanted and even diseased Orientalism is apparent as early as 'The Strayed Reveller', which includes some remarkable inversions of the characteristic motifs of Orientalism:

> They see the Indian
> On his mountain lake; but squalls
> Make their skiff reel, and worms
> In the unkind spring have gnawn
> Their melon-harvest to the heart.[17]

The melon, so often a symbol of the luxuriance and gaudiness of the East, is here 'gnawn' from within by a malign force analogous to the one which forces Arnold's 'Sick King in Bokhara' to execute a man against his own will, judgement, and better feelings.

The dissident and epicurean strain in Persian poetry found its most memorable expression in Edward Fitzgerald's *Rubáiyát of Omar Khayyám,* a very free adaptation of some of the verses attributed to the poet formerly known as 'Khiam'. This change to a more Oriental-looking name, complete with accents, is one indication of the aspiration towards scholarly integrity which characterizes Fitzgerald's poem. In preparing it he worked very closely with Edward Cowell (whom we have already encountered through his review of Costello's *Rose Garden of Persia*), following Cowell's relocation to India to take up the post of Professor of English History at Presidency College, Calcutta, in 1856. As Daniel Karlin points out in his recent edition of the *Rubáiyát,* Fitzgerald's commitment to and interest in questions of scholarly accuracy wavered throughout his lengthy involvement with Khayyám's poems; his famous determination to be 'orientally obscure rather than Europeanly clear' was, Karlin suggests, superseded by an even stronger determination to write living verse which would allow his countrymen to feel the force of Khayyám's alternately joyous and nihilistic vision of human life:[18]

> One Moment in Annihilation's Waste,
> One Moment, of the Well of Life to taste—
>   The Stars are setting and the Caravan
> Starts for the Dawn of Nothing—Oh, make haste!
>
>   (xxxviii)[19]

Fitzgerald's free and easy treatment of his source material, which extends to the imposition of a rudimentary narrative on a series of disconnected quatrains, has been seen by some critics as a prototypically Orientalist gesture, the appropriation and 'improvement' of an imperfectly understood original by a colonizing culture determined to fashion its own 'Orient'; and the subsequent history of the poem lends some credibility to this suggestion.[20] Following its failure to sell a single copy on first publication, it was discovered and championed by Rossetti, Swinburne, and others of the Pre-Raphaelite tendency, who recognized in its defiance of conventional piety and orthodoxy something analogous to their own revolt against the dominant values of mid-Victorian culture. Later in the century, it became the object of a different and more overtly Imperialist kind of attention from 'The Omar Khayyám Club of England', a specimen of the exotic East brought back to life by transplantation to the West; Annmarie Drury notes the symbolic significance of the Club members' not wholly successful attempts to plant a rosebush from Khayyám's grave at Naishapur on Fitzgerald's in Suffolk.[21] Both Karlin and Drury express some scepticism about this 'Orientalist' reading of the poem, with Drury pointing out Fitzgerald's own misgivings about the value of Empire; but Fitzgerald's own motives and views are, to a certain extent, beside the point.[22] The varying uses to which the poem was put in late-nineteenth-century British culture testify to the effectiveness of Fitzgerald's work of cultural appropriation; by importing and domesticating this very foreign product, he made it part of Britain's (or rather England's) continuing dialogue with itself about its own identity and values.

There is an interestingly parallel instance of collaboration between a poet and a scholar in Robert Browning's dealings with Charles James Lyall, the Orientalist and translator of Arabic poetry.[23] As the product of a very remote and austere culture, bound up almost from the moment of its origin with the development and spread of Islam, the reality of Arabic poetry (as opposed to the fantasy of the *Arabian Nights*) proved more resistant to European appropriation than its Persian counterpart.[24] Lyall undertook to make its products better known, publishing a number of articles on and translations of early Arabic poetry in the *Journal of the Asiatic Society of Bengal* during the late 1870s, and eventually issuing them in book form in 1885.[25] His standing as a scholar is indicated by the fact that his translations were still used in the *Cambridge History of Arabic Literature*, published a century later.[26] He seems to have been prompted to write to Browning in June 1878 by his discovery of a remarkable metrical coincidence between one of Browning's poems and the traditional Arabic form of the 'Tawil' during his translation of 'The Mo'allaqah of Zuheyr' into English:

> In the English an attempt has been made to imitate the metre of the original. The measure adopted is not entirely unknown in our language; it is to be found in many lines of that wonderful organ-swell, Browning's *Abt Vogler*; the seventh stanza of that poem in particular is almost entirely in the *Tawìl*.[27]

This resemblance goes beyond mere surface similarities, according to Lyall: Browning has used licences allowed in the Arabic metre, such as the addition or subtraction of an additional unstressed syllable at the beginning of each line, which imply an understanding of its fundamental principles.[28]

Browning was no doubt charmed to receive a letter from Simla, but his initial response to Lyall's assertion about his own indebtedness to Arabic poetry seems to have been one of polite bewilderment: 'I was surprised indeed, and no little flattered by your kind mention of a poem of my own, which oddly coincides in measure with what you inform me is an old and honoured one. Mine has indeed been "Poetry of the Ignorance", but I am glad to have struck into a path already traversed by the "slit-eared camels" who move so picturesquely in your translation.' ('Poetry of the Ignorance' is an Arabic expression, which Lyall cites on a number of occasions, for poetry produced before the revelation of Islam.)[29] He was, though, clearly intrigued by Lyall's suggestion, and it became, as he pointed out in a subsequent letter to Lyall, the catalyst for a late flowering of Eastern-inspired poems in his own work:

> [Your] poems are to me fuller of Arabian spice than any I have come upon before—the 'Time of the Ignorance' concerning Arabic only getting a little light of the 'True Faith' through your admirable notes. These,—in the former collection,—struck me so much,—together with your assurance that in 'Abt Vogler' I had somehow managed, like M. Jourdain, to compose Tawîl without knowing it,—that I dressed up an Arab story, I read in my boyhood, in the 'words and names'—and a good deal more—which were supplied by your erudition: I could not else have ventured on a single touch of local colour, or given a proper-name with its true spelling and accent.[30]

The 'Arab story' referred to here is 'Muléykeh', first published in the second series of *Dramatic Idyls* in 1880. As E. A. Khattab has demonstrated, this poem is explicitly indebted to Lyall's translations, making deliberate (rather than accidental) use of the 'Tawil' metre, and employing several other devices and motifs identified by Lyall as typical of the 'Mo'allaqah of Zuheyr'; even the 'slit-eared camels' make an appearance.[31] There is further evidence of collaboration between Browning and Lyall in connection with the Persian-inspired *Ferishtah's Fancies* (1884); Lyall's advice does not seem to have been solicited before publication, but he took it upon himself to write to Browning shortly after the publication of the first edition pointing out some errors in the names used in the poems:

> I am truly grateful to you for correcting so kindly my bad spelling in the two or three Persian names I was obliged to introduce, since Persian the poem professed to be—*not* on account of any pretence to scholarship, but because there was no other way of avoiding enunciation of European dogmas: I wished this slight disguise to be seen through, and was at no pains to verify the ordinary spelling of such travel-books, poems &c as were quite ready to my memory.[32]

Notwithstanding his insistence that he had no 'pretence to scholarship', Browning decided to incorporate all of Lyall's suggestions (with one exception) into subsequent editions.[33]

In the case of both Fitzgerald and Browning, collaboration with an 'Orientalist' seems to have opened up a new imaginative realm for intellectual appropriation, and at the same time acted as a constraint on the freedom of the imagination; in his letter to Lyall on 'Muléykeh', Browning expresses relief that he has not blundered in providing the horse in question with a 'bridle' rather than a 'rein'. Both also illustrate the increasing tendency to associate the Oriental with the archaic. The language used by Fitzgerald in the *Rubáiyát*, and by Browning in 'Muléykeh' and *Ferishtah's Fancies*, is self-consciously and even ostentatiously archaic in register, calling to mind the cadences of the Authorized Version:

> And lo, in the sunrise, still sat Hóseyn upon the ground
> Weeping; and neighbours came, the tribesmen of Bénu-Asád
> In the vale of green Er-Rass, and they questioned him of his grief[.][34]

This association between the Oriental and the biblical becomes a staple of the representation of Oriental language in literary texts of the period—think of the bizarre dialect invented by Rider Haggard for the 'Amahagger' in *She*—and it has a number of interesting implications. In the first place, it highlights the extent to which the Bible was increasingly seen as a document of Oriental literature. This is certainly the impulse behind Matthew Arnold's re-readings of the Bible in *Literature and Dogma* and elsewhere, an enterprise connected with his attempt to make the 'Semitic' origins of Christianity more palatable to the 'Indo-European' sensibility.[35] It also serves as a reminder of the enduring Western determination to see Oriental lands (in Whitman's memorable phrase) as 'realms of budding Bibles', endlessly renewed founts of spiritual wisdom for jaded Westerners.[36] This 'spiritual' East moves steadily further and further eastwards throughout the century, prompting interest in Indian religions (linked more and more closely to the West by the discovery of linguistic affinities between European languages and Sanskrit) and vast, unreadable tomes like Sir Edwin Arnold's translation of the Buddhist scriptures, *The Light of Asia* (1879).

This archaizing tendency also has a more directly ideological dimension, as Said and many other critics have pointed out; the powerful illusion of a non-progressive and unvarying East obscures the West's view of the current social and political reality of the Orient, and can even become an instrument of political control.[37] This is not to argue that all of the poets involved in the development and propagation of this image of the East were convinced Imperialists, or aware of an ideological motive behind their work; in the case of Fitzgerald and Browning this is demonstrably not the case. But the power of this general cultural movement towards placing the East firmly and immovably in the past is illustrated by some of the shifts in Browning's work. The interest in the Orient apparent in the poetry of the 1870s and 1880s was, in fact, a return to a subject that had fascinated him much earlier in his career. The Eastern-inspired pieces of the 1830s and 40s had, though, largely taken the form of reflections on the process of colonization, refracted through the era of the Crusades (in *The Return of the Druses*) and, most remarkably, written from the viewpoint of a contemporary fighter in an anti-colonial struggle ('Through the Metidja to Abd-el-Kadr').[38] This last poem in fact suggests that Browning might not have been entirely candid with Lyall about the extent to which his poetry on Arabic subjects was 'Poetry of the Ignorance'. The Arabic ode (*kasidah*) follows a strict sequence of subjects, according to Lyall; the main object is 'a panegyric on [the poet's] tribe, himself, or some other person, the description of some scene of travel or war', while 'the swiftness of the beast he rides is compared to that of the wild kine of the desert, the wild ass, or the ostrich'. The verse itself is 'made up either of couplets or single lines, the same rhyme being preserved from the beginning to the end of the poem', and, where single lines are used, 'each line ends with the same rhyme'.[39] It is difficult to imagine that Browning could have imitated both the form and the subject of this traditional Arabic poetry without some knowledge of it:

> As I ride, as I ride,
> Ne'er has spur my swift horse plied,
> Yet his hide, streaked and pied,
> As I ride, as I ride,

> Shows where sweat has sprung and dried,
> —Zebra-footed, ostrich-thighed—
> How has vied stride with stride
> As I ride, as I ride![40]

What sets 'Through the Metidja' apart from 'Muléykeh', though, is that Browning is aiming here not at antiquarian accuracy, but at the lively and sympathetic representation of a movement of resistance to French colonization. The energy of the Arabic verse form is transferred into the present, not confined to the safety of the remote past.

Browning's interest in the process of colonization also extended to the colonizers. His early verse includes 'Waring', the story of a failed scribbler who tires of '[pacing] up and down' in London and chooses instead to become an 'Avatar' in 'Vishnu-land', a 'God' to '[millions] of the wild made tame'.[41] Waring is the progenitor of a whole series of rakish colonial adventurers, from Kipling's 'Giffen' (of 'Giffen's Debt') all the way through to Evelyn Waugh's Basil Seal.[42] The impulse to colonize is regularly presented in Victorian poetry as an escape from Britain's intractable social evils (as in the emigration of Philip and Elspie at the end of Clough's *Bothie of Toper-na-Fuosich* [1848]), or as the acting out of an impulse towards heroic action denied an adequate outlet at home: 'We were dreamers, dreaming greatly, in the man-stifled town; / We yearned beyond the sky-line where the strange roads go down'.[43]

It is this latter note which becomes dominant towards the end of the century, in poetry celebrating the labours of the imperial heroes who had 'Conquered and annexed and Englished' a significant portion of the world.[44] At its worst, this Imperialist poetry is mere propaganda, playing on notions of racial superiority and solidarity, and appealing to a mythologized and romanticized 'England' of shires and sturdy yeomen. There are versions of this myth for the officer class, such as Henry Newbolt's much-anthologized 'Vitaï Lampada', with its mendaciously sentimental comparison between a cricket match with '[an] hour to play and the last man in' and the final stand of a broken British 'square' in some unnamed desert.[45] There are also versions by and for the other ranks, most conspicuously in the 'jingoism' of the late-Victorian music hall. Kipling, uniquely, is a master of both of these registers. His more formal reflections on Imperialism, such as 'Recessional' and the notorious 'White Man's Burden', are, though, weighed down by a portentous sense of the duties and responsibilities of Empire;[46] and his exercises in the demotic are often characterized by a recognition of the less glorious aspects of Imperial expansion, and an acknowledgement of affinities between the subalterns of the British army and the subject peoples of Empire.[47] In some of the poems, such as 'Mandalay', the world 'East of Suez' becomes a kind of paradise, making the ordinary British Tommy discontented with the 'gritty pavin' stones' and 'blasted English drizzle' that he finds on his return home:

> Ship me somewheres East of Suez, where the best is like the worst,
> Where there aren't no Ten Commandments an' a man can raise a thirst;
> For the temple-bells are callin', an' it's there that I would be—
> By the old Moulmein Pagoda, lookin' lazy at the sea[.][48]

Many of Kipling's contemporaries heard in this kind of poetry what Robert Buchanan called 'the voice of the hooligan', an attempt to lend cultural respectability to a boorish and philistine version of Englishness.[49] In his 'Ballad of Kiplingson', which imagines the poet robustly questioning St Peter's refusal to open the pearly gates for him, Buchanan demonstrates that this 'voice' is all too easy to parody:

> Wherever the Flag of England waves, down go all other flags;
> Wherever the thin black line is spread, the Bulldog bites and brags!
> And I warn you now, if you close that Gate, the moment it is done,
> I'll summon an army of Cockney Gents, with a great big Gatling gun!
> O Gawd, beware of the Jingo's wrath! the Journals of Earth are mine!
> Across the plains of the earth still creeps the thin black penny-a-line![50]

Recent criticism, however, influenced by the emphasis in postcolonial theory on the 'the interaction, the borrowings and lendings, the appropriations in both directions which trouble any binary oppositions between Europe and its "others"', has become attentive to the multiplicity of voices in Kipling's demotic verse, and in particular to the ways in which the different languages represented engage with and transform one another.[51] Kipling's ostentatious use of loan words from Indian languages, and his interest in the mutations these words undergo when refracted through the consciousness of the ordinary soldier, produces a poetry alert to (and often amused by) the hybrids generated in the 'contact zones' of colonization and conquest.[52]

By the end of the nineteenth century, these 'borrowings and lendings' were beginning to include the appropriation of the English language and English literary idioms by colonized peoples. This kind of 'writing back', as it is usually designated, has attracted a great deal of attention in recent years, not least because of the desire of postcolonial critics to find examples of 'the colonial encounter' in which colonized peoples do not figure exclusively as the objects of European oppression and domination. There are Indian poets writing in English from the early nineteenth century onwards; the dominant British attitude to them is indicated by Kipling's scornful description of Henry Derozio as 'the man who imitated Byron'.[53] Mimicry has, however, been identified by postcolonial critics as one of the most powerful and unsettling of the strategies available to the writer forced to adopt an alien literary and cultural tradition, and some of the resources it offers are visible in the work of the Bengali poet Toru Dutt. Her poetry, much of which deals with the question of translation, draws on some of the dominant metaphors of the colonial encounter to reflect on the complexities of representing one culture in the language of another. The concluding sonnet to her collection of translations from French poetry begins: 'The flowers look loveliest in their native soil / Amid their kindred branches; plucked, they fade'.[54] And her most substantial (posthumously published) collection, *Ancient Ballads and Legends of Hindustan*, continues this horticultural metaphor in its reflections on her Calcutta garden:

> A sea of foliage girds our garden round,
>   But not a sea of dull unvaried green,

> Sharp contrasts of all colours here are seen;
> The light-green graceful tamarinds abound
> Amid the mangoe clumps of green profound,
>   And palms arise, like pillars gray, between;
>   And o'er the quiet pools the seemuls lean,
> Red,—red, and startling like a trumpet's sound.
> But nothing can be lovelier than the ranges
>   Of bamboos to the eastward, when the moon
> Looks though their gaps, and the white lotus changes
>   Into a cup of silver. One might swoon
>   Drunken with beauty then, or gaze and gaze
>   On a primeval Eden, in amaze.[55]

This is not so much an attempt at hybridization as a reversal of the usual cultural hierarchy: the exotic vocabulary of the oriental garden, with its 'tamarinds', 'mangoes' and 'seemuls', has been transplanted into an English sonnet, adding vibrancy and colour to what would otherwise be 'a sea of dull unvaried green'. In seeming to challenge the primacy of European representations of nature, however, Dutt also illustrates the force of the European construction of the Orient, representing her own homeland as a 'primeval Eden' upon which the visitor might 'gaze' in wonder. She is, that is to say, conscious throughout this poem, not just of the way in which the garden appears to her, but also, and perhaps primarily, of the way in which it would appear to a European viewer—a graphic instance of the 'self-division' so often identified as one of the principal psychological consequences of colonization.[56] In the essay he wrote introducing *Ancient Ballads* to the British public, Edmund Gosse, picking up on Dutt's insistent use of flower symbolism, described the collection as a 'fragile exotic blossom of song'.[57] Literature written by the colonized was acceptable as long as it was ancient, exotic, and fragile— like the rose-bush planted on Fitzgerald's grave.

The transformations in Orientalism and the poetry of Empire during the Victorian period are summed up most neatly in the sequel to 'Locksley Hall' that Tennyson wrote nearly half a century after the original.[58] Tennyson's responsibilities as Laureate, and his own political convictions, led towards the end of his career to the publication of a number of poems in which the new certainties and stridencies of Empire are clearly audible. In 'The Defence of Lucknow', for instance, the defining event of the Indian Mutiny (or Revolt) of 1857 is recast in stark and schematic terms as a series of contrasts between 'brown' and 'white', East and West, health and disease:

> Heat like the mouth of a hell, or a deluge of cataract skies,
> Stench of old offal decaying, and infinite torment of flies,
> Thoughts of the breezes of May blowing over an English field,
> Cholera, scurvy and fever, the wound that *would* not be healed[.] [59]

This vision of England (not Britain) as a kind of rural idyll is an increasingly common one in late-nineteenth-century poetry—it stands behind Housman's mythical 'Shropshire', and Hopkins's impossibly sturdy (and highly eroticized) blacksmiths and ploughmen—and, in this poem, it heralds the arrival of the 'wholesome white faces' of Havelock's fusiliers.

There is a similar use of crudely racial language in 'Locksley Hall Sixty Years After', not least in the notorious line about 'the black Australian' whose dying wish is to 'return, a white'. This strand of Tennyson's later poetry unquestionably reflects the increasing importance of racial thinking in late-Victorian intellectual life, which often had a fairly straightforward connection with the ideology of imperial domination and control. In fact, the sequel to 'Locksley Hall' is riddled with anxieties about the deterioration of the English 'race', and the possible dereliction of its imperial duties. In the first 'Locksley Hall', the speaker's worries about the social organization of England, and especially the dominance of money, are epitomized by Amy's decision to marry for wealth rather than love: 'Cursed be the gold that gilds the straitened forehead of the fool!' In the later poem, this anxiety is given a more explicitly racial inflection. Addressing his grandson, who has suffered a similar disappointment in love to his own at the hands of 'Judith', the speaker reflects on the lessons offered by the tomb of one of their remote ancestors:

> She the worldling born of worldlings—father, mother—be content,
> Even the homely farm can teach us there is something in descent.
>
> Yonder in that chapel, slowly sinking now into the ground,
> Lies the warrior, my forefather, with his feet upon the hound.
>
> Crossed! for once he sailed the sea to crush the Moslem in his pride;
> Dead the warrior, dead his glory, dead the cause in which he died.[60]

The Crusader-ancestor is 'crossed' in a number of senses. He is a representative of the Christianity which is now, like the chapel, sinking into the ground; he has been thwarted in his aim of ensuring the victory of his cause; and, most significantly, his descendants have been 'crossed' with other and lesser specimens of humanity, leading to the gradual attenuation of the qualities which enabled him to subdue 'the Moslem in his pride'.[61] This is the lesson 'in descent' taught by the 'homely farm', and it makes the grandson's failure to marry the 'worldling' Judith a providential escape rather than a reason for lamentation.

This is, moreover, a lesson that England as a whole needs to learn if it intends to maintain its hold over its imperial possessions. Fears about Russian ambitions in the Indian subcontinent—a recurring theme of Imperial scaremongering during the 1880s and 1890s—are juxtaposed with worries about the spread of democracy:

> Russia bursts our Indian barrier; shall we fight her? shall we yield?
> Pause! before you sound the trumpet, hear the voices from the field.
>
> Those three hundred millions under one Imperial sceptre now,
> Shall we hold them? shall we loose them? take the suffrage of the plow.

This looks, at first sight, like a suggestion that the 'suffrage of the plow'—the extension of the franchise—is inconsistent with the kind of decisive action required to keep India under the 'Imperial sceptre', but it is quickly followed by a recollection of the native nobility apparent in many sons of the soil. What is needed, the speaker suggests, is a form of social organization which will allow a natural rather than an imposed hierarchy to manifest itself.[62] This is the only way to prevent the kind of 'crossing' which has led to the deterioration of the race since the days of the Crusaders, and to make sure that the forward movement of Evolution is not thwarted by its adversary Reversion, which is always 'dragging Evolution in the mud'.

It is tempting (if perhaps a little too neat) to see Tennyson's movement from the 'crescent promise' of the first 'Locksley Hall' to the 'Crossed' knight of the second as symptomatic of the general coarsening of poetic interaction with the East during the Victorian period. The rise of academic Orientalism, and the increasing stridency of Imperialism, with its attendant fixations on race and cultural difference, all served to limit the space available to the Orient within the poetic imagination. One response to this was to move 'the Orient' further and further east, as evidenced by the *fin-de-siècle* cult of Japan; another was to dematerialize the idea of the Orient into a kind of spiritual principle or ideal rather than a physical location. These transformations are an important part of the legacy of Victorian poetry for its Modernist successors, the influence of which can be seen in the interest shown by Fenellosa and Pound in the poetic potential of the Chinese ideogram, and in Eliot's invocation of the *Upanishads* at the end of *The Waste Land*.

NOTES

1. Christopher Ricks in *Tennyson: A Selected Edition*, ed. Christopher Ricks (Harlow: Pearson Longman, 2007), 182–3. Jones's translation was first published in 1782, one of a series of translations from Oriental literature which had an enormous influence on the Western understanding of Eastern literature; see Garland Cannon, 'Sir William Jones and Literary Orientalism', in C. C. Barfoot and Theo D'Haen, eds., *Oriental Prospects: Western Literature and the Lure of the East* (Amsterdam and Atlanta, GA: Rodopi, 1998), 27–41. The *Mu'allakat* are discussed in more detail below; see n27.
2. The Mahratta Empire succeeded the Mughals, and dominated most of the Indian subcontinent throughout the eighteenth century. The British (under the auspices of the East India Company) fought three wars with the Mahrattas, the last and most decisive of which was in 1817–18. 'Mahratta' (with various spellings) became a kind of code-word for undisciplined native resistance to British rule: see, for instance, Kipling's reference to 'a fine Maratha fury' in his poem 'A Legend of the Foreign Office'.
3. Said notes the importance of the Romantic idea of the Orient as a site of spiritual and civilizational renewal for the West; see Said, *Orientalism* (London: Penguin, 1987; 1st pub. 1978), esp. 113–123.
4. Said, *Orientalism*, 73.
5. J. R. Seeley, *The Expansion of England* (London: Macmillan, 1895; 1st pub. 1883), 44. In his preface, Seeley thanks 'Professor Cowell' for his assistance with the sections of the book dealing with India; this is Edward Byles Cowell, who provided Fitzgerald with the raw material for the *Rubáiyát* (see below).

6. Louisa Stuart Costello, *The Rose Garden of Persia* (London: Longman, Brown, Green and Longmans, 1845), vi. Costello is not alone in comparing the Islamic conquest of Persia to the Norman conquest of England in its social and historical results.

7. First published in 1819. The names of the Persian, Arabic, and other poets mentioned in this essay have been variously rendered into English; I give the transliterations used by the writers under discussion, unless otherwise indicated.

8. Costello, *Rose Garden*, 18–19.

9. Costello, *Rose Garden*, 66-67.

10. William Jones quoted in Costello, *Rose Garden*, 2.

11. *The Westminster Review*, 93 (July 1847), 145. This review is attributed to Cowell in the *Wellesley Index*.

12. *The Westminster Review*, 145, 146; compare Toru Dutt's reflections on the same topic below.

13. *The Westminster Review*, 150.

14. *The Westminster Review*, 150.

15. *Sohrab and Rustum* was the main poem in Arnold's 1853 *Poems*, in the famous Preface to which he explained his reasons for omitting *Empedocles on Etna* and some other early poems in which he had allowed 'the dialogue of the mind with itself' to predominate.

16. Arnold claimed, typically, to have come to Firdusi via a French rather than an English source, namely, Sainte-Beuve's essay 'Le livre des Rois, par Firdousi' reprinted in his *Causeries du Lundi* in December 1850. According to Miriam Allott's edition of Arnold's *Poems*, he also consulted Sir John Malcolm's *History of Persia* and other prose sources; see *Arnold: The Complete Poems*, ed. Miriam Allott (London and New York: Longman, 1979), 319–22.

17. Arnold, 'The Strayed Reveller', in *The Complete Poems*, 77.

18. Fitzgerald's statement comes from a letter to Cowell of 7 May 1855; cited in *The Rubáiyát of Omar Khayyám*, ed. Daniel Karlin (Oxford: Oxford University Press, 2009), xlii.

19. Fitzgerald, *Rubáiyát*, 35.

20. Edward Said notes that the series of extracts or anthology is the quintessential Orientalist form, paraphrasing the views of the French Orientalist Silvestre de Sacy: 'Not only are Oriental literary productions essentially alien to the European; they also do not contain a sustained enough interest, nor are they written with enough "taste and critical spirit," to merit publication except as extracts': *Orientalism*, 128.

21. Annmarie Drury, 'Accident, Orientalism, and Edward Fitzgerald as Translator', *Victorian Poetry*, 46 (2008), 37–53.

22. Drury, 'Accident', especially 47-8. Karlin reads the poem as a non-hierarchical fusion of Eastern and Western elements.

23. Lyall (1845-1920) worked as a civil servant in India throughout the 1870s and 1880s, pursuing his interest in early Arabic literature alongside his official duties, and producing useful books on such matters as *The Transliteration of Hindu and Muhammedan Names* (1885).

24. Lyall emphasizes this 'realistic' quality in the introduction to his *Translations of Ancient Arabian Poetry, Chiefly Præ-Islamic, with an Introduction and Notes* (London and Edinburgh: Williams and Norgate, 1885): 'No poetry better fulfils Mr. Matthew Arnold's definition of "a criticism of life"' (xviii).

25. Lyall's contributions to the journal appeared in vol. 46 (1877), part 1, 61–96, 168–73, and 437–61; and in vol. 47 (1878), part 1, 1–25. These versions appeared in slightly revised form in the 1885 *Translations*.

26. See A. F. L. Beeston et al. eds., *The Cambridge History of Arabic Literature: Arabic Literature to the End of the Umayyad Period* (Cambridge: Cambridge University Press, 1983), 111–3.

27. *Journal of the Asiatic Society of Bengal*, xlvii (1878), Part 1, 15. The 'Tawîl' is the traditional verse form in question. 'Mo'allaqah' is the singular from which the plural 'Mu'allaqat' is formed; the word means 'suspended' in Arabic, a fact which may have given rise to the myth (debunked by Lyall in his *Translations*) that the poems in question were originally written in gold and hung up in the Kaabah in Mecca.

28. The letter is dated 3 June 1878; see A. J. Armstrong, ed., *Intimate Glimpses from Browning's Letter File* (Waco: Baylor University, 1934), 78.

29. Previously unpublished letter of 8 July 1878 (Somerville College MS). I am grateful to Dr Anne Manuel of Somerville College Oxford for locating these letters for me, and to the governing body of the college for permission to quote from them in this essay. Lyall has a scholarly note on the 'slit-eared camels' on pages 19–20 of his translation of 'The Mo'allaqah of Zuheyr'.

30. Letter of 13 Nov. 1881 (Somerville College MS). Browning is responding at the beginning of this letter to a set of translations by Lyall from Hamâseh published in the *Journal of the Asiatic Society of Bengal* vol. 50 (1881), Part 1, 107–147.

31. E. A. Khattab, 'Assimilation and Transformation: Browning's "Muléykeh"', *Journal of Arabic Literature*, 15 (1984), 45–57.

32. For Lyall's letter of 13 Dec. 1884, see *Intimate Glimpses*, 100–1; Browning's reply of 16 Dec. 1884 is at Somerville College.

33. The exception concerned the pronunciation of 'Hakim', which Browning felt would involve too much rewriting. In fact, his suggested changes did not get to the printers in time for the second edition, and had to wait for the third; see letter of 18 Dec. 1884 (Somerville College MS).

34. Robert Browning, 'Muléykeh', in *Dramatic Idyls, Second Series* (London: Smith, Elder and Co., 1880), 58.

35. See Arnold's letter to his mother of 25 December 1867: 'Bunsen used to say that our great business was to get rid of all that was purely Semitic in Christianity, and make it Indo-European'; *Letters of Matthew Arnold*, 2 vols., ed. G. W. E. Russell (London: Macmillan, 1901), i. 443.

36. Walt Whitman, 'Passage to India', in *Leaves of Grass* (Philadelphia: David McKay, 1891–2), 320.

37. In his critique of Said, David Cannadine points out the tendency of the British Empire to reinforce archaic forms of social organization in India as a way of consolidating Imperial control; Cannadine, *Ornamentalism* (Oxford: Oxford University Press, 2001), 42–43.

38. I discuss Browning's earlier poetry, and its intellectual and cultural affiliations with the liberal Imperialism of the early Victorian period, in my 'Robert Browning and Colonialism', *Journal of Victorian Culture*, 8 (2003), 80–107.

39. Lyall, *Translations*, xix, xlv.

40. Browning, 'Through the Metidja to Abd-el-Kadr', in *The Poems of Browning*, 4 vols., ed. John Woolford and Daniel Karlin (London: Longman, 1991), ii. 156.

41. Browning, 'Waring', in *Poems*, ii. 144, 148.

42. Seal first appears in *Black Mischief* (1932).

43. From 'The Song of the Dead' (9–10), part of Kipling's 1893 *A Song of the English*, in *A Choice of Kipling's Verse*, ed. T. S. Eliot (London: Faber and Faber, 1973), 90.

44. Browning, 'Clive', in *Dramatic Idyls, Second Series*, 12. This poem immediately precedes 'Muléykeh' in the volume, and its typically oblique (and not completely flattering)

reflection on the character of an imperial hero might have been intended as a comment on the increasing tendency towards glamorization of these characters.

45. Henry Newbolt, 'Vitaï Lampada', in *Empire Writing: An Anthology of Colonial Literature 1870–1918*, ed. Elleke Boehmer (Oxford: Oxford University Press, 1998), 287–8.

46. 'The White Man's Burden' is, of course, about the United States and the Philippines; as its title implies, the poem attempts to represent Imperial domination as the ineluctable 'burden' of the whole 'white' race.

47. It is, perhaps, this feeling of affinity that underlies the confusing use of the term 'subaltern' in postcolonial criticism to mean the subjects of colonization.

48. Kipling, 'Mandalay', in *Kipling's Verse*, 189.

49. 'The voice of "The Hooligan"' is the title of 'a discussion of Kiplingism' by Robert Buchanan and Sir Walter Besant in the *Contemporary Review* LXXVI (Dec. 1899), 776–789.

50. Robert Buchanan, 'Ballad of Kiplingson', in *The New Rome: Poems and Ballads of Our Empire* (London: Walter Scott, 1898), 67.

51. Ania Loomba, *Colonialism/Postcolonialism* (London: Routledge, 1998), 68.

52. On this aspect of Kipling's work, see Simon Dentith, *Epic and Empire in Victorian Britain* (Cambridge: Cambridge University Press, 2006), especially 165.

53. From the (repugnant) short story 'His Chance in Life'; see *Empire Writing*, 100.

54. Toru Dutt, *Empire Writing*, 69.

55. Dutt, 'Baugmaree', *Ancient Ballads and Legends of Hindustan* (London: Kegan, Paul, Trench, Trübner and Co., 1927), 135.

56. 'The battle lines *between* native and invader are also replicated *within* native and invader . . . the crisis produced by this self-division is at least as psychologically significant as those which attended the more visible contestations of coloniser and colonised', Leela Gandhi, *Postcolonial Theory* (Edinburgh: Edinburgh University Press, 1998), 11–12. For a reading of Dutt's translations from French as an exercise in 'colonial mimicry', see Tricia Lootens, 'Bengal, Britain, France: The Locations and Translations of Toru Dutt', *Victorian Literature and Culture*, 34 (2006), 573–590.

57. Edmund Gosse quoted in *Empire Writing*, 480.

58. According to Ricks's edition, the first 'Locksley Hall' was probably written 1837–8; the second was published in 1886, roughly fifty years later. The 'Sixty Years After' in the title probably alludes to Walter Scott's *Waverley; or, 'Tis Sixty Years Since*.

59. Tennyson, 'The Defence of Lucknow' (1879), in *Empire Writing*, 62.

60. Tennyson, 'Locksley Hall Sixty Years After', in *Tennyson*, 642.

61. For the use of 'crossed' in this sense, as a metaphor drawn from the farm (or the racecourse), see Joseph Phelan, 'Ethnology and Biography: The Case of the Brownings', *Biography*, 26 (2003), 270.

62. This is the relatively common reactionary fantasy of the 'organic society', which also animated some of the poetry of Hopkins and the impassioned prose of Ruskin; see Joseph Phelan, *The Nineteenth-Century Sonnet* (Houndmills: Palgrave, 2005), especially 75–78.

SELECT BIBLIOGRAPHY

Bhabha, Homi, *The Location of Culture* (London: Routledge, 1994).

Boehmer, Elleke, *Colonial and Postcolonial Writing* (Oxford: Oxford University Press, 1995).

——*Empire Writing: An Anthology of Colonial Literature 1870–1918* (Oxford: Oxford University Press, 1998).

Brantlinger, Patrick, *Victorian Literature and Postcolonial Studies* (Edinburgh: Edinburgh University Press, 2009).

Cannadine, David, *Ornamentalism: How the British Saw Their Empire* (Oxford: Oxford University Press, 2001).

Dentith, Simon, *Epic and Empire in Nineteenth-Century Britain* (Cambridge: Cambridge University Press, 2006).

Haddad, Emily, *Orientalist Poetics: The Islamic Middle East in Nineteenth-Century English and French Poetry* (Aldershot: Ashgate, 2002).

Leask, Nigel, *British Romantic Writers and The East: Anxieties of Empire* (Cambridge: Cambridge University Press, 1992).

Loomba, Ania, *Colonialism/Postcolonialism* (London: Routledge, 1998).

Said, Edward, *Culture and Imperialism* (New York: Knopf, 1993).

—— *Orientalism* (London: Penguin, 1987; 1st pub. 1978).

Young, Robert, *Colonial Desire: Hybridity in Theory, Culture and Race* (London: Routledge, 1995).

CHAPTER 50

....

THE JOKES IN THE
MACHINE: COMIC VERSE

....

JAMES WILLIAMS

WHATEVER we take 'comic verse' to mean, we probably don't understand it to be the verse of a type of play distinct from tragedy, as it would have struck a sixteenth-century reader.[1] 'Comedy', like 'heterosexuality' and 'altruism', was a Victorian invention, at least in the common modern sense of 'the action or quality of being amusing'. The *OED* first finds the word so used in 1877, and the citation shows that, as it came to take on its now familiar meaning, 'comedy' was bound up with important ethical and social values. The citation is from George Meredith's essay *On the Idea of Comedy and the Uses of the Comic Spirit*: '[c]omedy is the fountain of sound sense'.[2] Meredith may have been stretching a word here, but he was not, of course, creating a concept out of thin air. Other terms were possible for thinking and talking about what caused laughter and amusement, and any discussion of Victorian 'comic verse' must sooner or later, and preferably sooner, acknowledge the location of its subject matter amidst these shifting vocabularies.

Earlier nineteenth-century writers were more likely to speak in terms of 'humour', especially when they were making elevated claims for it. 'Humour has justly been regarded as the finest perfection of the poetic genius,' wrote Carlyle in 1831,[3] and Tennyson concurred: 'I dare not tell how high I rate humour'.[4] Humour struck serious-minded writers as ethical because it presupposed a kind of sympathetic identification with the source of the amusement. Similar to humour insofar as it tended to produce laughter, but often seen as opposed to it, was 'wit', a form of purely intellectual amusement with no presupposition of sympathy, whose jokes tended to be sharp-edged, cruel, and morally doubtful. Essays on 'Wit and Humour', differentiating and demarcating the terms, occur frequently in nineteenth-century periodicals. As formulaic and commonplace as they often are, these essays bear eloquent testimony to two significant facts: first, that the distinction was of at least notional philosophical significance, and second, that in practice it tended to collapse, hence the perceived need to keep reaffirming it.

Critics have seen the relationships between these terms as part of a bigger cultural history of comedy, recognizable in its outlines, and capable of being narrated. As Stuart M. Tave has shown, the Victorian understanding of humour was the outcome of at least a century and a half of evolution, and a 'part of the larger histories of aesthetics, of nature and of human nature, of man's relation to his fellow man and to God'.[5] The comedy of the Restoration stage was essentially invective, a witty satirizing of folly and wickedness which condemned what it laughed at. The eighteenth century, Tave argued, beat a complex retreat from this understanding of the comic, and by the early nineteenth century a model of 'amiable humour' prevailed which found the roots of comedy in a benevolent appreciation of eccentricity and incongruity. It was in the hands of Romantic writers that this blossomed (or perhaps sprawled) into a model of sympathy itself, a way of reconciling human limitation with intuition of the infinite. 'Man is the only animal that laughs and weeps,' wrote Hazlitt, 'for he is the only animal that is struck with the difference between what things are, and what they ought to be'.[6]

In practice, the high claims made for humour by essayists and moral philosophers could and did coexist with plenty of less earnest laughs, including a good deal of sharp-edged satire (in the likes of Byron, Gilray, or Rowlandson) which showed that the spirit of Restoration wit had not been entirely quashed. Nonetheless it was essentially a worldly, genial, often melancholic model of humour which early Victorian writing inherited from its immediate precursors. John Bowen, acknowledging the work of Vic Gatrell, argues that while the 'forces of respectability' conspired in the 1820s to rein in the bawdier elements of Regency wit, the comedy of Dickens and Thackeray has a recognizably eighteenth-century sensibility, and it was not until the mid-century that the mood of English letters underwent a 'sharp, indeed epochal' shift. The mainstream of English literature becomes 'darker, more pessimistic, less funny', and comic writing drops away from the century's dominant literary form, the novel, and moves into 'what appeared to be minor or marginal modes'.[7] Around the same time, 'amiable humor' could be seen giving way to a 'comedy of the intellect', a resurgence of witty cynicism which Robert Martin saw as a necessary corrective to 'the unrelieved sentimentality of what had been passing as comedy'.[8]

The composite account offered by the historians of Victorian comedy (of which this is a mere sketch) vouches for the importance of comedy to nineteenth-century culture, not just as a source of idle amusement, but as an introspective mode by which Victorian writers investigated questions of moral and social weight, in which they asked themselves who they were and what they valued. It serves as a corrective against an inherited modernist cliché of Victorianism, in which, as Walter Murdoch put it: '[t]he silly nineteenth century seems to have been devised by kindly Providence as a butt for the laughter of the twentieth. We, thank heaven, have a sense of humour (though it is hard to see from whom we have inherited it)'.[9] Ours is a twenty-first century 'we', and hopefully the chips on our shoulders have fallen a little differently. All the same, even the best efforts to historicize or theorize Victorian comedy fall short as hermeneutic keys to unlock the workings of comic writing. To turn from the histories of comedy to examples of Victorian comic verse at work is to encounter the untidy relationship between literary texts and even the most elegant scholarly accounts of their contexts.

What this essay sets out to argue is that for the Victorians comic verse was primarily a matter of text, and only secondarily of context, because it was essentially an exploitation of the comedy inherent in the machinery of poetic form. Here is Clough:

> As I sat in the Café I said to myself,
> They may talk as they please about what they call pelf,
> They may sneer as they like about eating and drinking,
> But help it I cannot, I cannot help thinking,
>> How pleasant it is to have money, heigh-ho!
>> How pleasant it is to have money.
>
> I sit at my table *en grande seigneur,*
> And when I have done, throw a crust to the poor;
> Not only the pleasure itself of good living,
> But also the pleasure of now and then giving:
>> So pleasant it is to have money, heigh-ho!
>> So pleasant it is to have money.[10]

Valentine Cunningham has observed that 'one of the great attractions of Victorian poetry is precisely its impurity, the way it is so open to the new and the newly felt multitudinousness of the Victorian experience,'[11] and Clough's comedy here is brilliantly impure, resisting easy identification with either of the inherited categories of 'humour' or 'wit'. The poem's bluff is that it ventriloquizes the selfish attitudes of the *nouveaux riches* while at the same time drawing us into its charm and brio. The satire is sharply witty, becoming more cynical later, yet the form of the verse is otherwise: there is a winning humour in its brisk rhythms, and its final refrain, however unsympathetic, courts sympathy because a refrain is always an invitation to join in. Its 'heigh-ho!' is easy, 'amiable' even: it takes a double-take to realize that it is in fact the opposite. The poem is open to 'multitudinousness' of tone: its quality is not just in the way it draws on multiple sources of comedy, but the delicate balance in which they are held by the texture of the verse. It is a masterpiece of poise. Affectedly aloof from the world, Clough's speaker might be called a *flâneur* in a modernist poem ('As I sat in the Café I said to myself...'). But the detachment is skin deep: he is also utterly worldly, entangled at the most basic material level in the economic nexus of production and consumption upon which he passes comment.

Clough's complexities show up all the more sharply the limitations of a too rigid critical vocabulary, whether Victorian or contemporary, in the face of the multitudinous impurity of Victorian comic verse. In this light, the late Victorian extension of the word 'comedy' into its roomy modern sense, accommodating both 'humour' and 'wit', signifies a recognition at a cultural level of how far the real phenomenon of comic literature had become unyoked from generic and formulaic constraints. Clough's work shows, too, that Victorian comic verse was sustained, not just by a widening sense of 'comedy', but by the contemporary proliferation of invention and experimentation in poetic form. The poem is a skilful exploitation of the resources of verse, setting refrain and metre in comic tension with the moral qualities of the poem's speaker. Clough's speaker is not like that of a Browning monologue, though he may be just as self-deceiving: the regularity and rhythm of the poem curtails psychological realism, protecting comic verse from reaching for a profundity which would turn it into something else. The task at hand, then, is not merely finding Victorian ideas of comedy reflected in examples of verse, but considering how Victorian poets made use of verse per se to achieve comedy, what it was about verse which made it funny in a different way from prose.

The comic potential of verse was not constrained to poems which set out to be comic. If comedy could be heard in aspects of versification, then it could belong to the hearer as much as to the speaker:

> By the shores of Gitchee Gumee
> By the shining Big-Sea-Water,
> At the doorway of his wigwam,
> In the pleasant Summer morning,
> Hiawatha stood and waited.[12]

Few poems have ever had such serious intentions as Longfellow's *Song of Hiawatha* (1855); yet the Victorians, with their gifts for high drama, high seriousness, and high sentiment, can appear most comic where they themselves least intended it, both to us and to each other. Oscar Wilde's famous quip that '[o]ne must have a heart of stone to read the death of Little Nell without laughing'[13] is both wholly in character, and representative of a more widespread mischief which complicates the boundaries of the comic in the period. Victorian energies, more than a century of criticism attests, have their counter-energies: doubt and faith, prudery and licence, progress and degeneration. The anarchic comedy which offset Victorian earnestness was drawn to those liminal places where the sublime shades into the ridiculous, the tipping points where high moral and cultural aspiration topples into spectacular pratfall. From the moment of its publication, *Hiawatha* fitted the bill:

> He killed the noble mudjokivis,
> With the skin he made him mittens,
> Made them with the fur side inside,
> Made them with the skin side outside,
> He, to get the warm side inside,
> Put the inside skin side outside [14]

Edward Wagenknecht has called *Hiawatha* 'the most parodied poem in the English language'.[15] It was certainly one of the most quickly parodied: this offering by the Reverend George A. Strong appeared within a year of its publication. What Strong responded to, like every parodist after him, was the facile lolloping of the poem's metre. Here, emphasized and reduced to a kind of numbing repetitiousness, the metre is made to beat time for a corresponding reduction of the poem's epic pretensions.

Another Reverend, Charles Lutwidge Dodgson ('Lewis Carroll') published his own parody of the poem, and acknowledged, in some prefatory remarks, his easy and irresistible target:

> In these days of imitation, I can claim no sort of merit for this slight attempt at doing what is known to be so easy. Anyone who knows what verse is, with the slightest ear for rhythm, can throw off a composition in the easy running metre of 'The Song of Hiawatha'.[16]

Carroll's apparent modesty is questionable: it was a touch of *bravura* to bury, just beneath the surface of his prose, the very metre he was discussing ('Ín these dáys of ímitátion, / Í can cláim no sórt of mérit / fór this slíght attémpt at dóing / whát is knówn to bé so éasy...'). The point is persuasively self-demonstrating. No parody of *Hiawatha* could be regarded as successful simply for aping the metre of the original, but must find in that metre some distinctive comic use. For Carroll, it afforded a kind of comic frame, a viewfinder through which to reveal the absurdities of the bourgeois Victorians who were his photographic subjects:

> First the Governor, the Father: ...
> He would hold a scroll of something,
> Hold it firmly in his left-hand;
> He would keep his right-hand buried
> (Like Napoleon) in his waistcoat;
> He would contemplate the distance
> With a look of pensive meaning,
> As of ducks that die in tempests.
> He would gaze into the distance—
>   Grand, heroic was the notion:
> Yet the picture failed entirely:
> Failed because he moved a little [17]

'Grand, heroic was the notion' is the key line here, and it is *Hiawatha*'s aspirations to grandeur and heroism that are satirized and put to service. Longfellow's metre, modelled loosely on that of the Finnish epic *Kalevala* and unnatural to English, was deliberately estranging, intended to create the impression of a culturally remote and primitive civilization. Coupled with the poem's *outré* diction, it can sometimes verge on collapsing into a kind of inspired nonsense ('Like a bowstring snapped asunder, / Came the wild goose, Waw-be-wawa; /...Mahng the loon, with clangorous pinions, / The blue heron, the Shuh-shuh-gah...'),[18] yet it is rarely outright funny, and is capable of moments of strange beauty. Lewis Carroll brought to the poem a finely tuned gift for, in Gillian Beer's words, 'viewing askance the assumptions buried in poetic forms'.[19] Precisely those epic, unfamiliar, far-away qualities which Longfellow strove to signify with his poem's drumbeat are humorously conferred upon the modern family. Their putting on airs is given a metrical embodiment, and the result is bathetic, just as the transposition of the vigorous rhythm to the technical process of photography—'Finally he fixed each picture / With a saturate solution / Of a certain salt of Soda...'—implicitly contrasts the modern banal with the ancient heroic.

The parodic afterlife of *Hiawatha* is important for comic verse because it turns so unmistakably on the comedy the Victorians heard in metre, especially when unusual, or unusually emphasized. In an age of expansive metrical and formal experimentation, this meant a widening field of possibilities for comedy. It may not have been metre alone which made Tennyson's 'The Higher Pantheism' ripe for parody, full as it is of earnest, self-conscious searching: 'Is not the Vision He? tho' He be not that which He seems? / Dreams are true while they last, and do we not live in dreams?'[20] Nevertheless it was the poem's metre, its strained and straining heptameters, in which Swinburne heard the authentic ring of absurdity, and which gives his 'Higher Pantheism in a Nutshell' purchase: 'God, whom we see not, is, and God, who is not, we see: / Fiddle, we know, is diddle: and diddle, we take it, is dee'.[21] The vogue around the mid-century for the hexameter serves as a further case in point. Put to the service of serious poetic experiment in Longfellow's *Evangeline,* the young Lewis Carroll found it pregnant with humour when matched with the rising and falling of a more worldly, chatty voice:

> Well, *if* you must know all the facts, I was merely reading a pamphlet
> When what should I hear at the door but a knock as soft as a Zephyr.
> I listened and heard it again, so, as loud as I possibly *could* call,
> I shouted, 'Don't stand waiting there, come in, let me know who you are, sir!'[22]

What Longfellow sought, with some success, to reclaim as a serious cadence for English verse, a clever student, well-drilled in Latin, was already adept at parodying. The finest Victorian hexameters, those of Clough's *The Bothie of Tober-na-Vuolich* (1848) and *Amours de Voyage* ten years later, were brilliant precisely for their assured seriocomic balance, the way they take the weight of their own comic potential without ever fully yielding to it.[23]

Lewis Carroll's example brings this potential to the fore, and we see it in the italics into which he strains, signalling points of stress where the voice must be made to fit the metre. William Empson observed that most poetry exhibits 'a tension between the pronunciation demanded by the form and that demanded by the feeling', and he draws attention to the double-consciousness with which we read under the obligation of both demands: '[t]wo rival ways of scanning the line are both being used at once'.[24] If Empson is right then all metrical verse must find accommodation between the demands of form and of feeling, but the distinction of comic metre is in the way it exploits the implications of that word 'rival'. Comedy seeks out this rivalry and plays it up for effect. The overwhelming majority of Victorian comic verse is written with a prominent metrical beat, and it makes us hear metre as something at odds with feeling, an anarchic energy working against sincerity and seriousness. It puts the rivalry between metre and feeling at the centre of the poet's art.

A celebrated patter song from W. S. Gilbert's *Iolanthe* (1882), for example, contains plenty of distress but very little pathos:

When you're lying awake with a dismal headache, and repose is taboo'd by anxiety,
I conceive you may use any language you choose to indulge in, without impropriety;
For your brain is on fire—the bedclothes conspire of usual slumber to plunder you:
First your counterpane goes, and uncovers your toes, and your sheet slips
demurely from under you;
Then the blanketing tickles—you feel like mixed pickles—so terribly sharp is the
pricking,
And you're hot, and you're cross, and you tumble and toss till there's nothing
'twixt you and the ticking.[25]

The Lord Chancellor's stock comic role, that of licentious old man, makes his sleepless nights of unrequited passion fair game: he is someone whose feelings we do not need to take very seriously. This effect is underscored by the way Gilbert's lyrics, running along in their dactylic rattle, set up a stock pattern in which the emotionally real can be simultaneously flirted with and cancelled. A lot is off-key here—the Lord Chancellor's love for Phyllis, his ward, really is 'taboo'd'; there is the queasy sense that perhaps more than just his brain is 'on fire'. Then there is the awkward semantic penumbra of 'pricking'— the subject-matter, coldly stated, causes 'anxiety' on multiple levels, but such trouble can never gather tragic dignity so long as it keeps running up against the unrelenting diddly-diddle of Gilbert's metre. This is not merely comedy in verse but comic verse, because it exploits what the Victorians found most comical in versification: the resistance of metre to feeling. As with many qualities which are comic, this could be darkly troubling; contrary to the implication of Bowen's 'darker . . . less funny', perhaps darkest when funniest.

Comic verse in many periods is metrically patterned, but the consciousness of that metre as something alien, a rival to feeling, is particularly nineteenth-century. The Victorians were inheritors of a Romantic debate between a Coleridgean view of metre as expressive of emotion, and a Wordsworthian account which saw it as containing or counterbalancing emotion. In a celebrated passage of the 'Preface' to *Lyrical Ballads* (1800), Wordsworth set out the view which ultimately won out in Victorian prosody, that metre was something which holds feeling in check:

> if the words by which this excitement is produced are in themselves powerful, or the images and feelings have an undue proportion of pain connected with them, there is some danger that the excitement may be carried beyond its proper bounds. Now the co-presence of something regular, something to which the mind has been accustomed when in an unexcited or a less exciting state, cannot but have great efficacy in tempering and restraining the passion by an intertexture of ordinary feeling.[26]

Wordsworth's 'intertexture' sees metre as something 'regular', 'ordinary', not opposed to emotion per se; yet the implication was there that the measured patterns of verse might be something quite removed from the communicative and expressive aspects of language.

What Wordsworth saw as well-tempered emotion had other qualities in other hands. Byron, in *Don Juan* (1819–24), makes frequent sport with the disparity between content and printed form:

> Her memory was a mine: she knew by heart
>   All Calderon and greater part of Lope,
> So that if any actor miss'd his part
>   She could have served him for the prompter's copy;
> For her Feinagle's were an useless art,
>   And he himself obliged to shut up shop—he
> Could never make a memory so fine as
> That which adorn'd the brain of Donna Inez.[27]

The rhyme of 'Lope' with 'copy' sends us back two lines, readjusting our natural pronunciation towards 'Loppy' and exaggerating the metrical shape; reading forward, the eye encounters 'shop—he', an awkward collision of words which pulls the rhythm away from natural speech and towards 'shoppy', again making us more aware of the 'feminine' falling-off (/ x)which shapes the line ending. Insist on a correct pronunciation of 'Inez', and the rhyme is out of kilter: it must fall in line, as 'Eye-nez', if the couplet is to work. Byron's verse delights in these moments where what the poem says strains against the form in which it says it: there is a curious sense, which Richard Cronin has argued is characteristic of Victorian poetry, 'that the metre seems self-conscious, as if imposed on the poem'.[28]

In a typical Byronic paradox, this dimension of his verse is both part of the snook *Don Juan* cocks at Wordsworthian poetics, and one of the major channels through which that poetics was inherited by his successors. Byron anticipates the direction of Victorian poetry in that his versification makes us repeatedly aware of form as a restraint upon voice, something pressing on it from without. The poem demands and employs what Eric Griffiths has called a 'doubled consciousness of metrical language',[29] the consequences of which for Victorian poetry are profound. Yet humour was among its first effects. Byron's 'doubled consciousness' reads, as often as not, like a comic double-act with real back-and-forward repartee. It was this rollicking doggerel quality which Byron bequeathed to the poets of the 1820s and 30s. A stanza by his contemporary, Horatio Smith, shows it becoming part of the stock-in-trade of poetical comedy:

> One of the Kings of Scanderoon,
>   A Royal Jester,
> Had in his train a gross buffoon,
>   Who used to pester
> The Court with tricks inopportune,
> Venting on the highest folks his
> Scurvy pleasantries and hoaxes.[30]

The final couplet, finding 'hoaxes' at the last minute to rhyme with 'folks his', is recognizably Byronic, though it is something of an automatic flourish, like a rabbit pulled from a hat, by contrast with the sustained high-wire act of *Don Juan*. In Smith's work, Byron's wit is being assimilated into what would become a standard comic style in which metre is played up for laughs (and, given its title, 'The Jester Condemned to Death', potentially anxious laughs).

Byron's comic legacy was a self-awareness of verse as verse, and part of the joy of comic verse, for the Victorians as for us, was the ingenuity of saying something in verse at all. Put this way, verse starts to look a good deal like the Victorian account of 'wit', and in much comic poetry there is a sense that the thrill of formal manipulation has become something of an intellectual game. Here, for example, is the forgotten Reverend Orlando Thomas Dobbins, one of the few contemporaries William Michael Rossetti included in his anthology of *Humorous Poems* (1872), but whom the *Dictionary of National Biography* now passes over in silence:

> Confound their saucy-looking whiskers!
> Confound them whether staid or friskers!
> Confound their midnight squeally discourse!
>   Confound the Cats!
> Confound their roof-ridge caterwaulings—
> Their spittings, hissings, skirlings, squallings,
> And their still more lugubrious miaulings—
>   Confound the Cats!
> Confound all Cats ! Whate'er the fashion—
> Persian, Manx, Maltese, or Circassian,
> The sleek young Kit, or skinny passé one—
>   Confound the Cats![31]

The wit here is largely in keeping so constrictive a frame going for so long (it continues for many more stanzas). Victorian prosodists, Yopie Prins has observed, 'increasingly conceptualized meter as a formal grid or pattern of spacing',[32] an abstract paradigm which could easily seem unsettlingly perfect and inhuman. Poetry demanded a moderation, a softening of this abstraction if it was not to be pulled down into banality; but comic verse offered another way out, by rising to the challenge of that rigidity with dexterous ingenuity, pushing 'passé one' in line with 'Circassian', or 'friskers' with 'discourse' in order to keep its plates spinning.

For Victorian poets, comedy was a potential inherent in the very act of versifying, something prompted by the metrical arrangement of words. Wordsworth's account of metre as the 'co-presence of something regular' refracted through the lens of Victorian comic verse finds an illuminating echo a century later in Henri Bergson's *Laughter* (1900). For Bergson, 'any arrangement of acts and events is comic which gives us, in a single combination, the illusion of life and the distinct impression of a mechanical arrangement'.[33] The 'mechanical' is that which creates patterns and rhythms, and comedy is the result when human beings get caught up in them. The man in the street who slips on a banana skin is comical, in this view, because he cannot adapt his movements quickly enough to his change of circumstances: his involuntary forward momentum is characterized by 'a certain *mechanical inelasticity*, just where one would expect to find the wide awake adaptability and the living pliableness of a human being'.[34]

Whatever the limitations of Bergson's view as an account of the universal phenomenon of the comic, it describes with remarkable accuracy the relationship between voice and metre which we encounter in Victorian comic verse. Bergson's 'mechanical' corresponds to Wordsworth's 'regular', and that tempering 'co-presence', when played for laughs, is the imposition of a kind of rigidity onto what ought to be the living, pliable voice. 'A comic effect is always obtainable', observes Bergson, 'by transposing the natural expression of ideas into another key'.[35] 'Another key' here suggests 'other than natural': it catches metre's contrast between the humane and the abstract, and comedy frequently demands that the latter triumph over, or at least rein in, the former, as in Gilbert's account of the Lord Chancellor's sufferings. Comic verse is not a welcoming habitat for pathos, and when it touches on raw emotion it typically deadens it: a quality 'something like a momentary anesthesia of the heart', which Bergson saw as fundamental to all comedy.[36]

Bergson's metaphor of the 'mechanical' was a product of the larger nineteenth-century experience of living in an industrialized society. Although *Laughter* does not explicitly discuss metre, there is in all the arts, as Valéry pointed out, 'a physical component which can no longer . . . remain unaffected by our modern knowledge and power',[37] and Victorian prosody too was post-industrial. The perception of metre as abstract sequence generates a conception of verse as a kind of machinery, a formal contraption into which the writer can pour the raw materials of thought and feeling. This resonated with the Victorian double-mindedness about the mechanical: attraction to the sheer thrill of industrial clatter, and repulsion by its dehumanizing potential. John Hollander has written that 'to analyze the meter of a poem is not so much to scan it, as to show with what other poems its . . . formal elements associate it'.[38] Victorian poetry readily confirms the truth of this remark while querying its limits: why stop at 'other poems', when the rhythms of verse rang with other 'associations', such as the ambient noise of machinery?

> A tune was born in my head last week,
> Out of the thump-thump and shriek-shriek
> Of the train, as I came by it, up from Manchester;
> And when, next week, I take it back again,
> My head will sing to the engine's clack again,
> While it only makes my neighbour's haunches stir,
> —Finding no dormant musical sprout
> In him, as in me, to be jolted out.

Browning's poem brilliantly stage-manages 'thump-thump and shriek-shriek' without merely aping it. It holds back from too easily aligning the rhythms of the train and the verse, though this trick would be easy to do (it was the just-post-Victorian Charles Wing who, in 1906, published the 'Story of the Engine that Thought It Could', its famous mechanical-metrical refrain passing into American popular culture like a self-help *Hiawatha*). Browning's poem's comedy is exquisitely subtle. When the verse pulls in line with the engine's regularity it is to emphasize the modern comedy of life lived to railway timetables ('. . . And when, next week, I take it back again, / My head will sing to the engine's clack again'). Yet Browning feels too acutely the 'multitudinousness of the Victorian experience', and his metrical train is not machinery as imagined perfection ('it runs like clockwork...'), but the lived experience of machinery, sensitive to its little irregularities, 'jolted' as it passes over poorly laid track, registering the stirring of the passengers' haunches.[39]

A Bergsonian account of metre offers a way of theorizing the essential intuitions of Victorian comic verse, but the very best examples of the genre will always test the limits of theorizing. The ideal of 'amiable humour' stressed the element of incongruity in human behaviour, which metre, with its tensions between rigidity and flexibility, offered a way of modelling. If that is the only incongruity on offer, though, the result rapidly becomes too congruous. In the poems of Thomas Hood, incongruities of different kinds are finely cross-hatched, as in the ballad spoken by 'Toby, the Sapient Pig', a real pig celebrated in London in 1817 for feats ranging from writing to mind-reading, and thereafter retired, so Hood imagines, to a less celebrated end:

> Of what avail that I could spell
>   And read, just like my betters,
> If I must come to this at last,
>   To litters, not to letters?
>
> O, why are pigs made scholars of?
>   It baffles my discerning,
> What griskins, fry, and chittlerings,
>   Can have to do with learning.
>
> Alas! My learning once drew cash,
>   But public fame's unstable,
> So I must turn a pig again,
>   And fatten for the table.[40]

The prima facie incongruity of a learned pig is only the start. Toby pointedly draws our attention to the discrepancy of a scholar fattened for the table, and if the historical Toby was not quite so brilliant as Hood's speaker, he was at least a real prodigy. The sense of Toby's preternatural articulacy is compounded by the poem's formal elegance, and metre and rhyme once again lend pattern and order humorously at odds with subject matter. Those same prosodic features give a weight and a particular shape to Toby's fate: heard through these ballad stanzas, the learned pig is already on his way to being immortalized even as he contemplates his impending mortality. Metrical pattern is emphasized and regular, and this is not incidental in a poem whose central lament is that the speaker's life is conforming, with accursed inevitability, to an expected pattern. That sense is underscored by the poem's rhymes snapping shut, locking each stanza into place: the complaint that 'public fame's unstable' is met with 'fatten for the table', and in the following stanza 'my eyes get red and leaky' sets up what 'red and white, and streaky' knocks down.

In spite of this, what we learn from 'Toby' is not simply that shape (whether anatomical or poetical) is destiny. Like so much fine Victorian comic verse there is a liberty, and levity, at work precisely where ingenuity of language meets constraints of form. The comic doubling of metre and meaning has its back-and-forth banter which, in Hood, gathers around his irrepressible, sometimes acrobatic, punning. 'Good bye to the poetic Hogg! / The philosophic Bacon!' does double work as illustrative analogy and sharply fleshly description, and the slide from 'litters…to letters' enacts that paradox of proximity and disparity at the heart of what makes Toby's tale comic. Empson made a good point when he observed how Victorian verse 'uses puns to back away from the echoes and implications of words, to distract your attention by insisting on its ingenuity, so that you can escape from sinking into the meaning'.[41] Hood's ingenuity undercuts real pathos, the verse finding comedy where the sentiments pull another way. It is not only words which have 'echoes and implications', however, but forms of speech too: the fiction that Toby might wittily play off 'litters' against 'letters' at the same time renders him absurdly comic and makes his impending slaughter obscene. Ingenuity here is both 'wit' and 'humour': distraction from meaning, and an uncomfortable dimension of it.

I have argued that the very fabric of comic verse conspires to make certain conjunctions of form and feeling impossible. Tragedy demands emotional engagement, it insists that suffering be accorded dignity and weight: comic metres keep the voice bouncing along with an implication of weightlessness. A tragic limerick, then, should be impossible. Yet in the hands of Edward Lear this axiom is pushed to its limits:

> There was an Old Man of Cape Horn,
> Who wished he had never been born;
> So he sat on a chair, till he died of despair,
> That dolorous Man of Cape Horn.[42]

Lear's verse harmonizes at a profound level with some of the most melancholy poetical impulses of the age, and in particular with a Tennysonian poetics of belated despair. The Old Man of Cape Horn is another 'Mariana', whose story is similarly unresolved and unresolvable. Lear makes the limerick form a strange ally here: in the hands of a gifted practitioner it was one of the battery of exquisite contraptions available to Victorian poets for modelling incompleteness and inaction. With its return to the A-rhyme, it has, like the stanza of *In Memoriam,* an inbuilt collapse of momentum, falling back to return to where it started.

In Lear's case this effect is exaggerated, since a feature of his limericks was always to end by repeating the last word of the first line—the earliest printed limericks, such as the *Anecdotes and Adventures of Fifteen Gentlemen* (1822) do not do this, and most later limerick writers have not emulated it. On the contrary, the genius of the limerick form is often seen as residing precisely in that final line and its capacity to set up a punch. Once again, parody provides an example which sheds light on the outlines, and fault-lines, of the Victorian sense of humour:

> There was a young man of Cape Horn
> Who wished he had never been born;
>   Nor would he have been
>   If his father had seen
> That the end of the rubber was torn.[43]

For many modern aficionados, Swinburne's parody (if it is Swinburne's) stands up as a much better limerick than Lear's original. It is funny, for starters; and edgy, irreverent, and end-weighted in the way that Emile Cammaerts described as 'staking its all on the *witticism* disclosed by the strong line and on the *ingenuity* of the rhyme'.[44] It packs the expected punch. In the words of one of the numerous Victorian essays on 'Wit and Humour', wit 'marries ideas, lying wide apart, by a sudden jerk of the understanding'.[45]

R. L. Mégroz wrote that Edward Lear's custom of repeating the rhyming word in limericks was a way of avoiding the shift 'from pure nonsense to wit'.[46] This stands as one of the finest critical observations on Lear, because it recognizes in his limericks not merely a failure to be witty, but an active rejection of the impulse to wit. The pointedness of that clever final line was, for Lear, too close to the business of making a point. His limericks are deliberately blunt things, which may offer none of the pleasures of wit, but which court none of its vices either: attitudinizing, moralizing, reducing complexity to neat maxims. Wit is intellectual comedy, and to intellectualize is usually to pronounce judgement. Those cutting final lines always walk on a tightrope between comic dexterity and mere glibness.

Swinburne's tale of the 'young man of Cape Horn' (with the certainty of youth, perhaps) is explained for us neatly. The 'Old Man of Cape Horn' is verse that keeps plenty of things up in the air, but it would be hard to call it 'light'. An earlier draft, now in the Koch collection at Yale, suggested a way out: 'He sate on a chair and behaved like a bear, / That intrinsic old man of Cape Horn'.[47] 'Intrinsic' is a favourite Lear adjective meaning nothing at all and at the same time pregnant with the suggestion of inscrutable complexity. Simply the thing he is will make the Old Man live: but when Lear revised the poem in the 1846 *Book of Nonsense,* that 'intrinsic' is somehow not enough. Another 'Old Man', of Peru, takes on the bear-like traits, and the Old Man of Cape Horn can do nothing but sit and expire.

Lear was a life-long depressive, and the frequent flirtation of his nonsense with mortality tests the edges of what comic verse might be. In his limericks we often find him articulating, with deftness and charm, a suicidal impulse which he both courted and resisted. His early comic verse (the limericks are mostly from the 1830s to the 1850s) is in this respect recognizably marked by eighteenth-century and Romantic ideas of comedy, both in remaining benign and 'amiable', however dark its hints, and for its conformity with Coleridge's dictum (following the German humourist and critic Jean Paul Richter) that 'Humour and pathos are generally blended together'.[48] In this connection, Lear represents a distinctively early nineteenth-century tradition with long repercussions throughout Victorian verse, but to contrast Lear's amiable, melancholic, early Victorian 'humour' with Swinburne's barbed, late Victorian 'wit' is too simple. In many of the limericks Lear employs wordplay, a characteristic weapon of wit, to create carefully poker-faced ambiguities which embody the very questions of feeling upon which his Romantic humour rests. Consider, for example, the 'Old Person of Tartary': 'Who divided his jugular artery; / But he screeched to his wife, and she said, "Oh, my life! / Your death will be felt by all Tartary!"'[49] Lear's keynote here may be sympathy, but there is a recognizable wit in the manipulation of 'will be felt'. It means both 'will affect emotionally' (all Tartary will grieve for you), 'will be perceived' (all Tartary heard that 'screech'), and 'will have dire repercussions for' (all Tartary must pay for driving you to this). Writing a limerick about a brutal suicide throws into the air so many mixed feelings that only a stroke of cool genius would make its final line pivot on an ambiguity around the word 'felt'. The playful dance of related senses goes on, comically and emotionally alive, apparently unaffected by Bergson's anaesthesia.

This strain of dark foolery in Lear links his work to that of his close contemporary, Thomas Lovell Beddoes, which represents a strain in Romantic comedy that forms a bridge between the mordant stage nonsense of the Shakespearean fools, and the verse of the Victorians. The song of Isbrand, the court fool, was written in 1825–9, but first published in 1850. In Edmund Gosse's edition of 1890 it appeared as follows:

> I'll not be a fool, like the nightingale
> Who sits up all midnight without any ale,
>   Making a noise with his nose;
> Nor a camel, though 'tis a beautiful back;
> Nor a duck, notwithstanding the music of quack,
>   And the webby, mud-patting toes.
> I'll be a new bird with the head of an ass,
>   Two pigs' feet, two men's feet, and two of a hen;
> Devil-winged; dragon-bellied; grave-jawed, because grass
>   Is a beard that's soon shaved, and grows seldom again
>   Before it is summer; so cow all the rest;
>   The new Dodo is finished. O! Come to my nest.[50]

Reading Beddoes alongside Lear offers a sense of the counterbalance that humour offers to violent emotion. There is, at the heart of this song, a longing for extinction, a self-conscious identification with a zoological dead end. 'The new Dodo is finished' doesn't quite play off the idiom 'dead as a dodo' (which enters English at the start of the twentieth century), but it assumes the knowledge that the bird was long extinct, and dodos came in the Victorian period to refer to anything so ill-adapted to survival as to be moribund. As in Lear, nonsensical humour subordinates wit while keeping it nonetheless in play. Isbrand's final flourish, 'the new Dodo is finished. O! Come to my nest' is a rhetorical turn full of both creation and destruction. With the slippery wordplay of a stage fool, he lends to 'finished' a double sense of 'perfected', 'passed through the last … stage of manufacture', and more bluntly, 'ended'. There is a slyly blasphemous echo, too, of Christ's last words from the cross: 'It is finished' (John 19:30).

What Beddoes shares with Lear is the lightness of touch which his verse brings to bear on this apparent death-wish. These poems appear early in Victoria's reign, but we find the same quality at the end of the century, too, for example in the darkly droll dialect verse of Kipling's *Barrack-room Ballads* (1892).[51] For the finest comic poets, the 'co-presence' of metre is something permissive, a kind of folly which begs pardon for the darkest, but most human, desires: neither a Wordsworthian tranquillity in which to recollect emotion, nor quite a Bergsonian mechanism with which to cancel it. Theorists of humour from Kant to Freud have imagined jokes as sudden releases of tension, but Victorian comic verse at its subtlest is something richer, discovering in the nexus of verse a battery of devices which permit feeling to be contained without depreciation of its force and put into play without becoming the only game in town. The overlay of metre on the voice, for Victorian poetry, generates tension, but the best comic verse helps us live with the tension without being overwhelmed by it. It is a way of learning, in other words, how to be human: as Meredith put it, 'the fountain of sound sense'.[52]

NOTES

1. *OED* 'comic', adj., 1.
2. *OED* 'comedy', n.¹, 2c.
3. Thomas Carlyle, 'Schiller', in H. D. Traill, ed., *The Works of Thomas Carlyle*, 30 vols. (London: Chapman & Hall, 1896–99), xxvii. 200–201.
4. Hallam Tennyson, *Alfred, Lord Tennyson: A Memoir by his Son*, 2 vols. (London: Macmillan, 1897), i. 167.
5. Stuart M. Tave, *The Amiable Humorist: A Study in the Comic Theory and Criticism of the 18th and Early 19th Centuries* (Chicago: University of Chicago Press, 1960), vii.
6. William Hazlitt, in, P. P. Howe, ed., *Complete Works*, (London and Toronto: J. M. Dent & Sons, 1930), 68.
7. John Bowen, 'Comic and Satirical', in Kate Flint, ed., *The Cambridge History of Victorian Literature* (Cambridge: Cambridge University Press, 2012), 266–267.
8. Robert Bernard Martin, *The Triumph of Wit: A Study of Victorian Comic Theory* (Oxford: Clarendon Press, 1974), 38.
9. Walter Murdoch, 'Laughing at Tennyson', cited in Matthew Bevis, 'Tennyson's Humour', in Robert Douglas-Fairhurst and Seamus Perry, eds., *Tennyson Among the Poets* (Oxford: Oxford University Press, 2009), 231–232.
10. Arthur Hugh Clough, from *Dipsychus*, in A. L. P. Norrington, ed., *The Poems of Arthur Hugh Clough* (Oxford: Clarendon Press, 1968), 242.
11. Valentine Cunningham, ed., *The Victorians: An Anthology of Poetry and Poetics* (Oxford: Blackwell, 2000), xxxv.
12. Henry Wadsworth Longfellow, *The Song of Hiawatha*, in *Longfellow: Poetical Works* (London: Oxford University Press, 1904), 269.
13. Ada Leverson, *Letters to the Sphinx: From Oscar Wilde, with Reminiscences of the Author* (London: Duckworth, 1930), 39–40.
14. George A. Strong, 'The Modern Hiawatha', in John Gross, ed., *The Oxford Book of Comic Verse* (Oxford: Oxford University Press, 1994), 176.
15. Cited in Jack Sullivan, *New World Symphonies* (New Haven and London: Yale University Press, 1999), 47–48.
16. Lewis Carroll, *Jabberwocky and Other Nonsense: Collected Poems*, ed. Gillian Beer (London: Penguin, 2012), 129.
17. Carroll, 'Hiawatha's Photographing', in *Jabberwocky and Other Nonsense*, 130.
18. Longfellow, *Poetical Works*, 266.
19. Gillian Beer (ed. and notes) in Carroll, *Jabberwocky and Other Nonsense*, xi.
20. Alfred Lord Tennyson, 'The Higher Pantheism', in *Tennyson: The Major Works*, ed. Adam Roberts (Oxford: Oxford University Press, 2000), 379.

21. Algernon Charles Swinburne, 'The Higher Pantheism in a Nutshell', in *Collected Poetical Works*, 2 vols. (London: William Heinemann, 1924), ii. 787–788.

22. Carroll, 'A Visitor', in *Jabberwocky and Other Nonsense*, 23.

23. For a fuller account of Clough's metre, see Yopie Prins, 'Victorian meters', in Joseph Bristow, ed., *The Cambridge Companion to Victorian Poetry* (Cambridge: Cambridge University Press, 2006), 102–106.

24. William Empson, 'Rhythm and Imagery in English Poetry', *British Journal of Aesthetics*, 2 (1962), 42.

25. W. S. Gilbert, 'Song' from *Iolanthe* in Ed Glinert, ed., *The Complete Gilbert and Sullivan* (London: Penguin, 2006), 289.

26. William Wordsworth, 'Preface to *Lyrical Ballads*' (1800), in W. J. B. Owen and Jane Worthington Smyser, eds., *The Prose Works of William Wordsworth*, 3 vols. (Oxford: Clarendon Press, 1974), i. 146.

27. Lord Byron, *Don Juan* I.xi, in Frederick Page and John D. Jump, eds. *Byron: Complete Poetical Works*, ed. (Oxford: Oxford University Press, 1970), 638.

28. Richard Cronin, *Reading Victorian Poetry* (Malden, Mass and Oxford: Wiley-Blackwell, 2012), 68.

29. Eric Griffiths, *The Printed Voice of Victorian Poetry* (Oxford: Clarendon Press, 1989), 73.

30. Horace Smith, 'The Jester Condemned to Death', in *Gaieties and Gravities: A Series of Sketches, Comic Tales, and Fugitive Vagaries* (London: Henry Colburn, 1825), ii. 219.

31. Orlando Dobbin, 'A Dithyramb on Cats', in William Michael Rossetti, ed., *Humorous Poems*, ed. (London: E. Moxon, Son, & Company, 1872), 354.

32. Prins, 'Victorian meters', 90.

33. Henri Bergson, *Laughter: An Essay on the Meaning of the Comic* (Mineola NY: Dover Publications, 2005), 34.

34. Bergson, *Laughter*, 5.

35. Bergson, *Laughter*, 60–1.

36. Bergson, *Laughter*, 3.

37. Paul Valéry, 'La conquête de l'ubiquité', quoted in Walter Benjamin, *Illuminations*, trans. Harry Zorn, ed. Hannah Arendt (London: Jonathan Cape, 1970), 211.

38. John Hollander, *Vision and Resonance: Two Senses of Poetic Form*, 2nd edn. (New Haven and London: Yale University Press, 1985), 162.

39. Robert Browning, 'Christmas-Eve', in John Pettigrew and Thomas J. Collins, eds., *Robert Browning: The Poems* (Harmondsworth: Penguin, 1981), i. 469.

40. Thomas Hood, 'Toby, the Sapient Pig', in Susan J. Wolfson and Peter J. Manning, eds. *Selected Poems of Thomas Hood, Winthrop Mackworth Praed and Thomas Lovell Beddoes*, ed. (London: Penguin, 2000), 64.

41. William Empson, *Seven Types of Ambiguity* (Harmondsworth: Penguin, 1972; 1st pub. 1930), 137.

42. Edward Lear, 'There was an Old Man of Cape Horn', in *The Complete Verse and Other Nonsense* (London: Penguin, 2001), 97.

43. Attributed to Algernon Charles Swinburne, in E. O. Parrott, ed., *The Penguin Book of Limericks* (London: Allen Lane, 1983), 28.

44. Emile Cammaerts, *The Poetry of Nonsense* (London: Routledge, 1925), 5.

45. Edwin Whipple, 'Wit and Humour', *Hogg's Weekly Instructor*, 5 (1850), 167.

46. R. L. Mégroz, ed., *The Lear Omnibus* (London: Thomas Nelson and Sons, 1938), 18.

47. Lear, *The Complete Verse and Other Nonsense*, 485.

48. Samuel Taylor Coleridge, lecture on 'Wit and Humour' (1818), in Thomas Middleton Raysor, ed., *Miscellaneous Criticism* (Cambridge, Mass: Harvard University Press, 1936), 113.

49. Edward Lear, 'There was an Old Person of Tartary', in *Complete Verse and Other Nonsense*, 77.

50. Thomas Lovell Beddoes, 'Song by Isbrand', in Wolfson and Manning, eds., *Selected Poems of Thomas Hood, Winthrop Mackworth Praed and Thomas Lovell Beddoes*, 289.

51. Try, for example, Rudyard Kipling, 'Danny Deever', in Daniel Karlin, ed., *The Oxford Authors: Rudyard Kipling* (Oxford: Oxford University Press, 1999), 433–434.

52. George Meredith, *An Essay on Comedy and the Uses of the Comic Spirit*, standard edn. (London: Constable, 1919), 28.

SELECT BIBLIOGRAPHY

Bowen, John, 'Comic and Satirical', in Kate Flint, ed., *The Cambridge History of Victorian Literature* (Cambridge: Cambridge University Press, 2012).

Carroll, Lewis, *Jabberwocky and Other Nonsense: Collected Poems*, ed. Gillian Beer (London: Penguin, 2012).

Glinert, Ed, ed., *The Complete Gilbert and Sullivan* (London: Penguin, 2006).

Gross, John, ed., *The Oxford Book of Comic Verse* (Oxford: Oxford University Press, 1994).

Lear, Edward, *The Complete Verse and Other Nonsense*, ed. Vivian Noakes (London: Penguin, 2001).

Martin, Robert Bernard, *The Triumph of Wit: A Study of Victorian Comic Theory* (Oxford: Clarendon Press, 1974).

Rossetti, William Michael, ed., *Humorous Poems* (London: E. Moxon, Son, & Company, 1872).

Sypher, Wylie, ed., *Comedy* (Baltimore and London: Johns Hopkins University Press) [contains both George Meredith, *On the Idea of Comedy*, and Henri Bergson, *Laughter*].

Tave, Stuart M., *The Amiable Humorist: A Study in the Comic Theory and Criticism of the 18th and Early 19th Centuries* (Chicago: University of Chicago Press, 1960).

Wolfson, Susan J. and Manning, Peter, eds., *Selected Poems of Thomas Hood, Winthrop Mackworth Praed and Thomas Lovell Beddoes* (London: Penguin, 2000).

CHAPTER 51

....

'THE SONG-BIRD WHOSE NAME IS LEGION': BAD VERSE AND ITS CRITICS

....

DANIEL KARLIN

AT the mention of 'bad Victorian verse', two Leviathans swim into our ken: Martin Farquhar Tupper and William McGonagall. But both are red herrings. Tupper's *Proverbial Philosophy* had a popular energy no one in Britain knew what to do with; it took the genius of Walt Whitman to harness its mighty stream of commonplace. By the mid-century Tupper had become merely a bogey-man for 'respectable' poetic aspirants.[1] He is no longer with us; McGonagall, by contrast, is our Kitsch Poet Laureate:

> Beautiful Railway Bridge of the Silv'ry Tay!
> Alas! I am very sorry to say
> That ninety lives have been taken away
> On the last Sabbath day of 1879,
> Which will be remember'd for a very long time.[2]

McGonagall's awfulness was relished in his own lifetime, and the cruel side to such 'homage' has died away: he is affectionately tagged as a Great British Eccentric.[3] McGonagall's fame, like that of most 'naïve' artists, may be perverse, but it is real, because it is founded on something solid and enduring, the smugness of his 'admirers'. This essay is concerned with judgements of 'badness' that are less self-pleasing.

I begin with a necessary distinction between two kinds of bad verse. The first—on which this essay will concentrate—is poetry which represents the mediocre accomplishment of its day. The second comprises work by poets we now think of as 'major' figures. The hostile reviews of Tennyson's *Poems, Chiefly Lyrical* (1830) and *Poems* (1832), of Robert Browning's *Sordello* (1840), and of Swinburne's *Poems and Ballads* (1866), are examples of such attacks at the outset of a poet's career; there were also outbreaks of dissent against established figures, such as Alfred Austin's against both Tennyson and

Browning in 1870.[4] With regard to the early reviews, hindsight is a mixed blessing. We tend to forget, for example, that the critics whose blindness we disparage were reading poems later suppressed by their authors because they deserved the ridicule to which they had been subjected. The first volume of Christopher Ricks's edition of Tennyson offers dozens of examples of poems published in 1830 or 1832 and not reprinted, or relegated, sometimes in heavily revised forms, to 'Juvenilia' in later collected editions.[5] We need to remember, therefore, that J. W. Croker, reviewing the *Poems* of 1832, had to encounter, as well as 'Oenone' and 'The Lady of Shalott', 'O Darling Room':

> O darling room, my heart's delight,
> Dear room, the apple of my sight,
> With thy two couches soft and white,
> There is no room so exquisite,
> No little room so warm and bright,
> Wherein to read, wherein to write.[6]

'O Darling Room' would have suffered whoever its author had been. But the fact that some bad verse by good poets resembled the bad verse of bad poets should not be confused with the fact that critics applying the same criteria to two poems were often unable to distinguish between good and bad. Compare, for example, the following judgements:

> We complain, then, of a strange construction of language, by which many parts of his poem are disfigured, and which the author seems to have adopted, with the zeal— not of a poet, but of a workman. The beauties of composition in poetry are too fine, too subtle, too delicate, to be made the direct object of an author's care: they must rather be unintentional, the natural and unconstrained result of thought, feeling, and imagination. Mr. — has forgotten this: he has apparently searched everywhere around him, for a heavy and massive frame-work wherein to deposit his poetry; he has sacrificed, in many places, the harmony and music within, to a strange metrical garb without; he throws behind him that simple eloquence which belongs essentially to the breathings of a poet's thoughts, and adopts instead, big, rough, Cyclopean words, which, by their rumbling noise, divert our attention from the beauties of conception and of sense...

> If it were Mr. —'s desire to withdraw himself from the inquest of criticism, he could scarcely have effected that purpose better than by the impenetrable veil, both of manner and language, in which he has contrived to wrap up whatever truths or beauties this volume may contain...[E]ven if his truths and beauties lay nearer to the surface than they do, they would recommend themselves far more agreeably in the accepted grammatical forms . . . Euphony is one of the conditions of poetry, which, as a sort of usher to the rest, is less safely neglected than some of its higher and more essential qualities. The reader's attention, during the first half of this volume, is necessarily occupied in mastering those novelties of mere construction.

One of these passages refers to Browning's *Sordello*, the other to *Mount Sinai*, by 'William Phillips, of the Middle Temple'. But which is which?[7] They are founded on the same critical assumptions about what makes for good poetry: 'euphony', clarity, the conveyance of vaguely specified 'beauties'. If both these poems were lost, and we had only such critical accounts to go by, how might we tell that one is a masterpiece and the other—not? *Mount Sinai* is, indeed, a very bad poem—the reviewer in *Fraser's Magazine* called it, only a little harshly, 'the gesticulations of an ape'—but people were equally harsh about *Sordello* ('unintelligible oozings of nonsense'), and Ezra Pound's scorn for those who 'grin[ned] through the horse-collar' at the poem's difficulty misses the point.[8] The problem is not simply that there were no readers capable of understanding *Sordello* when it appeared, but that the ordinary principles of critical judgement with which most reviewers were equipped, and which they saw no reason to question ('harmony and music', 'accepted grammatical forms'), were not adequate in themselves to distinguish between the density of a genius and that of a dunce. It follows that the condemnation of bad verse was often enforced by contrast, not with good verse, but with verse equally bad.

One further restriction on the material discussed in this essay concerns ideologically motivated criticism: that is, the bias which leads a critic to depreciate *as verse* the work of a poet whose opinions he or she opposes. In 1857, for example, the *Literary Gazette* reviewed *The Revolt of Hindostan* by the former Chartist leader and radical author Ernest Jones. To a conservative supporter of British colonial policy, Jones's 'two aspects of poet and socialist' were conjoined: a passage is cited to illustrate both the 'senseless jargon' of his political views and the 'clumsy artifice' of his verse.[9] Again, an article by a Catholic writer on 'The Vices of Agnostic Poetry' affirms that 'The agnostic theory of human life being eminently superficial, it follows of necessity that the poetry of its adherents, when they indulge in verse, must be superficial, and in many cases obscure.'[10] Such criticism, interesting though it is on other grounds, is to one side of my subject here, the match between mediocre verse and conventional criticism.

The protest of the latter against the former runs with little change of tone throughout the period. According to the established evolutionary narrative of Victorian criticism, the coarser, more partisan traits belong to the earlier part of the period, when the Victorians were still extricating themselves from Regency frivolity and viciousness; criticism came of age in the 1860s and 1870s.[11] This narrative, though convincing in outline, does not tell the whole story. It is naturally biased towards the major figures, and towards the relatively lengthy articles devoted to them. Serious critical engagement with a writer's work requires space, and implies some leisure for the critic. It also assumes the importance of the writer whose work is being addressed. No such assumption applies to mediocrity. It is summarily treated by critics who have neither the leisure nor the incentive to develop new theoretical perspectives. The constriction of space exerts a pressure on critical language, shaping it into ready-made formulas; but it also has another effect, that of condensed passionate utterance. The formulas come out of the furnace at white heat. The violence of some of the criticism of bad verse in the period is perhaps a sign of the persistence of Regency habits, but it is also a sign of entrenched popular beliefs. Such beliefs are not always consistent, but they are deeply held, and many of them survive to this day, disdained by academic criticism but forming the fundamental orientation of the reading public.

I propose to look in some detail at the coverage of minor poetry in the *Athenaeum* and other periodicals, in the period between 1840 and 1870. I single out the *Athenaeum* for two reasons: first, because its column 'Poetry of the Million' represents a deliberate effort to 'notice' such work; second, because from 1854 it employed Gerald Massey, one of the great self-taught Victorian men of letters, as its poetry reviewer. Massey offers a picture of the 'jobbing' critic at work, plying his trade at speed and with recourse to the tools at hand.

'Poetry of the Million' was launched on 25 April 1846, shortly before Thomas Kibble Hervey took over the editorship of the magazine, and ran for seven years, almost to the day.[12] Hervey himself wrote the first article in the series, a manifesto against mediocrity. The huge surplus of poetry means that it has become impossible for a journal such as the *Athenaeum* to cope: 'Our resources break down, like the strength of the Roman matron beneath the heap of poetical trinkets which are tossed at us.'[13] Hervey plays with the legend of Tarpeia—a maiden (not matron) who betrayed Rome to the Sabines, and named as her price 'what they bore on their left arms', meaning their gold bracelets; they repaid her instead by crushing her to death with their shields. He casts the *Athenaeum* as a beleaguered emblem of virtue who does *not* covet the 'trinkets' which come her way. What of the owners of the 'poetical trinkets'? It is they who are the traitors, opening the gates of the city to the barbarians. Hervey's facetiousness is not really playful: 'None but ourselves, or others so circumstanced, *can* know the weight', he goes on. And the tone deepens into indignation, linked to a profound anxiety:

> There is some peculiar element of ponderosity in the metal of verse, where it is not gold, that increases in a ratio far beyond that of the quality—and so, defies the language of calculation. It is by similitudes only that we can reach its idea. Itself a nothing, or a less than nothing, like the nightmare—the creature of mental crudeness or indigestion—it yet sits with the imponderable weight of a nightmare on literature; and though nothing be so buoyant or elastic as the genius of a people...yet we can conceive of a poetical age of lead, too long protracted and too easily endured, which should bear down the resistance of the national springs, and crush out the finer spiritualities of a people forever.

The weight of a heap of trinkets becomes, first, 'the imponderable weight of a nightmare' (in the older sense of a succubus, literally suffocating the sleeper she sits astride); then gold is transformed to 'a poetical age of lead', of Saturnian dullness, capable of bringing about a *Dunciad*-like cultural apocalypse.

What can 'Poetry of the Million' do, faced with this prospect? Hervey wishes to teach his readers to avoid bad poetry 'by the lesson of multiplied example', but the lesson must be kept within bounds: the solution is an occasional and representative series. 'The mechanical difficulty of increasing number will be met, to all the extent necessary for our purpose, by ticketing this class of books in occasional lots—introducing our versifiers to the public by the dozen or half-dozen at a time', he writes. This formula set the pattern followed by 'Poetry of the Million' over the lifetime of the series—the first attempt, no matter how partial and unsystematic, to keep track of 'minor' poetry as a distinct category.[14]

Hervey tried to maintain that 'Poetry of the Million' would not simply be a negative voice, and that while 'reject[ing] the absolutely worthless' it would also 'prevent the waste of small and improvable values' by nurturing 'the germ of something better [which] is found, at times, lying idly among the mass'. But the title inclines towards satire: it remembers Hamlet's praise of the play which 'pleas'd not the million', only now it is the million who do not please: the multitude of vulgar spectators has become a multitude of vulgar producers.[15] There was, however, some uncertainty as to how to characterize this profusion. Here, for example, is the opening of the column for 15 January 1848 (written by Hervey):

> If our readers imagine that because we are in mid-winter there has been a suspension of the music of the song-bird whose name is Legion, they have extracted from the mere exigencies of our columns a speculative good in which we have not been permitted to share. With us, the singing 'Million' have had for the time to give place to that speciality of the season the Christmas carollers, in verse and prose; but we have them about us, nevertheless,—caged in bindings of all gay forms and hues, and uttering every variety of note save the higher ones. Our library-table is vocal with the chirp of the small poets…The leaf falls not in the grove where they learn their singing,—and their Helicon never freezes over. 'No song no supper' is a threat which in the Little Britain of poetry implies a danger so remote as would make the term of the proposition ridiculous. The rule of political economy is defied in that world—the supply is infinitely beyond the demand. Its population seems to grow and multiply upon neglect.[16]

'The song-bird whose name is Legion' conflates a conventional image of the poet with the episode of the Gadarene swine (Luke 8: 26–36), in which Jesus casts a 'legion' of devils out of a lunatic and into a herd of pigs. The suggestion is that the 'poets of the million' are possessed, and are in fact more like pigs than birds; and since the biblical pigs 'ran violently down a steep place into the lake and were choked' (33), there may also be a wish for the 'song-birds' to be stifled. At this point the metaphor shifts its ground. The 'singing Million' now appear as caged birds, each poet imprisoned in a physical book whose gaudy appearance derives from new printing technology which enabled the commercial production of elaborately decorated bindings, hitherto the preserve of wealthy individual purchasers. Within this economy of vulgar display, however, the comparison of the poet to a *caged* song-bird creates a problem for Hervey, both because birds don't choose to sing in cages, and because they are kept solely to entertain their owners: the 'singing Million' must therefore be giving pleasure, and are innocent of vain ambition. As though realizing that he has tripped himself up, Hervey now returns the caged birds to the wild ('the grove where they learn their singing'), then he simply abandons the metaphor altogether. A rapid transit takes him from the classical Helicon to 'the Little Britain of poetry'. 'Little Britain', in the City of London, had been celebrated by Washington Irving as an epitome of old-fashioned Englishness, 'the heart's core of the city; the stronghold of true John Bullism…a fragment of London as it was in its better days, with its antiquated folks and fashions'. But as Irving also noted, Little Britain had once been 'the great mart of learning…peopled by the busy and prolific race of booksellers'.[17] The real business of publishing has moved on; 'the Little Britain of poetry' represents a fantasy-space in which the normal rules of commercial enterprise are suspended. Poetry does not belong to the real world, ruled by 'political economy'; or rather it is a burlesque of that world—hence the allusion to *No song, no supper*, the title of a popular operatic 'afterpiece'.[18]

What are we to make of the conflicting images of poetry in this passage? With some hesitation, I would argue that the final image is the strongest, at least as far as the 'poetry of the million' is concerned. The fact that the decorative volumes on the 'Library table' do not represent a serious business is itself a serious matter, a crisis caused by the huge increase in opportunities to compose and publish poetry in the century between (say) the death of Byron and that of Hardy. The growth of literacy, the expansion of the book-publishing industry, and the multiplication of its forms (annuals, gift-books, albums, particularly important for women), the proliferation of newspapers and magazines (especially in the second half of the century, following the removal of stamp duty and other tariffs)—these developments allowed more individuals who wrote poetry to circulate their poems in print. And since most poetry (in all periods) is bad poetry, what this effectively meant was a huge increase in, and diversification of, the market for mediocrity. There were ill-advised young ladies and gentlemen ('a collection avowedly made up of poems by a young lady in her sixteenth year and poems by a young gentleman *written during tea* "immediately after the excitement of a long and very fatiguing walk"'); there were innumerable clergymen, including the Lord Bishop of Down, Connor, and Dromore, whose volume *The Sun-dial of Armoy* 'evinces classic taste as well as pious feeling' but is the work of 'a bard made to order'; there were lawyers, naval officers, and military men (Gerald Massey remarked of Col. James Abbott's *Prometheus' Daughter* that it offered 'another proof that the gallantry of British soldiers is equal to any need', since men prepared to 'charge the guns at Balaclava…might have quailed before writing these 878 pages of verse on such a subject'); there were deluded relatives ('The editor's belief that his father was a poet is delightfully filial'); there were Americans, Canadians, even Australians (Gerald Massey on *The Australian Sacred Lyre*, by James Sinclair of Melbourne: 'sacred lyre it is not, unless the word is wrongly spelt').[19] There had always been amateurs, tyros, and poetasters, but in the Victorian period there were not only more of them, but their presence became more visible, and to critics it seemed more urgent to stem their flow.

Material conditions alone do not, of course, account for the vast over-production of poems in the period: it is also linked, paradoxically, to the decline of poetry as a major cultural force, its mutation into a pastime or an occasion for self-display. Gerald Massey has a bitter joke at the expense of J. H. R. Bayley's *Oscar; and Autumnal Gleanings*, which came recommended by 'a long list of patrons, which includes Dukes, Duchesses, Bishops, Marquises, and Earls in abundance': 'Talk of poetry not being patronized in England! That is no longer a true bill:—it is a libel. Talk of the *decline* of poetry! Why the fact is it must be in a rapid *consumption* if this sort of stuff sells'.[20] Massey's working-class origins would make him especially sensitive to any revival of the old alliance between poetry and aristocratic patronage. But he was equally capable of scorning such pretension lower down the social scale. He remarked of one poor specimen: 'The volume…appeals exclusively to the admiration of any friends who may be willing to vote a crown to the poet of their parlour-circle'.[21] The vanity of those who took themselves (rather than their art) seriously, and the lack of self-knowledge of those who simply mistook themselves for poets, were recurring targets for satire; but behind the satire there is anger at the lack of respect that bad poets showed for the art they were bringing into disrepute, and at the fact that they kept on coming.

The Athenaeum, in common with other journals, shows a persistent hostility towards poets who crossed the line separating the private from the public. What might be indulged as a foible among one's family and friends became censurable when it became, to use Massey's term, an object of *consumption*—that is, when it entered the market, whether for fame or cash. Here is the greeting (again, the entire review) given to one volume in 'Poetry of the Million':

> *Lyra Rudis*, by Mr. Frank Browne…bears upon its title-page the motto
>   A book's a book, although there's nothing in it
> —and accordingly, this is—a book.[22]

Browne had thought to shield himself with Byron's self-deprecation:

> I, too, can scrawl, and once upon a time
> I poured along the town a flood of rhyme,
> A schoolboy freak, unworthy praise or blame;
> I printed—older children do the same.
> 'Tis pleasant, sure, to see one's name in print;
> A Book's a Book, altho' there's nothing in't.[23]

But the modesty topos receives short shrift, even when accompanied by a plea for sympathy on other grounds, as the author of *The Isle of Arran*, reviewed in the same issue as Browne, would have discovered:

> Few Poets of the Million come before the public with a frank simplicity like that which speaks by the preface to *The Isle of Arran*. The author does not venture out of cover of the anonymous—describes his rhymes as singing for his own sick room— and hints a suspicion that he may be writing only verse when he is aiming at poetry. If that wholesome distrust had carried him one step further and prevented his publishing, he would have had an added title to our esteem…

The brisk callousness of the tone springs from the stringent 'test' of publication, a test (supposedly) of objective merit, taking no account of personal circumstances or any other extraneous factor. Inevitably there were exceptions: poems on religious subjects, for example, or on topics aligned with the magazine's political views, might be let off lightly. The theme of John Burbidge's *The Slave Trade* 'so directly claim[s] the protection of the Muse that the very fact of the appeal itself pleads against imperfect execution'.[24] Profits from the Rev. Alexander Wallace's *Poems and Sketches* were to be donated to a fund for church-building in the east end of Glasgow, a cause dear to Gerald Massey's heart: the poems are 'hopeless enough in a literary point of view, but Charity is good-natured enough to lend its golden smile to very leaden things'.[25] But in general the *Athenaeum*, and other periodicals, insist that the *opportunity* to publish is not an *excuse*. Hervey's review of *Polynesia: a Sketch in Verse*, by Joseph P. Gibbins, begins:

> In his preface to this little volume, the writer tells us that he is just seventeen, that he is conscious that his poems are devoid of 'purity of diction, and elegance of style,' but he submits them with diffidence to the critics, hoping for indulgence on account of youth.
> This is a plea which we cannot admit. It concerns not the reader of a poem, save as a matter of curiosity, what is the age of the writer. He reads to improve or amuse himself, not to gratify the author, and if the writing be neither improving nor amusing, the author is amenable to censure, whatever his age; publication was a voluntary act, and he thereby submits, not himself, but his book, as a book, to the judgment of the reviewers.[26]

Notice the absoluteness with which the line between 'author' and 'book' is drawn, as though it were always clear and easy to maintain; yet it is hard to think of a more problematic distinction in the period, if only on the ground of gender. Five years later a different reviewer makes the same point in near-identical terms:

> It would appear that every young master or miss who perpetrates rhyme deems it necessary to rush into print, as if the fire would not be a better place of consignment for their nonsense than the grocer or the butterman to whom their sheets are universally consigned. And still they continue to plead youth as an excuse for writing badly—forgetful that if youth be an excuse for making stupid verses, it is no excuse for printing them.[27]

The 'young master' in question had made the mistake of advertising his youth on the title page of his volume: *Poems. By John Harwood, a Minor*. The reviewer was unmoved; but in his condemnation there is also a note of unease, a need to justify his own virulence:

> Now here again we have 'a minor,' perpetrating rhymes, and doubtless believing that his minority is a plea on behalf of their manifest imperfections. But it is a plea we can never admit, and we feel that we should be doing irreparable mischief often, if, from any misjudged feeling of kindness, we were to offer the slightest encouragement to those who have not the genius for it, to pursue a career in which failure is certain, and ruin of fortune, health, and happiness the too probable result.

Is John Harwood merely indulging his youthful vanity by 'rushing into print', or is he seriously 'pursuing a career'? The reviewer is unsure: at first Harwood seems to be one of a crowd of silly youngsters, then to be mistaking himself for a real poet. The defensive tone, marked by the exaggerated claim that the young author is truly risking 'ruin', conjures up the counter-image of Harwood as Keats, whose 'fortune, health, and happiness' had indeed been 'ruined' by his pursuit of his vocation, though not in the sense here intended. Richard Monckton Milnes's immensely influential biography of Keats had just appeared, and the reviewer in *The Critic* may have had at the back of his mind the memory that Keats had been given the same sneeringly 'salutary' advice to give up poetry for his own good.[28]

There were in fact few agreed criteria for distinguishing a dunce from a genius—leaving aside the overwhelming likelihood that any given volume was the work of the former. One of the safest seemed to be that of imitation:

> Miss Marianne Pennington is of that innumerable class of writers who have gone for inspiration to the full fountain of Mrs. Hemans. They who go to foreign fountains, however, even when most successful, commonly bring away all but the essential spirit of the poetical waters at which they drink. The spirit of assimilation wanting to secure the rest is the same spirit which would have rendered the borrowed draught unnecessary. That only is poetry which wells up within the singer's own heart and wanders into flow and motion of its own.[29]

The flat assertion in the last sentence exemplifies the kind of critical commonplace that emerges, shorn of nuance, in such reviews: it brushes aside any notion that the question of imitation and influence might be more complex than *that*. (The metaphor of the 'fountain' and the well of feeling is unconsciously determined by another received idea, which associates poetry, and women's poetry in particular, with *flow*, both of the voice and of tears, and thus doubly identifies Felicia Hemans's poetry as a 'source'.) For this critic, the mere fact of imitation is a fatal sign of weakness. Another unfavourable comparison with Hemans, in Hervey's review of Annie Tinsley's *Lays for the Thoughtful & the Solitary*, makes the same point:

> Mrs. Tinsley is one of those poetesses whom the world owes to Mrs. Hemans. If Mrs. Hemans had never sung, it is probable that neither would Mrs. Tinsley; and the loss which the world would have sustained in the first case would have been far too great to receive any material accession from the loss in the second. Many of the former's melodies the latter borrows; but the rich tones, the voice at once sweet and full that carried them to the heart—awakening at once the feelings and imagination—are in the grave with the first singer. Mrs. Tinsley's imitation is cold and colourless beside the original,—yet she plays rather a distinguished part in a chorus of 'the Million.'[30]

That last *arrière-pensée* acknowledges that Tinsley has at least some technical proficiency; but to be placed 'beside the original' is enough to condemn her. We might say with equal justice that Christina Rossetti is one of those poets whom the world owes to Tennyson; yet Gerald Massey wields the Tennysonian stick as a blunt instrument:

> There can be no doubt but that Mr. Tennyson is a great mistake for some of our minor minstrels. By some means or other,—we imagine it to be the 'weird seizure' that he hints at in *The Princess*,—he forestalls them in what they were going to say, and in the very way in which they were about to say it.[31]

The humour of this is gentle compared to the rebuke administered to William Lancaster's *Eclogues and Monodramas*, which begins by citing Tennyson's 'The Flower' ('Read my little fable: / He that runs may read. / Most can raise the flowers now, / For all have got the seed'), and 'warn[s] young rhymesters that they had better steal seed from anywhere and almost anything in literature than the Tennysonian flower':

> We are heartily sick of this continual feasting of our juveniles on dainties too rich for their stomachs, and then asking us to call their pukings poetry. Mr. Lancaster is one of the worst offenders amongst recent verse-writers. His painful mimicry of the noble music; his 'damnable iteration' of the well-known manner; his repetitions of tricks that we see through, in place of the old miracles that we did not see through: his flashy gilt instead of the fine gold, are almost sufficient to weary the reader into forswearing the original poetry altogether until he can get this lacquer-ware out of sight, and the monotonous drone of the sham music out of his ears.[32]

Massey cleverly iterates Falstaff's complaint to Prince Hal, but inverts its meaning:

> O, thou hast damnable iteration, and art indeed able to corrupt a saint. Thou hast done much harm upon me, Hal, God forgive thee for it! Before I knew thee, Hal, I knew nothing, and now am I, if a man should speak truly, little better than one of the wicked.[33]

Lancaster is travestied as Falstaff, complaining to Hal-Tennyson that he has been drawn into his orbit; yet it is Lancaster who has 'done much harm' to Tennyson, by threatening to 'weary the reader into forswearing the original poetry altogether'. It is witty, but it is not, as it happens, a just criticism. 'William Lancaster' was one of the pen-names of John Byrne Leicester Warren, 3rd Baron de Tabley, a good if not a great poet whom Massey badly misrepresents here (in part because we 'owe' him to Browning as much as to Tennyson). This is an admittedly rare example of a 'minor' poet being hastily or thoughtlessly misread, but it illustrates the vagueness with which criteria such as 'imitation' were applied.

There is the same problem with judgements of poetic language, put forward with confidence by so many critics of bad verse in the period. To return to Joseph P. Gibbins's *Polynesia*, Hervey, picking up the author's disclaimer as to his 'purity of diction and elegance of style', remarks that, on the contrary, he possesses these qualities in suspicious abundance, and that 'if he were more rude and rough of speech, we should have more hope of him'. Gibbins's 'fatal copiousness of expression' is in fact a sign of mental vacuity:

> from the first to the last page of the volume we have been unable to find one original idea, one thought that is not commonplace and hackneyed...Far more hopefully should we have discovered the harshest rhymes, the most imperfect metres, the worst language, clothing some rough earth-incrusted gems of thought, which time and the world will polish, than the smooth metrical array of choice words, that sound sweetly but embody nothing.[34]

The notion that originality consists in having original ideas is a familiar one: Massey, reviewing J. P. Robson's *Hermione the Beloved, and Miscellaneous Poems*, states it baldly: 'We do not deny to Mr. Robson the faculty of expression; but what is the use of expression if you have nothing to say?'[35] Yet this view was not universally held; as many accusations of want of originality focus on manner, not matter. The value placed on 'earth-incrusted gems of thought' sounds like a manifesto for Browning, until we remember that it was precisely for his harsh rhymes, imperfect metres, and rebarbative language that Browning was denied the title of poet by critics early and late in his career. The reviewer of *Sordello*, cited earlier, who maintained that 'euphony is one of the conditions of poetry' represents a stubborn, an inveterate attachment to the *intrinsic* value of polish, of harmony, of 'surface'. William Allingham reports a wholly typical exchange with Thackeray about Browning's lack of these qualities:

> [Thackeray] 'I can't manage his poetry. What do you say?'
> (I spoke highly of it.)
> 'Well, you see, I want poetry to be musical, to run sweetly.'
> 'So do I' ----
> 'Then that *does for* your friend B.!'
> I spoke of Browning's other qualities as so splendid as to make him, as it were, a law in himself. But Thackeray only smiled and declined further discussion.[36]

Examples of critics 'declining further discussion' of poets far less formidable than Browning, on just these grounds, are not hard to find. Other criteria, as we have seen, are equally likely to be applied without 'discussion', on the assumption that critic and reader share common ground, that the appeal to 'nature' or 'poetical spirit', or 'inner fire' is self-evident. The poor Bishop who was deemed 'a bard made to order' 'proves over again what has been proved a hundred times before—that while Art can cultivate, it cannot create, genius. Study may form a tasteful rhymester,—but Nature only has the making of the poet'.[37] The critical orthodoxy by which the Bishop is judged here may be as 'made to order' as anything in his book: that does not mean that the judgement is wrong, only that a cliché is deemed adequate to the purpose.

In many cases the verdict on a 'poet of the million' is delivered by quip rather than quotation; but quotation itself is often equivalent to a quip, since it is usually unaccompanied by any kind of justificatory analysis. A few lines are tied around the poet's neck, and the critic simply kicks away the chair. The problem of judgement is thrown into sharp relief by this practice—dictated in part by pressure of space, but revelatory in what it takes for granted. I shall conclude with some representative examples, and in keeping with the spirit of the originals, I shall present them with a minimum of comment, except for the final one—which will allow readers of this essay, like their counterparts in 1848, to take part in an interactive exercise of practical criticism.

The reviewer of *The Last Crusader* quotes Dryden and Shakespeare in his assault on the anonymous author, who, he claims, must have sung for the same reason that Dryden's boy whistled. 'Words, words, words,' was Hamlet's decision upon the book he was reading; and 'Words, words, words'—including rhyme—must be our decision upon the 'Last Crusader.' Seventy-two pages of stuff like this—

> 'Quoth the harper haughtilie
> "This horrid nuptial shall not be!
> When strikes the hour, speedilie
> And surely I shall be with thee!"
> "Grammercie, heaven! grammercie," cried
> In ecstacy, the grateful bride'—

is what the "Last Crusader is made up of. No doubt the author and his friends think it poetry...[38]

More readers knew their Dryden then than now, though fewer than knew their Shakespeare; the reviewer is offering an extra thrill to those who recognized the allusion to *Cymon and Iphigenia* ('He trudg'd along unknowing what he sought, / And whistled as he went, for want of Thought', ll. 84-5) and who would relish its aptness. The next reviewer confidently anticipates his readers' reaction to the (unconscious) depiction of juvenile snobbery in *Gwen: a Drama in Monologue*:

Mere pensiveness, such as the author affects and maintains throughout, was not enough. His heir to an earldom soliloquises in this style, and manages to nauseate the reader once and for ever:—

> For she tripped round the hill
> To visit some cottage lowly;
> *With her basket of food on her arm,*
> *She looked like Artemis holy;*
> *And I doffed to her,* and she knew
> The stranger of yesternight,
> And her soft eyes showed more blue
> As the rose in her cheek grew bright;
> *And, some power impelling me, I—*
> *I who was always counted so shy—*
> *I walked by her side a little,* &c.

Again—

> She is perfect, I hold, from the crown of her hair
> To the dainty sole of her delicate foot;
> And her hand and her voice are as soft as silk,
> *And she comes hour by hour with a tender care,*
> *With my draught or my food, or with rich cool milk.*

> Ah! if only—what, am I then worse than the brute,
> That I stoop to thoughts I loathe and hate—
> *I, a great peer's only son?*

> It is conceivable that such a snob should write bad verses, but scarcely possible that
> the critic should follow him with any patience.[39]

The italics here perform the critic's wordless scorn, but there might be some debate as
to what, exactly, he is pointing at. Are the 'bad verses' defective in technique, or in tone?
The clumsiness of the 'I' rhymes in the first passage might be defended as appropriate
to the context; and without knowing more of the poem it is hard to judge whether the
speaker's description of himself as 'a great peer's only son' really is as insufferable as it is
made to appear.

From nausea we pass to an even more extreme reaction:

> No language can do justice to *The Prince of Panama*, by Capt. Adderley Sleigh, but
> its own.

> #### Reply to Reflection
>
> There is another world for man—
>   There is a life of joy—of happiness—
> Such as no mind conceives—or can
>   Imagine how those joys are endless:—
>   But what's on earth?
> Alas! dull drear monotony of daily life—
>   The chill repulse—the keen retort—
> The doubt—deceit—malignant strife—
>   Thank God!—existence is but short.

> If existence is to be spent in uttering poetical outpourings like this, we agree with
> Capt. Adderley Sleigh that it might as well be short. There should be a time of
> compensation somewhere for the reading of such poetry. Where it is a duty, as with
> us, it may well rank with the heroisms of private life. Short as existence is, the task is
> enough to drive the critic into suicide.[40]

A sharp note of anguish breaks through the mask of facetiousness in that last paragraph. It is not the only example of a review of bad verse in which an appeal is made
to the reader to sympathize with the critic's suffering. But after all there is something
odd about such reviewing being presented as a 'duty' or 'task'—imposed by whom? and
accepted for what reason? Perhaps it is a moral imperative to expose Capt. Adderley
Sleigh for the clumsy bathetic bore he is; but perhaps the reviewer has to perform the
task in order to earn a crust.

My last example contains an appeal to the reader of a different kind. The reviewer of Edwin Lawrence's *Xamayca*, a 'romantic poem in six cantos', is presented with a gift by his author's preface:

> 'Popular opinion,' he says, 'has decided that in these days a writer's railroad to fame is prose; and yet the author of this work obstinately selects the now unhonoured and unfrequented pathway, Poetry.' And here, as we have said, it is remarkable how the stars that took care of M. Jourdain have kept Mr. Lawrence right in spite of himself— how, having set his face towards the poetical pole, he has unconsciously walked direct backwards till he reached the opposite one of prose. He may satisfy himself of this by taking any verse of his poem that he pleases and sacrificing the measures— which by the by are very unevenly applied. We will set him a copy...
>
> 'Two youthful travellers had climbed a rugged steep, and laid their wearied limbs upon the soft green moss o'ergrowing it, lost in admiration deep as their eyes wander'd o'er the enraptured scene expanding to their sight; a scene beheld by few. There art with nature was so matchlessly combined that where'er the eye roved there opened to the view all that could please the fancy or enthral the mind.'
>
> We challenge our readers—and the author too—to cut this into the proper lengths again, without the help of the book.[41]

I took up this challenge; readers may like to try it for themselves before going further. I began by identifying the end-rhymes, and came up with the following result, though it took me some time to accept that it must be so:

> Two youthful travellers had climbed a rugged steep,
> And laid their wearied limbs upon the soft green
> Moss o'ergrowing it, lost in admiration deep
> As their eyes wander'd o'er the enraptured scene
> Expanding to their sight; a scene beheld by few.
> There art with nature was so matchlessly combined
> That where'er the eye roved there opened to the view
> All that could please the fancy or enthral the mind.

I found it hard to believe that the *Athenaeum* had not misprinted the second and third lines: there is a missing syllable in line 2, and the only way to avoid a clashing sequence of three strong stresses running across the line break ('sóft gréen / Móss') would be to place an absurd stress on the 'up' of 'upon'; in any case the unavoidable strong stress on 'Moss' at the start of line 3 makes this line impossible to scan. Line 7 poses a further, though less acute difficulty, which can be resolved by placing the stress on the first syllable of 'where'er' instead of, as is more usual, the second. I ventured further into the poem, and can confirm that the sample is representative enough. The verse of *Xamayca* is, indeed, atrociously bad. The poem, and its author, have sunk into deserved oblivion.[42] Hervey's case is proved.

At this point I went back to the preface which gave Hervey his tactical advantage. And reading this preface in full, I began to have second thoughts, not about the badness of

Lawrence's verse, but about the virulence of Hervey's response. Lawrence is full of vanity and folly, and easy to laugh at—but so is Malvolio, who is both justly exposed and unjustly baited—and Malvolio, after all, 'thinks nobly of the soul'.[43] Edwin Lawrence, too, thinks nobly of his art, though he cannot practise it to any purpose, and though even his praise of it is excruciating. He ends the preface with a bathetic flourish:

> With these remarks the Author launches his bark on the waves of opinion, to float in pride or sink in disgrace, according to its merit. He may wish, but can scarce expect that the first will be its happy destiny. . .
>
> His failure will not change his opinion that the embers of Poetry still live in the human heart, and that a master spirit will yet, from time to time, arise and fan these embers into flame, while the contemners of Poetry will be taught to know that Poets do not vegetate like cucumbers; they bloom like the aloe, an age only produces a blossom.[44]

It took a kind of genius to produce a mixed metaphor as deflating as that. Yet it seems clear that Lawrence does not think himself this 'master spirit'—that something like humility underlies his pompous and painfully funny gesticulation. He bears witness against the 'contemners of Poetry' in his generation; not many poets as bad as he is, in his time or ours, can say as much.

ACKNOWLEDGEMENT

I should like to acknowledge the work of my research assistant, Elizabeth Hammond, a doctoral student in the Department of English at the University of Bristol, especially with regard to the 'Poetry of the Million' series in the *Athenaeum*, whose start- and end-dates she is (I believe) the first to have documented.

NOTES

1. The first edition of *Proverbial Philosophy* appeared in 1837; like *Leaves of Grass* it went through successive expanded editions (four, to 1876). In 1857 the *Literary Gazette* reviewed *Miching Mallecho; and other Poems*, by Paul Richardson, and reported the author's fury at having been compared to Tupper by a reviewer of his previous volume: 'We must concede to the irritated poet that this last accusation was a piece of unexampled malignity. It is humiliating enough to be told that one's measure halts, that one's poems are a compound of treason and folly, and whatever insignificant capacity one has, is abused and misdirected; but to be compared to Tupper, is an indignity beyond which it would seem to be impossible for critical scorn to go' (*The Literary Gazette*, 19 Dec. 1857, 1207).
2. William McGonagall, 'The Tay Bridge Disaster', in *Poetic Gems selected from the Works of William McGonagall*(Dundee: David Winter & Co., 1890).

3. See Thomas M. Disch, 'Inverse Genius: On the Greatness of William McGonagall', *Parnassus: Poetry in Review*, 24 (1999), 199. There is a William McGonagall Appreciation Society in his home town of Dundee, and a McGonagall website (<http://www.mcgonagall-online.org.uk> (accessed 25 January 2012.); 'tributes' regularly appear in the media (e.g. Andy McSmith, 'The story of William McGonagall, the worst poet in the history of the English language', *The Independent*, 17 May 2008). A contrasting case is that of Theo Marzials (1850–1920), whose poem 'A Tragedy' ('Death! / Plop. / The barges down in the river flop. / Flop, plop. / Above, beneath', etc.) now features on websites as 'the worst poem in the English language'; but Marzials is not amenable to being McGonagallized, and the plopping and flopping has been ably defended by Valentine Cunningham in *Victorian Poetry Now: Poets, Poems and Poetics* (Oxford: Wiley-Blackwell, 2011), 89–90.

4. See Alfred Austin, *The Poetry of the Period* (London: Richard Bentley, 1870), 1–37 (Tennyson) and 38–76 (Browning); Algernon Charles Swinburne, *Under the Microscope* (London: D. White, 1872), 34–42.

5. Christopher Ricks, ed., *The Poems of Tennyson*, 3 vols., 2nd ed. (Harlow: Longman, 1987). Of the 55 poems in *Poems, Chiefly Lyrical*, 23 were never reprinted, 31 were eventually classed as 'Juvenilia', and 1, 'National Song', was adapted for Tennyson's play *The Foresters* (completed 1881, published 1892; Ricks, i. 275).

6. Croker's review appeared in the *Quarterly Review*, 49 (1833), 81–96; it is reprinted in John D. Jump, ed., *Tennyson: the Critical Heritage* (London: Routledge & Kegan Paul, 1967), 66–83; the comments on 'O Darling Room' are on 81.

7. The first passage comes from the review of *Mount Sinai* in *The Dublin Literary Gazette*, 14 (1830), 215; the second from the review of *Sordello* in *The Athenaeum*, 657 (1840), 431; reprinted in Boyd Litzinger and Donald Smalley, eds., *Browning: the Critical Heritage* (London: Routledge & Kegan Paul, 1970), 62. The review of *Sordello* was unsigned but the author has been identified as Thomas Kibble Hervey, later editor of the magazine; the source for this, as for other identifications of contributors, is *The Athenaeum Index of Reviews and Reviewers 1830–1870*, an online archive compiled from marked volumes in the City University Library, in a project sponsored by the British Library Research & Development Department and The Pilgrim Trust, and directed by Professor Micheline Beaulieu: [<http://athenaeum.soi.city.ac.uk/reviews/home.html>]. Unless otherwise noted, all other articles are anonymous. *Athenaeum* articles are located by issue number, not volume.

8. The review of Phillips's poem is in *Fraser's Magazine*, 1 (1830), 349–52. The contemptuous dismissal of *Sordello* is from *The Metropolitan Magazine*, 27 (1840), 109 (in *Browning: the Critical Heritage*, 66). Ezra Pound's scorn for the scorners of *Sordello* is in his *ABC of Reading* (London: Routledge, 1934).

9. *The Literary Gazette*, 2135 (19 Dec. 1857), 1209-10.

10. John Charles Earle, 'The Vices of Agnostic Poetry', *The Dublin Review*, 8 (1882), 108.

11. See John Woolford, 'Periodicals and the Practice of Literary Criticism 1855–64', in Joanne Shattock and Michael Wolff, eds., *The Victorian Periodical Press: Samplings and Soundings* (Leicester: Leicester University Press, 1982), 109–42. See also Joanne Shattock, 'The Culture of Criticism', in Joanne Shattock, ed., *The Cambridge Companion to English Literature, 1830–1914* (Cambridge: Cambridge University Press, 2010).

12. The last article in the series is in issue 1327 (2 Apr. 1853), though it is not a valedictory piece; the series seems simply to have stopped, probably coinciding with the departure of Hervey as editor in Dec. 1853. Nearly a year later, 'Poetry of the Million' was replaced by another

occasional feature, 'Minor Minstrels' (starting with no. 1375, 4 Mar. 1854). An effort was made to begin a 'Novels of the Million' series (no.1331, 30 Apr. 1853) but it was confined to this issue.

13. *The Athenaeum*, 965 (25 Apr. 1846), 419. The first three volumes reviewed were all anonymous: *Barnard; a Modern Romance*; *Rhymes by a Poetaster*; and *Humbug; an Illiberal Satire, by a Bigot*.

14. Its two most notable accidental 'catches' were a brief review (not unfavourable) of the Brontë sisters' first, and only, published volume of verse, *Poems by Currer, Ellis, and Acton Bell* (no. 975 [4 July 1846], 682–683), and a lukewarm mention of Matthew Arnold's *Empedocles on Etna, and Other Poems*, in a list with five other volumes, in the final article in the series (see n.12).

15. Hence the importance of the preposition: in his only mention of the column in *The Athenaeum: A Mirror of Victorian Culture* (Chapel Hill: University of North Carolina Press, 1941), Leslie Marchand makes a significant error in calling it 'Poetry *for* the Million' (60, my emphasis).Hamlet's speech is in Act II. i. 436–40 in *The Riverside Shakespeare*, 2nd edn. (Boston: Houghton Mifflin, 1997).

16. Thomas Kibble Hervey, 'Poetry of the Million', *The Athenaeum*, 1055 (15. Jan 1848), 56.

17. Washington Irving, 'Little Britain', in *History, Tales and Sketches* (Cambridge: Cambridge University Press [Library of America], 1983), 970–1, 969.

18. *No song, no supper* (composer Stephen Sorace; librettist Prince Hoare) was first produced in 1790 and frequently revived.

19. All these quotations are from the *Athenaeum*: both the tea-time poet (Stafford Reeves, *A Voice from the North*) and the Bishop are from the 'Poetry of the Million' article in 1069 (22 Apr. 1848), 411 and 412, written by Dinah Maria Mulock (see n.22); Col. Abbott, 1759 (13 July 1861), 50; *The Poems of Francis Hingeston. Edited by his Son*, 1583 (27 Feb. 1858), 272; *The Australian Sacred Lyre*, 1580 (6 Feb. 1858), 176.

20. Gerald Massey, *The Athenaeum*, 1869 (22 Aug. 1863), 237.

21. 'Jos', *Sketches: being Poems*, *The Athenaeum*, 1063 (1858), 80.

22. Dinah Maria Mulock, 'Poetry of the Million', *The Athenaeum*, 1069(22 Apr. 1848), 411. Dinah Mulock, later Craik (1826–1887), was on the brink of a successful career as a novelist; she contributed a number of 'Poetry of the Million' columns in 1848, all of them in this caustic tone, piquantly at odds with the image conveyed by her *DNB* entry ('the tender and philanthropic, and at the same time energetic and practical womanhood of ordinary life has never had a more sufficient representative').

23. George Gordon Byron, *English Bards and Scotch Reviewers in Lord Byron: The Major Works*, ed. Jerome McGann (Oxford: Oxford University Press, 2000), 3.

24. *The Athenaeum*, 1069 (22 Apr. 1848), 412; the reviewer was Dinah Mulock.

25. Gerald Massey, 'Our Library Table', *The Athenaeum*, 1794 (15 Mar. 1862), 361.

26. Hervey, review of *Polynesia: a Sketch in Verse*, *The Critic*, 1.10 (1844), 210.

27. *The Critic*, 9.21 (1850), 18.

28. Richard Monckton Milnes (later Lord Houghton), *Life, Letters, and Literary Remains of John Keats*, 2 vols. (London: Moxon, 1848). As it happens, John Berwick Harwood (1828–1886) did have a literary career—not as a poet, but a minor novelist: see JoanneShattock, ed., *Cambridge Bibliography of English Literature*, 3rd ed., vol. 4 (Cambridge: Cambridge University Press, 1999), 1306.

29. Mulock, *The Athenaeum*, 1069 (22 Apr. 1848), 411.

30. Hervey, review of *Lays for the Thoughtful & the Solitary*, *The Athenaeum*, 1055 (15 Jan. 1848), 58. Annie Tinsley (1808–1885), minor novelist and poet, is 'Mrs. Charles Tinsley' on the

title page of the volume. The *Athenaeum*'s charge that Tinsley is 'cold and colourless' is unjust. Hervey would have noted that 'A Mother's Thoughts Amidst Her Children' has a motto from Hemans.

31. Review of E. J. Reed, *Corona, and other Poems*, *The Athenaeum*, 1583 (27 Feb. 1858), 272.

32. Review of *Eclogues and Monodramas*, *The Athenaeum*, 1933 (12 Nov. 1864), 365. Tennyson's 'The Flower' had recently been published in *Enoch Arden and other Poems* (1864); see Ricks, *Tennyson*, ii. 684–5.

33. *1 Henry IV* I. ii. 90–95 in Riverside edition (see n.15). Note that one of the—minor—characters is a 'Lancaster' (Lord John of Lancaster, Prince Hal's brother).

34. Hervey, review of *Polynesia: a Sketch in Verse*, *The Critic*, 1 (1844), 210.

35. Massey, review of *Hermione the Beloved, and Miscellaneous Poems*, *The Athenaeum*, 1583 (27 Feb. 1858), 271.

36. *William Allingham's Diary* (London: Centaur Press, 1967), 76–7, a re-issue of the 1907 edition by H. Allingham and D. Radford; also repr. in *Browning: the Critical Heritage*, 200–1.

37. 'Poetry of the Million', *The Athenaeum*, 1069 (1848), 411 and 412. The reviewer is presumably Dinah Mulock, to whom other items in the column for this date are attributed, but this one does not appear in the *Athenaeum* index (see n.7).

38. *The London Review* 15.368 (20 July 1867), 80.

39. *The Examiner*, 3078 (22 Feb. 1879), 247.

40. 'Poetry of the Million', *The Athenaeum*, 1063 (11 Mar. 1848), 267. The reviewer is presumably Dinah Mulock, to whom other items in the column for this date are attributed, but this one does not appear in the Athenaeum index (see n.7).

41. 'Poetry of the Million', *The Athenaeum*, 1059 (12 Feb. 1848),160 (Hervey). The poem is an exotic romance-cum-travelogue set in 'Xamayca' (i.e. Jamaica). 'M. Jourdain' is the hero of Molière's *Le Bourgeois gentilhomme*, who discovers to his amazement that he has been speaking prose all his life (II. vi). The extract from *Xamayca* is from Canto I.v; 'enraptur'd' in line 4 is a misprint for 'enrapturing', but this does not (much) affect the scansion.

42. The only trace I could find of Edwin Lawrence online was in a posting by the ethnomusicologist Daniel T. Neely on the 'merry wang', an apparently apocryphal name for a type of banjo, which Lawrence mentions in Canto V. xv (a stanza which, by the way, makes the *Athenaeum*'s sample sound like Spenser). [<http://danieltneely.com/?p=300>] (accessed 25 January 2012>

43. *Twelfth Night* IV.ii. 50–6, in *Riverside Shakespeare*(see n.15): '[Clown] What is the opinion of Pythagoras concerning wild-fowl? [Malvolio] That the soul of our grandam might haply inhabit a bird. [Clown] What think'st thou of his opinion? [Malvolio] I think nobly of the soul, and in no way approve his opinion.'

44. Edwin Lawrence, *Xamayca* (London: William Pickering, 1847), vii; the book is accessible online: [<http://books.google.co.uk/books/about/Xamayca_a_romantic_poem.html> (accessed 25 January 2012).].

Select Bibliography

Armstrong, Isobel, *Victorian Scrutinies: Reviews of Poetry 1830–1870* (London: Athlone Press, 1972).

Brake, Laurel, 'Literary Criticism and the Victorian Periodicals', *Yearbook of English Studies*, 16 (1986), 92–116.

Bristow, Joseph, ed., *The Victorian Poet: Poetics and Persona* (Beckenham: Croom Helm, 1987).

Gross, John, *The Rise and Fall of the Man of Letters: English Literary Life since 1800* (Harmondsworth: Penguin, 1991; 1st pub. 1969).

Shattock, Joanne, 'The Culture of Criticism', in Joanne Shattock, ed., *The Cambridge Companion to English Literature, 1830–1914* (Cambridge: Cambridge University Press, 2010).

—— and Wolff, Michael, eds., *The Victorian Periodical Press: Samplings and Soundings* (Leicester: Leicester University Press, 1982).

Small, Ian, *Conditions of Criticism: Authority, Knowledge, and Literature in the Late Nineteenth Century* (Oxford: Clarendon Press, 1990).

Treglown, Jeremy and Bennett, Bridget, eds., *Grub Street and the Ivory Tower: Literary Journalism and Literary Scholarship from Fielding to the Internet* (Oxford: Clarendon Press, 1998).

Woodfield, Malcolm, 'Reviews and Reviewing after 1860: R. H. Hutton and the "Spectator"', *Yearbook of English Studies*, 16 (1986), 74–91.

Woolford, John, 'Periodicals and the Practice of Literary Criticism 1855–64' in Shattock, J. and Wolff, M. eds., *The Victorian Periodical Press: Samplings and Soundings* (Leicester: Leicester University Press, 1982), 109–42.

INDEX

Note: page numbers in *italic* refer to illustration; page numbers in **bold** indicate a major discussion.

Lightning Source UK Ltd.
Milton Keynes UK
UKOW07f0129271115

263492UK00003B/4/P